$217
moving
exp.

University Casebook Series

April, 1992

ACCOUNTING AND THE LAW, Fourth Edition (1978), with Problems Pamphlet (Successor to Dohr, Phillips, Thompson & Warren)

George C. Thompson, Professor, Columbia University Graduate School of Business.
Robert Whitman, Professor of Law, University of Connecticut.
Ellis L. Phillips, Jr., Member of the New York Bar.
William C. Warren, Professor of Law Emeritus, Columbia University.

ACCOUNTING FOR LAWYERS, MATERIALS ON (1980)

David R. Herwitz, Professor of Law, Harvard University.

ADMINISTRATIVE LAW, Eighth Edition (1987), with 1989 Case Supplement and 1983 Problems Supplement (Supplement edited in association with Paul R. Verkuil, Dean and Professor of Law, Tulane University)

Walter Gellhorn, University Professor Emeritus, Columbia University.
Clark Byse, Professor of Law, Harvard University.
Peter L. Strauss, Professor of Law, Columbia University.
Todd D. Rakoff, Professor of Law, Harvard University.
Roy A. Schotland, Professor of Law, Georgetown University.

ADMIRALTY, Third Edition (1987), with 1991 Statute and Rule Supplement

Jo Desha Lucas, Professor of Law, University of Chicago.

ADVOCACY, see also Lawyering Process

AGENCY, see also Enterprise Organization

AGENCY—PARTNERSHIPS, Fourth Edition (1987)

Abridgement from Conard, Knauss & Siegel's Enterprise Organization, Fourth Edition.

AGENCY AND PARTNERSHIPS (1987)

Melvin A. Eisenberg, Professor of Law, University of California, Berkeley.

ANTITRUST: FREE ENTERPRISE AND ECONOMIC ORGANIZATION, Sixth Edition (1983), with 1983 Problems in Antitrust Supplement and 1991 Case Supplement

Louis B. Schwartz, Professor of Law, University of Pennsylvania.
John J. Flynn, Professor of Law, University of Utah.
Harry First, Professor of Law, New York University.

BANKRUPTCY, Second Edition (1989), with 1991 Case Supplement

Robert L. Jordan, Professor of Law, University of California, Los Angeles.
William D. Warren, Professor of Law, University of California, Los Angeles.

BANKRUPTCY AND DEBTOR–CREDITOR LAW, Second Edition (1988)

Theodore Eisenberg, Professor of Law, Cornell University.

BUSINESS ASSOCIATIONS, AGENCY, PARTNERSHIPS, AND CORPORATIONS (1991)

William A. Klein, Professor of Law, University of California, Los Angeles.
Mark Ramseyer, Professor of Law, University of California, Los Angeles.

BUSINESS CRIME (1990), with 1991 Case Supplement

Harry First, Professor of Law, New York University.

BUSINESS ORGANIZATION, see also Enterprise Organization

BUSINESS PLANNING (1991)

Franklin Gevurtz, Professor of Law, McGeorge School of Law.

BUSINESS PLANNING, Temporary Second Edition (1984)

David R. Herwitz, Professor of Law, Harvard University.

BUSINESS TORTS (1972)

Milton Handler, Professor of Law Emeritus, Columbia University.

CHILDREN IN THE LEGAL SYSTEM (1983), with 1990 Supplement (Supplement edited in association with Elizabeth S. Scott, Professor of Law, University of Virginia)

Walter Wadlington, Professor of Law, University of Virginia.
Charles H. Whitebread, Professor of Law, University of Southern California.
Samuel Davis, Professor of Law, University of Georgia.

CIVIL PROCEDURE, see Procedure

CIVIL RIGHTS ACTIONS (1988), with 1991 Supplement

Peter W. Low, Professor of Law, University of Virginia.
John C. Jeffries, Jr., Professor of Law, University of Virginia.

CLINIC, see also Lawyering Process

COMMERCIAL AND DEBTOR–CREDITOR LAW: SELECTED STATUTES, 1991 EDITION

COMMERCIAL LAW, Third Edition (1992)

Robert L. Jordan, Professor of Law, University of California, Los Angeles.
William D. Warren, Professor of Law, University of California, Los Angeles.

COMMERCIAL LAW, Fourth Edition (1985), with 1991 Case Supplement

E. Allan Farnsworth, Professor of Law, Columbia University.
John Honnold, Professor of Law, University of Pennsylvania.

COMMERCIAL PAPER, see also Negotiable Instruments

COMMERCIAL PAPER, Third Edition (1984), with 1991 Case Supplement

E. Allan Farnsworth, Professor of Law, Columbia University.

COMMERCIAL PAPER AND BANK DEPOSITS AND COLLECTIONS (1967), with Statutory Supplement

William D. Hawkland, Professor of Law, University of Illinois.

COMMERCIAL TRANSACTIONS—Principles and Policies, Second Edition (1991)

Alan Schwartz, Professor of Law, Yale University.
Robert E. Scott, Professor of Law, University of Virginia.

UNIVERSITY CASEBOOK SERIES—Continued

COMPARATIVE LAW, Fifth Edition (1988)

Rudolf B. Schlesinger, Professor of Law, Hastings College of the Law.
Hans W. Baade, Professor of Law, University of Texas.
Mirjan P. Damaska, Professor of Law, Yale Law School.
Peter E. Herzog, Professor of Law, Syracuse University.

COMPETITIVE PROCESS, LEGAL REGULATION OF THE, Revised Fourth Edition (1991), with 1991 Selected Statutes Supplement

Edmund W. Kitch, Professor of Law, University of Virginia.
Harvey S. Perlman, Dean of the Law School, University of Nebraska.

CONFLICT OF LAWS, Ninth Edition (1990), with 1992 Supplement

Willis L. M. Reese, Professor of Law, Columbia University.
Maurice Rosenberg, Professor of Law, Columbia University.
Peter Hay, Professor of Law, University of Illinois.

CONSTITUTIONAL LAW, Eighth Edition (1989), with 1991 Case Supplement

Edward L. Barrett, Jr., Professor of Law, University of California, Davis.
William Cohen, Professor of Law, Stanford University.
Jonathan D. Varat, Professor of Law, University of California, Los Angeles.

CONSTITUTIONAL LAW, CIVIL LIBERTY AND INDIVIDUAL RIGHTS, Second Edition (1982), with 1991 Supplement

William Cohen, Professor of Law, Stanford University.
John Kaplan, Professor of Law, Stanford University.

CONSTITUTIONAL LAW, Twelfth Edition (1991), with 1991 Supplement (Supplement edited in association with Frederick F. Schauer, Professor, Harvard University)

Gerald Gunther, Professor of Law, Stanford University.

CONSTITUTIONAL LAW, INDIVIDUAL RIGHTS IN, Fifth Edition (1992), (Reprinted from CONSTITUTIONAL LAW, Twelfth Edition), with 1991 Supplement (Supplement edited in association with Frederick F. Schauer, Professor, Harvard University)

Gerald Gunther, Professor of Law, Stanford University.

CONSUMER TRANSACTIONS, Second Edition (1991), with Selected Statutes and Regulations Supplement

Michael M. Greenfield, Professor of Law, Washington University.

CONTRACT LAW AND ITS APPLICATION, Fourth Edition (1988)

Arthur Rosett, Professor of Law, University of California, Los Angeles.

CONTRACT LAW, STUDIES IN, Fourth Edition (1991)

Edward J. Murphy, Professor of Law, University of Notre Dame.
Richard E. Speidel, Professor of Law, Northwestern University.

CONTRACTS, Fifth Edition (1987)

John P. Dawson, late Professor of Law, Harvard University.
William Burnett Harvey, Professor of Law and Political Science, Boston University.
Stanley D. Henderson, Professor of Law, University of Virginia.

CONTRACTS, Fourth Edition (1988)

E. Allan Farnsworth, Professor of Law, Columbia University.
William F. Young, Professor of Law, Columbia University.

CONTRACTS, Selections on (statutory materials) (1988)

UNIVERSITY CASEBOOK SERIES—Continued

CONTRACTS, Second Edition (1978), with Statutory and Administrative Law Supplement (1978)

Ian R. Macneil, Professor of Law, Cornell University.

COPYRIGHT, PATENTS AND TRADEMARKS, see also Competitive Process; see also Selected Statutes and International Agreements

COPYRIGHT, PATENT, TRADEMARK AND RELATED STATE DOCTRINES, Third Edition (1990), with 1991 Selected Statutes Supplement and 1981 Problem Supplement

Paul Goldstein, Professor of Law, Stanford University.

COPYRIGHT, Unfair Competition, and Other Topics Bearing on the Protection of Literary, Musical, and Artistic Works, Fifth Edition (1990), with 1991 Statutory and Case Supplement

Ralph S. Brown, Jr., Professor of Law, Yale University.
Robert C. Denicola, Professor of Law, University of Nebraska.

CORPORATE ACQUISITIONS, The Law and Finance of (1986), with 1991 Supplement

Ronald J. Gilson, Professor of Law, Stanford University.

CORPORATE FINANCE, Third Edition (1987)

Victor Brudney, Professor of Law, Harvard University.
Marvin A. Chirelstein, Professor of Law, Columbia University.

CORPORATION LAW, BASIC, Third Edition (1989), with Documentary Supplement

Detlev F. Vagts, Professor of Law, Harvard University.

CORPORATIONS, see also Enterprise Organization and Business Organization

CORPORATIONS, Sixth Edition—Concise (1988), with 1991 Case Supplement and 1991 Statutory Supplement

William L. Cary, late Professor of Law, Columbia University.
Melvin Aron Eisenberg, Professor of Law, University of California, Berkeley.

CORPORATIONS, Sixth Edition—Unabridged (1988), with 1991 Case Supplement and 1991 Statutory Supplement

William L. Cary, late Professor of Law, Columbia University.
Melvin Aron Eisenberg, Professor of Law, University of California, Berkeley.

CORPORATIONS AND BUSINESS ASSOCIATIONS—STATUTES, RULES, AND FORMS (1991)

CORRECTIONS, SEE SENTENCING

CREDITORS' RIGHTS, see also Debtor-Creditor Law

CRIMINAL JUSTICE ADMINISTRATION, Fourth Edition (1991), with 1991 Supplement

Frank W. Miller, Professor of Law, Washington University.
Robert O. Dawson, Professor of Law, University of Texas.
George E. Dix, Professor of Law, University of Texas.
Raymond I. Parnas, Professor of Law, University of California, Davis.

CRIMINAL LAW, Fifth Edition (1992)

Andre A. Moenssens, Professor of Law, University of Richmond.
Fred E. Inbau, Professor of Law Emeritus, Northwestern University.
Ronald J. Bacigal, Professor of Law, University of Richmond.

FAMILY PROPERTY LAW, Cases and Materials on Wills, Trusts and Future Interests (1991)

Lawrence W. Waggoner, Professor of Law, University of Michigan.
Richard V. Wellman, Professor of Law, University of Georgia.
Gregory Alexander, Professor of Law, Cornell Law School.
Mary L. Fellows, Professor of Law, University of Minnesota.

FEDERAL COURTS, Eighth Edition (1988), with 1991 Supplement

Charles T. McCormick, late Professor of Law, University of Texas.
James H. Chadbourn, late Professor of Law, Harvard University.
Charles Alan Wright, Professor of Law, University of Texas, Austin.

FEDERAL COURTS AND THE FEDERAL SYSTEM, Hart and Wechsler's Third Edition (1988), with 1992 Case Supplement, and the Judicial Code and Rules of Procedure in the Federal Courts (1991)

Paul M. Bator, Professor of Law, University of Chicago.
Daniel J. Meltzer, Professor of Law, Harvard University.
Paul J. Mishkin, Professor of Law, University of California, Berkeley.
David L. Shapiro, Professor of Law, Harvard University.

FEDERAL COURTS AND THE LAW OF FEDERAL–STATE RELATIONS, Second Edition (1989), with 1991 Supplement

Peter W. Low, Professor of Law, University of Virginia.
John C. Jeffries, Jr., Professor of Law, University of Virginia.

FEDERAL PUBLIC LAND AND RESOURCES LAW, Second Edition (1987), with 1990 Case Supplement and 1990 Statutory Supplement

George C. Coggins, Professor of Law, University of Kansas.
Charles F. Wilkinson, Professor of Law, University of Oregon.

FEDERAL RULES OF CIVIL PROCEDURE and Selected Other Procedural Provisions, 1991 Edition

FEDERAL TAXATION, see Taxation

FIRST AMENDMENT (1991)

William W. Van Alstyne, Professor of Law, Duke University.

FOOD AND DRUG LAW, Second Edition (1991), with Statutory Supplement

Peter Barton Hutt, Esq.
Richard A. Merrill, Professor of Law, University of Virginia.

FUTURE INTERESTS (1970)

Howard R. Williams, Professor of Law, Stanford University.

FUTURE INTERESTS AND ESTATE PLANNING (1961), with 1962 Supplement

W. Barton Leach, late Professor of Law, Harvard University.
James K. Logan, formerly Dean of the Law School, University of Kansas.

GENDER DISCRIMINATION, see Women and the Law

GOVERNMENT CONTRACTS, FEDERAL, Successor Edition (1985), with 1989 Supplement

John W. Whelan, Professor of Law, Hastings College of the Law.

GOVERNMENT REGULATION: FREE ENTERPRISE AND ECONOMIC ORGANIZATION, Sixth Edition (1985)

Louis B. Schwartz, Professor of Law, Hastings College of the Law.
John J. Flynn, Professor of Law, University of Utah.
Harry First, Professor of Law, New York University.

JUVENILE JUSTICE PROCESS, Third Edition (1985)

Frank W. Miller, Professor of Law, Washington University.
Robert O. Dawson, Professor of Law, University of Texas.
George E. Dix, Professor of Law, University of Texas.
Raymond I. Parnas, Professor of Law, University of California, Davis.

LABOR LAW, Eleventh Edition (1991), with 1991 Statutory Supplement

Archibald Cox, Professor of Law, Harvard University.
Derek C. Bok, President, Harvard University.
Robert A. Gorman, Professor of Law, University of Pennsylvania.
Matthew W. Finkin, Professor of Law, University of Illinois.

LABOR LAW, Second Edition (1982), with Statutory Supplement

Clyde W. Summers, Professor of Law, University of Pennsylvania.
Harry H. Wellington, Dean of the Law School, Yale University.
Alan Hyde, Professor of Law, Rutgers University.

LAND FINANCING, Third Edition (1985)

The late Norman Penney, Professor of Law, Cornell University.
Richard F. Broude, Member of the California Bar.
Roger Cunningham, Professor of Law, University of Michigan.

LAW AND MEDICINE (1980)

Walter Wadlington, Professor of Law and Professor of Legal Medicine, University
  of Virginia.
Jon R. Waltz, Professor of Law, Northwestern University.
Roger B. Dworkin, Professor of Law, Indiana University, and Professor of
  Biomedical History, University of Washington.

LAW, LANGUAGE AND ETHICS (1972)

William R. Bishin, Professor of Law, University of Southern California.
Christopher D. Stone, Professor of Law, University of Southern California.

LAW, SCIENCE AND MEDICINE (1984), with 1989 Supplement

Judith C. Areen, Professor of Law, Georgetown University.
Patricia A. King, Professor of Law, Georgetown University.
Steven P. Goldberg, Professor of Law, Georgetown University.
Alexander M. Capron, Professor of Law, University of Southern California.

LAWYERING PROCESS (1978), with Civil Problem Supplement and Criminal Problem Supplement

Gary Bellow, Professor of Law, Harvard University.
Bea Moulton, Professor of Law, Arizona State University.

LEGAL ETHICS (1992)

Deborah Rhode, Professor of Law, Stanford University.
David Luban, Professor of Law, University of Maryland.

LEGAL METHOD (1980)

Harry W. Jones, Professor of Law Emeritus, Columbia University.
John M. Kernochan, Professor of Law, Columbia University.
Arthur W. Murphy, Professor of Law, Columbia University.

LEGAL METHODS (1969)

Robert N. Covington, Professor of Law, Vanderbilt University.
E. Blythe Stason, late Professor of Law, Vanderbilt University.
John W. Wade, Professor of Law, Vanderbilt University.
Elliott E. Cheatham, late Professor of Law, Vanderbilt University.
Theodore A. Smedley, Professor of Law, Vanderbilt University.

UNIVERSITY CASEBOOK SERIES—Continued

LEGAL PROFESSION, THE, Responsibility and Regulation, Second Edition (1988)

Geoffrey C. Hazard, Jr., Professor of Law, Yale University.
Deborah L. Rhode, Professor of Law, Stanford University.

LEGISLATION, Fourth Edition (1982) (by Fordham)

Horace E. Read, late Vice President, Dalhousie University.
John W. MacDonald, Professor of Law Emeritus, Cornell Law School.
Jefferson B. Fordham, Professor of Law, University of Utah.
William J. Pierce, Professor of Law, University of Michigan.

LEGISLATIVE AND ADMINISTRATIVE PROCESSES, Second Edition (1981)

Hans A. Linde, Judge, Supreme Court of Oregon.
George Bunn, Professor of Law, University of Wisconsin.
Fredericka Paff, Professor of Law, University of Wisconsin.
W. Lawrence Church, Professor of Law, University of Wisconsin.

LOCAL GOVERNMENT LAW, Second Revised Edition (1986)

Jefferson B. Fordham, Professor of Law, University of Utah.

MASS MEDIA LAW, Fourth Edition (1990)

Marc A. Franklin, Professor of Law, Stanford University.
David A. Anderson, Professor of Law, University of Texas.

MUNICIPAL CORPORATIONS, see Local Government Law

NEGOTIABLE INSTRUMENTS, see Commercial Paper

NEGOTIABLE INSTRUMENTS AND LETTERS OF CREDIT (1992) (Reprinted from Commercial Law) Third Edition (1992)

Robert L. Jordan, Professor of Law, University of California, Los Angeles.
William D. Warren, Professor of Law, University of California, Los Angeles.

NEGOTIATION (1981) (Reprinted from THE LAWYERING PROCESS)

Gary Bellow, Professor of Law, Harvard Law School.
Bea Moulton, Legal Services Corporation.

NEW YORK PRACTICE, Fourth Edition (1978)

Herbert Peterfreund, Professor of Law, New York University.
Joseph M. McLaughlin, Dean of the Law School, Fordham University.

OIL AND GAS, Sixth Edition (1992)

Richard C. Maxwell, Professor of Law, Duke University.
Stephen F. Williams, Judge of the United States Court of Appeals.
Patrick Henry Martin, Professor of Law, Louisiana State University.
Bruce M. Kramer, Professor of Law, Texas Tech University.

ON LAW IN COURTS (1965)

Paul J. Mishkin, Professor of Law, University of California, Berkeley.
Clarence Morris, Professor of Law Emeritus, University of Pennsylvania.

PENSION AND EMPLOYEE BENEFIT LAW (1990), with 1991 Supplement

John H. Langbein, Professor of Law, University of Chicago.
Bruce A. Wolk, Professor of Law, University of California, Davis.

PLEADING AND PROCEDURE, see Procedure, Civil

POLICE FUNCTION, Fifth Edition (1991), with 1991 Supplement

Reprint of Chapters 1–10 of Miller, Dawson, Dix and Parnas's CRIMINAL JUSTICE ADMINISTRATION, Fourth Edition.

PREPARING AND PRESENTING THE CASE (1981) (Reprinted from THE LAW-YERING PROCESS)

Gary Bellow, Professor of Law, Harvard Law School.
Bea Moulton, Legal Services Corporation.

PROCEDURE (1988), with Procedure Supplement (1991)

Robert M. Cover, late Professor of Law, Yale Law School.
Owen M. Fiss, Professor of Law, Yale Law School.
Judith Resnik, Professor of Law, University of Southern California Law Center.

PROCEDURE—CIVIL PROCEDURE, Sixth Edition (1990), with 1991 Supplement

Richard H. Field, late Professor of Law, Harvard University.
Benjamin Kaplan, Professor of Law Emeritus, Harvard University.
Kevin M. Clermont, Professor of Law, Cornell University.

PROCEDURE—CIVIL PROCEDURE, Successor Edition (1992)

A. Leo Levin, Professor of Law Emeritus, University of Pennsylvania.
Philip Shuchman, Professor of Law, Rutgers University.
Charles M. Yablon, Professor of Law, Yeshiva University.

PROCEDURE—CIVIL PROCEDURE, Fifth Edition (1990), with 1991 Supplement

Maurice Rosenberg, Professor of Law, Columbia University.
Hans Smit, Professor of Law, Columbia University.
Rochelle C. Dreyfuss, Professor of Law, New York University.

PROCEDURE—PLEADING AND PROCEDURE: State and Federal, Sixth Edition (1989), with 1991 Case Supplement

David W. Louisell, late Professor of Law, University of California, Berkeley.
Geoffrey C. Hazard, Jr., Professor of Law, Yale University.
Colin C. Tait, Professor of Law, University of Connecticut.

PROCEDURE—FEDERAL RULES OF CIVIL PROCEDURE, 1991 Edition

PRODUCTS LIABILITY AND SAFETY, Second Edition (1989), with 1989 Statutory Supplement

W. Page Keeton, Professor of Law, University of Texas.
David G. Owen, Professor of Law, University of South Carolina.
John E. Montgomery, Professor of Law, University of South Carolina.
Michael D. Green, Professor of Law, University of Iowa

PROFESSIONAL RESPONSIBILITY, Fifth Edition (1991), with 1992 Selected Standards on Professional Responsibility Supplement

Thomas D. Morgan, Professor of Law, George Washington University.
Ronald D. Rotunda, Professor of Law, University of Illinois.

PROPERTY, Sixth Edition (1990)

John E. Cribbet, Professor of Law, University of Illinois.
Corwin W. Johnson, Professor of Law, University of Texas.
Roger W. Findley, Professor of Law, University of Illinois.
Ernest E. Smith, Professor of Law, University of Texas.

PROPERTY—PERSONAL (1953)

S. Kenneth Skolfield, late Professor of Law Emeritus, Boston University.

PROPERTY—PERSONAL, Third Edition (1954)

Everett Fraser, late Dean of the Law School Emeritus, University of Minnesota.
Third Edition by Charles W. Taintor, late Professor of Law, University of Pittsburgh.

UNIVERSITY CASEBOOK SERIES—Continued

PROPERTY—INTRODUCTION, TO REAL PROPERTY, Third Edition (1954)

Everett Fraser, late Dean of the Law School Emeritus, University of Minnesota.

PROPERTY—FUNDAMENTALS OF MODERN REAL PROPERTY, Third Edition (1992)

Edward H. Rabin, Professor of Law, University of California, Davis.
Roberta Rosenthal Kwall, Professor of Law, DePaul University.

PROPERTY, REAL (1984), with 1988 Supplement

Paul Goldstein, Professor of Law, Stanford University.

PROSECUTION AND ADJUDICATION, Fourth Edition (1991), with 1991 Supplement

Reprint of Chapters 11–26 of Miller, Dawson, Dix and Parnas's CRIMINAL JUSTICE ADMINISTRATION, Fourth Edition.

PSYCHIATRY AND LAW, see Mental Health, see also Hinckley, Trial of

PUBLIC UTILITY LAW, see Free Enterprise, also Regulated Industries

REAL ESTATE PLANNING, Third Edition (1989), with Revised Problem and Statutory Supplement (1991)

Norton L. Steuben, Professor of Law, University of Colorado.

REAL ESTATE TRANSACTIONS, Revised Second Edition (1988), with Statute, Form and Problem Supplement (1988)

Paul Goldstein, Professor of Law, Stanford University.

RECEIVERSHIP AND CORPORATE REORGANIZATION, see Creditors' Rights

REGULATED INDUSTRIES, Second Edition (1976)

William K. Jones, Professor of Law, Columbia University.

REMEDIES, Third Edition (1992)

Edward D. Re, Professor of Law, St. John's University.
Stanton D. Krauss, Professor of Law, University of Bridgeport.

REMEDIES (1989)

Elaine W. Shoben, Professor of Law, University of Illinois.
Wm. Murray Tabb, Professor of Law, Baylor University.

SALES, Third Edition (1992)

Marion W. Benfield, Jr., Professor of Law, Wake Forest University.
William D. Hawkland, Professor of Law, Louisiana State Law Center.

SALES (1992) (Reprinted from Commercial Law) Third Edition (1992)

Robert L. Jordan, Professor of Law, University of California, Los Angeles.
William D. Warren, Professor of Law, University of California, Los Angeles.

SALES AND SALES FINANCING, Fifth Edition (1984)

John Honnold, Professor of Law, University of Pennsylvania.

SALES LAW AND THE CONTRACTING PROCESS, Second Edition (1991) (Reprinted from Commercial Transactions) Second Edition (1991)

Alan Schwartz, Professor of Law, Yale University.
Robert E. Scott, Professor of Law, University of Virginia.

TAXATION, FEDERAL INCOME, OF BUSINESS ORGANIZATIONS (1991), with 1991 Supplement

Paul R. McDaniel, Professor of Law, Boston College.
Hugh J. Ault, Professor of Law, Boston College.
Martin J. McMahon, Jr., Professor of Law, University of Kentucky.
Daniel L. Simmons, Professor of Law, University of California, Davis.

TAXATION, FEDERAL INCOME, OF PARTNERSHIPS AND S CORPORATIONS (1991), with 1991 Supplement

Paul R. McDaniel, Professor of Law, Boston College.
Hugh J. Ault, Professor of Law, Boston College.
Martin J. McMahon, Jr., Professor of Law, University of Kentucky.
Daniel L. Simmons, Professor of Law, University of California, Davis.

TAXATION, FEDERAL INCOME, OIL AND GAS, NATURAL RESOURCES TRANSACTIONS (1990)

Peter C. Maxfield, Professor of Law, University of Wyoming.
James L. Houghton, CPA, Partner, Ernst and Young.
James R. Gaar, CPA, Partner, Ernst and Young.

TAXATION, FEDERAL WEALTH TRANSFER, Successor Edition (1987)

Stanley S. Surrey, late Professor of Law, Harvard University.
Paul R. McDaniel, Professor of Law, Boston College.
Harry L. Gutman, Professor of Law, University of Pennsylvania.

TAXATION, FUNDAMENTALS OF CORPORATE, Third Edition (1991)

Stephen A. Lind, Professor of Law, University of Florida and University of California, Hastings.
Stephen Schwarz, Professor of Law, University of California, Hastings.
Daniel J. Lathrope, Professor of Law, University of California, Hastings.
Joshua Rosenberg, Professor of Law, University of San Francisco.

TAXATION, FUNDAMENTALS OF PARTNERSHIP, Third Edition (1992)

Stephen A. Lind, Professor of Law, University of Florida and University of California, Hastings.
Stephen Schwarz, Professor of Law, University of California, Hastings.
Daniel J. Lathrope, Professor of Law, University of California, Hastings.
Joshua Rosenberg, Professor of Law, University of San Francisco.

TAXATION OF CORPORATIONS AND THEIR SHAREHOLDERS (1991)

David J. Shakow, Professor of Law, University of Pennsylvania.

TAXATION, PROBLEMS IN THE FEDERAL INCOME TAXATION OF PARTNER-SHIPS AND CORPORATIONS, Second Edition (1986)

Norton L. Steuben, Professor of Law, University of Colorado.
William J. Turnier, Professor of Law, University of North Carolina.

TAXATION, PROBLEMS IN THE FUNDAMENTALS OF FEDERAL INCOME, Second Edition (1985)

Norton L. Steuben, Professor of Law, University of Colorado.
William J. Turnier, Professor of Law, University of North Carolina.

TORT LAW AND ALTERNATIVES, Fifth Edition (1992)

Marc A. Franklin, Professor of Law, Stanford University.
Robert L. Rabin, Professor of Law, Stanford University.

TORTS, Eighth Edition (1988)

William L. Prosser, late Professor of Law, University of California, Hastings.
John W. Wade, Professor of Law, Vanderbilt University.
Victor E. Schwartz, Adjunct Professor of Law, Georgetown University.

TORTS, Third Edition (1976)

Harry Shulman, late Dean of the Law School, Yale University.
Fleming James, Jr., Professor of Law Emeritus, Yale University.
Oscar S. Gray, Professor of Law, University of Maryland.

TRADE REGULATION, Third Edition (1990)

Milton Handler, Professor of Law Emeritus, Columbia University.
Harlan M. Blake, Professor of Law, Columbia University.
Robert Pitofsky, Professor of Law, Georgetown University.
Harvey J. Goldschmid, Professor of Law, Columbia University.

TRADE REGULATION, see Antitrust

TRANSNATIONAL BUSINESS PROBLEMS (1986)

Detlev F. Vagts, Professor of Law, Harvard University.

TRANSNATIONAL LEGAL PROBLEMS, Third Edition (1986), with 1991 Revised Edition of Documentary Supplement

Henry J. Steiner, Professor of Law, Harvard University.
Detlev F. Vagts, Professor of Law, Harvard University.

TRIAL, see also Evidence, Making the Record, Lawyering Process and Preparing and Presenting the Case

TRUSTS, Sixth Edition (1991)

George G. Bogert, late Professor of Law Emeritus, University of Chicago.
Dallin H. Oaks, President, Brigham Young University.
H. Reese Hansen, Dean and Professor of Law, Brigham Young University.
Claralyn Martin Hill, J.D. Brigham Young University.

TRUSTS AND ESTATES, SELECTED STATUTES ON, 1992 Edition

TRUSTS AND WILLS, See also Decedents' Estates and Trusts, and Family Property Law

UNFAIR COMPETITION, see Competitive Process and Business Torts

WATER RESOURCE MANAGEMENT, Third Edition (1988), with 1992 Supplement

The late Charles J. Meyers, formerly Dean, Stanford University Law School.
A. Dan Tarlock, Professor of Law, IIT Chicago-Kent College of Law.
James N. Corbridge, Jr., Chancellor, University of Colorado at Boulder, and Professor of Law, University of Colorado.
David H. Getches, Professor of Law, University of Colorado.

WOMEN AND THE LAW (1992)

Mary Joe Frug, late Professor of Law, New England School of Law.

WILLS AND ADMINISTRATION, Fifth Edition (1961)

Philip Mechem, late Professor of Law, University of Pennsylvania.
Thomas E. Atkinson, late Professor of Law, New York University.

WRITING AND ANALYSIS IN THE LAW, Second Edition (1991)

Helene S. Shapo, Professor of Law, Northwestern University.
Marilyn R. Walter, Professor of Law, Brooklyn Law School.
Elizabeth Fajans, Writing Specialist, Brooklyn Law School.

University Casebook Series

CASES AND MATERIALS

ON

FUNDAMENTALS

OF

FEDERAL INCOME TAXATION

By

JAMES J. FREELAND

Distinguished Service Professor of Law, University of Florida

STEPHEN A. LIND

Professor of Law, University of Florida and Professor
of Law, Hastings Law School

RICHARD B. STEPHENS

Professor of Law, Emeritus, University of Florida

SEVENTH EDITION

Westbury, New York
THE FOUNDATION PRESS, INC.
1991

Library of Congress Cataloging-in-Publication Data

Freeland, James J., 1927–
    Cases and materials on fundamentals of federal income taxation /
by James J. Freeland, Stephen A. Lind, Richard B. Stephens. — 7th
ed.
        p.   cm. — (University casebook series)
    Includes index.
    ISBN 0–88277–891–9
    1. Income tax—Law and legislation—United States—Cases.
I. Lind, Stephen A.   II. Stephens, Richard B.   III. Title.
IV. Series.
KF6368.F69   1991
343.7305'2—dc20
[347.30352]   91–13884

F., L. & S. Fed.Income Tax. 7th Ed. UCB
1st Reprint—1992

∞

This book is dedicated to our co-author
RICHARD B. STEPHENS
in appreciation for all that he taught us about taxation,
about writing and about life itself.

*

PREFACE

During the lifespan of the Sixth Edition of this book, our co-author, RICHARD B. STEPHENS, died. This book is dedicated to him. Dick's gift with words is demonstrated by the Preface that he wrote to the Sixth Edition which is substantially republished as the Preface to this Seventh Edition. Dick's words, cogent and timely then, remain so today:

Tar, pitch, and turpentine, all begins with a. Look again. Tricky, isn't it? The federal income tax law is tricky, too. Confronted by protesting students, a colleague used to say, "It's the law that's tricky, not I." You are about to begin to enjoy learning some of the tricks.

The Internal Revenue Code, the glue that holds together the pages of this book, is complex. Perhaps it is the Rubik's Cube of legislation. But even the marvels of the prestidigitator lose their mystery when some of his methods are disclosed.

Tax books are perishable—not much affected by freeze but fragile when it comes to political heat. The law has been called evanescent, fleeting. And in some respects the description is apt when Congress changes its mind as often as it has in the past decade or so. If we could we would call: "Time out!" But that is why we are here soon after an earlier edition, at the beginning of the Sixth Edition of this book, which is responsive to very comprehensive legislation that makes it no longer possible to "Take the Fifth."

If tax law is tricky, complex, and perishable, do we suggest despair? By no means! For one thing, our national fiscal system, at least until such time as we can adopt a better one, has a very great need for lawyers who are competent in the area of taxation. A plug here for "the arts:" We think the best professional is one who has had a broad education, followed by comprehensive legal study, capped by technical tax training. But whatever! The object of this book is to aid in your technical tax training.

Moreover, the *fundamentals* of federal taxation have a very long shelf life: One *could* profitably study now the First Edition of this book. *Basic* concepts of income, deduction, rates, and credits appear there in some cases with astonishing similarity and in all cases in a manner that would aid in the understanding of today's concepts. Although we watch frequent additions, corrections, and amendments, they are rather like hanging meat on the skeleton of the Brontesaurus; underneath the structure remains much the same.

As its title indicates, the purpose of this book is to aid in the teaching of the fundamentals of the federal income tax. The accomplishment of such a purpose involves, first, a selective determination of basic principles and concepts and, second, a decision of the manner and depth of treatment of the matters that are deemed fundamental. There is wide room for disagreement on both points. Nevertheless, the authors are confident that a thoughtful study of the materials presented in this book will afford the student a good income tax foundation. Those who do not proceed beyond the fundamentals may not be "tax experts," but at least they will have a useful awareness of how the federal income tax impinges on practically everything that goes on in our society and economy. Others will have a good basis for enlarging their tax knowledge through advanced law school courses, or graduate study, or practice, or some combination of all three.

Although the major tax legislation of 1986 is called "reform," it [and we would add, subsequent legislation] moves us further away from the dream of simplicity, even fails to effect any simplification. The demands made of the tax lawyer are heavy; but legal educators need to keep in mind that a practitioner must be a lawyer first and a tax lawyer only second. The tax lawyer should receive the bulk of his specialized training either through graduate study or, in the time-honored tradition of the legal profession, through his own scholarly efforts in practice. In law school some tax study may be essential for all, but not to the point that law school becomes trade school at the expense of the study of jurisprudence, comparative law and other courses needed to develop perspective.

The approach taken in this book to various aspects of the income tax varies from one of great attention to detail to one of very general descriptive notes. These differences are not haphazard. For one thing, the authors, although aware of time limitations, are certain that to present a uniformly general survey approach to income taxation would be a meaningless exercise, a serious disservice to students and a waste of faculty energy and time. A substantial amount of detailed study and analysis, selectively presented, is the only way to achieve a basic understanding of what federal taxation is all about.

What we have done is attempt to make the detailed study portions of the book serve a second purpose of giving the student a tight grasp of tax concepts and principles that are of wide application and importance. For example, the "gotcha" (I.R.C. Section 1245, the first broad recapture provision which makes its appearance in Chapter 22) is examined closely both as to purpose and effect, because both it and other related recapture provisions crop up repeatedly, and they frequently affect all types of taxpayers, individuals, trusts, partnerships, corporations, and so forth. Section 1245 is primarily a characterization provision and although the concept of characterization is not as significant as in the past, it still retains some vitality. On the other hand, with regard to restrictions on deductions (considered in Chapter 17) the effect of illegality or impropriety on the deductibility of an expenditure, although it has been the subject of several interesting and highly "teachable" Supreme Court decisions, is relegated to an explanatory note that discusses the cases, because the problem is of far less frequent occurrence. We are content to present the constitutional status of the income tax by way of a note. When the modern income tax was first enacted in 1913, almost every conceivable constitutional objection was raised against it; and various objections dealt with in the note should be known to the student, even though they do not have much current importance. There is a current need to guard against constitutional tax principles falling into a state of innocuous desuetude.

Students should also have some understanding of tax procedure, which they can get from Chapters 28, 29 and 30, presented as text, even if busy instructors find no class time for this material.

There are some matters that must be classified as important which are not dealt with in detail. For example, deferred compensation arrangements, touched on in Chapter 20, affect the lives of millions of taxpaying employers and employees. And the tax rules applicable to trusts, partnerships, and corporations accorded only sparing recognition in Chapter 13 with regard to problems of assignment of income, also must be classified as important on the basis of any similar numerical test. Nevertheless, it simply cannot all be done in a basic course. And so, of necessity, some important matters are alluded to in notes but not considered in detail and are left for development in additional income tax courses at the J.D. or LL.M. level. The first edition of this book anticipated this trend which continues. A study of the taxation of individuals is the beginning, and it will serve as the cornerstone on which additional income tax courses can rest.

Brief note treatment of some matters not presented in detail reflects an effort to resist the academic compulsion to appear erudite. The purpose of such notes is only to create a general awareness. We know more about some of these matters, but it is more than we choose to tell. In this spirit we have resisted the inclination to let the book "grow." Nevertheless, references are often included to more nourishing books and articles that may be of assistance if, at another time, the student would undertake his own detailed exploration of an area.

The authors have attempted to take account of the fact that students arrive at their first law school tax course with a wide variety of educational and other experiences. Those who have little accounting background are apprehensive and likely to feel they "will not like tax." This attitude, as we know, is not fully justified, and experience has shown that many of these people will find a new dimension in tax law. Nevertheless, in many instances in which instruction is bound to encroach on the domain of the accountant, an effort is made, sometimes through informative comment such as the note on depreciation in Chapter 22 and on inventories in Chapter 19, to render the material manageable regardless of the student's background knowledge. Sometimes we are sneaky too, for example, by using the caption "Timing," rather than the intimidating term "Accounting." Moreover if, partly due to past lack of experience, the present study seems to get off to a slow beginning, the student may anticipate a quickening pace as later chapters unfold. In fact, most students will discern a mounting crescendo with something in the nature of fireworks at the end of the show. If an instructor deems procedure (Chapters 28 through 30) too unlike fireworks, he can select his own high note on which to end.

Many of the judicial opinions and other documents quoted in this work have fallen prey to our editorial license. Deletions are indicated conventionally by the use of ellipses and asterisks, and editorial additions are bracketed. Where necessary, footnotes are renumbered to take account of omissions. In general, the materials included are based on the status of the law [in early 1991.]

The authors acknowledge an indebtedness to the hundreds of law students who have passed through their classes over a combined teaching period approaching 100 years. Not only have these young men and women served as guinea pigs for various experiments; their perception and insight have been a part of the continuing education of their instructors, making former students substantial contributors to the form and substance of this book.

Over the years, numerous intelligent and industrious students at law schools where the authors were teaching have served as assistants in the preparation of the several prior editions of this book. It may not be sufficient but we seek to preserve a sign of our gratitude to them by listing their names at the end of this preface. Students who have worked with us on this edition and to whom our thanks are due are: Mike Brittingham, Mari Gaines, Jay Katz, Mike Little and Phil Tingle.

PREFACE

The essential procedure of mind to machine to publisher was accomplished by Jude Gilbert, Lena Hinson and Lorraine White.

Students to whom our thanks are due for assistance on prior editions are: Jeff Anthony, Bernie Barton, Craig Bonnell, David Bowen, David Brownhill, Andrew Coblentz, Chris Detzel, Nat Doliner, Mary Sue Donsky, Bruce Ellisen, Susan Elsey, Alan Friedman, Paul Johnson, Garo Kalfayan, Robin Kaufman, Kevin Keenan, Peter Kirkwood, Mel Knotts, Jack Levine, Steve Looney, Paul Lundberg, Tom McClendon, Michael O'Leary, Tim Patterson, Kendall Patton, Greg Rovenger, Sharon Selk, Chuck Tallant, Steve Voglesang, Kenneth Wheeler and Sue York.

RICHARD B. STEPHENS

June, 1987

JAMES J. FREELAND
and
STEPHEN A. LIND

May, 1991

*

SUMMARY OF CONTENTS

xi

TABLE OF CONTENTS

PART ONE: INTRODUCTION

PART TWO: IDENTIFICATION OF INCOME SUBJECT TO TAXATION

PART THREE: IDENTIFICATION OF THE PROPER TAXPAYER

PART SEVEN: DEFERRAL AND NONRECOGNITION OF INCOME AND DEDUCTIONS

PART EIGHT: CONVERTING TAXABLE INCOME INTO TAX LIABILITY

TABLE OF INTERNAL REVENUE CODE SECTIONS

TABLE OF INTERNAL REVENUE CODE SECTIONS

TABLE OF INTERNAL REVENUE CODE SECTIONS

xxii

TABLE OF INTERNAL REVENUE CODE SECTIONS

TABLE OF INTERNAL REVENUE CODE SECTIONS

TABLE OF INTERNAL REVENUE CODE SECTIONS

xxix

TABLE OF INTERNAL REVENUE CODE SECTIONS

TABLE OF INTERNAL REVENUE CODE SECTIONS

TABLE OF INTERNAL REVENUE CODE SECTIONS

TABLE OF INTERNAL REVENUE CODE SECTIONS

xl

TABLE OF INTERNAL REVENUE CODE SECTIONS

TABLE OF INTERNAL REVENUE CODE SECTIONS

TABLE OF INTERNAL REVENUE CODE SECTIONS

xlix

TABLE OF INTERNAL REVENUE CODE SECTIONS

1

TABLE OF TREASURY REGULATIONS

TABLE OF TREASURY REGULATIONS

liv

TABLE OF TREASURY REGULATIONS

*

TABLE OF INTERNAL REVENUE RULINGS

Rulings with accompanying text are indicated by italic type.

lix

TABLE OF MISCELLANEOUS RULINGS

*

TABLE OF CASES

Principal cases are in italic type. Non-principal cases are in roman type. References are to Pages.

*

TABLE OF AUTHORITIES

References are to Pages

*

CASES AND MATERIALS

ON

FUNDAMENTALS

OF

FEDERAL INCOME
TAXATION

*

PART ONE: INTRODUCTION

CHAPTER 1. ORIENTATION

A. A LOOK FORWARD

The question is: What can you tell a law student that will help to make him a good tax student? We have no universal *vade mecum* and no hope to emulate the wisdom of Polonius in his advice to Laertes. Nevertheless, having watched hundreds of law students in the beginning, middle, and never-ending process of learning about the federal income tax, the authors offer a few remarks that may be helpful.

A student may find unexpected excitement in the study of the income tax. The uninitiated are likely to think of taxes as a kind of sterile game of questions and answers, largely involving only arithmetic and little philosophy. Forget it! Nice reasoning and a careful consideration of underlying (often non-tax) policy considerations lurk behind every legislative tax effort, every administrative determination of the Treasury Department, every judicial decision in cases of tax controversy, and all but routine struggles of taxpayers, their counsel, and students to arrive at proper tax conclusions.

You are undertaking a study in communication. English majors take heart; the use of the language is as important here as it is in any area of the law. But of course other prior training and experience are likewise helpful. There is no such thing as pure tax law. Instead, tax principles relate to events and transactions that would go on even if there were no federal income tax, although many events and transactions are shaped by an awareness of relevant tax principles. There is a clue here to the nature of your study. You must be sure you understand what it is that is happening which gives rise to the tax question. You may have to learn a little (or a little more) about the respective rights and obligations of a mortgagor and mortgagee before you can properly appraise the tax consequences of their transactions; you may have to ponder the nature of interspousal payments in cases of divorce or separation before you can attempt to say how the tax laws will treat either spouse; and you must learn about annuity and endowment contracts if you would like to discover how Congress taxes (or relieves from tax) amounts that are received under such agreements. In the pages that follow, a case or a note will often be of assistance in this subordinate but important endeavor. As you know, taxes are so pervasive that the above examples could be extended indefinitely. But, while these remarks are intended as a word of caution to the neophyte, an encouraging note should also be detected. It is the very diversity of

1

circumstances giving rise to tax questions that makes tax study appealing to many. It is difficult to imagine any more broadening endeavor, for tax questions lead one into all segments of law and society often raising, at least indirectly, broad social, economic, and political considerations. Every substantive course in any law school's curriculum has an outer ripple of tax ramifications.

The communications study being undertaken is learning to decipher the messages of the Internal Revenue Code. This is not quite akin to foreign language study for, after all, the Code is written in English, and it is quite correct in matters of grammar and syntax. If it falters occasionally rhetorically, this is not the usual rule. The messages are there, in general written with about as much clarity as is possible, allowing for the complexity of the thoughts expressed. The origin of the present statute, indicated briefly in the next part of this chapter, may increase your respect for the document with which you are dealing. Our suggestion here, then, is not to throw down the statute in exasperation when an initial look at a provision does not provide much nourishment. Struggle with the language, rejecting the notion that it is not understandable and with confidence that persistence will pay off. This is an essential part of your training. The cryptic language of the Code has a key, a style which you, as have others before you, can learn to decipher.

We wrote the foregoing paragraph almost twenty years ago in the first edition of this book. It is essentially still true; but successive legislative events in recent years have strained our patience and somewhat dampened our conviction. The Code, formerly a carefully crafted document has succumbed to an assembly-line type of product of political and economic expediency. As one might expect, quality control in drafting and substantive content have suffered. The assembly-line product of 1986 is the law. The messages are still there and are understandable but so is the plastic dashboard. Your persistence, but lots of it, will pay off.

Just reading the Internal Revenue Code in cold blood is neither very much fun nor very productive. It must be read with an eye toward the circumstances to which its messages are directed. As you move into this course you will quickly see how hopeless it would be to try to teach the fundamentals of federal income taxation with the Code as the only material to be studied by students. Among other things, this explains repeated references in the pages that follow to selected provisions in the Regulations. For there, sometimes by way of narrative and often by way of illustration, you will gain an understanding of what the cryptic statutory rules are all about. We venture this prediction concerning the progress of a student who goes about his study in the right way: (1) He will read the assigned provision in the statute without very much comprehension. (2) He will study the assigned material in the Regulations with growing awareness. (3) He will return to what seems almost new statutory language, even discovering words in the statute which initially he did not realize were there.

This third phrase involves what German psychologists call a "gestalt." A student once more quaintly characterized the third stage as "hitting the Ah hah! button."

The process just described suggests growth but not maturity and admittedly the "gestalt" does not always arrive on schedule. Moreover, even as general awareness grows, different people will derive somewhat different meanings from the same language, much as two cooks following the same recipe will bake rather different cakes. And so there is need for further effort toward understanding. The materials that appear in the following pages of this book, cases, rulings, committee reports, notes, problems, etc., are presented as an aid to that effort.

Tax practice is of two main types: (1) An application of tax principles to past events or transactions, and (2) Advice as to how tax principles will apply to proposed events or transactions. The more interesting and rewarding activity is of the latter, planning type. But in either case, a prediction is called for. The tax practitioner must attempt to say how the administration and the courts will deal with the circumstances with which he is presented; indeed he must often, also, attempt to foresee possible *legislative* change. We now begin to see the need for a kind of two-phase approach to tax study—what may be called a Why? Why? approach.[1]

Why do we postulate a particular answer to a tax probem? The bible tells us so. That is, the Code provides, or seems to provide, this answer. But then *why* did Congress write this provision into the Code? Here we are in the realm of policy; why are we concerned with this second "why?" To be sure, a great many tax questions can be answered routinely without major struggle. But by his second year a law student is aware of the frailities of the language, of the necessarily short-hand nature of statutory language, of substantial uncertainties as to meaning in varying circumstances. The second "why?" calls for knowledge that may bear heavily on meaning in cases of obscurity; and it also has a direct bearing on the matter of predicting possible legislative change. For example: Why did Congress provide the regular investment tax credit in 1962? Why did Congress terminate it in 1969? Was its restoration in 1971 predictable? What about further tinkering with the credit in 1975, a gloomy economic year? Why did the Tax Reform Act of 1976 extend the 10 percent credit for four years and make other minor changes? Why did the Economic Recovery Tax Act of 1981 retain and further liberalize the credit provisions? Why did the Tax Equity and Fiscal Responsibility Act of 1982 impose some restrictions on use of the credit? Why were further restrictions imposed on the credit in the Tax Reform Act of 1984? Why did Congress again repeal it in 1986. Will it be resurrected in our next serious economic downturn?

1. Since the first edition of this book was published, the authors have learned that, while the normal owl says "Who? Who?, the psychotic owl says "Why? Why?" but we persist.

There are several by-products to seeking an understanding of the reasons behind tax legislation. For one thing, it makes the study far more interesting; a comparison might be the appeal of Euclidian geometry over elementary arithmetic. Secondly, the knowledge acquired has much longer life and usefulness. Finally, this is the *only* way to develop any comfortable feel for prediction in areas that cannot properly be regarded as settled. Of course, the policy reasons behind a statutory provision are not always discernible; one recalls the tradesman's classic reply: "There's no reason for it; it's just our policy!" But if there really is no reason (or perhaps no longer is any reason) for a legislative rule, is this in itself a basis for predicting legislative change, or at least narrow judicial interpretation?

It is also a truism that "the life of the law is not logic but experience." Judicial notions of what is sound policy often affect the way in which statutory language is read and not infrequently present the student with surprise interpretations quite at variance with his own possibly reasonable, literal reading of the statute. Thus, experience is essential to tax practice but, on any given matter, some experience can be gained quite quickly vicariously. As a student you begin the process of gaining experience by reliving the tax controversies of others, which are presented in numerous cases and rulings that appear in the pages that follow. The controversies of others serve as a catalyst to your analysis of the Code.

In most parts of this book problems appear, which the student is expected to work out. Usually, he can arrive at supportable answers on the basis of the related assigned materials. Proper effort in this regard teaches the required close reading of the statute and, gradually, yields a more comfortable feeling about wading into fresh thickets of Code verbiage. But enough difficult questions and questions to which authoritative answers seem surprising are included to create also a healthy skepticism. In many instances in which answers are elusive or unexpected a case or ruling is cited, which may be considered when the student has attempted his own analysis. The discovery, appraisal and persuasive use of precedent are as important in tax cases as in others.

Now it must be admitted that tax study presents the student with a mass of material, statutory and otherwise. Practice is of course no different in this respect. It is equally obvious that not everything can be learned at the same time, and the authors feel that initial study must be episodic rather than comprehensive. As in other law school courses, you must constantly ask yourself where you are. And you may not always be quite sure, just as the blind man's initial impression of an elephant depends upon whether he first grasps the trunk or the tail. We venture three suggestions here. After examining the brief historical, constitutional and policy discussions that follow in the next three segments of this chapter, study the last portion entitled "The Road Ahead". An effort is made there to give you an overview of the areas covered by this book. It would then be wise to take a careful look at the table of contents. While it will not now be perfectly meaningful, it will give you a start toward orientation. And, as you proceed with your study, pay attention to chapter headings and subheadings. This is obviously good practice in any course as an aid to directing pre-class efforts. Finally, as you go along consciously prepare your own notes for subsequent review. Again this is not a novel thought. But it can well be said that in the course of tax study knowledge grows with geometric rather than arithmetic progression; and the more you learn the greater your learning capacity. That which is obscure and difficult at the beginning of the course will become relatively clear and easy toward the end, as broader comprehension aids perception. Hours spent in review at the end may provide a greater yield than hours spent at the beginning, but only if the requisite hours *were* spent at the beginning.

B. A GLIMPSE BACKWARD

Historians often give too little recognition to the federal income tax despite its profound impact on political, economic, and social developments in the United States.[1] We do not attempt in any comprehensive way to fill that gap. An excellent brief "Historical Overview" appears in Surrey, McDaniel, Ault and Koppelman, Federal Income Taxation: Cases and Materials, vol. 1, pp. 1–17 (Foundation Press 1986), which includes references to principal historical source materials; and a useful "Brief History" of early developments may be found in Griswold and Graetz, *Federal Income Taxation: Principles and Policies*, pp. 2–6 (2d Ed. Foundation Press 1988). Among other works looking back more comprehensively at income taxation in the United States are Paul, Taxation in the United States (1954), and Blakey, The Federal Income Tax (1940). Probing the legislative history of specific statutory provisions is facilitated by Seidman, Legislative History of Federal Income Tax Laws, 1953–1939 (1954); Seidman, Legislative History of Federal Income Tax Laws, 1938–1861 (1938); Goldstein, Barton's Federal Tax Laws Correlated (1968). There are numerous historical references in subsequent chapters of this book, which are an aid to understanding specific provisions in the income tax laws. Some further comments are in order here regarding the origin of the present income tax statute.

The Congressional Joint Committee on Internal Revenue Taxation has summarized the first one hundred and fifty years of internal revenue taxation as follows:[2]

LAWS PRIOR TO 1939

The first internal-revenue tax law was enacted on March 3, 1791, and imposed a tax on distilled spirits and stills. This was followed by legislation imposing taxes upon carriages, retail dealers in wines and foreign spirituous liquors, snuff, refined sugar, property sold at auction, legal instruments, real

---

1. See, e.g., Samuel Eliot Morison's otherwise excellent History of the American People (1965).

2. "Codification of Internal Revenue Law," p. IX (1939), reproduced at 26 U.S.C.A. XIX–XX.

estate and slaves. All of these taxes and the offices created for their enforcement were abolished in 1802. During this first era of taxation the internal-revenue receipts amounted to only $6,758,764.26. Comparing this with the receipts for the fiscal year 1938, amounting to $5,658,765,314, it will be noted that the Internal Revenue Service collects at the present time more than twice as much from internal-revenue taxes in one day as the original organization collected in 10 years. [The "present time" was 1939. Collections now approach seven hundred and fifty billion dollars annually. Ed.]

Due to the necessities occasioned by the War of 1812, internal-revenue taxes were again imposed in 1813. These taxes were levied on refined sugar, carriages, distillers, sales at auction, distilled spirits, manufactured articles, household furniture, watches, gold, silver, plated ware, jewelry, real estate, and slaves. An officer known as the Commissioner of Revenues was in charge of the administration of such taxes. All these taxes were repealed by the act of December 23, 1817, and the office of Commissioner of Revenues was discontinued, effective upon the completion of the collection of the outstanding taxes. The collections during the 5–year period from 1813 to 1818 amounted to $25,833,449.43.

For a period of 43 years, namely, 1818 to 1861, no internal-revenue taxes were imposed. On July 6, 1861, an act was passed imposing a tax on incomes and real property. No income tax was ever collected under this act, and all of the tax collected on real property was returned to the States under authority of the act of March 2, 1891.

The act of July 1, 1862, is largely the basis of our present system of taxation. It contained the first law under which any income tax was collected, and it created the office of Commissioner of Internal Revenue. It taxed practically everything which Congress thought was susceptible of yielding revenue. The three sources of revenue which remained for a long time the backbone of the internal revenue system, namely, spirits, tobacco, and beer, received particular attention from the lawmakers.

The internal-revenue laws were first codified in the Revised Statutes of 1873, Title XXXV, which was made absolute law. A perfected edition of the Revised Statutes was prepared in 1878, but was only prima facie, not absolute law. The internal-revenue laws were again codified in Title 26 of the United States Code, which was enacted as prima facie law in 1924. Scrutiny of the Code was invited in its preface for the purpose of correcting errors, eliminating obsolete matter, and restatement.

In 1930, the Joint Committee on Internal Revenue Taxation published a complete substitute for Title 26 of the United States Code, containing all the law of a permanent character, relating exclusively to internal revenue, in force on December 1, 1930. This was not a mere duplication of the old Title, for in addition to correcting errors and eliminating obsolete matter, certain omitted provisions were added and the Title completely rearranged in a manner considered logical and useful.

In 1933, a new edition was published containing the internal-revenue laws in force on July 16, 1932. This edition was substituted for Title 26 of the United States Code, and was prima facie law. A third edition was published in 1938, containing the internal-revenue laws in force at the beginning of that year.

Prior to 1939, the mere ascertainment of statutory provisions that might affect the determination of a tax question threw the tax practitioner into the hodge-podge of the Statutes at Large. Happily, a 1939 development relieved the practitioner (but not necessarily the scholar) from this awkwardness, except as regards transitional problems that reached back to earlier years. The Report of the Ways and Means Committee on the Bill that became the Internal Revenue Code of 1939 [3] included the following statement:

THE NEED OF AN INTERNAL REVENUE CODE

The need for enactment into absolute law of a codification of internal revenue laws has long been recognized. The last such enactment was in 1874, when the Revised Statutes were adopted. If the need for enactment into law of a codification was recognized in 1874, when only 17 volumes of the Statutes at Large had been published and our internal revenue was derived almost entirely from taxes on liquor and tobacco, that need must be much greater today, when 34 additional volumes have been published and our internal revenue is derived from more than a hundred separate sources.

The United States Code is itself the culmination of more than 30 years' effort. Due to the mass of legislation contained in that Code, it was thought best by the Congress to put it through a testing period before its enactment into law. It was, therefore, made only prima facie evidence of the law, and scrutiny of it was invited for the purpose of correcting errors, eliminating obsolete matter, and restatement.

The review and correction of the internal revenue title was begun by the staff of the Joint Committee on Internal Revenue Taxation after the enactment of the Revenue Act of 1928. The first edition of the work was published in 1930 and the second,

3. H.Rep. No. 6, 76th Cong., 1st Sess.
(1939) 1939–2 C.B. 532–533.

in 1933. The second edition was substituted for Title 26 of the United States Code and became, therefore, prima facie evidence of the law.

It has now been nearly 13 years since the United States Code was enacted as prima facie law and more than 8 years since the first edition of the Internal Revenue Code was published by the staff of the joint committee. However, because the internal revenue title is not the law, but only prima facie evidence thereof, it can not be relied upon and it is still necessary to go to the many volumes of the Statutes at Large to determine what the law actually is. The great mass of internal revenue legislation since 1873, scattered through 34 volumes of the Statutes at Large, makes such a recourse an exceedingly difficult undertaking, even for the most experienced lawyer. Statutes are repeated in subsequent Acts in almost identical language, with no reference to prior Acts or any expressed intention to amend or repeal. Provisions of a permanent character are included in riders and provisos and are hidden in various Acts. Amendments are often involved and obscure. Inconsistencies and duplications abound.

The only practical way to determine with certainty that the Internal Revenue Code is actually the law is to enact it, as was done with the Revised Statutes of 1873. It is believed that it has had a sufficient testing period to make it acceptable as free from error.

* * *

This Code contains all the law of a general and permanent character relating exclusively to internal revenue in force on January 2, 1939. In addition, it contains the internal revenue law relating to temporary taxes, the occasion for which arises after the enactment of the Code. The following should be noted in connection with the general character of the Code:

First. It makes no changes in existing law.

Second. It makes liberal use of catchwords, headlines, different types, indentations, and other typographical improvements.

Third. By a system of cross-references, it correlates not only its own provisions but also provisions of the United States Code not relating exclusively to internal revenue.

Fourth. To obviate confusion with the law itself, the cross-references are in type different from that containing the law.

Fifth. It is arranged with a view of giving prominence to matters which concern the ordinary transactions of the ordinary classes of taxpayers.

The preparation of this Code began with the collection and examination of all original statutes relating to internal revenue, without reference to the United States Code. This procedure allowed an independent check to be made subsequently against that Code. The next step was the elimination of obsolete matter and those temporary provisions relating to taxes the occasion for which arose prior to the effective date of the Code. The most striking examples of the temporary laws which are omitted are the income tax provisions of the Revenue Act of 1936 and prior Revenue Acts. While these provisions remain in force for the purpose of administering the taxes for the earlier years, they do not affect the current tax situation.

After the elimination of the obsolete and temporary provisions from the whole body of internal revenue law, the remaining provisions were checked against the United States Code. The care in the preparation of the United States Code and in the present codification gives assurance of the accuracy of the final product. Moreover, every provision has been carefully reviewed and checked by the Treasury Department and conferences have been held and agreements reached on all issues.

There are many laws of a general character which, though relating to internal revenue, apply also to other objects. To codify such laws under internal revenue, however, would disrupt the entire title structure of the United States Code and render complete codification of Federal law impossible. In only a few instances has any provision been taken from any title of the United States Code other than the internal revenue title, and then only for the reason that such provision relates exclusively to internal revenue. The great value of the United States Code is thus preserved. Moreover, detailed cross-references compensate for any deficiency due to such a procedure by acquainting the reader both with the general subject of the provision referred to and its location in the United States Code.

The 1939 effort was largely a matter of sorting and putting together currently operative internal revenue statutes—*codification*. Even so, the result was the tax practitioner's "bible," the Internal Revenue Code of 1939. Wholesale *revision* of the internal revenue laws was first accomplished in 1954, yielding a new (King James Version?) "bible" for the practitioner. When the 1954 legislation was presented to the Senate, Senator Millikin, Chairman of the Senate Finance Committee said: [4]

INTERNAL REVENUE CODE OF 1954

Mr. President, the Senate has before it H.R. 8300, a bill to revise the internal revenue laws of the United States. The bill contains over 820 pages.

4. 100 Cong.Rec. 8536 (1954), reproduced at 26 U.S.C.A. XXI.

The need for revenue revision is evident from the fact that many of our revenue statutes are antiquated and ill-adapted to present-day conditions. Some have not been changed since the days of the Civil War. We have not had a complete revision of the internal revenue laws since 1875, more than 79 years ago.

In 1939, Congress enacted a codification of existing internal revenue laws. The 1939 code collected all the internal revenue laws in one document, eliminated obsolete matter and made typographical improvements in titles and cross-references. That code did not change the existing law, so that many of the complications and inequities of existing law were continued. It has been over 15 years since the 1939 code was enacted.

Since 1939, over 200 internal revenue statutes have been enacted, including 14 major revenue acts. I cannot too strongly emphasize the value of the 1939 code, which was enacted with the unanimous support of both parties. Without the basic work undertaken in the 1939 code, it would not have been possible to have H.R. 8300 ready for enactment at this time.

H.R. 8300 is the culmination of studies on tax revision extending over a period of nearly 2½ years. The Joint Committee on Taxation instructed its staff to make a study of tax revision in the spring of 1952. In July of that year, the staff prepared a questionnaire seeking suggestions from farm, labor and business groups, and from individual taxpayers, on how to improve the internal revenue laws. Over 17,000 replies were received from this questionnaire, coming from every State in the country.

The answers to this questionnaire were digested, and the staff of the Joint Committee on Internal Revenue Taxation and the Treasury Department began a study of this digest and other suggestions early in 1953. Groups in various sections of the country became revision conscious, and were encouraged to submit plans and make suggestions to improve the internal revenue laws.

The Ways and Means Commitee began hearings on revenue revision on June 16, 1953. A total of 504 witnesses were heard; and, in addition, 1,000 statements were submitted for the record. All this data was assembled and analyzed by the staffs of the Joint Committee on Internal Revenue Taxation and the Treasury.

The Committee on Ways and Means began its executive sessions on the revenue revision bill on January 13, 1954; and those sessions continued until March 9, 1954. On January 20, 1954, the President in his budget message made 25 recommendations for tax revision, 23 of which were incorporated in the House version of the bill.

The bill passed the House on March 18, 1954, by a majority of [sic] 259 votes—309 yeas, 80 nays. The bill was referred to the Senate Finance Committee on March 23, 1954. The Senate Finance Committee held public hearings from April 7 to April 23. A total of 130 witnesses were heard and approximately 420 statements were submitted for the record. The executive sessions by the committee lasted 5 weeks. In our deliberations, care was given toward meeting the objections of the witnesses to the House version of the bill. Suggestions not submitted to the Ways and Means Committee were also considered, and the Senate Finance Commitee amendments contain many of these suggestions.

I believe this bill has had the most thorough study and analysis of any tax bill ever presented to the Congress. Testimony had not been taken in the Ways and Means Committee on the text of the House version of the bill. Before our committee, witnesses were given an opportunity to raise objections to the final text of the House version.

Constructive criticisms were received from business, agricultural, labor, law, accounting, and engineering groups. Our committee gave particular attention to the criticisms of the technical provisions of the bill; for example, the provisions relating to corporate distributions and reorganizations have been completely revised, to meet constructive objections. I believe that the committee amendments considerably improve the provisions of the House version of the bill, and remove meritorious objections developed in the testimony. In cases where it was not possible to find an adequate solution to meet the criticism of a House provision, your committee has restored existing law. * * *

As in the case of its predecessor, the 1954 Code was amended many times. A major revision occurred in 1969. The Staff of the Joint Committee on Internal Revenue Taxation has said of the 1969 revision: [5]

The Tax Reform Act of 1969 (H.R. 13270) is a substantive and comprehensive reform of the income tax laws. As the House and Senate Committee Reports suggest, there was no prior tax reform bill of equal substantive scope.

The congressional consideration of this Act lasted eleven months and one day. * * *

From time to time, since the enactment of the present income tax over 50 years ago, various tax incentives or preferences have been added to the internal revenue laws. Increasingly in recent years, taxpayers with substantial incomes have found ways of gaining tax advantages from the provisions that

5. "General Explanation of the Tax Reform Act of 1969," p. 1 (1970).

were placed in the code primarily to aid limited segments of the economy. In fact, in many cases these taxpayers have found ways to pile one advantage on top of another. The House and Senate agreed that this was an intolerable situation. It should not have been possible for 154 individuals with adjusted gross incomes of $200,000 or more to pay no Federal income tax on 1966 income. Ours is primarily a self-assessment system. If taxpayers are generally to pay their taxes on a voluntary basis, they must feel that these taxes are fair. Moreover, only by sharing the tax burden on an equitable basis is it possible to keep the tax burden at a level which is tolerable for all taxpayers. It is for these reasons that the amendments in this Act contain some 41 categories of tax reform provisions described in summary fashion at the end of this section.

Despite the comprehensive scope of the Tax Reform Act of 1969, the committees recognized that much remains to be done. In some cases, income tax problems had to be postponed for further analysis and study. Moreover, the entire area of estate and gift tax reform lies outside the scope of this Act and remains an area for future consideration. * * *

Despite the enactment of the Tax Reform Act of 1976 and rather extensive changes in the estate and gift taxes, general tax reform of the kind contemplated by the Committee was left undone for many years. Since the publication of the first edition of this book there were eight significant revisions of the 1954 code. Three were undertaken in an effort to stimulate the economy. The Revenue Act of 1971 provided tax reductions for individuals and tax incentives for business to give a shot in the arm to a then sagging economy.[6] The Tax Reduction Act of 1975 provided further reductions for individuals and corporations in an attempt to check the sharpest economic decline since the 1930s,[7] and the Revenue Adjustment Act of 1975 extended the Reduction Act's relief into 1976.[8] Despite the broader scope of the 1976 legislation, it also included tax cuts designed to stimulate business. The Tax Reduction and Simplification Act of 1977[9] and the Revenue Act of 1978[10] afforded additional reductions and reforms designed to stimulate investment and consumer spending. The largest tax reduction in history was provided by the Economic Recovery Tax Act of 1981[11] in a further effort to encourage Economic growth by increasing savings and spurring investment. The Recovery Act included rate reductions for all

6. Pub.Law 92–178. See H.Rep. No. 92–533, 92d Cong., 1st Sess. (1971), 1972–1 C.B. 498.

7. Pub.Law 94–12. See H.Rep. No. 94–19, 94th Cong., 1st Sess. (1975), 1975–1 C.B. 569.

8. Pub.Law 94–164. See Sen.Rep. No. 94–548, 94th Cong., 1st Sess. (1975), 1976–1 C.B. 496.

9. Pub.Law 95–30. See Sen.Rep. No. 95–66, 95th Cong., 1st Sess. (1977), 1977–1 C.B. 469.

10. Pub.Law 95–600. See Sen.Rep. No. 95–1263, 95th Cong, 2d Sess. (1978), 1978–3 C.B. (Vol. 1) 315.

11. Pub.Law 97–34. See Sen.Rep. No. 97–144, 97th Cong., 1st Sess. (1981).

individuals, marriage penalty relief for working couples, accelerated depreciation schedules for businesses and a liberalization of estate and gift tax provisions. The Tax Equity and Fiscal Responsibility Act of 1982 [12] was an effort to increase revenues in a fashion to insure that all individuals and businesses would pay a fair share of the tax burden. It was followed by the Tax Reform Act of 1984 [13] which had four objectives: to reduce budget deficits; to prevent erosion of the tax base by tax sheltering activities; to insure all taxpayers pay a fair share of the tax burden; and to improve administration and efficiency of the tax system.[14]

The Internal Revenue Code of 1954 was replaced by the Internal Revenue Code of 1986. The 1986 legislation, it was said, was to be *broad-based, simple, fair, and revenue neutral* (not productive of greater or less amounts of revenue). Toward that end the 1986 Act reallocated the tax burden, subjected more items to taxation and, at the same time, reduced tax rates, essentially from a maximum rate of 50 percent to a maximum rate of 28 percent. The goals of the 1986 legislation (we sometimes refer to it as the Tax Obfuscation Act of 1986) were not achieved. The 1986 Code is more complex not more simple than its predecessor. A failure to achieve simplification dooms efforts toward fairness. It may be true that the elimination of some escape hatches has subjected more transactions to tax and some transactions to more tax accomplishing a base-broadening effect. But even so, a broader tax base does not necessarily translate to *simple* or *fair* for either Archie Bunker or high income taxpayers. The reduced rates are illusory because the taxable base is increased. The 1986 legislation has been followed by further tinkering of the 1986 Code in 1987,[15] 1988,[16] 1989 [17] and most recently in 1990.[18] But recent legislation, including the massive 1986 legislation, has not been accompanied with the type of careful, extensive studies that preceded the 1939 and 1954 legislation.

Haste has been the hallmark of the 1986 and more recent tax legislation. There must be some way to link that up with *waste.* In any event, as these remarks indicate, "What's past is prologue," and our income tax provisions should be expected to undergo further and

12. Pub.Law 97–248. See Sen.Rep. No. 97–494, 97th Cong., 2d Sess. (1982).

13. Pub.Law 98–369. See H.Rep. No. 98–432, 98th Cong., 2d Sess. (1984).

14. Several other recent acts which have had an effect on this text are the Technical Corrections Act of 1979, Pub.Law 96–222, 96th Cong., 2d Sess. 1980); the Windfall Profit Tax Act of 1980, Pub.Law 96–223, 96th Cong., 2d Sess. (1980); the Installment Sales Revision Act of 1980, Pub.Law 96–471, 96th Cong., 2d Sess. (1980); the Bankruptcy Tax Act of 1980, Pub.Law 96–589, 96th Cong., 2d Sess. (1980); the Miscellaneous Revenue Act of 1982, Pub.Law 97–362, 97th Cong., 2d Sess. (1982); and the Technical Corrections Act

of 1982, Pub.Law 97–448, 97th Cong., 2d Sess. (1982).

15. The Revenue Act of 1987, Pub.Law No. 100–203. See Conf.Rep. No. 100–495, 100th Cong., 1st Sess (1987), 1987–3 C.B. 193.

16. The Technical and Miscellaneous Revenue Act of 1988, Pub.Law No. 100–647. See Conf.Rep. No. 100–1104, 100th Cong., 2d Sess. (1988), 1988–3 C.B. 473.

17. The Revenue Reconciliation Act of 1989, Pub.Law No. 101–239. See Conf.Rep. No. 101–386, 101st Cong., 1st Sess. (1989).

18. The Revenue Reconciliation Act of 1990, Pub.Law No. 101–508. See Conf.Rep. No. 101–964, 101st Cong., 2d Sess. (1990).

perhaps constant and very likely extensive change. Nevertheless, students should not feel that their learning in this area is evanescent. The fundamentals of federal income taxation remain remarkably constant. And that is what this book is about. Certainly many of the details presented will be altered and some soon. But the student should join the authors in a search for basic concepts and policy considerations supporting basic principles. Such an approach is not only an aid in predicting change but also in understanding changes as they occur. This seventh edition of The Fundamentals is not published to present *new* fundamentals but, instead, to facilitate the study of long-standing fundamentals realistically in a setting that involves many new details.

C. THE INCOME TAX AND THE UNITED STATES CONSTITUTION

The very limited purpose of this note is to present what every good Boy Scout should know about the constitutional aspects of the federal income tax. The treatment of the subject is neither comprehensive nor detailed and, indeed, may reasonably be termed superficial. Nevertheless, these matters are relatively quiescent these days and for most purposes the elementary thoughts presented may be sufficient. The investigation and prosecution of tax fraud are not given detailed consideration in this book; but of course they are areas in which constitutional issues are constantly at the forefront.[1]

THE POWER TO TAX

The federal government's power to tax is derived from Article 1, Section 8, clause 1 of the Constitution of the United States, which confers on Congress the "power to lay and collect taxes, duties, imposts and excises * * *." If no other constitutional provision affected the taxing power, this would clearly be enough to authorize the imposition of an income tax. However, Section 2, clause 3 and Section 9, clause 4 of Article 1 require that "direct" taxes be apportioned among the several states in accordance with their respective populations. Further, Article 1, Section 8, clause 1 reads: "all duties, imposts, and excises shall be uniform throughout the United States." These provisions provide the substance for Mr. Justice Chase's famous quote: "[T]he power of Congress to tax is a very extensive power. It is given in the Constitution, with only * * * two qualifications. Congress * * * must impose direct taxes by the rule of apportionment, and indirect taxes by the rule of uniformity."[2]

1. See Crowley and Manning, *Criminal Tax Fraud—Representing the Taxpayer before Trial* (P.L.I.1976); Balter, *Tax Fraud and Evasion,* (Warren, Gorham and Lamont 5th Ed.1983); Lipton, "Constitutional Protection for Books and Records in Tax Fraud Investigations," *Tax Fraud,* p. 75 (I.C.L.E.1973). A brief note on procedure in tax fraud cases appears in Chapter 28, infra, at page 1010.

2. License Tax Cases, 72 U.S. (5 Wall.) 462, 471 (1866).

What is the difference between a "direct" tax and an "indirect" tax? A direct tax is a tax demanded from the very person who is intended to pay it. An indirect tax is a tax paid primarily by a person who can shift the burden of the tax to someone else or who at least is under no legal compulsion to pay the tax.[3] By way of example, a tax at a flat rate on all persons is a direct tax. In contrast, a sales tax is an indirect tax, because it is imposed on the seller who may shift it to the purchaser. A person may avoid an indirect tax by not buying the article subject to the tax.

APPORTIONMENT AMONG THE STATES

The rule of apportionment to which direct taxes must conform requires that, after Congress has established a sum to be raised by direct taxation, the sum must be divided among the states in proportion to their respective populations. This determines the share that must be collected within each particular state. There would be no inequality (but query as to unfairness) *among the states* in a tax at a flat rate on all persons, because a capitation tax is self-apportioning. But inequality of a sort would result if an unapportioned direct tax were levied on all carriages within the United States and a particular state had only 5% of the population but 10% of the carriages. Of course one might wonder today whether it was bad for a small state with many carriages to bear more of the federal tax burden than a more populous state with few.

Congress once did enact an unapportioned tax on carriages—hence this seemingly quaint example—which appeared to be a direct tax. However, it was held not to be direct but rather an excise tax on the *use* of carriages and therefore valid.[4] The court was influenced by dicta in prior opinions indicating direct taxes are only capitation taxes or taxes on land.

As one ponders the possible use of direct taxes as federal revenue raising measures, he is likely to come to the conclusion that (1) a failure to provide an apportionment rule might make it possible for a central taxing authority improperly to burden some states to the great advantage of others, but (2) application of an apportionment rule might create inter-personal inequities at least as bad as the interstate inequities sought to be avoided. Perhaps, it is for these reasons that Congress does not enact direct taxes, unless the income tax is still properly so classified.

What is the proper classification of the income tax? Prior to the enactment of the Income Tax Act of 1894 the United States Supreme Court had found that a tax on the premiums received by an insurance

3. Pollock v. Farmers' Loan & Trust Co., 157 U.S. 429, 558, 15 S.Ct. 673, 680–681 (1895).

4. Hylton v. U.S., 3 U.S. (3 Dall.) 171 (1796).

company [5] and a tax on income which an individual derived in part from professional earnings and in part from the interest on bonds [6] were not direct taxes. In the landmark case of Pollock v. Farmers' Loan & Trust Co.,[7] the Court was asked to decide the constitutionality of an income tax statute that included as income rents from real estate. On the principle that substance must prevail over form, the Court held that a tax on the income from property so burdened the property as to be the equivalent of a tax on the property. The Court held the intention of the drafters of the Constitution was to prevent the imposition of tax burdens on accumulations of property, except in accordance with the rule of apportionment,[8] and for this reason invalidated the tax. This decision was met with great criticism. At the time individual incomes varied sharply from state to state and it was observed that the effect of the decision, if income taxes had to be subject to the rule of apportionment, might be to cause a citizen in Massachusetts to pay only 2.8 percent of his income while a citizen in Minnesota had to pay 32.9 percent of his income.[9] There is also language in later Supreme Court opinions criticizing the *Pollock* case as an erroneous application of a principle of constitutional law.[10]

THE 16TH AMENDMENT

The foregoing capsule tax history may help in understanding the 16th Amendment. In the Amendment, emphasis is to be placed on the phrase "from whatever source derived," not on the "power" language. The power was already reposed in Congress by Article I. What the 16th Amendment provides is that income taxes shall not be subject to the rule of apportionment regardless of the *sources* from which the taxed income is derived.[11] With appropriate emphasis the Amendment reads:

AMENDMENT XVI

The Congress shall have power to lay and collect taxes on incomes, *from whatever source derived,* without apportionment among the several States, and without regard to any census or enumeration.

It matters not that a tax on salary income may be an excise and a tax on rental income a direct tax; Congress may enact a statute that taxes both without concern for the apportionment requirement.

5. Pacific Ins. Co. v. Soule, 74 U.S. (7 Wall.) 433 (1868).

6. Springer v. U.S., 102 U.S. (12 Otto) 586 (1880).

7. Supra note 3.

8. Supra note 3 at 583.

9. Seligman, *The Income Tax,* p. 587 (MacMillan Company 1914).

10. E.g., Graves v. People of New York ex rel. O'Keefe, 306 U.S. 466, 480, 59 S.Ct. 595, 598 (1939), citing People of New York ex rel. Cohn v. Graves, 300 U.S. 308, 313, 57 S.Ct. 466, 467 (1937).

11. Brushaber v. Union Pac. R. Co., 240 U.S. 1, 36 S.Ct. 236 (1916).

Another reason it is important not to look at the 16th Amendment as an isolated power-granting provision is that, if it were so read, it might appear to authorize an unapportioned tax on incomes only if Congress taxed *all* incomes regardless of source. This would invalidate a provision granting an exemption of some income, such as municipal bond interest, or perhaps invalidate an entire taxing act making such an exemption, an argument which the Supreme Court has rejected.[12] The primary message of the 16th Amendment is that, for future income taxes, the principle (apportionment) upon which the *Pollock* case invalidated the 1894 income tax statute shall be laid aside.

Despite the relatively minor role that constitutional issues such as apportionment now play in federal tax practice, reference may be made here to one interesting issue that seems to loom on the horizon. In 1974 Congress added Section 84 to the Internal Revenue Code, which treats as income subject to tax appreciation inherent in property, if a taxpayer gives the property to a political organization. A possible related future development has been the repeated proposal to tax pre-death appreciation in a decedent's property upon its transmission at the time of his death.[13] It can be argued that provisions of this type attempt to tax property rather than income, because under traditional notions the gain, which could become income, has not been "realized" by the taxpayer. The conclusion could be that the attempted tax is direct and therefore invalid because not apportioned.

At an early date the concept of realization entered the federal tax picture when the Supreme Court stressed that the 16th Amendment applied to gains *derived* from capital or labor and that, with respect to gains on property, income included profit gained through a sale or conversion of the property.[14] A later opinion added: [15]

> While it is true that economic gain is not always taxable as income, * * * [g]ain may occur as a result of exchange of property, payment of taxpayer's indebtedness, relief from a liability, or other profit realized from the completion of a transaction.

It has never been determined, however, that mere appreciation in property that continues to be held by the taxpayer is within the "incomes" concept of the 16th Amendment and, indeed, to this time it has been generally supposed that appreciation or gain is not "realized" and thus not brought within the "incomes" concept by a mere gift of appreciated property.[16] If Section 84 is to be sustained, it will be under

---

12. Id. at 21, 36 S.Ct. at 243.

13. The possibility of this seems remote in view of the repeal of I.R.C. (1954) § 1023. See Chapter 6 B 4, infra.

14. Eisner v. Macomber, 252 U.S. 189, 207, 40 S.Ct. 189 (1920).

15. Helvering v. Bruun, 309 U.S. 461, 469, 60 S.Ct. 631 (1940).

16. Compare Helvering v. Horst, 311 U.S. 112, 61 S.Ct. 144 (1940), with Campbell v. Prothro, 209 F.2d 331 (5th Cir.1954). Dicta in *Horst* seems to imply that the concept of "realization" may be a matter of administrative convenience only supporting a postponement of tax to the final event of enjoyment of the income by the taxpayer. Helvering v. Horst, supra at 116. One commentator, embracing the

judicial tax doctrine newly announced, because Section 84 pretty much requires that we treat any *disposition* of appreciated property,[17] not just its "sale or conversion", as giving rise to realized gain within the "incomes" concept of the 16th Amendment.[18]   Old constitutional lawyers never die; they just flail away.   Do we flail a dead horse in persisting upon the importance of "realization" to the concept of income.   To be impartial we must say here that some young Turks think so.   Will that change as the Supreme Court continues to edge to starboard?   Academicians don't always answer all the questions they raise.

Perhaps we have waded in a little too deep here for this introductory discussion; a briefer look now at the uniformity requirement.

UNIFORMITY AMONG THE STATES

The other qualification imposed by the Constitution on the federal taxing power is the rule of uniformity.   Article 1, Section 8, clause 1 states:

> * * * but all duties, imposts, and excises shall be uniform
> throughout the United States.

This provision does not expressly mention "taxes"; can it successfully be argued that a direct "tax" is to be differentiated from "Duties, Imposts, and Excises" and is therefore free from the uniformity requirement?   No.   An income tax is in the nature of an excise, the government literally "excising" and taking for its use a portion of the taxpayer's gain.   If as when it taxes rental income from property the present income tax may be termed direct, it does not escape the uniformity requirement.   Of course, a direct tax that had to be apportioned could not be imposed uniformly, a temporary effect of *Pollock,* criticized at the time.   But when the 16th Amendment removed the income tax from the apportionment requirement, it clearly left it fully subject to the constitutional requirement of uniformity.[19]

If it follows that all federal income taxation must be uniform throughout the United States, what then is the meaning of the constitutional term "uniform?"   It might appear that if both A and B have $10,000 of income but A is taxed on her *salary* income and B is not

---

Horst dicta, suggested some years ago that therefore the doctrine of realization is not a constitutional mandate at all, but only one of expedience, inviting administrative discretion.   Surrey, "The Supreme Court and the Federal Income Tax: Some Implications of the Recent Decisions," 35 Ill.L.Rev. 779, 791 (1941).

17. The question here must not be confused with the assignment of income issue principally involved in Helvering v. Horst, supra note 16.   Mere appreciation in property is certainly not ripe "fruit" which when later plucked by another to whom it

has been given may be attributed to the transferor.   See Helvering v. Horst and other materials at page 275, infra.   When the transferee disposes of the property the gain may indeed have vanished.   Helvering v. Bruun, supra note 15, may be similarly differentiated.

18. The somewhat parallel treatment under I.R.C. § 170(e), reducing the deduction allowed for charitable contributions of appreciated property, avoids the realization issue.

19. See Seligman, supra note 9 at 622.

taxed on his municipal bond *interest*,[20] the income tax is not being imposed in a uniform manner. However, it is well settled that the Constitution requires only geographic uniformity.[21] Although under principles dating back at least to *Brushaber*[22] certain exemptions may be constitutional, this does not mean that Congress may exempt the state bond interest of New Yorkers while taxing that kind of income of California residents. Similarly, the incomes of A and B may be subjected to different rates of tax; if A is taxed on part of her income at a higher rate than B pays, the constitutional uniformity requirement is not offended if it is because of different income levels and a graduated rate table and not because A and B are merely in different places.[23] Whenever some manner or mode of taxation is used somewhere in the United States, the same manner or mode must be used everywhere throughout the United States.[24]

Notwithstanding the constitutional fiat of uniformity, in the practical application of the income tax laws some lack of uniformity creeps in, even in the geographical sense. There are always uncertainties in the interpretation of statutes, tax or otherwise, but perhaps more in the tax area than in others. Crystallized differences in meaning develop in various parts of the country. A New York district judge may hold a person taxable on an alleged item of income which is held *not* taxable by a district judge in California. On appeal, the 2nd and 9th Circuits may similarly differ. Unless the matter goes to the Supreme Court, in a practical sense the law is different on the east and west coasts and possibly different in one trial forum from another.

Prior to 1970, the Tax Court said it was never bound to follow decisions of the Courts of Appeal as to issues of law when the same issue appeared before the Tax Court for later decision.[25] This was the Court's settled view even when the appeal in the later case would be to an appellate court that had previously expressly overruled the Tax Court.[26] The Tax Court advanced an important argument that a part of its mission as a court not subject to geographic division was to work towards a uniform interpretation of the tax laws throughout the nation, a mission best accomplished by adhering to its own views until the Supreme Court took a hand in the matter. However, the Tax Court has changed its position and now decides cases on the basis of the law in the circuit to which an appeal will lie.[27]

In recent years even the Treasury has indicated it will sometimes apply different tax principles in different circuits depending on the law

---

20. Compare I.R.C. § 61 with § 103.

21. Knowlton v. Moore, 178 U.S. 41, 20 S.Ct. 747 (1900).

22. Supra note 11.

23. Cf. Knowlton v. Moore, supra note 21 at 84, 20 S.Ct. at 764.

24. Ibid.

25. Arthur Lawrence, 27 T.C. 713 (1957).

26. Harold Holt, 23 T.C. 469, 473 (1954).

27. Jack E. Golsen, 54 T.C. 742 (1970), affirmed 445 F.2d 985 (10th Cir.1971), cert. denied 404 U.S. 940, 92 S.Ct. 284 (1971). See Patterson and Hughes, "The Golsen Rule 18 Years Later" 20 Tax Adv. 123 (1989).

as determined by the controlling Court of Appeals.[28] These disparities are hardly more palatable than direct geographic discrimination by Congress, which the Constitution expressly condemns. Can it be said that, even if a taxing *statute* is seemingly untainted, an unconstitutional lack of uniformity may arise by virtue of inconsistent *judicial* and *administrative* action?

DUE PROCESS

Congress sometimes makes use of its taxing power in a retrospective manner, but this generally does not offend any constitutional proscription. It has long been settled that Congress may impose an income tax measured by the income of a prior year or by income of the year of the enactment earned before the enactment date.[29] In fact, the 16th Amendment became operative March 1, 1913, and the imposition of a tax on income earned after that date was upheld even though the taxing *statute* was not enacted until October 3, 1913.[30] If question can be raised about retrospective taxation, the Fifth Amendment seems the likely weapon. But in *Brushaber*[31] the Court expressly held that the due process clause of the Fifth Amendment "is not a limitation upon the taxing power conferred upon Congress by the Constitution * * *,". Although the Fifth Amendment may not limit the taxing power, it can vitiate a statute which, while masquerading as a tax, in reality amounts to confiscation. If a supposed taxing statute is so arbitrary or capricious as to amount to spoliation or confiscation it may be held invalid as a denial of due process. Dicta in *Brushaber*[32] supports this proposition.[33]

The principal message here is that most taxing statutes are not vulnerable to constitutional attack. The Supreme Court will clearly not attempt to determine in the countless circumstances that arise whether Congress has nicely balanced the tax burden or is instead depriving some taxpayers of property in such a discriminatory manner that it might be considered denial of due process. But there is always the chance that Congress may go too far.[34]

SELF–INCRIMINATION

One of the vexatious problems in current tax litigation arises out of the Fifth Amendment provision that "[n]o person * * * shall be compelled in any criminal case to be a witness against himself." It is of course well-settled that requiring a taxpayer to file an income tax

---

28. E.g., Rev.Rul. 72–583, 1972–2 C.B. 534, no longer of substantive significance because of the addition of I.R.C. § 2501(a)(5).

29. Stockdale v. Atlantic Ins. Companies, 87 U.S. (20 Wall.) 323, 331 (1874).

30. Supra note 11.

31. Id. at 24, 36 S.Ct. at 237.

32. Ibid.

33. Ibid.; and see Heiner v. Donnan, 285 U.S. 312, 52 S.Ct. 358 (1932); Nichols v. Coolidge, 274 U.S. 531, 542, 47 S.Ct. 710, 713–714 (1926).

34. A Pennsylvania income tax statute was surprisingly held to offend the state constitution and therefore to be invalid in Amidon v. Kane, 444 Pa. 38, 279 A.2d 53 (1971).

return does not violate that Fifth Amendment privilege; rather, the proper place to raise the objection is in the return itself.[35] But to what extent, if at all, does the Fifth Amendment privilege apply in tax investigations? A summary analysis of this question appears in Part B of Chapter 28 infra, beginning at page 1010.

D. THE TAX PRACTITIONER'S TOOLS

In any matter governed by statutory law, as are all federal tax questions, the approach to an answer is two-fold. (1) The statutory law, all such law that bears on the problem must first be found. (2) The proper meaning must be ascribed to such law.[1] The first step *can* always be accomplished and very well better be. The second step involves opinion, judgment, and often controversy, but there are guides, sometimes controlling, that must be discovered and appraised.

To some extent this course emphasizes well-settled tax principles of wide application, basic statutory concepts that have a well-burnished gloss. But an effort is made as well to help the student develop a technique for proceeding with some assurance when, as is so often the case, answers are elusive or obscure. A feel for a tax solution is not an innate gift so much as it is a result of a broad understanding of the phenomena of our federal taxing system. A beginning toward such understanding can be made by attaining an awareness of legislative, administrative, and judicial procedures that affect federal taxes, identifying the products of such procedures, and pondering the effect such products have on the solution of a tax problem. When we speak of such "products" we are referring to the *primary* materials of federal taxation, which are discussed immediately below. Secondary (unofficial) materials, often indispensible in the proper use of the primary materials, are discussed more briefly at the end of this chapter.

1. LEGISLATIVE MATERIALS

a. **The Code.** The taxing power of the federal government is vested in Congress. Congress exercises its power by enacting legislation. Therefore, the exercise of the federal taxing power is by *statute* and, as far as internal taxes are concerned, the current statutory document is the Internal Revenue Code of 1986. It is fair to say in this area that the Code is *the* law; other materials to which the researcher resorts are only aids to establishing the meaning of the Code, sometimes challenging, at times persuasive, and occasionally controlling. All tax decisions and controversies center around the meaning of provisions of the Code.[2]

---

35. U.S. v. Sullivan, 274 U.S. 259, 47 S.Ct. 607 (1927); Garner v. U.S., 424 U.S. 648, 96 S.Ct. 1178 (1976).

1. There is a third facet to which most students receive a jolting introduction when they enter practice; all the relevant facts must be *ascertained*.

2. The improvement in tax teaching in the law schools has been dramatic in the past fifty years. Much credit for this goes to Erwin Griswold, one time professor and long time dean of the Harvard Law School, and more recently Solicitor General of the United States. And one of the world's few

Of course the plenary taxing power of Congress is subject to some restraints; federal taxing statutes must square with the requirements of the Constitution much the same as any other federal statute. However, beyond the brief comments in Chapter 1, discussion of the point will not be extended here because only infrequently in recent years has a civil tax case turned on a constitutional issue.

Not all the statutory law of federal income taxation can be found in the Internal Revenue Code. Some provisions affecting tax liability appear in other federal statutes.[3] But this is highly unusual, and the Code is the basic, and often the only relevant statutory document. By-products of the legislative process should now be briefly noted.

b. **Bills.** The formal beginning of the tax legislative process is the introduction of a bill in the House of Representatives where, under the Constitution, bills for raising revenue are supposed to originate.[4] As a matter of fact, most bills involving comprehensive tax legislation have had their origin in the Treasury Department, but they enter the legislative branch when they are introduced by a member of the House. The introduction of a tax bill, which is given publicity by the press and tax informational services, alerts the public to proposed changes in the law. But post-enactment examination of the bills introduced and the changes made in them as they passed through Congress rarely sheds much light on the final statutory product.

c. **Hearings.** Upon submission, in both the Senate and the House tax bills are usually referred to committees. In the House the Ways and Means Committee to which a tax bill is referred may hold quite extensive hearings on the proposed legislation. Important officials of the Treasury Department appear with a prepared statement and are questioned by committee members. But many others may also appear, some merely representing themselves and others representing various trade associations, industry groups, professional societies, etc. Similar proceedings may take place in the Finance Committee in the Senate.

possessors of a solid gold golf putter. In broadest outline, the organization of this book is similar to his innovative casebook, Cases on Federal Taxation, first published by Foundation Press in 1940. Moreover, present day stress on THE STATUTE (and the regulations) also largely originated with him. Whether known or acknowledged, many tax practitioners trained in the past three decades, and most tax instructors who have come along in that period, all are to some extent indebted to Erwin Griswold.

3. Pub.L. 93–490, 1974–2 C.B. 451, without amending the Code fixed some special rules for the deductibility of moving expenses of armed forces personnel at variance with I.R.C. § 217. Rev.Rul. 76–2, 1976–1 C.B. 82. Section 506(c) of the Tax Reform Act of 1976 added subsection 217(g) which deals with moving expenses of the armed forces. Section 2117 of the same act, however, limits tax liability potentially arising out of cancellation of certain student loans, without amending the Code. The 1984 Act subsequently added I.R.C. § 108(f) to the Code to incorporate this rule.

4. A sophisticated analysis of the tax legislative process appears in Surrey, "The Congress and the Tax Lobbyist—How Special Tax Provisions Get Enacted," 70 Harv.L.Rev. 1145 (1957), reprinted in Sander and Westfall, Readings in Federal Taxation, 3 (1970) and in Graetz, "Reflections on the Tax Legislative Process: Prelude to Reform," 58 Virg.L.Rev. 1389 (1972). See also Shaviro, "Beyond Public Choice and Public Interest: A Study of the Legislative Process as Illustrated by Tax Legislation in the 1980s," 139 U.Penn.L.R. 1 (1990).

Transcripts of these hearings are published and can be the source of much interesting material reflecting both private and governmental policy views on tax matters. But the hearings are only rarely useful in attempting to give meaning to the statutes ultimately enacted.

d. Committee Reports. When the Ways and Means Committee brings a bill back to the floor of the House, a report accompanies the bill. Basically, the report seeks to explain to the other House members just what the bill is designed to do, usually with illustrations. Later, when the Finance Committee reports its bill to the Senate another committee report emerges. These reports are the most important part of the so-called "legislative history" of a statute and, in this country, practitioners, the Treasury, and the courts often resort to them as guides to the meaning of the legislation. As a matter of fact, a good bit of approved literary piracy goes on here. The House committee report may borrow heavily from statements before the committee by Treasury officials. When the Senate committee prepares its report with respect to parts of the bill that have not been altered, the Senate report comments are likely to be identical to the comments in the House report. This custom-sanctioned plagiarism is usually carried one step further when the Treasury issues new regulations under the statute as enacted, echoing the language of the committee reports.

Usually a tax bill emerges from the Senate in a form somewhat different from the form in which it was passed by the House. Before such a bill can go to the president, the disagreeing votes of the two houses must be reconciled. This task is undertaken by a conference committee, made up of Senate and House members. When agreement is reached in the committee, the managers report the bill back to their respective houses, generally resulting in passage in the newly agreed form. The conference committee report is often a rather brief and cryptic document, mainly identifying the areas of disagreement on which each house receded. But it may be accompanied by a statement on the part of the managers of the bill which is informative as to the reasons for action taken in conference. And the conference committee may also issue an explanation of the bill as it has been developed by the committee members. There is always the possibility that such reports and explanations will afford some insight into the meaning of new legislation, which would be missed upon a reading of the bare words of the statute.

Distinct from *ad hoc* conference committees is the permanent Joint Committee on Internal Revenue Taxation, made up of five members of the Finance Committee and five members of the Ways and Means Committee. Its role in Congress is collateral to the formal legislative process.[5] Nevertheless, it has a staff of experts and authority, among other things, to investigate the tax laws and their administration, and some of its publications are enlightening as to the likelihood of changes in the law or as to the meaning of recent statutory changes.

---

5. See I.R.C. §§ 8001–8023.

e. **Debates.** Our legislative process contemplates parliamentary debate of proposed legislation. A tax bill is no exception. Congressional proceedings, including such debates, are published in the Congressional Record. This product of the legislative process may also have a bearing on the meaning ultimately accorded a new statute. But, of all the subordinate legislative materials mentioned, the committee reports are clearly the most significant.

f. **Prior Laws.** The modern income tax dates from 1913, the year in which the Sixteenth Amendment was ratified. From then until 1939, Congress enacted numerous internal revenue acts among which the controlling statutory law was scattered. In 1939, the internal revenue laws were codified, first as the Internal Revenue Code of 1939. Thereafter, for fifteen years, internal revenue legislation took the form of additions to or other changes in that Code. Wholesale revision in 1954 produced the Internal Revenue Code of 1954 which was the subject of many additions, deletions, and other changes over a thirty-two year span until the 1986 Act replaced it with the Internal Revenue Code of 1986. Shop talk about this or that section was greatly hampered by enactment of the 1954 Code as all but one of the 1939 Code section numbers were changed. Although the most recent changes are both broad and deep, most friendly old sections of the 1954 Code retain numerical identity in the 1986 version.

Statutory changes present two special problems for the student and practitioner. (1) If we are not talking about tax liability for the current year (questions controlled by the Code most recently enacted or as most recently amended), what was the status of the statutory law as of the year with which we are concerned? (2) If we find a case bearing on a tax problem, a current problem, did the decision in that case rest on provisions of statutory law that are the same as or at least similar to the current provisions? If not, the case is obviously irrelevant. Generally, the opinion will set out the pertinent statute, either in the text or in the margin, so that it can be compared with the current provisions. Where the problem arises otherwise, the so-called "Cumulative Changes Service," published by Prentice-Hall may save time that otherwise would have to be spent searching for the effective date provisions of numerous amendatory acts.

g. **Treaties.** In the hierarchy of laws in the United States, a federal statute and a treaty enjoy equal status. Treaties made under the authority of the United States are the supreme law of the land, along with laws made in pursuance of the Constitution and the Constitution itself. Consequently, a tax treaty, of which we now have many can supersede a provision of the Internal Revenue Code. The point is made as a precautionary gesture but will not be further explored here.

Generally it is the practice in this casebook to delete from a judicial opinion or its footnotes the quotation of statutory language that is essentially the same as that appearing in the Code in its present form. When that is done a reference to the current Code provision replaces the footnote, as it is assumed that students will have the Code available. Opinions quoting language no longer in the Code or substantially different from the Code's present language are not changed in this respect. A comparative analysis may have to be undertaken by the student to see what current relevance the case may have despite the statutory changes, an effort that has educational value in and of itself. Statutory assignments throughout the book will usually quickly bring the student to the current provisions with which the old should be compared. The matter discussed here is illustrated in *Glenshaw Glass* set out in Chapter 2, where the Court quotes I.R.C. (1939) Section 22(a) in the text and then in footnote 11 discusses a minor change of language in the parallel I.R.C. (1954) Section 61(a).

2. ADMINISTRATIVE MATERIALS

a. **Regulations.** The Secretary of the Treasury is given general authority to "prescribe all needful rules and regulations for the enforcement" of the Internal Revenue Code.[6] This is a lawful congressional delegation of subordinate legislative authority. Under it the regulations promulgated become a kind of proliferation of the statute. But all three branches of government may play a part here. In the final analysis, the *judiciary* has the right to say whether the regulations promulgated by the *executive* conform to the statute enacted by the *legislature*. Interpretative regulations may be dismissed as not the law if they are at variance with the statute. However, the student should not lightly assume that a regulation is invalid. Even where a provision in the "Regs." seems to stretch the statute pretty far, it will likely be sustained if it reflects a consistent, long-standing interpretation by the Treasury or, as a practical matter, if it happens to coincide with a judge's notions of sound policy and is reasonable.[7] Not infrequently courts have accorded interpretative regulations "force of law" status.[8]

In this course, principal emphasis is placed on the Code and the Regulations. And students should learn at once to think of the initial approach to a tax question as follows: (1) What Code provisions bear on

---

6. I.R.C. § 7805. Regulations which are initially issued as temporary regulations must also be issued as proposed regulations to ensure that they are the subject of public comment. I.R.C. § 7805(e)(1). Such regulations, if not finalized, expire 3 years after their issuance. I.R.C. § 7805(e)(2).

7. See e.g., Bingler v. Johnson, 394 U.S. 741, 89 S.Ct. 1439 (1969).

8. See e.g., Helvering v. Winmill, 305 U.S. 79, 59 S.Ct. 45 (1938); Crane v. Commissioner, 331 U.S. 1, 67 S.Ct. 1047 (1947), upholding a provision of the Regulations, stating: "As the * * * provision of the Regulations has been in effect since 1918, and as the relevant statutory provison has been repeatedly re-enacted since then in

substantially the same form, the * * * [Regulation] may itself be considered to have the force of law." 331 U.S. at 7 and 8, 67 S.Ct. at 1051; Fribourg Navigation Co. v. Commissioner, 383 U.S. 272, 283, 86 S.Ct. 862, 868, 869 (1966); Century Elec. Co. v. Commissioner, 192 F.2d 155 (8th Cir.1951), cert. denied 342 U.S. 954, 72 S.Ct. 625 (1952). Perhaps the highwater mark appears in U.S. v. Correll, 389 U.S. 299, 88 S.Ct. 445 (1967), in which the Supreme Court said: "The role of the judiciary in cases of this sort begins and ends with assuring that the Commissioner's regulations fall within his authority to implement the congressional mandate in some reasonable manner." 389 U.S. at 307, 88 S.Ct. at 450.

the problem? (2) Do the Regs. shed any light on their meaning in the setting at hand? This is not the end, but it is the right beginning for the solution of a tax problem.

Some Treasury Regulations are more than mere interpretations of the statute. Congress sometimes carves out areas in which the Treasury can actually make, not merely interpret, the rules.[9] Such qualified or restricted delegations of legislative power seem no longer to be subject at all to attack on constitutional grounds (the separation of powers doctrine), and consequently regulations of this sort are even less vulnerable in the courts than are interpretative regulations.

The Regulations are especially valuable to the student, often enabling him to move from the general and abstract language of the statute to a specific, concrete example of its application. The practitioner, as a student, is of course accorded the same opportunity. Nevertheless, in using the Regulations it is well to remember that they are generally subordinate to the statute and, in any instance in which an exact answer must be achieved, it is entirely improper to rely on the Regulations (or on instructions on a tax form, which generally have about the same status) as a substitute for the statute. Indeed, it may well be necessary to go beyond both, as further comments below will indicate.

b. **Rulings.** The Regulations are not the only income tax documents emanating from the Treasury Department. However, at this point we discuss only one other, the Revenue Ruling (others are Revenue Procedures and Technical Information Releases). Revenue Rulings are issued under the same statutory authority as the Regulations. They are generally the Treasury's answer to a specific question raised by a taxpayer concerning his tax liability. In the interest of a uniform application of the tax laws, they are published to provide precedents for use in the disposition of like cases. While they do not have the force and effect of regulations, they do at least reflect the current policies of the Internal Revenue Service. The Service will not invariably respond to a request for a ruling. See Rev.Proc. 91–1, 1991–1 C.B. ___ (procedure for rulings, determination letters and closing agreements),[10] and Rev.Proc. 91–3, 1991–1 C.B. ___ ("no ruling" areas). Published Revenue Rulings appear first in the weekly Internal Revenue Bulletin and then, in more permanent form, in the semi-annual Cumulative Bulletin. See Rev.Proc. 89–14, 1989–1 C.B. 814. Since 1939, the Cumulative Bulletin has also been a source for the tax legislation committee reports, otherwise rather elusive documents. A student should not delay in making the acquaintance of "C.B.".

The great majority of rulings are not officially published and thus remain "private" in the sense that they are issued in response to the request of a taxpayer and are officially kept confidential. However, as part of the Tax Reform Act of 1976, Congress added Section 6110 to the

---

9. See I.R.C. § 1017; Reg. § 1.1017–1.

10. See § 8.02(4) of the ruling for accelerated responses to ruling requests.

Code generally to require that many such private "letter rulings" be open to public inspection. This provision is intended to assure that all taxpayers have access to the rulings positions of the Service as well as to increase the public's confidence that the tax system operates in a fair and even-handed manner.[11] Congress was also motivated by judicial decisions that private letter rulings were subject to disclosure under the Freedom of Information Act,[12] and hence Congress chose to establish some legislative guidelines to the disclosures. The relevant regulations explain that the text of the rulings to which this disclosure provision applies will be located in the National Office Reading Room during regular hours of business of the Internal Revenue Service and copies of material will be furnished to any person requesting them.[13] Although letter rulings may not be relied upon as authority by anyone other than the taxpayer to whom the ruling was issued, they serve a useful function as planning tools especially in light of the announced policy of the Service that only rulings that involve important substantive tax questions and issues of widespread interest will be officially published as Revenue Rulings in the future.[14]

c. **Acquiescences.** The Internal Revenue Service publishes its acquiescence or nonacquiescence in the Tax Court's determination of issues adverse to the government. Such actions do not of course affect the taxpayer who has just won his case but, in essence, the Service is saying either we will or we will not continue to contest the point as it arises in *other* cases. Less methodically, notice is given from time to time whether the Treasury will follow a decision of the Claims Court, a district court, or court of appeals; obviously, Supreme Court decisions are controlling. These indications of adherence to or shifts in Treasury views, first published in the Internal Revenue Bulletin and eventually appearing in the Cumulative Bulletin, are of course of great importance in tax planning.

In addition to its essentially legislative and administrative activities, the Treasury performs a quasi-judicial function as well. If a deficiency in tax is asserted by the Treasury, or if the taxpayer claims a refund on the ground he has overpaid his tax, the initial decision of any ensuing controversy must be made by the Treasury. But such determinations give rise to no published opinions or reports, and procedures for judicial review always take the form of trials *de novo*. It will be important at another time to consider intra-agency procedures [15] but, as we are here mainly concerned with the *materials* of federal taxation

11. House Rep. No. 94–658, 94th Cong., 1st Sess. (1975), 1976–3 (vol. 2) C.B. 1006.

12. 5 U.S.C.A. § 552 (1967). See e.g. Fruehauf Corp. v. Internal Revenue Serv., 566 F.2d 574 (6th Cir.1977).

13. Reg. § 301.6110–1(c).

14. This change in policy was announced during "The Federal Tax Process"

conference (May 18–19, 1980), presented jointly by the Tax Section of the ABA and The Tax Division of the American Institute of Certified Public Accountants.

15. See Part Nine, Federal Tax Procedures, Chapters 28–30, infra.

and no such *materials* are generated by such procedures, we turn now
to the judicial process.

3. JUDICIAL MATERIALS

The decisional process serves to put the meat on the skeletal law of
the statute.[16] In broad perspective the Code lays down bare legal
norms and cursory fact norms, sometimes clearly and separately identifiable and sometimes coalescing and indistinguishable. When a tax
controversy gets into court, the court's function, at least at the trial
level, is to identify the problem, determine the relevant facts (findings
of fact) and interpret and apply the Code provisions. In essence the
tribunal must draw a line in each case; that is the primary job of the
courts. The growing body of decisions in many areas of the tax law
takes on a meaningful profile which can have significant value as an
aid in predicting the outcome of future controversies involving similar
issues. Thus lines drawn by the courts in prior decisions can be plotted
and are useful tools to the tax practitioner planning prospective transactions and are essential to the practitioner in deciding whether to
litigate an issue that is the subject of current administrative controversy.

An appellate tribunal can of course review the findings of fact as
determined by the trial court, but in general it cannot reject such
findings unless they are virtually entirely unsupported by evidence.
Hence the function of the appellate process is not so much fact line
drawing as it is interpretation. You will discover that appellate courts
are rather adept at enunciating legal norms or rules or tests, which are
then applied by trial courts in specific factual settings. Generally
speaking, the appellate tribunal is at its best when the issue before it is
a question of law. Thus, for example in Williams v. McGowan [17] the
only issue the Court of Appeals had to decide was whether the sale of a
proprietorship business was a sale of an entity or whether such a sale
was a sale of each constituent asset separately. The facts were clear
and undisputed. The Code did not provide a ready answer. The Court
held as a matter of law that a proprietorship is simply an aggregate of
many things, not an entity.

The cases presented in this casebook are representative, not only of
the substantive areas of tax law, but also of what courts do. In your
study of other law school courses you have become generally aware of
the federal court structure—district courts, courts of appeals and the
Supreme Court. You now meet two new federal courts, perhaps for the
first time: The United States Tax Court and the United States Claims
Court.

16. See Ginsberg, "Making Tax Law
Through the Judicial Process," 70 A.B.A.J.
(No. 3) 74 (1984).

17. 152 F.2d 570 (2d Cir.1945), set out
infra at page 777.

a. Trial Courts

(1) *Tax Court Decisions.* If the Commissioner of Internal Revenue asserts a deficiency in income tax (charges in effect that the taxpayer has paid less than he owed) for any year, one thing the taxpayer can do is petition the Tax Court for a redetermination of the deficiency (or hopefully, a decision that no additional tax is due). As such suits are always between the taxpayer and the Commissioner (who is represented by attorneys in the office of the Chief Counsel of the Treasury Department), prior to 1977 such cases were often referred to only by the taxpayer's name, e.g., Nora Payne Hill, 13 T.C. 291 (1949). The adversarial nature of Tax Court cases is now clearly indicated by the inclusion of "Commissioner" in the style of the cases, e.g., Diedrich v. Commissioner, 39 T.C.M. 433 (1979). The Tax Court, created as the Board of Tax Appeals in 1924 and changed in name only in 1942 was, until 1970, an independent administrative agency in the executive branch of the government. The Tax Reform Act of 1969 established the Tax Court as an Article I Court to be known as the United States Tax Court. Though not an Article III Court (the judiciary article of the Constitution) the United States Tax Court is now a de jure court albeit under the Legislative Article of the Constitution.[18]

It may be well to recognize three categories of Tax Court decisions. (1) The Court sits in divisions so that only one of the nineteen regular judges hears and decides a case. A Tax Court case is always tried without a jury before one of the judges. Such cases *may* be officially reported in the Tax Court (formerly B.T.A.) Reports, after required review by the Chief Judge. (2) The decision may not be officially reported if it involves primarily factual determinations and the application only of settled legal principles. Commerce Clearing House and Prentice-Hall, however, do publish such so-called "Memorandum Decisions." (3) Some officially reported decisions are, upon determination of the Chief Judge prior to publication, reviewed by the entire court. In such instances, the Court can reject the decision of the judge who heard the case. Constitutional challenge to this procedure has been rejected.[19] In any event, a decision that has the concurrence of all the judges of the Tax Court (or which has at least been considered by all) may have somewhat greater weight than the decision of a single judge. Still in the final analysis, it will usually be the judge's insight and the persuasiveness of his opinion, whether the case is reported, reviewed by the Court or merely a memorandum decision, which will determine whether it will be followed administratively and by other courts.

(2) *District Court Decisions.* When a tax deficiency is asserted the taxpayer's judicial remedy is not limited to suit in the Tax Court. He

---

18. This action was held constitutional in Burns, Stix, Friedman and Co., Inc., 57 T.C. 392 (1971); and it is fairly clear the Tax Court now has power to punish for contempt and to enforce its orders. See Dubroff, "The United States Tax Court: An Historical Analysis," 40 Albany L.Rev. 7 (1975).

19. Estate of Varian v. Commissioner, 396 F.2d 753 (9th Cir.1968).

can pay the deficiency, file an administrative claim for refund and, upon its denial or prolonged administrative inaction, file suit in the district court for a refund. Fact issues may be determined by a jury if the plaintiff demands a jury trial. The same procedure is open to him even if he merely asserts that initially he overpaid his tax.[20] The tax decisions in the district courts emerge in the Federal Supplement.

(3) *Claims Court Decisions.* An alternative forum for refund suits is the United States Claims Court, a new Article I trial forum replacing the Court of Claims.[21] The court is composed of sixteen judges who are authorized to sit nationwide. It resembles the Tax Court in organization and procedure. It is similar to the District Court in that it is a forum for refund claims, but no jury trial is available in the Claims Court. Decisions of the Claims Court appear in the Federal supplement and in a separate claims court reporter published by West Publishing Co.

b. Appellate Courts

(1) *Court of Appeals Decisions.* Tax decisions of the district courts and of the Tax Court can be appealed (as of right) by either party to the courts of appeal, and tax decisions of the Claims Court are appealable to the Court of Appeals for the Federal Circuit. Decisions on such appeals are of course reported in the Federal Reporter. It is not uncommon, as such appeals fan out to the eleven circuits, to find divergent views expressed on like questions in the several courts of appeal. This is often unsettling in matters of tax planning and often a factor taken into account in the forum-shopping stage of tax litigation.[22]

(2) *Supreme Court Decisions.* Many tax decisions in the Supreme Court represent that Court's determination (upon petition for certiorari) to settle a point on which the courts of appeal have taken divergent positions. Even so, the activities of the Tax Court, although its decisions are sometimes upset on judicial review, are so much more extensive that they clearly have more positive effect on the development of the tax law and on a uniform administration of the tax laws than the occasional forays of the Supreme Court.

Judicial decisions in federal tax cases (*except* those of the Tax Court) are collected in two important series of reports: (1) *United States Tax Cases* (cited, e.g., 88–2 U.S.T.C. para. ___) published by Commerce Clearing House, Inc., and (2) *American Federal Tax Reports* (cited ___ A.F.T.R. ___) published by Prentice-Hall, Inc. Thus, in contrast to the space now occupied by complete sets of the Federal Supplement, the Federal Reporter and the United States Reports, a complete set of

---

20. See Chapter 29, infra.

21. Pub.Law No. 97–164 (1982). See Sen.Rep. No. 97–275, 97th Cong., 2d Sess. (1984). See also the fourth edition of this text for a discussion of the Court of Claims.

22. Consider again the Constitutional requirement that federal taxes be uniform throughout the United States discussed in Chapter 1 at page 18, supra.

federal tax (other than Tax Court) cases is compressed into about 25 feet of bookshelf space.

4. UNOFFICIAL TAX MATERIALS

Federal tax practice would be almost impossible without the help of the major tax services. This is partly because of the bulk of material and partly because in detail tax principles are constantly changing. The Standard Federal Tax Reporter of Commerce Clearing House, Inc., and Federal Taxes published by Prentice-Hall, Inc., both do an elaborate job of indexing and digesting tax materials and keep their subscribers current by way of weekly advance sheet reports. Prentice-Hall publishes separately a Federal Tax Citator, which is the most comprehensive tool for "Shepardizing" tax cases. A more modest, selective citator volume is included in the C.C.H. service. *Tax Notes* published by Tax Analysts provides a weekly update of tax matters. Somewhat similar research assistance may be found in the *Federal Tax Coordinator,* published by the Research Institute of America, and *Bender's Federal Tax Service* published by Matthew Bender & Co. A tax research tool that has recently emerged, which can be of valuable assistance to beginning students as well as seasoned tax attorneys, is Bittker and Lokken's *Federal Taxation of Income, Estates and Gifts* published by Warren, Gorham & Lamont. A helpful guide to fundamental income tax concepts is Chirelstein's *Federal Income Tax* published by Foundation Press.

An important income tax encyclopedia is Mertens, Law of Federal Income Taxation, now published in loose-leaf form and kept current by fairly frequent supplements. The Bureau of National Affairs, Inc. publishes an extensive series of Tax Management portfolios, which are constantly revised.

There is a great deal of excellent literature available on federal income tax problems. As would be expected, all the major law reviews publish tax articles from time to time. The Tax Law Review (a New York University Law School publication) is made up exclusively of tax writing, generally of a detailed and scholarly nature, and the University of Florida Law Review publishes a similar annual tax issue. Other tax periodicals more practitioner oriented are The Journal of Taxation, Taxes, and The Review of Taxation of Individuals. Commerce Clearing House publishes, and keeps up to date, a loose-leaf volume entitled Federal Tax Articles. The indexing—by subject, Code section and author—is good, and a brief description of the subject matter of each listed article is presented. A similar Index to Federal Tax Articles is published by Warren, Gorham & Lamont. For tax articles, all that these volumes purport to cover, these services are somewhat superior to the better-known Index to Legal Periodicals.

Annual Institutes, such as the New York University Institute on Federal Taxation, the Southern Federal Tax Institute, and the Tax Institute of the University of Southern California yield volumes of papers usually addressed to current tax problems. And there are numerous useful treatises on special areas of tax law.

Further specific reference is made in the chapters that follow to helpful unofficial materials. The literature cited is of varying quality and depth and, as to some that may be classified as superficial, the editors' objective is to identify materials that may be helpful to the beginning student.

E. TAX POLICY CONSIDERATIONS

Every tax has an inescapable regulatory effect. To impose a tax on a transaction is to some extent to discourage it. To relieve from tax a transaction otherwise subject to the exaction tends on the other hand to encourage it. The present income tax statute has many special provisions in the form of exceptions and preferences that, according to some, defeat the laudable objective of a "comprehensive tax base" and an even-handed tax treatment of all financial increments that can properly be called income. To those who do not benefit from a particular special provision it is usually a "loophole." [1] Yet there may be no complete escape from this, and the elusive comprehensive tax base may not be realistically attainable although a step in that direction was attempted in the 1986 legislation.[2] In any event, the point is the federal income tax is far from a neutral, revenue raising device; it has a profound impact on what people do. Whether its regulatory aspects are deliberate or incidental, Congress sometimes uses the carrot and sometimes the stick that brings about a certain result through the use of the taxing power. Students should consider these possibilities as they work their way through this book.[3]

Revenue raising measures are condemned almost as incessantly as the weather. Reform measures are continually being urged ostensibly to make adjustment for inequities or hardships in the taxing system or, even more boldly, to create favored status for some interests. In recent years, federal administrations have sought to alleviate national economic and social ills by tinkering with the tax laws. In his 1984 State of the Union Address President Reagan asked the Treasury Department to conduct a thorough review of our federal tax system. This

---

1. See Blum, "The Effects of Special Provisions in the Income Tax on Taxpayer Morale," Joint Committee on the Economic Report Federal Tax Policy for Economic Growth and Stability 251 (1955), reprinted in Sander and Westfall, Readings in Federal Taxation 41 (Foundation Press 1970).

2. See Bittker, "A 'Comprehensive Tax Base' as a Goal of Income Tax Reform," 80 Harv.L.Rev. 925 (1967), reprinted in Sander and Westfall, Readings in Federal Taxation 91 (Foundation Press 1970).

3. See Surrey, "Tax Incentives as a Device for Implementing Government Policy: A Comparison with Direct Government Ex-

penditures," 83 Harv.L.Rev. 705 (1970), reprinted in Sander and Westfall, Readings in Federal Taxation 153 (Foundation Press 1970). See also Bittker, "Accounting for Federal 'Tax Subsidies' in the National Budget," 22 Nat. Tax J. 244 (1969); Surrey and Hellmuth, "The Tax Expenditure Budget—Response to Professor Bittker," 22 Nat. Tax J. 528 (1969) and, generally, Klein, *Policy Analysis of the Federal Income Tax,* c. 4 (Foundation Press 1976); and Bittker, "Income Tax 'Loopholes' and Political Rhetoric," 71 Mich.L.Rev. 1099 (1973).

request came less than five months after the enactment of the 1984 Act, which made numerous changes in the Internal Revenue Code. Nevertheless, on November 27, 1984 the Treasury issued its *Report on Tax Simplification and Reform*, commonly referred to as "Treasury One."

Any good cat-skinner knows the present federal income tax is not the only way to do it. The huge sums for which the federal government hungers can be raised in other ways. Treasury One analyzed the need for and goals of tax reform. The Treasury Report went on to consider four taxing methods as alternatives to the then current federal income tax: (1) a flat tax: a tax with a broad base (few or no deductions) on which tax is imposed at a single low rate; (2) a modified flat tax: a tax on a tax base containing more deductions but imposed at modestly graduated low rates;[4] (3) a consumption tax:[5] a personal tax at graduated rates on consumption, or consumed income, levied by exempting all savings from tax, allowing a deduction for repayment of debt, and taxing all borrowing and withdrawals from savings; and (4) a general sales tax: either a familiar retail sales tax or a value-added tax[6] (in effect a multistage sales tax that is collected at each stage in the production or distribution process). The Report concluded that a modified flat rate tax was the preferable alternative and superior to the tax system at the time, stating:[7]

> By combining a more comprehensive definition of income than under current law with modestly graduated low rates, modified flat tax proposals are able to achieve gains in simplicity, economic neutrality, equal tax treatment of families with equal incomes, and economic growth, without sacrificing distributional equity.

Unless you were living under a rock or in outer space between the 1984 announcement of Treasury One and October, 1986, when the Tax Reform Act of 1986 was signed, you are aware that Treasury One was the first step in one of the most substantial tax reform undertakings in the United States in the past fifty years. In the Chapters of this book

4. See Bradley, *The Fair Tax* (Pocket Books N.Y.1984). For three policy articles in a single journal, see Graetz and McDowell, "Tax Reform 1985: The Quest for a Fairer, More Efficient and Simpler Income Tax," 3 Yale Law and Pol.Rev. 5 (1984); Bradley and Gebhardt, "Fixing the Income Tax with the Fair Tax," 3 Yale Law and Pol.Rev. 41 (1984); Rosow, "The Treasury's Tax Reform Proposals: Not a 'Fair' Tax," 3 Yale Law and Pol.Rev. 58 (1984). See also Hall, Rabushka, and Simmons, "Low Tax, Simple Tax, Flat Tax," 17 U.C. Davis L.Rev. 1009 (1984).

5. See Andrews, "A Consumption-Type or Cash Flow Personal Income Tax," 87 Harv.L.Rev. 1113 (1974); Warren, "Would a Consumption Tax be Fairer Than an Income Tax?" 89 Yale L.J. 1081 (1980); Graetz, "Implementing a Progressive Consumption Tax," 92 Harv.L.Rev. 1575 (1979); Gunn, "The Case for an Income Tax," 46 U.Chi.L.Rev. 370 (1979).

6. Turnier, "Designing an Efficient Value Added Tax," 39 Tax L.Rev. 435 (1984); Brannon, "The Value Added Tax is a Good Utility Infielder," 37 Nat'l Tax J. 303 (1984); Wright, "Personal, Living or Family Matters and the Value Added Tax," 82 Mich.L.Rev. 419 (1983); Fuller, "The Proposed Value-Added Tax and the Question of Tax Reform," 34 Rutgers L.Rev. 50 (1981); Spizer, "The Value Added Tax and Other Proposed Tax Reforms: A Critical Assessment," 54 Tulane L.Rev. 194 (1979).

7. Treasury Report on Tax Simplification and Reform p. 23 (Report to the President, November 27, 1984).

which follow, you will encounter many of the changes made by the 1986 legislation. While there has been subsequent tax legislation in each year between 1986 and 1990, including the 1990 rate changes,[8] the 1986 legislation is the platform for our current tax structure. To help you understand the impetus for that legislation, even though the congressional product did not slavishly adhere to proposals, here are some significant portions of Treasury One.

EXCERPT FROM THE TREASURY REPORT ON TAX SIMPLIFICATION AND REFORM *

THE NEED FOR TAX REFORM: BACK TO BASICS

The present income tax is badly in need of fundamental simplification and reform. It is too complicated, it is unfair, and it interferes with economic choices and retards saving, investment and growth.

In a real sense, the U.S. income tax has grown without any conscious design or overall planning since it was enacted in 1913. It was originally imposed at low rates and applied to fewer than 400,000 individuals with very high incomes. The need to finance World War II and expanded non-defense expenditures turned the individual income tax into a levy paid by most Americans. Tax rates were increased during World War II, and at their peak individual income tax rates reached 94 percent. The original income tax had serious flaws, and while some of these have been corrected over time, others have grown worse. With over 90 million individual tax returns now being filed, it is important to address these problems.

It is one thing to decide to tax "income," and quite another to decide how to define taxable income. If inadequate attention is devoted to establishing a uniform and consistent definition of income, some sources and uses of income will escape tax, and others will be taxed twice, as in the United States. The result may or may not be a simple tax system, but it is certain that the tax system will contain inequities and interfere with the economic behavior of taxpayers.

The U.S. income tax is not used simply to raise revenue. Instead, it is used to subsidize a long list of economic activities through exclusions from income subject to tax, adjustments to income, business deductions unrelated to actual expenses, deferral of tax liability, deductions for personal consumption expenditures, tax credits, and preferential tax rates. In some cases, deviations from a comprehensive definition of income originated in incomplete understanding of the concept of income or in outmoded ideas about the proper fiscal relationship between the Federal Government and state and local govern-

---

8. See Chapter 27A, infra.   * Pages 1–11.

ments. But whatever its origin, in many cases bad public policy has become accepted—virtually enshrined—as appropriate.

For seven decades, the Treasury Department has fought to protect Federal revenues and the fairness and economic neutrality of the tax system from those seeking to create and exploit gaps and inconsistencies in the definition of taxable income. As loopholes have been discovered or created, exploited, and then plugged, techniques of tax avoidance have become increasingly sophisticated and the complexity of the incme tax has grown, in a never-ending cycle.

The resulting tax system is both unfair and needlessly complex. Moreover, it interferes with economic behavior and, thus, prevents markets from allocating economic resources to their most productive uses. Perhaps worse, the complexity and inequity of the tax system undermine taxpayer morale—a valuable, yet fragile, national asset and a prerequisite for a tax system based on voluntary compliance.

During the past year, the Treasury Department has undertaken a thorough review of the U.S. tax system. The object has been to determine how to reduce the complexities, inequities, and economic distortions in the tax system and make it more conducive to economic growth. Although the present report was prepared internally by the Treasury Department, it draws heavily on a vast national storehouse of knowledge about the tax system and its effects on the economy. The report also reflects information, views, and concerns which the Treasury Department received from taxpayers in the course of public hearings, meetings, and discussions, and in correspondence and in more formal written statements.

The Federal Income Tax in 1954

To understand better the need for tax reform, it is useful to compare our present income tax system with the one that prevailed in the late 1950s, after enactment of the 1954 Internal Revenue Code. Though the 1954 income tax system exhibited some serious problems, it was relatively simple, it was more nearly neutral toward many economic decisions, and most citizens probably thought it was reasonably fair.

Today the American economy is far more complex than it was 30 years ago. The financial affairs of the typical American family are far more complicated than in previous generations. Ownership of both financial and nonfinancial assets is more widespread and varied. Families have a greater quantity and variety of income, both taxed and untaxed. Business transactions are more complicated, financial intermediation is more highly developed, and taxpayers are more sophisticated and better advised. We also know more about the adverse effects of taxation than 30 years ago. Therefore, it would not be desirable—nor would it be possible—simply to reinstate an earlier tax law that was not designed to deal with the more complex economy of the 1980s. But a useful perspective on the current need for tax reform and simplification can be gained by considering how the tax law—and its impact on taxpayers—has changed over the past three decades.

One important defect of the 1954 income tax was a schedule of marginal rates that reached 91 percent for a small number of taxpayers. Besides creating severe disincentives for saving, investment, and work effort, the confiscatory rates may have spawned many of the vexing tax avoidance schemes that now riddle the income tax. But the advantages of the earlier income tax were also manifest. Virtually all taxpayers below the top 10 percent of the income distribution paid tax at an essentially uniform marginal rate of about 20 percent. Only at the very top of the income distribution did rates become steeply progressive. The income tax was still being used primarily to raise public revenues, and not to guide households and private business enterprises into a multitude of activities—some of dubious value—through preferential tax treatment. With notable exceptions, the income tax was levied on a base that included most income. The erosion of that base by a multitude of exclusions, adjustments, deductions, and credits not required to measure income accurately had not reached its present stage.

Compared to today, the 1954 income tax was simpler, more neutral, and fairer, in many respects. Perhaps as importantly, it was probably seen to be fair by most taxpayers, and the perception of fairness helped maintain the voluntary compliance so crucial to the American system of taxation.

The Decline in Simplicity

In 1954 the income tax was simpler for most taxpayers, in part because incomes were lower and the financial affairs of most families were simpler. There was little need for most taxpayers to work through a variety of complicated forms—and even more complicated instructions—to determine eligibility for a particular tax benefit. Only 25 percent of taxpayers itemized deductions in 1955, compared to 35 percent in 1982. Thus, fewer taxpayers found it necessary to save receipts verifying a multitude of expenditures accorded tax-preferred status. There was also little need to engage the services of a tax professional to file an individual income tax return. Tax planning—the rearrangement of one's economic affairs to minimize taxes—was the concern of only a few. Most taxpayers did not even feel the need to consider the tax consequences of major decisions, much less everyday transactions.

Today the proliferation and expansion of exclusions, adjustments to income, deductions, and credits create a major burden of paperwork and make part-time bookkeepers of many Americans. At present, about 100 different Federal tax forms are used by individuals. Many decisions—for example, whether and how to make a charitable contribution, whether to participate in insurance plans offered by an employer, and whether to contribute to a political party—all have tax consequences. Ordinary citizens are confronted with the alternatives of using a professional tax preparer, becoming knowledgeable in arcane tax law, running afoul of the tax administration, or possibly passing up available tax benefits. Today, over 40 percent of all individual income tax returns—and some 60 percent of all long forms (form 1040s)—are prepared by paid professionals. So-called tax shelters, once known only to the wealthy, are now attracting increasing numbers of middle-income Americans, many of whom do not have access to sophisticated tax advice and are misled by the misrepresentations of unscrupulous promoters of illegal shelters, often with disastrous effects. Legislative response to the tax shelter problem over the last 15 years has involved a patchwork of solutions that has generally increased the complexity of the tax system without correcting the underlying causes of tax shelters.

Erosion of the Tax Base

In 1954, the income tax did favor certain economic activities over others. For example, even then, tax experts criticized the fact that income from oil and gas properties, interest on state and local securities, and appreciation on capital assets were accorded preferential tax treatment. These "loopholes," as they were called, created inequities and distorted the use of the Nation's resources. By comparison, most interest, dividend, and labor income was taxed in full, and few forms of personal expenditure were tax deductible. The most important itemized deductions were for state and local taxes, charitable contributions, interest payments, and medical expenses; some of these had valid or easily understood justifications.

The last three decades have seen enormous erosion of the tax base. Compensation has increasingly taken the form of tax-free fringe benefits and legally taxable "perks" that many taxpayers improperly treat as tax-exempt. Interest on bonds issued by state and local governments has long been tax exempt, but recently these governments have increasingly used tax-exempt bonds to finance private investments. The investment tax credit greatly reduces the effective tax rate on income generated by business equipment, and accelerated depreciation and the deduction for interest expense combine to eliminate most taxes on income from debt-financed investments in real estate. In extreme cases these and other features of the tax law create losses for tax purposes that can be used to shelter other income. Exclusions, itemized deductions, and the deduction value of credits offset about 34 percent of personal income in 1982, as opposed to only 18 percent in 1954.

Economic Distortions

The lack of a comprehensive income tax base has two obvious and important adverse effects on the ability of the marketplace to allocate capital and labor to their most productive uses. First, the smaller the tax base, the higher tax rates must be to raise a given amount of revenue. High tax rates discourage saving and investment, stifle work effort, retard invention and innovation, encourage unproductive investment in tax shelters, and needlessly reduce the Nation's standard of living and growth rate.

Second, tax-preferred activities are favored relative to others, and tax law, rather than the market, becomes the primary force in determining how economic resources are used. Over the years, the tax system has come to exert a pervasive influence on the behavior of private decision-makers. The resulting tax-induced distortions in the use of labor and capital and in consumer choices have severe costs in terms of lower productivity, lost production, and reduced consumer satisfaction.

The existing taxation of capital and business income is particularly non-neutral. It favors capital-intensive industries over others, such as services. The tax system favors industries that are unusually dependent on equipment over those—such as wholesale and retail trade—that rely more heavily on other forms of capital, including inventories and structures. High technology companies are put at a particular disadvantage. Since they do not require large capital investments that benefit from preferential tax treatment they bear the full brunt of high tax rates. A tax system that interferes less with market forces in the determination of what business should produce—and how—would be more conducive to productive investment and economic growth.

Inequities

Erosion of the tax base also creates inequities. Most obviously, it is unfair that two households with equal incomes should pay different amounts of tax, simply because one receives or spends its income in ways that are tax-preferred. There is, for example, no reason that employees should be allowed to escape tax on fringe benefits and entertainment provided by their employers, while others must buy the same benefits and entertainment with after-tax dollars. Even at moderate income levels, taxpayers with similar incomes can incur tax liabilities that differ by thousands of dollars. Moreover, gaps in the tax base create inequities across income clases, as well as within income classes. Some of the most important tax preferences—those that give rise to tax shelters—benefit primarily those with high incomes.

Unfair Treatment of the Family

Thirty years ago the personal exemption for the taxpayer, spouse, and each dependent was $600, and there was a standard deduction of 10 percent of adjusted gross income, up to $1,000. Thus a family of four would pay no tax until income exceeded $2,675. Even though the personal exemption is now $1,000 and a larger "zero-bracket amount" has replaced the standard deduction, inflation has resulted in a substantial decline in the real value of the "tax-free amount," the level of income at which tax is first paid. Some families with incomes below the poverty level have become subject to tax. Tax burdens have increased relatively more for large families with many dependents than for other taxpayers.

The tax law was designed for a society in which dependents are generally present as part of a family with both parents present. Some groups with greater-than-average proportions of poor families, such as the elderly and the disabled, receive special tax treatment, but this treatment is often arbitrary and random, and depends on the source of the income, not on the need of the family. Until recently, the working poor have almost always been excluded from such special treatment. The special burdens faced by many single heads of households—especially those caring for dependents and trying to work at the same time—have been addressed inadequately.

* * *

The Decline in Taxpayer Morale

The United States has long been proud of the "taxpayer morale" of its citizens—the willingness to pay voluntarily the income taxes necessary to finance government activities. Taxpayer morale ultimately depends, however, on the belief that taxes are fair. If the basis for this belief comes under suspicion, voluntary compliance with the tax laws is jeopardized. Thus, the perceived lack of fairness of the income tax may be as important as actual complexities, economic distortions, and inequities. Taxpayers resent paying substantially more tax than their neighbors who have equal or higher incomes. This is true even if the neighbor reduces taxes through commonly available and perfectly legal exclusions, adjustments, deductions, and credits, rather than by questionable or illegal means. Many witnesses at tax reform hearings the Treasury Department held throughout the country during June 1984 emphasized that tax should be collected on virtually all income, with little regard to how the income is earned or spent. Taxation can be thought to be unfair because the basic tax structure is defective, as well as because taxpayers who do not comply with the law are not penalized. The proliferation and publicity of tax shelters has a particularly pernicious effect on taxpayer morale.

Needed: Taxes That are Broad-Based, Simple, and Fair

Fundamental reform of the tax system is required to correct the problems just described. The tax system must be made simpler, more economically neutral, fairer, and more conducive to economic growth. These objectives are described more fully in the next chapter. The key to their achievement is to define real taxable income comprehensively, to exempt families with poverty-level incomes from tax, and to subject taxable income to a rate structure that, while mildly progressive, avoids rates so high that they stifle incentives and prevent economic growth. In short, the income tax should be broad-based, simple, and fair.

F. THE ROAD AHEAD

Although Woodsworth's ambling dreamer happily happened upon a host of golden daffodils, one better embarks on a journey or project with a destination or goal clearly in mind. The goal in this course is to expose the fundamentals of income taxation by exploring the manner in which many basic transactions and events bear upon an individual's liability for income tax. This note summarizes the steps by which this book works toward that goal; a course has been set for which this note is a skeletal road map to the destination.

You have survived the scattered but important introductory material in most of Part One, although there may be some things to return to there. Part Two of this book seeks to corral all items required to be included in a taxpayer's gross income. Listing of course is impossible. Instead, an examination is made of judicial and administrative interpretation of the broad congressional language "income from whatever source derived" and its constitutional counterpart. This is followed by a detailed study of the Code sections by which Congress specifically excludes from or includes in gross income all or parts of specified items. The purpose here is not to memorize a laundry list, but much more to learn to manage the language of the Code, really a new language or at least *patois*.

After learning to identify gross income, a question may be: Who is to pay tax on it? Part Three of the book examines the so-called assignment-of-income doctrine which is aimed at preventing the artificial shifting of tax liability among individuals and other taxable entities. All right! Macy's won't pay Gimbel's tax. But there are challenging problems here which will unfold in due time.

Once one has gathered all items of income and assigned them to the proper taxpayer (in tax parlance, has determined his gross income for the year), various deductions are allowed to reach the net figure "taxable income", the base to which the tax rates are applied. Congress might have imposed a tax on gross income but, after all, fair is fair and almost as a required matter of legislative grace it determined instead to allow numerous statutory deductions. Part Four of this book considers these deductions.

Individuals are not the only taxpayers under our federal taxing system. Corporations, trusts, and estates pay income taxes as well and, while not actually taxed as an entity, a partnership also must determine its "taxable income". While this book emphasizes individual income tax liability, nevertheless, principles and concepts involved in determining tax liability (gross income, taxpayer identification, taxable income, rates, credits, etc.) are often similar or the same for all affected entities. Some of this spill-over is especially apparent in Part Four which treats deductions in five chapters dealing respectively with: business deductions; deductions for profit-making, non-business activities; deductions not limited to business or profit-making activities; limitations on deductions; and deductions for individuals only. The material includes cases and rulings relevant to but not specifically directed to individual taxpayers.

In determining taxable income for the year, three additional questions must be considered with respect to each item of income or deduction. They are: (1) For what taxable year is an item income or deductible? This will soon be seen to be quite important when rate tables and statutes limiting the period of liability or of refund recovery are considered. (2) What is the character (capital gain or loss, or ordinary income or loss) of various items? Tax advantages and limitations too attend such determinations. (3) Is gain or loss immediately to be recognized? Some items seemingly taxable or deductible get a deferment, sometimes essential or at least helpful and at others disadvantageous or even disastrous.

The timing matters identified in number (1), above, are considered in Part Five of the book. Conventional usage might cause the first chapter there to be entitled Tax Accounting, which normally puts the fear of God into Political Science majors who conjure up thoughts of balance sheets, debits and credits, and electronic calculators. The concepts involved will prove much less frightening when actually encountered. Our income taxing system is based on annual reporting (tax liability is determined and paid on a twelve month basis), and principles of tax accounting seek to say into what annual period an income or deduction item is properly included. These matters can be wonderfully complex; but the fundamental rules, the things with which we are concerned here, are really pretty simple.

The second question mentioned above is known as characterization of income and deductions. Although Congress has determined that income from some sources is no longer to be given significant preferential treatment (taxed at lower rates), it has put a 28 percent rate ceiling on some capital gains while subjecting other income to a maximum 31 percent rate, and it has continued to mandate that deductions of losses from such sources are to be subject to limitations. Part Six of the book illustrates that one must characterize each item of income or deduction and see whether the items when combined are to be given preferential treatment or subjected to limitations. Some deductions are not considered until Part Six because they cannot be intelligently considered separately from the characterization concept. Also, beware! Part Six is the den of the "Gotcha!" Enter with care, at your own risk. The "Gotcha!" is a sneaky kind of character assassin.

In some situations, even though one has income or loss, even *realized* income or loss, nevertheless Congress has seen fit not immediately to accord it tax consequences. Part Seven examines the nonrecognition or deferral of some gains and the non-recognition or sometimes outright disallowance of some losses.

Consideration of all of the above leads to the determination of taxable income, next to be converted into tax liability. Part Eight of the book explains that conversion. Different rates of tax are applied to various classifications of taxpayers. Corporations are taxed at essentially stepped rates found in Section 11, while estates and trusts are taxed at the essentially flat rates in Section 1(e). Individuals are further classified into various categories: married taxpayers filing joint returns and surviving spouses in Section 1(a), heads of households in Section 1(b), unmarried individuals in Section 1(c), and married individuals filing separately in Section 1(d), for which modified flat tax rate tables are provided. Part Eight studies the development of these individual classifications and the tax rates applicable to them.

Part Eight also introduces tax credits. Tax credits are subtracted from the amount of tax otherwise actually to be paid. They are therefore preferred by the taxpayer over deductions used to determine taxable income. Credits reduce tax dollar for dollar, while deductions are effective in reducing tax only to the extent of one's marginal tax rates.

Finally, Part Eight also introduces the Alternative Minimum Tax, an essentially separate and complicated taxing scheme. Under this tax, taxpayers compute their taxable income in a manner different from the regular tax system and pay tax at rates different from the regular rates. This tax applies in any year only if it generates greater revenue from the taxpayer than the regular tax.

We have reached the Moon but not the Millenium. Nobody is perfect, and mistakes are made in federal taxes as much or more as anywhere. Tax procedures are available for correcting mistakes and by administrative and judicial proceedings for settling inevitable controversies. Still in a fundamental way Part Nine, the last three chapters of this book, deals with these phenomena.

From here, in the words of your favorite Baedeker, as the sun settles softly behind the blue mountains that reach down to the shimmering sea, it's off to Part Two and Gross Income!

Bon voyage!

PART TWO: IDENTIFICATION OF INCOME SUBJECT TO TAXATION

CHAPTER 2. GROSS INCOME: THE SCOPE OF SECTION 61

A. INTRODUCTION TO INCOME

Internal Revenue Code: Section 61.

The federal income tax is imposed annually on a net figure known as "taxable income." Taxable income is "gross income" less certain authorized deductions. The scope of the gross income concept is taken as the starting point for this course, just as gross income is the starting point in the computation of tax liability.

Code Section 61 defines gross income as "all *income* from whatever source derived." It may appear that Congress has violated a cardinal principle against defining a word in terms of the very word being defined—"water" means "water". But this of course is not the case. "Gross income" is a distinct statutory concept which could as well have been called "gross take" or something of the sort. If it wished to, which of course it does not, Congress could define gross income to include only amounts received as salary or wages or as dividends or in some other very restricted manner. Under the statutory definition, the meaning of the term "gross income" depends initially upon the meaning accorded "income." According to the legislative history of Section 61,[1] "the word income is used as in section 22(a) [Section 61 of the 1954 and 1986 Codes] in its constitutional sense. It [was] not intended [in Section 61 of the 1954 and 1986 Codes] to change the concept of income that obtains under section 22(a) [of the 1939 Code]." A long standing question has therefore been: What is "income"?

The term "income" in the Code, "incomes" in the Sixteenth Amendment, has a tax meaning that may vary from the meaning accorded the term in other contexts. A finder's treasure trove may not be "income" to the economist because it is not a recurring kind of receipt; but is it "income" in the tax sense? It may be that for some purposes one has income if his wealth increases by way of an appreciation in his investments; but does such appreciation constitute income

---

1. S.Rep. No. 1622, 83rd Cong., 2d Sess. 168 (1954).

for tax purposes? Still it should not be understood that the question is always broad and elusive. The statute itself offers some illustrations in Section 61; and there are two important series of statutory rules of inclusion and exclusion which are taken up beginning with Chapter 3. Moreover, in recent years important court decisions have greatly narrowed the area of uncertainty, and long-standing administrative practice has added some clarification.[2]

B. EQUIVOCAL RECEIPT OF FINANCIAL BENEFIT

Internal Revenue Code: Section 61.

Regulations: Sections 1.61–1, –2(a)(1), –2(d)(1), –14(a).

CESARINI v. U.S.

District Court of the United States, Northern District of Ohio, 1969.
296 F.Supp. 3, affirmed per curiam 428 F.2d 812
(6th Cir.1970).

YOUNG, District Judge. This is an action by the plaintiffs as taxpayers for the recovery of income tax payments made in the calendar year 1964. Plaintiffs contend that the amount of $836.51 was erroneously overpaid by them in 1964, and that they are entitled to a refund in that amount, together with the statutory interest from October 13, 1965, the date which they made their claim upon the Internal Revenue Service for the refund.

Plaintiffs and the United States have stipulated to the material facts in the case, and the matter is before the Court for final decision. The facts necessary for a resolution of the issues raised should perhaps be briefly stated before the Court proceeds to a determination of the matter. Plaintiffs are husband and wife, and live within the jurisdiction of the United States District Court for the Northern District of Ohio. In 1957, the plaintiffs purchased a used piano at an auction sale for approximately $15.00, and the piano was used by their daughter for piano lessons. In 1964, while cleaning the piano, plaintiffs discovered the sum of $4,467.00 in old currency, and since have retained the piano instead of discarding it as previously planned. Being unable to ascertain who put the money there, plaintiffs exchanged the old currency for new at a bank, and reported the sum of $4,467.00 on their 1964 joint income tax return as ordinary income from other sources. On October 18, 1965, plaintiffs filed an amended return with the District Director of Internal Revenue in Cleveland, Ohio, this second return eliminating the sum of $4,467.00 from the gross income computation, and requesting a refund in the amount of $836.51, the amount allegedly overpaid as a result of the former inclusion of $4,467.00 in the original return for the calendar year of 1964. On January 18, 1966, the Commissioner of

---

2. There is a comprehensive analysis of the concept of gross income in Magill, Taxable Income (1945); see also Sneed, "The Configurations of Gross Income" (1967) and Lowndes, "Current Conceptions of Taxable Income," 25 Ohio St.L.J. 151 (1964).

Internal Revenue rejected taxpayers' refund claim in its entirety, and plaintiffs filed the instant action in March of 1967.

Plaintiffs make three alternative contentions in support of their claim that the sum of $836.51 should be refunded to them. First, that the $4,467.00 found in the piano is not includable in gross income under Section 61 of the Internal Revenue Code. (26 U.S.C.A. § 61) Secondly, even if the retention of the cash constitutes a realization of ordinary income under Section 61, it was due and owing in the year the piano was purchased, 1957, and by 1964, the statute of limitations provided by 26 U.S.C.A. § 6501 had elapsed. And thirdly, that if the treasure trove money is gross income for the year 1964, it was entitled to capital gains treatment under Section 1221 of Title 26. The Government, by its answer and its trial brief, asserts that the amount found in the piano is includable in gross income under Section 61(a) of Title 26, U.S.C.A., that the money is taxable in the year it was actually found, 1964, and that the sum is properly taxable at ordinary income rates, not being entitled to capital gains treatment under 26 U.S.C.A. §§ 1201 et seq.

After a consideration of the pertinent provisions of the Internal Revenue Code, Treasury Regulations, Revenue Rulings, and decisional law in the area, this Court has concluded that the taxpayers are not entitled to a refund of the amount requested, nor are they entitled to capital gains treatment on the income item at issue.

The starting point in determining whether an item is to be included in gross income is, of course, Section 61(a) of Title 26 U.S.C.A., and that section provides in part:

> "Except as otherwise provided in this subtitle, *gross income means all income from whatever source derived,* including (but not limited to) the following items: * * *" (Emphasis added.)

Subsections (1) through (15) of Section 61(a) then go on to list fifteen items specifically included in the computation of the taxpayer's gross income, and Part II of Subchapter B of the 1954 Code (Sections 71 et seq.) deals with other items expressly included in gross income. While neither of these listings expressly includes the type of income which is at issue in the case at bar, Part III of Subchapter B (Sections 101 et seq.) deals with items specifically *excluded* from gross income, and found money is not listed in those sections either. This absence of express mention in any of the code sections necessitates a return to the "all income from whatever source" language of Section 61(a) of the code, and the express statement there that gross income is "not limited to" the following fifteen examples. Section 1.61–1(a) of the Treasury Regulations, the corresponding section to Section 61(a) in the 1954 Code, reiterates this broad construction of gross income, providing in part:

> "Gross income means all income from whatever source derived, unless excluded by law. *Gross income includes income*

realized in any form, whether in money, property, or services.
*   *   *" (Emphasis added.)

The decisions of the United States Supreme Court have frequently stated that this broad all-inclusive language was used by Congress to exert the full measure of its taxing power under the Sixteenth Amendment to the United States Constitution. Commissioner of Internal Revenue v. Glenshaw Glass Co., 348 U.S. 426, 429, 75 S.Ct. 473 (1955); Helvering v. Clifford, 309 U.S. 331, 334, 60 S.Ct. 554 (1940); Helvering v. Midland Mutual Life Ins. Co., 300 U.S. 216, 223, 57 S.Ct. 423 (1937); Douglas v. Willcuts, 296 U.S. 1, 9, 56 S.Ct. 59 (1935); Irwin v. Gavit, 268 U.S. 161, 166, 45 S.Ct. 475 (1925).

In addition, the Government in the instant case cites and relies upon an I.R.S. Revenue Ruling which is undeniably on point:

> "The finder of treasure-trove is in receipt of taxable income, for Federal income tax purposes, to the extent of its value in United States currency, for the taxable year in which it is reduced to undisputed possession." Rev.Rul. 61, 1953–1, Cum.Bull. 17.

The plaintiffs argue that the above ruling does not control this case for two reasons. The first is that subsequent to the Ruling's pronouncement in 1953, Congress enacted Sections 74 and 102 of the 1954 Code, § 74, expressly *including* the value of prizes and awards in gross income in most cases, and § 102 specifically *exempting* the value of gifts received from gross income. From this, it is argued that Section 74 was added because prizes might otherwise be construed as non-taxable gifts, and since no such section was passed expressly taxing treasure-trove, it is therefore a gift which is non-taxable under Section 102. This line of reasoning overlooks the statutory scheme previously alluded to, whereby income from all sources is taxed unless the taxpayer can point to an express exemption. Not only have the taxpayers failed to list a specific exclusion in the instant case, but also the Government *has* pointed to express language covering the found money, even though it would not be required to do so under the broad language of Section 61(a) and the foregoing Supreme Court decisions interpreting it.

The second argument of the taxpayers in support of their contention that Rev.Rul. 61, 1953–1 should not be applied in this case is based upon the decision of Dougherty v. Commissioner, 10 T.C.M. 320, P–H Memo. T.C., ¶ 51,093 (1951). In that case the petitioner was an individual who had never filed an income tax return, and the Commissioner was attempting to determine his gross income by the so-called "net worth" method. Dougherty had a substantial increase in his net worth, and attempted to partially explain away his lack of reporting it by claiming that he had found $31,000.00 in cash inside a used chair he had purchased in 1947. The Tax Court's opinion deals primarily with the factual question of whether or not Dougherty actually *did* find this money in a chair, finally concluding that he did not and from this petitioners in the instant case argue that if such found money is clearly gross income, the Tax Court would not have reached the fact question, but merely included the $31,000.00 as a matter of law. Petitioners argue that since the Tax Court did not include the sum in Dougherty's gross income until they had found as a fact that it *was not* treasure trove, then by implication such discovered money is not taxable. This argument must fail for two reasons. First, the *Dougherty* decision precedes Rev.Rul. 61, 1953–1 by two years, and thus was dealing with what then was an uncharted area of the gross income provisions of the Code. Secondly, the case cannot be read as authority for the proposition that treasure trove is not includable in gross income, even if the revenue ruling had not been issued two years later.[1]

In partial summary, then, the arguments of the taxpayers which attempt to avoid the application of Rev.Rul. 61, 1953–1 are not well taken. The *Dougherty* case simply does not hold one way or another on the problem before this Court, and therefore petitioners' reliance upon it is misplaced. The other branch of their argument, that found money must be construed to be a gift under Section 102 of the 1954 Code since it is not expressly included as are prizes in Section 74 of the Code, would not even be effective were it being urged at a time prior to 1953, when the ruling had not yet been promulgated. In addition to the numerous cases in the Supreme Court which uphold the broad sweeping construction of Section 61(a) found in Treas.Reg. § 1.61–1(a), other courts and commentators writing at a point in time before the ruling came down took the position that windfalls, including found monies, were properly includable in gross income under Section 22(a) of the 1939 Code, the predecessor of Section 61(a) in the 1954 Code. See, for example, the decision in Park & Tilford Distillers Corp. v. United States, 107 F.Supp. 941, 123 Ct.Cl. 509 (1952); [2] and Comment, "Taxation of Found Property and Other Windfalls," 20 U.Chi.L.Rev. 748, 752 (1953).[3] While it is generally true that revenue rulings may be disre-

---

1. The Dougherty Court, after carefully considering the evidence before it on the factual question of whether or not the taxpayer actually found the $31,000.00 as claimed, stated:

"In short, we do not believe the money was in the chair when the chair was acquired by the petitioner.

"Where the petitioner got the money which he later took from the chair and in what manner it was obtained by him, we do not know. It is accordingly impossible for us to conclude and hold the $31,000 here in question was not acquired by him in a manner such as would make it income to him within the meaning of the statute. Such being the case, *we do not reach the question whether money, if acquired in the manner claimed by the petitioner, is income under the statute.*" (Emphasis added.) 10 T.C.M. 320 at 323 (1951).

2. In this taxpayer's suit for a refund of corporation taxes, Judge Madden of the Court of Claims stated at pages 943–944: "* * * It is not, and we think could not rationally be, suggested that Congress lacks the power to tax windfalls as income. * * * A windfall may, of course, be a gift, and thus expressly exempt from income tax. But if, as in the instant case, the windfall is clearly not a gift, but a payment required by a statute * * * we do not see how its exemption could be reconciled with the reiterated statements that Congress intended, by Section 22(a), to tax income to the extent of its constitutional power." 107 F.Supp. at 943, 944.

3. This article, after stating arguments both ways on the question, and thus suggesting by implication that the area was not clearly defined at that time, went on to state at page 752: "Perhaps a more appropriate interpretation of Section 22(a) would be to hold that all windfalls * * * are

garded by the courts if in conflict with the code and the regulations, or with other judicial decisions, plaintiffs in the instant case have been unable to point to any inconsistency between the gross income sections of the code, the interpretation of them by the regulations and the courts, and the revenue ruling which they herein attack as inapplicable. On the other hand, the United States *has* shown a consistency in letter and spirit between the ruling and the code, regulations, and court decisions.

Although not cited by either party, and noticeably absent from the Government's brief, the following Treasury Regulation appears in the 1964 Regulations, the year of the return in dispute:

"§ 1.61–14   Miscellaneous items of gross income.

"(a) In general.   In addition to the items enumerated in section 61(a), there are many other kinds of gross income * * *. *Treasure trove, to the extent of its value in United States currency, constitutes gross income for the taxable year in which it is reduced to undisputed possession.*" (Emphasis added.)

Identical language appears in the 1968 Treasury Regulations, and is found in all previous years back to 1958. This language is the same in all material respects as that found in Rev.Rul. 61–53–1, Cum.Bull. 17, and is undoubtedly an attempt to codify that ruling into the Regulations which apply to the 1954 Code. This Court is of the opinion that Treas.Reg. § 1.61–14(a) is dispositive of the major issue in this case if the $4,467.00 found in the piano was "reduced to undisputed possession" in the year petitioners reported it, for this Regulation was applicable to returns filed in the calendar year of 1964.

This brings the Court to the second contention of the plaintiffs: that if any tax was due, it was in 1957 when the piano was purchased, and by 1964 the Government was blocked from collecting it by reason of the statute of limitations. Without reaching the question of whether the voluntary payment in 1964 constituted a *waiver* on the part of the taxpayers, this Court finds that the $4,467.00 sum was properly included in gross income for the calendar year of 1964. Problems of when title vests, or when possession is complete in the field of federal taxation, in the absence of definitive federal legislation on the subject, are ordinarily determined by reference to the law of the state in which the taxpayer resides, or where the property around which the dispute centers is located. Since both the taxpayers and the property in question are found within the State of Ohio, Ohio law must govern as to when the found money was "reduced to undisputed possession" within the meaning of Treas.Reg. § 1.61–14 and Rev.Rul. 61–53–1, Cum.Bull. 17.

taxable income under its sweeping language. * * * Insofar as the policy of Section 22(a) is to impose similar tax burdens on persons in similar circumstances, there is no basis for distinguishing value received as windfall and * * * value received as salary." Footnote 50 of the Comment indicates that the article was in printing when Rev.Rul. 61–53–1 came out.

In Ohio, there is no statute specifically dealing with the rights of owners and finders of treasure trove, and in the absence of such a statute the common-law rule of England applies, so that "title belongs to the finder as against all the world except the true owner." Niederlehner v. Weatherly, 78 Ohio App. 263, 69 N.E.2d 787 (1946), appeal dismissed, 146 Ohio St. 697, 67 N.E.2d 713 (1946). The *Niederlehner* case held, *inter alia,* that the owner of real estate upon which money is found does not have title as against the finder. Therefore, in the instant case if plaintiffs had resold the piano in 1958, not knowing of the money within it, they later would not be able to succeed in an action against the purchaser who *did* discover it. Under Ohio law, the plaintiffs must have actually *found* the money to have superior title over all but the true owner, and they did not discover the old currency until 1964. Unless there is present a specific state statute to the contrary,[4] the majority of jurisdictions are in accord with the Ohio rule.[5] Therefore, this Court finds that the $4,467.00 in old currency was not "reduced to undisputed possession" until its actual discovery in 1964, and thus the United States was not barred by the statute of limitations from collecting the $836.51 in tax during that year.

Finally, plaintiffs' contention that they are entitled to capital gains treatment upon the discovered money must be rejected. * * *

[This portion of the opinion is omitted. The characterization of income and its tax significance are considered in Chapter 21, infra. Ed.]

OLD COLONY TRUST CO. v. COMMISSIONER

Supreme Court of the United States, 1929.
279 U.S. 716, 49 S.Ct. 499.

Mr. Chief Justice TAFT delivered the opinion of the Court.

* * *

William M. Wood was president of the American Woolen Company during the years 1918, 1919 and 1920. In 1918 he received as salary and commissions from the company $978,725, which he included in his federal income tax return for 1918. In 1919 he received as salary and commissions from the company $548,132.27, which he included in his return for 1919.

August 3, 1916, the American Woolen Company had adopted the following resolution, which was in effect in 1919 and 1920:

"Voted: That this company pay any and all income taxes, State and Federal, that may hereafter become due and payable upon the salaries of all the officers of the company, including

4. See, for example, United States v. Peter, 178 F.Supp. 854 (E.D.La.1959) where it is held that under the Louisiana Civil Code and the Code D'Napolean the finder of treasure does not own it, and can only become the owner if no one else can prove that the treasure is his property.

5. See Weeks v. Hackett, 104 Me. 264, 71 A. 858, 860 (1908) for a review of the authorities in jurisdictions where the finder is the owner as against all but the true owner. Also, see Finding Lost Goods 36A C.J.S. § 5, p. 422 (1961).

the president, William M. Wood; the comptroller, Parry C. Wiggin; the auditor, George R. Lawton; and the following members of the staff, to wit: Frank H. Carpenter, Edwin L. Heath, Samuel R. Haines, and William M. Lasbury, to the end that said persons and officers shall receive their salaries or other compensation in full without deduction on account of income taxes, State or Federal, which taxes are to be paid out of the treasury of this corporation."

This resolution was amended on March 25, 1918, as follows:

"Voted: That, in referring to the vote passed by this board on August 3, 1916, in reference to income taxes, State and Federal, payable upon the salaries or compensation of the officers and certain employees of this company, the method of computing said taxes shall be as follows, viz:

" 'The difference between what the total amount of his tax would be, including his income from all sources, and the amount of his tax when computed upon his income excluding such compensation or salaries paid by this company.' "

Pursuant to these resolutions, the American Woolen Company paid to the collector of internal revenue Mr. Wood's federal income and surtaxes due to salary and commissions paid him by the company, as follows:

Taxes for 1918 paid in 1919_____ $681,169.88
Taxes for 1919 paid in 1920_____ 351,179.27

The decision of the Board of Tax Appeals here sought to be reviewed was that the income taxes of $681,169.88 and $351,179.27 paid by the American Woolen Company for Mr. Wood were additional income to him for the years 1919 and 1920.

The question certified by the Circuit Court of Appeals for answer by this Court is:

"Did the payment by the employer of the income taxes assessable against the employee constitute additional taxable income to such employee?"

* * *

Coming now to the merits of this case, we think the question presented is whether a taxpayer, having induced a third person to pay his income tax or having acquiesced in such payment as made in discharge of an obligation to him, may avoid the making of a return thereof and the payment of a corresponding tax. We think he may not do so. The payment of the tax by the employers was in consideration of the services rendered by the employee and was a gain derived by the employee from his labor. The form of the payment is expressly declared to make no difference. Section 213, Revenue Act of 1918, c. 18, 40 Stat. 1065.* It is therefore immaterial that the taxes were

---

* The legislative history of the 1954 Code makes it clear that, while § 61 omits the phrase "in whatever form paid," the defini-

tion of gross income still includes "income realized in any form." Sen.Rep. No. 1622, 83d Cong., 2d Sess. 168 (1954). Ed.

directly paid over to the Government. The discharge by a third person of an obligation to him is equivalent to receipt by the person taxed. The certificate shows that the taxes were imposed upon the employee, that the taxes were actually paid by the employer and that the employee entered upon his duties in the years in question under the express agreement that his income taxes would be paid by his employer. This is evidenced by the terms of the resolution passed August 3, 1916, more than one year prior to the year in which the taxes were imposed. The taxes were paid upon a valuable consideration, namely, the services rendered by the employee and as part of the compensation therefor. We think therefore that the payment constituted income to the employee.

This result is sustained by many decisions. * * *

Nor can it be argued that the payment of the tax * * * was a gift. The payment for services, even though entirely voluntary, was nevertheless compensation within the statute. This is shown by the case of Noel v. Parrott, 15 F.2d 669. There it was resolved that a gratuitous appropriation equal in amount to $3 per share on the outstanding stock of the company be set aside out of the assets for distribution to certain officers and employees of the company and that the executive committee be authorized to make such distribution as they deemed wise and proper. The executive committee gave $35,000 to be paid to the plaintiff taxpayer. The court said, p. 672:

> "In no view of the evidence, therefore, can the $35,000 be regarded as a gift. It was either compensation for services rendered, or a gain or profit derived from the sale of the stock of the corporation, or both; and, in any view, it was taxable as income."

It is next argued against the payment of this tax that if these payments by the employer constitute income to the employee, the employer will be called upon to pay the tax imposed upon this additional income, and that the payment of the additional tax will create further income which will in turn be subject to tax, with the result that there would be a tax upon a tax. This it is urged is the result of the Government's theory when carried to its logical conclusion and results in an absurdity which Congress could not have contemplated.

In the first place, no attempt has been made by the Treasury to collect further taxes, upon the theory that the payment of the additional taxes creates further income, and the question of a tax upon a tax was not before the Circuit Court of Appeals and has not been certified to this Court. We can settle questions of that sort when an attempt to impose a tax upon a tax is undertaken, but not now. United States v. Sullivan, 274 U.S. 259, 264, 47 S.Ct. 607; Yazoo & Mississippi Valley R. R. v. Jackson Vinegar Co., 226 U.S. 217, 219, 33 S.Ct. 40. It is not, therefore, necessary to answer the argument based upon an algebraic formula to reach the amount of taxes due. The question in this case is, "Did the payment by the employer of the income taxes assessable against the employee constitute additional taxable income to such employee?" The answer must be "Yes."

[The separate opinion of Mr. Justice McReynolds has been omitted. Ed.]

COMMISSIONER v. GLENSHAW GLASS CO.*

Supreme Court of the United States, 1955.
348 U.S. 426, 75 S.Ct. 473, rehearing denied, 349 U.S. 925,
75 S.Ct. 657 (1955).

Mr. Chief Justice WARREN delivered the opinion of the Court.

This litigation involves two cases with independent factual backgrounds yet presenting the identical issue. The two cases were consolidated for argument before the Court of Appeals for the Third Circuit and were heard *en banc*. The common question is whether money received as exemplary damages for fraud or as the punitive two-thirds portion of a treble-damage antitrust recovery must be reported by a taxpayer as gross income under § 22(a) of the Internal Revenue Code of 1939.[1] In a single opinion, 211 F.2d 928, the Court of Appeals affirmed the Tax Court's separate rulings in favor of the taxpayers. 18 T.C. 860; 19 T.C. 637. Because of the frequent recurrence of the question and differing interpretations by the lower courts of this Court's decisions bearing upon the problem, we granted the Commissioner of Internal Revenue's ensuing petition for certiorari. 348 U.S. 813.

The facts of the cases were largely stipulated and are not in dispute. So far as pertinent they are as follows:

> Commissioner v. Glenshaw Glass Co.—The Glenshaw Glass Company, a Pennsylvania corporation, manufactures glass bottles and containers. It was engaged in protracted litigation with the Hartford-Empire Company, which manufacturers machinery of a character used by Glenshaw. Among the claims advanced by Glenshaw were demands for exemplary damages for fraud[2] and treble damages for injury to its business by reason of Hartford's violation of the federal antitrust laws.[3] In December, 1947, the parties concluded a settlement of all pending litigation, by which Hartford paid Glenshaw approximately $800,000. Through a method of allocation which was approved by the Tax Court, 18 T.C. 860, 870–872, and which is no longer in issue, it was ultimately determined that, of the total settlement, $324,529.94 represented payment of punitive damages for fraud and antitrust violations. Glenshaw did not

---

* See Wright, "The Effect of the Source of Realized Benefits upon the Supreme Court's Concept of Taxable Receipts," 8 Stan.L.Rev. 164 (1956). Ed.

1. 53 Stat. 9, 53 Stat. 574, 26 U.S.C.A. § 22(a). [See note 11, infra. Ed.]

2. For the bases of Glenshaw's claim for damages from fraud, see Shawkee Manu-

facturing Co. v. Hartford-Empire Co., 322 U.S. 271, 74 S.Ct. 1014, Hazel-Atlas Glass Co. v. Hartford-Empire Co., 322 U.S. 238, 64 S.Ct. 997.

3. See Hartford-Empire Co. v. United States, 323 U.S. 386, 65 S.Ct. 373, 324 U.S. 570, 65 S.Ct. 815.

report this portion of the settlement as income for the tax year involved. The Commissioner determined a deficiency claiming as taxable the entire sum less only deductible legal fees. As previously noted, the Tax Court and the Court of Appeals upheld the taxpayer.

Commissioner v. William Goldman Theatres, Inc.—William Goldman Theatres, Inc., a Delaware corporation operating motion picture houses in Pennsylvania, sued Loew's, Inc., alleging a violation of the federal antitrust laws and seeking treble damages. After a holding that a violation had occurred, William Goldman Theatres, Inc. v. Loew's, Inc., 150 F.2d 738, the case was remanded to the trial court for a determination of damages. It was found that Goldman had suffered a loss of profits equal to $125,000 and was entitled to treble damages in the sum of $375,000. William Goldman Theatres, Inc. v. Loew's, Inc., 69 F.Supp. 103, aff'd, 164 F.2d 1021, cert. denied, 334 U.S. 811. Goldman reported only $125,000 of the recovery as gross income and claimed that the $250,000 balance constituted punitive damages and as such was not taxable. The Tax Court agreed, 19 T.C. 637, and the Court of Appeals, hearing this with the *Glenshaw* case, affirmed. 211 F.2d 928.

It is conceded by the respondents that there is no constitutional barrier to the imposition of a tax on punitive damages. Our question is one of statutory construction: are these payments comprehended by § 22(a)?

The sweeping scope of the controverted statute is readily apparent:

1434 Code

"SEC. 22. GROSS INCOME.

"(a) GENERAL DEFINITION.—'Gross income' includes gains, profits, and income derived from salaries, wages, or compensation for personal service * * * of whatever kind and in whatever form paid, or from professions, vocations, trades, businesses, commerce, or sales, or dealings in property, whether real or personal, growing out of the ownership or use of or interest in such property; also from interest, rent, dividends, securities, or the transaction of any business carried on for gain or profit, *or gains or profits and income derived from any source whatever.* * * *" (Emphasis added.)[4]

This Court has frequently stated that this language was used by Congress to exert in this field "the full measure of its taxing power." Helvering v. Clifford, 309 U.S. 331, 334, 60 S.Ct. 554, 556; Helvering v. Midland Mutual Life Ins. Co., 300 U.S. 216, 223, 57 S.Ct. 423, 425; Douglas v. Willcuts, 296 U.S. 1, 9, 55 S.Ct. 346; Irwin v. Gavit, 268 U.S. 161, 166, 45 S.Ct. 475. Respondents contend that punitive damages, characterized as "windfalls" flowing from the culpable conduct of third parties, are not within the scope of the section. But Congress applied

---

4. See note 1, supra.

no limitations as to the source of taxable receipts, nor restrictive labels as to their nature. And the Court has given a liberal construction to this broad phraseology in recognition of the intention of Congress to tax all gains except those specifically exempted. Commissioner v. Jacobson, 336 U.S. 28, 49, 69 S.Ct. 358, 369; Helvering v. Stockholms Enskilda Bank, 293 U.S. 84, 87–91, 55 S.Ct. 50, 53. Thus, the fortuitous gain accruing to a lessor by reason of the forfeiture of a lessee's improvements on the rented property was taxed in Helvering v. Bruun, 309 U.S. 461, 60 S.Ct. 631. Cf. Robertson v. United States, 343 U.S. 711, 72 S.Ct. 994; Rutkin v. United States, 343 U.S. 130, 72 S.Ct. 571; United States v. Kirby Lumber Co., 284 U.S. 1, 52 S.Ct. 4. Such decisions demonstrate that we cannot but ascribe content to the catchall provision of § 22(a), "gains or profits and income derived from any source whatever." The importance of that phrase has been too frequently recognized since its first appearance in the Revenue Act of 1913[5] to say now that it adds nothing to the meaning of "gross income."

Nor can we accept respondents' contention that a narrower reading of § 22(a) is required by the Court's characterization of income in Eisner v. Macomber, 252 U.S. 189, 207, 40 S.Ct. 189, as "the gain derived from capital, from labor, or from both combined."[6] The Court was there endeavoring to determine whether the distribution of a corporate stock dividend constituted a realized gain to the shareholder, or changed "only the form, not the essence," of his capital investment. Id., at 210. It was held that the taxpayer had "received nothing out of the company's assets for his separate use and benefit." Id., at 211. The distribution, therefore, was held not a taxable event. In that context—distinguishing gain from capital—the definition served a useful purpose. But it was not meant to provide a touchstone to all future gross income questions. Helvering v. Bruun, supra, at 468–469; United States v. Kirby Lumber Co., supra, at 3.

Here we have instances of undeniable accessions to wealth, clearly realized, and over which the taxpayers have complete dominion. The mere fact that the payments were extracted from the wrongdoers as punishment for unlawful conduct cannot detract from their character as taxable income to the recipients. Respondents concede, as they must, that the recoveries are taxable to the extent that they compensate for damages actually incurred. It would be an anomaly that could not be justified in the absence of clear congressional intent to say that a recovery for actual damages is taxable but not the additional amount

5. 38 Stat. 114, 167.

6. The phrase was derived from Stratton's Independence, Ltd. v. Howbert, 231 U.S. 399, 415, 34 S.Ct. 136, 140, and Doyle v. Mitchell Bros. Co., 247 U.S. 179, 185, 38 S.Ct. 467, 469, two cases construing the Revenue Act of 1909, 36 Stat. 11, 112. Both taxpayers were "wasting asset" corporations, one being engaged in mining, the other in lumbering operations. The definition was applied by the Court to demonstrate a distinction between a return on capital and "a mere conversion of capital assets." Doyle v. Mitchell Bros. Co., supra, at 184. The question raised by the instant case is clearly distinguishable.

extracted as punishment for the same conduct which caused the injury. And we find no such evidence of intent to exempt these payments.

It is urged that re-enactment of § 22(a) without change since the Board of Tax Appeals held punitive damages nontaxable in Highland Farms Corp., 42 B.T.A. 1314, indicates congressional satisfaction with that holding. Re-enactment—particularly without the slightest affirmative indication that Congress ever had the Highland Farms decision before it—is an unreliable indicium at best. Helvering v. Wilshire Oil Co., 308 U.S. 90, 100–101, 60 S.Ct. 18, 24; Koshland v. Helvering, 298 U.S. 441, 447, 56 S.Ct. 767, 770. Moreover, the Commissioner promptly published his nonacquiescence in this portion of the Highland Farms holding [7] and has, before and since, consistently maintained the position that these receipts are taxable.[8] It therefore cannot be said with certitude that Congress intended to carve an exception out of § 22(a)'s pervasive coverage. Nor does the 1954 Code's [9] legislative history, with its reiteration of the proposition that statutory gross income is "all-inclusive," [10] give support to respondents' position. The definition of gross income has been simplified, but no effect upon its present broad scope was intended.[11] Certainly punitive damages cannot reasonably be classified as gifts, cf. Commissioner v. Jacobson, 336 U.S. 28, 47–52, 69 S.Ct. 358, 369, nor do they come under any other exemption provision in the Code. We would do violence to the plain meaning of the statute and restrict a clear legislative attempt to bring the taxing power to bear upon all receipts constitutionally taxable were we to say that the payments in question here are not gross income. See Helvering v. Midland Mutual Life Ins. Co., supra, at 223.

Reversed.

Mr. Justice DOUGLAS dissents.

Mr. Justice HARLAN took no part in the consideration or decision of this case.

---

7. 1941–1 Cum.Bull. 16.

8. The long history of departmental rulings holding personal injury recoveries nontaxable on the theory that they roughly correspond to a return of capital cannot support exemption of punitive damages following injury to property. See 2 Cum.Bull. 71; I–1 Cum.Bull. 92, 93; VII–2 Cum.Bull. 123; 1954–1 Cum.Bull. 179, 180. Damages for personal injury are by definition compensatory only. Punitive damages, on the other hand, cannot be considered a restoration of capital for taxation purposes.

9. 68A Stat. 3 et seq. Section 61(a) of the Internal Revenue Code of 1954, 68A Stat. 17, is the successor to § 22(a) of the 1939 Code.

10. H.R.Rep. No. 1337, 83d Cong., 2d Sess. A18; S.Rep. No. 1622, 83d Cong., 2d Sess. 168.

11. In discussing § 61(a) of the 1954 Code, the House Report states:

"This section corresponds to section 22(a) of the 1939 Code. While the language in existing section 22(a) has been simplified, the all-inclusive nature of statutory gross income has not been affected thereby. Section 61(a) is as broad in scope as section 22(a).

"Section 61(a) provides that gross income includes 'all income from whatever source derived.' This definition is based upon the 16th Amendment and the word 'income' is used in its constitutional sense." H.R.Rep. No. 1337, supra, note 10, at A18.

A virtually identical statement appears in S.Rep. No. 1622, supra, note 10, at 168.

NOTE

definition of gross income

The Supreme Court in *Glenshaw Glass* attempts to define gross income or at least to indicate some criteria for gross income [1] when it refers to "undeniable accessions to wealth, clearly realized, and over which the taxpayers have complete dominion." Within these requirements, do borrowers have income on the receipt of loans? Clearly not; loans are based on concurrently acknowledged obligations to repay which, offsetting the receipt, negate any accession to wealth.[2] A security deposit may be likened to a loan for tax purposes. In Commissioner v. Indianapolis Power & Light Company,[3] the Supreme Court concluded that the contractual arrangement between the customers and the power company cast the deposit as a loan to the company. Of course if the borrower has no intent to repay a "loan" and the lender is unaware of that fact, the "loan" is not a loan but an illegal appropriation of the would-be creditor's property, which is income to the so-called borrower under Section 61.[4]

At one time the line between loans and illegal income was difficult to draw. Initially, in Commissioner v. Wilcox [5] the Supreme Court did not tax embezzlers, because they could be compelled by victims to return the property involved. It analogized embezzlers to borrowers who, as suggested above, achieved no accession to wealth. Would a burglar's status be the same? Later in Rutkin v. United States,[6] the Court distinguished the receipts of an extortionist from those of an embezzler on the ground that an extortionist is less likely to be asked for repayment, taxing that kind of illegal loot. Still later, however, in James v. United States [7] the Court overruled *Wilcox* outright, deciding that illegal gain is income despite a legal obligation to make restitution.[8]

Beginning students in income taxation or anyone else for that matter may reasonably question whether gross income includes wealth acquired by illegal means, but the Supreme Court has left little doubt. Supplying an affirmative answer in *James,* the Court provided the following convenient summary of the area: [9]

> It had been a well-established principle * * * that unlawful, as well as lawful gains are comprehended within the term "gross income". Section 11B of the Income Tax Act of

1. In other opinions the Supreme Court has not attempted an all encompassing definition of gross income. See, for example, Commissioner v. Wilcox, 327 U.S. 404, 407, 66 S.Ct. 546, 548–549 (1946).

2. Lorenzo C. Dilks, 15 B.T.A. 1294 (1929); William H. Stayton, Jr., 32 B.T.A. 940 (1935).

3. 493 U.S. 203, 110 S.Ct. 589 (1990).

4. U.S. v. Rochelle, 384 F.2d 748 (5th Cir.1967), cert. denied 390 U.S. 946, 88 S.Ct. 1032 (1968).

5. Supra, note 1.

6. 343 U.S. 130, 72 S.Ct. 571 (1952).

7. 366 U.S. 213, 81 S.Ct. 1052 (1961).

8. The series of cases is discussed in Libin and Haydon, "Embezzled Funds as Taxable Income: A Study in Judicial Footwork," 61 Mich.L.Rev. 425 (1963) and Bittker, "Taxing Income from Unlawful Activities," 25 Case West.L.Rev. 130 (1974).

9. Supra note 7 at 218, 81 S.Ct. at 1054. See also Reg. § 1.61–14.

1913 provided that "the net income of a taxable person shall include gains, profits, and income * * * from * * * the transaction of any *lawful* business carried on for gain or profit, or gains or profits and income derived from any source whatever. * * *" (Emphasis supplied.) 38 Stat. 167. When the statute was amended in 1916, the one word "lawful" was omitted. This revealed, we think, the obvious intent of that Congress to tax income derived from both legal and illegal sources, to remove the incongruity of having the gains of the honest laborer taxed and the gains of the dishonest immune. Rutkin v. United States, supra, at p. 138; United States v. Sullivan, 274 U.S. 259, 263, 47 S.Ct. 607. Thereafter, the Court held that gains from illicit traffic in liquor are includible within "gross income". Ibid. * * * And, the Court has pointed out, with approval, that there "has been a widespread and settled administrative and judicial recognition of the taxability of unlawful gains of many kinds," Rutkin v. United States, supra, at p. 137. These include protection payments made to racketeers, ransom payments paid to kidnappers, bribes, money derived from the sale of unlawful insurance policies, graft, black market gains, funds obtained from the operation of lotteries, income from race track bookmaking and illegal prize fight pictures. Ibid.[10]

The taxation of illegal gains has caused some interesting results. It was the evasion of income tax laws and not a conviction of murder, robbery, or some similar crime that led to the conviction and imprisonment of gangster Al Capone in 1931.[11] A taxpayer's attempt to create some black letter law (bathed perhaps in red light) failed when the Tax Court said, in effect: Madame, the wages of sin are not exempt from taxation![12] One judge who disagreed with treating illegal pilfering the same as legal profiting was Judge Martin Manton of the Second Circuit Court of Appeals who felt such action was degrading to the government.[13] Ironically, the same Judge Manton was later held liable for tax on bribes accepted to influence his decisions,[14] after having been convicted,[15] imprisoned and disbarred for accepting the bribes. The Commissioner has been successful in taxing some scurrilous swindlers. In Akers v. Scofield[16] an ingenious scheme involving maps, hidden "gold" bars, and an intrigued and probably greedy widow was successful up to

10. Reporting of such gains can raise important 5th Amendment self-incrimination questions. See U.S. v. Sullivan, 274 U.S. 259, 47 S.Ct. 607 (1927), and Chapter 28 B, infra page 1010.

11. See Bittker, supra note 8.

12. Blanche E. Lane, 15 T.C.M. 1088 (1956).

13. The argument was offered in his concurring opinion in Steinberg v. U.S., 14 F.2d 564, 569 (2d Cir.1926).

14. Martin T. Manton, 7 T.C.M. 937 (1948). Judge Manton's philosophy is considered in greater detail in the Bittker article cited supra note 8.

15. U.S. v. Manton, 107 F.2d 834 (2d Cir.1939), cert. denied 309 U.S. 664, 60 S.Ct. 590 (1940).

16. 167 F.2d 718 (5th Cir.1948), cert. den. 335 U.S. 823, 69 S.Ct. 47 (1948).

a point but hit the fiscal fan when the Commissioner successfully taxed the swindler's proceeds. In a more timely vein, the Commissioner has been successful in taxing gains on the illegal sale of narcotics.[17]

Although the judicial opinions speak in terms of the question whether an illegal receipt is gross income and, if so, when, a third dimension of this problem is less often expressed. If a pickpocket's daily take is gross income, his failure to report it ultimately on his Form 1040 is itself a crime.[18] And it is of course a federal crime. One wonders therefore how much a desire to add a federal sanction to existing state sanctions for various offenses may affect the seeming effort to define and time the receipt of gross income.

PROBLEMS

1. Would the results to the taxpayer in the *Cesarini* case be different if, instead of discovering $4467 in old currency in the piano, he discovered that the piano, a Steinway, was the first Steinway piano ever built and it is worth $500,000?

2. Winner attends the opening of a new department store. All persons attending are given free raffle tickets for a digital watch worth $200. Disregarding any possible application of I.R.C. § 74, must Winner include anything within gross income when she wins the watch in the raffle?

3. Employee has worked for Employer's incorporated business for several years at a salary of $40,000 per year. Another company is attempting to hire Employee but Employer persuades him to agree to stay for at least two more years by giving him 2% of the company's stock, which is worth $20,000, and by buying Employee's spouse a new car worth $15,000. How much income does Employee realize from these transactions?

4. Insurance Adjuster refers his clients to an auto repair firm that gives him a kickback of 10% of billings on all referrals.

   (a) Does Adjuster have gross income?

   (b) Even if the arrangement violates local law?

5. Owner agrees to rent Tenant his lake house for the summer for $4000.

   (a) How much income does Owner realize if he agrees to charge only $1000 if Tenant makes $3000 worth of improvements to the house?

   (b) Is there a difference in result to Owner in (a), above, if Tenant effects exactly the same improvements but does all the labor himself and incurs a total cost of only $500?

   (c) Are there any tax consequences to Tenant in part (b), above?

---

17. Farina v. McMahon, 1958–2 U.S. T.C. para. 9938 (D.N.Y.1958).

18. See, e.g., I.R.C. §§ 7201 and 7206.

6. Under a nationally advertised plan, Consumer purchases a new automobile from Dealer at a cost of $10,000 and subsequently receives a $500 cash rebate from the manufacturer.

(a) Must Consumer include the $500 rebate in income? See Rev. Rul. 76–96, 1976–1 C.B. 23.

(b) What result if Consumer decides against purchasing the car but Dealer pays Consumer $50 simply for agreeing to look at his cars when Consumer decides to purchase another make of car?

C. INCOME WITHOUT RECEIPT OF CASH OR PROPERTY

Internal Revenue Code: Section 61.

Regulations: Sections 1.61–2(a)(1), –2(d)(2)(i).

HELVERING v. INDEPENDENT LIFE INS. CO.*

Supreme Court of the United States, 1934.
292 U.S. 371, 54 S.Ct. 758.

[This case raised the question whether a taxpayer must include in gross income the rental value of a building owned and occupied by the taxpayer. Whether or not the statute purported to subject that value to the income tax, it was the taxpayer's position that such a tax was foreclosed by Article I, § 9, cl. 4 of the Constitution, which requires the apportionment of direct taxes. See the discussion of basic constitutional principles in Chapter 1 at page 14. The Court sustained this position, saying in part:]

If the statute lays taxes on the part of the building occupied by the owner or upon the rental value of that space, it cannot be sustained, for that would be to lay a direct tax requiring apportionment. * * * The rental value of the building used by the owner does not constitute income within the meaning of the Sixteenth Amendment.

REVENUE RULING 79–24

1979–1 Cum.Bull. 60.

FACTS

Situation 1. In return for personal legal services performed by a lawyer for a housepainter, the housepainter painted the lawyer's personal residence. Both the lawyer and the housepainter are members of a barter club, an organization that annually furnishes its members a directory of members and the services they provide. All the members of the club are professional or trades persons. Members contact other

---

* See Goode, The Individual Income Tax, pp. 120–129 (1964), reprinted in Sander and Westfall, Readings in Federal Taxation, 290 (Foundation Press 1970); Marsh, "The Taxation of Imputed Income," 58 Pol. Sci.Q. 514 (1943). Ed.

members directly and negotiate the value of the services to be performed.

Situation 2. An individual who owned an apartment building received a work of art created by a professional artist in return for the rent-free use of an apartment for six months by the artist.

LAW

The applicable sections of the Internal Revenue Code of 1954 and the Income Tax Regulations thereunder are 61(a) and 1.61–2, relating to compensation for services.

Section 1.61–2(d)(1) of the regulations provides that if services are paid for other than in money, the fair market value of the property or services taken in payment must be included in income. If the services were rendered at a stipulated price, such price will be presumed to be the fair market value of the compensation received in the absence of evidence to the contrary.

HOLDINGS

Situation 1. The fair market value of the services received by the lawyer and the housepainter are includible in their gross incomes under section 61 of the Code.

Situation 2. The fair market value of the work of art and the six months fair rental value of the apartment are includible in the gross incomes of the apartment-owner and the artist under section 61 of the Code.

DEAN v. COMMISSIONER

United States Court of Appeals, Third Circuit, 1951.
187 F.2d 1019.

GOODRICH, Circuit Judge.

This appeal from the Tax Court raises the question of the correctness of a claim for income tax against the taxpayer based on the rental value of property held in the name of a corporation of which the taxpayer and his wife are the sole shareholders. The facts are simple and undisputed.

The taxpayer and his wife are the sole shareholders in a personal holding company called the Nemours Corporation. The wife owns 80% of the stock. The real estate which is the subject matter of this controversy was owned by the taxpayer's wife prior to her marriage. She and the taxpayer continued to occupy it after their marriage and the taxpayer's wife expended and has continued to expend appreciable sums in keeping up and beautifying the property. In 1931 the Nemours Corporation was indebted to a bank for a large sum. The bank insisted that the residence property above mentioned be transferred to the corporation. This was done. The parties continued to occupy the place as a home following the transfer. The taxpayer was in military service during the late war, but received from the corporation the difference between his military pay and the salary he had previously received. He also shared in the occupancy of the home at such times as he was free to do so.

The Commissioner takes the position that the fair rental value of the residence property is to be included in the taxpayer's gross income under the general provisions of Section 22 of the Internal Revenue Code, 26 U.S.C.A. § 22. The Tax Court agreed with the Commissioner. We do likewise. Although the taxpayer endeavors to distinguish it, we think our decision in Chandler v. Commissioner, 3 Cir., 1941, 119 F.2d 623, governs this case and the discussion therein is, for the most part, applicable here. It was the taxpayer's legal obligation to provide a family home and if he did it by the occupancy of a property which was held in the name of a corporation of which he was president, we think the fair value of that occupancy was income to him.

The fact that the corporation was simply a means by which the taxpayer and his wife carried on certain business activities does not change the case. We have no reason for thinking that the corporate existence was anything but bona fide. And we think that the real estate deeded to the corporation would clearly have been held to belong to it had the bank had occasion, which it did not, to take advantage of the corporation's title to the property. Our position is not based upon any thought that there is in this case any suggestion of tax evasion or avoidance. It is instead based upon taxpayer's valuable occupation of the corporation real estate.

The decision of the Tax Court will be affirmed.

PROBLEMS

1. Vegy grows vegetables in his garden. Does Vegy have gross income when:

   (a) Vegy harvests his crop?

   (b) Vegy and his family consume $100 worth of vegetables?

   (c) Vegy sells vegetables for $100? yes

   (d) Vegy exchanges $100 worth of vegetables with Charlie for $100 worth of tuna which Charlie caught? yes

   (e) Vegy agrees with Grocer to sell his vegetables in Grocer's market which previously did not have a vegetable section. Grocer pays $50 per month to landlord for the portion of the market used by Vegy but Grocer does not charge Vegy any rent. Vegy keeps all proceeds from his sales.

2. Doctor needs to have his income tax return prepared. Lawyer would like a general physical check up. Doctor would normally charge $200 for the physical and Lawyer would normally charge $200 for the income tax return preparation.

(a) What tax consequences to each if they simply swap services without any money changing hands?

(b) Does Lawyer realize any income when he fills out his own tax return?

a — must claim $200.00 — fair mkt value

b— no, he has a legal obligation to do this

CHAPTER 3. THE EXCLUSION OF GIFTS AND INHERITANCES

A. RULES OF INCLUSION AND EXCLUSION

Internal Revenue Code: Section 102(a) and (b) first sentence.
Regulations: Sections 1.102–1(a) and (b).

As Chapter 2 illustrates, gross income is a very broad concept. Over the years, numerous administrative and judicial decisions have gone a long way toward delineating its scope. Nevertheless, partly because of past uncertainties and partly because of a desire to accord special treatment for some types of receipts or benefits, Congress has been unwilling to rely on gross income, unexplained or only generally defined, as the starting point in the computation of federal income tax liability. Instead, two series of sections have undertaken to say that certain items are specifically includable in gross income, or partially includable, Sections 71–90, and other items are specifically excludable from gross income, or partially excludable, Sections 101–135. As cases such as *Cesarini* and *Glenshaw Glass* set out in Chapter 2 indicate, these special statutory rules do not purport to be exhaustive; some questions remain to be answered without special statutory help under the general definition of gross income in Section 61. But of course when an explicit statutory provision is applicable it takes precedence over the general definition. For example, interest is an illustration of an item of gross income specified in Section 61(a)(4), but according to Section 103(a) gross income does not include interest on some State and local bonds. In the materials that follow, be sure to differentiate exclusions from gross income from deductions available in determining taxable income which have a similar but not identical effect.

It is not possible to present a definition of gross income that will answer all questions which may arise. But here is a kind of checklist that may be helpful and which will be more meaningful as the study of gross income progresses:

Gross income includes the receipt of any financial benefit which is:

1. Not a mere return of capital, and

2. Not accompanied by a contemporaneously acknowledged obligation to repay, and

3. Not excluded by a specific statutory provision.

A comparatively simple, long-standing exclusionary rule is found in Section 102. We begin with it. It often comes as a surprise to a taxpayer who has grown accustomed to the income tax bite to learn that when Uncle Harry died and left him securities worth $10,000 the amount will not appear at all on his Form 1040. The section may safely be read fairly literally and is as generous as it sounds. Could Congress tax such receipts as income?

Of course if the securities received produce dividends for the taxpayer, the dividends must be treated as income. Perhaps redundantly, the statute makes this clear in Section 102(b)(1).

Somewhat less certain at an earlier time was the taxpayer's status if Uncle Harry left him the right only to the income from securities, perhaps by way of a trust under which the securities themselves were to be retained for a remainderman who would get them upon the taxpayer's death. In the famous case of Irwin v. Gavit,[1] the Supreme Court held, in effect, that language such as now appears in Section 102(a), excluding from gross income property acquired by bequest, did not exclude a gift *of the income* from property. A codification of that principle now appears in Section 102(b)(2).

We are steering you away from the last two sentences of Section 102(b). A gift, perhaps in trust, may assure the taxpayer of a steady flow of money over a period of years or for his life. A question then arises whether this is an excluded gift of property or an included gift of the income from property, or partly each. These last two sentences are a partial answer to the question; but the final answer is left to Subshapter J, Sections 641–692. The broad outline of Subchapter J is suggested in Chapter 13, infra; but its provisions must be studied in detail before the full significance of the last two sentences of Section 102(b) can be grasped. Such study is generally undertaken in a separate course on the income taxation of trusts and estates.

Some other questions that arise in the application of Section 102 are manageable here and are suggested in the materials that follow in this chapter.

B. THE INCOME TAX MEANING OF GIFT

Internal Revenue Code: Section 102(a).

––––––

COMMISSIONER v. DUBERSTEIN*

Supreme Court of the United States, 1960.
363 U.S. 278, 80 S.Ct. 1190.

Mr. Justice BRENNAN delivered the opinion of the Court.

These two cases concern the provision of the Internal Revenue Code which excludes from the gross income of an income taxpayer "the value of property acquired by gift."[1] They pose the frequently recurrent question whether a specific transfer to a taxpayer in fact amount-

1. 268 U.S. 161, 45 S.Ct. 475 (1924).

* See Klein, "An Enigma in the Federal Income Tax: The Meaning of the Word 'Gift'," 48 Minn.L.Rev. 215 (1963). Ed.

1. The operative provision in the cases at bar is § 22(b)(3) of the 1939 Internal Revenue Code. The corresponding provision of the present Code is § 102(a).

ed to a "gift" to him within the meaning of the statute. The importance to decision of the facts of the cases requires that we state them in some detail.

No. 376, Commissioner v. Duberstein. The taxpayer, Duberstein,[2] was president of the Duberstein Iron & Metal Company, a corporation with headquarters in Dayton, Ohio. For some years the taxpayer's company had done business with Mohawk Metal Corporation, whose headquarters were in New York City. The president of Mohawk was one Berman. The taxpayer and Berman had generally used the telephone to transact their companies' business with each other, which consisted of buying and selling metals. The taxpayer testified, without elaboration, that he knew Berman "personally" and had known him for about seven years. From time to time in their telephone conversations, Berman would ask Duberstein whether the latter knew of potential customers for some of Mohawk's products in which Duberstein's company itself was not interested. Duberstein provided the names of potential customers for these items.

One day in 1951 Berman telephoned Duberstein and said that the information Duberstein had given him had proved so helpful that he wanted to give the latter a present. Duberstein stated that Berman owed him nothing. Berman said that he had a Cadillac as a gift for Duberstein, and that the latter should send to New York for it; Berman insisted that Duberstein accept the car, and the latter finally did so, protesting however that he had not intended to be compensated for the information. At the time Duberstein already had a Cadillac and an Oldsmobile, and felt that he did not need another car. Duberstein testified that he did not think Berman would have sent him the Cadillac if he had not furnished him with information about the customers. It appeared that Mohawk later deducted the value of the Cadillac as a business expense on its corporate income tax return.

Duberstein did not include the value of the Cadillac in gross income for 1951, deeming it a gift. The Commissioner asserted a deficiency for the car's value against him, and in proceedings to review the deficiency the Tax Court affirmed the Commissioner's determination. It said that "The record is significantly barren of evidence revealing any intention on the part of the payor to make a gift. * * * The only justifiable inference is that the automobile was intended by the payor to be remuneration for services rendered to it by Duberstein." The Court of Appeals for the Sixth Circuit reversed. 265 F.2d 28.

No. 546, Stanton v. United States. The taxpayer, Stanton, had been for approximately 10 years in the employ of Trinity Church in New York City. He was comptroller of the Church corporation, and president of a corporation, Trinity Operating Company, the church set up as a fully owned subsidiary to manage its real estate holdings, which

2. In both cases the husband will be referred to as the taxpayer, although his wife joined with him in joint tax returns.

were more extensive than simply the church property. His salary by the end of his employment there in 1942 amounted to $22,500 a year. Effective November 30, 1942, he resigned from both positions to go into business for himself. The Operating Company's directors, who seem to have included the rector and vestrymen of the church, passed the following resolution upon his resignation: "Be it Resolved that in appreciation of the services rendered by Mr. Stanton * * * a gratuity is hereby awarded to him of Twenty Thousand Dollars, payable to him in equal instalments of Two Thousand Dollars at the end of each and every month commencing with the month of December, 1942; provided that, with the discontinuance of his services, the Corporation of Trinity Church is released from all rights and claims to pension and retirement benefits not already accrued up to November 30, 1942."

The Operating Company's action was later explained by one of its directors as based on the fact that, "Mr. Stanton was liked by all of the Vestry personally. He had a pleasing personality. He had come in when Trinity's affairs were in a difficult situation. He did a splendid piece of work, we felt. Besides that * * * he was liked by all of the members of the Vestry personally." And by another: "[W]e were all unanimous in wishing to make Mr. Stanton a gift. Mr. Stanton had loyally and faithfully served Trinity in a very difficult time. We thought of him in the highest regard. We understood that he was going in business for himself. We felt that he was entitled to that evidence of good will."

On the other hand, there was a suggestion of some ill-feeling between Stanton and the directors, arising out of the recent termination of the services of one Watkins, the Operating Company's treasurer, whose departure was evidently attended by some acrimony. At a special board meeting on October 28, 1942, Stanton had intervened on Watkins' side and asked reconsideration of the matter. The minutes reflect that "resentment was expressed as to the 'presumptuous' suggestion that the action of the Board, taken after long deliberation, should be changed." The Board adhered to its determination that Watkins be separated from employment, giving him an opportunity to resign rather than be discharged. At another special meeting two days later it was revealed that Watkins had not resigned; the previous resolution terminating his services was then viewed as effective; and the Board voted the payment of six months' salary to Watkins in a resolution similar to that quoted in regard to Stanton, but which did not use the term "gratuity." At the meeting, Stanton announced that in order to avoid any such embarrassment or question at any time as to his willingness to resign if the Board desired, he was tendering his resignation. It was tabled, though not without dissent. The next week, on November 5, at another special meeting, Stanton again tendered his resignation which this time was accepted.

The "gratuity" was duly paid. So was a smaller one to Stanton's (and the Operating Company's) secretary, under a similar resolution, upon her resignation at the same time. The two corporations shared the expense of the payments. There was undisputed testimony that there were in fact no enforceable rights or claims to pension and retirement benefits which had not accrued at the time of the taxpayer's resignation, and that the last proviso of the resolution was inserted simply out of an abundance of caution. The taxpayer received in cash a refund of his contributions to the retirement plans, and there is no suggestion that he was entitled to more. He was required to perform no further services for Trinity after his resignation.

The Commissioner asserted a deficiency against the taxpayer after the latter had failed to include the payments in question in gross income. After payment of the deficiency and administrative rejection of a refund claim, the taxpayer sued the United States for a refund in the District Court for the Eastern District of New York. The trial judge, sitting without a jury, made the simple finding that the payments were a "gift,"[3] and judgment was entered for the taxpayer. The Court of Appeals for the Second Circuit reversed. 268 F.2d 727.

The Government, urging that clarification of the problem typified by these two cases was necessary, and that the approaches taken by the Court of Appeals for the Second and Sixth Circuits were in conflict, petitioned for certiorari in No. 376, and acquiesced in the taxpayer's petition in No. 546. On this basis, and because of the importance of the question in the administration of the income tax laws, we granted certiorari in both cases. 361 U.S. 923, 80 S.Ct. 291.

The exclusion of property acquired by gift from gross income under the federal income tax laws was made in the first income tax statute[4] passed under the authority of the Sixteenth Amendment, and has been a feature of the income tax statutes ever since. The meaning of the term "gift" as applied to particular transfers has always been a matter of contention.[5] Specific and illuminating legislative history on the point does not appear to exist. Analogies and inferences drawn from other revenue provisions, such as the estate and gift taxes, are dubious. See Lockard v. Commissioner, 166 F.2d 409. The meaning of the statutory term has been shaped largely by the decisional law. With this, we turn to the contentions made by the Government in these cases.

First. The Government suggests that we promulgate a new "test" in this area to serve as a standard to be applied by the lower courts and by the Tax Court in dealing with the numerous cases that arise.[6] We reject this invitation. We are of opinion that the governing principles are necessarily general and have already been spelled out in the opinions of this Court, and that the problem is one which, under the present statutory framework, does not lend itself to any more definitive

3. See note 14, infra.

4. § II.B., c. 16, 38 Stat. 167.

5. The first case of the Board of Tax Appeals officially reported in fact deals with the problem. Parrott v. Commissioner, 1 B.T.A. 1.

6. The Government's proposed test is stated: "Gifts should be defined as transfers of property made for personal as distinguished from business reasons."

statement that would produce a talisman for the solution of concrete cases. The cases at bar are fair examples of the settings in which the problem usually arises. They present situations in which payments have been made in a context with business overtones—an employer making a payment to a retiring employee; a businessman giving something of value to another businessman who has been of advantage to him in his business. In this context, we review the law as established by the prior cases here.

The course of decision here makes it plain that the statute does not use the term "gift" in the common-law sense but in a more colloquial sense. This Court has indicated that a voluntary executed transfer of his property by one to another, without any consideration or compensation therefor, though a common-law gift, is not necessarily a "gift" within the meaning of the statute. For the Court has shown that the mere absence of a legal or moral obligation to make such a payment does not establish that it is a gift. Old Colony Trust Co. v. Commissioner, 279 U.S. 716, 730, 49 S.Ct. 499, 504. And, importantly, if the payment proceeds primarily from "the constraining force of any moral or legal duty," or from "the incentive of anticipated benefit" of an economic nature, Bogardus v. Commissioner, 302 U.S. 34, 41, 58 S.Ct. 61, 64, it is not a gift. And, conversely, "[w]here the payment is in return for services rendered, it is irrelevant that the donor derives no economic benefit from it." Robertson v. United States, 343 U.S. 711, 714, 72 S.Ct. 994, 996.[7] A gift in the statutory sense, on the other hand, proceeds from a "detached and disinterested generosity," Commissioner v. LoBue, 351 U.S. 243, 246, 76 S.Ct. 800, 802; "out of affection, respect, admiration, charity or like impulses." Robertson v. United States, supra, 343 U.S. at 714, 72 S.Ct. at 996. And in this regard, the most critical consideration, as the Court was agreed in the leading case here, is the transferor's "intention." Bogardus v. Commissioner, 302 U.S. 34, 43, 58 S.Ct. 61, 65. "What controls is the intention with which payment, however voluntary, has been made." Id., 302 U.S. at 45, 58 S.Ct. at 66 (dissenting opinion).[8]

The Government says that this "intention" of the transferor cannot mean what the cases on the common-law concept of gift call "donative intent." With that we are in agreement, for our decisions fully support this. Moreover, the *Bogardus* case itself makes it plain that the donor's characterization of his action is not determinative—that there must be

---

7. The cases including "tips" in gross income are classic examples of this. See, e.g., Roberts v. Commissioner, 176 F.2d 221.

8. The parts of the *Bogardus* opinion which we touch on here are the ones we take to be basic to its holding, and the ones that we read as stating those governing principles which it establishes. As to them we see little distinction between the views of the Court and those taken in dissent in *Bogardus*. The fear expressed by the dissent at 302 U.S., at 44, 58 S.Ct., at 66, that the prevailing opinion "seems" to hold "that every payment which in any aspect is a gift is * * * relieved of any tax" strikes us now as going beyond what the opinion of the Court held in fact. In any event, the Court's opinion in *Bogardus* does not seem to have been so interpreted afterwards. The principal difference, as we see it, between the Court's opinion and the dissent lies in the weight to be given the findings of the trier of fact.

an objective inquiry as to whether what is called a gift amounts to it in reality. 302 U.S., at 40, 58 S.Ct. at 64. It scarcely needs adding that the parties' expectations or hopes as to the tax treatment of their conduct in themselves have nothing to do with the matter.

It is suggested that the *Bogardus* criterion would be more apt if rephrased in terms of "motive" rather than "intention." We must confess to some skepticism as to whether such a verbal mutation would be of any practical consequence. We take it that the proper criterion, established by decision here, is one that inquires what the basic reason for his conduct was in fact—the dominant reason that explains his action in making the transfer. Further than that we do not think it profitable to go.

Second. The Government's proposed "test," while apparently simple and precise in its formulation, depends frankly on a set of "principles" or "presumptions" derived from the decided cases, and concededly subject to various exceptions; and it involves various corollaries, which add to its detail. Were we to promulgate this test as a matter of law, and accept with it various presuppositions and stated consequences, we would be passing far beyond the requirements of the cases before us, and would be painting on a large canvas with indeed a broad brush. The Government derives its test from such propositions as the following: That payments by an employer to an employee, even though voluntary, ought, by and large, to be taxable; that the concept of a gift is inconsistent with a payment's being a deductible business expense; that a gift involves "personal" elements; that a business corporation cannot properly make a gift of its assets. The Government admits that there are exceptions and qualifications to these propositions. We think, to the extent they are correct, that these propositions are not principles of law but rather maxims of experience that the tribunals which have tried the facts of cases in this area have enunciated in explaining their factual determinations. Some of them simply represent truisms: it doubtless is, statistically speaking, the exceptional payment by an employer to an employee that amounts to a gift. Others are over-statements of possible evidentiary inferences relevant to a factual determination on the totality of circumstances in the case: it is doubtless relevant to the over-all inference that the transferor treats a payment as a business deduction, or that the transferor is a corporate entity. But these inferences cannot be stated in absolute terms. Neither factor is a shibboleth. The taxing statute does not make nondeductibility by the transferor a condition on the "gift" exclusion; nor does it draw any distinction, in terms, between transfers by corporations and individuals, as to the availability of the "gift" exclusion to the transferee. The conclusion whether a transfer amounts to a "gift" is one that must be reached on consideration of all the factors.

Specifically, the trier of fact must be careful not to allow trial of the issue whether the receipt of a specific payment is a gift to turn into a trial of the tax liability, or of the propriety, as a matter of fiduciary or corporate law, attaching to the conduct of someone else. The major corollary to the Government's suggested "test" is that, as an ordinary matter, a payment by a corporation cannot be a gift, and, more specifically, there can be no such thing as a "gift" made by a corporation which would allow it to take a deduction for an ordinary and necessary business expense. As we have said, we find no basis for such a conclusion in the statute; and if it were applied as a determinative rule of "law," it would force the tribunals trying tax cases involving the donee's liability into elaborate inquiries into the local law of corporations or into the peripheral deductibility of payments as business expenses. The former issue might make the tax tribunals the most frequent investigators of an important and difficult issue of the laws of the several States, and the latter inquiry would summon one difficult and delicate problem of federal tax law as an aid to the solution of another.[9] Or perhaps there would be required a trial of the vexed issue whether there was a "constructive" distribution of corporate property, for income tax purposes, to the corporate agents who had sponsored the transfer.[10] These considerations, also, reinforce us in our conclusion that while the principles urged by the Government may, in non-absolute form as crystallizations of experience, prove persuasive to the trier of facts in a particular case, neither they, nor any more detailed statement than has been made, can be laid down as a matter of law.

Third. Decision of the issue presented in these cases must be based ultimately on the application of the fact-finding tribunal's experience with the mainsprings of human conduct to the totality of the facts of each case. The nontechnical nature of the statutory standard, the close relationship of it to the data of practical human experience, and the multiplicity of relevant factual elements, with their various combinations, creating the necessity of ascribing the proper force to each, confirm us in our conclusion that primary weight in this area must be given to the conclusions of the trier of fact. Baker v. Texas & Pacific R. Co., 359 U.S. 227, 79 S.Ct. 664; Commissioner v. Heininger, 320 U.S. 467, 475, 64 S.Ct. 249, 254; United States v. Yellow Cab Co., 338 U.S. 338, 341, 70 S.Ct. 177, 179; Bogardus v. Commissioner, supra, at 45 (dissenting opinion).[11]

9. Justice Cardozo once described in memorable language the inquiry into whether an expense was an "ordinary and necessary" one of a business:

"One struggles in vain for any verbal formula that will supply a ready touchstone. The standard set up by the statute is not a rule of law; it is rather a way of life. Life in all its fullness must supply the answer to the riddle." Welch v. Helvering, 290 U.S. 111, 115, 54 S.Ct. 8, 9. The same comment well fits the issue in the cases at bar.

10. Cf., e.g., Nelson v. Commissioner, 203 F.2d 1.

11. In *Bogardus,* the Court was divided 5 to 4 to the scope of review to be extended the fact-finder's determination as to a specific receipt, in a context like that of the instant cases. The majority held that such a determination was "a conclusion of law or at least a determination of a mixed question of law and fact." 302 U.S., at 39, 58 S.Ct. at 64. This formulation it took as justifying it in assuming a fairly broad standard of review. The dissent took a contrary view. The approach of this part of the Court's ruling in *Bogardus,* which we think was the only part on which there was real division among the Court, see note 8, supra, has not been afforded subse-

This conclusion may not satisfy an academic desire for tidiness, symmetry and precision in this area, any more than a system based on the determinations of various fact-finders ordinarily does. But we see it as implicit in the present statutory treatment of the exclusion for gifts, and in the variety of forms in which federal income tax cases can be tried. If there is fear of undue uncertainty or overmuch litigation, Congress may make more precise its treatment of the matter by singling out certain factors and making them determinative of the matter, as it has done in one field of the "gift" exclusion's former application, that of prizes and awards.[12] Doubtless diversity of result will tend to be lessened somewhat since federal income tax decisions, even those in tribunals of first instance turning on issues of fact, tend to be reported, and since there may be a natural tendency of professional triers of fact to follow one another's determinations, even as to factual matters. But the question here remains basically one of fact, for determination on a case-by-case basis.

One consequence of this is that appellate review of determinations in this field must be quite restricted. Where a jury has tried the matter upon correct instructions, the only inquiry is whether it cannot be said that reasonable men could reach differing conclusions on the issue. Baker v. Texas & Pacific R. Co., supra, 359 U.S. at 228, 79 S.Ct. at 665. Where the trial has been by a judge without a jury, the judge's findings must stand unless "clearly erroneous." Fed.Rules Civ.Proc., 52(a). "A finding is 'clearly erroneous' when although there is evidence to support it, the reviewing court on the entire evidence is left with the definite and firm conviction that a mistake has been committed." United States v. United States Gypsum Co., 333 U.S. 364, 395, 68 S.Ct. 521, 542. The rule itself applies also to factual inferences from undisputed basic facts, id., at 394, as will on many occasions be presented in this area. Cf. Graver Tank & Mfg. Co. v. Linde Air Products Co., 339 U.S. 605, 609–610, 70 S.Ct. 854, 856, 857. And Congress has in the most explicit terms attached the identical weight to the findings of the Tax Court. I.R.C., § 7482(a).[13]

---

quent respect here. In *Heininger*, a question presenting at the most elements no more factual and untechnical than those here—that of the "ordinary and necessary" nature of a business expense—was treated as one of fact. Cf. note 9, supra. And in Dobson v. Commissioner, 320 U.S. 489, 498, n. 22, 64 S.Ct. 239, 245, *Bogardus* was adversely criticized, insofar as it treated the matter as reviewable as one of law. While *Dobson* is, of course, no longer the law insofar as it ordains a greater weight to be attached to the findings of the Tax Court than to those of any other fact-finder in a tax litigation, see note 13, infra, we think its criticism of this point in the *Bogardus* opinion is sound in view of the dominant importance of factual inquiry to decision of these cases.

12. I.R.C., § 74, which is a provision new with the 1954 Code. Previously, there had been holdings that such receipts as the "Pot O' Gold" radio giveaway, Washburn v. Commissioner, 5 T.C. 1333, and the Ross Essay Prize, McDermott v. Commissioner, 80 U.S.App.D.C. 176, 150 F.2d 585, were "gifts." Congress intended to obviate such rulings. S.Rep. No. 1622, 83d Cong., 2d Sess., p. 178. We imply no approval of those holdings under the general standard of the "gift" exclusion. Cf. Robertson v. United States, supra.

13. "The United States Courts of Appeals shall have exclusive jurisdiction to review the decisions of the Tax Court * * * in the same manner and to the same extent as decisions of the district courts in civil actions tried without a jury.

Fourth. A majority of the Court is in accord with the principles just outlined. And, applying them to the *Duberstein* case, we are in agreement, on the evidence we have set forth, that it cannot be said that the conclusion of the Tax Court was "clearly erroneous." It seems to us plain that as trier of the facts it was warranted in concluding that despite the characterization of the transfer of the Cadillac by the parties and the absence of any obligation, even of a moral nature, to make it, it was at bottom a recompense for Duberstein's past services, or an inducement for him to be of further service in the future. We cannot say with the Court of Appeals that such a conclusion was "mere suspicion" on the Tax Court's part. To us it appears based in the sort of informed experience with human affairs that fact-finding tribunals should bring to this task.

As to *Stanton*, we are in disagreement. To four of us, it is critical here that the District Court as trier of fact made only the simple and unelaborated finding that the transfer in question was a "gift."[14] To be sure, conciseness is to be strived for, and prolixity avoided, in findings; but, to the four of us, there comes a point where findings become so sparse and conclusory as to give no revelation of what the District Court's concept of the determining facts and legal standard may be. See Matton Oil Transfer Corp. v. The Dynamic, 123 F.2d 999, 1000–1001. Such conclusory, general findings do not constitute compliance with Rule 52's direction to "find the facts specially and state separately * * * conclusions of law thereon." While the standard of law in this area is not a complex one, we four think the unelaborated finding of ultimate fact here cannot stand as a fulfillment of these requirements. It affords the reviewing court not the semblance of an indication of the legal standard with which the trier of fact has approached his task. For all that appears, the District Court may have viewed the form of the resolution or the simple absence of legal consideration as conclusive. While the judgment of the Court of Appeals cannot stand, the four of us think there must be further proceedings in the District Court looking toward new and adequate findings of fact. In this, we are joined by Mr. Justice Whittaker, who agrees that the findings were inadequate, although he does not concur generally in this opinion.

* * *" The last words first came into the statute through an amendment to § 1141(a) of the 1939 Code in 1948 (§ 36 of the Judicial Code Act, 62 Stat. 991). The purpose of the 1948 legislation was to remove from the law the favored position (in comparison with District Court and Court of Claims rulings in tax matters) enjoyed by the Tax Court under this Court's ruling in Dobson v. Commissioner, 320 U.S. 489, 64 S.Ct. 239. Cf. note 11, supra. See Grace Bros., Inc. v. Commissioner, 173 F.2d 170, 173

14. The "Findings of Fact and Conclusions of Law" were made orally, and were simply: "The resolution of the Board of Directors of the Trinity Operating Company, Incorporated, held November 19, 1942, after the resignations had been accepted of the plaintiff from his positions as controller of the corporation of the Trinity Church, and the president of the Trinity Operating Company, Incorporated, whereby a gratuity was voted to the plaintiff, Allen [sic] D. Stanton, in the amount of $20,000 payable to him in monthly installments of $2,000 each, commencing with the month of December, 1942, constituted a gift to the taxpayer, and therefore need not have been reported by him as income for the taxable years 1942, or 1943."

Accordingly, in No. 376, the judgment of this Court is that the judgment of the Court of Appeals is reversed, and in No. 546, that the judgment of the Court of Appeals is vacated, and the case is remanded to the District Court for further proceedings not inconsistent with this opinion.

It is so ordered.

[Concurring and dissenting opinions of Messrs. Justice HARLAN, WHITTAKER, DOUGLAS and BLACK have been omitted. Ed.]

Mr. Justice FRANKFURTER, concurring in the judgment in No. 376 and dissenting in No. 546, [said in part:]

* * *

The Court has made only one authoritative addition to the previous course of our decisions. Recognizing Bogardus v. Commissioner, 302 U.S. 34, 58 S.Ct. 61, as "the leading case here" and finding essential accord between the Court's opinion and the dissent in that case, the Court has drawn from the dissent in *Bogardus* for infusion into what will now be a controlling qualification, recognition that it is "for the triers of the facts to seek among competing aims or motives the ones that dominated conduct." 302 U.S. 34, 45, 58 S.Ct. 61, 66 (dissenting opinion). All this being so in view of the Court, it seems to me desirable not to try to improve what has "already been spelled out" in the opinions of this Court but to leave to the lower courts the application of old phrases rather than to float new ones and thereby inevitably produce a new volume of exegesis on the new phrases.

Especially do I believe this when fact-finding tribunals are directed by the Court to rely upon their "experience with the mainsprings of human conduct" and on their "informed experience with human affairs" in appraising the totality of the facts of each case. Varying conceptions regarding the "mainsprings of human conduct" are derived from a variety of experiences or assumptions about the nature of man, and "experience with human affairs," is not only diverse but also often drastically conflicting. What the Court now does sets fact-finding bodies to sail on an illimitable ocean of individual beliefs and experiences. This can hardly fail to invite, if indeed not encourage, too individualized diversities in the administration of the income tax law. I am afraid that by these new phrasings the practicalities of tax administration, which should be as uniform as is possible in so vast a country as ours, will be embarrassed. By applying what has already been spelled out in the opinions of this Court, I agree with the Court in reversing the judgment in Commissioner v. Duberstein.

But I would affirm the decision of the Court of Appeals for the Second Circuit in Stanton v. United States.

* * *

NOTE

The Supreme Court's decision in *Duberstein*, agrees with the trial court's (Tax Court) decision in the case. The Court holds that the question whether a transfer of money or property constitutes a gift within the exclusion of Section 102(a) is an issue of fact to be determined by the trial court trier of fact. In Stanton v. United States, the Supreme Court considered the findings of fact, as determined by the district court sitting without a jury, to be inadequate. The case was therefore remanded. The district court, on remand with more detailed findings of facts, held that Stanton had received a gift,[1] and the court of appeals affirmed.[2]

There are two interesting side effects of the *Duberstein* case. First, the Supreme Court in U.S. v. Kaiser,[3] decided on the same day as *Duberstein*, upheld a jury verdict of gift largely on the basis of its *Duberstein* rationale. In this case Kaiser, a non-union member, received strike benefits (subsistence payments) from the union which was striking the Kohler Company in Wisconsin. The district court entered judgment N.O.V. for the United States.[4] The court of appeals reversed, upholding the verdict for the taxpayer.[5] The Supreme Court, affirming the court of appeals, again emphasized the factual nature of the issue. On the other hand, in Madonna J. Colwell[6] the Tax Court differentiated *Kaiser* in a similar setting. Strike benefits received by a non-union member who honored a picket line but did not participate in strike activities were included in his income. Based primarily on the factor that the payments were made without union awareness of taxpayer's financial status, the Tax Court concluded that the union's interest was not charitable but to further the effectiveness of the strike. The final message should be clear. In this area, the law (Section 102(a)) is simple and concise. The facts give rise to the complexity, and cases such as these are generally won or lost at the trial level. This is the result in the trilogy of *Duberstein*, *Stanton* and *Kaiser*.

The second point is now relevant. Recall that in the *Duberstein* opinion, the Supreme Court expressly refused to lay down a test for determining whether a payment or transfer of property constitutes a gift, aware that its "conclusion may not satisfy an academic desire for tidiness, symmetry and precision in this area * * *".[7] However, earlier in its opinion, the Court, quoting language from some of its own decisions handed down many years ago involving this same issue, gratuitously said: "A gift in the statutory sense * * * proceeds from a 'detached and disinterested generosity,' * * * 'out of affection, respect, admiration, charity or like impulses' * * *, the most critical

---

1. 186 F.Supp. 393 (E.D.N.Y.1960).

2. U.S. v. Stanton, 287 F.2d 876 (2d Cir.1961).

3. 363 U.S. 299, 80 S.Ct. 1204 (1960).

4. Kaiser v. U.S., 158 F.Supp. 865 (E.D.Wis.1958).

5. Kaiser v. U.S., 262 F.2d 367 (7th Cir.1958).

6. 64 T.C. 584 (1975). Compare also Rev.Rul. 63–136, 1963–2 C.B. 19, welfare payments not for services and those made under work training programs are not income, with Rev.Rul. 71–425, 1971–2 C.B. 76, which while generally excluding amounts received under work training programs, taxes the entire amount if it exceeds the welfare payment that would be made absent the program, except such part as exceeds the value of the services performed.

7. Commissioner v. Duberstein, 363 U.S. 278, 290, 80 S.Ct. 1190, 1199 (1960); see page 65, supra.

consideration * * * is the transferor's 'intention'." [8] Perhaps the message was not intended as the formulation of criteria. But even so, it is a test of sorts, and the lower courts use those criteria in resolving the factual controversy of gift or no gift in cases decided subsequent to *Duberstein*.[9]

PROBLEM

Our system of self-assessment requires the taxpayer to make the initial determination of gift or income, and tax administration procedures give the Commissioner the power to challenge that decision. If judicial controversy develops, why is the decision of the trial court so important, and what role may an appellate court play?

C. EMPLOYEE GIFTS

Internal Revenue Code: Sections 101(b)(1) and (b)(2)(A); 102(c); 274(b). See Sections 74(c); 132(e); 274(j).

Prior to 1987, many cases turned on the possible application of the "gift" exclusion to transfers between persons in employer-employee relationships. Such cases typically arose on a payment or property transfer by an employer in one of three general contexts: to an employee during an ongoing employment relationship; [1] to an employee upon or after retirement; [2] and to survivors upon the death of an employee.[3]

The issue in these cases was whether the recipient had gross income as a result of the purported "gift".[4] Prior to the Tax Reform Act of 1986, Section 102 did not address specifically any amounts transferred by employers to employees.[5] Section 102(c) was added by the Act as an exception to the broad exclusionary rule of Section 102(a).[6] The message of Section 102(c)(1) is fairly straight forward. An employee "shall not exclude from gross income any amount transferred by or for an employer to, or for the benefit of, an employee." [7] The legislative history of the 1986 Act makes no specific mention of Section 102(c) and it mentions Section 102 only in passing, as follows: [8]

8. Id. at 285, 80 S.Ct. at 1197; see page 69, supra.

9. E.g. Max Kralstein, 38 T.C. 810 (1962); acq., 1963–2 C.B. 4.

1. See Fisher v. Commissioner, 59 F.2d 192 (2d Cir.1932); Painter v. Campbell, 110 F.Supp. 503 (N.D.Tex.1953).

2. See Hubert v. Commissioner, 212 F.2d 516 (5th Cir.1954); Stanton v. U.S., 363 U.S. 278, 80 S.Ct. 1190 (1960).

3. See Bausch's Estate v. Commissioner, 186 F.2d 313 (2d Cir.1951); Bounds v. U.S., 262 F.2d 876 (4th Cir.1958), and United States v. Allinger, 275 F.2d 421 (6th Cir.1960).

4. For example, see Fisher, supra note 1, in which the United States Court of Appeals, Second Circuit, rejected contentions that a $6,000 payment by an employer to the taxpayer, made because "it would do something for" the employee, actually was a gift and not compensation for services.

5. See I.R.C. § 102.

6. Pub.L. No. 99–514, 99th Cong., 2d Sess. § 112(b) (1986).

7. I.R.C. § 102(c)(1).

8. Sen.Rep. No. 99–313, 99th Cong., 2d Sess. 53 (1986).

Except to the extent that the new section 74(c) exclusion or section 132(e) applies, the fair market value of an employee award (whether or not satisfying the definition of an employee achievement award) is includible in the employee's gross income under section 61, and is not excludible under section 74 (as amended by the bill) or section 102 (gifts).

While legislative history is lacking, the statute seems to indicate a broad congressional intent to deny "gift" classification to all transfers by employers to employees. Although the motivation of an employer to make a transfer or payment to his employee might well be gratitude or affection alone, seemingly, that doesn't matter. Under the language of the statute "*any*" transfer to an employee is required to be included in his gross income under Section 102(c).

As the legislative history quoted above reports, the Code does provide two limited exceptions to the Section 102(c) inclusion rule. First, under Section 132(e) certain traditional retirement gifts are treated as de minimis fringe benefits; and second, under Section 74(c) certain employee achievement awards are freed from tax. Both exceptions are examples of a specific statutory rule of exclusion overriding a broader statutory rule of inclusion and both are considered in upcoming chapters.[9]

Finally a related exclusion, Section 101(b)(2)(A), presents a statutory dispensation that is framed differently from the two above. Section 101(b) places a limited portion of employee death benefits on an equal footing with regular life insurance benefits and, accordingly, it starts with a broad rule of exclusion. Under Section 101(b)(1), an employee's estate or beneficiaries may exclude from gross income amounts received that are paid by reason of the employee's death. However, Section 101(b)(2)(A) limits Section 101(b)(1) by imposing an aggregate $5,000 ceiling on amounts excludable.

In general, Section 101(b)(2)(A) imposes a two part requirement to satisfy the $5,000 exclusion. The employee's death must create the right to the amount received by the beneficiaries or the estate, and the amount received must not represent benefits the employee could have enjoyed had he lived.[10] Thus, Section 101(b)(1) has no application to payments made at an employee's death representing mere liquidation of nonforfeitable retirement benefits the deceased employee would have received personally had he survived.[11] For example, assume an employee has an arrangement with his employer providing a vested right to receive $1,200 per year for 10 years. The arrangement calls for continuation of the payments to the employee's estate upon the employee's premature death. If the employee dies six years into the arrange-

---

9. See respectively Chapters 4 and 5, infra.

10. See I.R.C. § 101(b)(2)(B). Regulations imposing this two part requirement under I.R.C. § 101(b)(1) prior to the 1954

addition of § 101(b)(2) were upheld in Hess v. Commissioner, 271 F.2d 104 (3d Cir.1959).

11. See I.R.C. § 101(b)(2)(B), first sentence.

ment, the remaining $4,800 payable to the employee's estate is not excludable under Section 101(b)(1).[12]

Section 101(b) overrides Section 102 and allows a $5,000 exclusion for employee death benefits without the need to classify them as gifts. Prior to the 1986 Act, an issue was whether excess payments (over $5,000) could sometimes qualify for Section 102 exclusion as gifts. This required a Section 102(a) factual determination.[13] The addition of Section 102(c) suggests that Congress settled any such gift controversy in the negative; and the excess over $5,000 is seemingly now required to be included in gross income.

Section 274(b)(1) generally limits the deductible amount of business gifts to $25 per donee per year; [14] but it defines the term "gift", with minor exceptions, as items excludable from the recipient's gross income under Section 102. As employee "gifts" now are includible in gross income under Section 102(c),[15] they are not subject to the Section 274(b)(1) ceiling. That ceiling is applicable only to non-employee business gifts.

PROBLEMS

1. Employer gives all of his employees, except his son, a black and white television set at Christmas, worth $100. He gives Son, who also is an employee, a color television set, worth $500. Does Son have gross income?

2. At the Heads Eye Casino in Vegas, Lucky Louie gives the maitre d' a $50 tip to assure a good table, and gives the croupier a $50 "toke" after a good night with the cubes. Does either the maitre d' or the croupier have gross income?

3. The congregation for whom Reverend serves as a minister gives him a check for $5,000 on his retirement. Does Reverend have gross income?

4. Retiree receives a $5,000 trip on his retirement. To pay for the cost of the trip, Employer contributed $2,000, and fellow employees of Retiree contributed $3,000. Does Retiree have gross income?

5. Employee was employed by Corporation for a good many years. When Employee died, the corporate board took note of his death. They agreed with the suggestion of one board member that although the corporation paid Employee his full salary under his contract, Employee had been sadly undercompensated. The board voted $15,000 to Em-

---

12. Ibid.; Reg. § 1.101–2(d)(2) Ex. 1. However, even if the deceased employee had a nonforfeitable right to payment, I.R.C. § 101(b)(2)(B) permits the $5,000 exclusion for certain lump sum distributions under various qualified plans and employee annuities. I.R.C. §§ 101(b)(2)(B)(i)–(iii), 402(e)(4). For the tax treatment of amounts not excluded, see Ferguson, Freeland and Stephens, Federal Income Taxation of Estates and Beneficiaries, 171–75 (Little, Brown 1970).

13. Rev.Rul. 62–102, 1962–2 C.B. 37.

14. Although discussion of deductions generally comes later in the text in Chapters 14 through 18, consideration of the deductibility of business gifts is relevant here.

15. I.R.C. § 102(c).

ployee's widow, Mary, and promptly paid such sum to her. What tax treatment should Mary accord the $15,000?

D. THE INCOME TAX MEANING OF INHERITANCE

Internal Revenue Code: Section 102(a), (b) first sentence, (c).

Regulations: Section 1.102–1(a), (b).

LYETH v. HOEY

Supreme Court of the United States, 1938.
305 U.S. 188, 59 S.Ct. 155.

Mr. Chief Justice HUGHES delivered the opinion of the Court.

The question presented is whether property received by petitioner from the estate of a decedent in compromise of his claim as an heir is taxable as income under the Revenue Act of 1932.

Petitioner is a grandson of Mary B. Longyear who died in 1931, a resident of Massachusetts, leaving as her heirs four surviving children and the petitioner and his brother, who were sons of a deceased daughter. By her will, the decedent gave to her heirs certain small legacies and the entire residuary estate, amounting to more than $3,000,000, was bequeathed to trustees of a so-called Endowment Trust, created April 5, 1926, the income from which was payable to another set of trustees under another trust described as the Longyear Foundation. The main purpose of the latter trust was to preserve "the records of the earthly life of Mary Baker Eddy," the founder of the Christian Science religion.

When the will was offered for probate in Massachusetts there was objection by the heirs upon the grounds, among others, of lack of testamentary capacity and undue influence. After hearing, at which a statement was made by the respective parties of their proposed evidence, the probate court granted a motion for the framing of issues for trial before a jury. In that situation a compromise agreement was entered into between the heirs, the legatees, the devisees and the executors under the will, and the Attorney General of Massachusetts. This agreement provided that the will should be admitted to probate and letters testamentary issued; that the specific and pecuniary bequests to individuals should be enforced; that the bequest of the residuary estate to the Endowment Trust should be disregarded; that $200,000 should be paid to the heirs and a like amount to the Endowment Trust, and that the net residue of the estate, as defined, should be equally divided between the trustees of the Endowment Trust and the heirs. The net residue to which the heirs were thus entitled was to be payable in units of stock owned by the decedent in certain corporations, Longyear Estate, Inc., Longyear Corporation and Longyear Realty Corporation, and for that purpose a unit was to consist of three shares, one share of each corporation.

The compromise was approved by the probate court pursuant to a statute of Massachusetts (Mass.Gen.Laws 1932, c. 204, §§ 15–17) and a decree was entered on April 26, 1932, admitting the will to probate, issuing letters testamentary to the executors and directing them "to administer the estate of said deceased in accordance with the terms of said will and said agreement of compromise." Owing to the Depression and the necessity of discharging pecuniary legacies amounting to about $300,000, which were entitled to priority in payment before distribution of the residue, the heirs undertook to finance one-half of these legacies and the residuary legatees the other one-half. For this purpose the heirs formed a corporation known as Longyear Heirs, Inc., to which they assigned their interests in the estate in exchange for common stock. Preferred stock was issued to the pecuniary legatees.

In July, 1933, the executors distributed to Longyear Heirs, Inc., as assignee of the petitioner, his distributable share of the estate, consisting of $80.17 in cash and a certificate of deposit for 358 units, each unit representing one share of each of the three corporations mentioned in the compromise agreement. The Commissioner of Internal Revenue valued this distributable share at $141,484.03 and treated the whole amount as income for the year 1933 in which it was received. An additional tax of $56,389.65 was assessed, which petitioner paid in October, 1936, with interest. Claim for refund was then filed and on its rejection this suit was brought against the collector.

On motion of petitioner the District Court entered a summary judgment in his favor, 20 F.Supp. 619, which the Circuit Court of Appeals reversed. 96 F.2d 141. Because of a conflict with the decision of the Circuit Court of Appeals of the Fourth Circuit in Magruder v. Segebade, 94 F.2d 177, certiorari was granted.

The Court of Appeals overruled the contentions of petitioner that the property he received was within the statutory exemption (§ 22(b)(3) of the Revenue Act of 1932) and, further, that the property was not income either under the statute or under the Sixteenth Amendment of the Federal Constitution. As the view of the Court of Appeals upon these questions determined the rights of the parties, it was found unnecessary to discuss certain affirmative defenses set up by the answer of the respondent and these defenses are not pressed in this court.

First. By § 22(b)(3) of the Revenue Act of 1932, there is exempted from the income tax—

> "The value of property acquired by gift, bequest, devise, or inheritance. * * *"

Whether property received by an heir from the estate of his ancestor is acquired by inheritance, when it is distributed under an agreement settling a contest by the heir of the validity of the decedent's will, is a question upon which state courts have differed. The question has arisen in the application of state laws of taxation. In Massachusetts, the rule is that when a will is admitted to probate under a compromise agreement, the state succession tax is applied to the property "that passes by the terms of the will as written and not as changed by any agreement for compromise." Baxter v. Treasurer, 209 Mass. 459, 463; 95 N.E. 854, 856. Although under the Massachusetts statute relating to compromise [1] it is the practice to insert a clause in the court's decree that the estate is to be administered in accordance with the agreement, "yet the rights of the parties so far as they rest upon the agreement are contractual and not testamentary." Ellis v. Hunt, 228 Mass. 39, 43; 116 N.E. 956. See, also, Brandeis v. Atkins, 204 Mass. 471, 474; 90 N.E. 861; Copeland v. Wheelwright, 230 Mass. 131, 136; 119 N.E. 667. Thus, when a contest was withdrawn under a compromise and the residuary estate was divided equally between the legatee and the heirs, it was held that the tax was properly levied upon the entire residuary legacy and that the administrators with the will annexed had no right to pay out of the share transferred to the heirs one-half of the tax thus collectible from the legatee unless the compromise agreement expressly or impliedly so provided. Brown v. McLoughlin, 287 Mass. 15, 17; 190 N.E. 795. Several States have a similar rule.[2] In other States the amount received by an heir under an agreement compromising a contest of his ancestor's will is considered to be received by virtue of his heirship and is subject to an inheritance tax unless the statute exempts him.[3]

In the instant case, the Court of Appeals applied the Massachusetts rule, holding that whether the property was received by way of inheritance depended "upon the law of the jurisdiction under which this taxpayer received it." We think that this ruling was erroneous. The question as to the construction of the exemption in the federal statute is not determined by local law. We are not concerned with the peculiarities and special incidences of state taxes or with the policies they reflect. Undoubtedly the state law determines what persons are qualified to inherit property within the jurisdiction. Mager v. Grima, 8 How. 490, 493; Maxwell v. Bugbee, 250 U.S. 525, 536, 537, 40 S.Ct. 2, 5. The local law determines the right to make a testamentary disposition of such property and the conditions essential to the validity of wills, and the state courts settle their construction. Uterhart v. United States, 240 U.S. 598, 603, 36 S.Ct. 417, 418. The State establishes the procedure governing the probate of wills and the processes of administration. Petitioner's status as heir was thus determined by the law of Massachusetts. That law also regulated the procedure by which his rights as an heir could be vindicated. The state law authorized its courts to supervise the making of agreements compromising contests by heirs of the validity of an alleged will of their ancestor, in order that such compromises shall be just and reasonable with respect to all persons in interest.[4] But when the contestant is an heir and a valid

---

1. Massachusetts General Laws 1932, Chap. 204, §§ 13–18.

2. [Citations omitted. Ed.]

3. [Citations omitted. Ed.]

4. See Note 1. Such agreements are "entirely valid outside of the statute." Ellis v. Hunt, 28 Mass. 39, 44, 116 N.E. 956.

compromise agreement has been made and there is a distribution to the heir from the decedent's estate accordingly, the question whether what the heir has thus received has been "acquired by inheritance" within the meaning of the federal statute necessarily is a federal question. It is not determined by local characterization.

In dealing with the meaning and application of an act of Congress enacted in the exercise of its plenary power under the Constitution to tax income and to grant exemptions from that tax, it is the will of Congress which controls, and the expression of its will, in the absence of language evidencing a different purpose, should be interpreted "so as to give a uniform application to a nationwide scheme of taxation." Burnet v. Harmel, 287 U.S. 103, 110, 53 S.Ct. 74. Congress establishes its own criteria and the state law may control only when the federal taxing act by express language or necessary implication makes its operation dependent upon state law. Burnet v. Harmel, supra. See Burk-Waggoner Oil Assn. v. Hopkins, 269 U.S. 110, 111, 114, 46 S.Ct. 48; Weiss v. Wiener, 279 U.S. 333, 337, 46 S.Ct. 48; Morrissey v. Commissioner, 296 U.S. 344, 356, 56 S.Ct. 289, 294. Compare Crooks v. Harrelson, 282 U.S. 55, 59, 51 S.Ct. 49; Poe v. Seaborn, 282 U.S. 101, 109, 110, 51 S.Ct. 58; Blair v. Commissioner, 300 U.S. 5, 9, 10, 57 S.Ct. 330, 332. There is no such expression or necessary implication in this instance. Whether what an heir receives from the estate of his ancestor through the compromise of his contest of his ancestor's will should be regarded as within the exemption from the federal tax should not be decided in one way in the case of an heir in Pennsylvania or Minnesota and in another way in the case of an heir in Massachusetts or New York,[5] according to the differing views of the state courts. We think that it was the intention of Congress in establishing this exemption to provide a uniform rule.

Second. In exempting from the income tax the value of property acquired by "bequest, devise, or inheritance," Congress used comprehensive terms embracing all acquisitions in the devolution of a decedent's estate. For the word "descent," as used in the earlier acts,[6] Congress substituted the word "inheritance" in the 1926 Act and the subsequent revenue acts as "more appropriately including both real and personal property."[7] Thus the acquisition by succession to a decedent's estate whether real or personal was embraced in the exemption. Further, by the "estate tax," Congress has imposed a tax upon the transfer of the entire net estate of every person dying after September 8, 1916,[8] allowing such exemptions as it sees fit in arriving at the net estate. Congress has not indicated any intention to tax again the value of the property which legatees, devisees or heirs receive from the decedent's estate.

---

5. See Notes 2 and 3.

6. See Act of October 3, 1913, c. 16, § II, 38 Stat. 167; Revenue Acts of 1918, 1921 and 1924, § 213(b)(3).

7. Revenue Act of 1926, § 213(b)(3); Acts of 1928 and 1932, § 22(b)(3). Sen.Rep. No. 52, 69th Cong., 1st Sess., p. 20.

8. Act of September 8, 1916, c. 463, Title II, 39 Stat. 777.

Petitioner was concededly an heir of his grandmother under the Massachusetts statute. It was by virtue of that heirship that he opposed probate of her alleged will which constituted an obstacle to the enforcement of his right. Save as heir he had no standing. Seeking to remove that obstacle, he asserted that the will was invalid because of want of testamentary capacity and undue influence. In accordance with local practice, he asked the probate court to frame these issues for a jury trial. It then became necessary for him to satisfy the court that the issues were substantial. Issues are not to be framed unless it appears from statements by counsel of expected evidence or otherwise that there is a "genuine question of fact supported by evidence of such a substantial nature as to afford ground for reasonable expectation of a result favorable to the party requesting the framing of issues." Briggs v. Weston, 294 Mass. 452, 2 N.E.2d 466; Smith v. Patterson, 286 Mass. 356, 190 N.E. 536. Petitioner satisfied that condition and the probate court directed the framing of jury issues. It was in that situation, facing a trial of the issue of the validity of the will, that the compromise was made by which the heirs, including the petitioner, were to receive certain portions of the decedent's estate.

There is no question that petitioner obtained that portion, upon the value of which he is sought to be taxed, because of his standing as an heir and of his claim in that capacity. It does not seem to be questioned that if the contest had been fought to a finish and petitioner had succeeded, the property which he would have received would have been exempt under the federal act. Nor is it questioned that if in any appropriate proceeding, instituted by him as heir, he had recovered judgment for a part of the estate, that part would have been acquired by inheritance within the meaning of the act. We think that the distinction sought to be made between acquisition through such a judgment and acquisition by a compromise agreement in lieu of such a judgment is too formal to be sound, as it disregards the substance of the statutory exemption. It does so, because it disregards the heirship which underlay the compromise, the status which commanded that agreement and was recognized by it. While the will was admitted to probate, the decree also required the distribution of the estate in accordance with the compromise and, so far as the latter provided for distribution to the heirs, it overrode the will. So far as the will became effective under the agreement it was because of the heirs' consent and release and in consideration of the distribution they received by reason of their being heirs. Respondent agrees that the word "inheritance" as used in the federal statute is not solely applicable to cases of complete intestacy. The portion of the decedent's property which petitioner obtained under the compromise did not come to him through the testator's will. That portion he obtained because of his heirship and to that extent he took in spite of the will and as in case of intestacy. The fact that petitioner received less than the amount of his claim did not alter its nature or the quality of its recognition through the distribution which he did receive.

We are not convinced by the argument that petitioner had but "the expectations" of an heir and realized on a "bargaining position." He was heir in fact. Whether he would receive any property in that capacity depended upon the validity of his ancestor's will and the extent to which it would dispose of his ancestor's estate. When, by compromise and the decree enforcing it, that disposition was limited, what he got from the estate came to him because he was heir, the compromise serving to remove *pro tanto* the impediment to his inheritance. We are of the opinion that the exemption applies.

In this view we find it unnecessary to consider the other questions that have been discussed at the bar.

The judgment of the Circuit Court of Appeals is reversed and that of the District Court is affirmed.

Reversed.

WOLDER v. COMMISSIONER *

United States Court of Appeals, Second Circuit, 1974.
493 F.2d 608.

OAKES, Circuit Judge: These two cases, involving an appeal and cross-appeal in the individual taxpayers' case and an appeal by the Commissioner in the estate taxpayer's case, essentially turn on one question: whether an attorney contracting to and performing lifetime legal services for a client receives income when the client, pursuant to the contract, bequeaths a substantial sum to the attorney in lieu of the payment of fees during the client's lifetime. In the individual taxpayer's case, the Tax Court held that the fair market value of the stock and cash received under the client's will constituted taxable income under § 61, Int.Rev.Code of 1954, and was not exempt from taxation as a bequest under § 102 of the Code. From this ruling the individual taxpayers, Victor R. Wolder, the attorney, and his wife, who signed joint returns, appeal.

* * *

There is no basic disagreement as to the facts. On or about October 3, 1947, Victor R. Wolder, as attorney, and Marguerite K. Boyce, as client, entered into a written agreement which, after reciting Mr. Wolder's past services on her behalf in an action against her ex-husband for which he had made no charge, consisted of mutual promises, first on the part of Wolder to render to Mrs. Boyce "such legal services as she shall in her opinion personally require from time to time as long as both * * * shall live and not to bill her for such services," and second on the part of Mrs. Boyce to make a codicil to her last will and testament giving and bequeathing to Mr. Wolder or to his estate "my 500 shares of Class B common stock of White Laboratories, Inc." or "such other * * * securities" as might go to her in the event of a

---

* See Kemp, "Federal Tax Aspects of Will Contests," 23 U.Miami L.Rev. 72 (1968); Schenk, "Tax Effects of Will Contests and Compromises," 10 Tulane Tax Inst. 214 (1961). Ed.

merger or consolidation of White Laboratories. Subsequently, in 1957, White Laboratories did merge into Schering Corp. and Mrs. Boyce received 750 shares of Schering common and 500 shares of Schering convertible preferred. In 1964 the convertible preferred was redeemed for $15,845. In a revised will dated April 23, 1965, Mrs. Boyce, true to the agreement with Mr. Wolder, bequeathed to him or his estate the sum of $15,845 and the 750 shares of common stock of Schering Corp. There is no dispute but that Victor R. Wolder had rendered legal services to Mrs. Boyce over her lifetime (though apparently these consisted largely of revising her will) and had not billed her therefor so that he was entitled to performance by her under the agreement, on which she had had a measure of independent legal advice. At least the New York Surrogate's Court (DiFalco, J.) ultimately so found in contested proceedings in which Mrs. Boyce's residuary legatees contended that the will merely provided for payment of a debt and took the position that Wolder was not entitled to payment until he proved the debt in accordance with § 212, New York Surrogate's Court Act.[1]

*   *   *

Wolder argues that the legacy he received under Mrs. Boyce's will is specifically excluded from income by virtue of § 102(a), Int.Rev.Code of 1954, which provides that "Gross Income does not include the value of property acquired by gift, bequest, devise or inheritance * * *" See also Treas.Reg. 1.102–1(a). The individual taxpayer, as did dissenting Judge Quealy below, relies upon United States v. Merriam, 263 U.S. 179, 44 S.Ct. 69 (1923), and its progeny for the proposition that the term "bequest" in § 102(a) has not been restricted so as to exclude bequests made on account of some consideration flowing from the beneficiary to the decedent. In *Merriam* the testator made cash bequests to certain persons who were named executors of the estate, and these bequests were " 'in lieu of all compensation or commissions to which they would otherwise be entitled as executors or trustees.' " 263 U.S. at 184, 44 S.Ct. at 70. The Court held nevertheless that the legacies were exempt from taxation, drawing a distinction—which in a day and age when we look to substance and not to form strikes us as of doubtful utility— between cases where "compensation [is] fixed by will for services to be rendered by the executor and [where] a legacy [is paid] to one upon the implied condition that he shall clothe himself with the character of executor." 263 U.S. at 187, 44 S.Ct. at 71. In the former case, Mr. Justice Sutherland said, the executor "must perform the services to earn the compensation" while in the latter case "he need do no more than in good faith comply with the condition [that he be executor] in order to receive the bequest." The Court went on to take the view that the provision in the will that the bequest was in lieu of commissions was simply "an expression of the testator's will that the executor shall not receive statutory allowances for the services he may render."

---

1. Subsequently another surrogate held that the estate would not be obligated under the so-called tax clause in Mrs. Boyce's will to reimburse Mr. Wolder for any income tax payable by him by reason of the bequest made to him in accordance with the 1947 contract.

While the distinction drawn in the *Merriam* case hardly stands economic analysis, Bank of New York v. Helvering, 132 F.2d 773 (2d Cir.1943), follows it on the basis that it is controlling law.[2]

But we think that *Merriam* is inapplicable to the facts of this case, for here there is no dispute but that the parties did contract for services and—while the services were limited in nature—there was also no question but that they were actually rendered. Thus the provisions of Mrs. Boyce's will, at least for federal tax purposes, went to satisfy her obligation under the contract. The contract in effect was one for the postponed payment of legal services, i.e., by a legacy under the will for services rendered during the decedent's life.

Moreover, the Supreme Court itself has taken an entirely different viewpoint from *Merriam* when it comes to interpreting § 102(a), or its predecessor, § 22(b)(3), Int.Rev.Code of 1939, in reference to what are gifts. In Commissioner v. Duberstein, 363 U.S. 278, 80 S.Ct. 1190 (1960), the Court held that the true test is whether in actuality the gift is a bona fide gift or simply a method for paying compensation. This question is resolved by an examination of the intent of the parties, the reasons for the transfer, and the parties' performance in accordance with their intentions—"what the basic reason for [the donor's] conduct was in fact—the dominant reason that explains his action in making the transfer." 363 U.S. at 286, 80 S.Ct. at 1197. See also Carrigan v. Commissioner, 197 F.2d 246 (2d Cir.1952); Fisher v. Commissioner, 59 F.2d 192 (2d Cir.1932). There are other cases holding testamentary transfers to be taxable compensation for services as opposed to tax-free bequests. Cotnam v. Commissioner, 263 F.2d 119 (5th Cir.1959); Mariani v. Commissioner, 54 T.C. 135 (1970); Cohen v. United States, 241 F.Supp. 740 (E.D.Mich.1965); Davies v. Commissioner, 23 T.C. 524 (1954). True, in each of these cases the testator did not fulfill his contractual obligation to provide in his will for payment of services rendered by the taxpayer, forcing the taxpayers to litigate the merits of their claims against the estates, whereas in the case at bar the terms of the contract were carried out. This is a distinction without a difference, and while we could decline to follow them in the case at bar, we see no reason to do so.

Indeed, it is to be recollected that § 102 is, after all, an exception to the basic provision in § 61(a) that "Except as otherwise provided in this subtitle, gross income means all income from whatever source derived, including * * * (1) Compensation for services, including fees, commissions and similar items * * *." The congressional purpose is to tax

---

2. One also doubts the present day validity of the underlying philosophical premise of Merriam, that "If the words are doubtful, the doubt must be resolved against the government and in favor of the taxpayer." 263 U.S. at 188, 44 S.Ct. at 71. In White v. United States, 305 U.S. 281, 292, 59 S.Ct. 179, 184 (1938), after noting for the majority that it was not "impressed" by this very argument, Mr. Justice Stone said, "It is the function and duty of courts to resolve doubts. We know of no reason why that function should be abdicated in a tax case more than in any other where the rights of suitors turn on the construction of a statute and it is our duty to decide what that construction fairly should be."

income comprehensively. Commissioner v. Jacobson, 336 U.S. 28, 49, 69 S.Ct. 358 (1949). A transfer in the form of a bequest was the method that the parties chose to compensate Mr. Wolder for his legal services, and that transfer is therefore subject to taxation, whatever its label whether by federal or by local law may be. See also Hort v. Commissioner, 313 U.S. 28, 31, 61 S.Ct. 757 (1941).

Taxpayer's argument that he received the stock and cash as a "bequest" under New York law and the decisions of the surrogates is thus beside the point. New York law does, of course, control as to the extent of the taxpayer's legal rights to the property in question, but it does not control as to the characterization of the property for federal income tax purposes. United States v. Mitchell, 403 U.S. 190, 197, 91 S.Ct. 1763 (1971); Commissioner v. Duberstein, 363 U.S. at 285, 44 S.Ct. at 69; Morgan v. Commissioner, 309 U.S. 78, 80–81, 60 S.Ct. 424 (1940); Higt v. United States, 256 F.2d 795, 800 (2d Cir.1958). New York law cannot be decisive on the question whether any given transfer is income under § 61(a) or is exempt under § 102(a) of the Code. We repeat, we see no difference between the transfer here made in the form of a bequest and the transfer under Commissioner v. Duberstein, supra, which was made without consideration, with no legal or moral obligation, and which was indeed a "common-law gift," but which was nevertheless held not to be a gift excludable under § 102(a).

PROBLEMS

1. Consider whether it is likely that § 102 applies in the following circumstances:

    (a) Father leaves Daughter $20,000 in his will.

    (b) Father dies intestate and Daughter receives $20,000 worth of real estate as his heir.

    (c) Father leaves several family members out of his will and Daughter and others attack the will. As a result of a settlement of the controversy Daughter receives $20,000.

    (d) Father leaves Daughter $20,000 in his will stating that the amount is in appreciation of Daughter's long and devoted service to him.

    (e) Father leaves Daughter $20,000 pursuant to a written agreement under which Daughter agreed to care for Father in his declining years.

    (f) Same agreement as in (e), above, except that Father died intestate and Daughter successfully enforced her $20,000 claim under the agreement against the estate.

    (g) Same as (f), above, except that Daughter settles her $20,000 claim for a $10,000 payment.

    (h) Father appointed Daughter executrix of his estate and Father's will provided Daughter was to receive $20,000 for services as executrix. *according to Merriam — it is exempt / may not be good law today*

(1)   Father appointed Daughter executrix of his estate and made a $20,000 bequest to her in lieu of all compensation or commissions to which she would otherwise be entitled as executrix.

2.   Boyfriend who has a "mental problem" with marriage agrees with Taxpayer that he will leave her "everything" at his death in return for her staying with him without marriage.   She does, he doesn't, she sues his estate on a theory of quantum meruit and settles her claim.   Is her settlement excludable under § 102?

3.   If the *Wolder* case arose after 1986, would § 102(c) apply to resolve the issue?

CHAPTER 4. LIMITATIONS IN EMPLOYMENT RELATIONSHIPS

A. FRINGE BENEFITS*

Internal Revenue Code: Section 132 (omit (h)(2)). See Sections 61(a)(1); 79; 83; 112; 117(d); 120; 125; 127; 129.

Regulations: Sections 1.61–1(a), –2T(b)(1) and (2). See Section 1.132–1 through 8.

Chapter Two of this book presents the standard broad definition of gross income under Section 61. Section 61(a)(1) specifically includes in gross income "compensation for services". Such compensation may take the form of property as well as cash,[1] and it can be indirectly as well as directly paid.[2] The Supreme Court has stated that Section 61(a) (1) "is broad enough to include in taxable income any economic or financial benefit conferred on the employee as compensation, whatever the form or mode by which it is effected." [3]

Technically, then, whether an employee is paid in dollars, property or use of property, any form of compensation is gross income. But comes now the fringe benefit which seems to challenge this broad, established concept. For example, employer has an office coffee maker and employees are allowed to consume all the free coffee they want. Technically, each cup is income. Realistically, reporting and enforcing the reporting of such income is impossible. Similar conclusions can be reached with respect to a secretary's typing of a personal letter for her boss or either's occasional personal use of the company copying machine. Such items are de minimis anyway and no big deal; but what happens when a so-called fringe becomes more substantial, such as travel passes to airline stewards or courtesy discounts to department store clerks?

All the above items are commonly known as fringe benefits. Although their value is conceptually gross income, nevertheless to some extent over the years the Service, even without statutory authorization, has allowed taxpayers not to report them. The exact scope of such administratively created exclusions has been vague. Occasionally Congress has enacted a statute specifically to exclude a fringe benefit from

---

* See Simon, "Fringe Benefits and Tax Reform Historical Blunders and a Proposal for Structural Change," 36 U.Fla.L.Rev. 871 (1984); Halperin, "Broadening the Base—The Case of Fringe Benefits," 37 Nat'l Tax J. 271 (1984).

1. Reg. § 1.61–1(a).

2. E.g., A may have income if B discharges a debt of A to C. Old Colony Trust Co. v. Commissioner, 279 U.S. 716, 49 S.Ct. 499 (1929).

3. Commissioner v. Smith, 324 U.S. 177, 181, 65 S.Ct. 591, 593 (1945).

gross income[4] or to include or partly include a fringe within gross income.[5] In other areas, vagueness as to the inclusion of fringes in gross income has led to inconsistency in the administration of the tax laws and perhaps sometimes to taxpayer misconception that any non-cash fringe benefit may be excluded.

In 1975, the Treasury Department issued a tentative proposal, a "Discussion Draft of Proposed Regulations," which contained a number of rules for determining whether questionable compensatory items were to be included in gross income.[6] In response, in 1978, Congress prohibited the Treasury from issuing or proposing regulations;[7] seemingly Congress chose to enact legislation unimpeded by possibly conflicting administrative action. The moratorium was extended with no governmental action whatever until 1984 when Congress enacted specific legislation to deal with fringes. The House Committee Report,[8] below, provides the reasons for and a summary of the legislation:

REASONS FOR CHANGE

In providing statutory rules for exclusion of certain fringe benefits for income and payroll tax purposes, the committee has attempted to strike a balance between two competing objectives.

First, the committee is aware that in many industries, employees may receive, either free or at a discount, goods and services which the employer sells to the general public. In many cases, these practices are long established, and have been treated by employers, employees, and the IRS as not giving rise to taxable income. Although employees may receive an economic benefit from the availability of these free or discounted goods or services, employers often have valid business reasons, other than simply providing compensation, for encouraging employees to avail themselves of the products which they sell to the public. For example, a retail clothing business will want its salespersons to wear, when they deal with customers, the clothing which it seeks to sell to the public. In addition, the fact that the selection of goods and services usually available from a particular employer usually is restricted makes it appropriate to provide a limited exclusion, when such discounts are generally made available to employees, for the income employees realize from obtaining free or reduced-cost goods or services. The committee believes, therefore, that many present practices under which employers may provide to

4. See I.R.C. § 106, excluding employer contributions to employee accident and health plans.

5. See I.R.C. § 79, classifying employer payment for group term life insurance.

6. See the Summary and Explanation of Discussion Draft of Proposed Regula-tions on Fringe Benefits published in the Federal Register September 5, 1975.

7. P.L. No. 95–427, 95th Cong., 2d Sess. (1978).

8. H.Rep. No. 98–432, 98th Cong., 2d Sess. 1591-2 (1984).

a broad group of employees, either free or at a discount, the products and services which the employer sells or provides to the public do not serve merely to replace cash compensation. These reasons support the committee's decision to codify the ability of employers to continue these practices without imposition of income or payroll taxes.

The second objective of the committee's bill is to set forth clear boundaries for the provision of tax-free benefits. Because of the moratorium on the issuance of fringe benefit regulations, the Treasury Department has been precluded from clarifying the tax treatment of many of the forms of noncash compensation commonly in use. As a result, the administrators of the tax law have not had clear guidelines in this area, and hence taxpayers in identical situations have been treated differently. The inequities, confusion, and administrative difficulties for business, employees, and the IRS resulting from this situation have increased substantially in recent years. The committee believes that it is unacceptable to allow these conditions—which have existed since 1978—to continue any longer.

In addition, the committee is concerned that without any well-defined limits on the ability of employers to compensate their employees tax-free by using a medium other than cash, new practices will emerge that could shrink the income tax base significantly, and further shift a disproportionate tax burden to those individuals whose compensation is in the form of cash. [Students may wish to let their imaginations run with this. Ed.] A shrinkage of the base of the social security payroll tax could also pose a threat to the viability of the social security system above and beyond the adverse projections which the Congress recently addressed in the Social Security Amendments of 1983. Finally, an unrestrained expansion of noncash compensation would increase inequities among employees in different types of business, and among employers as well.

The nondiscrimination rule is an important common thread among the types of fringe benefits which are excluded under the bill from income and employment taxes. Under the bill, most fringe benefits may be made available tax-free to officers, owners, or highly compensated employees only if the benefits are also provided on substantially equal terms to other employees. The committee believes that it would be fundamentally unfair to provide tax-free treatment for economic benefits that are furnished only to highly paid executives. Further, where benefits are limited to the highly paid, it is more likely that the benefit is being provided so that those who control the business can receive compensation in a nontaxable form; in that situation, the reasons stated above for allowing tax-free treatment would not be applicable. Also, if highly paid executives could receive free from taxation economic benefits that are denied to lower-paid employees, while the latter are compensated only in fully taxable cash, the committee is concerned that this situation would exacerbate problems of noncompliance among taxpayers. In this regard, some commentators argue that the current situation—in which the lack of clear rules for the tax treatment of nonstatutory fringe benefits encourages the nonreporting of many types of compensatory benefits—has led to nonreporting of types of cash income which are clearly taxable under present-law rules, such as interest and dividends.

In summary, the committee believes that by providing rules which essentially codify many present practices under which employers provide their own products and services tax-free to a broad group of employees, and by ending the uncertainties arising from a moratorium on the Treasury Department's ability to clarify the tax treatment of these benefits, the bill substantially improves the equity and administration of the tax system.

EXPLANATION OF PROVISIONS

Overview

Under the bill, certain fringe benefits provided by an employer are excluded from the recipient employee's gross income for Federal income tax purposes and from the wage base (and, if applicable, the benefit base) for purposes of income tax withholding, FICA, [Federal Insurance Contributions Act. Ed.] FUTA, [Federal Unemployment Tax Act. Ed.] and RRTA [Railroad Retirement Tax Act. Ed.]

The excluded fringe benefits are those benefits that qualify under one of the following five categories as defined in the bill: (1) a no-additional-cost service, (2) a qualified employee discount, (3) a working condition fringe, (4) a de minimis fringe, and (5) a qualified tuition reduction. Special rules apply with respect to certain parking or eating facilities provided to employees, on-premises athletic facilities, and demonstration use of an employer-provided car by auto salespersons. Some of the exclusions under the bill apply to benefits provided to the spouse and dependent children of a current employee, to former employees who separated from service because of retirement or disability (and their spouses and dependent children), and to the widow(er) of a deceased employee (and the dependent children of deceased employees).

In the case of a no-additional-cost service, a qualified employee discount, employee * * * eating facilities, or a qualified tuition reduction, the exclusion applies with respect to benefits provided to officers, owners, or highly compensated employees only if the benefit is made available to employees on a basis which does not discriminate in favor of officers, owners, or highly compensated employees.

Any fringe benefit that does not qualify for exclusion under the bill (for example, free or discounted goods or services which are limited to corporate officers) and that is not excluded under another statutory fringe benefit provision of the Code is taxable to the recipient under Code sections 61 and 83, and is includible in wages for employment tax purposes, at the excess of its fair market value over any amount paid by the employee for the benefit.

The provisions of the bill generally take effect on January 1, 1984, [changed before enactment to January 1, 1985. Ed.] except that the tuition reduction exclusion applies with respect to education furnished after June 30, 1984.

As the above quotation from the House Report indicates, the tax law on fringe benefits is now completely statutory and, while subject of course to customary administrative [9] and judicial interpretative refinements, it is not to be *created* administratively. If an employee benefit is not specifically excluded from gross income, its value must be included within gross income [10] under Section 61.[11]

Congress had previously enacted other Code sections that expressly include or exclude some equivocal benefits from gross income.[12] Most of the exclusionary rules of the 1984 Act appear in Code Section 132. But that section is not exclusive; and other sections may overlap to exclude a particular benefit from gross income.[13] Section 132 excludes from gross income the five categories of fringes identified in the committee report above. A brief examination of those five classifications of excludable fringe benefits follows.

In all cases, Section 132 excludes fringes provided to "employees". In the first two classifications of fringe benefits (no-additional-cost services and qualified employee discounts[14]) the definition of an employee is expanded to include not only persons currently employed but also retired and disabled ex-employees and the surviving spouses of employees or retired or disabled ex-employees [15] as well as spouses and dependent children of employees.[16]

---

9. I.R.C. § 132(k).

10. As income, it is also subject to withholding tax and social security and unemployment insurance payroll taxes (FICA and FUTA) to be paid by the employer.

11. See also I.R.C. § 83, which establishes the amount and timing of such income.

12. Some of those sections are discussed below.

13. I.R.C. § 132(j).

14. I.R.C. § 132(a)(1) and (2). See infra.

15. I.R.C. § 132(f)(1).

16. I.R.C. § 132(f)(2). The regulations provide that the term employee includes a partner rendering services to a partnership. Reg. § 1.132–1(b)(1). See also I.R.C. § 132(f)(3).

Section 132 excludes the first two classifications of fringes [17] and employee eating facilities [18] provided to highly compensated employees only if those fringes are offered to all employees on a nondiscriminatory basis.[19] The nondiscrimination requirement permits highly compensated employees no exclusion for those fringes unless the fringes are provided on substantially the same terms to a broad group of employees.[20] If a classification of fringes is discriminatory, highly compensated employees have gross income, but the exclusion still applies to those employees (if any) who receive the benefit and who are not members of the highly compensated group.[21]

Section 132(a)(1): No-Additional-Cost Services. The first type of fringe benefit excluded from an employee's gross income under Section 132 is services provided to an employee by an employer. Their value escapes gross income if the services are offered for sale to customers in the same line of business as that in which the employee is performing services,[22] the employer incurs no substantial additional cost in providing the service to the employee [23] and, in the case of highly compensated employees, the services are provided on a nondiscriminatory basis.[24] The amount of revenue an employer loses because of providing the service to the employee rather than to a paying customer and the amount of time spent by the other employees in providing a service for the employer are factors taken into consideration to determine whether there is substantial additional cost.[25] Examples of no-additional-cost services that are given in the legislative history of the new section include airline, railroad, or subway seats and hotel rooms furnished to employees, if they are working in those respective businesses, in a way that does not displace non-employee customers, and free telephone service to telephone employees within existing capacity of the employer company.[26] The exclusion is allowed whether the services are provided free of charge, at cost or some partial charge, or under a cash rebate program.[27]

As previously stated, the services must be provided in the same line of business as that in which the employee is employed. Thus, if an employee is a steward for an airline owned by a company that also owns a cruise ship, free standby airline flights for the employee, his spouse and his dependents are excludable but a free cruise is not. This restriction is framed carefully to preclude an unfair advantage for employees of conglomerates.[28] On the other hand, if two companies

17. See note 14, supra.

18. I.R.C. § 132(e)(2).

19. I.R.C. § 132(h)(1) and (7) and (e), last sentence. See also I.R.C. § 414(q).

20. Id.

21. Id.

22. I.R.C. § 132(b)(1). Cf. I.R.C. § 132(i).

23. I.R.C. § 132(b)(2).

24. I.R.C. § 132(h)(1).

25. Reg. § 1.132–2(a)(5)(i).

26. H.Rep. No. 98–432, supra note 8 at 1594. See also Reg. § 1.132–2(a)(2).

27. Cf. I.R.C. § 132(b)(2). Reg. § 1.132–2(a)(3).

28. If an employee were employed by the conglomerate in a position related to both businesses, perhaps as an accountant for both businesses, he would qualify for exclusions in each line of business if he performed substantial services in each line of business. Reg. § 1.132–4(a)(1)(iv)(A).

have a written reciprocal agreement that makes the services of one available to the employees of the other, employees of one company may exclude, as no-additional-cost services, services provided by the other, if the services in question are in the employee's line of business.[29] Thus a steward could exclude the value of standby flights on another airline, if there is the requisite written agreement between the airlines and neither airline incurs any substantial additional cost in providing standby flights pursuant to the agreement.

Section 132(a)(2): Qualified Employee Discounts. Historically, an employee has been allowed to exclude from gross income the value of "courtesy discounts" on items purchased from his employer for use by the employee.[30] Subject to some restrictions, this exclusion continues under the new section. As in the case of the no-additional-cost services exclusion, both the nondiscrimination[31] and the same-line-of-business[32] limitations apply.[33] The exclusion applies to purchases of both property (other than real property and personal property held for investment)[34] and purchases of services which includes, the legislative history indicates,[35] purchases of insurance policies,[36] but does not include loans to employees of financial institutions. The discount may take the form of either a price reduction or a rebate.[37]

The Code imposes a ceiling on the amount of the exclusion. In the case of services the exclusion may not exceed 20% of the price at which the services are offered by the employer to customers.[38] The maximum discount for property is essentially the employer's "gross profit percentage"[39] on goods in the employee's line of business. That percentage expressed as a fraction is:

$$\frac{\text{aggregate sales price reduced by cost}}{\text{aggregate sales price}}$$

The fraction is based on sales of all property in the employee's line of business (not just the discounted item) taking into account the employer's experience during a representative period.[40] Thus, if an employee works for a home appliance store and his employer has total sales for

---

29. I.R.C. § 132(g)(2). See I.R.C. § 132(b)(1).

30. Cf. Reg. § 31.3401(a)–1(b)(10).

31. I.R.C. § 132(h)(1).

32. I.R.C. § 132(c)(4). See also § 132(h)(2) which under some circumstances allows employees of lessees of department store space (concessions) to be treated as employees of the department store itself, if the store allows discounts to their employees.

33. The reciprocal agreement allowance is inapplicable to employee discounts. I.R.C. § 132(g) applies only to § 132(a)(1) fringes. See Reg. § 1.132–3(a)(3).

34. I.R.C. § 132(c)(4). Such property may be either tangible or intangible property. Reg. § 1.132–3(a)(2)(ii).

35. H.Rep. No. 98–432, supra note 8 at 1600, n. 12.

36. Cf. Commissioner v. Minzer, 279 F.2d 338 (5th Cir.1960).

37. Reg. § 1.132–3(a)(4).

38. I.R.C. § 132(c)(1)(B).

39. I.R.C. § 132(c)(1)(A).

40. I.R.C. § 132(c)(2)(B).

the entire year of $800,000 and paid $600,000 for the goods sold, the gross profit percentage is 25% determined as follows:

$$\frac{\$800,000 \text{ less } \$600,000}{\$800,000} = \frac{\$200,000}{\$800,000} = 25\%$$

If an employer allows an employee to buy an appliance regularly selling for $1,000 for a price of $750 or more, the full discount is subject to the exclusion. If the price is below $750 the exclusion is limited to $250, and the employee must report some income from the transaction (the excess over the permitted exclusion).[41]

Section 132(a)(3): Working Condition Fringe. Congress allows an exclusion for any property or services provided to an employee the cost of which, if the employee had paid for the property or services, would have been deductible by the employee as a business expense or by way of depreciation deductions.[42] At this point, it is premature to consider either Section 162 business expenses which are discussed in Chapter 14 or Section 167 depreciation deductions which are treated in Chapter 22. A rationale for the exclusion is that there would possibly be a "wash" (inclusion with matching deduction) on the employee's tax return if the exclusion were not allowed.[43] There is no discrimination limitation on this exclusion [44] and probably none is needed.

Examples of items that qualify under the working condition exclusion, as recounted in the legislative history,[45] are: use of a company car or airplane for business purposes; an employer's subscription to a business periodical for the employee; a bodyguard provided to an employee for security reasons; and on-the-job training provided by an employer.

The Code adds two items as working condition fringes even though they would not be fully deductible as business expenses if their costs were incurred by an employee. Under Section 132(h)(3) a full time auto salesperson can exclude the use value of an employer-provided demonstration car if the car is used primarily to facilitate the salesperson's performance of services for the employer and there are substantial restrictions on the personal use of the car by the salesperson.[46] Under Section 132(h)(4) free or reduced-cost parking provided an employee on or near the employer's business premises is also excludable as a working condition fringe benefit even though parking charges are not normally deductible by an employee.

Section 132(a)(4): De Minimis Fringes. This exclusion is very much in keeping with the original administrative allowance of fringe benefits. Any property or service whose value is so small as to make required

---

41. Reg. § 1.132–3(e).

42. I.R.C. § 132(d).

43. A wash is not guaranteed. Such expenses are itemized deductions subject to a two percent floor. See I.R.C. §§ 62, 63, and 67 and Chapter 18E, infra. Such expenses may also be subject to the overall

limitation on itemized deductions. See I.R.C. § 68 and Chapter 27A, infra.

44. Reg. § 1.132–5(q).

45. H.Rep. No. 98–432, supra note 8 at 1601–1602.

46. I.R.C. § 132(h)(3)(B).

accounting for it unreasonable or administratively impracticable is excluded as a fringe benefit.[47] In determining whether an item is within the de minimis concept, the frequency with which similar fringes are provided by an employer to his employees must be taken into account.[48]

Again the legislative history assists with examples of benefits that may be excluded.[49] Listed are: typing of personal letters by a company secretary; occasional personal use of the company copying machine; occasional cocktail parties or picnics for employees; occasional supper money or taxi fare advanced because of overtime work; coffee and doughnuts furnished to employees; occasional theater or sporting event tickets; low value holiday gifts; and monthly transit passes provided at a discount not exceeding $15 per employee per month. The legislative history of the 1986 Act states that also excluded are "traditional retirement gifts presented to an employee on his or her retirement after completing lengthy service."[50]

In addition the statute provides that bargains at employer-operated eating facilities will be treated as de minimis fringes if they are located on or near the employer's business premises and the revenue generated from their operation *normally* equals or exceeds their operating costs.[51] The exclusion dealing with eating facilities is restricted in the case of upper echelon employees by certain non-discrimination requirements.[52] And it does not apply to food and other items furnished to spouses and dependent children.[53]

Section 132(h)(5); Athletic Facilities. Tucked away in the depths of Section 132 is the fifth classification of excludable fringe benefits allowed under the section. Employees may exclude from gross income the value of the use of any on-premises athletic facility.[54] The exclusion applies to a gym, pool, golf course, tennis courts or other athletic facility [55] located on the employer's premises and operated by the employer, if substantially all the facility's use is by employees, their spouses, and their dependent children.[56]

After many years of stumbling inaction, one may applaud the enactment of Section 132 in an effort to bring some order to the tax treatment of employees' fringe benefits. Especially is this so when chaos gives way to principles and policies that are to be commended as they seek a nice balance of fairness and practicability. But statutory change is almost always high caloric and, here again, the Code has

47. I.R.C. § 132(e)(1).

48. Id. Reg. § 1.132–6(b)

49. H.Rep. No. 98–432, supra note 8 at 1603.

50. Sen.Rep. No. 99–313, 99th Cong., 2d Sess. 53 (1986).

51. I.R.C. § 132(e)(2)(A) and (B).

52. I.R.C. § 132(e)(2) last sentence. See note 19, supra.

53. See I.R.C. § 132(f) whose rules apply only to § 132(a)(1) and (2) fringes.

54. I.R.C. § 132(h)(5).

55. Reg. § 1.132–1(e)(1).

56. I.R.C. § 132(h)(5)(B). There is no nondiscriminatory restriction imposed because, under a related self-policing provision, if the facility is used discriminatorily the employer receives no deduction. See I.R.C. § 274(e)(4).

gained quite a few clauses. If the statute also has seemed further to gain in complexity, perhaps the answer to that is that Section 132 seeks only to answer complicated questions that Congress has previously swept under the rug.

The Statutory Exclusion of Other Fringe Benefits. As stated above, Section 132 is not the only section that provides for the exclusion of fringe benefits from gross income.[57] Some employee exclusions are the subject of other chapters of this book.[58] Others are considered more generally below. An important point to recall is that, after the 1984 Act, generally only fringes that are expressly excluded by statute are tax-free fringes. Section 132 indicates that if another Code section provides an exclusion for a type of benefit, Section 132 is generally inapplicable to that type; an ad hoc provision prevails over the general rules of Section 132.[59] For example, as seen below, the value of day care services is excludable only under Section 129, which is discussed below; if for some reason they are not excluded under that section, Section 132 cannot be invoked to exclude them.

Prior to 1984 when the tax treatment of fringe benefits was more an administrative matter, if an area threatened to get out of hand Congress sometimes stepped in with express legislation. Thus, in 1964, Section 79 was added to impose a limit on the amount of group term life insurance an employer can provide tax-free for an employee.[60] Group term life insurance premiums had been fully excluded and, while Congress recognized the desirability of encouraging employers to provide employee protection, the amount of coverage on many employees was so uneven and so great that Congress determined its compensatory nature should not be entirely ignored. A maximum of $50,000 was and still is imposed on the amount of employer-paid coverage that may be provided tax free.[61] Section 79 also contains a nondiscrimination requirement similar to the one in Section 132.[62]

Congress has enacted other fringe benefit exclusions that are not considered elsewhere in this book. For example, Section 120 provides

57. See I.R.C. § 132(j).

58. See I.R.C. § 117(d) excluding qualified tuition reductions and I.R.C. § 127 dealing with employer funded educational assistance programs, both considered in Chapter 5, infra, and see I.R.C. § 106, excluding employer contributions to employee accident and health plans, considered in Chapter 9, infra.

59. I.R.C. § 132(j). See I.R.C. § 132(e) and see H.Rep. No. 98–432, supra note 8 at 1608.

60. See Walker, "Group Life Insurance," 23 N.Y.U.Inst. on Fed.Tax. 153 (1965).

61. I.R.C. § 79(a). But see I.R.C. § 125(f). In effect, the ceiling is raised to the extent that the employee contributes to

the cost of the insurance. I.R.C. § 79(a)(2). For purposes of determining the taxable portion of premium payments, the cost of group insurance is determined under uniform tables provided in the regulations. Reg. § 1.79–3(d). The ceiling limitation does not apply: (1) if the premiums are paid for individuals whose employment has been terminated and who have either reached retirement age or are disabled, § 79(b)(1), or (2) if the employer or a charity is the beneficiary of the proceeds of the policy. I.R.C. § 79(b)(2). See also § 79(b)(3), providing a further exception in the case of insurance purchased under a qualified employer's benefit plan described in § 72(m)(3).

62. I.R.C. § 79(d).

an exclusion through 1991 for group legal services. The section excludes from an employee's gross income amounts contributed by an employer on behalf of an employee, his spouse or dependents under a funded or insured "qualified group legal service plan"[63] and also the value of legal services provided or paid for the employee by the employer or the fund under such a plan.[64] Subsection 120(b) defines a "qualified group legal services plan" which, in general, is one that does not discriminate in favor of upper echelon employees. In addition, as suggested above, Section 129 provides for an exclusion from gross income of up to $5,000[65] of amounts paid by an employer for an employee's "dependent care assistance."[66]

There have been numerous statutory and nonstatutory exclusions of military benefits from gross income.[67] In the 1986 Act Congress specifically consolidated all such exclusions under Section 134. Any military benefit not specifically excluded by a law or regulation or another Code section in effect at the time of the enactment of the 1986 Act is required to be included in gross income. Some military benefits are excluded under the general rules of Section 132 and others by Section 112. Under Section 112 military personnel below the rank of commissioned officers, but including warrant officers, may exclude all compensation received for services in a combat zone and compensation for periods during which the serviceman is hospitalized as a result of wounds, disease, or injury incurred while serving in a combat zone. A similar exclusion for commissioned officers is limited to $500 per month.[68]

The Revenue Act of 1978 liberalized rules of taxation on so-called "Cafeteria Plans."[69] These are plans, having of course nothing to do with food, under which employees may choose various types of qualified benefits[70] or cash. Qualified benefits include group term life insurance coverage up to and *in excess of* $50,000,[71] accident and health benefits,[72] group legal services,[73] and dependent care assistance programs.[74] The plan, however, may not offer certain other types of fringe benefits.[75]

---

63. I.R.C. § 120(a)(1).

64. I.R.C. § 120(a)(2).

65. I.R.C. § 129(a)(2). The limit is $2,500 for a married individual filing separately.

66. I.R.C. § 129(d). See also I.R.C. § 129(e)(1).

67. See Conf.Rep. No. 99–841, 99th Cong., 2d Sess. II–549 (1986), for a list of such exclusions.

Some tax benefits for military personnel, not limited to those expressed in the Internal Revenue Code, are discussed in Weiss, "Tax Problems of the Serviceman," 34 Taxes 277 (1956); on the deduction side, see also Behren, "Many Tax Deductions Are Overlooked by Military Reservists," 16 J.Tax 232 (1962).

68. I.R.C. § 112(b). In addition, I.R.C. § 112(d) excludes compensation of members of the armed forces of the United States and of civilian governmental employees for periods during which they were prisoners of war, missing in action, or in a detained status during the Viet Nam conflict.

69. See I.R.C. § 125.

70. I.R.C. § 125(f).

71. Id. See I.R.C. § 79(a)(1).

72. See I.R.C. §§ 105 and 106.

73. See I.R.C. § 120.

74. See I.R.C. § 129.

75. I.R.C. § 125(d)(2) and (f). See I.R.C. §§ 117, 127, and 132.

Prior to 1978, when an employee could elect either taxable or nontaxable benefits under such plans, the employee was required to include employer contributions in gross income to the extent the employee could have elected taxable benefits even though he did not actually choose taxable benefits. Section 125, which contains nondiscrimination rules,[76] changes the rule to allow an employee to exclude from gross income the value of the nontaxable benefits actually chosen, regardless of alternatives.[77] The cafeteria creeps closer to a smorgasboard.[78]

PROBLEMS

Consider whether or to what extent the fringe benefits listed below may be excluded from gross income and, where possible, support your conclusions with statutory authority:

   (a) Employee of a national hotel chain stays in one of the chain's hotels in another town rent-free on his vacation. The hotel has several empty rooms.

   (b) Same as (a), above, except that the desk clerk bounces a paying guest so Employee can stay rent-free.

   (c) Same as (a), above, except that Employee pays the bill and receives a cash rebate from the chain.

   (d) Same as (a), above, except that Employee's spouse and dependent children travelling without Employee use the room on their vacation.

   (e) Same as (a), above, except that Employee stays in the hotel of a rival chain under a written reciprocal agreement under which employees pay 50% of the normal rent.

76. I.R.C. § 125(b). See I.R.C. § 125(e) and (g).

77. See I.R.C. § 125(a).

78. Prior to 1984, restrictions on the scope of allowable fringe benefits were also imposed administratively. An example was the treatment of so-called "split-dollar" life insurance arrangements between employers and employees. Under such arrangements, which are outside the group insurance rule of I.R.C. § 79, an insurance contract is purchased on the life of the employee. The employer provides the funds to pay the annual premium to the extent of the increase in cash surrender value each year and the employee pays the balance of the premium. At the employee's death the amount of the cash surrender value of the policy is paid to the employer and any excess benefits go to the employee's designated beneficiary. While the initial cost of the policy falls primarily on the employee, subsequent premiums are paid principally by the employer. Initially the Service regarded such transactions as merely interest-free loans to the employee which did not then constitute income to him. Rev.Rul. 55–713, 1955–2 C.B. 23. In a change of administrative policy, the Service treated the transaction as one in which the earnings on the employer's investment in the contract are "applied to provide current life insurance protection to the employee from year to year, without cost to the employee." Rev.Rul. 64–328, 1964–2 C.B. 11, 13. The Service ruled that, since the effect of the "split-dollar" arrangement is "to provide an economic benefit to the employee represented by the amount of the annual premium cost that he should bear and of which he is relieved," the employee has income to that extent. Id. at 13 and 15. Rev.Rul. 64–328 is modified by Rev.Rul. 66–110, 1966–1 C.B. 12. See also Rev.Rul. 79–50, 1979–1 C.B. 138. Such amounts continue to be income under post 1983 law.

(f) Same as (a), above, except that Employee is an officer in the hotel chain and rent-free use is provided only to officers of the chain and all other employees pay 60% of the normal rent.

(g) Hotel chain is owned by a conglomerate which also owns a shipping line. The facts are the same as in (a), above, except that Employee works for the shipping line.

(h) Same as (g), above, except that Employee is comptroller of the conglomerate.

(i) Employee sells insurance and employer Insurance Company allows him 20% off the $1,000 cost of his policy.

(j) Employee is a salesman in a home electronics appliance store. During the year the store has $1,000,000 in sales and a $600,000 cost of goods sold. Employee buys a $2,000 video casette recorder from Employer for $1,000.

(k) Employee is an officer of corporation which pays his parking fees at a lot one block from the corporate headquarters. Non-officers pay their own parking fees.

(l) Employee and wife attend a business convention in another town. Employer picks up their costs.

(m) Employer has a bar and provides the employees with happy hour cocktails at the end of each week's work.

(n) Employer gives Employee a case of scotch each Christmas.

(o) Employer puts in a gym at the business facilities for the use of the employees and their families.

B. EXCLUSIONS FOR MEALS AND LODGING

Internal Revenue Code: Sections 107; 119(a). See Section 119(d).
Regulations: Section 1.119–1.

HERBERT G. HATT*

Tax Court of the United States, 1969.
28 T.C.M. 1194, affirmed per curiam 457 F.2d 499 (7th Cir.1972).

Findings of Fact

Hatt was a legal resident of Evansville, Indiana, at the time his petition was filed. He did not file income tax returns for 1957, 1958, 1959, and 1960. He filed timely income tax returns for 1961 and 1962.

Johann is a corporation organized under the laws of the State of Indiana. At the time its petition was filed its principal place of business was Evansville, Indiana. Johann filed corporation income tax returns for the calendar years 1955 and 1957 through 1961 with the district director of internal revenue, Indianapolis, Indiana. During the

* Footnotes omitted.

years in issue Johann operated a funeral home and embalming business.

Hatt was born July 9, 1932. He finished grade school, attended high school for four or five months, and then entered the Army in 1952, being discharged therefrom in August or September 1954. Prior to his military service he had held numerous jobs, such as delivering newspapers, picking up and delivering laundry and dry cleaning, and working as a helper for a lathe operator. Upon his discharge from the Army he worked in California for a short time as a taxicab driver and as a salesman in a jewelry store. Thereafter, in late 1954, he returned to Indianapolis, Indiana, where he had resided as a child, and started working for Household Sewing Machine Company as a salesman.

In the fall of 1955 Hatt opened a place of business known as the "Select Sewing Center," an individual proprietorship located in Evansville, Indiana, which engaged in the business of selling sewing machines. The business consisted primarily of contacting customers in their homes after they had answered advertisements.

Prior to 1957 Hatt became acquainted with Dorothy Echols (hereinafter Dorothy), the president and majority stockholder of Johann. They were married on March 2, 1957, at which time Hatt was approximately 25 years of age and she was about 43. Pursuant to an antenuptial agreement she then transferred to him 130 shares, a majority, of the stock of Johann, and he became the president and general manager of the corporation.

* * *

Issue 4. *The Apartment*

Immediately after his marriage to Dorothy, Hatt moved into an apartment located in the building used by Johann for its funeral home business, and he resided there during the years 1957 through 1962. Dorothy had resided in the same apartment prior to her marriage to Hatt. In addition to this apartment the building contained another apartment, which was rented, and a dormitory to house the ambulance crew. The telephone used by Johann rang in Hatt's apartment as well as in the business office. He answered the telephone in the apartment when the office was closed, and met there with customers who came to the home to discuss service after regular business hours. It is customary in the Evansville area for the manager or another employee authorized to deal with customers to live on the premises of a funeral home.

* * *

Issue 4. *The Apartment*

Section 119 grants an exclusion from gross income of the value of lodging furnished to an employee if three conditions are met: (1) The lodging is on the business premises of the employer; (2) the employee is "required to accept such lodging * * * as a condition of his employment"; and (3) the lodging is furnished for the convenience of the employer. Respondent does not question petitioner's compliance with the first condition, but contends that neither of the last two conditions has been met and that, therefore, Johann is not entitled to deductions for maintenance of Hatt's apartment and that Hatt is taxable on its fair rental value as a constructive dividend. The issue is primarily factual, and petitioners, of course, have the burden of proof. George I. Stone, 32 T.C. 1021 (1959).

The "condition of his employment" requirement of section 119 means that the employee must "be required to accept the lodging in order to enable him properly to perform the duties of his employment. Lodging will be regarded as furnished to enable the employee properly to perform the duties of his employment when, for example, the lodging is furnished because the employee is required to be available for duty at all times * * *." Sec. 1.119–1(b), Income Tax Regs.

The "convenience of the employer" test and the "condition of his employment" test prescribed by section 119 are basically similar, United States Junior Chamber of Commerce v. United States, 334 F.2d 660, 663 (Ct.Cl.1964), as are the arguments made by respondent under those tests—that Hatt was president and majority stockholder of Johann, thus enabling him to determine the "convenience" of Johann and the "conditions" of his own employment, and that one or more members of the ambulance crew was available at all times to take calls or answer the telephone, thus eliminating the necessity of Hatt's presence on the premises of Johann.

The facts that Hatt was the president and majority stockholder of Johann necessitate careful scrutiny of the arrangement but, in our view, do not alone disqualify Hatt for the exclusion or Johann for the claimed deductions. Cf. Armstrong v. Phinney, 394 F.2d 661 (C.A.5, 1968). Hatt also is not disqualified for the exclusion merely because the apartment was a convenience for him. William I. Olkjer, 32 T.C. 464, 469 (1959).

The funeral business is of such character that it requires someone to be in attendance 24 hours a day to answer telephone calls, to meet the family members of decedents, and to make financial arrangements, as well as to arrange to pick up the bodies of decedents. Family members of decedents in the Evansville area expect someone to be in the funeral home at all times. The undisputed testimony is that the manager or some other designated employee lived on the premises of every other funeral home in Evansville. In addition, supervision of the 24-hour ambulance service maintained by Johann during this period, a source of funeral business, was also required. The telephone in Johann's business office rang in Hatt's apartment, and, as manager of the funeral home, he took calls and handled business with customers. While the ambulance crew could have received the calls, they were not authorized to handle funeral business, particularly its financial aspects. Finally, we note that Dorothy, the president of Johann before Hatt, had lived in the same apartment for several years without paying rent to the corporation, and the corporation had deducted depreciation on the apartment's furnishings and related utility costs.

We think that petitioners have made the requisite showings for the claimed exclusion under section 119 and the deductions for utilities expense claimed by Johann under section 162(a).

NOTE

The "on the business premises" requirement of Section 119(a)(1) and (2) was not at issue in the *Hatt* case. But it has been stage center in litigation in other cases. In Commissioner v. Anderson[1] a motel manager was always "on call" at a residence owned by the motel owner two blocks from the motel. The court concluded that ownership was not the test of business premises and that the term means "either at a place where the employee performs a significant portion of his duties or where the employer conducts a significant portion of his business."[2] Section 119 was held inapplicable because the "on call" status did not constitute a significant portion of the taxpayer employee's duties. Compare Jack B. Lindeman[3] which held that a residence adjacent to the motel (across the street) was not geographically separated from the motel and was therefore "on the business premises."

Section 119(d) allows an employee of an educational institution[4] to exclude from gross income the value of lodging, not otherwise excluded under Section 119(a), if the lodging is located on or in the proximity of the campus of the educational institution.[5] The lodging may be used as a residence by the employee, his spouse, and any of his dependents.[6] There is a ceiling on the amount of the exclusion.[7]

Housing benefits provided to a "minister of the gospel"[8] are excluded from the minister's gross income by Section 107 but, somewhat anomalously, they must be furnished to him "as compensation." The exclusion applies not only to the fair rental value of a home actually provided for the minister's use, similar to Section 119, but also to a rental allowance. In order to qualify an allowance must be specifically earmarked in the minister's employment contract, the church minutes, or some similar documents,[9] and then it is excluded only to the extent that it is actually used to rent or provide a home.

1. 371 F.2d 59 (3d Cir.1966), cert. denied 387 U.S. 906, 87 S.Ct. 1687 (1967).

2. Id. at 67.

3. 60 T.C. 609 (1973), acq. 1973–2 C.B. 2.

4. I.R.C. § 119(d)(4). See I.R.C. § 170(b)(1)(A)(ii).

5. I.R.C. § 119(d)(3)(A).

6. I.R.C. § 119(d)(3)(B).

7. I.R.C. § 119(d)(2).

8. Reg. § 1.107–1(a). Compare Silverman v. Commissioner, 1973–2 USTC para. 9546 (8th Cir.1973), § 107 applied to a cantor in the Jewish faith who, although unordained, had duties essentially the same as a minister in non-Jewish faith, with Marc H. Tanenbaum, 58 T.C. 1 (1972), ordained rabbi employed as the National Director of Interreligious Affairs by the American Jewish Committee who did not have sacerdotal duties and was not a minister. See Block, "Who is a 'Minister of the Gospel' for Purposes of the Parsonage Exclusion?" 51 Taxes 47 (1973).

9. Reg. § 1.107–1(a). See Rev.Rul. 72–462, 1972–2 C.B. 76.

Congress may have made Section 107[10] more liberal than Section 119, because ministers are more likely to use their homes in conjunction with church activities than are other employees in their business activities.

PROBLEMS

1.　Employer provides Employee and wife and child a residence on Employer's business premises, having a rental value of $5000 per year, but charging Employee only $2000.

　(a)　What result if the nature of Employee's work does not require him to live on the premises as a condition of his employment? *taxable income of $3,000*

　(b)　What result if Employer and Employee simply agreed to a clause in the employment contract requiring Employee to live in the residence? *not enough—where does EE perform significant portion of duties?*

2 whether it is for convenience of ER

　(c)　What result if Employee's work and contract require him to live on the premises and Employer furnishes Employee and family $3000 worth of groceries during the year? *lodging—deductible $3,000 for groceries taxable groceries ≠ meals*

　(d)　What result if Employer transferred the residence to Employee in fee simple in the year that Employee accepted the position and commenced work? Does the value of the residence constitute excluded lodging? *no ⇒ no longer the ER'S premises §102(c) EE gift*

2.　Planner incorporated his motel business and the corporation purchased a piece of residential property adjacent to the motel. The corporation by contract "required" Planner to use the residence and also furnished him meals. Planner worked at the motel and was on call 24 hours a day. May Planner exclude the value of the residence or the meals or both from his gross income? *similar to Hatt　Planner = corporation*

3.　State highway patrolman is required to be on duty from 8 a.m. to 5 p.m. At noon he eats lunch at various privately owned restaurants which are adjacent to the state highway. At the end of each month the state reimburses him for his luncheon expenses. Are such cash reimbursements included in his gross income? See Commissioner v. Kowalski, 434 U.S. 77, 98 S.Ct. 315 (1977). *cash reimbursement = income*

10.　Cf. I.R.C. § 265(a)(6)(B), which provides that ministers receiving excludible parsonage allowances, as well as military personnel receiving excludible military housing allowances, are not precluded by § 265(a)(1) from deducting mortgage interest or real property taxes on their residences.

business premises not determined by ownership
— place where EE performs significant portion of duties
or— ER conducts a significant portion of business

"on-call" may not be significant portion of EE's duties

CHAPTER 5. AWARDS

A. PRIZES

Internal Revenue Code: Section 74. See Sections 102(c); 132(a)(4), (e); 274(j). Regulations: Section 1.74–1.

As asserted in the first chapter of this book,[1] two major congressional goals in enacting the 1986 revenue-neutral tax legislation were to broaden the tax base (increase the amount of income subject to the income tax) and to lower the income tax rates. There are two principal ways to broaden the tax base: one is to increase items included in gross income, and the other is to decrease items allowed as deductions. Gross income is of course increased by the reduction of items that are excluded from gross income. This chapter examines two exclusionary areas that were substantially reduced by the 1986 legislation in order to broaden the tax base, i.e. prizes and awards, and scholarships and fellowships.

Prizes and awards are considered first. The Section 74 income tax rules on prizes and awards relate to such things as receipts for winning a company's sales or other contest,[2] the Nobel Peace Prize, the Pulitzer Prize, the Hickok belt, a contest to guess the most jelly beans in a jar, to mention just a few of the many items covered. Awards of a different nature such as scholarships and fellowships are subject to separate legislation in Section 117.

Prior to the enactment of the 1954 Code there were no statutory provisions that dealt expressly with prizes and awards. Controversy arose whether prizes and awards were excluded from gross income as gifts under the 1939 Code predecessor to Section 102.[3] In 1954, Congress enacted Section 74 expressly including prizes and awards in gross income but, in Section 74(b), carved out an exception for a prize or award made primarily to recognize achievement in one of several specified fields (religious, charitable, scientific, educational, artistic, literary, or civic) if the recipient was selected without any action on his part to enter the contest or proceeding and was not required to render substantial future services as a condition to receiving the prize or award. As a part of its 1986 base-broadening action, Congress substantially curtailed the achievement exclusion.

The statute now excludes prizes and awards from gross income only in two limited circumstances. First, under current Section 74(b) prizes

---

1. See Chapter 1 D, supra.

2. Cf. Allen J. McDonell at page 108, infra.

3. Pauline C. Washburn, 5 T.C. 1333 (1945); McDermott v. Commissioner, 150 F.2d 585 (D.C.Cir.1945). See also Sen.Rep.No. 1622, 83rd Cong., 2d Sess. 178–179 (1954).

and awards that satisfy the requirements of old Section 74(b) are excluded from gross income only if the taxpayer winner designates a governmental unit or a Section 170(c)(1) or (2) charity [4] to receive the award and if the award is transferred directly to the designee without any use or enjoyment of it by the taxpayer.[5] Thus the only way the winner can escape an inclusion in gross income is never to receive the award. However, the designation of the recipient can be made before or after the taxpayer is aware that he is the recipient of the award.

Second, Section 74(c) creates an exclusion for "employee achievement awards".[6] This narrow exclusion is best understood when examined in conjunction with several other Code sections. Recall that Section 102(c) does not include gifts from an employer to an employee within the Section 102(a) gift exclusion rule, thus requiring inclusion of such gifts in an employee's gross income. However, a gift from an employer to an employee such as a retirement gift after a long period of service [7] may escape gross income inclusion by qualifying as a Section 132(a)(4) de minimis fringe benefit.[8] Section 74(c) adds an exclusion or partial exclusion from gross income for the value of certain employee achievement awards. An award may qualify if it relates to length of service or to safety.[9] It must be in the form of tangible personal property, be awarded as part of a meaningful ceremony, and not be mere disguised compensation.[10] A length of service award does not qualify unless the employee has been in the employer's service for five years or more and has not received a length of service award for the current or any of the prior four years.[11] A safety achievement award qualifies only if made to other than a manager, administrator, clerical employee or other professional employee [12] and only if 10 percent or less of an employer's qualified employees receive such awards during the year [13] so that it is discriminating and not just a part of the general pay scale. The *amount* of employee exclusion [14] is geared to the extent to which the employer qualifies for a deduction for the awards under Section 274(j),[15] a section full of ifs, ands, and buts that are not "fundamental."

A final thought: Do you think Nobel (Pulitzer, etc.) would have set up his handsomely remunerative devices if told that the sums involved were to be divided by the winners and the United States government on an essentially 69 to 31 ratio? [16]

---

4. See Chapter 23 B, infra, which discusses charitable contributions.

5. I.R.C. § 74(b)(3).

6. I.R.C. § 274(j)(3)(A).

7. H.Rep. No. 3838, 99th Cong., 1st Sess. 106 (1985).

8. See I.R.C. § 132(e).

9. I.R.C. § 274(j)(3)(A)(i).

10. I.R.C. § 274(j)(3)(A).

11. I.R.C. § 274(j)(4)(B). If such an award was received but was excluded from gross income by I.R.C. § 132(e)(1), it will not disqualify the subsequent award. Id.

12. I.R.C. § 274(j)(4)(C)(ii).

13. I.R.C. § 274(j)(4)(C)(i).

14. I.R.C. § 74(c).

15. See I.R.C. § 274(j)(1), (2) and (3)(B).

16. See I.R.C. § 1(a)–(e).

ALLEN J. McDONELL

Tax Court of the United States, 1967.
26 T.C.M. 115.

Memorandum Findings of Fact and Opinion

TANNENWALD, Judge: Respondent determined a deficiency in income tax and an addition to tax under section 6653(a) [1] for 1960 in the amounts of $246.83 and $12.34, respectively.

Because of concessions by respondent, the only issue remaining for decision is whether all or any portion of expenses of a trip taken by petitioners and paid for by petitioner Allen's employer are includable in petitioners' income or, if so, are deductible in arriving at adjusted gross income.

Findings of Fact

Some of the facts are stipulated and are found accordingly.

Allen J. and Jeanne M. McDonell, husband and wife, residing at 5505 Russett Road, Madison, Wisconsin, filed their joint tax return for 1960 with the district director of internal revenue, Milwaukee, Wisconsin.

Allen was employed by Dairy Equipment Co. (hereinafter referred to as DECO) in 1956 as assistant sales manager and he continued in that position through the taxable year in question. At the time of hiring Allen DECO pursuant to established policy, interviewed Jeanne. The purpise of interviewing the wife of a potential home office salesman was to be sure the wife understood that her husband would be required to do considerable traveling for the company and to evaluate her capacity to discharge social responsibilities required in connection with the company's business activities.

At no time did either of the petitioners own any stock in DECO.

DECO is a sales company, distributing bulk milk coolers manufactured for it on a subcontract basis. During the period in question, DECO coolers were sold through territorial salesmen and independent distributors. They handled other products dissimilar to those of DECO but competitive in terms of demand upon their time and effort.

Sales supervision was provided by home office salesmen. Allen, as assistant sales manager, was one of eight home office salesmen. None of the home office salesmen was assigned to a specific territory; each would be sent into the field when and where needed.

Beginning in 1959, DECO initiated an incentive sales contest for its 31 distributors and 9 territorial salesmen. The prize in 1959 for achieving an established sales quota was a trip to Hawaii for each winner and his wife. Home office salesmen did not participate.

---

1. All references are to the Internal Revenue Code of 1954.

There were 11 winners. They had produced $3,929,690.62 in gross sales, representing 56 percent of the total sales volume generated by the company during the period of the contest. Of the 11 winners in 1959, 10 decided to take the trip.

At the time of initiating the contest, DECO management decided to send one home office salesman and his wife for each of three contest winners. This decision was based upon the company's past experience that unguided gatherings of salesmen and distributors often turned into complaint sessions and were otherwise damaging to the company's business interests. DECO assigned four home office salesmen and their wives to the trip. They were selected by placing the names of all the home office salesmen in a hat and drawing out four names. This random method was used to avoid discontent and dissatisfaction. The same random method was used for selecting home office personnel to represent the company on subsequent similar trips. A home office salesman chosen one year was eligible the next year. Those selected to go on a particular trip received no cut in pay and did not lose vacation time. Those not chosen received no substitute benefit.

Allen was one of the four chosen. At the time of drawing the names, the home office salesmen were told that those selected and their wives were expected to go, although they would have been excused for good reasons. They were instructed that they should consider the trip as an assignment and not as a vacation and that their job was to stay constantly with the contest winners, to participate in all the scheduled activities, and not to go off alone. Their objective was not only to make sure that every winner enjoyed himself but to guide anticipated informal discussion relating to DECO's business in order to protect and enhance DECO's image with its distributors and territorial salesmen. The wives were considered essential participants in the achievement of this objective. DECO felt it would be impossible for stag salesmen to host a trip for couples.

The contest winners and the home office personnel departed from Madison, Wisconsin, on February 4, 1960, arriving in Honolulu on February 5. They left Hawaii on February 14, returning to Madison on February 15. Aside from one day which was devoted to a sales meeting, there were no direct business activities on the trip.

Petitioners performed their assigned duties, which consumed substantially all of the trip time. Neither had any spare time, as they had hoped to have, to go swimming or shopping.

The portion of the trip costs paid by DECO and attributable to petitioners was $1,121.96.

Petitioners reported $600 as miscellaneous commissions in their tax return for 1960 as the estimated cost to DECO attributable to Jeanne's presence on the trip.

Respondent determined a deficiency based on the entire cost of the trip.[2] Petitioners now claim that they erroneously reported the $600 and seek a refund in addition to the determination that respondent's deficiency was in error.

Opinion

The battle lines in this case are clearly drawn. Petitioners assert that they took the trip in order to carry out duties required of them by virtue of Allen's employment by DECO. Respondent counters that the trip represented an award, taxable to petitioners under section 74, or additional compensation, taxable under section 61. We agree with petitioners.

The mere fact that petitioners were selected by a random drawing does not make the trip a taxable prize or award under section 74. Surely there would have been no question if the drawing had been designed to choose a home office salesman to take a trip without his wife to handle a disgruntled customer. The method of selection was founded on a sound business reason, namely, to choose those who were to serve DECO's business objectives on a basis which would obviate any feeling of discrimination. The situation of petitioners is to be distinguished from that of the contest winners, whose tax liability is not before us and for whom the trip was both a reward and an incentive.

Similarly, the fact that the trip was a vacation for the contest winners does not necessarily make it a vacation for petitioners. Unlike the contest winners, petitioners were expected to go as an essential part of Allen's employment. The right to go carried with it the duty to go. The trip was not a vacation for the petitioners. It was realistically a command performance to work. What was a social benefit to the contest winners was a work obligation to these petitioners. More importantly, petitioners herein were expected to devote substantially all of their time on the trip to the performance of duties on behalf of DECO in order to achieve, albeit subtly, DECO's well-defined business objectives. In this respect, the situation is unlike that in Patterson v. Thomas, 289 F.2d 108 (C.A.5, 1961), certiorari denied 368 U.S. 837, 82 S.Ct. 35 (1961); where the Court found that, although the taxpayer had an obligation to attend the convention, his work responsibility was minimal.

Nor do we consider it material that petitioners enjoyed the trip. Pleasure and business, unlike oil and water, can sometimes be mixed. See Wilson v. Eisner, 282 F. 38, 42 (C.A.2, 1922). Similarly, although the fact that the trip involved a resort area is an element to be taken into account, cf. Patterson v. Thomas, supra, it is not conclusive. A resort may be heaven to certain people but something less than that to others, depending on the circumstances. See Mr. Justice Douglas

---

2. Respondent concedes that the deficiency is partially in error because of the amount reported by petitioners.

dissenting in Rudolph v. United States, 370 U.S. 269, 280, 82 S.Ct. 1277, 1283 (1962). It is noteworthy that neither of petitioners went swimming or shopping during their entire stay, two activities for which Hawaii is famous.

Again, unlike the taxpayer in Patterson v. Thomas, supra, petitioners' right to go on the trip was not determined by any standard of work performance. In addition, home office salesmen who did not go on the trip received no substitute compensation and those who did go were not eliminated from consideration for trips in subsequent years. There is not the slightest suggestion that the trip which the petitioners took was conceived of as disguised remuneration to them. On the contrary, DECO had sound business reasons for them to go. We recognize that the presence of an employer business purpose does not thereby preclude a finding of compensation to the employee. Patterson v. Thomas, supra. But such business reasons, when coupled with the equally compelling business circumstances involving these petitioners' participation, made the trip no different from any other business trip requiring their services—including Jeanne, whose duties were substantial and could not have been performed by stag men. Cf. Gotcher v. United States, 259 F.Supp. 340 (E.D.Tex.1966); Warwick v. United States, 236 F.Supp. 761 (E.D.Va.1964).

We hold that, under all the facts and circumstances herein, the expenses of the trip are not includable in the gross income of petitioners. In view of this holding, we need not consider an alternative argument of petitioners that the trip had no fair market value to them. See, e.g., Lawrence W. McCoy, 38 T.C. 841 (1962).

Decision will be entered under Rule 50.

PROBLEMS

1. Each year national sportswriters get together and select the single most outstanding amateur athlete in the country and award that person a check for $5,000. Carl, a talented sprinter, has been selected for this year's award. The award is given with the stipulation that the winner deliver a 15 minute "acceptance speech" at an awards banquet. Carl, essentially delivering an acceptable rejection "acceptance speech," designates the International Track and Field Federation, a recognized charity under § 170, to receive the $5,000 award. The sportswriters send the check to the Federation. Will Carl be able to exclude the $5,000 from his gross income?   *yes*

2. Gusher Oil desires to make its employees feel more appreciated. To implement this desire, Gusher creates an awards program whereby employees are given awards for achieving certain lengths of service. In each case, determine the extent to which employee, Cliff Hanger, is able to exclude the award from gross income.

    (a) Cliff has been working for Gusher for 12 years. Announcing Cliff's retirement at the Oil Baron's Ball, Gusher Oil gives him a $300 gift certificate.   *totally excludable*

   (b) Cliff (who is continuing to work for Gusher) receives a gold watch worth $300 for his twelve years of service, presented at the Oil Baron's Ball. *excludable*

   (c) Same as (b), above, except that Cliff has worked for Gusher for only four years. *must claim*

B. SCHOLARSHIPS AND FELLOWSHIPS

Internal Revenue Code: Sections 117; 127(a) and (b)(1).

Regulations: Section 1.117–1(a), –3, –4(c).

BINGLER v. JOHNSON *

Supreme Court of the United States, 1969.
394 U.S. 741, 89 S.Ct. 1439.

Mr. Justice STEWART delivered the opinion of the Court.

We are called upon in this case to examine for the first time § 117 of the Internal Revenue Code of 1954, which excludes from a taxpayer's gross income amounts received as "scholarships" and "fellowships." The question before us concerns the tax treatment of payments received by the respondents [1] from their employer, the Westinghouse Electric Corporation, while they were on "educational leave" from their jobs with Westinghouse.

During the period here in question the respondents held engineering positions at the Bettis Atomic Power Laboratory in Pittsburgh, Pennsylvania, which Westinghouse operates under a "cost-plus" contract with the Atomic Energy Commission. Their employment status enabled them to participate in what is known as the Westinghouse Bettis Fellowship and Doctoral Program. That program, designed both to attract new employees seeking further education and to give advanced training to persons already employed at Bettis, offers a two-phase schedule of subsidized postgraduate study in engineering, physics, or mathematics.

Under the first, or "work-study," phase, a participating employee holds a regular job with Westinghouse and in addition pursues a course of study at either the University of Pittsburgh or Carnegie-Mellon University. The employee is paid for a 40-hour work week, but may receive up to eight hours of "release time" per week for the purpose of attending classes. "Tuition remuneration," as well as reimbursement for various incidental academic expenses, is provided by the company.

When an employee has completed all preliminary requirements for his doctorate, he may apply for an educational leave of absence, which constitutes the second phase of the Fellowship Program. He must

---

* Some footnotes omitted.

1. We refer only to respondents Richard E. Johnson, Richard A. Wolfe, and Martin L. Pomerantz; their wives are parties to this action solely because joint tax returns were filed for the years in question.

submit a proposed dissertation topic for approval by Westinghouse and the AEC. Approval is based, *inter alia,* on a determination that the topic has at least some general relevance to the work done at Bettis. If the leave of absence is secured, the employee devotes his full attention, for a period of at least several months,[5] to fulfilling his dissertation requirement. During this period he receives a "stipend" from Westinghouse, in an amount based on a specified percentage (ranging from 70% to 90%) of his prior salary plus "adders," depending upon the size of his family. He also retains his seniority status and receives all employee benefits, such as insurance and stock option privileges. In return he not only must submit periodic progress reports, but under the written agreement that all participants in the program must sign, also is obligated to return to the employ of Westinghouse for a period of at least two years following completion of his leave.[7] Upon return he is, according to the agreement, to "assume * * * duties commensurate with his education and experience," at a salary "commensurate with the duties assigned."

The respondents all took leaves under the Fellowship Program at varying times during the period 1960–1962, and eventually received their doctoral degrees in engineering. * * *

Westinghouse, which under its own accounting system listed the amounts paid to the respondents as "indirect labor" expenses, withheld federal income tax from those amounts. The respondents filed claims for refund, contending that the payments they had received were "scholarships," and hence were excludable from income under § 117 of the Code, which provides in pertinent part:

"(a) General rule.

"In the case of an individual, gross income does not include—

"(1) any amount received—

"(A) as a scholarship at an educational institution (as defined in section 151(e)(4)), or

"(B) as a fellowship grant * * *."[10]

When those claims were rejected, the respondents instituted this suit in the District Court for the Western District of Pennsylvania, against the District Director of Internal Revenue. After the basically undisputed evidence regarding the Bettis Program had been presented, the trial judge instructed the jury in accordance with Treas.Reg. on Income Tax (1954 Code) § 1.117–4(c), 26 CFR § 1.117–4(c), which provides that amounts representing "compensation for past, present, or future em-

---

5. The ordinary leave period is nine months.

7. Respondent Wolfe began his leave at a time when Westinghouse did not require agreement in writing to the two-year "return" commitment. He was formally advised before he went on leave, however, that he was "expected" to return to Westinghouse for a period of time equal to the duration of his leave, and he in fact honored that obligation.

10. The entire section reads as follows: [I.R.C. § 117 is omitted. Ed.]

ployment services," and amounts "paid * * * to * * * an individual to enable him to pursue studies or research primarily for the benefit of the grantor," are not excludable as scholarships.[11] The jury found that the amounts received by the respondents were taxable income. Respondents then sought review in the Court of Appeals for the Third Circuit, and that court reversed, holding that the Regulation referred to was invalid, that the jury instructions were therefore improper, and that on the essentially undisputed facts it was clear as a matter of law that the amounts received by the respondents were "scholarships" excludable under § 117. 396 F.2d 258.

The holding of the Court of Appeals with respect to Treas.Reg. § 1.117–4(c) was contrary to the decisions of several other circuits—most notably, that of the Fifth Circuit in Ussery v. United States, 296 F.2d 582, which explicitly sustained the Regulation against attack and held amounts received under an arrangement quite similar to the Bettis Program to be taxable income. Accordingly, upon the District Director's petition, we granted certiorari to resolve the conflict and to determine the proper scope of § 117 and Treas.Reg. § 1.117–4(c) with respect to payments such as those involved here. 393 U.S. 949.

In holding invalid the Regulation that limits the definitions of "scholarship" and "fellowship" so as to exclude amounts received as "compensation," the Court of Appeals emphasized that the statute itself expressly adverts to certain situations in which funds received by students may be thought of as remuneration. After the basic rule excluding scholarship funds from gross income as set out in § 117(a), for instance, subsection [(c)] stipulates:

* * *

Congress' express reference to the limitations just referred to concededly lends some support to the respondents' position. The difficulty with that position, however, lies in its implicit assumption that those limitations are limitations on an exclusion of *all funds* received by students to support them during the course of their education. Section 117 provides, however, only that amounts received as "scholarships" or "fellowships" shall be excludable. And Congress never defined what it meant by the quoted terms. As the Tax Court has observed:

> "[A] proper reading of the statute requires that before the exclusion comes into play there must be a determination that the payment sought to be excluded has the normal characteristics associated with the term 'scholarship.'" Reese v. Commissioner, 45 T.C. 407, 413, aff'd, 373 F.2d 742.

The regulation here in question represents an effort by the Commissioner to supply the definitions that Congress omitted.[14] And it is

---

11. [Reg. § 1.117–4(c) is omitted. Ed.]

14. See also Treas.Reg. on Income Tax (1954 Code) §§ 1.117–3(a), (c), 26 CFR §§ 1.117–3(a), (c), which set out the "nor-

mal characteristics" associated with scholarships and fellowships: * * *

[Reg. §§ 1.117–3(a) and (c) are omitted. Ed.]

fundamental, of course, that as "contemporaneous constructions by those charged with administration of" the Code, the Regulations "must be sustained unless unreasonable and plainly inconsistent with the revenue statutes," and "should not be overruled except for weighty reasons." Commissioner v. South Texas Lumber Co., 333 U.S. 496, 501. In this respect our statement last Term in United States v. Correll, 389 U.S. 299, bears emphasis:

> "[W]e do not sit as a committee of revision to perfect the administration of the tax laws. Congress has delegated to the Commissioner, not to the courts, the task of prescribing 'all needful rules and regulations for the enforcement' of the Internal Revenue Code, 26 U.S.C. § 7805(a). In this area of limitless factual variations, 'it is the province of Congress and the Commissioner, not the courts, to make the appropriate adjustments.'" Id., at 306–307.

Here, the definitions supplied by the Regulation clearly are prima facie proper, comporting as they do with the ordinary understanding of "scholarships" and "fellowships" as relatively disinterested, "no-strings" educational grants, with no requirement of any substantial *quid pro quo* from the recipients.

The implication of the respondents' *expressio unius* reasoning is that any amount paid for the purpose of supporting one pursuing a program of study or scholarly research should be excludable from gross income as a "scholarship" so long as it does not fall within the specific limitations of § 117(b). Pay received by a $30,000 per year engineer or executive on a leave of absence would, according to that reasoning, be excludable as long as the leave was granted so that the individual could perform work required for a doctoral degree. This result presumably would not be altered by the fact that the employee might be performing, in satisfaction of his degree requirements, precisely the same work which he was doing for his employer prior to his leave and which he would be doing after his return to "employment"—or by the fact that the fruits of that work were made directly available to and exploited by the employer. Such a result would be anomalous indeed, especially in view of the fact that under § 117 the comparatively modest sums received by part-time teaching assistants are clearly subject to taxation.[15] Particularly in light of the principle that exemptions from taxation are to be construed narrowly,[16] we decline to assume that Congress intended to sanction—indeed, as the respondents would have it, to compel—such an inequitable situation.

The legislative history underlying § 117 is, as the Court of Appeals recognized, "far from clear."[18] We do not believe, however, that it

We are not concerned in this case with distinctions between the terms "scholarship" and "fellowship."

15. Cf. 1 J. Mertens, Law of Federal Income Taxation § 7.42, p. 110 (P. Zimet & W. Oliver rev. ed. 1962).

16. See Commissioner v. Jacobson, 336 U.S. 28, 48–49; Helvering v. Northwest Steel Rolling Mills, Inc., 311 U.S. 46, 49.

18. 396 F.2d, at 263.

precludes, as "plainly inconsistent" with the statute, a definition of "scholarship" that excludes from the reach of that term amounts received as compensation for services performed. The 1939 Internal Revenue Code, like predecessor Codes, contained no specific provision dealing with scholarship grants. Whether such grants were includable in gross income depended simply upon whether they fell within the broad provision excluding from income amounts received as "gifts." Thus case-by-case determinations regarding grantors' motives were necessary. The cases decided under this approach prior to 1954 generally involved two types of financial assistance: grants to research or teaching assistants—graduate students who perform research or teaching services in return for their stipends—and foundation grants to post-doctoral researchers. In cases decided shortly before the 1954 Code was enacted, the Tax Court, relying on the "gift" approach to scholarships and fellowships, held that amounts received by a research assistant were taxable income, but reached divergent results in situations involving grants to post-doctoral researchers.

In enacting § 117 of the 1954 Code, Congress indicated that it wished to eliminate the necessity for reliance on "case-by-case" determinations with respect to whether "scholarships" and "fellowships" were excludable as "gifts." Upon this premise the respondents hinge their argument that Congress laid down a standard under which all case-by-case determinations—such as those that may be made under Treas.Reg. § 1.117–4(c)—are unnecessary and improper. We have already indicated, however, our reluctance to believe that § 117 was designed to exclude from taxation all amounts, no matter how large or from what source, that are given for the support of one who happens to be a student. The sounder inference is that Congress was merely "recogni[zing] that scholarships and fellowships are sufficiently unique * * * to merit [tax] treatment separate from that accorded gifts,"[22] and attempting to provide that grants falling within those categories should be treated consistently—as in some instances, under the generic provisions of the 1939 Code, they arguably had not been. Delineation of the precise contours of those categories was left to the Commissioner.

Furthermore, a congressional intention that not all grants received by students were necessarily to be "scholarships" may reasonably be inferred from the legislative history. In explaining the basis for its version of § 117(b)(2),[23] the House Ways and Means Committee stated that its purpose was to "tax those grants which are in effect merely payments of a salary during a period while the recipient is on leave from his regular job."[24] This comment related, it is true, to a specific exception to the exclusion from income set out in subsection (a). But, in view of the fact that the statute left open the definitions of "scholar-

---

22. Gordon, Scholarship and Fellowship Grants as Income: A Search for Treasury Policy, 1960 Wash. U.L.Q. 144, 151.

23. * * * See H.R.Rep. No. 1337, 83d Cong., 2d Sess., 17; S.Rep. No. 1622, 83d Cong., 2d Sess., 18.

24. H.R.Rep. No. 1337, supra, n. 23, at 17.

ship" and "fellowship," it is not unreasonable to conclude that in adding subsection (b) to the statute Congress was merely dealing explicitly with those problems that had come explicitly to its attention—*viz.*, those involving research and teaching assistantships and post-doctoral research grants—without intending to forbid application to similar situations of the general principle underlying its treatment of those problems. One may justifiably suppose that the Congress that taxed funds received by "part-time" teaching assistants, presumably on the ground that the amounts received by such persons really represented compensation for services performed, would also deem proper a definition of "scholarship" under which comparable sorts of compensation—which often, as in the present case, are significantly greater in amount—are likewise taxable.[26] In providing such a definition, the Commissioner has permissibly implemented an underlying congressional concern. We cannot say that the provision of Treas.Reg. § 1.117–4(c) that taxes amounts received as "compensation" is "unreasonable or plainly inconsistent with the * * * statut[e]." [28]

Under that provision, as set out in the trial court's instructions, the jury here properly found that the amounts received by the respondents were taxable "compensation" rather than excludable "scholarships." [30] The employer-employee relationship involved is immediately suggestive, of course, as is the close relation between the respondents' prior salaries and the amount of their "stipends." In addition, employee benefits were continued. Topics were required to relate at least generally to the work of the Bettis Laboratory. Periodic work reports were to be submitted. And, most importantly, Westinghouse unquestionably extracted a *quid pro quo.* The respondents not only were required to hold positions with Westinghouse throughout the "work-study" phase of the program, but also were obligated to return to Westinghouse's employ for a substantial period of time after completion of their leave. The thrust of the provision dealing with compensation is that bargained-for payments, given only as a *"quo"* in return for the *quid* of services rendered—whether past, present, or future—should not be

26. In connection with the question of what Congress may have intended to denote by the terms "scholarship" and "fellowship," it is noteworthy that the House Report stated, "Such grants generally are of small amount and are usually received by individuals who would have little or no tax liability in any case." H.R.Rep. No. 1337, supra, n. 23, at 17.

28. The Court of Appeals seems to have recognized that in some circumstances the Commissioner's approach is justified. Its opinion stated:

"A significant commitment by the student in return for a grant would, of course, place that grant outside the category 'scholarship,' at least to the extent of the value of that commitment. For if

the grantee had to barter for his stipend, giving full value for it, this arrangement would hardly serve the primary purpose of the § 117 exclusion: to encourage financial aid to education through tax relief." 396 F.2d, at 262.

It is not clear how this position can be squared with the Court of Appeals' holding that Treas.Reg. § 1.117–4(c) is invalid. In any event, as we suggest infra, we cannot agree with the conclusion of the Court of Appeals that the grants received by the respondents were not "bartered for."

30. We thus endorse the decisions of the Fifth and Sixth Circuits in Ussery v. United States, 296 F.2d 582, and Stewart v. United States, 363 F.2d 355. * * *

excludable from income as "scholarship" funds.[32] That provision clearly covers this case.

Accordingly, the judgment of the Court of Appeals is reversed, and that of the District Court reinstated.

It is so ordered.

Mr. Justice DOUGLAS would affirm the judgment for the reasons stated by the Court of Appeals in 396 F.2d 258.

NOTE

As the opinion in *Johnson* points out, prior to the enactment of the 1954 Internal Revenue Code there was no statutory provision that dealt expressly with the taxability of scholarships or fellowships. The basis for the sometimes exclusion of such grants from gross income under the 1939 Code was the treatment accorded amounts received as "gifts". Outside of routine matters, factual variations in the "gift" area required that the tax status of scholarships and fellowships be determined largely on a case by case approach. In 1954 Congress enacted Section 117 with the express purpose of providing a clear-cut method for distinguishing between taxable and nontaxable educational grants.[1] As a part of the 1986 movement to broaden the tax base and reduce tax rates, Congress severely restricted the scope of the Section 117 exclusion.[2] Thus, as in the case of the exclusion for prizes and awards, the exclusion for scholarships and fellowships is substantially curtailed under the new legislation.

Section 117 fails to define the terms "scholarship" and "fellowship". The regulations attempt to fill the statutory gap. They define a scholarship generally as an amount paid for the benefit of either an undergraduate or graduate student to aid him in his studies, and a fellowship as an amount paid for the benefit of an individual to aid him in the pursuit of study or research.[3] As seen in the *Johnson* case, the United States Supreme Court upheld the definitions that appear in the Regulations, specifically the compensation restrictions imposed by Reg. Section 1.117–4(c) which rule out of the definition any amount that

---

32. We accept the suggestion in the Government's brief that the second paragraph of Treas.Reg. § 1.117–4(c)—which excepts from the definition of "scholarship" any payments that are paid to an individual "to enable him to pursue studies or research primarily for the benefit of the grantor"—is merely an adjunct to the initial "compensation" provision:

"By this paragraph, the Treasury has supplemented the first in order to impose tax on bargained-for arrangements that do not create an employer-employee relation, as, for example, in the case of an independent contractor. But the general idea is the same: 'scholarship' or 'fellowship' does not include arrange-

ments where the recipient receives money and in return provides a *quid pro quo*." Brief for Petitioner 22. * * *

1. Sen.Rep. No. 1622, 83rd Cong., 2d Sess. 17 (1954).

2. H.Rep. No. 3838, 99 Cong., 2d Sess. 101 (1985). One rationale for the reduction of the exclusion under the new legislation was that many scholarship and fellowship recipients would not be taxed anyway as a result of the increase in the threshold of income level at which individuals become subject to tax.

3. Reg. §§ 1.117–3(a) and (c). See also Reg. § 1.117–4(c).

represents either "compensation for past, present or future employment services or represents payment for services which are subject to the direction or supervision of the grantor."[4] There must be a gratuity flavor to the grant similar to the gift concept as developed in the well-known *Duberstein*[5] opinion. Accordingly, amounts paid to enable an individual to pursue his studies or research "primarily for the benefit of the grantor" reap no tax benefit under Section 117.[6] In *Johnson*, the Supreme Court accepted the government's contention that the "primarily for the benefit of the grantor" language of Reg. Section 1.117–4(c)(2) is merely an adjunct to the "compensation" provision of Reg. Section 1.117–4(c)(1).[7] The "grantor" language was added to insure that "bargained for" arrangements, even outside the employer-employee relationship, would be taxed. Thus, following the *Johnson* case, the predominant issue in determining "scholarship" status under Section 117 has become whether a grant has the indicia of compensation.[8] As a result, even after the 1986 legislative changes, the *Johnson* case upholds the definitional regulations which must be satisfied prior to qualifying for any exclusion under Section 117(a).

The problem of distinguishing nontaxable scholarships from taxable compensation has been rife in several circumstances. Educational grants made by an employer to a current or former employee, as in the *Johnson* case, have generally been held taxable because they represent compensation for past, present or future services.[9] This result has been reached even in cases in which the employee has no contractual obligation to render future services if there is a "clear expectation" that the employment relationship will continue.[10]

As amended by the 1986 Act, Section 117(a) excludes from gross income amounts received as a "qualified scholarship"[11] by a degree candidate[12] at an educational organization.[13] The principal require-

---

4. Reg. § 1.117–4(c)(1).

5. Commissioner v. Duberstein, 363 U.S. 278, 80 S.Ct. 1190 (1960).

6. Reg. § 1.117–4(c)(2). See Rev.Rul. 57–560, 1957–2 C.B. 108.

7. 394 U.S. 741 at 758, 89 S.Ct. 1439 at 1449 (1969).

8. Comment, "Excludability of Scholarship and Fellowship Grants Under Section 117 of the Internal Revenue Code of 1954," 31 Ohio St.L.J. 186, 192 (1970).

9. See, e.g., Leonard T. Fielding, 57 T.C. 761 (1972). But see Ltr.Rul. 8335008 (1983).

10. John E. MacDonald, Jr., 52 T.C. 386 (1969); see also Ehrhart v. Commissioner, 470 F.2d 940 (1st Cir.1973).

11. This term is defined in I.R.C. § 117(b).

12. The regulations define the term "candidate for a degree" as one who is "pursuing studies or conducting research

to meet the requirements for an academic or professional degree conferred by colleges or universities." Reg. § 1.117–3(e). Conf.Rep. No. 99–841, 99 Cong., 2d Sess. II–16 (1986), extends this definition and provides "in the case of individuals other than students attending a primary or secondary school or pursuing a degree at a college or university, the term candidate for a degree means a student (whether full-time or part-time) who receives a scholarship for study at an educational institution (described in sec. 170(b)(1)(A)(ii)) that (1) provides an educational program that is acceptable for full credit toward a bachelor's or higher degree, or offers a program of training to prepare students for gainful employment in a recognized occupation, and (2) is authorized under Federal or State law to provide such a program and is accredited by a nationally recognized accreditation agency."

13. I.R.C. § 117(a) adopts the definition of "educational organization" contained in

ments of the exclusion are found in the definition of a qualified scholarship, which is defined as any amount received as a scholarship or fellowship grant [14] that in accordance with the grant [15] is used for "qualified tuition and related expenses," which encompass only tuition and enrollment fees at the educational organization [16] as well as fees, books, supplies and equipment required for courses of instruction.[17]

The 1986 Act severely restricted the scope of Section 117 by making the current exclusion inapplicable to several types of benefits that qualified as exclusions under pre-1986 law. The exclusion is totally inapplicable to non-degree candidates. With respect to degree candidates, it provides no exclusion for amounts to cover personal living expenses such as meals and lodging or for travel or research.[18] In addition, under Section 117(c) a portion of an otherwise excluded scholarship or fellowship is required to be included in the recipient's gross income to the extent that the portion represents a payment for teaching, research or other services by the student required as a condition for receiving the otherwise excludable amount. Inclusion is required even though such services are required of all persons (regardless of whether they are receiving a scholarship or fellowship) qualifying for the degree, which is a conceptual difference from prior law.

The Code contains two additional exclusions of educational benefits neither of which is subject to the *Johnson* case "scholarship" definitional hurdle. Section 117(d) allows a "qualified tuition reduction" [19] to be excluded from gross income in the case of education below the graduate level[20] or at the graduate level if the graduate student is engaged in teaching or research activities.[21] The reduction may be available to the employees of the educational organization granting the reduction or to employees of some other educational organization as well.[22] The term "employee" is defined by reference to the broad definition of employee in Section 132(f), which includes the employee, his spouse and dependent children and, in some circumstances, the surviving spouse of a deceased employee.[23] The exclusion invokes the Section 132 concept of nondiscrimination: Section 117(d) is applicable to highly compensated employees only if the reductions are offered to all employees on a

---

§ 170(b)(1)(A)(ii), which provides that an "educational organization" is an institution which maintains a regular faculty and curriculum and has a regularly enrolled body of students in attendance at a place where the educational activities are regularly carried on.

14. See note 3, supra.

15. This Conference Report requirement is met if the terms of the grant do not earmark it for other purposes (such as room or board) and do not specify that it cannot be used for tuition or course related expenses. Conf.Rep. No. 99-841, supra note 12 at II-16.

16. I.R.C. § 117(b)(2)(A).

17. I.R.C. § 117(b)(2)(B).

18. Some grants for travel or research may be deductible, however, under I.R.C. § 162.

19. I.R.C. § 117(d)(2) defines this term.

20. See I.R.C. § 117(d)(2) (1st parenthetical).

21. I.R.C. § 117(d)(4).

22. I.R.C. § 117(d)(2) (2nd parenthetical).

23. I.R.C. § 117(d)(2)(B). See page 93, supra.

nondiscriminatory basis.[24] Moreover, similar to Section 117(a), Section 117(d) provides no exclusion for the portion of any amount which represents payment for teaching, research or other services required of the student in order to receive the qualified tuition reduction.[25]

Section 127 permits an employee to exclude up to $5,250 from gross income for amounts paid by the employer for educational assistance,[26] provided the educational assistance program meets certain requirements[27] related primarily to nondiscrimination in favor of highly compensated employees. Educational assistance under Section 127 includes tuition, books, supplies and an employer provided educational course. By its very nature the educational assistance is compensation; thus, as in the case of the Section 117(d) exclusion, one is not required to jump the *Johnson* case scholarship definitional hurdle to qualify for an exclusion under Section 127.[28]

PROBLEMS

1. Student working toward an A.B. degree is awarded a scholarship of $6,000 for full tuition and for room and board during the academic year. The tuition, including the cost of books, is $3,000, and the room and board costs $3,000. As a scholarship recipient, Student is required to do about 300 hours of research for the professor to whom he is assigned. Nonscholarship students, if hired, receive $10.00 per hour for such work.

(a) What tax consequences to Student?

(b) What tax consequences to Student if all students are required to do 300 hours of research for faculty?

(c) What result if Student is not required to do any research but receives the $6,000 as a football scholarship?

(d) What tax consequences to Student if he receives only a tuition scholarship worth $2,500 (no books) because his spouse is an employee at a neighboring educational institution and the tuition scholarship is part of a nondiscriminatory plan between several institutions applicable to all employees of such institutions?

2. Lawyer, an associate in a large tax law firm, receives a $10,000 stipend from her firm to assist her while on a leave of absence to obtain her LL.M. degree in taxation. The stipend is part of a firm plan under which all recipients are required to return to the firm following their educational leave.

(a) What tax consequences to Lawyer?

24. I.R.C. § 117(d)(3). See page 94, supra.

25. I.R.C. § 117(c).

26. I.R.C. § 127(c)(1). Amounts in excess of the maximum or which are disqualified by the last sentence of I.R.C. § 127(c)(1)

may qualify for an exclusion as a working condition fringe under § 132(d). I.R.C. § 132(h)(9).

27. I.R.C. § 127(b)(2)–(5).

28. I.R.C. § 127 is scheduled to expire on Dec. 31, 1991.

(b) What tax consequences to Lawyer if she is not required to return to the firm after completing her LL.M. degree?   *not taxable*

(c) What are the tax consequences to Lawyer if she is not an employee, but instead receives the stipend as a prize in an essay contest?

prize

only excluded for educational purposes

CHAPTER 6. GAIN FROM DEALINGS
IN PROPERTY

A. FACTORS IN THE DETERMINATION OF GAIN

Internal Revenue Code: Sections 1001(a), (b) first sentence, (c); 1011(a); 1012.
Regulations: Section 1.1001–1(a).

If T lends B money and later B pays it back no one would suppose that T has gross income upon the mere repayment of the principal amount of the loan. In tax parlance, the reason for this conclusion is that the repayment constitutes a mere *return of capital* to T. There is no element of gain in such a transaction and, consequently, this exclusionary rule has always been recognized just as if the principle were spelled out in the statutory provisions.

But the return-of-capital concept is by no means restricted to the loan repayment area. It arises in many more sophisticated ways, both as a kind of common law rule and as a statutory principle. In other circumstances, it may be more difficult to say to what extent the taxpayer's capital is merely being returned. In general the device adopted for aid in measuring this is "basis." Basis, unadjusted, essentially answers the question: How much have I got in it? Thus, if T buys property for $10,000, he has that amount in it, and his basis is $10,000. Basis and value must be carefully differentiated. If the property so acquired is securities that increase in *value* to $15,000, *basis* is still only $10,000. Avoid the student inclination to use these terms indiscriminately.

If the value of the property increases to $15,000 and T sells the property for $15,000 he has made $5,000 on his investment because the property has appreciated in value to that extent and because he has liquidated his investment. This rather obvious result is translated into tax terminology by Section 1001(a), which identifies gain on the disposition of property as the excess of the "amount realized" over the "adjusted basis". The "amount realized" is defined in Section 1001(b) as the amount of money received and the fair market value of property (other than money) received on the disposition. Here the amount realized by T is $15,000 (only money was received) and, if his basis is $10,000, his § 1001(a) realized gain is $5,000. Section 1001(c) requires gain realized to be recognized unless otherwise provided by another code section. Current attention is directed only to the "amount" of gain; Part Six of this book is addressed to the "character" of gain and the tax consequences of such characterization and Part Seven is addressed to possible "nonrecognition" of gain. What would be the result to T under Section 1001(a) if, instead of appreciating, the property had declined in value and he had sold it for $8,000 cash? Again, characterization and final tax consequences are intended to be deferred.

Determination of the "amount realized" on a disposition of property and of the property's "adjusted basis" are not always as simple as in the hypothetical posed above. The materials that follow suggest ways, other than by purchase, in which basis is established and circumstances calling for adjustment in basis, both upward and downward. They also present some less obvious circumstances in which the "amount realized" must be determined as a factor in the measurement of gain on a sale or other disposition of property.

B. DETERMINATION OF BASIS

1. COST AS BASIS*

Internal Revenue Code: Sections 109; 1012; 1016(a)(1); 1019.
Regulations: Sections 1.61–2(d)(2)(i); 1.1011–1; 1.1012–1(a).

PHILADELPHIA PARK AMUSEMENT CO. v. U.S.
Court of Claims of the United States, 1954.
130 Ct.Cl. 166, 126 F.Supp. 184.

[In 1889, the taxpayer had been granted a 50-year franchise to operate a passenger railway in Fairmount Park, Philadelphia. At a cost of $381,000, it built the Strawberry Bridge over the Schuylkill River, which was used by its streetcars. In 1934, it deeded the bridge to the city in exchange for a ten year extension of its franchise. In 1946 when the extended franchise still had several years to run, it was abandoned, and the taxpayer arranged bus transportation for visitors to its amusement park. The taxpayer's basis for the ten year extension of its franchise became important when the taxpayer asserted depreciation deductions based on the cost of the extension and a loss upon abandonment of the franchise. Basis questions for these purposes are essentially the same as those that arise in the determination of gain or loss on the disposition of an asset. Ed.]

LARAMORE, Judge.

* * *

This brings us to the question of what is the cost basis of the 10-year extension of taxpayer's franchise. Although defendant contends that Strawberry Bridge was either worthless or not "exchanged" for the 10-year extension of the franchise, we believe that the bridge had some

---

* There is an early but comprehensive discussion of cost as basis in Greenbaum, "The Basis of Property Shall Be the Cost of Such Property: How is Cost Defined?" 3 Tax.L.Rev. 351 (1948); See also Kohl, "The Identification Theory of Basis," 40 Tax L.Rev. 623 (1985).

value, and that the contract under which the bridge was transferred to the City clearly indicates that the one was given in consideration of the other. * * *

The gain or loss, whichever the case may have been, should have been recognized, and the cost basis under section 113(a) [4] of the Code, of the 10-year extension of the franchise was the cost to the taxpayer. The succinct statement in section 113(a) that "the basis of property shall be the cost of such property" although clear in principle, is frequently difficult in application. One view is that the cost basis of property received in a taxable exchange is the fair market value of the property *given* in the exchange.[5] The other view is that the cost basis of property received in a taxable exchange is the fair market value of the property *received* in the exchange.[6] As will be seen from the cases and some of the Commissioner's rulings [7] the Commissioner's position has not been altogether consistent on this question. The view that "cost" is the fair market value of the property given is predicated on the theory that the cost to the taxpayer is the economic value relinquished. The view that "cost" is the fair market value of the property received is based upon the theory that the term "cost" is a tax concept and must be considered in the light of the * * * prime role that the basis of property plays in determining tax liability. We believe that when the question is considered in the latter context that the cost basis of the property received in a taxable exchange is the fair market value of the property *received* in the exchange.

When property is exchanged for property in a taxable exchange the taxpayer is taxed on the difference between the adjusted basis of the property given in exchange and the fair market value of the property received in exchange. For purposes of determining gain or loss the fair market value of the property received is treated as cash and taxed accordingly. To maintain harmony with the fundamental purpose of these sections, it is necessary to consider the fair market value of the property received as the cost basis to the taxpayer. The failure to do so would result in allowing the taxpayer a stepped-up basis, without paying a tax therefor, if the fair market value of the property received is less than the fair market value of the property given, and the taxpayer would be subjected to a double tax if the fair market value of the property received is more than the fair market value of the property given. By holding that the fair market value of the property received in a taxable exchange is the cost basis, the above discrepancy is avoided and the basis of the property received will equal the adjusted basis of the property given plus any gain recognized, or that should

---

4. Section 113(a) provides: "Basis, (unadjusted) of property. The basis of property shall be the cost of such property; except that * * *." 26 U.S.C.A. § 113. [See I.R.C. § 1012. Ed.]

5. [Citations omitted. Ed.]

6. [Citations omitted. Ed.]

7. Compare I.T. 2212, IV–2 C.B. 118 with I.T. 3523, 1941–2 C.B. 124 and the Commissioner's equivocal acquiescence in Estate of Isadore L. Myers case, supra, 1943–1 C.B. 17.

have been recognized, or minus any loss recognized, or that should have been recognized.

Therefore, the cost basis of the 10-year extension of the franchise was its fair market value on August 3, 1934, the date of the exchange. The determination of whether the cost basis of the property received is its fair market value or the fair market value of the property given in exchange therefor, although necessary to the decision of the case, is generally not of great practical significance because the value of the two properties exchanged in an arms-length transaction are either equal in fact, or are presumed to be equal.[8] The record in this case indicates that the 1934 exchange was an arms-length transaction and, therefore, if the value of the extended franchise cannot be determined with reasonable accuracy, it would be reasonable and fair to assume that the value of Strawberry Bridge was equal to the 10-year extension of the franchise. The fair market value of the 10-year extension of the franchise should be established but, if that value cannot be determined with reasonable certainty, the fair market value of Strawberry Bridge should be established and that will be presumed to be the value of the extended franchise. This value cannot be determined from the facts now before us since the case was prosecuted on a different theory.

The taxpayer contends that the market value of the extended franchise or Strawberry Bridge could not be ascertained and, therefore, it should be entitled to carry over the undepreciated cost basis of the bridge as the cost of the extended franchise under section 113(b)(2).[9] If the value of the extended franchise or bridge cannot be ascertained with a reasonable degree of accuracy, the taxpayer is entitled to carry over the undepreciated cost of the bridge as the cost basis of the extended franchise. Helvering v. Tex-Pen Oil Co., 300 U.S. 481, 499, 57 S.Ct. 569; Gould Securities Co. v. United States, 2 Cir., 96 F.2d 780. However, it is only in rare and extraordinary cases that the value of the property exchanged cannot be ascertained with reasonable accuracy. We are presently of the opinion that either the value of the extended franchise or the bridge can be determined with a reasonable degree of accuracy. Although the value of the extended franchise may be difficult or impossible to ascertain because of the nebulous and intangible characteristics inherent in such property, the value of the bridge is subject to more exact measurement. Consideration may be given to expert testimony on the value of comparable bridges, Strawberry Bridge's reproduction cost and its undepreciated cost, as well as other relevant factors.

8. [Reference omitted. Ed.]

9. Section 113(b)(2) provides: "Substituted basis. The term 'substituted basis' as used in this subsection means a basis determined under any provision of subsection (a) of this section or under any corresponding provision of a prior income tax law, providing that the basis shall be determined—(A) by reference to the basis in the hands of a transferor, donor, or grantor, or (B) by reference to other property held at any time by the person for whom the basis is to be determined."

Therefore, because we deem it equitable, judgment should be suspended and the question of the value of the extended franchise on August 3, 1934, should be remanded to the Commissioner of this court for the taking of evidence and the filing of a report thereon.

The failure of taxpayer to properly record the transaction in 1934 and thereafter does not prevent the correction of the error, especially under the circumstances of this case. Countway v. Commissioner, 1 Cir., 127 F.2d 69.

* * *

We, therefore, conclude that the 1934 exchange was a taxable exchange and that the taxpayer is entitled to use as the cost basis of the 10-year extension of its franchise its fair market value on August 3, 1934, for purposes of determining depreciation and loss due to abandonment, as indicated in this opinion.

Accordingly, judgment will be suspended and the question of the value of the extended franchise on August 3, 1934, is remanded to the Commissioner of this court for the taking of evidence and the filing of a report thereon.

JONES, Chief Judge, and MADDEN, WHITAKER, and LITTLETON, Judges, concur.

PROBLEMS

1. Owner purchases some land for $10,000 and later sells it for $16,000.

$16,000 - 10,000 = 6,000$

(a) Determine the amount of Owner's gain on the sale.

(b) What difference in result in (a), above, if Owner purchased the land by paying $1000 for an option to purchase the land for an additional $9000 and subsequently exercised the option?

$16,000 - 10,000$ (9+1) $= \$6,000$

(c) What result to Owner in (b), above, if rather than ever actually acquiring the land Owner sold the option to investor for $1500?

$1500 - 1000 = \$500$

(d) What result in (a), above, if Owner purchased the land for $10,000, spent $2000 in clearing the land prior to its sale, and sold it for $18,000?

$18,000 - 12,000 = 6,000$

(e) What difference in result in (a), above, if when the land had a value of $10,000, Owner, a real estate salesman, received it from his employer as a bonus for putting together a major real estate development, and Owner's income tax was increased $3,000 by reason of his receipt of the land?

$16,000 - 10,000 = \$6,000$

(f) What difference in result in (a), above, if Owner had previously rented the land to Lessee for five years for $1000 per year cash rental and permitted Lessee to expend $2000 clearing the property? Assume that, although Owner properly reported the cash rental payments as gross income, the $2000 expenditures were properly excluded under § 109. See § 1019.

$L \rightarrow 6$ $\$1,000/yr$ rent

$\$2,000$ clearing

Gain $16,000 - 10,000 = 6,000$

$§109$ F.I. does not include improvements on land done by lease.

(g) What difference if Owner is a salesperson in an art gallery and she purchases a $10,000 painting from the art gallery, but she is required to pay only $9000 for it (instead of $10,000 because she is allowed a 10% employee discount which is excluded from her gross income under § 132(a)(2)), and she later sells the painting for $16,000?

16,000 − 9,000 = 7,000

2. PROPERTY ACQUIRED BY GIFT

Internal Revenue Code: Section 1015(a). See Section 1015(d)(1)(A), (4) and (6).

Regulations: Sections 1.1001–1(e); 1.1015–1(a), –4.

TAFT v. BOWERS

Supreme Court of the United States, 1929.
278 U.S. 470, 49 S.Ct. 199.

Mr. Justice McREYNOLDS delivered the opinion of the Court.

Petitioners, who are donees of stocks, seek to recover income taxes exacted because of advancement in the market value of those stocks while owned by the donors. The facts are not in dispute. Both causes must turn upon the effect of paragraph (2), § 202, Revenue Act, 1921, (c. 136, 42 Stat. 227) which prescribes the basis for estimating taxable gain when one disposes of property which came to him by gift. The records do not differ essentially and a statement of the material circumstances disclosed by No. 16 will suffice.

During the calendar years 1921 and 1922, the father of petitioner Elizabeth C. Taft, gave her certain shares of Nash Motors Company stock then more valuable than when acquired by him. She sold them during 1923 for more than their market value when the gift was made.

The United States demanded an income tax reckoned upon the difference between cost to the donor and price received by the donee. She paid accordingly and sued to recover the portion imposed because of the advance in value while the donor owned the stock. The right to tax the increase in value after the gift is not denied.

Abstractly stated, this is the problem—

In 1916 A purchased 100 shares of stock for $1,000 which he held until 1923 when their fair market value had become $2,000. He then gave them to B who sold them during the year 1923 for $5,000. The United States claim that, under the Revenue Act of 1921, B must pay income tax upon $4,000, as realized profits. B maintains that only $3,000—the appreciation during her ownership—can be regarded as income; that the increase during the donor's ownership is not income assessable against her within intendment of the Sixteenth Amendment.

The District Court ruled against the United States; the Circuit Court of Appeals held with them.

Act of Congress approved November 23, 1921, Chap. 136, 42 Stat. 227, 229, 237—

"Sec. 202. (a) That the basis for ascertaining the gain derived or loss sustained from a sale or other disposition of property, real, personal, or mixed, acquired after February 28, 1913, shall be the cost of such property; except that—

"(1) * * *

"(2) In the case of such property, acquired by gift after December 31, 1920, the basis shall be the same as that which it would have in the hands of the donor or the last preceding owner by whom it was not acquired by gift. * * * [See Section 1015(a). Ed.]

"Sec. 213. That for the purposes of this title (except as otherwise provided in section 233) the term 'gross income'—

"(a) * * *

"(b) Does not include the following items, which shall be exempt from taxation under this title;

"(1) * * * (2) * * *

"(3) The value of property acquired by gift, bequest, devise, or descent (but the income from such property shall be included in gross income); * * *" [See Section 102. Ed.]

We think the manifest purpose of Congress expressed in paragraph (2), Sec. 202, supra, was to require the petitioner to pay the exacted tax.

The only question subject to serious controversy is whether Congress had power to authorize the exaction.

It is said that the gift became a capital asset of the donee to the extent of its value when received and, therefore, when disposed of by her no part of that value could be treated as taxable income in her hands.

The Sixteenth Amendment provides—

"The Congress shall have power to lay and collect taxes on incomes from whatever source derived, without apportionment among the several States, and without regard to any census or enumeration."

Income is the thing which may be taxed—income from any source. The Amendment does not attempt to define income or to designate how taxes may be laid thereon, or how they may be enforced.

Under former decisions here the settled doctrine is that the Sixteenth Amendment confers no power upon Congress to define and tax as income without apportionment something which theretofore could not have been properly regarded as income.

Also, this Court has declared—"Income may be defined as the gain derived from capital, from labor, or from both combined, provided it be understood to include profit gained through a sale or conversion of capital assets." Eisner v. Macomber, 252 U.S. 189, 207, 40 S.Ct. 189, 193. The "gain derived from capital," within the definition, is "not a gain accruing to capital, nor a growth or increment of value in the investment, but a gain, a profit, something of exchangeable value proceeding from the property, severed from the capital however invested, and coming in, that is, received or drawn by the claimant for his separate use, benefit and disposal." United States v. Phellis, 257 U.S. 156, 169, 42 S.Ct. 63, 65.

If, instead of giving the stock to petitioner, the donor had sold it at market value, the excess over the capital he invested (cost) would have been income therefrom and subject to taxation under the Sixteenth Amendment. He would have been obliged to share the realized gain with the United States. He held the stock—the investment—subject to the right of the sovereign to take part of any increase in its value when separated through sale or conversion and reduced to his possession. Could he, contrary to the express will of Congress, by mere gift enable another to hold this stock free from such right, deprive the sovereign of the possibility of taxing the appreciation when actually severed, and convert the entire property into a capital asset of the donee, who invested nothing, as though the latter had purchased at the market price? And after a still further enhancement of the property, could the donee make a second gift with like effect, etc.? We think not.

In truth the stock represented only a single investment of capital—that made by the donor. And when through sale or conversion the increase was separated therefrom, it became income from that investment in the hands of the recipient subject to taxation according to the very words of the Sixteenth Amendment. By requiring the recipient of the entire increase to pay a part into the public treasury, Congress deprived her of no right and subjected her to no hardship. She accepted the gift with knowledge of the statute and, as to the property received, voluntarily assumed the position of her donor. When she sold the stock she actually got the original sum invested, plus the entire appreciation; and out of the latter only was she called on to pay the tax demanded.

The provision of the statute under consideration seems entirely appropriate for enforcing a general scheme of lawful taxation. To accept the view urged in behalf of petitioner undoubtedly would defeat, to some extent, the purpose of Congress to take part of all gain derived from capital investments. To prevent that result and insure enforcement of its proper policy, Congress had power to require that for purposes of taxation the donee should accept the position of the donor in respect of the thing received. And in so doing, it acted neither unreasonably nor arbitrarily.

*   *   *

There is nothing in the Constitution which lends support to the theory that gain actually resulting from the increased value of capital can be treated as taxable income in the hands of the recipient only so far as the increase occurred while he owned the property. And Irwin v. Gavit, 268 U.S. 161, 167, 45 S.Ct. 475, 476, is to the contrary.

The judgments below are

Affirmed.

The CHIEF JUSTICE took no part in the consideration or decision of these causes.

FARID–ES–SULTANEH v. COMMISSIONER

United States Court of Appeals, Second Circuit, 1947.
160 F.2d 812.

CHASE, Circuit Judge. The problem presented by this petition is to fix the cost basis to be used by the petitioner in determining the taxable gain on a sale she made in 1938 of shares of corporate stock. She contends that it is the adjusted value of the shares at the date she acquired them because her acquisition was by purchase. The Commissioner's position is that she must use the adjusted cost basis of her transferor because her acquisition was by gift. The Tax Court agreed with the Commissioner and redetermined the deficiency accordingly.

The pertinent facts are not in dispute and were found by the Tax Court as they were disclosed in the stipulation of the parties substantially as follows:

The petitioner is an American citizen who filed her income tax return for the calendar year 1938 with the Collector of Internal Revenue for the Third District of New York and in it reported sales during that year of 12,000 shares of the common stock of the S.S. Kresge Company at varying prices per share, for the total sum of $230,802.36 which admittedly was in excess of their cost to her. How much this excess amounted to for tax purposes depends upon the legal significance of the facts now to be stated.

In December 1923 when the petitioner, then unmarried, and S.S. Kresge, then married, were contemplating their future marriage, he delivered to her 700 shares of the common stock of the S.S. Kresge Company which then had a fair market value of $290 per share. The shares were all in street form and were to be held by the petitioner "for her benefit and protection in the event that the said Kresge should die prior to the contemplated marriage between the petitioner and said Kresge." The latter was divorced from his wife on January 9, 1924, and on or about January 23, 1924 he delivered to the petitioner 1800 additional common shares of S.S. Kresge Company which were also in street form and were to be held by the petitioner for the same purposes as were the first 700 shares he had delivered to her. On April 24, 1924, and when the petitioner still retained the possession of the stock so delivered to her, she and Mr. Kresge executed a written ante-nuptial agreement wherein she acknowledged the receipt of the shares "as a gift made by the said Sebastian S. Kresge, pursuant to this indenture, and as an ante-nuptial settlement, and in consideration of said gift and said ante-nuptial settlement, in consideration of the promise of said Sebastian S. Kresge to marry her, and in further consideration of the consummation of said promised marriage" she released all dower and other marital rights, including the right to her support to which she otherwise would have been entitled as a matter of law when she became his wife. They were married in New York immediately after the ante-nuptial agreement was executed and continued to be husband and wife until the petitioner obtained a final decree of absolute divorce from him on, or about, May 18, 1928. No alimony was claimed by, or awarded to, her.

The stock so obtained by the petitioner from Mr. Kresge had a fair market value of $315 per share on April 24, 1924, and of $330 per share on, or about May 6, 1924, when it was transferred to her on the books of the corporation. She held all of it for about three years, but how much she continued to hold thereafter is not disclosed except as that may be shown by her sales in 1938. Meanwhile her holdings had been increased by a stock dividend of 50 per cent, declared on April 1, 1925; one of 10 to 1 declared on January 19, 1926; and one of 50 per cent, declared on March 1, 1929. Her adjusted basis for the stock she sold in 1938 was $10.66⅔ per share computed on the basis of the fair market value of the shares which she obtained from Mr. Kresge at the time of her acquisition. His adjusted basis for the shares she sold in 1938 would have been $0.159091.[1]

When the petitioner and Mr. Kresge were married he was 57 years old with a life expectancy of 16½ years. She was then 32 years of age with a life expectancy of 33¾ years. He was then worth approximately $375,000,000 and owned real estate of the approximate value of $100,000,000.

The Commissioner determined the deficiency on the ground that the petitioner's stock obtained as above stated was acquired by gift within the meaning of that word as used in § 113(a)(2) of the Revenue Act of 1938, 26 U.S.C.A. Int.Rev.Acts, page 1048, and, as the transfer to her was after December 31, 1920, used as the basis for determining the gain on her sale of it the basis it would have had in the hands of the donor.[2] This was correct if the just mentioned statute is applicable, and the Tax Court held it was on the authority of Wemyss v. Commissioner, 324 U.S. 303, 65 S.Ct. 652, 156 A.L.R. 1022, and Merrill v. Fahs, 324 U.S. 308, 65 S.Ct. 655.

The issue here presented cannot, however, be adequately dealt with quite so summarily. The Wemyss case determined the taxability to the transferor as a gift, under §§ 501 and 503 of the Revenue Act of 1932, 26 U.S.C.A. Int.Rev.Acts, pages 580, 585, and the applicable regulations, of property transferred in trust for the benefit of the prospective wife of the transferor pursuant to the terms of an ante-nuptial agreement. It

---

1. Current rules for allocation of basis in the case of stock dividends appear in I.R.C. § 307. Ed.

2. See I.R.C. (1986) § 1015(a). Ed.

was held that the transfer, being solely in consideration of her promise of marriage, and to compensate her for loss of trust income which would cease upon her marriage, was not for an adequate and full consideration in money or money's worth within the meaning of § 503 of the statute, the Tax Court having found that the transfer was not one at arm's length made in the ordinary course of business. But we find nothing in this decision to show that a transfer, taxable as a gift under the gift tax, is ipso facto to be treated as a gift in construing the income tax law.

In Merrill v. Fahs, supra, it was pointed out that the estate and gift tax statutes are in pari materia and are to be so construed. Estate of Sanford v. Commissioner of Internal Revenue, 308 U.S. 39, 44, 60 S.Ct. 51. The estate tax provisions in the Revenue Act of 1916 required the inclusion in a decedent's gross estate of transfers made in contemplation of death, or intended to take effect in possession and enjoyment at or after death except when a transfer was the result of "a bona fide sale for a fair consideration in money or money's worth." Sec. 202(b), 39 Stat. 756, 777. The first gift tax became effective in 1924, and provided inter alia, that where an exchange or sale of property was for less than a fair consideration in money or money's worth the excess should be taxed as a gift. Rev.Act of 1924, § 320, 43 Stat. 314, 26 U.S.C.A. Int. Rev.Acts, page 81. While both taxing statutes thus provided, it was held that a release of dower rights was a fair consideration in money or money's worth. Ferguson v. Dickson, 3 Cir., 300 F. 961, certiorari denied 266 U.S. 628, 45 S.Ct. 126; McCaughn v. Carver, 3 Cir., 19 F.2d 126. Following that, Congress in 1926 replaced the words "fair consideration" in the 1924 Act limiting the deductibility of claims against an estate with the words "adequate and full consideration in money or money's worth" and in 1932 the gift tax statute as enacted limited consideration in the same way. Rev.Act 1932, § 503. Although Congress in 1932 also expressly provided that the release of marital rights should not be treated as a consideration in money or money's worth in administering the estate tax law, Rev.Act of 1932, § 804, 26 U.S.C.A. Int.Rev.Acts, page 642, and failed to include such a provision in the gift tax statute, it was held that the gift tax law should be construed to the same effect.[3] Merrill v. Fahs, supra.

We find in this decision no indication, however, that the term "gift" as used in the income tax statute should be construed to include a transfer which, if made when the gift tax were effective, would be taxable to the transferor as a gift merely because of the special provisions in the gift tax statute defining and restricting consideration for gift tax purposes. A fortiori, it would seem that limitations found in the estate tax law upon according the usual legal effect to proof that a transfer was made for a fair consideration should not be imported into the income tax law except by action of Congress. In our opinion the income tax provisions are not to be construed as though they were

3. See I.R.C. (1986) §§ 2043(b) and 2512(b). Ed.

in pari materia with either the estate tax law or the gift tax statutes. They are aimed at the gathering of revenue by taking for public use given percentages of what the statute fixes as net taxable income. Capital gains and losses are, to the required or permitted extent, factors in determining net taxable income. What is known as the basis for computing gain or loss on transfers of property is established by statute in those instances when the resulting gain or loss is recognized for income tax purposes and the basis for succeeding sales or exchanges will, theoretically at least, level off tax-wise any hills and valleys in the consideration passing either way on previous sales or exchanges. When Congress provided that gifts should not be treated as taxable income to the donee there was, without any correlative provisions fixing the basis of the gift to the donee, a loophole which enabled the donee to make a subsequent transfer of the property and take as the basis for computing gain or loss its value when the gift was made. Thus it was possible to exclude from taxation any increment in value during the donor's holding and the donee might take advantage of any shrinkage in such increment after the acquisition by gift in computing gain or loss upon a subsequent sale or exchange. It was to close this loophole that Congress provided that the donee should take the donor's basis when property was transferred by gift. Report of Ways and Means Committee (No. 350, P. 9, 67th Cong., 1st Sess.). This change in the statute affected only the statutory net taxable income. The altered statute prevented a transfer by gift from creating any change in the basis of the property in computing gain or loss on any future transfer. In any individual instance the change in the statute would but postpone taxation and presumably would have little effect on the total volume of income tax revenue derived over a long period of time and from many taxpayers. Because of this we think that a transfer which should be classed as a gift under the gift tax law is not necessarily to be treated as a gift income-tax-wise. Though such a consideration as this petitioner gave for the shares of stock she acquired from Mr. Kresge might not have relieved him from liability for a gift tax, had the present gift tax then been in effect, it was nevertheless a fair consideration which prevented her taking the shares as a gift under the income tax law since it precluded the existence of a donative intent.

Although the transfers of the stock made both in December 1923, and in the following January by Mr. Kresge to this taxpayer are called a gift in the ante-nuptial agreement later executed and were to be for the protection of his prospective bride if he died before the marriage was consummated, the "gift" was contingent upon his death before such marriage, an event that did not occur. Consequently, it would appear that no absolute gift was made before the ante-nuptial contract was executed and that she took title to the stock under its terms, viz: in consideration for her promise to marry him coupled with her promise to relinquish all rights in and to his property which she would otherwise acquire by the marriage. Her inchoate interest in the property of her affianced husband greatly exceeded the value of the stock transferred to her. It was a fair consideration under ordinary legal concepts of that term for the transfers of the stock by him. Ferguson v. Dickson, supra; McCaughn v. Carver, supra. She performed the contract under the terms of which the stock was transferred to her and held the shares not as a donee but as a purchaser for a fair consideration.

As the decisive issue is one of law only, the decision of the Tax Court interpreting the applicable statutory provisions has no peculiar finality and is reviewable. Bingham v. Commissioner, 325 U.S. 365, 65 S.Ct. 1232.

Decision reversed.

[The dissenting opinion of Circuit Judge CLARK has been omitted. Ed.]

PROBLEMS

1. Donor gave Donee property under circumstances that required no payment of gift tax. What gain or loss to Donee on the subsequent sale of the property if:

(a) The property had cost Donor $20,000, had a $30,000 fair market value at the time of the gift, and Donee sold it for:

(1) $35,000? *35,000 - 20,000 = 15,000 gain*

(2) $15,000? *20,000 - 15,000 = 5,000 loss*

(3) $25,000? *25000 - 20000 = 5,000 gain*

(b) The property had cost Donor $30,000, had a $20,000 fair market value at the time of the gift, and Donee sold it for:

(1) $35,000? *35,000 - 30,000 = 5,000 gain*

(2) $15,000? *20,000 - 15,000 = 15,000 loss*

(3) $24,000? *30,000 - 24,000 = 6,000 loss*

2. Father had some land that he had purchased for $120,000 but which had increased in value to $180,000. He transferred it to Son for $120,000 in cash in a transaction properly identified as in part a gift and in part a sale.* Assume no gift tax was paid on the transfer.

(a) What gain to Father and what basis to Son under Reg. §§ 1.1001–1(e) and 1.1015–4? *no gain to father - no loss* *basis = 120,000*

(b) Suppose the transaction were viewed as a sale of two thirds of the land for full consideration and an outright gift of the other one third. How would this affect Father's gain and Son's basis? Is it a more realistic view than that of the Regulations? Cf. §§ 170(e)(2) and 1011(b), relating to bargain sales to charities.

---

* See Wurzel, "The Tax Basis for Assort- Cost of 'Ersatz' Legislation," 20 Tax L.Rev. ed Bargain Purchases, or: The Inordinate 165 (1964).

3. PROPERTY ACQUIRED BETWEEN SPOUSES OR INCIDENT TO DIVORCE

Internal Revenue Code: Section 1041.

Regulations: Section 1.1041–1T(a) and (d).

Property acquired by purchase has a cost basis to the buyer in the amount of what he paid for it.[1] Depending on the nature of the property, the seller's gain or loss is determined by whether the amount realized[2] by him exceeds or is less than his basis in the property.[3] In general and in contrast to the gift of property, the sale or exchange of property is not a tax neutral transaction.

Property that is acquired by gift costs the donee nothing; it is not even includable in his gross income.[4] Therefore, the donee's basis in property acquired solely by gift is never a cost or quasi-cost basis.[5] A special provision generally accords the donee a transferred basis in such property.[6] Except for purposes of determining a loss on the sale of the property, the basis of property in the hands of a donee is the same basis the property had in the hands of the donor.[7] A consequence of this transferred basis rule is that pre-gift appreciation remains taxable in the event of a subsequent sale or exchange of the property by the donee. For purposes of determining gain (and sometimes loss), the donee steps into the basis shoes of the donor. The transfer of property by gift between the donor and the donee can properly be said to have neutral income tax consequences.

Prior to the Tax Reform Act of 1984, the transfer of appreciated property to a spouse in a sale or exchange for full value resulted in a gain to the transferor[8] and the transferee spouse was accorded a "cost" basis equal to the fair market value of the property received. The above gain recognition rules also applied if the transfer of appreciated property to a spouse (or former spouse) was in exchange for the release of marital claims,[9] and the transferee spouse again was accorded a "cost" basis of full fair market value in the property but with no income tax price to pay for such basis.[10] The results, however, were not uniform as the various states have differing types of property ownership within a marriage.[11] For these and other reasons, Congress considered it inappropriate to tax transfers of property between spouses or former spouses. The policy implemented here reflects the attitude that a husband and wife are a single economic unit, and the tax laws

---

1. I.R.C. § 1012.

2. I.R.C. § 1001(b).

3. I.R.C. § 1001(a).

4. I.R.C. § 102(a).

5. Cf. Reg. § 1.1015–4.

6. I.R.C. § 1015(a).

7. Id. See also I.R.C. § 1015(d).

8. I.R.C. § 267 disallowed losses on sales or exchanges between spouses. I.R.C.

§ 276(a)(1), (b)(1), (c)(4). See Chapter 25A, infra and see I.R.C. § 267(g) making § 267 inapplicable to transfers within § 1041.

9. See, e.g., United States v. Davis, 370 U.S. 65, 82 S.Ct. 1190 (1962), at page 228, infra; Cf. note 8, supra.

10. Rev.Rul. 67–221, 1967–2 C.B. 63.

11. See page 234, infra.

governing transfers of property between spouses and sometimes between former spouses should be as unintrusive as possible.[12]

Section 1041 accords almost complete tax neutrality to transfers of property between spouses and between former spouses if, in the latter instance, the transfer is incident to divorce.[13] No gain or loss is recognized.[14] This rule applies whether the transfer of property is for cash or other property, for the relinquishment of marital rights or for any other consideration [15] or for the assumption of liabilities in excess of basis (unless the transfer is to a trust).[16] So now we are finally able to answer the Trivial Pursuit game question: When is a sale-purchase not a sale-purchase? Answer: When Section 1041 applies. We do not mean to imply that this is trivial, for Section 1041 is amazingly generous in most circumstances.

It is premature at this point, but a student should be warned of circumstances in which a taxpayer is adversely affected by the rules of Section 1041. The key is the attending basis provision. In the case of any transfer of property between spouses or former spouses, the transferee is treated as if the property were acquired by gift,[17] and the basis of the property in the hands of the transferee is the same as the basis of the property in the hands of the transferor.[18] Unlike the gift basis rule,[19] the Section 1041 transferee spouse or former spouse *always* takes a transferred basis,[20] even for computing loss.

Query: Do the rules of Section 1041 apply to transfers of property after marriage which are incident to an antenuptial agreement executed by an engaged couple? And what if they do? Look again at *Farid-Es-Sultaneh.* Would Section 1041 apply to both Farid and Kresge?

4. PROPERTY ACQUIRED FROM A DECEDENT

Internal Revenue Code: Sections 1014(a), (b)(1) and (6), (e).
Regulations: Section 1.1014–1(a), –3(a).

———

While property that is the subject of a gift receives what is commonly referred to as a carry-over or transferred basis, the same is not true of property acquired by bequest or inheritance. Under Section 1014(a) property acquired from a decedent receives a basis equal to its fair market value on the date on which it was valued for federal estate tax purposes.[1] The effect of this basis rule is to give property that

---

12. H.Rep. No. 98–432, Part 2, 98th Cong., 2d Sess. 1491–1492 (1984).

13. This aspect of I.R.C. § 1041 is considered in more detail in Chapter 10. See page 235, infra.

14. I.R.C. § 1041(a). This is an example of a non-recognition provision. Other such provisions are considered in Chapter 26, infra.

15. Note 12, supra.

16. I.R.C. § 1041(e). Cf. Diedrich v. Commissioner, page 159, infra.

17. I.R.C. § 1041(b)(1); see also I.R.C. § 1015(e).

18. I.R.C. § 1041(b)(2).

19. I.R.C. § 1015(a).

20. I.R.C. § 1015(e).

1. The estate tax is usually based on date of death value, but the executor may sometimes use an alternate valuation date,

appreciated during the decedent's ownership a "stepped-up" basis with no income tax cost to anyone. Of course a "stepped-down" basis results without deductible loss if property declined in value during decedent's ownership.

Section 1014 applies not only to property held by the decedent at his death, but also to some property that he transferred during his life if the value of the property is nevertheless required to be included in his estate for federal estate tax purposes.[2]

The Revenue Act of 1948 brought into the Code a number of provisions designed, at least roughly, to equalize the tax status of persons in noncommunity property and community property states.[3] As a part of that enactment Congress added Section 1014(b)(6), which gives a Section 1014 basis to a surviving spouse's one-half share of community property, if at least one-half of the whole of the community interest in such property was included in the decedent spouse's estate (whether or not the estate was of sufficient size to require an estate tax return or payment of tax).[4] This is a somewhat perplexing provision, because the surviving spouse's share is not subjected to estate tax on the decedent's death. However, an examination of Section 2056 will reveal that in a common law state a decedent's property that passes to his spouse, which automatically gets a Section 1014 basis, also may escape tax by way of the estate tax marital deduction.

The Section 1014 basis rule is an important element in estate planning. It means that, although appreciated property is fully subjected to the estate tax, the appreciation itself entirely escapes the income tax. Thus, elderly people with substantially appreciated property often choose not to sell such property in order to avoid income taxation and are said to be "locked-in" to their positions.

Prior to 1982, Section 1014 was potentially subject to abuse. If a younger person who owned appreciated property gave it to an elderly or ill relative or friend and then, at death, the property passed from the elderly or ill person back to the younger person, she received it with a

usually the date six months after decedent's death but sometimes a date within that six months period. I.R.C. §§ 2031 and 2032. The date-of-death value basis rule was often criticized. See "Taxation of Appreciation of Assets Transferred at Death or by Gift," United States Treasury Dept., Tax Reform Studies and Proposals, 91st Cong., 1st Sess., Pt. 3, at 331–340 (1969), reprinted in Sander and Westfall, Readings in Federal Taxation 542 (Foundation Press 1970); see also Waterbury, "A Case for Realizing Gains at Death in Terms of Family Interests," 52 Minn.L.Rev. 1 (1967); Slawson, "Taxing as Ordinary Income the Appreciation of Publicly Held Stock," 76 Yale L.J. 623 (1967), reprinted in part in Sander and Westfall, Readings in Federal Taxation 495 (Foundation Press 1970); Castruccio, "Becoming More Inevitable? Death and Taxes ∗ ∗ ∗ and Taxes," 17 U.C.L.A.L.Rev. 459 (1970); Heckerling, "The Death of the 'Stepped-Up' Basis at Death," 37 S.Cal.L.Rev. 247 (1964).

2. See I.R.C. § 1014(b)(2)–(10). See Stephens, Maxfield, Lind, & Calfee, *Federal Estate and Gift Taxation*, ¶ 4.07 through ¶ 4.16 (6th Ed. Warren, Gorham & Lamont, 1991), which criticizes different treatment of direct transfers from transfers in trust in this respect.

3. See Chapter 27, infra at page 971.

4. Reg. § 1.1014–2(a)(5).

Section 1014 stepped-up basis.[5] Quite possibly the Commissioner could have successfully attacked this gambit upon a showing of collusion. Section 1014(e), effective after 1981, prevents this abuse mechanically without the need to show culpability. If "appreciated property"[6] is acquired by a decedent within the one-year period ending on the decedent's death and if the property (or property acquired with the proceeds from its sale by the estate) passes from the decedent back to the donor or the donor's spouse, the basis in the property is the adjusted basis of the property in the hands of the decedent immediately before his death.[7] Thus if Son owns some land that he purchased for $20,000 which is worth $100,000 and he gives it to his ill Father who dies within a year devising the property back to Son, under Section 1014(e) upon reacquisition Son's basis in the land is still $20,000, rather than $100,000.

The step-up in basis has been attacked both on economic and social policy grounds,[8] and there have been proposals for legislation either to provide a transferred basis at death, to subject the appreciation to income tax at death, or to provide an estate tax surcharge measured by the amount of untaxed appreciation.[9] In 1976 Congress chose a version of the carryover basis approach when it enacted Section 1023.[10] That section generally provided a carryover basis to property which was acquired from a decedent after 1976; thus the section was similar to Section 1015.[11] Reacting to a public outcry that Section 1023 imposed an onerous burden on executors and attorneys to ascertain a decedent's basis,[12] Congress initially postponed implementation of the provision[13] and finally put it to rest in 1980.[14] In its place Congress resurrected Section 1014, which for all practical purposes remained applicable throughout the Section 1023 era.

C. THE AMOUNT REALIZED

Internal Revenue Code: Section 1001(b).

Regulations: Section 1.1001–1(a), –2(b).

---

5. The decedent may have had to pay an estate tax on the property. See I.R.C. § 2001(c). But see I.R.C. § 2010.

6. I.R.C. § 1014(e)(2)(A).

7. I.R.C. § 1014(e)(1) and (2)(B).

8. See references cited at note 1, supra.

9. See Graetz, "Taxation of Unrealized Gains at Death—An Evaluation of the Current Proposals," 59 Virg.L.R. 830 (1973); but see G. Break and J. Pechman, Tax Reform: The Impossible Dream, pp. 13–18 (1975).

10. Tax Reform Act of 1976 § 2005(a).

11. I.R.C. § 1023 allowed a "fresh start" adjustment to the carryover basis. I.R.C. § 1023(h). That adjustment general-

ly stepped up the basis of property to its December 31, 1976 value if the decedent owned the property on that date. The adjustment was the result of a compromise to the straight carryover basis rule to insure passage of § 1023.

12. See a student note on some of the problems with I.R.C. § 1023; Blum, "Carryover Basis: The Case for Repeal," 57 Texas L.R. 204 (1979).

13. In the Revenue Act of 1978 Congress originally postponed the effective date of I.R.C. § 1023 from January 1, 1977 to January 1, 1980. P.L. 95–600 § 702(c)(1) (1978).

14. Windfall Profit Tax Act of 1980, P.L. 96–223 § 401.

INTERNATIONAL FREIGHTING CORPORATION, INC.
v. COMMISSIONER

United States Court of Appeals, Second Circuit, 1943.
135 F.2d 310.

Before L. HAND, CHASE and FRANK, Circuit Judges.

During the years 1933 to 1935, inclusive, E.I. duPont deNemours and Company, Inc., owned all of taxpayer's stock and during the year 1936 it owned two-thirds of taxpayer's stock, the balance being owned by the General Motors Corporation. During the years 1933 to 1936, inclusive, taxpayer informally adopted the bonus plan of the duPont Company as its own bonus plan. Class A or class B bonus awards, or both, might be made to employees under that plan. Class B bonus awards (the only ones here involved) might be granted to those employees who, by their ability, efficiency and loyalty, had contributed most in a general way to the taxpayer's success, and were to be made from the portion of taxpayer's profits which its finance committee had set aside in the class B bonus fund. Only those employees were eligible for class B awards who on January first of the year in which the awards were made had been in the continuous employ of taxpayer at least two years. Recommendations for bonuses were to be made by the president or the heads of departments and were to be acted on by the executive committee or the board of directors. It was not incumbent on the executive committee or the board of directors to distribute the entire amount available in the fund. The taxpayer reserved the right at any time to discontinue the awarding of any bonuses.

Bonuses were in the form of common stock of the duPont Company or in the form of cash to be invested in such stock.

* * *

During the calendar year 1936 taxpayer paid over and distributed to the beneficiaries of its class B bonus award, certificates representing 150 shares of the common stock of the duPont Company, whose cost to taxpayer at the date of delivery was $16,153.36 and whose market value was then $24,858.75. Each of the employees receiving those shares in 1936 paid a tax thereon, computing the market value at the time of delivery as taxable income.

Taxpayer took a deduction of $24,858.75 in its income tax return for 1936 on account of the 150 shares of stock distributed in that year to its employees. In a notice of deficiency the Commissioner reduced the deduction from $24,858.75 to $16,153.35, a difference of $8,705.39, determining that, as the bonus was paid in property, "the basis for calculation of the amount thereof is the cost of such property and not its market value as claimed on the return." This was the only adjustment which the Commissioner made to taxpayer's return and, as a result, the Commissioner determined a deficiency in the amount of $2,156.76, in taxpayer's tax liability for the year. Taxpayer filed a petition with the Tax Court for a redetermination of the deficiency thus determined. By an amended answer, the Commissioner, in the alternative, alleged that if it were held that taxpayer was entitled to a deduction in the amount of $24,858.75 on account of the payment of bonus in stock, then taxpayer realized a taxable profit of $8,705.39 on the disposition of the shares, and taxpayer's net taxable income otherwise determined should be increased accordingly.

The Tax Court held that taxpayer was entitled to a deduction for compensation paid in the year 1936 in the amount of $24,858.75. The Tax Court decided for the Commissioner, however, on the defense set forth in the Commissioner's amended answer, holding that taxpayer realized a gain of $8,705.39 in 1936 by paying the class B bonus in stock which had cost taxpayer $8,705.39 less than its market value when taxpayer transferred the stock to its employees. The deficiency resulting from this decision was $2,156.76. From that decision taxpayer seeks review.

FRANK, Circuit Judge.

1. Up to the time in 1936 when the shares were delivered to the employees, the taxpayer retained such control of the shares that title had not passed to the employees.[1] We think the Tax Court correctly held that the market value at the time of delivery was properly deducted by the taxpayer as an ordinary expense of the business under [Section 162(a), Ed.] because that delivery was an additional reasonable compensation for past services actually rendered. Cf. Lucas v. Ox Fibre Brush Co., 281 U.S. 115, 50 S.Ct. 273.[2] The payment depleted the taxpayer's assets in an amount equal to that market value fully as much as if taxpayer had, at the time of delivery, first purchased those shares.

2. We turn to the question whether the transaction resulted in taxable gain to taxpayer. We think that the Tax Court correctly held that it did. The delivery of those shares was not a gift, else (1) it would have been wrongful as against taxpayer's stockholders, (2) the value of the shares could not have been deducted as an expense under § 23(a), and (3) the employees as donees would not be obliged to pay, as they must,[3] an income tax on what they received. It was not a gift precisely because it was "compensation for services actually rendered," i.e., because the taxpayer received a full quid pro quo. Accordingly, cases holding that one is not liable for an income tax when he makes a gift of shares are not in point.

But, as the delivery of the shares here constituted a disposition for a valid consideration, it resulted in a closed transaction with a consequent realized gain. It is of no relevance that here the taxpayer had

1. Cf. Olson v. Commissioner, 7 Cir., 67 F.2d 726, 729.

2. § [162(a). Ed.] permits deduction of "all the ordinary and necessary expenses paid or incurred during the taxable year in carrying on any trade or business, including a reasonable allowance for salaries or other compensation for personal services actually rendered."

3. Old Colony Trust Co. v. Commissioner, 279 U.S. 716, 49 S.Ct. 499; Fisher v. Commissioner, 2 Cir., 59 F.2d 192; Olson v. Commissioner, supra.

not been legally obligated to award any shares or pay any additional compensation to the employees; bonus payments by corporations are recognized as proper even if there was no previous obligation to make them; although then not obligatory, they are regarded as made for a sufficient consideration.[4] Since the bonuses would be invalid to the extent that what was delivered to the employees exceeded what the services of the employees were worth, it follows that the consideration received by the taxpayer from the employees must be deemed to be equal at least to the value of the shares in 1936. Here then, as there was no gift but a disposition of shares for a valid consideration equal at least to the market value of the shares when delivered, there was a taxable gain equal to the difference between the cost of the shares and that market value.

For [Section 1001(a). Ed.] provides that the gain from "the sale or other disposition of property" shall be the excess of "the amount realized therefrom" over "the adjusted basis" provided in [Section 1016. Ed.] in the light of [Section 1012. Ed.] —makes the "basis" the cost of such property. True, [Section 1001(b). Ed.] provides that "the amount realized" is the sum of "any money received plus the fair market value of the property (other than money) received." Literally, where there is a disposition of stock for services, no "property" or "money" is received by the person who thus disposes of the stock. But, in similar circumstances, it has been held that "money's worth" is received and that such a receipt comes within [Section 1001(b). Ed.]. See Commissioner v. Mesta, 3 Cir., 123 F.2d 986, 988; cf. Commissioner v. Halliwell, 2 Cir., December 1, 1942, 131 F.2d 642; Kenan v. Commissioner, 2 Cir., 114 F.2d 217.[5]

The taxpayer properly asks us to treat this case "as if there had been no formal bonus plan" and as if taxpayer "had simply paid outright 150 shares of duPont stock to selected employees as additional compensation." On that basis, surely there was a taxable gain. For to shift the equation once more, the case supposed is the equivalent of one in which the taxpayer in the year 1936, without entering into a previous contract fixing the amount of compensation, had employed a transposition expert for one day and, when he completed his work, had paid him 5 shares of duPont stock having market value at that time of $500 but which it had bought in a previous year for $100. There can be no doubt that, from such a transaction, taxpayer would have a taxable gain. And so here.

The order of the Tax Court is affirmed.

4. Cf. the cases cited in the preceding footnote.

5. In these cases the taxpayer paid a money claim by delivering stock. What the taxpayer received was literally neither property nor money, yet it was held that there was a taxable transaction under § [1001(b). Ed.].

CRANE v. COMMISSIONER*

Supreme Court of the United States, 1947.
331 U.S. 1, 67 S.Ct. 1047.

[The Crane case, which follows, is hard going at best. One key to understanding the concepts that are developed in the opinion is some understanding of the income tax aspects of depreciation and consequent basis adjustments. If this is a new problem for you, as a student, you may benefit from a reading of the note on depreciation in Chapter 22 at page 740. Ed.]

Mr. Chief Justice VINSON delivered the opinion of the Court.

The question here is how a taxpayer who acquires depreciable property subject to an unassumed mortgage, holds it for a period, and finally sells it still so encumbered, must compute her taxable gain.

Petitioner was the sole beneficiary and the executrix of the will of her husband, who died January 11, 1932. He then owned an apartment building and lot subject to a mortgage,[1] which secured a principal debt of $255,000.00 and interest in default of $7,042.50. As of that date, the property was appraised for federal estate tax purposes at a value exactly equal to the total amount of this encumbrance. Shortly after her husband's death, petitioner entered into an agreement with the mortgagee whereby she was to continue to operate the property— collecting the rents, paying for necessary repairs, labor, and other operating expenses, and reserving $200.00 monthly for taxes—and was to remit the net rentals to the mortgagee. This plan was followed for nearly seven years, during which period petitioner reported the gross rentals as income, and claimed and was allowed deductions for taxes and operating expenses paid on the property, for interest paid on the mortgage, and for the physical exhaustion of the building. Meanwhile, the arrearage of interest increased to $15,857.71. On November 29, 1938, with the mortgagee threatening foreclosure, petitioner sold to a third party for $3,000.00 cash, subject to the mortgage, and paid $500.00 expenses of sale.

Petitioner reported a taxable gain of $1,250.00. Her theory was that the "property" which she had acquired in 1932 and sold in 1938 was only the equity, or the excess in the value of the apartment building and lot over the amount of the mortgage. This equity was of zero value when she acquired it. No depreciation could be taken on a

---

* See Bittker, "Tax Shelter, Nonrecourse Debt, and the *Crane* Case," 33 Tax L.Rev. 277 (1978); Simmons, "Nonrecourse Debt and Basis: Mrs. Crane Where Are You Now?" 53 So.Cal.L.Rev. 1 (1979); Del Cotto, "Basis and Amount Realized Under Crane: A Current View of Some Tax Effects in Mortgage Financing," 118 U. of Pa. L.Rev. 69 (1969); Adams, "Exploring the Outer Boundaries of the Crane Doctrine; An Imaginary Supreme Court Opinion," 21 Tax L.Rev. 159 (1966), reprinted in Sander and Westfall, Readings in Federal Taxation at page 325 (Foundation Press 1970); Cooper, "Negative Basis," 75 Harv.L.Rev. 1352 (1962); White, "Realization, Recognition, Reconciliation, Rationality and the Structure of the Federal Income Tax System," 88 Mich.L.Rev. 2034 (1990). Ed.

1. The record does not show whether he was personally liable for the debt.

zero value.[2] Neither she nor her vendee ever assumed the mortgage, so, when she sold the equity, the amount she realized on the sale was the net cash received, or $2,500.00. This sum less the zero basis constituted her gain, of which she reported half as taxable on the assumption that the entire property was a "capital asset."[3]

The Commissioner, however, determined that petitioner realized a net taxable gain of $23,767.03. His theory was that the "property" acquired and sold was not the equity, as petitioner claimed, but rather the physical property itself, or the owner's rights to possess, use, and dispose of it, undiminished by the mortgage. The original basis thereof was $262,042.50, its appraised value in 1932. Of this value $55,000.00 was allocable to land and $207,042.50 to building.[4] During the period that petitioner held the property, there was an allowable depreciation of $28,045.10 on the building,[5] so that the adjusted basis of the building at the time of sale was $178,997.40. The amount realized on the sale was said to include not only the $2,500.00 net cash receipts, but also the principal amount[6] of the mortgage subject to which the property was sold, both totaling $257,500.00. * * *

The Tax Court * * * [essentially] adopted petitioner's contentions, and expunged the deficiency.[9] * * * [T]he Circuit Court of Appeals reversed, one judge dissenting.[10] We granted certiorari because of the importance of the questions raised as to the proper construction of the gain and loss provisions of the Internal Revenue Code.[11]

The 1938 Act,[12] § 111(a), defines the gain from "the sale or other disposition of property" as "the excess of the amount realized therefrom over the adjusted basis provided in section 113(b) * * *." It proceeds,

2. This position is, of course, inconsistent with her practice in claiming such deductions in each of the years the property was held. The deductions so claimed and allowed by the Commissioner were in the total amount of $25,500.00.

3. See § 117(a), (b), Revenue Act of 1938, c. 289, 52 Stat. 447. Under this provision only 50% of the gain realized on the sale of a "capital asset" need be taken into account, if the property had been held more than two years.

4. The parties stipulated as to the relative parts of the 1932 appraised value and of the 1938 sales price which were allocable to land and building.

5. The parties stipulated that the rate of depreciation applicable to the building was 2% per annum.

6. The Commissioner explains that only the principal amount, rather than the total present debt secured by the mortgage, was deemed to be a measure of the amount realized, because the difference was attributable to interest due, a deductible item.

9. 3 T.C. 585. The Court held that the building was not a "capital asset" within the meaning of § 117(a) and that the entire gain on the building had to be taken into account under § 117(b), because it found that the building was of a character subject to physical exhaustion and that petitioner had used it in her trade or business.

But because the Court accepted petitioner's theory that the entire property had a zero basis, it held that she was not entitled to the 1938 depreciation deduction on the building which she had inconsistently claimed.

For these reasons, it did not expunge the deficiency in its entirety.

10. 153 F.2d 504.

11. 328 U.S. 826, 66 S.Ct. 980.

12. All subsequent references to a revenue act are to this Act unless otherwise indicated. The relevant parts of the gain and loss provisions of the Act and Code are identical.

§ 111(b), to define "the amount realized from the sale or other disposition of property" as "the sum of any money received plus the fair market value of the property (other than money) received." [See Sections 1001(a) and (b). Ed.] Further, in § 113(b), the "adjusted basis for determining the gain or loss from the sale or other disposition of property" is declared to be "the basis determined under subsection (a), adjusted * * * [(1) (B)] * * * for exhaustion, wear and tear, obsolescence, amortization * * * to the extent allowed (but not less than the amount allowable) * * *." [See Section 1016(a)(2). Ed.] The basis under subsection (a) "if the property was acquired by * * * devise * * * or by the decedent's estate from the decedent," § 113(a) (5), is "the fair market value of such property at the time of such acquisition." [See Section 1014(a)(1). Ed.]

Logically, the first step under this scheme is to determine the unadjusted basis of the property, under § 113(a)(5), and the dispute in this case is as to the construction to be given the term "property." If "property," as used in that provision, means the same thing as "equity," it would necessarily follow that the basis of petitioner's property was zero, as she contends. If, on the contrary, it means the land and building themselves, or the owner's legal rights in them, undiminished by the mortgage, the basis was $262,042.50.

We think that the reasons for favoring one of the latter constructions are of overwhelming weight. In the first place, the words of statutes—including revenue acts—should be interpreted where possible in their ordinary, everyday senses.[13] The only relevant definitions of "property" to be found in the principal standard dictionaries [14] are the two favored by the Commissioner, i.e., either that "property" is the physical thing which is a subject of ownership, or that it is the aggregate of the owner's rights to control and dispose of that thing. "Equity" is not given as a synonym, nor do either of the foregoing definitions suggest that it could be correctly so used. Indeed, "equity" is defined as "the value of a property * * * above the total of the liens. * * *" [15] The contradistinction could hardly be more pointed. Strong countervailing considerations would be required to support a contention that Congress, in using the word "property," meant "equity," or that we should impute to it the intent to convey that meaning.[16]

In the second place, the Commissioner's position has the approval of the administrative construction of § 113(a)(5). With respect to the valuation of property under that section, Reg. 101, Art. 113(a)(5)–1, promulgated under the 1938 Act, provided that "the value of property as of the date of the death of the decedent as appraised for the purpose of the Federal estate tax * * * shall be deemed to be its fair market

---

13. Old Colony R. Co. v. Commissioner, 284 U.S. 552, 560, 52 S.Ct. 211, 213.

14. See Webster's New International Dictionary, Unabridged, 2d Ed.; Funk & Wagnalls' New Standard Dictionary; Oxford English Dictionary.

15. See Webster's New International Dictionary, supra.

16. Crooks v. Harrelson, 282 U.S. 55, 59, 51 S.Ct. 49, 50.

value ✶ ✶ ✶." The land and building here involved were so appraised
in 1932, and their appraised value—$262,042.50—was reported by peti-
tioner as part of the gross estate. This was in accordance with the
estate tax law [17] and regulations,[18] which had always required that the
value of decedent's property, undiminished by liens, be so appraised
and returned, and that mortgages be separately deducted in computing
the net estate.[19] As the quoted provision of the Regulations has been in
effect since 1918,[20] and as the relevant statutory provision has been
repeatedly reenacted since then in substantially the same form,[21] the
former may itself now be considered to have the force of law.[22]

Moreover, in the many instances in other parts of the Act in which
Congress has used the word "property," or expressed the idea of
"property" or "equity," we find no instances of a misuse of either word
or of a confusion of the ideas.[23] In some parts of the Act other than the
gain and loss sections, we find "property" where it is unmistakably
used in its ordinary sense.[24] On the other hand, where either Congress
or the Treasury intended to convey the meaning of "equity," it did so by
the use of appropriate language.[25]

A further reason why the word "property" in § 113(a) should not
be construed to mean "equity" is the bearing such construction would
have on the allowance of deductions for depreciation and on the
collateral adjustments of basis.

Section 23(*l*) permits deduction from gross income of "a reasonable
allowance for the exhaustion, wear and tear of property. ✶ ✶ ✶"
Sections 23(n) and 114(a) declare that the "basis upon which exhaustion, wear and tear ✶ ✶ ✶ are to be allowed" is the basis "provided in
section 113(b) for the purpose of determining the gain upon the sale" of
the property, which is the § 113(a) basis "adjusted ✶ ✶ ✶ for exhaus-

---

17. See §§ 202 and 203(a)(1) Revenue
Act of 1916; §§ 402 and 403(a)(1), Revenue
Acts of 1918 and 1921; §§ 302, 303(a)(1),
Revenue Acts of 1924 and 1926; § 805,
Revenue Act of 1932.

18. See Reg. 37, Arts. 13, 14, and 47;
Reg. 63, Arts. 12, 13, and 41; Reg. 68, Arts.
11, 13, and 38; Reg. 70, Arts. 11, 13, and
38; Reg. 80, Arts. 11, 13, and 38.

19. See City Bank Farmers' Trust Co. v.
Bowers, 68 F.2d 909, cert. denied, 292 U.S.
644, 54 S.Ct. 778; Rodiek v. Helvering, 87
F.2d 328; Adriance v. Higgins, 113 F.2d
1013.

20. [Citations omitted. Ed.]

21. [Citations omitted. Ed.]

22. Helvering v. Reynolds Co., 306 U.S.
110, 114, 59 S.Ct. 423.

23. Cf. Helvering v. Stockholms Bank,
293 U.S. 84, 87, 55 S.Ct. 50, 51.

24. Sec. 23(a)(1) permits the deduction
from gross income of "rentals ✶ ✶ ✶ required to be made as a condition to the
continued use ✶ ✶ ✶ for purposes of the
trade or business, of *property* ✶ ✶ ✶ in
which he [the taxpayer] has no *equity*."
(Italics supplied.)

Sec. 23(*l*) permits the deduction from
gross income of "a reasonable allowance
for the exhaustion, wear and tear of *property* used in the trade or business ✶ ✶ ✶."
(Italics supplied.)

See also § 303(a)(1), Revenue Act of
1926, c. 27, 44 Stat. 9; § 805, Revenue Act
of 1932, c. 209, 47 Stat. 280.

25. See § 23(a)(1), supra, note 24;
§ 805, Revenue Act of 1932, supra, note 24;
§ 3482, I.R.C.; Reg. 105, § 81.38. This provision of the Regulations, first appearing in
1937, T.D. 4729, 1937–1 Cum.Bull. 284, 289,
permitted estates which were not liable on
mortgages applicable to certain of decedent's property to return "only the value of
the equity of redemption (or value of the
property, less the indebtedness) ✶ ✶ ✶."

tion, wear and tear ＊　＊　＊ to the extent allowed (but not less than the amount allowable). ＊　＊　＊"＊ [See Section 167. Ed.]

Under these provisions, if the mortgagor's equity were the § 113(a) basis, it would also be the original basis from which depreciation allowances are deducted. If it is, and if the amount of the annual allowances were to be computed on that value, as would then seem to be required,[26] they will represent only a fraction of the cost of the corresponding physical exhaustion, and any recoupment by the mortgagor of the remainder of that cost can be effected only by the reduction of his taxable gain in the year of sale.[27] If, however, the amount of the annual allowances were to be computed on the value of the property, and then deducted from an equity basis, we would in some instances have to accept deductions from a minus basis or deny deductions altogether.[28] The Commissioner also argues that taking the mortgagor's equity as the § 113(a) basis would require the basis to be changed with each payment on the mortgage,[29] and that the attendant problem of repeatedly recomputing basis and annual allowances would be a tremendous accounting burden on both the Commissioner and the taxpayer. Moreover, the mortgagor would acquire control over the timing of his depreciation allowances.

Thus it appears that the applicable provisions of the Act expressly preclude an equity basis, and the use of it is contrary to certain implicit principles of income tax depreciation, and entails very great administrative difficulties.[30] It may be added that the Treasury has never furnished a guide through the maze of problems that arise in connection with depreciating an equity basis, but, on the contrary, has consistently permitted the amount of depreciation allowances to be

---

＊ In the Internal Revenue Code of 1986, as compared with earlier Acts cited here, the depreciation deduction is authorized by § 167(a); § 167(g) makes reference to § 1011 for a determination of the basis upon which deductions are to be claimed. Detailed differences are not of significance here. Ed.

26. Secs. 23(n) and 114(a), in defining the "basis upon which" depreciation is "to be allowed," do not distinguish between basis as the minuend from which the allowances are to be deducted, and as the dividend from which the amount of the allowance is to be computed. The Regulations indicate that the basis of property is the same for both purposes. Reg. 101, Art. 23(*l*)–4, 5.

27. This is contrary to Treasury practice, and to Reg. 101, Art. 23(*l*)–5, which provides in part:

"The capital sum to be recovered shall be charged off over the useful life of the property, either in equal annual installments or in accordance with any other recognized trade practice, such as an ap-

portionment of the capital sum over units of production."

See Detroit Edison Co. v. Commissioner, 319 U.S. 98, 101, 63 S.Ct. 902, 903.

28. So long as the mortgagor remains in possession, the mortgagee can not take depreciation deductions, even if he is the one who actually sustains the capital loss, as § 23(*l*) allows them only on property "used in the trade or business."

29. Sec. 113(b)(1)(A) requires adjustment of basis "for expenditures ＊　＊　＊ properly chargeable to capital account ＊　＊　＊."

30. Obviously we are not considering a situation in which a taxpayer has acquired and sold an equity of redemption only, i.e., a right to redeem the property without a right to present possession. In that situation, the right to redeem would itself be the aggregate of the taxpayer's rights and would undoubtedly constitute "property" within the meaning of § 113(a). No depreciation problems would arise. See note 28.

computed on the full value of the property, and subtracted from it as a basis. Surely, Congress' long-continued acceptance of this situation gives it full legislative endorsement.[31]

We conclude that the proper basis under § 113(a)(5) is the value of the property, undiminished by mortgages thereon, and that the correct basis here was $262,042.50. The next step is to ascertain what adjustments are required under § 113(b). As the depreciation rate was stipulated, the only question at this point is whether the Commissioner was warranted in making any depreciation adjustments whatsoever.

Section 113(b)(1)(B) provides that "proper adjustment in respect of the property *shall in all cases be made* * * * for exhaustion, wear and tear * * * to the extent allowed (but not less than the amount allowable). * * * (Italics supplied.)** The Tax Court found on adequate evidence that the apartment house was property of a kind subject to physical exhaustion, that it was used in taxpayer's trade or business, and consequently that the taxpayer would have been entitled to a depreciation allowance under § 23(1), except that, in the opinion of that Court, the basis of the property was zero, and it was thought that depreciation could not be taken on a zero basis. As we have just decided that the correct basis of the property was not zero, but $262,042.50, we avoid this difficulty, and conclude that an adjustment should be made as the Commissioner determined.

Petitioner urges to the contrary that she was not entitled to depreciation deductions, whatever the basis of the property, because the law allows them only to one who actually bears the capital loss,[32] and here the loss was not hers but the mortgagee's. We do not see, however, that she has established her factual premise. There was no finding of the Tax Court to that effect, nor to the effect that the value of the property was ever less than the amount of the lien. Nor was there evidence in the record, or any indication that petitioner could produce evidence, that this was so. The facts that the value of the property was only equal to the lien in 1932 and that during the next six and one-half years the physical condition of the building deteriorated and the amount of the lien increased, are entirely inconclusive, particularly in the light of the buyer's willingness in 1938 to take subject to the increased lien and pay a substantial amount of cash to boot. Whatever may be the rule as to allowing depreciation to a mortgagor on property in his possession which is subject to an unassumed mortgage and clearly worth less than the lien, we are not faced with that problem and see no reason to decide it now.

At last we come to the problem of determining the "amount realized" on the 1938 sale. Section 111(b), it will be recalled, defines

31. See note 22.

** See I.R.C. (1986) § 1016(a)(2); refinements in the amounts of the adjustments in basis required do not affect the principles for which the case is studied here. Ed.

32. See Helvering v. Lazarus & Co., 308 U.S. 252, 60 S.Ct. 209; Duffy v. Central R. Co., 268 U.S. 55, 64, 45 S.Ct. 429.

the "amount realized" from "the sale * * * of property" as "the sum of any money received plus the fair market value of the property (other than money) received," and § 111(a) defines the gain on "the sale * * * of property" as the excess of the amount realized over the basis. Quite obviously, the word "property" used here with reference to a sale, must mean "property" in the same ordinary sense intended by the use of the word with reference to acquisition and depreciation in § 113, both for certain of the reasons stated heretofore in discussing its meaning in § 113, and also because the functional relation of the two sections requires that the word mean the same in one section that it does in the other. If the "property" to be valued on the date of acquisition is the property free of liens, the "property" to be priced on a subsequent sale must be the same thing.[33]

Starting from this point, we could not accept petitioner's contention that the $2,500.00 net cash was all she realized on the sale except on the absurdity that she sold a quarter-of-a-million dollar property for roughly one per cent of its value, and took a 99 per cent loss. Actually, petitioner does not urge this. She argues, conversely, that because only $2,500.00 was realized on the sale, the "property" sold must have been the equity only, and that consequently we are forced to accept her contention as to the meaning of "property" in § 113. We adhere, however, to what we have already said on the meaning of "property," and we find that the absurdity is avoided by our conclusion that the amount of the mortgage is properly included in the "amount realized" on the sale.

Petitioner concedes that if she had been personally liable on the mortgage and the purchaser had either paid or assumed it, the amount so paid or assumed would be considered a part of the "amount realized" within the meaning of § 111(b).[34] The cases so deciding have already repudiated the notion that there must be an actual receipt by the seller himself of "money" or "other property," in their narrowest senses. It was thought to be decisive that one section of the Act must be construed so as not to defeat the intention of another or to frustrate the Act as a whole,[35] and that the taxpayer was the "beneficiary" of the payment in "as real and substantial [a sense] as if the money had been paid it and then paid over by it to its creditors."[36]

Both these points apply to this case. The first has been mentioned already. As for the second, we think that a mortgagor, not personally liable on the debt, who sells the property subject to the mortgage and

---

33. See Maguire v. Commissioner, 313 U.S. 1, 8, 61 S.Ct. 789, 794.

We are not troubled by petitioner's argument that her contract of sale expressly provided for the conveyance of the equity only. She actually conveyed title to the property, and the buyer took the same property that petitioner had acquired in 1932 and used in her trade or business until its sale.

34. United States v. Hendler, 303 U.S. 564, 58 S.Ct. 655; Brons Hotels, Inc., 34 B.T.A. 376; Walter F. Haass, 37 B.T.A. 948. See Douglas v. Willcuts, 296 U.S. 1, 8, 56 S.Ct. 59, 62.

35. See Brons Hotels, Inc., supra, 34 B.T.A. at 381.

36. See United States v. Hendler, supra, 303 U.S. at 566, 58 S.Ct. at page 656.

for additional consideration, realizes a benefit in the amount of the mortgage as well as the boot.[37] If a purchaser pays boot, it is immaterial as to our problem whether the mortgagor is also to receive money from the purchaser to discharge the mortgage prior to sale, or whether he is merely to transfer subject to the mortgage—it may make a difference to the purchaser and to the mortgagee, but not to the mortgagor. Or put in another way, we are no more concerned with whether the mortgagor is, strictly speaking, a debtor on the mortgage, than we are with whether the benefit to him is, strictly speaking, a receipt of money or property. We are rather concerned with the reality that an owner of property, mortgaged at a figure less than that at which the property will sell, must and will treat the conditions of the mortgage exactly as if they were his personal obligations.[38] If he transfers subject to the mortgage, the benefit to him is as real and substantial as if the mortgage were discharged, or as if a personal debt in an equal amount had been assumed by another.

Therefore we conclude that the Commissioner was right in determining that petitioner realized $257,500.00 on the sale of this property.

The Tax Court's contrary determinations, that "property," as used in § 113(a) and related sections, means "equity," and that the amount of a mortgage subject to which property is sold is not the measure of a benefit realized, within the meaning of § 111(b), announced rules of general applicability on clear-cut questions of law.[39] The Circuit Court of Appeals therefore had jurisdiction to review them.[40]

Petitioner contends that the result we have reached taxes her on what is not income within the meaning of the Sixteenth Amendment. If this is because only the direct receipt of cash is thought to be income in the constitutional sense, her contention is wholly without merit.[41] If it is because the entire transaction is thought to have been "by all dictates of common sense * * * a ruinous disaster," as it was termed in her brief, we disagree with her premise. She was entitled to depreciation deductions for a period of nearly seven years, and she actually took them in almost the allowable amount. The crux of this case, really, is whether the law permits her to exclude allowable

---

37. Obviously, if the value of the property is less than the amount of the mortgage, a mortgagor who is not personally liable cannot realize a benefit equal to the mortgage. Consequently, a different problem might be encountered where a mortgagor abandoned the property or transferred it subject to the mortgage without receiving boot. That is not this case. [But see the *Tufts* case at page 152, infra and problem 3(b) at page 166, infra. Ed.]

38. For instance, this petitioner returned the gross rentals as her own income, and out of them paid interest on the mortgage, on which she claimed and was allowed deductions. See Reg. 77, Art. 141; Reg. 86, Art. 23(b)–1; Reg. 94, Art. 23(b)–1 Reg. 101, Art. 23(b)–1.

39. See Commissioner v. Wilcox, 327 U.S. 404, 410, 66 S.Ct. 546, 550; Trust of Bingham v. Commissioner, 325 U.S. 365, 369–372, 62 S.Ct. 1232, 1234–1236. Cf. John Kelley Co. v. Commissioner, 326 U.S. 521, 527, 698, 66 S.Ct. 299, 302; Dobson v. Commissioner, 320 U.S. 489, 64 S.Ct. 239.

40. Ibid; see also § 1141(a) and (c), I.R.C.

41. Douglas v. Willcuts, supra, 296 U.S. at 9, 56 S.Ct. 62; Burnet v. Wells, 289 U.S. 670, 677, 53 S.Ct. 761, 763.

deductions from consideration in computing gain.[42] We have already showed that, if it does, the taxpayer can enjoy a double deduction, in effect, on the same loss of assets. The Sixteenth Amendment does not require that result any more than does the Act itself.

Affirmed.

Mr. Justice JACKSON, dissenting.

The Tax Court concluded that this taxpayer acquired only an equity worth nothing. The mortgage was in default, the mortgage debt was equal to the value of the property, any possession by the taxpayer was forfeited and terminable immediately by foreclosure, and perhaps by a receiver *pendente lite*. Arguments can be advanced to support the theory that the taxpayer received the whole property and thereupon came to owe the whole debt. Likewise it is argued that when she sold she transferred the entire value of the property and received release from the whole debt. But we think these arguments are not so conclusive that it was not within the province of the Tax Court to find that she received an equity which at that time had a zero value. Dobson v. Commissioner, 320 U.S. 489, 64 S.Ct. 239; Commissioner v. Scottish American Investment Co., Ltd., 323 U.S. 119, 65 S.Ct. 169. The taxpayer never became personally liable for the debt, and hence when she sold she was released from no debt. The mortgage debt was simply a subtraction from the value of what she did receive, and from what she sold. The subtraction left her nothing when she acquired it and a small margin when she sold it. She acquired a property right equivalent to an equity of redemption and sold the same thing. It was the "property" bought and sold as the Tax Court considered it to be under the Revenue Laws. We are not required in this case to decide whether depreciation was properly taken, for there is no issue about it here.

We would reverse the Court of Appeals and sustain the decision of the Tax Court.

Mr. Justice FRANKFURTER and Mr. Justice DOUGLAS join in this opinion.

---

42. In the course of the argument some reference was made, as by analogy, to a situation in which a taxpayer acquired by devise property subject to a mortgage in an amount greater than the then value of the property, and later transferred it to a third person, still subject to the mortgage, and for a cash boot. Whether or not the differ- ence between the value of the property on acquisition and the amount of the mortgage would in that situation constitute either statutory or constitutional income is a question which is different from the one before us, and which we need not presently answer.

COMMISSIONER v. TUFTS *

Supreme Court of the United States, 1983.**
461 U.S. 300, 103 S.Ct. 1826.

Justice BLACKMUN delivered the opinion of the Court.

Over 35 years ago, in Crane v. Commissioner, 331 U.S. 1, 67 S.Ct. 1047 (1947), this Court ruled that a taxpayer, who sold property encumbered by a nonrecourse mortgage (the amount of the mortgage being less than the property's value), must include the unpaid balance of the mortgage in the computation of the amount the taxpayer realized on the sale. The case now before us presents the question whether the same rule applies when the unpaid amount of the nonrecourse mortgage exceeds the fair market value of the property sold.

I

On August 1, 1970, respondent Clark Pelt, a builder, and his wholly owned corporation, respondent Clark, Inc., formed a general partnership. The purpose of the partnership was to construct a 120-unit apartment complex in Duncanville, Tex., a Dallas suburb. Neither Pelt nor Clark, Inc., made any capital contribution to the partnership. Six days later, the partnership entered into a mortgage loan agreement with the Farm & Home Savings Association (F & H). Under the agreement, F & H was committed for a $1,851,500 loan for the complex. In return, the partnership executed a note and a deed of trust in favor of F & H. The partnership obtained the loan on a nonrecourse basis: neither the partnership nor its partners assumed any personal liability for repayment of the loan. Pelt later admitted four friends and relatives, respondents Tufts, Steger, Stephens, and Austin, as general partners. None of them contributed capital upon entering the partnership.

The construction of the complex was completed in August 1971. During 1971, each partner made small capital contributions to the partnership; in 1972, however, only Pelt made a contribution. The total of the partners' capital contributions was $44,212. In each tax year, all partners claimed as income tax deductions their allocable shares of ordinary losses and depreciation. The deductions taken by the partners in 1971 and 1972 totalled $439,972. Due to these contributions and deductions, the partnership's adjusted basis in the property in August 1972 was $1,455,740.

---

* See Turner, "Nonrecourse Liabilities as Tax Shelter Devices After *Tufts*: Elimination of Fair Market Value and Contingent Liability Defenses," 35 U.Fla.L.Rev. 904 (1983); Blackburn, "Important Common Law Developments for Nonrecourse Notes: Tufting It Out," 18 Geo.L.Rev. 1 (1983); Narciso, "Some Reflections on Commission-er v. Tufts: Mrs. Crane Shops at Kirby Lumber," 35 Rutgers L.Rev. 929 (1983); and Simmons, "Tufts v. Commissioner: Amount Realized Limited to Fair Market Value," 15 U.C. Davis L.Rev. 577 (1982) (discussing the Fifth Circuit opinion).

** Some footnotes omitted.

In 1971 and 1972, major employers in the Duncanville area laid off significant numbers of workers. As a result, the partnership's rental income was less than expected, and it was unable to make the payments due on the mortgage. Each partner, on August 28, 1972, sold his partnership interest to an unrelated third party, Fred Bayles. As consideration, Bayles agreed to reimburse each partner's sale expenses up to $250; he also assumed the nonrecourse mortgage.

On the date of transfer, the fair market value of the property did not exceed $1,400,000. Each partner reported the sale on his federal income tax return and indicated that a partnership loss of $55,740 had been sustained.[1] The Commissioner of Internal Revenue, on audit, determined that the sale resulted in a partnership capital gain of approximately $400,000. His theory was that the partnership had realized the full amount of the nonrecourse obligation.[2]

Relying on Millar v. Commissioner, 577 F.2d 212, 215 (CA3), cert. denied, 439 U.S. 1046, 99 S.Ct. 721 (1978), the United States Tax Court, in an unreviewed decision, upheld the asserted deficiencies. 70 T.C. 756 (1978). The United States Court of Appeals for the Fifth Circuit reversed. 651 F.2d 1058 (1981). That court expressly disagreed with the *Millar* analysis, and, in limiting Crane v. Commissioner, supra, to its facts, questioned the theoretical underpinnings of the *Crane* decision. We granted certiorari to resolve the conflict. 456 U.S. 960, 102 S.Ct. 2034 (1982).

II

*   *   * Section 1001 governs the determination of gains and losses on the disposition of property. Under § 1001(a), the gain or loss from a sale or other disposition of property is defined as the difference between "the amount realized" on the disposition and the property's adjusted basis. Subsection (b) of § 1001 defines "amount realized": "The amount realized from the sale or other disposition of property shall be the sum of any money received plus the fair market value of the property (other than money) received." At issue is the application of the latter provision to the disposition of property encumbered by a nonrecourse mortgage of an amount in excess of the property's fair market value.

A

In Crane v. Commissioner, supra, this Court took the first and controlling step toward the resolution of this issue.   *   *   *

1. The loss was the difference between the adjusted basis, $1,455,740, and the fair market value of the property, $1,400,000. On their individual tax returns, the partners did not claim deductions for their respective shares of this loss. In their petitions to the Tax Court, however, the partners did claim the loss.

2. The Commissioner determined the partnership's gain on the sale by subtracting the adjusted basis, $1,455,740, from the liability assumed by Bayles, $1,851,500. *   *   *

1,851,500
1,455,740
———————
395,760

F., L. & S. Fed.Income Tax. 7th Ed. UCB—9

* * *

In a footnote, pertinent to the present case, the Court observed:

"Obviously, if the value of the property is less than the amount of the mortgage, a mortgagor who is not personally liable cannot realize a benefit equal to the mortgage. Consequently, a different problem might be encountered where a mortgagor abandoned the property or transferred it subject to the mortgage without receiving boot. That is not this case." Id., at 14, n. 37, 67 S.Ct., at 1054–55, n. 37.

B

This case presents that unresolved issue. We are disinclined to overrule *Crane,* and we conclude that the same rule applies when the unpaid amount of the nonrecourse mortgage exceeds the value of the property transferred. *Crane* ultimately does not rest on its limited theory of economic benefit; instead, we read *Crane* to have approved the Commissioner's decision to treat a nonrecourse mortgage in this context as a true loan. This approval underlies *Crane's* holdings that the amount of the nonrecourse liability is to be included in calculating both the basis and the amount realized on disposition. That the amount of the loan exceeds the fair market value of the property thus becomes irrelevant.

When a taxpayer receives a loan, he incurs an obligation to repay that loan at some future date. Because of this obligation, the loan proceeds do not qualify as income to the taxpayer. When he fulfills the obligation, the repayment of the loan likewise has no effect on his tax liability.

Another consequence to the taxpayer from this obligation occurs when the taxpayer applies the loan proceeds to the purchase price of property used to secure the loan. Because of the obligation to repay, the taxpayer is entitled to include the amount of the loan in computing his basis in the property; the loan, under § 1012, is part of the taxpayer's cost of the property. Although a different approach might have been taken with respect to a nonrecourse mortgage loan,[5] the

---

5. The Commissioner might have adopted the theory, implicit in Crane's contentions, that a nonrecourse mortgage is not true debt, but, instead, is a form of joint investment by the mortgagor and the mortgagee. On this approach, nonrecourse debt would be considered a contingent liability, under which the mortgagor's payments on the debt gradually increase his interest in the property while decreasing that of the mortgagee. [Citations omitted. Ed.] Because the taxpayer's investment in the property would not include the nonrecourse debt, the taxpayer would not be permitted to include that debt in basis. [Citations omitted. Ed.]

We express no view as to whether such an approach would be consistent with the statutory structure and, if so, and *Crane* were not on the books, whether that approach would be preferred over *Crane's* analysis. We note only that the *Crane* Court's resolution of the basis issue presumed that when property is purchased with proceeds from a nonrecourse mortgage, the purchaser becomes the sole owner of the property. 331 U.S., at 6, 67 S.Ct., at 1050. Under the *Crane* approach, the mortgagee is entitled to no portion of the basis. Id., at 10, n. 28, 67 S.Ct., at 1052, n. 28. The nonrecourse mortgage is part of the mortgagor's investment in the proper-

Commissioner has chosen to accord it the same treatment he gives to a recourse mortgage loan. The Court approved that choice in *Crane,* and the respondents do not challenge it here. The choice and its resultant benefits to the taxpayer are predicated on the assumption that the mortgage will be repaid in full.

When encumbered property is sold or otherwise disposed of and the purchaser assumes the mortgage, the associated extinguishment of the mortgagor's obligation to repay is accounted for in the computation of the amount realized. See United States v. Hendler, 303 U.S. 564, 566–567, 58 S.Ct. 655, 656 (1938). Because no difference between recourse and nonrecourse obligations is recognized in calculating basis,[7] *Crane* teaches that the Commissioner may ignore the nonrecourse nature of the obligation in determining the amount realized upon disposition of the encumbered property. He thus may include in the amount realized the amount of the nonrecourse mortgage assumed by the purchaser. The rationale for this treatment is that the original inclusion of the amount of the mortgage in basis rested on the assumption that the mortgagor incurred an obligation to repay. Moreover, this treatment balances the fact that the mortgagor originally received the proceeds of the nonrecourse loan tax-free on the same assumption. Unless the outstanding amount of the mortgage is deemed to be realized, the mortgagor effectively will have received untaxed income at the time the loan was extended and will have received an unwarranted increase in the basis of his property.[8] The Commissioner's interpretation of § 1001(b) in this fashion cannot be said to be unreasonable.

C

The Commissioner in fact has applied this rule even when the fair market value of the property falls below the amount of the nonrecourse obligation. Treas.Reg. § 1.1001–2(b), 26 CFR § 1.1001–2(b) (1982);[9]

ty, and does not constitute a coinvestment by the mortgagee. * * *

7. The Commissioner's choice in *Crane* "laid the foundation stone of most tax shelters," Bittker, Tax Shelters, Nonrecourse Debt, and the *Crane* Case, 33 Tax.L.Rev. 277, 283 (1978), by permitting taxpayers who bear no risk to take deductions on depreciable property. Congress recently has acted to curb this avoidance device by forbidding a taxpayer to take depreciation deductions in excess of amounts he has at risk in the investment. Pub.L. 94–455, § 204(a), 90 Stat. 1531 (1976), 26 U.S.C. § 465; Pub.L. 95–600, §§ 201–204, 92 Stat. 2814–2817 (1978), 26 U.S.C. § 465(a) (1976 ed., Supp. V). Real estate investments, however, are exempt from this prohibition. § 465(c)(3)(D) (1976 ed., Supp. V). Although this congressional action may foreshadow a day when nonrecourse and recourse debts will be treated differently,

neither Congress nor the Commissioner has sought to alter *Crane's* rule of including nonrecourse liability in both basis and the amount realized.

8. Although the *Crane* rule has some affinity with the tax benefit rule, see Bittker, supra, at 232; Del Cotto, Sales and Other Dispositions of Property Under Section 1001: The Taxable Event, Amount Realized and Related Problems of Basis, 26 Buffalo L.Rev. 219, 323–324 (1977), the analysis we adopt is different. Our analysis applies even in the situation in which no deductions are taken. It focuses on the obligation to repay and its subsequent extinguishment, not on the taking and recovery of deductions. See generally Note, 82 Colum.L.Rev., at 1526–1529.

9. The regulation was promulgated while this case was pending before the Court of Appeals for the Fifth Circuit.

Rev.Rul. 76–111, 1976–1 Cum.Bull. 214. Because the theory on which the rule is based applies equally in this situation, see Millar v. Commissioner, 67 T.C. 656, 660 (1977), aff'd on this issue, 577 F.2d 212, 215–216 (CA3), cert. denied, 439 U.S. 1046, 99 S.Ct. 721 (1978); [10] * * * we have no reason, after *Crane,* to question this treatment.

Respondents received a mortgage loan with the concomitant obligation to repay by the year 2012. The only difference between that mortgage and one on which the borrower is personally liable is that the mortgagee's remedy is limited to foreclosing on the securing property. This difference does not alter the nature of the obligation; its only effect is to shift from the borrower to the lender any potential loss caused by devaluation of the property.[12] If the fair market value of the property falls below the amount of the outstanding obligation, the mortgagee's ability to protect its interests is impaired, for the mortgagor is free to abandon the property to the mortgagee and be relieved of his obligation.

This, however, does not erase the fact that the mortgagor received the loan proceeds tax-free and included them in his basis on the understanding that he had an obligation to repay the full amount. See Woodsam Associates, Inc. v. Commissioner, 198 F.2d 357, 359 (CA2 1952); Bittker, 33 Tax.L.Rev., at 284. When the obligation is canceled, the mortgagor is relieved of his responsibility to repay the sum he originally received and thus realizes value to that extent within the meaning of § 1001(b). From the mortgagor's point of view, when his obligation is assumed by a third party who purchases the encumbered property, it is as if the mortgagor first had been paid with cash borrowed by the third party from the mortgagee on a nonrecourse basis, and then had used the cash to satisfy his obligation to the mortgagee.

Moreover, this approach avoids the absurdity the Court recognized in *Crane.* Because of the remedy accompanying the mortgage in the nonrecourse situation, the depreciation in the fair market value of the property is relevant economically only to the mortgagee, who by lending on a nonrecourse basis remains at risk. To permit the taxpayer to limit his realization to the fair market value of the property would be

T.D. 7741, 45 Fed.Reg. 81743, 1981–1 Cum. Bull. 430 (1980). It merely formalized the Commissioner's prior interpretation, however.

10. The Court of Appeals for the Third Circuit in *Millar* affirmed the Tax Court on the theory that inclusion of nonrecourse liability in the amount realized was necessary to prevent the taxpayer from enjoying a double deduction. 577 F.2d, at 215; cf. n. 4, supra. Because we resolve the question on another ground, we do not address the validity of the double deduction rationale.

12. In his opinion for the Court of Appeals in *Crane,* Judge Learned Hand observed:

"[The mortgagor] has all the income from the property; he manages it; he may sell it; any increase in its value goes to him; any decrease falls on him, until the value goes below the amount of the lien. * * * When therefore upon a sale the mortgagor makes an allowance to the vendee of the amount of the lien, he secures a release from a charge upon his property quite as though the vendee had paid him the full price on condition that before he took title the lien should be cleared. * * *" 153 F.2d 504, 506 (CA2 1945).

to recognize a tax loss for which he has suffered no corresponding economic loss.[13] Such a result would be to construe "one section of the Act * * * so as * * * to defeat the intention of another or to frustrate the Act as a whole." 331 U.S., at 13, 67 S.Ct., at 1054.

In the specific circumstances of *Crane,* the economic benefit theory did support the Commissioner's treatment of the nonrecourse mortgage as a personal obligation. The footnote in *Crane* acknowledged the limitations of that theory when applied to a different set of facts. *Crane* also stands for the broader proposition, however, that a nonrecourse loan should be treated as a true loan. We therefore hold that a taxpayer must account for the proceeds of obligations he has received tax-free and included in basis. Nothing in either § 1001(b) or in the Court's prior decisions requires the Commissioner to permit a taxpayer to treat a sale of encumbered property asymmetrically, by including the proceeds of the nonrecourse obligation in basis but not accounting for the proceeds upon transfer of the encumbered property. See Estate of Levine v. Commissioner, 634 F.2d 12, 15 (CA2 1980).

IV

When a taxpayer sells or disposes of property encumbered by a nonrecourse obligation, the Commissioner properly requires him to include among the assets realized the outstanding amount of the obligation. The fair market value of the property is irrelevant to this calculation. We find this interpretation to be consistent with Crane v. Commissioner, 331 U.S. 1, 67 S.Ct. 1047 (1947), and to implement the statutory mandate in a reasonable manner. National Muffler Dealers Assn. v. United States, 440 U.S. 472, 476, 99 S.Ct. 1304, 1306 (1979).

The judgment of the Court of Appeals is therefore reversed.

It is so ordered.

Justice O'CONNOR, concurring.

I concur in the opinion of the Court, accepting the view of the Commissioner. I do not, however, endorse the Commissioner's view. Indeed, were we writing on a slate clean except for the *Crane* decision, I would take quite a different approach—that urged upon us by Professor Barnett as *amicus.*

Crane established that a taxpayer could treat property as entirely his own, in spite of the "coinvestment" provided by his mortgagee in

---

13. In the present case, the Government bore the ultimate loss. The nonrecourse mortgage was extended to respondents only after the planned complex was endorsed for mortgage insurance under §§ 221(b) and (d)(4) of the National Housing Act, 12 U.S.C. § 1715*l*(b) and (d)(4) (1976 ed. and Supp. V). After acquiring the complex from respondents, Bayles operated it for a few years, but was unable to make it profitable. In 1974, F & H foreclosed, and the Department of Housing and Urban Development paid off the lender to obtain title. In 1976, the Department sold the complex to another developer for $1,502,000. The sale was financed by the Department's taking back a note for $1,314,800 and a nonrecourse mortgage. To fail to recognize the value of the nonrecourse loan in the amount realized, therefore, would permit respondents to compound the Government's loss by claiming the tax benefits of that loss for themselves.

the form of a nonrecourse loan. That is, the full basis of the property, with all its tax consequences, belongs to the mortgagor. That rule alone, though, does not in any way tie nonrecourse debt to the cost of property or to the proceeds upon disposition. I see no reason to treat the purchase, ownership, and eventual disposition of property differently because the taxpayer also takes out a mortgage, an independent transaction. In this case, the taxpayer purchased property, using nonrecourse financing, and sold it after it declined in value to a buyer who assumed the mortgage. There is no economic difference between the events in this case and a case in which the taxpayer buys property with cash; later obtains a nonrecourse loan by pledging the property as security; still later, using cash on hand, buys off the mortgage for the market value of the devalued property; and finally sells the property to a third party for its market value.

The logical way to treat both this case and the hypothesized case is to separate the two aspects of these events and to consider, first, the ownership and sale of the property, and, second, the arrangement and retirement of the loan. Under *Crane,* the fair market value of the property on the date of acquisition—the purchase price—represents the taxpayer's basis in the property, and the fair market value on the date of disposition represents the proceeds on sale. The benefit received by the taxpayer in return for the property is the cancellation of a mortgage that is worth no more than the fair market value of the property, for that is all the mortgagee can expect to collect on the mortgage. His gain or loss on the disposition of the property equals the difference between the proceeds and the cost of acquisition. Thus, the taxation of the transaction *in property* reflects the economic fate of the *property.* If the property has declined in value, as was the case here, the taxpayer recognizes a loss on the disposition of the property. The new purchaser then takes as his basis the fair market value as of the date of the sale. [Citations omitted. Ed.]

In the separate borrowing transaction, the taxpayer acquires cash from the mortgagee. He need not recognize income at that time, of course, because he also incurs an obligation to repay the money. Later, though, when he is able to satisfy the debt by surrendering property that is worth less than the face amount of the debt, we have a classic situation of cancellation of indebtedness, requiring the taxpayer to recognize income in the amount of the difference between the proceeds of the loan and the amount for which he is able to satisfy his creditor. 26 U.S.C. § 61(a)(12). The taxation of the financing transaction then reflects the economic fate of the loan.

The reason that separation of the two aspects of the events in this case is important is, of course, that the Code treats different sorts of income differently. A gain on the sale of the property may qualify for capital gains treatment, §§ 1202, 1221 (1976 ed. and Supp. V), while the cancellation of indebtedness is ordinary income, but income that the taxpayer may be able to defer. §§ 108, 1017 (1976 ed. Supp. V). Not only does Professor Barnett's theory permit us to accord appropriate treatment to each of the two types of income or loss present in these sorts of transactions, it also restores continuity to the system by making the taxpayer-seller's proceeds on the disposition of property equal to the purchaser's basis in the property. Further, and most important, it allows us to tax the events in this case in the same way that we tax the economically identical hypothesized transaction.

Persuaded though I am by the logical coherence and internal consistency of this approach, I agree with the Court's decision not to adopt it judicially. We do not write on a slate marked only by *Crane.* The Commissioner's longstanding position, Rev.Rul. 76–111, 1976–1 C.B. 214, is now reflected in the regulations. Treas.Reg. § 1.1001–2, 26 CFR § 1.1001–2 (1982). In the light of the numerous cases in the lower courts including the amount of the unrepaid proceeds of the mortgage in the proceeds on sale or disposition, [Citations omitted. Ed.] it is difficult to conclude that the Commissioner's interpretation of the statute exceeds the bounds of his discretion. As the Court's opinion demonstrates, his interpretation is defensible. One can reasonably read § 1001(b)'s reference to "the amount realized *from* the sale or other disposition of property" (emphasis added) to permit the Commissioner to collapse the two aspects of the transaction. As long as his view is a reasonable reading of § 1001(b), we should defer to the regulations promulgated by the agency charged with interpretation of the statute. [Citations omitted. Ed.] Accordingly, I concur.

DIEDRICH v. COMMISSIONER *

Supreme Court of the United States, 1982.*
457 U.S. 191, 102 S.Ct. 2414.

Chief Justice BURGER delivered the opinion of the Court.

We granted certiorari to resolve a Circuit conflict as to whether a donor who makes a gift of property on condition that the donee pay the resulting gift tax receives taxable income to the extent that the gift tax paid by the donee exceeds the donor's adjusted basis in the property transferred. 454 U.S. 813, 102 S.Ct. 89 (1981). The United States Court of Appeals for the Eighth Circuit held that the donor realized income. 643 F.2d 499 (1981). We affirm.

I

A

Diedrich v. Commissioner of Internal Revenue

In 1972 petitioners Victor and Frances Diedrich made gifts of approximately 85,000 shares of stock to their three children, using both a direct transfer and a trust arrangement. The gifts were subject to a

---

* Section 1026 of the Tax Reform Act of 1984, not a part of the Code, provides amnesty from the *Diedrich* holding but only for gifts made prior to March 4, 1981.

** Some footnotes omitted.

condition that the donees pay the resulting federal and state gift taxes. There is no dispute concerning the amount of the gift tax paid by the donees. The donors' basis in the transferred stock was $51,073; the gift tax paid in 1972 by the donees was $62,992. Petitioners did not include as income on their 1972 federal income tax returns any portion of the gift tax paid by the donees. After an audit the Commissioner of Internal Revenue determined that petitioners had realized income to the extent that the gift tax owed by petitioners but paid by the donees exceeded the donors' basis in the property. Accordingly, petitioners' taxable income for 1972 was increased by $5,959.[1] Petitioners filed a petition in the United States Tax Court for redetermination of the deficiencies. The Tax Court held for the taxpayers, concluding that no income had been realized. 39 TCM 433 (1979).

B

United Missouri Bank of Kansas City v.
Commissioner of Internal Revenue

In 1970 and 1971 Mrs. Frances Grant gave 90,000 voting trust certificates to her son on condition that he pay the resulting gift tax. Mrs. Grant's basis in the stock was $8,742.60; the gift tax paid by the donee was $232,620.09. As in *Diedrich,* there is no dispute concerning the amount of the gift tax or the fact of its payment by the donee pursuant to the condition.

Like the Diedrichs, Mrs. Grant did not include as income on her 1970 or 1971 federal income tax returns any portion of the amount of the gift tax owed by her but paid by the donee. After auditing her returns, the Commissioner determined that the gift of stock to her son was part gift and part sale, with the result that Mrs. Grant realized income to the extent that the amount of the gift tax exceeded the adjusted basis in the property. Accordingly, Mrs. Grant's taxable income was increased by approximately $112,000.[2] Mrs. Grant filed a petition in the United States Tax Court for redetermination of the deficiencies. The Tax Court held for the taxpayer, concluding that no income had been realized. Grant v. Commissioner, 39 TCM 1088 (1980).

C

The United States Court of Appeals for the Eighth Circuit consolidated the two appeals and reversed, concluding that "to the extent the

1. Subtracting the stock basis of $51,073 from the gift tax paid by the donees of $62,992, the Commissioner found that petitioners had realized a long-term capital gain of $11,919. After a 50% reduction in long-term capital gain, 26 U.S.C. § 1202, the Diedrichs' taxable income increased by $5,959. [I.R.C. (1954) § 1202 was repealed by the 1986 Act. Ed.]

2. The gift taxes were $232,630.09. Subtracting the adjusted basis of $8,742.60,

the Commissioner found that Mrs. Grant realized a long-term capital gain of $223,887.49. After a 50% reduction for long-term capital gain, 26 U.S.C. § 1202, Mrs. Grant's taxable income increased by $111,943.75.

During pendency of this lawsuit, Mrs. Grant died and the United Missouri Bank of Kansas City, the decedent's executor, was substituted as petitioner.

gift taxes paid by donees" exceeded the donors' adjusted bases in the property transferred, "the donors realized taxable income." 643 F.2d, at 504. The Court of Appeals rejected the Tax Court's conclusion that the taxpayers merely had made a "net gift" of the difference between the fair market value of the transferred property and the gift taxes paid by the donees. The court reasoned that a donor receives a benefit when a donee discharges a donor's legal obligation to pay gift taxes. The Court of Appeals agreed with the Commissioner in rejecting the holding in Turner v. Commissioner, 49 T.C. 356 (1968), aff'd per curiam, 410 F.2d 752 (CA6 1969), and its progeny, and adopted the approach of Johnson v. Commissioner, 59 T.C. 791 (1973), aff'd, 495 F.2d 1079 (CA6), cert. denied, 419 U.S. 1040, 95 S.Ct. 527 (1974), and Estate of Levine v. Commissioner, 72 T.C. 780 (1979), aff'd, 634 F.2d 12 (CA2 1980). We granted certiorari to resolve this conflict, and we affirm.

II

A

Pursuant to its constitutional authority, Congress has defined "gross income" as income "from whatever source derived," including "[i]ncome from discharge of indebtedness." 26 U.S.C. § 61(12). This Court has recognized that "income" may be realized by a variety of indirect means. In Old Colony Trust Co. v. Commissioner, 279 U.S. 716, 49 S.Ct. 499 (1929), the Court held that payment of an employee's income taxes by an employer constituted income to the employee. Speaking for the Court, Chief Justice Taft concluded that "[t]he payment of the tax by the employe[r] was in consideration of the services rendered by the employee and was a gain derived by the employee from his labor." Id., at 729. The Court made clear that the substance, not the form, of the agreed transaction controls. "The discharge by a third person of an obligation to him is equivalent to receipt by the person taxed." Ibid. The employee, in other words, was placed in a better position as a result of the employer's discharge of the employee's legal obligation to pay the income taxes; the employee thus received a gain subject to income tax.

The holding in *Old Colony* was reaffirmed in Crane v. Commissioner, 331 U.S. 1, 67 S.Ct. 1047 (1947). In *Crane* the Court concluded that relief from the obligation of a nonrecourse mortgage in which the value of the property exceeded the value of the mortgage constituted income to the taxpayer. The taxpayer in *Crane* acquired depreciable property, an apartment building, subject to an unassumed mortgage. The taxpayer later sold the apartment building, which was still subject to the nonrecourse mortgage, for cash plus the buyer's assumption of the mortgage. This Court held that the amount of the mortgage was properly included in the amount realized on the sale, noting that if the taxpayer transfers subject to the mortgage, "the benefit to him is as real and substantial as if the mortgage were discharged, or as if a personal debt in an equal amount had been assumed by another." Id., at 14.

Again, it was the "reality," not the form, of the transaction that governed. Ibid. The Court found it immaterial whether the seller received money prior to the sale in order to discharge the mortgage, or whether the seller merely transferred the property subject to the mortgage. In either case the taxpayer realized an economic benefit.

B

The principles of *Old Colony* and *Crane* control.[5] A common method of structuring gift transactions is for the donor to make the gift subject to the condition that the donee pay the resulting gift tax, as was done in each of the cases now before us. When a gift is made, the gift tax liability falls on the donor under 26 U.S.C. § 2502(d). When a donor makes a gift to a donee, a "debt" to the United States for the amount of the gift tax is incurred by the donor. Those taxes are as much the legal obligation of the donor as the donor's income taxes; for these purposes they are the same kind of debt obligation as the income taxes of the employee in *Old Colony,* supra. Similarly, when a donee agrees to discharge an indebtedness in consideration of the gift, the person relieved of the tax liability realizes an economic benefit. In short, the donor realizes an immediate economic benefit by the donee's assumption of the donor's legal obligation to pay the gift tax.

An examination of the donor's intent does not change the character of this benefit. Although intent is relevant in determining whether a gift has been made, subjective intent has not characteristically been a factor in determining whether an individual has realized income.[7] Even if intent were a factor, the donor's intent with respect to the condition shifting the gift tax obligation from the donor to the donee

---

5. Although the Commissioner has argued consistently that payment of gift taxes by the donee results in income to the donor, several courts have rejected this interpretation. See, e.g., Turner v. Commissioner, 49 T.C. 356 (1968), aff'd per curiam, 410 F.2d 752 (CA6 1969); Hirst v. Commissioner, 572 F.2d 427 (CA4 1978) (en banc). Cf. Johnson v. Commissioner, 495 F.2d 1079 (CA6), cert. denied, 419 U.S. 1040, 95 S.Ct. 527 (1974).

It should be noted that the *gift* tax consequences of a conditional gift will be unaffected by the holding in this case. When a conditional "net" gift is given, the gift tax attributable to the transfer is to be deducted from the value of the property in determining the value of the gift at the time of transfer. See Rev.Rul. 75–72, 1975–1 Cum. Bull. 310 (general formula for computation of gift tax on conditional gift); Rev.Rul. 71–232, 1971–1 Cum.Bull. 275.

7. Several courts have found it highly significant that the donor intended to make a gift. Turner v. Commissioner, supra; Hirst v. Commissioner, supra. It is not enough, however, to state that the donor intended simply to make a gift of the amount which will remain after the donee pays the gift tax. As noted above, subjective intent has not characteristically been a factor in determining whether an individual has realized income. In Commissioner v. Duberstein, 363 U.S. 278, 286, 80 S.Ct. 1190, 1197 (1960), the Court noted that "the donor's characterization of his action is not determinative." See also Minnesota Tea Co. v. Helvering, 302 U.S. 609, 613, 58 S.Ct. 393, 394 (1938) ("A given result at the end of a straight path is not made a different result because reached by following a devious path").

was plainly to relieve the donor of a debt owed to the United States; the choice was made because the donor would receive a benefit in relief from the obligation to pay the gift tax.[8]

Finally, the benefit realized by the taxpayer is not diminished by the fact that the liability attaches during the course of a donative transfer. It cannot be doubted that the donors were aware that the gift tax obligation would arise immediately upon the transfer of the property; the economic benefit to the donors in the discharge of the gift tax liability is indistinguishable from the benefit arising from discharge of a pre-existing obligation. Nor is there any doubt that had the donors sold a portion of the stock immediately before the gift transfer in order to raise funds to pay the expected gift tax, a taxable gain would have been realized. 26 U.S.C. § 1001. The fact that the gift tax obligation was discharged by way of a conditional gift rather than from funds derived from a pregift sale does not alter the underlying benefit to the donors.

C

Consistent with the economic reality, the Commissioner has treated these conditional gifts as a discharge of indebtedness through a part gift and part sale of the gift property transferred. The transfer is treated as if the donor sells the property to the donee for less than the fair market value. The "sale" price is the amount necessary to discharge the gift tax indebtedness; the balance of the value of the transferred property is treated as a gift. The gain thus derived by the donor is the amount of the gift tax liability less the donor's adjusted basis in the entire property. Accordingly, income is realized to the extent that the gift tax exceeds the donor's adjusted basis in the property. This treatment is consistent with § 1001 of the Internal Revenue Code, which provides that the gain from the disposition of property is the excess of the amount realized over the transferor's adjusted basis in the property.

III

We recognize that Congress has structured gift transactions to encourage transfer of property by limiting the tax consequences of a transfer. See, e.g., 26 U.S.C. § 102 (gifts excluded from donee's gross income). Congress may obviously provide a similar exclusion for the conditional gift. Should Congress wish to encourage "net gifts," changes in the income tax consequences of such gifts lie within the legislative responsibility. Until such time, we are bound by Congress'

---

8. The existence of the "condition" that the gift will be made only if the donee assumes the gift tax consequences precludes any characterization that the payment of the taxes was simply a gift from the donee back to the donor.

A conditional gift not only relieves the donor of the gift tax liability, but also may enable the donor to transfer a larger sum of money to the donee than would otherwise be possible due to such factors as differing income tax brackets of the donor and donee.

mandate that gross income includes income "from whatever source derived." We therefore hold that a donor who makes a gift of property on condition that the donee pay the resulting gift taxes realizes taxable income to the extent that the gift taxes paid by the donee exceed the donor's adjusted basis in the property.

The judgment of the United States Court of Appeals for the Eighth Circuit is affirmed.

Justice REHNQUIST, dissenting.

It is a well-settled principle today that a taxpayer realizes income when another person relieves the taxpayer of a legal obligation in connection with an otherwise taxable transaction. See Crane v. Commissioner, 331 U.S. 1, 67 S.Ct. 1047 (1947) (sale of real property); Old Colony Trust Co. v. Commissioner, 279 U.S. 716, 49 S.Ct. 499 (1929) (employment compensation). In neither *Old Colony* nor *Crane* was there any question as to the existence of a taxable transaction; the only question concerned the amount of income realized by the taxpayer as a result of the taxable transaction. The Court in this case, however, begs the question of whether a taxable transaction has taken place at all when it concludes that "[t]he principles of *Old Colony* and *Crane* control" this case. Ante, at 196.

In *Old Colony*, the employer agreed to pay the employee's federal tax liability as part of his compensation. The employee provided his services to the employer in exchange for compensation. The exchange of compensation for services was undeniably a taxable transaction. The only question was whether the employee's taxable income included the employer's assumption of the employee's income tax liability.

In *Crane*, the taxpayer sold real property for cash plus the buyer's assumption of a mortgage. [The buyer took the property subject to a mortgage. Ed.] Clearly a sale had occurred, and the only question was whether the amount of the mortgage assumed by the buyer should be included in the amount realized by the taxpayer. The Court rejected the taxpayer's contention that what she sold was not the property itself, but her equity in that property.

Unlike *Old Colony* or *Crane*, the question in this case is not the amount of income the taxpayer has realized as a result of a concededly taxable transaction, but whether a taxable transaction has taken place at all. Only *after* one concludes that a partial sale occurs when the donee agrees to pay the gift tax do *Old Colony* and *Crane* become relevant in ascertaining the amount of income realized by the donor as a result of the transaction. Nowhere does the Court explain why a gift becomes a partial sale merely because the donor and donee structure the gift so that the gift tax imposed by Congress on the transaction is paid by the donee rather than the donor.

In my view, the resolution of this case turns upon congressional intent: whether Congress intended to characterize a gift as a partial sale whenever the donee agrees to pay the gift tax. Congress has determined that a gift should not be considered income to the donee.

26 U.S.C. § 102. Instead, gift transactions are to be subject to a tax system wholly separate and distinct from the income tax. See 26 U.S.C. § 2501 et seq. Both the donor and the donee may be held liable for the gift tax. §§ 2502(d), 6324(b). Although the primary liability for the gift tax is on the donor, the donee is liable to the extent of the value of the gift should the donor fail to pay the tax. I see no evidence in the tax statutes that Congress forbade the parties to agree among themselves as to who would pay the gift tax upon pain of such an agreement being considered a taxable event for the purposes of the income tax. Although Congress could certainly determine that the payment of the gift tax by the donee constitutes income to the donor, the relevant statutes do not affirmatively indicate that Congress has made such a determination.

I dissent.

PROBLEMS

1. Chuck purchased some land ten years ago for $4,000 cash. The property appreciated to $7,000 at which time Chuck sold it to his wife Di for $7,000 cash, its fair market value.

   (a) What are the income tax consequences to Chuck? *gain of 3,000*

   (b) What is Di's basis in the property? *7,000*

   (c) What gain to Di if she immediately resells the property? *∅ if she resells at 7,000*

   (d) What results in (a)–(c), above, if the property had declined in value to $3,000 and Chuck sold it to Di for $3,000? *loss of 1,000   basis = 3,000   ∅ gain if resold at 3,000*

   (e) What results (gains, losses, and bases) to Chuck and Di if Di transfers other property with a basis of $5,000 and value of $7,000 (rather than cash) to Chuck in return for his property?

2. Mortgagor owns property with a basis of $2,000 and value of $10,000. Bank later lends him $4,000 on a loan in which he incurs no personal liability (although the property is subject to the liability). The $4,000 loan is used for another investment. Two years later, having paid nothing on the loan and in circumstances that because of the dollar amounts involved require payment of no gift tax, he transfers the property subject to the mortgage gratuitously to his Daughter.

   (a) Does Mortgagor have income when he borrows the $4,000? *No* See Woodsam Associates, Inc. v. Commissioner, 198 F.2d 357 (2d Cir.1952).

   (b) What tax consequences to Mortgagor on the transfer? *gain 10,000 − (2,000 4,000) = 4,000*

   (c) What is Daughter's basis in the property? Cf. § 1015(b). *,000*

   (d) If Daughter immediately sells the property subject to the mortgage to Purchaser, how much cash may she expect to receive?

   (e) What is Daughter's gain on the sale?

   (f) What is Purchaser's basis for the property?

(g) What result in (b)–(e), above, if Mortgagor transfers the property subject to the $4,000 mortgage to his spouse?

(h) What consequences to Mortgagor and Spouse if Spouse retains the property but pays off the $4,000 mortgage?

3. The facts are the same as the original facts in problem 2, above: Mortgagor owns property with a basis of $2,000 subject to a liability of $4,000 with a value of $10,000.

(a) Some years later when the liability is still $4,000 the land declines in value to $4,000. Does Mortgagor have income if he transfers the property by means of a quitclaim deed to Lender? See Parker v. Delaney, 186 F.2d 455 (1st Cir.1950).

(b) The facts are the same as in (a), above, except the property has a value of $3,500 at the time of the quitclaim deed.

4. Investor purchased three acres of land, each acre worth $10,000 for $30,000. Investor sold one of the acres in year one for $14,000 and a second in year two for $16,000. The total amount realized by Investor was $30,000 which is not in excess of his total purchase price. Does Investor have any gain or loss on the sales? See Reg. § 1.61–6(a).

5. Gainer acquired an apartment in a condominium complex by intervivos gift from Relative. Both used it only as a residence. It had been purchased by Relative for $20,000 cash and was given to Gainer when it was worth $30,000. Relative paid a $6,000 gift tax on the transfer. Gainer later sells the apartment to Shelterer.

(a) What gain or loss to Gainer on his sale to Shelterer for $32,000?

(b) What is Shelterer's basis in the apartment?

(c) Same questions now assuming that Relative acquired the property for $8,000 cash, but subject to a $12,000 mortgage on which neither he nor Gainer was ever personally liable or ever paid any amount of principal, and that Relative paid $3,000 tax on the gift. See § 1015(d)(6). Upon purchase, Shelterer merely took the property subject to the mortgage, paying $20,000 cash for it.

CHAPTER 7. ANNUITIES AND LIFE INSURANCE PROCEEDS

Internal Revenue Code: Sections 72(a), (b), (c); 101(a), (c) and (d).

Regulations: Sections 1.72–4(a), –9 (Table V), 1.101–1(a)(1), (b)(1), –4(a)(1)(i), (b) (1), (c).

It should be acknowledged at the beginning that the tax picture presented here of life insurance and annuities is no more than a long-range photograph taken without the benefit of a telephoto lens. This is for two reasons: (1) the presentation is in only one dimension ignoring, as it does, related estate and gift tax considerations that are likely to be of even more importance here than in other portions of this book; and (2) many details are set aside as out of keeping with the objective of this book to try to establish a good grounding in income tax fundamentals. The student should, nevertheless, emerge with an understanding of basic congressional policy in the area, an ability to apply the statute in routine circumstances, and a foundation for grappling with complexities that arise in other situations.

Insurance Proceeds. A common element of all life insurance policies is the agreement by the insurer to make payments upon the insured's death to his estate or to others whom he may designate as beneficiaries. The plain thrust of Section 101(a)(1) is to exclude the proceeds of such policies from the gross income of the recipients.[1] There are, however, two important conditions to this result.

First of all, Section 101(a) applies only to amounts "paid by reason of the death of the insured." It is possible, for example, that after a policy has been in effect for some time the cash surrender value of the policy (the amount the insurer will pay the policy owner *during* the insured's life in discharge of all rights under the policy) will exceed the net premiums paid. If the insured elects to take the cash surrender value, he may realize an amount in excess of basis, which is a taxable gain to him unprotected by the exclusionary rules of Section 101(a), because it is an amount *not* paid by reason of his death. Perhaps more important, an insurance policy that guarantees payments on the insured's death often contains alternative lifetime benefits that may be

---

1. One restriction on the exclusion arises in cases in which the policy has been the subject of a transfer for valuable consideration. See I.R.C. § 101(a)(2) which requires the excess of the proceeds received over the costs incurred (i.e. the gain on the policy) to be included in gross income. Congress enacted § 101(a)(2) to discourage speculation on the death of an insured. S.Rep. No. 1622, 83d Cong., 2d Sess. 14 (1954). The § 101(a)(2) income rule does not apply if the transfer for consideration is to a transferee who acquired the policy with a transferred basis, § 101(a)(2)(A), or is to the insured, a partner of the insured, or a partnership or corporation in which the insured has an interest, § 101(a)(2)(B). See Lawthers, "Income Tax Aspects of Transfers of Life Insurance Policies and of Various Forms of Settlement Options," 22 N.Y.U.Inst. on Fed.Tax. 1299 (1964).

elected. For example, the insured may be able to demand the payment of fixed annual sums for his life in lieu of and upon cancellation of any right to death benefits. If such a demand is made the receipts are obviously not paid by reason of the insured's death and, again, are not within the Section 101(a) exclusion.[2]

Secondly, although it might appear Section 101(a) excludes from gross income *whatever* amount is paid by reason of the insured's death, the introductory reference to subsection (d) calls attention to an important limitation. Usually an insurance policy will identify a fixed sum to be paid at death (the "face amount" of the policy). Essentially, it is this amount that is to be received tax-free. We might pause to wonder why this amount should not be taxed to the recipient. Consider the possibility that Young Married took out a $100,000 term policy on his life paying only the initial premium of $100. A week later he was killed in an automobile accident, and the insurer paid Mrs. Married $100,000. Neither of the Marrieds will ever be taxed on a clear gain (crass thought) of $99,900. Is this a reflection of a "suffered enough" notion?[3] Consider the relationship of the philosophy behind Sections 102 and 1014.

Under most life insurance policies Mrs. Married would have an option to accept something different from the $100,000, the face amount of the policy. She might, instead, be entitled to elect fixed monthly payments of amounts, determined with reference to her age and life expectancy, for the rest of her life. Without close regard to mortality tables and actuarial principles, let us assume that she can and does elect to be paid $250 each month ($3000 per year) for life and that her life expectancy is 50 years. If she should live just that long she will receive, overall, $150,000 (50 × $3000).[4] What, now, should be excluded? Until 1954, the entire $150,000 was excluded on these facts. But is this also consistent with the basic policy behind the exclusion? Congress has decided that it is not, and that is what Section 101(d) is all about.

If there are reasons for allowing an exclusion of $100,000 on the above facts, is it not just as clear that amounts that may be paid in excess of that sum represent amounts earned after the death of the insured on property of the beneficiary, much the same as on any other investment? With this much background, attack Section 101(d) to determine the congressional answer to this problem. You should conclude that Mrs. Married would in each of the 50 years of her remaining life exclude $2000 from and include $1000 in gross income.

2. But see the comments below on the exclusionary rules of I.R.C. § 72.

3. See Note on I.R.C. § 104 at page 193, infra; see also Swihart, "Federal Taxation of Life Insurance Wealth," 37 Ind.L.J. 167 (1962).

4. Obviously, an insurer will agree to pay a larger sum over a long time than the amount to be paid as a lump sum immediately, because he has the use of much of the money over the long period.

Logical?[5] If she lived years beyond her life expectancy the same exclusionary rule would apply in all those years.[6]

An insurance beneficiary may have the right to leave the entire proceeds with the insurer, drawing only interest on the amount that otherwise would be paid as a lump sum. Section 101(c) specifies that such interest payments are fully taxable. In general, Sections 101(c) and (d) are mutually exclusive; whenever any recurring payments substantially eat into the principal amount of the insurance (d), not (c), applies.[7]

Annuity Payments. Broadly speaking, an annuity is an arrangement under which one buys a right to future money payments. Being a mere matter of contract, the variety of such arrangements is limited only by the scope of human ingenuity. But there are some common classes: (1) A single-life annuity calls for fixed money payments to the annuitant for his life after which all rights under the contract cease. (2) Under a self-and-survivor annuity, fixed payments are made to an annuitant during his life and are then continued to another (in the same or a different amount) after his death. (3) The joint-and-survivor type annuity pays amounts jointly to two annuitants while both are living, and then payments are continued (in the same or a different amount) to the survivor. It is also not uncommon for the agreement to contain a refund feature; the contract may guarantee the payment of a sum certain to assure against severe loss through the premature death of the annuitants. Moreover the payments may be for a term certain, rather than for the life or lives of individuals. That is, the purchaser may buy the right to receive $1000 per month for twenty years, in which case payments would continue to his designee in the event of his death before expiration of the term. Such arrangements are sometimes called endowment contracts, and at an earlier time they were differentiated from annuities for tax purposes,[8] but both types of arrangements are now treated alike under Section 72.

In recent years the practice has developed of combining the annuity with the mutual fund concept to produce what is called the variable annuity.[9] Under one form of variable annuity, the annuitant in effect acquires an interest (generally described as a certain number of "units") in a diversified investment portfolio. When he starts receiving payments his rights are defined in terms of the number of units credited to him which are to be distributed to him or his survivors over

---

5. Cf. I.R.C. § 102(b)(1).

6. Reg. § 1.101–4(c); and see Sen.Rep. No. 1622, 83rd Cong., 2d Sess., 181 (1954).

7. Reg. § 1.101–3(a); but see § 1.101–4(h).

See Irenas, "Life Insurance Interest Income Under the Federal Income Tax," 21 Tax.L.Rev. 297 (1966).

8. See I.R.C. (1939) § 22(b)(2) and Reg. § 39.22(b)(2)–2.

9. Cf. I.R.C. § 817(d). Earlier, some employees' annuities were made variable in accordance with the Cost of Living Index. See Kern, "The Income Taxation of Variable Annuities," 55 A.B.A.J. 369 (1969); and see, generally, Bartlett, "Variable Annuities: Evolution and Analysis," 19 Stan.L.Rev. 150 (1966), a non-tax treatment.

the pay-out period. But the amount he receives each time varies with the investment experience of the fund—hence the term "variable". The use of variable annuities is becoming fairly common under qualified employee's pension plans [10] in an effort to provide against the ravages of inflation.[11] Variable annuities outside the qualified plan area present some tax difficulties not expressly answered in Section 72 and are the subject of special rules in the Regulations [12] which, however, are not discussed here.

Most annuity arrangements are made with insurance companies, although the rules of Section 72 are equally applicable to contracts between individuals.[13]

Even these brief remarks on annuities suggest the complexity of the area. Any attempt to explore the tax aspects of all the variations would of course be out of keeping with the objectives of this book. Accordingly, we turn now in as simple a setting as possible to the fundamental questions: How are annuities taxed and why? The keys to basic understanding are that (1) Income connotes gain and (2) A mere return of capital is not income. These are concepts that are familiar from the preceding chapter.

Assume now that Abouto Retire pays an insurance company $60,000 for their agreement to pay her $5000 each year for the rest of her life. Payments begin and Retire receives $5000 in the current year. Does this, or some part of it, represent income? If there were no special statutory rule applicable, we might say that Retire has just received a partial return of her capital which should go untaxed. Indeed, that was the law until 1934. Of course its corollary was that after 12 years when Retire had fully recovered her capital (12 × $5000 = $60,000), any further payments she received would be fully taxable and, under facts such as these, Retire might have a life expectancy of twenty years when the annuity payments began.

The Revenue Act of 1934 [14] took account of a deficiency in this taxing plan. It was recognized that there was really an income element in *each* annuity payment from the outset. Somewhat arbitrarily, that element was identified as an amount equal to 3% of the cost of the contract. Congress decided to tax that amount and to exclude from gross income the balance of each year's receipts. Thus, one in Retire's circumstances became taxable, as to each $5000 payment, on $1800 (3%

---

10. See Goodman, "Planning for Maximum Tax Benefits with Variable Annuities in Qualified Pension Plans," 30 J.Tax. 300 (1969).

11. Employees' annuities are not further discussed here, but it might be noted that, except where an employee has contributed his own taxed dollars to the purchase of an annuity under a qualified plan, his receipts under the annuity whether variable or fixed will generally be fully taxable to him as ordinary income. I.R.C. §§ 72(d) and 402(a)(1); but see § 402(a)(2).

12. Reg. § 1.72–2(b)(3) and see Reg. § 1.72–4(d)(3) Example.

13. So-called "private" annuities present some special tax considerations, which are explored in Ellis, Private Annuities, 195 Tax Management (1969); see also Vernava, "Tax Planning for the Not-so-Rich: Variable and Private Annuities," 11 Wm. and Mary L.Rev. 1 (1969). See note 20, infra.

14. § 22(b)(2), 48 Stat. 680, 686 (1934).

of $60,000) and could exclude from gross income $3200 ($5000 – $1800). Under this statutory approach the exclusions continued until the tax-free portions of her receipts equalled the cost of the contract. In Retire's case this might work out pretty well. That is, it would take about 19 years (19 × $3200 = $60,800) for her to recover her investment tax free, and we have assumed Retire might have a life expectancy of twenty years. But the 3% rule was subject to criticism in that it did not purport to fix the amount of the tax-free receipt with respect to the relationship of the cost of the annuity and the life expectancy and probable return to the annuitant. In some circumstances it was quite possible that one who had little or no chance for a full tax-free recovery of her investment was, nevertheless, taxed on portions of her annual receipts.[15]

The philosophy of present Section 72, enacted in 1954, is not sharply different from the provision it replaced. Congress still attempts properly to accord tax neutrality to the taxpayer's return of capital. Examine the statute. It allows a recovery of capital over the expected life of the contract by excluding the portion of each payment which is in the ratio of the "investment in the contract"[16] to the "expected return under the contract."[17] The excess receipt is taxed as the income element in each payment.[18] Assuming Abouto Retire, under the facts above, under tables provided in the regulations[19] has a 20 year life expectancy,[20] she would include $2000 of each $5000 payment in income, excluding 60,000/100,000 of each $5000 payment.

What if Abouto Retire lives beyond her life expectancy and receives a $5,000 payment in year 21? What if, in the alternative, she lives less than 20 years? Prior to 1987, a taxpayer merely was subject to the luck of the draw and the rules were like the life insurance rules, allowing the exclusion to continue even though the taxpayer lived beyond her life expectancy, denying a deduction if she died prior to her life expectancy.[21] But in the 1986 Act Congress added two special rules to Section 72(b). If an annuitant lives beyond her life expectancy and fully recovers her investment in the contract, the *full* amount of any subsequent annuity payment is included in her gross income.[22] In the

---

15. See Vernava, supra note 13, at 10.

16. I.R.C. § 72(c)(1) defines this term as cost less recoveries of such cost under the pre-1954 code.

17. I.R.C. § 72(c)(3).

18. I.R.C. § 72(a).

19. See Reg. § 1.72–9 Table V.

20. These tables (V–VIII) are applicable to post-June 1986 investment in the contract and are not based on the sex of the taxpayer. The Supreme Court has held that retirement benefits based on the recipient's sex violate Title VII. Arizona Governing Committee, Etc. v. Norris, 463 U.S. 1073, 103 S.Ct. 3492 (1983). The Service has also issued unisex tables under

Reg. §§ 20.2031–7 and 25.2512–5 for valuing income interests and remainders. Rev. Rul. 84–162, 1984–2 C.B. 200, makes those valuations applicable to I.R.C. § 72. Reg. § 1.72–9 Tables I–IV are based on the sex of the taxpayer and are applicable to pre-July 1986 investment in the contract. See Reg. § 1.72–6(d)(3).

21. See note 6, supra. Recall that life benefits under a life insurance policy are subject to tax under I.R.C. § 72, rather than § 101, because they are not received by reason of the death of the insured. But when § 101 applies, § 72 is inapplicable. Reg. § 1.72–2(b)(1).

22. I.R.C. § 72(b)(2) and (4).

alternative, if she dies without fully recovering her investment, i.e., with an unrecovered investment in the contract, the amount of the unrecovered investment is allowed as a deduction on her last income tax return.[23]

One must question the policy of the 1986 Act change. If one lives beyond his life expectancy and is accustomed to receiving an annuity only *part* of which is taxed, is it appropriate when the annuitant has reached an elderly age to begin then to tax the *full* amount of the annuity payment? Admittedly, an income tax deduction on one's final return is beneficial; but to whom? Certainly not the annuitant. On the law of averages the Treasury should reap the same amount of revenue under either approach, but isn't the prior law fairer and more appropriate?

Annuities are not all as simple as those above. For example, if Abouto purchased again for $60,000 a self and survivor annuity that paid $5000 per year until the survivor of Abouto and her spouse died and we assume this creates a payment expectancy of 30 years,[24] then each $5000 payment would include $3000 of taxable income, after excluding 60,000/150,000 of each $5000 payment.[25] Some annuities contain what are known as "refund features." One example of a refund occurs if any annuity is paid to an annuitant for her life, but if the annuity payments made prior to the annuitant's death do not equal the premiums paid for the contract, the excess is refunded.[26] In such a situation Section 72(c)(2) requires that the value of the potential refund (based on the annuitant's life expectancy) be subtracted from the "investment in the contract," which has of course the intended effect of increasing the income portion of each annuity payment.[27] The legislative history indicates that, as the refund itself is exempt from tax,[28] the purpose of Section 72(c)(2) is to avoid a double exclusion from tax.[29]

That is not to imply that all refunds are exempt from tax. Refunds may be totally or partially included in income under Section 72(e). For example, Les Abouto Retire at age 55 pays $60,000 for an annuity

---

23. I.R.C. § 72(b)(3).

24. See Reg. § 1.72–9 Tables II and VI. See note 20, supra.

25. Another alternative here is an annuity in which the survivorship annuity payments are only one-half the regular payments ($2500). If such an assumption were cranked into our text hypothetical, obviously the "investment in the contract" and the "expected return" would be less. However, whatever exclusion ratio is established by those factors remains constant over the life of the contract, whether the full or reduced payments are being received.

26. Reg. § 1.72–7(a).

27. See Reg. § 1.72–7(b). A taxpayer, age 57 with a 20 year life expectancy might be entitled to receive $5000 per year under a single life annuity but, if he died prior to recovering the $60,000 premium paid, his estate would receive a payment equal to the excess of the premium over prior annuity payments received. As computed under Reg. §§ 1.72–7(b) and 1.72–9 Table VII, the refund feature would amount to $2400. The "investment in the contract" would be reduced to $57,600 and his exclusion ratio would be $57,600/100,000. He would include 42.4% of each $5000 payment in income or $2120 (as compared with $2000 above). See note 20, supra.

28. It would be excluded from gross income under I.R.C. § 72(e) or as an insurance payment under § 101(a).

29. S.Rep. No. 1622, 83rd Cong., 2d Sess. 11 (1954).

which is to begin payment of $6000 per year to him at age 65 but, after a time, he may cancel the contract prior to age 65 and receive back amounts in excess of $60,000, more the longer he waits. Les has purchased a single premium deferred life annuity with a refund feature and if he cancels at age 62 receiving $66,000 he has $6,000 of gross income.[30] There are numerous other possible types of refunds.[31]

If a beneficiary who has a right to a lump sum refund not fully tax exempt, instead exercises an option to receive a second annuity in lieu of such refund and does so within 60 days of the lump sum refund becoming payable, then no part of the lump sum refund is included in income.[32] The annuity payments are then included in income to the extent they constitute Section 72 income.

Now, after a careful examination of the statute, test your grasp of the basic working of these principles by way of the problems below.

PROBLEMS

1. Insured died in the current year owning a policy of insurance that would pay Beneficiary $100,000 but under which several alternatives were available to Beneficiary.

    (a) What result if Beneficiary simply accepts the $100,000 in cash? *≠ income*

    (b) What result in (a), above, if Beneficiary instead leaves all the proceeds with the company and they pay him $10,000 interest *10,000 = income* in the current year? *set up annuity*

    (c) What result if Insured's Daughter is Beneficiary of the policy and, in accordance with an option that she elects, the company pays her $12,000 in the current year? Assume that such *4,000 non tax* payments will be made annually for her life and that she has a *8,000 taxed* 25 year life expectancy. *25 (12,000) = 300,000*

100,000
300,000
⅓(12,000)= 4000 exclude

    (d) What result in (c), above, if Insured's Daughter lives beyond her 25 year life expectancy and receives $12,000 in the twenty-sixth year? *12,000 fully taxed.*

2. Jock agreed to play football for Pro Corporation. Pro, fearful that Jock might not survive, acquired a $1 million insurance policy on Jock's life. If Jock dies during the term of the policy and the proceeds of the policy are paid to Pro, what different consequences will Pro incur under the following alternatives?

    (a) With Jock's consent Pro took out and paid $20,000 for a two year term policy on Jock's life.

    (b) Jock owned a paid-up two year term $1 million policy on his life which he sold to Pro for $20,000, Pro being named beneficiary of the policy.

    (c) Same as (b), above, except that Jock was a shareholder of Pro Corporation.

30. I.R.C. § 72(e).   32. I.R.C. § 72(h).
31. See Reg. § 1.72–11(c)(2).

3.   Wife purchases a single premium $100,000 life insurance policy on her life for $40,000. When its value increases to $45,000, she sells it to Husband for $45,000 cash. Wife dies several years later, and Husband collects the $100,000 of proceeds. Does Husband have gross income?

4.   In the current year, T purchases a single life annuity with no refund feature for $48,000. Under the contract T is to receive $3000 per year for life. T has a 24 year life expectancy.

(a) To what extent, if at all, is T taxable on the $3000 received in the first year?

(b) If the law remains the same and T is still alive, how will T be taxed on the $3000 received in the thirtieth year of the annuity payments?

(c) If T dies within ten years will T or T's estate be allowed an income tax deduction?

(d) To what extent are T and T's spouse taxable on the $3000 received in the current year if at a cost of $76,500 they purchase a joint and survivorship annuity to pay $3000 per year as long as either lives and they have a joint life expectancy of 34 years?

CHAPTER 8. DISCHARGE OF INDEBTEDNESS

Internal Revenue Code: Sections 61(a)(12); 102(a); 108(a), (b)(1)–(3), (d)(1)–(5), (e) (1), (5) and (6); 1017(a), (b)(1), (2), (3)(A) and (B). See Sections 108(f) and (g); 385.

Regulations: Section 1.61–12(a). See Section 1.1017–1(a).

U. S. v. KIRBY LUMBER CO.*
Supreme Court of the United States, 1931.
284 U.S. 1, 52 S.Ct. 4.

Mr. Justice HOLMES delivered the opinion of the Court.

In July, 1923, the plaintiff, the Kirby Lumber Company, issued its own bonds for $12,126,800 for which it received their par value. Later in the same year it purchased in the open market some of the same bonds at less than par, the difference of price being $137,521.30. The question is whether this difference is a taxable gain or income of the plaintiff for the year 1923. By the Revenue Act of (November 23,) 1921, c. 136, § 213(a) gross income includes "gains or profits and income derived from any source whatever," and by the Treasury Regulations authorized by § 1303, that have been in force through repeated reenactments, "If the corporation purchases and retires any of such bonds at a price less than the issuing price or face value, the excess of the issuing price or face value over the purchase price is gain or income for the taxable year." Article 545(1)(c) of Regulations 62, under Revenue Act of 1921. See Article 544(1)(c) of Regulations 45, under Revenue Act of 1918; Article 545(1)(c) of Regulations 65, under Revenue Act of 1924; Article 545(1)(c) of Regulations 69, under Revenue Act of 1926; Article 68(1)(c) of Regulations 74, under Revenue Act of 1928. We see no reason why the Regulations should not be accepted as a correct statement of the law.

In Bowers v. Kerbaugh-Empire Co., 271 U.S. 170, 46 S.Ct. 449, the defendant in error owned the stock of another company that had borrowed money repayable in marks or their equivalent for an enterprise that failed. At the time of payment the marks had fallen in value, which so far as it went was a gain for the defendant in error, and it was contended by the plaintiff in error that the gain was taxable income. But the transaction as a whole was a loss, and the contention was denied. Here there was no shrinkage of assets and the taxpayer made a clear gain. As a result of its dealings it made available $137,521.30 assets previously offset by the obligation of bonds now extinct. We see nothing to be gained by the discussion of judicial definitions. The defendant in error has realized within the year an

---

* See Bittker and Thompson, "Income From the Discharge of Indebtedness: The Progeny of United States v. Kirby Lumber Co.," 66 Calif.L.Rev. 1159 (1978).

accession to income, if we take words in their plain popular meaning, as they should be taken here. Burnet v. Sanford & Brooks Co., 282 U.S. 359, 364, 51 S.Ct. 150.

Judgment reversed.

ZARIN v. COMMISSIONER*

United States Court of Appeals, Third Circuit, 1990.**
916 F.2d 110.

COWEN, Circuit Judge: David Zarin ("Zarin") appeals from a decision of the Tax Court holding that he recognized $2,935,000 of income from discharge of indebtedness resulting from his gambling activities, and that he should be taxed on the income. This Court has jurisdiction to review the Tax Court's decision under section 7482 of the Internal Revenue Code (1954) (the "Code"). After considering the issues raised by this appeal, we will reverse.

I.

Zarin was a professional engineer who participated in the development, construction, and management of various housing projects. A resident of Atlantic City, New Jersey, Zarin occasionally gambled, both in his hometown and in other places where gambling was legalized. To facilitate his gaming activities in Atlantic City, Zarin applied to Resorts International Hotel ("Resorts") for a credit line in June, 1978. Following a credit check, Resorts granted Zarin $10,000 of credit. Pursuant to this credit arrangement with Resorts, Zarin could write a check, called a marker,[2] and in return receive chips, which could then be used to gamble at the casino's tables.

Before long, Zarin developed a reputation as an extravagant "high roller" who routinely bet the house maximum while playing craps, his game of choice. Considered a "valued gaming patron" by Resorts, Zarin had his credit limit increased at regular intervals without any further credit checks, and was provided a number of complimentary services and privileges. By November, 1979, Zarin's permanent line of credit had been raised to $200,000. Between June, 1978, and December, 1979, Zarin lost $2,500,000 at the craps table, losses he paid in full.

Responding to allegations of credit abuses, the New Jersey Division of Gaming Enforcement filed with the New Jersey Casino Control Commission a complaint against Resorts. Among the 809 violations of casino regulations alleged in the complaint of October, 1979, were 100 pertaining to Zarin. Subsequently, a Casino Control Commissioner issued an Emergency Order, the effect of which was to make further extensions of credit to Zarin illegal.

---

* See Shaviro, "The Man Who Lost Too Much: *Zarin v. Commissioner* and the Measurement of Taxable Consumption," 45 Tax.L.Rev. 215 (1990).

2. A "marker" is a negotiable draft payable to Resorts and drawn on the marker's bank.

** Some footnotes omitted.

Nevertheless, Resorts continued to extend Zarin's credit limit through the use of two different practices: "considered cleared" credit and "this trip only" credit.[3] Both methods effectively ignored the Emergency Order and were later found to be illegal.

By January, 1980, Zarin was gambling compulsively and uncontrollably at Resorts, spending as many as sixteen hours a day at the craps table.[5] During April, 1980, Resorts again increased Zarin's credit line without further inquiries. That same month, Zarin delivered personal checks and counterchecks to Resorts which were returned as having been drawn against insufficient funds. Those dishonored checks totaled $3,435,000. In late April, Resorts cut off Zarin's credit.

Although Zarin indicated that he would repay those obligations, Resorts filed a New Jersey state court action against Zarin in November, 1980, to collect the $3,435,000. Zarin denied liability on grounds that Resort's claim was unenforceable under New Jersey regulations intended to protect compulsive gamblers. Ten months later, in September, 1981, Resorts and Zarin settled their dispute for a total of $500,000.

The Commissioner of Internal Revenue ("Commissioner") subsequently determined deficiencies in Zarin's federal income taxes for 1980 and 1981, arguing that Zarin recognized $3,435,000 of income in 1980 from larceny by trick and deception. After Zarin challenged that claim by filing a Tax Court petition, the Commissioner abandoned his 1980 claim, and argued instead that Zarin had recognized $2,935,000 of income in 1981 from the cancellation of indebtedness which resulted from the settlement with Resorts.

Agreeing with the Commissioner, the Tax Court decided, eleven judges to eight, that Zarin had indeed recognized $2,935,000 of income from the discharge of indebtedness, namely the difference between the original $3,435,000 "debt" and the $500,000 settlement. Zarin v. Commissioner, 92 T.C. 1084 (1989). Since he was in the seventy percent tax bracket, Zarin's deficiency for 1981 was calculated to be $2,047,245. With interest to April 5, 1990, Zarin allegedly owes the Internal Revenue Service $5,209,033.96 in additional taxes. Zarin appeals the order of the Tax Court.

II.

The sole issue before this Court is whether the Tax Court correctly held that Zarin had income from discharge of indebtedness. Section 108 and section 61(a)(12) of the Code set forth "the general rule that gross income includes income from the discharge of indebtedness."

---

3. Under the "considered cleared" method, Resorts would treat a personal check as a cash transaction, and would therefore not apply the amount of the check in calculating the amount of credit extended Zarin. "This trip only" credit allowed Resorts to grant temporary increases of credit for a given visit, so long as the credit limit was lowered by the next visit.

5. Zarin claims that at the time he was suffering from a recognized emotional disorder that caused him to gamble compulsively.

I.R.C. § 108(e)(1). The Commissioner argues, and the Tax Court agreed, that pursuant to the Code, Zarin did indeed recognize income from discharge of gambling indebtedness.

Under the Commissioner's logic, Resorts advanced Zarin $3,435,000 worth of chips, chips being the functional equivalent of cash. At that time, the chips were not treated as income, since Zarin recognized an obligation of repayment. In other words, Resorts made Zarin a tax-free loan. However, a taxpayer does recognize income if a loan owed to another party is cancelled, in whole or in part. I.R.C. §§ 61(a)(12), 108(e). The settlement between Zarin and Resorts, claims the Commissioner, fits neatly into the cancellation of indebtedness provisions in the Code. Zarin owed $3,435,000, paid $500,000, with the difference constituting income. Although initially persuasive, the Commissioner's position is nonetheless flawed for two reasons.

III.

Initially, we find that sections 108 and 61(a)(12) are inapplicable to the Zarin/Resorts transaction. Section 61 does not define indebtedness. On the other hand, section 108(d)(1), which repeats and further elaborates on the rule in section 61(a)(12), defines the term as any indebtedness "(A) for which the taxpayer is liable, or (B) subject to which the taxpayer holds property." I.R.C. § 108(d)(1). In order to come within the sweep of the discharge of indebtedness rules, then, the taxpayer must satisfy one of the two prongs in the section 108(d)(1) test. Zarin satisfies neither.

Because the debt Zarin owed to Resorts was unenforceable as a matter of New Jersey state law,[7] it is clearly not a debt "for which the taxpayer is liable." I.R.C. § 108(d)(1)(A). Liability implies a legally enforceable obligation to repay, and under New Jersey law, Zarin would have no such obligation.

---

7. The Tax Court held that the Commissioner had not met its burden of proving that the debt owed Resorts was enforceable as a matter of state law. *Zarin*, 92 T.C. at 1090. There was ample evidence to support that finding. In New Jersey, the extension of credit by casinos "to enable [any] person to take part in gaming activity as a player" is limited. N.J.Stat.Ann. § 5:12–101(b) (1988). Under N.J.Stat.Ann. § 5:12–101(f), any credit violation is "invalid and unenforceable for the purposes of collection . . . ." In Resorts Int'l Hotel, Inc. v. Salomone, 178 N.J.Super. 598, 429 A.2d 1078 (App.Div.1981), the court held that "casinos must comply with the Legislature's strict control of credit for gambling purposes. Unless they do, the debts reflected by players' checks will not be enforced . . . ." Id. at 607, 429 A.2d at 1082.

With regards to the extension of credit to Zarin after the Emergency Order of October, 1979, was issued, Resorts did not comply with New Jersey regulations. The Casino Control Commission specifically stated in 1983 "that Resorts was guilty of infractions, violations, improprieties, with the net effect that [Zarin] was encouraged to continue gambling long after, one, his credit line was reached, and exceeded; two, long after it became apparent that the gambler was an addicted gambler; three, long after the gambler had difficulty in paying his debts; and four, Resorts knew the individual was gambling when he should not have been gambling." Appendix at 325–326. It follows, therefore, that under New Jersey law, the $3,435,000 debt Zarin owed Resorts was totally unenforceable.

Moreover, Zarin did not have a debt subject to which he held property as required by section 108(d)(1)(B). Zarin's indebtedness arose out of his acquisition of gambling chips. The Tax Court held that gambling chips were not property, but rather, "a medium of exchange within the Resorts casino" and a "substitute for cash." Alternatively, the Tax Court viewed the chips as nothing more than "the opportunity to gamble and incidental services . . ." *Zarin*, 92 T.C. at 1099. We agree with the gist of these characterizations, and hold that gambling chips are merely an accounting mechanism to evidence debt.

Gaming chips in New Jersey during 1980 were regarded "solely as evidence of a debt owed to their custodian by the casino licensee and shall be considered at no time the property of anyone other than the casino licensee issuing them." N.J.Admin.Code tit. 19k, § 19:46–1.5(d) (1990). Thus, under New Jersey state law, gambling chips were Resorts' property until transferred to Zarin in exchange for the markers, at which point the chips became "evidence" of indebtedness (and not the property of Zarin).

Even were there no relevant legislative pronouncement on which to rely, simple common sense would lead to the conclusion that chips were not property in Zarin's hands. Zarin could not do with the chips as he pleased, nor did the chips have any independent economic value beyond the casino. The chips themselves were of little use to Zarin, other than as a means of facilitating gambling. They could not have been used outside the casino. They could have been used to purchase services and privileges within the casino, including food, drink, entertainment, and lodging, but Zarin would not have utilized them as such, since he received those services from Resorts on a complimentary basis. In short, the chips had no economic substance.

Although the Tax Court found that theoretically, Zarin could have redeemed the chips he received on credit for cash and walked out of the casino, *Zarin*, 92 T.C. at 1092, the reality of the situation was quite different. Realistically, before cashing in his chips, Zarin would have been required to pay his outstanding IOUs. New Jersey state law requires casinos to "request patrons to apply any chips or plaques in their possession in reduction of personal checks or Counter Checks exchanged for purposes of gaming prior to exchanging such chips or plaques for cash or prior to departing from the casino area." N.J. Admin.Code tit. 19k, § 19:45–1.24(s) (1979) (currently N.J.Admin.Code tit. 19k, § 19:45–1.25(o) (1990) (as amended)). Since his debt at all times equalled or exceeded the number of chips he possessed, redemption would have left Zarin with no chips, no cash, and certainly nothing which could have been characterized as property.

Not only were the chips non-property in Zarin's hands, but upon transfer to Zarin, the chips also ceased to be the property of Resorts. Since the chips were in the possession of another party, Resorts could no longer do with the chips as it pleased, and could no longer control the chips' use. Generally, at the time of a transfer, the party in possession of the chips can gamble with them, use them for services, cash them in, or walk out of the casino with them as an Atlantic City souvenir. The chips therefore become nothing more than an accounting mechanism, or evidence of a debt, designed to facilitate gambling in casinos where the use of actual money was forbidden.[8] Thus, the chips which Zarin held were not property within the meaning of I.R.C. § 108(d)(1)(B).[9]

In short, because Zarin was not liable on the debt he allegedly owed Resorts, and because Zarin did not hold "property" subject to that debt, the cancellation of indebtedness provisions of the Code do not apply to the settlement between Resorts and Zarin. As such, Zarin cannot have income from the discharge of his debt.

IV.

Instead of analyzing the transaction at issue as cancelled debt, we believe the proper approach is to view it as disputed debt or contested liability. Under the contested liability doctrine, if a taxpayer, in good faith, disputed the amount of a debt, a subsequent settlement of the dispute would be treated as the amount of debt cognizable for tax purposes. The excess of the original debt over the amount determined to have been due is disregarded for both loss and debt and accounting purposes. Thus, if a taxpayer took out a loan for $10,000, refused in good faith to pay the full $10,000 back, and then reached an agreement with the lendor that he would pay back only $7,000 in full satisfaction of the debt, the transaction would be treated as if the initial loan was $7,000. When the taxpayer tenders the $7,000 payment, he will have been deemed to have paid the full amount of the initially disputed debt. Accordingly, there is no tax consequence to the taxpayer upon payment.

The seminal "contested liability" case is N. Sobel, Inc. v. Commissioner, 40 B.T.A. 1263 (1939). In *Sobel*, the taxpayer exchanged a $21,700 note for 100 shares of stock from a bank. In the following year, the taxpayer sued the bank for recision, arguing that the bank loan was violative of state law, and moreover, that the bank had failed to perform certain promises. The parties eventually settled the case in

---

8. Although, as noted above, Zarin would not have been able to leave the casino with cash or chips, and probably would not have used the chips for services, these facts do not change the character of the chips. Despite the aforementioned limitations upon Zarin's use of the chips, they remain an accounting mechanism or evidence of a debt. Resorts' increased interest in Zarin's chips does not rise to the level of a property interest, since Zarin still has dominion over the chips within the casino.

9. The parties stipulated before the Tax Court that New Jersey casino "chips are property which are not negotiable and may not be used to gamble or for any other purpose outside the casino where they were issued." It could be argued that we are bound by this stipulation to accept the proposition that chips are property. We do not dispute the notion that chips are property, but as discussed above, they are only property in the hands of the casino. The stipulation is consistent with this idea. In fact, both parties agreed in their briefs that chips are property of the casino. Moreover, during oral arguments, both parties agreed that chips were not property when held by the gambler.

1935, with the taxpayer agreeing to pay half of the face amount of the note. In the year of the settlement, the taxpayer claimed the amount paid as a loss. The Commissioner denied the loss because it had been sustained five years earlier, and further asserted that the taxpayer recognized income from the discharge of half of his indebtedness.

The Board of Tax Appeals held that since the loss was not fixed until the dispute was settled, the loss was recognized in 1935, the year of the settlement, and the deduction was appropriately taken in that year. Additionally, the Board held that the portion of the note forgiven by the bank "was not the occasion for a freeing of assets and that there was no gain . . ." Id. at 1265. Therefore, the taxpayer did not have any income from cancellation of indebtedness.

There is little difference between the present case and *Sobel.* Zarin incurred a $3,435,000 debt while gambling at Resorts, but in court, disputed liability on the basis of unenforceability. A settlement of $500,000 was eventually agreed upon. It follows from *Sobel* that the settlement served only to fix the amount of debt. No income was realized or recognized. When Zarin paid the $500,000, any tax consequence dissolved.[10]

Only one other court has addressed a case factually similar to the one before us. In United States v. Hall, 307 F.2d 238 (10th Cir.1962), the taxpayer owed an unenforceable gambling debt alleged to be $225,000. Subsequently, the taxpayer and the creditor settled for $150,000. The taxpayer then transferred cattle valued at $148,110 to his creditor in satisfaction of the settlement agreement. A jury held that the parties fixed the debt at $150,000, and that the taxpayer recognized income from cancellation of indebtedness equal to the difference between the $150,000 and the $148,110 value affixed to the cattle. Arguing that the taxpayer recognized income equal to the difference between $225,000 and $148,000, the Commissioner appealed.

The Tenth Circuit rejected the idea that the taxpayer had any income from cancellation of indebtedness. Noting that the gambling debt was unenforceable, the Tenth Circuit said, "The cold fact is that taxpayer suffered a substantial loss from gambling, the amount of which was determined by the transfer." Id. at 241. In effect, the Court held that because the debt was unenforceable, the amount of the loss and resulting debt cognizable for tax purposes were fixed by the settlement at $148,110. Thus, the Tenth Circuit lent its endorsement to the contested liability doctrine in a factual situation strikingly similar to the one at issue.[11]

---

10. Had Zarin not paid the $500,000 dollar settlement, it would be likely that he would have had income from cancellation of indebtedness. The debt at that point would have been fixed, and Zarin would have been legally obligated to pay it.

11. The Commissioner argues that the decision in *Hall* was based on United States Supreme Court precedent since overruled, and therefore *Hall* should be disregarded. Indeed, the *Hall* court devoted a considerable amount of time to Bowers v. Kerbaugh–Empire Co., 271 U.S. 170, 46 S.Ct. 449 (1926), a case whose validity is in question. We do not pass on the question of whether or not *Bowers* is good law. We do note that *Hall* relied on *Bowers* only for the proposition that " 'a court need not

The Commissioner argues that *Sobel* and the contested liability doctrine only apply when there is an unliquidated debt; that is, a debt for which the amount cannot be determined. See Colonial Sav. Ass'n v. Commissioner, 85 T.C. 855, 862–863 (1985) (*Sobel* stands for the proposition that "there must be a liquidated debt"), aff'd, 854 F.2d 1001 (7th Cir.1988). See also N. Sobel, Inc. v. Commissioner, 40 B.T.A. at 1265 (there was a dispute as to "liability and the amount" of the debt). Since Zarin contested his liability based on the unenforceability of the entire debt, and did not dispute the amount of the debt, the Commissioner would have us adopt the reasoning of the Tax Court, which found that Zarin's debt was liquidated, therefore barring the application of *Sobel* and the contested liability doctrine. *Zarin*, 92 T.C. at 1095 (Zarin's debt "was a liquidated amount" and "[t]here is no dispute about the amount [received].").

We reject the Tax Court's rationale. When a debt is unenforceable, it follows that the amount of the debt, and not just the liability thereon, is in dispute. Although a debt may be unenforceable, there still could be some value attached to its worth. This is especially so with regards to gambling debts. In most states, gambling debts are unenforceable, and have "but slight potential . . ." United States v. Hall, 307 F.2d 238, 241 (10th Cir.1962). Nevertheless, they are often collected, at least in part. For example, Resorts is not a charity; it would not have extended illegal credit to Zarin and others if it did not have some hope of collecting debts incurred pursuant to the grant of credit.

Moreover, the debt is frequently incurred to acquire gambling chips, and not money. Although casinos attach a dollar value to each chip, that value, unlike money's, is not beyond dispute, particularly given the illegality of gambling debts in the first place. This proposition is supported by the facts of the present case. Resorts gave Zarin $3.4 million dollars of chips in exchange for markers evidencing Zarin's debt. If indeed the only issue was the enforceability of the entire debt, there would have been no settlement. Zarin would have owed all or nothing. Instead, the parties attached a value to the debt considerably lower than its face value. In other words, the parties agreed that given the circumstances surrounding Zarin's gambling spree, the chips he acquired might not have been worth $3.4 million dollars, but were worth something. Such a debt cannot be called liquidated, since its exact amount was not fixed until settlement.

To summarize, the transaction between Zarin and Resorts can best be characterized as a disputed debt, or contested liability. Zarin owed an unenforceable debt of $3,435,000 to Resorts. After Zarin in good

in every case be oblivious to the net effect of the entire transaction.' " United States v. Hall, 307 F.2d at 242, quoting Bradford v. Commissioner, 233 F.2d 935, 939 (6th Cir.1956). *Hall*'s reliance on *Bowers* did not extend to the issue of contested liability, and even if it did, the idea that "Courts need not apply mechanical standards which smother the reality of a particular transaction," Id. at 241, is hardly an exceptional concept in the tax realm. See Commissioner v. Tufts, 461 U.S. 300, 103 S.Ct. 1826 (1983); Hillsboro Nat'l Bank v. Commissioner, 460 U.S. 370, 103 S.Ct. 1134 (1983).

faith disputed his obligation to repay the debt, the parties settled for $500,000, which Zarin paid. That $500,000 settlement fixed the amount of loss and the amount of debt cognizable for tax purposes. Since Zarin was deemed to have owed $500,000, and since he paid Resorts $500,000, no adverse tax consequences attached to Zarin as a result.[12]

V.

In conclusion, we hold that Zarin did not have any income from cancellation of indebtedness for two reasons. First, the Code provisions covering discharge of debt are inapplicable since the definitional requirement in I.R.C. section 108(d)(1) was not met. Second, the settlement of Zarin's gambling debts was a contested liability. We reverse the decision of the Tax Court and remand with instructions to enter judgment that Zarin realized no income by reason of his settlement with Resorts.

Dissenting Opinion

STAPLETON, Circuit Judge, dissenting: I respectfully dissent because I agree with the Commissioner's appraisal of the economic realities of this matter.

Resorts sells for cash the exhilaration and the potential for profit inherent in games of chance. It does so by selling for cash chips that entitle the holder to gamble at its casino. Zarin, like thousands of others, wished to purchase what Resorts was offering in the marketplace. He chose to make this purchase on credit and executed notes evidencing his obligation to repay the funds that were advanced to him by Resorts. As in most purchase money transactions, Resorts skipped the step of giving Zarin cash that he would only return to it in order to pay for the opportunity to gamble. Resorts provided him instead with chips that entitled him to participate in Resorts' games of chance on the same basis as others who had paid cash for that privilege.[1] Whether viewed as a one or two-step transaction, however, Zarin received either $3.4 million in cash or an entitlement for which others would have had to pay $3.4 million.

Despite the fact that Zarin received in 1980 cash or an entitlement worth $3.4 million, he correctly reported in that year no income from

12. The Commissioner argues in the alternative that Zarin recognized $3,435,000 of income in 1980. This claim has no merit. Recognition of income would depend upon a finding that Zarin did not have cancellation of indebtedness income solely because his debt was unenforceable. We do not so hold. Although unenforceability is a factor in our analysis, our decision ultimately hinges upon the determination that the "disputed debt" rule applied, or alternatively, that chips are not property within the meaning of I.R.C. section 108.

1. I view as irrelevant the facts that Resorts advanced credit to Zarin solely to enable him to patronize its casino and that the chips could not be used elsewhere or for other purposes. When one buys a sofa from the furniture store on credit, the fact that the proprietor would not have advanced the credit for a different purpose does not entitle one to a tax-free gain in the event the debt to the store is extinguished for some reason.

his dealings with Resorts. He did so *solely* because he recognized, as evidenced by his notes, an offsetting obligation to repay Resorts $3.4 million in cash. See, e.g., Vukasovich, Inc. v. Commissioner, 790 F.2d 1409 (9th Cir.1986); United States v. Rochelle, 384 F.2d 748 (5th Cir. 1967), cert. denied, 390 U.S. 946 (1968); Bittker and Thompson, Income From the Discharged Indebtedness: The Progeny of United States v. Kirby Lumber Co., 66 Calif.L.Rev. 159 (1978). In 1981, with the delivery of Zarin's promise to pay Resorts $500,000 and the execution of a release by Resorts, Resorts surrendered its claim to repayment of the remaining $2.9 million of the money Zarin had borrowed. As of that time, Zarin's assets were freed of his potential liability for that amount and he recognized gross income in that amount. Commissioner v. Tufts, 461 U.S. 300 (1983); United States v. Kirby Lumber Company, 284 U.S. 1 (1931); Vukasovich, Inc. v. Commissioner, 790 F.2d 1409 (9th Cir.1986). But see United States v. Hall, 307 F.2d 238 (10th Cir.1962).[2]

The only alternatives I see to this conclusion are to hold either (1) that Zarin realized $3.4 million in income in 1980 at a time when both parties to the transaction thought there was an offsetting obligation to repay or (2) that the $3.4 million benefit sought and received by Zarin is not taxable at all. I find the latter alternative unacceptable as inconsistent with the fundamental principle of the Code that anything of commercial value received by a taxpayer is taxable unless expressly excluded from gross income.[3] Commissioner v. Glenshaw Glass Co., 348 U.S. 426 (1955); *United States v. Kirby Lumber Co.,* supra. I find the former alternative unacceptable as impracticable. In 1980, neither party was maintaining that the debt was unenforceable and, because of the settlement, its unenforceability was not even established in the litigation over the debt in 1981. It was not until 1989 in this litigation over the tax consequences of the transaction that the unenforceability was first judicially declared. Rather than require such tax litigation to resolve the correct treatment of a debt transaction, I regard it as far preferable to have the tax consequences turn on the manner in which the debt is treated by the parties. For present purposes, it will suffice

2. This is not a case in which parties agree subsequent to a purchase money transaction that the property purchased has a value less than thought at the time of the transaction. In such cases, the purchase price adjustment rule is applied and the agreed-upon value is accepted as the value of the benefit received by the purchaser; see e.g., Commissioner v. Sherman, 135 F.2d 68 (6th Cir.1943); Commissioner v. N. Sobel, Inc., 40 B.T.A. 1263 (1939). Nor is this a case in which the taxpayer is entitled to rescind an entire purchase money transaction, thereby to restore itself to the position it occupied before receiving anything of commercial value. In this case, the illegality was in the extension of credit by Resorts and whether one views the benefit received by Zarin as cash or the

opportunity to gamble, he is no longer in a position to return that benefit.

3. As the court's opinion correctly points out, this record will not support an exclusion under § 108(a) which relates to discharge of debt in an insolvency or bankruptcy context. Section 108(e)(5) of the Code, which excludes discharged indebtedness arising from a "purchase price adjustment" is not applicable here. Among other things, § 108(e)(5) necessarily applies only to a situation in which the debtor still holds the property acquired in the purchase money transaction. Equally irrelevant is § 108(d)'s definition of "indebtedness" relied upon heavily by the court. Section 108(d) expressly defines that term solely for the purposes of § 108 and not for the purposes of § 61(a)(12).

to say that where something that would otherwise be includable in gross income is received on credit in a purchase money transaction, there should be no recognition of income so long as the debtor continues to recognize an obligation to repay the debt. On the other hand, income, if not earlier recognized, should be recognized when the debtor no longer recognizes an obligation to repay and the creditor has released the debt or acknowledged its unenforceability.

In this view, it makes no difference whether the extinguishment of the creditor's claim comes as a part of a compromise. Resorts settled for 14 cents on the dollar presumably because it viewed such a settlement as reflective of the odds that the debt would be held to be enforceable. While Zarin should be given credit for the fact that he had to pay 14 cents for a release, I see no reason why he should not realize gain in the same manner as he would have if Resorts had concluded on its own that the debt was legally unenforceable and had written it off as uncollectible.[5]

I would affirm the judgment of the Tax Court.

KIRBY LUMBER EXCEPTIONS

If Holmes, J., can be characteristically succinct, perhaps so can we. We seek to emulate him with some *brief* comments on the *Kirby* area.

The *Kirby Lumber* case accords some meaning to the cryptic language of Section 61(a)(12), requiring that income from the discharge of indebtedness be included within gross income. The simplest view of *Kirby* is that it reflects the corollary of the 34th Street lullabye, "buy low-sell high;" with respect to one's obligations, if he sells high and then buys back low, he can profit equally. The receipt of money in the form of a loan has, by itself, no income tax consequences. To be sure, the taxpayer derives an economic benefit from the funds obtained through a loan; however, the obligation to repay, whether in the form of a note, account payable or a simple "I.O.U.", offsets the receipt of the loan proceeds, effecting a "wash" for tax purposes. No income is realized. But if a taxpayer pays off a debt for less than the amount owing, the difference constitutes income to him, because he realizes an economic benefit by way of an increase in his net worth much as if he had sold property at a profit. The taxable event is the freeing of assets that previously were held subject to the obligation. However, the *Kirby Lumber* doctrine is subject to exceptions most of which were judicially developed.[1] Many of the exceptions were codified upon enactment of

---

5. A different situation exists where there is a bona fide dispute over the amount of a debt and the dispute is compromised. Rather than require tax litigation to determine the amount of income received, the Commission treats the compromise figure as representing the amount of the obligation. I find this sensible and consistent with the pragmatic approach I would take.

1. See Eustice, "Cancellation of Indebtedness and the Federal Income Tax: A Problem of Creeping Confusion," 14 Tax L.Rev. 225 (1959) and Stone, "Cancellation of Indebtedness," 34 N.Y.U.Inst. on Fed. Tax. 555 (1976).

[handwritten:] Taxable Event = freeing of assets that previously were held subject to the obligation.

the Bankruptcy Tax Act of 1980.[2]   A portion of the Senate Finance Committee Report [3] explaining the background of the judicial exceptions and a part of the codification appears below.   Much of the legislation is too detailed for consideration here.   Nevertheless the assigned portion of the statutes (Sections 108 and 1017), a glimpse into the Congressional mind through the window of a Committee Report, and problems two and three (which follow the Report) should provide a feel for the fundamental aspects of the *Kirby Lumber* exceptions.

SENATE FINANCE COMMITTEE REPORT

A.   Tax Treatment of Discharge of Indebtedness

Present Law

In General.—Under present law, income is realized when indebtedness is forgiven or in other ways cancelled (sec. 61(a) (12) of the Internal Revenue Code).   For example, if a corporation has issued a $1,000 bond at par which it later repurchases for only $900, thereby increasing its net worth by $100, the corporation realizes $100 of income in the year of repurchase (United States v. Kirby Lumber Co., 284 U.S. 1 (1931)).

There are several exceptions to the general rule of income realization.   Under a judicially developed "insolvency exception," no income arises from discharge of indebtedness if the debtor is insolvent both before and after the transaction; [1] and if the transaction leaves the debtor with assets whose value exceeds remaining liabilities, income is realized only to the extent of the excess.[2]   Treasury regulations provide that the gratuitous cancellation of a corporation's indebtedness by a shareholder-creditor does not give rise to debt discharge income to the extent of the principal of the debt, since the cancellation amounts to a contribution to capital of the corporation.[3]

* * *

A debt cancellation which constitutes a gift or bequest is not treated as income to the donee debtor (Code sec. 102).[6]

* * *

2.   P.L. No. 96–589, 96th Cong., 2d Sess. (1980).   A statutory exception in a solvency situation was repealed in the 1986 legislation.   P.L. No. 99–514, 99th Cong., 2d Sess. § 822 (1986).   But see I.R.C. § 108(g).   See Heinlen, "The ABCs of Cancellation of Indebtedness Income and Attribute Reduction," 40 N.Y.U.Inst. on Fed. Tax'n Ch. 42 (1982); Asofsky and Tatlock, "Bankruptcy Tax Act Radically Alters Treatment of Bankruptcy and Discharging Debts," 54 J.Tax. 106 (1981).

3.   Sen.Rep.No. 96–1035, 96th Cong., 2d Sess. 8 (1980), 1980–2 C.B. 620 at 623.

1.   Treas.Reg. § 1.61–12(b)(1); Dallas Transfer & Terminal Warehouse Co. v. Commissioner, 70 F.2d 95 (5th Cir.1934).

2.   Lakeland Grocery Co., 36 B.T.A. 289 (1937).

3.   Treas.Regs. § 1.61–12(a).

6.   Debt discharge that is only a medium for some other form of payment, such as a gift or salary, is treated as that form of payment rather than under the debt discharge rules.   Treas.Regs. § 1.61–12(a). [This continues to be so even after the 1980 changes.   Ed.]

Reasons for Change

Overview.—In P.L. 95–598, Congress repealed provisions of the Bankruptcy Act governing Federal income tax treatment of debt discharge in bankruptcy, effective for cases instituted on or after October 1, 1979. The committee's bill provides tax rules in the Internal Revenue Code applicable to debt discharge in the case of bankrupt or insolvent debtors, and makes related changes to existing Code provisions applicable to debt discharge in the case of solvent debtors outside bankruptcy.

* * *

Explanation of Provisions

Debt Discharge in Bankruptcy.—*In General.*—Under the bill, no amount is to be included in income for Federal income tax purposes by reason of a discharge of indebtedness in a bankruptcy case.[11] Instead, the amount of discharged debt which is excluded from gross income by virtue of the bill's provisions (the "debt discharge amount") is to be applied to reduce certain tax attributes.

Unless the taxpayer elects first to reduce basis in depreciable assets (or in real property held primarily for sale to customers in the ordinary course of a trade or business), the debt discharge amount is applied to reduce the taxpayer's tax attributes in the following order:

(1) net operating losses and carryovers;

(2) carryovers of the [general business credit. Ed.];

(3) capital losses and carryovers;

(4) the basis of the taxpayer's assets (both depreciable and nondepreciable); and

(5) carryovers of the foreign tax credit.[12]

* * *

After reduction of the attributes specified in categories (1), (2), and (3) above, any remaining debt discharge amount is applied to reduce asset basis, but not below the amount of the taxpayer's remaining undischarged liabilities. [See Section 1017(b)(2). Ed.] (Thus, a sale of all the taxpayer's assets

---

11. For purposes of these rules, the term "bankruptcy case" (referred to in the bill as a "title 11 case") means a case under new title 11 of the U.S. Code, but only if the taxpayer is under the jurisdiction of the court in the case and the discharge of indebtedness is granted by the court or is pursuant to a plan approved by the court. [See I.R.C. § 108(d)(2). Ed.]

12. For purposes of the attribute reduction rules, credits are reduced at the rate of 50 cents [33⅓ cents after 1986. Ed.] for each dollar of debt discharge amount. This flat-rate reduction avoids the complexity of determining a tax on the debt discharge amount and determining how much of the amount would be used up by the credits for purposes of determining other reductions. Except for reductions in credit carryovers, the specified tax attributes are reduced one dollar for each dollar of debt discharge amount. [See I.R.C. § 108(b)(3). Ed.]

immediately after the discharge generally will not result in income tax liability unless the sale proceeds and cash on hand exceed the amount needed to pay off the remaining liabilities.) Any amount of debt discharge which remains after such reduction in asset basis, including any debt discharge amount which remains unapplied solely by virtue of the limitation just described with respect to undischarged liabilities, is applied to reduce carryovers of the foreign tax credit.

Any amount of debt discharge which is left after attribute reduction under these rules is disregarded, i.e., does not result in income or have other tax consequences.

*   *   *

Debt Discharge Outside Bankruptcy—Insolvent Debtors.—The bill provides that if a discharge of indebtedness occurs when the taxpayer is insolvent (but is not in a bankruptcy case), the amount of debt discharge is excluded from gross income up to the amount by which the taxpayer is insolvent.[16] The excluded amount is applied to reduce tax attributes in the same manner as if the discharge had occurred in a bankruptcy case. Any balance of the debt discharged which is not excluded from gross income (because it exceeds the insolvency amount) is treated in the same manner as debt cancellation in the case of a wholly solvent taxpayer.

*   *   *

Certain Reductions as Purchase Price Adjustments.— The bill provides that if the seller of specific property reduces the debt of the purchaser which arose out of the purchase, and the reduction to the purchaser does not occur in a bankruptcy case or when the purchaser is insolvent, then the reduction to the purchaser of the purchase money is to be treated (for both the seller and the buyer) as a purchase price adjustment on that property. This rule applies only if but for this provision the amount of the reduction would be treated as income from discharge of indebtedness.

This provision [see Section 108(e)(5). Ed.] is intended to eliminate disagreements between the Internal Revenue Service and the debtor as to whether, in a particular case to which the provision applies, the debt reduction should be treated as discharge income or a true price adjustment. If the debt has been transferred by the seller to a third party (whether or not related to the seller), or if the property has been transferred by the buyer to a third party (whether or not related to the

---

16. The bill defines "insolvent" as the excess of liabilities over the fair market value of assets, determined with respect to the taxpayer's assets and liabilities immediately before the debt discharge. [See I.R.C. § 108(d)(3). Ed.] The bill provides that except pursuant to section 108(a)(1)(B) of the Code (as added by the bill), there is to be no insolvency exception from the general rule that gross income includes income from discharge of indebtedness.

buyer), this provision does not apply to determine whether a reduction in the amount of purchase-money debt should be treated as discharge income or a true price adjustment. Also, this provision does not apply where the debt is reduced because of factors not involving direct agreements between the buyer and the seller, such as the running of the statute of limitations on enforcement of the obligation.

Equity-for-Debt Rules.—*Issuance of Stock**—The committee bill generally does not change the present law rule developed by the courts governing whether income is recognized if a corporation issues its own stock to its creditor for outstanding debt (whether or not the debt constitutes a security for tax purposes). Therefore, no attribute reduction generally will be required where such stock is issued to discharge the debt. [See Section 108(e)(6). Ed.]

* * *

As originally enacted, the 1980 legislation contained a broad elective exception to the *Kirby Lumber* doctrine which was applicable to any solvent individual who incurred a debt on property used in his trade or business and to solvent corporations.[4] The exception was repealed in the 1986 legislation.[5] However, in 1986 a special exception to the *Kirby Lumber* rule was created under Section 108(g), allowing some solvent farmers [6] essentially to use the insolvency exception to the *Kirby Lumber* doctrine to exclude income from the relief from debts incurred in their farming businesses.[7]

Another *Kirby Lumber* exception, enacted prior to the 1980 changes, appears in Section 108(f). It relates to the relief from obligations to repay student loans. It differs from the exceptions above, because it does not require the usual basis adjustments. If pursuant to the terms of a student loan [8] a person, such as a doctor, nurse, or teacher is relieved of the obligation to repay a student loan upon fulfillment of his agreement to work in a rural or low-income area, Section 108(f) applies. Although the amount of the obligation discharged constitutes gross income under *Kirby Lumber,* Section 108(f) excludes it from gross income without any basis or other adjustment. Subsidy is the word here, not mere postponement.

---

* See Bryan, "Cancellation of Indebtedness by Issuing Stock in Exchange: Challenging the Congressional Solution to Debt—Equity Swaps," 63 Texas L.Rev. 89 (1984). Ed.

4. I.R.C. (1954) § 108(a)(1)(C), (c), and (d)(4). A similar exception was incorporated into the statute even prior to 1980.

5. P.L. No. 99–514, 99th Cong., 2d Sess. § 405 (1986).

6. The taxpayer must be a "qualified person" as defined in I.R.C.

§ 49(a)(1)(D)(iv), and at least 50 percent of his average gross receipts for the prior three years must have been attributable to farming operations. I.R.C. § 108(g)(1)(B) and (2). See also I.R.C. § 1017(b)(4).

7. I.R.C. § 108(g)(2)(A).

8. I.R.C. § 108(f)(2). In order to qualify for the exclusion, the loan must have been made by one of the lenders described in I.R.C. § 108(f)(2)(A) through (D).

PROBLEMS

1. Poor borrowed $10,000 from Rich several years ago. What tax consequences to Poor if he pays off the so far undiminished debt with:

(a) A settlement of $7000 of cash? *G.I. = 3000*

(b) A painting with a basis and fair market value of $8000? *2,000 G.I.*

(c) A painting with a value of $8000 and a basis of $5000? *G.I. = 5000*

(d) Services, in the form of remodeling Rich's office, which are worth $10,000? *wash*

(e) Services that are worth $8000? *G.I. = 7000*

(f) Same as (a), above, except that Poor's Employer makes the $7000 payment to Rich, renouncing any claim to repayment by Poor. *GI = 10,000*

2. Businessman borrows $100,000 from Creditor to start an ambulance service. He then purchases ambulances for use in his business at a cost of $100,000. Assume the ambulances are his only depreciable property and, unrealistically, that after some time their adjusted basis and value are still $100,000. What consequences under § 108 and § 1017 in the following circumstances:

(a) Businessman is solvent but is having financial difficulties and Creditor compromises the debt for $60,000. *G.I. 40,000*

(b) Same as (a), above, except that Creditor is also the ambulance dealer who sold the ambulances to Businessman and, as a result of depreciation deductions, the adjusted basis of the ambulances is $35,000. *no change to G.I.*

Businessman is insolvent
liabilities > assets
60,000 > 35,120

(c) Assume the same facts as in (a) above, except that Businessman is insolvent and his liabilities of $225,000 exceed his assets (the ambulances worth $100,000) by $125,000. Further assume Businessman has no net operating losses, general business credit carryovers, capital loss carryovers, or foreign tax credit carryovers. Creditor discharges $40,000 of the $100,000 loan without any payment. *evenso liabilities > assets* *no change to G.I.*

depreciation 5,000

(d) Same as (c), above, except that Businessman has a $30,000 net operating loss. *insolvent before a after = no income*

100,000 asset
-125,000 liability
-40
85,000

(e) Same as (c), above, except Businessman's liabilities exceed his assets by $25,000. *G.I. of 15,000 b/c that is amt that exceeds insolvency*

3. Decedent owed Friend $5000 and Nephew owed Decedent $10,000.

(a) At Decedent's death Friend neglected to file a claim against Decedent's estate in the time allowed by state law and Friend's claim was barred by the statute of limitations. (Let's defer our concern for Nephew.) What result to Decedent's estate?

(b) What result to the estate in (a), above, (with Nephew still in cold storage) if instead Friend simply permitted the statute to run stating that he felt sorry for Decedent's widow, the residuary beneficiary of his estate?

(c) Now, what result to Nephew if Decedent's will provided that his estate not collect Nephew's debt to the estate?

#3   Nephew $\xrightarrow{\text{owed }10,000}$ Decedent $\xrightarrow{\text{owed }5000}$ Friend

(a) G.I. 5000 to estate

(b) gift by Friend to widow ⇒ no tax consequences to estate

(c) G.I. of nephew = 10,000

CHAPTER 9. DAMAGES AND RELATED RECEIPTS

Internal Revenue Code: Sections 104(a); 105(a)–(c) and (e); 106.

Regulations: Sections 1.104–1(a), (c), (d); 1.105–1(a), –2, –3; 1.106–1.

INTRODUCTION

An on-going effort to enable students to determine what is and what is not gross income has indicated by this time that the identification of basic principles in tax law is much the same as in other fields of law. A tax *common law* rule may develop: Is there any element of gain in a receipt? If not, the receipt falls outside the income concept, as in the case of the payment of principal on a loan. There may be a controlling *statutory* rule: How sweet it is to receive a gift, the essence of gain! And yet by statutory proscription, Section 102, property received by gift is excluded from gross income.

Amounts received as damages or reimbursements for damages are governed in part by statute. Code Sections 104–106, discussed in Part A of this chapter immediately below, contain most of the tax rules on compensation for injuries and sickness.[1] But some other similar receipts are not accorded express congressional recognition and so their treatment must be worked out under more general tax principles. It is these general principles that, for example, add gloss to the phrase "income from whatever source derived" in Section 61, which are referred to as the common law of federal taxation.[2] Of course, federal taxation is not a common law subject and the statute is "the thing." But when a statutory term is general a body of case law soon grows around it which is not unlike the growth of the common law and so it is with the kinds of receipts that are the subject of discussion in this chapter.

A detailed study of the area covered by this chapter could well be justified. But by now an inescapable fact of life must be plain to the student: It is impossible in any course or even a series of courses to cover in detail *all* facets of federal taxation. Federal taxation is the life-size shadow of "life in all its fullness"; and who can ever know *all*

1. A number of other Code sections deal with the includibility as gross income of damages or settled recoveries of other types or with other special rules regarding such recoveries. Not discussed in this note are: I.R.C. § 71, Alimony and separate maintenance payments; § 80, Restoration of value of certain securities; § 111, Recovery of tax benefit items; § 1341, Computation of tax where taxpayer recovers substantial amount held by another under a claim of right; § 1351, Treatment of recoveries of foreign expropriation losses.

2. See Ericksen, "The Common Law of Federal Taxation," 7 U. of Fla.L.Rev. 178 (1954); see also Frolik, "Personal Injury Compensation as a Tax Preference," 37 Maine L.Rev. 1 (1985).

about life, much less its tax shadow? These comments of course again explain why there are scattered notes throughout this book which are intended to be read and to be informative without making the related statute the subject of detailed examination.

A. COMPENSATION FOR INJURIES OR SICKNESS: STATUTORY EXCLUSIONS

Some benevolent provisions of the Internal Revenue Code rest simply on the compassionate thought that the taxpayer has suffered enough. Sections 104–106 are of this order. In broad outline they say that a taxpayer who has incurred personal injury should not additionally suffer injury to his purse in the form of tax liability, if he achieves some financial recompense.

Section 104 is the principal provision. Its exclusionary rules are limited to amounts recovered for injuries, physical or mental, to the person or for sickness. Five areas of exclusion are expressly identified, covering amounts received (1) under workmen's compensation acts, (2) as damages for injuries or sickness, (3) as benefits under health and accident insurance policies purchased by the taxpayer, (4) as disability pensions arising out of some types of governmental service, but limited by subsection (b), and (5) disability income received by United States officials who are violently attacked outside the Country.

All exclusions under Section 104 are restricted by an "except" clause which is echoed in Section 105(b). It reads:

> Except in the case of amounts attributable to (and not in excess of) deductions allowed under section 213 (relating to medical, etc., expenses) for any prior taxable year, ∗ ∗ ∗

The general effect of this exception is to *include* in gross income any amount, otherwise excluded, which constitutes reimbursement of a medical expense that served as the basis of a Section 213 deduction in a prior year. The obvious objective is to dovetail the exclusionary rule with the medical expense deduction. Assume in year one T incurred $500 of *deductible* medical expenses that were reimbursed in year two. If he were allowed to claim the deduction in year one and exclude the reimbursement in year two, he would have a *double* tax benefit, a $500 deduction with no out-of-pocket expense.[3]

If reimbursement is received in the same year the expense is incurred, the exclusion applies, as there has been no deduction with respect to that amount in any "prior taxable year." This fits well, however, with Section 213(a) which denies the deduction for expenses of medical care which are "compensated for by insurance or otherwise." That is, the medical expense deduction will not have been allowed for such reimbursed amounts. The Sections 104 and 105 exceptions are statutory expressions of the tax benefit doctrine, partially codified more

---

3. This disregards, as it seems we should, the 7½% floor under the medical expense deduction. I.R.C. § 213(a). See Chapter 18C, infra.

broadly in Section 111.[4] The related principles of Sections 104 and 105 and Section 213 are rather well illustrated in the regulations.[5]

Section 104(a)(1). In most states, statutes assure employees compensation for injuries and illnesses arising out of and in the course of their employment. These are the classic "workmen's compensation acts" contemplated by Section 104(a)(1). Section 104(a)(1) is interpreted literally to exclude benefits paid to an employee's survivors under workmen's compensation acts and similar statutes in the case of job-related death, not mere injury.[6] However, to be excluded under Section 104(a)(1) the amount in question must be paid for death or injury that *is* job-related, not merely under a statute entitled "workmen's compensation law." Nonoccupational benefits, such as amounts paid for disability during employment but not caused by injury or sickness related to the employment, are not covered by Section 104(a)(1).[7]

Section 104(a)(2). Here we find excluded from gross income recoveries for both intentional and unintentional torts "received * * * on account of personal injury or sickness."[8] The statute makes it clear by a parenthetical phrase that an amount received by way of settlement is to be treated the same as damages judicially determined.[9]

Very large sums of money may change hands outside the reach of the tax gatherer as a result of Section 104(a)(2); and questions can be raised about the policy behind the provision. On the one hand, one hardly thinks in terms of *gain* in connection with compensatory damages for injuries suffered, say, in an automobile accident that caused a broken leg or a whip-lash injury to the spine. But neither is there any *tax basis* for what is lost or relinquished, and cash flows which is difficult to identify as a return of capital. The exclusions go back to a time when multi-million dollar damages were generally unknown and must be viewed as compassionate in nature. Would Congress adopt a different policy if the matter came up afresh? If damages were taxed, would the settlements and judgments soon increase to take account of the tax attrition? And how might that affect insurance rates that have already skyrocketed?

One of the major problems of the day is the rising number and amount of medical malpractice recoveries which have generated hard questions for doctors practically required to purchase insurance against such recoveries, even though the premiums paid are deductible ex-

---

4. See Chapter 20, infra.

5. See Reg. § 1.213–1(g)(1)–(3)(iii). Other portions of this regulation, which are more complex, may not be of much concern as they reflect the dollar limitation on the medical expense deduction which was repealed for years beginning in 1967 and later.

6. Reg. § 1.104–1(b).

7. See Rev.Rul. 85–104, 1985–2 C.B. 52; Rev.Rul. 83–77, 1983–1 C.B. 37. These amounts may however qualify fully or par-

tially for exclusion under § 105, discussed below.

8. I.R.C. § 104(a)(2).

9. It was recognized in Dudley G. Seay, 58 T.C. 32 (1972), that damages awarded in a single case might be partly for breach of contract and unaffected by § 104(a)(2) and partly for personal injury and therefore within the exclusion. See Burken, "Tax Treatment of Post-Termination Personal Injury Settlements," 61 Calif.L.Rev. 1237 (1973).

penses under Section 162. There is a surprising lack of authority on the tax consequences of such recoveries to the victim. Apparently they are excluded from gross income under Section 104(a)(2). This would appear to be the case regardless of the nature of the claim of recovery, tort or contract; [10] although if the recovery were for breach of contract the application of Section 104(a)(2) might be questioned on the ground that the damages are on account of breach of contract rather than "on account of personal injuries or sickness." [11] The forgotten surgical sponge sewed up in the victim rather clearly is a negligent "injury" of the kind contemplated by Section 104. Negligent advice that the tumorous lump is innocuous and benign probably produces the kind of tortiously caused "sickness" for which recovery is intended to be excluded from gross income by the section. [12]

Whether damages are computed by judge or jury or merely by the parties in an out-of-court settlement, it may be important to allocate the total award among two or more causes of action. Dudley G. Seay [13] involved an allocation between alleged personal injuries and damages for breach of an employment contract to which Section 104 is inapplicable. [14]

Much is unclear under Section 104(a)(2). A series of recent cases have excluded recoveries for defamation, [15] First Amendment rights, [16] and sex and age discrimination [17] from gross income even though the recoveries were based at least in part on lost business profits or underpaid wages. Is exclusion appropriate under Section 104(a)(2) or should Congress redraft the provision? [18] Section 104(a)(2) applies to "*any* damages received . . . on account of personal injuries or sickness" (emphasis added). Does this include punitive damages? Congress has specifically stated that Section 104(a)(2) is inapplicable to punitive damages recovered in a case "not involving physical injury or

---

10. See Epstein, "Medical Malpractice: The Case for Contract," 1976 Amer.Bar. Found.Research J. 87 (1976).

11. See Reg. § 1.104–1(c) stating that § 104(a)(2) applies to actions "based upon tort or tort-type rights." Cf. Burford v. United States, at page 207, infra.

12. This seems so, even though as is commonly said: "The physician did not *give* the patient cancer." Epstein, supra note 10.

13. Supra, note 9.

14. Cf. Thompson v. Commissioner, 866 F.2d 709 (4th Cir.1989), discussed infra at page 206.

15. See Roemer v. Commissioner, 716 F.2d 693 (9th Cir.1983); Threlkeld v. Commissioner, 848 F.2d 81 (6th Cir.1988). See also Rev.Rul 85–143, 1985–2 C.B. 55, in which the Service announced that it will not follow the *Roemer* decision, and Willoughby, "The Taxation of Defamation Re-

coveries: Toward Establishing Its Reputation," 37 Vand.L.Rev. 621 (1984).

16. Bent v. Commissioner, 835 F.2d 67 (3d Cir.1987).

17. See Byrne v. Commissioner, 883 F.2d 211 (3d Cir.1989) (sex discrimination); Rickel v. Commissioner, 900 F.2d 655 (3d Cir.1990) (age discrimination); Pistillo v. Commissioner, 912 F.2d 145 (6th Cir.1990) (age discrimination). Cf. Thompson v. Commissioner, supra note 14 (sex discrimination).

18. See Helleloid and Turner, "Tax Status of Employment Discrimination Awards and Settlements," 15 Rev.Tax'n Ind. 127 (1991); Burke and Friel, "Tax Treatment of Employment–Related Personal Injury Awards: The Need for Limits," 50 Mont.L. Rev. 13 (1989); Cochran, "Should Personal Injury Awards be Taxed?" 38 Case W.Res. 43 (1987).

physical sickness." [19]   Does this mean that punitive damages received in conjunction with physical injuries are excluded? [20]   If so, *should* such punitive damages be excluded from gross income? [21]   If a physical injury recovery is based on the degree of fault of the wrongdoer, is the recovery mere punitive damages?   If so, is it excluded from gross income?   Many of these issues are explored in the *Pistillo* and *Burford* cases which appear at the end of this Note and the problems at the end of the Chapter.

Section 104(a)(3).   The third paragraph of Section 104(a) excludes from gross income amounts received under accident and health insurance policies for personal injuries or sickness. [22]   However, this rule is limited to the proceeds of policies paid for by the individual himself and should be compared with the treatment of certain employee health and accident benefits under Section 105, described below.   Being subject to the general prefatory exception of Section 104(a), the exclusion does not cover amounts attributable to medical expense deductions for prior years. [23]

It appears that Section 104(a)(3) holds out an opportunity for a tax-free profit in health and accident insurance.   Some policies pay a stated number of dollars per day for hospitalized illness and will pay even if other policies in effect have already defrayed the charges.   It is curious that Congress invites this kind of tax-free profiteering, even if it may occur only infrequently.

Under Section 106 the gross income of employees does not include an employer's contributions to accident and health insurance plans or other payments made to compensate or reimburse his employees for injuries or sickness.   However, Section 105(e) does treat amounts *paid out* by such plans, [24] as well as by sickness and disability funds of states

---

19. I.R.C. § 104(a)(2) last sentence.

20. The Service would argue no.   See Rev.Rul. 84–108, 1984–2 C.B. 32, holding that no punitive damages are excludable under I.R.C. § 104(a)(2) and reversing Rev. Rul. 75–45, 1975–1 C.B. 47, excluding punitive damages within the "any" damages clause of § 104(a)(2).

21. See Cochran, "1989 Tax Act Compounds Confusion Over the Tax Status of Personal Injury Damages," 49 Tax Notes 1565 (1990).

22. This has been held to include "no fault" insurance disability benefits received for loss of income or earning capacity.   Rev.Rul. 73–155, 1973–1 C.B. 50.

23. This exception is clear enough in one respect and fuzzy in another.   It nails as includible in gross income insurance reimbursements for explicit previously deducted medical expenses.   For example, if the proceeds are obtained only after having been deducted as a medical expense in a prior year, to the extent that they have

been previously deducted they are knocked out of the exclusion by the exception and are includible in income.   It may also be true that the proceeds *escape* tax (are not within the exception) if they are payable merely in case of certain injury or illness without regard to expenses incurred in connection therewith.   This seems to be the Tax Court's view.   Cf., Robert O. Deming, Jr., 9 T.C. 383 (1947).   It is uncertain, however, whether premiums paid for the health and accident insurance and deducted in a prior year or years as medical expenses operate to reduce the exclusion. The insurance proceeds would probably be attributable to the deducted premiums and to that extent should not be excluded.

24. An employer's health care plan need not be detailed in a formal written document in order to qualify as an "accident or health plan" under § 105(e).   If an employer has a "policy or custom" of providing benefits and employees are aware of their availability, then there is a plan despite the absence of a written plan.   See

and the District of Columbia as amounts received through accident and health insurance. This would be awkward and inappropriate except that the Section 105(e) rule does not bring such amounts under the protective umbrella of Section 104(a)(3) (see the parenthetical exception in paragraph (3)). Both direct payments by employers of accident and health benefits to employees and indirect payments funded by amounts not taxed to the employees are placed outside Section 104(a)(3). This is not to say they will always be taxed, but only that their tax status must be tested under Section 105. It is realistic to differentiate insurance proceeds paid by policies bought with the recipient's own taxed or partially taxed dollars from amounts simply paid directly by employers or paid under arrangements that have been without cost, tax or otherwise, to the recipient.[25]

Section 106. This seems the best place to take brief further account of the enigmatic sentence which is Section 106, excluding from an employee's gross income an employer's contributions to accident and health plans set up to pay compensation to employees for injuries or sickness. The function of Section 106 is to equalize the tax status of employees (1) whose employers undertake to pay health or accident benefits to employees directly, and employees (2) whose employers accomplish the same results through the purchase of insurance or the funding of benefit plans. Before the enactment of the 1954 Code, an employer's payment of a premium for an individual health and accident policy for an employee resulted in income taxable to the employee.[26] But the employee was in the same situation as an employee whose employer himself would pay benefits like those purchased under the insurance contract and, in the second case, the employee realized no income from his employer's direct assumption of this obligation. There was no reason why one should incur tax liability and the other not, and Section 106 eliminates the difference by way of its further exclusionary rule. It may be well to emphasize that the exclusion under Section 106 relates, not to amounts paid to employees who are sick or injured, but to amounts paid by employers for insurance premiums or into funded plans to set up benefits for employees in case of future sickness or injury.

Section 104(a)(4). Section 104(a)(4) excludes disability pensions of members of the armed forces and certain other governmental units.[27] Although subsection (b) of Section 104 now limits the application of

---

John L. Greer, 70 T.C. 294 (1978), following Reg. § 1.105–5(a).

25. In a highly technical fashion, the penultimate sentence of § 104(a) fits quasi-employees (self-employed persons given employee status for purposes of tax benefits) into this scheme of things. See Reg. § 1.72–15(g). Although the self-employed person's payments would be deductible under § 404(a), making the introductory reference to § 213 irrelevant, the general effect, nevertheless, is again to deny the

double benefit of an exclusion for amounts attributable to deductible payments.

26. See Sen.Rep. No. 1622, 83rd Cong., 2d Sess., 185–186 (1954).

27. Although this note makes no pretense at being exhaustive, note that § 1403 of Title 10 U.S.C.A. expressly provides: "That part of the retired pay of a member of an armed force computed ∗ ∗ ∗ on the basis of years of service, which exceeds the retired pay that he would receive if it were computed on the basis of disability is not

Section 104(a)(4) in general, it "grandfathers" in persons who were receiving benefits excluded under Section 104(a)(4) in 1975 and continues its application to persons receiving compensation for combat-related injuries or who would, upon application, be entitled to disability compensation from the Veterans' Administration.

Section 104(a)(5). Section 104(a)(5) excludes disability income attributable to injuries incurred as a result of terrorist attacks on United States employees performing official duties outside the United States.

Section 105(a). Section 105(a) addresses taxpayers who *as employees* receive some financial benefit arising out of their employer's concern for their health. Some comments above, explaining the limited scope of Section 104(a)(3) which generally excludes amounts received through accident and health plans,[28] serve as an introduction to this provision. Its first thrust is generally to label *includible* gross income amounts that an employee [29] receives through accident or health insurance. These amounts are expressly includible if (1) attributable to an employer's contributions to a plan which were not taxed to the employee or (2) simply paid by the employer. It will be recalled that these are the very amounts that failed to be excluded under Section 104(a)(3). Is all lost? No. The main messages of Section 105 are in subsections (b) and (c), which back off from the general rule of inclusion provided in subsection (a).

Section 105(b). If an employer directly or indirectly reimburses an employee for expenses of medical care [30] for himself, his spouse or his dependents,[31] the amount received is excluded from gross income under Section 105(b). Of course it was noted earlier in the chapter that the prefatory exception in Section 104(a) is echoed in Section 105(b). Thus, an employee's medical expense deductions for a prior year may reduce the excludible amount of his later reimbursement, just as in the case of exclusions under Section 104(a)(3). The tax benefit concept requires this limitation on the exclusions.

Note that here it is the amount of medical care actually paid for which measures the exclusion, in contrast to the possibility (maybe even likelihood) under Section 104(a)(3) that the amounts received under a health or accident policy, which measure the exclusions, may exceed the medical expenses incurred. Under this scheme of things an obvious problem arises if an individual has two accident and health insurance policies, the premiums of one being paid by the individual and the other by his employer, and both compensate him for the same illness. Assume, for example, that an employee had $900 of medical expenses related to an illness and that he received $800 from an

---

considered as a pension * * * under section 104(a) of Title 26."

28. See note 24, supra.

29. Quasi-employees, see note 25, above, are not "employees" here. I.R.C. § 105(g).

30. The I.R.C. § 213(d) definition is expressly adopted.

31. The I.R.C. § 152 definition of dependent is expressly adopted, although for purposes of this section any child to whom § 152(e) (concerning children of divorced parents) applies is treated as a dependent.

employer funded policy and $400 from his own policy. Under Section 104(a)(3), all proceeds from his own policy are excluded from income, but Section 105(b) limits the exclusion for his other benefit to amounts which reimburse him for his medical care. Thus, the question arises as to what amount of the $800 received from the employer funded policy may be excluded. *Revenue Ruling 69–154* [32] indicates that the amount of medical expense to be considered paid by each policy is proportionate to the benefits received from each policy. Under this approach, if the employee received $800 from the employer's policy and $400 from his own policy (a total of $1200), 800/1200 or two-thirds of the medical expense is deemed paid by the employer's policy. Therefore, two-thirds of the $900 of medical expenses, or $600, will be considered as paid for out of the proceeds of the employer policy. It follows that of the $800 received from the employer funded policy only $600 is excluded by Section 105(b), because the exclusion under Section 105(b) is limited to the amount of reimbursement for actual expenses. $200 of the $800 received is included in the employee's gross income.[33] Of course, the full $400 received from the employee's policy is excluded under Section 104(a)(3) which has no such limitation. Even if the taxpayer who is self-supporting in this respect may deserve some kind of acclaim, the exclusion of "profits" on health and accident policies under Section 104(a)(3) may still be questioned. More complex problems sometimes arise regarding the interrelationship of Sections 104(a)(3) and 105(b).[34]

Section 105(c). This subsection provides that, if an employee receives payments through health or accident insurance [35] provided by his employer without tax cost to him for loss of a member or function of the body or for disfigurement, not just of himself but also of his spouse or a dependent,[36] and if the amount is computed only with regard to the nature of the injury and not to the period the employee is absent from work,[37] the amount is excluded from gross income.[38] Of course, as a rule the employee himself will receive payment for casualties of this type under workmen's compensation legislation and can exclude the receipts under Section 104(a)(1). When this is so Section 104(a)(1) preempts Section 105(c), according to the Service.[39] This seems to make little difference, however, because amounts that are of the type received under workmen's compensation acts but are outside Section 104 because they exceed what is provided for *are* permitted to be excluded under Section 105(c).[40] And of course nonoccupational injuries and disfigurement and also injuries and disfigurement of an employee's

---

32. 1969–1 C.B. 46.

33. Rev.Rul. 69–154, Situation 3, supra note 32.

34. Rev.Rul. 69–154, Situation 4, supra note 32.

35. Recall the broad definition in I.R.C. § 105(e).

36. The § 152 definition of dependent is expressly adopted.

37. See Rev.Rul. 74–603, 1974–2 C.B. 35.

38. Receipts of this kind do not affect the amount of a taxpayer's medical expense deduction. See I.R.C. § 105(f).

39. Reg. § 1.105–3, last sentence.

40. Reg. § 1.104–1(b).

spouse and dependents may produce financial compensation outside Section 104 which is excluded from gross income by Section 105(c).[41]

PISTILLO v. COMMISSIONER *
United States Court of Appeals, Sixth Circuit, 1990.
912 F.2d 145.

KEITH, Circuit Judge:

On April 30, 1982, petitioner Carmen Pistillo ("Pistillo") received $58,000 from his former employer, pursuant to the settlement of an age discrimination lawsuit. See Age Discrimination in Employment Act ("ADEA"), 29 U.S.C. §§ 621–634. This appeal requires us to decide whether the United States Tax Court ("the Tax Court") properly determined that Pistillo's settlement award is taxable. Because we conclude that Pistillo's settlement award is excludable from his taxable income pursuant to § 104(a)(2) of the Internal Revenue Code ("IRC"), 26 U.S.C. § 104(a)(2), we REVERSE the order of the Tax Court.

I.

For over ten years, Pistillo was employed by the Cleveland Tool & Supply Company ("Cleveland Tool") as a commissioned salesman. A Cleveland Tool managerial employee, Harry Parks, often made disparaging remarks about Pistillo's work and reputation, including statements that he was "old"; had "gray hair"; and was unable to relate to his younger clients. On April 6, 1979, when Pistillo was 57 years old, Cleveland Tool terminated his employment and replaced him with a younger employee. Pistillo has remained unemployed.

After the termination of his employment by Cleveland Tool, Pistillo concluded that he had been a victim of age discrimination. On July 27, 1979, Pistillo filed a timely notice of his intent to sue Cleveland Tool with the Wage and Hour Division of the United States Department of Labor. See ADEA, 29 U.S.C. § 626(d). On June 5, 1980, the Equal Employment Opportunity Commission ("the E.E.O.C.") notified Pistillo that its efforts to resolve his dispute with Cleveland Tool through informal methods of conciliation, conference and persuasion had been unsuccessful. See id. The E.E.O.C. advised Pistillo of his right to institute an independent civil action against Cleveland Tool. See ADEA, 29 U.S.C. § 626(c).[1]

In October 1980, Pistillo filed a complaint against Cleveland Tool in the United States District Court for the Northern District of Ohio. Initiating his suit in equity and at law, Pistillo alleged that the true reason for the termination of his employment was his age, in violation

---

41. Ibid.

* Some footnotes omitted.

1. 29 U.S.C. § 626(c)(1) provides:

Any person aggrieved may bring a civil action in any court of competent jurisdiction for such legal or equitable relief as will effectuate the purposes of this chapter. *Provided,* That the right of any person to bring such action shall terminate upon the commencement of an action by the Equal Employment Opportunity Commission to enforce the right of such employee under this chapter.

of the ADEA, 29 U.S.C. §§ 621–634 [2]; 42 U.S.C. §§ 1981 and 1988; and the fifth and fourteenth amendments to the United States Constitution. Pistillo sought an order: (1) declaring that Cleveland Tool had discriminated against him on the basis of his age; (2) granting him a preliminary and permanent injunction enjoining Cleveland Tool from abridging his rights; (3) requiring Cleveland Tool to reinstate him to the position he had held on April 6, 1979, and to pay him all wages, including overtime, that he would have received in the normal course of his employment from April 6, 1979 to the date of his reinstatement; and (4) granting him reasonable attorneys fees.

TX prayer

Pistillo's age discrimination suit was tried before a jury. The district court instructed the jury that if it found that Cleveland Tool had discriminated against Pistillo on the basis of his age, it could award compensation for back pay, including the amount of sales commissions Pistillo did not receive because of his discharge. The district court also instructed the jury that it could award Pistillo liquidated damages and compensatory damages. The district court further instructed the jury that any award of damages to Pistillo would not be taxed; therefore, the jury should not consider taxes in awarding damages.

On March 13, 1981, the jury found for Pistillo and awarded him $55,000 in compensatory damages. The district court awarded Pistillo attorneys fees in the amount of $22,432.83. On August 6, 1981, the judgement was filed. Cleveland Tool appealed to this court on January 13, 1982.

While the appeal was pending, Cleveland Tool initiated settlement negotiations with Pistillo. On April 30, 1982, the parties settled the litigation by executing a document entitled "Release and Settlement." [3] On the same day, Cleveland Tool paid Pistillo $81,562.58, which was

---

2. 29 U.S.C. § 623(a) provides:

(a) Employer practices.

It shall be unlawful for an employer—

(1) to fail or refuse to hire or discharge any individual or otherwise discriminate against any individual with respect to his compensation, terms, conditions, or privileges of employment, because of such individual's age;

(2) to limit, segregate, or classify his employees in any way which would deprive or tend to deprive any individual of employment opportunities or otherwise adversely affect his status as an employee, because of such individual's age; or

(3) to reduce the wage rate of any employee in order to comply with this chapter.

3. The Release and Settlement between Pistillo and Cleveland Tool provided:

For the sole consideration of the payment of the sum of Eighty–One Thousand Five Hundred Sixty–Two Dollars

and Fifty–Eight Cents ($81,562.58) by Cleveland Tool, the receipt of which is hereby acknowledged, [Pistillo] does hereby forever release and discharge Cleveland Tool . . . from any and all judgments, claims, demands, actions, causes of action, wages, damages, costs, claims of reinstatement, claims of interest, awards of attorneys' fees, expenses and compensation or suits of law or equity of whatsoever kind of nature, which he . . . may now or hereafter have or assert against Cleveland Tool, . . . growing out of or resulting from his employment at Cleveland Tool, whether now existing or hereafter developing, and whether now known or unknown, including but not limited to, any claims he had asserted or judgments he had been awarded in Case No. C80–1941, United States District Court for the Northern District of Ohio, Eastern Division, entitled 'Carmen Pistillo, Plaintiff, v. Cleveland Tool and Supply Co., Defendant.'

allocated as follows: $58,000 was paid to Pistillo; $22,706.18 was paid for his attorney fees; and $856.40 was paid for court reporter fees. In accordance with the release and settlement, Cleveland Tool dismissed its appeal.

Pistillo did not include the $58,000 received by him from Cleveland Tool in his gross income for 1982. Pistillo reasoned that the settlement proceeds were excludable from his gross income under § 104(a)(2), which excludes from gross income damages received on account of personal injuries. 26 U.S.C. § 104(a)(2). On November 6, 1986, the Commissioner of Internal Revenue ("the Commissioner") issued a Notice of Deficiency to Pistillo. In the notice, the Commissioner stated that Pistillo had a tax deficiency of $22,131.90. The Commissioner explained that Pistillo should have included the $58,000 settlement award in his gross income for the 1982 taxable year because the suit was brought to secure lost wages, as opposed to damages for personal injuries.

On January 29, 1987, Pistillo petitioned the Tax Court seeking a redetermination of the deficiency. On July 11, 1989, the Tax Court issued its opinion, adopted the position advanced by the Commissioner, and concluded that Pistillo's settlement was taxable income. See Pistillo v. Commissioner, 57 T.C.M. (CCH) 874, 881 (1989). . . .

II.

On appeal, Pistillo argues that the Tax Court erred in holding that his $58,000 settlement award was not excludable from his taxable income under § 104(a)(2). In response, the Commissioner contends that the Tax Court correctly concluded that Pistillo's settlement award: (1) represented compensatory damages awarded to him under the ADEA; (2) redressed his claim for lost wages resulting from the termination of his employment; (3) did not reflect a tort claim for personal injuries; and (4) did not warrant exclusion from his taxable income pursuant to § 104(a)(2). Relying substantially upon our holding in Threlkeld v. Commissioner, 87 T.C. 1294 (1986) aff'd, 848 F.2d 81 (6th Cir.1988), and the Third Circuit's recent opinion in Rickel v. Commissioner, 92 T.C. 510 (1989) aff'd in part and rev'd in part, 900 F.2d 655 (3rd Cir.1990), we conclude that under § 104(a)(2), the $58,000 paid by Cleveland Tool to Pistillo in settlement of his age discrimination suit was excludable from his taxable income as damages received on account of personal injuries.

The IRC states: "[e]xcept as otherwise provided . . . ., gross income means all income from whatever source derived. . . ." 26 U.S.C. § 61(a). All accessions to wealth are presumed to be gross income, unless the taxpayer can demonstrate that the accessions qualify for specific exclusions created by the IRC. See Commissioner v. Glenshaw Glass Co., 348 U.S. 426, 430, 75 S.Ct. 473, 476, 99 L.Ed. 483 (1955).

Pistillo v. Commissioner, 57 T.C.M. (CCH) 874, 877 (1989) (quoting "Release and Settlement").

Section 104(a)(2), the exclusion at issue here, provides that "gross income does not include . . . the amount of any damages received (whether by suit or agreement and whether as lump sums or as periodic payments) on account of personal injuries or sickness. . . ." For purposes of § 104(a)(2), several courts have explained that the meaning of "personal injuries" encompasses both physical and nonphysical injuries. See *Rickel,* 900 F.2d at 658; Bent v. Commissioner, 835 F.2d 67, 70 (3d Cir.1987); Roemer v. Commissioner, 716 F.2d 693, 697 (9th Cir. 1983); *Threlkeld,* 87 T.C. at 1297. As defined by the Treasury regulations, a claim for an exclusion based on a personal injury award must assert violations of tort or tort-type rights. 26 C.F.R. § 1.104–1(c). See Byrne v. Commissioner, 883 F.2d 211, 214 (3d Cir.1989). The essential element, however, of an "exclusion under section 104(a)(2) is that the income involved must derive from some sort of tort claim against the payor." Glynn v. Commissioner, 76 T.C. 116, 119 (1981).

In Threlkeld v. Commissioner, 87 T.C. 1294 (1986), aff'd, 848 F.2d 81 (6th Cir.1988), the Tax Court held that a portion of a malicious prosecution settlement was attributable to injury to the taxpayer's professional reputation; constituted damages received on account of personal injuries; and thus, was excludable from the taxpayer's gross income. See 87 T.C. at 1308. With a 15–1 vote, the Tax Court established the prevailing test to determine whether a specific damage award qualifies for the exclusion:

> Section 104(a)(2) excludes from income amounts received as damages on account of personal injuries. *Therefore, whether the damages received are paid on account of "personal injuries" should be the beginning and end of the inquiry.* To determine whether the injury complained of is personal, we must look to the origin and character of the claim . . ., and not to the consequences that result from the inquiry.
>
> * * *
>
> Exclusion under section 104 will be appropriate if compensatory damages are received on account of any invasion of the rights an individual is granted by virtue of being a person in the sight of the law.

Id. at 1299, 1308 (citations omitted) (emphasis added).

Affirming the Tax Court in *Threlkeld,* we held that the "nonpersonal consequences of a personal injury, such as a loss of future income are often the most persuasive means of proving the extent of the injury that was suffered, [but] the personal nature of an injury should not be defined by its effect." 848 F.2d at 84. For purposes of § 104(a)(2), the Third, Ninth and Tenth Circuits also have concluded that to determine whether damages received by a taxpayer were paid on account of personal injuries, courts must look to the nature of the claim and not to the consequences that result from the injury. See Wulf v. City of Wichita, 883 F.2d 842, 872–73 (10th Cir.1989) (where taxpayer was wrongfully discharged in violation of the first amendment under

§ 1983, held that his settlement award compensated him for personal injuries and was nontaxable under § 104(a)(2)); Metzger v. Commissioner, 88 T.C. 834 (1987), aff'd without published opinion, 845 F.2d 1013 (3d Cir.1988) (concluding that even though taxpayer sought an award of back pay under Title VII, sex discrimination was deemed a personal injury and a substantial portion of the damage award was excludable under § 104(a)(2)); Bent v. Commissioner, 835 F.2d 67, 70 (3rd Cir.1987) (explaining that even though the settlement was based in part on taxpayer's lost wages, the damage award for the violation of his first amendment rights compensated him for his personal injuries and thus, was excludable under § 104(a)(2)); Roemer v. Commissioner, 716 F.2d 693, 700 (9th Cir.1983) (holding that compensatory and punitive damages received in taxpayer's defamation suit were excludable from gross income, since under California law, defamation of an individual is a personal injury.) * See also Byrne v. Commissioner, 883 F.2d 211, 216 (3d Cir.1989) (extending the analysis of *Bent* and *Roemer* both to a retaliatory discharge claim under the Fair Labor Standards Act and a wrongful discharge claim under state law).

In Rickel v. Commissioner, 92 T.C. 510 (1989), aff'd in part and rev'd in part, 900 F.2d 655 (3rd Cir.1990), the Third Circuit explained that because an age discrimination claim is an assertion of a tort or tort-type right, rather than an economic right arising out of a contract, the taxpayer's entire settlement award was excludable from his gross income. 900 F.2d at 661. In *Rickel,* as in the case at bar, the taxpayer sued his former employer in federal court, alleging a violation of the ADEA. . . . While the jury was deliberating, the parties entered into a settlement agreement that obligated the employer to pay $105,000 to the taxpayer. The taxpayer did not report the settlement amount in his gross income. The Commissioner, however, determined that the $105,000 was taxable. After the taxpayer filed his petition for a re-determination of the tax deficiency, the Tax Court found that one-half of the settlement was taxable income and one-half was excludable under § 104(a)(2).

On appeal, the order of the Tax Court was reversed. The Third Circuit found that: (1) age discrimination was more analogous to a personal injury claim than a breach of contract action, as it alleged a violation of a duty owed to the taxpayer by his employer which arose by operation of law; (2) the taxpayer's ADEA action amounted to an assertion of a tort or tort-type right; and (3) all damages flowing from the taxpayer's age discrimination claim were excludable under § 104(a)(2). See *Rickel,* 900 F.2d at 661–62. The Third Circuit then emphasized that all employers have a statutory duty to refrain from discriminating against employees on the basis of their age. "Society has made the moral and economic determination that as a matter of law it will not abide such discrimination. Such a duty arises even in the absence

---

* [The holding in *Roemer* regarding punitive damages has been statutorily reversed. See I.R.C. § 104(a) last sentence. Ed.]

of a written employment contract. . . ." Id. at 662. Consistent with prevailing judicial views, the Third Circuit concluded that a workplace discrimination suit may be most appropriately characterized as the assertion of a tort-type right to redress for personal injuries. Id. at 662. See e.g., Goodman v. Lukens Steel Co., 482 U.S. 656, 661, 107 S.Ct. 2617, 2621, 96 L.Ed.2d 572 (1987) (describing § 1981 as "part of a federal law barring racial discrimination, which . . . is a fundamental injury to the individual rights of a person"); Wilson v. Garcia, 471 U.S. 261, 277, 105 S.Ct. 1938, 1947, 85 L.Ed.2d 254 (1985) (analogizing a violation of § 1983 to a violation of the fourteenth amendment which "is an injury to the individual rights of the person").

Reviewing the nature of Pistillo's claim, we conclude that his age discrimination lawsuit is analogous to the assertion of a tort-type right to redress personal injuries. Cleveland Tool discriminated against Pistillo on the basis of his age and invaded the rights Pistillo "is granted by virtue of being a person in the sight of the law." *Threlkeld,* 87 T.C. at 1308. Contrary to the arguments of the Commissioner, Pistillo has not brought separate actions to seek back pay damages for his pain and suffering.[6] Pistillo merely sought the remedies afforded by the ADEA as compensation for the *personal injury* he suffered as a result of his employer's invidious age discrimination. Pistillo's loss of wages—a substantial nonpersonal consequence of his employer's age discrimination—did not transform the discrimination into a nonpersonal injury. See *Rickel,* 900 F.2d at 663. Therefore, we conclude that the entire settlement award received by Pistillo, on account of his age discrimination lawsuit against Cleveland Tool, is excludable from his taxable income under § 104(a)(2).

Given the result we reach today, Pistillo will have less federal tax liability than if he had not suffered age discrimination in the first place. The reality, however, as opposed to the hypothetical, is that Pistillo did suffer invidious age discrimination. Pistillo endured his employer's indignities, insults and age discrimination; suffered a dignitary tort; and was personally injured. Cf. Curtis v. Loether, 415 U.S.

---

6. Relying upon our decisions in Bowman v. United States, 824 F.2d 528 (6th Cir.1987), and Hill v. Spiegel, Inc., 708 F.2d 233 (6th Cir.1983), the Commissioner argues that the order of the Tax Court should be affirmed. We do not find the Commissioner's arguments to be persuasive. First, in *Bowman,* both parties agreed, prior to trial, that the taxpayer's race discrimination settlement award constituted back wages for past employment. See *Bowman,* 824 F.2d at 529. In the present case, the parties have not reached such an agreement. Second, in *Hill,* we held that plaintiff's award for pain and suffering fell outside the scope of the ADEA. See *Hill,* 708 F.2d at 235. Pistillo, however, remains entitled to his settlement award which reflects all "the reme-dies afforded by the [ADEA] as compensation for the personal injury he suffered as a result of his employer's act of discrimination." *Rickel,* 900 F.2d at 663. Third, whether Cleveland Tool paid Pistillo a portion of the settlement award to compensate him for pain and suffering or lost back pay is irrelevant to the § 104(a)(2) inquiry. See *Threlkeld,* 87 T.C. at 1299 (determining whether or not the damages were paid on account of a personal injury is "the beginning and the end" of the § 104(a)(2) inquiry). See also *Roemer,* 716 F.2d at 699 ("The nonpersonal consequences of a personal injury, such as a loss of future income, are often the most persuasive means of proving the extent of the injury that was suffered. The personal nature of an injury should not be defined by its effect.").

189, 195 n. 10, 94 S.Ct. 1005, 1009 n. 10, 39 L.Ed.2d 260 (1974) (dictum) (analogizing an action to redress racial discrimination to an action for defamation or the intentional infliction of emotional distress). Pistillo is now entitled to receive federal tax treatment *equal* to that received by the typical tort victim who suffers a physical injury and, as a result, receives a settlement award. See *Rickel,* 900 F.2d at 664 ("[T]he successful ADEA plaintiff is being treated no better . . . than the typical tort victim who suffers a physical injury. We see no reason to treat one personal injury victim any differently than another."); Miller v. Commissioner, 93 T.C. 330, 337 (1989) ("Section 104 does not distinguish between physical and nonphysical injuries, and we see no sound reason to construe the statute in such a way as to not afford the same tax treatment to recoveries for all types of 'personal' injury regardless of consequences.") (citation omitted).

Congress enacted the ADEA "to promote employment of older persons based on their ability rather than age; to prohibit arbitrary age discrimination in employment; [and] to help employers and workers find ways of meeting problems arising from the impact of age on employment." 29 U.S.C. § 621(b). Just as the common law punishes tort-feasors, the ADEA punishes employers who practice age discrimination—regardless of whether the discrimination manifests itself in express acts of ageism or through more subtle and evasive forms. To effectuate the purposes of both the ADEA and the IRC, we must make the victims of arbitrary age discrimination whole by providing equal recognition to the substantial indignities and personal injuries they have suffered.

Thus, we hold that the age discrimination settlement award received by Pistillo qualifies for the § 104(a)(2) exclusion. Accordingly, we reverse the order of the Tax Court and remand for entry of an order consistent with this opinion.

NOTE

The recent approach of the courts interpreting Section 104(a)(2) is first to examine the nature of the claim. If the recovery is for personal injury, whether physical or nonphysical, then Section 104(a)(2) operates to preclude federal taxation of the amounts received.[1] However, if the recovery is found to be contractual in nature, the Section 104(a)(2) exclusion does not operate to prevent inclusion in gross income.[2]

For example, in Thompson v. Commissioner,[3] a female employee prevailed in an action alleging that she was paid less than male employees in a similar position. She recovered back pay equal to the wage differential alleged plus an amount equal to the back pay as

---

1. See the *Pistillo* and *Burford* cases at pages 200 supra and 207, infra.

2. Kurowski v. Commissioner, 917 F.2d 1033 (7th Cir.1990). See Dudley G. Seay, 58 T.C. 32 (1972).

3. 866 F.2d 709 (4th Cir.1989).

liquidated damages.[4]   The Fourth Circuit affirmed the Tax Court's holding that the liquidated damages were excluded from the taxpayer's gross income but that the back pay was included in her gross income. The court reasoned: [5]

> After analyzing the statutory scheme we conclude that Thompson received the liquidated damages through prosecution of a tort-type claim for personal injuries. We conclude, however, that the claim for back pay was essentially a contractual claim for accrued wages.

Is the Fourth Circuit analysis consistent with that of the Sixth Circuit in *Pistillo?*

BURFORD v. UNITED STATES

United States District Court, Northern District of Alabama, 1986.
642 F.Supp. 635.

LYNNE, District Judge: This action comes before the Court on cross motions for summary judgment. The plaintiff has brought this action for a refund of federal income tax. She contends that settlement proceeds of an Alabama wrongful death claim are excludable from gross income under Internal Revenue Code § 104(a)(2), despite a Revenue Ruling that holds such proceeds to be taxable income. The Court agrees with plaintiff's contention that Alabama wrongful death proceeds fall within the plain language of Section 104(a)(2) and grants her motion for summary judgment.

Factual Background

The facts that give rise to this action are neither complex nor disputed. Plaintiff Ann Burford pursued a wrongful death claim against the University of Alabama–Birmingham after her husband died during treatment at the U.A.B. Hospital. On August 15, 1984, the claim was settled before any lawsuit was filed; Mrs. Burford received $62,203.00 from the settlement after deduction of attorney's fees and costs.

Mrs. Burford included the settlement amount on her 1984 federal income tax return, then later amended her return to exclude that amount and claim a refund of $19,961.00. Mrs. Burford waited for more than six months for some indication from the Internal Revenue Service whether her claim would be allowed, then filed this suit.

Discussion

The Internal Revenue Service's refusal to allow Mrs. Burford's claim is grounded upon the Service's recent Revenue Ruling 84–108, 1984–29 I.R.B. 5. This Ruling reversed the previous position of the IRS

---

4. The back pay was recovered under the Equal Pay Act of 1963 and Title VII of the Civil Rights Act of 1964. The liquidated damages were recovered under the Equal Pay Act of 1963.

5. 866 F.2d 709 at 712.

and stated that proceeds of a claim obtained under Alabama's wrongful death statute [1] are includable in the gross income of the recipient. The Court is of the opinion that Revenue Ruling 84–108 constitutes an unwarranted administrative amendment of the clear language of the Internal Revenue Code and cannot stand.

A. "Amounts received . . . on account of personal injury"

The Internal Revenue Code broadly defines "gross income" to mean all income from whatever source derived, except for those categories of income specifically excluded by other Code sections. I.R.C. § 61(a). Section 104(a)(2) defines one of these statutory exceptions, excluding from gross income "the amount of any damages received (whether by suit or agreement, and whether as lump sums or as periodic payments) on account of personal injuries or sickness." The dispositive question, therefore, is whether wrongful death proceeds fall within the "personal injuries" exception provided in Section 104(a)(2).

Issue

The starting place in the construction of any statute is with the language of the statute itself. The clear import of "any damages received . . . on account of personal injuries" would seem to express clearly the Congressional intent to exclude wrongful death proceeds— regardless of whether those proceeds are classified as compensatory or punitive—from gross income. Indeed, this was the position of the Internal Revenue Service from its inception until July 16, 1984. See Revenue Ruling 75–47, 1975–1 C.B. 47. The Service's traditional position on punitive wrongful death proceeds was that "any damages, whether compensatory or punitive and whether a substitute for income or not, received on account of personal injuries or sickness are excludable from gross income." G.C.M. 35967 at 3, 4.[2]

The Service's position was reversed, however, with the publication of Revenue Ruling 84–108, which specifically discussed Alabama's wrongful death statute and concluded that proceeds under that statute did not fit within the exception of Section 104(a)(2).[3] The Service noted that Alabama caselaw construing the wrongful death statute consistently has labeled damages obtained under that statute as punitive in nature. Revenue Ruling 84–108 concluded that proceeds are received under the statute "on account of" the enormity of the tortfeasor's wrongful act and not "on account of . . . personal injury," as required by Section 104(a)(2).

1. Ala.Code § 6–5–410 (1975). *Wrongful act, omission or negligence causing death.* "A personal representative may commence an action and recover such damages as the jury may assess in a court of competent jurisdiction within the State of Alabama, and not elsewhere, for the wrongful act, omission or negligence of any person, persons or corporations, his or their servants or agents, whereby the death of his testator or intestate was caused . . ."

2. The Court recognizes that General Counsel Memoranda have no precedential value and quotes the above language only to demonstrate the Service's prior interpretation of Section 104(a)(2).

3. Rev.Rul. 84–108 also considered the wrongful death statute of Virginia, which it interpreted as allowing only compensatory damages, and stated that proceeds received under that statute were excludable from gross income.

Revenue Ruling 84–108 relies in large part upon Glenshaw Glass Co. v. Commissioner, 348 U.S. 426 (1955), which held that the punitive damage portion of a fraud and antitrust settlement constituted gross income. Such reliance is misplaced. In Glenshaw Glass the Service contended that, where the plaintiff had settled his claim against the defendant for $800,000, almost $325,000 of the total amount represented punitive damages. The Supreme Court agreed that the punitive damage portion of the settlement did constitute gross income. *Glenshaw Glass* based this classification on the fact that such damages were paid *in addition to* the amount necessary to compensate the plaintiff for its losses, holding that "it would be an anomaly that could not be justified in the absence of clear congressional intent to say that a recovery for actual damages is taxable but not the additional amount extracted as punishment for the same conduct which caused the injury." 348 U.S. at 431.

The Court is of the opinion that Section 104(a)(2) is the "clear congressional intent" required by *Glenshaw Glass,* making the Service's reliance upon that decision misplaced. Only a contorted reading of that Section can lead to the interpretation that wrongful death actions are not received on account of a personal injury. To contend that such proceeds are received only because of the tortfeasor's wrongful conduct and not because of a personal injury is neither logical nor realistic.[4]

The exclusion of damages received on account of personal injuries must extend to amounts received for one's death. The Service is correct in its statement that Alabama wrongful death proceeds are intended to punish and deter wrongdoers. This characterization does not alter the inescapable fact that a wrongful death action arises only upon a person's death. Other Alabama cases have recognized that a wrongful death action essentially is one for personal injuries. American Fidelity & Casualty Co. v. Werfel, 162 So. 103 (Ala.1935), involved a statute allowing successful plaintiffs in actions for "bodily injuries" to require the defendant's insurer to satisfy the judgment. The court held that the statute applied to punitive damages obtained under Alabama's wrongful death act, rejecting the precise argument advanced in this case—that such damages are obtained for punitive rather than compensatory purposes. 162 So. at 106. In so holding, the *Werfel* case recognized the wrongful death action as one for personal injuries.[5]

---

4. Under the Service's present interpretation of Section 104(a)(2), the personal representative of a decedent killed in Alabama will see the settlement or damages proceeds cut in half (assuming a 50% tax rate) by federal taxes. Those same proceeds would be obtained tax-free if the decedent was killed: (1) in another state, or (2) in Alabama under circumstances giving rise to a claim under the Federal Tort Claims Act.

Nor does this Court accept the Service's contention that footnote eight of the *Glenshaw Glass* opinion serves as authority for Rev.Rul. 84–108. The footnote is nothing more than dicta concerning punitive damages in a business context and offers no precedential or persuasive support for defendant's position.

5. Related statute and case law support the determination that wrongful death proceeds are the result of personal injury. Ala.Code § 6–5–440 prohibits simultaneous actions "for the same cause and against the same party." This statute has been construed as prohibiting a personal repre-

The plain language of Section 104(a)(2) therefore leads to the conclusion that damages received under any wrongful death act are personal injury proceeds and are excludable from gross income.[6] Accordingly, plaintiff's motion for summary judgment is due to be granted and defendant's cross-motion for summary judgment is due to be overruled.

B. RECOVERIES FOR INJURIES TO BUSINESS OR TO PROPERTY

Even though this chapter is entitled Damages and Related Receipts, it is not appropriate here to attempt a broad description of the tax treatment of recoveries for injuries to business and to property. The reason is that there are necessarily involved characterization questions.[1] All these matters are the subject of detailed consideration in Parts Six and Seven of this book and they cannot sensibly be fully anticipated here. Nevertheless, a few comments are advanced.

As a general proposition, taxability of a recovery can be determined by an identification of the nature of the injury.[2] If an injured party receives damages on a claim nonpersonal in nature for loss of profits in his business the damages, being a substitute for the profits, are fairly easily identified as gross income.[3] Of course this basic principle may be altered by statute. In some instances if there is a recovery for patent infringement, breach of contract or of a fiduciary duty, or violations of the antitrust laws, a compensating deduction may nullify the inclusion in gross income.[4]

---

sentative from simultaneously pursuing recovery for personal injuries and wrongful death when both result from the same wrongful conduct. See, e.g., Simmons v. Pulmosan Safety Equipment Corp., 471 F.Supp. 999, 1001–1002 (S.D.Ala.1979). Nor does the Alabama survival statute, Ala.Code § 6–5–462, allow an action or cause of action for personal injuries to survive the plaintiff's death, when death is caused by those injuries. See Price v. Southern Railway Co., 470 So.2d 1125, 1128 (Ala.1985). Lastly, the Alabama Supreme Court has held that a wrongful death action is equivalent to a personal injury action for purposes of determining venue. See, e.g. Harris v. Elliott, 277 Ala. 421, 423, 171 So.2d 237, 239 (1965). These decisions reinforce the common sense conclusion that wrongful death proceeds result from personal injuries.

6. This conclusion is supported by the *Code's* treatment of similar proceeds obtained as a result of another's death: § 101(a) excludes life insurance proceeds from gross income; § 101(b) excludes employee death benefits up to $5,000; and § 102 excludes property acquired by devise or inheritance. These sections demon-

strate a general policy of excluding from taxable income amounts received because of the death of another.

1. These include the capital gain or loss, ordinary income or loss dichotomy, see, e.g., I.R.C. §§ 1201–1223; special rules on sales or exchanges of business property and involuntary conversions of that and also capital assets, see the I.R.C. § 1231 "hotchpot"; the depreciation recapture concept, e.g., the I.R.C. §§ 1245 and 1250 "gotchas"; and principles, e.g., I.R.C. §§ 1033 and 1034.

2. Pistillo v. Commissioner, 912 F.2d 145 (6th Cir.1990).

3. See Raytheon Products Corp. v. Commissioner, 144 F.2d 110 (1st Cir. 1944), cert. denied 323 U.S. 779, 65 S.Ct. 192 (1944) which at page 113 poses the question: "In lieu of what were the damages awarded?" Taxable recovery for average profits whaling vessel might have made if not detained by United States, J. R. Knowland, 29 B.T.A. 618 (1933); recovery for profits lost in sealing operations because of improper interference by the U.S., H. Liebes & Co. v. Commissioner, 90 F.2d 932 (9th Cir.1937).

4. See I.R.C. § 186.

We have known since 1955, or maybe in your case since page 53,[5] that punitive or exemplary damages, even if they are properly characterized as a windfall, may be fully taxable.[6]

Generally, damages or other recoveries for the improper taking of or injury to physical property operate simply to reduce the loss deduction otherwise potentially available,[7] but they become gross income subject to tax under special rules where the amounts received exceed the basis for the property.

As in the case of personal injuries, damages recovered in a single suit may rest on several grounds.[8] Tax analysis requires allocation of the award in such circumstances.[9]

A contract for the sale of property may contain a clause anticipating the possibility of breach and expressing the consequences. If amounts are then required to be paid as liquidated damages, not penalties, do the recipients have income? While arguably the transaction represents a mere recovery of capital with a concurrent basis reduction, nevertheless the recoveries are treated as income.[10] And properly so, as the seller is left where he began, having given up no property or property interests. The recovery is most appropriately treated as a "windfall." [11]

Professional people these days are appropriately held to a reasonably high standard of performance and may incur liability for failure to attain it, as mentioned above in the discussion of medical malpractice. It is a shattering thought to a young tax lawyer that his bad advice to a client might give rise to personal liability for tax costs unnecessarily incurred by the client. Should such an event occur, *Edward H. Clark* [12] is authority for the client's exclusion from gross income of his recovery from the lawyer. This old opinion seems erroneously to rest on the notion that the recovery is not "derived from capital or from labor or from both combined." While *Glenshaw Glass* [13] repudiated this rationale, it may still be true that in some circumstances such awards lack any element of gain, which is an essential characteristic of gross income.[14]

---

5. Commissioner v. Glenshaw Glass Co., 348 U.S. 426, 75 S.Ct. 473 (1955), rehearing denied, 349 U.S. 925, 75 S.Ct. 657 (1955).

6. Cf. Burford v. United States, at page 207, supra.

7. See page 415, infra. Cf. I.R.C. § 123, considered page 859, infra.

8. Thompson v. Commissioner, 866 F.2d 709 (4th Cir.1989).

9. Compare State Fish Corp., 48 T.C. 465 (1967), acq. 1968–2 C.B. 3, amounts received for damages to goodwill escaped tax as not in excess of taxpayer's basis for goodwill, with Raytheon Products Corp. v. Commissioner, supra note 3, recovery for destruction of business and goodwill fully taxable for failure to establish any basis for the business and goodwill of the company.

10. Harold S. Smith, 50 T.C. 273 (1968), affirmed per curiam 418 F.2d 573 (9th Cir.1969); Meyer Mittleman, 56 T.C. 171 (1971).

11. The recovery also has characterization consequences. If a "windfall", the gain should be ordinary income, Harold S. Smith and Meyer Mittleman, supra note 9. But see Alvin G. Lowe, 44 T.C. 363 (1965).

12. 40 B.T.A. 333 (1939), acq., 1944 C.B. 5.

13. Supra, note 5.

14. If the award were made for a medical malpractice recovery, it is seemingly

PROBLEMS

1. Plaintiff brought suit and unless otherwise indicated successfully recovered. Discuss the tax consequences in the following alternative
situations:

(a) Plaintiff's suit was based on a recovery of an $8,000 loan that
she made to Debtor. Plaintiff recovered $8,500 cash, $8,000 for
the loan plus $500 in interest.   *500 = G.I.*

(b) What result to Debtor under the facts of (a), above, if instead
he transferred some land worth $8,500 with a basis of $2,000 to
Plaintiff to satisfy the obligation?   *↑ of 8000 -2000 = 6,000 = G.I.*

(c) Plaintiff's suit was for a refund of a $2,000 overpayment of her
federal income taxes for a prior year. She received cash of
$2,240 which included the refund and $240 of interest.
240 = G.I.

(d) Plaintiff's suit was based on a breach of a business contract
and she won a judgment for $8,000 for lost profits.

(e) What result in (d), above, if Plaintiff also recovered $6,000 of
punitive damages?

(f) Plaintiff's suit was based on a claim of injury to the goodwill of
her business arising from a breach of a business contract.
Plaintiff had a $4,000 cost basis for the goodwill (the amount
she paid for the goodwill when she purchased the business).
She recovered $10,000 damages for injury to goodwill which
she had built up over the years.

(g) Plaintiff was injured in an automobile accident and settled the
suit the day of the trial for $20,000?

(h) Defendant in (g), above, satisfies the obligation with stock
worth $20,000 in which Defendant has a $5,000 basis. What
result to Defendant and what is Plaintiff's basis in the stock?

2. Plaintiff brought suit and successfully recovered. Discuss the
tax consequences in the following alternative situations.

(a) Plaintiff, a surgeon, suffers the loss of a finger in an automobile accident and is awarded damages of $100,000.

(b) What result in (a), above, if $50,000 of the award is specifically
identified by the jury as compensation for income Plaintiff lost
as a result of the severed finger?

(c) What result in (a), above, if Plaintiff also recovers $100,000 of
punitive damages?

(d) Plaintiff, a surgeon, recovers $100,000 from Tortfeasor because
of the following slanderous statement made by Tortfeasor:
"Plaintiff cheats on his income taxes."

shielded from the Commissioner's grasp by
I.R.C. § 104(a)(2). See page 194, supra.

(e) What result in (d), above, if the jury specifically identifies $50,000 of Plaintiff's award as compensation for lost profits?

(f) What result if Plaintiff recovers $100,000 of lost profits when tortfeasor, a former patient of Plaintiff, stated that: "Plaintiff is an incompetent doctor"?

(g) What result in (f), above, if Tortfeasor stated instead that: "Plaintiff uses obsolete equipment"?

3. Injured and Spouse were injured in an automobile accident. Their total medical expenses incurred were $2,500.

(a) In the year of the accident they properly deducted $1,500 of the expenses on their joint income tax return and filed suit against Wrongdoer. In the succeeding year they settled their claim against Wrongdoer for $2,500. What income tax consequences on receipt of the $2,500 settlement?

(b) In the succeeding year Spouse was ill but, fortunately, they carried medical insurance and additionally Spouse had insurance benefits under a policy provided by Employer. Spouse's medical expenses totalled $4,000 and they received $3,000 of benefits under their policy and $2,000 of benefits under Employer's policy. To what extent are the benefits included in their gross income?

(c) Under the facts of (b), above, may Injured and Spouse deduct the medical expenses? (See § 213(a).)

CHAPTER 10. SEPARATION AND DIVORCE

A. ALIMONY AND SEPARATE MAINTENANCE PAYMENTS

1. DIRECT PAYMENTS

Internal Revenue Code: Sections 71 (omit (c)(2) and (3)); 215(a) and (b); 7701(a) (17).

Regulations: Section 1.71–1T(a) and (b) (omit Q 6 and 7).

Prior to 1942 in the absence of explicit statutory provisions, alimony payments were looked upon as nondeductible personal expenses of the payor spouse,[1] like family expenses in an unbroken home. Similarly, alimony was not required to be included in a divorced payee spouse's gross income, because it was considered merely an interest in the payor's property to which the payee was equitably entitled.[2] When World War II required a substantial escalation of income tax rates, it became possible for alimony and income taxes to exceed the entire net income of divorced payors. Even in less extreme circumstances, nondeductible alimony payments were very burdensome. Consequently, it is not surprising that in the 1942 Revenue Act Congress effected a statutory reversal of previously established principles; alimony would be included within the payee's gross income and, to the extent so included, would be deductible by the payor.[3]

This is the first place in this book that the deduction concept is prominently encountered. For the most part, deductions are deferred to Part Four, beginning with Chapter 14. Still most people have some notion of the concept of taxable (net) income, if only from hearing their fathers complain that the really good things always seem to turn out to be either immoral, illegal, fattening, or at best *nondeductible*. In any event Sections 71 (income rule) and 215 (deduction rule) are so interrelated that they must be viewed together. In some of the materials below they are referred to as Sections 22(k) and 23(u), their 1939 Code designations. In general, deductibility by the paying spouse is made dependent upon includability of the payment in the gross income of the recipient spouse. But this limited reciprocal principle should not be

1. See I.R.C. § 262.

2. Gould v. Gould, 245 U.S. 151, 38 S.Ct. 53 (1917).

3. The constitutional validity of the 1942 provision was sustained in Mahana v. U.S., 115 Ct.Cl. 716, 88 F.Supp. 285 (1950), which held that *Gould*, supra note 2, was not based on a decision that alimony was not income within the Sixteenth Amendment, but instead on a determination that the Income Tax Act of 1913 did not purport to tax it.

taken as a general rule applicable in areas other than divorce and separation. For example, when Viewer pays a television repairman $50, the repairman has $50 gross income even though Viewer has merely incurred a nondeductible personal expense.

The provisions of Sections 71 and 215 can well be viewed as a kind of income-splitting or tax allocation device, a proposition more directly recognized under recent amendments than it was under prior law.[4] That is, divorced or separated persons may in effect allocate taxability between them of some of the payor spouse's income by the payee assuming the tax burden for the amount received as alimony and the payor being accorded a deduction for that amount. Whether that is accomplished, however, depends upon how things are done. Thus, the manner in which interspousal payments are arranged becomes a bargaining matter in negotiations for any settlement, with a close eye on the tax consequences. Think of this in studying the materials in this Chapter. So you're not much interested in tax because you plan to be a general practitioner? This is one of several areas in which federal tax law has come to dominate "general practice" law.

The student should, however, avoid thinking of alimony payments as coming "out of" the payor's income. If the payor personally makes the payments, their origin is immaterial in determining their taxability to the payee and their deductibility by the payor. A payor might have no job and hold all his or her wealth in the form of a checking account and unproductive, speculative real estate and thus have no gross income. Still, if the payor pays the ex-spouse $1000 per month as alimony, the payee will be taxed on it; while it is deductible by the payor, the deduction would be wasted for lack of any income to be offset.

The Tax Reform Act of 1984, while substantially amending the Section 71 rules, continued the income-splitting or tax allocation scheme of prior tax law relating to divorce.[5] In general Section 71 applies to alimony and separate maintenance payments [6] made pursuant to a "divorce or separation instrument." [7] The instrument may be a decree of divorce or of legal separation, a written instrument incident to such a decree,[8] a written separation agreement, or a decree for

---

4. In Chapters 12 and 27 of this book you will come across the concept of income-splitting for *married* taxpayers. Its origin and purpose are, however, quite different. Still, it is related to the present problem inasmuch as the effective income-splitting rules of § 71(b)(2)(B) and (C) and § 215, applicable where the parties are still married, do not apply if the parties achieve income-splitting advantages under I.R.C. § 1(a), as they can by way of electing to file a joint return under § 6013. See I.R.C. § 71(e).

5. See Seago and O'Neill, "New Law Substantially Changes Treatment of Ali-

mony and Property Transfers at Divorce," 61 J.Tax. 202 (1984); Berman, "The Alimony Deduction: Time to Slaughter the Sacred Cow," 5 Amer.J.Tax Pol. 49 (1986); Hjorth, "Divorce, Taxes, and the 1984 Tax Reform Act: An Inadequate Response to an Old Problem," 61 Wash.L.Rev. 151 (1986).

6. I.R.C. § 71(b)(1) defines alimony or separate maintenance payments.

7. I.R.C. § 71(b)(2).

8. Cf. Newton v. Pedrick, 212 F.2d 357 (2d Cir.1954).

support. Alimony and separate maintenance payments are generally accorded the same treatment as under the prior law; i.e., payments that qualify as alimony or separate maintenance are gross income to the payee spouse [9] under Section 71(a) and deductible by the payor spouse under Section 215(a).[10] However, qualification criteria have been changed.

The prior income tax law definition of alimony generated needless uncertainties and litigation. It required that the payments be in discharge of a legal obligation imposed upon or incurred by a spouse because of a family or marital relationship; [11] and it also required that the payments be "periodic." [12] The current law, originating in the 1984 Act, abandons both of these criteria in favor of a new, more objective federal standard. The House Report suggests the reasons for the change: [13]

> The committee believes that the present law definition of alimony is not sufficiently objective. Differences in State laws create differences in Federal tax consequences and administrative difficulties for the I.R.S. The committee believes that a uniform Federal standard should be set forth to determine what constitutes alimony for Federal Tax purposes. This will make it easier for the Internal Revenue Service, the parties to a divorce, and the courts to apply the rules to the facts in any particular case and should lead to less litigation. The committee bill attempts to define alimony in a way that would conform to general notions of what type[s] of payments constitute alimony as distinguished from property settlements and to prevent the deduction of large, one-time lump-sum property settlements.

Rights, interests and liabilities inherent in the nature of alimony and separate maintenance payments are necessarily based on local law. Nevertheless, we now have an almost uniform federal definition of alimony and separate maintenance for purposes of the tax allocation of such payments.[14]

The current statute, similar in profile to the prior law, can be divided into three parts. The first part, identifies taxable and deductible alimony or separate maintenance payments.[15] The second part, by negative inference, identifies payments that are not treated as alimony or separate maintenance, which are accorded the non-taxable and non-

9. Cf. I.R.C. § 71(c).

10. See I.R.C. §§ 71(d) and 7701(a)(17).

11. Under prior law there was an issue whether payments met this requirement and constituted alimony or were instead property settlements. See, for example, Bernatschke v. United States, 176 Ct.Cl. 1234, 364 F.2d 400 (1966).

12. Former I.R.C. § 71(a)(1), (2) and (3).

13. H.Rep. No. 98–432, 98th Cong.2d Sess. 1495 (1984).

14. We say "almost" uniform because of the 1986 amendment to the fourth requirement. See the text at note 34, infra.

15. I.R.C. § 71(b)(1).

deductible status of property settlements.[16]   The third part, which is considered later in this Chapter, addresses child support payments.[17]

Requirements for Taxable and Deductible Alimony

Today, a payment that is made in *cash* (or check or money order) [18] qualifies as alimony or as separate maintenance, if five requirements are met:[19]

(1)   The payment is received by, or on behalf of,[20] a spouse under a divorce or separation instrument; [21]

(2)   The divorce or separation instrument does not designate the payment as a non-alimony payment; [22]

(3)   In the case of a decree of legal separation or of divorce, the parties are not members of the same household at the time the payment is made; [23]

(4)   There is no liability to make any payment in cash or property, after the death of the payee spouse; [24] and

(5)   The payment is not for child support.[25]

The first requirement is that payments be received pursuant to a divorce or separation instrument.   Thus Sections 71 and 215 are applicable only to taxpayers who find themselves in one of the following four differing situations: [26] (1) divorced; (2) legally separated by decree; (3) married but payments are directed by a written separation agreement;   or (4) married but payments are directed under a support decree.[27]

Under the second requirement,[28] the Code now permits all or seemingly any portion of a payment that qualifies in all other respects as alimony to be effectively labeled *non-alimony* in the divorce or separation instrument.   The designation of any payment as non-alimony generally yields tax relief to the recipient (no gross income under Section 71(a)) and an increased tax burden for the payor (no deduction under Section 215(a)).   This allows the parties to allocate the income tax consequences of the marital dissolution between themselves.   Depending on the relative income tax brackets of the parties, the forthright flexibility of the statute may encourage agreement between them, if only for tax purposes.   By the terms of the divorce or separation instrument, such non-alimony characterization can be made to apply to

---

16.   I.R.C. § 71(f).   See page 219, infra.

17.   I.R.C. § 71(c).   See page 238, infra.

18.   I.R.C. § 71(b)(1), Temp.Reg. 1.71–1T(b) at A–5.   Cash does not include a promissory note or any other property.   Id.

19.   But see I.R.C. § 71(f) discussed, infra.

20.   See page 224, infra.

21.   I.R.C. § 71(b)(1)(A).

22.   I.R.C. § 71(b)(1)(B).

23.   I.R.C. § 71(b)(1)(C).

24.   I.R.C. § 71(b)(1)(D).

25.   I.R.C. § 71(c).

26.   See I.R.C. § 71(b)(2).

27.   However, I.R.C. § 71 is not applicable to a married couple who file a joint return.   I.R.C. § 71(e).   See Chapter 27A, infra.

28.   I.R.C. § 71(b)(1)(B).

differing amounts for different designated years. By designating all or seemingly a portion of the payments as nonalimony, the parties are able to achieve a form of cash property settlement tax treatment for payments that would otherwise be accorded treatment as alimony or separate maintenance.[29]

The third requirement (separate households)[30] marks a change in congressional thinking. Under prior law, spouses who were still married were required to be "separated"[31] in order to invoke the rules of Sections 71 and 215.[32] No such requirement was imposed on divorced or legally separated couples. Congress has done an about-face and reversed the rules. Now, ex-spouses who are divorced or legally separated may not be members of the same household. Perhaps the non-application of this rule to non-divorced or legally separated spouses is an attempt to encourage their reconciliation. However, a still married couple does not come within Section 71 if they file a joint return.[33]

The fourth requirement is that the payor must have no obligation to pay after the death of the payee.[34] An implicit concept, not spelled out in the Section 71(a) gross income inclusion and Section 215(a) deduction statutory symmetry is that alimony is in the nature of support for the payee spouse.[35] Payments required to be made after the death of the payee spouse are not for support and they are not permitted to qualify as alimony or separate maintenance payments. In these circumstances the payments have the flavor of a property settlement, or perhaps of child support; and Congress has placed them beyond the scope of the inclusion-deduction statutory scheme.

This requirement may be expressly provided in the divorce instrument; but it is enough if termination is required by a state statute.[36] In bowing to local law the Code here makes a minor deviation from the policy of Congress to effect uniform national results.[37]

If payments that terminate at the payee's death are to be replaced by substitute payments to the spouse's estate or some third party, to the extent of the substitute payments the termination requirement is not met.[38] For example, if the payee spouse is to receive $35,000 a year for

---

29. Compare the effect of § 71(b)(1)(B) with the general rules of §§ 71(a) and 215(a).

30. I.R.C. § 71(b)(1)(C).

31. See, e.g., Sydnes v. Commissioner, 577 F.2d 60 (8th Cir.1978).

32. Former I.R.C. § 71(a)(2) and (3); see, e.g., Washington, 77 T.C. 601 (1981); Catherine M. Hertsch, 43 T.C.M. 703 (1982); M. LaBow, 46 T.C.M. 777 (1983).

33. I.R.C. § 71(e). See I.R.C. § 6013.

34. I.R.C. § 71(b)(1)(D).

35. Compare I.R.C. § 71(b)(1), first clause, and § 71(b)(1)(D) with § 71(c) and § 71(f).

36. See, for example, Calif. Civil Code § 4801(b).

37. See text at note 13, supra. As originally enacted I.R.C. § 71(b)(1)(D) required the divorce or separation instrument to provide expressly against any obligation of the payor spouse to continue making payments after the death of the payee spouse. The 1986 legislation retroactively removed the requirement of language in the instrument. Pub. Law No. 99–514, 99th Cong., 2d Sess. § 1843(b) (1986).

38. I.R.C. § 71(b)(1)(D). Temp.Reg. § 1.71–1T(b) at A–14 provides:

To the extent that one or more payments are to begin to be made, increase in amount, or become accelerated in

life but at the payee's death the payor is required to pay $15,000 a year to their child until majority, $15,000 of the $35,000 is a non-qualified payment. Only $20,000 terminates at the payee's death and only that amount qualifies as alimony.[39]

The fifth requirement, that the payment not be for child support, is considered later in this Chapter.[40]

From the foregoing discussion of the Section 71 requirements for statutory inclusion-deduction, various rules of disqualification are evident. For example, payments made other than in cash do not meet the federal definition of alimony and, even though incident to divorce, cannot be subject to the inclusion-deduction rules. Further, cash payments that would qualify as alimony but which are designated as non-alimony in the divorce or separation instrument are not considered taxable alimony. And, again, to the extent that there is a continuing obligation to make payments after the death of the payee spouse, payments, even if made during the life of the recipient spouse, are not accorded alimony status.[41] The persistent theme here is that such arrangements do not have the earmarks of support and hence should not qualify for alimony or separate maintenance tax treatment. Just as transfers and divisions of property between a husband and wife during marriage have no immediate income tax consequences today,[42] so a transfer of property that is made incident to a divorce is of no immediate consequence.[43] Most alimony and separate maintenance payments qualify for tax allocation but property settlements, whether in cash or other property, do not. But, as the income tax consequences of alimony payments and property settlements are vastly different, the obvious question is: How, beyond basic indicia stated above, do we identify a cash payment as alimony and differentiate it from a tax-free, non-deductible cash property settlement? Section 71(f) adds some refinements to the basic criteria of Section 71(b), discussed above.

The Section 71(f) Alimony Recapture Provision

Some divorce or separation instruments require the payor spouse to make a single, large cash payment to the payee spouse. This is not in the nature of a support payment and, we might agree, it should not be accorded alimony status. Even so, the payment could well be within the definition of alimony in Section 71(b) and, if so, the payee would have gross income and the payor a deduction in the amount of the

time as a result of the death of the payee spouse, such payments may be treated as a substitute for the continuation of payments terminating on the death of the payee spouse which would otherwise qualify as alimony or separate maintenance payments. The determination of whether or not such payments are a substitute for the continuation of payments which would otherwise qualify as alimony or separate maintenance payments, and of the amount of the otherwise qualifying alimony or separate maintenance payments for which any such payments are a substitute, will depend on all of the facts and circumstances.

39. Temp.Reg. § 1.71–1T(b) at Q–14.

40. I.R.C. § 71(c). See page 238, infra.

41. See note 38, supra.

42. See I.R.C. § 1041. See page 136, supra.

43. Id. See page 227, infra.

payment. To the initiated, a payment such as this essentially has the look and smell of a cash property settlement. Adopting that view, Congress decided upon Section 71(f) as a means to reduce the potential for abusive income allocation in transactions that in substance are property settlements made in cash.

A single lump sum payment is not the only type of payment which falls within Section 71(f). The subsection applies to situations where disproportionately large payments are made during the early years of payments, achieving a property settlement by way of *front loading*. For example, assume that under the divorce or separation instrument the following amounts of annual payments are made (all of which qualify under Section 71(b)):

Year	Payment
One:	$80,000
Two:	$80,000
Three:	$30,000
Four:	$30,000

Reflect on the support characteristic of alimony which differentiates it from cash property settlements generally. At least a portion of the total sum of $160,000 paid during the first two years has the flavor of a cash property settlement. Admittedly the exigencies of life and the needs of the parties should permit some flexibility in the amount of payments for any given year. On the other hand, where the amount of one or more of the payments is inordinately large in relation to the amount of payments for other years, something may be amiss.

In an effort to prevent the front-loading of alimony payments in what in substance is a cash property settlement,[44] Congress added a special recapture provision as a backup to the rules of Sections 71(a) and 215. Under Section 71(f) when inordinately large amounts of alimony and support are paid in the first or second year in relation to year three, an amount is recaptured in year three. That recapture takes the form of an amount included in the payor spouse's gross income for year three (offsetting prior deductions) and a deduction in the same year by the recipient spouse (offsetting prior inclusions).

Section 71(f) is a one shot deal; all the action occurs in year three although it is based on the amount of front loading in years one and two. The recapture rule does not reopen the preceding two years to which it relates. Recapture is a device that, when applicable, simply says that as the amount recaptured was not properly treated as alimony or separate maintenance for the earlier year, correction is in order. The correction effects a reversal of roles (now it is recipient deduction and payor inclusion) accomplished in the third year.

Congress seems to see more or less level payments as likely support or maintenance, which get inclusion-deduction treatment. But some

---

44. H.Rep. No. 98–432, 98th Cong., 2d Sess. 1496 (1984).

flexibility is needed. How much? The statute is intricate but precise; the general message is: fun, but not too much fun! Moreover the statute, so precise in addressing front-loading, is not concerned with potential cash rear-loading. Thus, for example, if payments which otherwise qualify as alimony equal $30,000 a year in each of two years, followed by a payment of $80,000 in the third year, all will qualify as alimony, even though the $80,000 payment seems in the nature of a cash property settlement.

When there is a sufficient reduction over the three years, the recapture rules come into play and the amount of recapture depends on the nature of the reduction. The computation is approached by first, determining the second year recapture under Section 71(f)(4), and then, by determining the first year recapture under Section 71(f)(3), because the first year recapture can be computed only after one ascertains the amount of the second year recapture.[45] If the payments in the second year exceed payments in the third year by more than $15,000, then there is a recapture of that excess [46] in the third year.[47] If the alimony payments in the first year exceed the average of the payments in the second year and the third year (after reducing second year excess payments as determined above) by more than $15,000,[48] that excess amount is also recaptured in the third year.[49]

To illustrate these rules we use the figures of $80,000, $80,000 and $30,000 from the illustration above. As the payments in the second year ($80,000) exceed the third year payments of $30,000 plus $15,000 (a total of $45,000), there is a $35,000 recapture of the year two excess in year three.[50] In addition, as the payment in the first year ($80,000) exceeds the average of the second year (as reduced by the second year recapture) and the third year or the average of $45,000 and $30,000, i.e., $37,500 *plus* $15,000 ($52,500), there is an additional $27,500 ($80,000 less $52,500) recapture from year one in year three.[51] Thus the total excess alimony payments from year one and year two is $62,500 ($35,000 plus $27,500) and that amount is recaptured (taxed to the payor and deducted by the payee) in year three.[52]

What, you may ask, is going on here? [53] Questions like this often should be asked. Sometimes, as here, the answers come with difficulty. One thing can be said with assurance: If the amounts paid within year one and two and three are all within $15,000 of each other, there will be no recapture. The reason? Relatively level payments for at least three years fit the congressional notion of alimony which, in turn, falls

---

45. I.R.C. § 71(f)(3)(B)(i)(I).

46. I.R.C. § 71(f)(4).

47. I.R.C. § 71(f)(1) and (2)(B).

48. I.R.C. § 71(f)(3).

49. I.R.C. § 71(f)(1) and (2)(A).

50. I.R.C. § 71(f)(4).

51. I.R.C. § 71(f)(3).

52. I.R.C. § 71(f)(1) and (2).

53. The I.R.C. § 71(f) rules grow out of the Senate Bill that preceded the 1984 Act, even though the current recapture rule did not enter the Code until the 1986 Act. Pub. Law No. 99–514, supra note 37, § 1843(c). The Senate Report of the 1984 Act leads no insight into the rationale for the specific lines drawn. See Sen. Rep. No. 98–160, 98th Cong., 2d Sess. 1946 (1984).

within the congressional inclusion-deduction policy of letting the income tax obligation tag along after the support roll. However, the statute does not go so far as to allow a $15,000 reduction in each year; i.e., $40,000, $25,000 and $10,000 payments result in $7,500 of recapture. Test this conclusion to see the working of the statute. And then give a moment's thought to whether there may be a better way to achieve the apparent Congressional objective.

Exceptions to the Section 71(f) Rules. There are various situations that should not trigger the Section 71(f) recapture rule and consequently the statute provides some exceptions. If the amount of payment in the second or third year is reduced because either spouse dies or the payee spouse remarries, the reduction is not taken into account in determining applicability of the rule.[54]

A mere decree for support or for temporary maintenance by its very nature is not a property settlement; it contemplates a situation where the parties are not divorced or legally separated [55] and simply requires the payor spouse to support the payee spouse. It generally does not require payments for a fixed term of years. Even if the decree should order that payments be reduced in excess of $15,000 in any year after the first year, the payments are in the nature of alimony and the statute appropriately places them outside the recapture rule.[56] Mere decrees for support are totally disregarded under the recapture rules.[57]

The final exception relates to contingent payments. Payments made under a continuing liability to pay a fixed portion of the income from a business, or from property, or from compensation from employment or self-employment, if they are to be made for at least three years, are not subject to the recapture rule.[58] These payments are subject to fluctuations in amount generally beyond the control of the payor and, consequently, Congress makes the recapture rule inapplicable if the payments are to be made for at least three years.

PROBLEMS

1. Determine whether the following payments are accorded "alimony or separate maintenance" status and therefore are includible in the recipient's gross income under § 71(a) and deductible by the payor under § 215(a). Unless otherwise stated, Donald and Ivana are divorced and payments are called for by the divorce decree.

§71 applies (a) The divorce decree directs Donald to make payments of $10,000 per year to Ivana for her life or until she remarries. Donald makes a $10,000 cash payment to Ivana in the current year.

Not cash so §71 doesn't apply (b) Same as (a), above, except that Donald, finding himself short on cash during the year, transfers his $10,000 promissory note to Ivana.

---

54. I.R.C. § 71(f)(5)(A)(i).

55. I.R.C. § 71(b)(2)(C).

56. I.R.C. § 71(f)(5)(B).

57. Id.

58. I.R.C. § 71(f)(5)(C).

not cash
no application

(c) Same as (b), above, except that instead of transferring his promissory note to Ivana, Donald transfers a piece of art work, having a fair market value of $10,000.

asymmetric

(d) Same as (a), above, except that in addition the decree provides that the payments are nondeductible by Donald and are excludible from Ivana's gross income.

(e) Would it make any difference in (d), above, if you learned that Donald anticipated that he would have little or no taxable income in the immediate future, making the § 215 deduction practically worthless to him, and as a consequence of this agreed to the "nondeductibility" provision in order to enable Ivana to avoid the imposition of federal income taxes on the payments?

looks like settlement
OK

(f) What result in (a), above, if the divorce decree directs Donald *that's* to pay $10,000 cash each year to Ivana for a period of 10 years? *if death occurs not $ support*

(g) Same as (f), above, except that under local law Donald is not required to make any post-death payments.

(h) Same as (a), above, except the divorce decree directs Donald to pay $10,000 cash each year to Ivana for a period of 10 years or her life, whichever ends sooner. Additionally, the decree requires Donald to pay $15,000 cash each year to Ivana or her estate for a period of 10 years. Donald makes a $25,000 cash payment to Ivana in the year.

(i) Same as (a), above, except that at the time of the payment, Donald and Ivana are living in the same house.

(j) Same as (i), above, except that Donald and Ivana are not divorced or legally separated and the payments are made pursuant to a written separation agreement instead of a divorce decree.

2. A divorce decree requires Tina to make the following payments (which meet all the requirements of § 71(b)) to Ike:

Year 1	$80,000	*∃ recapture*
Year 2	40,000	
Year 3	10,000	

(a) What are the tax consequences of these payments to Tina and Ike?

(b) What result if the payments are:

Year 1	$80,000	*no recapture*
Year 2	70,000	
Year 3	60,000	

(c) What result if the payments are:

Year 1	$30,000	
Year 2	40,000	*recapture*
Year 3	80,000	

(d) What result if the payments are:

Year 1 $80,000
Year 2   50,000
Year 3   80,000

(e) Suppose that instead of requiring Tina to make the payments set forth in (a), above, the divorce decree requires Tina to pay Ike 50 percent of the net income (before taxes) of her oil business for three years. The payments above represent 50 percent of the net income from the oil business for the respective years. What tax consequences to Tina and Ike?

(f) What are the tax consequences if the decree instead provides for level payments of $80,000 per year for three years, but Ike dies at the end of year 2 and the payments terminate at that time according to the express provisions of the instrument?

(g) What result in (a), above, if the payments are made pursuant to a § 71(b)(2)(C) decree for support?

(h) Tina and Ike are legally divorced and live in the same household in year one. Tina moves to a new apartment at the beginning of year two. Under the divorce decree, Tina makes payments to Ike of: *71,215 dont apply*

Year 1 $120,000
Year 2   80,000   *71,215 apply*
Year 3   70,000   *no recapture.*
Year 4   60,000

What results to Tina and Ike in each of the years?

2. INDIRECT PAYMENTS

Internal Revenue Code: Section 71(b)(1)(A).

Regulations: Section 1.71–1T(b)(Q6 and 7).

I.T. 4001

1950–1 Cum.Bull. 27.

Advice is requested whether premiums paid by a husband on (1) a life insurance policy assigned to his former wife and with respect to which she is the irrevocable beneficiary, and (2) a life insurance policy not assigned to the wife and with respect to which she is only the contingent beneficiary, are includible in the gross income of the wife under section 22(k) of the Internal Revenue Code [See Section 71(a) of the 1954 Code Ed.] and deductible by the husband under section 23(u) of the Code [See Section 215. Ed.]

In the instant case, the husband and his former wife entered into a property settlement agreement which provides, in addition to monthly payments for support of the wife and support, maintenance, and education of minor children, for the payment by the husband of premiums on two life insurance policies covering the husband's life. One of the policies is assigned absolutely to the wife. She is designated as the irrevocable beneficiary of such policy and the children as irrevocable contingent beneficiaries. Within a specified number of years from the date of issuance of such policy, the husband will exchange it for a whole life or endowment policy and deliver the policy received in exchange to the wife. With respect to the other life insurance policy, the husband, pursuant to the agreement with his wife, designated the children as beneficiaries and the wife as contingent beneficiary. This policy is not assigned to the wife, and its possession and control are retained by the husband. The property settlement agreement in question was entered into as an incident to a divorce action, and the divorce decree makes reference to and approves the terms of the agreement.

It is held that premiums paid by the husband on the life insurance policy absolutely assigned to his former wife and with respect to which she is the irrevocable beneficiary are includible in the gross income of the wife under section 22(k) of the Internal Revenue Code and deductible by the husband under section 23(u) of the Code. (See Anita Quinby Stewart v. Commissioner, 9 T.C. 195, acquiescence, C.B. 1947–2, 4, and Estate of Boies C. Hart et al. v. Commissioner, 11 T.C. 16, acquiescence, C.B. 1949–1, 2.) It is held further that the premiums paid by the husband on the life insurance policy which was not assigned to the wife and with respect to which she is only the contingent beneficiary are neither includible in the gross income of the wife nor deductible by the husband.

NOTE

The statutory definition of alimony expressly contemplates that payments can be made indirectly to the payee. Section 71(b)(1)(A) requires that payment be "∗ ∗ ∗ received by (*or on behalf of*) a spouse under a divorce or separation instrument." [1] The sparse legislative history states that "A payment can ∗ ∗ ∗ qualify as alimony, for example, where a cash payment is made to a third party for the benefit of the payee spouse." [2] And if all other requirements are met, indirect cash payments that are gross income to the payee spouse support a corresponding deduction for the payor spouse. [3]

The question raised is what types of indirect payments qualify as alimony. The answer turns on the nature of the payments, i.e., on the rights and legal interests of the payor and payee with respect to the payments. Just as in the case of the statute prior to the 1984 Act, to the extent that payments are made merely to maintain property owned by the payor spouse which is simply being used by the payee spouse, they do not qualify as indirect alimony payments. [4] Examples are

---

1. Emphasis supplied.

2. H.Rep. No. 68–432, 98th Cong., 2d Sess. 1496 (1984).

3. I.R.C. §§ 71(a), 215(a).

4. See, e.g., Seligmann v. Commissioner, 207 F.2d 489 (7th Cir.1953); Mandel v. Commissioner, 229 F.2d 382 (7th Cir.1956); Rev.Rul. 70–218, 1970–1 C.B. 19; James Parks Bradley, 30 T.C. 701 (1958).

premium payments on life insurance [5] or mortgage payments on real property [6] where the life insurance or the real property is owned by the payor spouse. But if the payments are in satisfaction of a legal obligation exclusively that of the payee spouse and are applicable with respect to property in which the payor has no legal interest, then such payments qualify as indirect alimony payments.[7] The Service's position echoes these observations.[8]

To the extent an indirect payment that qualifies as alimony [9] is in the nature of a capital expenditure,[10] the payee spouse should be viewed as having received the payment and used it, say, to pay principal on a mortgage or premiums on a life insurance policy. Principal payments on a mortgage do not increase the basis of the property,[11] but premium payments on a life insurance policy increase its basis. However, with respect to a life insurance contract, basis may prove to be irrelevant. If the proceeds are ultimately received by the spouse on the death of the insured they are tax-free anyway, the same as in the case of any other beneficiary.[12]

PROBLEMS

1. Ted and Joan are divorced. Pursuant to their written separation agreement incorporated in the divorce decree, Ted is required to make the following alternative payments which satisfy the § 71(b) requirements. Discuss the tax consequences to both Ted and Joan.

    (a) Rental payments of $1000 per month to Joan's landlord.

    (b) Mortgage payments of $1000 per month on their family home which is transferred outright to Joan in the divorce proceedings.

    (c) Mortgage payments of $1000 per month as well as real estate taxes and upkeep expenses on the house where Joan is living which is owned by Ted.

2. Sonny agrees to pay Cher $15,000 a year in alimony until the death of either or the remarriage of Cher. The alimony satisfies the § 71(b) requirements. After 3 years, Cher is concerned about Sonny's

---

5. Note 4, supra.

6. Del Vecchio, 32 T.C.M. 1153 (1973).

7. See, e.g., Melvin A. Christiansen, 60 T.C. 456 (1973); Stevens v. Commissioner, 439 F.2d 69 (2d Cir.1971).

8. Temp.Reg. § 1.71–1T(b) at A–6 provides:

    * * * cash payments of rent, mortgage, tax, or tuition liability of the payee spouse made under the terms of the divorce or separation instrument will qualify as alimony or separate maintenance payments. Any payments to maintain property owned by the payor spouse and used by the payee spouse (including mortgage payments, real estate taxes

and insurance premiums) are not payments on behalf of a spouse even if those payments are made pursuant to the terms of the divorce or separation instrument. Premiums paid by the payor spouse for term or whole life insurance on the payor's life made under the terms of the divorce or separation instrument will qualify as payments on behalf of the payee spouse to the extent that the payee spouse is the owner of the policy.

9. See I.R.C. §§ 71(b) and (f).

10. Cf. I.R.C. §§ 263(a), 1016(a).

11. Cf. Crane v. Commissioner, 331 U.S. 1, 67 S.Ct. 1047 (1947).

12. I.R.C. § 101(a).

life expectancy and they agree to reduce the alimony amount to $10,000 a year if Sonny provides Cher $100,000 of life insurance on his life.

(a) What are the tax consequences to Sonny and Cher if Sonny purchases a single premium $100,000 policy on his life for $60,000 and he transfers it to Cher?

(b) What result in (a), above, if Sonny instead pays Cher $60,000 cash and she purchases the policy for $60,000?

(c) What result if Sonny buys an ordinary policy on his life for $5,000, transfers it to Cher, and agrees to transfer $5,000 cash to her each year so she can pay the annual premiums on the policy?

(d) Same as (c), above, except that Sonny pays the $5,000 annual premiums directly to the insurance company.

(e) Same as (d), above, except that instead of transferring the policy to Cher, Sonny retains ownership of the policy but irrevocably names Cher as its beneficiary.

B. PROPERTY SETTLEMENTS

Internal Revenue Code: Section 1041; See Section 1015(e).

Regulations: Section 1.1041–1T(b).

　　As amended by 1984 legislation, the Code for the first time defines the tax meaning of alimony and separate maintenance payments in terms of objective criteria. The statutory criteria offer myriad choices that can affect the tax results of payments between separating parties. A favorable result can be obtained to the mutual satisfaction of each by an awareness of the criteria and careful drafting of the divorce or separation instrument. If the payments qualify as alimony or separate maintenance, the statute permits allocation (income-deduction treatment) of the tax in accordance with the expressed wishes of the parties; if not, there is no tax (tax neutral) splitting. It is as simple as that. Although the statute nowhere expressly uses the term "support" in these circumstances, the authors have used the support concept as a rationale or underlying theme that is useful in explaining most of the requirements that must be met for payments to constitute alimony or separate maintenance payments. With one exception,[1] all of the criteria for alimony classification taken together,[2] including the anti-abuse provisions,[3] point toward payments that are in the nature of support. Even though Congress has rejected the explicit support obligation requirement of the prior statute[4] the support flavor remains as a

---

1. See I.R.C. § 71(b)(1)(B). This provision is not contrary to the thesis expressed in the text. It merely permits the parties to elect to treat otherwise qualified payments as outside the scope of §§ 71 and 215.

2. See I.R.C. § 71(b).

3. I.R.C. § 71(f).

4. See H.Rep. No. 98–432, 98th Cong., 2d Sess. 1499 (1984).

common denominator of payments within the new definition. The corollary is that payments not meeting the criteria are simply a form of property settlement resulting in tax neutrality.[5]

Before the 1984 legislation it was well established that payments made to effect a division of property between the spouses and consequently not made for "support" were not within the tax allocation scheme of the statute.[6] A little more clearly under the current statute, payments of cash that fail to meet any of the objective statutory requirements for alimony or separate maintenance do not qualify for the tax allocation afforded by Sections 71(a) and 215(a). Therefore, depending on the facts, they are either for child support[7] or are in the nature of a property settlement, and in either instance they have neutral tax consequences.

With respect to any payments in cash, the alimony and separate maintenance provisions of current law are so objective that the parties can arrange these payments so that part or even all of essentially alimony or separate maintenance payments will be treated as a neutral cash property settlement and not taxable to the recipient.[8] Conversely, the parties can arrange what is essentially a "property settlement" so that for federal income tax purposes a portion of the payments (possibly all) will be treated as taxable alimony or separate maintenance[9] and the balance (if any) as a neutral property settlement.

UNITED STATES v. DAVIS

Supreme Court of the United States, 1962.
370 U.S. 65, 82 S.Ct. 1190. Rehearing denied 371 U.S. 854, 83 S.Ct. 14 (1962).

Mr. Justice CLARK delivered the opinion of the Court.

These cases involve the tax consequences of a transfer of appreciated property by Thomas Crawley Davis[1] to his former wife pursuant to a property settlement agreement executed prior to divorce, as well as the deductibility of his payment of her legal expenses in connection therewith. The Court of Claims upset the Commissioner's determination that there was taxable gain on the transfer but upheld his ruling that the fees paid the wife's attorney were not deductible. 152 Ct.Cl. 805, 287 F.2d 168. We granted certiorari on a conflict in the Court of Appeals and the Court of Claims on the taxability of such transfers.[2]

---

5. Such payment may be for child support. I.R.C. § 71(c); see discussion at page 238, infra.

6. See, e.g., Mills v. Commissioner, 442 F.2d 1149 (10th Cir.1971); Ann Hairston Ryker, 33 T.C. 924, 929 (1960).

7. I.R.C. § 71(c).

8. Thus, for example, if the divorce or separation instrument specifically treats all or a portion of the payments as "non-alimony," I.R.C. §§ 71(a) and 215(a) do not apply to the designated payments.

9. The three year rule of I.R.C. § 71(f) can be tailored so that each payment can qualify as alimony or separate maintenance, even though in substance the arrangement is a cash property settlement paid in three annual installments.

1. Davis' present wife, Grace Ethel Davis, is also a party to these proceedings because a joint return was filed in the tax year in question.

2. The holding in the instant case is in accord with Commissioner v. Marshman, 279 F.2d 27 (C.A.6th Cir.1960), but is con-

368 U.S. 813, 82 S.Ct. 60. We have decided that the taxpayer did have a taxable gain on the transfer and that the wife's attorney's fees were not deductible.

In 1954 the taxpayer and his then wife made a voluntary property settlement and separation agreement calling for support payments to the wife and minor child in addition to the transfer of certain personal property to the wife. Under Delaware law all the property transferred was that of the taxpayer, subject to certain statutory marital rights of the wife including a right of intestate succession and a right upon divorce to a share of the husband's property.[3] Specifically as a "division in settlement of their property" the taxpayer agreed to transfer to his wife, *inter alia,* 1,000 shares of stock in the E.I. du Pont de Nemours & Co. The then Mrs. Davis agreed to accept this division "in full settlement and satisfaction of any and all claims and rights against the husband whatsoever (including but not by way of limitation, dower and all rights under the laws of testacy and intestacy) * * *." Pursuant to the above agreement which had been incorporated into the divorce decree, one-half of this stock was delivered in the tax year involved, 1955, and the balance thereafter. Davis' cost basis for the 1955 transfer was $74,775.37, and the fair market value of the 500 shares there transferred was $82,250. The taxpayer also agreed orally to pay the wife's legal expenses, and in 1955 he made payments to the wife's attorney, including $2,500 for services concerning tax matters relative to the property settlement.

I.

The determination of the income tax consequences of the stock transfer described above is basically a two-step analysis: (1) Was the transaction a taxable event? (2) If so, how much taxable gain resulted therefrom? Originally the Tax Court (at that time the Board of Tax Appeals) held that the accretion to property transferred pursuant to a divorce settlement could not be taxed as capital gain to the transferor because the amount realized by the satisfaction of the husband's marital obligations was indeterminable and because, even if such benefit were ascertainable, the transaction was a nontaxable division of property. Mesta v. Commissioner, 42 B.T.A. 933 (1940); Halliwell v. Commissioner, 44 B.T.A. 740 (1941). However, upon being reversed in quick succession by the Courts of Appeals of the Third and Second Circuits, Commissioner v. Mesta, 123 F.2d 986 (C.A.3d Cir.1941); Commissioner v. Halliwell, 131 F.2d 642 (C.A.2d Cir.1942), the Tax Court accepted the position of these courts and has continued to apply these views in appropriate cases since that time, Hall v. Commissioner, 9 T.C. 53 (1947); Patino v. Commissioner, 13 T.C. 816 (1949); Estate of Stouffer v.

tra to the holdings in Commissioner v. Halliwell, 131 F.2d 642 (C.A.2d Cir.1942), and Commissioner v. Mesta, 123 F.2d 986 (C.A. 3d Cir.1941).

3. 12 Del.Code Ann. (Supp.1960) § 512; 13 Del.Code Ann. § 1531. In the case of realty, the wife in addition to the above has rights of dower. 12 Del.Code Ann. §§ 502, 901, 904, 905.

Commissioner, 30 T.C. 1244 (1958); King v. Commissioner, 31 T.C. 108 (1958); Marshman v. Commissioner, 31 T.C. 269 (1958). In Mesta and Halliwell the Courts of Appeals reasoned that the accretion to the property was "realized" by the transfer and that this gain could be measured on the assumption that the relinquished marital rights were equal in value to the property transferred. The matter was considered settled until the Court of Appeals for the Sixth Circuit, in reversing the Tax Court, ruled that, although such a transfer might be a taxable event, the gain realized thereby could not be determined because of the impossibility of evaluating the fair market value of the wife's marital rights. Commissioner v. Marshman, 279 F.2d 27 (1960). In so holding that court specifically rejected the argument that these rights could be presumed to be equal in value to the property transferred for their release. This is essentially the position taken by the Court of Claims in the instant case.

II.

We now turn to the threshold question of whether the transfer in issue was an appropriate occasion for taxing the accretion to the stock. There can be no doubt that Congress, as evidenced by its inclusive definition of income subject to taxation, i.e., "all income from whatever source derived, including * * * [g]ains derived from dealings in property," [4] intended that the economic growth of this stock be taxed. The problem confronting us is simply *when* is such accretion to be taxed. Should the economic gain be presently assessed against taxpayer, or should this assessment await a subsequent transfer of the property by the wife? The controlling statutory language, which provides that gains from dealings in property are to be taxed upon "sale or other disposition," [5] is too general to include or exclude conclusively the transaction presently in issue. Recognizing this, the Government and the taxpayer argue by analogy with transactions more easily classified as within or without the ambient of taxable events. The taxpayer asserts that the present disposition is comparable to a nontaxable division of property between two co-owners, [6] while the Government

---

4. Internal Revenue Code of 1954 § 61(a).

5. Internal Revenue Code of 1954 §§ 1001, 1002.

6. Any suggestion that the transaction in question was a gift is completely unrealistic. Property transferred pursuant to a negotiated settlement in return for the release of admittedly valuable rights is not a gift in any sense of the term. To intimate that there was a gift to the extent the value of the property exceeded that of the rights released not only invokes the erroneous premise that every exchange not precisely equal involves a gift but merely raises the measurement problem discussed in Part III, infra * * *. Cases in which this Court

has held transfers of property in exchange for the release of marital rights subject to gift taxes are based not on the premise that such transactions are inherently gifts but on the concept that in the contemplation of the gift tax statute they are to be taxed as gifts. Merrill v. Fahs, 324 U.S. 308, 65 S.Ct. 655 (1945); Commissioner v. Wemyss, 324 U.S. 303, 65 S.Ct. 652 (1945); see Harris v. Commissioner, 340 U.S. 106, 71 S.Ct. 181 (1950). In interpreting the particular income tax provisions here involved, we find ourselves unfettered by the language and considerations ingrained in the gift and estate tax statutes. See Farid-Es-Sultaneh v. Commissioner, 160 F.2d 812 (C.A.2d Cir. 1947).

contends it more resembles a taxable transfer of property in exchange for the release of an independent legal obligation. Neither disputes the validity of the other's starting point.

In support of his analogy the taxpayer argues that to draw a distinction between a wife's interest in the property of her husband in a common-law jurisdiction such as Delaware and the property interest of a wife in a typical community property jurisdiction would commit a double sin; for such differentiation would depend upon "elusive and subtle casuistries which * * * possess no relevance for tax purposes," Helvering v. Hallock, 309 U.S. 106, 118, 60 S.Ct. 444, 450 (1940), and would create disparities between common-law and community property jurisdictions in contradiction to Congress' general policy of equality between the two. The taxpayer's analogy, however, stumbles on its own premise, for the inchoate rights granted a wife in her husband's property by the Delaware law do not even remotely reach the dignity of co-ownership. The wife has no interest—passive or active—over the management or disposition of her husband's personal property. Her rights are not descendable, and she must survive him to share in his intestate estate. Upon dissolution of the marriage she shares in the property only to such extent as the court deems "reasonable." 13 Del. Code Ann. § 1531(a). What is "reasonable" might be ascertained independently of the extent of the husband's property by such criteria as the wife's financial condition, her needs in relation to her accustomed station in life, her age and health, the number of children and their ages, and the earning capacity of the husband. See, e.g., Beres v. Beres, 52 Del. 133, 154 A.2d 384 (1959).

This is not to say it would be completely illogical to consider the shearing off of the wife's rights in her husband's property as a division of that property, but we believe the contrary to be the more reasonable construction. Regardless of the tags, Delaware seems only to place a burden on the husband's property rather than to make the wife a part owner thereof. In the present context the rights of succession and reasonable share do not differ significantly from the husband's obligations of support and alimony. They all partake more of a personal liability of the husband than a property interest of the wife. The effectuation of these marital rights may ultimately result in the ownership of some of the husband's property as it did here, but certainly this happenstance does not equate the transaction with a division of property by co-owners. Although admittedly such a view may permit different tax treatment among the several States, this Court in the past has not ignored the differing effects on the federal taxing scheme of substantive differences between community property and common-law systems. E.g., Poe v. Seaborn, 282 U.S. 101, 51 S.Ct. 58 (1930). To be sure Congress has seen fit to alleviate this disparity in many areas, e.g., Revenue Act of 1948, 62 Stat. 110, but in other areas the facts of life are still with us.

Our interpretation of the general statutory language is fortified by the long-standing administrative practice as sounded and formalized by the settled state of law in the lower courts. The Commissioner's position was adopted in the early 40's by the Second and Third Circuits and by 1947 the Tax Court had acquiesced in this view. This settled rule was not disturbed by the Court of Appeals for the Sixth Circuit in 1960 or the Court of Claims in the instant case, for these latter courts in holding the gain indeterminable assumed that the transaction was otherwise a taxable event. Such unanimity of views in support of a position representing a reasonable construction of an ambiguous statute will not lightly be put aside. It is quite possible that this notorious construction was relied upon by numerous taxpayers as well as the Congress itself, which not only refrained from making any changes in the statutory language during more than a score of years but re-enacted this same language in 1954.

III.

Having determined that the transaction was a taxable event, we now turn to the point on which the Court of Claims balked, viz., the measurement of the taxable gain realized by the taxpayer. The Code defines the taxable gain from the sale or disposition of property as being the "excess of the amount realized therefrom over the adjusted basis. * * *" I.R.C. (1954) § 1001(a). The "amount realized" is further defined as "the sum of any money received plus the fair market value of the property (other than money) received." I.R.C. (1954) § 1001(b). In the instant case the "property received" was the release of the wife's inchoate marital rights. The Court of Claims, following the Court of Appeals for the Sixth Circuit, found that there was no way to compute the fair market value of these marital rights and that it was thus impossible to determine the taxable gain realized by the taxpayer. We believe this conclusion was erroneous.

It must be assumed, we think, that the parties acted at arm's length and that they judged the marital rights to be equal in value to the property for which they were exchanged. There was no evidence to the contrary here. Absent a readily ascertainable value it is accepted practice where property is exchanged to hold, as did the Court of Claims in Philadelphia Park Amusement Co. v. United States, 130 Ct. Cl. 166, 172, 126 F.Supp. 184, 189 (1954), that the values "of the two properties exchanged in an arms-length transaction are either equal in fact, or are presumed to be equal." Accord, United States v. General Shoe Corp., 282 F.2d 9 (C.A.6th Cir.1960); International Freighting Corp. v. Commissioner, 135 F.2d 310 (C.A.2d Cir.1943). To be sure there is much to be said of the argument that such an assumption is weakened by the emotion, tension and practical necessities involved in divorce negotiations and the property settlements arising therefrom. However, once it is recognized that the transfer was a taxable event, it is more consistent with the general purpose and scheme of the taxing statutes to make a rough approximation of the gain realized thereby than to ignore altogether its tax consequences. Cf. Helvering v. Safe Deposit & Trust Co., 316 U.S. 56, 67, 62 S.Ct. 925, 930 (1942).

Moreover, if the transaction is to be considered a taxable event as to the husband, the Court of Claims' position leaves up in the air the wife's basis for the property received. In the context of a taxable transfer by the husband,[7] all indicia point to a "cost" basis for this property in the hands of the wife.[8] Yet under the Court of Claims' position for cost for this property, i.e., the value of the marital rights relinquished therefor, would be indeterminable, and on subsequent disposition of the property she might suffer inordinately over the Commissioner's assessment which she would have the burden of proving erroneous, Commissioner v. Hansen, 360 U.S. 446, 468, 79 S.Ct. 1270, 1282 (1959). Our present holding that the value of these rights is ascertainable eliminates this problem; for the same calculation that determines the amount received by the husband fixes the amount given up by the wife, and this figure, i.e., the market value of the property transferred by the husband, will be taken by her as her tax basis for the property received.

Finally, it must be noted that here, as well as in relation to the question of whether the event is taxable, we draw support from the prior administrative practice and judicial approval of that practice. See p. 171, supra. We therefore conclude that the Commissioner's assessment of a taxable gain based upon the value of the stock at the date of its transfer has not been shown erroneous.[9]

IV.

The attorney-fee question is [omitted. Ed.]

Reversed in part and affirmed in part.

Mr. Justice FRANKFURTER took no part in the decision of these cases.

Mr. Justice WHITE took no part in the consideration or decision of these cases.

NOTE

The unscrambling of property interests in the case of divorce in a community property state may present a situation quite different from the *Davis* case. If one simply keeps that which is his or hers, no

---

7. Under the present administrative practice, the release of marital rights in exchange for property or other consideration is not considered a taxable event as to the wife. For a discussion of the difficulties confronting a wife under a contrary approach, see Taylor and Schwartz, Tax Aspects of Marital Property Agreements, 7 Tax L.Rev. 19, 30 (1951); Comment, The Lump Sum Divorce Settlement as a Taxable Exchange, 8 U.C.L.A.L.Rev. 593, 601–602 (1961).

8. Section 1012 of the Internal Revenue Code of 1954 provides that:

"The basis of property shall be the cost of such property, except as otherwise provided in this subchapter and subchapters C (relating to corporate distributions and adjustments), K (relating to partners and partnerships), and P (relating to capital gains and losses). * * *"

9. We do not pass on the soundness of the taxpayer's other attacks upon this determination, for these contentions were not presented to the Commissioner or the Court of Claims.

taxable event has occurred; and that would seem to be the effect of an *in kind* equal division of community property. This is indeed acknowledged in *Davis.* However, no reported cases reflect such equal in kind divisions, probably because they are a practical impossibility. That is, the bargaining will go: You take the business and I will take the farm and all the telephone stock, etc.; or the judge in the divorce case may make that decision. Even though all the property involved is community property, exchanges easily recognized by the tax lawyer are taking place. Nevertheless, in cases that involve only a scattering of community property between the spouses the courts [1] and the service [2] have long refused to require recognition of gain or loss under an administratively approved judicial nonrecognition rule. This is coupled with a rule that the basis of the property is carried over to the transferee, i.e. stays with the property.

Difficulties also surfaced regarding the nature of the spouses' property interests under state law. After a long series of litigation, in 1969 the Tenth Circuit decided that Oklahoma law created marital co-ownership interests that *could* be the subject of a tax-free division at the time of divorce.[3] A district court has differentiated *Davis* in a similar manner, finding that Colorado law also creates marital interests that fall on the community property rather than the common law side of the dividing line.[4] On the other hand, the Eighth Circuit has found that an Iowa wife's property interest in her husband's estate is inchoate, like the Delaware wife's interest in *Davis,* and treated the husband's transfer in satisfaction of the interest as a taxable event; [5] and the Tenth Circuit (which had, in effect, placed Oklahoma in the community property category) refused to find that Kansas law (even though it called for an equitable division of property upon divorce) created marital property interests like those in community property states.[6]

The *Davis* case concerned the tax consequences to the transferor husband. But what about his former wife who received the stock? Did she have income? She received property with a fair market value and so the answer would appear to depend on the amount of her basis in the

1. E.g. Jean C. Carrieres, 64 T.C. 959 (1975), acq. 1976–2 C.B. 1, affirmed per curiam 552 F.2d 1350 (9th Cir.1977); Osceola Heard Davenport, 12 T.C.M. 856 (1953); Clifford H. Wren, 24 T.C.M. 290 (1965); Frances R. Walz, 32 B.T.A. 718 (1935).

2. Rev.Rul. 76–83, 1976–1 C.B. 213. With respect to basis, the ruling holds that "the basis of each individual asset received in its entirety by one spouse or the other in the division will retain its present community basis in the hands of the spouse receiving it. The basis of each asset that will be partitioned will be the applicable percentage of the asset received multiplied by that asset's present basis to the community."

3. Collins v. Commissioner, 412 F.2d 211 (10th Cir.1969). See also Bosch v. U.S., 590 F.2d 165 (5th Cir.1979).

4. Imel v. U.S., 375 F.Supp. 1102 (D.Colo.1973).

5. Wallace v. U.S., 439 F.2d 757 (8th Cir.1971).

6. Wiles v. Commissioner, 499 F.2d 255 (10th Cir.1974), cert. denied 419 U.S. 996, 95 S.Ct. 310 (1974). See Lawson, "Tax Implications of Using Appreciated Property in a Property Settlement," 42 J.Tax. 58 (1975) and Glickfeld, Rabow, and Schwartz, "Federal Income Tax Consequences of Marital Property Settlements," 26 U.S.C.T.I. 307 (1974).

property interests she relinquished. Supported by footnote 7 of *Davis*, supra, Revenue Ruling 67–221[7] stated:

> Under the terms of a divorce decree and in accordance with a property settlement agreement, which was incorporated in the divorce decree, the husband transferred his interest in an apartment building to his former wife in consideration for and in discharge of her dower rights. The marital rights the former wife relinquished are equal in value to the value of the property she agreed to accept in exchange for those rights. *Held*, there is no gain or loss to the wife on the transfer and the basis of the property to the wife is its fair market value on the date of the transfer.

If Wife realized no income, is this because her basis in her marital rights was equal to their value? Where could such basis come from? This seems to be merely another judge-made rule but, again, one that appears fair when the *Davis* tax on the transferor is considered.

Almost fourteen years ago in the Second Edition of this casebook[8] and in all subsequent editions, we have stated:

> In view of the difference between community and noncommunity property states and the possible nonapplication of *Davis* in some noncommunity states one may question whether such a substantial difference in tax consequences should be left to be dependent upon state law. Certainly the *Davis* case imposes a tax in an already troubled divorce or legal separation situation where the transfer does not generate any liquidity, any funds with which to pay. Perhaps Congress should come to the rescue of noncommunity property states (as it did in 1948) and reverse the *Davis* result. If it does, it should also consider the consequences to the recipient spouse as well, expressly excluding receipts from income but providing suitable carryover basis provisions.

The Tax Reform Act of 1984 quieted this tumultuous area and rescues all noncommunity property taxpayers by reversing the holding in *Davis*.[9] We have previously seen that paradoxically[10] the new provision, Section 1041, actually reaches beyond the *Davis* facts, providing a clear nonrecognition rule for gains and losses with respect to *any* transfer of property between married persons[11] and also between formerly married persons.[12] In the latter instance, however, the non-

---

7. 1967–2 C.B. 63.

8. 2d Ed. Fundamentals of Income Taxation at page 168 (1978).

9. P.L. No. 98–369, § 421 98th Cong., 2d Sess. (1984). See Gabinet, "Section 1041: The High Price of Quick Fix Reform in Taxation of Interspousal Transfers," 5 Amer.J. of Tax Pol. 13 (1986); Lepow, "Tax Policy for Lovers and Cynics: How Divorce Settlement Became the Last Tax Shelter in America," 62 Notre Dame L.Rev. 32 (1986);

Asimow, "The Assault on Tax-Free Divorce: Carryover Basis and the Assignment of Income," 44 Tax.L.Rev. 65 (1989); Nunnallee, "The Assignment of Income Doctrine as Applied to Section 1041 Divorce Transfers: How the Service Got it Wrong," 68 Ore.L.Rev. 615 (1989).

10. See page 136, supra.

11. I.R.C. § 1041(a)(1).

12. I.R.C. § 1041(a)(2).

recognition rule applies only if the transfer is "incident to divorce." [13] Further, consistent with the Second Edition suggestion of the authors, the transferee spouse or former spouse takes the property with a transferred basis.[14]

The reasons for the change in the law and a brief explanation of the new provision are succinctly expressed in the House Report, as follows: [15]

Reasons for Change

The committee believes that, in general, it is inappropriate to tax transfers between spouses. This policy is already reflected in the Code rule that exempts marital gifts from the gift tax, and reflects the fact that a husband and wife are a single economic unit.

The current rules governing transfers of property between spouses or former spouses incident to divorce have not worked well and have led to much controversy and litigation. Often the rules have proved a trap for the unwary as, for example, where the parties view property acquired during marriage (even though held in one spouse's name) as jointly owned, only to find that the equal division of the property upon divorce triggers recognition of gain.

Furthermore, in divorce cases, the government often gets whipsawed. The transferor will not report any gain on the transfer, while the recipient spouse, when he or she sells, is entitled under the *Davis* rule to compute his or her gain or loss by reference to a basis equal to the fair market value of the property at the time received.

The committee believes that to correct these problems, and make the tax laws as unintrusive as possible with respect to relations between spouses, the tax laws governing transfers between spouses and former spouses should be changed.

Explanation of Provision

The bill provides that the transfer of property to a spouse incident to a divorce [16] will be treated, for income tax purposes, in the same manner as a gift. Gain (including recapture income) or loss will not be recognized to the transferor, and the transferee will receive the property at the transferor's basis (whether the property has appreciated or depreciated in value). A transfer will be treated as incident to a divorce if the transfer occurs within one year after the parties cease to be

transfer like a gift

---

13. See I.R.C. § 1041(c). The term incident to divorce is considered in more detail in the text at note 17, infra.

14. I.R.C. § 1041(b). Cf. I.R.C. § 1015(a) and (e).

15. H.Rep. No. 98–432, 98th Cong., 2d Sess., 1491 (1984).

16. For purposes of this provision, an annulment is treated as a divorce.

married or is related to the divorce.[17] This nonrecognition rule applies whether the transfer is for the relinquishment of marital rights, for cash or other property, for the assumption of liabilities in excess of basis, or for other consideration and is intended to apply to any indebtedness which is discharged. Thus, uniform Federal income tax consequences will apply to these transfers notwithstanding that the property may be subject to differing state property laws.

In addition, this nonrecognition rule applies in the case of transfers of property between spouses during marriage.

Where an annuity is transferred, or a beneficial interest in a trust is transferred or created, incident to divorce or separation, the transferee will be entitled to the usual annuity treatment, including recovery of the transferor's investment in the contract (under sec. 72), or the usual treatment as the beneficiary of a trust (by reason of sec. 682), notwithstanding that the annuity payments or payments by the trust qualify as alimony or otherwise discharge a support obligation.[18] The transfer of a life insurance contract to a spouse incident to a divorce or separation generally will no longer result in the proceeds of the policy later being includible in income, since the policy will have a carryover basis and therefore the transfer for value rules (sec. 101(a)(2)) will not apply. Also, the transfer of an installment obligation will not trigger gain and the transfer of investment credit property will not result in recapture if the property continues to be used in the trade or business.

The student is cautioned that the holding of *Davis* extends well beyond the context of a divorce property settlement situation. Although Section 1041 reverses the holding of *Davis* for a narrow situation including all interspousal transfers of property and transfers between nonspouses which are incident to divorce, the holding has

[handwritten marginalia: interspousal trans — trans between nonspouses incident to divorce]

---

17. [Temp.Regs. 1.1041–1T(b) at A–7 provides that:

A transfer of property is treated as related to the cessation of the marriage if the transfer is pursuant to a divorce or separation instrument, as defined in section 71(b)(2), and the transfer occurs not more than 6 years after the date on which the marriage ceases. A divorce or separation instrument includes a modification or amendment to such decree or instrument. Any transfer not pursuant to a divorce or separation instrument and any transfer occurring more than 6 years after the cessation of the marriage is presumed to be not related to the cessation of the marriage. This presumption may be rebutted only by showing that the transfer was made to effect the division of property owned by the former spouses at the time of the cessation of the marriage. For example, the presumption may be rebutted by showing that (a) the transfer was not made within the one- and six-year periods described above because of factors which hampered an earlier transfer of the property, such as legal or business impediments to transfer or disputes concerning the value of the property owned at the time of the cessation of the marriage, and (b) the transfer is effected promptly after the impediment to transfer is removed. Ed.]

18. This rule relates, in part, to amendments made to Code section 71 by section 423 of the bill. [See page 244, infra. Ed.]

continued vitality in all other situations involving the transfer of property in discharge of obligations. In these other circumstances whenever appreciated or loss property is transferred to satisfy an obligation, a gain subject to tax or possibly a deductible loss occurs.[19]

PROBLEMS

1. Johnny and Joanna's divorce decree becomes final on January 1, 1991. Discuss the tax consequences of the following transactions to both Johnny and Joanna:

(a) Pursuant to their divorce decree, Johnny transfers to Joanna in March, 1991 a parcel of unimproved land he purchased 10 years ago. The land has a basis of $100,000 and a fair market value of $500,000. Joanna sells the land in April, 1991 for $600,000.

(b) Same as (a), above, except that the land is transferred to satisfy a debt that Johnny owes Joanna. The land has a basis of $500,000 and a fair market value of $400,000 at the time of the transfer. Joanna sells the land for $350,000.

(c) What result if pursuant to the divorce decree, Johnny transfers the land in (a), above, to Joanna in March, 1996.

(d) Same as (c), above, except that the transfer is required by a written instrument incident to the divorce decree.

(e) Same as (c), above, except the transfer is made in March, 1998.

C. OTHER TAX ASPECTS OF DIVORCE

---

1. CHILD SUPPORT

Internal Revenue Code: Section 71(b)(1)(D); (c).

Regulations: See Section 1.71–1T(c).

COMMISSIONER v. LESTER

Supreme Court of the United States, 1961.
366 U.S. 299, 81 S.Ct. 1343.

Mr. Justice CLARK delivered the opinion of the Court.

The sole question presented by this suit, in which the Government seeks to recover personal income tax deficiencies, involves the validity of respondent's deductions from his gross income for the taxable years 1951 and 1952 of the whole of his periodic payments during those years to his divorced wife pursuant to a written agreement entered into by

---

19. See, e.g., International Freighting Corporation, Inc. v. Commissioner, 135 F.2d 310 (2d Cir.1943) at page 140, supra and Kenan v. Commissioner, 114 F.2d 217 (2d Cir.1940) at page 704, infra.

them and approved by the divorce court. The Commissioner claims that language in this agreement providing "[i]n the event that any of the [three] children of the parties hereto shall marry, become emancipated, or die, then the payments herein specified shall * * * be reduced in a sum equal to one-sixth of the payments which would thereafter otherwise accrue" sufficiently identifies one-half of the periodic payments as having been "payable for the support" of the taxpayer's minor children under § 22(k) of the Internal Revenue Code of 1939 and, therefore, not deductible by him under § 23(u) of the Code.[1] The Tax Court approved the Commissioner's disallowance, 32 T.C. 1156, but the Court of Appeals reversed, 279 F.2d 354, holding that the agreement did not "fix" with requisite clarity any specific amount or portion of the periodic payments as payable for the support of the children and that all sums paid to the wife under the agreement were, therefore, deductible from respondent's gross income under the alimony provision of § 23(u). To resolve a conflict among the Courts of Appeals on the question,[2] we granted certiorari. 364 U.S. 890, 81 S.Ct. 220. We have concluded that the Congress intended that, to come within the exception portion of § 22(k), the agreement providing for the periodic payments must specifically state the amounts or parts thereof allocable to the support of the children. Accordingly, we affirm the judgment of the Court of Appeals.

Prior to 1942, a taxpayer was generally not entitled to deduct from gross income amounts payable to a former spouse as alimony, Douglas v. Willcuts, 296 U.S. 1, 56 S.Ct. 59 (1935), except in situations in which the divorce decree, the settlement agreement and state law operated as a complete discharge of the liability for support. Helvering v. Fitch, 309 U.S. 149, 60 S.Ct. 427 (1940). The hearings, Senate debates and the Report of the Ways and Means Committee of the House all indicate that it was the intention of Congress, in enacting § 22(k) and § 23(u) of the Code, to eliminate the uncertain and inconsistent tax consequences resulting from the many variations in state law. "[T]he amendments are designed to remove the uncertainty as to the tax consequences of payments made to a divorced spouse * * *." S.Rep.No. 673, Pt. 1, 77th Cong., 1st Sess. 32. They "will produce uniformity in the treatment of amounts paid * * * regardless of variance in the laws of different States * * *." H.R.Rep. No. 2333, 77th Cong., 2d Sess. 72. In addition, Congress realized that the "increased surtax rates[3] would intensify" the hardship on the husband who in many cases, "would not have sufficient income left after paying alimony to meet his income tax obligations," H.R.Rep. No. 2333, 77th Cong., 2d Sess. 46, and perhaps also that, on the other hand, the wife, generally being in a lower income tax bracket than the husband, could more easily protect herself

---

1. [I.R.C. (1939) § 22(k) and 23(u) are omitted. See I.R.C. (1986) §§ 71(b) and 215. Ed.]

2. Both Metcalf v. Commissioner, 271 F.2d 288 (C.A.1st Cir.1959), and Eisinger v. Commissioner, 250 F.2d 303 (C.A.9th Cir.

1957), have arrived at conclusions contrary to those of the court below.

3. Sections 22(k) and 23(u) were enacted as part of the Revenue Act of 1942 which provided for greatly increased tax revenue to meet the expenses of World War II.

H may give more if deductible

in the agreement and in the final analysis receive a larger net payment from the husband if he could deduct the gross payment from his income.

The first version of § 22(k) was proposed by the Senate as an amendment to the Revenue Act of 1941. The sums going to child support were to be includible in the husband's gross income [sic] only if the amount thereof was "specifically designated as a sum payable for the support of minor children of the spouses." H.R. 5417, 77th Cong., 1st Sess., § 117. The proposed amendment thus drew a distinction between a case in which the amount for child support was "specifically designated" in the agreement, and one in which there was no such designation. In the latter event, "the whole of such amounts are includible in the income of the wife. * * *" S.Rep. No. 673, Pt. 1, 77th Cong., 1st Sess. 35. Action on the bill was deferred by the conference committee [4] and hearings on the measure were again held the following year. The subsequent Report of the Senate Finance Committee on § 22(k) carried forward the term "specifically designated," used in the 1941 Report (No. 673), with this observation:

> "If, however, the periodic payments * * * are received by the wife for the support and maintenance of herself and of minor children of the husband without such specific designation of the portion for the support of such children, then the whole of such amounts is includible in the income of the wife as provided in section 22(k). * * *" S.Rep. No. 1631, 77th Cong., 2d Sess. 86.*

As finally enacted in 1942, the Congress used the word "fix" instead of the term "specifically designated," but the change was explained in the Senate hearings as "a little more streamlined language." Hearings before Senate Committee on Finance on H.R. 7378, 77th Cong., 2d Sess. 48. As the Office of the Legislative Counsel reported to the Senate Committee:

> "If an amount is specified in the decree of divorce attributable to the support of minor children, that amount is not income of the wife. * * * If, however, that amount paid the wife includes the support of children, *but no amount is specified for the support of the children,* the entire amount goes into the income of the wife. * * *" *Ibid.* (Italics supplied).

This language leaves no room for doubt. The agreement must expressly specify or "fix" a sum certain or percentage of the payment for child support before any of the payment is excluded from the wife's income. The statutory requirement is strict and carefully worded. It does not say that "a sufficiently clear purpose" on the part of the parties is sufficient to shift the tax. It says that the "written instrument" must "fix" that "portion of the payment" which is to go to the support of the

---

4. H.R.Rep. No. 1203, 77th Cong., 1st Sess. 11.

* This Report and this quotation appear at 1942–2 C.B. 504, 570, respectively. Ed.

children.   Otherwise, the wife must pay the tax on the whole payment. We are obliged to enforce this mandate of the Congress.

One of the basic precepts of the income tax law is that "[t]he income that is subject to a man's unfettered command and that he is free to enjoy at his own option may be taxed to him as his income, whether he sees fit to enjoy it or not."   Corliss v. Bowers, 281 U.S. 376, 378, 50 S.Ct. 336, 337 (1930).   Under the type of agreement here, the wife is free to spend the monies paid under the agreement as she sees fit.   "The power to dispose of income is the equivalent of ownership of it."   Helvering v. Horst, 311 U.S. 112, 118, 61 S.Ct. 144, 147 (1940). Including the entire payments in the wife's gross income under such circumstances, therefore, comports with the underlying philosophy of the Code.   And, as we have frequently stated, the Code must be given "as great an internal symmetry and consistency as its words permit." United States v. Olympic Radio & Television, 349 U.S. 232, 236, 75 S.Ct. 733, 736 (1955).

It does not appear that the Congress was concerned with the perhaps restricted uses of unspecified child-support payments permitted the wife by state law when it made those sums includible within the wife's alimony income.   Its concern was with a revenue measure and with the specificity, for income tax purposes, of the amount payable under the terms of the written agreement for support of the children. Therefore, in construing that revenue act, we too are unconcerned with the variant legal obligations, if any, which such an agreement, by construction of its nonspecific provisions under local rules, imposes upon the wife to use a certain portion of the payments solely for the support of the children.   The Code merely affords the husband a deduction for any portion of such payment not specifically earmarked in the agreement as payable for the support of the children.

As we read § 22(k), the Congress was in effect giving the husband and wife the power to shift a portion of the tax burden from the wife to the husband by the use of a simple provision in the settlement agreement which fixed the specific portion of the periodic payment made to the wife as payable for the support of the children.   Here the agreement does not so specifically provide.   On the contrary, it calls merely for the payment of certain monies to the wife for the support of herself and the children.   The Commissioner makes much of the fact that the agreement provides that as, if, and when any one of the children married, became emancipated or died the total payment would be reduced by one-sixth, saying that this provision did "fix" one-half (one-sixth multiplied by three, the number of children) of the total payment as payable for the support of the children.   However, the agreement also pretermitted the entire payment in the event of the wife's remarriage and it is as consistent to say that this provision had just the opposite effect.   It was just such uncertainty in tax consequences that the Congress intended to and, we believe, did eliminate when it said that the child-support payments should be "specifically designated" or, as the section finally directed, "fixed."   It does not say that "a sufficiently clear purpose" on the part of the parties would satisfy. It says that the written instrument must "fix" that amount or "portion of the payment" which is to go to the support of the children.

The Commissioner contends that administrative interpretation has been consistently to the contrary. It appears, however, that there was such a contrariety of opinion among the Courts of Appeals that the Commissioner was obliged as late as 1959 to issue a Revenue Ruling which stated that the Service would follow the rationale of Eisinger v. Commissioner, 250 F.2d 303 (C.A.9th Cir.1957),[5] but that Weil v. Commissioner, 240 F.2d 584 (C.A.2d Cir.1957),[6] would be followed "in cases involving similar facts and circumstances." Rev.Rul. 59–93, 1959–1 Cum.Bull. 22, 23.

All of these considerations lead to the conclusion that if there is to be certainty in the tax consequences of such agreements the allocations to child support made therein must be "specifically designated" and not left to determination by inference or conjecture. We believe that the Congress has so demanded in § 22(k). After all, the parties may for tax purposes act as their best interests dictate, provided, as that section requires, their action be clear and specific. Certainly the Congress has required no more and expects no less.

Affirmed.

Mr. Justice DOUGLAS, concurring.

While I join the opinion of the Court, I add a few words. In an early income tax case, Mr. Justice Holmes said "Men must turn square corners when they deal with the Government." Rock Island, A. & L.R. Co. v. United States, 254 U.S. 141, 143, 41 S.Ct. 55, 56. The revenue laws have become so complicated and intricate that I think the Government in moving against the citizen should also turn square corners. The Act, 1939 I.R.C. § 22(k), makes taxable to the husband that part of alimony payments "which the terms of the decree or written instrument fix, in terms of an amount of money or a portion of the payment, as a sum" payable for support of minor children.

I agree with the Court that this agreement did not "fix" any such amount. To be sure, an amount payable in support of minor children may be inferred from the *proviso* that one-sixth of the payment shall no longer be due, if the children marry, become emancipated, or die. But Congress in enacting this law realized that some portion of alimony

---

5. The court there approved the rule that "when the settlement agreement, read as a whole, discloses that the parties have earmarked or designated * * * the payments to be made, one part to be payable for alimony, and another part to be payable for the support of children, with sufficient certainty and specificity to readily determine which is which, without reference to contingencies which may never come into being, then the 'part of any periodic payment' has been fixed 'by the terms of the decree or written instrument' * * *." 250 F.2d, at 308.

6. In that case the agreement provided for reductions only in the event the divorced wife remarried. The court stated that "[t]he fortuitous or incidental mention of a figure in a provision meant to be inoperative, unless some more or less probable future event occurs, will not suffice to shift the tax burden from the wife to the husband." 240 F.2d, at 588.

taxable to the wife might be used for support of the children, as the opinion of the Court makes clear.

The present agreement makes no specific designation of the portion that is intended for the support of the children. It is not enough to say that the sum can be computed. Congress drew a clear line when it used the word "fix." Resort to litigation, rather than to Congress, for a change in the law is too often the temptation of government which has a longer purse and more endurance than any taxpayer.

NOTE

All might well agree that payments to a payee spouse for child support should not be accorded the same treatment as alimony or separate maintenance payments. Such amounts received by the custodial parent have no gross income characteristics either to the parent or to the child. And, just as in the case of unbroken families, a parent furnishing child support should hardly be entitled to any deduction for such payments.[1] This result continues in the law after 1984 changes.[2] But the current statute, reversing *Lester*, redefines the meaning of an amount "fixed" for the support of children.[3] Thus, for example, assume the divorce or separation instrument requires the payor spouse to pay $12,000 each year for the life of the payee spouse for payee's support and for the support of their child. Assume, however, that when the child reaches majority, marries or dies, the annual sum is to be reduced to $8,000. The *Lester* court interpreting the prior statute concluded that no amount was *fixed* for the support of the child, with the result that the entire sum of $12,000 was accorded alimony (taxable) status. The entire amount of each payment was gross income to the payee and deductible by the payor. Although the *Lester* holding may have been questionable from a tax policy standpoint, it had the distinct advantage of providing an easy means to shift income tax liability to the recipient spouse who might well be in a lower tax bracket than the payor spouse. This would enable the payor to make larger payments at no greater cost because of the resulting tax leverage of the deduction. Moreover, the *Lester* arrangement served to satisfy the local divorce tribunals that the children of the marriage were actually supported after the divorce or separation. The chameleon nature of the *Lester* rule became well known to the matrimonial or family lawyers.

In 1984, Congress closed the door, expressly providing that, if any amount specified in the instrument [4] will be reduced on a child "attaining a specified age, marrying, dying, leaving school, or upon a similar contingency, or at a time which can clearly be associated with [such] a contingency," then the amount of the reduction will be treated as an amount "fixed" as payable for the support of the child of the payor

---

1. The dependency exemption authorized by I.R.C. § 151(c) is not a deduction for support payments. See page 548, infra.

2. I.R.C. § 71(c)(1).

3. I.R.C. § 71(c)(2).

4. See I.R.C. § 71(b)(2).

spouse.[5] Accordingly, in the earlier example, of the total $12,000 paid, $4,000 would now be deemed fixed for child support, and only $8,000 would be for alimony or separate maintenance.

PROBLEMS

Sean and Madonna enter into a written support agreement which is incorporated into their divorce decree at the time of their divorce. They have one child who is in Madonna's custody. Discuss the tax consequences in the following alternative situations:

(a) The agreement requires Sean to pay Madonna $10,000 per year and it provides that $4,000 of the $10,000 is for the support of their child.

(b) The agreement requires Sean to pay Madonna $10,000 per year, but when their child reaches age twenty-one, dies, or marries prior to reaching twenty-one, the amount is to be reduced to $6,000 per year.

(c) The agreement requires Sean to pay Madonna $10,000 per year but that the payments will be reduced to $8,000 per year on January 1, 1992, and to $6,000 per year on January 1, 1996. Sean and Madonna have two children: Daughter (born June 17, 1974), and son (born March 5, 1977).

(d) What result in (a), above, if Sean pays Madonna only $5,000 of the $10,000 obligation in the current year?

2. ALIMONY PAYMENTS MADE BY A THIRD PARTY

Internal Revenue Code: Sections 215; 682. See Sections 72; 1041.

The object here in part is to pull together some peripheral problems that arise in connection with payments, including indirect payments and property transfers, occasioned by separation and divorce. A modest excursion into the area of trusts is inescapable, and these comments may be more meaningful after one has explored the materials on trusts in Chapter 13[1] although even there the taxation of trusts is not considered in depth.

It is possible now to see an overall pattern in Sections 71 and 215. If a payor spouse hangs on to his or her property and makes piece-meal alimony or separate maintenance payments to a payee spouse, payee is taxed on such payments and payor may deduct them. If such payments do not qualify as alimony or separate maintenance[2] or are treated as non-alimony by the parties[3] then in either case, under the statute, the payments are without tax significance. Similarly, if instead a payor spouse discharges the obligation by transferring property to payee spouse the transfer is without tax significance to either of

if non alimony then no tax significance

---

5. I.R.C. § 71(c)(2).

1. See page 302 infra.

2. I.R.C. § 71(b), (f).

3. I.R.C. § 71(b)(1)(B).

them.[4] But as the transferred property produces income, it will be income taxable to the payee and not the payor. It is payee's property and consequently the income from the property is payee's income.[5] A lump sum settlement accomplishes an *actual* splitting of future income (with tax liability in accord with economic reality), making unnecessary the somewhat artificial splitting accomplished in other circumstances by Section 71(a) inclusion and Section 215(a) deduction.

Annuity Payments. The question dealt with here is: What are the consequences of a *lump sum transfer* by a payor spouse that does not go directly to payee spouse but which generates periodic income received by payee? In these circumstances, there is no payment by the payor, even indirectly to payee, which would qualify as alimony or separate maintenance.[6] Although the payor's investment via a lump sum expenditure to a third party, for example for an annuity contract, is the source of current income receipts by the payee, such receipts flow from the contract or other investment purchased by the payor.

The answer to the question is simple. The payee as owner of the investment is treated as any other taxpayer owner. The statutory allocation of tax provided by Sections 71 and 215 is not applicable to either the payee or the payor. The income generated by the investment is taxable to the payee in accordance with the taxing rules applicable to the nature of the property which generates the receipts.[7] Such income is not included in the payor's gross income, since payor does not own the property that produces it.[8] In these circumstances, whether the payee actually receives a lump sum amount which payee then invests in income producing property, or the payor makes the investment in property that payor then transfers to payee, the income from the property is payee's; payee is the owner of the property and the taxpayer with respect to generated income.[9] The allocation provisions of Sections 71 and 215 are not needed in these circumstances and are not applicable.[10] In the case of an annuity policy, the payee is taxed with respect to each annual receipt under the annuity rules of

---

4. See I.R.C. §§ 1041, 1015(e). Even gift tax neutrality can be assured. See I.R.C. § 2516.

5. I.R.C. § 102(b)(1).

6. See I.R.C. § 71(b)(1)(A) and Indirect Payments, page 224, supra. Technically, a lump sum cash payment by payor either directly to payee or to an annuity company could constitute alimony or separate maintenance in the unlikely event that it met the § 71(b) requirements.

7. P.L. No. 98–369, § 422(a), 98th Cong., 2d Sess. (1984), repealed I.R.C. §§ 71(d), 72(k), 101(e). See H.Rep. No. 98–432, 98th Cong., 2d Sess. 1491 (1984).

8. See note 10, infra. Cf. Helvering v. Horst, 311 U.S. 112, 61 S.Ct. 144 (1940).

9. P.L. No. 98–369, § 422, 98th Cong., 2d Sess. (1984), repealed I.R.C. § 71(d). It also eliminated the reference in § 215 of prior law to § 71(d). See note 7, supra.

10. While the principles of Old Colony Trust Co. v. Commissioner, 279 U.S. 716, 49 S.Ct. 499 (1929), may tax one on amounts paid in discharge of his obligation, the *annual* payments to the payee would discharge no such obligation; that obligation was eliminated with the purchase of the investment by the payor. But in any case, the payment of lump sum cash or the transfer of appreciated property cannot result in taxable gain. See I.R.C. § 1041.

Section 72,[11] not under Section 71. The payor has no income and is not entitled to any deduction.

Alimony Trusts. Outside the annuity area and similar arrangements effected by a transfer of investment property to a payee spouse incident to divorce, different but parallel rules apply with respect to alimony trusts. Suppose, for example, that the divorce or separation instrument [12] requires the payor to transfer a specified amount of property to a trust under the terms of which the income is to be paid to the payee for payee's life or until payee's remarriage with provision for distribution of the remainder to the payor or to others upon the payee's death or remarriage. Money or property placed in such a trust does constitute transferred property. But unlike the transfers of property discussed earlier in which the payee is the legal *owner* of the property, the payee in these circumstances is the beneficial owner of an *income interest* in a trust. This constitutes a transferred interest in property.[13] But, even so, the income paid to payee by the trust is not income spawned by *payee's* own property; it is income much like alimony in flavor, but paid to payee through the vehicle of a trust. Two questions must be considered. First, is such income taxable to the payor because it discharges payor's support obligation or because the payor retains a reversionary interest? [14] Second, is the income taxable to the payee as alimony under Section 71? The specific answer to both questions, found in Section 682, is no; [15] but we must not jump to final conclusions about the treatment of the payee.

Section 682, in contrast to prior law, pre-empts the area with respect to alimony trusts.[16] The income of such trusts, excluded from the payor's gross income, is taxable to the payee.[17] In fact, the payee in these circumstances is treated as the "beneficiary".[18] For purposes of computing the taxable income of the trust and of the payee, the special provisions of Subchapter J are applicable.[19] Therefore the allocation of tax liability here is between the trust and the payee as beneficiary. Section 71 is not applicable. The payee has gross income and the trust is entitled to a deduction to the extent of income of the trust that is required to be distributed currently or to the extent that income is paid

11. I.R.C. § 72; see page 169, supra.

12. I.R.C. § 71(b)(2).

13. Cf. Blair v. Commissioner, 300 U.S. 5, 57 S.Ct. 330 (1937). But cf. I.R.C. § 1001(e)(1).

14. I.R.C. §§ 673, 677(a) and (b); cf. Old Colony Trust Co. v. Commissioner, note 10, supra.

15. Prior to the 1984 Act, the entire alimony trust was handled under I.R.C. § 71. The income of the trust, not taxed to the payor under § 71(d), was taxable to the payee, outside the regular taxation of trusts rules, to the extent that the trust payments met the requirements of former

§ 71(a) and § 71(c)(2). P.L. No. 98–369, § 422(a), 98th Cong., 2d Sess. (1984), repealed § 71(d) and enlarged § 682 to cover alimony trusts. See H.Rep. No. 98–432, 98th Cong., 2d Sess. 1492 (1984). Cf. Ellis v. U.S., 416 F.2d 894 (6th Cir.1969) and Anita Quinby Stewart, 9 T.C. 195 (1947) both decided under prior law.

16. P.L. No. 98–369, § 422(a) repealed *inter alia* § 71(d); § 422(d)(2) amended § 682(b).

17. I.R.C. § 682(a); cf. I.R.C. § 215(d).

18. I.R.C. § 682(b).

19. I.R.C. §§ 641–692.

to payee.[20] This is all subject to the quantitative and qualitative limitations of "distributable net income" (D.N.I.).[21] In this setting, the payee as *beneficiary* is entitled to treat amounts received in a special way. Thus, tax exempt interest and other special trust receipts will retain their unique character under the conduit provisions of the trust distribution rules.[22] The tax advantages to the payee as beneficiary of an alimony trust governed by Subchapter J, in contrast to payee receiving alimony under Section 71 *from* payor, are numerous.[23] The payor is entitled to exclude the trust's income from gross income[24] and, therefore, is entitled to no deduction.[25]

Consistent with the notion of Section 71(c), concerning child support, Section 682(a) denies the payor an exclusion and relieves the payee of tax on amounts of trust income which are fixed as a sum payable for the support of minor children of the payor.[26] This means that the payor remains taxable on the amount of trust income used for child support.[27]

3. DIVORCE

Where a payor spouse makes alimony payments to a payee spouse under a decree of divorce or under a decree of separate maintenance, such payments constitute gross income to the payee under Section 71(a) and are deductible from the payor's gross income under Section 215(a). If the divorce decree is subsequently declared invalid by the jurisdiction which rendered the divorce, it is void everywhere,[1] and payments made thereafter, in the absence of a written separation agreement or decree for support,[2] are neither income to the payee nor deductible by the payor. Conversely, the Internal Revenue Service generally will not question the validity of any divorce decree for federal income tax purposes until a court of competent jurisdiction declares the divorce to be invalid.[3] The law is unsettled, however, when alimony or support

---

20. I.R.C. §§ 652, 651 or 662, 661.

21. I.R.C. § 643(a) defines distributable net income in terms of the taxable income of the trust, adjusted for certain receipts accorded special treatment elsewhere in the statute so as to effect a qualitative conduit, see, e.g., § 643(a)(5). For a discussion of D.N.I., see page 303, infra.

22. See note 20, supra; and see Ferguson, Freeland and Stephens, Federal Income Taxation of Estates and Beneficiaries, Ch. 7 (1970).

23. I.R.C. § 682 also applies in the case of decedents' estates which continue to make "alimony" type payments to a surviving payee after the death of the payor, so that the payee as *beneficiary* of the estate is subject to the same benefits as in the case of a trust; see note 21, supra.

24. I.R.C. § 682(a).

25. I.R.C. § 215(d).

26. The amount is fixed by the terms of the decree, written separation agreement or trust instrument. There is a curious omission here. See I.R.C. § 71(c)(2) which reverses the holding in Commissioner v. Lester, 366 U.S. 299, 81 S.Ct. 1343 (1961), and see page 238, supra. One can only speculate whether *Lester*-type facts built into an alimony trust, would be converted by the application of § 71(c)(2) *over* to § 682(a), construing the word "fix".

27. I.R.C. § 677(a) and (b).

1. Estate of Daniel Buckley, 37 T.C. 664 (1962).

2. I.R.C. § 71(a), (b)(2)(B) and (C) and § 215.

3. G.C.M. 25250, 1947–2 C.B. 32; Rev. Rul. 67–442, 1967–2 C.B. 65. This principle is further applied in Rev.Rul. 71–390, 1971–2 C.B. 82. However, if a divorce is obtained at the close of the tax year solely

payments are made under an ex parte divorce decree rendered by a court other than the court of marital domicile and that decree is subsequently declared invalid by a state court with jurisdiction over the parties or subject matter of the action.[4]

Assume the following hypothetical fact situation: Ex-husband and Ex-wife were married in State X in 1980. They separated in 1990; no separation agreement was signed, nor was a decree of support entered.[5] In 1991 Ex-husband obtained an ex parte Mexican divorce. The divorce decree provided for alimony payments to be made to Ex-wife. In 1993, Ex-wife obtained an ex parte decree in State X declaring the 1991 Mexican divorce to be invalid. Ex-husband took Section 215 deductions for alimony paid to Ex-wife for the years 1991 to 1994 inclusive.[6] Ex-wife never treated the payments as gross income. In 1995 the Commissioner filed deficiencies against Ex-husband for the years 1991 to 1994 on the ground that the Section 215 deductions for alimony payments were improper because the 1991 divorce was a nullity.

Faced with facts similar to those above, the Tax Court has consistently held that state law governs marital status and has denied the validity of an ex parte divorce decree for federal income tax purposes where that decree is subsequently invalidated by a court of competent jurisdiction.[7] The Tax Court would thus uphold all deficiencies entered against Ex-husband for the years 1991 to 1994. The Tax Court's position was adopted by the Internal Revenue Service in Revenue Ruling 67–442,[8] which states that where a state court of competent jurisdiction declares the prior divorce to be invalid, "the Service will usually follow the later court decision rather than the divorce decree for Federal income tax purposes for such years as may not be barred by the statute of limitations"[9] and deny Ex-husband a Section 215 deduction. Further, in the same Revenue Ruling the Service expressly declined to follow the decisions of the Court of Appeals for the Second

to enable separate return filings by a couple and remarriage is intended and actually follows in the next tax year, the I.R.S. will not recognize the divorce for federal income tax purposes. See Rev.Rul. 76–255, 1976–2 C.B. 40 and see page 956 infra.

4. See Lathrope, "State-Defined Marital Status: Its Future as an Operative Tax Factor," 17 U.C. Davis L.Rev. 257 (1983); Spolter, "Invalid Divorce Decrees," 24 Tax L.Rev. 163 (1969); Kapp, "Tax Aspects of Alimony Agreements and Divorce Decrees," 27 N.Y.U.Inst. on Fed. Tax. 1231 (1969); Currie, "Suitcase Divorce in the Conflict of Laws: Simons, Rosentiel and Borax," 34 U.Chi.L.Rev. 26 (1966) (considering the conflict of laws question).

5. Under I.R.C. § 71(b)(2)(B) and (C), respectively, alimony payments as defined in § 71(b)(1) made by Ex-husband to Ex-wife

under a written separation agreement or a court decree of support or maintenance, are includible in Ex-wife's gross income, and deductible to Ex-husband under § 215(a), regardless of whether a valid decree of divorce exists.

6. One can certainly question husband's motive in making the 1994 payments. If they were pursuant to a written separation agreement I.R.C. § 71(a) would be applicable as would § 215(a).

7. Ruth Borax, 40 T.C. 1001 (1963); Harold E. Wondsel, 23 T.C.M. 1278 (1964); Albert Gersten, 28 T.C. 756 (1957) (denying taxpayer joint income tax return with second wife); George J. Feinberg, 16 T.C. 1485 (1951).

8. Supra note 3.

9. Rev.Rul. 67–442, supra note 3 at 66.

Circuit in Estate of Herman Borax v. Commissioner [10] and Harold E. Wondsel v. Commissioner.[11]

The facts of *Borax* and *Wondsel* are very similar to the hypothetical facts posited above.[12] In both cases, however, the Court of Appeals reversed the Tax Court and held the divorce decrees to be valid for Federal income tax purposes, despite the subsequent invalidating decrees. The court concluded that the respective taxpayer husbands were entitled to deduct the alimony payments under Section 215.[13] If *Borax* and *Wondsel* are viewed as controlling, then Ex-husband in our hypothetical fact situation would be allowed Section 215 deductions for all years contested by the Commissioner, and Ex-wife would be required to include payments in her gross income.[14]

Cases subsequent to *Borax* and *Wondsel* have limited those cases to alimony situations, stating that marriage, for the purposes of filing joint returns [15] and allowing marital deductions for estate taxes,[16] is authorized and defined by state law alone. Contrary to the court's reasoning in *Borax* and *Wondsel,* certainty within the entire federal taxing structure requires that state law determine the validity of a marriage. It would seem that state law should therefore determine the validity of a divorce decree and be the basis for determining the deductibility of alimony payments made pursuant thereto. Furthermore, when an ex parte divorce decree is invalidated by a court having jurisdiction over the parties or subject matter of the action, in the absence of a written separation agreement or decree of support or maintenance, alimony paid by the payor spouse subsequent to the

---

10. 349 F.2d 666 (2d Cir.1965), cert. denied 383 U.S. 935, 86 S.Ct. 1064 (1966), reversing 40 T.C. 1001 (1963).

11. 350 F.2d 339 (2d Cir.1965), cert. denied 383 U.S. 935, 86 S.Ct. 1064 (1966), reversing 23 T.C.M. 1278 (1964).

12. In *Borax,* husband obtained a Mexican divorce, while in *Wondsel* the divorce decree was entered by a Florida court. Both husbands, prior to their respective ex parte divorces, had been making nondeductible support payments to their wives under *pre-1954* written separation agreements. In both cases each husband remarried. Their respective first wives subsequently obtained decrees invalidating the ex parte divorces from state courts of competent jurisdiction.

13. The cases further held that they were entitled to file joint income tax returns with their current wives. See I.R.C. § 6013.

14. In *Wondsel,* petitioner's ex-wife declared alimony received under the divorce decrees as gross income. In *Borax,* however, petitioner's ex-wife never declared alimony payments as gross income; as the litigation involved husband taxpayers the

Court of Appeals for the Second Circuit did not rule on this issue.

15. See Harold K. Lee, 64 T.C. 552 (1975), affirmed 550 F.2d 1201 (9th Cir.1977), limiting *Borax* and *Wondsel* to alimony situations and denying taxpayer the right to file a joint return with his current wife. See also I.R.C. § 152(b)(5), where local law determines the validity of a marital relationship for personal exemption deductions.

16. See Wesley A. Steffke's Estate, 64 T.C. 530 (1975), affirmed 538 F.2d 730 (7th Cir.1976); Estate of Leo J. Goldwater, 64 T.C. 540 (1975), affirmed 539 F.2d 878 (2d Cir.1976) (limiting *Borax* and *Wondsel* to alimony situations refusing to allow § 2056 marital deduction to decedent taxpayer's current wives). But see Estate of Spalding, 537 F.2d 666 (2d Cir.1976), allowing a California decedent's estate a § 2056 marital deduction for property passing to the surviving husband where husband's divorce from his first wife had been declared invalid by a New York court, because the divorce decree had not been invalidated by the state where the decedent's estate was being administered.

invalidation decree should not be income to the payee under Section 71(a), nor should payor be allowed a Section 215(a) deduction for the payment. However, until the date on which the divorce decree is invalidated, the divorce should be respected for federal income tax purposes, and Section 215 deductions taken by payor after the alleged divorce and prior to its invalidation should not be subject to attack by the Commissioner.

If the above suggested solution to the issue were adopted, the result on the hypothetical facts would allow Ex-husband Section 215 deductions for alimony payments made to Ex-wife in 1991 and 1992, subsequent to the divorce and prior to its invalidation. Likewise, Ex-wife should include the alimony payments received in 1991 and 1992 in her gross income for those years. For the years 1993 and 1994, Ex-husband should be denied a Section 215 deduction on the ground that the 1993 invalidation decree rendered the prior ex parte divorce decree void under state law, and thus a nullity for federal income tax purposes. Ex-wife need not include these payments in her gross income.

In another area related to the status of divorce in the application of Section 71 the courts, over the Commissioner's objection, have equated an annulment to a divorce with the usual inclusion and deduction consequences to the parties.[17] The commissioner now agrees.[18]

17. Anna E. Laster, 48 T.C. 178 (1967); George F. Reisman, 49 T.C. 570 (1968); Andrew M. Newburger, 61 T.C. 457 (1974).

18. Acquiescences in the *Laster, Reisman* and *Newburger* cases, supra note 2, appear at 1971–2 C.B. 3 and 1974–2 C.B. 3. Cf. H.Rep. No. 98–432, 98th Cong., 2d Sess. 1492, n. 6 (1984). Cf. Reg. § 1.1041–1T Q and A 8.

Up until the time that a divorce decree may be determined invalid the divorce will be respected for Fed tax purposes. After the invalidity is determined the pymts will not be treated as alimony under Fed tax law.

CHAPTER 11.　OTHER EXCLUSIONS FROM GROSS INCOME

Several statutory exclusions from gross income not identified elsewhere in the book are of sufficient significance to warrant brief discussion. Of course, not all exclusions from gross income occur as a result of a specific statutory provision. Most benefits received under federal Social Security legislation are administratively excluded from gross income by way of lenient interpretation of less than specific statutory language.[1] However, Section 86 expressly requires *inclusion* of some such benefits.[2] Items may also be excluded from gross income by federal legislation not within the Internal Revenue Code. For example, payments of benefits under any law administered by the Veteran's Administration are excluded from gross income by Title 38 of the United States Code.[3] This chapter considers only statutory exclusions under Section 911, excluding some income earned abroad, Section 135 excluding income from certain U.S. savings bonds essentially used to pay higher education tuition and fees, and Section 103, excluding interest paid on some governmental obligations which also has constitutional overtones. The latter is taken up along with other constitutional concepts.[4]

A.　INCOME EARNED ABROAD

Internal Revenue Code: See Section 911.

Income earned abroad is allowed special income tax treatment. This area is especially typical of the current congressional practice of continually changing the rules, which requires tax attorneys constantly to analyze and apply new statutes. Although the United States taxes both its citizens and mere residents on their worldwide income, historically there has been a limited exclusion from gross income for income earned abroad. Obviously, this is in anticipation of a tax on the income at its source as well.

1. Old age and survivors insurance benefit payments are excluded by Rev.Rul. 70–217, 1970–1 C.B. 12, and medicare benefits by Rev.Rul. 70–341, 1970–2 C.B. 31. See Reg. § 1.61–11(b). This includes educational assistance allowances. See Rev.Rul. 71–536, 1971–2 C.B. 78. Compare Rev.Rul. 76–121, 1976–1 C.B. 24, holding social security benefits paid by the United Kingdom to a resident of the United States includible in gross income and Rev.Rul. 66–34, 1966–1 C.B. 22, involving a similar payment by Germany to a United States resident.

2. See page 530, infra.

3. 38 U.S.C.A. § 3101(a). Cf. Strickland v. Commissioner, 540 F.2d 1196 (4th Cir.1976).

4. I.R.C. §§ 118, 122, 126, 130, 131, and 133 are not discussed in the book.

The current exclusion from gross income under Section 911 [1] may be substantial. To qualify for the exclusion an American citizen must be a bona fide resident of a foreign country or countries for an uninterrupted period that includes an entire taxable year, or an American citizen or resident must be present in a foreign country or countries for at least 330 days during any period of twelve consecutive months.[2] The exclusion applies only to foreign earned income which is defined as income from a foreign source which is attributable to the taxpayer's performance of services.[3] The maximum exclusion is $70,000.[4]

Section 911 also provides an exclusion for amounts paid as reimbursement of foreign "housing expenses" in excess of a statutorily provided base housing amount,[5] if the housing expenses are paid for by the taxpayer's employer. Qualified taxpayers whose housing costs are not paid for by employers may elect to deduct a limited amount of housing costs in computing adjusted gross income. Housing expenses include reasonable amounts paid for housing [6] (including utility bills and insurance) in a foreign country for the taxpayer and his family if they live together.[7]

Both the earned income and foreign housing cost exclusions are elective.[8] Elections for each are made separately [9] and, once made, remain in effect in future years unless revoked.[10] The exclusions are denied to a taxpayer for earned income and housing expenses in a foreign country in which travel by United States citizens and residents is restricted.[11]

1. P.L. No. 97–314, §§ 111, 112, 97th Cong., 1st Sess. (1981).

2. I.R.C. § 911(d)(1).

3. I.R.C. § 911(b)(1)(A). Foreign earned income does not include amounts received as a pension or annuity, amounts paid by the United States or its agencies to their employees, amounts received from certain trusts, or amounts received after the close of the taxable year in which the services to which the amounts are attributable are performed. I.R.C. § 911(b)(1)(B).

4. I.R.C. § 911(b)(2)(A). Specific dollar limitations on the exclusion have varied over time. They were provided to prevent abuses by highly paid persons (particularly entertainers and athletes) who might otherwise be tempted to move abroad to escape U.S. income tax. See Sen.Rep. No. 97–144, 97th Cong., 1st Sess. 36 (1981).

5. The base housing amount equals 16% of the salary of a U.S. employee at grade GS–14 on the federal payscale times the applicable period during the year. I.R.C. § 911(c)(1)(B).

6. Housing expenses do not include amounts paid as interest or taxes which are independently deductible. I.R.C. § 911(c)(2)(A)(ii). See I.R.C. §§ 163, 164.

7. If dangerous or other adverse conditions require the taxpayer to maintain a separate residence for his family overseas, the excess housing costs of both households are eligible for the exclusion. See also I.R.C. § 119(c) which provides an exclusion from gross income for employer-provided meals and lodging in remote "camps" in foreign countries.

8. I.R.C. § 911(a).

9. Id.

10. I.R.C. § 911(e).

11. I.R.C. § 911(d)(8).

B. SAVINGS BOND INCOME USED TO PAY HIGHER EDUCATION TUITION AND FEES

Internal Revenue Code: Section 135.

In an effort to help low and medium income taxpayers fund the cost of their or their dependents' higher education tuition payments, Congress allows taxpayers to exclude from gross income the discounted interest on certain Federal bonds the proceeds of which are directly or indirectly used to finance such educational costs.[1] Section 135(a) allows an exclusion from gross income for the gain[2] on the redemption of "qualified United States savings bonds"[3] to the extent that the taxpayer pays "qualified higher education expenses"[4] during the year. A United States savings bond is qualified if it is issued at a discount after 1989 to an individual who has attained age 24 before the date of the bond's issuance.[5] The exclusion is inapplicable if the bonds are purchased by a parent and put in the name of a child or are purchased by a child.[6]

Qualified higher education expenses include tuition and fees[7] of the taxpayer and the taxpayer's spouse and dependents[8] during the year of the bond redemption at an eligible higher educational institution.[9] The amount of tuition and fees is reduced by scholarships, fellowships, employer-funded educational assistance, and other tuition reductions.[10] No exclusion is allowed if the taxpayer is married and files a separate return.[11]

There are two special limitations on the exclusion. If the bond redemption proceeds in a year exceed the qualified higher education expenses for the year, only a portion of the interest income from the bonds is excluded equal to the ratio of the expenses to the proceeds.[12] For example, if a taxpayer redeems a bond in a year in which his dependent's qualified higher education expenses are $8,000 and the bond proceeds are $10,000, made up of $5,000 of the principal cost of the bond and $5,000 of accrued interest, only 80 percent of the proceeds

---

1. I.R.C. § 135. See Williams, "Financing a College Education: A Taxing Dilemma," 50 Ohio State L.J. 561 (1989); Sumutka, "Qualified U.S. Savings Bonds are a Viable Education Savings Alternative," 43 Tax'n for Accts 370 (1989).

2. The bonds are issued at a discount with the result that the gain is attributable to interest earned on the bonds over their lifetime. See I.R.C. § 135(c)(1)(C).

3. I.R.C. § 135(c)(1).

4. I.R.C. § 135(c)(2).

5. I.R.C. § 135(c)(1). The exclusion applies only to series EE bonds. I.R.C. § 135(c)(1)(C).

6. Conf.Rep. No. 100–1104, 100th Cong., 2d Sess. 141 (1988), reprinted in 1988–3 C.B. 631.

7. I.R.C. § 135(c)(2)(A).

8. I.R.C. § 135(c)(2)(A)(i)–(iii). The taxpayer must be allowed an I.R.C. § 151 deduction for the year with respect to a dependent. I.R.C. § 135(c)(2)(A)(iii). See Chapter 18D, infra.

9. I.R.C. § 135(c)(2)(A), (c)(3).

10. I.R.C. § 135(d)(1).

11. I.R.C. § 135(d)(2).

12. I.R.C. § 135(b)(1). The term proceeds includes the original cost of the bond as well as any income interest generated by the bond. Id.

are excluded and 20 percent of the interest ($1,000) must be included in the taxpayer's gross income for the year.[13]

The second limitation limits the exclusion to low and medium-income taxpayers. Under the limitation, there is a phase-out of the amount of exclusion if the taxpayer's "modified adjusted gross income" [14] exceeds $40,000 (or $60,000 in the case of a joint return),[15] with the dollar amounts adjusted for inflation for years after 1990.[16] The amount of the phase-out is determined by multiplying the exclusion times a fraction the numerator of which is the excess of the taxpayer's modified adjusted gross income over the $40,000 or $60,000 amount and the denominator is $15,000 in the case of a single taxpayer or $30,000 in the case of a taxpayer filing a joint return.[17] Thus there is no exclusion if the taxpayer's modified adjusted gross income exceeds $55,000 (or $90,000 in the case of a joint return), with those dollar amounts adjusted for inflation for years after 1990.[18]

PROBLEM

Several years ago in a year after 1989, Mother purchased some series EE bonds at a cost of $10,000. Mother was 35 years old at the time. She redeems the bonds in the current year for $25,000. Assume (for simplicity) that there is no post–1990 inflation. Does Mother who is a widow have gross income and, if so, how much, if:

   (a) Mother uses the proceeds to pay Daughter's $25,000 college tuition?

   (b) Mother uses the proceeds to buy a new car in a year in which she also pays Daughter's $25,000 college tuition?

   (c) Mother uses the proceeds to pay Daughter's $12,500 college tuition and Daughter's $12,500 rent and living expenses while Daughter attends college?

   (d) What results under the facts of (a), above, if Mother has modified adjusted gross income of $50,000?

   (e) What results under the facts of (a), above, if Mother instead gave Daughter, then aged 15, the $10,000 and Daughter purchased the bonds?

C. FEDERAL TAXES AND STATE ACTIVITIES

Internal Revenue Code: Sections 103; 115; 141(a) and (e). See Sections 141 through 150.

"The power to tax involves the power to destroy." So wrote Chief Justice Marshall in 1819 in McCulloch v. Maryland.[1] This classic dictum is the foundation of a doctrine of intergovernmental immunity.

---

13. See Conf.Rep. No. 100–1104, supra note 6.

14. I.R.C. § 135(c)(4).

15. I.R.C. § 135(b)(2)(A).

16. I.R.C. § 135(b)(2)(B).

17. I.R.C. § 135(b)(2)(A).

18. Id. I.R.C. § 135(b)(2)(B).

1. 17 U.S. (4 Wheat.) 316, 431 (1819).

That doctrine imposes some restraints upon federal and local government undertakings to impose taxes impinging upon each other.[2]

The doctrine finds no express support in the Constitution. It rests instead upon an implied guarantee of governmental self-preservation, and over the years, the courts have limited the scope of the doctrine. Even when the doctrine of intergovernmental immunity imposes no obstacles, important policy questions exist. The questions center on the extent to which the federal government should exercise restraint in imposing taxes that have an impact on state activities.

The Court applied the philosophy of *McCulloch* in reverse (applied it to a federal tax) in The Collector v. Day.[3] The Court in *Day* held invalid the imposition of a *federal* tax (the Civil War Income Tax) on the salary of a *state* judge. The Court reasoned that the tax threatened an essential function of the state. Later, the Court expressed the reciprocal nature of the intergovernmental immunity doctrine as follows: [4]

> As the States cannot tax the powers, the operations, or the property of the United States, nor the means which they employ to carry their powers into execution, so it has been held that the United States have no power under the Constitution to tax either the instrumentalities or the property of a State.

Intergovernmental immunity had bold beginnings and a vigorous early life but has suffered a marked decline over the past half century. Much of its attrition occurred around World War II. By 1939, Mr. Justice Frankfurter referred to Chief Justice Marshall's dictum, quoted above, as a mere "seductive cliche." [5] The Court rejected the reciprocal nature of the doctrine about this time: [6]

> [I]n laying a federal tax on state instrumentalities the people of the states, acting through their representatives, are laying a tax on their own institutions and consequently are subject to political restraints which can be counted on to prevent abuse. State taxation of national instrumentalities is subject to no such restraint, for the people outside the state have no representatives who participate in the legislation; and in a real sense, as to them, the taxation is without representation.

2. The actual holding of *McCulloch* repudiated a *state* tax imposed on the privilege of issuing bank notes, but applicable in fact only to national banks. The Court held the tax invalid as an improper interference with powers expressly granted to the federal government.

3. 78 U.S. (11 Wall.) 113 (1870).

4. Pollock v. Farmers' Loan & Trust Co., 157 U.S. 429, 584, 15 S.Ct. 673, 690 (1895).

5. Graves v. People of State of New York ex rel. O'Keefe, 306 U.S. 466, 489, 59 S.Ct. 595, 602 (1939). Earlier, Mr. Justice Holmes had delivered the classic comment: "The power to tax is not the power to destroy while this Court sits." Panhandle Oil Co. v. Mississippi ex rel. Knox, 277 U.S. 218, 223, 48 S.Ct. 451, 453 (1928).

6. Helvering v. Gerhardt, 304 U.S. 405, 412, 58 S.Ct. 969, 971–972 (1938).

Shortly thereafter, the Court nailed the coffin shut on reciprocity with the following: [7]

> The considerations bearing upon taxation by the states of activities or agencies of the Federal Government are not correlative with the considerations bearing upon federal taxation of state agencies or activities.

The question whether a tax has an adverse impact on an essential governmental function [8] has shifted to a consideration whether the tax applies even-handedly in a non-discriminatory fashion. The Court first differentiated *Day* in a decision involving a federal tax on a less-than-essential state employee.[9] Then, the Court overruled *Day*, holding: [10]

> So much of the burden of a non-discriminatory general tax upon the incomes of employees of a government, state or national, as may be passed on economically to that government, through the effect of the tax on the price level of labor or materials, is but the normal incident of the organization within the same territory of two governments, each possessing the taxing power.

Intergovernmental immunity still may generate nostalgic feelings in law professors at state universities. In the final analysis, however, neither state nor federal employees enjoy immunity from state or federal income taxes.[11]

The tattered doctrine of intergovernmental immunity long hovered over the taxation of interest paid on state and local obligations. There was little reason for this. In Pollock v. Farmers Loan & Trust, in which the Supreme Court nullified the 1894 federal income tax statute, there is dictum that Congress could not validly tax the interest on state bonds.[12] However, since 1894 the Court has condoned a federal tax on salaries of state employees which, by analogy, goes a long way to undermine the *Pollock* dictum. Arguably a state's activities are affected no differently if it must pay higher (taxable) interest on its bonds than if it must pay higher (taxable) salaries to its employees. The issue was put to rest by the holding of the Supreme Court in South Carolina v. Baker [13] that taxation of interest on state bonds did not violate the doctrine of intergovernmental tax immunity.[14]

The bond interest question is becoming less academic. States, of course, do not tax interest paid on federal bonds. But the federal income tax, has begun to recognize that some state bonds support private functions. Section 103(a) contains a deceptively broad state-

---

7. New York v. U.S., 326 U.S. 572, 577, 66 S.Ct. 310, 312 (1946).

8. See The Collector v. Day, supra note 3.

9. Helvering v. Gerhardt, supra note 6.

10. Graves, supra note 5.

11. See the Public Salary Tax Act of 1939, 53 Stat. 574.

12. Pollock v. Farmers' Loan & Trust Co., supra note 4.

13. 485 U.S. 505, 108 S.Ct. 1355 (1988).

14. The Court also held that such taxation did not violate the Tenth Amendment limitation on the authority of Congress to regulate state activities.

ment that excludes interest on *any* state or local bond from gross income.[15] But, the exclusion, historically intended to apply to interest on bonds the proceeds of which are used to finance operations of state and local governmental units, does not extend to interest paid on any state or local bond that is a "private activity bond", if it is not a "qualified bond", an "arbitrage bond", or a bond which is not in "registered form".[16]

Private activity bonds are obligations of state or local governments issued to finance nongovernmental undertakings. Thus a bond to raise money to build public buildings such as a courthouse, a library or a school is a public bond; but a bond to build a building for a private company to use tax-free, to encourage it to locate within a state or community, is a private activity bond. A private activity bond is any bond that is part of a bond issue where, in general, more than 10 percent of the proceeds are to be used for a private use,[17] and the payment of the principal or of interest on more than 10 percent of the proceeds of the issue is secured by an interest on private use property.[18] In the alternative, a bond is treated as a private activity bond if it is part of an issue of which more than 5 percent or $5 million of the proceeds, whichever is less, is used to finance direct or indirect loans to borrowers other than "governmental units" or to acquire "nongovernmental output property." [19]

Certain bonds, despite being classified as private activity bonds, may nevertheless receive the interest exclusion benefits of Section 103(a).[20] Such private activity bonds, known as "qualified bonds", are: exempt facility bonds, qualified mortgage bonds, qualified veteran's mortgage bonds, qualified small issue bonds, qualified student loan bonds, qualified redevelopment bonds, and bonds the proceeds of which are to benefit certain charitable organizations.[21] The restrictions applicable to each type of qualified bond are extremely intricate; and there are also volume limitations on the amount of such bonds an issuer may

15. I.R.C. § 103(a), stating "gross income does not include interest on any State or local bond."

16. I.R.C. § 103(b).

17. I.R.C. § 141(a)(1)(A). This is known as the "private business use" test. See I.R.C. § 141(b)(1).

18. I.R.C. § 141(a)(1)(B). This is known as the "private security or payment" test. See I.R.C. § 141(b)(2).

This 10% ceiling under both § 141(a)(1)(A) and (B) becomes 5% where the private use being financed is unrelated to the governmental use being financed. I.R.C. § 141(b)(3). For example, a privately operated newsstand located in a courthouse is related to the courthouse, and a privately operated school cafeteria is relat-

ed to the school in which it is located. Conf.Rep. No. 99–841, 99th Cong., 2d Sess. II–691 (1986). If, however, 6% of the proceeds of a school construction bond issue is used to build a privately operated cafeteria in the county's administrative office building the related use restriction is violated. Id. at Example 1.

19. I.R.C. § 141(c), (d). A governmental unit is defined to exclude any agency or instrumentality of the United States. I.R.C. § 150(a)(2). Nongovernmental output property is essentially property which before its acquisition was used by a nongovernmental unit in connection with an output facility. I.R.C. § 141(d)(2).

20. I.R.C. § 103(b)(1).

21. I.R.C. § 141(e)(1).

offer without loss of preferred status.[22]   What follows is a general description, only, of the various types of qualified bond issues.

Exempt facility bonds are bonds issued to finance airports, docks and wharves, mass commuting facilities, water facilities, sewage facilities, solid waste disposal facilities, certain qualified residential rental projects, local gas or electric facilities, local heating or cooling facilities, and qualified hazardous waste facilities, and high-speed intercity rail facilities.[23]   In order to qualify for the exemption, at least 95 percent of the net proceeds of the bond issue must be used for the exempt facility for which the bonds are issued.[24]

Qualified mortgage bonds are bonds issued to finance below market mortgage loans to single family home buyers.[25]   Several restrictions apply.   For example, at least 95 percent of the net proceeds of such bond issues must be used to finance mortgage loans to first-time home buyers purchasing a principal residence.[26]

A qualified veteran's mortgage bond is also related to the purchase of single family principal residences.   It is a bond 95 percent or more of the proceeds of which are used to finance loans to veterans for the purchase of such residences.[27]

Qualified small issue bonds are in general bonds forming part of an issue the face amount of which does not exceed $1 million,[28] where at least 95 percent of the proceeds are used to acquire business land or depreciable property.[29]   Loans to some types of businesses are disqualified.[30]

A qualified student loan bond is a bond where either 90 or 95 percent of the proceeds are used to finance student loans.[31]   Some federal loans are subject to the 90 percent limit; all others are subject to the 95 percent requirement.[32]

A qualified redevelopment bond is one where 95 percent or more of the bond issue proceeds are used for redevelopment of a designated

---

22. See I.R.C. §§ 141–147, especially § 141(e)(2) and § 146.

23. I.R.C. § 142(a).

24. Id. The term "net proceeds" is defined as gross proceeds of the issue less amounts placed in a reasonably required reserve or replacement fund.   I.R.C. § 150(a)(3).

25. I.R.C. § 143. Cf. I.R.C. § 25 which is discussed at page 984, infra.

26. I.R.C. § 143(c)(1), (d)(1). The special treatment afforded qualified mortgage bonds will not be available to bonds issued after December 31, 1991.   I.R.C. § 143(a)(1)(B).

27. I.R.C. § 143(b).

28. I.R.C. § 144(a)(1).   Subject to further restrictions, the authorized face

amount of a qualified small bond issue may be as high as $10 million.   I.R.C. § 144 (a)(4).

29. The tax exempt status of qualified small issue bonds is not available to bonds issued after December 31, 1986, except where 95% or more of the proceeds are used to finance manufacturing facilities or land purchases for first time farmers in which case the exemption is available to bonds issued before January 1, 1992. I.R.C. § 144(a)(12).

30. I.R.C. § 144(a)(8).

31. I.R.C. § 144(b).

32. I.R.C. § 144(b)(2).   See I.R.C. § 144(b)(1)(A) and (B).

blighted area.[33] The redevelopment may take the form of acquisition of land, clearing and preparation for redeveloping land, the rehabilitation of buildings, or the relocation of occupants.[34]

A qualified 501(c)(3) bond is, in general, a bond where at least 95 percent of the proceeds are to be used by either a charitable organization or a governmental unit.[35] Section 501(c)(3) charitable organizations are organizations organized and operated exclusively for the benefit of a religious, scientific, educational or related purpose.[36]

The exclusion of interest paid on state or local bonds under Section 103(a) does not extend to any "arbitrage bond".[37] Arbitrage occurs when any portion of the proceeds of a bond issue is used to acquire investment property which produces a yield that is "materially higher" than the return paid on the bond issue itself.[38] Prior to enactment of arbitrage restrictions, state and local governments issued tax exempt bonds, on which they paid low interest rates because of their tax exempt status, and invested the proceeds in other securities (generally taxable bonds) with a higher yield, thereby producing tax free income at the expense of the federal coffers. There are several exceptions to the current arbitrage rules.[39]

Finally, the Section 103 exclusion is not applicable to interest paid on state and local bonds that do not meet the registration requirements of Section 149.[40] Congress was concerned that the use of bearer (nonregistered) tax exempt bonds facilitated abuses within the tax system. Without registration of the bonds taxpayers could easily conceal from the Internal Revenue Service income tax gains on bearer bonds (which gains are taxable even if the interest they pay is not) and, for estate and gift tax purposes, could conceal the bonds themselves (or their transfer). Congress, generally, has required tax exempt bonds issued after June 30, 1983, to be in registered form in order to qualify for the Section 103(a) interest exclusion.[41] In addition, unregistered bonds are subject to various punitive provisions.[42]

Should Congress continue a provision that generates huge sources of untaxed income? Note that taxpayers in the 31 percent bracket receive a yield on a 10 percent tax-exempt bond worth the same as the

---

33. I.R.C. § 144(c).   See   I.R.C. § 144(c)(4) for the definition of a designated blighted area.

34. I.R.C. § 144(c)(3).

35. I.R.C. § 145(a).

36. I.R.C. § 501(c)(3).

37. I.R.C. § 103(b)(2).

38. I.R.C. § 148(a) and (b).

39. See I.R.C. §§ 148(c) through (f). For instance, a state or local government may save the tax exempt status of a bond issue by refunding to the federal government any arbitrage profits. I.R.C. § 148(f)(2). In addition, a small portion of the proceeds

(5% or $100,000 whichever is lesser) may be invested in higher yielding investments (§ 148(e)), a temporary investment may be made until the proceeds are needed for their specified purposes (§ 148(c)) or 10% of the proceeds may be placed in a reserve fund (§ 148(d)).

40. I.R.C. § 103(b)(3). The constitutionality of such taxation was upheld in South Carolina v. Baker, supra note 13.

41. Pub.Law No. 97–448, 97th Cong., 2d Sess. § 306(b)(2) (1982). Cf. I.R.C. § 149(c)(2)(A) and see I.R.C. (1954) § 103(j).

42. See, for example, I.R.C. §§ 163(f) and 165(j).

yield on a 14.5 percent taxable bond.[43]　Historically, Congressional efforts to eliminate the perceived inequity have been rebuffed.[44]　One problem is the extent to which any such change might be accorded retroactive effect to tax the interest on outstanding state bonds.　And of course a constant problem is the extent to which the fiscal situations could stand further complication by the increased costs of state borrowing, which would follow if the interest on state bonds were subject to the income tax.　There is the possibility that state losses could be made up by the *states* extending their income taxes to interest on federal obligations.[45]　Nevertheless the 1986 Act broke historic ground by indirectly subjecting some interest exempted from regular income tax by Section 103(a) to taxation under the alternative minimum tax.[46]

The foregoing comments all concern circumstances in which federal income taxes may impinge on the states only indirectly, by way of imposing a tax on an individual or other recipient on amounts *paid* by a state, such as salary or bond interest.　What about taxing the *state's* income?　From a legislative viewpoint, statutes handle this matter loosely.

A great many organizations enjoy express statutory exemption from Federal income tax.[47]　These provisions may encompass some state-owned instrumentalities, but they do not embrace the states as such.[48]　This does not mean, however, that the states are subject to tax on their net receipts.　Instead, it reflects a state exemption, generally assumed.　At one time, even the Treasury Department considered this exemption to rest on the constitutional doctrine of intergovernmental immunity.[49]　Treasury changed its position and later considered the

---

43. If a taxpayer receives 14.5% interest on a $10,000 taxable bond and pays tax at a 31% rate on that amount he will receive $1,450 of interest, pay $450 of tax, and net $1,000 after taxes, the same after-tax return as he would receive on 10% tax-exempt bond.　For a discussion written when tax rates were higher than after enactment of the Tax Reform Act of 1986, see generally, Surrey, "Federal Income Taxation of State and Local Government Obligation," 36 Tax Policy 3 (1969), reprinted in Sander and Westfall, Readings in Federal Taxation, page 277 (1970) and Morris, "Tax Exemption for State and Local Bonds," 42 Geo.Wash.L.Rev. 483 (1974).

44. See Maxwell, "Exclusion from Income of Interest on State and Local Government Obligations," House Comm. on Ways and Means, 86th Cong., 2d Sess., 1 Tax Revision Compendium 701, 702–703 (1959).　In 1969, an unsuccessful effort was made to bring such interest at least within the reach of the Minimum Tax for Tax Preferences, I.R.C. (1954) §§ 56–58. H.Rep. No. 91–413 (Part 1), 91st Cong., 1st Sess. (1969), 1969–2 C.B. 249.　But see note 46, infra.

45. This is one to conjure with. It is likely Congress could by legislation prohibit the imposition of state income taxes on the interest paid on federal obligations. Congressional power to protect its agencies and activities clearly extends beyond any automatic immunities inferred from the Constitution. See Graves v. New York ex rel. O'Keefe, supra note 5 at 478, 59 S.Ct. at 597, and cases there cited. However, to do so would seem to lend support to the argument of the states that the imposition of federal income tax on interest paid on state obligations should be precluded under remnants of the constitutional doctrine of intergovernmental immunity on a kind of fair's fair principle.

46. I.R.C. § 57(a)(5). See page 995, infra. See generally I.R.C. §§ 55–59 and Chapter 27C, infra.

47. See I.R.C. § 501(c) and (d).

48. See Rev.Rul. 60–351, 1960–2 C.B. 169, 173; but cf. Estate of Leslie E. Johnson, 56 T.C. 944 (1971).

49. G.C.M. 13745, XIII–2 C.B. 76 (1934).

state's exemption to rest on an interpretation of the Code, which failed to make the state a taxpayer.[50]

As to some types of income, Section 115(1) supports the state's exempt status. Section 115(1) excludes from gross income a state's receipts from any public utility and from the exercise of any "essential governmental function." [51] At present, there is only one instance in which amounts received by states or state agencies are in fact subjected to Federal income tax.[52] Obviously, as long as Congress and the Treasury do not attempt to subject a state's receipts to the Federal income tax, actual questions regarding the scope of the federal power to do so cannot arise. Should such questions arise, they probably will not be answered strictly on a state immunity basis.

Several decisions suggest that some state income may be vulnerable to the Federal income tax. One such decision is New York v. United States.[53] In that decision, the Court held that the State of New York, in its sale of mineral waters from Saratoga Springs, was not immune from a federal excise on the sale of soft drinks. In the employee salary cases, the Court finally rejected as a criterion of taxability the question whether the activity in which the employee was engaged constituted an essential governmental function, but the question of essentiality may still have some relevance. Sustaining the excise tax in *New York*,[54] the court stated:

> There are, of course, state activities and state-owned property that partake of uniqueness from the point of view of inter-governmental relations. These inherently constitute a class by themselves. Only a state can own a statehouse; only a state can get income by taxing. These could not be included for purposes of federal taxation in any abstract category of taxpayers without taxing the state as a state. But so long as Congress generally taps a source of revenue by whomsoever earned and not uniquely capable of being earned only by a state, the Constitution of the United States does not forbid it merely because its incidence falls also on a state.

Consider the retail liquor business against this background. In State A liquor stores are state-owned and operated. In State B they are publicly licensed but privately owned and operated. Under present circumstances does this appear to give rise to an inequitable application of the Federal income tax laws? [55] If you think so, what do you think should be done about it?

---

50. G.C.M. 14407, XIV–1 C.B. 103 (1935): and see Rev.Rul. 71–132, 1971–1 C.B. 29, superseding G.C.M. 13745, supra note 49, reaching the same result as the earlier G.C.M. but without reference to the immunity doctrine.

51. I.R.C. § 115(1).

52. See I.R.C. § 511(a)(2)(B) which taxes the "unrelated business income" of state colleges and universities.

53. 326 U.S. 572, 66 S.Ct. 310 (1946).

54. Id. at 582 and 66 S.Ct. at 314.

55. See Rev.Rul. 71–132, supra note 50.

These are at best fragmentary comments on a tax area that produces very great amounts of administrative, judicial and academic literature.[56]

56. Some important articles that examine the cases and competing philosophies in depth include: (1) The classic analysis of the intergovernmental immunities doctrine up to 1946, in Powell, "The Waning of Intergovernmental Tax Immunities," 58 Harv.L.Rev. 633 (1945), and Powell, "The Remnant of Intergovernmental Tax Immunities," 58 Harv.L.Rev. 757 (1945); (2) Frank, "Reciprocal Taxation of Governments," 40 Taxes 468 (1962); (3) Ratchford, "Intergovernmental Tax Immunities in the United States," 6 Nat.Tax.J. 305 (1953); (4) Surrey, "Federal Income Taxation of State and Local Government Obligations," 36 Tax Policy 3 (May-June 1969).

PART THREE: IDENTIFICATION OF THE PROPER TAXPAYER

CHAPTER 12. ASSIGNMENT OF INCOME

A. INTRODUCTION

Internal Revenue Code: Sections 1(a), (c), (e), (h); 6013(a). See Sections 63, 66; 73.

Until the 1986 legislation, the United States imposed taxes on "taxable income" [1] at "progressive" rates under which increasing rates were applicable to additional increments of taxable income.[2] For many years the rates were spread among fifteen separate tax brackets. For a long period prior to 1981 the maximum noncorporate tax rate was 70 percent; then until 1987 it was 50 percent. The progressive income tax rates provided a strong inducement to the fragmentization of income.[3] Thus, if a taxpayer in a 50 percent tax rate bracket could transfer some of his income to another individual or entity in an 11 percent bracket, he would reduce the amount of tax on the income by 78 percent. In many instances it was a matter of indifference to a taxpayer whether he himself actually received an item of income or whether it went instead to a related individual or an economically related entity such as a trust or a corporation. In a sense, the game was have-your-cake and eat-it, and the temptation was great to spread income among family members or entities or both in an effort to reduce total tax liability.

With its introduction of the modified flat tax rate system, with some variations considered below, Congress took much of the sport out of the "assignment of income" game. Beginning in 1991, with respect to noncorporate taxpayers the modified flat rate system imposes tax at 15 percent, 28 percent and 31 percent with the 28 percent and 31 percent rates phased in at various levels depending upon the classification of the taxpayer.[4] To the extent that one is successful in shifting

---

1. Taxable income, defined in I.R.C. § 63, is essentially the taxpayer's gross income reduced by all allowable deductions. Credits are ignored here.

2. See Blum and Kalven, "The Uneasy Case for Progressive Taxation," 19 U. of Chi.L.Rev. 417 (1952), Smith, "High Pro-

gressive Tax Rates: Inequity and Immorality?" 20 U. of Fla. L.Rev. 451 (1968).

3. Often *estate tax* planning is a motivation for transactions that raise *income tax* assignment or shifting of income questions.

4. See Chapter 27A, infra.

income say from the 31 percent to the 15 percent bracket, there is a more than 50 percent saving in the amount of taxes paid.[5]

Successfully achieving a 50 percent saving is often easier said than done. Congress has added some "rules" to the game (beyond the modified flat tax rates) which affect the degree of success one can achieve by assignments. For example, a child under the age of 14 years is generally taxed on almost all of his *unearned* income at his parent's tax rate, nullifying the tax advantage in assignment of income to such minors.[6] This is commonly referred to as "the kiddie tax." Similarly Congress has sharply curtailed the incentives to assign income to entities (see Chapter 13) by limiting the 15 and 28 percent tax rates on trusts to their first $3300 and $9900 of taxable income respectively[7] and by generally imposing higher maximum tax rates on corporate taxpayers (34 percent) than on noncorporate taxpayers (31 percent).

Although the spoils of victory are not as great as before the 1986 legislation, nevertheless some will persist in playing the game. In the income tax area there are both statutory and judge-made restraints on the efficacy of "assignment of income," the subject of this and the next Chapter. This Chapter deals with assignments of income to other individuals; Chapter 13 concerns assignments of income when artificial entities, as well as other individuals, enter the picture.

In one instance the Code itself provides a mandatory rule that has the computational consequence of an effective assignment of income. The rule is Section 73. Under some state laws income arising out of the *services* of a minor child is deemed to be the property of the parents. Such income probably could be taxed to the parents as *theirs*.[8] However, Section 73 provides that "amounts received in respect of the services of a child shall be included in his gross income * * *." Thus, a uniform rule is provided for federal tax purposes, which operates independently of the vagaries of state property laws. Obviously, the rule is generally favorable to taxpayers.[9] The tax rule of course does not bear on who ultimately gets to keep the income but, instead, only on how the tax on it is to be determined.[10]

So-called "income-splitting" provisions available on an elective basis to married taxpayers are of greater significance. If they elect to file a joint return,[11] their combined taxable income is taxed at rates provided in Section 1(a). If they file separately, each is taxed at rates provided in Section 1(d). A comparison of the two rate tables will show

5. A reduction from 31 percent to 15 percent would constitute a 51.61 percent saving. A reduction from 28 percent to 15 percent would constitute a 46.43 percent saving.

6. This provision is considered in more detail in Chapters 13 and 27A, infra.

7. I.R.C. § 1(e). Cf. I.R.C. § 1(f).

8. But compare Lucas v. Earl with Commissioner v. Giannini, both infra, this Chapter.

9. But see I.R.C. § 6201(c), sometimes making a parent liable for the child's tax on income included in gross income by § 73.

10. See I.R.C. § 66 which applies a similar type rule to some community property.

11. I.R.C. § 6013 permits this, even if one of the spouses has no gross income.

1948 income-splitting provision

that, the tax on the combined taxable income of husband and wife under Section 1(a) is twice the tax on one-half their combined taxable income using 1(d) rates. Consequently, the filing of a joint return, even where one spouse has all the income, produces the same tax as if the income were equally divided and each half were taxed under the Section 1(d) rates.[12]

We retain historical coverage of the concepts of assignment of income in this edition of the book fully recognizing that for various reasons the game will not be played as it was in years past. Lucas v. Earl, which follows immediately, is a landmark case. It involved a husband and wife but a tax year before 1948 when income splitting was enacted. What is the present importance of the case? Was the assignment in Lucas v. Earl effected for tax reasons? Note the date of the contract in the case.

B. INCOME FROM SERVICES

LUCAS v. EARL

Supreme Court of the United States, 1930.
281 U.S. 111, 50 S.Ct. 241.

Mr. Justice HOLMES delivered the opinion of the Court.

Issue *tax Earl on all or part of income*

This case presents the question whether the respondent, Earl, could be taxed for the whole of the salary and attorney's fees earned by him in the years 1920 and 1921, or should be taxed for only a half of them in view of a contract with his wife which we shall mention. The Commissioner of Internal Revenue and the Board of Tax Appeals imposed a tax upon the whole, but their decision was reversed by the Circuit Court of Appeals, 30 F.2d 898. A writ of certiorari was granted by this Court.

Commissioner Board of Tax App taxed whole

Cir. Ct App reversed

Sup Ct held to tax all

By the contract, made in 1901, Earl and his wife agreed "that any property either of us now has or may hereafter acquire * * * in any way, either by earnings (including salaries, fees, etc.), or any rights by contract or otherwise, during the existence of our marriage, or which we or either of us may receive by gift, bequest, devise, or inheritance, and all the proceeds, issues, and profits of any and all such property shall be treated and considered and hereby is declared to be received, held, taken, and owned by us as joint tenants, and not otherwise, with the right of survivorship." The validity of the contract is not questioned, and we assume it to be unquestionable under the law of the State of California, in which the parties lived. Nevertheless we are of opinion that the Commissioner and Board of Tax Appeals were right.

Commis + B. Tax App affirmed tax the whole

---

12. This is an artificial splitting only for tax purposes. Before 1971, the statutory splitting device was more apparent in the statute. Pre-1971, I.R.C. § 2(a) provided that, if a joint return was filed, "the tax imposed by section 1 shall be twice the tax which would be imposed if the taxable income were cut in half." The change was required by a reduction in tax rates applicable to unmarried taxpayers. See I.R.C. § 1(c). The origin of this statutory income-splitting device and computation questions concerning the several § 1 rate tables are further explored in Chapter 27A, infra.

H & W had a K → any property whenever acquired, owned in joint tenancy w/ r/b of survivorship.

The Revenue Act of 1918 approved February 24, 1919, c. 18, §§ 210, 211, 212(a), 213(a), 40 Stat. 1057, 1062, 1064, 1065, imposes a tax upon the net income of every individual including "income derived from salaries, wages, or compensation for personal service * * * of whatever kind and in whatever form paid," § 213(a). The provisions of the Revenue Act of 1921, c. 136, 42 Stat. 227, in sections bearing the same numbers are similar to those of the above. A very forcible argument is presented to the effect that the statute seeks to tax only income beneficially received, and that taking the question more technically the salary and fees became the joint property of Earl and his wife on the very first instant on which they were received. We well might hesitate upon the latter proposition, because however the matter might stand between husband and wife he was the only party to the contracts by which the salary and fees were earned, and it is somewhat hard to say that the last step in the performance of those contracts could be taken by anyone but himself alone. But this case is not to be decided by attenuated subtleties. It turns on the import and reasonable construction of the taxing act. There is no doubt that the statute could tax salaries to those who earned them and provide that the tax could not be escaped by anticipatory arrangements and contracts however skilfully devised to prevent the salary when paid from vesting even for a second in the man who earned it. That seems to us the import of the statute before us and we think that no distinction can be taken according to the motives leading to the arrangement by which the fruits are attributed to a different tree from that on which they grew.

Judgment reversed.

The CHIEF JUSTICE took no part in this case.

COMMISSIONER v. GIANNINI

United States Court of Appeals, Ninth Circuit, 1942.
129 F.2d 638.

STEPHENS, Circuit Judge. Petition by the Commissioner of Internal Revenue for a review of a decision of the Board of Tax Appeals which is reported at 42 B.T.A. 546 to the effect that there is no deficiency in taxpayer's federal income tax for the year 1928.

The facts upon which the Commissioner relies in claiming a deficiency are as follows:

The taxpayer and his wife at all relevant times were husband and wife and were residents of California. The taxpayer was a Director and President of Bancitaly Corporation from 1919 until its dissolution after the tax year in question. From 1919 to 1925 he performed the services of these offices without compensation, and on January 22, 1925, the Board of Directors authorized a committee of three to devise a plan to compensate him, he in the meantime to have the privilege of drawing upon the corporation for his current expenditures.

On April 19th, 1927, the committee reported and on June 27th, 1927, the Directors unanimously approved the report. It was: "The

[handwritten top margin: Tax Yr in ? 1927]

committee as above met on Wednesday, April 13, 1927, at 2:00 o'clock, in Mr. Fagan's office, in the Crocker First National Bank, San Francisco, and unanimously agreed to, and hereby do, recommend to the directors of the Bancitaly Corporation that Mr. A.P. Giannini, for his services as President of your Corporation, be given 5% of the net profits each year, with a guaranteed minimum of $100,000 per year, commencing January 1, 1927, in lieu of salary." *

[handwritten margin note: withdrawal acct credited with... being used for the... past 8 years]

On November 20, 1927, the withdrawal account of taxpayer showed an indebtedness to the corporation of $215,603.76, and on that date his account was credited and the salary account on the books of the corporation was debited with the amount of $445,704.20, being the equivalent of 5% of the corporation net profits from January 1, 1927, to July 22, 1927.

In 1927 after the taxpayer learned the amount of the profits from January to July of that year and that he would receive $445,704.20 as his 5% thereof, the taxpayer informed members of the Board of Directors of the corporation that he would not accept any further compensation for the year 1927, and suggested that the corporation do something worthwhile with the money. The finding of the Board in this respect is that the refusal was "definite" and "absolute", and there is ample evidence in the record to support such finding.

[handwritten margin note: T.P. refused compensation]

The corporation never credited to the taxpayer or his wife any portion of the 5% of the net profits for the year 1927, other than the $445,704.20 above referred to, nor did it set any part of the same aside for the use of the taxpayer or his wife. The only action of the corporation in this respect is as follows:

On January 20, 1928, the Board of Directors of Bancitaly Corporation adopted a resolution reading in part as follows:

"Whereas, this Corporation is prepared now to pay to Mr. A.P. Giannini for his services as its President and General Manager five per cent (5%) of the net profits of this Corporation computed from July 23, 1927 to the close of business January 20, 1928, which five percent (5%) amounts to the sum of One Million Five Hundred Thousand Dollars ($1,500,000.00); and

"Whereas, Mr. A.P. Giannini refuses to accept any part of said sum but has indicated that if the Corporation is so minded he would find keen satisfaction in seeing it devote such a sum or any lesser adequate sum to the objects below enumerated or kindred purposes; and

"Whereas, we believe that this Corporation would do a great good and derive a great benefit from the establishment of a Foundation of Agricultural Economics at the University of California, and we believe that something should be done by

* About twenty years earlier the directors had voted Mr. Giannini, as founder and vice-president, a salary of $200 a month. Thomas and Witts, The San Francisco Earthquake, 41 (1971). Ed.

this Corporation to evidence its appreciation of the fact that without the general confidence and hearty cooperation of the people of the State of California the great success of this Corporation would not have been possible * * *;

* * *

"Now, Therefore, Be it Resolved, by the Board of Directors of this Corporation, that the aforesaid sum of One Million Five Hundred Thousand Dollars ($1,500,000.00) be set apart from the undivided profits of this Corporation in a Special Reserve Account for the purpose hereinafter described, and the whole of said sum be donated to the Regents of the University of California for the purpose of establishing a Foundation of Agricultural Economics; and

"Be it Further Resolved, that said donation be made in honor of Mr. A.P. Giannini, and that said Foundation shall be named after him; and

"Be it Further Resolved, that a Committee consisting of James A. Bacigalupi, P.C. Hale and A. Pedrini be appointed to confer with the President of the University of California, for the purpose of discussing and determining upon the general scope of said Foundation, and with full power of settling all details in connection therewith; * * *".

In accordance with said resolution the Corporation in February, 1928, submitted a written offer of contribution to the Regents of the University of California, and the offer was accepted. One deviation occurred in carrying out the plan, however, in that 5% of the profits of the Bancitaly Corporation for the period January 1, 1927, to January 20, 1928, less the sum of $445,704.20 credited to taxpayer amounted to $1,357,607.40 instead of the estimated $1,500,000.00, and the difference of $142,392.60 was paid by the taxpayer personally. There is no question in this appeal concerning this $142,392.60.

The taxpayer and his wife in reporting their income for taxation purposes in 1928 did not report any portion of the $1,357,607.40 paid to the Regents of the University of California by the Bancitaly Corporation as aforesaid, and it is the Commissioner's contention that one-half of said sum should be reported by each.* Based upon this theory the Commissioner assessed a deficiency of $137,343.50 in the case of the taxpayer in this appeal and a deficiency of $123,402.71 in the case of his wife. Separate appeals have been taken by each party, but it is stipulated by the parties that the decision in the wife's case is to abide the final decision in the case now before this court.

The Commissioner's argument in support of the claimed deficiency may be summarized as follows: That actual receipt of money or property is not always necessary to constitute taxable income; that it is

---

* [Between the tax year involved in *Earl,* a principal case above, and this case, California became a community property state. The effect, reflected here, was actual income-splitting between husband and wife. Ed.]

T.P.'s unqualified refusal to take compensation

the "realization" of taxable income rather than actual receipt which gives rise to the tax; that a taxpayer "realizes" income when he directs the disposition thereof in a manner so that it reaches the object of his bounty; that in the instant case the taxpayer had a right to claim and receive the whole 5% of the corporation profit as compensation for his services; and that his waiver of that right with the suggestion that it be applied to some useful purpose was such a disposition thereof as to render the taxpayer taxable for income "realized" in the tax year in which the suggestion is carried out. In connection with this latter argument the Commissioner states in his opening brief that "For the purposes of income tax it would seem immaterial whether the taxpayer waived his compensation, thus in effect giving it to Bancitaly Corporation, with the suggestion that it be applied to some useful purpose, or whether he failed to waive the right to receive the compensation and directed that it be paid to a donee of his choice." Again it is stated by the Commissioner, "Insofar as the question of taxation is concerned it would not seem to make much difference whether he directed Bancitaly Corporation to pay his compensation to the University of California or whether he merely told his employer to keep it."

Supplemental to the argument as above summarized, the Commissioner urges that the Board's finding that the money paid to the Foundation of Agricultural Economics as above set forth "was the property of Bancitaly and the petitioner [taxpayer] had no right, title or interest therein" is unsupported by the evidence; and that in any event such finding is an "ultimate finding" and therefore reviewable by this court under the rule announced in Commissioner v. Boeing, 9 Cir., 106 F.2d 305 and cases therein cited. We agree that the question of the effect of the taxpayer's unqualified refusal to take the compensation for *ISSUE* his services is a question of law subject to review by this court. That question is the sole question presented by this appeal.

The taxpayer, on the other hand, urges that "A person has the right to refuse property proffered to him, and if he does so, absolutely and unconditionally, his refusal amounts to a renunciation of the proffered property, which, legally, is an abandonment of right to the property without a transfer of such right to another. Property which is renounced (i.e. abandoned) cannot be 'diverted' or 'assigned' by the renouncer, and cannot be taxed upon the theory that it was received."

The Commissioner takes issue with the argument of the taxpayer as above quoted by arguing that the amount involved was more than "property proffered to" the taxpayer, but was instead compensation which the taxpayer had a contractual right to receive. The point is that any disposition of this contractual right, whether it be by waiver, transfer, assignment or any other means, and whether it be before or after the rendition of the services involved, results in taxable income under the rules announced in the cases of Lucas v. Earl, 281 U.S. 111, 50 S.Ct. 241; Helvering v. Horst, 311 U.S. 112, 61 S.Ct. 144, 131 A.L.R. 655; Helvering v. Eubank, 311 U.S. 122, 61 S.Ct. 149; and Harrison v. Schaffner, 312 U.S. 579, 61 S.Ct. 759.

The *Earl* case arises out of an assignment of salary and attorneys fees by a husband to his wife in advance of the rendition of the services. It was claimed that the husband never beneficially received them, but the Court refused to follow this reasoning and held that "the tax could not be escaped by anticipatory arrangements and contracts however skillfully devised to prevent the salary when paid from vesting even for a second in the man who earned it". The gist of the decision appears to be that the salary was accepted, and the employee's dominance over it amounted to his receipt of it.

In the *Horst* case the taxpayer gave away interest bearing coupons, and the donee collected the interest during the taxpayer's taxable year. A conflict was asserted between the Circuit Court decision and the case of Lucas v. Earl, supra. In commenting upon the rule that income is not taxable until "realized", the Court [311 U.S. 122, 61 S.Ct. 147, 131 A.L.R. 655] asserted that such rule is a rule of postponement of the tax to the final event of enjoyment, saying "income is 'realized' by the assignor * * * who owns or controls the source * * * controls the disposition * * * and diverts. * * * The donor [taxpayer] here, * * * has * * * by his act, procured payment of the interest, as a valuable gift * * *. Such a use * * * would seem to be the enjoyment of the income * * *."

In the *Eubank* case a life insurance agent, after terminating agency contracts, made assignments of renewal commissions payable to him for services rendered in procuring policies. The Court held the renewal commissions taxable to the assignor. Here again [in *Eubank*], the dominance over the fund by the assignor was shown.

In the *Schaffner* case the life beneficiary of a trust assigned to children income from the trust for the year following the assignment. In holding that the income was taxable to the assignor the Court analyzes and compares these three cited cases. The Court said [312 U.S. 579, 61 S.Ct. 760],

> "Since granting certiorari we have held, following the reasoning of Lucas v. Earl, supra, that one who is entitled to receive, at a future date, interest or compensation for services and who makes a gift of it by an anticipatory assignment, realizes taxable income quite as much as if he had collected the income and paid it over to the object of his bounty. Helvering v. Horst, 311 U.S. 112, 61 S.Ct. 144, 131 A.L.R. 655; Helvering v. Eubank, 311 U.S. 122, 61 S.Ct. 149."

Here again [in *Schaffner*] the dominance over the fund and taxpayer's direction show that he beneficially received the money by exercising his right to divert it to a use.

Now, turning again to the instant case. The findings of the Board, supported by the evidence, are to the effect that the taxpayer did not receive the money, and that he did not direct its disposition. All that he did was to unqualifiedly refuse to accept any further compensation for his services with the suggestion that the money be used for some worthwhile purpose. So far as the taxpayer was concerned, the corporation could have kept the money. All arrangements with the University of California regarding the donation to the Foundation were made by the corporation, the taxpayer participating therein only as an officer of the corporation.

In this circumstance we cannot say as a matter of law that the money was beneficially received by the taxpayer and therefore subject to the income tax provisions of the statute. It should be kept in mind that there is no charge of fraud in this case. It would be impossible to support the Commissioner in his contention that the money was received by the taxpayer without arriving at the conclusion that the taxpayer was acting in less than full and open frankness.[1] The Board rejects this suggestion and we see no occasion for drawing inferences from the evidence contrary to the plain intent of the testimony which is not disputed. To support the Commissioner's argument we should have to hold that only one reasonable inference could be drawn from the evidence, which is that the donation is but a donation of the taxpayer masquerading as a creature of the corporation to save the true donors [taxpayer and his wife] some tax money. The circumstances do not support this contention. In our opinion the inferences drawn by the Board are more reasonable and comport with that presumption of verity that every act of a citizen of good repute should be able to claim and receive.

Affirmed.

[The concurring opinion of Circuit Judge HEALY is omitted. Ed.]

REVENUE RULING 66–167

1966–1 Cum.Bull. 20.

In the instant case, the taxpayer served as the sole executor of his deceased wife's estate pursuant to the terms of a will under which he and his adult son were each given a half interest in the net proceeds thereof. The laws of the state in which the will was executed and probated impose no limitation on the use of either principal or income for the payment of compensation to an executor and do not purport to deal with whether a failure to withdraw any particular fee or commission may properly be considered as a waiver thereof.

The taxpayer's administration of his wife's estate continued for a period of approximately three full years during which time he filed two annual accountings as well as the usual final accounting with the

---

1. We say that the Commissioner's argument compels this conclusion for the reason that the claimed deficiency is for the tax year in which the donation was actually made to the Foundation. It should be recalled that the taxpayer's unqualified refusal to take any further compensation for his services in 1927 was made prior to December 31, 1927. If the Commissioner were earnestly taking the position that a waiver of compensation, with nothing more, is such an exercise of dominion over the moneys to be received as to render it taxable, it seems apparent that the deficiency if any would be in the year of the waiver, rather than some subsequent year in which the corporation disposes of the fund in some other manner.

probate court, all of which reported the collection and disposition of a substantial amount of estate assets.

At some point within a reasonable time after first entering upon the performance of his duties as executor, the taxpayer decided to make no charge for serving in such capacity, and each of the aforesaid accountings accordingly omitted any claim for statutory commissions and was so filed with the intention to waive the same. The taxpayer-executor likewise took no other action which was inconsistent with a fixed and continuing intention to serve on a gratuitous basis.

The specific questions presented are whether the amounts which the taxpayer-executor could have received as fees or commissions are includible in his gross income for Federal income tax purposes and whether his waiver of the right to receive these amounts results in a gift for Federal gift tax purposes.

In Revenue Ruling 56-472, the executor of an estate entered into an agreement to serve in such capacity for substantially less than all of the statutory commissions otherwise allowable to him and also formally waived his right to receive the remaining portion thereof. The basic agreement with respect to his acceptance of a reduced amount of compensation antedated the performance of any services and the related waiver of the disclaimed commissions was signed before he would otherwise have become entitled to receive them. Under these circumstances, the ruling held that the difference between the commissions which such executor could have otherwise acquired an unrestricted right to obtain and the lesser amount which he actually received was not includible in his income and that his disclaimer did not effect any gift thereof.

In Revenue Ruling 64-225, the trustees of a testamentary trust in the State of New York waived their rights to receive one particular class of statutory commissions. This waiver was effected by means of certain formal instruments that were not executed until long after the close of most of the years to which such commissions related. This circumstance, along with all the other facts described therein, indicated that such trustees had not intended to render their services on a gratuitous basis. The Revenue Ruling accordingly held that such commissions were includible in the trustees' gross income for the taxable year when so waived and that their execution of the waivers also effected a taxable gift of these commissions.

The crucial test of whether the executor of an estate or any other fiduciary in a similar situation may waive his right to receive statutory commissions without thereby incurring any income or gift tax liability is whether the waiver involved will at least primarily constitute evidence of an intent to render a gratuitous service. If the timing, purpose, and effect of the waiver make it serve any other important objective, it may then be proper to conclude that the fiduciary has thereby enjoyed a realization of income by means of controlling the disposition thereof, and at the same time, has also effected a taxable gift by means of any resulting transfer to a third party of his contingent beneficial interest in a part of the assets under his fiduciary control * * *.

The requisite intention to serve on a gratuitous basis will ordinarily be deemed to have been adequately manifested if the executor or administrator of an estate supplies one or more of the decedent's principal legatees or devisees, or of those principally entitled to distribution of decedent's intestate estate, within six months after his initial appointment as such fiduciary, with a formal waiver of any right to compensation for his services. Such an intention to serve on a gratuitous basis may also be adequately manifested through an implied waiver, if the fiduciary fails to claim fees or commissions at the time of filing the usual accountings and if all the other attendant facts and circumstances are consistent with a fixed and continuing intention to serve gratuitously. If the executor or administrator of an estate claims his statutory fees or commissions as a deduction on one or more of the estate, inheritance, or income tax returns which are filed on behalf of the estate, such action will ordinarily be considered inconsistent with any fixed or definite intention to serve on a gratuitous basis. No such claim was made in the instant case.

Accordingly, the amounts which the present taxpayer-executor would have otherwise become entitled to receive as fees or commissions are not includible in his gross income for Federal income tax purposes, and are not gifts for Federal gift tax purposes.

Revenue Ruling 56–472 is clarified to remove any implication that, although an executor effectively waives his right to receive commissions, such commissions are includible in his gross income unless the waiver is executed prior to performance of any service.

Revenue Ruling 64–225 is distinguished.

REVENUE RULING 74–581
1974–2 Cum.Bull. 25.

Advice has been requested concerning the Federal income tax treatment of payments received for services performed by a faculty member or a student of a university's school of law under the circumstances described below.

The university's school of law has as part of its regular teaching curriculum several clinical programs. The clinics include programs in Constitutional Litigation, Urban Legal Problems, Women's Rights, Prisoner's Rights and Corrections, and from time to time other clinical programs as well. Each program is supervised and conducted by full-time faculty members of the school of law's teaching staff.

At times, various clinics in the law school program handle criminal matters wherein faculty members are assigned as counsel. On occasion, the faculty member is appointed by a Federal District Court, * * * pursuant to the provisions of the Criminal Justice Act of 1964, as amended, 18 U.S.C.A. 3006A ("Criminal Justice Act"), which authorizes the payment of compensation of attorneys appointed to represent indigent defendants. In the cases for which an appointment under the Criminal Justice Act is made, the students in the clinical programs assist the attorney-faculty member in investigation of the case, research of the case, and preparation of the litigation papers as the case may require. In other circumstances, the individual student may be able to participate directly in the legal representation of the client pursuant to the newly promulgated rule of the United States Court of Appeals for the Third Circuit (Local Rule 9(2), Entry of Appearance by Eligible Law Students), or under similar rules in other jurisdictions.

When an attorney-faculty member is appointed in a criminal case by the Federal Courts pursuant to the Criminal Justice Act, the attorney is entitled to submit a voucher for the expenditure of time and for disbursements incident to the representation. With regard to the clinical programs of the law school, each faculty member has agreed, as a condition of participation in the program, that since the time spent in supervising work of students on these cases and in the representation of the client is part of the faculty member's teaching duties for which the faculty member is compensated by a total annual salary, all amounts received under the Criminal Justice Act will be endorsed over to the law school. The attorney-faculty members involved are working solely as agents of the law school, while supervising the law students within the scope of the clinical programs, and realize no personal gain from payments for their services in representing the indigent defendants.

Although the Criminal Justice Act itself does not specify that the monies may not be paid directly to the law school, the Clerk of the District Court has taken the generally acknowledged position that under the Criminal Justice Act payment cannot be arranged through the law school or its clinical programs. Therefore, as a matter of practice, the vouchers would be submitted by the attorney-faculty member to the appropriate Federal court in the name of the faculty member, and upon receipt of the check, he would endorse it over to the university's law school accounts.

Section 61(a) of the Internal Revenue Code of 1954 provides that, unless excluded by law, gross income means all income from whatever source derived including (but not limited to) compensation for services, including fees and similar items.

The Supreme Court of the United States has stated that the dominant purpose of the revenue laws is the taxation of income to those who earn or otherwise create the right to receive it and enjoy the benefit of it when paid. Helvering v. Horst, 311 U.S. 112 (1940), 1940–2 C.B. 296. Consistent with this, it is well established that a taxpayer's anticipatory assignment of a right to income derived from the ownership of property will not be effective to redirect that income to the assignee for tax purposes. See the *Horst* case and Lucas v. Earl, 281 U.S. 111 (1930).

However, the Internal Revenue Service has recognized that amounts that would otherwise be deemed income are not, in certain unique factual situations, subject to the broad rule of inclusion provided by section 61(a) of the Code.

For example, Rev.Rul. 65–282, 1965–2 C.B. 21, holds that statutory legal fees received by attorneys for representing indigent defendants are not includible in gross income where the attorneys, pursuant to their employment contracts, immediately turn the fees over to their employer, a legal aid society.

Rev.Rul. 58–220, 1958–1 C.B. 26, holds that the amount of the checks received by a physician from patients he has treated in the hospital by which he is employed full-time, which checks he is required to endorse over to the hospital, is not includible in his gross income.

Similarly, Rev.Rul. 58–515, 1958–2 C.B. 28, considers a situation where a police officer, in the performance of duties as an employee of the police department, entered into private employment for the purpose of obtaining certain information for the department. Pursuant to the rules and procedures of the department, the officer remitted to the police pension fund the compensation he received from the private employer. That Revenue Ruling holds that the officer was acting as an agent of the department while privately employed and that the compensation remitted to the pension fund is not includible in his gross income.

In similar circumstances, Rev.Rul. 69–274, 1969–1 C.B. 36, holds that faculty physicians of a medical school who provide medical services to indigent patients at a hospital are not required to include in their income fees collected and remitted to the university in accordance with the university policy and agreement.

Accordingly, in the instant case, amounts received for services performed by a faculty member or a student of the university's school of law under the clinical programs and turned over to the university are not includible in the recipient's income.

C. INCOME FROM PROPERTY

HELVERING v. HORST

Supreme Court of the United States, 1940.
311 U.S. 112, 61 S.Ct. 144.

Mr. Justice STONE delivered the opinion of the Court.

The sole question for decision is whether the gift, during the donor's taxable year, of interest coupons detached from the bonds, delivered to the donee and later in the year paid at maturity, is the realization of income taxable to the donor.

In 1934 and 1935 respondent, the owner of negotiable bonds, detached from them negotiable interest coupons shortly before their due date and delivered them as a gift to his son who in the same year collected them at maturity. The Commissioner ruled that under the applicable § 22 of the Revenue Act of 1934, 48 Stat. 680, 686, the interest payments were taxable, in the years when paid, to the respondent donor who reported his income on the cash receipts basis. The Circuit Court of Appeals reversed the order of the Board of Tax Appeals sustaining the tax. 107 F.2d 906; 39 B.T.A. 757. We granted certiorari, 309 U.S. 650, 60 S.Ct. 807, because of the importance of the question in the administration of the revenue laws and because of an asserted conflict in principle of the decision below with that of Lucas v. Earl, 281 U.S. 111, 50 S.Ct. 241, and with that of decisions by other circuit courts of appeals. See Bishop v. Commissioner, 54 F.2d 298; Dickey v. Burnet, 56 F.2d 917, 921; Van Meter v. Commissioner, 61 F.2d 817.

The court below thought that as the consideration for the coupons had passed to the obligor, the donor had, by the gift, parted with all control over them and their payment, and for that reason the case was distinguishable from Lucas v. Earl, supra, and Burnet v. Leininger, 285 U.S. 136, 52 S.Ct. 345, where the assignment of compensation for services had preceded the rendition of the services, and where the income was held taxable to the donor.

The holder of a coupon bond is the owner of two independent and separable kinds of right. One is the right to demand and receive at maturity the principal amount of the bond representing capital investment. The other is the right to demand and receive interim payments of interest on the investment in the amounts and on the dates specified by the coupons. Together they are an obligation to pay principal and interest given in exchange for money or property which was presumably the consideration for the obligation of the bond. Here respondent, as owner of the bonds, had acquired the legal right to demand payment at maturity of the interest specified by the coupons and the power to command its payment to others, which constituted an economic gain to him.

Admittedly not all economic gain of the taxpayer is taxable income. From the beginning the revenue laws have been interpreted as defining "realization" of income as the taxable event, rather than the acquisition of the right to receive it. And "realization" is not deemed to occur until the income is paid. But the decisions and regulations have consistently recognized that receipt in cash or property is not the only characteristic of realization of income to a taxpayer on the cash receipts basis. Where the taxpayer does not receive payment of income in money or property realization may occur when the last step is taken by which he obtains the fruition of the economic gain which has already accrued to him. Old Colony Trust Co. v. Commissioner, 279 U.S. 716, 49 S.Ct. 499; Corliss v. Bowers, 281 U.S. 376, 378, 50 S.Ct. 336. Cf. Burnet v. Wells, 289 U.S. 670, 53 S.Ct. 761.

In the ordinary case the taxpayer who acquires the right to receive income is taxed when he receives it, regardless of the time when his right to receive payment accrued. But the rule that income is not taxable until realized has never been taken to mean that the taxpayer, even on the cash receipts basis, who has fully enjoyed the benefit of the economic gain represented by his right to receive income, can escape taxation because he has not himself received payment of it from his obligor. The rule, founded on administrative convenience, is only one of postponement of the tax to the final event of enjoyment of the income, usually the receipt of it by the taxpayer, and not one of exemption from taxation where the enjoyment is consummated by some event other than the taxpayer's personal receipt of money or property. Cf. Aluminum Castings Co. v. Routzahn, 282 U.S. 92, 98, 51 S.Ct. 11, 13. This may occur when he has made such use or disposition of his power to receive or control the income as to procure in its place other satisfactions which are of economic worth. The question here is, whether because one who in fact receives payment for services or interest payments is taxable only on his receipt of the payments, he can escape all tax by giving away his right to income in advance of payment. If the taxpayer procures payment directly to his creditors of the items of interest or earnings due him, see Old Colony Trust Co. v. Commissioner, supra; Bowers v. Kerbaugh-Empire Co., 271 U.S. 170, 46 S.Ct. 449; United States v. Kirby Lumber Co., 284 U.S. 1, 52 S.Ct. 4, or if he sets up a revocable trust with income payable to the objects of his bounty, §§ 166, 167, Revenue Act of 1934, Corliss v. Bowers, supra; cf. Dickey v. Burnet, 56 F.2d 917, 921, he does not escape taxation because he did not actually receive the money. Cf. Douglas v. Willcuts, 296 U.S. 1, 56 S.Ct. 59; Helvering v. Clifford, 309 U.S. 331, 60 S.Ct. 554.

Underlying the reasoning in these cases is the thought that income is "realized" by the assignor because he, who owns or controls the source of the income, also controls the disposition of that which he could have received himself and diverts the payment from himself to others as the means of procuring the satisfaction of his wants. The taxpayer has equally enjoyed the fruits of his labor or investment and obtained the satisfaction of his desires whether he collects and uses the income to procure those satisfactions, or whether he disposes of his right to collect it as the means of procuring them. Cf. Burnet v. Wells, supra.

Although the donor here, by the transfer of the coupons, has precluded any possibility of his collecting them himself, he has nevertheless, by his act, procured payment of the interest as a valuable gift to a member of his family. Such a use of his economic gain, the right to receive income, to procure a satisfaction which can be obtained only by the expenditure of money or property, would seem to be the enjoyment of the income whether the satisfaction is the purchase of goods at the corner grocery, the payment of his debt there, or such nonmaterial satisfactions as may result from the payment of a campaign or community chest contribution, or a gift to his favorite son. Even though he never receives the money, he derives money's worth from the disposition of the coupons which he has used as money or money's worth in the procuring of a satisfaction which is procurable only by the expenditure of money or money's worth. The enjoyment of the economic benefit accruing to him by virtue of his acquisition of the coupons is realized as completely as it would have been if he had collected the interest in dollars and expended them for any of the purposes named. Burnet v. Wells, supra.

In a real sense he has enjoyed compensation for money loaned or services rendered, and not any the less so because it is his only reward for them. To say that one who has made a gift thus derived from interest or earnings paid to his donee has never enjoyed or realized the fruits of his investment or labor, because he has assigned them instead of collecting them himself and then paying them over to the donee, is to affront common understanding and to deny the facts of common experience. Common understanding and experience are the touchstones for the interpretation of the revenue laws.

The power to dispose of income is the equivalent of ownership of it. The exercise of that power to procure the payment of income to another is the enjoyment, and hence the realization, of the income by him who exercises it. We have had no difficulty in applying that proposition where the assignment preceded the rendition of the services, Lucas v. Earl, supra; Burnet v. Leininger, supra, for it was recognized in the Leininger case that in such a case the rendition of the service by the assignor was the means by which the income was controlled by the donor and of making his assignment effective. But it is the assignment by which the disposition of income is controlled when the service precedes the assignment, and in both cases it is the exercise of the power of disposition of the interest or compensation, with the resulting payment to the donee, which is the enjoyment by the donor of income derived from them.

This was emphasized in Blair v. Commissioner, 300 U.S. 5, 57 S.Ct. 330, on which respondent relies, where the distinction was taken between a gift of income derived from an obligation to pay compensation and a gift of income-producing property. In the circumstances of that case, the right to income from the trust property was thought to be so identified with the equitable ownership of the property, from which alone the beneficiary derived his right to receive the income and his power to command disposition of it, that a gift of the income by the beneficiary became effective only as a gift of his ownership of the property producing it. Since the gift was deemed to be a gift of the property, the income from it was held to be the income of the owner of the property, who was the donee, not the donor—a refinement which was unnecessary if respondent's contention here is right, but one clearly inapplicable to gifts of interest or wages. Unlike income thus derived from an obligation to pay interest or compensation, the income of the trust was regarded as no more the income of the donor than would be the rent from a lease or a crop raised on a farm after the leasehold or the farm had been given away. Blair v. Commissioner, supra, 12, 13 and cases cited. See also Reinecke v. Smith, 289 U.S. 172, 177, 53 S.Ct. 570, 572. We have held without deviation that where the donor retains control of the trust property the income is taxable to him although paid to the donee. Corliss v. Bowers, supra. Cf. Helvering v. Clifford, supra.

The dominant purpose of the revenue laws is the taxation of income to those who earn or otherwise create the right to receive it and enjoy the benefit of it when paid. See, Corliss v. Bowers, supra, 378; Burnet v. Guggenheim, 288 U.S. 280, 283, 53 S.Ct. 369, 370. The tax laid by the 1934 Revenue Act upon income "derived from * * * wages, or compensation for personal service, of whatever kind and in whatever form paid, * * *; also from interest * * *" therefore cannot fairly be interpreted as not applying to income derived from interest or compensation when he who is entitled to receive it makes use of his power to dispose of it in procuring satisfactions which he would otherwise procure only by the use of the money when received.

It is the statute which taxes the income to the donor although paid to his donee. Lucas v. Earl, supra; Burnet v. Leininger, supra. True, in those cases the service which created the right to income followed the assignment, and it was arguable that in point of legal theory the right to the compensation vested instantaneously in the assignor when paid, although he never received it; while here the right of the assignor to receive the income antedated the assignment which transferred the right and thus precluded such an instantaneous vesting. But the statute affords no basis for such "attenuated subtleties." The distinction was explicitly rejected as the basis of decision in Lucas v. Earl. It should be rejected here; for no more than in the Earl case can the purpose of the statute to tax the income to him who earns, or creates and enjoys it be escaped by "anticipatory arrangements however skilfully devised" to prevent the income from vesting even for a second in the donor.

Nor is it perceived that there is any adequate basis for distinguishing between the gift of interest coupons here and a gift of salary or commissions. The owner of a negotiable bond and of the investment which it represents, if not the lender, stands in the place of the lender. When, by the gift of the coupons, he has separated his right to interest payments from his investment and procured the payment of the interest to his donee, he has enjoyed the economic benefits of the income in the same manner and to the same extent as though the transfer were of earnings, and in both cases the import of the statute is that the fruit is not to be attributed to a different tree from that on which it grew. See Lucas v. Earl, supra, 115.

Reversed.

[The dissenting opinion of Mr. Justice REYNOLDS, in which the CHIEF JUSTICE and Mr. Justice ROBERTS concurred, has been omitted. Ed.]

BLAIR v. COMMISSIONER

Supreme Court of the United States, 1937.
300 U.S. 5, 57 S.Ct. 330.

Mr. Chief Justice HUGHES delivered the opinion of the Court.

This case presents the question of the liability of a beneficiary of a testamentary trust for a tax upon the income which he had assigned to his children prior to the tax years and which the trustees had paid to them accordingly.

The trust was created by the will of William Blair, a resident of Illinois who died in 1899, and was of property located in that State. One-half of the net income was to be paid to the donor's widow during her life. His son, the petitioner Edward Tyler Blair, was to receive the other one-half and, after the death of the widow, the whole of the net income during his life. In 1923, after the widow's death, petitioner assigned to his daughter, Lucy Blair Linn, an interest amounting to $6000 for the remainder of that calendar year, and to $9000 in each calendar year thereafter, in the net income which the petitioner was then or might thereafter be entitled to receive during his life. At about the same time, he made like assignments of interests, amounting to $9000 in each calendar year, in the net income of the trust to his daughter Edith Blair and to his son, Edward Seymour Blair, respectively. In later years, by similar instruments, he assigned to these children additional interests, and to his son William McCormick Blair other specified interests, in the net income. The trustees accepted the assignments and distributed the income directly to the assignees.

The question first arose with respect to the tax year 1923 and the Commissioner of Internal Revenue ruled that the income was taxable to the petitioner. The Board of Tax Appeals held the contrary. 18 B.T.A. 69. The Circuit Court of Appeals reversed the Board, holding that under the law of Illinois the trust was a spendthrift trust and the assignments were invalid. Commissioner v. Blair, 60 F.2d 340. We denied certiorari. 288 U.S. 602, 53 S.Ct. 386.

Thereupon the trustees brought suit in the Superior Court of Cook County, Illinois, to obtain a construction of the will with respect to the power of the beneficiary of the trust to assign a part of his equitable interest and to determine the validity of the assignments he had made. The petitioner and the assignees were made defendants. The Appellate Court of Illinois, First District, after a review of the Illinois decisions, decided that the trust was not a spendthrift trust and upheld the assignments. Blair v. Linn, 274 Ill.App. 23. Under the mandate of the appellate court, the Superior Court of Cook County entered its décree which found the assignments to be "voluntary assignments of a part of the interest of said Edward Tyler Blair in said trust estate" and as such adjudged them to be valid.

At that time there were pending before the Board of Tax Appeals proceedings involving the income of the trust for the years 1924, 1925,

1926 and 1929. The Board received in evidence the record in the suit in the state court and, applying the decision of that court, the Board overruled the Commissioner's determination as to the petitioner's liability. 31 B.T.A. 1192. The Circuit Court of Appeals again reversed the Board. That court recognized the binding effect of the decision of the state court as to the validity of the assignments but decided that the income was still taxable to the petitioner upon the ground that his interest was not attached to the corpus of the estate and that the income was not subject to his disposition until he received it. Commissioner v. Blair, 83 F.2d 655, 662.

Because of an asserted conflict with the decision of the state court, and also with decisions of circuit courts of appeals, we granted certiorari. October 12, 1936.

* * *

Second. The question of the validity of the assignments is a question of local law. The donor was a resident of Illinois and his disposition of the property in that State was subject to its law. By that law the character of the trust, the nature and extent of the interest of the beneficiary, and the power of the beneficiary to assign that interest in whole or in part, are to be determined. The decision of the state court upon these questions is final. Spindle v. Shreve, 111 U.S. 542, 547, 548, 4 S.Ct. 522; Uterhart v. United States, 240 U.S. 598, 603, 36 S.Ct. 417; Poe v. Seaborn, 282 U.S. 101, 110, 51 S.Ct. 58; Freuler v. Helvering, supra, p. 45. It matters not that the decision was by an intermediate appellate court. Compare Graham v. White-Phillips Co., 296 U.S. 27, 56 S.Ct. 21. In this instance, it is not necessary to go beyond the obvious point that the decision was in a suit between the trustees and the beneficiary and his assignees, and the decree which was entered in pursuance of the decision determined as between these parties the validity of the particular assignments. Nor is there any basis for a charge that the suit was collusive and the decree inoperative. Freuler v. Helvering, supra. The trustees were entitled to seek the instructions of the court having supervision of the trust. That court entertained the suit and the appellate court, with the first decision of the Circuit Court of Appeals before it, reviewed the decisions of the Supreme Court of the State and reached a deliberate conclusion. To derogate from the authority of that conclusion and of the decree it commanded, so far as the question is one of state law, would be wholly unwarranted in the exercise of federal jurisdiction.

In the face of this ruling of the state court it is not open to the Government to argue that the trust "was, under the Illinois law, a spendthrift trust." The point of the argument is that, the trust being of that character, the state law barred the voluntary alienation by the beneficiary of his interest. The state court held precisely the contrary. The ruling also determines the validity of the assignment by the beneficiary of parts of his interest. That question was necessarily presented and expressly decided.

Third. The question remains whether, treating the assignments as valid, the assignor was still taxable upon the income under the federal income tax act. That is a federal question.

Our decisions in Lucas v. Earl, 281 U.S. 111, 50 S.Ct. 241, and Burnet v. Leininger, 285 U.S. 136, 52 S.Ct. 345, are cited. In the Lucas case the question was whether an attorney was taxable for the whole of his salary and fees earned by him in the tax years or only upon one-half by reason of an agreement with his wife by which his earnings were to be received and owned by them jointly. We were of the opinion that the case turned upon the construction of the taxing act. We said that "the statute could tax salaries to those who earned them and provide that the tax could not be escaped by anticipatory arrangements and contracts however skilfully devised to prevent the same when paid from vesting even for a second in the man who earned it." That was deemed to be the meaning of the statute as to compensation for personal service, and the one who earned the income was held to be subject to the tax. In Burnet v. Leininger, supra, a husband, a member of a firm, assigned future partnership income to his wife. We found that the revenue act dealt explicitly with the liability of partners as such. The wife did not become a member of the firm; the act specifically taxed the distributive share of each partner in the net income of the firm; and the husband by the fair import of the act remained taxable upon his distributive share. These cases are not in point. The tax here is not upon earnings which are taxed to the one who earns them. Nor is it a case of income attributable to a taxpayer by reason of the application of the income to the discharge of his obligation. Old Colony Trust Co. v. Commissioner, 279 U.S. 716, 49 S.Ct. 499; Douglas v. Willcuts, 296 U.S. 1, 9, 56 S.Ct. 59; Helvering v. Stokes, 296 U.S. 551, 56 S.Ct. 308; Helvering v. Schweitzer, 296 U.S. 551, 56 S.Ct. 304; Helvering v. Coxey, 297 U.S. 694, 56 S.Ct. 498. See, also, Burnet v. Wells, 289 U.S. 670, 677, 53 S.Ct. 761, 763. There is here no question of evasion or of giving effect to statutory provisions designed to forestall evasion; or of the taxpayer's retention of control. Corliss v. Bowers, 281 U.S. 376, 50 S.Ct. 336; Burnet v. Guggenheim, 288 U.S. 280, 53 S.Ct. 369.

In the instant case, the tax is upon income as to which, in the general application of the revenue acts, the tax liability attaches to ownership. See Poe v. Seaborn, supra; Hoeper v. Tax Commission, 284 U.S. 206, 52 S.Ct. 120.

The Government points to the provisions of the revenue acts imposing upon the beneficiary of a trust the liability for the tax upon the income distributable to the beneficiary.[1] But the term is merely descriptive of the one entitled to the beneficial interest. These provisions cannot be taken to preclude valid assignments of the beneficial interest, or to affect the duty of the trustee to distribute income to the owner of the beneficial interest, whether he was such initially or

---

1. Revenue Acts of 1921, § 219(a)(d); 1924 and 1926, § 219(a)(b); 1928, § 162(a) (b). [See I.R.C. (1986) §§ 652(a) and 662(a) (1). Ed.]

becomes such by valid assignment. The one who is to receive the income as the owner of the beneficial interest is to pay the tax. If under the law governing the trust the beneficial interest is assignable, and if it has been assigned without reservation, the assignee thus becomes the beneficiary and is entitled to rights and remedies accordingly. We find nothing in the revenue acts which denies him that status.

The decision of the Circuit Court of Appeals turned upon the effect to be ascribed to the assignments. The court held that the petitioner had no interest in the corpus of the estate and could not dispose of the income until he received it. Hence it was said that "the income was *his*" and his assignment was merely a direction to pay over to others what was due to himself. The question was considered to involve "the date when the income became transferable." 83 F.2d, p. 662. The Government refers to the terms of the assignment,—that it was of the interest in the income "which the said party of the first part now is, or may hereafter be, entitled to receive during his life from the trustees." From this it is urged that the assignments "dealt only with a right to receive the income" and that "no attempt was made to assign any equitable right, title or interest in the trust itself." This construction seems to us to be a strained one. We think it apparent that the conveyancer was not seeking to limit the assignment so as to make it anything less than a complete transfer of the specified interest of the petitioner as the life beneficiary of the trust, but that with ample caution he was using words to effect such a transfer. That the state court so construed the assignments appears from the final decree which described them as voluntary assignments of interests of the petitioner "in said trust estate," and it was that aspect that petitioner's right to make the assignments was sustained.

The will creating the trust entitled the petitioner during his life to the net income of the property held in trust. He thus became the owner of an equitable interest in the corpus of the property. Brown v. Fletcher, 235 U.S. 589, 598, 599, 35 S.Ct. 154, 157; Irwin v. Gavit, 268 U.S. 161, 167, 168, 45 S.Ct. 475, 476; Senior v. Braden, 295 U.S. 422, 432, 433, 55 S.Ct. 800, 803; Merchants' Loan & Trust Co. v. Patterson, 308 Ill. 519, 530, 139 N.E. 912. By virtue of that interest he was entitled to enforce the trust, to have a breach of trust enjoined and to obtain redress in case of breach. The interest was present property alienable like any other, in the absence of a valid restraint upon alienation. Commissioner v. Field, 42 F.2d 820, 822; Shanley v. Bowers, 81 F.2d 13, 15. The beneficiary may thus transfer a part of his interest as well as the whole. See Restatement of the Law of Trusts, §§ 130, 132 et seq. The assignment of the beneficial interest is not the assignment of a chose in action but of the "right, title and estate in and to property." Brown v. Fletcher, supra; Senior v. Braden, supra. See Bogert, "Trusts and Trustees," vol. 1, § 183, pp. 516, 517; 17 Columbia Law Review, 269, 273, 289, 290.

We conclude that the assignments were valid, that the assignees thereby became the owners of the specified beneficial interests in the income, and that as to these interests they and not the petitioner were taxable for the tax years in question. The judgment of the Circuit Court of Appeals is reversed and the cause is remanded with direction to affirm the decision of the Board of Tax Appeals.

Reversed.

NOTE

The court's discussion in *Blair* on the effect in a tax controversy of a local court's determination of a related property issue has been substantially modified by later decisions in Commissioner v. Bosch's Estate and Second Nat. Bank of New Haven, Executor v. U.S.[1]

SUSIE SALVATORE

Tax Court of the United States, 1970.
29 T.C.M. 89.

FEATHERSTON, Judge: Respondent determined a deficiency in petitioner's income tax for 1963 in the amount of $31,016.60. The only issue presented for decision is whether petitioner is taxable on all or only one-half of the gain realized on the sale of certain real property in 1963.

Findings of Fact

Petitioner was a legal resident of Greenwich, Connecticut, at the time her petition was filed. She filed an individual Federal income tax return for 1963 with the district director of internal revenue, Hartford, Connecticut.

Petitioner's husband operated an oil and gas service station in Greenwich, Connecticut, for a number of years prior to his death on October 7, 1948. His will, dated December 6, 1941, contained the following pertinent provisions:

SECOND: I give devise and bequeath all of my estate both real and personal of whatsoever the same may consist and wheresoever the same may be situated of which I may die possessed or be entitled to at the time of my decease, to my beloved wife, SUSIE SALVATORE, to be hers absolutely and forever.

I make no provision herein for my beloved children because I am confident that their needs and support will be provided for by my beloved wife.

* * *

FOURTH: I hereby give my Executors full power to sell any and all of my property in their discretion and to execute any and all

---

1. 387 U.S. 456, 87 S.Ct. 1776 (1967). See Ferguson, Freeland, and Stephens, Federal Income Taxation of Estates and Beneficiaries, c. 2, "Local Law and Local Adjudications in Federal Tax Cases," 25–47 (1970).

necessary deed or deeds of conveyance of my said property or any part or parts thereof, and which said deed or deeds, conveyance or assignment so executed by my Executors shall be as good and effectual to pass the title to the property therein described and conveyed as if the same had been executed by me in my lifetime.

For several years after her husband's death petitioner's three sons, Amedeo, Eugene, and Michael, continued operating the service station with the help of her daughter Irene, who kept the books of the business. Sometime prior to 1958, however, Michael left the service station to undertake other business endeavors; and in 1958 Eugene left to enter the real estate business, leaving Amedeo alone to manage and operate the service station.

During this period and until 1963, petitioner received $100 per week from the income of the service station. This sum was not based on the fair rental of the property, but was geared to petitioner's needs for her support. The remaining income was divided among the family members who worked in the business.

The land on which the service station was located became increasingly valuable. Several major oil companies from time to time made purchase proposals, which were considered by members of the family. Finally, in the early summer of 1963 representatives of Texaco, Inc. (hereinafter Texaco), approached Amedeo regarding the purchase of the service station property. Petitioner called a family conference and asked for advice on whether the property should be sold. Realizing that Amedeo alone could not operate the station at peak efficiency, petitioner and her children decided to sell the property if a reasonable offer could be obtained.

Amedeo continued his negotiations with Texaco and ultimately received an offer of $295,000. During the course of the negotiations Eugene discovered that tax liens in the amount of $8,000 were outstanding against the property. In addition, there was an outstanding mortgage, securing a note held by Texaco, on which approximately $50,000 remained unpaid. The family met again to consider Texaco's offer.

As a result of the family meeting (including consultation with petitioner's daughter Geraldine, who lived in Florida), it was decided that the proposal should be accepted and that the proceeds should be used, first, to satisfy the tax liens and any other outstanding liabilities. Second, petitioner was to receive $100,000, the estimated amount needed to generate income for her life of about $5,000 per year—the approximate equivalent of the $100 per week she previously received out of the service station income. Third, the balance was to be divided equally among the five children. To effectuate this family understanding, it was agreed that petitioner would first convey a one-half interest in the property to the children and that deeds would then be executed by petitioner and the children conveying the property to Texaco.

On July 24, 1963, petitioner formally accepted Texaco's offer by executing an agreement to sell the property to Texaco for $295,000, the latter making a down payment of $29,500. Subsequently, on August 28, 1963, petitioner executed a warranty deed conveying an undivided one-half interest in the property to her five children. This deed was received for record on September 6, 1963. By warranty deeds dated August 28 and 30, 1963, and received for record on September 6, 1963, petitioner and her five children conveyed their interest in the property to Texaco; Texaco thereupon tendered $215,582.12, the remainder of the purchase price less the amount due on the outstanding mortgage.

Petitioner filed a Federal gift tax return for 1963, reporting gifts made to each of her five children on August 1, 1963, of a 1/10 interest in the property and disclosing a gift tax due in the amount of $10,744.35.

After discharge of the mortgage and the tax liens the remaining proceeds of the sale (including the down payment) amounted to $237,082, of which one-half, $118,541, was paid to petitioner. From the other half of the proceeds the gift tax of $10,744.35 was paid and the balance was distributed to the children.

In her income tax return for 1963 petitioner reported as her share of the gain from the sale of the service station property a long-term capital gain of $115,063 plus an ordinary gain of $665. Each of the children reported in his 1963 return a proportionate share of the balance of the gain.

In the notice of deficiency respondent determined that petitioner's gain on the sale of the service station property was $238,856, all of which was taxable as long-term capital gain. Thereafter each of petitioner's children filed protective claims for refund of the taxes which they had paid on their gains from the sale of the service station property.

Opinion

The only question is whether petitioner is taxable on all or only one-half of the gain realized from the sale of the service station property. This issue must be resolved in accordance with the following principle stated by the Supreme Court in Commissioner v. Court Holding Co., 324 U.S. 331, 334, 65 S.Ct. 707, (1945):

"The incidence of taxation depends upon the substance of a transaction. The tax consequences which arise from gains from a sale of property are not finally to be determined solely by the means employed to transfer legal title. Rather, the transaction must be viewed as a whole, and each step, from the commencement of negotiations to the consummation of the sale, is relevant. *A sale by one person cannot be transformed for tax purposes into a sale by another by using the latter as a conduit through which to pass title.* To permit the true nature of a transaction to be disguised by mere formalisms, which exist solely to alter tax liabilities, would seriously impair the effective administration of the tax policies of Congress." [Footnote omitted. Emphasis added.]

See Harry C. Usher, Sr., 45 T.C. 205 (1965); John E. Palmer, 44 T.C. 92 (1965), affirmed per curiam 354 F.2d 974 (C.A.1, 1965).

The evidence is unmistakably clear that petitioner owned the service station property prior to July 24, 1963, when she contracted to sell it to Texaco. Her children doubtless expected ultimately to receive the property or its proceeds, either through gifts or inheritance, and petitioner may have felt morally obligated to pass it on to them. But at that time the children "held" no property interest therein.[1] Petitioner's subsequent conveyance, unsupported by consideration, of an undivided one-half interest in the property to her children—all of whom were fully aware of her prior agreement to sell the property—was merely an intermediate step in the transfer of legal title from petitioner to Texaco; petitioner's children were only "conduit[s] through which to pass title." That petitioner's conveyance to the children may have been a bona fide completed gift prior to the transfer of title to Texaco, as she contends, is immaterial in determining the income tax consequences of the sale, for the form of a transaction cannot be permitted to prevail over its substance. In substance, petitioner made an anticipatory assignment to her children of one-half of the income from the sale of the property.

The artificiality of treating the transaction as a sale in part by the children is confirmed by the testimony by petitioner's witnesses that the sum retained by her from the sale was a computed amount—an amount sufficient to assure that she would receive income in the amount of approximately $5,000 annually. If the sales price had been less, petitioner would have retained a larger percentage of the proceeds; if more, we infer, she would have received a smaller percentage.[2] While the children's desire to provide for their mother's care and petitioner's willingness to share the proceeds of her property with her children during her lifetime may be laudable, her tax liabilities cannot be altered by a rearrangement of the legal title after she had already contracted to sell the property to Texaco.

All the gain from sale of the service station property was taxable to petitioner. We find nothing in Oscar Deinert, 11 B.T.A. 651 (1928), or

---

1. Sec. 1221, I.R.C.1954, defines the term "capital asset" to mean "property held by the taxpayer."

2. Eugene Salvatore testified as follows:

Q. You stated that you wanted one hundred thousand dollars for your mother. That is, this was to be her share, more or less?

A. Yes.

Q. If the property was sold for one hundred thousand dollars would your mother have kept all the money?

A. She had to.

Q. She would have?

A. She would have kept all the money.

Q. Because she needed the money to live on the interest?

A. Because we felt she needed it to live on.

Q. The children would have got nothing?

A. If she got $90 a week the five children would have made up the difference. We felt she needed the money to live on.

Charles W. Walworth, 6 B.T.A. 788 (1927), cited by petitioner, which requires an opposite conclusion.

Decision will be entered for the respondent.

REVENUE RULING 69–102
1969–1 Cum.Bull. 32.

Advice has been requested by an individual with respect to the Federal income tax consequences to him upon the maturity and surrender for their cash surrender values of an endowment life insurance contract and an annuity contract under the circumstances described below.

In the instant case, the taxpayer sold an unencumbered endowment life insurance contract to a charitable organization described in section 170(c) of the Internal Revenue Code of 1954 for an amount equal to his basis therein, net aggregate of premiums or other consideration paid less dividends received, donating his remaining interest to the charity. [Since 1969 such a transaction would require an allocation of taxpayer's basis between the portion sold to a charity and the portion given so that there would be a taxable gain on these facts at the time of the transfer. Section 1011(b). See Section 1011(b) and Chapter 23, infra at page 836. Ed.] At the same time he made a gift of an unencumbered annuity contract to his son. In the donor's succeeding taxable year both contracts matured and were surrendered by the donees to the insurance company for their then cash surrender values. The cash surrender value of each contract at the time of the transfers to the donees exceeded the amount of the donor's basis. In accordance with the terms of the policy, the insurance company was notified of its assignment and provided with the name and address of the new owners.

Section 1.61–1 of the Income Tax Regulations provides, in part, that gross income includes income realized in any form. It is well established that income is taxable to the person who realizes it, the incidence of the tax not being shifted by a gift thereof to another. Lucas v. Guy C. Earl, 281 U.S. 111 (1930). Also, it has been pointed out that "one who is entitled to receive at a future date, interest or compensation for services and who makes a gift of it by an anticipatory assignment, realizes taxable income quite as much as if he had collected the income and paid it over to the object of his bounty" and "the power to dispose of income is the equivalent of ownership of it and * * * the exercise of the power to procure its payment to another, whether to pay a debt or to make a gift, is within the reach of the statute taxing income 'derived from any source whatever.'" Harrison v. Sarah H. Schaffner, 312 U.S. 579 (1941), Ct.D. 1503, C.B. 1941–1, 321, 322. The Tax Court of the United States has held that "The theory of the cases dealing with anticipatory assignment of income by gift has not been concerned with when the income was accrued in a legal sense of accrual but rather with whether the income has been earned so that the right to the payment at a future date existed when the gift was made.

* * * It is the giving away of this right to income in advance of payments which has been held not to change the *incidence* of the tax." (Emphasis added.) S.M. Friedman v. Commissioner, 41 T.C. 428, 435, affirmed 346 F.2d 506 (1965).

As to the time of realization, the Supreme Court of the United States has said, "Where the taxpayer does not receive payment of income in money or property realization may occur when the last step is taken by which he obtains the fruition of the economic gain *which has already accrued to him*." (Emphasis added.) Helvering v. Paul R.G. Horst, 311 U.S. 112, 115 (1940), Ct.D. 1472, C.B. 1940–2, 206, 207. It follows that the time of the gift is not determinative of the time when income is realized. It has been consistently held that a gift of income does not operate to accelerate the year of taxability. See the *Friedman* case, above, wherein the following was said (p. 436):

"A cash basis taxpayer is not taxable on income until he receives it actually or constructively. The making of a gift of his right to receive income does not cause such income to be received until the donor derives the economic benefit of having the income received by his donee. * * *"

See also Helvering v. Gerald A. Eubank, 311 U.S. 122 (1940), Ct.D. 1473, C.B. 1940–2, 209; Abraham E. Duran et al., v. Commissioner, 123 F.2d 324 (1941); and Annie A. Colby v. Commissioner, 45 B.T.A. 536 (1941), acquiescence C.B. 1942–2, 4.

In the instant case, it is held that the taxpayer is in receipt of taxable income for the taxable year in which the endowment and annuity contracts were surrendered for their cash surrender values by the recipients, the amount of such income being the excess of the cash surrender value of each contract at the time of gift over the taxpayer's basis in that contract. The gain realized through the transfer of the contracts is ordinary income. Commissioner v. Percy W. Phillips, et al., 275 F.2d 33 (1960).

The excess of the fair market value of the endowment contract sold to the charitable organization over the amount received therefor is the measure of the charitable contribution for the taxable year in which the contract was transferred.

* * *

NOTE

The "fruit-tree" tax area is a very large orchard indeed, stretching out over many acres not visible from the vantage point of materials included in this Chapter.[1]

At this point of time the *Horst* case seems easy. The owner of the tree picks some fruit and gives it to another who converts it to cash.

1. The classic work in the orchard is Lyon and Eustice, "Assignment of Income: Fruit and Tree as Irrigated by the P.G. Lake Case," 17 Tax L.Rev. 293 (1962); sup- plemented in Eustice, "Contract Rights, Capital Gain, and Assignment of Income— The Ferrer Case," 20 Tax L.Rev. 1 (1964).

As the owner has kept the tree that produces the fruit, the tree's produce (interest later paid) remains his for tax purposes, even though economically it has become the property of another. Rev.Rul. 69–102, set out above, is illuminating as to the period for which the owner must report the income thus attributed to him.

If the owner gives away the tree (the bond itself in the *Horst* setting), the donee in general is taxable on fruit subsequently produced (later interest payments), because he has become the owner of the income-producing property itself. But what if there is ripe fruit hanging on the tree at the time of the gift? Rev.Rul. 69–102, set out above, has a message here, also, and see Austin v. Commissioner.[2] In many instances, however, it is difficult to say what should be regarded as fruit. Mere appreciation in the value of the property (the tree) is not fruit until it is realized. What further concept was applied, then, to tax Susie Salvatore on the gain on the sale of the property? Can appreciation ripen into fruit?

In Campbell v. Prothro[3] the taxpayer raised calves. On May 7 he transferred 100 head of calves by written instrument to a charitable donee.[4] The donated calves were never physically separated from the rest of the calves. On June 8 taxpayer and the charitable donee entered into a contract to sell the entire calf crop to a third party. The court held that gain on the sale of the calves given to the charity could not be attributed to the donor. Rejecting the Commissioner's argument that no gift in fact occurred prior to the sale, the court went on to say:[5]

> We find ourselves in agreement with appellees' views. In the Horst case, the father, when the coupons on the bonds involved had become, or were about to become due, gave them to his son who collected them, and the court there properly held that the gift constituted an anticipatory assignment of the interest as income, within the Lucas-Earl rule (Lucas v. Earl, 281 U.S. 111, 50 S.Ct. 241). It was not there held, nor has any case cited to or found by us held that if both principal and interest are given, and the principal matures in the year of the assignment, there would be an anticipatory assignment of income as to the principal, so as to make the giver taxable on unrealized appreciation in its value, or on interest accruing in successive years. Indeed, the contrary has been held in Austin v. Commissioner of Internal Revenue, 6 Cir., 161 F.2d 666.

> Here the facts are entirely different from those of any of the cited cases. Here not interest due on choses in action in the year in which the assignment is made, but calves, chattels, whose value would be realized only by a sale, were given. We

---

2. 161 F.2d 666 (6th Cir.1947), cert. denied 332 U.S. 767, 68 S.Ct. 75 (1947).

3. 209 F.2d 331 (5th Cir.1954).

4. The fact that the donee was a charity makes no difference with respect to the ripeness of income issue raised by the case.

However, since 1969 the charitable deduction question in cases of this sort is sharply affected by I.R.C. § 170(e)(1)(A). See Chapter 23B, infra.

5. Campbell v. Prothro, supra note 3 at 335–336.

have found no case, we have been referred to none holding that
unrealized appreciation in the value of cattle given away would
be regarded as ordinary income merely because they had no
base, were kept for sale in the ordinary course of business, and
when sold by the taxpayer would have been ordinary income.
Cf. Visintainer v. Commissioner of Internal Revenue, 10 Cir.,
187 F.2d 519 and White v. Brodrick, D.C., 104 F.Supp. 213 to
the contrary.

*   *   *

Were the calves when transferred by gift to the Y.M.C.A.
realized income to the appellees in the taxable sense? We
think it clear that they were not. If they were, then every
appreciation in value of property passing by gift is realized
income. We know that this is not so, and that, though it is and
has been the contention of the Bureau that it ought to be,
Congress has never enacted legislation so providing.

If appellant's position is sustained here, it must be because
the calves were already income to the taxpayers. If in their
hands the calves were then their income, of course the making
of the gift did not change this status. If they were not income
in taxpayers' hands, their gift of them could not, in the present
state of the law, result in the receipt of income by them. It is
true that efforts have been made to procure the enactment of
statutes to change the rule that a gift does not make the donor
taxable on unrealized appreciation in the value of the property
given. Congress has so far not adopted, indeed has declined to
adopt that view. Under the statutes as they exist, the court
may not do so. The judgment is right. It is affirmed.

The opposite result was reached in the distinguishable case of
Tatum v. Commissioner.[6] In *Tatum* taxpayers owned land which they
leased to sharecroppers who paid their rent in the form of a portion of
the crops produced. Had the rent been payable in cash or in any form
other than crop shares, the landlord would have had to report the rent
as gross income for the year of receipt. However, Reg. § 1.61–4(a), a
reporting regulation, permits a landlord to defer reporting crop share
rent until the year in which such crops are reduced to money or the
equivalent of money. Taxpayer landlords upon receiving the crops
immediately transferred them to a charitable donee, which sold them
in the same year. The court agreed with the Commissioner that the
value of the crops was required to be included in taxpayers' income and
differentiated Campbell v. Prothro, saying:[7]

Turning to the question of law we conclude that crop
shares in the hands of the landlord essentially are income
assets, taxable when reduced to money or the equivalent of
money, rather than, like crops in the hands of a farmer,

6. 400 F.2d 242 (5th Cir.1968).   7. Id. at 246–248.

appreciated property items not taxable if assigned to a third party prior to the realization of any income.

An operating farmer who donates crops to a third party prior to a taxable event, and prior to the point at which he must recognize income, is not required to include the value of the crops in gross income. Rev.Rul. 55–138, supra; Rev.Rul. 55–531, supra. The farmer has done nothing more than assign to another a property asset which has appreciated in value. There has been no taxable event. Neither the harvesting of the crop nor the donative transfer is a taxable event. E.g., Campbell v. Prothro, supra. Thus far Congress has not seen fit to tax unrealized appreciation in property value.

The share-crop landlord, on the other hand, enters an agreement with his tenant whereby the tenant is given the use of the land in return for a share of the crops produced. When the crops are harvested and delivered the landlord has been paid in kind for the use of his land. Crop shares representing payment by the tenant for the use of the land are rental income assets no less than money paid for the same purpose.

* * *

For present purposes it is enough to say that crop shares are potential income assets, not property, and that a landlord may not avoid taxation by assigning his rights to the income prior to the reduction of the crop shares to money or its equivalent. The assignment of income principles of Helvering v. Horst, supra, and the rule of Treas.Reg. § 1.61(a) are applicable to this case and dispositive of the issues it presents.

The *Tatum* case was followed in Parmer v. Commissioner;[8] and now the Treasury also accepts the timing principles expressed in *Tatum*.[9] Usually, of course, realization of income by the donee fixes the donor's time of reporting in assignment of income cases. The *Tatum* case and its followers differentiate *Horst* on this issue, which at least subsumed that the donor of income (ripe fruit) property should take it into income just as and when he would if he had made no gift and had in fact received the income. The difference lies in the peculiar nature of crop shares which *are* realized income but which, as a matter of administrative convenience, are not required to be reported until converted into money or its equivalent.

Under an extension of the fruit-tree metaphor, it is not just fruit but *ripe* fruit that may leave a donor taxable on post-transfer income. Generally a determination of ripeness is simple, at least once we get the hang of it. Thus in *Tatum,* crop shares in hand represent realized income just waiting around to be taxed. If the income generated by property accrues ratably over time, that portion accrued at the time of the gift is likewise ripe. For example, if interest on a coupon bond is

8. 468 F.2d 705 (10th Cir.1972); cf. Harold N. Sheldon, 62 T.C. 96 (1974).

9. Rev.Rul. 75–11, 1975–1 C.B. 27, partially repudiating Rev.Rul. 63–66, 1963–1 C.B. 13.

payable semi-annually on January 1 and July 1 and a donor transfers the bond (not just the coupon) on April 1 midway between payment dates, one-half of the current interest coupon is "ripe" as of the time of the transfer and one-half the amount of the coupon is taxed to the donor and the other one-half is taxed to the donee, generally upon payment.[10] This same principle applies to rents, interest on bank accounts and other items that accrue or are generated merely by the passage of time. Dividends on stock create a more difficult problem. They do not automatically accrue with time but are dependent on a decision by the Board of Directors to issue dividends. Consequently, for business purposes a relevant date must be determined on which ownership of the stock fixes the right to the dividend, the so-called "record" date. There are normally four important dates with respect to the issuance of dividends: the declaration date, the record date, the payment date and the date of actual receipt. Sometimes, especially in a closely held corporation,[11] two dates, possibly the record and payment dates, coincide. In one such case [12] the court held that the fruit ripened on the declaration date, taxing the dividend to a donor who made a gift of the stock the day before the record date. But the case involved a small, closely held corporation. In contrast, in Bishop v. Shaughnessy,[13] involving a minority shareholder of a more widely held corporation, the court reached the conclusion that the fruit ripened on the record date because no enforceable right accrued to any shareholder at the time of the dividend declaration. Is this distinction between closely held and more widely held corporations justified? Are we confronted with conflicting doctrines on assignment of dividend income or merely with divergent tax results sometimes called for, especially in close family circumstances, under the broad rubric of sham transactions?

D. ANTICIPATORY ASSIGNMENT FOR VALUE

ESTATE OF STRANAHAN v. COMMISSIONER

United States Court of Appeals, Sixth Circuit, 1973.
472 F.2d 867 (6th Cir.1973).*

PECK, Circuit Judge: This appeal comes from the United States Tax Court, which partially denied appellant estate's petition for a redetermination of a deficiency in the decedent's income tax for the taxable period January 1, 1965 through November 10, 1965, the date of decedent's death.

The facts before us are briefly recounted as follows: On March 11, 1964, the decedent, Frank D. Stranahan, entered into a closing agreement with the Commissioner of Internal Revenue Service (IRS) under which it was agreed that decedent owed the IRS $754,815.72 for interest

10. The timing depends upon the donor's and donee's accounting methods. See Ch. 19, infra.

11. E.g. Smith's Estate v. Commissioner, 292 F.2d 478 (3d Cir.1961).

12. Ibid.

13. 195 F.2d 683 (2d Cir.1952).

* Some footnotes omitted.

due to deficiencies in federal income, estate and gift taxes regarding several trusts created in 1932. Decedent, a cash-basis taxpayer, paid the amount during his 1964 tax year. Because his personal income for the 1964 tax year would not normally have been high enough to fully absorb the large interest deduction, decedent accelerated his future income to avoid losing the tax benefit of the interest deduction. To accelerate the income, decedent executed an agreement dated December 22, 1964, under which he assigned to his son, Duane Stranahan, $122,820 in anticipated stock dividends from decedent's Champion Spark Plug Company common stock (12,500 shares). At the time both decedent and his son were employees and shareholders of Champion. As consideration for this assignment of future stock dividends, decedent's son paid the decedent $115,000 by check dated December 22, 1964. The decedent thereafter directed the transfer agent for Champion to issue all future dividend checks to his son, Duane, until the aggregate amount of $122,820 had been paid to him. Decedent reported this $115,000 payment as ordinary income for the 1964 tax year and thus was able to deduct the full interest payment from the sum of this payment and his other income. During decedent's taxable year in question, dividends in the total amount of $40,050 were paid to and received by decedent's son. No part of the $40,050 was reported as income in the return filed by decedent's estate for this period. Decedent's son reported this dividend income on his own return as ordinary income subject to the offset of his basis of $115,000, resulting in a net amount of $7,282 of taxable income.

Subsequently, the Commissioner sent appellant (decedent's estate) a notice of deficiency claiming that the $40,050 received by the decedent's son was actually income attributable to the decedent. After making an adjustment which is not relevant here, the Tax Court upheld the deficiency in the amount of $50,916.78. The Tax Court concluded that decedent's assignment of future dividends in exchange for the present discounted cash value of those dividends "though conducted in the form of an assignment of a property right, was in reality a loan to [decedent] masquerading as a sale and so disguised lacked any business purpose; and, therefore, decedent realized taxable income in the year 1965 when the dividend was declared paid."

As pointed out by the Tax Court, several long-standing principles must be recognized. First, under Section 451(a) of the Internal Revenue Code of 1954, a cash basis taxpayer ordinarily realizes income in the year of receipt rather than the year when earned. Second, a taxpayer who assigns future income for consideration in a bona fide commercial transaction will ordinarily realize ordinary income in the year of receipt. Commissioner v. P.G. Lake, Inc., 356 U.S. 260, 78 S.Ct. 691 (1958); Hort v. Commissioner, 313 U.S. 28, 61 S.Ct. 757 (1941). Third, a taxpayer is free to arrange his financial affairs to minimize his tax liability; [1] thus, the presence of tax avoidance motives will not

---

1. "Any one may so arrange his affairs that his taxes shall be as low as possible; he is not bound to choose that pattern which will best pay the Treasury; there is

nullify an otherwise bona fide transaction.[2] We also note there are no claims that the transaction was a sham, the purchase price was inadequate or that decedent did not actually receive the full payment of $115,000 in tax year 1964. And it is agreed decedent had the right to enter into a binding contract to sell his right to future dividends. 12 Ohio Jur.2d, Corporations, Sec. 604.

Comm'r

The Commissioner's view regards the transaction as merely a temporary shift of funds, with an appropriate interest factor, within the family unit. He argues that no change in the beneficial ownership of the stock was effected and no real risks of ownership were assumed by the son. Therefore, the Commissioner concludes, taxable income was realized not on the formal assignment but rather on the actual payment of the dividends.

It is conceded by taxpayer that the sole aim of the assignment was the acceleration of income so as to fully utilize the interest deduction. Gregory v. Helvering, 293 U.S. 465, 55 S.Ct. 266 (1935), established the landmark principle that the substance of a transaction, and not the form, determines the taxable consequences of that transaction. See also Higgins v. Smith, 308 U.S. 473, 60 S.Ct. 355 (1940). In the present transaction, however, it appears that both the form and the substance of the agreement assigned the right to receive future income. What was received by the decedent was the present value of that income the son could expect in the future. On the basis of the stock's past performance, the future income could have been (and was) estimated with reasonable accuracy. Essentially, decedent's son paid consideration to receive future income. Of course, the fact of a family transaction does not vitiate the transaction but merely subjects it to special scrutiny. Helvering v. Clifford, 309 U.S. 331, 60 S.Ct. 554 (1940).

family txn subject to special scrutiny

We recognize the oft-stated principle that a taxpayer cannot escape taxation by legally assigning or giving away a portion of the income derived from income producing property retained by the taxpayer. Lucas v. Earl, 281 U.S. 111, 50 S.Ct. 241 (1930); Helvering v. Horst, 311 U.S. 112, 61 S.Ct. 144 (1940); Commissioner v. P.G. Lake, Inc., supra. Here, however, the acceleration of income was not designed to avoid or escape recognition of the dividends but rather to reduce taxation by fully utilizing a substantial interest deduction which was available. As stated previously, tax avoidance motives alone will not serve to obviate the tax benefits of a transaction. Further, the fact that this was a transaction for good and sufficient consideration, and not merely gratu-

not even a patriotic duty to increase one's taxes." Helvering v. Gregory, 69 F.2d 809, 810 (2d Cir.1934) (Hand, J. Learned), aff'd 293 U.S. 465, 55 S.Ct. 266.

2. "As to the astuteness of taxpayers in ordering their affairs so as to minimize taxes, we have said that 'the very meaning of a line in the law is that you intentionally may go as close to it as you can if you do

not pass it.' Superior Oil Co. v. Mississippi, 280 U.S. 390, 395–396, [50 S.Ct. 169]. This is so because 'nobody owes any public duty to pay more than the law demands; taxes are enforced exactions, not voluntary contributions.'" Atlantic Coast Line v. Phillips, 332 U.S. 168, 172–173, 67 S.Ct. 1584, 1587 (1947) (Frankfurter, J.).

itous, distinguishes the instant case from the line of authority beginning with Helvering v. Horst, supra.

The Tax Court in its opinion relied on three cases. In Fred W. Warner, 5 B.T.A. 963 (1926), which involved an assignment by taxpayer to his wife of all dividend income respecting his 12,500 shares of General Motors Corporation stock, it was held the dividends were income to the taxpayer and were not diverted to the wife through the purported assignment. However, this was a mere gratuitous assignment of income since apparently the only consideration for the assignment was ten dollars. Alfred LeBlanc, 7 B.T.A. 256 (1927), involved a shareholder-father assigning dividends to his son for as long as the son remained with the father's corporation. The Court held that in effect the father postdated his assignment to the dates when he was to receive dividends and hence the dividends were income to the father. However, here again it is apparent that at the time of the assignment there was no consideration.

*   *   *

[The third case is omitted. Ed.]

Hence the fact that valuable consideration was an integral part of the transaction distinguishes this case from those where the simple expedient of drawing up legal papers and assigning income to others is used. The Tax Court uses the celebrated metaphor of Justice Holmes regarding the "fruit" and the "tree", and concludes there has been no effective separation of the fruit from the tree. Judge Cardozo's comment that "[m]etaphors in law are to be narrowly watched, for starting as devices to liberate thought, they end often by enslaving it" (Berkey v. Third Avenue Railway Co., 244 N.Y. 84, 94, 155 N.E. 58, 61 (1926)) is appropriate here, as the genesis of the metaphor lies in a gratuitous transaction, while the instant situation concerns a transaction for a valuable consideration.

The Commissioner also argues that the possibility of not receiving the dividends was remote, and that since this was particularly known to the parties as shareholders and employees of the corporation, no risks inured to the son. The Commissioner attempts to bolster this argument by pointing out that consideration was computed merely as a discount based on a prevailing interest rate and that the dividends were in fact paid at a rate faster than anticipated. However, it seems clear that risks, however remote, did in fact exist. The fact that the risks did not materialize is irrelevant. Assessment of the risks is a matter of negotiation between the parties and is usually reflected in the terms of the agreement. Since we are not in a position to evaluate those terms, and since we are not aware of any terms which dilute the son's dependence on the dividends alone to return his investment, we cannot say he does not bear the risks of ownership.

Accordingly, we conclude the transaction to be economically realistic, with substance, and therefore should be recognized for tax purposes even though the consequences may be unfavorable to the Commissioner. The facts established decedent did in fact receive payment. Decedent deposited his son's check for $115,000 to his personal account on December 23, 1964, the day after the agreement was signed. The agreement is unquestionably a complete and valid assignment to decedent's son of all dividends up to $122,820. The son acquired an independent right against the corporation since the latter was notified of the private agreement. Decedent completely divested himself of any interest in the dividends and vested the interest on the day of execution of the agreement with his son.

The Commissioner cites J.A. Martin, 56 T.C. 1255 (1972), aff'd No. 72–1416 (5th Cir., August 18, 1972), to show how similar attempts to accelerate income have been rejected by the courts. There taxpayer assigned future rents in return for a stated cash advance. Taxpayer agreed to repay the principal advanced plus a 7% per annum interest. These facts distinguish this situation from the instant case as there the premises were required to remain open for two years' full rental operation, suggesting a guarantee toward repayment. No such commitment is apparent here.

The judgment is reversed and the cause remanded for further proceedings consistent with this opinion.

PROBLEMS

1. Executive has a salaried position with Hi Rolling Corporation under which he earns $80,000 each calendar year.

(a) Who is taxed if Executive, at the beginning of the year, directs that $20,000 of his salary be paid to his aged parents?

(b) Who is taxed if Executive at the beginning of the year directs that $20,000 of his salary be paid to any charity the Board of Directors of Hi Rolling selects? (Executive is not a member of the Board.)

(c) Same as (b), above, except that Executive makes the same request with respect to a $10,000 year-end bonus which Corporation has announced toward the end of the year, based on services rendered during the year?

(d) Who is taxed if Executive, in his corporate role, gives a series of lectures on corporate finance at a local business school and, pursuant to his contract with Hi Rolling, turns his $1000 honorarium over to Corporation?

2. Father owns a corporate coupon bond which he purchased several years ago for $8000. It has a $10,000 face amount and is to be paid off in 2000. The current fair market value of the bond is $9,000. The bond pays 8% interest, semi-annually April 1st and October 1st (i.e., $400 each payment). What tax consequences to Father and Daughter in the following alternative situations?

(a) On April 2 of the current year, Father gives Daughter all the interest coupons.

(b) On April 2, Father gives Daughter the bond with all interest coupons attached.

(c) On April 2, Father gives Daughter a one-half interest in the bond and all the interest coupons.

(d) On April 2, Father sells Daughter two succeeding interest coupons for $500, their fair market value as of the time of sale.

(e) On December 31, Father gives Daughter the bond with all interest coupons attached.

(f) On April 2, Father sells the bond and directs that the $9,000 sale price be paid to Daughter.

(g) Prior to April 2, Father negotiates the above sale and on April 2 he transfers the bond to Daughter who transfers the bond to Buyer who pays Daughter the $9,000.

3. In the financial page of the San Francisco *CHRONICLE* it was reported:

Playboy Enterprises Inc. declared a semiannual dividend of six cents a share Tuesday, but the company said its president, Hugh Hefner, decided to give his back.

A spokesman said Hefner's dividend would have totaled more than $380,000. He holds more than six million of the total shares in the company, or 72 percent of the stock.

"It was a gesture of his faith in the company," the spokesman said. "It will go back to the company for its use."

How will Mr. Hefner's gesture be treated by the Commissioner? What additional facts do you want to know?

4. Inventor develops a new electric switch which he patents. Who is taxed on the proceeds of its subsequent sale if:

(a) The patent is transferred gratuitously to Son who sells it to Buyer?

(b) Inventor transfers all his interest in the patent to Buyer for a royalty contract and then transfers the contract gratuitously to Son prior to receiving any royalties? See Heim v. Fitzpatrick, 262 F.2d 887 (2d Cir.1959).

CHAPTER 13. INCOME PRODUCING ENTITIES

A. INTRODUCTION

The Internal Revenue Code recognizes three principal types of income producing entities: partnerships, corporations and trusts. To what extent do they lend themselves to income fragmentation with an eye toward tax savings? As seen in Chapter 12, prior to the Tax Reform Act of 1986, individual taxpayers encountered a progressive tax rate structure of fifteen separate graduated rates, ranging from a low of 11 percent to a top rate of 50 percent of taxable income.[1] The graduated rates provided incentive to shift income producing assets to family members subject to lower rates and to utilize partnerships, corporations and trusts as vehicles to fragmentize income so as to sidestep the higher rates.[2]

The 1986 Act reduced much of the tax incentive for fragmentizing income either directly as seen in Chapter 12 or through the use of a partnership, a corporation or a trust, as seen in this Chapter. The rate structures[3] have been flattened and are now compressed into three rates (15, 28 and 31 percent) with respect to individuals[4] and trusts[5] and into three rates (15, 25 and 34 percent) in the case of corporations. The reduced flattened rates plus the special provision for taxing the passive income of a child under fourteen[6] serve to reduce, if not eliminate, much of the tax benefit of fragmentizing income. And while some tax saving may be possible under the current law,[7] one can generally conclude that for the future tax incentive will not be the primary reason for the use of partnerships, corporations and trusts.[8] The routine tax treatment of and detailed measures designed to prevent the tax abuse of each entity are large areas of study usually relegated to separate courses. This part of this Chapter describes the basic tax

1. I.R.C. § 1. For taxable years beginning after 1983, the 14 graduated rates were 11%, 12%, 14%, 16%, 18%, 22%, 25%, 28%, 33%, 38%, 42%, 45%, 49% and 50%.

2. If a taxpayer in a 50% tax rate bracket could transfer some of his income to another individual or entity in an 11% bracket, he would reduce the amount of tax on the income by 78%.

3. I.R.C. §§ 1(a), 11.

4. I.R.C. § 1(a).

5. I.R.C. § 1(e). Beginning in taxable years after December 31, 1990, the first $3,300 of income of a trust or estate is taxed at a rate of 15%, income in excess of $3,300 is taxed at 28%, and income in excess of $9,900 is taxed at 31%, although the dollar amounts are to be adjusted for post-1989 inflation. I.R.C. § 1(f).

6. I.R.C. § 1(g). See page 978, infra.

7. To the extent that one is successful in shifting income say from the 31% to the 15% bracket, there is a more than 50% saving in the amount of taxes paid.

8. See Sen.Rep.No. 99–313, 99th Cong., 2d Sess. 868 (1986).

characteristics of each entity, and the parts that follow explore some income assignment questions with respect to each.

Partnerships. The Internal Revenue Code provisions that present special rules for income earned by partnerships appear in Subchapter K, Sections 701 through 761. A partnership is essentially a conduit for income tax purposes, because it is required to file only an information return reporting its annual income or loss,[9] and the income is taxed to, or the loss deducted by the various partners, individually.[10] A partnership's "taxable income" is computed under Section 703, but this is for the purpose of allocating taxable amounts among the members, as "[p]ersons carrying on business as partners shall be liable for income tax only in their separate or individual capacities."[11] In general, the tax impact of partnership transactions on each individual partner is determined by the partnership agreement. With some exceptions, such private agreements fix a "partner's distributive share of income, gain, loss, deduction, or credit * * *."[12] Certain "publicly traded partnerships" are not treated as partnerships but are instead classified as corporations for tax purposes with the same tax consequences as are applicable to corporations.[13] The partnership form of doing business is of course very flexible; almost everything depends upon what is agreed to by the members. The tax laws take account of such flexibility and, to a great extent, give effect to the private agreements made. When transactions are at arm's length, this works rather well. But the obvious question here is to what extent family members may make agreements at variance with economic reality and then seek to insist that such agreements be accorded tax recognition. Is there, at least at first blush, an invitation to income assignment?

Corporations. The Internal Revenue Code provisions that provide special rules for the income taxation of corporations and shareholders appear in Subchapter C, Sections 301 through 385. A corporation is at the opposite end of the tax spectrum from a partnership. A corporation is an entity that is taxed under Section 11 at special rates

---

9. Form 1065 required by I.R.C. § 6031. See I.R.C. § 6698 imposing a penalty for failure to file a timely partnership tax return even though the return is only informational.

A partnership may be treated as an entity for procedural purposes. See I.R.C. §§ 6221–6232. These rules are designed to assure uniformity of treatment of items by all members of a single partnership. Small partnerships are generally exempted from the rules unless they elect to be included within them. I.R.C. § 6231(a)(1).

10. I.R.C. § 701.

11. Ibid.

12. I.R.C. § 704(a).

13. I.R.C. § 7704. A publicly traded partnership is any partnership whose in-

terests are traded on an established securities market or are readily tradeable on a secondary market (or its substantial equivalent). I.R.C. § 7704(b). There is an important exception to such reclassification if 90 percent or more of the partnership's gross income for all years after 1987 consists of various types of passive income items (interest, dividends, rent from real property, gains from the sale of real property, and income and gains from certain natural resource activities). I.R.C. § 7704(c). Publicly traded partnerships in existence as of December 17, 1987 are generally allowed a ten year deferral from corporate treatment (until after 1997). Rev.Act of 1987, P.L. No. 100–203 § 10211(c).

applicable only to corporations. When corporate after-tax income is distributed as dividends to shareholders, it is taxed (again?) to the shareholders in their individual capacities.[14] Dividends are taxed as ordinary income, however, only to the extent of the corporation's "earnings and profits," earnings of the current year or accumulated from prior years.[15]

While a partner is not insulated from partnership income for tax purposes, a shareholder usually is insulated from the income of a corporation. In general, a corporation is an entity separate and apart from its shareholders.[16] Therefore, the incorporation of a partnership or sole proprietorship is itself a fragmentation device, because a new taxpayer has come upon the scene. But is this invariably a tax advantage? Recall the tax treatment of corporate distributions. Also note that under current law, the corporate tax rates often exceed those applicable to individuals. In any event, corporate distributions are generally taxed to the owners of the stock on which the dividends are paid. Are there, then, double fragmentization possibilities with respect to income earned by corporations? [17]

A corporation that qualifies as a "small business corporation" [18] can elect, with unanimous shareholder consent, to be an S corporation.[19] The provisions of Subchapter S, while quite complex in detail, can be summarized in a simple fashion. In general, with two exceptions,[20] an S corporation is not subject to income tax; [21] it simply pays no tax on its income.[22] In this respect it is much like a partnership. Each shareholder must take into account his pro rata share of the S corporation's income for the shareholder's taxable year in which the taxable year of the S corporation ends.[23] Since there is in general no corporate tax on such income, what we have here then is a quantitative and qualitative [24] conduit whereby the income constructively passes through the S corporation to be taxed to the shareholders ratably for each taxable year. There need not be any actual distribution of any

14. I.R.C. §§ 61(a)(7), 301.

15. I.R.C. § 316.

16. The exceptions are a corporation that is treated as a mere sham and ignored, U.S. v. McGuire, 249 F.Supp. 43 (S.D.N.Y.1965), and a so-called "tax-option" corporation. Tax option corporations that elect to be S corporations achieve more nearly conduit status. I.R.C. §§ 1361–1379.

17. The student should be fully aware that many assignment of income problems in the business area are largely ignored here. E.g., I.R.C. § 482, authorizing the commissioner to reallocate income, deductions, etc., among related taxpayers; § 269, disallowing some expected tax benefits questionably sought by way of corporate acquisitions and transfers; § 1561, denying surtax exemptions to some multiple incorporations.

18. See I.R.C. § 1361(b). See Coven and Hess, "The Subchapter S Revision Act: An Analysis and Appraisal," 50 Tenn.L.Rev. 569 (1983); Grant, "Subchapter S Corporations vs. Partnerships as Investment Vehicles," 36 U.S.C. Inst. on Fed. Tax'n 13 (1984).

19. Subchapter S, I.R.C. §§ 1361–1379, govern the tax treatment of S corporations. See I.R.C. § 1362(a).

20. I.R.C. §§ 1374 and 1375.

21. I.R.C. § 1363(a).

22. See I.R.C. § 1363(b).

23. I.R.C. § 1366(a). Similarly if an S corporation has a loss, it passes through to the shareholders. Id.

24. Id.; see I.R.C. § 1366(d).

amount of income to any shareholder. The amount of S corporation income that the shareholder is required to include in his gross income effects an increase in the basis of his stock.[25] And the symmetry is complete when we consider actual S corporation distribution of money to its respective shareholders. In that circumstance, its distribution serves to reduce the shareholder's basis in his stock.[26]

The point can now be made that with respect to S corporations and their shareholders there is no double taxation. There is only one tax and that is at the shareholder level. Further since after 1987 the maximum tax rates at the shareholder level are less than those at the corporate level,[27] there is added incentive to elect S corporation status. This means that, even within the current compacted flattened income tax rates, the S corporation continues as a viable tool for family tax planning.

Trusts. For tax purposes a trust falls between a partnership and a corporation. Depending upon the circumstances, the income from a trust may be taxed to the beneficiaries, to the trust, or in part to each. The Internal Revenue Code provisions that present special rules for the determination of tax liability on income earned by trusts (and decedents' estates) appear in Subchapter J, Sections 641 through 692. While quite successful in fitting trusts and estates into a comprehensive scheme of federal taxation, the provisions are highly complex. But this is not to say the area should be completely ignored in a course on tax fundamentals. The objectives here are two-fold: first, to describe very generally the way in which trust and estate income is taxed and second, as in the partnership and corporate area, to look in just a little more detail at specified circumstances in which Congress prescribes a departure from the usual trust rules in order to prevent tax abuses that could arise out of questionable income assignment devices.

Congress has identified a trust as a tax-paying entity whose tax liability is generally determined in a manner similar to that of individuals.[28] On the other hand, a basic aspect of congressional policy is that trust income is to be taxed only once on its way into the hands of its beneficial owners. A further aspect of the plan, seemingly inconsistent with the objective of taxing trust income but once, is to tax trust beneficiaries on amounts of trust income to which they are entitled or which are in fact properly distributed to them.[29] If income may be taxed to the beneficiaries *and* to the trust, how is the one tax objective to be accomplished? The answer is a distribution deduction for the trust, commensurate with the amount of its income which is distributed and taxed to the beneficiaries.[30] In determining the *taxable* income of

25. I.R.C. § 1367(a).

26. I.R.C. § 1368(b)(1). Since it is regarded as a tax-free recovery of tax-paid dollars with respect to the shareholder, only to the extent that a distribution by an S corporation exceeds stock basis is the shareholder subjected to income tax with respect to distributions. I.R.C. § 1368(b)(2).

27. I.R.C. §§ 1(a)–(e) and 11(a).

28. I.R.C. § 641.

29. I.R.C. §§ 652, 662.

30. I.R.C. §§ 651, 661.

the trust, a deduction is allowed generally for amounts required to be, or otherwise properly paid to beneficiaries. In effect, *such* income escapes tax at the trust level but is taxed to the beneficiaries.[31]

It will be observed that in the case of what is called a "simple" trust (essentially one required to distribute all its income currently) the trust, while a *potential* taxable entity, serves as little more than a conduit for both tax and non-tax purposes, simply funneling income to the trust beneficiaries. In other trusts, known as "complex" trusts, where all or a part of the trust income may be accumulated, all or a part of the income may be taxed to the trust and none or only a part of the income to beneficiaries. Consider, then, how a trust appears to present a double fragmentization opportunity somewhat similar to that noted with respect to corporations.

This general description can be extended without getting into too much detail. Outside the "throw-back" area,[32] the statute operates with regard to trust income for the taxable year of the trust. The objective is a division of the tax on such *annual* income between the trust and its beneficiaries. Some students will see a difference from the corporate approach in which previously accumulated (not just current) earnings and profits affect the taxability of corporate distributions.

In another respect, however, the trust provisions resemble the corporate rules. For trust purposes a "distributable net income" of the trust is determined annually,[33] which is somewhat similar to *current* corporate earnings and profits in its regulation of the *amount* on which distributees may be subject to tax.[34] In effect D.N.I., as it is often called, identifies a kind of net income for the year, which could be taxed entirely to the trust or partly or entirely to beneficiaries. However, in the trust (and estate) area, this quantitative objective is not the sole function of D.N.I. In keeping with an essentially conduit approach to the taxation of trust income, D.N.I. is seen as made up of the various *kinds* of income received by the trust, and distributions are considered to consist of ratable portions of each *kind* of income.[35] In this respect, D.N.I. serves a characterization or *qualitative* function in addition to its quantitative function. Thus, if a trust properly distributes half its income to a beneficiary and if half of the trust's income is tax-exempt interest, one half of what the beneficiary receives retains its tax-exempt character in his hands.[36]

One laudable objective of the D.N.I. device is to eliminate the need for tracing. There are circumstances in which a trust instrument may direct income of a particular kind to a specified beneficiary;[37] but, in

---

31. These broad comments apply equally to the income of estates and their beneficiaries. See I.R.C. § 641.

32. There are possible abusive uses of the trust not discussed here. See I.R.C. §§ 665–668.

33. I.R.C. § 643(a).

34. I.R.C. §§ 651(b), 652(a), 661(a), 662(a).

35. I.R.C. §§ 652(b), 662(b); see also § 661(b) and Reg. § 1.651(b)–1.

36. Recall, e.g., the tax-exempt nature of some bond interest under I.R.C. § 103.

37. See Reg. §§ 1.652(b)–2, 1.662(b)–1.

the ordinary case, where income is simply to be divided no tracing is required. Instead, each beneficiary reports a ratable share of all trust income items.[38] Similarly, it is no longer open to argument whether a particular distribution was of principal or of income; the question is immaterial, in the determination of tax liability, as a distribution is deemed to be out of distributable net income to the extent of D.N.I. Distributions that exceed D.N.I. are generally received as tax-free gifts or, in case of an estate, bequests.[39]

The student should note the compressed tax rate schedule applicable to trusts (and estates) in Section 1(e) and compare that with the rate schedule applicable to individuals generally in Section 1(a) through (d). In this respect, the legislative history states: [40]

> The committee believes that the tax benefits which result from the ability to split income between a trust or estate and its beneficiaries should be eliminated or significantly reduced. On the other hand, the committee believes that significant changes in the taxation of trusts and estates are unnecessary to accomplish this result. Accordingly, the bill attempts to reduce the benefits arising from the use of trusts and estates by revising the rate schedule applicable to trusts and estates so that retained income of the trust or estate will not benefit significantly from a progressive tax rate schedule that might otherwise apply. This is accomplished by reducing the amount of income that must be accumulated by a trust or estate before that income is taxed at the top marginal rate. The committee believes that these changes will significantly reduce the tax benefits inherent in the present law rules of taxing trusts and estates while still retaining the existing structure of taxing these entities.[41]

The Tax Reform Act of 1986 added the so-called "kiddie tax" [42], considered here because most income subject to the tax will likely be income distributions from a trust. Under current Section 1(g), net unearned income of a child under 14 years of age who has at least one living parent at the close of the taxable year is taxed to the child at the greater of the child's top tax rate or the parent's top rate.[43] Net unearned income means unearned income [44] generally reduced by $1,000.[45] The "kiddie tax" is considered in Chapter 27A, infra.

---

38. I.R.C. §§ 652(b), 662(b).

39. See I.R.C. § 102.

40. Sen.Rep.No. 99–313, 99th Cong., 2d Sess. 868 (1986).

41. The current revised tax rate schedule is discussed in note 5, supra. Ed.

42. Pub.L.No. 99–514, 99th Cong., 2d Sess. § 1411(a) (1986).

43. I.R.C. § 1(g)(1) and (2).

44. Unearned income is income excluding wages, salaries, or professional fees and other amounts received as compensation for personal services actually rendered. I.R.C. §§ 1(g)(4)(A)(i) and 911(d)(2).

45. I.R.C. § 1(g)(4)(A)(ii). If the child itemizes deductions for the year (see Chapter 18, infra) the $1,000 amount is increased by the amount of the itemized deductions connected with the production of the unearned income in excess of $500. I.R.C. § 1(g)(4)(A)(ii)(II).

The amount of net unearned income for any taxable year cannot exceed the child's

A detailed description of the federal income tax characteristics of each of these three types of entities is beyond the scope of this book. Such details, however, are well supplied in McKee, Nelson and Whitmire, *Federal Taxation of Partnerships and Partners* (2d Ed. Warren, Gorham, and Lamont, 1990); Willis, Pennell and Postlewaite, *Partnership Taxation* (3rd Ed. McGraw-Hill 1981); Bittker and Eustice, *Federal Income Taxation of Corporations and Shareholders* (5th Edition, Warren, Gorham and Lamont, 1987); Ferguson, Freeland, and Stephens, *Federal Income Taxation of Estates and Beneficiaries* (Little, Brown and Company, 1970), in large part as applicable to trusts as to estates.

B. TRUSTS AND ESTATES

Internal Revenue Code: Sections 644(a), (b), (e); 671; 672(a), (b), (e); 673; 676; 677. See Sections 1(g); 641(c); 672(c), (d); 674; 675; 678; 691.

Regulations: Sections 1.671–1; 1.673(a)–1 (omit 1.673(a)–1(a)(2)); 1.676(a)–1; 1.676(b)–1.

CORLISS v. BOWERS

Supreme Court of the United States, 1930.
281 U.S. 376, 50 S.Ct. 336.

Mr. Justice HOLMES delivered the opinion of the Court.

This is a suit to recover the amount of an income tax paid by the plaintiff, the petitioner, under the Revenue Act of 1924, June 2, 1924, c. 234, § 219, (g)(h), 43 Stat. 253, 277. (U.S.C.A., Tit. 26, § 960.) The complaint was dismissed by the District Court, 30 F.2d 135, and the judgment was affirmed by the Circuit Court of Appeals, 34 F.2d 656. A writ of certiorari was granted by this Court.

The question raised by the petitioner is whether the above section of the Revenue Act can be applied constitutionally to him upon the following facts. In 1922 he transferred the fund from which arose the income in respect of which the petitioner was taxed, to trustees, in trust to pay the income to his wife for life with remainder over to their children. By the instrument creating the trust the petitioner reserved power "to modify or alter in any manner, or revoke in whole or in part, this indenture and the trusts then existing, and the estates and interests in property hereby created" &c. It is not necessary to quote more words because there can be no doubt that the petitioner fully reserved the power at any moment to abolish or change the trust at his will. The statute referred to provides that "when the grantor of a trust has, at any time during the taxable year, * * * the power to revest in himself title to any part of the corpus of the trust then the income of such part of the trust for such taxable year shall be included in computing the net income of the grantor." § 219(g) with other similar provisions as to income in § 219(h). [See Sections 676 and 677. Ed.] There can be no doubt either that the statute purports to tax the

taxable income for such taxable year.
I.R.C. § 1(g)(4)(B).

plaintiff in this case. But the net income for 1924 was paid over to the petitioner's wife and the petitioner's argument is that however it might have been in different circumstances the income never was his and he cannot be taxed for it. The legal estate was in the trustee and the equitable interest in the wife.

But taxation is not so much concerned with the refinements of title as it is with actual command over the property taxed—the actual benefit for which the tax is paid. If a man directed his bank to pay over income as received to a servant or friend, until further orders, no one would doubt that he could be taxed upon the amounts so paid. It is answered that in that case he would have a title, whereas here he did not. But from the point of view of taxation there would be no difference. The title would merely mean a right to stop the payment before it took place. The same right existed here although it is not called a title but is called a power. The acquisition by the wife of the income became complete only when the plaintiff failed to exercise the power that he reserved. Saltonstall v. Saltonstall, 276 U.S. 260, 271, 48 S.Ct. 225; Chase National Bank v. United States, 278 U.S. 327, 49 S.Ct. 126; Reinecke v. Northern Trust Co., 278 U.S. 339, 49 S.Ct. 123. Still speaking with reference to taxation, if a man disposes of a fund in such a way that another is allowed to enjoy the income which it is in the power of the first to appropriate it does not matter whether the permission is given by assent or by failure to express dissent. The income that is subject to a man's unfettered command and that he is free to enjoy at his own option may be taxed to him as his income whether he sees fit to enjoy it or not. We consider the case too clear to need help from the local law of New York or from arguments based on the power of Congress to prevent escape from taxes or surtaxes by devices that easily might be applied to that end.

Judgment affirmed.

The CHIEF JUSTICE took no part in this case.

MORRILL v. UNITED STATES

District Court of the United States, Southern District of Maine, 1964.
228 F.Supp. 734.

GIGNOUX, District Judge. This is an action for refund of federal income taxes for the years 1959, 1960 and 1961 in the amounts of $1,736.75, $2,344.50 and $3,064.63, respectively. The only question presented is whether the amounts of the income of four trusts established by George B. Morrill, Jr., which the trustees applied to the payment of the tuition and room charges of the taxpayers' four minor children at private schools and colleges, were taxable as income to him under the provisions of Section 677(a) of the Internal Revenue Code of 1954, 26 U.S.C.A. § 677(a).

The relevant facts, which have been stipulated, may be briefly stated: In April, 1959 Mr. Morrill established four short-term trusts, one for the benefit of each of his four minor children, and named a corporate trustee of each trust. The income of each trust was to be accumulated until the child became 21 years of age, at which time the accumulated income, and thereafter during the remaining term of the trust any current income, was to be distributed to the beneficiary. Ten years after the date of their creation, the trusts were to terminate and the corpus of each was to revert to Mr. Morrill. Each of the trusts also provided that during the minority of the beneficiary, the trustee might, in its discretion, use the trust income "for the payment of room, tuition, books and travel to and from any private school, college or other institution of learning at home or abroad."

During the tax years in question, the taxpayers' children attended Vassar College, Connecticut College, Brown University, The Holderness School and The Waynflete School. Mr. Morrill expressly assumed responsibility for the payment of the tuition, room, board and other expenses of his children at Vassar College and Connecticut College.[1] There was no express agreement between Mr. Morrill and Brown University, The Holderness School or The Waynflete School regarding the payment of the expenses of his children at those schools. However, each school submitted its bills to Mr. Morrill. He then wrote out a personal check to the institution for that portion of the bill other than room and tuition, sent the bill with his personal check to the trustee of the appropriate trust, and requested the trustee to pay from the trust the room and tuition charges on the bill. The trustee then mailed to the institution its check in payment of the room and tuition charges, together with Mr. Morrill's check for the balance of the bill involved.

George B. Morrill, Jr. and Elizabeth H. Morrill, as husband and wife, filed joint federal income tax returns for the calendar years 1959, 1960 and 1961. They did not include in the returns any of the income of the four children's trusts. Upon audit of the returns, the Commissioner determined that the amounts of trust income which had been applied in payment of the children's tuition and room charges had been used to satisfy legal obligations of Mr. Morrill, as father of the children, and were therefore taxable as income to him under Section 677 of the 1954 Code.[2] Plaintiffs paid under protest the resulting deficiency

1. Mr. Morrill signed the following agreement with Vassar College: "In consideration of the acceptance by Vassar College of Bonnie Elizabeth Morrill I agree to be responsible for her tuition, room and board, and other incidental expenses, in accordance with the terms and conditions stated in the current catalogue." He signed the following agreement with Connecticut College: "Bills may be sent to me and I assume responsibility for their payment until further notice."

2. The Commissioner initially based his assessment on Section 677(b). The Government later shifted its ground for asserting taxability to Section 677(a). During legal argument before the Court, counsel for the

Government and for the taxpayers conceded that Section 677(b) has no application to the facts of this case. In this they were correct because Subsection (b) merely limits the tax, imposed by Subsection (a), on trust income which may be applied for the support or maintenance of a beneficiary whom the grantor is legally obligated to support or maintain, to that portion of the trust income which is so applied. Here the Government has not attempted to tax that part of the trust income which was not used to pay the school and college bills in issue. Congress enacted what is now Subsection (b), 58 Stat. 51 (1944), to change the law established by the holding in Helvering v. Stuart, 317 U.S. 154, 63 S.Ct. 140

assessments, and instituted this suit after their claims for refund were disallowed. For reasons which it will state briefly, this Court has concluded that the Commissioner was correct.

Section 671 of the Internal Revenue Code of 1954, 26 U.S.C.A. § 671, provides that the income of a trust is taxable to the person specified in the Code as the owner of the trust. Section 677(a) of the Code provides in relevant part:

"§ 677. Income for benefit of grantor

"(a) General rule.—The grantor shall be treated as the owner of any portion of a trust * * * whose income without the approval or consent of any adverse party is, or, in the discretion of the grantor or a nonadverse party, or both, may be—

"(1) distributed to the grantor [or the grantor's spouse * * *; (as amended in 1969). Ed.]"

A long line of judicial decisions applying Section 677(a) and its predecessor statutes has established that trust income which is used to satisfy a legal obligation of the grantor is, in effect, distributed to him and is, therefore, taxable to him. Douglas v. Willcuts, 296 U.S. 1, 56 S.Ct. 59 (1935) (trust income used to discharge divorced settlor's alimony obligation); Helvering v. Stokes, 296 U.S. 551, 56 S.Ct. 308 (1935), reversing, C.I.R. v. Stokes, 3 Cir., 79 F.2d 256 (trust income used to discharge settlor's legal obligation to support, educate and maintain his minor children); Helvering v. Schweitzer, 296 U.S. 551, 56 S.Ct. 304 (1935), reversing 7 Cir., 75 F.2d 702 (trust income used to discharge settlor's legal obligation to support, educate and maintain his minor children); Helvering v. Blumenthal, 296 U.S. 552, 56 S.Ct. 305 (1935), reversing 2 Cir., 76 F.2d 507 (trust income used to discharge settlor's debt); Helvering v. Coxey, 297 U.S. 694, 56 S.Ct. 498 (1936), reversing 3 Cir., 79 F.2d 661 (trust income used to discharge settlor's alimony and support obligation); Helvering v. Fitch, 309 U.S. 149, 60 S.Ct. 427 (1940) (trust income used to discharge divorced settlor's alimony obligation); Helvering v. Stuart, 317 U.S. 154, 63 S.Ct. 140 (1942) (trust income used to discharge settlor's legal obligation to support, educate and maintain his minor children); Mairs v. Reynolds, 120 F.2d 857 (8th Cir.1941) (trust income used to discharge settlor's legal obligation to support and educate his minor children); Hamiel's Estate v. Comm'r, 253 F.2d 787 (6th Cir.1958) (trust income used for the support, maintenance and education of settlor's minor child); Sheaffer's Estate v. Comm'r, 313 F.2d 738 (8th Cir.), cert. denied, 375 U.S. 818, 84 S.Ct. 55 (1963) (trust income used to discharge settlor's primary obligation to pay gift taxes arising from transfers in creation of the trust.) The Treasury Regulations reflect this fundamental principle. Treas.Reg. § 1.677(a)–1(d).

(1942). See 6 Mertens, Federal Income Taxation § 37.21 (1948).

Despite the Government's change of theory, the burden of proof in this tax refund suit remains on the taxpayers to show that they have overpaid their taxes for the years in question. Lewis v. Reynolds, 284 U.S. 281, 52 S.Ct. 145 (1932); Roybark v. United States, 218 F.2d 164 (9th Cir.1954); Maine Steel, Inc. v. United States, 174 F.Supp. 702, 715 (D.Me.1959).

The transaction is regarded "as being the same in substance as if the money had been paid to the taxpayer and he had transmitted it to his creditor." Douglas v. Willcuts, supra, 296 U.S. at 9, 56 S.Ct. at 63. The income is taxable to the grantor when used to discharge his individual obligation, whether imposed by law or by contract. 6 Mertens, Federal Income Taxation § 37.06 at 434 (1948); compare Douglas v. Willcuts, supra with Helvering v. Blumenthal, supra.

In the present case, the trust income paid to each of the schools and colleges was used to defray expenses for which Mr. Morrill was legally liable. The taxpayers concede that Mr. Morrill was personally obligated for payment of his children's expenses at Vassar College and Connecticut College, because he had expressly assumed that responsibility. It also seems very evident that Mr. Morrill had impliedly obligated himself to pay his children's bills at Brown University, The Holderness School and The Waynflete School. It is a settled principle of contract law that when one renders services to another at the request, or with the knowledge and consent, of the other, and the surrounding circumstances make it reasonable for him to believe that he will receive payment therefor from the other, and he does so believe, a promise to pay will be inferred, and there is an implied contract. 3 Corbin, Contracts, § 566 (1960); Restatement, Contracts § 72 (1932); Saunders v. Saunders, 90 Me. 284, 38 A. 172 (1897); Leighton v. Nash, 111 Me. 525, 90 A. 385 (1914); Gordon v. Keene, 118 Me. 269, 107 A. 849 (1919); Stinson v. Bridges, 152 Me. 306, 129 A.2d 203 (1957). The implied obligation to pay arises whether the services are rendered directly to the other person or to a third person at the request of the other. 3 Corbin, op. cit. supra, § 566 at 312–14. The application of this principle to the determination of Mr. Morrill's obligations with reference to payment of the children's expenses at Brown University, The Holderness School and The Waynflete School is clear. Mr. Morrill was the parent and natural guardian of the children, and insofar as the record shows, approved of their enrollment in these institutions. The record is devoid of evidence that the schools were asked, or agreed, to accept the children with the understanding that they would look only to the trusts for the payment of their room and tuition charges—in fact, there is no evidence that the schools were even aware of the existence of the trusts when they accepted the children. Nor is there any suggestion that the schools looked to the children themselves for the payment of these bills. In each instance the institutions sent their bills to Mr. Morrill. Not once did they submit their bills to the trustees or to the children. Under these circumstances, the only reasonable conclusion is that the schools believed that Mr. Morrill was to be responsible for payment of any bills incurred on behalf of his children. In this they were clearly justified, as it was reasonable for them to expect, in the absence of an express disclaimer by him of an intention to be responsible for the bills, that he would pay for his children's education.

Plaintiffs argue that Mr. Morrill at most undertook, as a party secondarily liable, to guarantee payment of the schools' bills by the children, as the primary obligors. In this view, they assert that the payments by each trustee satisfied the child's obligation and merely extinguished that of Mr. Morrill. The fallacy in this argument is that it presupposes the existence of contracts between the schools and the children. There is no indication that there were any such express contracts; nor is there any showing of circumstances from which a court could imply such contracts. Indeed, it is incredible that these institutions were looking to the children, all of whom were minors without any apparent assets of their own, for payment of these bills. The facts of the case clearly establish that Mr. Morrill, rather than his children, expressly or impliedly undertook to assume primary responsibility for the payment of the school bills here in issue, and that he, and he alone, was legally liable therefor.

The Court holds that the amounts of trust income which the trustees applied in payment of the tuition and room charges of the taxpayers' four minor children at the private schools and colleges which they attended during the tax years in question were used to satisfy express or implied contractual obligations of Mr. Morrill, the grantor of the trusts, and were therefore taxable as income to him under the provisions of Section 677(a) of the 1954 Code. In view of this disposition of the case, it is unnecessary for the Court to consider the Government's alternative contention that such income was taxable to Mr. Morrill, also under Section 677(a), on the theory that Mr. Morrill, as a parent, was under a duty imposed by Maine law to pay the school and college bills of his children. Compare Mairs v. Reynolds, supra.

Judgment will be entered for the defendant against the plaintiffs, with costs.

HELVERING v. CLIFFORD

Supreme Court of the United States, 1940.
309 U.S. 331, 60 S.Ct. 554.

Mr. Justice DOUGLAS delivered the opinion of the Court.

In 1934, respondent declared himself trustee of certain securities which he owned. All net income from the trust was to be held for the "exclusive benefit" of respondent's wife. The trust was for a term of five years, except that it would terminate earlier on the death of either respondent or his wife. On termination of the trust the entire corpus was to go to respondent, while all "accrued or undistributed net income" and "any proceeds from the investment of such net income" was to be treated as property owned absolutely by the wife. During the continuance of the trust respondent was to pay over to his wife the whole or such part of the net income as he in his "absolute discretion" might determine. And during that period he had full power (a) to exercise all voting powers incident to the trusteed shares of stock; (b) to "sell, exchange, mortgage, or pledge" any of the securities under the declaration of trust "whether as part of the corpus or principal thereof or as investments or proceeds and any income therefrom, upon such terms and for such consideration" as respondent in his "absolute discretion may deem fitting"; (c) to invest "any cash or money in the trust estate or any income therefrom" by loans, secured or unsecured, by deposits in banks, or by purchase of securities or other personal property "without restriction" because of their "speculative character" or "rate of return" or any "laws pertaining to the investment of trust funds"; (d) to collect all income; (e) to compromise, etc., any claims held by him as trustee; (f) to hold any property in the trust estate in the names of "other persons or in my own name as an individual" except as otherwise provided. Extraordinary cash dividends, stock dividends, proceeds from the sale of unexercised subscription rights, or any enhancement, realized or not, in the value of the securities were to be treated as principal, not income. An exculpatory clause purported to protect him from all losses except those occasioned by his "own wilful and deliberate" breach of duties as trustee. And finally it was provided that neither the principal nor any future or accrued income should be liable for the debts of the wife; and that the wife could not transfer, encumber, or anticipate any interest in the trust or any income therefrom prior to actual payment thereof to her.

It was stipulated that while the "tax effects" of this trust were considered by respondent they were not the "sole consideration" involved in his decision to set it up, as by this and other gifts he intended to give "security and economic independence" to his wife and children. It was also stipulated that respondent's wife had substantial income of her own from other sources; that there was no restriction on her use of the trust income, all of which income was placed in her personal checking account, intermingled with her other funds, and expended by her on herself, her children and relatives; that the trust was not designed to relieve respondent from liability for family or household expenses and that after execution of the trust he paid large sums from his personal funds for such purposes.

Respondent paid a federal gift tax on this transfer. During the year 1934 all income from the trust was distributed to the wife who included it in her individual return for that year. The Commissioner, however, determined a deficiency in respondent's return for that year on the theory that income from the trust was taxable to him. The Board of Tax Appeals sustained that redetermination. 38 B.T.A. 1532. The Circuit Court of Appeals reversed. 105 F.2d 586. We granted certiorari because of the importance to the revenue of the use of such short term trusts in the reduction of surtaxes.

Sec. 22(a) of the Revenue Act of 1934, 48 Stat. 680, includes among "gross income" all "gains, profits, and income derived * * * from professions, vocations, trades, businesses, commerce, or sales, or dealings in property, whether real or personal, growing out of the ownership or use of or interest in such property; also from interest, rent, dividends, securities, or the transaction of any business carried on for gain or profit, or gains or profits and income derived from any source whatever." The broad sweep of this language indicates the purpose of

Congress to use the full measure of its taxing power within those definable categories. Cf. Helvering v. Midland Mutual Life Insurance Co., 300 U.S. 216, 57 S.Ct. 423. Hence our construction of the statute should be consonant with that purpose. Technical considerations, niceties of the law of trusts or conveyances, or the legal paraphernalia which inventive genius may construct as a refuge from surtaxes should not obscure the basic issue. That issue is whether the grantor after the trust has been established may still be treated, under this statutory scheme, as the owner of the corpus. See Blair v. Commissioner, 300 U.S. 5, 12, 57 S.Ct. 330, 333. In absence of more precise standards or guides supplied by statute or appropriate regulations,[1] the answer to that question must depend on an analysis of the terms of the trust and all the circumstances attendant on its creation and operation. And where the grantor is the trustee and the beneficiaries are members of his family group, special scrutiny of the arrangement is necessary lest what is in reality but one economic unit be multiplied into two or more[2] by devices which, though valid under state law, are not conclusive so far as § 22(a) is concerned.

In this case we cannot conclude, as a matter of law that respondent ceased to be the owner of the corpus after the trust was created. Rather, the short duration of the trust, the fact that the wife was the beneficiary, and the retention of control over the corpus by respondent all lead irresistibly to the conclusion that respondent continued to be the owner for purposes of § 22(a).

So far as his dominion and control were concerned it seems clear that the trust did not effect any substantial change. In substance his control over the corpus was in all essential respects the same after the trust was created, as before. The wide powers which he retained included for all practical purposes most of the control which he as an individual would have. There were, we may assume, exceptions, such as his disability to make a gift of the corpus to others during the term of the trust and to make loans to himself. But this dilution in his control would seem to be insignificant and immaterial, since control over investment remained. If it be said that such control is the type of dominion exercised by any trustee, the answer is simple. We have at best a temporary reallocation of income within an intimate family group. Since the income remains in the family and since the husband retains control over the investment, he has rather complete assurance that the trust will not effect any substantial change in his economic position. It is hard to imagine that respondent felt himself the poorer after this trust had been executed or, if he did, that it had any rational foundation in fact. For as a result of the terms of the trust and the intimacy of the familial relationship respondent retained the substance

---

1. We have not considered here Art. 166-1 of Treasury Regulations 86 promulgated under § 166 of the 1934 Act and in 1936 amended (T.D. 4629) so as to rest on § 22(a) also, since the tax in question arose prior to that amendment.

2. See Paul, The Background of the Revenue Act of 1937, 5 Univ.Chic.L.Rev. 41.

of full enjoyment of all the rights which previously he had in the property. That might not be true if only strictly legal rights were considered. But when the benefits flowing to him indirectly through the wife are added to the legal rights he retained, the aggregate may be said to be a fair equivalent of what he previously had. To exclude from the aggregate those indirect benefits would be to deprive § 22(a) of considerable vitality and to treat as immaterial what may be highly relevant considerations in the creation of such family trusts. For where the head of the household has income in excess of normal needs, it may well make but little difference to him (except income-tax-wise) where portions of that income are routed—so long as it stays in the family group. In those circumstances the all-important factor might be retention by him of control over the principal. With that control in his hands he would keep direct command over all that he needed to remain in substantially the same financial situation as before. Our point here is that no one fact is normally decisive but that all considerations and circumstances of the kind we have mentioned are relevant to the question of ownership and are appropriate foundations for findings on that issue. Thus, where, as in this case, the benefits directly or indirectly retained blend so imperceptibly with the normal concepts of full ownership, we cannot say that the triers of fact committed reversible error when they found that the husband was the owner of the corpus for the purposes of § 22(a). To hold otherwise would be to treat the wife as a complete stranger; to let mere formalism obscure the normal consequences of family solidarity; and to force concepts of ownership to be fashioned out of legal niceties which may have little or no significance in such household arrangements.

The bundle of rights which he retained was so substantial that respondent cannot be heard to complain that he is the "victim of despotic power when for the purpose of taxation he is treated as owner altogether." See DuPont v. Commissioner, 289 U.S. 685, 689, 53 S.Ct. 766, 767.

We should add that liability under § 22(a) is not foreclosed by reason of the fact that Congress made specific provision in § 166 for revocable trusts [Section 676. Ed.], but failed to adopt the Treasury recommendation in 1934, Helvering v. Wood, post, p. 344, that similar specific treatment should be accorded income from short term trusts. [See Section 673, not added until 1954. Ed.] Such choice, while relevant to the scope of § 166, Helvering v. Wood, supra, cannot be said to have subtracted from § 22(a) what was already there. Rather, on this evidence it must be assumed that the choice was between a generalized treatment under § 22(a) or specific treatment under a separate provision [3] (such as was accorded revocable trusts under

---

3. As to the disadvantage of a specific statutory formula over more generalized treatment see Vol. I, Report, Income Tax Codification Committee (1936), a committee appointed by the Chancellor of the Ex-

chequer in 1927. In discussing revocable settlements the Committee stated, p. 298:

"This and the three following clauses reproduce section 20 of the Finance Act, 1922, an enactment which has been the

§ 166); not between taxing or not taxing grantors of short term trusts. In view of the broad and sweeping language of § 22(a), a specific provision covering short term trusts might well do no more than to carve out of § 22(a) a defined group of cases to which a rule of thumb would be applied. The failure of Congress to adopt any such rule of thumb for that type of trust must be taken to do no more than to leave to the triers of fact the initial determination of whether or not on the facts of each case the grantor remains the owner for purposes of § 22(a).

In view of this result we need not examine the contention that the trust device falls within the rule of Lucas v. Earl, 281 U.S. 111, 50 S.Ct. 241 and Burnet v. Leininger, 285 U.S. 136, 52 S.Ct. 345, relating to the assignment of future income; or that respondent is liable under § 166, taxing grantors on the income of revocable trusts.

The judgment of the Circuit Court of Appeals is reversed and that of the Board of Tax Appeals is affirmed.

Reversed.

Mr. Justice ROBERTS, dissenting:

I think the judgment should be affirmed.

The decision of the court disregards the fundamental principle that legislation is not the function of the judiciary but of Congress. * * *

Mr. Justice McREYNOLDS joins in this opinion.

NOTE

The student should note that in *Clifford* the settlor assigned *property* to the trust, not mere naked rights to income as was the case involving an outright assignment in Helvering v. Horst.[1] The trust was irrevocable; otherwise Section 676 would have been enough to tax the settlor on the trust income.[2] Also, in *Clifford* the government stipulated that the income of the trust was not used for the support of the settlor's wife; for, if the income were so used, it would have been taxable to Clifford under Section 677, and it is doubtful the case would have reached the Supreme Court.[3] Thus one can surmise that, in frustration resulting from the failure of Congress to enact specific Code provisions dealing with short-term, family control trusts, the government, in a calculated risk, sought to combat such devices in a maneuver relying solely on the vagueness of Section 61; and it paid off. It is clear that the settlor's retention of control over the property was the basis for the court's decision. The short duration of the trust is properly

subject of much litigation, is unsatisfactory in many respects, and is plainly inadequate to fulfill the apparent intention to prevent avoidance of liability to tax by revocable dispositions of income or other devices. We think the matter one which is worthy of the attention of Parliament."

1. 311 U.S. 112, 61 S.Ct. 144 (1940), Chapter 12, supra at page 275.

2. Cf., Corliss v. Bowers, 281 U.S. 376, 50 S.Ct. 336 (1930), supra at page 305.

3. See Morrill v. United States, 228 F.Supp. 734 (D.C.Me.1964), supra page 306.

regarded as one of the settlor's retained strings of control. Following *Clifford*, the question became how many and what strings of control could a settlor of a trust retain without incurring tax liability on income that is payable to others. The answers were forthcoming, but over a period of more than forty years in several separate stages.

The immediate impact of *Clifford* was confusion because, while Clifford himself may have retained enough of the bundle of rights to be held to "own" the trust property, the outer limits of the *Clifford* doctrine were very obscure. In 1945, the Treasury sought to accord some definition to the doctrine by elaborate and expansive regulations, promulgated under the generic provision of what is now Section 61.[4] In the enactment of the Internal Revenue Code of 1954, Congress undertook to give the grantor trust area a more substantial statutory underpinning by the enactment of Sections 671–675 and 678. The Tax Reform Act of 1976 added Section 679 to deal with problems arising under some foreign trusts. As indicated in *Clifford*, Sections 676 and 677 had a much earlier origin.[5] What is the scope and effect of the restrictive language in the last sentence of Section 671?

Some feel for the grantor trust area can be attained by a look at Sections 673 through 677. A general feel for the area is all that is intended to be gleaned from an examination of the problems in this book. However, here are a few comments on the so-called "grantor trust" provisions, which may help to round out the broad picture.

Section 673. The grantor trust rules were tightened up considerably by the Tax Reform Act of 1986. The significant changes here affect the reversionary interest rule of Section 673. Prior to 1986, the grantor of a trust was taxed on the income from the trust (see Section 671) if he retained a reversionary interest in corpus or income which might reasonably be expected to revert to him within ten years.[6] Thus the law provided a safe and easily determinable harbor for a temporary transfer of income-producing property where certain powers and interests retained by the grantor did not become operative for a period of ten years.[7] Moreover, the 1954 version of Section 673 contained an exception to the ten year reversionary interest rule if the expectation of reversion depended only on the life expectancy of the income beneficiary.[8] And the former statute did virtually nothing with respect to the

---

4. Treas.Reg. 111, § 29.22(a)–21 (1943); see Alexandre, "Case Method Restatement of The New Clifford Regulations," 3 Tax L.Rev. 189 (1947).

5. See Revenue Act of 1924, §§ 219(g) and (h), 43 Stat. 253, 277 (1942); and see Corliss v. Bowers set out at page 296, supra. An early basic discussion of the 1954 legislative changes appears in Greenberger, "Changes in the Income Taxation of Clifford Type Trust", 13 N.Y.U.Inst. on Fed.Tax. 165 (1955), and see Yohlin, "The Short-Term Trust—A Respectable Tax-Saving Device," 14 Tax L.Rev. 109 (1958).

6. I.R.C. § 673(a). Prior to the enactment of I.R.C. § 7872 under the 1984 Act (see page 456 infra), old I.R.C. § 673 was easily circumvented by interest-free loans whose use was judicially approved by J. Simpson Dean, 35 T.C. 1083 (1961), and other cases. See page 451 infra. Interest-free loans are considered in Chapter 17B, infra.

7. See I.R.C. §§ 674(b)(2); 676(b); 677(a), last flush sentence.

8. I.R.C. § 673(c).

avoidance possibilities of a spousal remainder trust, pursuant to which the grantor retained no reversionary interest but on termination of the trust, the remainder would pass to the grantor's spouse.[9]

Today, a grantor is treated as holding any power or interest that is held by an individual who was the spouse of the grantor at the creation of the power or interest or who became the spouse of the grantor after the creation of the power or interest, but only for periods after the individual became the grantor's spouse.[10] Note that this provision appears in Section 672, which means that it applies to each of the substantive provisions found in Sections 673 through 678.

Under Section 673, as amended in 1986, the grantor is treated as the owner of any portion of a trust (possibly all) in which he has a reversionary interest in either the corpus or the income, if the value of the reversionary interest exceeds 5 percent of the value of that portion of the trust.[11] The value of the reversionary interest is measured as of the inception of that portion of the trust in which the grantor has an interest. This provision replaces the "ten year" reversionary interest rule of prior law.[12] There is an exception to the 5 percent reversionary interest rule if the grantor's reversion can take effect only upon the death of a lineal descendant under twenty-one years of age.[13] But, for the exception to apply, the beneficiary whose life is used must have the entire present interest in the trust or trust portion.[14] Two concepts both of which have roots in the estate and gift tax area have been imported here into Section 673: the reversionary interest rule [15] and the present interest exception.[16]

The five percent reversionary interest rule treats the grantor as owner of any portion of a trust with respect to which he has a reversionary interest in excess of five percent of the value of that interest. The application of the rule may require an actuarial determination of the grantor's chances of surviving others who have beneficial interests in the trust and a valuation of those chances in relation to the value of the property in the trust.[17] In very general terms, if the amount a third party would pay the grantor for a reversionary interest that *might* vest in the grantor a portion of the trust property is more than five percent of the value of that portion of the trust, then the grantor is treated as the owner of such portion and must pay the tax on

---

9. See e.g. Sen.Rep. No. 99–313, 99th Cong., 2d Sess. 871 (1986).

10. I.R.C. § 672(e)(1). Individuals are not considered married if they are legally separated under a decree of divorce or separate maintenance. I.R.C. § 672(e)(2).

11. I.R.C. § 673(a). Any postponement of the date for the reversionary interest is treated as a new transfer in trust commencing with the date the postponement is effective. I.R.C. § 673(d).

12. I.R.C. § 673(a).

13. I.R.C. § 673(b).

14. I.R.C. § 673(b)(2).

15. See I.R.C. § 2037. Under I.R.C. § 2037(b), "reversionary interest" includes a possibility that the property transferred may return to the decedent transferor or to his estate, or a possibility that it may become subject to a power of disposition by him.

16. See I.R.C. § 2503(b) and (c).

17. See Stephens, Maxfield, Lind and Calfee, *Federal Estate and Gift Taxation,* § 4.09[4][d] (6th Ed. Warren, Gorham & Lamont, 1991).

the income generated by that portion of the trust. The value of the grantor's reversionary interest is determined by assuming the maximum exercise of discretion in favor of the grantor.[18]

The limited exception to the reversionary interest rule applies if the reversionary interest will take effect only by reason of the death of a minor lineal descendant of the grantor before reaching age 21. But this is so only if the descendant is a beneficiary who has all of the present interest in the portion of the trust in question. The "present interest" concept, borrowed from the federal gift tax, in general requires that the beneficiary have an immediate, in contrast to a future interest, in the trust or a portion of the trust.[19]

Section 674. Under Section 674(a), the grantor of a trust is taxed on the income from the trust if he or a nonadverse party [20] holds a power to determine who, other than the grantor,[21] will receive the income or the corpus of the trust. Subsections (b), (c) and (d) provide exceptions to the general rule of Section 674(a) identifying groups of situations in which the grantor is not taxed even though such powers are held. The exceptions look to two factors, the nature of the power held and the person holding the power. Generally very indirect or weak powers to alter the beneficial enjoyment may be held by anyone, including the grantor, without invoking Section 674(a).[22] As the scope of the power increases, it will render the grantor taxable unless it is held by someone not closely associated with him.[23]

Section 675. This section may apply if a grantor or a nonadverse party holds merely administrative powers over the trust corpus. For example, a power to dispose of trust property for less than full consideration is proscribed; and so is a power to borrow trust corpus or income without payment of adequate interest or the posting of adequate security. Generally, Section 675 may apply in situations in which normal stringent fiduciary standards are waived by the trust instrument.

Section 677. The income from a trust need not be actually paid to the grantor to provide benefits to him and if the income from a trust may benefit the grantor, directly or indirectly, Congress has provided in Section 677 that he may be taxed on the income. In 1969, Congress decided that the same result should follow if the income may be used directly or indirectly for the grantor's spouse.[24] In general, the provisions of Section 677 apply if the income "may be" used for the proscribed purposes, regardless of how it is in fact used.[25]

18. I.R.C. § 673(c).

19. See Stephens, Maxfield, Lind and Calfee, supra note 17 at § 9.04[5].

20. See I.R.C. § 672(a) and (b).

21. I.R.C. § 677(a) controls if the income may be used for the grantor's benefit.

22. I.R.C. § 674(b).

23. I.R.C. § 674(c) and (d). See Westfall, "Trust Grantors and Section 674:

Adventures in Income Tax Avoidance," 60 Colum.L.Rev. 326 (1960), reprinted in Sander and Westfall, Readings in Federal Taxation 471 (Foundation Press 1970).

24. Tax Reform Act of 1969, § 332.

25. But see I.R.C. § 677(b), relieving the grantor of tax on income that may be used to support a dependent (other than his spouse) except to the extent it is so used; and see Morrill v. U.S., supra at page 306.

Section 678.   This section presents a new twist to the so-called grantor provisions.   Under this section a third person (not the grantor), not necessarily a beneficiary, may be taxed on the income of a trust, if the grantor escapes the other grantor trust provisions [26] and the third person has a power to obtain the income or corpus for his own benefit.[27]

NOTE

As suggested in the Note introducing this Chapter, for tax purposes trusts fall between partnerships (individual partners usually taxed) and corporations (the entity usually taxed), because they provide a dual possibility for assignment of income either to their beneficiaries or to the trust entity itself.   For example, in the case of a "simple" trust, income generated by corpus is taxed to beneficiaries while gains on the corpus itself are taxed to the trust.

Prior to 1976 [1] gains on sales of appreciated property made by a trust were taxed to the trust at its applicable rate even though they occurred shortly after the grantor had transferred the property.[2]   However, in 1976 Congress enacted a special rule providing a different computation of tax under Section 644 for sales of appreciated property by a trust within two years of the property's transfer to the trust.[3] Section 644 essentially is a statutory adoption of a "ripeness" concept under which sales of such property made by the trust (to the extent of appreciation on the property at the time of the transfer to the trust) are treated for rate purposes as though made by the grantor [4] of the trust. In essence the trust acts as the grantor's agent with respect to precontribution gain and that gain, although taxed to the trust, is taxed at the grantor's rates in the year of the sale.   Mechanically, Section 644 does this by adding to the trust's regular income tax an additional tax equal to the amount of additional tax the grantor would have paid if the grantor, rather than the trust, had sold the property in the year of the

---

26.   See I.R.C. § 678(b).

27.   A person's possession of a power, as a fiduciary, merely to have trust income used for the support of his dependents does not invite tax, except to the extent the income is so used.   I.R.C. § 678(c); and cf. § 677(b).   One might escape § 678 by reason of a trust requirement that *another* person join in the exercise of his power. Reg. § 1.678(c)–1(b).   However, the Treasury holds that one whose obligations are discharged by trust distributions is taxable as a beneficiary under §§ 652 or 662.   See Reg. § 1.662(a)–4.

1.   I.R.C. § 644 applies to transfers made to trusts after May 21, 1976.

2.   This assumes no "prearranged sales."   Cf. Commissioner v. Court Holding Co., 324 U.S. 331, 65 S.Ct. 707 (1945) and problem 2(g) at page 298, supra.

3.   Sales beyond two years after the property's transfer to the trust are not affected by § 644.   See, however, § 644(f) related to § 453 sales which requires gains on installments recognized beyond the two year period to be taxed under § 644 if the sale itself occurred within the two year period.   See Rosen and Botkin, "Can Trusts Still be Used to Avoid Realization of Gain by Grantor Despite Section 644?"   7 Tax. for Lawyers 14 (1978), discussing § 644.

4.   The statute makes it clear the § 644 rule may be invoked by a sale or exchange by a distributee trust as well as the original trust.   I.R.C. § 644(a)(1)(A).

Although this note refers to the "grantor" of the trust, the section applies to sales of property transferred by *any* transferor to the trust.

sale.[5] The section limits the "includible gain" to the lesser of the appreciation on the property at the time of its transfer to the trust or the trust's gain on the property [6] conventionally determined. That amount of gain is then *excluded* from the trust's taxable income so that it is not taxed twice.[7]

Consequently, if in year one grantor transfers property with a $100,000 adjusted basis and $300,000 value to a trust and the trust sells it in the succeeding year for $350,000, the trust will pay the tax on the entire gain of $250,000. But the tax is an amount equal to the amount of tax the grantor would have paid if he (rather than the trust) had sold the property in that year for *$300,000* plus the tax the trust would pay on the remaining $50,000. Thus, the total gain is $250,000, $200,000 of which, called "includible gain", is subjected to the grantor's tax rates; $50,000, the post contribution appreciation, is simply taxed along with other trust gains.[8] If the trust had sold the property for $250,000, the tax imposed on the trust would have been computed as if the grantor had realized the entire gain of $150,000. Problem 3, below, tests your understanding of the Section 644 concept.

Section 644 is not a dead duck, but it is definitely a lame duck since the 1986 Act. Because of the 31 percent ceiling on tax rates and the $3,300 phase-in of the 28 percent rates under Section 1(e), it seems unlikely that Section 644 will often generate additional tax revenue for the Treasury. As Section 644 simply uses the grantor's rates (and not the greater of the rates of trust or the grantor), it is possible that in some instances less tax would be due. Section 644 was a good idea at the time it was enacted, but with recent legislation, its time has passed. Congress should have taken a small step to simplify the Code by knocking off this lame duck.

PROBLEMS

1. Grantor who is a lawyer creates a trust for the benefit of his adult Son with income to Son for life, remainder to Son's children. Who is taxed on the income paid to Son in the following circumstances:

    (a) Grantor transfers to the trust accounts receivable for services which have never been included in his gross income. The clients pay the fees represented by the receivables in the succeeding year.

5. To the extent that gain is attributed to the transferor it is characterized as if the sale were made by him. See I.R.C. § 644(c).

6. I.R.C. § 644(b). The special tax of § 644 is inapplicable to transfers from a decedent or to sales occurring after the death of the transferor.

7. See I.R.C. § 641(c). The overall effect of this is that part or all of the gain is taxed at the transferor's tax rates, and any remaining gain is included in the trust's income and characterized at the trust level.

8. The trust's taxable income would, in effect, include only $50,000 of gain attributable to the post transfer appreciation on the property. See note 7, supra.

(b) Grantor owns a building subject to a long term lease. He transfers the right to future rentals under the lease to the trust.

(c) Same as (b), above, except that he transfers the building along with the right to the rentals at a time when no rent has accrued.

(d) Same as (c), above, except that six months' rent has accrued on the lease at the time of Grantor's transfer.

(e) Same as (c), above, except that Grantor retains the right to revoke the trust at any time.

(f) Same as (c), above, except that Grantor holds liberal powers to change the income beneficiary of the trust from Son to anyone other than Grantor.

(g) Same as (c), above, except that at Son's death the property reverts to Grantor if Grantor is then living. The value of the reversionary interest exceeds 5% of the value of the trust corpus.

(h) Same as (g), above, except that Son is a 15 year old minor.

(i) Same as (h), above, except that the trust instrument provides that the corpus shall revert to Grantor only if Son dies prior to reaching 21 years of age.

(j) Same as (c), above, except that Grantor may direct the sale of the trust corpus to any person including himself for any price he wishes.

(k) Same as (c), above, except that Son is a minor and the income from the trust while Son is a student is used to pay Son's tuition at a private high school which Son attends.

(l) Same as (c), above, except that under the terms of the trust, Wife may require the trustee to pay the income from the trust to her in any year.

2. Do you see a relationship between the results in problem one and the messages of the *Earl, Horst,* and other cases of Chapter 12? What additional concept does the Grantor trust provisions add?

3. Funder transfers stock to an irrevocable "simple" trust which provides income to Child for life with a remainder to the children of Child. Funder purchased the stock several years ago at a cost of $40,000 and it is worth $100,000 at the date of its transfer to the trust.

(a) If the trust immediately sells the stock and reinvests the proceeds in other stock how is the gain on the stock taxed? See §§ 644(a) and (b) and 641(c).

(b) How is the gain taxed in (a), above, if the sale occurs in the third year after the stock's transfer to the trust?

(c) What consequences in (a), above, if the trust sells the stock for $120,000 in the year it is transferred to the trust?

(d) What consequences in (c), above, if the sale is for $80,000?

(e) How is the gain taxed in (a), above, if the trust sells the stock within one year of the transfer in trust but after the death of Funder?

Income in Respect of Decedents

Questions arise upon the death of a taxpayer which involve, not only the issue of *who* is taxable on income (the major question in this Chapter) but also *when* the income is taxed and the *character* of the income; and there are related issues with respect to deductions. Fundamental consideration is given later in this book to questions of timing, characterization, and deductions, but these phenomena cannot properly be injected here. Moreover, more knowledge on the income taxation of trusts and estates than is presented in this book is needed for a full grasp of the area. Nevertheless a brief note on income in respect of decedents is presented here. It might, at most, be skimmed at this time. Later, it might be reviewed as a general introduction to a very difficult area.

Section 691 addresses itself to some of the transitional problems that arise because a person's financial affairs, instead of terminating neatly at the time of his death, linger on, sometimes for a considerable period after his demise. An executor marshalling the decedent's assets will usually find that his efforts involve the collection of amounts that would have been gross income to the decedent had he collected them and the payment of amounts that would have been tax deductions if paid by the decedent. What should be the post-death tax consequences of such transactions? *Possible* answers to this question are suggested by a brief review of three legislative approaches that Congress has, at different times, taken to the matter of income and deductions in respect of decedents.

From the inception of the individual income tax in 1913 to 1934, Congress did not legislate specifically on the subject. But of course such inaction itself had important tax consequences. The principal result was for much income constitutionally subject to tax to escape the federal exaction. This came about by way of the treatment of income rights as a part of the corpus of a decedent's estate entitled, along with all other property owned by him, to a new date-of-death value basis, which foreclosed the imposition of income tax upon its post-death collection. Of course, at the same time, expenses incurred before death that could not under the decedent's accounting method be deducted on his final return also lost their potential for tax reduction when paid.

The two main problems with the pre-1934 approach were: (1) substantial revenue loss through the escape from income taxation of transitional income items and (2) quite unequal treatment of accrual and cash method taxpayers. With regard to the second difficulty, it is obvious that some transitional income items, such as a decedent's unpaid salary, interest, and gain on the sale of property, were either *taxed or not* according to the decedent's accounting method,[1] whereas in the case of living taxpayers accounting methods generally affect only timing and do not govern whether an item is subject to tax at all.

To overcome these problems, Congress in 1934 in effect put all final returns of decedents on the accrual method. Thus, notwithstanding the fact that a decedent had been a cash method taxpayer, his *final* return included accrued items of income and deduction. This stemmed the revenue loss and eliminated the discriminatory advantage previously enjoyed by estates and beneficiaries of cash method taxpayers. But it was soon evident that there were equally strong objections to the new approach. Especially when the courts gave support to a broad administrative interpretation of what income items could be treated as accrued by reason of death, there was great possibility that substantial previously untaxed income would be bunched in the final return of a cash method taxpayer.

The origin of the present congressional approach to the problem was the Revenue Act of 1942, which first presented the concept of income and deductions in respect of decedents. If it can be capsulized, the intended thrust of Section 691 is insofar as possible to neutralize the tax consequences of a person's death. Thus, income generated by him, but untaxed to him, is to be taxed to others when received by them, not in the decedent's final return. And some potential deductions of the decedent may be claimed by others when they pay the related pre-death expenses of the decedent. In general, this will be seen: (1) To prevent revenue loss which, pre-1934, was a sometimes result of death, (2) To let accounting method continue to affect the timing of income and deductions, but not to affect the questions whether income would be taxed or whether deductions could be claimed, also pre-1934 inequities, and (3) To avoid the bunching problem inherent in the 1934 legislation.[2]

Together with Sections 451 and 1014(c), Section 691(a) taxes a decedent's transitional income items to the one who receives the item after a decedent's death. When death terminates his taxable year,

---

1. See Chapter 19, infra.

2. There are estate tax problems intimately related to the question of income in respect of decedents. At a time when the statute was silent on this income tax matter, it was apparently deemed inappropriate to impose both income and estate taxes with respect to the same transitional income items. Perhaps it was sound not to assume a congressional intent to impose such "double taxation" in the absence of a clear congressional mandate. Nevertheless, a decedent's untaxed right to income is clearly an interest in property subject to estate tax under I.R.C. § 2033. And there is no good reason why estate taxation should turn on whether the right has been subjected to income tax in a return of the decedent or is only to be taxed to another after the decedent's death. In fact, § 691 now carries the clear inference that such "double taxation" *is* intended. The inference is found in provisions of § 691 allowing a deduction for estate taxes that are attributable to the inclusion in the gross estate of items of income in respect of decedents, and it is no longer open to question that income in respect of decedents can be subjected to both income and estate taxes after death. There is a comprehensive examination of I.R.C. § 691 in Ferguson, Freeland, and Stephens, Federal Income Taxation of Estates and Beneficiaries, c. 4, "Income in Respect of Decedents," 139–300 (1970).

income inclusions in the decedent's final return are determined by his established accounting method under Section 451(a).[3] The full income component of post-death receipts is preserved by Section 1014(c), which denies the usual date-of-death value basis to any right to receive income in respect of a decedent, commonly called I.R.D.

I.R.D. items [4] are to be included "when received," which makes the recipient's accounting method immaterial with respect to such items.[5] The statute is explicit as regards who may be taxed upon receipt of I.R.D. If, as is usually the case with respect to unpaid salary, the executor collects the amount, it is an item of gross income to the estate.[6]

Finally, upon acquisition of an I.R.D. item as a part of the decedent's estate, the executor or administrator may transmit it, before collection, to one who is entitled to it by reason of bequest, devise, or inheritance. In such a case, the one to whom it is transmitted takes it into account as I.R.D. when payment is received.[7] However, some transmissions of I.R.D. items are far from neutral events. Instant tax liability results to the transferor if, for example, the executor sells an I.R.D. item or a beneficiary who acquired it innocuously from the executor makes a gift of it.[8]

The neutralization objective of Section 691 is further carried out by provisions that *characterize* I.R.D. when received in accordance with the nature of the income that would have been realized by the decedent had he collected the item during life.[9] Thus, gain on the sale of a capital asset, taxed as I.R.D. when the proceeds are collected after

---

3. Thus, receipt prior to death (or constructive receipt) is the test for inclusions for cash method taxpayers. In the case of accrual method decedents, the usual "all events" test will control, especially since I.R.C. § 451(b) forecloses accrual only by reason of death in the case of such taxpayers.

4. The examples in Reg. § 1.691(a)–2 are helpful as illustrations of what constitutes an I.R.D. item. See Furr, "Determining When Sales Proceeds are Income in Respect of a Decedent," 19 Wake Forest L.Rev. 993 (1983).

5. Some variations in the "when received" rule, such as may be necessary in the case of the death of a partner, see Reg. § 1.753–1(b), are not discussed here.

6. I.R.C. § 691(a)(1)(A). This of course does not answer the ultimate question regarding the incidence of the tax, however, which will depend in part on distributions by the executor and the usual deduction and inclusion rules for estates and beneficiaries under §§ 661 and 662. Thus, even when the executor collects the item, the tax bite may fall on estate beneficiaries.

7. I.R.C. § 691(a)(1)(C). It should be noted that such transmission of an I.R.D. item takes place outside the usual distribution rules of §§ 661 and 662. That is, it does not give rise to a distribution deduction for the estate, and it is not regarded as an "amount properly paid" (not a distribution in kind) such as would cause tax liability to the beneficiary within limitations of the estate's distributable net income. See Ferguson, Freeland and Stephens, Federal Income Taxation of Estates and Beneficiaries, c. 7, p. 533 (Little, Brown 1970). The result is in keeping with the § 691 objective to neutralize the effect of death with respect to I.R.D. items, and Rollert Residuary Trust v. Commissioner, 752 F.2d 1128 (6th Cir.1985), so held.

8. I.R.C. § 691(a)(2). These acceleration rules are somewhat analogous to the more familiar principles that apply to the disposition of installment obligations under § 453B. See Chapter 24, infra at page 868.

9. I.R.C. § 691(a)(3). See Chapter 21, infra.

death, is capital gain to the recipient.   Salary collected after death is ordinary income.   And so forth.

The deductions side of Section 691 in effect passes through to the decedent's estate or beneficiaries the tax benefit of certain deductible expenses incurred by the decedent but not properly taken into account in his final, or any earlier return.   However, only expenses that are of a business nature within Section 162 or are non-trade expenses within Section 212, plus interest under Section 163 and taxes under Section 164, qualify as deductions in respect of decedents for this purpose.[10]   In general as regards expenses that may be deducted as deductions in respect to decedents, a "when paid" test parallels the "when received" test that applies to I.R.D.   Section 691(b)(1)(A) accords the right to the deduction to the estate but, under subparagraph (B), if the estate is not liable to discharge the obligation, one who by bequest, devise or inheritance acquires property subject to the obligation, succeeds to the right to the deduction.

A minor breakdown in the neutralization objective of Section 691 occurs with respect to estate taxes.   When the value of an I.R.D. item included in the decedent's gross estate is later subjected to an income tax imposed on someone else, the estate tax on the decedent's estate may be larger than it would have been if the decedent had collected the item himself.   Had he collected the item, his taxable estate would have been smaller by the amount of income tax *he* paid upon the receipt, or by the amount of deduction for income tax due that could have been claimed for estate tax purposes under Section 2053.   It might appear that some adjustment could be made in estate tax liability to take into account this phenomenon.   But that is not practicable.   In fact, a hypothetical determination of the income tax that the decedent might have paid is at odds with the objective of Section 691 *not* to tax him on I.R.D. items.   Congress has settled for an acceptable rough and ready answer to this recognized problem.

Section 691(c) allows one who is taxed on an I.R.D. item, upon receipt, an *income* tax deduction for *estate* tax attributable to the inclusion of the item in the decedent's estate.   This is obviously not precisely responsive to the problem that seems to call for some adjustment;   but is there any better way to handle the problem?[11]   The

---

10. The omission of depreciation from this list is logical. Depreciation is not an expense to be paid; and pre-death depreciation on the decedent's property will be taken into account on the final return. Post-death depreciation will be allocated between the estate and beneficiaries in accordance with § 167(h). However, § 691(b) (2) undertakes to match a depletion deduction with related I.R.D. that is taxed to the one who receives it. And § 691(b) also attempts to match the § 27 credit for tax on foreign income against such income taxed as I.R.D. when received.

11. The general principle of I.R.C. § 691(c) can be expressed quite simply. The complexities of the provision, not discussed here in detail, are needed to answer questions such as (1) What portion of the estate tax is attributable to all I.R.D. items?   § 691(c)(2).   (2) How is that amount to be allocated as deductions available to each recipient of I.R.D.?   § 691(c)(1) (A), formula.   (3) If the deduction becomes available to an estate or a trust, how is it to be divided between the estate or trust and its beneficiaries?   I.R.C. § 691(c)(1)(B).

Section 691(c) deduction creates a situation where it was sometimes advantageous to the taxpayer to have an income item classified as I.R.D.

C. PARTNERSHIPS *

Internal Revenue Code: Sections 701; 704(e). See Sections 1(g); 707(c).
Regulations: Sections 1.704–1(e)(1), –1(e)(2)(i), (viii), –1(e)(3)(i).

COMMISSIONER v. CULBERTSON

Supreme Court of the United States, 1949.
337 U.S. 733, 69 S.Ct. 1210.

Mr. Chief Justice VINSON delivered the opinion of the Court.

This case requires our further consideration of the family partnership problem. The Commissioner of Internal Revenue ruled that the entire income from a partnership allegedly entered into by respondent and his four sons must be taxed to respondent,[1] and the Tax Court sustained that determination. The Court of Appeals for the Fifth Circuit reversed. 168 F.2d 979. We granted certiorari, 335 U.S. 883, to consider the Commissioner's claim that the principles of Commissioner v. Tower, 327 U.S. 280, 66 S.Ct. 532 (1946), and Lusthaus v. Commissioner, 327 U.S. 293, 66 S.Ct. 539 (1946), have been departed from in this and other courts of appeals decisions.

Respondent taxpayer is a rancher. From 1915 until October 1939, he had operated a cattle business in partnership with R.S. Coon. Coon, who had numerous business interests in the Southwest and had largely financed the partnership, was 79 years old in 1939 and desired to dissolve the partnership because of ill health. To that end, the bulk of the partnership herd was sold until, in October of that year, only about 1,500 head remained. These cattle were all registered Herefords, the brood or foundation herd. Culbertson wished to keep these cattle and approached Coon with an offer of $65 a head. Coon agreed to sell at that price, but only upon condition that Culbertson would sell an undivided one-half interest in the herd to his four sons at the same price. His reasons for imposing this condition were his intense interest in maintaining the Hereford strain which he and Culbertson had developed, his conviction that Culbertson was too old to carry on the work alone, and his personal interest in the Culbertson boys. Culbertson's sons were enthusiastic about the proposition, so respondent thereupon bought the remaining cattle from the Coon and Culbertson partnership for $99,440. Two days later Culbertson sold an undivided one-half interest to the four boys, and the following day they gave their

---

* See Note, "Family Partnerships and the Federal Income Tax," 41 Ind.L.J. 684 (1966); Lifton, "The Family Partnership: Here We Go Again," 7 Tax L.Rev. 461 (1952).

1. Gladys Culbertson, the wife of W.O. Culbertson, Sr., is joined as a party because of her community of interest in the property and income of her husband under Texas law.

father a note for $49,720 at 4 per cent interest due one year from date. Several months later a new note for $57,674 was executed by the boys to replace the earlier note. The increase in amount covered the purchase by Culbertson and his sons of other properties formerly owned by Coon and Culbertson. This note was paid by the boys in the following manner:

Credit for overcharge	$ 5,930
Gifts from respondent	21,744
One-half of a loan procured by Culbertson & Sons partnership	30,000

The loan was repaid from the proceeds from operation of the ranch.

The partnership agreement between taxpayer and his sons was oral. The local paper announced the dissolution of the Coon and Culbertson partnership and the continuation of the business by respondent and his boys under the name of Culbertson & Sons. A bank account was opened in this name, upon which taxpayer, his four sons and a bookkeeper could check. At the time of formation of the new partnership, Culbertson's oldest son was 24 years old, married, and living on the ranch, of which he had for two years been foreman under the Coon and Culbertson partnership. He was a college graduate and received $100 a month plus board and lodging for himself and his wife both before and after formation of Culbertson & Sons and until entering the Army. The second son was 22 years old, was married and finished college in 1940, the first year during which the new partnership operated. He went directly into the Army following graduation and rendered no services to the partnership. The two younger sons, who were 18 and 16 years old respectively in 1940, went to school during the winter and worked on the ranch during the summer.[2]

The tax years here involved are 1940 and 1941. A partnership return was filed for both years indicating a division of income approximating the capital attributed to each partner. It is the disallowance of this division of the income from the ranch that brings this case into the courts.

First. The Tax Court read our decisions in Commissioner v. Tower, supra, and Lusthaus v. Commissioner, supra, as setting out two essential tests of partnership for income-tax purposes: that each partner contribute to the partnership either vital services or capital originating with him. Its decision was based upon a finding that none of respondent's sons had satisfied those requirements during the tax years in question. Sanction for the use of these "tests" of partnership is sought in this paragraph from our opinion in the *Tower* case:

"There can be no question that a wife and a husband may, under certain circumstances, become partners for tax, as for

---

2. A daughter was also made a member of the partnership some time after its formation upon the gift by respondent of one-quarter of his one-half interest in the partnership. Respondent did not contend before the Tax Court that she was a partner for tax purposes.

other, purposes. If she either invests capital originating with her or substantially contributes to the control and management of the business, or otherwise performs vital additional services, or does all of these things she may be a partner as contemplated by 26 U.S.C. §§ 181, 182. The Tax Court has recognized that under such circumstances the income belongs to the wife. A wife may become a general or a limited partner with her husband. But when she does not share in the management and control of the business, contributes no vital additional service, and where the husband purports in some way to have given her a partnership interest, the Tax Court may properly take these circumstances into consideration in determining whether the partnership is real within the meaning of the federal revenue laws." 327 U.S. at 290, 66 S.Ct. at 537.

It is the Commissioner's contention that the Tax Court's decision can and should be reinstated upon the mere reaffirmation of the quoted paragraph.

The Court of Appeals, on the other hand, was of the opinion that a family partnership entered into without thought of tax avoidance should be given recognition tax-wise whether or not it was intended that some of the partners contribute either capital or services during the tax year and whether or not they actually made such contributions, since it was formed "with the full expectation and purpose that the boys would, in the future, contribute their time and services to the partnership." [3] We must consider, therefore, whether an intention to contribute capital or services sometime in the future is sufficient to satisfy ordinary concepts of partnership, as required by the *Tower* case. The sections of the Internal Revenue Code involved are §§ 181 and 182,[4] which set out the method of taxing partnership income, and §§ 11 and 22(a),[5] which relate to the taxation of individual incomes.

In the *Tower* case we held that, despite the claimed partnership, the evidence fully justified the Tax Court's holding that the husband, through his ownership of the capital and his management of the business, actually created the right to receive and enjoy the benefit of the income and was thus taxable upon that entire income under §§ 11 and 22(a). In such case, other members of the partnership cannot be considered "Individuals carrying on business in partnership" and thus "liable for income tax * * * in their individual capacity" within the meaning of § 181. If it is conceded that some of the partners contributed neither capital nor services to the partnership during the tax years in question, as the Court of Appeals was apparently willing to do in the

---

3. 168 F.2d 979 at 982. The court further said: "Neither statute, common sense, nor impelling precedent requires the holding that a partner must contribute capital or render services to the partnership prior to the time that he is taken into it. These tests are equally effective whether the cap- ital and the services are presently contributed and rendered or are later to be contributed or to be rendered." Id. at 983. See Note, 47 Mich.L.Rev. 595.

4. 26 U.S.C.A. §§ 181, 182.

5. 26 U.S.C.A. §§ 11, 22(a).

present case, it can hardly be contended that they are in any way responsible for the production of income during those years.[6]   The partnership sections of the Code are, of course, geared to the sections relating to taxation of individual income, since no tax is imposed upon partnership income as such.   To hold that "Individuals carrying on business in partnership" includes persons who contribute nothing during the tax period would violate the first principle of income taxation: that income must be taxed to him who earns it.   Lucas v. Earl, 281 U.S. 111, 50 S.Ct. 241 (1930); Helvering v. Clifford, 309 U.S. 331, 60 S.Ct. 554 (1940); National Carbide Corp. v. Commissioner, 336 U.S. 422, 69 S.Ct. 726 (1949).

Furthermore, our decision in Commissioner v. Tower, supra, clearly indicates the importance of participation in the business by the partners during the tax year.   We there said that a partnership is created "when persons join together their money, goods, labor, or skill for the purpose of carrying on a trade, profession, or business and when there is community of interest in the profits and losses."   Id. at 286.   This is, after all, but the application of an often iterated definition of income—the gain derived from capital, from labor, or from both combined [7]—to a particular form of business organization.   A partnership is, in other words, an organization for the production of income to which each partner contributes one or both of the ingredients of income—capital or services.   Ward v. Thompson, 22 How. 330, 334 (1859).   The intent to provide money, goods, labor or skill sometime in the future cannot meet the demands of §§ 11 and 22(a) of the Code that he who presently earns the income through his own labor and skill and the utilization of his own capital be taxed therefor.   The vagaries of human experience preclude reliance upon even good faith intent as to future conduct as a basis for the present taxation of income.[8]

Second.   We turn next to a consideration of the Tax Court's approach to the family partnership problem.   It treated as essential to membership in a family partnership for tax purposes the contribution of either "vital services" or "original capital." [9]   Use of these "tests" of

---

6. Of course one who has been a bona fide partner does not lose that status when he is called into military or government service, and the Commissioner has not so contended.   On the other hand, one hardly becomes a partner in the conventional sense merely because he might have done so had he not been called.

7. Eisner v. Macomber, 252 U.S. 189, 207, 40 S.Ct. 189 (1920); Merchants Loan & Trust Co. v. Smietanka, 255 U.S. 509, 519, 41 S.Ct. 386 (1921).   See Treas.Reg. 101, Art. 2(a)–1.   See 1 Mertens, Law of Federal Income Taxation, 159 et seq.

8. The *reductio ad absurdum* of the theory that children may be partners with their parents before they are capable of being entrusted with the disposition of

partnership funds or of contributing substantial services occurred in Tinkoff v. Commissioner, 120 F.2d 564, where a taxpayer made his son a partner in his accounting firm the day the son was born.

9. While the Tax Court went on to consider other factors, it is clear from its opinion that a contribution of either "vital services" or "original capital" was considered essential to membership in the partnership.   After finding that none of respondent's sons had, in the court's opinion, contributed either, the court continued: "In addition to the above inquiry as to the presence of those elements deemed by the *Tower* case essential to partnerships recognizable for Federal tax purposes, * * *."

partnership indicates, at best, an error in emphasis. It ignores what we said is the ultimate question for decision, namely, "whether the partnership is real within the meaning of the federal revenue laws" and makes decisive what we described as "circumstances [to be taken] into consideration" in making that determination.[10]

The *Tower* case thus provides no support for such an approach. We there said that the question whether the family partnership is real for income-tax purposes depends upon

> "whether the partners really and truly intended to join together for the purpose of carrying on business and sharing in the profits or losses or both. And their intention in this respect is a question of fact, to be determined from testimony disclosed by their 'agreement, considered as a whole, and by their conduct in execution of its provisions.' Drennen v. London Assurance Co., 113 U.S. 51, 56, 5 S.Ct. 341; Cox v. Hickman, 8 H.L.Cas. 268. We see no reason why this general rule should not apply in tax cases where the Government challenges the existence of a partnership for tax purposes." 327 U.S. at 287, 66 S.Ct. at page 536.

The question is not whether the services or capital contributed by a partner are of sufficient importance to meet some objective standard supposedly established by the *Tower* case, but whether, considering all the facts—the agreement, the conduct of the parties in execution of its provisions, their statements, the testimony of disinterested persons, the relationship of the parties, their respective abilities and capital contributions, the actual control of income and the purposes for which it is used, and any other facts throwing light on their true intent—the parties in good faith and acting with a business purpose intended to join together in the present conduct of the enterprise.[11] There is

6 CCH TCM 692, 699. Again, the court commented:

> "Though, the petitioner urges that many cattle businesses are composed of fathers and sons, and that the nature of the industry so requires, we think the same is probably equally true of other industries where men wish to take children into business with them. Nevertheless, we think that fact does not override the many decisions to the general effect that partners must contribute capital originating with them, or vital services." Id. at 700.

10. See Mannheimer and Mook, A Taxwise Evaluation of Family Partnerships, 32 Iowa L.Rev. 436, 447–48.

11. This is not, as we understand it, contrary to the approach taken by the Bureau of Internal Revenue in its most recent statement of policy. I.T. 3845, 1947 Cum. Bull. 66, states at p. 67:

"Where persons who are closely related by blood or marriage enter into an agreement purporting to create a so-called family partnership or other arrangement with respect to the operation of a business or income-producing venture, under which agreement all of the parties are accorded substantially the same treatment and consideration with respect to their designated interests and prescribed responsibilities in the business as if they were strangers dealing at arm's length; where the actions of the parties as legally responsible persons evidence an intent to carry on a business in a partnership relation; and where the terms of such agreement are substantially followed in the operation of the business or venture, as well as in the dealings of the partners or members with each other, it is the policy of the Bureau to disregard the close family relationship existing between the parties and to recognize, for Federal income tax purposes,

nothing new or particularly difficult about such a test. Triers of fact are constantly called upon to determine the intent with which a person acted.[12] The Tax Court, for example, must make such a determination in every estate tax case in which it is contended that a transfer was made in contemplation of death, for "The question, necessarily, is as to the state of mind of the donor." United States v. Wells, 283 U.S. 102, 117, 51 S.Ct. 446 (1931). See Allen v. Trust Co. of Georgia, 326 U.S. 630, 66 S.Ct. 389 (1946). Whether the parties really intended to carry on business as partners is not, we think, any more difficult of determination or the manifestations of such intent any less perceptible than is ordinarily true of inquiries into the subjective.

But the Tax Court did not view the question as one concerning the bona fide intent of the parties to join together as partners. Not once in its opinion is there even an oblique reference to any lack of intent on the part of respondent and his sons to combine their capital and services "for the purpose of carrying on the business." Instead, the court, focusing entirely upon concepts of "vital services" and "original capital," simply decided that the alleged partners had not satisfied those tests when the facts were compared with those in the *Tower* case. The court's opinion is replete with such statements as "we discern nothing constituting what we think is a requisite contribution to a real partnership," "we find no son adding 'vital additional service' which would take the place of capital contributed because of formation of a partnership," and "the sons made no capital contribution, within the sense of the *Tower* case."[13]   6 CCH TCM 698, 699.

Unquestionably a court's determination that the services contributed by a partner are not "vital" and that he has not participated in "management and control of the business"[14] or contributed "original

the division of profits as prescribed by such agreement. However, where the instrument purporting to create the family partnership expressly provides that the wife or child or other member of the family shall not be required to participate in the management of the business, or is merely silent on that point, the extent and nature of the services of such individual in the actual conduct of the business will be given appropriate evidentiary weight as to the question of intent to carry on the business as partners."

12. Nearly three-quarters of a century ago, Bowen, L.J., made the classic statement that "the state of a man's mind is as much a fact as the state of his digestion." Edgington v. Fitzmaurice, 29 L.R.Ch.Div. 459, 483. State of mind has always been determinative of the question whether a partnership has been formed as between the parties. See, e.g., Drennen v. London Assurance Co., 113 U.S. 51, 56, 5 S.Ct. 341 (1885); Meehen v. Valentine, 145 U.S. 611,

621, 12 S.Ct. 972 (1892); Barker v. Kraft, 259 Mich. 70, 242 N.W. 841 (1932); Zuback v. Bakmaz, 346 Pa. 279, 29 A.2d 473 (1943); Kennedy v. Mullins, 155 Va. 166, 154 S.E. 568 (1930).

13. In the *Tower* case the taxpayer argued that he had a right to reduce his taxes by any legal means, to which this Court agreed. We said, however, that existence of a tax avoidance motive gives some indication that there was no bona fide intent to carry on business as a partnership. If *Tower* had set up objective requirements of membership in a family partnership, such as "vital services" and "original capital," the motives behind adoption of the partnership form would have been irrelevant.

14. Although "management and control of the business" was one of the circumstances emphasized by the *Tower* case, along with "vital services" and "original capital," the Tax Court did not consider it an alternative "test" of partnership. See

capital" has the effect of placing a heavy burden on the taxpayer to show the bona fide intent of the parties to join together as partners. But such a determination is not conclusive, and that is the vice in the "tests" adopted by the Tax Court. It assumes that there is no room for an honest difference of opinion as to whether the services or capital furnished by the alleged partner are of sufficient importance to justify his inclusion in the partnership. If, upon a consideration of all the facts, it is found that the partners joined together in good faith to conduct a business, having agreed that the services or capital to be contributed presently by each is of such value to the partnership that the contributor should participate in the distribution of profits, that is sufficient. The *Tower* case did not purport to authorize the Tax Court to substitute its judgment for that of the parties; it simply furnished some guides to the determination of their true intent. Even though it was admitted in the *Tower* case that the wife contributed no original capital, management of the business, or other vital services, this Court did not say as a matter of law that there was no valid partnership. We said, instead, that "There was, thus, more than ample evidence to support the Tax Court's finding that no genuine union for partnership business purposes *was ever intended* and that the husband earned the income." 327 U.S. at 292, 66 S.Ct. at page 538. (Italics added.)

Third. The Tax Court's isolation of "original capital" as an essential of membership in a family partnership also indicates an erroneous reading of the *Tower* opinion. We did not say that the donee of an intra-family gift could never become a partner through investment of the capital in the family partnership, any more than we said that all family trusts are invalid for tax purposes in Helvering v. Clifford, supra. The facts may indicate, on the contrary, that the amount thus contributed and the income therefrom should be considered the property of the donee for tax, as well as general law, purposes. In the *Tower* and *Lusthaus* cases this Court, applying the principles of Lucas v. Earl, supra; Helvering v. Clifford, supra; and Helvering v. Horst, 311 U.S. 112, 61 S.Ct. 144, found that the purported gift, whether or not technically complete, had made no substantial change in the economic relation of members of the family to the income. In each case the husband continued to manage and control the business as before, and income from the property given to the wife and invested by her in the partnership continued to be used in the business or expended for family purposes. We characterized the results of the transactions entered into between husband and wife as "a mere paper reallocation of income among the family members," noting that "The actualities of their relation to the income did not change." 327 U.S. at 292, 66 S.Ct. at page 538. This, we thought, provided ample grounds for the finding that no true partnership was intended; that the husband was still the true earner of the income.

discussion, infra, at part *Third,* and note 17.

But application of the *Clifford-Horst* principle does not follow automatically upon a gift to a member of one's family, followed by its investment in the family partnership. If it did, it would be necessary to define "family" and to set precise limits of membership therein. We have not done so for the obvious reason that existence of the family relationship does not create a status which itself determines tax questions,[15] but is simply a warning that things may not be what they seem. It is frequently stated that transactions between members of a family will be carefully scrutinized. But, more particularly, the family relationship often makes it possible for one to shift tax incidence by surface changes of ownership without disturbing in the least his dominion and control over the subject of the gift or the purposes for which the income from the property is used. He is able, in other words, to retain "the substance of full enjoyment of all the rights which previously he had in the property." Helvering v. Clifford, supra, at 336.[16]

The fact that transfers to members of the family group may be mere camouflage does not, however, mean that they invariably are. The *Tower* case recognized that one's participation in control and management of the business is a circumstance indicating an intent to be a bona fide partner despite the fact that the capital contributed originated elsewhere in the family.[17] If the donee of property who then invests it in the family partnership exercises dominion and control over that property—and through that control influences the conduct of the partnership and the disposition of its income—he may well be a true partner. Whether he is free to, and does, enjoy the fruits of the partnership is strongly indicative of the reality of his participation in the enterprise. In the *Tower* and *Lusthaus* cases we distinguished between active participation in the affairs of the business by a donee of a share in the partnership on the one hand, and his passive acquiescence to the will of the donor on the other.[18] This distinction is of

15. Except, of course, when Congress defines "family" and attaches tax consequences thereto. See, e.g. 26 U.S.C.A. § 503(a)(2).

16. It is not enough to say in this case, as we did in the *Clifford* case, that "It is hard to imagine that respondent felt himself the poorer after this [partnership agreement] had been executed or, if he did, that it had any rational foundation in fact." 309 U.S. at 336, 60 S.Ct. at 557. Culbertson's interest in his partnership with Coon was worth about $50,000 immediately prior to dissolution of the partnership. In order to sustain the Tax Court, we would have to conclude that he felt himself worth approximately twice that much upon his purchase of Coon's interest, even though he had agreed to sell that interest to his sons at the same price.

17. As noted above (note 13), participation in control and management of the business, although given equal prominence with contributions of "vital services" and "original capital" as circumstances indicating an intent to enter into a partnership relation, was discarded by the Tax Court as a "test" of partnership. This indicates a basic and erroneous assumption that one can never make a gift to a member of one's family without retaining the essentials of ownership, if the gift is then invested in a family partnership. We included participation in management and control of the business as a circumstance indicative of intent to carry on business as a partner to cover the situation in which active dominion and control of the subject of the gift had actually passed to the donee. It is a circumstance of prime importance.

18. There is testimony in the record as to the participation by respondent's sons in the management of the ranch. Since such evidence did not fall within either of the "tests" adopted by the Tax Court, it failed to consider this testimony. Without inti-

obvious importance to a determination of the true intent of the parties. It is meaningless if "original capital" is an essential test of membership in a family partnership.

The cause must therefore be remanded to the Tax Court for a decision as to which, if any, of respondent's sons were partners with him in the operation of the ranch during 1940 and 1941. As to which of them, in other words, was there a bona fide intent that they be partners in the conduct of the cattle business, either because of services to be performed during those years, or because of contributions of capital of which they were the true owners, as we have defined that term in the *Clifford, Horst,* and *Tower* cases? No question as to the allocation of income between capital and services is presented in this case, and we intimate no opinion on that subject.

The decision of the Court of Appeals is reversed with directions to remand the cause to the Tax Court for further proceedings in conformity with this opinion.

Reversed and remanded.

[The separate concurring opinions of Justices BLACK and RUTLEDGE, BURTON, JACKSON, and FRANKFURTER have been omitted. Ed.]

PROBLEMS

1. Section 704(e)(1) recognizes as a partner in a family partnership one who "owns a capital interest in a partnership in which capital is a material income-producing factor." Consider whether the following situations meet the statutory requirement:

(a) Father is a doctor who makes his Son (a law student) a partner in his practice, assuming applicable state law does not prohibit such associations.

(b) Father is a doctor who makes his Daughter (a recent medical school graduate) a partner in his practice.

(c) Father owns a shopping center where the stores are subject to long-term leases and he transfers the leases to a partnership with Son and Daughter.

(d) Father transfers both the shopping center and the leases in (c), above, to the partnership with Son and Daughter.

(e) Same as (d), above, except that Father retains the right to make all business decisions with respect to the shopping center and to use income from the center to expand the center.

(f) Do you see a relationship between § 704(e) and the messages in both Chapter 12 and the *Clifford* case in Chapter 13?

2. Father owns a group of apartments which he transfers to a partnership with Son and two Daughters who provide no consideration

mating any opinion as to its probative value, we think that it is clearly relevant evidence of the intent to carry on business as partners.

for their ¼ interests in the partnership. The income from the partnership is $100,000.

(a) What result if Father renders services worth $20,000 to the partnership, but the partnership agreement merely calls for splitting the income ¼ each and each partner actually receives $25,000?

(b) What result if Father renders no services but the agreement provides the income is to be divided 10% to Father and 30% each to Son and each of his Daughters?

(c) What result if Father and Son both render services worth $20,000 and the agreement is the same as in part (b), above. See Reg. § 1.704–1(e)(3)(i)(b).

D. CORPORATIONS

Internal Revenue Code: Sections 11(a) and (b); 482.

OVERTON v. COMMISSIONER

United States Court of Appeals, Second Circuit, 1947.
162 F.2d 155.

SWAN, Circuit Judge. These appeals involve gift tax liability of petitioner Overton for the years 1936 and 1937 and income tax liability of petitioner Oliphant for the year 1941. Each petitioner was held liable on the theory that dividends received by his wife in the year in question on stock registered in her name on the books of Castle & Overton, Inc., a New York corporation, were income of the husband for tax purposes. No gift tax return with respect to such dividends was filed by Mr. Overton in 1936 or 1937, and the dividends received by Mrs. Oliphant in 1941 were not included in her husband's return for that year.

There is no dispute as to the evidentiary facts. They are stated in detail in the opinion of the Tax Court, 6 T.C. 304, and will be here repeated only so far as may be necessary to render intelligible the discussion which follows. On May 26, 1936 the corporation had outstanding 1,000 shares of common stock without par value but having a liquidating value of at least $120 per share. On that date, pursuant to a plan devised to lessen taxes, the certificate of incorporation was amended to provide for changing the outstanding common stock into 2,000 shares without par value, of which 1,000 were denominated Class A and 1,000 Class B. The old stock was exchanged for the new, the shareholders then gave the B stock to their respective wives, and new certificates therefor were issued to the wives. The B stock had a liquidating value of one dollar per share; everything else on liquidation was to belong to the holders of the A stock, who had also the sole voting rights for directors and on all ordinary matters.[1] By virtue of an agreement made in April 1937 restricting alienation of their stock, the wives were precluded from realizing more than one dollar a share by selling their shares. The A stock was to receive noncumulative dividends at the rate of $10 a share per year before payment of any dividend on the B stock; if dividends in excess of $10 per share were paid on the A stock in any year, such excess dividends were to be shared by both classes of stock in the ratio of one-fifth thereof for the A stock and four-fifths for the B stock. During the six year period ending in December 1941, the dividends paid on B stock totaled $150.40 a share as against $77.60 a share paid on A stock. In 1941 the A stock had a book value of $155 per share.

The Tax Court was of opinion that the 1936 arrangement, though made in the form of a gift of stock, was in reality an assignment of part of the taxpayers' future dividends. Unless form is to be exalted above substance this conclusion is inescapable. Since the total issue of B stock represented only $1,000 of the corporate assets, it is plain that the property which earned the large dividends received by the B shareholders was the property represented by the A stock held by the husbands. In transferring the B shares to their wives they parted with no substantial part of their interest in the corporate property. Had they been content to transfer some of the original common stock, they could have accomplished their purpose of lessening taxes on the family group,[2] but they would then have made substantial gifts of capital. The arrangement they put into effect gave the wives nothing, or substantially nothing, but the right to future earnings flowing from property retained by the husbands. That anticipatory assignments of income, whatever their formal cloak, are ineffective taxwise is a principle too firmly established to be subject to question. See Lucas v. Earl, 281 U.S. 111, 50 S.Ct. 241; Helvering v. Horst, 311 U.S. 112, 61 S.Ct. 144; Helvering v. Eubank, 311 U.S. 122, 61 S.Ct. 149; Harrison v. Schaffner, 312 U.S. 579, 61 S.Ct. 759; Commissioner v. Tower, 327 U.S. 280, 66 S.Ct. 532; Lusthaus v. Commissioner, 327 U.S. 293, 66 S.Ct. 539; Hyman v. Nunan, 2 Cir., 143 F.2d 425. We think the Tax Court correctly applied this principle to the facts of the case at bar.

Orders affirmed.

McGUIRE v. UNITED STATES

District Court of the United States, Southern District of New York (1969).
1969–1 USTC para. 9279. Aff'd 1971–1 USTC para. 9304, 2d Cir.1971.

TYLER, JR., District Judge. The Court: Miss McBryant and ladies and gentlemen, now that you have heard the arguments of the lawyers,

1. Whether the amendment of the certificate of incorporation excluded B shareholders from voting on extraordinary matters specified in section 51 of the Stock Corporation Law of New York, McK.Consol.Laws, c. 59, in effect on May 26, 1937, the Tax Court did not find it necessary to determine; nor do we.

2. See Blair v. Commissioner, 300 U.S. 5, 57 S.Ct. 330.

Mr. Cohen and Mr. Hering in this case, the time has come for me, as you know, to give you the rules of law which will be applicable to your deliberations here.

* * *

Now as you are well aware from the submissions of counsel, the plaintiffs, the three McGuire sisters, sue here for refund of income taxes paid by them as individuals for the tax years of 1955 and 1956.

As I recall it, the combined total refunds claimed by the three sisters for each of these tax years is the sum of $33,232.95.

As you know, they paid their taxes, which include these claims, under protest; and under the law they filed this civil suit to collect these sums by way of refunds when their protests, copies of which, by the way, are in evidence, were rejected by the Commissioner of Internal Revenue.

Simply stated, this case, that is, the claims of the plaintiffs and the defenses thereto by the government, can be simply summarized as presenting the question of whether or not certain income earned by the group known as the McGuire Sisters, was income earned by them as individuals or was it properly earned by two corporations which were set up by them in 1955, which, as you know, had the names of McGuire Sisters Corporation and McGuire Sisters Productions, Inc.

That is a simple statement of the basic dispute between the parties.

However, of course, as I think you are also aware, the specific claims of the plaintiffs and the defense thereto of the government raise a number of questions. * * * I have determined to put these * * * basic questions, if you will, to you in the form of special questions which are susceptible of a simple yes-or-no answer.

Thus your verdict in this case will take the form of a simple yes-or-no answer to these * * * basic questions, which I now intend to articulate for you, and beyond that, to discuss in relation to those questions the rules of law and other considerations which either are or may be relevant to your deliberations in an effort to answer these * * * questions.

The first of these * * * questions cast up by this case can be posed essentially as follows:

Were the corporations formed by the plaintiffs actually engaged in a valid business or commercial or industrial activity as opposed to some non-business or non-commercial activity, as, for example, merely to avoid paying certain taxes or to save certain taxes?

Now on this question plaintiffs, at least initially, as I understand them, argue that the two corporations which they formed in September of 1955 or at least caused to be formed in that month, were valid firms actually engaged in a valid business.

Specifically, as I understand the plaintiffs, they contend that those corporations were formed for the business purpose of realizing, at least initially, income from the entertainment services of the three sisters, and then taking that income and investing it in income-producing real estate properties.

But the United States, as you know, argues that the evidence shows that the corporations never got close to investing in any income-producing real estate or in any commercial real estate, as it is sometimes called; or doing any other valid business or commercial activities.

Thus, this first question can be simply related thus:

Did the two corporations in fact engage in any business or were they just depositories for the income earned by the plaintiffs as the well-known entertainers that they were in the years in question?

Keep in mind, ladies and gentlemen, that here the plaintiffs have the burden by the preponderance of the evidence of proving to your satisfaction that these two corporations in fact engaged in some valid business or commercial purpose.

Now in considering this first question there are some rules and considerations which are or may be relevant here and indeed on the other questions which I am going to discuss with you in a few moments.

I start out, for example, by observing that under our law it is true a taxpayer has the right to organize and run his business in a way which will avoid certain taxes or minimize federal income taxes.

However, a taxpayer is not permitted by our law to use the corporate organization or the corporate form, if you will, for no other activity than tax avoidance or tax reduction or tax minimization.

Now in considering this first question I pose to you and which we are going to ask you to answer, and the contentions of the parties on this first question which you have just heard from Mr. Cohen and Mr. Hering, bear in mind that corporate or business or commercial formalities and labels are not necessarily determinative of this first question, or indeed any other basic question in this case.

That is, ladies and gentlemen, you should examine entire transactions as they are shown by the evidence during the trial in order to get the substance of the transaction, that is to say, in order to determine what really happened in a particular activity or transaction.

For example, you should, of course, consider documents which were put in evidence here, such as the corporate records of these two corporations formed by the ladies McGuire. You should consider the books and records of these two corporations, and the facsimile stock certificates, for example, which I recall were placed in evidence.

However, you may also consider other things about these corporations, again as shown by the evidence.

To illustrate, how did these corporations operate? Or in fact did they operate at all?

How did the suppliers of goods and services to these corporations or to the McGuire sisters deal with the corporations or the McGuire sisters?

For example, did the suppliers think they were dealing with the sisters as individuals? Or did they think they were dealing with two corporations or one corporation?

Another question you might ask yourself is: Did these corporations have a place of business? And, if so, what kind of place of business was it?

Did these corporations have employees? If they did, how were these employees compensated?

Who were the stockholders of these corporations? Who were the officers of these corporations? What were the activities of these officers and stockholders, as shown by the evidence?

The point I am trying to get across is a simple one. These and similar questions are the kind of questions to ask yourselves in the course of deciding whether or not the two corporations formed in September, 1955, were engaged in a valid business or commercial purpose.

I should say before I conclude on this first question, by the way, ladies and gentlemen, that the intention or purpose of the three McGuire sisters, is, strictly speaking, not really too important or important at all here.

That is to say, the main point raised by this first question is: What in fact did these two corporations do or what in fact did they not do?

[L]et me pose the [final] question [this way]: Was the Internal Revenue Service, or, as it is sometimes put, the Commissioner of Internal Revenue, arbitrary or capricious in allocating or apportioning income from the corporation contracts with the Copacabana Club, for example, and all those other clubs as shown in the evidence, in 1955 and 1956 to the three plaintiffs rather than to the two corporations?

Now, ladies and gentlemen, let me explain that this question comes up in this case because of one of the government's arguments, which is based upon the statute known to lawyers at least as Section 482 of the Internal Revenue Code of 1954.

Very simply, that statute states in words or substance, that where two or more organizations, or businesses, if you will, whether or not incorporated, are owned and controlled by the same person or persons, the Commissioner or the Internal Revenue Service is authorized to apportion or allocate gross income for tax purposes between or among such businesses or entities or persons as the Commissioner deems necessary to clearly reflect income as it was actually earned or to prevent improper avoidance of income tax.

Now in certain respects, as some of you may have divined, this question does cast up similar issues as were implicit in the first two basic questions.

However, there are some other elements here involved and the emphasis is somewhat different.

To explain, I start off by observing that plaintiffs here must prove by a preponderance of the evidence that the Internal Revenue Service was arbitrary or capricious, that is to say, that the Internal Revenue Service acted without any factual basis whatsoever in allocating income from the singing engagements, not to the corporations or one of them, but to the three ladies McGuire as individual taxpayers.

In other words, if you find from the evidence before you that the Internal Revenue Service had justification, factually, for deciding that it was the plaintiffs rather than the corporations who were the real earners of the income in question, or for deciding that the corporations were set up solely to avoid paying income taxes at a higher personal rate, then the plaintiffs would not have carried their burden on this issue and you would be obliged to answer this third and last question "No."

On the other hand, if you determine that the corporations and not the ladies McGuire, as individuals, earned these engagement fees at such clubs as, for example, the Copacabana here in New York City, then you would be entitled to find further that the Internal Revenue Service acted arbitrarily, that is, without foundation in fact, in allocating this income to the plaintiffs, and not to the two corporations.

Now from what I have just been saying, ladies and gentlemen, you should note that the question here is not whether you would have allocated the income as the Commissioner did; rather, it is [did] the Commissioner have factual justification for making the allocation he did even though you might decide you would have done it otherwise?

* * *

Written Questions and Jury's Answers

1. Q. Were the two corporations formed by plaintiffs actually engaged in a valid business or commercial activity, as opposed to merely a tax-saving activity?

A. NO.

* * *

BORGE v. COMMISSIONER *

United States Court of Appeals, Second Circuit, 1968.
405 F.2d 673, cert. denied 395 U.S. 933, 89 S.Ct. 1994, 1969.

HAYS, Circuit Judge: Petitioners seek review of a decision of the Tax Court sustaining the Commissioner's determination of deficiencies in their income tax payments for the years 1958 through 1962, inclusive. The Tax Court upheld * * * the Commissioner's allocation to Borge [1] under Section 482 of the Internal Revenue Code of 1954, 26 U.S.

---

* See Katz, "Can Section 482 Be Used to Negate the Tax Effect of a Bona Fide Corporation?" 28 J.Tax. 2 (1968). Ed.

1. "Borge" refers herein to Victor Borge. His wife has been included as a party to the action solely because of the filing of joint returns. [Discussion in the opinion of an alternative issue of tax liability under I.R.C. § 269 has been deleted. Ed.]

C.A. § 482 (1964), of a portion of the compensation received by Danica Enterprises, Inc., Borge's wholly owned corporation, for services performed by Borge as an entertainer. * * * We affirm.

[From 1952 to 1958 Borge, as an individual, operated ViBo Farms where he developed, produced, processed and sold quality chickens known as rock cornish hens. He had substantial losses each year which he deducted against the substantial income he earned as an entertainer. Ed.]

* * *

* * * Borge organized Danica, and, on March 1, 1958, transferred to the corporation, in exchange for all of its stock and a loan payable, the assets of the poultry business (except the farm real property).

Borge is a well-known professional entertainer. During the years preceding the organization of Danica he made large sums from television, stage and motion picture engagements.

Since Danica had no means of meeting the expected losses from the poultry business, Borge and Danica entered into a contract at the time of the organization of the corporation under which Borge agreed to perform entertainment and promotional services for the corporation for a 5-year period for compensation from Danica of $50,000 per year. Danica offset the poultry losses [3] against the entertainment profits, which far exceeded the $50,000 per year it had contracted to pay Borge.[4] Borge obviously would not have entered into such a contract with an unrelated party.

Danica did nothing to aid Borge in his entertainment business. Those who contracted with Danica for Borge's entertainment services required Borge personally to guarantee the contracts. Danica's entertainment earnings were attributable solely to the services of Borge, and Danica's only profits were from the entertainment business.

The only year during the period in dispute in which Danica actually paid Borge anything for his services was 1962, when Borge was paid the full $50,000.

The issues in controversy are (1) whether the Commissioner, acting under Section 482 of the Internal Revenue Code of 1954, 26 U.S.C.A. § 482 (1964), properly allocated to Borge from Danica $75,000 per year from 1958 through 1961 and $25,000 for 1962, * * *

I.

When two or more organizations, trades or businesses, whether or not incorporated, are owned or controlled by the same interests, Section 482 of the Internal Revenue Code of 1954, 26 U.S.C.A. § 482 (1964), authorizes the Commissioner to apportion gross income between or among such organizations, trades or businesses if he deems that appor-

---

3. [Details of the poultry losses are omitted. Ed.]

4. [Details of Danica's net entertainment income are omitted. Ed.]

tionment is necessary clearly to reflect income or to prevent evasion of tax.[5] We conclude that the Commissioner could properly have found that for purposes of Section 482 Borge owned or controlled two businesses, an entertainment business and a poultry business, and that the allocation to Borge of part of the entertainment compensation paid to the corporation was not error.[6]

We accept, as supported by the record, the Tax Court's finding: that Borge operated an entertainment business and merely assigned to Danica a portion of his income from that business; that Danica did nothing to earn or to assist in the earning of the entertainment income; that Borge would not have contracted for $50,000 per year with an unrelated party to perform the services referred to in his contract with Danica. Thus Borge was correctly held to be in the entertainment business.

At the same time Danica, Borge's wholly owned corporation, was in the poultry business.

Petitioners, relying primarily on Whipple v. Commissioner, 373 U.S. 193, 83 S.Ct. 1168 (1963), argue that Borge is not an "organization, trade or business" and that Section 482 is therefore inapposite.

In *Whipple* the Supreme Court held only that where one renders services to a corporation as an investment, he is not engaging in a trade or business:

"Devoting one's time and energies to the affairs of a corporation is not of itself, and without more, a trade or business of the person so engaged. Though such activities may produce income, profit or gain in the form of dividends or enhancement in the value of an investment, this return is distinctive to the process of investing and is generated by the successful operation of the corporation's business as distinguished from the trade or business of the taxpayer himself. When the only return is that of an investor, the taxpayer has not satisfied his burden of demonstrating that he is engaged in a trade or business since investing is not a trade or business and the return to the taxpayer, though substantially the product of his services, legally arises not from his own trade or business but from that of the corporation." 373 U.S. at 202, 83 S.Ct. at 1174.

Here, however, Borge was in the business of entertaining. He was not devoting his time and energies to the corporation; he was carrying on his career as an entertainer, and merely channeling a part of his entertainment income through the corporation.

Moreover, in *Whipple* petitioner was devoting his time and energies to a corporation in the hope of realizing capital gains treatment from the sale of appreciated stock. When the hoped-for appreciation did not materialize he attempted to deduct his losses as ordinary losses. The

5. [I.R.C. § 482 is omitted. Ed.]

6. We agree with petitioners' contention that since Borge's employment contract with Danica went into effect on March 1, 1958, the 1958 allocation should have been only $62,500 (⅚ of $75,000). A recomputation of Borge's deficiency to this extent should be made.

Court decided that where one stands to achieve capital gains through an investment, any losses incurred in connection with the investment are capital losses. Borge is clearly earning ordinary income; the only question is who should pay the taxes on it. Thus, *Whipple* is not apposite.

For somewhat similar reasons we find Commissioner v. Gross, 236 F.2d 612 (2d Cir.1956), on which petitioner also seeks to rely, also inapposite.

Nor do we consider the other cases cited by petitioners persuasive. The Commissioner is not arguing here, as he did, for example, in Charles Laughton, 40 B.T.A. 101 (1939), remanded, 113 F.2d 103 (9th Cir.1940), that the taxpayer should be taxed on the entire amount paid into the wholly owned corporation, i.e. that the corporation should be ignored. See also Pat O'Brien, 25 T.C. 376 (1955); Fontaine Fox, 37 B.T.A. 271 (1938). Instead he recognizes the existence of the corporation, but under Section 482 allocates a portion of its income to its sole shareholder who alone was responsible for the production of such income.

Petitioner contends that the Congress, in enacting the personal holding company and collapsible corporation provisions of the Code, precluded the Commissioner's action in this case under Section 482. We do not read those provisions, however, as the only available methods for dealing with the situations there involved. As the Third Circuit said in National Sec. Corp. v. Commissioner, 137 F.2d 600, 602 (3d Cir.), cert. denied, 320 U.S. 794, 64 S.Ct. 262:

"In every case in which [Section 482] is applied its application will necessarily result in an apparent conflict with the literal requirements of some other provision of the [Internal Revenue Code]. If this were not so Section [482] would be wholly superfluous."

The fact that similar, but not identical, factual situations have been dealt with by legislation does not mean that this situation, because it was not also specifically dealt with by legislation, cannot be reached even by a general code provision.

We thus conclude that the Tax Court was correct in upholding the Commissioner's ruling that Borge controlled two separate businesses. See Pauline W. Ach, 42 T.C. 114 (1964), aff'd, 358 F.2d 342 (6th Cir.), cert. denied, 385 U.S. 899, 87 S.Ct. 205.

The Commissioner's action in allocating a part of Danica's income to Borge was based upon his conclusion that such allocation was necessary in order clearly to reflect the income of the two businesses under Borge's common control. The Commissioner's allocation has received the approval of the Tax Court. As this Court held in dealing with the predecessor of Section 482, "Whether the Tax Court was correct in allocating income to the petitioner under § 45 [of the Internal Revenue Code of 1939] is essentially one of fact and the decision below must be affirmed if supported by substantial evidence." Advance Mach. Exch. v. Commissioner, 196 F.2d 1006, 1007–08 (2d Cir.), cert.

denied, 344 U.S. 835, 73 S.Ct. 45. See Int.Rev.Code of 1954, § 7482(a), 26 U.S.C.A. § 7482(a) (1964). Here the determination of the Commissioner and the decision of the Tax Court are supported by substantial evidence that the income of Borge's two businesses has been distorted through Borge's having arranged for Danica to receive a large part of his entertainment income although Danica did nothing to earn that income, and the sole purpose of the arrangement was to permit Danica to offset losses from the poultry business with income from the entertainment business. The amount allocated by the Commissioner ($75,000 per year) was entirely reasonable—indeed, generous—in view of the fact that Danica's annual net income from Borge's entertainment services averaged $166,465 during the years in question.

* * *

PROBLEMS

1. Following the Tax Reform Act of 1986, which party would benefit from the application of the rationale of the *McGuire* case to set aside a corporation and why?

2. Father runs his own hardware store and has income far in excess of his needs. Several years ago he started a small manufacturing company that produces video tapes. For the first few years of operation, the business operated at a loss, but with the recent V.C.R. craze, business is booming. Father has no need for all of this income and in fact has considered transferring the business to Son and Daughter. Father ultimately decides that by incorporating the video tape business, electing S Corporation status, and retaining 51% of the stock, he can maintain control of the business and still transfer part of the business (and hence the income) to Son and Daughter. Will Father's plan successfully rid him of the surplus income? Is there another vehicle (other than a corporation) that Father can use to effectuate his plan?

PART FOUR: DEDUCTIONS IN COMPUTING TAXABLE INCOME

CHAPTER 14. BUSINESS DEDUCTIONS

A. INTRODUCTION

Internal Revenue Code: See Sections 1; 63.

There is no constitutional obstacle to a tax on *gross* income. This is not to say the 16th Amendment would support an unapportioned tax on gross receipts, for the term "incomes" as used there connotes *gain* at least to the extent that a mere return of capital is not "income." But expenses incurred earning income might constitutionally be disregarded in the computation of the tax. For this reason, deductions are spoken of as a matter of "legislative grace;" and it is at least true that, as a taxpayer has no constitutional right to a deduction,[1] he must find a statutory provision that specifically allows the deduction claimed.

Is the "grace" aspect of deduction provisions of importance in their interpretation? There may be some notion that by allowing a deduction Congress bestows a *special* benefit that should be narrowly construed. Consider whether this is a proper view of any or all the deduction provisions presented in this Part. At least where it is not, should not the courts seek to give meaning to a deduction provision in the same manner as they approach any other congressional product?[2]

Since the statute is all-important in the deduction area, its basic design should be noted. The individual income tax rates[3] are applied to "taxable income."[4] In general, under Section 63 taxable income is gross income minus the deductions provided in the statute.[5]

This Part of the book divides deductions allowed in computing taxable income into four groups. Chapter 14 is concerned with trade and business deductions; and these provisions apply alike to individuals and corporations, although sometimes with variations. For individuals only, Congress identifies a kind of sub-business category in which some

---

1. First Nat. Bank & Trust Co. v. U.S., 115 F.2d 194 (5th Cir.1940).

2. See Griswold, "An Argument Against the Doctrine that Deductions Should Be Narrowly Construed as a Matter of Legislative Grace," 56 Harv.L.Rev. 1142 (1943).

3. I.R.C. § 1.

4. See I.R.C. § 63. Consideration must be given later to (1) computation of tax in the case of joint returns, I.R.C. § 1(a), and certain other special circumstances, and (2) to the tax tables for low-income taxpayers, I.R.C. § 3.

5. See Chapter 18E, infra.

expenditures that are not incurred in "business" are considered sufficiently connected with income or profit-seeking activities to warrant their deduction. Chapter 15 is addressed to the deductibility of these expenditures.

A general appreciation of the dichotomy recognized in Chapters 14 and 15 can be gleaned from an examination of some of the Code sections making use of the differing concepts. For example, Sections 162 (expenses), 165(c)(1) (losses), and 167(a)(1) (depreciation) all relate specifically to "trade or business" activities. In contrast Sections 165(c)(2) (losses), 167(a)(2) (depreciation), and 212(1) and (2) are all concerned with activities directed toward the "production of income," the "collection of income" or "transactions entered into for profit" without regard to whether the activity involved can be classified as a trade or business.

A third group of deductions available alike to individuals and corporations are allowed without regard to whether they have a business, or income, or profit connection. These are presented in Chapter 16. Finally, Chapter 18 identifies a group of deductions, also outside the business, or income, or profit area which, however, are available only to individuals.

In the deduction area, there are some negative provisions that sometimes countermand what seems to be clear statutory allowance. Thus a practitioner (and of course a student) must be on the alert for congressional finger-crossing. Throughout these Chapters, references are made to these negative provisions, many of which (but not all, see, e.g., Sections 183, 465 and 469) are grouped in the Code at Sections 261–280G. A glance at the headings of those sections might be in order at this point. Chapter 17 considers some of the negative statutory limitations imposed on the deductions examined in Chapters 14, 15 and 16.

This Chapter begins with Section 162 which is the most comprehensive of the sections concerning business deductions. By this stage a student knows that he does not read the Code the way he does a novel and will appreciate therefore a kind of pondering analysis of the opening clause of Section 162(a). Significant words and phrases will light up as if electrified by the push of a button. For example, it will appear that it is "expenses" that are allowed as deductions by the section. What kinds of expenditures are properly classified as expenses? It will appear further that it is only "ordinary and necessary" expenses that are to be deducted. Does "ordinary" have its ordinary meaning here? And does "necessary" mean absolutely necessary? Further, the expenses that are deductible are only those that relate to "carrying on" a trade or business. Are we "carrying on" when we are getting ready to do business?

The next three segments of this Chapter are addressed directly to the questions just raised. Of course, that does not exhaust the interesting words and phrases of the introductory clause of Section 162(a). For example, it is expenses "paid or incurred" that may be deducted and of course the question further arises whether an expense was paid or incurred "during the taxable year." These are timing questions and, while they necessarily arise here in some circumstances, their development is reserved for later treatment in Chapter 19.

Obviously, deduction under Section 162 also hinges on the expenses involved being related to a "trade or business." This Chapter devotes no separate treatment to that concept because, as indicated above, it arises in numerous contexts throughout the tax areas to which this book is addressed. Accordingly, Part B of this Chapter develops three crucial factors in the application of Section 162 ("ordinary and necessary," "expenses," and "carrying on") and then examines specific expenditures that the statute identifies as deductible business expenses when all requirements of Section 162 are met.

B. THE ANATOMY OF THE BUSINESS DEDUCTION WORKHORSE: SECTION 162

---

1. "ORDINARY AND NECESSARY"

Internal Revenue Code: Section 162(a).

Regulations: Sections 1.162–1(a); –17(b).

WELCH v. HELVERING

Supreme Court of the United States, 1933.
290 U.S. 111, 54 S.Ct. 8.

Mr. Justice CARDOZO delivered the opinion of the Court.

The question to be determined is whether payments by a taxpayer, who is in business as a commission agent, are allowable deductions in the computation of his income if made to the creditors of a bankrupt corporation in an endeavor to strengthen his own standing and credit.

In 1922 petitioner was the secretary of the E.L. Welch Company, a Minnesota corporation, engaged in the grain business. The company was adjudged an involuntary bankrupt, and had a discharge from its debts. Thereafter the petitioner made a contract with the Kellogg Company to purchase grain for it on a commission. In order to reestablish his relations with customers whom he had known when acting for the Welch Company and to solidify his credit and standing, he decided to pay the debts of the Welch business so far as he was able. In fulfilment of that resolve, he made payments of substantial amounts during five successive years. In 1924, the commissions were $18,028.20; the payments $3,975.97; in 1923, the commissions $31,377.07; the payments $11,968.20; in 1926, the commissions $20,925.25; the payments $12,815.72; in 1927, the commissions $22,119.61; the payments $7,379.72; and in 1928, the commissions $26,177.56, the payments

$11,068.25. The Commissioner ruled that these payments were not deductible from income as ordinary and necessary expenses, but were rather in the nature of capital expenditures, an outlay for the development of reputation and good will. The Board of Tax Appeals sustained the action of the Commissioner (25 B.T.A. 117), and the Court of Appeals for the Eighth Circuit affirmed. 63 F.2d 976. The case is here on certiorari.

"In computing net income there shall be allowed as deductions * * * all the ordinary and necessary expenses paid or incurred during the taxable year in carrying on any trade or business." Revenue Act of 1924, c. 234, 43 Stat. 253, 269, § 214; 26 U.S.C.A. § 955; Revenue Act of 1926, c. 27, 44 Stat. 9, 26, § 214; 26 U.S.C.A.App. § 955; Revenue Act of 1928, c. 852, 45 Stat. 791, 799, § 23; cf. Treasury Regulations 65, Arts. 101, 292, under the Revenue Act of 1924, and similar regulations under the Acts of 1926 and 1928.

We may assume that the payments to creditors of the Welch Company were necessary for the development of the petitioner's business, at least in the sense that they were appropriate and helpful. McCulloch v. Maryland, 4 Wheat. 316. He certainly thought they were, and we should be slow to overide his judgment. But the problem is not solved when the payments are characterized as necessary. Many necessary payments are charges upon capital. There is need to determine whether they are both necessary and ordinary. Now, what is ordinary, though there must always be a strain of constancy within it, is none the less a variable affected by time and place and circumstance. Ordinary in this context does not mean that the payments must be habitual or normal in the sense that the same taxpayer will have to make them often. A lawsuit affecting the safety of a business may happen once in a lifetime. The counsel fees may be so heavy that repetition is unlikely. None the less, the expense is an ordinary one because we know from experience that payments for such a purpose, whether the amount is large or small, are the common and accepted means of defense against attack. Cf. Kornhauser v. United States, 276 U.S. 145, 48 S.Ct. 219. The situation is unique in the life of the individual affected, but not in the life of the group, the community, of which he is a part. At such times there are norms of conduct that help to stabilize our judgment, and make it certain and objective. The instance is not erratic, but is brought within a known type.

The line of demarcation is now visible between the case that is here and the one supposed for illustration. We try to classify this act as ordinary or the opposite, and the norms of conduct fail us. No longer can we have recourse to any fund of business experience, to any known business practice. Men do at times pay the debts of others without legal obligation or the lighter obligation imposed by the usages of trade or by neighborly amenities, but they do not do so ordinarily, not even though the result might be to heighten their reputation for generosity and opulence. Indeed, if language is to be read in its natural and common meaning (Old Colony R. Co. v. Commissioner, 284 U.S. 552,

560, 52 S.Ct. 211; Woolford Realty Co. v. Rose, 286 U.S. 319, 327, 52 S.Ct. 568), we should have to say that payment in such circumstances, instead of being ordinary is in a high degree extraordinary. There is nothing ordinary in the stimulus evoking it, and none in the response. Here, indeed, as so often in other branches of the law, the decisive distinctions are those of degree and not of kind. One struggles in vain for any verbal formula that will supply a ready touchstone. The standard set up by the statute is not a rule of law; it is rather a way of life. Life in all its fullness must supply the answer to the riddle.

The Commissioner of Internal Revenue resorted to that standard in assessing the petitioner's income, and found that the payments in controversy came closer to capital outlays than to ordinary and necessary expenses in the operation of a business. His ruling has the support of a presumption of correctness, and the petitioner has the burden of proving it to be wrong. Wickwire v. Reinecke, 275 U.S. 101, 48 S.Ct. 43; Jones v. Commissioner, 38 F.2d 550, 552. Unless we can say from facts within our knowledge that these are ordinary and necessary expenses according to the ways of conduct and the forms of speech prevailing in the business world, the tax must be confirmed. But nothing told us by this record or within the sphere of our judicial notice permits us to give that extension to what is ordinary and necessary. Indeed, to do so would open the door to many bizarre analogies. One man has a family name that is clouded by thefts committed by an ancestor. To add to his own standing he repays the stolen money, wiping off, it may be, his income for the year. The payments figure in his tax return as ordinary expenses. Another man conceives the notion that he will be able to practice his vocation with greater ease and profit if he has an opportunity to enrich his culture. Forthwith the price of his education becomes an expense of the business, reducing the income subject to taxation. There is little difference between these expenses and those in controversy here. Reputation and learning are akin to capital assets, like the good will of an old partnership. Cf. Colony Coal & Coke Corp. v. Commissioner, 52 F.2d 923. For many, they are the only tools with which to hew a pathway to success. The money spent in acquiring them is well and wisely spent. It is not an ordinary expense of the operation of a business.

Many cases in the federal courts deal with phases of the problem presented in the case at bar. To attempt to harmonize them would be a futile task. They involve the appreciation of particular situations, at times with borderline conclusions. Typical illustrations are cited in the margin.[1]

The decree should be

Affirmed.

---

1. Ordinary expenses: Commissioner v. People's-Pittsburgh Trust Co., 60 F.2d 187, expenses incurred in the defense of a criminal charge growing out of the business of the taxpayer; American Rolling Mill Co. v. Commissioner, 41 F.2d 314, contributions to a civic improvement fund by a corporation employing half of the wage earning population of the city, the payments being made, not for charity, but to add to the

PROBLEMS

1. Taxpayer is a businessman, local politician who is also an officer-director of a savings and loan association of which he was a founder. When, partially due to his mismanagement, the savings and loan began to go under, he voluntarily donated nearly one half a million dollars to help bail it out. Is the payment deductible under § 162? See Elmer W. Conti, 31 T.C.M. 348 (1972).

2. Employee incurred ordinary and necessary expenses on a business trip for which he was entitled to reimbursement upon filing a voucher. However, Employee did not file a voucher and was not reimbursed but, instead, deducted his costs on his income tax return. Is Employee entitled to a § 162 deduction? See Heidt v. Comm'r, 274 F.2d 25 (7th Cir.1954).

3. Suppose on the facts of problem 2, above, Employee, having accounted to Employer for the expenses incurred, was fully reimbursed by Employer.

   (a) How may he treat this expense and the reimbursement? See Reg. § 1.162–17(b)(1).

   (b) What if the amount paid to the Employee as reimbursement exceeds his actual expenses? See Reg. § 1.162–17(b)(2).

   (c) What if actual expenses exceed his reimbursement? See Reg. § 1.162–17(b)(3).

2. "EXPENSES"

Internal Revenue Code: Sections 162(a); 263(a).

Regulations: Sections 1.162–4; 1.263(a)–2.

---

skill and productivity of the workmen (cf. the decisions collated in 30 Columbia Law Review 1211, 1212, and the distinctions there drawn); Corning Glass Works v. Lucas, 59 App.D.C. 168; 37 F.2d 798, donations to a hospital by a corporation whose employes with their dependents made up two thirds of the population of the city; Harris v. Lucas, 48 F.2d 187, payments of debts discharged in bankruptcy, but subject to be revived by force of a new promise. Cf. Lucas v. Ox Fibre Brush Co., 281 U.S. 115, 50 S.Ct. 273, where additional compensation, reasonable in amount, was allowed to the officers of a corporation for services previously rendered.

Not ordinary expenses: Hubinger v. Commissioner, 36 F.2d 724, payments by the taxpayer for the repair of fire damage, such payments being distinguished from those for wear and tear; Lloyd v. Commissioner, 55 F.2d 842, counsel fees incurred by the taxpayer, the president of a corporation, in prosecuting a slander suit to protect his reputation and that of his business; 105 West 55th Street v. Commissioner, 42 F.2d 849, and Blackwell Oil & Gas Co. v. Commissioner, 60 F.2d 257, gratuitous payments to stockholders in settlement of disputes between them, or to assume the expense of a lawsuit in which they had been made defendants; White v. Commissioner, 61 F.2d 726, payments in settlement of a lawsuit against a member of a partnership, the effect being to enable him to devote his undivided efforts to the partnership business and also to protect its credit.

MIDLAND EMPIRE PACKING CO.

Tax Court of the United States, 1950.
14 T.C. 635.

ARUNDELL, Judge: The issue in this case is whether an expenditure for a concrete lining in petitioner's basement to oilproof it against an oil nuisance created by a neighboring refinery is deductible as an ordinary and necessary expense under section 23(a) of the Internal Revenue Code, on the theory it was an expenditure for a repair, or, in the alternative, whether the expenditure may be treated as the measure of the loss sustained during the taxable year and not compensated for by insurance or otherwise within the meaning of section 23(f) of the Internal Revenue Code.

The respondent has contended, in part, that the expenditure is for a capital improvement and should be recovered through depreciation charges and is, therefore, not deductible as an ordinary and necessary business expense or as a loss.

It is none too easy to determine on which side of the line certain expenditures fall so that they may be accorded their proper treatment for tax purposes. Treasury Regulations 111,* from which we quote in the margin, is helpful in distinguishing between an expenditure to be classed as a repair and one to be treated as a capital outlay. In Illinois Merchants Trust Co., Executor, 4 B.T.A. 103, at page 106, we discussed this subject in some detail and in our opinion said:

> "It will be noted that the first sentence of the article [now Regulations 111, sec. 29.23(a)–4] relates to repairs, while the second sentence deals in effect with replacements. In determining whether an expenditure is a capital one or is chargeable against operating income, it is necessary to bear in mind the purpose for which the expenditure was made. To repair is to restore to a sound state or to mend, while a replacment connotes a substitution. A repair is an expenditure for the purpose of keeping the property in an ordinarily efficient operating condition. It does not add to the value of the property, nor does it appreciably prolong its life. It merely keeps the property in an operating condition over its probable useful life for the uses for which it was acquired. Expenditures for that purpose are distinguishable from those for replacements, alterations, improvements, or additions which prolong the life of the property, increase its value, or make it adaptable to a different use. The one is a maintenance charge,

---

* Sec. 29.23(a)–4. Repairs.—The cost of incidental repairs which neither materially add to the value of the property nor appreciably prolong its life, but keep it in an ordinarily efficient operating condition, may be deducted as expense, provided the plant or property account is not increased by the amount of such expenditures. Repairs in the nature of replacements, to the extent that they arrest deterioration and appreciably prolong the life of the property, should be charged against the depreciation reserve if such account is kept. (See sections 29.23(1)–1 to 29.23(1)–10, inclusive.) [The similar current provision is Reg. § 1.162–4. Ed.]

while the others are additions to capital investment which should not be applied against current earnings."

It will be seen from our findings of fact that for some 25 years prior to the taxable year petitioner had used the basement rooms of its plant as a place for the curing of hams and bacon and for the storage of meat and hides. The basement had been entirely satisfactory for this purpose over the entire period in spite of the fact that there was some seepage of water into the rooms from time to time. In the taxable year it was found that not only water, but oil, was seeping through the concrete walls of the basement of the packing plant and, while the water would soon drain out, the oil would not, and there was left on the basement floor a thick scum of oil which gave off a strong odor that permeated the air of the entire plant, and the fumes from the oil created a fire hazard. It appears that the oil which came from a nearby refinery had also gotten into the water wells which served to furnish water for petitioner's plant, and as a result of this whole condition the Federal meat inspectors advised petitioner that it must discontinue the use of the water from the wells and oilproof the basement, or else shut down its plant.

To meet this situation, petitioner during the taxable year undertook steps to oilproof the basement by adding a concrete lining to the walls from the floor to a height of about four feet and also added concrete to the floor of the basement. It is the cost of this work which it seeks to deduct as a repair. The basement was not enlarged by this work nor did the oilproofing serve to make it more desirable for the purpose for which it had been used through the years prior to the time that the oil nuisance had occurred. The evidence is that the expenditure did not add to the value or prolong the expected life of the property over what they were before the event occurred which made the repairs necessary. It is true that after the work was done the seepage of water, as well as oil, was stopped, but, as already stated, the presence of the water had never been found objectionable. The repairs merely served to keep the property in an operating condition over its probable useful life for the purpose for which it was used.

While it is conceded on brief that the expenditure was "necessary," respondent contends that the encroachment of the oil nuisance on petitioner's property was not an "ordinary" expense in petitioner's particular business. But the fact that petitioner had not theretofore been called upon to make a similar expenditure to prevent damage and disaster to its property does not remove that expense from the classification of "ordinary" for, as stated in Welch v. Helvering, 290 U.S. 111, "ordinary in this context does not mean that the payments must be habitual or normal in the sense that the same taxpayer will have to make them often. * * * the expense is an ordinary one because we know from experience that payments for such a purpose, whether the amount is large or small, are the common and accepted means of defense against attack. Cf. Kornhauser v. United States, 276 U.S. 145, 48 S.Ct. 219. The situation is unique in the life of the individual affected, but not in the life of the group, the community, of which he is a part." Steps to protect a business building from the seepage of oil from a nearby refinery, which had been erected long subsequent to the time petitioner started to operate its plant, would seem to us to be a normal thing to do, and in certain sections of the country it must be a common experience to protect one's property from the seepage of oil. Expenditures to accomplish this result are likewise normal.

In American Bemberg Corporation, 10 T.C. 361, we allowed as deductions, on the ground that they were ordinary and necessary expenses, extensive expenditures made to prevent disaster, although the repairs were of a type which had never been needed before and were unlikely to recur. In that case the taxpayer, to stop cave-ins of soil which were threatening destruction of its manufacturing plant, hired an engineering firm which drilled to the bedrock and injected grout to fill the cavities where practicable, and made incidental replacements and repairs, including tightening of the fluid carriers. In two successive years the taxpayer expended $734,316.76 and $199,154.33, respectively, for such drilling and grouting and $153,474.20 and $79,687.29, respectively, for capital replacements. We found that the cost (other than replacement) of this program did not make good the depreciation previously allowed, and stated in our opinion:

> "In connection with the purpose of the work, the Proctor program was intended to avert a plant-wide disaster and avoid forced abandonment of the plant. The purpose was not to improve, better, extend, or increase the original plant, nor to prolong its original useful life. Its continued operation was endangered; the purpose of the expenditures was to enable petitioner to continue the plant in operation not on any new or better scale, but on the same scale and, so far as possible, as efficiently as it had operated before. The purpose was not to rebuild or replace the plant in whole or in part, but to keep the same plant as it was and where it was."

The petitioner here made the repairs in question in order that it might continue to operate its plant. Not only was there danger of fire from the oil and fumes, but the presence of the oil led the Federal meat inspectors to declare the basement an unsuitable place for the purpose for which it had been used for a quarter of a century. After the expenditures were made, the plant did not operate on a changed or larger scale, nor was it thereafter suitable for new or additional uses. The expenditure served only to permit petitioner to continue the use of the plant, and particularly the basement for its normal operations.

In our opinion, the expenditure of $4,868.81 for lining the basement walls and floor was essentially a repair and, as such, it is deductible as an ordinary and necessary business expense. This holding makes unnecessary a consideration of petitioner's alternative contention that the expenditure is deductible as a business loss, nor need we heed the respondent's argument that any loss suffered was compensated for by "insurance or otherwise."

Decision will be entered under Rule 50.

NOTE

Tax Lawyer (T.L.) kept at the side of his bed a collection of cases carefully selected for him by his law clerk to be used by him as a substitute for Nytol when sleep was elusive. He had just finished reading *Midland Empire Packing Co.* and was comfortably close to dozing when his eye caught *Mt. Morris Drive-In Theatre Co.*[1] Hastily scanning the one-page Tax Court opinion, he discovered that when the Theatre Company was required by threat of a lawsuit by adjacent property owners to expend money for a drainage system that would protect the Company's neighbors from the flow of water from its land, it had made a nondeductible capital expenditure. He noticed also that when the Tax Court opinion was reviewed, one judge concurred in two sentences, to which when read by another he said, "uh huh." On the other hand, another judge spent four sentences dissenting and picked up four of his brethren as followers. But T.L. was not sure he could see a difference in the expenditures to prevent liquid incursion by an offended flowee from those of an offending flow-er.

T.L. had a bad night. He *could* see, as did the concurring Tax Court judge, that if the drainage expenditure had been undertaken initially when the drive-in theatre had been first built, it certainly would have been a capital cost of construction, not an expense. However, he felt most frustrated by not being able to ask the concurring Tax Court judge how the *Midland Empire* expenditure would have been treated if it, too, had been made at the time the packing plant was being built. He found very little tranquility in the comment in the Tax Court opinion that in the business expense, capital expenditure area, "The decisive test is * * * the character of the transaction which gives rise to the payment."

After a wholly sleepless night, T.L.'s first action at the office in the morning was to dictate a memorandum to his law clerk directing him to select no more cases for him dealing with the question whether an expenditure is an expense or one to be capitalized.[2]

1. Mt. Morris Drive-In Theatre Co. v. Commissioner, 25 T.C. 272 (1955), affirmed 238 F.2d 85 (6th Cir.1956).

2. The dilemma reflected in *Midland Empire* and *Mt. Morris Drive-In* can be elaborated to present a possible *three-way* tax view of a single expenditure. In Hochschild v. Commissioner, 161 F.2d 817 (2d Cir.1947), a taxpayer had paid attorneys' fees defending a stockholders' derivative suit. The Tax Court in the later income tax case treated the fees in part as capital expenditures, a cost of defending title to the taxpayer's stock (see page 423, infra) and in part as deductible expense incurred for the collection of income (see I.R.C. § 212(1) and the text infra at page 422). Could at least a part, as the taxpayer argued, have been treated as a § 162 business expense, sufficiently related to the taxpayer's business as a corporate employee? Indeed, it does not upset the purpose of this example to state that in reversing the Tax Court the Second Circuit, noting the taxpayer was defending a charge of malfeasance in his position as a director and officer, treated the *entire* fee as a § 162 expense.

And so it is with equivocal expenditures such as those in *Midland Empire* and *Mt. Morris*. We are here of course only beginning to examine the way in which costs are taken into account in arriving at the *net* figure now called "taxable income" to which income tax rates are applied. We should say, therefore, that the present problem is really only one of timing because, as a rule the cost incurred will be either deducted immediately, "expensed" as the accountants say, or capitalized and written off over a period of time by way of depreciation or amortization deductions. But of course timing is important. Here it determines whether the taxpayer will continue to have the use of dollars at least momentarily saved by way of a deduction for an expense or whether he must let the government have the use of the money paid as tax when the expense deduction is disallowed and get back his costs piecemeal by way of deductions in future years. It is therefore not surprising, although it is unfortunate, to discover much controversy and expensive litigation in this area and too little light for sound prediction.

The regulations[3] attempt to differentiate deductible expenses from capital expenditures somewhat enigmatically. Thus they place in the immediately deductible "expense" category of Section 162 "repairs which neither materially add to the value of the property nor appreciably prolong its life, but keep it in efficient operating condition * * *." This is certain to be perplexing to the neophyte. For example, in *Midland Empire* one asks himself: (1) Was not the property more valuable when the basement was lined? (2) Would not use of the basement have ceased, shortening its useful life, except for the expenditure which thus "prolonged" useful life? These questions misconstrue the controlling concepts. Consider this comment in a very early B.T.A. opinion:[4]

> In determining whether an expenditure is a capital one or is chargeable against operating income, it is necessary to bear in mind the purpose for which the expenditure was made. To repair is to restore to a sound state or to mend, while a replacement connotes a substitution. A repair is an expenditure for the purpose of keeping the property in an ordinarily efficient operating condition. It does not add to the value of the property nor does it appreciably prolong its life. It merely keeps the property in an operating condition over its probable useful life for the uses for which it was acquired. Expenditures for that purpose are distinguishable from those for replacements, alterations, improvements or additions which prolong the life of the property, increase its value, or make it adaptable to a different use. The one is a maintenance charge, while the others are additions to capital investment which should not be applied against current earnings.

3. Reg. § 1.162–4.

4. Appeal of Illinois Merchants Trust Co., Executor, 4 B.T.A. 103, 106 (1926).

This may be somewhat enlightening but, even so, we are dealing with concepts with edges no more sharp than those of "fraud", "proximate cause" or "reasonably prudent person". Decisions in the area often defy reconciliation. Should we throw up our hands and seek academic fun and satisfaction in a parade of judicial inconsistencies?[5] Even if specific cases are difficult to analyze, it seems more profitable to strive for an understanding of the basic criteria for decision.

Section 263(a), one of the negative Code provisions, is somewhat more precise than the Section 162 regulations in disallowing deductions for "permanent improvement or betterments" and for "any amount expended in restoring property or making good the exhaustion thereof for which an allowance is or has been made." The Section 263 regulations [6] also nail as capital expenditures amounts spent "to adapt property to a new or different use."

The general idea is that the cost of property acquired for business use is a charge against income that it helps to earn, ratably over the expected useful life of the property.[7] Expenditures made to enable the taxpayer to use the property for *that* expected period and for the planned purpose are deductible expenses. Thus he can paint and patch and repaper and add some new shingles to the roof and charge the costs against ordinary income;[8] but if he undertakes the same activities as a part of the overall restoration of a building, which will extend its use beyond the period originally expected, he must capitalize these and related expenditures.[9]

Perhaps it is a mistake to attempt to talk about property generally in this context. If the property concerned is complex, like a building consisting of walls and floors and roof and foundation and fixtures and elevators and heating and cooling equipment and so forth, it is probably necessary to think in terms of the various components. Shoring up a floor to achieve continuing utility *may* be a deductible expense, but the replacement of a floor, or possibly even of an important door, is a capital expenditure.[10]

In thinking of the useful life of a building, does one anticipate only the replacement of a few shingles or that the entire roof may have to be renewed? This *question* may be wrong, if we should think in terms of the roof as one component. In thinking of the life of a roof, one expects to replace a few shingles.

---

5. Compare Zimmern v. Commissioner, 28 F.2d 769 (5th Cir.1928) reversing 9 B.T.A. 1382, allowing business expense deductions of $20,000 for refurbishing a barge that had been sunk in a storm, with P. Dougherty Co. v. Commissioner, 159 F.2d 269 (4th Cir.1946), affirming 5 T.C. 791 (1945), requiring capitalization of $17,000 spent to rebuild the stern of a barge where timbers and planks had rotted out.

6. Reg. § 1.263(a)–1(b).

7. See text at page 740, infra.

8. Chesapeake Corp. of Virginia, 17 T.C. 668 (1951), acq. Rev.Rul. 65–13, 1965–1 C.B. 87.

9. Regenstein v. Edwards, 121 F.Supp. 952 (M.D.Ga.1954).

10. See Alabama-Georgia Syrup Co., 36 T.C. 747 (1961), reversed on other issue, sub nom. L.B. Whitfield, Jr., 311 F.2d 640 (5th Cir.1962).

Do we get some better idea now of what is meant by prolonging useful life as that concept is expressed in the regulations? If so, what about increases in value? Have you increased the value of your car when you put in a new set of spark plugs? Certainly, in a sense; but not in the sense of the Section 162 and 263 regulations. Nor is that an "improvement" or "betterment" in the sense in which those terms are used in Section 263(a)(1). But if a building that was improperly built is given a going over by shoring up the walls with steel rods, inserting new beams to support the roof, and replacing an inadequate foundation with cinder block, it is "improved", and the costs must be capitalized.[11]

Nor is it material that the work is done under compulsion, as pursuant to the order of the city building commissioner,[12] or under threat of an injunction.[13]

Attention should be drawn to the fact that some Code sections make expensing or capitalizing expenditures elective.[14] These provisions are conveniently collected in the regulations.[15]

Much more could be said here about the expense, capital expenditure dichotomy. But it would probably not be profitable. Many matters are crisp and clean, as just a little research will show. The gray areas are best approached by a wide reading of the cases; it may be more a matter of developing a "feel" for the problems than just acquiring some knowledge.[16]

3. "CARRYING ON" BUSINESS

Internal Revenue Code: Sections 162(a); 195; 262.

Regulations: Section 1.162–6.

---

11. J.L. Boland, 19 T.C.M. 1030 (1960).

12. Ibid.

13. See Woolrich Woolen Mills v. U.S., 289 F.2d 444 (3d Cir.1961), addition of filtration plant required by state antipollution law.

14. For a short period of time Congress even reduced the repair expense deduction question to a mathematical formula under a "reasonable repair allowance" rule that was contained in I.R.C. § 263(e). That rule, which helped to reduce uncertainty, controversy, and litigation, was a part of a depreciation system known as A.D.R. (asset depreciation range). See page 743 infra. Both were repealed by the Economic Recovery Act of 1981 § 201(c).

15. Reg. § 1.263(a)–3. See also I.R.C. § 190, Expenditures to remove architectur-

al and transportation barriers to the handicapped and elderly.

16. This note deals with the expense, capital expenditure dichotomy largely on the basis of whether something is a repair or an improvement. The problem is of course very much broader as the *Welch* case, supra page 346 indicates. And compare e.g., Zimmerman & Sons, Inc. v. U.S., 1972–2 USTC para. 9585 (E.D.Wis.1972), subscription lists costs expensed, with Manhattan Co. of Virginia, 50 T.C. 78 (1968), purchased customer lists were partly nondepreciable goodwill that could not be expensed and partly intangibles with useful lives subject only to the allowance for depreciation.

MORTON FRANK

Tax Court of the United States, 1953.
20 T.C. 511.

The respondent determined an income tax deficiency against the petitioners for the year 1946 in the amount of $2,914.92. The only issue presented is whether the petitioners are entitled to deduct traveling expenses and legal fees in the amount of $5,965 in the taxable year.

Findings of Fact

Morton Frank and Agnes Dodds Frank, the petitioners, are husband and wife who filed a joint income tax return for 1946 with the collector of internal revenue for the eighteenth district of Ohio. In November 1945, Morton Frank was released from the Navy. His place of residence during the period of his service was Pittsburgh, Pennsylvania. Prior to the war, he had been employed by such newspapers as The Pittsburgh Press, The Braddock Free Press, The Braddock Daily News Herald, and The Michigan Daily. His wife, an attorney, had no experience in the newspaper business and during the war had been employed by several government agencies. During and prior to his service in the Navy, Morton Frank was interested in purchasing and operating a newspaper or radio station. Near the end of November 1945, the petitioners began a trip to examine newspapers and radio properties throughout the country. The purpose of the trip was to investigate, and, if possible, acquire a newspaper or radio enterprise to operate.

The trip took both petitioners westward from Pittsburgh through Ohio, Indiana, Michigan, Minnesota, Wisconsin, Oklahoma, and New Mexico. They interviewed persons in these states with respect to local newspapers and radio stations. On January 1, 1946, the petitioners were in San Diego, California. They then traveled through California, New Mexico, Texas, and Arizona. They arrived in Phoenix, Arizona, on February 12, 1946. The taxpayers estimated that their travel and communication expenses from January 1 to February 12, 1946, aggregated $1,596.44.

The petitioners took employment in Phoenix with The Arizona Times and remained in that city from February to Mid-July 1946. While working in Phoenix, the petitioners made several trips to various cities throughout the country in search of a newspaper plant to purchase. They traveled to Los Angeles and Santa Barbara, California, Yuma, Arizona, Pittsburgh, Pennsylvania, and Wilmington, Delaware. Offers of purchase were made to the owners of several newspapers. While in Phoenix, the petitioners lived first in a hotel and later in a house which they acquired. The petitioners estimated their traveling, telephone, and telegraph expenses from March through December 1946, at $5,027.94. Included within this total was a legal fee of $1,000 paid to an attorney for services rendered in connection with unsuccessful negotiations to purchase a newspaper in Wilmington, Delaware. None of these claimed expenses were incurred in connection with the petitioners' employment in Phoenix, Arizona. A portion of it was based on estimated allowances of mileage at 6 cents per mile, lodging at $5 per day per person, and other costs at comparable rates, the whole expenditures reasonably aggregating $5,027.94. In November 1946, the petitioners purchased a newspaper in Canton, Ohio, and commenced publication of the Canton Economist in that month.

Opinion

VAN FOSSAN, Judge: The only question presented is whether the petitioners may deduct $5,965 in the determination of their net income for the year 1946 as ordinary and necessary business expenses or as losses. The petitioners base their claim for deductions upon section 23(a)(1) and (2) and (e)(2) of the Internal Revenue Code.[1] The evidence reasonably establishes that the petitioners expended the amount of expenses stated in our Findings of Fact during the taxable year in traveling, telephone, telegraph, and legal expenses in the search for and investigation of newspaper and radio properties. This total amount was spent by the petitioners in their travels through various states in an endeavor to find a business which they could purchase and operate. These expenses do not include amounts spent while living in Phoenix, Arizona.

The travel expenses and legal fees spent in searching for a newspaper business with a view to purchasing the same cannot be deducted under the provisions of section 23(a)(1), Internal Revenue Code. The petitioners were not engaged in any trade or business at the time the expenses were incurred. The trips made by the taxpayers from Phoenix, Arizona, were not related to the conduct of the business that they were then engaged in but were preparatory to locating a business venture of their own. The expenses of investigating and looking for a new business and trips preparatory to entering a business are not deductible as an ordinary and necessary business expense incurred in carrying on a trade or business. George C. Westervelt, 8 T.C. 1248. The word "pursuit" in the statutory phrase "in pursuit of a trade or business" is not used in the sense of "searching for" or "following after," but in the sense of "in connection with" or "in the course of" a trade or business. It presupposes an existing business with which petitioner is connected. The fact that petitioners had no established home during the period of their travels further complicates the question and alone may be fatal to petitioners' case. If they had no home, how could they have expenses "away from home"? The issue whether all or part of the expenses so incurred were capital expenditures is not raised or argued and we do not pass judgment on such question.

* * *

1. [The 1939 Code section cited is omitted. See I.R.C. (1986) §§ 162(a), 165(a) and (c)(2), 212. The portion of the opinion dealing with §§ 165 and 212 has been deleted. Ed.]

We conclude that the petitioners may not deduct the expenses claimed for 1946 under the applicable provisions of the Internal Revenue Code.

Decision will be entered for the respondent.

NOTE

Section 162(a) provides: "There shall be allowed as a deduction all the ordinary and necessary expenses paid or incurred during the taxable year in carrying on any trade or business * * *" The corresponding clause in Section 23(a)(1) of the Internal Revenue Code of 1939, which controlled in *Morton Frank*, supra, was identical. Reference in the opinion to the phrase "in pursuit of a trade or business" may be confusing. It appears in Section 162(a)(2) and its predecessor, Section 23(a)(1)(A) of the 1939 Code, in connection with the specific provision on business travel. Even so, the "pursuit" phrase takes color from the more general "carrying on" expression and, as the opinion in *Frank* suggests, both phrases have about the same meaning.

It seems almost axiomatic that one cannot be "carrying on" a business unless he *has* a business, a frailty in the *Frank* circumstances which, among other factors,[1] foreclosed any Section 162 deduction. Nevertheless, the opinion should not be read so broadly as to suggest all costs incurred in seeking employment can never give rise to a Section 162 deduction. If *Frank* had been in a trade or business and was seeking to expand that business or some branch of it, his position would have been stronger.[2]

The Tax Court has also distinguished *Frank* in situations where the taxpayer has proceeded beyond an initial investigation stage and has entered a transactional stage.[3] The transactional stage is reached at the point where the preliminary investigation has led to the decision to purchase a specific business, but further investigation of the business continues.[4] If subsequent developments compel the taxpayer to abandon the venture prior to engaging in it, this is not necessarily a bar to a deduction of such transactional stage expenses, but the deduction claimed should be for a loss on a transaction entered into for profit allowed by Section 165(c)(2), not a business expense under Section 162.[5]

In order to clarify the treatment of expenses incurred prior to the establishment of a trade or business ("start-up expenditures"), Congress enacted Section 195 in 1980. Section 195 permits a taxpayer to elect to amortize start-up expenditures over a period of not less than 60 months.[6] The amortization period runs from the month in which the

---

1. See the discussion of the meaning of "away from home", infra page 373.

2. Colorado Springs Nat. Bank v. U.S., 505 F.2d 1185 (10th Cir.1974); First Nat. Bank of South Carolina v. U.S., 558 F.2d 721 (4th Cir.1977); but see Central Texas Savings & Loan Ass'n v. U.S., 731 F.2d 1181 (5th Cir.1984).

3. Johan Domenie, 34 T.C.M. 469 (1975); Harris W. Seed, 52 T.C. 880 (1969).

4. Id. at 472 and 885, respectively.

5. See page 444, infra, and see note 14, infra.

6. I.R.C. § 195(b)(1).

business "begins";[7] consequently, the taxpayer must actually enter a trade or business successfully to elect Section 195.[8]

Start-up expenditures are defined in Section 195(c)(1)(A) as amounts incurred with respect to:

(i) investigating the creation or acquisition of an active trade or business;

(ii) creating an active trade or business; or

(iii) activities engaged in for profit * * * before the day on which the active trade or business begins, in anticipation of such activity becoming an active trade or business.

Additionally, the expenditures must be of the type that would be allowable as a deduction if paid or incurred by an existing trade or business.[9] Eligible expenditures thus include both "investigatory costs" incurred before reaching a final decision to acquire or enter into a business (e.g., costs for market studies, evaluation of products and labor supplies) and "start-up" costs incurred after a decision to establish a business but before the business begins operation (e.g., costs for advertising, training employees, lining up distributors or potential customers and fees for professional services in setting up books).[10] However, the statute specifically provides that amounts deductible under Sections 163 (interest), 164 (taxes), and 174 (research expenses) do not constitute start-up expenditures. As such, these expenses need not be amortized but instead may be deducted currently to the extent allowable under the respective sections.[11]

Prior to the amendment of Section 195 by the Tax Reform Act of 1984, uncertainty existed with respect to the treatment of start-up expenditures in cases where the taxpayer chose not to make an election under Section 195. While the Internal Revenue Service felt that such costs should be treated as nondeductible capital expenditures, taxpayers argued that such expenditures should be currently deductible under the general provisions of Section 162 or 212.[12] The Tax Reform Act of 1984 resolved the controversy by amending Section 195 to provide that all start-up expenditures must be either amortized over the requisite

---

7. Id.

8. Expenditures attributable to the acquisition of an investment are not eligible for amortization under § 195. See also I.R.C. §§ 248 and 709 which provide for the amortization of corporate and partnership "organizational expenditures" over periods of not less than 60 months.

9. Ordinary and necessary expenditures incurred in the expansion of an existing business are currently deductible under I.R.C. § 162. Expenditures that are not deductible by an existing trade or business under § 162 are ineligible for amortization under § 195. See note 2, supra. Ineligible expenditures include amounts paid for the acquisition of property held for sale or depreciable property, amounts paid as part of the acquisition cost of a trade or business and amounts paid in connection with the sale of stock, securities or partnership interests (e.g., securities registration expenses, underwriter's commissions). See Sen.Rep. No. 96–1036, 96th Cong., 2d Sess. (1980).

10. Id.

11. I.R.C. § 195(c)(1). Cf. I.R.C. § 263A.

12. Sen.Rep. No. 98–169, 98th Cong., 2d Sess. 282–283 (1984). Cf. Hoopengarner v. Commissioner, 80 T.C. 538 (1983).

period or capitalized and treated as nondeductible expenditures, i.e., in no event "expensed." [13]

The Tax Reform Act of 1984 also enacted a new subsection which sets forth the manner in which start-up expenditures are to be treated in cases where the business is terminated before the close of the amortization period. Section 195(b)(2) provides that where a business is completely disposed of prior to the completion of the amortization period, any start-up expenditures not previously deducted may be deducted to the extent provided in Section 165.[14]

Though Section 195 clarifies the extent to which start-up expenses may be deducted, it has no application to an individual having employee status with respect to his deduction of expenses incurred in seeking new employment. Instead, the general provisions of Sections 162 and 212 must be relied on in order to determine whether, and to what extent, such expenses are deductible. It is well settled that being an employee constitutes carrying on a trade or business,[15] but in recent years question has arisen whether a prospective employee is in a trade or business [16] and whether new employment, perhaps of short duration, prevents one from continuing to be considered as carrying on his former trade, and whether lack of employment ends a trade altogether. As the Section 162 statutory language is the same for an employee as for a self-employed person, the deductibility of expenses ought to be the same.

Now a person who has never before "carried on" a particular trade or business as an employee or otherwise, may be permitted a deduction for expenses incurred in entering that trade or business. Although it might seem that pre-employment expenses could never be deductible under Section 162 because not incurred in carrying on a trade or business, the Tax Court earlier sensibly made an exception in a situation where services were rendered to one who was to become the employee of a third party prior to the commencement of his employment, but payment for those services was contingent upon his becoming employed [17] as he later did. In *Hundley,* the petitioner who later became employed as a major league baseball player, was earlier taught the tools of his trade by his father, a former semi-professional baseball player. As compensation for those services, it had been agreed that the petitioner (son) would pay his father fifty percent of any bonus that might be paid to the petitioner under the terms of a professional

---

13. I.R.C. § 195(a).

14. Seemingly, all start-up expenses would be deductible under I.R.C. § 165(c)(1).

15. David J. Primuth, 54 T.C. 374 (1970); U.S. v. Generes, 405 U.S. 93, 92 S.Ct. 827 (1972).

16. Rev.Rul. 75–120, 1975–1 C.B. 55, 56. Cf. Reg. § 1.162–5(b)(2)(i) and (3)(i). The Service had previously ruled that fees paid

to employment agencies for actually securing an initial employment (as distinguished from merely seeking employment) were deductible. Rev.Rul. 60–223, 1960–1 C.B. 57. The Ruling, conditioning deductibility on success, not properly a condition to the deduction, was revoked in Rev.Rul. 75–120, supra.

17. C.R. Hundley, Jr., 48 T.C. 339 (1967).

baseball contract if one should later be signed.[18] The petitioner eventually signed a bonus contract with a professional baseball club and paid one half of the bonus to his father. The Tax Court found that this expense was not paid or incurred prior to petitioner's entering into the business of baseball, because the payment of compensation to the father was not due or incurred or payable until the petitioner was engaged in the business of baseball.[19] The court concluded that the payments made under the terms of the agreement were paid for services actually rendered in carrying on a trade or business and thus were deductible,[20] and the Commissioner has acquiesced.[21] The rationale of the *Hundley* decision could extend to any situation in which payment for employment-seeking services is contingent upon employment and does not become due until employment is secured.

Once an employee has entered a trade or business one issue is: How long does one remain in that trade or business during periods of unemployment or diversification into other businesses? It is becoming clear that, once having entered a trade or business, being unemployed does not prevent one from still being considered in a trade or business,[22] but there are qualifications. A prolonged length of time away from one's usual employment is a factor that may be considered in determining he is no longer carrying on that employment as a trade or business. In James D. Protiva,[23] the Tax Court held that the petitioner was not entitled to deduct the cost of newspaper advertisements that were unsuccessful in locating him a new teaching position. He had previously held a teaching position for several years, but not during the year of the advertisements, and the court found that he was not in that trade or business at any time during the year at issue. The Tax Court also denied a taxpayer a deduction for education expenses where over a four year period up to the time of litigation, the taxpayer did no teaching while obtaining a graduate degree.[24]

The Treasury states the position in Revenue Ruling 75–120 [25] that it will not allow deductions under Section 162 for expenses incurred by individuals who have been unemployed for such a period of time that there is a substantial lack of continuity between their past employments and their endeavors to find new employments, but the length of time necessary to establish this substantial lack of continuity remains uncertain.

Another factor bearing on whether an unemployed person is in a trade or business is the length of time he has been employed before becoming unemployed. However, in Albert Ruehmann, III,[26] a law

---

18. Id. at 340.

19. Id. at 348.

20. Id. at 349. With Hundley, id., compare Richard A. Allen, 50 T.C. 466 (1968).

21. 1967–2 C.B. 2.

22. Furner v. Commissioner, 393 F.2d 292 (7th Cir.1968); Harold Haft, 40 T.C. 2 (1963); Rev.Rul. 75–120, supra note 16.

23. 29 T.C.M. 1318 (1970).

24. Corbett v. Commissioner, 55 T.C. 884 (1971).

25. Supra note 16 at 56. See Rev.Rul. 77–32, 1977–1 C.B. 38.

26. 30 T.C.M. 675 (1971).

student who had passed his state's bar examination and had worked as an attorney for only three months with a law firm was (surprisingly?) held to be carrying on a trade or business when he went back to graduate school. In contrast, an engineering student who worked for a year after graduation prior to doing graduate work in engineering was found not to have entered a trade or business that he could be carrying on to make his education expenses deductible.[27]

Even if it is clear an individual is engaged in a trade or business, question may be raised under Section 162 whether his expenses were incurred in carrying on *that* trade or business, which of course they must be to be deductible.

After some extensive judicial battering,[28] the Treasury conceded [29] that an employee's expenses in seeking employment elsewhere but in the same trade are deductible whether or not successful. This determination does not of course extend to first jobs, lengthy unemployment, or new trades or businesses.[30] This concession by the Treasury followed on the heels of several cases holding that success is not an element in the deductibility of employment-seeking expenses,[31] the Commissioner finally conceding the issue by acquiescing in Leonard Cremona.

Although Revenue Ruling 75–120 and Section 195 appear to clear the air with regard to the question of deductibility of employment-seeking expenses, some trouble spots remain. The courts have taken the position that in the case of a position obtained by public election, the incumbent's trade or business is concluded at the end of the elective term. Under this view, election and re-election expenses are not differentiated, and neither are deductible. Thus, in McDonald v. U.S., the Supreme Court of the United States disallowed a deduction for a judge's re-election expenses because the expenses were not incurred in being a judge but "in trying to be a judge." [32] The Commissioner seeks to distinguish political campaign expenses from other employment-seeking expenses in Revenue Ruling 75–120 [33] and continues successfully to challenge the deductibility of campaign expenses.[34] Similarly, Vice President Nelson Rockefeller's estate was denied a deduction for expenses incurred in his congressional confirmation proceedings to

---

27. Barry Reisine, 29 T.C.M. 1429 (1970). Business deductions for education expenses are considered further, infra at page 399.

28. David J. Primuth, 54 T.C. 374 (1970); Kenneth R. Kenfield, 54 T.C. 1197 (1970); Roy E. Blewitt, Jr., 31 T.C.M. 1225 (1972); Leonard F. Cremona, 58 T.C. 219 (1972).

29. Leonard F. Cremona, supra note 28, acq., 1975–1 C.B. 1. See Rev.Rul. 75–120, supra note 16.

30. Ibid.

31. Ibid. See note 16, supra.

32. McDonald v. Commissioner, 323 U.S. 57, 60, 65 S.Ct. 96 (1944).

33. Supra note 16 at 56.

34. Nichols v. Commissioner, 1975–1 USTC para. 9404 (C.A.–5); Joseph W. Martino, 62 T.C. 840 (1974); Carey v. Commissioner, 460 F.2d 1259 (4th Cir.1972), cert. denied 409 U.S. 990, 93 S.Ct. 325 (1972). Court decisions have not only denied a § 162 deduction for campaign expenses but also have held that these expenses may not be amortized over the term of office, Maness v. U.S., 367 F.2d 357 (5th Cir.1966); Levy v. U.S., 210 Ct.Cl. 97, 535 F.2d 47 (1976), cert. denied 429 U.S. 885, 97 S.Ct. 236 (1976), although capitalized replacements of a physical nature are depreciable. See page 740, infra.

become vice president.[35] In contrast, Rev.Rul. 71–470[36] properly allows a deduction for expenses incurred in fighting a recall procedure which would have removed a judge from office, obviously keeping him from carrying on his judicial duties.

PROBLEMS

1. Determine the deductibility under §§ 162 and 195 of expenses incurred in the following situations.

    (a) Tycoon, a salesman, unexpectedly inherited a sizeable amount of money from an eccentric millionaire. Tycoon decided to invest a part of his fortune in the development of industrial properties and he incurred expenses in making a preliminary investigation.

    (b) The facts are the same as in (a), above, except that Tycoon, rather than having been a salesman, was a successful developer of residential and shopping center properties.

    (c) The facts are the same as in (b), above, except that Tycoon, desiring to diversify his investments, incurs expenses in investigating the possibility of purchasing a professional sports team.

    (d) The facts are the same as in (a), above, except that Tycoon then begins developing industrial properties. Tycoon is advised by his lawyer that his prior expenses qualify as § 195 "start-up expenditures." Since Tycoon has commenced developing the properties, may he forego a § 195 election and deduct his prior expenses under § 162?

    (e) The facts are the same as in (d), above. However, after two years Tycoon's fortunes turn sour and he sells the business at a loss. What happens to the deferred investigation expenses?

2. Law student's Spouse completed secretarial school just prior to student entering law school. Consider whether Spouse's employment agency fees are deductible in the following circumstances:

    (a) Agency is unsuccessful in finding Spouse a job.

    (b) Agency is successful in finding Spouse a job.

    (c) Same as (b), above, except that Agency's fee was contingent upon its securing employment for Spouse and the payments will not become due until Spouse has begun working.

    (d) Same as (a) and (b), above, except that Spouse previously worked as a secretary in Old Town and seeks employment in New Town where student attends law school.

---

35. Estate of Nelson A. Rockefeller, 83 T.C. 368 (1984). Burke and Friel, "Recent Developments in the Income Taxation of Individuals; Rockefeller v. Commissioner: Deducting Employment-Seeking Expenses," 10 Rev. Tax'n Individ. 182 (1986).

36. 1971–2 C.B. 121. See Rev.Rul. 84–110, 1984–2 C.B. 35, allowing a public official to deduct as business expenses out-of-pocket expenses necessary for the proper performance of his duties. See also I.R.C. § 7701(a)(26).

(e) Same as (d), above, except that Agency is successful in finding Spouse a job in New Town as a bank teller.

C. SPECIFIC BUSINESS DEDUCTION

---

1. "REASONABLE" SALARIES

Internal Revenue Code: Section 162(a)(1).

Regulations: Section 1.162–7, –8, –9.

HAROLDS CLUB v. COMMISSIONER *

United States Court of Appeals, Ninth Circuit, 1965.
340 F.2d 861.

Raymond Smith
Harold / another
proprietorship son
partnership

HAMLEY, Circuit Judge.

[In the years 1952 to 1956 Harolds Club, an incorporated gaming establishment in Nevada, paid Raymond I. Smith salary in annual amounts ranging from about $350,000 to $560,000. The Commissioner disallowed in part the corporation's deductions based on these payments. Smith was not a shareholder in the corporation all the stock of which was owned by his two sons. However, the business was essentially a continuation of one that Smith had earlier operated illegally in California but which, upon the move to Nevada, became at first that of son Harold, as a proprietorship, and later in 1938 a partnership owned by Harold and another son of Smith. The partnership was incorporated in 1946. The scope of the business is suggested by the fact that by 1952 there were seven bars in the Club. Harolds Club did not prosper initially but in 1935 Smith, while not an owner as indicated, agreed to take over management of the Club. Ed.]

Cal—>Nev

* * *

At the outset, Smith was paid a salary, plus a bonus which was determined at the end of each year. In the early part of January, 1941, Smith and his sons decided upon a fixed percentage arrangement, Smith suggesting that he be paid twenty percent of the profits. Since Smith was running the club at this time and was the "brains" of the organization, his sons had no objection. Percentage employment contracts were not uncommon in the gaming business. On January 15, 1941, Smith and his sons entered into a formal written contract, under which Smith would receive an annual salary of ten thousand dollars plus twenty percent of the yearly net profits accruing from the operation of the club.

K – 10,000 annually
+ 20% profits

* * *

* See Sugarman, "Contingent Compensation Agreement Leads to Disallowance of Corporate Deduction," 53 Calif.L.Rev. 1544 (1965); Ford and Page, "Reasonable Compensation: Continuous Controversy," 5 J.Corp.Tax 307 (1979); Footer and Sczepanski, "Current Factors Being Used to Determine When Compensation is Deductible as Reasonable," 32 Tax'n for Acct's. 226 (1984). Ed.

By 1952, Harolds Club was employing approximately eight hundred people. Harold was then an assistant manager and Raymond was in the bookkeeping department. The club also employed a business manager and a casino manager, both of whom reported directly to Smith. On several occasions between 1941 and 1956, one or the other of the three Smiths proposed to expand gaming activities into other areas. A majority vote decided against each of the proposals, Smith sometimes thereby getting his way, and sometimes not.

* * *

For the tax years 1952 through 1956 the annual net income of Harolds Club ranged from $1,367,029.88 to $2,098,906.01. The amounts paid to Smith for those years have already been indicated. Harold and Raymond each received salaries of from sixty thousand to seventy-five thousand dollars a year during this period.

Competitors testified that, in their opinion, the salary contract between Smith and Harolds Club was reasonable, and that he was worth all that was paid to him. As before noted however, Harolds Club does not here challenge the Tax Court's implicit finding that annual amounts paid to Smith in excess of ten thousand dollars plus fifteen percent of yearly net profits constituted unreasonable compensation for the years 1952 to 1956.

Petitioner predicates its claimed business expense deductions for the entire amounts paid to Smith during these years upon section 162(a) of the 1954 Code and section 23(a)(1)(A) of the 1939 Code.[1] Since the amount of compensation was contingent upon the amount of net profits of the business, petitioner also relied on Treasury Regulations 111, § 29.23(a)(6) and Treasury Regulations 118, § 39.23(a)(6) for the years 1952 and 1953, and Treasury Regulations § 1.162–7(b) for the remaining years.[2]

Under the quoted regulations contingent compensation, generally speaking, should be allowed as a deduction even though it may prove to be greater than the amount which would ordinarily be paid, if paid pursuant to a "free bargain" between the employer and the individual, and if the contract for compensation was reasonable under the circumstances "existing at the date when the contract for services was made."

The Tax Court determined that the amount paid to Smith as compensation in the years 1952 to 1956, under the contract for contingent compensation, was greater than the amount which would ordinarily be paid in those years, a conclusion which is not here disputed. The Court then proceeded to determine whether the deduction was nevertheless allowable under Regulation § 1.162–7(b), because such compensation resulted from a "free bargain" which, when entered into, was reasonable. It concluded that the 1941 salary agreement was not the result of a "free bargain" within the meaning of the quoted regulation, and that therefore reasonableness must be judged as of the time the

1. [I.R.C. § 162(a)(1) is omitted. Ed.]   2. [Reg. § 1.162–7(b)(2) and (3) are omitted. Ed.]

compensation was paid. In reaching this conclusion the Court placed primary reliance upon the family relationship between Smith and his employers in 1941, and circumstances indicating that he dominated them at that time.[3]

In contesting this conclusion petitioner first points out that the Commissioner, after audit, agreed that the salaries paid to Smith under the 1941 formula in the years 1941 through 1949 were reasonable. Petitioner reasons from this that if the contract was reasonable and entitled to recognition when the owners-sons were younger and more likely to be dominated by their father than when they themselves were over forty, "* * * it would seem that logically the contract would not become unreasonable as the domination abated."

The precise question before us, however, is not as to the Tax Court determination concerning the reasonableness of the contract at any particular time, but as to its determination that the contract was not the result of a "free bargain" in 1941. The Internal Revenue Service had no occasion to look into the latter question until it first determined that the compensation was unreasonable for a particular tax year. Since the agency determined that the compensation was in fact reasonable for the years 1941 through 1949, it made no determination for those years as to whether the 1941 contract resulted from a "free bargain." [4]

IRS held compensation was reasonable

Tax Ct held K was not free bargain

Petitioner next contends that the Tax Court erred in attributing adverse significance to the family relationship between Smith and the 1941 owners of the business, in view of the fact that the owners-sons were adults and legally competent.

The question of whether the 1941 compensation agreement resulted from a "free bargain," is one of fact. In determining that question all circumstances bearing upon the ability of the employer to exercise a free and independent judgment are relevant.

One such circumstance is family relationship. The fact that Harold and Raymond were competent adults at the time they entered into the 1941 contract tends to minimize the significance which should be attached to the fact, standing alone, that they were the sons of Smith. But that fact did not stand alone. The record fully supports the Tax Court's finding that Smith dominated the sons, notwithstanding their

3. The Tax Court said, in part:

"In view of the family relationship existing between Harold and Raymond, the employers, and Smith, the employee; the ages and experience of the employers; Smith's domination over his sons in the past; the respective roles and duties of the sons and Smith in Harolds Club's creation and organization; and the reasons offered by Harold and Raymond for agreeing to Smith's 'suggested' compensation, we cannot say that petitioner has established that the original employment contract (1941) between Harolds Club and Smith was the product of a free bargain or arm's-length transaction."

4. Even if the reasonableness of Smith's compensation were here in question we fail to see how its solution is promoted by considering the likelihood that Smith's domination decreased as the years went by. Reasonableness of compensation for services depends upon the value of the services rendered. Under that test, compensation could be reasonable or unreasonable wholly apart from any factor of domination.

adulthood and competency. Indeed, the latter finding is not challenged on this review. Where there is such domination, lack of abililty to bargain freely may exist even as between competent adults.

Petitioner asserts that in concluding that the 1941 agreement did not result from a free bargain, the Tax Court applied a standard which is the exact and precise opposite of the correct standard. Petitioner asserts that the statute permitting business expense deductions is designed to prevent deduction for salaries in excess of the employee's true worth. The Tax Court therefore erred, petitioner urges, in accepting the Commissioner's argument that Smith's services were so essential to the success of his sons' business that the sons could not bargain with him on equal terms, hence the "bargain" was not "free." Under this reasoning, petitioner argues, only drones can bargain freely for their compensation.

Whatever the Commissioner may have argued in the Tax Court, we find no indication that the Court predicated its resolution of the "free bargain" question upon the theory that the sons felt obliged to enter into the 1941 agreement because of their belief that Smith's services were indispensable. The only court finding which might imply such a view is the statement that since Smith was running the club in 1941 and was the "brains" of the organization, his sons had no objection to the percentage arrangement. In our opinion this finding tends more to show that the sons surrendered their judgments to that of their father's because he exerted control rather than because he was indispensable.[5]

The Tax Court did consider the value of Smith's services in deciding what compensation for the years in question was reasonable. But the question now under discussion is the entirely different one of whether the 1941 contract resulted from a free bargain.

Petitioner argues, additionally, that apart from the above-discussed regulation pertaining to contingent compensation, the statute does not authorize the "double taxation" of payments made solely as compensation for personal services and not as disguised dividends or as the purchase price of property. By "double taxation" petitioner refers to the fact that Smith has paid personal income taxes on the full amount paid to him and, to the extent that such compensation is not allowed as a business expense deduction, petitioner must also pay a corporate income tax thereon.

Petitioner acknowledges that there is good reason to set reasonable bounds upon ostensible salaries paid to employees who are also shareholders or who are selling property to the corporation. Regulation

---

5. As indicated in the Tax Court findings quoted in note 3, one of the factors which the Court took into account in determining that the 1941 bargain was not "free," was "＊ ＊ ＊ the reasons offered by Harold and Raymond for agreeing to Smith's 'suggested' compensation, ＊ ＊ ＊"

We have examined that part of Harold's and Raymond's testimony contained in the excerpted record before us and find nothing therein to indicate that they agreed to the 1941 arrangement because of Smith's indispensability.

§ 1.162–7(b)(1), quoted in the margin, gives recognition to this need.[6] But petitioner argues that Congress did not intend to authorize the Commissioner to sit in judgment on salaries paid to nonshareholders. This is true, petitioner reasons, because such salaries are, unless the disguised purchase price of property, paid solely to obtain personal services. No revenue purpose is served, petitioner urges, because the progressive tax structure on individuals goes higher than the corporate tax rate, consequently what is gained in corporate income taxes will be more than lost in reduced personal income taxes.

Whatever practical effect the disallowance of salary as a corporate business expense deduction may have upon the tax revenue,[7] the statute in question admits of no such qualification. Under section 162(a)(1) of the 1954 Code, only "reasonable" compensation is made deductible. Petitioner's thesis would read "reasonable" out of the statute, for it would sanction disallowance only where the payment was not compensation at all, but was really disguised dividends, property payments or gifts. The Tax Court, however, has been sustained in disallowing what was held to be unreasonable compensation which could not have been a dividend or purchase price of property. See Patton v. Commissioner, 6 Cir., 168 F.2d 28.

The fact that the regulation quoted in note 6 singles out cases where a salary is disallowed in part because it is a disguised dividend or payment for property does not alter the requirement that the salary must be reasonable to be deductible. The regulation purports only to give illustrative examples of the practical application of the Code and not to define the limits of its application.

Petitioner contends that to interpret and apply the Code section as is here done makes it a regulatory provision to control salary and wage scales. Congress, petitioner argues, intended no such regulation.

Section 162(a)(1) is designed to define which expenses are deductible. To the extent that a salary is unreasonable it is not deductible. The disallowance of a deduction for an unreasonable salary with resulting adverse tax effects to the business has a regulatory effect to the extent that it discourages the employer from disbursing, as salaries to employees what, if disbursed at all, should be distributed to such employees or others as dividends or gifts. But this regulatory effect is unavoidably incident to the tax scheme whereby only necessary business expenses may be deducted in calculating the employer's income tax.

Other arguments advanced by petitioner have been examined but are without merit.

---

6. [Reg. § 1.162–7(b)(1) is omitted. Ed.]

7. Petitioner's argument as to the practical effect of the Tax Court ruling is open to question. Corporate net income withheld from disbursement as compensation for services, because in excess of reasonable compensation, would ordinarily be distributed, to a large extent, as dividends. To this extent it would be subject to both corporate and personal income taxes, whereas if disbursed as compensation for services, with an offsetting business expense deduction, it would be subject only to personal income taxes.

The Tax Court's construction of the Code provisions and regulations is correct and its determination based thereon is affirmed.

NOTE

Oftentimes when ownership of a corporation changes hands through a takeover, merger, or otherwise, a key executive may "bail out," either voluntarily or involuntarily. His landing back into the job market may be cushioned by a stack of dollar bills, required by an employment contract granting him considerable severance pay under such circumstances, a "parachute payment." When generous, these severance packages are known as golden parachutes.[1] The Tax Reform Act of 1984[2] let the air out of the golden parachutes by adding to the Code Section 280G which prohibits a Section 162 deduction to the payor corporation for excess parachute payments[3] and by tagging the recipient of such payments with a 20 percent excise tax[4] in addition to income and social security taxes.

A parachute payment[5] is any payment in the nature of compensation made to a "disqualified" individual. A disqualified individual is an employee, independent contractor or other person specified in regulations who performs personal services for the corporation *and* who is an officer, shareholder, or highly compensated individual[6] of such corporation.[7] The payment must be contingent[8] on a change in the ownership or effective control of a corporation, and the aggregate present value[9] of all such payments[10] must equal or exceed three times the disqualified individual's base amount.[11] A disqualified individual's base

1. Advisory Comm. on Tender Offers, U.S. Sec. and Exchange Comm., Report of Recommendations (July 8, 1983).

2. P.L. No. 98–369, 98 Cong., 2d Sess. § 67 (1984). See Hood and Benge, "Golden Parachute Agreements: Reasonable Compensation or Disguised Bribery?" 53 U.M.K.C.L.Rev. 199 (1985).

3. I.R.C. § 280G(a). See text at note 14, infra.

4. I.R.C. § 4999.

5. I.R.C. § 280G(b)(2)(A). A compensation payment to a disqualified individual automatically qualifies as a parachute payment if it violates any general enforced securities laws or regulations. I.R.C. § 280G(b)(2)(B).

6. A highly compensated individual is an individual who is a member of the group consisting of the highest paid 1 percent of the employees of the corporation or, if less, the highest paid 250 employees of the corporation. I.R.C. § 280G(c).

7. I.R.C. § 280G(c). All members of the same affiliated group (defined in I.R.C. § 1504, determined without regard to I.R.C. § 1504(b)), are treated as a single

corporation for purposes of the golden parachute provision. I.R.C. § 280G(d)(5). Thus, any person who is an officer or highly compensated individual of any member of the affiliated group is treated as an officer or highly compensated individual of such single corporation. I.R.C. § 280G(d)(5).

8. I.R.C. § 280G(b)(2)(A)(i). If payments are made pursuant to a contract formed or amended within one year of a change of ownership they are presumed to be contingent upon the change. I.R.C. § 280G(b)(2)(C). The amendment must be significant. H.Rep. No. 98–861, 98th Cong., 2d Sess. 851 (1984).

9. Present value is determined by using a discount rate equal to 120% of the § 1274(d) applicable Federal rate, compounded semiannually. I.R.C. § 280G(d)(4).

10. Transfers of property are treated as payments and are taken into account at fair market value. I.R.C. § 280G(d)(3).

11. I.R.C. § 280G(b)(2)(A)(ii). The base amount is defined in § 280G(b)(3)(A) and (d)(1) and (2).

amount is essentially the average annual income received from the corporation for the five years preceding the taxable year in which the contingency occurs.[12]

If a parachute payment meets the threshold requirements above, then to the extent that the payment in any year exceeds the individual's base amount [13] (not three times that amount) the excess is presumed to be an unreasonable amount of compensation.[14] The payor can rebut, through clear and convincing evidence, the presumption of unreasonableness for payments for (1) personal services to be rendered on or after the date of the change in ownership or control or (2) personal services actually rendered before the date of the change in ownership or control.[15] To the extent that the taxpayer fails to rebut the presumption that the payment is unreasonable compensation, the Section 162 deduction is disallowed.[16]

The statute provides exemptions from the golden parachute rules for payments to disqualified individuals from two types of corporations. The first type of corporation from which an exempt payment can be made is one that was, immediately before the change in control, a small business corporation as defined in Section 1361(b).[17] The second type of corporation from which an exempt payment can be made is one which has no stock, immediately before the change in control, readily tradable on an established securities market.[18] In addition, for this second type of corporation, shareholder approval must be obtained with respect to the payment.[19] Payments from either type of corporation are not taken into account in determining whether a payment exceeds three times the base amount.[20]

The section also provides an exemption from the golden parachute rules for payments from: (1) a qualified pension, profit-sharing, or stock bonus plan described in Section 401(a), (2) a qualified annuity plan described in Section 403(a) or (3) a simplified employee pension, as

---

12. I.R.C. § 280G(b)(3)(A) and (d)(1) and (2). If there is more than one parachute payment the base amount is allocated among the payments. I.R.C. § 280G(b)(3)(B).

13. I.R.C. § 280G(b)(1).

14. I.R.C. § 280G(b)(4).

15. Id. If the payments are reasonable compensation for personal services to be rendered on or after the date of change in ownership or control, the payment is not taken into consideration in determining whether a payment exceeds three times the base amount. I.R.C. §§ 280G(b)(4)(A) and 280G(b)(2). However, if the payments are reasonable compensation for personal services actually rendered before the date of the change in ownership or control, the payments are first offset against the base amount and then against the parachute payments. I.R.C. § 280G(b)(4).

16. I.R.C. § 280G(b)(4). Cf. I.R.C. § 4999(b) and (c)(2).

17. I.R.C. § 280G(b)(5)(A)(i). I.R.C. § 1361(b)(1)(C) is disregarded in determining whether the § 1361(b) definition is satisfied.

18. I.R.C. § 280G(b)(5)(A)(ii)(I).

19. I.R.C. § 280G(b)(5)(A)(ii)(II). The shareholder approval requirement is met with respect to any payment if (1) the payment is approved by a vote of shareholders owning more than 75 percent of the voting power of all outstanding stock immediately before the change in control and (2) there was adequate disclosure to all shareholders of the material facts concerning a payment that would be a parachute payment without the exception. I.R.C. § 280G(b)(5)(B).

20. I.R.C. § 280G(b)(2).

defined in Section 408(k).[21] Such payments are not taken into account in determining whether a payment exceeds three times the base amount.[22]

The following example taken from the legislative history [23] demonstrates the computational aspects of Section 280G:

> * * * Assume that the disqualified individual's base amount is $100,000. Assume further that a payment totalling $400,000, which is contingent on a change in control, is made to the disqualified individual on the date of the change. Under the Act, parachute payments total $400,000, and the provisions apply because $400,000 exceeds $300,000 (3 times the base amount). Excess parachute payments are as much as $300,000 ($400,000 less $100,000, the base amount). Assume that the taxpayer by clear and convincing evidence establishes that reasonable compensation for services compensated for by the parachute payment totals $150,000. Under the Act, excess parachute payments equal $250,000 ($300,000 less ($150,000 less $100,000)).[24]

If, in the above example, payments contingent on the change in ownership or control totalled $290,000, the provisions of the Act would not apply. In that case, those payments would not equal or exceed $300,000 (3 times the base amount). This result would follow even if the taxpayer was unable to establish that any of the $290,000 was reasonable compensation for personal services actually rendered. The tax consequences of the payment of the $290,000 would be determined under prior law.

PROBLEM

Employee is the majority shareholder (248 of 250 outstanding shares) and president of Corporation. Shortly after Corporation was incorporated, its Directors adopted a resolution establishing a contingent compensation contract for Employee. The plan provided for Corporation to pay Employee a nominal salary plus an annual bonus based on a percentage of Corporation's net income. In the early years of the plan, payments to Employee averaged $50,000 annually. In recent years, Corporation's profits have increased substantially and, as a consequence, Employee has received payments averaging more than $200,000 per year.

21. I.R.C. § 280G(b)(6).

22. I.R.C. § 280G(b)(2).

23. See H.Rep. No. 98–861, 98th Cong., 2d Sess. 852 (1984).

24. It must be assumed in this example that the $150,000 payment is for services rendered before the date of the change in ownership or control. Thus, the amount that the disqualified individual can prove is reasonable compensation is first offset against the base amount, then against the parachute payments. I.R.C. § 280G(b)(4). This requires the disqualified individual first to justify his base amount, usually his annual salary. In the example it is assumed that the disqualified individual also establishes that his $100,000 annual salary is reasonable compensation. Ed.

(a) What are Corporation's possible alternative tax treatments for the payments?

(b) What factors should be considered in determining the proper tax treatment for the payments?

(c) The problem assumes Employee *always* owned 248 of the Corporation's 250 shares. Might it be important to learn that the compensation contract was made at a time when Employee held only 10 out of the 250 outstanding shares?

2. TRAVEL "AWAY FROM HOME" *

Internal Revenue Code: Sections 162(a)(2); 274(n)(1). See Sections 162(h); 274(c), (h) and (m)(1).

Regulations: Sections 1.162–2; 1.262–1(b)(5).

ROSENSPAN v. UNITED STATES **

United States Court of Appeals, Second Circuit, 1971.
438 F.2d 905, cert. denied 404 U.S. 864, 92 S.Ct. 54, 1971.

FRIENDLY, Circuit Judge: This appeal is from the dismissal on the merits of an action for refund of income taxes, brought in the District Court for the Eastern District of New York. The taxes were paid as a result of the Commissioner's disallowance of deductions for unreimbursed expenses for meals and lodging allegedly incurred "while away from home in the pursuit of a trade or business," I.R.C. § 162(a)(2), in 1962 and 1964.

Plaintiff, Robert Rosenspan, was a jewelry salesman who worked on a commission basis, paying his own traveling expenses without reimbursement. In 1962 he was employed by one and in 1964 by two New York City jewelry manufacturers. For some 300 days a year he traveled by automobile through an extensive sales territory in the Middle West, where he would stay at hotels and motels and eat at restaurants. Five or six times a year he would return to New York and spend several days at his employers' offices. There he would perform a variety of services essential to his work—cleaning up his sample case, checking orders, discussing customers' credit problems, recommending changes in stock, attending annual staff meetings, and the like.

Rosenspan had grown [up] in Brooklyn and during his marriage, had maintained a family home there. After his wife's death in 1948, he

---

* See Tallant, Logan and Milton, "The Travelling Taxpayer: A Rational Framework for His Deductions," 29 U.Fla.L.R. 119 (1976); Klein, "Income Taxation and Commuting Expenses: Tax Policy and the Need for Nonsimplistic Analysis of 'Simple' Problems," 54 Cornell L.Rev. 871 (1969); Klein, "The Deductibility of Transportation Expenses of a Combination Business and Pleasure Trip—A Conceptual Analysis," 18 Stan.L.Rev. 1099 (1966); Rose, "The Deductibility of Daily Transportation Expenses To and From Distant Temporary Worksites," 36 Vanderbilt L.Rev. 541 (1983).

** Note, "Section 162(a)(2): Resolving the Tax Home Dispute," 2 Va.Tax.Rev. 153 (1982).

abandoned this. From that time through the tax years in question he used his brother's Brooklyn home as a personal residential address, keeping some clothing and other belongings there, and registering, voting, and filing his income tax returns from that address. The stipulation of facts states that, on his trips to New York City, "out of a desire not to abuse his welcome at his brother's home, he stayed more often" at an inn near the John F. Kennedy Airport. It recites also that "he generally spent his annual vacations in Brooklyn, where his children resided, and made an effort to return to Brooklyn whenever possible," but affords no further indication where he stayed on such visits. In 1961 he changed the registration of his automobile from New York to Ohio, giving as his address the address of a cousin in Cincinnati, where he also received mail, in order to obtain cheaper automobile insurance. Rosenspan does not contend that he had a permanent abode or residence in Brooklyn or anywhere else.

The basis for the Commissioner's disallowance of a deduction for Rosenspan's meals and lodging while in his sales territory was that he had no "home" to be "away from" while traveling. Not denying that this would be true if the language of § 162(a)(2) were given its ordinary meaning, Rosenspan claimed that for tax purposes his home was his "business headquarters," to wit, New York City where his employers maintained their offices, and relied upon the Commissioner's long advocacy of this concept of a "tax home," see e.g., G.C.M. 23672, 1943 Cum.Bull. 66–67. The Commissioner responded that although in most circumstances "home" means "business headquarters," it should be given its natural meaning of a permanent abode or residence for purposes of the problem here presented. Rosenspan says the Commissioner is thus trying to have it both ways.

The provision of the Internal Revenue Code applicable for 1962 read:

> "SEC. 162. TRADE OR BUSINESS EXPENSES.
>
> (a) In general.—There shall be allowed as a deduction all the ordinary and necessary expenses paid or incurred during the taxable year in carrying on any trade or business, including—
>
> * * *
>
> (2) traveling expenses (including the entire amount expended for meals and lodging) while away from home in the pursuit of a trade or business; * * *"

For 1964 the statute remained the same except for the interpolation in the parenthesis after "lodging" of the words "other than amounts which are lavish or extravagant under the circumstances"—a change not relevant in this case.

What is now § 162(a)(2) was brought into the tax structure by § 214 of the Revenue Act of 1921, 42 Stat. 239. Prior to that date, § 214 had permitted the deduction of "ordinary and necessary expenses paid or incurred * * * in carrying on any trade or business," Revenue

Act of 1918, 40 Stat. 1066 (1918), without further specification. In a regulation, the Treasury interpreted the statute to allow deduction of "traveling expenses, including railroad fares, and meals and lodging *in an amount in excess of any expenditures ordinarily required for such purposes when at home,*" T.D. 3101, amending Article 292 of Regulations 45, 3 Cum.Bull. 191 (1920) (emphasis supplied). A formula was provided for determining what expenditures were thus "ordinarily required"; the taxpayer was to compute such items as rent, grocery bills, light, etc. and servant hire for the periods when he was away from home, and divide this by the number of members of his family. Mim. 2688, 4 Cum.Bull. 209–11 (1921). The puzzlement of the man without a home was dealt with in a cryptic pronouncement, O.D. 905, 4 Cum.Bull. 212 (1921):

Living expenses paid by a single taxpayer who has no home and is continuously employed on the road may not be deducted in computing net income.

The 1921 amendment, inserting what is now § 162(a)(2)'s allowance of a deduction for the entire amount of qualified meals and lodging, stemmed from a request of the Treasury based on the difficulty of administering the "excess" provision of its regulation. See United States v. Correll, 389 U.S. 299, 301 n. 6, 88 S.Ct. 445 (1967). While the taxpayer cites statements of legislators in the 1921 Congress that the amendment would provide "a measure of justice" to commercial travelers,[1] there is nothing to indicate that the members making or hearing these remarks were thinking of the unusual situation of the traveler without a home. There is likewise nothing to indicate that the Treasury sought, or that Congress meant to require, any change in the ruling that disallowed deductions for living expenses in such a case. The objective was to eliminate the need for computing the expenses "ordinarily required" at home by a taxpayer who had one, and the words used were appropriate to that end. If we were to make the unlikely assumption that the problem of the homeless commercial traveler ever entered the legislators' minds, the language they adopted was singularly inept to resolve it in the way for which plaintiff contends. Thus, if the literal words of the statute were decisive, the Government would clearly prevail on the simple ground that a taxpayer cannot be "away from home" unless he has a home from which to be away, cf. Haddleton, Traveling Expenses "Away from Home," 17 Tax.L.Rev. 261, 263, 286 (1962); 49 Va.L.Rev. 125, 126–28 (1963). Although that is our ultimate conclusion, the Supreme Court has wisely admonished that "More than a dictionary is thus required to understand the provision here involved, and no appeal to the 'plain language' of the section can obviate the need for further statutory construction," United States v. Correll, supra, 389 U.S. at 304 n. 16, 88 S.Ct. at 448. We turn, therefore, in the first instance to the Court's decisions.

---

1. Representative Hawley, a member of the Committee on Ways and Means, 61 Cong.Rec. 5201 (1921); see also the re-marks of Senator Walsh, a member of the Committee on Finance, 61 Cong.Rec. 6673 (1921).

The initial Supreme Court decision bearing on our problem is C.I.R. v. Flowers, 326 U.S. 465, 66 S.Ct. 250 (1946). Flowers, a lawyer, had a "home" in the conventional sense in Jackson, Mississippi, but his principal post of business was at the main office of his employer, the Gulf, Mobile & Ohio Railroad in Mobile, Alabama. Flowers sought to deduct the cost of transportation for his trips to Mobile and the meal and lodging expenses which he incurred in that city. In upholding the Commissioner's disallowance of these deductions, the Court said that "three conditions must thus be satisfied before a traveling expense deduction may be made" under what was substantially the present statute, 326 U.S. at 470, 66 S.Ct. at 252. These were:

(1) The expense must be a reasonable and necessary traveling expense, as that term is generally understood. This includes such items as transportation fares and food and lodging expenses incurred while traveling.

(2) The expense must be incurred "while away from home."

(3) The expense must be incurred in pursuit of business. This means that there must be a direct connection between the expenditure and the carrying on of the trade or business of the taxpayer or of his employer. Moreover, such an expenditure must be necessary or appropriate to the development and pursuit of the business or trade.

It noted that "The meaning of the word 'home' * * * with reference to a taxpayer residing in one city and working in another has engendered much difficulty and litigation," with the Tax Court and the administrative officials having "consistently defined it as the equivalent of the taxpayer's place of business" and two courts of appeals having rejected that view and "confined the term to the taxpayer's actual residence," 326 U.S. at 471–72, 66 S.Ct. at 253. The Court found it "unnecessary here to enter into or to decide this conflict," 326 U.S. at 472. This was because the Tax Court had properly concluded "that the necessary relationship between the expenditures and the railroad's business was lacking." The railroad's interest was in having Mr. Flowers at its headquarters in Mobile; it "gained nothing" from his decision to continue living in Jackson, 326 U.S. at 472–74, 66 S.Ct. at 253–254; hence, the third condition the *Flowers* Court had enunciated as a prerequisite to deductibility was absent. Mr. Justice Rutledge dissented. He did not believe that when Congress used the word "home," it meant "business headquarters," and thought the case presented no other question, 326 U.S. at 474, 66 S.Ct. 250. The most that Rosenspan can extract from *Flowers* is that it did not decide *against* his contention that the employer's business headquarters is the employee's tax home.

The Court's next venture into this area was in Peurifoy v. C.I.R., 358 U.S. 59, 79 S.Ct. 104 (1958). That case dealt with three construction workers employed at a site in Kinston, North Carolina, for periods of 20½, 12½, and 8½ months respectively, who maintained permanent residences elsewhere in the state. The Tax Court had allowed them deductions for board and lodging during the employment at Kinston and expenses in regaining their residences when they left, apparently of their own volition and before completion of the project.[2] The Fourth Circuit had reversed, C.I.R. v. Peurifoy, 254 F.2d 483 (1957). After having granted certiorari "to consider certain questions as to the application of § 23(a)(1)(A) of the Internal Revenue Code of 1939 raised by the course of decisions in the lower courts since our decision in Commissioner v. Flowers," 358 U.S. at 59–60, 79 S.Ct. at 105, the Court announced in a *per curiam* opinion that it had "found it inappropriate to consider such questions." It read *Flowers* as establishing that "a taxpayer is entitled to deduct unreimbursed travel expenses * * * only when they are required by 'the exigencies of business,'" a "general rule" which the majority seemed to feel would mandate disallowance of the deductions under consideration. However, the Court went on to acknowledge an exception to this rule engrafted by the Tax Court, which would have allowed the claimed deductions if the taxpayer's employment were shown to be "temporary" rather than "indefinite" or "indeterminate." Nevertheless, even within this framework, the majority thought that the Court of Appeals had been justified in holding the Tax Court's finding of temporary employment to be clearly erroneous. Mr. Justice Douglas, joined by Justices Black and Whittaker, dissented. Adopting Mr. Justice Rutledge's position in *Flowers*, they disagreed "with the Commissioner's contention that 'home' is synonymous with the situs of the employer's business." While adhering to "the exigencies of business" test announced in *Flowers* they thought this requirement was satisfied by the fact that, in view of the impracticability of construction workers' moving their homes from job to job, "the expenses incurred were necessary, not to the business of the contractor for whom the taxpayers worked, but for the taxpayers themselves in order to carry on their chosen trade," 358 U.S. at 62–63 n. 6, 79 S.Ct. at 107. While the three dissenting Justices thus rejected the Commissioner's identification of "home" with "the situs of the employer's business," the majority did not adopt it and, so far as our problem is concerned, that matter remained in the state of indecision where *Flowers* had left it.

We come finally to C.I.R. v. Stidger, 386 U.S. 287, 87 S.Ct. 1065 (1967), where the Court sustained the disallowance of the expense for meals incurred by a Marine Corps captain who had been assigned to a base in Japan, while his wife and children—prohibited from accompanying him to that post—remained near his previous duty station in California. After noting that in this case there could be no question of the "direct connection between the expenditure and the carrying on of the trade or business of the taxpayer or of his employer," 386 U.S. at 289–90, 87 S.Ct. at 1067, the Court reviewed the continuing disagreement among the circuits over the Commissioner's view "that 'home'

---

2. The Court of Appeals explicitly so found with respect to two of the three. 254 F.2d 483, 485 (4 Cir.1957).

meant the taxpayer's principal place of business or employment whether or not it coincided with his place of residence,"[3] and took note of a ruling of the Board of Tax Appeals that members of Congress could not deduct living expenses incurred in Washington, D.C.,[4] and of Congress' response by enacting a special provision making the legislator's place of residence within the district that he represents his home but limiting the amount of deductible living expenses to $3,000, 66 Stat. 467 (1952), now codified in I.R.C. § 162(a). However, the Court again found it unnecessary either to approve or to disapprove the Commissioner's interpretation of "home," since it found that "in the context of the military taxpayer, the Commissioner's position has a firmer foundation." 386 U.S. at 292, 87 S.Ct. at 1069. This built "on the terminology employed by the military services to categorize various assignments and tours of duty, and also on the language and policy of the statutory provisions prescribing travel and transportation allowance for military personnel," id. The Court particularly stressed "the fact that Congress traditionally has provided a special system of tax-free allowances for military personnel," 386 U.S. at 294, 87 S.Ct. at 1070. Mr. Justice Douglas, who had written the dissent in *Peurifoy*, again joined by Justice Black and now by Justice Fortas, dissented. He thought it was "clear that home means residence, with the qualification that a taxpayer should establish his residence as near to his place of employment as is reasonable," 386 U.S. at 297, 87 S.Ct. at 1071.[5] The fact that Congress provides special allowances for military personnel did not, in Justice Douglas' view, call for what he deemed an unnatural reading of § 162(a)(2) even in that context.

Proper analysis of the problem has been beclouded, and the Government's position in this case has been made more difficult than it need be, by the Commissioner's insistence that "home" means "business headquarters," despite the Supreme Court's having thrice declined to endorse this, and its rejection by several courts of appeals, see Flowers v. C.I.R., 148 F.2d 163 (5 Cir.1945), rev'd on other grounds, 326 U.S. 465, 66 S.Ct. 250 (1946); United States v. LeBlanc, 278 F.2d 571 (5 Cir.1960); Burns v. Gray, 287 F.2d 698 (6 Cir.1961); James v. United States, 308 F.2d 204 (9 Cir.1962). But cf. C.I.R. v. Mooneyhan, 404 F.2d 522 (6 Cir.1968), cert. denied, 394 U.S. 1001, 89 S.Ct. 1593 (1969); Wills v. C.I.R., 411 F.2d 537, 540 (9 Cir.1969). When Congress uses such a nontechnical word in a tax statute, presumably it wants administrators and courts to read it in the way that ordinary people would understand, and not "to draw on some unexpressed spirit outside the bounds of the normal meaning of words," Addison v. Holly Hill Fruit Prods., Inc., 322

---

3. Although the opinion lists this circuit as having subscribed to the Commissioner's definition of "home," citing O'Toole v. C.I.R., 243 F.2d 302 (2 Cir.1957), and a sentence in our per curiam opinion does read that way, the facts of O'Toole presented a typical Flowers situation and the ratio decidendi was the same as in that case, namely, that "The job, not the tax-

payer's pattern of living, must require the traveling expenses," 243 F.2d at 303.

4. Lindsay v. C.I.R., 34 B.T.A. 840 (1936). This had long been the Commissioner's position. O.D. 864, 4 Cum.Bull. 211 (1921).

5. Perhaps more accurately, he should be treated as if he had done so.

U.S. 607, 617, 64 S.Ct. 1215 (1944). The construction which the Commissioner has long advocated not only violates this principle but is unnecessary for the protection of the revenue that he seeks. That purpose is served, without any such distortion of language, by the third condition laid down in *Flowers,* supra, 326 U.S. at 470, 66 S.Ct. at 252, namely, "that there must be a direct connection between the expenditure and the carrying on of the trade or business of the taxpayer or of his employer" and that "such an expenditure must be necessary or appropriate to the development and pursuit of the business or trade." These requirements were enough to rule out a deduction for Flowers' lodging and meals while in Mobile even if he was "away from home" while there. The deduction would not have been available to his fellow workers living in that city who obtained similar amenities in their homes or even in the very restaurants that Flowers patronized, and Flowers was no more compelled by business to be away from his home while in Mobile than were other employees of the railroad who lived there.

Since the Commissioner's definition of "home" as "business headquarters" will produce the same result as the third *Flowers* condition in the overwhelming bulk of cases arising under § 162(a)(2), courts have often fallen into the habit of referring to it as a ground or an alternate ground of decision, as this court did in O'Toole v. C.I.R., 243 F.2d 302 (1957), see fn. 3. But examination of the string of cases cited by plaintiff as endorsing the "business headquarters" test has revealed almost none, aside from the unique situations involving military personnel considered above, which cannot be explained on the basis that the taxpayer had no permanent residence, or was not away from it, or maintained it in a locale apart from where he regularly worked as a matter of personal choice rather than business necessity.[6] This principle likewise affords a satisfactory rationale for the "temporary" employment cases, see 49 Va.L.Rev., supra, at 162–63. When an assignment is truly temporary, it would be unreasonable to expect the taxpayer to move his home, and the expenses are thus compelled by the "exigencies of business"; when the assignment is "indefinite" or "indeterminate," the situation is different and, if the taxpayer decides to

---

6. Whether the "personal choice" principle has not sometimes been pressed too far is another matter. The case of a Congressman, see fn. 4, may have been one such instance. It is also hard to be completely satisfied with the distinction between Barhill v. C.I.R., 148 F.2d 913 (4 Cir.1945), disallowing meals and lodging deductions while in the state capital to justices of the Supreme Court of North Carolina who spent approximately 7 months a year there, but maintained their residences elsewhere, in deference to a custom that, at the time of selection, the justices should be fairly distributed throughout the state and a decision allowing such a deduction in the case of a justice of the Supreme Court of Louisiana who spent 9 months at the Court's headquarters in New Orleans but who, in contrast to the unwritten North Carolina practice, was required by the state constitution to maintain his residence in his own parish. United States v. LeBlanc, 278 F.2d 571 (5 Cir.1960). England v. United States, 345 F.2d 414 (7 Cir.1965), cert. denied, 382 U.S. 986, 88 S.Ct. 537 (1966), is another case in which the "personal choice" principle scarcely provides a satisfactory basis of decision if it suffices that the expenses be necessary to the taxpayer-employee's "trade or business" as distinguished from his employer's. As to this, see the discussion in the text, infra.

leave his home where it was, disallowance is appropriate, not because he has acquired a "tax home" in some lodging house or hotel at the worksite but because his failure to move his home was for his personal convenience and not compelled by business necessity. Under the facts here presented, we need not decide whether in the case of a taxpayer who is not self-employed the "exigencies of business" which compel the traveling expenses away from home refer solely to the business of his employer or to the business of the taxpayer as well. We note only that the latter contention is surely not foreclosed by decisions to date. See Peurifoy v. C.I.R., 358 U.S., supra, at 62–63, 79 S.Ct. at 107, n. 6 (Douglas, J., dissenting); Rev.Rul. 60–189, 1960–1 Cum.Bull. 60; see generally 49 Va.L.Rev., supra, at 136–45; and Trent v. C.I.R., 291 F.2d 669, and cases cited, especially at 674 (2 Cir.1961).

Shifting the thrust of analysis from the search for a fictional "tax home" to a questioning of the business necessity for incurring the expense away from the taxpayer's permanent residence thus does not upset the basic structure of the decisions which have dealt with this problem. Compare 49 Va.L.Rev., supra, at 162–63, with Haddleton, supra, at 286. It merely adopts an approach that better effectuates the congressional intent in establishing the deduction and thus provides a sounder conceptual framework for analysis while following the ordinary meaning of language. Cf. 19 U.Chi.L.Rev. 534, 545 (1952); 49 Va.L.Rev., supra, at 163. We see no basis whatever for believing that when the 1921 Congress eliminated the requirement for determining the excess of the costs of meals and lodging while on the road over what they would have been at home, it meant to disallow a deduction to someone who had the expense of maintaining a home from which business took him away but possessed no business headquarters. By the same token we find it impossible to read the words "away from home" out of the statute, as Rosenspan, in effect, would have us do and allow a deduction to a taxpayer who had no "home" in the ordinary sense. The limitation reflects congressional recognition of the rational distinction between the taxpayer with a permanent residence—whose travel costs represent a duplication of expense or at least an incidence of expense which the existence of his permanent residence demonstrates he would not incur absent business compulsion—and the taxpayer without such a residence. Cf. James v. United States, supra, 308 F.2d at 207. We fail to see how Rosenspan's occasional trips to New York City, assuming for the sake of argument that his "business headquarters" was in New York rather than in his sales territory, differentiate him economically from the homeless traveling salesman without even the modicum of a business headquarters Rosenspan is claimed to have possessed. Yet we approved disallowance of the deduction in such a case many years ago. Duncan v. C.I.R., 17 B.T.A. 1088 (1929), aff'd per curiam, 47 F.2d 1082 (2 Cir.1931), as the Ninth Circuit has done more recently, James v. United States, supra, 308 F.2d 204.

It is enough to decide this case that "home" means "home" and Rosenspan had none. He satisfied the first and third conditions of Flowers, supra, 326 U.S. at 470, 66 S.Ct. 250, but not, on our reading of the statute, the second. The judgment dismissing the complaint must therefore be affirmed.

REVENUE RULING 75–432 [1]
1975–2 Cum.Bull. 60.

The purpose of this Revenue Ruling is to update and restate, under the current statute and regulations, the position set forth in Rev.Rul. 54–497, 1954–2 C.B. 75, at 77–81, with regard to the principles applicable in determining when an employee may deduct expenses for meals and lodging incurred while traveling on business.

The courts in considering questions involving deductions for traveling expenses have frequently stated that each case must be decided on its own particular facts. Furthermore, there appears to be no single rule that will produce the correct result in all situations.

Section 162(a)(2) of the Internal Revenue Code of 1954 provides that a deduction shall be allowed for all the ordinary and necessary expenses paid or incurred during the taxable year in carrying on any trade or business, including traveling expenses (including amounts expended for meals and lodging other than amounts which are lavish or extravagant under the circumstances) while away from home in the pursuit of a trade or business. On the other hand, section 262 of the Code states that, except as otherwise expressly provided, no deduction shall be allowed for personal, living, or family expenses.

A taxpayer cannot deduct the cost of meals and lodging while performing duties at a principal place of business, even though the taxpayer maintains a permanent residence elsewhere. Congress did not intend to allow as a business expense those outlays that are not caused by the exigencies of the business but by the action of the taxpayer in having a home, for the taxpayer's convenience, at a distance from the business. Such expenditures are not essential for the conduct of the business and were not within the contemplation of Congress, which proceeded on the assumption that a person engaged in business would live within reasonable proximity of the business. See Barnhill v. Commissioner, 148 F.2d 913 (4th Cir.1945), 1945 C.B. 96; Commissioner v. Stidger, 386 U.S. 287 (1967), 1967–1 C.B. 32.

It is therefore the long-established position of the Internal Revenue Service that the "home" referred to in section 162(a)(2) of the Code as the place away from which traveling expenses must be incurred to be deductible is, as a general rule, the place at which the taxpayer conducts the trade or business. If the taxpayer is engaged in business at two or more separate locations, the "tax home" for purposes of section 162(a)(2) is located at the principal place of business during the

---

1. Prepared pursuant to Rev.Proc. 67–6, 1967–1 C.B. 576.

taxable year. Markey v. Commissioner, 490 F.2d 1249 (6th Cir.1974); Rev.Rul. 60–189, 1960–1 C.B. 60. It should, of course, be emphasized that the location of an employee's tax home is necessarily a question of fact that must be determined on the basis of the particular circumstances of each case.

In the rare case in which the employee has no identifiable principal place of business, but does maintain a regular place of abode in a real or substantial sense in a particular city from which the taxpayer is sent on temporary assignments, the tax home will be regarded as being that place of abode. This should be distinguished from the case of an itinerant worker with neither a regular place of business nor a regular place of abode. In such case, the home is considered to go along with the worker and therefore the worker does not travel away from home for purposes of section 162(a)(2) of the Code, and may not deduct the cost of meals or lodging. Rev.Rul. 73–529, 1973–2 C.B. 37; Rev.Rul. 71–247, 1971–1 C.B. 54.

The tax home rule may be illustrated by its application to railroad employees. The principal or regular post of duty of a member of a train crew is not regarded as being aboard the train, but at the terminal where such member ordinarily, or for an indefinite period (as distinguished from a temporary period, discussed below), begins and ends actual train runs. This terminal is referred to, for tax purposes, as that employee's tax home, the location of which may or may not coincide with the railroad's designation of the home terminal for a particular run.

Whether an employee's current post of duty is that employee's tax home depends on whether that individual is assigned there temporarily or permanently (an assignment for an indefinite period is regarded as a permanent assignment for section 162(a)(2) of the code purposes). The basic principle is that an employee is considered to maintain a residence at or in the vicinity of that employee's principal place of business. See *Markey*. An employee who is temporarily transferred to a different area is not expected to move to the new area, and is therefore considered away from home and "in a travel status" while at his temporary post. Truman C. Tucker, 55 T.C. 783 (1971); Rev.Rul. 60–189. However, an employee who is permanently transferred to a new area is considered to have shifted the home to the new post, which is the employee's new tax home. See Commissioner v. Mooneyhan, 404 F.2d 522 (6th Cir.1968), cert. denied, 394 U.S. 1001. The maintenance of the old residence where the taxpayer's family resides, and the taxpayer's travel back and forth, are strictly personal expenses that, under the provisions of section 262, are not deductible. See Commissioner v. Flowers, 326 U.S. 465, 1946–1 C.B. 57.

An exception to this rule exists in those unusual situations when the employee maintains a permanent residence for that employee's family at or near the minor or temporary post of duty, and another residence at or near the principal post of duty. Since the employee is traveling away from the principal post of duty on business where the employee also maintains a residence, the cost of meals and lodging at the minor or temporary post of duty is allowed as a deduction. Of course, the deduction is limited to that portion of the family expenses for meals and lodging that is properly attributable to the employee's presence there in the actual performance of business duties. Rev.Rul. 61–67, 1961–1 C.B. 25; Rev.Rul. 54–147, 1954–1 C.B. 51, 53.

An employee whose assignment away from that employee's principal place of business is strictly temporary (that is, its termination is anticipated within a fixed or reasonably short period of time) is considered to be in a travel status for the entire period during which duties require the employee to remain away from the regular post of duty. For example, if a member of a railroad train crew receives a temporary assignment to a run (whether or not "overnight," a rule discussed below) that begins and ends at a terminal situated at a distance from the tax home, the member may deduct not only the expenses for meals and lodging while making runs from and to that terminal, but all such expenses for the entire time during which duties prevent such member from returning to the regular post of duty. Typical of temporary assignments necessitating such an absence from the employee's regular post of duty are replacement or relief jobs during sick or vacation leave of the employees who regularly perform those duties.

Another kind of temporary assignment away from an employee's regular post of duty is a seasonal job that is not ordinarily filled by the same individual year after year. For example, during seasonal shipping periods for the marketing of crops, an employee may be assigned for several months to one or more places that are located at a distance from the regular place of employment. Such an employee is generally regarded as being in a travel status for the duration of such a temporary assignment.

The same rule would be true even if the seasonal job is not temporary, but a regularly recurring post of duty. A seasonal job to which an employee regularly returns, year after year, is regarded as being permanent rather than temporary employment. For example, a railroad employee might habitually work eight or nine months each year transporting ore from the same terminal, maintaining a residence for the employee's family at or near such work location. During the winter, when the ore-hauling service is suspended, the same employee might also be employed for three or four months each year at another regular seasonal post of duty, taking up residence at or near such employment. The ordinary rule is that when an employee leaves one permanent job to accept another permanent job, such employee is regarded as abandoning the first job for the second, and the principal post of duty shifts from the old to the new place of employment. The employee in the above example, however, is not regarded as having abandoned the ore-hauling assignment during the period in which that service is suspended, since the employee reasonably expects to return to it during the appropriate following season. The employee is conducting a trade or business each year at the same two recurring, seasonal places of employment, and under these circumstances the tax home does not shift during alternate seasons from one business location to the other, but remains stationary at the principal post of duty throughout the taxable year. In each case of this nature, a factual determination must be made in order to establish which of the seasonal posts of duty is the principal post of duty. Of course, the employee may only deduct the cost of the meals and lodging at the minor place of employment while duties there require such employee to remain away from the principal post of duty.

The rule known as the "overnight rule" or the "sleep or rest rule" is used to determine whether an employee whose duties require that employee to leave the principal post of duty during all or part of actual working hours is considered to be in a travel status. An employee may deduct the expenses for meals and lodging on a business trip away from the principal post of duty only when the trip lasts substantially longer than an ordinary day's work, the employee cannot reasonably be expected to make the trip without being released from duty for sufficient time to obtain substantial sleep or rest while away from the principal post of duty, and the release from duty is with the employer's tacit or express acquiescence, or is required by regulations of a governmental agency regulating the activity involved. The overnight rule is discussed in Rev.Rul. 75–170, 1975–19 I.R.B. 14, as are the requirements for substantiating claims for deductions for the cost of meals and lodging under section 274 of the Code.

When expenses are incurred for meals and lodging by an employee "while away from home" in the course of business duties, they are deductible as traveling expenses under section 162(a)(2) of the Code, subject to the substantiation requirements of section 274. * * * Such expenses are deductible under section 62(2)(B) in computing adjusted gross income * * *.

The portion of Rev.Rul. 54–497 regarding the principles applicable in determining when an employee may deduct expenses for meals and lodging incurred while traveling on business is superseded.

PROBLEMS

1. Commuter owns a home in Suburb of City and drives to work in City each day. He eats lunch in various restaurants in City.

    (a) May Commuter deduct his costs of transportation and/or meals? See Reg. § 1.162–2(e).

    (b) Same as (a), above, but Commuter is an attorney and often must travel between his office and the City Court House to file papers, try cases, etc. May Commuter deduct all or any of his costs of transportation and meals?

    (c) Commuter resides and works in City, but occasionally must fly to Other City on business for his employer. He eats lunch in

Other City and returns home in the late afternoon or early evening. May he deduct all or a part of his costs?

2. Taxpayer lives with her husband and children in City and works there.

(a) If her employer sends her to Metro on business for two days and one night each week and if Taxpayer is not reimbursed for her expenses, what may she deduct? See § 274(n)(1).

(b) Same as (a), above, except that she works three days and spends two nights each week in Metro and maintains an apartment there.

(c) Taxpayer and Husband own a home in City and Husband works there. Taxpayer works in Metro, maintaining an apartment there, and travels to City each weekend to visit her husband and family. What may she deduct? See Robert A. Coerver, 36 T.C. 252 (1961), affirmed per curiam 297 F.2d 837 (3d Cir.1962), and Virginia Foote, 67 T.C. 1 (1976).

3. Burly is a professional football player for the City Stompers. He and his wife own a home in Metro where they reside during the 7-month "off season."

(a) If Burly's only source of income is his salary from the Stompers, may Burly deduct any of his City living expenses which he incurs during the football season? See Ronald L. Gardin, 64 T.C. 1079 (1975).

(b) Would there be any difference in result in (a), above, if during the 7-month "off season" Burly worked as an insurance salesman in Metro? See George R. Lanning, 34 T.C.M. 1366 (1975).

4. Temporary works for Employer in City where Temporary and his family live.

(a) Employer has trouble in Branch City office in another state. He asks Temporary to supervise the Branch City office for nine months. Temporary's family stays in City and he rents an apartment in Branch City. Are Temporary's expenses in Branch City deductible?

(b) What result in (a), above, if Temporary and his family had lived in a furnished apartment in City and he and family gave the apartment up and moved to Branch City where they lived in a furnished apartment for the nine months? Compare J.B. Stewart, 30 T.C.M. 1316 (1971), with Alvin L. Goldman, 32 T.C.M. 574 (1973).

5. Traveler flies from his personal and tax home in New York to a business meeting in Florida on Monday. The meeting ends late Wednesday and he flies home on Friday afternoon after two days in the sunshine.

(a) To what extent are Traveler's transportation, meals, and lodging deductible? See Reg. § 1.162–2(a) and (b).

(b) May Traveler deduct any of his wife's expenses if she joins him on the trip. See Reg. § 1.162–2(c) and U.S. v. Disney, 413 F.2d 783 (9th Cir.1969).

(c) What result in (a), above, if Traveler stays in Florida until Sunday afternoon?

(d) What result in (a), above, if Traveler takes a cruise ship leaving Florida on Wednesday night and arriving in New York on Friday? See § 274(m)(1).

(e) What result in (a), above, if Traveler's trip is to Mexico City rather than Florida? See § 274(c).

(f) What result in (e), above, if Traveler went to Mexico City on Thursday and conducted business on Thursday, Friday, Monday, and Tuesday, and returned to New York on the succeeding Friday night? See Reg. § 1.274–4(d)(2)(v).

(g) What result in (e), above, if Traveler's trip to Mexico City is to attend a business convention? See § 274(h).

3. NECESSARY RENTAL AND SIMILAR PAYMENTS

Internal Revenue Code: Section 162(a)(3).

Regulations: Section 1.162–11.

STARR'S ESTATE v. COMMISSIONER

United States Court of Appeals, Ninth Circuit, 1959.
274 F.2d 294.

CHAMBERS, Circuit Judge. Yesterday's equities in personal property seem to have become today's leases. This has been generated not a little by the circumstance that one who leases as a lessee usually has less trouble with the federal tax collector. At least taxpayers think so.

But the lease still can go too far and get one into tax trouble. While according to state law the instrument will probably be taken (with the consequent legal incidents) by the name the parties give it, the internal revenue service is not always bound and can often recast it according to what the service may consider the practical realities.[1] We have so held in Oesterreich v. Commissioner, 9 Cir., 226 F.2d 798, and Commissioner of Internal Revenue v. Wilshire Holding Corporation, 9 Cir., 244 F.2d 904, certiorari denied 355 U.S. 815, 78 S.Ct. 16. The principal case concerns a fire sprinkler system installed at the taxpayer's plant at Monrovia, California, where Delano T. Starr,[2] now deceased, did business as the Gross Manufacturing Company. The "lessor" was "Automatic" Sprinklers of the Pacific, Inc., a California

---

[1.] Thus it shifts rental payments of a business (fully deductible) to a capital purchase for the business. If the nature of the property is wasting, then depreciation may be taken, but usually not all in one year.

[2.] Presumably the plant and the business were California community property of Starr and his wife, Mary W. Starr. For each of the calendar years 1951 and 1952, they filed joint tax returns.

corporation. The instrument entitled "Lease Form of Contract" (hereafter "contract") is just about perfectly couched in terms of a lease for five years with annual rentals of $1,240. But it is the last paragraph thereof, providing for nominal rental for five years, that has caused the trouble. It reads as follows:

> "28. At the termination of the period of this lease, if Lessee has faithfully performed all of the terms and conditions required of it under this lease, it shall have the privilege of renewing this lease for an additional period of five years at a rental of $32.00 per year. If Lessee does not elect to renew this lease, then the Lessor is hereby granted the period of six months in which to remove the system from the premises of the Lessee."

Obviously, one renewal for a period of five years is provided at $32.00 per year, if Starr so desired. Note, though, that the paragraph is silent as to status of the system beginning with the eleventh year. Likewise the whole contract is similarly silent.

The tax court sustained the commissioner of internal revenue, holding that the five payments of $1,240, or the total of $6,200, were capital expenditures and not pure deductible rental.[3] Depreciation of $269.60 was allowed for each year. Generally, we agree.

Taxpayers took the deduction as a rental expense under trade or business pursuant to Section 23(a) of the Internal Revenue Code, as amended by Section 121(a) of the Revenue Act of 1942.[4]

The law in this field for this circuit is established in Oesterreich v. Commissioner, supra, and Robinson v. Elliot, 9 Cir., 262 F.2d 383. There we held that for tax purposes form can be disregarded for substance and, where the foreordained practical effect of the rent is to produce title eventually, the rental agreement can be treated as a sale.

In this, Starr's case, we do have the troublesome circumstance that the contract does not by its terms ever pass title to the system to the "lessee." Most sprinkler systems have to be tailor-made for a specific piece of property and, if removal is required, the salvageable value is negligible. Also, it stretches credulity to believe that the "lessor" ever intended to or would "come after" the system. And the "lessee" would be an exceedingly careless businessman who would enter into such contract with the practical possibility that the "lessor" would reclaim the installation. He could have believed only that he was getting the system for the rental money. And we think the commissioner was entitled to take into consideration the practical effect rather than the legal, especially when there was a record that on other such installations the "lessor", after the term of the lease was over, had not reclaimed from those who had met their agreed payments. It is

---

3. Starr, Estate of v. Commissioner, 30 T.C. 856.

4. [I.R.C. (1939) § 23(a) is omitted. See I.R.C. (1986) § 162(a). Ed.]

obvious that the nominal rental payments after five years of $32.00 per year were just a service charge for inspection.[5]

Recently the Court of Appeals for the Eighth Circuit has decided Western Contracting Corporation v. Commissioner, 1959, 271 F.2d 694, reversing the tax court in its determination that the commissioner could convert leases of contractor's equipment into installment purchases of heavy equipment. The taxpayer believes that case strongly supports him here. We think not.[6]

There are a number of facts there which make a difference. For example, in the contracts of Western there is no evidence that the payments on the substituted basis of rent would produce for the "lessor" the equivalent of his normal sales price plus interest. There was no right to acquire for a nominal amount at the end of the term as in Oesterreich and the value to the "lessor" in the personalty had not been exhausted as in Starr's case. And there was no basis for inferring that Western would just keep the equipment for what it had paid. It appears that Western paid substantial amounts to acquire the equipment at the end of the term. There was just one compelling circumstance against Western in its case: What it had paid as "rent" was apparently always taken into full account in computing the end purchase price. But on the other hand, there was almost a certainty that the "lessor" would come after his property if the purchase was not eventually made for a substantial amount. This was not even much of a possibility in Oesterreich and not a probability in Starr's case.

In Wilshire Holding Corporation v. Commissioner, 9 Cir., 262 F.2d 51, we referred the case back to the tax court to consider interest as a deductible item for the lessee. We think it is clearly called for here. Two yardsticks are present. The first is found in that the normal selling price of the system was $4,960 while the total rental payments for five years were $6,200. The difference could be regarded as interest for the five years on an amortized basis. The second measure is in clause 16 (loss by fire), where the figure of six per cent per annum discount is used. An allowance might be made on either basis, division of the difference (for the five years) between "rental payments" and "normal purchase price" of $1,240, or six per cent per annum on the normal purchase price of $4,960, converting the annual payments into amortization. We do not believe that the "lessee" should suffer the pains of a loss for what really was paid for the use of another's money, even though for tax purposes his lease collapses.

5. It is true that the normal inspection fee would be $64.00. However, the difference between $32.00 and $64.00 would not seem to ruin the tax court's determination for income tax purposes that there was a sale.

6. It is unnecessary to determine here whether the Ninth Circuit would follow the decision of the Eighth Circuit or the decision of the tax court. (Western Contracting Corp. v. Commissioner, 17 TCM 371, T.C.Memo. 1958–77, CCH Dec. 22, 1960 [M]). It is enough here to say that the Ninth Circuit regards the Eighth Circuit's opinion distinguishable from Starr's case and not inconsistent with the holding herein.

We do not criticize the commissioner. It is his duty to collect the revenue and it is a tough one. If he resolves all questions in favor of the taxpayers, we soon would have little revenue. However, we do suggest that after he has made allowance for depreciation, which he concedes, and an allowance for interest, the attack on many of the "leases" may not be worth while in terms of revenue.

Decision reversed for proceedings consistent herewith.

WHITE v. FITZPATRICK

United States Court of Appeals, Second Circuit, 1951.
193 F.2d 398, cert. denied 343 U.S. 928, 72 S.Ct. 762, 1952.

CLARK, Circuit Judge. Involved in this appeal is the recurring problem of tax savings claimed as a consequence of a transfer of property from husband to wife with resulting lease or license back. Here neither the Commissioner of Internal Revenue nor the district court has accepted the taxpayer's view of the transactions; and he now appeals from the judgment against him in his action for a refund of the deficiency assessed against him by the Commissioner upon his income and victory taxes for the years 1941, 1943, and 1944. [All years are prior to the 1984 enactment of Section 1041. Ed.]

The following are the facts of the case as stipulated by the parties and found by the trial court. During the years in question and for some time prior thereto, plaintiff engaged in the manufacture of chokes for use on the barrels of shotguns, as sole proprietor of the Poly Choke Company, an unincorporated business. Beginning in 1939 the company occupied certain properties—land, three factories, a garage, and an office—under a lease coupled with a nontransferable option to purchase for $15,370. Plaintiff had developed the basic invention for this device himself and obtained a United States patent for it on December 27, 1932.

On January 21, 1941, he entered into a written agreement with his wife, transferring "the entire right, title and interest in and to" the patent, "to the full end of the term of said patent," for a stated consideration of $10. The following day his wife licensed the exclusive manufacturing right back to him "to the full end of the entire term of said patent." The assignment back was subject to cancellation only if (a) payments fell into sixty days' arrears, or (b) receivership, bankruptcy, forced assignment, or other financial difficulty made it impossible for her husband to carry on his manufacturing concern. It provided for royalties of $1 on each product marketed. Plaintiff filed a gift tax return for the year declaring the fair market value of the patent to be $10,000 and for the next four years, 1941–1944 inclusive, paid his wife some $60,000 as royalties.

At about the same time, December 27, 1940, plaintiff's wife also purchased the property on which the company was located for $16,800 and immediately leased it to her husband orally. On the next day plaintiff made a gift to his wife of $16,175 to cover the purchase price and filed a gift tax return for that amount. Rental payments for the years 1941–1944 inclusive were $1,500 a year, which was the amount that plaintiff had been paying to the original lessor; in 1944, plaintiff in addition paid his wife some $5,000 as "an adjustment in rent."

During the years in question plaintiff deducted both rental payments and royalties as business expenses. After investigation and audit, the Commissioner of Internal Revenue issued a deficiency notice disallowing the deductions in 1948. Plaintiff paid the total deficiency of about $47,000 thus assessed and brought this action for refund. The district court found (1) that the plaintiff's motivation was to make good certain losses in the value of securities held by his wife and to minimize income taxes for the family group, but (2) that "it was the taxpayer's expectation that no action would be taken by the wife in exercise of her rights of ownership of the patent or real property which would be detrimental to the plaintiff's interest." The court then concluded that by the gifts and license and lease back "by reason of the family relationship the husband retains effective control of the patent and real property, while valid transfers for other purposes, will not form a valid basis for deduction of royalties and rent paid by the husband to the wife as business expenses in arriving at the taxpayer's net income for income tax purposes."

The bare assignment of the patent was legally adequate to transfer all rights adhering thereto to the wife. Likewise the land was purchased in the name of the wife alone. From this plaintiff contends on appeal that the wife's legal title and power were absolute and subject to no conditions or future claims whatsoever. Moreover, there is no evidence, nor does defendant contend, that the plaintiff derived any direct benefit in the form of income from these transactions. Therefore, plaintiff argues that, since the royalties and rents were both ordinary in nature for his type of business and reasonable in amount, they constitute valid business expenses under I.R.C. § 23(a)(1)(A), 26 U.S.C.A. § 23(a)(1)(A), which authorizes the deduction from gross income of "ordinary and necessary expenses" paid "in carrying on any trade or business." See Welch v. Helvering, 290 U.S. 111, 54 S.Ct. 8; Deputy v. DuPont, 308 U.S. 488, 60 S.Ct. 363.

Underlying reality, however, contradicts this appearance of a complete assignment. "Title" to the patent and land may legally reside in the plaintiff's wife; practically and actually, as the district court concluded, control rests with the husband as effectively as if he had never made the gift of the patent to his wife or given her the money with which to buy the property. Assignment and gift cannot be divorced for tax purposes from their accompanying agreements whereby the husband retained dominion. And in fact plaintiff never intended that it should be; he admitted the impossibility of conducting the business without this basic patent or of finding a comparable factory site in Connecticut. His wife was neither equipped nor evinced any desire to exercise or transfer any rights to the use of either of the properties; in the case of the patent at least, it is clear that she had no legal right to do so, save in the unlikely event of the husband's default. The sole practical effect of these transactions, therefore, was to create a right to income in the wife, while leaving untouched in all practical reality the husband-donor's effective dominion and control over the properties in question. It is not without significance on this point that the arrangement made was actually disadvantageous to the business. For it passed over the reduction of land charges which the taxpayer might have made by taking up his option to purchase in order to create the income right in the donor's wife, and that, too, at a greater capital cost. For the statutory purposes, the mere creation of a legal obligation to pay is not controlling. Interstate Transit Lines v. C.I.R., 8 Cir., 130 F.2d 136, affirmed 319 U.S. 590, 63 S.Ct. 1279.

In this respect, then, the case before us does not involve the definite problem presented by the completed assignment of a created product which divided our court and the Fourth Circuit, both inter- and extra-murally, in the two cases of Wodehouse v. C.I.R., 2 Cir., 177 F.2d 881, Id., 4 Cir., 178 F.2d 987. Gift and retained control must be regarded as inseparable parts of a single transaction, especially since it was only in their sum total that they had any reality in regard to the conduct of plaintiff's business. To isolate them, as would be necessary to bring them within the rationale of our own majority ruling in Wodehouse v. C.I.R., supra, is to hide business reality behind paper pretense.

For the question here is as to the tax consequences of a formal gift of certain income-producing properties by the husband to his wife coupled with the informal retention of administrative control—the transfer, in effect, of the right to receive income and the retention of those complex of "use rights" which are usually compressed in the term "ownership." In the context of I.R.C. § 23(a)(1)(A), the question is a rather new one; under I.R.C. § 22(a), 26 U.S.C.A. § 22(a), [See Section 61. Ed.] where it arises in the definition of gross income problems, it is not. And we think the line drawn in the precedents under the latter section is the same as that in the field of deductibility of business expenses. Plaintiff here, for example, accepts as his own the income he has received on the patent equivalent to the royalties he is paying his wife, but then seeks to deduct it as a business expense; in effect this is not different from claiming that the gift itself made the original income hers in the first place.

We think, therefore, that the principles governing the intermarital transfer of income enunciated in Helvering v. Clifford, 309 U.S. 331, 60 S.Ct. 554, and re-enforced by later cases, are also decisive here. In the case at bar, plaintiff assigned the "legal title" to the patent and provided for his wife's assumption of the "legal title" to the land; but he retained, by formal agreement in the first case, by informal arrangement in the second, the administrative control of these properties. His wife had the right to income, but he had a right to the use of the patent and land. Henson v. C.I.R., 5 Cir., 174 F.2d 846, is thus distinguishable. The Clifford rule is clear, that this direct control, when fused with the indirect control which we must imply from a formal but unsubstantial assignment within the closed family group displaying no obvious business purpose, renders the assignment ineffective for federal tax purposes. The same result should obtain whether the question arises under § 22(a) or 23(a)(1)(A) of the Internal Revenue Code.

Plaintiff relies heavily on Skemp v. C.I.R., 7 Cir., 168 F.2d 598, and Brown v. C.I.R., 3 Cir., 180 F.2d 926, certiorari denied C.I.R. v. Brown, 340 U.S. 814, 71 S.Ct. 42. These cases, which are criticized in reasoned discussions in 51 Col.L.Rev. 247 and 59 Yale L.J. 1529, may be thought to go to the verge of the law in support of what are essentially intrafamily transfers. But both, being to trustees, were sufficiently outright, to be distinguishable from our present case. Both involved claimed deductions under I.R.C. § 23(a)(1)(A). In the first, a plaintiff-physician had deeded the building in which he had his office in irrevocable trust for twenty years or until the prior deaths of both himself and his wife, with their children as beneficiaries. He then leased the building back for ten years. In the second, there were two trusts, also irrevocable, terminating on the majority of the beneficiaries who were children of the settlor, coupled with an immediate leaseback of the corpus properties. In upholding the deductions, both courts expressly emphasized the independence of the trustees. It is probable that a like result would probably have obtained had the question been one of gross income under I.R.C. § 22(a). For three factors determine attributability of income to the settlor of a family trust. Whether these are conjunctive tests, see Helvering v. Clifford, supra, 309 U.S. at 335, 60 S.Ct. 554, or alternative, under the new Clifford regulations, U.S.Treas.Reg. No. 111, § 29.22(a)–21; Kay v. C.I.R., 3 Cir., 178 F.2d 772, it seems likely that in both the cases relied on, income would have been attributable to the trusts and thus to the beneficiaries, rather than the settlors. For (1) the settlors retained no reversionary interests; (2) they retained no dispositive power over either corpus or income;[1] and (3) administrative control was not exercisable primarily for the benefit of the settlors.[2] See Alexandre, Case Method Restatement of the New Clifford Regulations, 3 Tax L.Rev. 189.

The Supreme Court has long emphasized the test of retention of practical ownership in passing on the tax consequences of intra-family assignment. Soll, Intra-Family Assignments: Attribution and Realization of Income, 6 Tax L.Rev. 435. In the recent case of C.I.R. v. Sunnen, 333 U.S. 591, 68 S.Ct. 715, involving the assignment by the inventor-husband of patent licensing contracts to his wife, the court said, "The crucial question remains whether the assignor retains sufficient power and control over the assigned property or over receipt of

---

1. In the Skemp case, 7 Cir., 168 F.2d 598, 599, the "taxpayer * * * did reserve the right to rent all or a part of the building 'at a rental to be determined by the trustee'"; but this does not constitute "beneficial enjoyment" of the property in the Clifford sense. Moreover, both leases

back were for a term and were not coextensive with the life of the trust.

2. Here the factor of independent trusteeship is crucial. And it is in this respect that the instant case differs on its facts from the Skemp and Brown results.

the income to make it reasonable to treat him as the recipient of the income for tax purposes," 333 U.S. at page 604, 68 S.Ct. at page 722, and went on to note that "The taxpayer's controlling position in the corporation also permitted him to regulate the amount of royalties payable to his wife." 333 U.S. at page 609, 68 S.Ct. at page 725. In essence the assignment in the present case was effective only to the extent of transferring the single right to receive income. It is now too late to question the well-established proposition that mere assignment of such a right will not suffice to insulate the grantor from tax liability under § 22(a), and we think like tax results must obtain under § 23(a)(1)(A). See Lucas v. Earl, 281 U.S. 111, 50 S.Ct. 241; Helvering v. Horst, 311 U.S. 112, 61 S.Ct. 144; Helvering v. Eubank, 311 U.S. 122, 61 S.Ct. 149. The recent case of C.I.R. v. Culbertson, 337 U.S. 733, 69 S.Ct. 1210, has established the test in the family-partnership field, whether or not there existed as part of the arrangement a "bona fide intent" to have the donee exercise a real part in management, thus giving a final blessing to the doctrine that "true ownership" is decisive in matters of federal taxation. See also C.I.R. v. Tower, 327 U.S. 280, 66 S.Ct. 532; Harrison v. Schaffner, 312 U.S. 579, 61 S.Ct. 759; Ingle Coal Corp. v. C.I.R., 7 Cir., 174 F.2d 569.

Since here we find no evidence of a potential exercise of "control and management" on the part of the donee, only of "passive acquiescence to the will of the donor," C.I.R. v. Culbertson, supra, 337 U.S. at pages 747, 748, 69 S.Ct. at page 1217, since the transaction is in all practical respects a "mere paper reallocation of income among the family members," C.I.R. v. Tower, supra, 327 U.S. at page 292, 66 S.Ct. at page 538, and since the husband has remained the actual enjoyer and owner of the property, payments to the wife do not constitute valid business deductions within the statute. See Johnson v. C.I.R., 2 Cir., 86 F.2d 710; W.H. Armston Co. v. C.I.R., 5 Cir., 188 F.2d 531.

Affirmed.

CHASE, Circuit Judge (dissenting). Perhaps it would be desirable to protect the revenue by amending Sec. 23(a)(1)(A) to exclude from the business expense deductions now allowed those which become necessary only because of intrafamily gifts of property used, or to be used, in the business. But that is a matter to be determined by Congress and, until it acts, I think courts are bound to give effect taxwise to gifts which are fully effective otherwise.

There is, I think, some distinction between the disallowance of the royalty and the disallowance of the rent deductions. It is that the transfer of the patent by gift to the wife was a transfer of needed business property already owned by the taxpayer which was intended to, and did, make it necessary to pay her the royalties. The gift of the money, however, which she used together with some of her own to buy the building never owned by the taxpayer was not shown to have been of money which had any connection with the business at all and the net result from the standpoint of the taxpayer and his business was merely a change in landlord. However, as I view this case, it is not necessary to rely upon this distinction.

In respect to the claimed deductions, the decisive factor as the statute is now, is whether the rent and royalty payments were "required to be made as a condition to the continued use or possession, for purposes of the trade or business, of property to which the taxpayer has not taken or is not taking title or in which he had no equity." Sec. 23(a)(1)(A). The findings, based on evidence adequately supporting them, show that everything was done to transfer the legal and equitable titles both to the patent and to the building absolutely to the wife, and the ownership she thereby acquired gave her the right to whatever she could get by way of royalties and rents which were, of course, taxable to her as income. And, as Sec. 23(a)(1)(A) is now so broad that no exception is made because of the way in which business expenses become necessary, i.e., by gift or otherwise, the reasonable royalties and rents the husband paid her were, I think, well within the scope of the statute, being "required" by the license and lease arrangements, and therefore deductible. Skemp v. Commissioner, 7 Cir., 168 F.2d 598; Brown v. Commissioner, 3 Cir., 180 F.2d 926, certiorari denied, 340 U.S. 814, 71 S.Ct. 42. See also Henson v. Commissioner, 5 Cir., 174 F.2d 846. The fact that in the Skemp and Brown cases the transfers were to independent trustees for the benefit of family members is a distinction without a difference since that bore only on the completeness of the gifts and reasonableness of the royalties and rentals paid, both here shown and found. W.H. Armston Co. v. Commissioner, 5 Cir., 188 F.2d 531, is distinguishable as an instance of a disguised transfer of dividends to a large stockholder of the corporation.

The cases dealing with problems arising under Sec. 22(a), I.R.C. as to the identity of the taxpayer liable for taxes payable by some one, on which my brothers so much rely, help little, if any, in determining what deductions an identified taxpayer may take under Sec. 23(a)(1)(A) in computing his net income. Assuming, arguendo, that these cases are relevant [1] factually they are inapplicable. The only basis pointed out by the majority for applying these cases to the facts before us is that the license of the patent and the lease of the buildings given to the taxpayer left "untouched in all practical reality the husband-donor's effective dominion and control over the properties in question." But whatever control the taxpayer received was the control of a licensee and lessee and was conditioned upon making the payments here claimed to be deductible. It would seem erroneous, therefore, to deny the claimed deduction on this basis.

1. The only issue to which these cases could be relevant is whether or not the taxpayer was "required" to pay the royalties and rents as a condition to using the property since that is the test set forth in the statute. In order to be relevant to this issue, and to hold as the majority does, it would seem that one must accept the premise that a donor who retains sufficient control over property transferred by him so as to make any income from that property includible in the donor's gross income under Sec. 22(a), is not, as a matter of law, "required" to pay the donee for its use even though he has entered into a firm, and legally enforceable, obligation so to do.

One other point warrants brief mention. My brothers apparently think that the taxpayer is no longer entitled to any rent deduction because, presumably, he could have used the money he gave his wife to buy the building himself and then he would have had no rent to pay. If he had done so, no doubt he would have been allowed as deductions the maintenance costs, taxes, etc., which must have been included in the rent he paid his wife to make it reasonable over all but the effect of this decision may deprive him of even them. I cannot help but think that my brothers have mistakenly applied the business purpose rule of cases like Gregory v. Helvering, 293 U.S. 465, 55 S.Ct. 266, to a situation where what the taxpayer did was merely to use permissible business judgment as to whether he would increase his business investment or continue to pay reasonable rent.

I would reverse and remand for a judgment for the appellant.

NOTE

A thoughtful student when he reads White v. Fitzpatrick will see, not an isolated business deduction issue, but a new facet of the assignment of income problem to which attention is directed principally in Chapters 12 and 13. Income may be fragmented among an intimate group as much by way of deductible payments that are taxable to the recipients as by more direct devices suggested by the familiar *Earl,* *Horst,* and *Clifford* cases. The analogy is so pat that one might confidently expect like administrative, judicial, and legislative attacks on the problem. In contrast, however,[1] Congress has been relatively inactive in the deduction sector, which has encouraged an aggressive posture by the Commissioner; and some courts at least have been led far afield by a spurious but aromatic red herring.[2] In the typical or at least *early* typical case,[3] where a plan was prepared to yield maximum tax benefits, possibly though with a high risk of failure, a doctor, say, would transfer his office and equipment to a trust under which Doctor was trustee for his child as the income beneficiary and provide for a reversion to Doctor in 122 months, carefully avoiding also any control or other arrangement that would offend the then grantor trust sections. (Such a reversion would now violate the grantor trust rules.)[4] The trust as owner would then lease office and equipment to Doctor for its fair rental value. As rent was paid it would be distributed to and taxed to Child, with the usual attending deduction for the trust.[5] Meanwhile, Doctor would claim a Section 162(a)(3) deduction for rent. Abstractly, the matter would look like this:

1. Compare, e.g., I.R.C. §§ 671–678 and 704(e), dealing with income assignment, with § 267(a)(2), mildly restraining deduction for some intrafamily payments.

2. E.g., Mathews v. Commissioner, 520 F.2d 323 (5th Cir.1975), reflecting one court's enchantment with a questionable "business purpose" doctrine.

3. See Van Zandt v. Commissioner, 341 F.2d 440 (5th Cir.1965), cert. denied 382 U.S. 814, 86 S.Ct. 32 (1965).

4. See I.R.C. § 673. See page 315, supra.

5. I.R.C. §§ 651 and 652, 661 and 662.

BEFORE

Doctor: Income, $100,000 (Ignoring depreciation deductions).

AFTER

Doctor				
Income	$100,000	*Trust*		
Rent	−20,000 .... Income	$ 20,000		
Income taxed	$ 80,000 ..... Distribution		*Child*	
	deduction	−20,000	Income taxed	$20,000
	Income taxed	0		

With $20,000 peeled off the top of Doctor's income, escaping tax to the trust by way of Section 651 or Section 661, and subjected to possibly lower rates as income of Child, the scene would be:

Doctor: Taxable Income, $80,000. *Child:* Taxable Income, $20,000.[6]

Use of these arrangements has been substantially curtailed by the 1986 legislation. As seen in the Introduction to Chapter 12, the modified flat tax rates and the enactment of "the kiddie tax" (generally taxing unearned income of minors under age 14 at their parents' rates) should result in fewer attempted direct assignments of income and, as here, the somewhat similar contrived generation of deductions. In addition, most assignments of income attempted by means of deductions were carried out through *Clifford* trusts in which the grantor retained a reversion at the end of a ten plus year period. With the 1986 amendment to Section 673, considered in Chapter 13, the successful use of reversionary *Clifford* trusts is also essentially eliminated. Thus we will likely see substantially fewer transfer and leasebacks by means of the use of trusts. Nevertheless, we perceive sufficient dying gasps in this and related areas to feel impelled to consider them below.

The viability of this type of grantor trust-leaseback arrangement should be (but are not) tested against the rules, statutory and now quite specific, for more direct income assignment through the use of trusts [7] or under the *Horst* doctrine which addresses directly the taxation of income from property.[8] Of course, taxation is properly interested in things only as they *are*, not as they *seem*. Consequently, an alleged transfer and leaseback that lacked reality, possibly shown to be a sham by unrealistic rental payments, could properly be disregarded merely by refusing to exalt form over substance.[9] But assuming that all *t*'s are crossed and all *i*'s dotted, and that judicial supervision of a trustee

---

6. In the typical case, Child's taxable income will be reduced by depreciation deductions on the trust property which would have been available to Doctor if the trust had not been created. I.R.C. §§ 167(a) and (h), 168(a).

7. I.R.C. §§ 671–678.

8. Cf., I.R.C. § 704(e).

9. Kirschenmann v. Westover, 225 F.2d 69 (9th Cir.1955), cert. denied 350 U.S. 834, 76 S.Ct. 70 (1955); and cf. Armston Co. v. Commissioner, 188 F.2d 531 (5th Cir.1951).

under local law assures regularity, it is difficult to see from a policy point of view why the asserted rental deduction is vulnerable. At present, however, results in this area are not uniform.[10]

It seems that the major difficulties stem from a failure to recognize that it is the owner of property who should be taxed on the income from the property. Sham transactions should always be disregarded. But if one effectively transfers ownership of his property to another, the other becomes the taxpayer on the property's income. This is what makes relevant in this case the preoccupation in the trust, partnership and corporate area with determination of ownership for tax purposes. The trust rules are most elaborate and should control when a trust is involved.[11] Partnership provisions recognize that an interest carrying income sharing rights in a partnership, where capital is a substantial income-producing factor, may arise by gift;[12] but the regulations caution against purported transfers of interests which lack reality.[13] And although no *Clifford* trust or family partnership doctrine has developed formally in the corporate area, assignments of interests in corporate businesses which are mere sham and lack substance are not accorded recognition.[14]

Assuming that a *real* ownership interest is created in another of property that a taxpayer uses in his business, payment of fair rental for his use of the property should accord the taxpayer a business deduction under Section 162. Only one respectable question can be raised about this conclusion. Section 162 permits the deduction of "necessary" expenses: Is an expense unnecessary if it arises only because the taxpayer gives away (directly or to a trust) or sells[15] the property to one to whom it must *then* pay rent for its use?

In *Mathews,*[16] fusing the gift and the lease agreement, the Fifth Circuit has found a lack of necessity for the rental payments in the absence of any "business purpose" for the arrangement.[17] Other courts, viewing the gift and the rental agreement as separate transactions have been willing to find the requisite necessity for the rental payment after the property in question has been placed in the hands of a trustee for the benefit of others.[18] Whether the unified or separate view is more appropriate seems a better question for Congress than for the courts. Nevertheless, as there are several clear ways to skin this very cat and apt analogies regarding the treatment of *income* from

---

10. Compare Brooke v. U.S., 468 F.2d 1155 (9th Cir.1972), allowing the deduction, with Mathews v. Commissioner (reversing T.C.) supra note 2, deduction disallowed.

11. I.R.C. §§ 671–678 are given some consideration in Chapter 13, supra.

12. I.R.C. § 704(e).

13. Reg. § 1.704–1(e)(2)(i)–(iii).

14. E.g., Overton v. Commissioner, 162 F.2d 155 (2d Cir.1947).

15. See Sun Oil Co., 35 T.C.M. 173 (1976).

16. Supra note 2; accord, Perry v. U.S., 520 F.2d 235 (4th Cir.1975).

17. Accord, Frank L. Butler, 65 T.C. 327 (1975), denying the rental deduction, but under the *Golsen* principle requiring the court merely to analyze and apply the teachings of the Fifth Circuit; contra, Albert T. Felix, 21 T.C. 794 (1954).

18. E.g., Rosenfeld v. Commissioner, 706 F.2d 1277 (2d Cir.1983); Skemp v. Commissioner, 168 F.2d 598 (7th Cir.1948); Brown v. Commissioner, 180 F.2d 926 (3d Cir.1950).

property that has been the subject of a gift, it seems the unified view of the Fifth Circuit should be rejected and the deduction more freely allowed. It would be well for Congress to so specify along the lines of the language in Section 704(e).

Within the history of this litigious area are distinctions based on (1) whether more property was transferred than was leased back by the taxpayer, (2) whether (in pre-1987 cases) the transferor retained a reversionary interest or, when a trust was used, put the remainder in others, (3) whether, when the transfer was in trust, the trustee was independent and (4) whether the transferor-lessee had an equity interest in the property.[19] There is no agreement, however, on the effect of these various factors and they might all well be regarded as irrelevant.

One may validly make a direct gift of property to a relative and thereafter lease it from him, paying deductible rent. One may also effectively transfer the income from property to another who will be taxed on it, if he does it by giving the other person a trust interest that does not run afoul of the grantor trust provisions. Other income splitting possibilities arise through the use of partnerships and corporations, as seen in Chapter 13. All these possibilities are within the teachings of the *Horst* case, as embellished in some instances by statute. Consequently, one may well ask: What's the big deal about some similar income splitting by way of deductions? Clearly Congress should answer this question but, until it does, controversy should be resolved with a clear view of the analogy between the income and deduction areas.[20]

One final point should be made. The *Clifford* or Grantor Trust area of the statute is fairly well worked out to answer related questions. When its provisions bite in, Section 671 treats the grantor as the *owner* of the property involved. The expressed consequence is to tax him on the income from the trust property and to allow him deductions otherwise available to the trust. The income beneficiary is treated as receiving amounts free of tax by way of the gift exclusion.[21] Thus, a trust grantor taxed on income under the grantor trust provisions is entitled to depreciation on the trust property. It is fairly clear that in cases such as *Mathews*[22] the Commissioner will not seek to tax the

---

19. This last issue rests on the express statutory proscription that a lessee who would claim a deduction for rent may do so only with respect to property "in which he has no equity." I.R.C. § 162(a)(3). Although there is some authority for the notion that a reversionary interest may be an "equity", e.g., dictum in Alden B. Oaks, 44 T.C. 524, 531 (1965), the phrase is properly applied only in cases such as Starr's Estate v. Comm'r, supra page 386, in which it is uncertain whether one making payments for the use of property is paying deductible rent or is purchasing the property. For an excellent discussion of the broad scope of this area, see Bittker and Merrikoff, "Restructuring Business Transactions for Federal Income Tax Purposes," 1978 Wis.L.Rev. 715 (1978).

20. See Peroni, "Untangling the Web of Gift-Leaseback Jurisprudence," 68 Minn.L.R. 735 (1984); Eller, "The Second Circuit Approves Intrafamily Gift-Leaseback, But Fails to Scrutinize Strictly the Underlying Clifford Trust," 50 Brooklyn L.Rev. 839 (1984).

21. See § 102(a) and the negative inference of § 102(b).

22. Supra note 2.

trust beneficiary when the grantor's rental deduction is denied.[23]　It seems clear too that, if the transferor-lessee is to be treated as owner under Rev.Rul. 54–9,[24] it is he who will be entitled to depreciation and maintenance expense deductions for the property,[25] which is only fair.[26]

4.　EXPENSES FOR EDUCATION *

Internal Revenue Code: Sections 162(a);　262;　274(m)(2).

Regulations: Section 1.162–5.

INTRODUCTION

There are two cases presented in this segment, *Hill* and *Coughlin*. They were decided by the Fourth Circuit and the Second Circuit in 1950 and 1953, respectively.　Each seems to clash with a dictum in Justice Cardozo's 1933 opinion in Welch v. Helvering: [1]

> [A] man conceives the notion that he will be able to practice his vocation with greater ease and profit if he has an opportunity to enrich his culture.　Forthwith the price of his education becomes [the Justice is being facetious] an expense of the business, reducing the income subject to taxation.

The clash is apparent only, and *Hill* and *Coughlin* can now be found in distilled form as paragraphs (1) and (2) (but in reverse order) of Reg. § 1.162–5(a), an affirmative general rule on the deductibility of expenses for education.

The two basic concepts expressed in the general rule of the regulations are fairly simple and forthright and answer a great many questions.　Even so, nice distinctions have been drawn in numerous circumstances: How do we decide whether an Internal Revenue Agent should be allowed to deduct the expenses he incurs in obtaining a law degree? [2]

Recent developments have made the area one of greater concern to lawyers with respect to their own personal tax liability not just that of their clients.　Some states are now requiring continuing education for

----

23. See Rev.Rul. 54–9, 1954–1 C.B. 20; and cf. Rev.Rul. 57–315, 1957–2 C.B. 624 which, while specifically addressed to gift tax liability and modifying the earlier ruling in this respect, leaves intact the income tax rulings of Rev.Rul. 54–9.

24. See note 23, supra.

25. Cf. Frank Lyon Co. v. U.S., 435 U.S. 561, 98 S.Ct. 1291 (1978).　See also Weinstein and Silvers, "The Sale and Leaseback Transaction after Frank Lyon Company," 24 N.Y.L.S.L.Rev. 337 (1978) and Massey, "Sale-Leaseback Transactions: Loss Realization—The Neglected Issue," 6 J.Real Est.Tax. 308 (1979).

26. The authors have had the use of a research paper prepared by Peter J.

Losavio, Jr., an LL.M. student at the University of Florida, in the writing of this Note.　His thoughts were helpful; responsibility for comments appearing here, however, is assumed by the authors.

* See McNulty, "Tax Policy and Tuition Credit Legislation: Federal Income Tax Allowances for Personal Costs of Higher Education," 61 Calif.L.Rev. 1 (1973); Schoenfeld, "The Educational Expense Deduction: The Need for a Rational Approach," 27 Villanova L.Rev. 237 (1982).

1. See page 348, supra.

2. See Melnik v. U.S., 521 F.2d 1065 (9th Cir.1975), cert. denied 425 U.S. 911, 96 S.Ct. 1506 (1976).

the bar. Others are permitting specialty designation or certification by lawyers who can establish expertise in various areas of the law, either by way of experience or education.[3] As more lawyers will be getting more formal education and spending more for it, and as similar developments are taking place in other disciplines, the importance of studying the tax aspects of education expenses is obvious.

HILL v. COMMISSIONER

United States Court of Appeals, Fourth Circuit, 1950.
181 F.2d 906.

DOBIE, Circuit Judge. This is an appeal by Nora Payne Hill (hereinafter called taxpayer) from a decision of the Tax Court of the United States entered on September 7, 1949, affirming a determination of the Commissioner of Internal Revenue that there is a deficiency in the income tax due by taxpayer in the amount of $57.52 for the calendar year 1945.

During the taxable year and for twenty-seven years prior thereto, taxpayer was engaged in the business of teaching school in the State of Virginia. During the taxable year in question, she attended summer school at Columbia University in New York City, for which she incurred expenses in an amount of $239.50, which she deducted in computing her net income on her federal income tax return for the year 1945. These expenses were disallowed upon the grounds that they were personal expenses and were not deductible for federal income tax purposes. The only question for decision by us is: Was the taxpayer correct in deducting those expenses as ordinary and necessary expenses incurred in carrying on her trade or business? We think this question must be answered in the affirmative. The reasonableness of the amount of these expenses is not disputed.

* * *

[The Court quotes here I.R.C. (1939) Sections 23(a)(1)(A), 23(a)(2) and 24(a)(1) which for purposes of this case are essentially the same as I.R.C. (1986) Section 162(a), concerning trade or business expenses, Section 212, concurring expenses for the production of income and Section 262, disallowing any deduction for personal expenses. Ed.]

The pertinent provisions of the Virginia Code Annotated, 1942, applicable to the issues before us, are as follows:

Title 11, Chapter 33, Section 660

* * * No teacher shall be employed or paid from the public funds unless such teacher holds a certificate in full force in accordance with the rules of certification laid down by the State Board of Education, provided, that, where a teacher holding a certificate in force is not available, a former teacher

---

3. See Kalb and Roberts, "The Deductibility of Post-graduate Legal Education Expenses," 27 U.Fla.L.Rev. 995 (1975), written in partial satisfaction of requirements for the LL.M. degree at the University of Florida and Mock "Deductibility of Educational Expenses for Full Time Graduate Study," 25 Okla.L.R. 582 (1972).

holding an expired certificate may be employed temporarily as a substitute teacher to meet an emergency * * *.

Title 11, Chapter 35, Section 786(b)(3)

* * * provided, that no school board shall employ or pay any teacher from the public funds unless the teacher shall hold a certificate in full force, according to the provisions of section six hundred and sixty of the laws relating to the public free schools in counties; * * *.

The Regulations Governing the Certification of Teachers and the Qualifications of Administrators and Supervisors in Virginia required for the renewal of a teacher's certificate that taxpayer present evidence that she had been a successful teacher, had read at least five books on the Teachers' Reading Course during the life of her certificate and also must either (a) present evidence of college credits in professional or academic subjects earned during the life of the certificate or (b) pass an examination on five books selected by the State Department of Education from the Teachers' Reading Course for the year in which her license expired.

In 1945, taxpayer was head of the Department of English and a teacher of English and Journalism at the George Washington High School in Danville, Virginia. A Master of Arts of Columbia University, she held the Collegiate Professional Certificate, the highest certificate issued to public school teachers by the Virginia State Board of Education. She was notified of the expiration of her certificate and that the certificate could not be renewed unless she complied with the Regulations set out above.

The alternatives required for the renewal of taxpayer's certificate were: (a) acquiring college credits or (b) passing an examination on five selected books. She elected (a) and attended the Summer School of Columbia University. We hardly think it open to question that she chose the alternative which would most effectively add to her efficiency as a teacher. At Columbia she took two courses: one on the technique of short story writing, which was right in her alley; another in abnormal psychology, which would be most useful to a teacher whose pupils were adolescents.

It is clear that to be deductible as a business expense the item must be—(a) "paid or incurred" within the taxable year; (b) incurred in carrying on a "trade or business"; and (c) both "ordinary and necessary." As a corollary, the expenses must not be personal in their nature. We think taxpayer has completely satisfied all these requisites, so that the decision of the Tax Court must be reversed.

In its opinion, the Tax Court stated:

We cannot assume that public school teachers *ordinarily* attend summer school to renew their certificates when alternative methods are available. The record does not show that the course pursued by petitioner was the usual method followed by

[handwritten margin note: Tax Ct held this course taking was not ordinary nor necessary]

teachers in obtaining renewals of their certificates or that it was necessary so to do. * * *

The record is devoid of any showing that petitioner was employed to continue in her position as teacher at the time she attended summer school in 1945 and made the expenditures in connection therewith for which she seeks a deduction. The inference may well be that she took the summer course to obtain a renewal of her certificate that would qualify her for reemployment. The expense incurred was more in the nature of a preparation to qualify her for teaching in the High School in Danville, Virginia.

Also, in support of its decision, the Tax Court quoted O.D. 892, 4 C.B. 209 (1921): "The expenses incurred by schoolteachers in attending summer school are in the nature of personal expenses incurred in advancing their education and are not deductible in computing net income."

[handwritten margin note: unreasonable to make T.P. show % of teachers who take courses or take exam]

As to the first of these statements, we think it is quite unreasonable to require a statistical showing by taxpayer of the comparative number of Virginia teachers who elect, for a renewal of their certificates, the acquisition of college credits rather than the much less desirable alternative of standing an examination on the five selected books. The existence of two methods for the renewal of these certificates, one or the other of which is compulsory, is not in itself vital in this connection. If the particular course adopted by the taxpayer is a response that a reasonable person would normally and naturally make under the specific circumstances, that would suffice. Even if a statistical study actually revealed that a majority of Virginia teachers adopted the examination on the selected books, in order to renew their certificates, rather than the method of acquiring college credits, our conclusion here would be the same. Manifestly, the added expense of attending a summer school, in the light of the slender salaries paid to teachers, would deter many teachers from such a course, however strong might be their predilections in favor of such a procedure. We note that the statistical requirement does not seem to have been enforced in the cases subsequently cited in this opinion—cases, we think, far less meritorious than the one before us.

[handwritten margin note: even if > # took exam rather than course no change in outcome.]

[handwritten margin note: she did not need to show that she was actually employed for the next year.]

Nor do we approve the reasoning of the Tax Court that the taxpayer's failure to show by positive evidence that she was employed to continue in her position as teacher when she incurred the summer school expenses should negative the deduction of these expenses. She did prove to the Tax Court that she had been continuously so engaged for consecutive decades. She had not resigned her position and no practical advantage would accrue to her upon a renewal of her certificate other than the privilege and power to continue as a teacher. Clearly, the very logic of the situation here shows that she went to Columbia to maintain her present position, not to attain a new position; to preserve, not to expand or increase; to carry on, not to commence.

Any other view seems to us unreal and hypercritical. And taxpayer, in her petition to the Tax Court for a review of its decision, showed conclusively that when she went to Columbia University in the summer of 1945, she was then under contract with the Danville School Board to teach for the ensuing session of 1945–1946 and that to carry out this existing contract, she was obligated to renew her certificate by complying with the pertinent regulations.

* * *

Dictionary definitions of the words "ordinary," "necessary," and "personal" afford scant assistance in the solution of our problem. Quite helpful, though, are the opinions in the decided cases. Frequently quoted is the observation of Mr. Justice Cardozo, in Welch v. Helvering, 290 U.S. 111, 113, 54 S.Ct. 8, 9: "Now, what is ordinary, though there must always be a strain of constancy within it, is none the less a variable affected by time and place and circumstance. Ordinary in this context does not mean that the payments must be habitual or normal in the sense that the same taxpayer will have to make them often. A lawsuit affecting the safety of a business may happen once in a lifetime. The counsel fees may be so heavy that repetition is unlikely. None the less, the expense is an ordinary one because we know from experience that payments for such a purpose, whether the amount is large or small, are the common and accepted means of defense against attack. Cf. Kornhauser v. United States, 276 U.S. 145, 48 S.Ct. 219. The situation is unique in the life of the individual affected, but not in the life of the group, the community, of which he is a part. At such times there are norms of conduct that help to stabilize our judgment, and make it certain and objective. The instance is not erratic, but is brought within a known type."

* * *

Said Mr. Justice Douglas, in Deputy v. DuPont, 308 U.S. 488, 496, 60 S.Ct. 363: "One of the extremely relevant circumstances is the nature and scope of the particular business out of which the expense in question accrued. The fact that an obligation to pay has arisen is not sufficient. It is the kind of transaction out of which the obligation arose and its *normalcy in the particular business* which are crucial and controlling." (Italics ours.)

* * *

We quote a trenchant critique on the decision of the Tax Court from Maguire, Individual Federal Income Tax in 1950, 35 American Association of University Professors Bulletin, 748, 762: "As to the matters just discussed, Nora P. Hill, 13 T.C. [291] No. 41 (1949), is an interesting decision, if scarcely an encouragement. The taxpayer, a Virginia public school teacher, sought to deduct as an ordinary and necessary business expense for 1945 the cost of attending summer courses in Columbia University. Her teaching certificate, the highest granted by the State Board of Education, came up for renewal in 1945. Virginia law required for renewal of teaching certificates either the taking of professional or academic courses for credit or the passing of examinations on prescribed reading. The Tax Court denied the claim of deduction. Part of its reasoning was that because the Virginia legal requirements might be satisfied by pursuing either of the two alternatives, the showing was insufficient that what the taxpayer had done was the ordinary method of satisfaction. Another part of the reasoning was that the taxpayer had not explicitly shown she was employed to continue as a teacher at the time she took the summer school courses. Hence, said the Court, it might be inferred that the taxpayer was seeking to qualify for reemployment as distinguished from merely maintaining an employed status. While these views seem hypercritical and are an invitation to the same teacher or another teacher to try again with more carefully detailed proof, the tone of the opinion hints at strong distaste for this sort of deduction."

Our conclusion is that the expenses incurred by the taxpayer here were incurred in carrying on a trade or business, were ordinary and necessary, and were not personal in nature. She has, we think, showed that she has complied with both the letter and the spirit of the law which permits such expenses to be deducted for federal income tax purposes. We do not hold (and it is not necessary for us to hold) that all expenses incurred by teachers in attending summer schools are deductible. Our decision is limited to the facts of the case before us. The decision of the Tax Court of the United States is, accordingly, reversed and the case is remanded to that Court with instructions to allow taxpayer as a deduction the expenses which she claims.

Reversed.

COUGHLIN v. COMMISSIONER *
United States Court of Appeals, Second Circuit, 1953.
203 F.2d 307.

CHASE, Circuit Judge. The petitioner has been a member of the bar for many years and in 1944 was admitted to practice before the Treasury Department. In 1946 he was in active practice in Binghamton, N.Y., as a member of a firm of lawyers there. The firm engaged in general practice but did considerable work which required at least one member to be skilled in matters pertaining to Federal taxation and to maintain such skill by keeping informed as to changes in the tax laws and the significance of pertinent court decisions when made. His partners relied on him to keep advised on that subject and he accepted that responsibility. One of the various ways in which he discharged it was by attending, in the above mentioned year, the Fifth Annual Institute on Federal Taxation which was conducted in New York City under the sponsorship of the Division of General Education of New York University. In so doing he incurred expenses for tuition, travel, board and lodging of $305, which he claimed as an allowable deduction under section 23(a)(1)(A) I.R.C., as ordinary and necessary expenses

* See Niswander, "Tax Aspects of Education: When Ordinary and Necessary; When Personal," 26 N.Y.U.Inst. on Fed. Tax. 27 (1968). Ed.

incurred in carrying on a trade or business and no question is raised as to their reasonableness in amount. The Commission[er] disallowed the deduction and the Tax Court, four judges dissenting, upheld the disallowance on the ground that the expenses were non-business ones "because of the educational and personal nature of the object pursued by the petitioner."

The Tax Court found that the Institute on Federal Taxation was not conducted for the benefit of those unversed in the subject of Federal taxation and students were warned away. In 1946, it was attended by 408 attorneys, accountants, trust officers, executives of corporations and the like. In 1947, over 1500 of such people from many states were in attendance. It was "designed by its sponsors to provide a place and atmosphere where practitioners could gather trends, thinking and developments in the field of Federal taxation from experts accomplished in that field."

Thus there is posed for solution a problem which involves no dispute as to the basic facts but is, indeed, baffling because, as is so often true of legal problems, the correct result depends upon how to give the facts the right order of importance.

We may start by noticing that the petitioner does not rely upon section 23(a)(2) which permits the deduction of certain non-trade or non-business expenses, but rests entirely upon his contention that the deduction he took was allowable as an ordinary and necessary expense incurred in the practice of his profession. The expenses were deductible under section 23(a)(1)(A) if they were "directly connected with" or "proximately resulted from" the practice of his profession. Kornhauser v. United States, 276 U.S. 145, 153, 48 S.Ct. 219, 220. And if it were usual for lawyers in practice similar to his to incur such expenses they were "ordinary." Deputy v. DuPont, 308 U.S. 488, 495, 60 S.Ct. 363. They were also "necessary" if appropriate and helpful. Welch v. Helvering, 290 U.S. 111, 54 S.Ct. 8. But this is an instance emphasizing how dim a line is drawn between expenses which are deductible because incurred in trade or business, i.e., because professional, and those which are nondeductible because personal. Section 24(a)(1) of Title 26.

The respondent relies upon T.R. 111, § 29.23(a)–15, which provides that "expenses of taking special courses or training" are not allowable as deductions under section 23(a)(2). But section 23(a)(2) concerns non-trade or non-business expenses. It is not necessary to decide whether, in the light of the regulation, an expense of the nature here involved would be deductible if incurred in connection with a profit-making venture that is not a trade or business. It will suffice to say that, since the expense was incurred in a trade or business within the meaning of section 23(a)(1)(A), the regulation interpreting section 23(a)(2) is not a bar to allowance here.

In Welch v. Helvering, supra, 290 U.S. at page 115, 54 S.Ct. at page 9, there is a dictum that the cost of acquiring learning is a personal expense. But the issue decided in that case is far removed from the one involved here. There the taxpayer paid debts for which he was not legally liable whose payment enhanced his reputation for personal integrity and consequently the value of the good will of his business, and it was held that these payments were personal expenses. The general reference to the cost of education as a personal expense was made by way of illustrating the point then under decision, and it related to that knowledge which is obtained for its own sake as an addition to one's cultural background or for possible use in some work which might be started in the future. There was no indication that an exception is not to be made where the information acquired was needed for use in a lawyer's established practice.

T.R. 111, § 29.23(a)–5, makes clear that among the expenses which a professional man may deduct under Section 23(a)(1)(A) are dues to professional societies, subscriptions to professional journals, and amounts currently expended for books whose useful life is short. Such expenses as are here in question are not expressly included or excluded, but they are analogous to those above stated which are expressly characterized as allowable deductions.

This situation is closely akin to that in Hill v. Commissioner, 4 Cir., 181 F.2d 906, where the expenses incurred by a teacher in attending a summer school were held deductible. The only difference is in the degree of necessity which prompted the incurrence of the expenses. The teacher couldn't retain her position unless she complied with the requirements for the renewal of her teaching certificate; and an optional way to do that, and the one she chose, was to take courses in education at a recognized institution of learning. Here the petitioner did not need a renewal of his license to practice and it may be assumed that he could have continued as a member of his firm whether or not he kept currently informed as to the law of Federal taxation. But he was morally bound to keep so informed and did so in part by means of his attendance at this session of the Institute. It was a way well adapted to fulfill his professional duty to keep sharp the tools he actually used in his going trade or business. It may be that the knowledge he thus gained incidentally increased his fund of learning in general and, in that sense, the cost of acquiring it may have been a personal expense; but we think that the immediate, over-all professional need to incur the expenses in order to perform his work with due regard to the current status of the law so overshadows the personal aspect that it is the decisive feature.

It serves also to distinguish these expenditures from those made to acquire a capital asset. Even if in its cultural aspect knowledge should for tax purposes be considered in the nature of a capital asset as was suggested in Welch v. Helvering, supra, the rather evanescent character of that for which the petitioner spent his money deprives it of the sort of permanency such a concept embraces.

Decision reversed and cause remanded for the allowance of the deduction.

PROBLEMS

1. Alice, Barbara, Cathy, and Denise were college roommates who after graduating went on to become a doctor, a dentist, an accountant (C.P.A.), and a lawyer, respectively. In the current year, after sometime in practice as an orthopedic surgeon, Alice, who was often called upon to give medical testimony in malpractice suits, decided to go to law school so as to better understand this aspect of her medical practice. Barbara enrolled in a course of postgraduate study in orthodontics, intending to restrict her dental practice to that specialty in the future. Cathy enrolled part time in law school (with eventual prospects of attaining a degree) so as better to perform her accounting duties in areas in which law and accounting tend to overlap. And Denise took a leave of absence from her firm to enroll in an LL.M. course in taxation, intending to practice exclusively in the tax area. Which, if any, is incurring deductible expenses of education?

2. Assume Denise's expenses in problem 1, above, are deductible. If she is a practitioner in Seattle, Washington, who travels to Gainesville, Florida for a year to participate in their LL.M. program, what expenses, in addition to tuition and books, may she deduct? See Reg. § 1.162–5(e) and I.R.C. § 274(n).

3. Carl earned a bachelor's degree in education and he teaches world history in a junior high school. In the current year he contemplates a summer European tour doing things that will be beneficial to his teaching efforts. He wishes to know if he may deduct his expenses. What do you advise?

4. Dentist attends a five day dental seminar at a ski resort. All of the seminar proceedings are taped and Dentist skis on clear days and watches all of the tapes on snowy days or in other off-the-slopes time prior to his return home. Are Dentist's travel, meal and lodging deductible?

D. MISCELLANEOUS BUSINESS DEDUCTIONS

---

1. INTRODUCTION

Internal Revenue Code: Sections 162(a); 274(a), (d), (e), (k), (*l*) and (n).
Regulations: See Sections 1.162–20(a)(2); 1.274–2(a), (c), (d).

The three business expense deductions listed in paragraphs (1) through (3) of Section 162(a) are illustrative only and by no means exclusive. The statute specifically states that *all* ordinary and necessary business expenses are deductible *including* those specifically listed, and it is similar in that regard to Section 61.[1] It would be impossible to list every conceivable type of deduction within the section, especially since the test varies among different businesses. This note will, however, attempt to highlight some of the more important business expense deductions.

Business Meals and Entertainment. Business meals and entertainment expenses may be deductible. Waiters often overhear someone say: "Have another—it's deductible!" or "Don't worry, I can write it off on my income tax!" Certainly to furnish meals and entertainment is an accepted practice and expense in carrying on many businesses. But when such expenses fall within Section 162(a) are there not obvious possibilities for abuse? Prior to 1962 there were few restrictions on the deductibility of business meals and entertainment expenses, either as to the scope of items which were considered within permissible meals or entertainment or as to the amount of proof or substantiation of expenses incurred. The question of substantiation was raised in the case of Cohan v. Commissioner,[2] in which the actor, George M. Cohan, attempted to deduct large unsubstantiated travel and entertainment expenses. The Second Circuit instructed that in such cases the trial court should approximate the expenses stating:[3]

> In the production of his plays Cohan was obliged to be freehanded in entertaining actors, employees, and, as he naively adds dramatic critics. He had also to travel much, at times with his attorney. These expenses amounted to substantial sums but he kept no account and probably could not have done so. At the trial before the Board [Tax Court] he estimated that he had spent eleven thousand dollars in this fashion during the six months of 1921, twenty-two thousand dollars, between July 1, 1921 and June 30, 1922, and as much for his following fiscal year, fifty five thousand dollars in all. The Board refused to allow him any part of this, on the ground that it was impossible to tell how much he had in fact spent, in the absence of any items or details. The question is how far this refusal is justified, in view of the finding that he had spent much and that the sums were allowable expenses. Absolute certainty in such matters is usually impossible and is not necessary; the Board should make as close an approximation as it can, bearing heavily if it chooses upon the taxpayer whose inexactitude is of his own making. But to allow nothing at all appears to us inconsistent with saying that something was spent. True, we do not know how many trips Cohan made, nor how large his entertainments were; yet there was obviously some basis for computation, if necessary by drawing upon the Board's personal estimates of the minimum of such expenses. The amount may be trivial and unsatisfactory, but there was basis for some

---

1. On the Code meaning of "including,"   **3.** Id. at 543–544.
see I.R.C. § 7701(b).

2. 39 F.2d 540 (2d Cir.1930).

allowance, and it was wrong to refuse any, even though it were the travelling expenses of a single trip. It is not fatal that the result will inevitably be speculative; many important decisions must be such.

Prior to 1962, the *Cohan* rule was often applied to allow some deduction in the absence of proof.[4] A fairly easy atitude on the scope of deductions for meals and entertainment and the fluidity of the *Cohan* rule caused many to wonder whether, by way of "business" deductions, taxpayers generally were being called upon to pay for the enjoyments of a relatively select few in the business community. The limiting concepts of "ordinary" and "necessary" under Section 162(a) and Section 262 seemed not to do the job.[5]

In 1962, Congress enacted Section 274 in an attempt to muffle the cry: "It's deductible!" After some amendments, the effect of current Section 274 is to narrow the scope of Section 162 with respect to expenses for business meals, entertainment, gifts, employee awards, and travel[6] by imposing some limitations and requiring substantiation.[7] Section 274 imposes two principal limitations on the deductibility of *business meals and entertainment.* First, to the extent that such expenses (including the cost of facilities used in connection with entertainment) are otherwise deductible after any other statutory limitations (as discussed below), Section 274(n)(1) places another restriction on the deduction allowing only 80 percent of the otherwise deductible amount. The 80 percent limitation extends to *all deductible meals,* not just business meals; although there are some exceptions.[8] Second, Section 274 also provides that expenses related to any business meals or entertainment, amusement, or recreational activity are deductible, only if the meal or activity is "directly related to" or "associated with" the taxpayer's trade or business.[9] The regulations grapple with these concepts.[10] Essentially, the phrase "directly related to" requires that business go on *during* the entertainment for which an expense deduction is claimed (sales pitch during the ball game?); and the phrase "associated with" requires that the entertainment have a business purpose and either immediately precede or follow a bona fide business

---

4. See James Schulz, 16 T.C. 401 (1951); Harold A. Christensen, 17 T.C. 1456 (1952); Richard A. Sutter, 21 T.C. 170 (1953).

5. See Caplan, "The Travel and Entertainment Expense Problem," 30 Taxes 947 (1961).

6. I.R.C. § 274 also limits deductions under § 212 and other sections such as § 170 and § 217.

I.R.C. § 274(b) limitations on business gifts; § 274(c) limitations on deductibility of foreign travelling expenses; § 274(h) limitations on conventions, § 274(j) limitations on employee achievements awards, § 274(m)(1) limitations or cruise ship travel, and § 274(m)(2) limitations on travel as

a form of education have previously been referred to.

7. I.R.C. § 274(d).

8. I.R.C. § 274(n)(2). Thus, the 80% limitation is applicable to meals related to educational expenses, § 217 moving expenses, etc.

9. I.R.C. § 274(a)(1)(A). Although § 274(a)(1)(A) does not specifically include business meals, the 1986 legislation repealed an exclusion for them under § 274(e) and the legislative history of the 1986 Act specifically includes them within the limitation. Query the need for a technical amendment to § 274(a)(1)?

10. Reg. § 1.274–2(c) and (d).

discussion (lunch and ball game after office conference?)[11] The legislative history suggests that meals while travelling on business away from home are not subject to these requirements and may be eaten alone or with nonbusiness meal partners.[12]

Some additional restrictions are imposed on the deductibility of business meals. Most business meals generate deductible expenses only if they are not "lavish or extravagant" [13] and only if the deducting taxpayer or an employee of the taxpayer is present at the meal.[14]

One problem with respect to business meals is the deductibility of the taxpayer's own meals and those of his wife. In pure theory, if a taxpayer takes a customer to dinner to talk business and the taxpayer's wife goes along the amount that it would have cost husband and wife to eat anyway, is a nondeductible personal expense under Section 262. Along this line, in Richard A. Sutter [15] the court sustained the Commissioner's disallowance of a deduction for the taxpayer's own meals at business lunches where the taxpayer could not prove that the expenses incurred exceeded his normal meal costs. It is the Service's position that the portion of the taxpayer's meal which exceeds the amount which he would have normally spent is deductible; however, the Service applies the *Sutter* doctrine "only to abuse cases where taxpayers claim deductions for substantial amounts of personal living expenses."[16] Would it be administratively feasible to apply the *Sutter* doctrine comprehensively? Similarly, the regulations under Section 274 allow the taxpayer to deduct his wife's expenses if they are closely connected to the business activity.[17]

Expenses related to entertainment *facilities*,[18] such as yachts, summer homes and club dues, are often only remotely related to the furtherance of a taxpayer's business; the potential for writing off nondeductible personal expenses is especially great in this area. As such, expenditures for entertainment facilities have been subject to even closer tax scrutiny than entertainment activity expenses. Prior to 1979 Section 274(a)(1)(B) provided that no deduction was allowed for such expenses unless the use of the facility was "directly related to" the

---

11. Under I.R.C. § 274(e), various inherently business activities (typical business meals) and expenditures for employees are excepted from the requirements of I.R.C. § 274(a)(1).

12. Conf. Rep. No. 99–841, 99th Cong., 2d Sess. II–27 (1986). The meals remain subject to the I.R.C. § 274(n) 80% limitation.

13. I.R.C. § 274(k)(1)(A). There are several exceptions to the application of this limitation. See I.R.C. § 274(k)(2) and (e)(2), (3), (4), (7), (8), and (9).

14. I.R.C. § 274(k)(1)(B). The legislative history indicates that an independent contractor who renders significant services to the taxpayer, such as his attorney, may be treated as an employee under this sec-

tion if he attends the meeting in connection with the performance of services. Conf. Rep. No. 99–841, supra note 12 at II–26.

15. Supra note 4.

16. Rev.Rul. 63–144, Question 31, 1963–2 C.B. 129, 135. See however Letter Ruling 8006004, 10/26/79, which may mark a departure from that administrative policy.

17. Reg. § 1.274–2(d)(4).

18. Reg. § 1.274–2(e)(2)(i) defines an entertainment facility as "any item of personal or real property owned, rented, or used by a taxpayer * * * if it is used * * * for, or in connection with, entertainment * * *." See also I.R.C. § 274(a)(2)(A).

taxpayer's trade or business and was primarily for business purposes.[19] Further, the deduction was limited to the business portion of the total expenditure.[20] As stringent as these requirements were, Congress felt they still provided encouragement to taxpayers "to attempt to deduct, as business expenses, items that essentially represented nondeductible personal expenses"[21] and in the Revenue Act of 1978 it amended Section 274(a)(1)(B) further to preclude facilities deductions. Thus, expenses respecting entertainment facilities are now non-deductible.[22]

Three aspects of this disallowance must be emphasized. First, expenses of facilities used in business for non-entertainment purposes remain deductible. Thus an airplane used for business travel as opposed to entertainment is outside the grasp of Section 274(a)(1)(B), and costs related to it (such as depreciation and repairs) are deductible to the extent of such non-entertainment business use.[23] Second, the payment of dues or fees to a social, athletic or sporting club are 80 percent deductible if the taxpayer establishes that the club is used primarily for furtherance of his trade or business and that the expenditure is "directly related to" the active conduct of a trade or business.[24] Finally, although expenditures for entertainment facilities are not deductible, nevertheless entertainment activities related to the use of such facilities remain 80 percent deductible if the rules for deduction of entertainment activity expenditures are satisfied.[25] For example, if a taxpayer takes a client skiing, staying several nights in taxpayer's ski home, 80 percent of expenses for lift tickets, ski rentals, and meals are likely deductible as an entertainment activity.[26] However, the costs related to the home even if it is used exclusively for business entertainment are disallowed under Section 274(a)(1)(B).[27]

19. In such instances the regulations prescribed a more than 50% test to meet the primary requirement. Reg. § 1.274–2(e)(4).

20. Thus if a businessman belonged to a country club and used it 40% of the time for business purposes, he could deduct none of the dues; but if he used it 60% of the time for business purposes, he could deduct 80% of 60% of the dues.

21. See Sen.Rep. No. 95–1263, 95th Cong., 2d Sess. 174 (1978), 1978–3 vol. 1 C.B. 472.

22. The disallowance is expressly made applicable to dues and fees paid to social, athletic, and sporting clubs. I.R.C. § 274(a)(2)(A). However, dues paid to professional organizations, such as bar fees, are still deductible.

23. Cf. Sharp v. U.S., infra at page 753. Further, the Conference Report states that inherently business activities (see note, 11 supra) continue to be excepted from I.R.C. § 274(a). See § 274(e).

24. I.R.C. § 274(a)(2)(C). See notes 19 and 20, supra, and note 47, infra, for rules applicable to such club dues or fees. Originally the § 274(a)(2)(C) exception applied only to country club dues; however, the Technical Corrections Act of 1979 increased the scope of the exception to include all social, athletic, and sporting clubs.

25. See Conf.Rep. No. 95–1800, 95 Cong., 2d Sess. 251 (1978).

26. This assumes the I.R.C. § 274(a)(1)(A) requirements are met. See note 9, supra.

27. For a comprehensive discussion of the effect of the Revenue Act of 1978 on deductions for entertainment facilities, see Bostick and Terr, "How the 1978 Act Affects T & E Deductions for Facilities: Implications and Planning," 59 J.Tax. 130 (1979); Schnee and Bates, "Entertainment Expense Under the Revenue Act of 1978," 57 Taxes 435–39 (July, 1979).

Section 274 also imposes some special limitations on the cost of certain entertainment expenses. For example, generally the deductible cost of an entertainment event is limited to 80 percent of the *face amount* of the ticket.[28] Thus the amount of any scalper's premiums on tickets is not deductible. Seemingly, the cost of skyboxes and private luxury boxes (beyond seat cost for a regular ticket) is categorized as a "facility" and is nondeductible under Section 274(a)(1)(B). However, until 1986 the cost of leasing such skyboxes for business purposes was deductible as an entertainment expense. In the 1986 legislation, the cost of leases on skyboxes for more than one event was made nondeductible subject to a phase-in for 1987 and 1988. Deductibility of 80 percent of the regular seat cost continues, subject of course to the usual general restraints.[29]

In addition to classifying some expenses, possibly within Section 162, as only 80 percent deductible or not deductible at all, subsection (d) of Section 274 also imposes substantiation requirements with respect to expenditures that are allowable as deductions.[30] The substantiation requirements apply to travel expenses (both foreign and domestic) including meals and lodging,[31] as well as to expenditures for business meals, entertainment, gifts, and "listed property." Listed property is considered in Chapter 22A2, infra. The regulations under Section 274(d),[32] which have received judicial blessing,[33] impose stringent documentation requirements, normally necessitating a receipt for expenditures in excess of $25. Rev.Rul. 63–144,[34] which is in the form of a detailed list of questions and answers, is helpful in understanding of the overall impact of Section 274.[35]

---

28. I.R.C. § 274(*l*)(1)(A), (n)(1). I.R.C. § 274(*l*)(1)(B) allows an exception for the cost of tickets to certain charitable fund-raising events.

29. I.R.C. § 274(*l*)(2)(A). There was a phase-in of the disallowance in 1987 and 1988; the phase-in resulted in a one-third disallowance in 1987, a two-thirds disallowance in 1988, and full disallowance in 1989. I.R.C. § 274(*l*)(2)(B).

30. In the areas affected by I.R.C. § 274 (but only those areas), § 274(d) overrules the long-established *Cohan* rule. With respect to substantiation of deductions not within the scope of § 274, the *Cohan* rule still applies. Ellery W. Newton, 57 T.C. 245 (1971), business use of an automobile other than in a travel status; William H. Green, 31 T.C.M. 592 (1972), wagering losses.

31. See Rev.Rul. 75–169, 1975–1 C.B. 59. See also I.R.C. § 274(h), sometimes wholly denying deductions for expenses incurred in attending foreign conventions.

32. Reg. § 1.274–5.

33. Sanford v. Commissioner, 412 F.2d 201 (2d Cir.1969), cert. denied 396 U.S. 841,

90 S.Ct. 104 (1969); Robert H. Alter, 50 T.C. 833 (1968); John Robinson, 51 T.C. 520 (1968), affirmed per curiam (this issue) 422 F.2d 873 (9th Cir.1970). The Fifth Circuit has ruled that each and every element of each expenditure must be adequately substantiated. Dowell v. U.S., 522 F.2d 708 (5th Cir.1975). There is a comment on the *Sanford* case by Aaron, "Substantiation Requirements for Travel, Entertainment and Gift Expenses," 35 Mo.L.Rev. 70 (1970); and see McNally, "Substantiation of Business Related Entertainment Expenses," 54 Marq.L.Rev. 347 (1971).

34. 1963–2 C.B. 129.

35. The ruling and articles cited below discuss the law prior to the 1978 and 1979 changes for facilities. For a discussion of those rules see the articles at note 27, supra. For further discussion of I.R.C. (26 U.S.C.A.) § 274, see Graichen, "Effect of T and E Disallowances Upon Employer, and Employee, Officer, Stockholder," 22 N.Y.U.Inst. on Fed.Tax 843 (1964); Emmanuel and Lipoff, "Travel and Entertainment: The New World of Section 274," 18 Tax L.Rev. 487 (1963); Axelrad, "An Evaluation of the New Rules Relating to the

Uniforms. Recall from prior consideration of the "carrying on" requirement that an employee is considered to be in a trade or business in his role as an employee.[36] Consequently, he may deduct unreimbursed expenses that he incurs which otherwise meet the Section 162 requirements. A common deduction for employees is the cost of obtaining and maintaining their uniforms. Deductions for uniforms are allowed only if "(1) the uniforms are specifically required as a condition of employment and (2) are not of a type adaptable to general or continued usage to the extent that they take the place of ordinary clothing."[37] Thus, policemen, firemen, baseball players, jockeys, etc. may deduct their uniform costs, because their required uniforms are not adaptable to personal use.[38] In one case the Tax Court held that the most advanced styles and fashions which the taxpayer, a fashion coordinator, was required to wear were not suitable for her personal use and hence were deductible.[39] The Treasury takes the position that uniforms of military personnel are for general use and generate no deductions, but recognizes an exception for uniforms of reservists that are worn only occasionally and also for swords, which can hardly be considered available for general use.[40]

Advertising. Generally advertising expenses of a business are deductible in the year in which they are incurred or paid even though the benefits may extend over several years.[41] On the other hand, an expenditure related to advertising can be capital in nature and thus fail to qualify as a Section 162 expense. For example, the purchase of a piece of property or the construction of a billboard or advertising sign which lasts several years involve capital expenditures, the latter to be written off by way of deductions under Section 167 or Section 168.[42] Generally, the cost of advertising in magazines, television, and sports programs is currently deductible.[43] A limitation is imposed on such advertising if it borders on the area of political contributions. Contributions directly or indirectly to political candidates and political parties are not allowed as deductions.[44] Consequently, to foreclose attempted subterfuge, deduction of the cost of advertising in convention programs or publications of political parties is expressly proscribed.[45]

Deductibility of Entertainment, Travel and Gifts: A Critical Look at Section 274," 16 U.S.C. Tax Inst. 345 (1964); Osborn, "Tax Problems of the Attorney and Other Professionals in Connection with Travel and Entertainment ∗ ∗ ∗" 11 Wake Forest L.Rev. 535 (1975).

36. Supra page 359.

37. Mim. 6463, 1950–1 C.B. 29.

38. Rev.Ruls. 70–474, 475, and 476, 1970–2 C.B. 35. See also Robert C. Fryer, 33 T.C.M. 403 (1974) where a commercial airline pilot was allowed to deduct the cost of his shoeshines but not the cost of his haircuts.

39. Betsy Lusk Yeomans, 30 T.C. 757 (1958).

40. Reg. § 1.262–1(b)(8).

41. G.G. Ebner, 17 T.C.M. 550 (1958).

42. Cf. Alabama Coca-Cola Bottling Co., 28 T.C.M. 635 (1969).

43. See Alexander Sprunt & Son, Inc., 24 B.T.A. 599 (1931).

44. I.R.C. § 162(e) and see § 271; Reg. § 1.162–20; and Holzman, "That Advertising Expense Deduction," 40 Taxes 555 (1962).

45. I.R.C. § 276(a)(1).

Dues. In general dues paid to organizations directly related to one's business are deductible under Section 162.[46] Thus, attorney's dues paid to the local bar are deductible and an employee's labor union dues are also deductible. Dues, like advertising, must be examined according to the substance of the payment to determine their deductibility. For example, dues to a social, athletic or sporting club are considered amounts paid for an entertainment facility under Section 274(a)(1)(B) and are generally not deductible unless the club is used primarily for the furtherance of the taxpayer's trade or business; and then only the portion of dues directly related to that trade or business are deductible.[47]

Some payments, such as those for interest and property taxes, which are deductible whether or not business oriented are reserved for consideration in Chapter 16.[48] Many of the deductions discussed above are allowed (along with several other "itemized deductions") only after the imposition of a floor of two percent of adjusted gross income. Consideration of this rule is deferred to Chapter 18E.

PROBLEMS

1. Employee spends $100 taking 3 business clients to lunch at a local restaurant to discuss a particular business matter. The $100 cost includes $5 in tax and $15 for a tip. They each have two martinis before lunch.

(a) To what extent are Employee's expenses deductible?

(b) To what extent are the meals deductible if the lunch is merely to touch base with the clients?

(c) What result if Employee merely sends the three clients to lunch without going himself but picks up their $75 tab?

(d) What result in (a), above, if, in addition, Employee incurs a $15 cab fare to transport the clients to lunch?

(e) What result in (a), above, if Employer reimburses Employee for the $100 tab?

2. Businessman who is in New York on business meets with two clients and afterward takes them to the Broadway production of The Phantom of the Opera. To what extent is the $300 cost of their tickets deductible if the marked price on the tickets is $50 each, but he buys them from the bellman at his hotel for $100 each?

3. Airline Pilot incurs the following expenses in the current year:

(1) $250 for the cost of a new uniform.

(2) $30 for dry cleaning the uniform.

---

46. Some restrictions on this general rule are expressed in Reg. § 1.162–20(c)(3).

47. I.R.C. § 274(a)(2)(A) and § 274(a)(2)(C).

48. Payments to organizations which may qualify for the charitable deduction under I.R.C. § 170 but for their connection with business are considered in Chapter 23B.

(3) $100 in newspaper ads to acquire a new job as a property manager in his spare time.

(4) $200 in union dues.

(5) $50 in political contributions to his local legislator who he hopes will push legislation beneficial to airline pilots.

(6) $500 in fees to a local gym to keep in physical shape for flying.

What is the total of Pilot's deductible § 162 expenses?

2. BUSINESS LOSSES

Internal Revenue Code: Sections 165(c)(1); 280B.

If a transaction or event produces a "loss", the threshold question *whether* the loss may be deductible must always be answered on the basis of the rules in Section 165. It is the Code's central switchboard for *all* losses. But statutory restrictions may be encountered elsewhere, and the *manner* in which the taxpayer may make use of loss deductions is the subject of a number of special provisions. The most recent restrictive developments are the subject of comment at the end of this brief note.

Although Section 165(a) seems to make all losses deductible,[1] attention is directed to Section 165(c). An individual taxpayer can deduct only such losses as are identified there. Section 165(c)(1) permits the deduction by an individual of any loss "incurred in a trade or business." As this Chapter is addressed to business deductions, we defer for later consideration other individual losses that may be deducted under Section 165(c)(2) or (3), and focus on business losses.[2]

What is a business "loss"?[3] At the outset, it must be stated that only "realized" losses are taken into account. The concept of realization is essentially the same here as in the income area. Just as mere appreciation in the value of property is not income subject to tax, so a mere decline in the value of the property is not a loss that can be deducted. To be deductible, a loss must be evidenced by a closed and completed transaction, such as a sale, or fixed by an identifiable event, such as a fire.[4]

Here are a few examples of deductible business losses. A buys a delivery truck for use in his business and sells it a year later for less than its adjusted basis. B buys a tractor for use on his farm and, when he determines it is completely worn out, abandons it—gives it to the junk man for no consideration. C pays $1000 for an option on a plant to be used in his business, but forfeits the $1000 when he decides not to

---

1. In general, they are for corporate taxpayers.

2. I.R.C. § 165(c)(2) and (3) losses are considered in Chapters 15 and 23, respectively.

3. The question whether the taxpayer is engaged in a "trade or business" is the same here as in I.R.C. § 162(a) and § 167(a)(1) and is not further explored at this point.

4. Reg. § 1.165–1(b).

exercise the option. D buys a Chris Craft which he operates for hire at a resort, but the boat which is not insured is demolished in a storm. The measurement of the loss deduction depends in part on the adjusted basis of the property.[5] Thus, A's loss will be the familiar difference between the amount realized and adjusted basis. In B's and C's cases the loss deduction will probably be the adjusted basis of the tractor or the option.[6] D's loss is a casualty loss and, since his boat is totally destroyed, his loss is the amount of his basis in the boat.[7] If the boat were only damaged, D's casualty loss would be measured by the difference between its fair market value before and after the storm limited however by the adjusted basis of the property.[8] To the extent that D's loss is compensated by insurance D's deductible loss is reduced;[9] if the insurance recovery exceeds D's adjusted basis in the boat he has a casualty gain.[10] To illustrate, if D had a $6,000 adjusted basis for his boat and it had a $10,000 value before the storm and its value after the storm (uncompensated by insurance) is $7,000 D has a $3,000 loss. If the uninsured boat is totally destroyed D would have a $6,000 loss. In the later case if D recovered $4,000 of insurance for the boat his loss would be limited to $2,000. Finally if the boat were fully insured, D's recovery of $10,000 of insurance would result in a $4,000 casualty gain.[11]

Each of the losses suggested above will ultimately have a direct impact on the taxable income reported by the individual. If the Section 165(c)(1) losses incurred in a business during the year, along with its other expenses, exceed its income, the business will be unprofitable and the owner will have an overall business loss for the year.[12] The business loss can be deducted against other types of income on his return such as income from investments, other businesses, or salaries. If he has a business loss and no other income (or if the business loss exceeds his other income) so that the loss cannot be fully utilized to reduce taxable income, he will get the benefit of a net operating loss carryback or carryover to another taxable year.[13]

Not every closed transaction that involves financial disadvantages supports a deductible tax loss. Congress has lately changed the criteria for one type of loss and has made, predictable even if they are questionable, complementary changes in attending basis rules.

If Simple Simon were around these days, he would probably claim recently added[14] and more recently amended[15] Section 280B as a

---

5. I.R.C. § 165(b).

6. Id. See, e.g., Reg. § 1.165–7(b)(1), last sentence.

7. I.R.C. § 165(b).

8. Reg. § 1.165–7(b)(1).

9. I.R.C. § 165(a).

10. I.R.C. § 1001(a).

11. For characterization of business casualty gains and losses see I.R.C. § 1231(a), especially (a)(4)(C) and page 770, infra.

12. Some gains and losses, even if incurred in a separate identifiable business, must be aggregated with the results of other transactions outside the business. See especially Chapter 21 at pages 663 and 668 and Chapter 22 at page 770.

13. See Chapter 20 at page 654.

14. Tax Reform Act of 1976, P.L.No. 94–455, § 2124, 90 Stat. 1520, 1918.

15. P.L.No. 98–369, § 1063 (1984).

"kissin' cousin", for simple it appears to be. *Prior* to Section 280B, the question whether a demolition loss deduction was allowed rested upon a subjective analysis of the taxpayer's motivation.[16] If there was an intent at the time of purchase of improved property immediately to demolish the building, no basis was allocated to the building and no loss deduction was allowed on its demolition.[17] Instead, the entire purchase price for the property was allocated to the land.[18] If no such intent existed or if there was an intent to demolish at a subsequent time, some basis was allocated to the building.[19] Thus, upon a later demolition of the building, a loss deduction would be allowed in the amount of the building's unamortized basis.[20]

Except for special equities involved in the cases, it was difficult to see any support for these decisions. Furthermore, inquiry into why one acquired real property and removed an existing structure on it was much more difficult than the mere objective question *whether* he had done so. Now under Section 280B, whether the property was newly acquired or held for some time even for varying purposes, the taxpayer is denied a loss deduction for the structure and denied any deduction for expenses incurred in the demolition. Instead of a deduction, any basis the taxpayer had in the removed structure and any cost incurred in its removal are simply added to the basis he has for the *land* on which the structure stood. When Section 280B was added, the change from the past was that sometimes these costs were allowed as deductions, instead of having to be capitalized and that sometimes the taxpayer's basis for the removed structure became a part of his basis for the replacement structure rather than merely having to be added to the land. As land is not depreciable, the effect of Section 280B is to place unamortized cost of razed buildings and of expenses of demolition as far as possible away from affording any benefit to the taxpayer as a charge in computing taxable income.

Is Section 280B simple? If so (*and* if it embodies good tax policy) it will have a wide support within the tax profession for no matter what others may think in terms of crass commercialism, thoughtful tax lawyers and accountants are much more aware than most persons believe in the need for simplification of the tax structure. But, even without undertaking a full analysis, one may wonder whether the simplicity is not more apparent than real. What, for example, is the meaning of "demolition of any structure"? Probably we speak here of *willful*, not merely accidental, razing of the entire structure (or perhaps just a portion)? And is a parking lot a "structure"? Statutory change

---

16. Reg. § 1.165–3.

17. Reg. § 1.165–3(a)(1). Time of purchase means the time equitable title passes (signing of a contract) not the later date of transfer of the deed. If an intent to demolish arises between such dates, a demolition loss is allowed. The First Nat. Bank & Trust Co. of Chickasha v. U.S., 462 F.2d 908 (10th Cir.1972).

18. Reg. § 1.165–3(a)(1).

19. Reg. § 1.165–3(a)(2); McBride v. Commissioner, 50 T.C. 1 (1968), acq., 1969–1 C.B. 21; Commissioner v. Appleby's Estate, 123 F.2d 700 (2d Cir.1941), affirming 41 B.T.A. 18, non acq., 1940–2 C.B. 9.

20. See, e.g., A.F. McBride, Jr., note 19, supra; J.A. Rider, 30 T.C.M. 188 (1971).

usually raises new interpretative questions; or it may raise old ones that have been snoozing comfortably for years under a comfy blanket of legalese.

What of the *policy* question? Every tax (and every exclusion or exemption or deduction from income) has some regulatory effect. If the Waldorf ever succumbs to the ravages of time, would anyone buy the Park Avenue block on which it stands knowing that the huge cost of removing it will all be buried in the ground rather than allocated to the cost of constructing another Waldorf to replace it, e.g., recoverable through depreciation? Indeed, is not the cost of removing an impediment to the construction of a building every bit as much a cost of the new building as the costs of brick and mortar and labor and all the other affirmative actions that go into its erection?

We do not raise a constitutional question; Section 280B seems invulnerable enough in that respect. Nor can we extend our comments here on the lesser question whether Congress has done well with the 1984 change in Section 280B.[21] We hope, however, to pass the latter baton on to a student or colleague fairly sure, even on superficial and inadequate analysis, that Section 280B is no big thing, as matters stand.

3. DEPRECIATION, DEPLETION, AND AMORTIZATION

Because these concepts are intimately related to the subject matter of Part six their analysis is deferred to Chapter 22, which is in that Part.

---

21. Supra note 15. The 1984 change made I.R.C. § 280B effective to all structures, not just certified historic structures.

CHAPTER 15. DEDUCTIONS FOR PROFIT-MAKING, NONBUSINESS ACTIVITIES

A. SECTION 212 EXPENSES

Internal Revenue Code: Section 212; 274(h)(7).

Regulations: Sections 1.212–1(g), (k), (l), (m); 1.262–1(b)(7).

HIGGINS v. COMMISSIONER

Supreme Court of the United States, 1941.
312 U.S. 212, 61 S.Ct. 475.

Mr. Justice REED delivered the opinion of the Court.

Petitioner, the taxpayer, with extensive investments in real estate, bonds and stocks, devoted a considerable portion of his time to the oversight of his interests and hired others to assist him in offices rented for that purpose. For the tax years in question, 1932 and 1933, he claimed the salaries and expenses incident to looking after his properties were deductible under § 23(a) of the Revenue Act of 1932.[1] The Commissioner refused the deductions. The applicable phrases are: "In computing net income there shall be allowed as deductions: (a) *Expenses.*—All the ordinary and necessary expenses paid or incurred during the taxable year in carrying on any trade or business * * *." There is no dispute over whether the claimed deductions are ordinary and necessary expenses. As the Commissioner also conceded before the Board of Tax Appeals that the real estate activities of the petitioner in renting buildings[2] constituted a business, the Board allowed such portions of the claimed deductions as were fairly allocable to the handling of the real estate. The same offices and staffs handled both real estate and security matters. After this adjustment there remained for the year 1932 over twenty and for the year 1933 over sixteen thousand dollars expended for managing the stocks and bonds.

Petitioner's financial affairs were conducted through his New York office pursuant to his personal detailed instructions. His residence was in Paris, France, where he had a second office. By cable, telephone and mail, petitioner kept a watchful eye over his securities. While he sought permanent investments, changes, redemptions, maturities and accumulations caused limited shiftings in his portfolio. These were made under his own orders. The offices kept records, received securities, interest and dividend checks, made deposits, forwarded weekly and

---

1. 47 Stat. 169, c. 209 [The parallel language in the 1986 Internal Revenue Code is of course found in § 162(a). Ed.]

2. Cf. Pinchot v. Commissioner, 113 F.2d 718.

419

annual reports and undertook generally the care of the investments as instructed by the owner. Purchases were made by a financial institution. Petitioner did not participate directly or indirectly in the management of the corporations in which he held stock or bonds. The method of handling his affairs under examination had been employed by petitioner for more than thirty years. No objection to the deductions had previously been made by the Government.

The Board of Tax Appeals [3] held that these activities did not constitute carrying on a business and that the expenses were capable of apportionment between the real estate and the investments. The Circuit Court of Appeals affirmed,[4] and we granted certiorari because of conflict.[5]

Petitioner urges that the "elements of continuity, constant repetition, regularity and extent" differentiate his activities from the occasional like actions of the small investor. His activity is and the occasional action is not "carrying on business." On the other hand, the respondent urges that "mere personal investment activities never constitute carrying on a trade or business, no matter how much of one's time or of one's employees' time they may occupy."

Since the first income tax act, the provisions authorizing business deductions have varied only slightly. The Revenue Act of 1913 [6] allowed as a deduction "the necessary expenses actually paid in carrying on any business." By 1918 the present form was fixed and has so continued.[7] No regulation has ever been promulgated which interprets the meaning of "carrying on a business," nor any rulings approved by the Secretary of the Treasury, i.e., Treasury Decisions.[8] Certain rulings of less dignity, favorable to petitioner,[9] appeared in individual cases but they are not determinative.[10] Even acquiescence [11] in some Board rulings after defeat does not amount to settled administrative practice.[12] Unless the administrative practice is long continued and substantially uniform in the Bureau and without challenge by the Government in the Board and courts, it should not be assumed, from rulings of this class, that Congressional reenactment of the language which they construed was an adoption of their interpretation.

3. 39 B.T.A. 1005.

4. 111 F.2d 795.

5. Kales v. Commissioner, 101 F.2d 35; DuPont v. Deputy, 103 F.2d 257.

6. 38 Stat. 167, § IIB.

7. 40 Stat. 1066, § 214(a)(1).

8. Cf. Helvering v. New York Trust Co., 292 U.S. 455, 467–468, 54 S.Ct. 806, 809–810.

9. O.D. 537, 2 C.B. 175 (1920); O.D. 877, 4 C.B. 123 (1921); I.T. 2751, XIII–1 C.B. 43 (1934). See also 1934 C.C.H. Federal Tax Service, Vol. 3, ¶ 6035, p. 8027.

10. Biddle v. Commissioner, 302 U.S. 573, 582, 58 S.Ct. 379, 383. Cf. Estate of Sanford v. Commissioner, 308 U.S. 39, 52, 60 S.Ct. 51, 59. But see Helvering v. Bliss, 293 U.S. 144, 151, 55 S.Ct. 17, 20, and McFeely v. Commissioner, 296 U.S. 102, 108, 56 S.Ct. 54, 57.

11. Kissel v. Commissioner, 15 B.T.A. 1270, acquiesced in VIII–2 C.B. 28 (1929); Croker v. Commissioner, 27 B.T.A. 588, acquiesced in XII–1 C.B. 4 (1933).

12. Higgins v. Smith, 308 U.S. 473, 478–479, 60 S.Ct. 355, 358.

While the Commissioner has combated views similar to petitioner's in the courts, sometimes successfully [13] and sometimes unsuccessfully, [14] the petitioner urges that the Bureau accepted for years the doctrine that the management of one's own securities might be a business where there was sufficient extent, continuity, variety and regularity. We fail to find such a fixed administrative construction in the examples cited. It is true that the decisions are frequently put on the ground that the taxpayer's activities were sporadic but it does not follow that had those activities been continuous the Commissioner would not have used the argument advanced here, i.e., that no amount of personal investment management would turn those activities into a business. Evidently such was the Government's contention in the *Kales,* cases, [15] where the things the taxpayer did met petitioner's tests, and in Foss v. Commissioner [16] and Washburn v. Commissioner [17] where the opinions turned on the extent of the taxpayer's participation in the management of the corporations in which investments were held. [18]

Petitioner relies strongly on the definition of business in Flint v. Stone Tracy Company: [19] " 'Business' is a very comprehensive term and embraces everything about which a person can be employed." This definition was given in considering whether certain corporations came under the Corporation Tax law which levies a tax on corporations engaged in business. The immediate issue was whether corporations engaged principally in the "holding and management of real estate" [20] were subject to the act. A definition given for such an issue is not controlling in this dissimilar inquiry. [21]

To determine whether the activities of a taxpayer are "carrying on a business" requires an examination of the facts in each case. As the Circuit Court of Appeals observed, all expenses of every business transaction are not deductible. Only those are deductible which relate to carrying on a business. The Bureau of Internal Revenue has this duty of determining what is carrying on a business, subject to reexamination of the facts by the Board of Tax Appeals [22] and ultimately to review on the law by the courts on which jurisdiction is conferred. [23] The Commissioner and the Board appraised the evidence here as insufficient to establish petitioner's activities as those of carrying on a business. The petitioner merely kept records and collected interest and dividends from his securities, through managerial attention for his investments. No matter how large the estate or how continuous or

13. Bedell v. Commissioner, 30 F.2d 622, 624; Monell v. Helvering, 70 F.2d 631; Kane v. Commissioner, 100 F.2d 382.

14. Kales v. Commissioner, 101 F.2d 35; DuPont v. Deputy, 103 F.2d 257, 259, reversed on other grounds, 308 U.S. 488, 60 S.Ct. 363.

15. Kales v. Commissioner, 34 B.T.A. 1046, 101 F.2d 35.

16. 75 F.2d 326.

17. 51 F.2d 949, 953.

18. Cf. Roebling v. Commissioner, 37 B.T.A. 82; Heilbroner v. Commissioner, 34 B.T.A. 1200.

19. 220 U.S. 107, 171, 31 S.Ct. 342, 357.

20. Id. 169.

21. Cohens v. Virginia, 6 Wheat. 264, 399; Puerto Rico v. Shell Co., 302 U.S. 253, 269, 58 S.Ct. 167, 174.

22. Revenue Act of 1932, 47 Stat. 169, § 272; Internal Revenue Code, § 272.

23. Internal Revenue Code, § 1141.

extended the work required may be, such facts are not sufficient as a matter of law to permit the courts to reverse the decision of the Board. Its conclusion is adequately supported by this record, and rests upon a conception of carrying on business similar to that expressed by this Court for an antecedent section.[24]

The petitioner makes the point that his activities in managing his estate, both realty and personalty, were a unified business. Since it was admittedly a business in so far as the realty is concerned, he urges, there is no statutory authority to sever expenses allocable to the securities. But we see no reason why expenses not attributable, as we have just held these are not, to carrying on business cannot be apportioned. It is not unusual to allocate expenses paid for services partly personal and partly business.[25]

Affirmed.

NOTE

The congressional reaction to the *Higgins* decision was negative. But, instead of attempting to mitigate the problem by defining a trade or business as including income-producing activity, Congress enacted what is now Section 212(1) and (2) as part of the Revenue Act of 1942.[1] Subparagraph (3) of Section 212 first appeared with the enactment of the Internal Revenue Code of 1954.[2]

If a bridge is needed here from a preoccupation with trade or business problems in Chapter 14, it is the question: All right, we do not fit the trade or business requirements of Section 162; so what? Is there, nevertheless a proper basis for asserting deductibility? Our inquiry here carries us primarily into Section 212 [3] where "the production [or collection] of income" test replaces that of the "trade or business" concept of Section 162. The *Higgins* background of Section 212 supports the other similarities of Sections 162 and 212; note especially that in either case it is only "expenses" that are "ordinary and necessary" which are deductible.

Other quasi-business deductions crop up in this chapter as well. A question may be whether a loss is one that, if not in business, arises out of a "transaction entered into for profit" as that phrase is used in Section 165(c)(2). If one is seeking income (Section 212), is he engaged in a transaction entered into for profit (Section 165(c)(2)), and vice versa? It is worth noting here that in other respects Section 165 clearly differs from Section 212 (and Section 162), not being concerned with "expenses" or the question whether what occurred was "ordinary"

---

24. Van Wart v. Commissioner, 295 U.S. 112, 115, 55 S.Ct. 660.

25. 3 Paul & Mertens, Law of Federal Income Taxation § 23.65; cf. National Outdoor Advertising Bureau v. Helvering, 89 F.2d 878, 881.

1. § 121, 55 Stat. 798, 819 (1942).

2. Paragraph (3) was prompted by the decision in Lykes v. U.S., 343 U.S. 118, 72 S.Ct. 585 (1952) which, essentially, it overruled.

3. Further possibilities are explored in Chapters 16, 18 and 23.

or "necessary." A related problem that appears somewhat prematurely here [4] is whether property is "held for the production of income" so
as to be subject to depreciation under Section 167(a)(2), even if not used
in a trade or business.[5]

Problems of the kind dealt with here cover a wide range of human
activity and, thinking in terms of two of the cases that follow, it may be
difficult to see that Mr. Surasky's proxy expenses (he won) have very
much in common with those involved in Mr. Fleischman's divorce (he
lost). However, if the following materials are approached with the
underlying statutory concepts in mind they will not only appear less
fragmentary, but they will also supply a basis for dealing with many
other problems not specifically presented here.

not a syllabus

BOWERS v. LUMPKIN

United States Court of Appeals, Fourth Circuit, 1944.
140 F.2d 927, cert. denied 322 U.S. 755, 64 S.Ct. 1266, 1944.

SOPER, Circuit Judge. This suit was brought by Mrs. Lumpkin to
recover individual federal income taxes alleged to have been overpaid
for the years 1936 and 1937. It was tried before the District Judge
without a jury and resulted in a judgment for the plaintiff in the sum of
$22,680.10. The taxpayer had a life interest under a trust created for
her benefit by the will of her former husband in one-half of the stock of
a corporation which owned valuable rights in the sale and distribution
of coca cola syrup in South Carolina. She purchased the remaining
stock of the corporation for $255,885 from trustees to whom it had been
bequeathed to establish and maintain an orphanage. The Attorney
General of South Carolina instituted an action to invalidate the sale
and require the taxpayer to account for profits and the taxpayer was
obliged to defend the suit in the courts of South Carolina where she
finally won a decision upholding the sale. In connection with this
litigation she incurred expenses of $250 in 1936 and $26,798.22 in 1937
which she deducted from gross income in preparing her income tax
returns for these years. The Commissioner of Internal Revenue disallowed the deductions and assessed additional taxes and interest of $155
for 1936 and $19,187.72 for 1937, which were paid under protest and
form the basis of the instant suit.

The taxpayer relies upon § 121(a) of the Revenue Act of 1942, 56
Stat. 798, 819, 26 U.S.C.A. Int.Rev.Code, § 23(a), which amended § 23(a)
of the Internal Revenue Code, 53 Stat. 12, whereby all the ordinary and
necessary expenses of carrying on a trade or business were allowed as
deductions from gross income. The Act of 1942 broadened the scope of
allowable deductions by adding amongst others the following subsection
to § 23(a):

4. See Note, "Depreciation," in Chapter
22, at page 740, infra.

5. These related concepts are ably discussed by Kilbourn, "Deductible Expenses:
Transactions Entered into for Profit: In-

come-Producing Property," 21 N.Y.U. Inst.
on Fed.Tax. 193 (1963). See also Lang,
"The Scope of Deductions Under Section
212," 7 Rev. of Tax. of Inds. 291 (1983).

"(2) Non-trade or non-business expenses. In the case of an individual, all the ordinary and necessary expenses paid or incurred during the taxable year for the production or collection of income, or for the management, conservation, or maintenance of property held for the production of income." *

This amendment was made retroactive by the following provision:

"(e) Retroactive Amendment to Prior Revenue Acts.—For the purposes of the Revenue Act of 1938 or any prior revenue Act the amendments made to the Internal Revenue Code by this section shall be effective as if they were a part of such revenue Act on the date of its enactment." 56 Stat. 819, 26 U.S.C.A.Int.Rev.Code, § 23 note.

The purpose of this amendment was to permit deductions for certain non-trade and non-business expenses and thereby enlarge the allowable deduction for expenses which under previous revenue acts had been confined to expenses paid or incurred in carrying on any trade or business. Under the earlier statutes it had been held that investors not engaged in the investment business could not deduct expenses such as salaries, clerk hire or office rent incurred in connection with the earning or collection of taxable income, or in looking after one's own investments in stocks and bonds. See, Higgins v. Commissioner, 312 U.S. 212, 61 S.Ct. 475, decided February 3, 1941. To mitigate the harshness of this rule Congress in 1942 eliminated the requirement that the expenses to be deductible must be incurred in connection with a trade or business. But, as the reports of Congressional committees show, it was not the intention of Congress to remove the other restrictions and limitations applicable to deductions under § 23(a) of the act. See S.Rep. No. 1683, 77th Cong., 2d Sess., 88; H.Rep. No. 2333, 77th Cong., 2d Sess., 75.

Under § 23(a), as it was prior to the amendment, it was firmly established that legal expenses involved in defending or protecting title to property are not "ordinary and necessary expenses" and are not deductible from gross income in order to compute the taxable net income, but constitute a capital charge which should be added to the cost of the property and taken into account in computing the capital gain or loss in case of a subsequent sale. The Treasury regulations throughout the years have consistently so provided;[1] the decisions of the courts have been to the same effect;[2] and Congress has retained

---

* See I.R.C. (1986) § 212(1) and (2). Ed.

1. Article 293 of Regulations 45 (1919 Ed.), and 62 (1922 Ed.), promulgated under the Revenue Acts of 1918 and 1921; Article 292 of Regulations 65 and 69, promulgated under the Revenue Acts of 1924 and 1926; Article 282 of Regulations 74 and 77, promulgated under the Revenue Acts of 1928 and 1932; Article 24–2 of Regulations 94 and 101, promulgated under the Revenue Acts of 1936 and 1938; Section 19, 24– 2 of Regulations 103 (1940 Ed.) promulgated under the Internal Revenue Code.

2. Jones' Estate v. Commissioner, 5 Cir., 127 F.2d 231; Murphy Oil Co. v. Burnett, 9 Cir., 55 F.2d 17, 26, affirmed 287 U.S. 299, 53 S.Ct. 161; Brawner v. Burnett, 61 App.D.C. 352, 63 F.2d 129, 131; Farmer v. Commissioner, 10 Cir., 126 F.2d 542, 544; Crowley v. Commissioner, 6 Cir., 89 F.2d 715, 718. Cf. Welch v. Helvering, 290 U.S. 111, 113, 114, 54 S.Ct. 8.

the same language in repeated reenactments with this interpretation in mind.

Hence it may not be doubted that Congress, in amending § 23 of the Internal Revenue Code by the Revenue Act of 1942, used the phrase "all the ordinary and necessary expenses" under the caption "Non-Trade or Non-Business Expenses" in the same sense and with the same limitations that it had previously used in connection with trade and business expenses. It is contended that the phrase "all the ordinary and necessary expenses" in the amendment covers more ground than it did in the original act because the amendment expressly authorizes a deduction for expenses paid "for the management, conservation, or maintenance of property held for the production of income"; and the word "conservation" is said to be particularly pertinent in the pending case where the expenses were incurred in the protection of income producing stock from adverse attack. But the term "conservation" can be given effect if it is limited to expenses ordinarily and necessarily incurred during the taxable year for the safeguarding of the property, such as the cost of a safe deposit box for securities. The term cannot be given the meaning contended for by the taxpayer without losing sight of the purpose which Congress intended to accomplish and the settled meaning that the phrase "ordinary and necessary expenses" has been given in the administration and re-enactment of the federal income tax statutes.

Treasury Regulations 103, as amended by T.D. 5196, 1942–2 "C.B." 96, 97–100, which were promulgated to cover the 1942 amendments, preserve the established interpretation. Section 19.23(a)–15 provides in part:

> "(b) Except for the requirement of being incurred in connection with a trade or business, a deduction under this section is subject to all the restrictions and limitations that apply in the case of the deductions under section 23(a)(1)(A) of an expense paid or incurred in carrying on any trade or business. This includes restrictions and limitations contained in section 24, as amended. ＊ ＊ ＊

> "Capital expenditures, and expenses of carrying on transactions which do not constitute a trade or business of the taxpayer and are not carried on for the production or collection of income or for the management, conservation, or maintenance of property held for the production of income, but which are carried on primarily as a sport, hobby, or recreation are not allowable as non-trade or non-business expenses.

> ＊ ＊ ＊

> "Expenditures incurred in defending or perfecting title to property, in recovering property (other than investment property and amounts of income which, if and when recovered, must be included in income), or in developing or improving

property, constitute a part of the cost of the property and are not deductible expenses."

The judgment of the District Court must be reversed.

ESTATE OF BAIER v. COMMISSIONER

United States Court of Appeals, Third Circuit, 1976.
533 F.2d 117.

Opinion of the Court

VAN DUSEN, Circuit Judge. The sole question presented on this appeal from the Tax Court is whether certain legal expenses incurred by the taxpayer during calendar years 1969–1971 qualify as an ordinary expense under § 212 of the Internal Revenue Code of 1954,[1] or whether those expenses must be treated as capital expenditures. The Tax Court held that the expenses have their origin in the disposition of a capital asset and, therefore, must be used to offset the realized capital gains. Baier v. Commissioner of Internal Revenue, 63 T.C. 513 (1975). We affirm.

Richard Baier was first employed by American Smelting and Refining Company (American) in 1933. In 1953, he became the chief engineer in a division of American's central research department. In conjunction with his promotion to this position, Baier signed an employment contract which contained the following provisions:

"7. [Employee] agrees that he will forthwith disclose and assign to the Company all discoveries, processes and inventions made or conceived in whole or in part by him * * * during his employment, relative to or useful in any business carried on by the Company * * * and the said discoveries, processes and inventions shall become and remain the property of the Company * * * Upon request of the Company * * * the [employee] agrees to make application * * * for letters patent of the United States and of any other countries where obtainable, on said discoveries, processes and inventions, and forthwith to assign all such applications and the letters patent thereon to the Company * * *

"8. Under the provisions of the Executive Committee Circular No. 605 * * * employees of the Company making inventions in the course of their employment useful in the business of the Company, may derive certain benefits therefrom in accordance with the terms and conditions in said circular set forth; but the granting of such benefits is discretionary with the Company and the provisions of such circular are subject to withdrawal or change without notice."

App. at 54a–55a. Circular No. 605, incorporated by reference into the contract, provided that, if American should grant to any person or corporation other than itself the right to make, use or vend the

1. 26 U.S.C.A. [I.R.C.] § 212 is omitted.

discovery, process, or invention, then the company would give to the employee or employees responsible a 15% share in the net proceeds realized.

In August 1961, Baier and a co-inventor reduced to practice a method and apparatus for melting copper which had a tremendous commercial potential. In May 1962, American amended Circular No. 605 by issuing Executive Committee Circular Letter No. 995. Circular No. 995 was identical to Circular No. 605 in all material respects except that the payments made to employees under its terms would be limited to $20,000 per year and would be paid only while the employee was actively employed by American. Baier was asked to sign a new employment contract incorporating Circular No. 995, but he refused.

In accordance with the terms of the 1953 employment contract, Baier applied for a patent to cover the method and apparatus for melting copper, and assigned this application to American. Beginning in November 1962, American licensed the invention to various unrelated corporations.

A dispute arose between American and Baier over whether the payments to Baier for the invention were to be determined under the terms of Circular No. 605 or under the terms of Circular No. 995. The licensing fees realized by American were of such magnitude that the difference to Baier was extremely large. To protect his interests, Baier retained legal counsel and then commenced suit. In February 1964, a settlement was reached, the terms of which were substantially more favorable to Baier than the terms of Circular No. 995.

The payments received from American have been properly reported by Baier as long-term capital gains. See Treas.Reg. § 1.1235–1(c)(2). His legal counsel was retained on a contingent fee basis, entitling such counsel to a percentage of the payments made by American to Baier. Payments were made by Baier to his attorney in the years 1969, 1970 and 1971 were claimed as an ordinary deduction for each year under 26 U.S.C.A. § 212. The Commissioner disallowed these payments as ordinary deductions and recharacterized them as capital expenditures, and ruled on the basis of 26 U.S.C.A. § 263 [2] that they were not deductible. Accordingly, the Commissioner assessed a deficiency for the years 1969–1971. Baier petitioned the Tax Court for a redetermination of the deficiencies. After the Tax Court upheld the Commissioner, Baier filed a timely notice of appeal.

2. 26 U.S.C. [I.R.C.] § 263 provides:

"(a) General rule.—No deduction shall be allowed for—

(1) Any amount paid out for new buildings or for permanent improvements or betterments made to increase the value of any property or estate. * * *"

This section has consistently been interpreted as requiring the capitalization of the costs incident to the acquisition or disposition of a capital asset. See Commissioner v. Idaho Power Co., 418 U.S. 1, 12–19, 94 S.Ct. 2757, 2764–2767 (1974); Woodward v. Commissioner, 397 U.S. 572, 575, 90 S.Ct. 1302, 1304 (1970); United States v. General Bancshares Corp., 388 F.2d 184, 187 (8th Cir.1968).

Baier contends that he incurred legal fees to enforce a fully executed contract, complete as to its terms, and not incident to the disposition of a capital asset (the invention underlying the patent). "Litigation was required not to fill in any missing terms [such as price] but to enforce the contract as written" (taxpayer's brief at p. 31). The Tax Court found that the terms of the contract were not final with respect to the invention disposition price, and therefore the legal expenses were incurred as the cost of setting that price. See United States v. Hilton Hotels Corp., 397 U.S. 580, 90 S.Ct. 1307 (1970). We believe it is unnecessary in this case to resolve the dispute over the construction of the employment contract.

It is clear that § 263 modifies § 212. See 26 U.S.C.A. § 211; Commissioner v. Idaho Power Co., 418 U.S. 1, 17, 94 S.Ct. 2757, 2759 (1974). The test for determining what a § 263 capital expenditure is has been described by the Supreme Court in Woodward v. Commissioner, 397 U.S. 572, 90 S.Ct. 1302 (1970), and United States v. Hilton Hotels Corp., supra:

> "[U]ncertainty is not called for in applying the regulation that makes the 'cost of acquisition' of a capital asset a capital expense. In our view application of [that] regulation to litigation expenses involves the simpler inquiry whether the origin of the claim litigated is in the process of acquisition itself."

Woodward, supra at 577.

> "The whole process of acquisition required both legal operations—fixing the price, and conveying title to the property—and we cannot see why the order in which these operations occurred * * * should make any difference in the characterization of the expenses * * *"

Hilton Hotels, supra, at 584. We are satisfied that the "origin of the claim test" applies to expenses incident to the disposition of property, as well as to the acquisition of property. See Munn v. United States, 455 F.2d 1028 (Ct.Cl.1972); Helgerson v. United States, 426 F.2d 1293 (8th Cir.1970). The origin of the litigation expenses at issue in this case was the disposition of a capital asset—the patent.[3] We hold that the costs of disposition include legal fees incurred incident to a dispute over what the terms of the disposition are. See Munn, supra at 1032.*

To make the federal tax treatment of legal expenses turn on the underlying merits of the dispute giving rise to the legal expenses in a case such as this would involve the Commissioner in an area of the law

---

3. See 26 U.S.C. [I.R.C.] § 1235(a); Treas.Reg. § 1.1235–1(c)(2). [The cited regulation is omitted. Ed.]

* In a recent case an employee received an Invention Achievement Award which was held to constitute ordinary income as compensation for services rather than a capital gain from the transfer of inventions under I.R.C. § 1235. The Award was held to be separate from the transfer of the inventions. William F. Beausoleil, 66 T.C. 244 (1976). If the taxpayer in *Beausoleil* had incurred legal expenses in recovering the award would his expenses have been deductible? And from an *income* standpoint, is not the employment agreement involved in *Baier* much more favorable to the employee? Ed.

far from his field of expertise. We can perceive no reason in law or policy to make the deductibility of legal expenses dependent upon the correct interpretation of a contract such as this involving the application of numerous rules of construction, see Restatement of Contracts §§ 235 and 236 (1932); Restatement of Contracts §§ 228 and 229 (Tent. Draft. No. 5, 1970). See Galewitz v. Commissioner of Internal Revenue, 411 F.2d 1374, 1377–78 (2d Cir.1969).

Appellants argue, however, that the Commissioner's interpretation of § 263 to encompass the legal fees involved in this case ignores the language and purpose of Treas.Reg. § 1.212–1(b). The text of this regulation is set out in the margin.[4] Reading the regulation as a whole, we are convinced that the regulation is not inconsistent with the Commissioner's position. We understand the regulation to mean that expenses which would be deductible from ordinary income if they were incurred in the maintenance or management of property ordinarily held for the production of income are deductible, even though the expenses were incurred in the management or maintenance of property not in fact producing ordinary income and not purchased for the purpose of producing ordinary income. The function of the regulation is to make unnecessary any investigation into the taxpayer's subjective purpose in procuring any property or in incurring any expense. We have concluded that the regulation was not intended to overcome the injunction of § 263 that capital expenditures are not deductible expenses.

The decision of the Tax Court will be Affirmed.

not syllabus

SURASKY v. UNITED STATES

United States Court of Appeals, Fifth Circuit, 1963.
325 F.2d 191.

TUTTLE, Chief Judge. This appeal challenges the correctness of the judgment of the district court holding that the sum of $17,000 contributed by the taxpayer to the Wolfson-Montgomery Ward Stockholders Committee as a part of a proxy battle during 1955 was not allowable as a deduction as an ordinary and necessary non-business expense.[1]

The facts are not in dispute since substantially all of the facts were either stipulated between the parties or proved by undisputed affidavit and a deposition which was not in any way countered.

The taxpayer purchased 4000 shares of stock of Montgomery Ward & Co. in 1954 and 1955, at a total cost of $296,870.20. In making the purchase, he acted on the recommendation of Louis E. Wolfson after he made a personal investigation of the financial condition of Montgomery Ward & Co. Taxpayer purchased the stock for the sole reason that he thought it was a good chance to make money, in that it was a good long term investment because of anticipated increased dividends and appre-

---

4. [Treas.Reg. § 1.212–1(b) is omitted. Ed.]   **1.** [I.R.C. § 212 is omitted. Ed.]

ciation in the value of the stock through improvements in the condition
of the company. Mr. Wolfson, who had purchased more than 50,000
shares of the stock, had laid out what he believed to be an aggressive
program which he testified he thought would improve the company and
greatly enhance the value of the stock. In pursuing his plans he
attempted, without success, to discuss his proposals with the management. Thereafter, the taxpayer and other stockholders formed a Committee known as the Wolfson-Montgomery Ward Stockholders Committee. The objectives of the Stockholders Committee were set out in a
document entitled "Let's Rebuild Montgomery Ward." [2] This document
made it clear that the Stockholders Committee advocated far-reaching
changes in the management of the company. It expressly called for the
establishment of new stores; relocating and modernizing or repairing
others; expanding manufacturing operations; developing private
brands; increasing inventory turnovers; obtaining the services of outstanding merchandising personnel; improving employee morale; and
generally, revamping and bringing up to date all policies touching on
advertising, merchandising, sales and corporate financing. The Committee expressly sought increased dividends and a stock split. The
Stockholders Committee sought to accomplish these objectives by
means of electing a new Board of Directors, or at least a majority of the
Board which would then provide new management. It started a proxy
campaign for the regular annual meeting of stockholders scheduled for
April 22, 1955. In this effort, it incurred substantial expense which
was financed by payments made from members of the Committee and
other stockholders.

The taxpayer paid the Stockholders Committee $17,000 in 1955,
which was expended for the purpose of the Committee during that year.
The taxpayer was not an officer, director or employee and did not seek
a position either as a director or as an officer or employee of the
company. His stated purpose for making the payments was that he
believed his opportunity to make more money from his stock invest-

---

2. Although the parties stipulated:

"The objectives of this Committee were
set forth in a document entitled 'Let's
Rebuild Montgomery Ward', * * *
which the Committee circulated, together with other similar material, to the
stockholders of Montgomery Ward & Co.
* * *," and although the document
clearly stated the objectives to include
the establishment of new stores, the relocating, modernizing or repairing of
others, expanding manufacturing operations, improving employee morale, and
making changes generally in advertising,
merchandising, sales, financial and personnel policies for the purpose of seeking
increased dividends and a stock split, the
Government, in its brief, states, "The
object of the Wolfson Committee was to
displace a majority of the Board of Direc-

tors and the existing management of
Ward and replace them with its own
nine candidates for the Board and new
management."

The court also, in its finding No. 4 stated, "The object of the Wolfson Committee
was to displace a majority of the Board of
Directors and the existing management of
Ward and replace them with its own nine
candidates for the Board and new management."

The stipulation further provides, "The
Committee proposed to *accomplish its
objectives* by displacing a majority of the
Board of Directors and existing management of the corporation with its own candidates for the Board and new management."

ment was much greater if the purposes of the Committee could be accomplished.

It turned out that, while the drive was unsuccessful in placing a majority of the Stockholders Committees' candidates on the Board of Directors, it was at least partially successful in that three of its nominees were placed on the board of nine directors. Also, immediately after the election the Chairman of the Board and the President resigned. The Chairman of the Board and President were the focus of the attack by the Committee in challenging the current management policies of the company. It also eventuated that sales and earnings of the company increased during the latter half of the fiscal year ended January 31, 1956; the regular quarterly dividend was increased by the Directors at a meeting held on November 28, 1955, from $.75 per share to $1.00 per share, and an extra dividend of $1.25 per share was voted on the common stock. At the same meeting, the Board recommended a two-for-one split of the common stock, which was accomplished the following year. The market quotations of the stock increased substantially during 1955.

The taxpayer's venture in Montgomery Ward stock was a profitable one in that he received dividends totalling $30,000 on the stock purchased by him in less than a two year period, and he sold his stock in the first eight months of 1956, realizing a capital gain of $50,929.55.

Trying the case without a jury, the trial court based its legal conclusion that the expenditures were not deductible on the following summarization of the facts:

"To summarize the facts, the plaintiff herein contributed $17,000 to a committee which was to use the money to solicit proxies from other shareholders of a large, publicly-held corporation, in the hope that the committee would be able to seat a sufficient number of its candidates on the board of directors so that new management policies could be carried out which might result in larger profits and larger dividends to the shareholders.

"The plaintiff had clear title to his Ward stock and was receiving dividend income therefrom. It was certainly most speculative whether his contribution to the Wolfson Committee would touch off a series of events culminating in the production of increased income to the plaintiff. Furthermore, the plaintiff was not a candidate for the board of directors nor does the record reflect that he anticipated obtaining a position in Ward's management.

* * *

"The Court specifically finds lacking the necessary proximate relationship between the expenditure and the production of income or the management of income producing property. At the time the plaintiff contributed his funds to the committee, it was pure speculation whether he would derive any monetary reward therefrom. At the time the expenditure was made, the Court would certainly not find that it was necessary, nor was it even ordinary, within the common meaning of that word.

"The Court is not unmindful of the fact that the plaintiff, at the time he contributed the $17,000 to the committee, did so with hopes of realizing a profit and that, as a matter of fact, the dividends on his stock increased following the election of three of the Wolfson Committee's candidates. However, it is necessary to view the instant transaction as of the time it occurred, without the benefit of hindsight. The record is completely devoid of any evidence of a direct proximate relationship between the plaintiff's expenditure and the increased dividends; the latter could have been caused by any one of a myriad of factors. As for the plaintiff's desire to make a profit, there are any number of transactions entered into by the parties with a profit motive which are not accorded preferential tax treatment. The Treasury cannot be expected to underwrite all profit seeking speculations."

The appellant here urges that in its stressing of the "speculative" nature of the expenditure and the court's apparent reliance on the theory that for an expense, to be deductible under subparagraph 2 of Section 212, i.e., "for the management, conservation, or maintenance of property held for the production of income," there must be some threat of the loss of the property by the taxpayer, the court has imposed too rigid a requirement. We agree.

There is one thing both parties here agree upon, that is, that it was to change the result of the distinction between "business" and "personal" expenses that Section 212 was added to the Internal Revenue Code in 1942. The United States, in its brief, cites the decision by the Supreme Court in McDonald v. Commissioner, 323 U.S. 57, 61, 65 S.Ct. 96, as authority for the following statement: "In order to correct the inequity of making non-trade or non-business income taxable, but not allowing non-trade or non-business expenses to be deducted, Congress allowed a deduction in the new subsection (a)(2) for 'all the ordinary and necessary expenses paid or incurred' (1) 'for the production or collection of income' or (2) 'for the management, conservation, or maintenance of property held for the production or collection of income.' "

The parties also agree that in construing the language of Section 212, it is to be taken in *pari materia* with Section 162 so far as relates to the language "ordinary and necessary business expenses." [3]

From the manner in which the trial court stressed the terms "speculative" and "speculation" it is apparent that the court may have been too greatly persuaded by the language of the income tax regulations declaring, in Section 1.212–1(d), that "expenses to be deductible

3. [I.R.C. § 162(a) is omitted. Ed.]

under Section 212, must be 'ordinary and necessary'. Thus, such expenses must be reasonable in amount and must bear a reasonable and proximate relation to the production or collection of taxable income or to the management, conservation, or maintenance of property held for the production of income." While we do not determine that this regulation is not warranted by the section of the statute with which we are involved, we think that it has been construed by the trial court to require much too difficult a showing of proximate cause in the common-law tort concept than is required by the statute.

It will be noted that nothing in the statute expressly requires a showing of a "proximate relation to the production or collection of taxable income." None of the cases cited to us by the United States contain such language. We think Congress had in mind allowing deduction of expenses genuinely incurred in the exercise of reasonable business judgment in an effort to produce income that may fall far short of satisfying the common law definition of proximate cause. Thus, we think the use of the term "speculative" is not an apt expression that would describe the determining factor in deciding this issue.

This Court has held in Harris & Co. v. Lucas, Commissioner, 5th Cir., 48 F.2d 187.

"It is evident that the words 'ordinary' and 'necessary' in the statute are not used conjunctively, and are not to be construed as requiring that an expense of a business to be deductible must be both ordinary and necessary in a narrow, technical sense. On the contrary, it is clear that Congress intended the statute to be broadly construed to facilitate business generally, so that any necessary expense, not actually a capital investment, incurred in good faith in a particular business, is to be considered an ordinary expense of that business. This in effect is the construction given the statute by the Treasury Department and the court. * * *" 48 F.2d 187, 188.

This Court has cited the Harris case a number of times with approval, most recently in Luta v. Commissioner of Internal Revenue, 5 Cir., 282 F.2d 614, 617.[4]

In dealing with the "necessary" part of the formula, the Supreme Court has indicated in Welch v. Helvering, 290 U.S. 111, at page 113, 54 S.Ct. 8, at page 9, that this requirement may be satisfied if the expenditures "were appropriate and helpful", saying as to the taxpayer, Welch, "He certainly thought they were, and we should be slow to override his judgment."

Then, dealing with the question of what expenses are "ordinary" the Supreme Court in the same opinion said, "here, indeed, as so often

---

4. The entire paragraph from the Harris & Co. case is quoted above although it is clear that the Supreme Court in Welch v. Helvering, 290 U.S. 111, 54 S.Ct. 8, has held that in order to qualify as a business deduction an expenditure must be *both* necessary *and* ordinary. However, we still believe that they need not be "both ordinary and necessary in a narrow, technical sense," as stated in the Harris & Co. case.

in other branches of the law, the decisive distinctions are those of degree and not of kind. One struggles in vain for any verbal formula that will supply a ready touchstone. The standard set up by the statute is not a rule of law; it is rather a way of life. Life in all its fullness must supply the answer to the riddle."

Here, it seems incontestable that the payments made by the taxpayer were made with the anticipation that profit to the taxpayer would result. It may have been a long chance that Mr. Surasky was taking. However, he testified he knew Mr. Wolfson well enough to know his ability and believed that there was reasonable likelihood of success. This testimony is undisputed. In point of fact, the activity resulting from the expenditures by the taxpayer and his associates did produce direct and tangible results in that three nominees of the Committee were elected to the Board of Directors, the President, who had been severely criticized by the Committee was caused to resign as was the Chairman of the Board, and many other actions which parallel those sought for by the Committee were undertaken by the corporation. Profits were increased; dividends were increased; the stock enhanced in value. We think that for a trial court to conclude that there was not sufficient connection between the expenditure to assist the Committee in its activities and the achievement of so many of its objectives was too remote to meet the test of what is reasonable and ordinary in this particular type of investor activity is to apply too rigid a standard in the application of a remedial statute.

While there are differences in the facts, as there must always be in different cases, we think that the Tax Court decision in Alleghany Corporation, 28 T.C. 298, acq. 1957–2 C.B. 3, points the direction in which the statute should be applied. The expenditures there sought to be deducted were for proxy solicitation and other committee activities in a railroad reorganization. To be sure, the proposal that was fought successfully in that case would have resulted in diluting the taxpayer's common stock possibly to the vanishing point. However, we think it immaterial whether the expenditure is directed towards an effort to prevent the loss or dilution of an equity interest or to cause an enhancement or increase of the equity value, as was the undoubted purpose in the case before us. The Tax Court there said, 28 T.C. page 304, "We think it is clear that the expenditures in question were made for no other purpose than to protect petitioner's business." See also Shoe Corporation of America, 29 T.C. 297, 1957, acq. 1958–2 C.B. 7, and Allied Chemical Corp. v. United States (Ct.Cl.1962), 305 F.2d 433.

It appearing, as we have noted above, that the decision of this case was based on undisputed evidence, most of which was stipulated, our review of the decision of the trial court is somewhat freed from the "clearly erroneous" rule. See Patterson v. Belcher, 5th Cir., 302 F.2d 289, 292, cert. denied, 371 U.S. 921, 83 S.Ct. 289; Galena Oaks Corporation v. Scofield, 5th Cir., 218 F.2d 217, 219.

The judgment is reversed and the case is remanded to the trial court for the entry of a judgment in favor of the appellant, taxpayer.

REVENUE RULING 64–236 [1]
1964–2 Cum.Bull. 64.

The Internal Revenue Service will follow the decision of the U.S. Court of Appeals for the Fourth Circuit in the case of R. Walter Graham, et ux. v. Commissioner, 326 F.2d 878 (1964).

This decision held that proxy fight expenditures are deductible by a stockholder under section 212 of the Internal Revenue Code of 1954, if such expenditures are proximately related to either the production or collection of income or to the management, conservation or maintenance of property held for the production of income.

The Service will also follow the decision of the U.S. Court of Appeals for the Fifth Circuit in Jack Surasky v. United States, 325 F.2d 191 (1963), a case involving a similar issue. Internal Revenue will not, however, follow this decision to the extent that the court in its opinion indicates that to be deductible proxy fight expenditures need not be proximately related to either the production or collection of income or to the management, conservation, or maintenance of property held for the production of income.

MEYER J. FLEISCHMAN
Tax Court of the United States, 1966.
45 T.C. 439.

SIMPSON, Judge: The Commissioner has determined a deficiency in the petitioner's income tax for 1962 in the amount of $725.60. The issue in this case is whether the petitioner may deduct legal expenses incurred in defending his wife's lawsuit to set aside their antenuptial contract.

Findings of Fact

Meyer J. Fleischman, the petitioner, is a physician in Cincinnati, Ohio. He reported his income on the cash method of accounting and filed his 1962 income tax return with the district director of internal revenue at Cincinnati, Ohio.

On February 25, 1955, petitioner entered into an antenuptial agreement with Joan Ruth Francis. That agreement was made in contemplation of marriage and provided: [that in case of divorce Meyer would pay Joan $5000, in consideration for which Joan released all interest in Meyer's property.]

Petitioner and Joan R. Francis were married on February 26, 1955. On December 20, 1961, Joan filed for a divorce in the Court of Common Pleas, Division of Domestic Relations, Hamilton County, Ohio. In her

1. Based on Technical Information Release 613, dated July 23, 1964.

suit for divorce the wife made the following prayer: [*inter alia*] That plaintiff be awarded a fair and equitable division of all properties, real and personal, of the defendant Meyer J. Fleischman, and for all such other and further relief to which she may be entitled in the premises, including her attorney fees and expenses.

On December 26, 1961, she filed another action in the Court of Common Pleas, Hamilton County, Ohio. The latter suit was instituted to set aside the antenuptial agreement and was necessary because the domestic relations division had no jurisdiction to declare the contract void and invalid. In her petition, she alleged that her husband had deceived her by false representations concerning the validity of the agreement, and that at the time of the agreement and at the time of filing suit she had no idea of the nature and extent of the defendant's property. She asserted that the provisions made for her under the agreement were grossly disproportionate to her husband's means.

A decree of divorce was entered on October 19, 1962. The suit to rescind and invalidate the antenuptial agreement was dismissed with prejudice on the plaintiff's application October 22, 1962.

Petitioner did not deduct the legal expenses incurred in connection with the divorce proceeding. Petitioner did deduct on his 1962 return $3,000 for legal expenses incurred in defending the suit to invalidate the antenuptial agreement signed on February 25, 1955. Respondent disallowed this deduction and determined a deficiency of $725.60. This deficiency is in issue here.

Opinion

The sole question in this case is whether petitioner is entitled to deduct $3,000 in legal expenses incurred in defending his wife's suit to set aside an antenuptial agreement.

We hold that he is barred from deducting these expenses by section 262 of the Internal Revenue Code of 1954[1] and the decision of the Supreme Court in United States v. Gilmore, 372 U.S. 39 (1963).

The petitioner's brief asserts first that his position was adequately set forth in the opinion of Carpenter v. United States, 338 F.2d 366 (Ct. Cl.1964). Second, he argues that Erdmand v. Commissioner, 315 F.2d 762 (C.A.7, 1963), affirming 37 T.C. 1119 (1962), supports his position. Lastly, petitioner suggests that the litigation giving rise to the legal expenses here in issue did not grow out of the marriage relationship, but sprang from rights excluded from that relationship. The respondent has countered that the *Carpenter* case is distinguishable; that *Erdman* is inapposite; and that the suggested distinction between rights flowing from the marriage relationship and rights flowing from an antenuptial agreement is one of form and should be rejected. In the alternative, respondent urges that the expenses were incurred in de-

---

1. All statutory references are to the Internal Revenue Code of 1954 unless oth- erwise indicated. [The 1986 Code cites are identical. Ed.]

fending title to property and should be capitalized, not allowed as a deduction.

We agree with all three of respondent's arguments and, therefore, do not reach his alternative proposition.

Petitioner's first contention, that his position is sustained by *Carpenter* is untenable. *Carpenter* involved a deduction for legal expenses paid for tax counsel in the course of a divorce proceeding. The court found these payments to be deductible under section 212(3) as an ordinary and necessary expense paid in connection with the determination of a tax. In Fleischman's case, there is no suggestion in the record that the legal expenses involved were for consultation and advice on tax matters. The stipulation clearly states that the expenses were incurred in defending a suit to set aside and declare void an antenuptial contract.

If petitioner means to rely on *Carpenter* to sustain his case under section 212(2) or 212(1), he is left with the liability that the case did not deal with those paragraphs. Paragraph (3) of section 212, as the *Carpenter* case holds, expresses a policy and has a meaning quite different from paragraphs (1) and (2). In fact, the court pointed out in *Carpenter* that the legal fees would not be deductible under section 212(2).

If petitioner cites *Carpenter* for the proposition that certain legal fees can be deducted even though incurred in connection with a divorce, he is certainly correct. This Court has so held in the case of Ruth K. Wild, 42 T.C. 706 (1964). The question in the case before us, however, is whether *these* legal expenses are deductible, and in resolving that issue, the *Carpenter* case is of no assistance.

The petitioner's second argument is that the case of Erdman v. Commissioner, may be pertinent. We do not agree. *Erdman* concerned the deductibility of legal expenses incurred by taxpayers defending their title to property as beneficiaries of a testamentary trust. In the alternative, it was contended that the trust was entitled to deduct these expenses. This Court held that the attorney's fees were an expenditure of the trust, not of the taxpayer. In addition, the trust was not permitted to deduct the fee currently as it was charged to trust corpus, not income. Calvin Pardee Erdman, 37 T.C. 1119 (1962).

On appeal, the Seventh Circuit upheld the Tax Court on both grounds and added that the taxpayer's expenses were capital in nature, being in defense of title, and not deductible for that reason as well. Erdman v. Commissioner, supra. It is our view that the factual and legal issues in *Erdman* are so significantly different from those in this case that it is of no assistance in reaching our decision.

The expenditures in question are deductible, if at all, only under section 212.[2] Since there is not the slightest indication in the record that the counsel fees concerned taxes, we do not consider this case

2. [I.R.C. § 212 is omitted. Ed.]

under section 212(3). In addition, there is no support for the view that the petitioner incurred the legal expenses for the production or collection of income, nor does he argue that he did; therefore, section 212(1) is not raised. The petition alleges that the expense was for the preservation and protection of taxpayer's real property inherited from his mother. This leaves only the suggestion that the expenses are deductible under section 212(2) as paid for the management, conservation, or maintenance of property held for the production of income.

In approaching the issue thus presented, it is helpful to consider the general purpose and history of section 212. Prior to 1942, legal expenses were deductible only if the suit occasioning them was directly connected with or proximately related to the taxpayer's trade or business. Sarah Backer, et al., Executors, 1 B.T.A. 214 (1924). Legal costs which were simply personal expenses were not deductible, although the line between personal and business expenses was sometimes difficult to draw. Kornhauser v. United States, 276 U.S. 145 (1928).

Certain investment activities conducted by the taxpayer might generate taxable income; however, the expenses attributable to these activities were not deductible where the activities did not constitute a trade or business. Higgins v. Commissioner, 312 U.S. 212 (1941). In order to equalize the treatment of these expenses with business expenses,[3] both of which produced taxable income, Congress added section 23(a)(2) to the 1939 Code by the Revenue Act of 1942 (56 Stat. 798, 819). That section provided as follows:

SEC. 23. DEDUCTIONS FROM GROSS INCOME.

In computing net income there shall be allowed as deductions:

(a) EXPENSES.—

* * *

(2) NON–TRADE OR NON–BUSINESS EXPENSES.—In the case of an individual, all the ordinary and necessary expenses paid or incurred during the taxable year for the production or collection of income, or for the management, conservation, or maintenance of property held for the production of income.

At the same time that Congress enacted section 23(a)(2), it also added sections 22(k) and 23(u) to the 1939 Code. In general, those sections required a divorced spouse to include alimony payments in her gross income and permitted the paying spouse to deduct the amounts paid from his taxable income. Thus, while the Congress increased the range of deductions by section 23(a)(2), it also provided for a new kind of taxable income to a divorced spouse. However, Congress left us with no guidance in the legislative history as to the relationship between the alimony provisions and section 23(a)(2).

---

3. H.Rept. No. 2333, 77th Cong., 2d Sess., p. 75 (1942), 1942–2 C.B. 372, 429.

Section 23(a)(2) was construed as enlarging the category of incomes with respect to which expenses were deductible. Deductions under that section were analogous to business expenses and were allowable or not in accordance with principles which had long controlled these expenses. McDonald v. Commissioner, 323 U.S. 57 (1944). In particular, legal expenses were allowable as investment expenses subject to the same limitations imposed on legal fees incurred in a trade or business. Trust of Bingham v. Commissioner, 325 U.S. 365 (1945).

Great difficulty was experienced in distinguishing deductible legal expenses from those which were purely personal. This Court found that a wife could deduct legal fees incurred to obtain alimony included in her gross income under the Revenue Act of 1942. Elsie B. Gale, 13 T.C. 661 (1949), affd. 191 F.2d 79 (C.A.2d, 1951), acq. 1952–1 C.B. 2; Barbara B. LeMond, 13 T.C. 670 (1949), acq. 1952–1 C.B. 3. On the other hand, the husband's legal expenses were regarded as personal even if he was compelled to pay his wife's counsel fees, or if his income-producing property was threatened with sequestration to pay alimony. Lindsay C. Howard, 16 T.C. 157 (1951), affd. 202 F.2d 28 (C.A.9, 1953); Robert A. McKinney, 16 T.C. 916 (1951); Thorne Donnelley, 16 T.C. 1196 (1951).

The Supreme Court in construing the new section found that Congress did not intend to permit taxpayers to deduct personal, living, or family expenses. Lykes v. United States, 343 U.S. 118, 125 (1952). In applying this rationale, the Court stated as follows:

> * * * Legal expenses do not become deductible merely because they are paid for services which relieve a taxpayer of liability. That argument would carry us too far. It would mean that the expense of defending almost any claim would be deductible by a taxpayer on the ground that such defense was made to help him keep clear of liens whatever income-producing property he might have. * * * Section 23(a)(2) never has been so interpreted by us. It has been applied to expenses on the basis of their immediate purposes rather than upon the basis of the remote contributions they might make to the conservation of a taxpayer's income-producing assets by reducing his general liabilities. See McDonald v. Commissioner, supra. * * *

In 1963, the Court undertook to explain the application of this rationale to a husband's legal expenses incurred in a divorce action. United States v. Gilmore, 372 U.S. 39 (1963).

The taxpayer in *Gilmore* owned a controlling interest in three corporations. The dividends and salary from these companies were his major source of income. In a divorce proceeding, his wife alleged that much of this property was community property and that more than half of the community property should be awarded to her. The taxpayer incurred substantial legal expenses in the course of successfully resisting these claims. He sought to deduct the expenses attributable to his defense against his wife's property claims under section 23(a)(2) of the 1939 Code. The Supreme Court sustained the Government's contention that deductibility depended upon the origin and nature of the claim giving rise to the legal expenses, rather than upon the consequences of such a claim to income-producing property.[4]

The Supreme Court reached this result for two basic reasons. First, the language of the statute "conservation of property" was said to refer to operations performed with respect to the property itself rather than the taxpayer's retention of ownership in it. Secondly, the Court examined the legislative history and discerned a congressional purpose to equalize treatment of expenditures for profit-seeking activities with those related to a trade or business. In order to achieve this result, any limitation or restriction imposed upon a business expense must be applied to section 23(a)(2) expenses. Among those restrictions was the rule, now embodied in section 262, that personal, living, or family expenses are not deductible. The characterization of litigation costs as personal or business depends upon whether the claim involved in the litigation arises in connection with the profit-seeking activities. A suit against a taxpayer must be directly connected with or proximately result from his business before it is a business expense. This being so, the "origin of claim" test used in the business deduction cases was selected as most consistent with the meaning of section 23(a)(2). The claim against the property in a divorce suit arises only from the marital relationship and is therefore personal. The wife's rights, if any, must have their source in the marriage.

Dispelling all doubts that the Supreme Court was passing only on community property claims was United States v. Patrick, 372 U.S. 53 (1963), decided the same day as *Gilmore*. The *Patrick* case dealt with a property settlement which was made prior to divorce and which was supposed to have preserved the husband's income-producing property. The Supreme Court found little or no difference between that situation and *Gilmore* where the issue concerned community property and the wife's claim to an award of more than her existing share of such property.

Gilmore was decided under the 1939 Code and *Patrick* under the 1954 Code. There was no suggestion in these cases that enactment of the 1954 Code changed the meaning of the statutory language. The 1954 Code divides the provisions formerly contained in section 23(a)(2) of the 1939 Code into two paragraphs. The first deals with expenses for the production of income, and the second with expenses for the management, conservation, or maintenance of property held for the production of income. In connection with section 212(1) and (2), the legislative history specifically states that no substantive change from section 23(a)

---

4. The Commissioner's regulations have long provided that expenses do not become deductible merely because incurred in defense of a claim which may result in income-producing property being sold or used to satisfy taxpayer's liability. Sec. 39.23(a)–15(k), Regs. 118; sec. 1.212–1(m), Income Tax Regs.

(2) of the Internal Revenue Code of 1939 was made. Thus, the Code simply puts in separate paragraphs what was once one sentence.

Scarcely had the *Gilmore* case been decided, when the Tax Court was again confronted with the issue of the deductibility of the wife's attorney fees expended to collect defaulted alimony payments. Jane U. Elliott, 40 T.C. 304 (1963), acq. 1964–1 C.B. (Part 1) 4. In accordance with prior law, the wife was allowed a deduction under section 212(1). The Court held that the legal fees in question were incurred for the production of her taxable income. *Gilmore* and *Patrick* were not cited in this opinion.

The following year the case of Ruth K. Wild, 42 T.C. 706 (1964), was presented for review by the whole Court. The wife sought a deduction for counsel fees under section 212(1) in reliance upon the *Elliott* case for expenses incurred in negotiating an alimony agreement and in hearings concerning this agreement. The respondent contended that *Gilmore* and *Patrick* required a contrary result since the expenses were attributable to a claim which was based on her marital rights and not on a profit-seeking activity. This Court distinguished *Gilmore* and *Patrick* upon the basis that both of those cases were decided under paragraph (2) of section 212 and the contention in the *Wild* case was that the legal fees were deductible under paragraph (1). The Commissioner's regulations permitting a deduction for legal costs attributable to the collection of taxable alimony had not been changed following the *Gilmore* decision. Neither had his acquiescence in *Elliott* been withdrawn. These two factors influenced the Court in holding that the wife could continue to deduct legal expenses related to alimony. Thus, she retained a deduction under section 212(1).

This Court has made it clear that the wife's deduction under section 212(1) is limited to expenses incurred in obtaining alimony includable in her gross income. There is no deduction for expenses related to property claims, even when incurred by the wife. Those claims grow out of the marital relationship and are covered by the rule in *Gilmore.* Georgia Leary Neill, 42 T.C. 793 (1964).

Turning to the case at hand, both petitioner and respondent have argued the case under section 212(2). In order to prevail, the petitioner must demonstrate how his expenses differ from those in *Gilmore* and *Patrick.* We find that he has failed in this task.

Petitioner suggests that his expenses differ from those at issue in *Gilmore* because his were caused by a separate suit to rescind a contract. In Joan Fleischman's second suit, she alleged that the provisions of the antenuptial agreement were disproportionate to her husband's means at the time the agreement was made and at the time of suit. Simultaneously, she had a divorce suit pending requesting support payments. Viewed in its entirety, her effort was one directed at obtaining support payments greater than those provided in the antenuptial agreement. In part, her claim to greater rights was founded upon facts existing or arising during the marriage. In this respect her claim was not unlike that involved in the *Gilmore* case. There, the claim was that certain community property belonging one-half to the husband should be awarded to the wife because of wrongs committed during the marital relationship. The Supreme Court rejected any distinction between legal expenses related to the issue of whether assets were community property and those related to an award of such property. Both issues have a common origin. In both *Gilmore* and here, the wife was requesting an award of property and her right was founded only upon the consequences that State law attaches to marriage. In petitioner's case, his wife made no claim to specific property except as a source of payment, hence his position is even weaker than that of the taxpayer in *Gilmore*.

The fact that Fleischman's wife first had to file a separate suit to invalidate the antenuptial agreement is solely the result of the restricted jurisdiction of the Ohio divorce courts. That fact alone is not a sound basis for a distinction in the field of Federal taxation.

For ascertaining the source of claims giving rise to legal expenses, the Supreme Court suggested a "but for" test. If the claim could not have existed but for the marriage relationship, the expense of defending it is a personal expense and not deductible. Applying that test, it is clear that but for her marriage to petitioner, the wife could have no claim to the property sought to be protected.

In deciding that the antenuptial agreement in this case is not significantly different from a property settlement incident to a divorce, we are aided in our reasoning by United States v. Patrick. In that case, complicated property adjustments were required so that the husband could retain controlling interest in a publishing business owned jointly with his wife. The legal fees involved were spent arranging a transfer of various stocks, leasing real property, and creating a trust, rather than conducting divorce litigation. The Supreme Court found no legal significance in these differences from *Gilmore*. The Court found that the transfers were incidental to the litigation which had its origin in taxpayer's personal life. It could be argued that we should take a narrow view and say that the suit to set aside petitioner's antenuptial agreement concerned contract rights. However, that view ignores the fact that marital rights were the subject of this contract and the fact that the second lawsuit was intimately bound up with the divorce litigation. In *Patrick*, the settlement agreement stated that it settled "rights growing out of the marital relationship." In the case at hand, the agreement states that the parties desire to agree to a distribution of property should their marriage be dissolved by divorce or annulment. We can perceive little or no difference between the two agreements when the question of deducting legal expenses is in issue.

A similar question was presented in David G. Joyce, 3 B.T.A. 393 (1926). The taxpayer there sought a deduction for legal expenses incurred in defending a postnuptial agreement from attack by his wife. The agreement was made in 1913 and governed rights upon death or divorce. In 1920 the wife instituted an action for divorce and for an award of maintenance in addition to the provisions of the postnuptial contract. The taxpayer sought to deduct the expenses related to defending the agreement as a business expense. He argued that the contract gave him greater freedom in managing his business property and that such property was the subject of the contract.

In holding that the expenses were personal, the Board stated that the husband's argument ignored the genesis of the rights he attempted to settle and limit by the postnuptial agreement. Those rights existed and would exist only by virtue of the marriage.[5]

In conclusion, we find no significant distinction between this case and the *Gilmore* and *Patrick* cases, and accordingly, we hold that the legal expenses incurred by the petitioner are not deductible.

Decision will be entered for the respondent.

PROBLEMS

1. Speculator buys 100 shares of Sound Company stock for $3000, paying his broker a commission of $50 on the purchase. Fourteen months later he sells the shares for $4000 paying a commission of $60 on the sale.

(a) He would like to treat $110 paid as commissions as § 212 expenses. Why? Can he? See Spreckles v. Helvering, 315 U.S. 626, 62 S.Ct. 777 (1942).

(b) What result in (a), above, if instead he sells the shares for $2500 paying a $45 commission on the sale? See § 165(c)(2).

(c) Speculator owned only one-tenth of one percent of the Sound Company stock but, being an eager investor during the time he owned the stock, he incurred $500 of transportation, meals and lodging expenses in traveling 1000 miles to New York City to attend Sound's annual shareholder meeting. May he deduct his costs under § 212(2)?

(d) What result in (c), above, if instead Speculator owned 10% of the total outstanding Sound stock, worth $300,000?

(e) What result to Speculator if he incurred the expenses in (c), above, to attend a seminar on investments?

(f) Speculator owns 10% of Sound's stock worth $300,000 and he incurs $10,000 in legal fees and personal costs investigating the operation of the business after the business has some serious setbacks. Is the $10,000 deductible?

(g) Speculator (a 10% shareholder) agrees to sell his stock in installments to Buyer at its price on the market at the time of

---

5. "It is hardly necessary to allude to the fact that marriage is a personal relationship, except for the purpose of pointing out that the legal rights and obligations annexed to the relationship are also personal and the expenses connected therewith would, we think, come within the classification of personal or family expenses." (David G. Joyce, 3 B.T.A. 393, 397.)

each sale, but subject to changes in valuation for blockage. A dispute arises over the "blockage" effects on value. May Speculator deduct his attorney's fees incurred in determining the "blockage" effect on his stock's value?

2. After reading the *Fleischman* case, consider in what situations:

(a) Husband's attorneys' fees incurred in getting a divorce are deductible by him.

(b) Wife's attorneys' fees incurred in getting a divorce are deductible by her.

(c) Wife's attorneys' fees incurred in getting a divorce are deductible by Husband if he pays them.

3. Planner consults his attorneys with respect to his estate plan. They decide to make various inter vivos gifts and draft his will. To what extent, if any, are Planner's legal fees deductible under § 212(3)? Under § 212(2)? See Rev.Rul. 72–545, 1972–2 C.B. 179, and Sidney Merians, 60 T.C. 187 (1973), acq., 1973–2 C.B. 2.

B. CHARGES ARISING OUT OF TRANSACTIONS ENTERED INTO FOR PROFIT

Internal Revenue Code: Sections 165(a), (b), (c)(2); 167(a)(2); 168(a); 212. See Sections 195; 280A.

Regulations: Sections 1.165–9(b); 1.167(g)–1; 1.212–1(h).

WILLIAM C. HORRMANN *

Tax Court of the United States, 1951.
17 T.C. 903(A).

[The Findings of Fact have been omitted.]

Opinion

BLACK, Judge: Three issues are presented in this proceeding. All issues relate to the real property, residence and garage, at 189 Howard Avenue, Staten Island, New York, which was acquired by petitioner by a devise from his mother upon her death in February 1940.

Petitioner redecorated the house and moved into it about October 1940. Shortly thereafter petitioner sold the residence in which he was living prior to October 1940. The property at 189 Howard Avenue was used by petitioner as his personal residence until October 1942, at which time petitioner abandoned the house. Petitioner, after living in

---

* Problems such as those presented here and in *Lowry,* infra page 447, are discussed in Erck, "And You Thought Moving Was Bad—Try Deducting Depreciation and Maintenance Expenses on Your Unsold Residence," 26 U.Fla.L.R. 587 (1974); Reese, "Maintenance and Depreciation De- ductions Are Not Available on a Residence Vacated and Offered for Sale But Not for Rent Unless Taxpayer Intends to Profit," 49 Texas L.Rev. 581 (1971); and Fasan, "Maintenance and Depreciation Deduc- tions for a Personal Residence Offered for Sale," 25 Tax L.Rev. 269 (1970). Ed.

the residence for awhile, considered the property too large and too expensive and when he left he planned never to use it again as his personal residence.

Petitioner considered converting the building into apartments, but this was found to be impractical. Numerous efforts were made to rent and to sell the property. The property was sold in June 1945, and the net proceeds from the sale were $20,800. At the time petitioner acquired the property its value was $60,000, and at the time it was abandoned by petitioner as a personal residence the value was $45,000, with $35,000 allocated to land and $10,000 to the buildings.

The issue which we shall first consider is whether petitioner is entitled to a deduction for depreciation on the property during the taxable years 1943, 1944, and 1945. The applicable provision of the Internal Revenue Code is set forth in the margin.[1]

Petitioner is entitled to a deduction for depreciation at the rate of $500 per year provided the property was *held for the production of income.* In determining whether the test prescribed by statute is satisfied the use made of the property and the owner's intent in respect to the future use or disposition of the property are generally controlling. Until November 1942, the property was used by petitioner solely as a personal residence, but thereafter that use was abandoned. The mere abandonment of such use does not mean that thereafter the property was held for the production of income. But when efforts are made to rent the property as were made by petitioner herein, the property is then being held for the production of income and this may be so even though no income is in fact received from the property, Mary Laughlin Robinson, 2 T.C. 305, and even though the property is at the same time offered for sale. While an intention not to rent the house was indicated in May 1943, on the brochure of the real estate clearing house, efforts to rent the property were made subsequent to that time. The evidence, when considered in its entirety, supports the conclusion that petitioner continuously offered to rent the property until it was sold. In the recomputation of tax for the years 1943, 1944, and 1945, petitioner is to be allowed depreciation at the rate of $500 per year until June 1945, when the property was sold.

The second issue is whether petitioner is entitled to a deduction for expenses incurred during the taxable years for the maintenance and conservation of the property. The applicable provision of the Internal Revenue Code is set forth in the margin.[2] The same phrase appearing in section 23(1)(2) of the Code, see footnote 1 of this Opinion, appears also in section 23(a)(2) of the Code, the requirement being that the property be *held for the production of income.* The taxpayer in Mary Laughlin Robinson, supra, claimed a deduction for depreciation on the property and expenses for services of a caretaker. Although the taxable year there was 1937, the sections of the Code applicable there

---

1. [I.R.C. (1939) § 23(*l*)(2) is omitted. See I.R.C. (1986) § 167(a)(2); 168(a). Ed.]   2. [I.R.C. (1939) § 23(a)(2) is omitted. See I.R.C. (1986) § 212(2). Ed.]

(see footnote 1 of that Opinion) contain the same standard, *property held for the production of income,* as is applicable here. We there held that the taxpayer was entitled to both the deductions at issue. In accordance with that Opinion, we hold that petitioner in the recomputation of tax for the years 1943 and 1944, is entitled to deductions for maintenance and conservation expenses of the property as itemized in our Findings of Fact.

The third issue is whether petitioner is entitled to a deduction for a long term capital loss arising from the sale in 1945 of the property at 189 Howard Avenue. Petitioner claims a deduction under the provisions of section 23(e)(2) of the Code which are set forth in the margin,[3] and he has computed the deduction in accordance with the limitations provisions of section 117 of the Code.

The language of the Code sections applicable in issues one and two was *property held for the production of income,* and the language of section 23(e)(2) of the Code is different. In order for a loss to be deductible under that section it must be incurred *in any transaction entered into for profit.* In a situation where the use of the property as a personal residence has been abandoned, and where the owner has offered the property for sale or for rent and finally sells the property at a loss, that distinction in language may result in allowing a deduction in one case and not allowing a deduction of another type. At least the cases have distinguished between the two statutory provisions, Warner v. Commissioner, 167 F.2d 633, affirming per curiam a Memorandum Opinion of this Court. We think that the facts in respect to this issue are not materially different from those in Allen L. Grammer, 12 T.C. 34, and those in Morgan v. Commissioner, 76 F.2d 390. When property has been used as a personal residence, in order to convert the transaction into one entered into for profit the owner must do more than abandon the property and list it for sale or rent, Allen L. Grammer, supra. See also Rumsey v. Commissioner, 82 F.2d 158. In that case, in denying the taxpayer any deduction for the loss so incurred, the Court said:

The taxpayer argues with considerable persuasive force that the fact that a man first rents his house before selling it is only significant as evidentiary of his purpose to abandon it as a residence and to devote the property to business uses; that renting is not the sole criterion of such purpose, as the regulations themselves imply by the words "rented or otherwise appropriated" to income producing purposes. But we think the argument cannot prevail over counter considerations. If an owner rents, his decision is irrevocable, at least for the term of the lease; and if he remodels to fit the building for business purposes, he has likewise made it impossible to resume residential uses by a mere change of mind. When, however, he only instructs an agent to sell or rent the property, its change of character remains subject to his

---

3. [I.R.C. (1939) § 23(e)(2) is omitted.
See I.R.C. (1986) § 165(c)(2). Ed.]

unfettered will; he may revoke the agency at any moment. Certainly it strains the language of Article 171, Regulations 74, to find that the property is "appropriated to" and "used for" income producing purposes by merely listing it with a broker for sale or rental. * * *

We have held that an actual rental of the property is not always essential to a conversion, Estate of Maria Assmann, 16 T.C. 632, but that case is not controlling here for the taxpayer there abandoned the residence only a few days after it was inherited, and then later demolished the residence. In Mary E. Crawford, 16 T.C. 678, which involved only the question of whether the loss was a section 23(e)(1) loss or a section 23(e)(2) loss, the owner-taxpayer had also demolished the residence. While we held in both cases that such action constituted an appropriation or conversion, in both cases the facts indicate that from the moment the properties were inherited the taxpayers did not intend to continue to occupy the property as their personal residence.

Here the situation is different. The petitioners in the instant case soon after the death of petitioner's mother took immediate and decisive action, fixing the character of the property in their hands as residential. The surrounding circumstances point to this conclusion; their expenditure of approximately $9,000 in redecorating the house in preparation for their use of it as a home; their moving into the property within nine months after they acquired it; the sale of their former residence at Ocean Terrace shortly after they had moved into the Howard Avenue property; and finally, their occupancy of the Howard Avenue property for a period of about two years as a home and residence. They could hardly have gone further more decisively to fix the character of this property, originally neutral in their hands, as personal residential property.

As to the third issue, we think there was no conversion of the property into a transaction entered into for profit. Respondent did not err in determining that petitioner was not entitled to the benefits of a capital loss carry-over to 1946 for the loss sustained upon the sale in 1945 of the property at 189 Howard Avenue. Allen L. Grammer, supra.

Decision will be entered under Rule 50.

LOWRY v. UNITED STATES

District Court of the United States, District of New Hampshire, 1974.
384 F.Supp. 257.

Opinion

BOWNES, District Judge. Plaintiffs bring this action to recover federal income taxes and interest, in the amount of $1,072, which they allege were erroneously or illegally assessed and collected. Jurisdiction is based on 28 U.S.C.A. § 1346(a)(1).

The issue is whether plaintiffs, who ceased to use their summer house as residential property in 1967 and immediately offered it for sale without attempting to rent the property, converted it into "income producing property," thereby entitling them to deduct the maintenance expenses incurred after it was put on the market and prior to its sale in 1973. The Internal Revenue Service allowed plaintiffs to take maintenance deductions in the tax years 1968 and 1969. They disallowed similar maintenance deductions in the tax year 1970. The only year in issue is 1970.[1]

Plaintiffs are husband and wife domiciled in Peterborough, New Hampshire. (Since Edward G. Lowry, Jr., is the principal party in this case, he alone will hereinafter be referred to as plaintiff.) Plaintiff filed a joint federal income tax return for 1970 with the District Director of Internal Revenue in Portsmouth, New Hampshire. On his 1970 income tax return, plaintiff deducted expenditures made for the care and maintenance of his former summer residence. He based these deductions upon the premise that the summer residence was no longer personal property, but was property "held for the production of income." Int.Rev.Code of 1954 § 212. The Internal Revenue Service disagreed with plaintiff and disallowed the deduction basing its decision on Internal Revenue Code of 1954 § 262 which provides:

> Except as otherwise expressly provided in this chapter, no deductions shall be allowed for personal, living, or family expenses.

On November 27, 1971, plaintiff paid the disputed $1,072 under written protest.

The property in question is plaintiff's former summer residence on Martha's Vineyard (hereinafter referred to as Vineyard property). The Vineyard property is part of a cooperative community known as Seven Gates Farm Corporation.

Seven Gates was formed in 1921 by five persons, one of whom was plaintiff's father. Upon forming the corporation, plaintiff's father acquired the Vineyard property. In 1942, plaintiff acquired "title" to the property by gift from his father.

Legal title to the Vineyard property is held by Seven Gates. In 1970, plaintiff had a lease for the Vineyard property and was a 3% stockholder in the corporation. The leasing arrangement treated plaintiff as the de facto owner of the property. It ran for the life of the corporation with the proviso that, upon dissolution of the corporation, it would automatically be converted into a fee title. No stockholder-lessee, however, could sell his stock and lease without the prior consent of 75% of the stockholder-lessees. Each lease further provided that a rental for a year or less required the prior consent of the Committee on Admissions and that a lease for more than a year required the prior consent of 75% of the other stockholder-lessees.

----

1. Plaintiff, due to his own mistake, failed to take the allowable depreciation deductions and that matter is not before this court.

In 1966, plaintiff owned three residential properties: he maintained his legal residence in Maryland; he had a winter residence in Florida; and the Vineyard property. During 1966, plaintiff sold his Maryland home and purchased a house in Peterborough, New Hampshire. Because the Peterborough house did "all the things that the house in Martha's Vineyard did," plaintiff decided, in 1967, to sell the Vineyard property and put a sales price on it of $150,000. From 1921 through 1967, plaintiff had spent nearly all of his summers at the Vineyard property.

After it was put on the market, the house was never again used as residential property. Each spring plaintiff went to Martha's Vineyard, opened the house, put up curtains, pruned the shrubbery, generally cleaned and spruced up the property, and then left. This took two or three days and plaintiff occupied the house during this period. Each fall plaintiff returned and closed the house for the winter. The closing also took two to three days and plaintiff stayed in the house. The only other time that plaintiff occupied the property was once a year, when the corporation had its annual meeting of stockholders. As evidence of his intent to treat the Vineyard property as a business asset, plaintiff testified that in 1971 his daughter, after returning from abroad, requested the use of the property. Plaintiff refused, stating that the property was a business proposition. As a fatherly gesture, however, he rented a summer home in Maine for her use.

Plaintiff made no attempt to rent the house for the following reasons: He believed that it would be easier to sell a clean empty house than one occupied by tenants; the house being suitable for summer occupancy only, would have had to have been rented completely equipped, which would have required the plaintiff to purchase linen, silver, blankets, and recreational equipment at a cost which would not have been justified by any possible rental; rental prices bore no reasonable relation to the value of the property and the expected sales price; and rental was complicated by the restrictive provisions of the corporation's bylaws.

In 1968, a prospective purchaser offered to buy the property for $150,000. Plaintiff, however, could not obtain the necessary 75% approval of the stockholders of Seven Gates and the sale was not completed. In 1973, plaintiff received a cash offer of $150,000 for the property and the sale was closed in September of 1973. Plaintiff's 1973 tax return showed a net long-term capital gain of $100,536.50, as a result of the sale.

Rulings of Law

The tax issue in this case is: When and how does residential property become converted into income producing property?

The Tax Court, in attempting to establish a clear guideline in a murky area, created a simple test: The taxpayer had to make a bona fide offer to rent in order to convert residential property into "income producing property." [2] The Tax Court's *sine qua non* was a product of administrative reality. There are three basic reasons why the Government established a rental prerequisite. First, it stemmed from a fear that taxpayers would countermand the listing for sale after taking a series of deductions and reoccupy the house on a personal basis. Mary Laughlin Robinson, 2 T.C. 305, 309 (1943). Second, the rental requisite provided a clear and convenient administrative test. Warren Leslie, Sr., 6 T.C. 488, 494 (1946). Third, the rental requirement found some implied support in Treas.Reg. § 1.212–1(h) (1954), which provides:

> Ordinary and necessary expenses paid or incurred in connection with the management, conservation, or maintenance of property held for use as a residence by the taxpayer are not deductible. However, ordinary and necessary expenses paid or incurred in connection with the management, conservation, or maintenance of property held by the taxpayer as rental property are deductible even though such property was formerly held by the taxpayer for use as a home.[3]

In Hulet P. Smith, 26 T.C.M. 149 (1967), aff'd 397 F.2d 804 (9th Cir. 1968), the Tax Court abandoned the rental test and held that an offer for sale plus an abandonment transformed the property into an investment asset. The Court of Appeals, in affirming, circumspectly stated:

> The Government makes a strong case for reversal. See Recent Development, Hulet P. Smith, 66 Mich.L.Rev. 562 (1968). Unusual circumstances are present, however, and we are not persuaded that the Tax Court's factual finding and its consequent conclusions are clearly wrong.[4] *Smith,* supra, 397 F.2d 804.

In a subsequent decision, the Tax Court was presented with a fact pattern which was similar to the one presented in *Smith* and came to the opposite conclusion. Frank A. Newcombe, 54 T.C. 1298 (1970). The court stated that *Smith* was "of little precedential value." Id. at 1303.

In *Newcombe* the taxpayers moved out of their personal residence and immediately offered it for sale. At no time was the property offered for rent. The taxpayers argued that, under the *Smith* doctrine, the property was being held for the production of income. The Government contended that the *Smith* case was erroneous and that property can only be converted into income producing property use when there has been a bona fide offer to rent.

In rejecting both parties' positions, the court stated:

2. See Note, Recent Developments, Hulet P. Smith, 66 Mich.L.Rev. 562, 564–65 n. 14 (1968), and numerous cases cited therein.

3. Id. at 566 where "[b]y implication, then the regulations require a rental offer to convert a former residence to income producing property."

4. It is unclear as to what "unusual circumstances" the Court of Appeals was referring to. See Note, 25 Tax L.Rev. 269, 272 (1970):

> [O]ne would especially like to know what "unusual circumstances" the appellate court thought were present, since this does not appear to be such a situation.

We do not share the penchant for polarization which the arguments of the parties reflect. Rather, we believe that a variety of factors must be weighed. * * * *Newcombe, supra,* 54 T.C. at 1299–1300.

The *Newcombe* court found that "[t]he key question, in cases of the type involved herein, is the purpose or intention of the taxpayer in light of all the facts and circumstances." Id. at 1303. The critical inquiry is, therefore, whether the taxpayer had or intended an "expectation of profit." To aid in its inquiry, the court took into account the following considerations: length of time the taxpayer occupied his former residence prior to abandonment; the availability of the house for the taxpayer's personal use while it was unoccupied; the recreational character of the property; attempts to rent the property; and, whether the offer to sell was an attempt to realize post-conversion appreciation. The court explained its final criterion as follows:

> The placing of property on the market for immediate sale, at or shortly after the time of its abandonment as a residence, will ordinarily be strong evidence that a taxpayer is not holding the property for post conversion appreciation in value. Under such circumstances, only a most exceptional situation will permit a finding that the statutory requirement has been satisfied. *On the other hand, if a taxpayer believes that the value of the property may appreciate and decides to hold it for some period in order to realize upon such anticipated appreciation, as well as an excess over his investment, it can be said that the property is being "held for the production of income."* Id. at 1302–1303 (emphasis added).

I rule that the Vineyard property was converted into income producing property in 1967 and that plaintiff was entitled to deduct his maintenance expenses. In ruling in plaintiff's favor, I adopt the approach taken by the *Newcombe* court and do not regard renting as the "litmus test" for conversion.[5]

Administrative difficulty in determining when personal property is transformed into investment property should not create a rigid and inflexible barrier to the benefits of conversion.[6] Plaintiff gave sound and substantial business reasons for his failure to rent. I also note that the rental rule does not provide an elixir to administrative ills, for it must be determined that the offer to rent is bona fide and not a sham. Paul H. Stutz, 1965 P–H Tax Ct.Mem. ¶ 65,166; S. Wise, 1945 P–H Tax Ct.Mem. ¶ 45,298. Finally, I do not believe that Treas.Reg. § 1.212–1(h) (1954) commands a rental offer as a prerequisite to converting a prior residence into income producing property. I find the language con-

---

5. I.J. Wagner, 33 T.C.M. 201 (February 19, 1974); Charles D. Mayes, 30 T.C.M. 363 (April 28, 1973); Raymond L. Opper, 31 T.C.M. 48 (May 25, 1972); Richard R. Riss, Sr., 56 T.C. 388 (May 24, 1971); Richard N. Newbre, 30 T.C.M. 705 (July 15, 1971); James J. Sherlock, 31 T.C.M. 383 (April 27, 1971).

6. See note 2, supra at 568.

tained therein, with regard to renting, to be illustrative and not an explicit statement of law.

In fact, another regulation provides that: "[t]he term 'income' for the purpose of section 212 * * * is not confined to recurring income but applies as well to gains from the disposition of property." Treas. Reg. § 1.212–1(b) (1954). The regulation further provides that the maintenance expenses of property held for investment are deductible; even if the property is not producing income, there is no likelihood of current income, and there is no likelihood of gain upon the sale of the property.

The determination of whether plaintiff's prior residence has been converted into income producing property is made by examining the taxpayer's purpose in light of all the facts and circumstances. Treas. Reg. § 1.212–1(c) (1954). I find that the facts and circumstances presented clearly indicate that plaintiff intended to benefit from post-abandonment appreciation.

I take judicial notice that the price for recreational property on Martha's Vineyard and everywhere else in New England has skyrocketted in the past decade. Plaintiff has had wide exposure to financial and real estate transactions. He was thoroughly exposed to the real estate world from 1934 to 1943. During that period, he liquidated about 15,000 properties in about 1,200 communities located in thirty-six states. He was specifically aware of Martha's Vineyard land values, having spent nearly all of his summers there. Plaintiff also testified that he was aware, during the latter half of the 1960's of changing economic conditions. As administrator of a large New York insurance company, he saw increasing cash flow and rising prosperity. He testified that, as a result of this exposure, he came to the conclusion, during the latter part of 1967, that we were in the beginning of an inflationary trend and that the value of land would appreciate markedly. Although the 1967 market value of the Vineyard property was $50,000, plaintiff's business acumen and experience suggested that he could obtain his list price of $150,000 if he kept the property visible and in good condition and waited for the anticipated real estate boom coupled with the anticipated inflation. After a period of five and one-half years, plaintiff did, in fact, sell the property in September of 1973, for his original list price. A capital gain of $100,536.50 appeared on his 1973 income tax return as a consequence of the sale.

The fact that plaintiff immediately listed the property does not negate his contention that he intended to capitalize on post-abandonment appreciation in land values. By an immediate listing, plaintiff made the property a visible commodity on a demanding market. He patiently waited until the economic forces pushed the market value of his property up to his list price.

Based on all the facts and circumstances, I find that plaintiff had a reasonable "expectation of profit" and that the Vineyard property was held as income producing property during 1967. Accordingly, I rule that plaintiff was entitled to deduct the property's maintenance expenses incurred during 1970.

Judgment for the plaintiffs.

So ordered.

PROBLEMS

1. Recall the *Morton Frank* case in Chapter 14 at page 357 supra.

(a) Should Frank's expenses have been deductible under § 212 or § 165(c)(2)?

(b) If Frank had decided to buy the newspaper and incurred capital expenditures to begin operations, but then abandoned his plans, would he have been allowed a deduction? See Johan Domenie, 34 T.C.M. 469 (1975) and Rev.Rul. 77–254, 1977–2 C.B. 63.

(c) If Frank entered the business and elected to use § 195 but ceased operations within the 60 month period, to what extent could he take a § 165(c) loss?

2. Homeowners purchased their residence for $80,000 ($10,000 of which was allocable to the land). When it was worth $60,000 ($10,000 of which was allocable to the land), they moved out and put it up for sale, but not rent, for $70,000.

(a) May they take deductions for expenses and depreciation on the residence? If so, what types of expenses would qualify?

(b) Assume instead that they rented the property and properly took $10,000 of depreciation on it. What result when they subsequently sell the property for

(1) $45,000?

(2) $75,000?

(3) $65,000?

CHAPTER 16. DEDUCTIONS NOT LIMITED TO BUSINESS OR PROFIT–SEEKING ACTIVITIES

A. INTRODUCTION

The preceding chapters have dealt with deductions that emanate from business and profit-seeking activities. The primary purposes for their allowance are to reflect accurately net income and profits from business and profit-seeking activities and to encourage investment in such activities.

Generally, Section 262 precludes deductions for personal, living or family expenses. The deductions allowed by the provisions considered in this chapter are exceptions to the general prohibition. Although the deduction provisions considered in this chapter apply to business, profit-seeking, *and* personal activities, as a practical matter the business and profit-seeking items would be deductible under Section 162 or Section 212 without assistance from the provisions examined here. Thus, the practical effect of the provisions considered here is to *create* deductions only for limited personal, living or family items.

As the comment below indicates, an effect of the allowance of an income tax deduction is a federal subsidy.[1] For example, the interest deduction may aid economic growth. The deduction for local taxes eases the pain of certain taxation and thus assists revenue raising by states and municipalities. Consider the excerpt below. Should the federal government pick up a higher percentage of the costs of some taxpayers than of others? Is there an alternative under which all taxpayers would be treated the same? To what extent is the problem alleviated by recent legislation lowering and flattening tax rates?

TAX SUBSIDIES AS A DEVICE FOR IMPLEMENTING GOVERNMENT POLICY: A COMPARISON WITH DIRECT GOVERNMENT EXPENDITURES *

Stanley S. Surrey.

* * *

1. See Surrey, "Tax Incentives as a Device for Implementing Government Policy: A Comparison with Direct Government Expenditures," 83 Harv.L.Rev. 705 (1970); Turnier and Kelly, "The Economic Equivalence of Standard Tax Credits, Deductions and Exemptions," 36 U.Fla.L.Rev. 1003 (1984).

* Excerpts from Hearings before the Subcommittee on Priorities and Economy in Government of the Joint Economic Committee, 92d Cong., 1st Sess. pp. 49–51 (1972).

1. THE NATURE AND EXTENT OF EXISTING TAX SUBSIDIES * * *

A. The Tax Expenditure Budget

The Federal Income tax system consists really of two parts: one part comprises the structural provisions necessary to implement the income tax on individual and corporate net income; the second part comprises a system of tax expenditures under which governmental financial assistance programs are carried out through special tax provisions rather than through direct government expenditures. The second system is simply grafted on to the structure of the income tax proper; it has no basic relation to that structure and is not necessary to its operation.

Instead, the system of tax expenditures provides a vast subsidy apparatus that uses the mechanics of the income tax as a method of paying the subsidies. The special provisions under which this subsidy apparatus functions take a variety of forms, covering exclusions from income, exemptions, deductions, credits against tax, preferential rates of tax, and deferrals of tax. The Tax Expenditure Budget * * * identifies and qualifies the existing tax expenditures. This Tax Expenditure Budget is essentially an enumeration of the present "tax incentives" or "tax subsidies" contained in our income tax system.

* * *

The Tax Expenditure Budget enables us to look at the income tax provisions reflected in that Budget in a new light. Once these tax provisions are seen not as inherent parts of an income tax structure but as carrying out programs of financial assistance for particular groups and activities, a number of questions immediately come into focus. Once we see that we are not evaluating technical tax provisions but rather expenditure programs, we are able to ask the traditional questions and use the analytical tools that make up the intellectual apparatus of expenditure experts.

We thus can put the basic question of whether we desire to provide that financial assistance at all, and if so in what amount—a stock question any budget expert would normally ask of any item in the regular Budget. We can inquire whether the program is working well, how its benefits compare with its costs, is it accomplishing its objectives—indeed, what are its objectives? Who is actually being assisted by the program and is that assistance too much or too little? Again, these are stock questions directed by any budget expert at existing programs. They all equally must be asked of the items and programs in the Tax Expenditure Budget.

* * *

The translation and consequent restatement of a tax expenditure program in direct expenditure terms generally show an upside-down result utterly at variance with usual expenditure policies. Thus, if cast in direct expenditure language, the present assistance for owner-occupied homes under the tax deductions for mortgage interest and property taxes would look as follows, envisioned as a HUD program:

> For a married couple with more than $200,000 in income, HUD would, for each $100 of mortgage interest on the couple's home pay $70 [after 1987, $28 or possibly $33. Ed.] to the bank holding the mortgage, leaving the couple to pay $30 [after 1987, $72 or possibly $67. Ed.]. It would also pay a similar portion of the couple's property tax to the State or city levying the tax.

> For a married couple with income of $10,000, HUD would pay the bank on the couple's mortgage $19 [after 1987, $15. Ed.] per each $100 interest unit, with the couple paying $81 [after 1987, $85. Ed.]. It would also pay a similar portion of the couple's property tax to the State or city levying the tax.

> For a married couple too poor to pay an income tax, HUD would pay nothing to the bank, leaving the couple to pay the entire interest cost. The couple would also have to pay the entire property tax.

One can assume that no HUD Secretary would ever have presented to Congress a direct housing program with this upside-down effect.

B. INTEREST *

Internal Revenue Code: Sections 163(a), (h); 280A(d)(1); 7872. See Sections 163(b), (d), and (f); 263A; 265(a)(2) through (4); 266; 461(g); 483.

Regulations: Section 1.163–1. See Proposed Sections 1.7872–1 through 14.

REVENUE RULING 69–188
1969–1 Cum.Bull. 54.

Advice has been requested whether for Federal income tax purposes, a payment made under the circumstances set forth below is considered to be interest.

A taxpayer on the cash receipts and disbursements method of accounting who wished to purchase a building, arranged with a lender to finance the transaction. A conventional mortgage loan of 1,000x dollars was negotiated, secured by a deed of trust on the building, and repayable in monthly installments over a ten-year period at a stated annual interest rate of 7.2 percent. In addition to the annual interest rate the parties agreed that the borrower would pay a "loan processing fee" of 70x dollars (sometimes referred to as "points") prior to receipt of the loan proceeds. The borrower established that this fee was not paid for any specific services that the lender had performed or had agreed to

---

* See Bedell, "The Interest Deduction: Its Current Status," 32 N.Y.U.Inst. on Fed. Tax. 1117 (1974), and Kanter, "Interest Deduction: Use, Ruse, and Refuse," 46 Taxes 794 (1968); a briefer discussion appears in Kanter, "The Interest Deduction: When and How Does It Work," 26 N.Y.U.Inst. on Fed.Tax. 87 (1968).

perform in connection with the borrower's account under the loan contract. The loan agreement provided for separate charges for these services. For example, separate charges were made for a preliminary title report, a title report, an escrow fee, the drawing of the deed and other papers, and insurance.

In determining the amount of this "loan processing fee" the lender considered the economic factors that usually dictate an acceptable rate of interest. That is, he considered the general availability of money, the character of the property offered as security, the degree of success that the borrower had enjoyed in his prior business activities, and the outcome of previous transactions between the borrower and his creditors.

The taxpayer tendered a check for $70x$ dollars drawn on a bank account owned by him, which contained a sufficient balance, in payment of the fee. The monies in this account were not originally obtained from the lender.

Section 163(a) of the Internal Revenue Code of 1954 provides that there shall be allowed as a deduction all interest paid or accrued within the taxable year on indebtedness.

Section 446(a) of the Code provides that taxable income shall be computed under the method of accounting on the basis of which the taxpayer regularly computes his income in keeping his books. Section 446(b) of the Code provides, in part, that if the method used does not clearly reflect income, the computation of taxable income shall be made under such method as, in the opinion of the Secretary of the Treasury or his delegate, does clearly reflect income.

For tax purposes, interest has been defined by the Supreme Court of the United States as the amount one has contracted to pay for the use of borrowed money, and as the compensation paid for the use or forbearance of money. See Old Colony Railroad Co. v. Commissioner, 284 U.S. 552 (1932), Ct.D. 456, C.B. XI–1, 274 (1932); Deputy v. Dupont, 308 U.S. 488 (1940), Ct.D. 1435, C.B. 1940–1, 118. The Board of Tax Appeals has stated that interest is the compensation allowed by law or fixed by the parties for the use, forbearance, or detention of money. Fall River Electric Light Co. v. Commissioner, 23 B.T.A. 168 (1931). A negotiated bonus or premium paid by a borrower to a lender in order to obtain a loan has been held to be interest for Federal income tax purposes. L–R Heat Treating Co. v. Commissioner, 28 T.C. 894 (1957).

The payment or accrual of interest for tax purposes must be incidental to an unconditional and legally enforceable obligation of the taxpayer claiming the deduction. Paul Autenreith v. Commissioner, 115 F.2d 856 (1940). There need not, however, be a legally enforceable indebtedness already in existence when the payment of interest is made. It is sufficient that the payment be a "prerequisite to obtaining borrowed capital." *L–R Heat Treating Co.* The fee of $70x$ dollars in the instant case was paid prior to the receipt of the borrowed funds;

however, this does not preclude the payment from being classified as interest.

It is not necessary that the parties to a transaction label a payment made for the use of money as interest for it to be so treated. See *L–R Heat Treating Co.* The mere fact that the parties in the instant case agreed to call the 70*x* dollars a "loan processing fee" does not in itself preclude this payment from being interest under section 163(a) of the Code. Further, this conclusion would not be affected by the fact that this payment is sometimes referred to as "points." Compare Revenue Ruling 67–297, C.B. 1967–2, 87, relating to the deductibility as interest of a loan origination fee paid by the purchaser of a residence to a lending institution in connection with the acquisition of a home mortgage. Also, compare Revenue Ruling 68–650, C.B. 1968–2, 78, relating to the deductibility as interest of the payment of a loan charge paid by the seller of a residence to assist the purchaser in obtaining a mortgage loan.

The method of computation also does not control its deductibility, so long as the amount in question is an ascertainable sum contracted for the use of borrowed money. See Kena, Inc. v. Commissioner, 44 B.T.A. 217 (1941). The fact that the amount paid in the instant case is a flat sum paid in addition to a stated annual interest rate does not preclude a deduction under section 163 of the Code.

To qualify as interest for tax purposes, the payment, by whatever name called, must be compensation for the use or forbearance of money per se and not a payment for specific services which the lender performs in connection with the borrower's account. For example, interest would not include separate charges made for investigating the prospective borrower and his security, closing costs of the loan and papers drawn in connection therewith, or fees paid to a third party for servicing and collecting that particular loan. See Workingmen's Loan Ass'n v. United States, 142 F.2d 359 (1944); Rev.Rul. 57–541, C.B. 1957–2, 319. Compare Revenue Ruling 57–540, C.B. 1957–2, 318, relating to the classification as interest of the fees imposed on borrowers by a mortgage finance company. Also, even where service charges are not stated separately on the borrower's account, interest would not include amounts attributable to such services. See Rev.Rul. 67–297; compare Norman L. Noteman, et al., Trustees v. Welch, 108 F.2d 206 (1939) relating to the classification as interest of the charges paid by borrowers to a personal finance company.

Accordingly, in the instant case, because the taxpayer was able to establish that the fee of 70*x* dollars was paid as compensation to the lender solely for the use or forbearance of money, and because he did not initially obtain the funds to pay this fee from the lender, the 70*x* dollars is considered to be interest.

J. SIMPSON DEAN

Tax Court of the United States, 1961.
35 T.C. 1083.

Opinion

RAUM, Judge: The Commissioner determined deficiencies in income tax against petitioners for 1955 and 1956 in the amounts of $13,875.61 and $16,383.86, respectively. Petitioners are husband and wife; they filed joint returns for 1955 and 1956 with the director of internal revenue at Wilmington, Delaware. To the extent that the deficiencies still remain in controversy they raise the question whether petitioners were entitled to deduct as interest the amounts of $9,243.38 in 1955 and $26,912.02 in 1956 representing interest on loans on life insurance policies which had accrued and which was paid by them after they had made irrevocable assignments of such policies to their children. An amended answer filed by the Commissioner claims increases in the deficiencies already determined by adding thereto the amounts of $105,181.50 and $119,796.78 for 1955 and 1956, respectively. Such increases raise a single issue, unrelated to the original deficiencies, namely, whether petitioners realized taxable income to the extent of the alleged economic benefit derived from the interest-free use of funds which they had borrowed from a family corporation controlled by them. The facts have been stipulated.

* * *

[Only the portion of the opinion dealing with the interest-free loans is presented. Ed.]

The Commissioner's amended answer charged petitioners with income equal to interest at the alleged legal rate in Delaware (6 percent) with respect to loans which they had obtained upon non-interest-bearing notes from their controlled corporation, Nemours Corporation, and which were outstanding during 1955 and 1956. The theory of the amended answer was that the petitioners realized income to the extent of the economic benefit derived from the free use of borrowed funds from Nemours, and that such economic benefit was equal to interest at the legal rate in Delaware, alleged to be 6 percent per annum. However, the Commissioner's brief has reduced the amount of his additional claim so that the income thus attributed to petitioners is measured, not by the legal rate of interest, but by the prime rate, since it is stipulated that petitioners could have borrowed the funds at the prime rate. As thus reduced, the additional income which the Commissioner seeks to charge to petitioners is $65,648.79 for 1955 and $97,931.71 for 1956. The facts in relation to this issue have been stipulated as follows:

9. Prior to December 17, 1954 the entire issued and outstanding capital stock of Nemours Corporation, hereinafter referred to as Nemours, organized under the laws of the State of Delaware with

principal office in Wilmington, Delaware, consisting of 36,172 shares of no par common, was owned by the petitioners, as follows:

J. Simpson Dean .... 7,249 shares

Paulina duPont Dean .... 28,923 shares

10. On December 17, 1954 each of the petitioners made a gift of 2,000 shares of the stock of Nemours to the above-mentioned trusts created by them in 1937 for the benefit of their children. In the years 1955 and 1956 the petitioners owned 32,172 shares of no par common of Nemours.

11. For the taxable year 1955 Nemours was a personal holding company under section 542 of the Internal Revenue Code of 1954 and filed its Federal income tax returns as such.

12. For the taxable year 1956 Nemours filed its Federal income tax return as a regular business corporation. By notice of deficiency dated March 2, 1960, respondent determined that Nemours was a personal holding company for the year 1956. An appeal from such determination was taken by Nemours and the matter is now pending before this Court in Docket No. 86863, entitled Nemours Corporation v. Commissioner of Internal Revenue.

13. Petitioner J. Simpson Dean owed Nemours on non-interest bearing notes the following amounts:

Period	Amount
January 1, 1955 to January 10, 1955	$302,185.73
January 11, 1955 to December 31, 1955	223,861.56
January 1, 1956 to December 31, 1956	357,293.41

14. Petitioner Paulina duPont Dean owed Nemours on non-interest bearing notes the following amounts:

Period	Amount
January 1, 1955 to December 31, 1955	$1,832,764.71
January 1, 1956 to December 31, 1956	2,205,804.66

15. The following are the prime rates of interest and the dates on which changes were made in such rates at which the petitioners could have borrowed money during the years 1955 and 1956:

January 1, 1955 .... 3%

August 15, 1955 .... 3¼%

October 20, 1955 .... 3½%

April 20, 1956 .... 3¾%

September 1, 1956 .... 4%

December 31, 1956 .... 4%

16. Interest computed at the prime rates shown in the preceding paragraph on the non-interest bearing notes of the petitioners for the taxable years 1955 and 1956 would be as follows:

Year 1955:	**Amount**
J. Simpson Dean	$ 7,203.98
Paulina duPont Dean	58,444.81
Total	$65,648.79

Year 1956:	**Amount**
J. Simpson Dean	$13,651.59
Paulina duPont Dean	84,280.12
Total	$97,931.71

[Paragraph 17 of the stipulation, objected to by respondent as to relevancy,[1] states that if petitioners had paid interest to Nemours, the corporation would have made dividend distributions to petitioners equal to the amount of such interest, and further sets forth the effect, taxwise and otherwise, upon petitioners, Nemours, and the trusts, based upon that hypothesis as well as certain other assumptions.]

The theory of the Commissioner's amended answer, as modified in his brief, undoubtedly had its origin in a statement by this Court in a Memorandum Opinion involving certain gift taxes of these taxpayers, Paulina duPont Dean, T.C.Memo. 1960–54, on appeal (C.A.3), where it was said:

> Viewed realistically, the lending of over two million dollars to petitioners without interest might be looked upon as a means of passing on earnings (certainly potential earnings) of Nemours in lieu of dividends, to the extent of a reasonable interest on such loans. * * *

The amended answer herein was filed within several months after the foregoing Memorandum Opinion had been promulgated. The statement quoted above was mere dictum and we have not been directed to any case holding or even suggesting that an interest-free loan may result in the realization of taxable income by the debtor, or to any administrative ruling or regulation taking that position. Although the question may not be completely free from doubt we think that no taxable income is realized in such circumstances.

In support of its present position, the Government relies primarily upon a series of cases holding that rent-free use of corporate property by a stockholder or officer may result in the realization of income. Charles A. Frueauff, 30 B.T.A. 449 (rent-free use of corporation's apartment); Reynard Corporation, 30 B.T.A. 451 (rent-free use of corporation's house); Percy M. Chandler, 41 B.T.A. 165, affirmed 119 F.2d 623 (C.A.3) (rent-free use of corporation's apartment and lodge); Paulina duPont Dean, 9 T.C. 256 (rent-free use of corporation's house); Dean v. Commissioner, 187 F.2d 1019 (C.A.3), affirming a Memorandum Opinion of this Court (rent-free use of corporation's house); Rodgers Dairy Co., 14 T.C. 66 (personal use of corporation's automobile). Cf.

---

1. We find it unnecessary to rule upon that objection, since we reach the result herein without reliance upon paragraph 17.

Louis Greenspon, 23 T.C. 138, affirmed on this point but reversed on other grounds 229 F.2d 947 (C.A.8) (farm expenses paid by corporation); Alex Silverman, 28 T.C. 1061, affirmed 253 F.2d 849 (C.A.8) (wife's travel expenses paid by corporation); Chester Distributing Co. v. Commissioner, 184 F.2d 514 (C.A.3), affirming per curiam a Memorandum Opinion of this Court (personal entertainment expenses paid by corporation). These cases bear a superficial resemblance to the present case, but reflection convinces us that they are not in point. In each of them a benefit was conferred upon the stockholder or officer in circumstances such that had the stockholder or officer undertaken to procure the same benefit by an expenditure of money such expenditure would not have been deductible by him. Here, on the other hand, had petitioners borrowed the funds in question on interest-bearing notes, their payment of interest would have been fully deductible by them under section 163, I.R.C. 1954. Not only would they not be charged with the additional income in controversy herein, but they would have a deduction equal to that very amount. We think this circumstance differentiates the various cases relied upon by the Commissioner, and perhaps explains why he has apparently never taken this position in any prior case.

We have heretofore given full force to interest-free loans for tax purposes, holding that they result in no interest deduction for the borrower, A. Backus, Jr. & Sons, 6 B.T.A. 590; Rainbow Gasoline Corporation, 31 B.T.A. 1050; Howell Turpentine Co., 6 T.C. 364, reversed on another issue 162 F.2d 316 (C.A.5); D. Loveman & Son Export Corporation, 34 T.C. 776, nor interest income to the lender, Combs Lumber Co., 41 B.T.A. 339; Society Brand Clothes, Inc., 18 T.C. 304; Brandtjen & Kluge, Inc., 34 T.C. 416. We think it to be equally true that an interest-free loan results in no taxable gain to the borrower,[2] and we hold that the Commissioner is not entitled to any increased deficiency based upon this issue.

Reviewed by the Court.

Decision will be entered under Rule 50.

FISHER, J., concurs in the result.

OPPER, J., concurring: The necessity is not apparent to me of deciding more on the second issue than that there can be no deficiency. If petitioners were in receipt of some kind of gross income, possibly comparable to that dealt with in such cases as Charles A. Frueauff, 30 B.T.A. 449 (1934), the corresponding interest deduction would perhaps exactly offset and nullify it. But because that would mean that there is

2. As recently as 1955, this was also the view of the Commissioner. In Rev.Rul. 55–713, 1955–2 C.B. 23, in sanctioning the so-called split-dollar insurance scheme, it is said at page 24: "In the instant case, the substance of the insurance arrangement between the parties is in all essential respects the same as if Y corporation makes annual loans without interest, of a sum of money equal to the annual increases in the cash surrender value of the policies of insurance taken out on the life of B. The mere making available of money does not result in realized income to the payee or a deduction to the payor."

no deficiency, it would not necessarily follow that there was no gross income, as the present opinion, in my view, gratuitously holds. Certainly the statement that "an interest-free loan results in no taxable gain to the borrower" is much too broad a generalization to make here.

Suppose, for example, that in such a case as Charles A. Frueauff, supra, the property made available without charge to the shareholder-officer was rented by him to another, instead of being occupied for personal use. Would the fact that he could presumably deduct as a business or nonbusiness expense the hypothetical rental value theoretically paid by him to the corporation, section 212, I.R.C. 1954, and thereby completely offset any gross income, lead us to conclude, as here, contrary to that whole line of cases, that there could be no gross income in the first place?

Or suppose the facts showed that the indebtedness was "incurred * * * to purchase or carry obligations * * * the interest on which is wholly exempt from * * * taxes." Sec. 265(2), I.R.C. 1954.

This being apparently a case of first impression, the present result seems peculiarly unfortunate in deciding a point that need not be passed on. To make matters worse, the burden here is on respondent, since the issue was first raised by his answer; [1] and thus in this leading case all factual conclusions and inferences must be favorable to petitioners. Cf., e.g., Spheeris v. Commissioner, 284 F.2d 928 (C.A.7, 1960), affirming a Memorandum Opinion of this Court. Disposition of the issue as one of generally applicable law is hence doubly unnecessary.

TIETJENS, WITHEY, and DRENNEN, JJ., agree with this concurring opinion.

BRUCE, J., dissenting: I respectfully dissent from the opinion of the majority with respect to the second issue. In my opinion the present case is not distinguishable in principle from such cases as Paulina duPont Dean, 9 T.C. 256; Chandler v. Commissioner, 119 F.2d 623 (C.A.3), affirming 41 B.T.A. 165, and other cases cited by the majority, wherein it was held that the rent-free use of corporate property by a stockholder or officer resulted in the realization of income. "Interest" in the sense that it represents compensation paid for the use, forbearance, or detention of money, may be likened to "rent" which is paid for the use of property.

I agree with Judge Opper in his concurring opinion that "the statement that 'an interest-free loan results in no taxable gain to the borrower' is much too broad a generalization to make here." I do not wish to infer that the interest-free loan of money should be construed as resulting in taxable income to the borrower in every instance. However, it is difficult to believe that the interest-free loan of in excess of $2 million ($2,563,098.07 throughout 1956) by a personal holding company to its majority stockholders (its only stockholders prior to

1. See, e.g., Rainbow Gasoline Corporation, 31 B.T.A. 1050 (1935), decided partly for petitioner and partly for respondent entirely on the question of burden of proof.

December 17, 1954) did not result in any economic benefit to the borrower.

In my opinion, the statement that "had petitioners borrowed the funds in question on interest-bearing notes, their payment of interest would have been fully deductible by them under section 163, I.R.C. 1954," is likewise too broad a generalization to make here.

Section 163(a) states the "General Rule" to be that "There shall be allowed as a deduction all interest paid or accrued within the taxable year on indebtedness." Section 265(2) provides, however, that—

No deduction shall be allowed for—

* * *

(2) INTEREST.—Interest on indebtedness incurred or continued to purchase or carry obligations * * * the interest on which is wholly exempt from the taxes imposed by this subtitle.

Section 265(2) is specifically included in the cross references contained in subsection (c) of section 163 and is therefore clearly intended as an exception to, or limitation upon, section 163(a). For obligations, the interest on which is wholly exempt from taxes, see section 103 of the Internal Revenue Code of 1954.

It is recognized that the burden with respect to the issue here presented by his amended answer is upon the respondent. This burden, however, was, in my opinion, discharged by the stipulated facts presented. It was incumbent upon the petitioners, if such were the facts, to plead and establish that had they been required to pay interest on the loans in question they would have been entitled to deduct such interest from their gross income. They have done neither. It is well established that deductions are matters of legislative grace and must be clearly established.

On the record presented herein, I do not agree that "had petitioners borrowed the funds in question on interest-bearing notes, their payment of interest would have been fully deductible by them under section 163," and that the inclusion in the gross income of the petitioners of an amount representing a reasonable rate of interest on the loans in question would therefore result in no deficiency.

NOTE

The *J. Simpson Dean* case involves a gross income issue but is placed here among deductions because it also indirectly involves deductibility of interest. Prior to the Tax Reform Act of 1984 interest-free loans were used in intra-family transactions to shift income from the lender to the borrower. They were especially helpful in avoiding the then existing ten year reversionary rule of Section 673 of the Clifford trust provisions.[1] For example, Parent, in a high income

---

1. The rule was amended by the 1986 legislation. See page 315, supra.

bracket, could make an interest-free loan to Child and thereafter the income earned by the principal of the loan would be taxed to Child. If the loan were a demand loan or a term loan for a period of less than ten years the transaction would escape Section 673, which would have defeated this device if it were handled by way of a trust.

Some 48 years elapsed between the advent of the federal income tax and the Service's first attempt to tax the benefit of interest-free loans as income. But now, despite the leisurely pace at which it initially pursued interest-free and below-market interest rate loans, the Service has lately been quite persistent in seeking to tax these transactions. That persistence earned congressional support in the Tax Reform Act of 1984 with the enactment of Section 7872.[2]

Congressional action was required because of the Tax Court's obstinate adherence to its errant rationale in *J. Simpson Dean.* The Tax Court clung to its reasoning in the *post-Dean* years, differentiating interest-free loans from the rent-free use of property, upon the basis of the deductibility of the benefits derived. Many recent cases continued the error.[3] For example, in Zager v. Commissioner,[4] the Tax Court noted that the Treasury had not attempted to tax interest-free loans until *Dean.* Troubled by the Treasury's abstaining on this issue for almost half a century, the Court in *Zager* searched for a distinction to "support the administrative practice which had endured for so long a period."[5] The distinction on which the Court rested its decision was again the *interest deduction* potentially available under Section 163 to recipients of interest-free loans.

In Greenspun v. Commissioner,[6] the Tax Court conceded that in certain instances very close to the *Dean* case there could be gross income to the borrower, i.e., no offsetting deduction. The most notable example discussed was a loan used by the recipient to invest in securities generating tax-exempt interest. In that instance, a loan recipient paying interest would be barred from an interest deduction by Section 265(a)(2).[7]

---

2. See Hartigan, "From *Dean* and Crown to the Tax Reform Act of 1984: Taxation of Interest-Free Loans," 60 Notre Dame L.Rev. 31 (1984); Bilter, "Interest-Free Loans—Boon or Bust?" 37 U.S.C. Inst. on Fed.Tax'n 23 (1985).

3. See, e.g., Albert Suttle, 37 T.C.M. 1638 (1978), affirmed 625 F.2d 1127 (4th Cir.1980), Martin v. Commissioner, 649 F.2d 1133 (5th Cir.1981), and Marsh v. Commissioner, 73 T.C. 317 (1979). These cases also reaffirmed *Dean* on the same issue.

4. 72 T.C. 1009 (1979), affirmed sub nom. Martin v. Commissioner, 649 F.2d 1133 (5th Cir.1981).

5. 72 T.C. at 1011.

6. 72 T.C. 931 (1979), affirmed 670 F.2d 123 (9th Cir.1982).

7. I.R.C. § 265(a)(2) prohibits deductions for interest paid on indebtedness incurred to purchase or carry obligations, the interest income from which is exempt from tax. The *Greenspun* court further stated that the non-inclusion of the economic benefit of an interest-free loan would also have an effect on deductions that are capped or floored by a percentage of adjusted gross income, e.g., the medical expense, charitable and casualty loss deductions.

The *Dean* issue has also arisen in the gift tax area. In Crown v. Commissioner [8] the Tax Court, following an earlier district court decision,[9] held that no taxable gift resulted from an interest-free demand loan. The Service's first breakthrough finally arrived with the Supreme Court's decision in Dickman v. Commissioner,[10] in which the Court held that an interest-free loan to a family member was a transfer of property by gift. The lender was treated as having made a taxable gift of the reasonable value of the use of the money.

Prompted perhaps by the *Dickman* decision,[11] Congress finally determined to recognize the economic reality of interest-free loan transactions. The House Ways and Means Committee acknowledged that: [12]

> [l]oans between family members (and other similar loans) are being used to avoid the assignment of income rules and the grantor trust rules. * * * [l]oans from corporations to shareholders are being used to avoid rules requiring the taxation of corporate income at the corporate level. * * * [and] [l]oans to persons providing services are being used to avoid rules requiring the payment of employment taxes and rules restricting the deductibility of interest in certain situations by the person providing the services.

The measures taken by Congress in the Tax Reform Act of 1984 [13] represented an all-inclusive attempt to stem taxpayer avoidance of these well-recognized rules of taxation.

Section 7872 of the Code generally divides loans with below-market interest rates [14] into two broad categories—gift loans and non-gift loans.[15] It then subdivides each category according to the terms of the repayment of the loan, i.e., term loans and demand loans. The treatment the loan receives under Section 7872 depends upon its category and subcategory. The classification of below-market interest rate loans by category and subcategory determines the nature and timing of the

8. 67 T.C. 1060 (1977), affirmed 585 F.2d 234 (7th Cir.1978).

9. Johnson v. U.S., 254 F.Supp. 73 (N.D. Tex.1966).

10. 465 U.S. 330, 104 S.Ct. 1086 (1984).

11. Congress may also have been nudged by admonitions such as that of the Ninth Circuit affirming the *Greenspun* case, that when "the Government seeks to modify a principle of taxation so firmly entrenched in our jurisprudence, it should turn to Congress, not to the courts." 670 F.2d at 126.

12. Staff of House Comm. on Ways and Means, 98th Cong., 2d Sess., Summary of Comm.Amendment to H.R. 4170, 1373–74 (Comm.Print 1984).

13. The Tax Reform Act of 1984 (T.R.A. '84) is actually only a section of a larger

piece of legislation; T.R.A. '84 is Division A of the Deficit Reduction Act of 1984.

14. I.R.C. § 7872(e)(1) defines below-market interest rate loans. Demand loans are below the market interest rate if the interest payable is less than the applicable Federal rate, see text at note 16, infra. Term loans are below the market interest rate if the amount loaned exceeds the present value of all payments required by the loan.

15. I.R.C. § 7872(a). Notwithstanding the title of paragraph (a) (treatment of gift loans and demand loans), the treatment of below-market interest rate loans is easier to understand if dichotomized between gift and nongift loans.

income or gift to the borrower, the timing of the possibly deductible payment of constructive interest by the borrower to the lender, and the inclusion of the mythical interest in gross income of the lender. Under Section 7872 all loans that carry a below-market interest rate (or charge no interest at all) are recharacterized to impute the payment of interest. Thus, for example, a $100,000 interest-free loan from a father to his son is transformed, for tax purposes, into a loan in which the father charges interest at a rate based upon the average market yield of outstanding marketable United States securities with maturities comparable to the term of the loan. This rate of interest is called the applicable Federal rate.[16] The son is presumed to pay this interest,[17] possibly generating an interest deduction for himself and generating interest income for his father.[18] The son's interest payment is deemed to have been made from a separate source of funds made available to him by his father. This constructive transmittal of funds from the father to his son to permit the son to pay the constructive interest is another taxable event and, depending on the identity of the taxpayers and the nature of the loan, generally is characterized as either a gift, a dividend, or compensation.

Gift Loans. The first major category, gift loans, consists of loans in which the lender's funding (foregoing) of the borrower's interest payments is characterized as a gift from the lender to the borrower.[19] If the gift loan is to be repaid on a specific date (i.e., a *term loan*),[20] the lender must recognize interest income and the borrower possibly earns an interest deduction.[21] Thus in our example above, let us assume that

---

16. The applicable Federal rates are determined by the Secretary on a monthly basis. I.R.C. § 1274(d)(1)(B). The rates in effect will reflect the average yields of outstanding marketable U.S. securities with comparable maturities. I.R.C. § 1274(d)(1)(C)(i). The applicable Federal rate to be applied to a particular loan is determined by reference to the term of that loan, as set forth below (see § 1274(d)(1)(A)):

In the case of a loan with a term of:	The applicable rate is:
Not over 3 years	The Federal short-term rate
Over 3 years but not over 9 years	The Federal mid-term rate
Over 9 years	The Federal long-term rate

The applicable Federal rate for a demand loan is always the federal short-term rate for each day the loan is unpaid. I.R.C. § 7872(f)(2)(B). See text at note 34, infra.

17. This constructive interest payment is subject to several exceptions. See text at notes 55–62, infra.

18. Through its recharacterization of the transaction I.R.C. § 7872 artificially turns what actually happened into what should have happened. Since the father

(the lender) never actually received this deemed interest payment, choosing instead to forego levying it upon his son, § 7872 labels this amount as "foregone interest." I.R.C. § 7872(e)(2). It is computed in accordance with principles of § 1272, which is also a product of the Tax Reform Act of 1984. See page 900, infra. "Foregone interest" is defined as the excess of the applicable Federal rate over any amounts of interest payable under the actual terms of the loan. I.R.C. § 7872(e)(2).

19. See I.R.C. § 7872(f)(3) and Chapter 3A, supra.

20. See I.R.C. § 7872(f)(6), which helpfully defines "term loan" as any loan that is not a demand loan.

21. The interest payment that is imputed to the borrower is possibly allowed as a deduction under I.R.C. § 163(a) if no disallowance is specified under some other section such as I.R.C. §§ 163(d), 163(h); 265(a)(2), etc. Whether a deduction is disallowed depends somewhat upon the borrower's use of the funds. See the note at pages 474–480 infra. Further, the question of deductibility also depends upon whether the interest is an above the line

the $100,000 loan from the father to his son on January 1, 1992, due four years later on January 1, 1995 was made with donative intent. We assume further (a dire assumption) that the Federal mid-term rate in effect on January 1, 1992 is 12 percent.

Under Section 7872 this loan would properly be characterized as a gift loan with the constructive interest (the amount treated as transmitted from the father to his son) taxed as a gift. The amount of the constructive interest is the amount loaned less the present value of all principal and all actual interest payments to be made under the loan.[22] In our example no interest payments are called for by the loan, so we calculate the present value of $100,000 for 4 years at 12 percent compounded semiannually,[23] which is $62,741.24, and subtract that amount from $100,000. The $37,258.76 difference is constructive interest, the amount of the gift from the father to his son. This gift is deemed to be made on the date the loan was made.[24]

The son's possible interest deduction and his father's corresponding interest income are computed annually for each calendar year the loan is outstanding.[25] The amount of interest that would have accrued for the year under the applicable Federal rate is reduced by any actual interest payable which is properly allocable to the year and the remainder is called foregone interest.[26] In the hypothetical above, since father's loan to his son called for no interest the foregone interest for each year of the loan is simply 12 percent interest compounded semiannually on $100,000, or $12,360.[27]

deduction or an itemized deduction. If it is an itemized deduction the borrower will receive no tax benefit from it unless the total of his itemized deductions, after some other itemized deductions are subjected to the 2 percent floor, exceeds his standard deduction. See Chapter 18E, infra.

22. The total payments are discounted using the appropriate applicable Federal rate. I.R.C. § 7872(f)(1).

Conceptually, a present value calculation asks the question, "how much money must I put into the bank today in order to have $X on a certain date in the future?" In order to make this calculation you must know the rate of interest your investment will earn, the period of time over which the investment will collect interest and the amount of money you want to have at the end of the investment period. In this case, we knew that the rate of interest was 12 percent compounded semiannually (this is equal to 6 percent interest for each of the several six-month periods, but adding all prior interest to the interest base each six months, see note 28, infra), that the investment was for a 4 year period and that at the end of the 4 years we wanted $100,000.

The solution, $62,741.24, can be derived through a somewhat complicated mathe-

matical formula, through the use of present value tables, or by using a financial calculator. We suggest one of the latter two methods.

23. Referring to note 16, supra, we see that loans of 3 to 9 years are subject to the Federal mid-term rate, which we assume to be 12 percent. Note that interest on a term loan at the applicable Federal rate is compounded semiannually. I.R.C. § 7872(f)(2)(A).

24. I.R.C. § 7872(d)(2), (b)(1).

25. I.R.C. § 7872(a). See also I.R.C. § 7872(d)(1) and the text beginning at note 58, infra.

26. I.R.C. § 7872(a)(2), (e)(2).

27. This amount is computed by imposing 6 percent of $100,000 or $6,000 for the first one-half of the year plus 6 percent of $106,000 or $6,360 for the second half of the year totalling $12,360 of interest for the year. But see the text at notes 58–62 infra.

Notice that the amount of the gift is computed under the provisions of § 7872(b), whereas the amount of the son's interest deduction and his father's corresponding interest income is computed under the provisions of § 7872(a). This bifur-

Foregone interest, the amount of the annual interest income and the potential corresponding deduction, is treated as having been paid by the borrower to the lender on the last day of each calendar year during which the loan is outstanding.[28] Thus on December 31, 1992, son is treated as having paid his father $12,360, possibly earning himself an interest deduction in that amount[29] and resulting in income to his father of a like amount. An exact duplicate of this transaction is deemed to occur on December 31 of each of the 3 subsequent years the loan is outstanding.[30]

If the gift loan is a *demand loan*,[31] rather than a term loan, a gift of the funds with which to pay the constructive interest is again deemed to be made by the lender to the borrower.[32] However, no separate calculation of the amount of the gift need be made here—both the amount of the gift and the borrower's potential interest deduction (and the lender's corresponding interest income) are simply determined by subtracting any actual interest payments due under the loan from the interest that would have accrued under the applicable Federal rate, (i.e., the foregone interest).[33]

Because the loan has no fixed date for repayment, the lender is deemed to make a gift on the last day of each of the lender's taxable years (or portion thereof) that the loan remains outstanding.[34] Similarly, the lender recognizes interest income and the borrower earns a possible interest deduction, in the amount of the gift, during each year that the loan is outstanding.[35]

In our example if father lends his son $100,000 interest-free, payable in full upon father's demand, and the loan remained outstanding throughout the entire calendar year, only one calculation is re-

cation is a result of § 7872(d)(2), which provides that in the case of a gift loan which is also a term loan, the *gift tax* consequences of such loan are to be determined by applying § 7872(b) instead of § 7872(a). But because the loan is also a gift loan, § 7872(a) will apply in determining the *income tax* consequences of the loan, i.e., the amount deemed to be retransferred from the borrower to the lender as interest. The Conference Report indicates that term gift loans are given the *income tax* treatment accorded demand loans because the close relationship of the parties that prompted the gift may well lead to disregard of the loan's maturity date. Additionally, if a term gift loan was treated as a term loan for *income tax* purposes, a complex original issue discount analysis, as required by § 7872(b)(2), would have to be made in order to determine the income tax consequences of the loan. H.Rep.No. 98–861, 98th Cong., 2d Sess. 1020 at n. 11 (1984). See also, Staff of the Joint Committee on Taxation, 98th Cong., 2d Sess., General Explanation of the Revenue Provi-

sions of the Deficit Reduction Act of 1984, 532–533 (Comm.Print 1984).

28. I.R.C. § 7872(a)(2).

29. Of course, the borrower possibly earns an I.R.C. § 163(a) deduction for any actual interest he may pay to the lender. See note 21, supra.

30. See note 27, supra.

31. A demand loan is generally "any loan which is payable in full at any time on the demand of the lender." I.R.C. § 7872(f)(5).

32. I.R.C. § 7872(a)(1)(A).

33. I.R.C. § 7872(a) and (e)(2).

34. I.R.C. § 7872(a)(2).

35. If Father were to have made a demand loan on January 1, 1992, and called it on June 30, 1992, with his son promptly repaying the principal, another $6,000 of interest would have accrued. This $6,000 would be deemed to be a gift from father to his son resulting in a corresponding $6,000 interest payment from son to his father, all on December 31, 1992.

quired. As the loan calls for no actual interest payments the determination of the interest on $100,000 at a 12 percent rate compounded semi-annually, or $12,360,[36] is all that is required. Father is deemed to make a gift to his son of $12,360 on December 31, 1992. Similarly, son is treated as paying that same amount back to his father as interest, possibly earning himself a deduction and creating income for his father, all on December 31st.

Nongift Loans. The rules applicable to nongift loans are somewhat different from those governing gift loans. Again, interest is deemed to be charged by the lender. The borrower is deemed to have paid that interest, generating income to the lender and a possible corresponding deduction for the borrower. The amount transmitted from the lender to the borrower to pay the constructive interest is characterized, not as a gift, but rather according to the nature of the relationship between the lender and the borrower. These various relationships are the subcategories of nongift loans.

Section 7872(c) identifies five subcategories of nongift loans: (1) loans between a corporation and one of its shareholders;[37] (2) loans between an employer and an employee or between an independent contractor and the person to whom he provides his services (all labelled "compensation-related" loans);[38] (3) loans with a principal purpose to avoid any federal tax;[39] (4) a catch-all subcategory of "other below-market loans,"[40] which are loans that do not fall within one of the preceding subcategories of nongift, loans yet their interest arrangements have a significant effect on any federal tax liability of the lender or the borrower; and (5) loans to a qualifying continuing care facility pursuant to a continuing care contract.[41]

Returning to our benevolent father and his needy son, let us assume that this time they are an unrelated employer and employee. The employee has worked overtime for the past several months without additional compensation,[42] so the employer lends him $100,000 interest-free on January 1, 1992, due four years later on December 31, 1995.

As this nongift loan is a *term loan,* both the amount treated as compensation by the employee and the amount of interest deemed paid by the employee to the employer are calculated by subtracting the present value of all principal and actual interest payments due under the loan from the amount loaned.[43] The entire amount treated as

---

36. See note 27, supra and I.R.C. § 7872(d)(1) considered in the text beginning at note 58, infra.

37. I.R.C. § 7872(c)(1)(C). But see I.R.C. § 7872(f)(11).

38. I.R.C. § 7872(c)(1)(B). Employee relocation loans are exempted from tax by temporary regulations. Reg. § 1.7872–5T(b)(6) and (c)(1).

39. I.R.C. § 7872(c)(1)(D).

40. I.R.C. § 7872(c)(1)(E). Congress left the skeleton of this fourth catch-all to be fleshed out by the regulations.

41. I.R.C. § 7872(c)(1)(F).

42. The Conference Committee Report explains that a loan will be treated as compensation-related only if a debtor-creditor relationship exists between the employer and employee when the loan is made. H.Rep.No. 98–861, 98th Cong., 2d Sess. 1018, 1019 (1984).

43. I.R.C. § 7872(b)(1).

compensation in this nongift term loan situation is viewed as having been received by the employee on the date the loan was made and must be included in the employee's gross income for that year.[44] The employer also gets an immediate deduction for the compensation attributable to all four years of the loan.[45]

Conversely, the constructive interest deemed to be paid by the employee to the employer is treated as being constantly paid and received over the term of the loan.[46] Thus, the employee may possibly take a deduction each year only for the amount of interest deemed paid in that year and the employer need include only that amount in his income for each corresponding year.

Applying these rules to our employer, we find that on January 1, 1992, he pays his employee $37,258.76 of compensation, calculated by subtracting the present value of $100,000 for 4 years at 12 percent compounded semiannually, $62,741.24, from the amount loaned, $100,000.[47] The employer receives a 1992 deduction of $37,258.76 for compensation paid, and the employee includes $37,258.76 in his 1992 gross income. The interest, however, is treated as earned and paid ratably over the course of the loan in accordance with the principles of Section 1272 (which deals with original issue discount).[48] Thus, employee is treated as paying employer a total of $37,258.76 of interest over the 4 year period.

If a nongift loan is a *demand loan,* the rules are the same as those established for gift demand loans.[49] Both the amount of compensation deemed to be paid by an employer to his employee in a compensation-related demand loan and the subsequent interest income and possible deduction are calculated by subtracting any interest payable under the *(foregone int.)* loan from the interest that would have accrued at the applicable Federal rate.[50] This amount is compensation paid by the employer and — *(actual int)* received by the employee on the last day of the calendar year.[51] An amount equal to this compensation is treated as interest paid by the

---

44. Id. The same treatment would be accorded to the amount treated as a dividend in the case of a loan from a corporation to one of its shareholders, and to the like amount regardless of the subcategory of nongift term loan applicable.

45. It is assumed that the expense is ordinary and necessary and that the compensation is reasonable in amount. I.R.C. § 162(a). Cf. I.R.C. § 461(h).

46. I.R.C. § 7872(b)(2). While this amount is truly foregone interest in the sense that it represents interest that could (or should) have been charged but was not, note that it does not fall within the definition of "foregone interest" as established in § 7872(e)(2). See text at note 18, supra. The treatment this amount receives is consistent with the rules governing original issue discount. I.R.C. § 1272. Again, similar treatment would be accorded to this

constructive interest regardless of the subcategory of nongift term loan that is applicable and the characterization based upon the subcategory of the loan involved (e.g., compensation, dividend, etc.).

47. See note 22, supra.

48. I.R.C. § 7872(b)(2)(A). See page 900, infra.

49. Here also the explanation given for a loan from an employer to his employee is applicable to all nongift demand loan situations. However, the amount treated as transferred by the lender to the borrower with which to pay the imputed interest will receive a characterization based upon the subcategory of the loan involved (e.g., compensation, dividend, etc.).

50. I.R.C. § 7872(a)(1).

51. I.R.C. § 7872(a)(2).

employee (borrower) to the employer (lender),[52] resulting in income to the lender and a possible deduction for the borrower, again on the last day of the calendar year.[53]

Thus if our employer lends his employee $100,000 interest-free on January 1, 1992, payable on demand, and the loan remains outstanding throughout all of 1992, the calculations required are identical to those made above for the gift demand loan.[54] On December 31, 1992, the employee is deemed to have received $12,360 of compensation and the employer earns a 1992 deduction of $12,360 for compensation paid. Also on December 31 the employee pays the employer $12,360 of interest, possibly earning an equal deduction for himself and resulting in income in that amount to the employer. These items of income and deduction for compensation-related loans result in a wash to the employer and possibly to the employee—neither is adversely affected by the imputed compensation and interest income if there are corresponding deductions.

However, if the loan is from a corporation to one of its shareholders a different result occurs. In the corporation-shareholder loan context, the corporation is deemed to have paid a dividend to the shareholder. The shareholder then pays interest to the corporation possibly earning himself an interest deduction (to offset his dividend income) but as the corporation earns no deduction for having paid the dividend, it cannot offset its interest income.

Exceptions for Gift Loans. Having explained income and gift taxes on the various types of below-market interest rate loans, we now encounter limitations that can prevent the imposition of these taxes in certain situations. In the case of any gift loans made between individuals,[55] the statute allows a de minimis exception: Section 7872 generally applies only to days when the aggregate amount of the loans between the individuals exceeds $10,000.[56] On days when the amount of the loans is $10,000 or less (including a situation where a loan or principal portion thereof has been paid off), Section 7872 does not apply except to a loan that is used to purchase income-producing assets.[57]

Another set of rules applies if gift loans between the borrower and lender do not exceed $100,000.[58] Generally the amount of imputed interest treated as retransferred from borrower to lender is limited to

---

52. I.R.C. § 7872(a)(1), (e)(2).

53. I.R.C. § 7872(a)(2).

54. See page 469, supra.

55. A husband and wife are treated as one person for purposes of I.R.C. § 7872. I.R.C. § 7872(f)(7); Cf. I.R.C. § 1041.

Although § 7872(c)(2)(A) provides that the $10,000 limitation applies to "individuals," the Senate Finance Committee Report chose to apply the limitation to "natural persons," adding in a footnote that loans to persons as custodians or guardians qualified as loans to "natural persons." S.Rep.

No. 98–160, 98th Cong., 2d Sess. 483 (1984). Is there a difference between an "individual" and a "natural person?"

56. I.R.C. § 7872(c)(2)(A).

57. I.R.C. § 7872(c)(2)(B). Additionally, in the case of gift term loans, if the aggregate amount of loans exceed $10,000 the parties cannot escape the gift tax consequences provided by Section 7872 by reducing one or more of the loans so that the total aggregates less than $10,000. I.R.C. § 7872(f)(10).

58. I.R.C. § 7872(d)(1)(D).

the borrower's net investment income (essentially the excess of investment income over investment related expenses) [59] for the year; [60] and if the borrower's net investment income for the year does not exceed $1,000, no interest is imputed. [61] If the borrower has loans from two or more lenders, a special allocation rule applies. [62]

Exception for Nongift Loans. Compensation-related and corporation-shareholder loans are also subject to a similar $10,000 de minimis exception as applies to gift loans. [63] However, there is no de minimis exception for other types of nongift loans. [64] The $10,000 exception does not apply to loans with a principal purpose of avoiding federal tax. [65] Just as with gift loans, compensation-related and corporation-shareholder loans between the same lender and borrower are aggregated to determine whether the $10,000 floor prevents the recognition of interest income by the lender. [66] However, in the case of term loans, once aggregate compensation-related or corporation-shareholder term loans exceed $10,000, the parties cannot subsequently escape the grasp of Section 7872 by reducing one or more of the loans so that the total aggregates less than $10,000; once subject to Section 7872 a compensation-related or corporate-shareholder loan is always subject to Section 7872. [67]

These below-market loan provisions have left *J. Simpson Dean* to die a natural death.

NOTE

The Creation of Interest. If interest is deductible a question is: What is "interest"? Rev.Rul. 69–188, set out above, [1] presents a basic definition. As the Ruling suggests, interest, like the rose, by any other name smells as sweet. The *J. Simpson Dean* saga demonstrates that the courts have been chary of finding imputed interest, [2] either as a gross income inclusion or as a deduction. Nevertheless at times, especially in recent times, Congress intervenes to create both interest

59. I.R.C. § 163(d)(4)(A).

60. I.R.C. § 7872(d)(1)(A). This rule does not apply if the interest arrangements on the loan have as one of their principal purposes the avoidance of federal tax. I.R.C. § 7872(d)(1)(B).

61. I.R.C. § 7872(d)(1)(E)(ii).

62. If any borrower has more than one gift loan outstanding during the year he must allocate his net investment income between the loans in proportion to the amounts that would otherwise be deemed as retransferred to the lender. This limitation has no effect upon the amount of interest the borrower is deemed to pay under I.R.C. § 7872. However, if the borrower has loans from 2 or more lenders outstanding at one time, § 7872(d)(1)(C) instructs the borrower how to allocate his net investment income between the lend-

ers, thus affecting the amount of interest income they must recognize.

63. I.R.C. § 7872(c)(3)(A). The exception is not identical because it is inapplicable where one of the principal purposes of the loan is tax avoidance (I.R.C. § 7872(c)(3)(B)) and there is no restriction related to use of the loan proceeds to purchase or carry income-producing assets (I.R.C. § 7872(d)(2)(B)).

64. Id. See I.R.C. § 7872(d)(1)(A).

65. I.R.C. § 7872(c)(3)(B).

66. Id.

67. I.R.C. § 7872(f)(10). This rule also applies to gift tax on gift term loans. See note 57, supra.

1. See page 456, supra.

2. See page 459, supra.

income and interest deductions, such as they did for parties involved in interest-free and below-market loans in the enactment of Section 7872.

In addition to the creation of interest under Section 7872, Congress has similarly taxed an unstated interest component in a variety of financial transactions. For example, a corporation sells its own bonds at a discount (face $5,000, price $4,600), the discount ($400) is actually disguised interest, for it represents a price the corporation will have to pay, along with current interest, as the cost of using the money. Congress recognizes this fact and under Section 1272 creates both interest income (to the bondholder) and interest deductions (for the corporation). If no interest or low interest is paid on the purchase of property, Congress imputes interest to both parties in the transaction in a series of provisions that are similar to Section 7872.[3] Both Section 1272 and the other provisions are intimately related to timing[4] and characterization[5] concepts, and so their consideration, is deferred to Chapter 24[6] after timing and characterization concepts have been examined.

Congress also "finds" deductible interest in other obscure places. For example, Section 163(c) places redeemable ground rents in that category.[7] In addition, recall[8] that Section 482 gives the Commissioner limited authority to allocate gross income, deductions, credits, or allowances among organizations controlled by the same persons. Although it may stretch the statute, this authority has been used to generate (a mere allocation?) interest payments on otherwise interest-free loans between such organizations.[9] When one is *taxed* on interest imputed to him by this strained application of Section 482, the other party gains a corresponding interest *deduction*.[10]

The Disallowance of Interest. At the other end of the spectrum is the disallowance of interest deductions. There are numerous statutory restrictions on the deductibility of interest, many of which are considered below. Nevertheless even without such legislative assistance, the courts have sometimes disallowed such deductions. Elaborate schemes have been attempted to generate an interest deduction in order to reduce taxes without the usual economic pain attached to paying for borrowed money. But not successfully if the device is tabbed a mere artifice.[11] In addition, as in many other areas, the Commissioner and the courts have refused to let taxpayers exalt form over substance. For example, in the corporate area, the "thin incorporation" has produced

3. See I.R.C. §§ 483 and 1274. See also I.R.C. §§ 1271–1286.

4. See Chapter 19, infra.

5. See Chapter 21, infra.

6. See page 893, infra.

7. See also I.R.C. § 1055.

8. See page 339, supra.

9. See, e.g., B. Forman Co. v. Commissioner, 453 F.2d 1144 (2d Cir.1972), cert. denied 407 U.S. 934, 92 S.Ct. 2458 (1972).

However, see page 464, supra and page 893, infra.

10. See Gerald F. Paduano, 34 T.C.M. 368, 370 note 9 (1975).

11. See Knetsch v. U.S., 364 U.S. 361, 81 S.Ct. 132 (1960), and Golsen v. Commissioner, 54 T.C. 742 (1970), affirmed 445 F.2d 985 (10th Cir.1971), both involving tax years unaffected by I.R.C. § 264(a)(3), briefly discussed, infra.

substantial litigation. Especially in a close corporation, if indebtedness is greatly disproportionate to equity capital, evidences of debt may be viewed instead as evidences of ownership and hoped-for deductible interest may become non-deductible dividends.[12]

Some interest that is not paid or incurred in business or profit seeking activities is deductible,[13] but much consumer or "personal" interest is not.[14] Prior to the 1986 legislation most interest, including personal interest was deductible. One could deduct the interest on a loan whose proceeds were used to purchase a residence, a car, a boat, or an excursion to Vegas and interest charged on credit card balances. However, Congress, in the 1986 effort to broaden the tax base,[15] enacted Section 163(h) which disallows deductions for most "personal" interest.[16]

A major exception to the Section 163(h) rule is the allowance of a deduction for "qualified residence interest."[17] The qualified residence need not be the principal residence of the taxpayer, but qualifying indebtedness is limited to a maximum of two residences and, if there are two, one must be the taxpayer's principal residence.[18] The term residence may be broadly interpreted to include mobile homes and live-in boats.[19] If either a mobile home or a live-in boat is used on a transient basis, it may qualify as a second residence.[20]

Interest paid on two categories of debt, "acquisition indebtedness" and "home equity indebtedness" secured by a qualified residence is fully deductible as qualified residence interest.[21] As its name implies, the term "acquisition indebtedness" refers to debt secured by a qualified residence, which is incurred by the taxpayer in acquiring, constructing, or substantially improving a qualified residence.[22] The term

---

12. E.g., Gooding Amusement Co. v. Commissioner, 236 F.2d 159 (6th Cir.1956), cert. denied 352 U.S. 1031, 77 S.Ct. 595 (1957). See I.R.C. § 385.

13. I.R.C. § 163(h)(2)(D) and (3)–(5).

14. I.R.C. § 163(h)(1).

15. See page 13, supra.

16. The disallowances of subsection (h) were subject to a phase-in rule under which 65% of endangered interest continued to be deductible for 1987, 40% for 1988, 20% for 1989, and 10% for 1990. I.R.C. § 163(h)(5) and (d)(6)(B). Full disallowance commenced with the year 1991.

17. I.R.C. § 163(h)(2)(D) and (3)–(5). The disallowance rule is also inapplicable to interest on loans incurred in a taxpayer's trade or business, interest on loans related to profit seeking activities or "passive activities" (see page 503, infra) of the taxpayer and certain interest on estate tax liability. I.R.C. § 163(h)(2)(A)–(C) and (E), respectively.

18. I.R.C. § 163(h)(4). To qualify a dwelling as a second residence, the taxpay-

er must use the dwelling as his residence for part of the year if it is rented to others during the year. I.R.C. § 163(h)(4)(A)(iii). Cf. I.R.C. § 280A(d)(1). No taxpayer use of a residence is required if it is not rented during the year.

In addition, if a taxpayer has more than two residences, in any year she may select any one of her non-principal residences to qualify as a qualified residence. I.R.C. § 163(h)(4)(A)(i)(II). See Reg. § 1.163–10T(p)(3)(i) and (iv).

19. See page 947, infra.

20. See Reg. § 1.163–10T(p)(3)(ii). Although the House of Representatives at one time disagreed with this conclusion, their thinking did not become law. Compare H.Rep. No. 100–391, 100th Cong., 1st Sess. 1032 (1987) with Conf.Rep. No. 100–495, 100th Cong., 1st Sess. 917 (1987). See also note 18, supra.

21. I.R.C. § 163(h)(3)(A).

22. I.R.C. § 163(h)(3)(B)(i).

also includes debt incurred as a result of refinancing acquisition indebtedness and any subsequent refinancing of such indebtedness.[23] However, the amount of refinancing debt that can subsequently qualify as acquisition indebtedness can never exceed the outstanding principal of the debt which is being refinanced.[24] For example, if a taxpayer reduces the principal balance of an acquisition debt from $200,000 to $150,000, the maximum amount of any subsequent refinancing debt which may then qualify as acquisition indebtedness is $150,000. In addition, the total amount a taxpayer may treat as acquisition indebtedness may not exceed $1 million ($500,000 in the case of a married person filing separately).[25]

The second category of debt which generates qualified residence interest is "home equity indebtedness." This type of debt loosely corresponds to a home equity loan now offered by many financial institutions. The term home equity indebtedness is defined as any debt (other than acquisition indebtedness), secured by a qualified residence, to the extent the aggregate amount of such debt does not exceed the fair market value of the residence reduced by the outstanding acquisition indebtedness incurred by the taxpayer with respect to such property.[26] Thus the maximum amount of debt which may be classified as home equity indebtedness is limited to the amount of "equity" a taxpayer has in his home. The use of the debt proceeds is irrelevant in classifying the debt as home equity indebtedness. The aggregate amount treated as home equity indebtedness may not exceed $100,000 ($50,000 in the case of a married filing separately).[27]

To illustrate the above rules, assume in 1991 a taxpayer purchases two qualified residences. If the first residence is subject to a $500,000 acquisition mortgage and the second residence is subject to a $600,000 acquisition mortgage, $100,000 of the total indebtedness will be disqualified as acquisition indebtedness because of the $1 million ceiling.[28] However, the $100,000 excess may qualify as home equity indebtedness if the fair market value of the residence securing the $100,000 loan exceeds the amount of acquisition indebtedness with respect to that residence by at least $100,000.[29] Thus, if the second acquired residence, which has a $600,000 acquisition mortgage, caused the $1 million limitation to be exceeded, then only $500,000 of the mortgage on the second residence would be treated as acquisition indebtedness (along with the $500,000 mortgage from the first residence).[30] The $100,000 of remaining debt from the second residence is home equity indebtedness whose interest is fully deductible if the second residence has a fair market value of at least $600,000.[31]

23. I.R.C. § 163(h)(3)(B)(i) flush language.

24. Id.

25. I.R.C. § 163(h)(3)(B)(ii).

26. I.R.C. § 163(h)(3)(C)(i).

27. I.R.C. § 163(h)(3)(C)(ii).

28. I.R.C. § 163(h)(3)(B)(ii).

29. I.R.C. § 163(h)(3)(C)(i).

30. I.R.C. § 163(h)(3)(B).

31. I.R.C. § 163(h)(3)(C).

Similarly, if a taxpayer has a single residence with a $600,000 fair market value and subject to a $300,000 acquisition indebtedness, and she takes out a second mortgage on the residence, the interest on up to $100,000 of the proceeds of the second mortgage is fully deductible as home equity indebtedness regardless of the use of such proceeds.[32] However, if the proceeds are used to substantially improve the residence, the indebtedness would then qualify as acquisition indebtedness.[33]

If the dollar limitations on acquisition or home equity indebtedness are exceeded, then the excess indebtedness is treated no differently from other personal loans, and any interest paid on such excess is personal interest that is non-deductible.[34] If the dollar ceilings are exceeded, it is necessary to determine which debt caused the excess so that the specific interest paid on such excess will be subject to the personal interest limitation. A chronological tracing of debt in order to determine which debt caused the excess would seem to provide the best method of allocation.[35]

Any debt incurred on or before October 13, 1987, if secured by a qualified residence on such date as well as at all times thereafter, is grandfathered into the new scheme of deductibility by being categorized as acquisition indebtedness.[36] Such "grandfathered debt" is not subject to the $1,000,000 limitation generally applicable to other acquisition indebtedness.[37] Therefore, the interest on any secured "pre-October 13, 1987, indebtedness" remains fully deductible regardless of the aggregate amount of the debt. Nevertheless, the amount of grandfathered debt does reduce the $1,000,000 ceiling on other acquisition indebtedness and, thereby, reduces the amount of post-October 13, 1987 debt which the taxpayer may treat as acquisition indebtedness.[38] As is the case with other acquisition debt, pre-October 13, 1987 debt may be refinanced, but not in excess of the outstanding principal just prior to refinancing; the resulting debt will continue to be treated as acquisition indebtedness.[39] However, the resulting debt, or any debt resulting from a subsequent refinancing of the grandfathered debt, will be treated as acquisition indebtedness only until the term of the "grandfathered" debt expires (or if the principal of the "grandfathered" debt is not amortized over its term, until the earlier of 30 years or the expiration of the first refinancing.)[40]

Section 163(d) imposes a limit on the deductibility of investment interest by noncorporate taxpayers. Investment interest is generally

---

32. Id.

33. I.R.C. § 163(h)(3)(B)(i). Such indebtedness is limited to the $1 million I.R.C. § 163(h)(3)(B)(ii) ceiling.

34. If the year involved is prior to 1990, see note 16, supra.

35. See H.Rep. No. 100–391, 100th Cong., 1st Sess. 1033 (1987). Future regulations should provide guidance here.

36. I.R.C. § 163(h)(3)(D)(i) and (iii)(I).

37. I.R.C. § 163(h)(3)(D)(i)(II).

38. I.R.C. § 163(h)(3)(D)(ii).

39. I.R.C. § 163(h)(3)(D)(iii)(II).

40. I.R.C. § 163(h)(3)(D)(iv).

deductible only to the extent that the taxpayer has net investment income.[41]

Investment interest is interest paid or accrued on indebtedness incurred to purchase or carry property held for investment.[42] It does not include any qualified residence interest which is limited by the Section 163(h) rules considered above,[43] or any interest that is taken into account in determining the taxpayer's income or loss from a passive activity, a concept to be considered later.[44]

Net investment income is, logically for a change, the excess of investment income over investment expenses.[45] Investment income is gross income *from* property held for investment plus any gain on the *sale* of such property, but only if the property is not a part of a trade or business [46] or an activity subject to the passive activity rules.[47] Investment expense is any deductible expense (other than interest) directly connected with the production of such investment income.[48]

The investment interest limitation is applicable to interest paid or accrued in or for taxable years beginning in or after 1987, regardless of when the obligation was incurred.[49] Interest disallowed as a deduction for any taxable year under the Section 163(d) limitation can be carried forward and is treated as investment interest in subsequent years until utilized.[50]

The Code also contains restrictions on the deduction of interest on loans related to life insurance. Section 264(a)(2) precludes a deduction for interest paid on debt incurred or continued to buy a "single premium" life insurance or endowment or annuity contract.[51] The reasons may be obvious. As regards life insurance, the purchaser is buying proceeds that will be received tax-free by beneficiaries.[52] It

---

41. I.R.C. § 163(d)(1).

42. I.R.C. § 163(d)(3)(A).

43. I.R.C. § 163(d)(3)(B)(i).

44. I.R.C. § 163(d)(3)(B)(ii). See I.R.C. § 469 and Chapter 17E, infra.

45. I.R.C. § 163(d)(4)(A).

46. I.R.C. § 163(d)(4)(B).

47. I.R.C. § 163(d)(4)(D). See note 17, supra. However passive losses allowed under the passive loss phase-in do reduce investment income. I.R.C. § 163(d)(4)(E).

48. I.R.C. § 163(d)(4)(C). Investment expenses are itemized deductions which may be subjected to the 2% floor of I.R.C. § 67(a) prior to being considered under this section; however, any other § 67(a) itemized deductions are disallowed prior to the disallowance of such investment expense. Conf.Rep. No. 99–841, 99th Cong., 2d Sess. at II–153–154 (1986). See Chapter 18E, infra.

49. The investment interest limitation was subject to a phase-in rule similar to the phase-in rule applicable to personal interest which was considered at note 16, supra, although here there was a ceiling on the amount of interest qualifying for the phase-in. I.R.C. § 163(d)(6)(C). I.R.C. § 163(d)(6)(A) is a disallowance provision. In essence, it allowed as a deduction a percentage of investment interest in excess of investment income up to a ceiling amount (generally $10,000 although $5,000 in the case of married taxpayers filing separately and zero in the case of a trust). I.R.C. § 163(d)(6)(C). The percentage is the same as is applicable to the personal interest phase-in—65% in 1987, 40% in 1988, 20% in 1989, and 10% in 1990. See I.R.C. § 163(d)(6)(B).

50. I.R.C. § 163(d)(2).

51. The "single premium" limitation is broader than it sounds. See I.R.C. § 264(b).

52. Recall I.R.C. § 101.

seems inappropriate to Congress to allow a deduction for interest paid on money used to purchase tax-free gain.[53] Annuity and endowment contracts produce funds also only partially taxed.[54] An offset against likely current high income (otherwise taxed at high rates) might be inappropriate looking ahead to the favorable tax treatment of the proceeds. At least so it seems to Congress.

A bootstrap operation may have been possible, at relatively little cost, to borrow from an insurer the periodic increases in cash surrender value (which mere increases are not taxed as income) and to pay only slightly higher interest than that in effect paid by the insurer. If this was possible and the interest paid was deductible, it was a very nice plan indeed.[55] Subject to some details and to some thoughtful exceptions expressed in Section 264(c), Congress now by Section 264(a)(3) expressly disallows the interest deduction in these circumstances.[56]

Suppose I borrow $5000 at the bank and use it to buy a municipal bond that pays tax-exempt [57] interest at 9%. If I also pay 9% interest at the bank, will the receipts on the bond and the interest paid merely wash? Not if I can deduct the interest from income otherwise taxed, say, at 31 percent.

Interest received		$450
Less interest paid	$450	
Reduced by tax saved (31% of $450)	−140	
After tax cost		310
Gain after tax		$140

But a long time ago Congress appropriately stopped this. Section 265(a)(2) disallows any deduction claimed for interest on indebtedness incurred or continued to purchase or carry tax-exempt obligations.[58] Whether indebtedness is "incurred or carried" for the proscribed purpose is a question that has produced much litigation. The basic problem is: How much of a connection need be shown between the loan and tax-exempt interest in order to invoke the proscription against the deduction of the interest on the loan?

It is settled that to disallow the interest deduction the Commissioner must show that "the relationship between the indebtedness and the

---

53. Cf. I.R.C. § 265(a)(2), noted below.

54. Recall I.R.C. § 72.

55. See, e.g., *Knetsch* and *Golsen*, supra note 11.

56. In addition, I.R.C. § 264(a)(4) sometimes denies an interest deduction to a taxpayer who owns a policy (not limited to a single premium policy) on the life of an officer or employee of, or one who is financially interested in the taxpayer's trade or business. If a loan on such a policy exceeds $50,000, a deduction is denied for the interest associated with the excess amount.

The legislative history indicates that the $50,000 limitation is applicable on a per person basis. Conf.Rep. No. 99–841, supra note 48 at II–340–341.

57. Recall I.R.C. § 103. Regulated investment companies may pay exempt-interest dividends which I.R.C. § 852(b)(5)(B) treats as tax exempt interest. TRA (1976) added I.R.C. § 265(a)(3) generally disallowing deductions for interest paid to purchase or carry securities in such companies.

58. See, e.g., I.R.C. §§ 103(c), 135.

tax-exempt securities involves more than their mere simultaneous existence in respect of a single taxpayer. * * *[59] [Section 265(a)(2)] applies when 'the *purpose* for which the indebtedness is incurred or continued is to purchase or carry tax-exempt obligations.' (Emphasis supplied.)"[60] Nevertheless, the courts appear to be more and more willing to find the required nexus. Of course direct evidence of purpose to buy tax-exempts with a loan is sufficient; and pledging currently owned tax-exempts for the loan has been held to be the equivalent of such direct evidence.[61] Beyond that several courts of appeal have found the connection in less compelling circumstances.[62]

In what might be called "operation smoke-out" (to restrict the use of unregistered bonds), Section 163(f) prohibits the deduction of a bond-issuer's interest payments unless the bonds are registered.[63]

Also in the corporate area, there developed a wide use of bonds and debentures by corporations to acquire the stock or assets of other corporations. The acquiring corporation was entitled to a deduction under Section 163 for the interest paid on this debt. In order to discourage the use of debt financing in corporate acquisitions, Congress enacted Section 279 imposing limitations on the deductibility of interest on this type of indebtedness, but it applies only when the stakes are high.[64]

Timing Restrictions. Restrictions on interest deductions often relate to timing. For example, the Tax Reform Act of 1986 added Section 263A disallowing the deduction of interest on debt incurred to finance the construction or production of certain property, requiring such interest to be capitalized as a part of the cost of the property. The restriction applies only to business or investment property[65] where amounts capitalized may later be deducted by way of depreciation. For example, the rule applies to interest costs on loans used in the construction of a building or for the production of inventory, but not to interest

---

59. Swenson Land and Cattle Co., 64 T.C. 687, 695 (1975). Cf. Rev.Rul. 79–272, 1979–2 C.B. 124, involving an interspousal transaction.

60. Swenson Land and Cattle Co., supra note 59 at 696, quoting Leslie v. Commissioner, 413 F.2d 636, 638 (2d Cir.1969), cert. denied 396 U.S. 1007, 90 S.Ct. 564 (1970). Further, a broker-dealer exception is recognized in Rev.Rul. 74–294, 1974–1 C.B. 71.

61. Wisconsin Cheeseman v. U.S., 388 F.2d 420 (7th Cir.1968); and see Rev.Proc. 72–18, 1972–1 C.B. 740.

62. Levitt v. U.S., 517 F.2d 1339 (8th Cir.1975); Israelson v. U.S., 508 F.2d 838 (4th Cir.1974); affirming per curiam, 367 F.Supp. 1104 (D.Md.1973); Mariorenzi v. Commissioner, 490 F.2d 92 (1st Cir.1974), affirming per curiam 32 TCM 681 (1973); Indian Trail Trading Post, Inc. v. Commissioner, 503 F.2d 102 (6th Cir.1974); but see Handy Button Machine Co., 61 T.C. 846

(1974), where tax-exempts purchased were held to meet recognized business needs, and Rev.Proc. 72–18, supra, indicating the required nexus will not be found if investment in tax-exempts is insubstantial. See Note, "The Deductibility of Interest Costs by a Taxpayer Holding Tax-Exempt Obligations: A Neutral Principle of Allocation," 61 Va.L.Rev. 211 (1975). See also Oliver, "Section 265(2): A Counterproductive Solution to a Nonexistent Problem," 40 Tax.L.Rev. 351 (1985), which is critical of I.R.C. § 265(a)(2).

63. See text at notes 40 and 42 at page 259, supra.

64. Bittker and Eustice, Federal Income Taxation of Corporations and Shareholders, § 4.21 (4th ed. 1979).

65. I.R.C. § 263A(c)(1). It is inapplicable to interest on a qualified residence as described under I.R.C. § 163(h). I.R.C. § 263A(f)(2)(B).

costs on personal use property such as a residence. There is an exception allowing an immediate deduction for interest costs on construction or production of property having a short life, a short production period, or a low cost.[66] The amount of interest that must be capitalized is limited to interest on loans directly or indirectly attributable to production or construction costs.[67] The rule generally applies to interest paid or incurred after December 31, 1986, but transitional rules inject some complexity.

In some instances a taxpayer has the option of deducting an expenditure or charging it to capital account so that it has a favorable impact ultimately on his tax liability by way of increasing his basis for property. If he elects to capitalize a deductible expenditure the obvious counterpart is a denial of the related deduction.[68] Interest paid on money borrowed to purchase property is one of the deductible casualties, if the taxpayer elects to capitalize the interest.[69]

In addition, another timing restriction on the deductibility of interest is found in Section 267(a)(2). The Section applies only to related taxpayers and is tied in with the payor and payee taxpayers' methods of accounting. Methods of accounting and Section 267(a)(2) are both considered in Chapter 19.[70]

PROBLEMS

1. Lender makes a $100,000 interest-free demand loan to Borrower on January 1 at a time when the applicable federal rate is 10 percent. The proceeds of the loan are used to purchase a principal residence for Borrower. Ten percent interest compounded semiannually on $100,000 is $10,250 per annum. Consider the tax consequences to both parties at the end of the year if the loan is still unpaid and is in the nature of:

    (a) A gift.

    (b) Compensation.

    (c) A dividend.

2. Mother makes an interest free demand loan to Daughter under the following alternative situations at a time when the applicable

---

66. I.R.C. § 263A(f)(1)(B). The interest capitalization rule applies only to property that has either (1) a long useful life (such as a building), (2) an estimated production period exceeding two years, or (3) an estimated production period exceeding one year and a cost exceeding one million dollars. Id.

67. I.R.C. § 263A(f)(2). See especially I.R.C. § 263A(f)(2)(A)(ii) which is known as the avoided cost rule. Under the rule, any interest expense incurred during the construction period that could have been avoided if funds had not been expended for construction must be capitalized.

68. I.R.C. § 266. Although phrased negatively, "no deduction * * * etc.", it is interpreted affirmatively to permit capitalization, as provided by the regulations.

69. Reg. § 1.266–1(b)(1). The regulations properly emphasize, § 1.266–1(b)(2), that "an item not otherwise deductible may not be capitalized under § 266." Thus, for example, the section does not apply to interest on money borrowed to buy tax-exempts.

70. See page 557, infra.

Federal rate is 10 percent. Discuss the tax consequences to Mother and Daughter.

(a) Mother loans Daughter $10,000 that Daughter uses as part of a down payment on Daughter's new residence.

(b) Mother loans Daughter $10,000 that Daughter invests in a residence that she rents to others.

(c) Mother loans Daughter $100,000 that Daughter uses as a down payment on Daughter's new residence at a time when Daughter has $20,000 of net investment income.

(d) Same as (c), above, except that Daughter has $1,000 of net investment income.

3. Taxpayer purchases a home in 1991 which he uses as his principal residence. Unless otherwise stated, he obtains a loan secured by the residence and uses the proceeds to acquire the residence. What portion of the interest paid on such loan may Taxpayer deduct in the following situations?

(a) The purchase price and fair market value of the home is $350,000. Taxpayer obtains a mortgage for $250,000 of the purchase price.

(b) The facts are the same as in (a), above, except that Taxpayer by 1996 has reduced the outstanding principal balance of the 1991 mortgage to $200,000 and the fair market value of the residence has increased to $400,000. In 1996, Taxpayer takes out a second mortgage for $100,000 secured by his residence to add a fourth bedroom and a den to the residence.

(c) The facts are the same as in (b), above, except that Taxpayer uses the proceeds of the $100,000 mortgage to buy a Ferrari.

(d) The facts are the same as in (a), above. By 2010, Taxpayer has paid off $200,000 of the $250,000 1991 mortgage and the residence is worth $500,000. In 2010, Taxpayer borrows $200,000 on the residence, $50,000 of which is used to pay off the remaining balance of the 1991 loan and the remainder is invested in stock.

(e) The facts are the same as in (a), above, but additionally, towards the end of 1991, Taxpayer's financial prospects improve dramatically and he purchases a luxury vacation residence in Florida for its fair market value of $1,250,000. He finances $950,000 of the purchase price with a note secured by a mortgage on the Florida house and elects to treat the residence as a qualified residence.

(f) The facts are the same as in (a), above, except that the year of acquisition of the $350,000 residence subject to the $250,000 mortgage was 1985. In addition, instead of using all of the loan proceeds to purchase the residence, Taxpayer applied $200,000 toward its cost and used the other $50,000 of the proceeds to buy a sailboat. By 1991, Taxpayer has reduced the outstanding principal of the 1985 loan to $175,000. In that year, he refinances the property (now worth $500,000) with a loan for $300,000 which is secured by the residence. He uses $175,000 of the proceeds from the 1991 loan to pay off the balance of the 1985 loan and the remaining $125,000 to pay off his childrens' educational loans.

4. Investor incurs investment interest of $100,000. To what extent is it deductible in a year after 1990 if:

(a) She sells stock during the year at a $60,000 gain, has $20,000 in dividends on all her stock, and has $10,000 in deductible investment adviser fees? Are there any other tax consequences to Investor?

(b) The interest of $100,000 is on loans whose proceeds are used to purchase tax exempt bonds?

(c) The facts are the same as in (a) and (b), above, except that the proceeds of the loans are used 50% to purchase tax exempt bonds and 50% to buy stock and the bonds and stock are her only investments?

C. TAXES

Internal Revenue Code: Sections 164(a), (b), (c), (d)(1); 275; 1001(b)(2).

Regulations: Section 1.164–1(a), –2, –3(a)–(d).

CRAMER v. COMMISSIONER *

Tax Court of the United States, 1971.
55 T.C. 1125.

FEATHERSTON, Judge: Respondent determined deficiencies in petitioner's income tax for 1964, 1965, and 1966 in the amounts of $257.62, $561.21, and $594.22, respectively. The issues presented for decision are:

* * *

(2) Whether the taxes which petitioner paid on certain real property during 1965 and 1966 are deductible under section 164;

* * *

FINDINGS OF FACT

Petitioner was a legal resident of Dearborn Heights, Mich., at the time she filed her petition. Her returns for 1964, 1965, and 1966 were filed with the district director of internal revenue, Detroit, Mich.

* * *

* Some footnotes omitted.

Real Property Issues

In August 1963, petitioner sold her residence located at 8247 Auburn Street (hereinafter the Auburn Street property) under a land sale contract to William S. Osborn (hereinafter Osborn). Under the terms of this agreement, Osborn agreed to make monthly payments on the sale price and to pay the property taxes. Record title to the residence remained in petitioner.

During 1964 and 1965, Osborn failed to pay the real property taxes, and petitioner paid them in the respective amounts of $264.68 and $255.98. Osborn also failed to make his monthly payments on the indebtedness to petitioner, and she instituted a foreclosure suit against him in the Circuit Court of Wayne County. She obtained a default judgment against him and recovered possession of the property on February 18, 1966.

Later in the same year, petitioner resold the property. * * * She also paid the real property taxes for 1966 in the amount of $259.06. No gain was realized on the sale, recovery, or resale of the residence.

During 1965 and 1966, petitioner's mother, Ann Marion Gay, owned a residence located at 720 Atkinson Street (hereinafter the Atkinson Street property). She was intermittently hospitalized from 1965 until June 7, 1968, when she died. Petitioner looked after her mother's residence during this period and paid, with her own money, taxes on the property for 1965 and 1966 in the amounts of $300.62 and $381.94, respectively. Her mother executed a quitclaim deed of the property to petitioner in 1967.

After petitioner sold her residence in 1963, she purchased a new one at 27314 Clearview Street (hereinafter the Clearview Street property). During 1964, 1965, and 1966, her new residence was subject to a mortgage which required petitioner to make monthly escrow payments of real property taxes. The escrow agent paid the property taxes for those years as follows: 1964—$0; 1965—$843.95; and 1966—$847.89.

On her 1965 and 1966 returns, petitioner deducted $1,144.87 and $915.39, respectively, as real property taxes; these amounts included the taxes paid on the Auburn Street, Atkinson Street, and Clearview Street properties. She also deducted $607.64 on her 1966 return as repairs on the property which she had repossessed during that year.

Respondent determined "that property tax deductions are allowable in the amount of $436.94 in 1965 and $470.88 in 1966."

* * *

Real Property Taxes

On brief, respondent has conceded the deductibility of the taxes which petitioner paid with respect to the Clearview Street property. Remaining in dispute are the taxes on the Atkinson and Auburn Street properties.

As to the Atkinson Street property, petitioner is not entitled to the disputed deductions. Section 164 allows a deduction for real property taxes; but they are, in general, "deductible only by the person upon whom they are imposed." Sec. 1.164–1(a), Income Tax Regs.; Magruder v. Supplee, 316 U.S. 394 (1942). During 1965 and 1966, the years in dispute, this property was owned by petitioner's mother, and was not deeded to petitioner until 1967. Prior to the delivery of this deed, she had no interest, legal or equitable, in the property, and the taxes for 1965 and 1966 were not imposed upon her. Her payments of the taxes for those years were, in substance, gifts or some other kind of advances for funds to, or for the benefit of, her mother and, consequently, are not deductible by petitioner.

The dispute as to the Auburn Street property taxes involves two periods: One during 1964 and 1965, prior to the time petitioner recovered possession of the property; the other during 1966, when she resold it. After petitioner first sold the property in 1961, record title remained in her name, and, we infer, the land sale contract with Osborn was not recorded. Under the Michigan statutes, real property taxes are assessed "to the owner if known, and also to the occupant." Mich.Stat.Ann. sec. 7.3 (1960). As the record owner of the property, petitioner was assessed for the property taxes, and they became a debt to the taxing entity for the collection of which her chattels, as well as the realty, could be seized and sold. Schaefer v. Woodmere Cemetery Ass'n., 256 Mich. 332, 239 N.W. 300, 301 (1931); see also Gulf Refining Co. v. Perry, 303 Mich. 487, 6 N.W.2d 756 (1942); Gilken Corp. v. Commissioner, 176 F.2d 141, 144 (C.A.6, 1949), affirming 10 T.C. 445 (1948). The parties have stipulated that petitioner actually paid the taxes even though Osborn was obligated by the land sale contract to pay them.[4] Consequently, petitioner, having been assessed for the taxes on the Auburn Street property and having paid them in order to discharge her debt and to protect her property interests, is entitled to deduct them on her income tax returns for 1964 and 1965. See, e.g., Theodore Milgroom, 31 T.C. 1256 (1959); William R. Tracy, 25 B.T.A. 1055 (1932), reversed on other grounds 70 F.2d 93 (C.A.6,1934), acq. XI–2 C.B. 10; Cornelia C.F. Horsford, 2 T.C. 826, 827 (1943) acq. 1943 C.B. 11. The case of Pacific Southwest Realty Co., 45 B.T.A. 426, 437–438 (1941), affd. 128 F.2d 815 (C.A.9,1942), involving California law, under which the real property taxes were assessed to the equitable owner of the property is inapposite.

As to 1966, section 164(d)(1) provides:

> (1) General Rule.—For purposes of subsection (a), if real property is sold during any real property tax year, then—
>
> (A) so much of the real property tax as is properly allocable to that part of such year which ends on the day before the

---

4. Of course, if petitioner were ever to recover on the judgment which she obtained against Osborn, that recovery would constitute income subject to the limitations of sec. 111.

date of the sale shall be treated as a tax imposed on the seller, and

   (B) so much of such tax as is properly allocable to that part of such year which begins on the date of the sale shall be treated as a tax imposed on the purchaser.

While the property taxes were assessed to petitioner for 1966, the statute quoted above provides that they will be treated as having been partially assessed to the buyer instead of her. This provision reflects the common practice of prorating property taxes as between the buyer and the seller, but it is not dependent on an actual proration. The section applies automatically to every sale and allows the buyer to deduct a portion of the property taxes, whether he actually pays them or not. * * * Consequently, petitioner is treated as having been assessed for, and as having paid, only the portion of the taxes for 1966 allocable to the period prior to the time she sold the property. Sec. 1.164–6(a), Income Tax Regs.

The record does not disclose when in 1966 she made the sale; however, from the fact that her income tax return for that year reflects that she received a substantial amount of interest income in respect of the sale of this property, we infer that the sale was made shortly after she recovered possession of it on February 18. For the portion of the year prior to the sale—not less than the 48 days prior to February 18— she is entitled to a deduction. Accordingly, we hold that she may deduct 48/365 of the $259.06 in taxes on the Auburn Street property for 1966, or $34.07. Rev.Rul. 67–31, 1967–1 C.B. 49.

PROBLEMS

   1. Which of the following taxes would be deductible *as such* under § 164?

   (a) A state sales tax imposed at a single rate on sellers but required to be separately stated and paid by purchasers to sellers, applicable to retail sales of any property except food, clothing, and medicine.

   (b) A state real property tax of $1000 for which A became liable as owner of Blackacre on January 1st but which B agreed to pay half of when he acquired Blackacre from A on July 1st.

   (c) A state income tax.

   (d) The federal income tax.

   (e) A state gasoline tax imposed on consumers.

   2. Which of the following expenditures would be deductible, if not as taxes, as § 162 or § 212 expenses within the second sentence of § 164(a)?

   (a) A state tax on cigarettes (imposed on their sale at a rate five times the rate of the general sales tax) paid for cigarettes provided by the taxpayer gratuitously to customers.

(b) A filing fee required to be paid to the State Democratic Party by candidates entering state primary elections. See Horace E. Nichols, 60 T.C. 236 (1973).

3. Son who is still in college owns substantial securities. Father, when paying his own intangibles tax to State X, pays the intangibles tax due by Son.

(a) May Father deduct the tax paid?

(b) Is it deductible by Son?

4. Dr. Medic employs Charles to work for her as receptionist. She pays Charles's salary but withholds X dollars to which she adds Y dollars all of which she pays to the federal government under the Federal Insurance Contributions Act (for "social security").

(a) Can Dr. Medic deduct amount X? Amount Y? X plus Y?

(b) Is Charles entitled to a deduction for the payments?

5. The City of Oz constructs a yellow brick road that runs past Woodman's property. He and other property owners adjacent to the road are assessed varying amounts by Oz, based on the relative values of their properties. Woodman elects to pay off the assessment over five years and pays $400 in the taxable year. Deductible?

D. BAD DEBTS, CHARITABLE CONTRIBUTIONS AND CASUALTY AND THEFT LOSSES

Because these types of deductions are intimately related to characterization principles, their analysis is deferred to Chapter 23.

CHAPTER 17. RESTRICTIONS ON DEDUCTIONS

A. INTRODUCTION

That which Congress giveth, Congress may also take away. In this Chapter we encounter examples of congressional finger crossing,—specific denials of deductions that seem to have been authorized. In general, the "give" provisions are in Sections 161 through 196, which prescribe deductions for individuals and corporations, and in Sections 211 through 220, authorizing additional deductions for individuals.[1] Most of the "take" provisions are in Sections 261 through 280H, specifying nondeductible items and carving out some no nos in the affirmative rules.

There are examples of takeaway rules in other parts of this book, many of which appear along with the affirmative deduction provisions to which they relate. For instance, interest expense generally is deductible under Section 163,[2] but Congress expressly limits or disallows some interest deductions[3] or requires the capitalizing of the interest rather than permitting it to be "expensed."[4] Similarly, as Congress allows deductions for bad debts[5] but not for political contributions,[6] it precludes an indirect deduction for political contributions by denying deductions for bad debts that are obligations of a political party to the taxpayer.[7] The foregoing are only illustrative of the many types of restrictions and limitations on deductions which are discussed throughout this text.

An important instance of congressional finger crossing occurs under Section 274, a broad disallowance provision which we have already encountered in several different chapters of this book. That section severely limits many of the deductions generally allowed by the broad Section 162 and 212 deduction provisions.[8] Chapter 3 disclosed the $25 limitation on the deduction for business gifts,[9] and Chapter 4 revealed that Section 274 also limits the deduction (and the Section 74(c) exclusion) for employee achievement awards.[10] Section 274 strongly asserts

1. See also I.R.C. §§ 241–250 providing special deductions for corporations.

2. See Chapter 16B, supra.

3. See I.R.C. §§ 163(d) and (h). See also I.R.C. §§ 264(a)(2)–(4), 265(a)(2), and 279. Limitations on the deduction of interest are discussed at page 474, supra.

4. I.R.C. § 263A.

5. I.R.C. § 166. See Chapter 23A, infra.

6. I.R.C. § 24 allowing a limited amount of credit for political contributions was repealed in the 1986 Act.

7. I.R.C. § 271.

8. Note that I.R.C. § 274 may limit deductions under other provisions. For example the § 274(n) 80% limitation on meals is applicable to meals deductible under other sections such as § 170 and § 217.

9. I.R.C. § 274(b)(1).

10. I.R.C. § 274(j).

itself with respect to the Section 162 deductions considered in Chapter 14, imposing numerous limitations on various ordinary and necessary business expenses. In general, it is a congressional attempt to call a halt to business persons (and even congressmen) living too high on the hog at government expense. The Section 274(n) disallowance of 20 percent of the cost of entertainment and most business meals [11] applies to meals incurred not only in business entertainment but in travel, education, and general business as well.[12] Section 274 also imposes numerous limitations on the deductibility of business entertainment [13] and business travel expenses,[14] including travel expenses as a form of education.[15] Sometimes Congress uncrosses its fingers by providing internal relief provisions within Section 274, lessening or negating its generally restrictive or prohibitive effects.[16]

The restrictions set out above are substantial, but Section 274 goes even further: it also contains substantiation and reporting requirements.[17] The reporting requirements generally concern reporting on attendance at conventions and seminars.[18] The substantiation requirements generally involve travel, entertainment and gifts.[19] Insufficiency of reporting or substantiation can cause total disallowance of deductions that might otherwise survive the give and take mechanism described above.

Many of the statutory restrictions on deductions are aimed at tax shelters. It's a safe bet that even before students take a tax course, they have already heard about tax shelters. "Tax shelter" can have various meanings, and tax shelters take various forms. Some would look upon the exclusion of interest on municipal bonds as a tax shelter.[20] The Section 1014 "step-up" in basis at death[21] can also be considered a form of tax shelter. Use of deferred compensation is an important form of tax shelter.[22] However, the term "tax shelter" is most frequently used in an invidious sense to describe a circumstance in which a taxpayer generates deductions in excess of income from one activity and uses that excess to avoid tax on some or all of the income from another unrelated activity. The unrelated income from the second activity is "sheltered" from tax liability by the excess deductions generated by the first. For example, a successful professional person or investor who has high-bracket income generated by services, or by dividends or interest on investments, may become a gentleman farmer in an enjoyable rural area. In the absence of statutory limitations, if

11. See I.R.C. § 274(n)(2) providing an exception for some business meals. See also I.R.C. § 274(k).

12. I.R.C. § 274(n)(1)(A).

13. I.R.C. § 274(a), (g), and (*l*).

14. I.R.C. § 274(c), (h), and (m).

15. I.R.C. § 274(m)(2).

16. I.R.C. § 274(a)(2)(C), (c)(2), (e), (k)(2), (*l*)(1)(B), (m)(1)(B), and (n)(2).

17. I.R.C. § 274(d) and (h)(5).

18. I.R.C. § 274(h)(5).

19. I.R.C. § 274(d). There are also substantiation requirements imposed on the depreciation of certain "listed property". See I.R.C. §§ 274(d)(4) and 280F(d)(4) and Chapter 22A 2, infra.

20. See Chapter 11C, supra.

21. See Chapter 6B 4, supra.

22. See Chapter 20C 3, infra.

the farm activity generates deductions in excess of income, the taxpayer can use excess deductions from the farm to reduce taxable income (and correspondingly the tax on the income) from other sources.

In recent years Congress, not unaware of such activities, has attacked shelters in two fashions: substantively, by limiting deductions and, procedurally, with special penalties and registration requirements. Substantively, Congress deals with what it deems artificial losses under several provisions. Under Section 465, the deduction of losses incurred by the gentleman farmer in the above example is, in general, limited to the amount he personally has "at risk" and could actually lose from engaging in his farming activity. Taking a different tack in limiting artificial loss deductions, Section 183, known as the "hobby loss" provision, raises the question whether a gentleman farmer's activity is actually engaged in for profit; if not, in general Section 183 limits the deduction of expenditures or losses of the farm to gross income derived from the farm, foreclosing use of the farm as an umbrella to shelter any other income. Similarly, Section 280A, limiting deductions related to a home that a taxpayer uses as a residence, generally allows those deductions only against gross income generated by the home. Finally Section 469 prohibits certain taxpayers from deducting losses from passive activities against income from other activities, except income from other passive activities.

The substantive provisions above are of two different types but have one common goal: limiting the use of artificial losses to prevent taxpayers from succeeding in tax sheltering schemes. The first type, a substantive takeaway provision, is one which disallows or partially disallows the use of what Congress considers artificial losses by simply *disallowing* in whole or in part the deductions from an activity. Limitation here is similar to disallowance under Section 274. Section 183 and, in most situations, Section 280A are takeaway provisions. In a second type of limitation, Congress limits the current deduction of losses or the assertion of credits by *postponing* them, i.e., disallowing their utilization in the current year but permitting them to be carried over to be used in future years. Sections 465, 469 and, in limited situations, 280A are postponement provisions.

In addition to its substantive attack on tax shelters, Congress also made a procedural assault on them in 1981 which was intensified in 1984 and 1986. Congress penalizes one who promotes or participates in the promotion of tax shelters by making false or fraudulent representations concerning the tax benefits from the shelter [23] or assertions of gross overvaluation of involved assets.[24]

---

23. I.R.C. § 6700(a)(2)(A).

24. I.R.C. § 6700(a)(2)(B). Such persons are penalized in an amount equal to the lesser of $1,000 or 100 percent of the gross income derived (or even just expected) from the arrangement. I.R.C. § 6700(a). Congress also grants the Service injunctive powers against such promoters. I.R.C. § 7408.

Congress became aware of an horrendous number of cases involving tax shelters at various stages of investigation.[25] And Congress, like Alcoa, can't wait! The large number of shelter cases awaiting attention suggests an even much greater number that have not come to light. The heinous nature of this tax dodge is indicated by the Senate Committee's assertion that:[26]

> These promoters know that even if a tax scheme they market is clearly faulty, some investors' incorrect returns will escape detection and many will enjoy a substantial deferral of tax while the Treasury searches for their returns and coordinates its handling of similar cases.

Consequently, Congress created the concept of the "potentially abusive tax shelter"[27] and imposed several requirements on promoters of such shelters. Promoters who organize or sell interests in such shelters are required to keep lists of customers.[28] In addition, if the abusive tax shelter requirements are met Congress requires registration of the shelters with the Service by the time sales of the interests occur.[29] The scheme is capped off by requiring the promoter of an abusive shelter to furnish each customer with the shelter's registration number and, in turn, requiring the customer to include the shelter's registration number on his tax return.[30] There are penalties for failure to satisfy the above requirements.[31]

In addition to the substantive provisions listed above as attacks on tax shelters, this chapter also considers some limitations on deductions aimed not at tax shelters, but at illegal activities. As should be anticipated, this final group of restrictions is in the form of total disallowance provisions.

---

25. Sen.Rep. No. 98–169, 98th Cong., 2d Sess. 436 (1984).

26. Sen.Rep. No. 98–169, note 25 supra at 425–426.

27. I.R.C. § 6112(b). I.R.C. § 6112(b)(1) defines a potentially abusive tax shelter as a tax shelter described in § 6111. I.R.C. § 6111(c)(1)(A) defines an abusive tax shelter essentially as one where an investor could reasonably infer from representation made that the tax shelter ratio (essentially the ratio that the amount of deductions and 200 percent of the credits potentially allowable bears to the investment base of the total amount of money and unconditional liabilities) for the year is greater than two to one for any of the first five years ending after the date the investment is offered for sale. In addition such shelters must be required to be registered under Federal or State securities law, sold under an exemption from registration requirements, or a substantial investment (one where the total amounts offered for sale exceed $250,000 and five or more investors are expected. I.R.C. § 6111(c)(4)).

I.R.C. § 6111(c)(1)(B). I.R.C. § 6112(b)(2) includes as a potentially abusive tax shelter any entity, investment plan or arrangement, or other plan or arrangement which the Service determines by regulations has a potential for tax avoidance or evasion. See Dellett, "Abusive Tax Shelters After the Tax Reform Act of 1984," 42 Wash. & Lee L.Rev. 247 (1985).

28. I.R.C. § 6112(a).

29. I.R.C. § 6111(a)(1). Registration must include information identifying and describing the shelter and the tax benefits represented to investors. I.R.C. § 6111(a)(2). Form 8264 is to be used for such registration.

30. I.R.C. § 6111(b). See also Rev.Proc. 84–84, 1984–2 C.B. 782, and Rev.Rul. 84–175, 1984–2 C.B. 296, announcing and illustrating the Service's policy to freeze refunds which are attributable to some abusive tax shelters. Cf. I.R.C. §§ 6221–6233.

31. See I.R.C. §§ 6708, 6707(a)(1), and 6707(b), respectively.

B. DEDUCTIONS LIMITED TO AMOUNT AT RISK

Internal Revenue Code: Section 465(a), (b), (c)(1) and (3), (d), (e).

Simply stated, Section 465 limits a taxpayer's deductible losses from a specific business or investment activity to the amount the taxpayer is personally "at risk" in that activity, in effect what he personally stands to lose from failure in the activity. Prior to 1976 the only general limitation on the amount of losses a taxpayer could claim from an activity was the taxpayer's cost or other *basis* in the activity.[1] The taxpayer's basis in an activity, however, includes, not only the taxpayer's actual investment and liabilities on which he is personally obligated but also nonrecourse liabilities for which he has no personal obligation.[2] A taxpayer could often deduct losses far in excess of the amount he was actually "at risk" in the given activity, in effect sheltering income earned in other activities from tax liability.

Congress reacted to this somewhat artificial loss situation by enacting Section 465 as a part of the Tax Reform Act of 1976.[3] It provides that the amount of loss, otherwise allowed the taxpayer in a given year, which may be deducted in connection with most activities engaged in for the production of income or in carrying on a trade or business, cannot exceed the aggregate amount with respect to which the taxpayer is "at risk" in each such activity at the close of the taxable year.[4] Generally, a taxpayer is considered to be at risk with respect to a given activity to the extent of the cash and the adjusted basis of other property he has contributed to the activity, and any amounts borrowed for use in that activity on which the taxpayer is personally liable.[5] In addition, he is at risk to the extent of other liabilities if he has pledged property other than that used in the activity as security, but only to the extent of the net fair market value of such pledged property.[6] A taxpayer is not considered to be at risk with respect to amounts protected against loss through nonrecourse financing, guarantees, or other agreements or arrangements[7] and to amounts borrowed from a person having an interest in the activity or from anyone "related" to such persons.[8] When the taxpayer has a loss from a Section 465

1. Staff of Joint Comm. on Taxation, 94th Cong. 2d Sess., General Explanation of the Tax Reform Act of 1976 (P.L. 94–455) at 33 et seq. (1976), 1976–3 vol. 2 C.B. 45 et seq.

2. Nonrecourse liabilities are generally treated the same as personal liabilities for federal tax purposes. Cf. Crane v. Commissioner, 331 U.S. 1, 67 S.Ct. 1047 (1947).

3. In 1976 there was a lion-like roar in Congress to impose substantive "limitations on artificial losses" (L.A.L.). However, the 1976 Act produced what in its original enactment was only a mouse-like squeak, I.R.C. § 465.

4. I.R.C. § 465(a)(1).

5. I.R.C. § 465(b)(1) and (2)(A).

6. I.R.C. § 465(b)(2)(B).

7. See I.R.C. § 465(b)(4). A taxpayer is not personally liable on nonrecourse obligations; the lender has recourse against only the property which secures the obligation, and not against the personal assets of the taxpayer.

8. I.R.C. § 465(b)(3). Related persons are defined by I.R.C. § 465(b)(3)(C), with reference to I.R.C. §§ 267(b) and 707(b)(1). See also § 465(b)(3)(B).

activity, the amount the taxpayer is considered to be at risk in subsequent taxable years with respect to the Section 465 activity will be reduced to the extent that his loss deduction was previously allowed.[9] Importantly, on the other hand, any disallowed losses in the taxable year can be carried over to a future year.[10] For example, if a taxpayer contributes cash of $10,000 and incurs personal liability of $20,000 on property used in an activity, and in the first two years he incurs a total of $18,000 of losses, in year three he will still have $12,000 at risk.[11] If, instead, the liability were a nonrecourse liability on property used in the activity, taxpayer would have only $10,000 at risk and Section 465 would deny a deduction for $8,000 of losses. However, those losses would be carried over to future years [12] to be deducted when the taxpayer increases his amounts at risk.[13]

Section 465 applies to all activities engaged in by a taxpayer in carrying on a trade or business or for the production of income [14] other than equipment leasing by closely held corporations.[15] Thus, the at risk rules apply to real estate activities [16] but with a major variation from the normal operation of the at risk rules. In general, a taxpayer *is* at risk with respect to *nonrecourse* financing of real estate activities if the financing is from the government, is guaranteed by the government, or is from a qualified person who is in the business of lending money.[17] In general, the qualified person must not be related to the taxpayer,[18] a person from whom the taxpayer acquired the property (i.e. the seller),[19] or a person who receives a fee for the taxpayer's investment in the property (i.e. the promoter of the activity).[20] The requirement that the qualified person be unrelated to the taxpayer is waived if the terms of the nonrecourse financing are commercially reasonable and on substantially the same terms as loans involving unrelated persons.[21]

Section 465 is applicable only to individuals and closely held C corporations.[22] Closely held C corporations are defined as corporations more than 50 percent of whose stock is owned directly or indirectly [23] by

---

9. I.R.C. § 465(b)(5).

10. I.R.C. § 465(a)(2).

11. I.R.C. § 465(b)(5).

12. I.R.C. § 465(a)(2).

13. An increase in the amount at risk could, for example,. occur by a direct cash contribution to the activity, an indirect cash contribution by paying off principal on the nonrecourse liability, or a contribution of more property to the activity.

14. I.R.C. § 465(c)(3)(A). This includes I.R.C. § 465(c)(1) activities to which the provision when originally enacted was applicable.

15. I.R.C. § 465(c)(4). See the discussion at notes 23–24, infra.

16. Pub.Law No. 99–514, 99th Cong., 2d Sess. § 503(a) (1986).

17. I.R.C. §§ 465(b)(6)(B) and 49(a)(1)(D)(iv).

18. I.R.C. § 49(a)(1)(D)(iv)(I). See I.R.C. § 465(b)(3)(C), which defines a related person.

19. I.R.C. § 49(a)(1)(D)(iv)(II).

20. I.R.C. § 49(a)(1)(D)(iv)(III).

21. I.R.C. § 465(b)(6)(D)(ii).

22. I.R.C. § 465(a)(1).

23. The attribution of ownership rules of I.R.C. § 544 are made applicable to § 465. See I.R.C. §§ 465(a)(1)(B), 542(a)(2) and 544(a); but see some limitations in the attribution rules provided in § 465(a)(3).

five or fewer individuals.[24]   Although Section 465 is inapplicable to partnerships and S corporations, it does apply to the partners and the S corporation shareholders at their individual levels.[25]

Section 465(e) provides for recapture of previously allowed loss deductions for taxable years beginning after December 31, 1978, in a situation where some event has caused a taxpayer's allowed losses in prior taxable years to exceed his amount currently at risk.   For example, if a taxpayer converts a recourse obligation (one on which he is personally liable) to a nonrecourse obligation creating a negative at risk situation, Section 465(e) requires a recapture of the excess loss deductions taken in prior years, and permits, as with any other loss disallowed under Section 465, a carryover of the disallowed loss to a future year.   Thus assume taxpayer paid $80 cash and incurred $320 of personal liability to acquire a business in 1984, and incurred and properly deducted $200 of loss in 1985.   If in 1986 he had not paid off any principal on the $320 personal liability and he converted it to a nonrecourse obligation, he would have been allowed deductions of $120 for which he is currently not at risk ($200 loss less $80 cash currently at risk); he must therefore recognize $120 of recapture income from the activity under Section 465(e) in 1986.[26]

PROBLEMS

1.   Discuss the extent to which § 465 limits Taxpayer's loss deductions, generates recapture income out of a previously allowed loss deductions, or allows the use of a loss carryover in the following situations:

(a)   Taxpayer purchased a farm for $50,000 cash and his personal note for $400,000 secured by a mortgage.   In the first two years of operation he put in an additional $50,000 each year, by way of cash and personal loans, for feed, fertilizer and other supplies; but things did not go well.   In the first year of operations his loss was $80,000 and he had another $80,000 loss in the second year of operations.   No principal was paid on the liability in either year.

(b)   The facts are the same as in (a), above, except that the farm was acquired for $50,000 cash and $400,000 of nonrecourse financing.

24. See I.R.C. §§ 465(a)(1)(B) and 542(a) (2).

25. Cf. Reg. § 1.465–1T. See August, "Navigating the At–Risk Waters After the Tax Reform Act of 1984," 63 Taxes 83 (1985).

26. See I.R.C. § 465(e)(1)(A). Phrased in the statutory terms, taxpayer is at risk to the extent of $80 (cash) reduced by the prior allowed deductions of $200 (see I.R.C.

§ 465(b)(5)) or a minus $120. Tracking the statute, and by the numbers, zero exceeds minus $120 by $120, which is the amount of the recapture income.

The legislative history suggests that other events triggering § 465(e) recapture are distributions to the taxpayer and the commencement of a guarantee or some similar arrangement which affects a taxpayer's risk of loss.

(c) The facts are the same as in (a), above, except that in the third year of operations when the farm broke even, Taxpayer converted his personal liability of $400,000 to a nonrecourse loan.

(d) The facts are the same as in (b), above, except that Taxpayer is a corporation whose stock is owned equally by ten unrelated shareholders.

(e) The facts are the same as in (b), above, except that Taxpayer is a corporation whose stock is owned equally by nine unrelated shareholders.

(f) The facts are the same as in (b), above, except that Taxpayer pays off $10,000 of the nonrecourse loan in year two.

(g) The facts are the same as in (b), above, except that the farm breaks even in year three and Taxpayer pays off $10,000 of the nonrecourse loan in year three.

2. Discuss the extent to which § 465 potentially applies to limit the deductions of Vestor who invests in an apartment house in the following situations:

(a) Vestor obtains a $200,000 nonrecourse loan from an unrelated commercial bank to purchase the apartment from Seller.

(b) The facts are the same as in (a), above, except that Vestor obtains the nonrecourse loan from Seller.

(c) The facts are the same as in (a), above, except that Vestor obtains the nonrecourse loan from his brother (a "related person" under § 465(b)(3)(C)) who is a commercial lender. The loan is at an interest rate 3 percent below the market rate of interest.

(d) The facts are the same as in (c), above, except the interest rate on the loan is equal to the market rate of interest.

C. ACTIVITIES NOT ENGAGED IN FOR PROFIT

Internal Revenue Code: Section 183(a)–(d).

Regulations: Section 1.183–2(a) and (b).

————

It may very well be that our gentleman farmer considered above in the Introduction is legitimately engaged in his farming activity to earn a profit and if so, his deductions should be fully allowed to the extent that he is at risk. If, however, he is not engaged in the activity for profit then excess deductions from the activity should not be permitted to shelter other sources of income. By statute the result depends upon whether the taxpayer's activity is one "engaged in for profit", a criterion easy to state but not easy to determine.

Congress initially provided the so-called "hobby loss" provisions [1] to test deductibility in such situations. However, because those provisions were weak and easy to manipulate, Congress in 1969 introduced Section 183.

Section 183 applies to individuals, S corporations, trusts and estates.[2] It creates a rebuttable presumption related to whether the activity is "engaged in for profit." [3] Specifically, Section 183(d) establishes the presumption that an activity is engaged in for profit in the current taxable year if, in three or more of the past five consecutive taxable years,[4] gross income derived from the activity exceeds deductions attributable to that activity.[5] For an activity the major part of which is breeding, training, showing, or racing horses, the critical question is whether there were two or more profitable years in a seven year period. Overall, these provisions, indicate that the presumption depends on the taxpayer's actual record in making profits.

Section 183(d) merely creates a presumption the Commissioner may overcome.[6] Even when facts are such that no presumption arises, the taxpayer still may qualify an activity as one "engaged in for profit". He may be able to show, using an objective standard, that he or she engaged in the activity, or the continuation of the activity, with the objective of making a profit.[7]

If the activity is engaged in for profit, then all items conventionally deductible are allowed, without limitation. If, on the other hand, the activity is not engaged in for profit, Section 183(b) comes into play, providing the extent to which deductions are allowed. Section 183(b) renders wholly deductible expenses that are deductible whether the activity is business, investment or personal in nature, such as interest

---

1. I.R.C. § 270, which was repealed by Tax Reform Act of 1959.

2. I.R.C. § 183(a); see I.R.C. § 641(b) and Reg. § 1.183–1(a). See I.R.C. § 1361 et seq. for the definition of a S corporation.

3. See Lee, "A Blend of Old Wines in a New Wineskin: Section 183 and Beyond," 29 Tax L.Rev. 347 (1974).

4. For a determination year prior to January, 1987, the presumption was met if there were two, rather than three, profitable years. However if the contested year is 1987 (or later) three of the years from 1983–1987 (or later) have to be profitable to generate the presumption.

5. All deductions attributable to the activity, other than allowable net operating loss carryovers, are taken into account in determining the applicability of the I.R.C. § 183(d) presumption. An amendment in 1971 added § 183(e) under which a taxpayer may defer the time for determination whether the statutory presumption applies. With respect to any such deferral, the Tax Reform Act of 1976 added

§ 183(e)(4) to protect the government against inappropriate running of the limitations period on deficiency assessments.

6. Reg. § 1.183–1(c)(i). See also Reg. § 1.183–2(b).

7. Reg. § 1.183–2(a). In determining whether a profit objective exists, a reasonable expectation of profit is not required; it may be sufficient that there is a small chance of making a large profit. Thus a taxpayer investing in a wildcat oil well may deduct his substantial expenditures incurred in the activity even though his expectation of profit might be considered unreasonable. See Reg. § 1.183–2(b) for factors relevant to determining whether an activity is engaged in for profit.

For examples of cases in this area, compare Engdahl v. Commissioner, 72 T.C. 659 (1979), and Appley v. Commissioner, 39 T.C.M. 386 (1979), with Golanty v. Commissioner, 72 T.C. 411 (1979), affirmed by 9th Cir. without opinion, 647 F.2d 170 (9th Cir. 1981). And see Posker, "Activity, Profit and Section 183," 56 Taxes 155 (1978).

and taxes.[8] The remainder of the total deductions allowed are deductions that would be fully allowed if the activity were engaged in for profit, but only to the extent that gross income from the activity exceeds the preferred deductions just indicated.[9]

D. RESTRICTIONS ON DEDUCTIONS OF HOMES

Internal Revenue Code: Sections 280A(a), (b), (c)(1) and (5), (d)(1), (e), (f) and (g).

Proposed Regulations: See Section 1.280A

Prior to 1976 the rules of Section 183, discussed above, were applicable in determining the extent of deductibility of expenses incurred in connection with the then-popular tax shelter device of vacation or second homes.[1] In 1976 Congress became concerned with the overall aspects of the deductibility of items related to a home used by a taxpayer both for business or investment and for residential purposes. In the Tax Reform Act of 1976 Congress responded to that concern by enacting Section 280A which provides specific rules limiting deductions on homes.[2] The rules of Section 280A and Section 183[3] apply to the same taxpayers and both sections impose similar limitations on deductions.[4] However, Section 280A applies in circumstances different from those to which Section 183 applies. With respect to vacation or second homes the Commissioner may assert the rules of Section 183 to limit deductions for those taxable years to which the limitations of Section 280A do not apply.[5]

Section 280A identifies three sets of circumstances relating to the deductibility of expenses connected primarily with vacation homes. First, Section 280A(g) provides that if the taxpayer's residence is rented for less than 15 days during the taxable year, no deductions attributable to the rental activity are allowed, *but* neither is income derived from such rental included in the taxpayer's gross income.[6]

Second, if the vacation home is rented for more than 14 days during the taxable year and the home is *not* used for personal pur-

---

8. I.R.C. § 183(b)(1). See Reg. § 1.183–1(d)(3) Example (ii) and Chapter 16, supra.

9. I.R.C. § 183(b)(2). Within this category of deductions the regulations give priority to deductions which do not reduce the basis of property. See Reg. § 1.183–1(b)(1) (ii) and (iii).

1. See Reg. § 1.183–1(d)(3) and Rev.Rul. 73–219, 1973–1 C.B. 134.

2. Kaplan, "Deductions for 'Vacation Homes' Under the Tax Reform Act of 1976," 63 A.B.A.J. 1302 (1977).

3. I.R.C. § 280A(a) and Reg. § 1.183–1(a).

4. See the discussion at notes 11 through 14, infra, and at notes 8 and 9, at page 497, supra.

5. I.R.C. § 280A(f)(3). See the discussion at notes 9 and 10, infra.

6. Deductions otherwise allowable for the home without respect to whether or not the home is rented out, such as property taxes and mortgage interest, are fully deductible. See I.R.C. § 280A(g)(1) and (b). See Rev.Rul. 80–55, 1980–1 C.B. 65. However, rental to a relative at fair market value for relative's use as a principal residence is not considered personal use by the taxpayer. § 280A(d)(3)(A). In addition, any day spent by the taxpayer substantially on repair and maintenance will not be considered a day of personal use. § 280A(d)(2), last sentence.

poses [7] *in excess* of the greater of 14 days or 10 percent of the actual rental period, the principal limitations of Section 280A do not apply.[8] Instead Section 183 determines deductibility. If, under Section 183, it is determined that rental of the vacation home is engaged in for profit, either by meeting the Section 183(d) presumption or by qualifying the activity as one objectively entered into with a profit-making goal, all *allocable* [9] expenses incurred in renting the home plus all expenses otherwise deductible (interest, property taxes) can be deducted. If, however, it is determined that the activity is not engaged in for profit, the limitations of Section 183 apply, and the taxpayer can take deductions only to the extent of gross income from the home.[10]

Finally if the vacation home is rented for more than 14 days during the taxable year and the home is used for personal purposes *in excess* of the greater of 14 days or 10 percent of the actual rental time, the limitations on deduction imposed by Section 280A(c)(5) apply. Section 280A(c)(5) limits deductions attributable to the rental activity to the amount by which gross income derived from the rental of the vacation home exceeds deductions that are allowable without respect to the rental of the home. These limitations are similar to the Section 183(b) limitations.[11]

This computation is trickier than first appears. It begins with the net rental income derived from the activity. Interest and taxes allocable to rental use of the property are deducted from that income. As interest and taxes are deemed to accrue daily throughout the year, the allocation is based on the *portion of the year* the property is rented.[12] Section 280A(c)(5) provides that the remaining deductions (for (1) maintenance and utilities and (2) depreciation, in that order [13]) allocable to rental use are limited to the difference between the rental income and allocable interest and taxes. A different fraction based on *proportionate business, non business actual use* of the property is computed to

---

7. Under I.R.C. § 280A(d)(2) a vacation home is considered to have been used for personal purposes if, for any part of a day, the home is used for personal purposes by the taxpayer, certain of his relatives, other persons owning an interest in the home, or any other individual using the home who has either not paid fair rental or used the home under the reciprocal use arrangement with the taxpayer.

8. The expense allocation limitation of I.R.C. § 280A(e) is, however, still applicable. See note 14, infra. The parenthetical language of § 280A(e)(1), "whether or not [the taxpayer] is treated under [§ 280A] as using such unit as a residence," indicates that the § 280A(e) limitation on deductions based on allocation of expenses continues to apply where the provisions of I.R.C. § 183, rather than § 280A, are controlling.

9. See I.R.C. § 280A(e) and note 8, supra.

10. See I.R.C. § 183(b) and notes 11 through 14, infra and see especially note 17, infra.

11. See the discussion at notes 8 and 9 at page 497, supra.

12. Bolton v. Commissioner, 694 F.2d 556 (9th Cir.1982); McKinney v. Commissioner, 732 F.2d 414 (10th Cir.1983). Compare the deductibility of these items under I.R.C. § 183. See Reg. § 1.183–1(d)(3) Example (ii).

13. I.R.C. § 183 would allow the deductions which do not result in a basis reduction (utility and maintenance expenses) to be taken before deductions requiring a basis reduction (depreciation). The same rule applies under § 280A. See Prop.Reg. § 1.280A–2(h), (i)(5) and Rev.Rul. 80–55, supra note 7.

determine what portion of those remaining deductions are allocable to rental use.[14]

The above rules are illustrated in the following example. Assume Taxpayer owns a vacation home that he rents for 60 days and personally uses for 30 days in a taxable year. Gross rental income from the vacation home is $5400. Taxpayer pays real estate taxes and mortgage interest on the home totaling $3600, and incurs other expenses related to the home (utility and maintenance expenses of $1500 and depreciation of $6300) totaling $7800 for the year. Taxpayer does *not* meet the minimal personal use requirements of Section 280A(d), because (1) the home was rented for more than 14 days during the taxable year (see Section 280A(g)) and (2) during the year the home is used for personal purposes in excess of the greater of 14 days or 10 percent of the actual rental time. Taxpayer's deductions (other than expenses deductible without regard to the rental activity) are limited by gross rental income as follows:

(1) Gross rental income $5400

(2) Less allocable portion of Interest and Taxes, $60/365$ of $3600 (*rounded off*) $ 600

(3) Section 280A(c)(5) limit on deductible rental income expenses other than Interest and Taxes $4800

(4) Allocable portion under Section 280A(e) of rental expenses other than depreciation,[15] $60/90$ of $1500 $1000

(5) Maximum depreciation deduction $3800

(6) Allocable portion under Section 280A(e) of depreciation deduction, $60/90$ of $6300 = $4200, but limited by Section 280A(c)(5) to $3800

Taxpayer can deduct only $4800 of his $5200 ($1000 plus $4200) of expenses allocable and related to the rental of his home,[16] but can deduct all $3600 of his interest and property tax expenses, because such expenses are deductible without regard to rental use.[17]

---

14. See I.R.C. § 280A(e) under which expenses allocable to rental use are limited to the amount which bears the same ratio to such expenses as the number of days during each year that the vacation home is actually rented out at a fair rental bears to the total number of days during the taxable year that the home is used for *all* purposes. Merely holding the property out for rental does not constitute actual rental. Personal use of the home for even one day requires that expenses be allocated under § 280A, although see the rule at note 6, supra.

15. See note 13, supra.

16. See (4) and (6) above.

17. I.R.C. § 280A(b). See Chapter 16, supra. If, instead, the taxpayer had used the home for personal purposes for only 10 days, the minimal personal use require-

ments of I.R.C. § 280A(d) would be met and § 183, rather than § 280A, would apply to potentially limit deductions. Assuming that the rental of the home is determined to be an activity *not* engaged in for profit under § 183, the taxpayer's allowable deduction will be determined as follows:

(1) Gross rental income $5400

(2) Less Interest and Taxes (see Reg. § 1.183–1(d) Example (ii)) $3600

(3) § 183(b) limit on deductible rental expenses other than Interest and Taxes $1800

(4) Allocable portion under § 280A(e) of rental expenses other than depreciation ($60/70$ of $1500 (see note 13, supra) $1286

Section 280A(d) is not limited to vacation homes and its restrictions can be applied to one's principal residence as well. Congress, not wishing to limit deductibility for a year when one's principal residence is legitimately converted to rental property, eased the restrictions on a principal residence by the addition in 1978 of Section 280A(d)(4). That section permits a disregard of personal use of one's principal residence in applying the Section 280A(d)(1) limitations if the personal use of the principal residence precedes or follows a "qualified rental period" as defined in Section 280A(d)(4)(B). In general, unless the period is shortened by a sale, a "qualified rental period" means rental of the property for twelve consecutive months to unrelated persons or a holding of the property for rental purposes for a like period. In both instances, the rental must be "fair."

As stated above, in 1976 Congress was concerned with deductible expenses related to all residences, not only vacation homes. One area of special concern was commonly referred to as the "office in home" situation, where taxpayers would attempt to deduct a portion of the expenses of operating their residences (owned or rented) as business expenses when they conducted business or business related activities in their homes. Case law was mixed as to both the tests for and the amount of deductibility.[18] Congress responded with a portion of Section 280A which provides both certainty and restrictions for deductibility of such expenses.[19] Section 280A(a) generally denies a taxpayer deductions for expenses attributable to the use of his home for business purposes,[20] but makes exception for the extent such deductions are attributable to a portion of the home [21] used *exclusively* and on a *regular basis:* (1) As the principal place of business for any trade or business of the taxpayer; [22] (2) as a place of business which is used by patients, clients, or customers in meeting or dealing with the taxpayer in the normal course of business,[23] or (3) as a separate structure not

(5) Maximum depreciation deduction	$ 514
(6) Allocable portion under § 280A(e) of depreciation deduction ($^{60}/_{70}$ of $6300) is $5400 but limited by § 183 to	$ 514

Under § 183, taxpayer can deduct only $1800 of his $6686 of expenses related to the rental of his home, subject to the rule in note 8 at page 497, supra.

18. E.g., Stephen E. Bodzin, 60 T.C. 820 (1973), reversed 509 F.2d 679 (4th Cir. 1975), and Paul J. O'Connell, 31 T.C.M. 837 (1972), cert. denied 423 U.S. 825, 96 S.Ct. 40 (1975), considering the propriety of and tests for deductibility. See also Alice Pauline Browne, 73 T.C. 723 (1980); Edwin R. Curphey, 73 T.C. 766 (1980), and Gino v. Commissioner, 538 F.2d 833 (9th Cir.1976), cert. denied 429 U.S. 979, 97 S.Ct. 490 (1976), considering possible amounts of the deduction.

19. See, de Guardiola, "Home Office Deductions Under the New Section 280A of the Internal Revenue Code," 6 F.S.U.L.Rev. 129 (1978).

20. Again note that I.R.C. § 280A(b) expressly excepts from limitation deductions allowable to the taxpayer without regard to their connection with his trade or business or income-producing activity, such as interest, state and local taxes, and casualty losses. See Chapter 16, supra.

21. A portion of a room even though not physically separated may qualify. Weightman v. Commissioner, 42 T.C.M. 104 (1981).

22. I.R.C. § 280A(c)(1)(A). See notes 27–33, infra.

23. I.R.C. § 280A(c)(1)(B). See Green v. Commissioner, 707 F.2d 404 (9th Cir.1983); Cousino v. Commissioner, 679 F.2d 604 (6th Cir.1982); Max Frankel, 82 T.C. 318 (1984).

attached to the dwelling unit used in connection with the taxpayer's trade or business.[24] In the case of an employee, the business use must be "for the convenience of his employer" if a deduction is to be allowed,[25] and the requirements cannot be circumvented by rental of the home or a portion of the home to one's employer.[26]

Much of the current litigation involving the "office in home" deduction involves the interpretation of the "principal place of business" test.[27] If a taxpayer is involved in more than one trade or business, one business may satisfy the test.[28] In interpreting the principal place of business test, the Tax Court originally applied a "focal point" test of taxpayer's activities, looking to the place where goods and services are provided to customers and revenues are generated.[29] After being reversed by two circuits,[30] the Tax Court has broadened its original test to apply a more nebulous facts and circumstances test [31] under which it looks at such factors as whether the home office is essential to the business, whether the taxpayer spends substantial time in the home office, and whether another location is available to perform the functions of the business.[32] The Service disagrees with the Tax Court's action, in part because the Service feels it is contrary to legislative intent and leads to an unclear standard.[33] Further litigation can be anticipated on the principal place of business issue.

---

24. I.R.C. § 280A(c)(1)(C). Heineman v. Commissioner, 82 T.C. 538 (1984). Where the dwelling unit is the sole fixed location of the taxpayer's trade or business consisting of selling products at wholesale or retail, and the taxpayer regularly uses a separate identifiable portion of his residence for inventory storage, § 280A(c)(2) excepts such activity from the exclusive use test. Further, the exclusive use test does not apply where the taxpayer uses his residence to provide qualified day care services. See § 280A(c)(4).

25. See I.R.C. § 280A(c)(1). The "convenience of the employer" test supersedes the "appropriate and helpful" test previously followed by some courts in this area. See note 18, supra.

26. I.R.C. § 280A(c)(6). Cf. Ira S. Feldman, 84 T.C. 1 (1985).

27. I.R.C. § 280A(c)(1)(A).

28. Curphey v. Commissioner, supra note 18. In Curphey, taxpayer had rental activities which constituted a business and which were carried on in addition to his other business of being a dermatologist. Regular use of a room in his residence exclusively as an office in connection with the rental activities fell within the subsection. If, however, a room is used for two businesses, one of which is taxpayer's principal place of business, but the other fails to satisfy the principal place of business test, a deduction is denied under the exclusivity test of I.R.C. § 280A(c)(1). Hamacher v. Commissioner, 94 T.C. 348 (1990).

29. Rudolph Baie, 74 T.C. 105 (1980); Ernest Drucker, 79 T.C. 605 (1982), reversed 715 F.2d 67 (2d Cir.1983); David J. Weissman, 47 T.C.M. 520 (1983), reversed 751 F.2d 512 (2d Cir.1984); John Meiers, 49 T.C.M. 136 (1984), reversed 782 F.2d 75 (7th Cir.1986).

30. See note 29, supra.

31. Soliman v. Commissioner, 94 T.C. 20 (1990), allowing an office-in-home deduction for an anesthesiologist who performed all administrative duties of his medical practice in a home office, while all revenues from the business were generated at various hospitals. See also Hamacher v. Commissioner, note 28, supra, Leroy K. Kahaku, 58 T.C.M. 1247 (1990), and Shore v. Commissioner, 59 T.C.M. 762 (1990) (all applying the *Soliman* test). See Pusker, "Home Office Deductions: Some Good News," 18 J.Real Est.Tax. 24 (1990); Zimmerman, "Abandonment of the Focal Point Test For Office-in-Home Deductions," 68 Taxes 434 (1990).

32. Id. See also Prop.Reg. § 1.280A-2(b)(3).

33. I.R.C. News Release, IR 90-55 (Mar. 27, 1990).

In addition to the "allocable portion" limitation on deductions under Section 280A, Section 280A(c)(5) further limits deductions attributable to the home office to the amount by which gross income from that use exceeds: (i) deductions allowed without respect to the home office (e.g., interest and taxes); and (ii) all other expenses attributable to the business activity but not allocable to the use of the home (e.g., expenditures for supplies and compensation paid to other persons).[34] Any home office deduction disallowed solely because of the income limitation may be carried forward to subsequent taxable years.[35]

PROBLEMS

1. T owns a two bedroom vacation home that he rents for 90 days and uses for personal purposes for 30 days during the taxable year. T receives gross rental income from the home of $3,000, pays property taxes and mortgage interest totalling $2,000, and incurs other expenses (including $2,000 of depreciation) of $3,600. Assume that the intrest is "qualified residence interest as defined in § 163(h)(3).

    (a) Will T's deductions be limited by §§ 183 or 280A?

    (b) What amount of expenses, other than property taxes and mortgage interest, may T deduct?

    (c) May T deduct all of his property taxes and mortgage interest? Why or why not?

    (d) Same facts, figures, and questions as in parts (a) through (c), above, except that T rents the home for only three weeks and vacations in it with his family for one week.

2. Taxpayer operates a consulting business out of his home. He uses an office in his home, exclusively and on a regular basis, as the principal place of business for his consulting business. Taxpayer has $2,000 gross income from his consulting business. He has business deductions of $1,600 for supplies and secretary expenses. Mortgage interest and real estate taxes allocable to his office total $400. Utilities and depreciation allocable to his office are $200 and $150, respectively.

How much of the utility expense and depreciation is deductible?

3. For a number of years Widow has rented three rooms in her large residence to three law students. Are her deductions related to the rooms (depreciation, utilities, repairs, interests and taxes) limited by § 280A? See Prop. Reg. § 1.280A–1(c).

4. T, a self-employed surgeon, generates all of his income by performing operations at several hospitals throughout the city. He maintains an office in his home where he keeps all patient records,

---

34. I.R.C. § 280A(c)(5). See especially I.R.C. § 280A(c)(5)(B)(ii) reversing the result reached in Charles A. Scott, 84 T.C. 683 (1985).

35. I.R.C. § 280A(c)(5), flush language. Such carryforward shall be allowable only to the income from the business in which it arose, whether or not the dwelling unit is used as a residence during such year. I.R.C. § 280A(c)(5), last sentence.

billing records, and correspondence with the hospital. T spends approximately 30 hours each week performing surgery at the various hospitals and 10 hours per week in his home office performing the administrative duties of his medical practice. He is not provided any space at any of the hospitals for his administrative duties. Is T entitled to a deduction for expenses incurred in connection with his home office?

E. PASSIVE ACTIVITY LIMITATIONS

Internal Revenue Code: Section 469.

Regulations: Sections 1.469–4T(a),–5T(a), (b)(2)(ii), (iii), (c), (d).

———

Introduction. The Tax Reform Act of 1986 added Code Section 469 which, for certain taxpayers, disallows the deduction of passive activity losses and the usage of passive activity credits.[1] Passive activity losses are the excess of losses from all passive activities over the income from such activities during a taxable year; and passive activity credits are the excess of credits from all passive activities over the tax liability for the year attributable to such activities.[2] The disallowed losses and credits are sometimes only postponed, not totally disallowed, because the loss deductions and credits disallowed by this limitation are carried forward and treated as losses and credits from passive activities in succeeding years.[3] Further, any disallowed *losses* (but not credits) are fully deductible when a taxpayer sells his interest in the passive activity.[4] Thus Section 469 is perhaps more appropriately described as a postponement provision than a disallowance provision.

In this Chapter we've seen Congress generally allow some deductions only with its fingers crossed, and restrict or disallow those very deductions in specific situations where it feels they are not warranted. Such piecemeal disallowances in specific situations usually seem justified. With the enactment of Section 469 Congress has taken a much broader step. The central congressional notion is that losses are not all birds of a feather; i.e., passive activity losses are second class citizens. The blacksmith's loss, which followed the efforts that raised the "honest sweat" on his brow, is seen by Congress as nicer (more worthy of deduction treatment) than the losses of a mere investor who does not work up the same sweat. But, as is so often the case, the ability to differentiate in a statutory setting between that which is nice and that which is vulgar is difficult. Wonder a little, also, whether this is one of the relatively rare instances of congressional moralizing creeping into the Code. At the same time consider whether the congressional action, which in effect involves the timing of losses (and generally credits), is justified.[5]

1. I.R.C. § 469(a)(1). Credits are discussed generally at Chapter 16A, supra and specifically at Chapter 27B, infra.

2. I.R.C. § 469(d).

3. I.R.C. § 469(b).

4. I.R.C. § 469(g)(1).

5. See Oberst, "The Passive Activity Provisions—A Tax Policy Blooper," 40 U.Fla.L.Rev. 641 (1988); Peroni, "A Policy

Taxpayers Subject to the Limitations. The passive activity rules apply to individuals, estates and trusts,[6] closely-held C corporations,[7] and personal service corporations.[8] Closely held C corporations are defined as corporations more than 50 percent of the value of whose stock is owned directly or indirectly [9] at any time during the last half of the taxable year by five or fewer individuals.[10] A personal service corporation is one whose principal activity is to offer personal services performed substantially by employee-owners.[11] Employee-owners are defined as employees who on any day during the taxable year were owners of any of the outstanding stock of the corporation.[12] A de minimis rule within the definition of "personal service corporation" excludes a corporation if only ten percent or less of the value of its stock is held by employee-owners.[13]

Although conduit-entities partnerships and S corporations, are not subject to the passive activity rules, the partners and shareholders of these entities who are individuals, estates, trusts, closely-held C corporations, and personal service corporations are governed by Section 469 with respect to any passive activity losses passed through to them.[14]

Definition of an "Activity". A passive activity is any business or profit seeking activity in which the taxpayer-owner does not materially participate.[15] An important feature of the passive loss rules (which is not specifically addressed in the statute) is the determination of what constitutes an "activity". Identifying an activity is important for several reasons. If two undertakings are merely parts of a single activity, the taxpayer need establish material participation only with respect to the overall activity to avoid passive classification.[16] If, however, they are separate activities, the taxpayer must establish material participation separately for each.[17] Another reason every activity must be identified is because, at the time of the sale of an activity, prior disallowed losses generated from that activity become currently deductible.[18] A narrow definition of an activity, if accepted, increases a taxpayer's flexibility in realizing suspended passive losses

Critique of the Section 469 Passive Loss Rules," 62 So.Cal.L.Rev. 1 (1988).

6. I.R.C. § 469(a)(2)(A).

7. I.R.C. § 469(a)(2)(B).

8. I.R.C. § 469(a)(2)(C).

9. The attribution of ownership rules of I.R.C. § 544 are applicable in determining stock ownership. See I.R.C. §§ 469(j)(1), 465(a)(1)(B), 542(a)(2) and 544(a); but see some limitations in the attribution rules provided in § 465(a)(3).

10. I.R.C. § 469 relies on the § 465 definition of a closely held corporation. I.R.C. §§ 469(j)(1), 465(a)(1)(B) and 542(a)(2).

11. I.R.C. §§ 469(j)(2) and 269A(b)(1).

12. I.R.C. §§ 469(j)(2)(A) and 269A(b)(2). The attribution of ownership rules of § 318 are applicable in determining stock owner-

ship except that "any" is substituted for "50 percent or more in value" in § 318(a)(2)(C). See I.R.C. § 469(j)(2)(B).

13. I.R.C. § 469(j)(2).

14. Cf. Reg. § 1.469–2T(e).

15. I.R.C. § 469(c)(1). See also I.R.C. § 469(c)(6) which provides that the term "trade or business" includes any activity in connection with a trade or business or any activity conducted for profit for which deductions are allowable under § 212.

16. Sen.Rep. No. 99–313, 99th Cong., 2d Sess. 738–739 (1986).

17. Id.

18. I.R.C. § 469(g)(1)(A). See page 511, infra, regarding the tax consequences from the disposition of an entire interest in a passive activity.

through dispositions of interests. However, a broad definition allows a taxpayer to combine undertakings that are actually separate to use material participation in one as a basis for currently claiming losses and credits from another.[19] To summarize with a mixed metaphor, this is another example of the commissioner/taxpayer polka where they change positions depending upon who is playing goose and who gander.

Section 469 authorizes the promulgation of regulations to specify what constitutes an activity; the legislative history also provides some guidance.[20] It indicates an activity consists of undertakings that are "an integrated and interrelated economic unit, conducted in coordination with or in reliance upon each other, and constituting an appropriate unit for the measurement of gain or loss."[21] It also states that what constitutes a separate activity is a determination to be made in a realistic economic sense considering all of the facts and circumstances, a phrase that grows more and more shop-worn.[22] The Service has promulgated temporary regulations which generally define the term "activity" in a broad sense[23] and use a building block approach. They begin with the concept of an "undertaking"[24] which is defined as business or rental operations[25] that are conducted at the same location and are owned by the same person.[26] An undertaking is the smallest unit that can constitute an activity.[27] The regulations then provide a series of rules under which undertakings are sometimes required to be aggregated[28] and at other times may be electively aggregated.[29] In addition, in some circumstances the building blocks can be dismantled under rules allowing an elective disaggregation of an activity.[30]

19. Sen.Rep. No. 99–313, supra note 16 at 739.

20. I.R.C. § 469(*l*)(1). Sen.Rep. No. 99–313, supra note 16 at 739.

21. Id.

22. Id.

23. Reg. § 1.469–4T. See Cuff, "Defining 'Activity' Under the Passive Loss Temp. Regs.," 71 J. Tax. 68 (1989); Evaul and Wallace, "Passive Activity Losses: Definition of Activity," 44 Tax Notes No. 11, 1257 (1989).

24. Reg. § 1.469–4T(a)(3).

25. The term business is broadly defined to include professional service activities and oil and gas operations. Cf. Reg. § 1.469–4T(a)(3)(v), (a)(4)(ii)(A), and (a)(4)(iii). However the regulations provide special aggregation rules for professional service undertakings (Reg. § 1.469–4T(a)(4)(iii) and (h)) and for oil and gas operations (Reg. § 1.469–4T(a)(3)(v) and (e)). See note 28, infra.

26. Reg. § 1.469–4T(a)(3)(ii). Generally, business or rental operations that constitute a separate source of income production are treated as a single undertaking

that is separate from other undertakings. Reg. § 1.469–4T(e)(1).

27. Reg. § 1.469–4T(a)(3)(i).

28. Reg. § 1.469–4T(a)(4)(i). See Reg. § 1.469–4T(f)–(m). For example, trade or business undertakings (other than oil and gas undertakings and professional service undertakings, see note 25, supra) generally must be aggregated if they are similar or integrated undertakings which are commonly controlled. Reg. § 1.469–4T(a)(4)(ii) (B), (C). A similar undertaking is one where the predominant operations of the undertakings are in the same line of business. Reg. § 1.469–4T(f)(4)(i). See Rev. Proc. 89–38, 1989–1 C.B. 920, 921 describing 79 different but fairly broad lines of business, one of which is, for example, communications. An integrated undertaking is defined in Reg. § 1.469–4T(g). Common control is defined in Reg. § 1.469–4T(j).

29. For example, rules for aggregating rental real estate are generally elective. Reg. § 1.469–4T(a)(4)(iv), (k)(2).

30. Nonrental undertakings may in some circumstances be treated as separate activities. Reg. § 1.469–4T(a)(4)(v) and (o). Generally, the election may be made either

Definition of a "Passive" Activity. As stated above, a passive activity is any activity that involves the conduct of a trade or business or a transaction entered into for profit in which the taxpayer does not materially participate.[31] In general, an interest in a limited partnership (other than as a general partner) is inherently passive, regardless of the taxpayer's actual level of participation,[32] as is a mere rental activity.[33] However, passive activity does not include a working interest in an oil or gas property owned (directly or indirectly) through entities that do not limit the taxpayer's liability.[34]

A taxpayer materially participates in an activity only if he is involved on a regular, continuous, and substantial basis in the operations of the activity.[35] Determination whether a taxpayer materially participates in the operations of an activity requires a look at the whole picture.[36] A taxpayer is most likely to be viewed as having materially participated in the operations of an activity if the activity is the taxpayer's principal business.[37] A taxpayer who is regularly present at the place where the principal operations of the activity are conducted is likely to be considered a material participant.[38] But one who has little or no knowledge or experience regarding the business activity is likely to be hard pressed to prove his material participation.[39]

Management functions generally are not treated differently from other services or the performance of physical work with respect to the activity.[40] A merely formal and nominal participation in management, not actually involving the exercise of independent discretion and judgment does not constitute material participation.[41] Nor does an active but only intermittent role in management conclusively establish material participation.[42] In addition, activities of one's agents are not attributed to a taxpayer in establishing material participation.[43] Finally, providing legal, tax or accounting services to a business as an independent contractor does not constitute material participation in that business.[44]

The Service has promulgated temporary regulations which provide a substantially mechanical set of rules to determine whether the

in the first year of operations of the undertaking or August 9, 1989, whichever is later. Reg. § 1.469–4T(o)(4).

31. I.R.C. § 469(c)(1). See note 15, supra.

32. I.R.C. § 469(h)(2). But see Reg. § 1.469–5T(e)(2) providing situations in which a limited partner is treated as materially participating. See also Reg. § 1.469–5T(e)(3)(ii).

33. I.R.C. § 469(c)(2). Cf. I.R.C. § 469(c)(4). See that text at note 60, infra.

34. I.R.C. § 469(c)(3).

35. I.R.C. § 469(h)(1).

36. Sen.Rep. No. 99–313, supra note 16 at 732.

37. Id. at 732–733. However this is not conclusive in and of itself. Id.

38. Id. at 733.

39. Id. at 734.

40. Id. But see Reg. § 1.469–5T(b)(2)(ii).

41. Id.

42. Id.

43. Id. at 735. But see I.R.C. § 469(h)(5) where a spouse's participation is given recognition.

44. Sen.Rep. No. 99–313, supra note 16 at 735.

material participation test is satisfied by individuals.[45] The regulations provide seven situations in which the test may be satisfied.[46] An individual materially participates in an activity if she participates [47] in the activity for more than 500 hours during the year,[48] if her participation constitutes substantially all of the participation in such activity of all individuals (including non-owners) during the year,[49] if her participation involves more than 100 hours during the year and is not less than the participation of any other individual (again including non-owners),[50] or if her aggregate participation in "significant participation activities" (those in which an individual participates for more than 100 hours but does not materially participate) [51] exceeds 500 hours for the year.[52] There are two situations in which material participation of prior years constitutes material participation in the current year.[53] The final situation provided by the regulations returns to the non-mechanical statutory test of whether the taxpayer participates in the activity on a regular, continuous, and substantial basis during the year.[54] However, for purposes of applying this final test, there is no material participation unless the taxpayer participates in the activity for more than 100 hours during the year,[55] and under certain circumstances, management services do not count toward hours of participation.[56]

Special rules determine whether an entity is materially participating in an activity. A closely held C corporation or a personal service corporation is treated as materially participating in an activity if one or more shareholders holding more than 50 percent of the value of outstanding stock of the corporation materially participate in the activity.[57] A closely held C corporation (other than a personal service corporation) is also treated as qualifying in some other circumstances.[58]

---

45. Reg. § 1.469–5T.

46. Reg. § 1.469–5T(a).

47. Reg. § 1.469–5T(f).

48. Reg. § 1.469–5T(a)(1).

49. Reg. § 1.469–5T(a)(2).

50. Reg. § 1.469–5T(a)(3).

51. Reg. § 1.469–5T(c).

52. Reg. § 1.469–5T(a)(4).

53. If the individual materially participated in the activity for any 5 years (not necessarily consecutive) during the immediately preceding 10 years or if the activity is a personal service activity (one in which capital is not a material income-producing factor) and the individual materially participated in the activity for any 3 prior years (not necessarily consecutive and not restricted to any particular time period), the material participation test is met. Reg. § 1.469–5T(a)(5) and (6).

54. Reg. § 1.469–5T(a)(7). See I.R.C. § 469(h)(1).

55. Reg. § 1.469–5T(b)(2)(iii).

56. Reg. § 1.469–5T(b)(2)(ii).

57. I.R.C. § 469(h)(4)(A).

58. I.R.C. § 469(h)(4)(B). Note the word "only" in § 469(h)(4), flush language. I.R.C. § 469(h)(4)(B) treats a closely held C corporation as materially participating if the requirements of I.R.C. § 465(c)(7)(C) (determined without regard to clause (iv)) are satisfied. The applicable requirements of § 465(c)(7)(C) are as follows:

(1) During the entire twelve-month period ending on the last day of the taxable year, such corporation had at least one full-time employee substantially all of whose services were in the active management of such business;

(2) During the entire twelve-month period ending on the last day of the taxable year, such corporation had at least three full-time, nonowner employees substantially all of whose services were directly related to such business; and

An estate or a trust is treated as materially participating in an activity if an executor or other fiduciary, in his capacity as such, materially participates in the activity.[59]

Rental activity is passive, even if a taxpayer materially participates in the activity.[60] Rental activity is that in which payments are made principally for the use of tangible property.[61] However, if substantial services are rendered in an activity that also involves payment for the use of property (e.g. the innkeeper versus the landlord), then the activity will not constitute a "rental activity" within the passive loss rules and the material participation test again becomes relevant.[62]

Passive Activity Losses and Credits. A net amount of income or loss is computed for the taxable year with respect to each passive activity. Then all such income and losses are combined. The limitation applies to the extent that losses from all passive activities exceed income from such activities for the year, or that credits from such activities exceed tax liability for the year attributable to such activities.[63]

In determining income or loss from a passive activity, portfolio income of the activity is excluded.[64] Portfolio income includes interest, dividends,[65] annuities and royalties not derived from ordinary trade or business.[66] Also included in portfolio income are gains and losses not derived in the ordinary course of a trade or business from the disposition of property that produces such interest, dividends, annuities and royalties and from the disposition of property that is held for investment,[67] even if it is not productive of current income. Portfolio income arising from an investment of working capital is treated the same as any other portfolio income.[68] Any gain or loss from the sale of an interest in a passive activity is deemed not to be part of portfolio income or loss.[69] The reason for expressly excluding portfolio income from passive income is that portfolio investments ordinarily give rise to income that could be sheltered by "vulgar" losses.[70] The legislative history states that "to permit portfolio income to be offset by passive

(3) The amount of the deductions attributable to such business which are allowable to the taxpayer solely by reason of I.R.C. §§ 162 and 404 for the taxable year exceeds 15% of the gross income from such business for such year.

59. Sen.Rep. No. 99–313, supra note 16 at 735.

60. I.R.C. § 469(c)(2), (4). See Reg. § 1.469–1T(e)(3).

61. I.R.C. § 469(j)(8).

62. Conf.Rep. No. 99–841, 99th Cong., 2d Sess. II–148 (1986). See Reg. § 1.469–1T(e)(3)(ii)(C) and (D), (v) and (vi).

63. I.R.C. § 469(a)(1) and (d).

64. I.R.C. § 469(e)(1).

65. Dividends included in portfolio income are net of the dividends received deduction under I.R.C. §§ 243, 244, and 245. I.R.C. § 469 (e)(4).

66. I.R.C. § 469(e)(1)(A)(i)(I).

67. I.R.C. § 469(e)(1)(A)(ii). Portfolio income is reduced by expenses, other than interest, which are clearly and directly allocable to portfolio income and interest expense properly allocable to portfolio income. I.R.C. § 469(e)(1)(A)(i)(II) and (III). The Treasury has issued regulations that provide the standards for allocating expenses and interest. Reg. §§ 1.163–8T, 1.469–2T(d)(4).

68. I.R.C. § 469(e)(1)(B).

69. I.R.C. § 469(e)(1)(A).

70. Sen.Rep. No. 99–313, supra note 16 at 728.

losses would create the inequitable result of restricting sheltering by individuals dependent for support on wages or active business income, while permitting sheltering by those whose income is derived from an investment portfolio."[71] A number of other special rules affect the computation of income or loss from a passive activity.[72]

Credits from passive activities [73] are also subject to limitations under Section 469. Such credits may reduce tax liability in a year only to the extent that there is net income and tax liability from all of the taxpayer's passive activities for the year.[74] Thus, if there is a net loss from all passive activities (and the loss limitations above apply), there is no tax generated and no credits are allowed. In a year when there is net income from all passive activities the amount of tax liability allocable to those activities equals the difference between (1) the tax liability for all income and (2) the tax liability for all income excluding passive activity income.[75] After it is determined that a credit is allowed under the passive loss rules, it still may be limited by other provisions of the Code.[76] However, once a credit is allowed under the passive loss rules, it is treated as an active credit arising in that year.[77]

Exceptions to Disallowance. The general rule of Section 469 provides a blanket disallowance of excess losses and credits for the current year. But seemingly for every rule in the Code there are exceptions. This is so here where there are two exceptions to the blanket disallowance of excess losses and credits.[78] The two special rules involve active participation in rental real estate and closely held corporations.

Active Participation in Rental Real Estate. For individuals, other than those with very large income, there is a limited exception to the general disallowance rule.[79] Up to $25,000 of losses and the "deduction equivalent" of passive activity credits [80] attributable to rental real

---

71. Id.

72. Earned income is not taken into account in computing income or loss from a passive activity. I.R.C. § 469(e)(3). See I.R.C. § 911(d)(2)(A) defining earned income.

Deductibility of qualified residence interest is not limited by the passive activity rules. I.R.C. § 469(j)(7). Qualified residence interest is defined in I.R.C. § 163(h)(3) and, subject to some limitations, means interest paid on indebtedness secured by taxpayer's principal or a second residence.

73. I.R.C. § 469(d)(2)(A). These credits are set forth in I.R.C. §§ 27(b), 28, 29, and 38 (which encompasses several other credits).

74. I.R.C. § 469(a)(1)(B), (d)(2).

75. Sen.Rep. No. 99–313, supra note 16 at 723–724.

76. Id at 724. For example, see I.R.C. § 38(c), which generally provides that cred-

its cannot offset more than $25,000 tax liability plus 75% of the tax liability for the year in excess of $25,000.

77. Conf.Rep. No. 99–841, supra note 62 at II–143.

78. Prior to 1991, there was a third exception under a pre-enactment phase-in rule. I.R.C. § 469(m). Deductions and credits attributable to a passive activity interest acquired before the enactment of I.R.C. § 469 (October 22, 1986) were deductible in part under a declining percentage applicable from 1987 to 1990. Such interests no longer receive any such preferential treatment.

79. I.R.C. § 469(i)(1). But see I.R.C. § 469(i)(4).

80. The deduction equivalent of passive activity credits is the amount which, if allowed as a deduction, would reduce regular tax liability by an amount equal to such credits. I.R.C. § 469(j)(5). The legislative history says that in utilizing the

estate activities can be offset against income from nonpassive activities if the taxpayer "*actively participates*" in the rental activity both in the year the deduction or credit arose and the year the deduction or credit is taken [81] *and* if he owns at least 10 percent of all interests in the activity.[82]

The active participation requirement is not as stringent as the material participation rule.[83] It can be satisfied without regular, continuous and substantial involvement in operations if the taxpayer participates in the making of significant management decisions.[84] Significant management decisions include approving new tenants, deciding on rental terms, approving capital or repair expenditures, and other similar determinations.[85] Thus, for example, a taxpayer who owns and rents to others an apartment that formerly was his primary residence, or which he uses as a part-time vacation home, may be treated as actively participating even if he hires a rental agent and others provide services such as repairs. As long as the taxpayer participates in the manner described above, a lack of participation in operations does not lead to the denial of allowances.[86] However, unless regulations provide otherwise, a taxpayer who is a limited partner is conclusively presumed to be passive with respect to a rental activity of the partnership, regardless of his actual level of participation in the activity.[87] In determining whether a taxpayer actively participates, the participation of the spouse of the taxpayer is also taken into account.[88]

The $25,000 exception is applicable to individuals other than those whose income is very large. It is an aggregate figure that takes account of both deductions and credits. However, the allowance is reduced by 50 percent of the amount by which a taxpayer's adjusted gross income for the year[89] exceeds $100,000.[90] Accordingly, the $25,000 allowance is eliminated for any taxpayer with an adjusted gross income of $150,000 or greater.[91]

$25,000 exemption, credits from a rental real estate activity are used after losses from a rental real estate activity. Sen.Rep. No. 99–313, supra note 16 at 724.

81. I.R.C. § 469(i)(1) and (2). The Conference Committee Report states that in determining the rental real estate loss eligible for the exemption, income from other passive activities must be netted against any rental real estate rental losses. Conf.Rep. 99–841, supra note 62 at II–141.

82. I.R.C. § 469(i)(6)(A).

83. The active participation requirement is waived for the credits under I.R.C. §§ 42 and 47. I.R.C. § 469(i)(6)(B).

84. Sen.Rep. No. 99–313, supra note 16 at 737.

85. Id. at 737–738.

86. Id. at 738.

87. I.R.C. § 469(i)(6)(C).

88. I.R.C. § 469(i)(6)(D).

89. Adjusted gross income is computed exclusive of taxable social security benefits, IRA's and passive losses. I.R.C. § 469(i)(3)(E).

90. I.R.C. § 469(i)(3)(A). The adjusted gross income for phasing out the $25,000 allowance is increased to $200,000 for rehabilitation investment credits and the phase-out is disregarded for the low-income housing credit. I.R.C. § 469(i)(3)(B) and (C).

91. For married individuals filing separate returns, the $25,000 allowance is reduced to $12,500 and is phased out for taxpayers with adjusted gross incomes in excess of $50,000. I.R.C. § 469(i)(5)(A). However, if married individuals do not live apart from each other for the entire year, the allowance is unavailable if separate returns are filed. I.R.C. § 469(i)(5)(B).

Closely Held C Corporations. A closely held C corporation that is not a personal service corporation is allowed to offset passive activity losses and credits against taxable income other than passive or portfolio income.[92] Thus, a closely held C corporation can offset income from its trade or business with losses from passive activities.

Release of Suspended Losses and Credits. Losses and credits disallowed in any year are carried forward to be used against net income or taxes from passive activities in subsequent years.[93] Two special rules come into play here when a taxpayer either converts a former passive activity to an active one or sells his entire interest in a passive activity.

Treatment of Former Passive Activities. A taxpayer's participation in an activity is determined annually.[94] One who was passive with respect to an activity in one year may begin materially participating in the activity in a later year. In such a case, previously suspended losses or credits remain suspended and continue to be treated as passive activity losses;[95] however, previously suspended losses can continue to be applied against net income (other than portfolio income) from the former passive (now active) activity and previously suspended credits can be offset against newly arising tax liability of the former passive activity.[96] The reason for this treatment is to avoid discouraging taxpayers from materially participating in activities.[97]

A similar situation arises when a taxpayer ceases to be a closely held C corporation or personal service corporation. If such a change in status occurs, previously suspended losses and credits remain suspended and Section 469 continues to apply to the suspended losses and credits as if the change in status had not occurred. Thus, the suspended losses and credits can continue to offset all income, other than portfolio income, of the taxpayer after the taxpayer ceases to be a closely held C corporation or personal service corporation.[98]

Dispositions of Entire Interests in Passive Activities. When a taxpayer disposes of his entire interest in a passive activity (or former passive activity) and all gain or loss realized on the disposition is recognized, any previously suspended losses from the activity are generally allowable as deductions against income.[99] They are allowed in the following order: first, against income or gain from the passive activity for the taxable year of disposition (including any gain recognized on the disposition); second, against net income or gain for the same year from all other passive activities; and the remainder, against any other income or gain for that year.[100]

---

92. I.R.C. § 469(e)(2).

93. I.R.C. § 469(b).

94. Sen.Rep.No. 99–313, supra note 16 at 731.

95. I.R.C. § 469(f)(1)(C).

96. I.R.C. § 469(f)(1)(A) and (B).

97. Sen.Rep.No. 99–313, supra note 16 at 727, footnote 15.

98. I.R.C. § 469(f)(2).

99. But see I.R.C. § 469(g)(1)(C) providing for regulations allowing the suspended losses to be reduced by income or gain realized by the activity in prior years.

100. I.R.C. § 469(g)(1)(A). These pecking order rules were clearer under the prior version of § 469(g)(1)(A), but they are

The rationale for activating suspended losses upon the fully taxable disposition of a taxpayer's entire interest in a passive activity is that, at that time, the actual economic gain or loss can be accurately computed.[101] Thus, as seen in the Introduction, as to *losses* (but sometimes not to credits) Section 469 generally acts as a mere postponement rather than a total disallowance provision.

The legislative history states that the type of disposition which generally releases suspended losses is a sale to a third party at arm's length and, thus, presumably for a price equal to its fair market value.[102] A transaction in the form of a sale does not release suspended losses if it is a sham or any other transaction not treated as a taxable disposition under tax law, including tax common law.[103]

The legislative history provides guidance in the identification of a disposition of a taxpayer's entire interest in an activity. If the activity is in the form of a sole proprietorship, the taxpayer must dispose of all assets used or created in the activity.[104] If a taxpayer holds an interest in a limited partnership that conducts two separate activities, the disposition by the limited partnership of one of the activities will release only suspended losses allocable to that activity.[105] Obviously, taxpayers must keep adequate records of suspended losses allocable to each activity to be eligible to claim deductions for such suspended losses.[106]

If a taxpayer sells his entire interest in an activity by way of an installment sale, suspended losses are released each year in which payments are made in the same ratio that gain reported in the year bears to the total gain on the sale.[107] A taxpayer may dispose of his interest in a passive activity in a nonrecognition transaction.[108] In such a case, suspended losses attributable to the passive activity remain suspended.[109] Any remaining suspended losses are deductible when the taxpayer disposes of his entire interest in the property received in the nonrecognition transaction.[110]

If a taxpayer disposes of his interest in a passive activity in an otherwise taxable transaction, but the transferee is a "related par-

retained under the current wording of the statute.

101. Sen.Rep.No. 99–313, supra note 16 at 725.

102. Id.

103. Conf.Rep.No. 99–841, supra note 62 at II–143. Thus, wash sales and transfers not properly treated as sales due to the existence of a put, call, or similar right relating to repurchase, do not release suspended losses. Id.

104. Sen.Rep.No. 99–313, supra note 16 at 725.

105. Conf.Rep.No. 99–841, supra note 62 at II–145.

106. Sen.Rep.No. 99–313, supra note 16 at 726.

107. I.R.C. § 469(g)(3).

108. See Chapter 26, infra.

109. Sen.Rep.No. 99–313, supra note 16 at 726–727. Cf. I.R.C. § 469(g)(1)(A). An example of a nonrecognition transaction is a like-kind exchange under I.R.C. § 1031. To the extent gain is recognized in the transaction e.g., boot received in a tax-free exchange, passive activity losses can be utilized. For further discussion on nonrecognition transactions, see Chapter 26B, infra.

110. Sen.Rep.No. 99–313, supra note 16 at 726–727.

ty," [111] suspended losses are not released under the disposition rule. Suspended losses remaining with the taxpayer are not triggered until the related transferee disposes of the entire interest in a taxable transaction to an unrelated party.[112]

A gift does not release suspended losses. However, if a taxpayer disposes of his interest in a passive activity by gift, the basis of the interest is increased by passive activity losses allocable to it.[113] For purposes of determining a donee's loss in a subsequent transaction, the donee's basis may not exceed fair market value of the interest at the time of the gift whatever the amount of the suspended losses.[114] Suspended losses are eliminated once they have played their role to increase the basis of the interest.[115]

If an interest in an activity is transferred by reason of death, suspended losses are deductible on the final return of the decedent. However, such losses are deductible only to the extent that they exceed the "step up" in the basis of the property allowable under Section 1014.[116]

In contrast to the sanctioned utilization of suspended losses upon a taxable disposition of an entire interest in a passive activity, suspended credits remain suspended.[117] Under such circumstances, the suspended credits can offset only tax liability attributable to income from other passive activities. Some relief is provided if a fully taxable disposition involves assets that were subject to a basis reduction from the claiming of tax credits. Upon such a disposition, the taxpayer may elect to increase the basis of the property by the amount of the previously suspended credits. However, the basis adjustment can not exceed the amount of the original basis reduction.[118] This election reduces the gain (or increases the loss) recognized on the taxable disposition of such property. Any passive activity credits used to increase the basis of property can no longer reduce tax liability.[119]

PROBLEMS

1. Lawyer earns $200,000 of taxable income from her practice in the current year. Discuss the extent to which the following transactions affect her taxable income in the current year.

111. A related party is defined in I.R.C. §§ 267(b) and 707(b)(1), including their applicable attribution rules. I.R.C. § 469(g)(1)(B).

112. I.R.C. § 469(g)(1)(B).

113. I.R.C. § 469(j)(6)(A).

114. Sen.Rep.No. 99–313, supra note 16 at 726, footnote 12. See I.R.C. § 1015(a).

115. I.R.C. § 469(j)(6)(B). Thus, some of the suspended losses may be lost. See note 114, supra.

116. I.R.C. § 469(g)(2). See page 137, supra. For example, if a taxpayer died

owning an interest in a passive activity with $40,000 of suspended losses with an adjusted basis of $75,000 prior to death which was stepped-up to $90,000 under § 1014 at death, $25,000 of the suspended losses ($40,000 less the differences between $90,000 and $75,000) would be deductible on the final income tax return of the deceased taxpayer.

117. Sen.Rep.No. 99–313, supra note 16 at 725.

118. I.R.C. § 469(j)(9).

119. Id.

(a) Lawyer also has $10,000 of dividends and interest in the year. She invests as a limited partner in a partnership that films and distributes movies. Her share of the partnership's movie losses for the year is $50,000.

(b) Same as (a), above, except that Lawyer also has a $30,000 gain from her investment in a windmill power tax shelter.

(c) Same as (a), above, except that in the succeeding year the movie limited partnership makes a gain of $90,000 as a result of a successful movie, "Alligator Allee."

(d) Same as (a), above, except that Lawyer sells her movie limited partnership interest at the beginning of the succeeding year at a gain.

(e) Same monetary figures as (a), above, except that Lawyer's limited partnership interest is in rental real estate rather than in a movie.

(f) Same as (e), above, except that Lawyer owns a 20 percent general (not limited) partnership interest in rental real estate in which she actively participates in the management decisions.

(g) Same as (f), above, except that Lawyer's adjusted gross income for the year from her law practice is $120,000 (rather than $200,000).

2. (a) In the current year Grocer purchases a grocery store and spends 35 hours per week operating it to the exclusion of all other business and investment activities. Grocer's loss from the grocery store business is $50,000. How much of his loss is deductible?

(b) Same as (a), above, except Grocer is only irregularly involved in the operation of the grocery store. Intermittently, Grocer makes significant management decisions.

(c) Same as (a), above, except that Grocer who is retired purchases the grocery store and hires a manager who has carte blanche power to make all business decisions.

(d) Grocer, upset with the $50,000 loss in (c), above, fires manager at the end of the year and in the succeeding year, Grocer manages the store on a full-time basis and in that year makes a $60,000 profit. What tax consequences to Grocer for the succeeding year?

3. (a) In 1991, Eileen purchases a house and uses it as her primary residence. In 1992, Eileen changes her primary residence and decides to rent out her former residence. Eileen hires a rental agent to handle day-to-day problems but she approves new tenants, sets rental terms and approves capital or repair expenditures. Eileen's loss from the apartment is $8,000 and her other adjusted gross income is $40,000. How much of the loss is deductible?

(b) Same as (a), above, except that in 1992, Eileen also purchases an undivided interest in a shopping mall. She purchased her interest from a promoter, based on a prospectus describing the investment opportunity and stressing the tax benefits. A professional management company makes all significant management decisions. Eileen's share of the shopping mall loss is $3,000. What amount of her total $11,000 of losses are deductible?

4. Investor is a limited partner in a partnership that is involved in two ventures. The first is the operation of a television station in New York. The second is the operation of a radio station in New Jersey. Investor's suspended passive losses are $5,000 from the television station and $25,000 from the radio station. Because of its large losses, the limited partnership sells the radio station. How much of investor's suspended passive losses are deductible upon the sale of the radio station?

5. In the current year, Dentist purchased two limited partnership interests. For the current year, Dentist had a $20,000 loss and a $7,000 credit from one of the passive activities. In the same year, she had $35,000 of income from the other passive activity. Excluding the passive income and loss amounts, Dentist had $110,000 of adjusted gross income in the current year. Assume all of Dentist's taxable income exceeding $47,050 falls in the 31 percent tax bracket.

(a) What is the amount of Dentist's passive activity credit for the current year?

(b) What result in (a), above, if, in addition, Dentist actively participates in a rental real estate activity in which she has a 20 percent interest and her share of the real estate activity loss is $20,000?

6. Doctor has a limited partnership interest. His passive activity carryover losses from the partnership are $60,000. Doctor's limited partnership interest has an adjusted basis of $50,000 and a fair market value of $100,000.

(a) What are the tax consequences if Doctor sells his interest to an unrelated third party for $100,000?

(b) What are the tax consequences in (a), above, if Doctor's adjusted basis for his partnership interest is $120,000?

(c) What are the tax consequences in (a), above, if Doctor gives his partnership interest to his son?

(d) What are the tax consequences in (a), above, if Doctor sells his partnership interest to his son for $100,000?

(e) What are the tax consequences in (a), above, if Doctor dies prior to any sale?

F. ILLEGALITY OR IMPROPRIETY

Internal Revenue Code: Section 162(c), (f), (g). See Sections 1(a); 152(b)(5); 165(d); 280E; 6013.

————

Although the first modern (post-16th Amendment) income tax act taxed income from the transaction of any "lawful" business, the term "lawful" was dropped quickly in 1916 and, since that time, the fact that income may somehow be tainted has had no bearing on its taxability. Thus, the Supreme Court early sustained a tax on the bootlegger's profits.[1] And much later the extortionist's plunder was held taxable.[2] Although the Supreme Court once refused to sustain a tax on embezzled income,[3] it was not because the income had a shady origin but, essentially, because such receipts were likened to loans. In any event, development of an "economic benefit" theory of income in James v. United States[4] enabled the Court to bring embezzled income into the area of taxability. It is unnecessary here to extend the discussion to other kinds of ill-gotten gains.

On the other hand, when the deduction question arises the propriety of an expenditure may be significant. Generally, the statute itself is free from moralizing restrictions, and the income tax is not a sanction against wrong-doing. Senator Williams, manager of the 1913 act, said to the Senate:[5]

> The object of this bill is to tax a man's net income; that is to say, what he has at the end of the year after deducting from his receipts his expenditures or losses. It is not to reform men's moral characters. * * * The tax is not levied for the purpose of restraining people from betting on horse races or upon "futures", but the tax is framed for the purpose of making a man pay upon his net income, his actual profit during the year.

Of course, over the years a little moralizing has crept in. Curiously, against the background of the Williams statement, Congress has decided to limit the deduction for wagering losses to an amount not in excess of gains from such transactions, possibly imposing a mild restraint on betting on the ponies.[6] Also, a man may find that Congress has expressly foreclosed a dependency deduction for his mistress, certainly a mild fiscal attack against such cohabitation.[7] It might be added, borrowing from Dorothy Parker, that the benefits of the joint return go along with the solid comforts of the double bed, not the hurly-burly of

1. U.S. v. Sullivan, 274 U.S. 259, 47 S.Ct. 607 (1927).

2. Rutkin v. U.S., 343 U.S. 130, 72 S.Ct. 571 (1952).

3. Commissioner v. Wilcox, 327 U.S. 404, 66 S.Ct. 546 (1946).

4. 366 U.S. 213, 81 S.Ct. 1052 (1961).

5. 50 (Part 4) Cong.Rec. 3849, 63d Cong., 2d Sess. (1913).

6. I.R.C. § 165(d).

7. I.R.C. § 152(b)(5). But see page 974, infra, indicating that unmarrieds living together may be more advantageous taxwise!

the chaise-lounge.[8] Perhaps more concretely, Congress also expressly disallows any deduction for bribes to government officials and, in some circumstances, for illegal bribes or kickbacks to anyone.[9] Fines and similar penalties are also now expressly proscribed as nondeductible,[10] as are certain payments required as sanctions under the antitrust laws.[11] In an effort to further attempt to deal with the underground dope economy, Congress in 1982 added Section 280E to the Code precluding any deduction or credit for expenses in carrying on the trade or business of trafficking in controlled substances.[12] But these statutory provisions are the exception rather than the rule.

The foregoing comments on the statute suggest a simplicity in this area which, however, does not exist. The courts have found that public policy (that "notoriously unruly horse, likely to carry its rider off in any direction") sometimes stands in the way of a deduction which, otherwise, would appear to be authorized by the statute. As a general proposition it may be said that expenditures that are against the law and others whose deduction would tend to frustrate sharply defined public policy are not deductible.[13] While there is still substantial uncertainty, confusion in the area shrinks as provisions such as those mentioned in the preceding paragraph are added to the Code. A few words of history may be enlightening.

The first Supreme Court decision in which a claimed business expense deduction was denied on public policy grounds was Textile Mills Securities Corp. v. Commissioner.[14] The expenditures in question included amounts paid to a publicist and lawyers to seek legislation that would enable German textile interests to recover properties seized during World War I. In part the decision was rested on a long-continued (since 1915) regulation denying any deduction for lobbying expenses. The court noted the lack of precision in the "ordinary and necessary" requirement of the statute which, it held, left room for administrative interpretation. And it accepted the interpretation denying deductions for lobbying expenses on public policy grounds, saying: [15]

> Contracts to spread such insidious influences through legislative halls have long been condemned. * * * Whether the

8. See I.R.C. §§ 1(a) and 6013.

9. I.R.C. § 162(c). See Lycan, "Public Policy and the Deductibility of Kickbacks Under § 162(c)(2)," 35 Ohio State L.J. 686 (1974).

10. I.R.C. § 162(f).

11. I.R.C. § 162(g); but see earlier Rev.Rul. 64–224, 1964–2 C.B. 52.

12. P.L.No. 97–248, § 351(a), 97th Cong., 2d Sess. (1982).

13. Although there is language in the legislative histories of the Code sections cited in footnotes 9–11, supra, indicating the statutory disallowances are "all inclusive" and are under the "control of Congress", [the most relevant comments can be found at 1972–1 C.B. 599 and 1969–3 C.B. 597.] nevertheless such statutory proscriptions have been held not to preclude a consideration whether public policy should stand in the way of a claimed § 165 deduction for theft where the claiming taxpayer was playing footsie with the thieves who were seemingly engaged in an illegal activity, counterfeiting currency. Raymond Mazzei, 61 T.C. 497 (1974).

14. 314 U.S. 326, 62 S.Ct. 272 (1941). Pre-1964 "public policy" cases are collected in Lamont, "Controversial Aspects of Ordinary and Necessary Business Expenses," 42 Taxes 808, 819–835 (1964).

15. Id. at 338–339, 62 S.Ct. at 279–280.

precise arrangement here in question would violate the rule of [such] cases is not material. The point is that the general policy indicated by those cases need not be disregarded by the rule-making authority in its segregation of non-deductible expenses.

From that point on the question has been to what extent administrative and judicial moralizing can be expected when Congress has engaged in none.

The fact that *Textile Mills* involved efforts on behalf of alien Germans and that it was decided just prior to the full-scale conflagration of World War II might leave its present effect in some doubt. However, in 1959, the Supreme Court refused to give a restrictive interpretation to its *Textile Mills* opinion. Expenses involved in an attempt to protect the business of bars and liquor wholesalers from threatening state action in the form of an initiative and referendum measure, which would have created a state monopoly for retail sales, were held non-deductible.[16] To the supporting factors of a longstanding regulation and the Court's own decision in *Textile Mills*, the Court could now add that the reenactment in 1954 of the "ordinary and necessary" rule without change was "significant as indicating [congressional] satisfaction with the interpretation consistently given the statute by the regulations * * * and in demonstrating its [Congress'] prior intent." [17]

The lobbying expense area is interesting in reflecting administrative, judicial, and legislative participation in the development of tax law. In 1962, Congress marked off a limited area in which lobbying expenses may now be deducted,[18] without however adopting a rule that would make deductible efforts to shape legislation through broad appeals to the public.

In some other cases the Commissioner has asserted different public policy reasons for the disallowance of deductions for attorneys fees incurred in connection with business activities. A reference to two Supreme Court cases will suffice. In Commissioner v. Heininger,[19] the taxpayer, a Chicago dentist, was in the false teeth business. The teeth were advertised, ordered, delivered and paid for by mail. Challenging his claims for his product, the Postmaster General issued a fraud order to the Chicago postmaster, interrupting the taxpayer's business. The taxpayer sought an injunction against enforcement of the order but, while initially successful, he lost on appeal. The *tax* litigation arose out of the Commissioner's disallowance of a claimed deduction for $36,000 representing admittedly reasonable attorney's fees incurred in contesting the fraud order. The Board of Tax Appeals agreed with the Commissioner's assertion that these were not "ordinary and necessary" business expenses. The idea seemed to be that dentists do not "ordina-

---

16. Cammarano v. U.S., 358 U.S. 498, 79 S.Ct. 524 (1959).

17. Id. at 510, 79 S.Ct. at 532.

18. I.R.C. § 162(e).

19. 320 U.S. 467, 64 S.Ct. 249 (1943).

rily" seek to sell false teeth fraudulently; therefore, expenses related to such activity (the legal expenses incurred) are not ordinary and not deductible. But the Supreme Court agreed with the Seventh Circuit's reversal, allowing the deduction, saying: [20]

> It has never been thought ∗ ∗ ∗ that the mere fact that an expenditure bears a remote relation to an illegal act makes it non-deductible. The language (of the statute) contains no express reference to the lawful or unlawful character of the business expenses which are declared to be deductible. And the brief of the government in the instant case expressly disclaims any contention that the purpose of the tax laws is to penalize illegal business by taxing gross income instead of net income. ∗ ∗ ∗
>
> ∗ ∗ ∗
>
> If the respondent's litigation expenses are to be denied deduction, it must be because allowance of the deduction would frustrate the sharply defined policies of [the statutes] which authorize the Postmaster General to issue fraud orders.

The Court found no such threatened frustration.

Heininger of course involved expenses incurred in an unsuccessful effort to resist a civil sanction, no matter how penal it might be in nature. The Commissioner thought it was still open to him to challenge a deduction for attorney's fees incurred in unsuccessfully attempting to defend a criminal prosecution that grew out of misconduct in the course of the taxpayer's business. But, although the Tax Court agreed, neither the Court of Appeals nor the Supreme Court did. One Tellier was convicted on several counts, including charges under the mail fraud provisions of the Securities Act of 1933, and sentenced to pay an $18,000 fine and to serve four and one half years in prison. En route, he incurred $23,000 in legal expenses which he sought to deduct. It is now settled that the legal expenses are deductible.[21] In the *Tellier* case the court said: [22]

> No public policy is offended when a man faced with serious criminal charges employs a lawyer to help in his defense. That is not 'proscribed conduct'. It is his constitutional right.

Note that this is not to say all legal expenses are deductible but only that, if otherwise within Section 162 or possibly Section 212, the fact that they relate to the defense of a criminal charge,[23] successful or unsuccessful, will not foreclose the deduction.

Meanwhile, between the decisions in *Heininger* and *Tellier*, some other more difficult public policy cases worked their way to the Supreme Court. In Lilly v. Commissioner,[24] the issue was the deductibility of kickbacks made by an optician to eye doctors who sent patients to

---

20. Id. at 474, 64 S.Ct. at 253, 254.

21. Commissioner v. Tellier, 383 U.S. 687, 86 S.Ct. 1118 (1966).

22. Id. at 694, 86 S.Ct. at 1122.

23. John Kurkjian, 65 T.C. 862 (1976).

24. 343 U.S. 90, 72 S.Ct. 497 (1952).

him to have their prescriptions filled. Probably most people would agree that such payments are contrary to public policy, and perhaps further, that it violates generally accepted notions of public policy to allow a tax deduction for such payments. However, differing with the Commissioner and both lower courts, the Supreme Court held such payments to be deductible. The reason advanced was that public policies that might preclude a deduction may do so only if they are "national or state policies evidenced by some governmental declaration of them." [25] Finding no such declaration applicable to the payments in *Lilly*, the amounts were held to be deductible.[26] The general effect of the decision, at least outside the lobbying area, is to relieve the taxpayer from the obligation of having to comply with the Commissioner's appraisal of public policy in order to justify a deduction.[27]

Dictum appears in *Lilly* to the effect that expenditures which themselves violate a federal or state law could be argued, by virtue of their illegality, not to be "ordinary and necessary." As a matter of fact in a later case Mr. Justice Clark said directly: "Certainly the frustration of state policy is most complete and direct when the expenditure for which deduction is sought is itself prohibited by statute." [28] Still, it is not the law that an illegal expenditure is never deductible. In Commissioner v. Sullivan,[29] salary and rental payments made in carrying on an illegal gambling business, which payments were themselves in violation of Illinois law, were held to be deductible. The case cannot easily be reconciled with other "public policy" decisions. In support, if not in logical explanation, of the result reached Mr. Justice Douglas said for the Court: [30]

> If we enforce as federal policy the rule espoused by the Commissioner in this case [denying the deductions], we would come close to making this type of business taxable on the basis of its gross receipts, while all other business would be taxable on the basis of net income.

On the other hand, this does seem consistent with the amoral role ascribed to the income tax statute by Senator Williams in 1913.

An understanding of *Sullivan* is rendered even more difficult by the decisions in two cases decided at the same time. Each involved the deductibility of state fines incurred by trucking companies for violation of state laws against overweight loads on the highways. Such fines, whether incurred wilfully or inadvertently, were held nondeductible.[31]

---

25. Id. at 97, 72 S.Ct. at 501. See also Bertolini Trucking Co. v. Commissioner, 736 F.2d 1120 (6th Cir.1984).

26. But see United Draperies v. Commissioner, 340 F.2d 936 (7th Cir.1964), cert. denied 382 U.S. 813, 86 S.Ct. 30 (1965), denying a deduction for kickbacks found to be not "ordinary" in the industry.

27. Note that the provision on illegal payments continues this philosophy by its requirement of a conviction in a criminal proceeding or a loss of license or privilege to engage in a trade or business. I.R.C. § 162(c)(2).

28. Tank Truck Rentals, Inc. v. Commissioner, 356 U.S. 30, 78 S.Ct. 507 (1958).

29. 356 U.S. 27, 78 S.Ct. 512 (1958).

30. Id. at 29, 78 S.Ct. at 514.

31. Tank Truck Rentals, Inc. v. Commissioner, supra note 28; Hoover Motor

The rationale of these cases is that to allow the deduction would frustrate state policy by diluting the penalty for violation of the law. The penalty is less if the amount paid reduces income otherwise taxable. Said Mr. Justice Clark for the Court: [32]

> Deduction of fines and penalties uniformly has been held to frustrate state policy in severe and direct fashion by reducing the "sting" of the penalty prescribed by the state legislature.

Thus, if in the case of the corporations involved their income was effectively taxed at about a 34 percent rate, allowance of the deduction would reduce each $1.00 of fine to 66 cents, net cost after taxes. A seeming answer on these facts would be to say that the state could increase the fine by 50 percent in order, after allowance of the deduction, to exact the full penalty. But this is an inadequate answer; consider in other circumstances how a low bracket individual (or a corporation subject only to the normal corporate tax) would incur a higher after tax penalty than a taxpayer whose deduction was in a sense more valuable because it would offset income otherwise to be subjected to higher rates.

In any event, fines are not deductible and Congress has now expressly said so.[33] In *Tellier* it was not contended that the taxpayer could deduct his $18,000 fine, only attorney's fees paid in seeking to avoid it. But this is another area of the law in which it is not always easy to differentiate an administrative requirement that is remedial in nature from the imposition of a fine or penalty, a sanction against wrongdoing. If fines may confidently be said generally to be nondeductible, what *is* a fine?[34] Congress, of course, has sought to avoid the "tyranny of labels" by disallowing deductions for "any fine *or similar penalty*."[35] Does this eliminate the problem?

Public policy problems such as are discussed in this note have evoked a substantial addition to the legal literature. There are perceptive discussions in Taggart, "Fines, Penalties, Bribes and Damage Payments," 25 Tax.L.Rev. 611 (1970); Scallen, "The Deductibility of Antitrust Treble Damage Payments," 52 Minn.L.Rev. 1149 (1968); Wright, "Tax Formula to Restore the Historical Effects of Antitrust Treble Damages Provisions," 65 Mich.L.Rev. 245 (1966); Tyler, "Disallowance of Deductions on Public Policy Grounds," 20 Tax L.Rev. 665 (1965). See also Note, "Cost of Unsuccessful Criminal Defense," 64

Exp. Co. v. U.S., 356 U.S. 38, 78 S.Ct. 511 (1958).

32. Tank Truck Rentals, Inc. v. Commissioner, supra note 28 at 35–36, 78 S.Ct. at 510.

33. I.R.C. § 162(f). However, if the fine is characterized in a settlement agreement as compensation for damages, the penalty may be deductible. See Middle Atlantic Distributors, Inc., 72 T.C. 1136 (1979). Compare this result to Adolf Meller Co. v.

U.S., 600 F.2d 1360 (Ct.Cl.1979), which held that amounts paid pursuant to a compromise settlement retained the character of the underlying potential civil liability and were nondeductible.

34. Compare Rossman Corp. v. Commissioner, 175 F.2d 711 (2d Cir.1949), with Lentin v. Commissioner, 226 F.2d 695 (7th Cir.1955), cert. denied 350 U.S. 934, 76 S.Ct. 305 (1956).

35. I.R.C. § 162(f).

Mich.L.Rev. 161 (1965); Note, "Business Expenses, Disallowance, and Public Policy: Some Problems of Sanctioning with the Internal Revenue Code," 72 Yale L.J. 108 (1962).

CHAPTER 18. DEDUCTIONS FOR INDIVIDUALS ONLY

A. MOVING EXPENSES *

Internal Revenue Code: Sections 82; 217(a)–(f); 274(n).

Regulations: Sections 1.82–1(a); 1.217–2(d)(2)(ii) and (3). See Section 1.217–2(b), (c), (d)(1).

EXCERPT FROM THE GENERAL EXPLANATION OF THE TAX REFORM ACT OF 1969

Staff of the Joint Committee on Internal Revenue Taxation.
Pp. 101–104 (1970).

MOVING EXPENSES

Prior Law.—Prior law allowed, under specified conditions, a deduction from gross income for the following job-related moving expenses: (1) the cost of transporting the taxpayer and members of his household from the old to the new residence; (2) the cost of transporting their belongings; and (3) the cost of meals and lodging en route. The deduction was available to new employees (whether or not reimbursed) and to unreimbursed transferred employees, but not to self-employed individuals.

For a deduction for moving expenses to be allowed, the taxpayer's new principal place of work had to be located at least 20 miles farther from his former residence than was his former principal place of work (if the taxpayer had no former place of work, then at least 20 miles from his former residence). In addition, to obtain the deduction the taxpayer had to be employed full-time during at least 39 weeks of the 52 weeks immediately following his arrival at the new place of work.

The position of the Service under prior law also allowed existing employees whose moving expenses were reimbursed to exclude reimbursements for the above categories of expense (to the extent of the expenses) whether or not they satisfied the tests prescribed by the law for the deduction of moving expenses by other employees.

Prior law did not specifically deal with other reimbursed moving expenses;[1] however, the courts generally held that reimbursements for

---

* See Allington, "Moving Expenses and Reimbursements," 56 A.B.A.J. 495 (1970); Youngman, "New Law Broadens Scope of Moving Expenses and Extends It to Self-Employed Individuals," 32 J.Tax. 292 (1970).

1. Prior law provided that no deduction was allowable for moving expenses for any item to the extent that the taxpayer received reimbursement or other expense allowance for such item unless the amount of the reimbursement or other expense allowance was included in the taxpayer's

moving expenses, other than those which were deductible, had to be included in gross income.

General Reasons for Change.—The mobility of labor is an important and necessary part of the nation's economy, since it reduces unemployment and increases productive capacity. It has been estimated that approximately one-half million employees are requested by their employers to move to new job locations each year. In addition, self-employed individuals relocate to find more attractive or useful employment. Substantial moving expenses often are incurred by taxpayers in connection with employment-related relocations, and these expenses may be regarded as a cost of earning income.

The Congress believed that more adequate recognition should be given in the tax law to expenses connected with job-related moves. In addition, the Congress concluded that equity required that the moving expense deduction be made available on a comparable basis for self-employed persons who move to a new work location. Finally, it was desired to equalize fully the tax treatment for the moving expenses of new employees and unreimbursed transferred employees with the treatment accorded reimbursed employees.

Explanation of Provision.—The Act broadens the categories of deductible moving expenses, provides that reimbursed taxpayers are to be treated in the same manner as unreimbursed taxpayers, increases the minimum 20-mile test to 50 [Reduced to 35 by TRA (1976). Ed.] miles, extends the moving expense deduction to the self-employed, and refines the application of the 39-week test which must be satisfied for the deduction to be available.

A moving expense deduction is allowed by the Act for three additional categories of expenses: (1) pre-move house-hunting trips; (2) temporary living expenses at the new job location; and (3) qualified expenses of selling, purchasing or leasing a residence. These additional moving expense deductions are subject to an overall limit of $2,500, with a $1,000 limit on the first two categories. [These figures became $3000 and $1500 under TRA (1976). Ed.]

The pre-move house-hunting trip expenses include the cost of transportation, meals [now 80 percent of the cost of meals—see Section 274(n). Ed.] and lodging for the taxpayer and members of his household paid for the principal purpose of searching for a new residence. The deduction is not available, however, unless the taxpayer (a) has obtained employment at a new principal place of work before the trip begins, and (b) travels from his former residence to the general area of his new principal place of work and returns.

The temporary living expenses at the new job location include costs of [now 80 percent of] meals and lodging for the taxpayer and members

gross income. Thus, if an employee had claimed a deduction for moving expenses and subsequently received a reimbursement for those expenses which he did not include in his gross income, then he had to file an amended return for the taxable year in which the deduction was claimed.

of his household at the new job location while waiting to move into permanent quarters. However, only those expenses incurred within 30 consecutive days after obtaining employment are deductible.

Residence sale and purchase expenses which qualify for the deduction are those reasonable expenses incident to the sale or exchange by the taxpayer (or his spouse) of his former residence and also expenses incident to his purchase of the new residence. Reasonable expenses incurred in settling an unexpired lease on an old residence or acquiring a lease on a new residence (except any amounts representing security deposits or payments or prepayments of rent) also may be deducted. The expenses related to the sale of the former residence include a real estate agent's commission, escrow fees, and similar expenses reasonably necessary to effect the sale or exchange of the residence. Expenses for fixing up a residence to assist in its sale are not in this category. The expenses related to purchasing the new residence include attorney's fees, escrow fees, appraisal fees, title costs, loan placement charges (which do not represent interest) and similar expenses reasonably necessary to effect the purchase of the new residence. These expenses do not include any portion of real estate taxes, any payments which represent interest, or any portion of the purchase price of the residence. A residence for this purpose includes a house, an apartment, a cooperative or condominium dwelling unit, or other similar dwelling.

The selling expenses on the former residence which are deductible under this provision do not reduce the amount realized on the sale of the residence for purposes of determining gain. Similarly, the expenses of purchasing a residence which have been deducted may not be added to the cost basis of the new residence for purposes of determining gain. These adjustments were necessary to prevent double tax benefits.

If a husband and wife both commence work at a new principal place of employment within the same general location, the $2,500 [now $3000] limit rule is to be applied as if there were only one commencement of work. Where a married couple files separate returns, the overall limit for these additional moving expenses is $1,250 [now $1500] for each, and the house-hunting trip and temporary living expenses are limited to $500 [now $750] out of the $1,250 [now $1500]. In those cases where the moving expenses (both those deductible under prior law and those for which a deduction is provided by the Act) relate to an individual other than the taxpayer, a deduction is to be allowed only if the individual lives in both the former and the new residence and is a member of the taxpayer's household.

The Act also provides that the reimbursement of expenses of moving from one residence to another are to be included in the taxpayer's gross income (as compensation for services). Under this provision, taxpayers include the reimbursements in gross income but then are permitted to take deductions to the extent permitted under the provisions for the deduction of moving expenses.

Since compensation for services is generally subject to the withholding of income tax, moving expense reimbursements are subject to the general withholding rules. However, the withholding provisions (sec. 3401(a)) do not apply to reimbursements to the extent it is reasonable to believe that a moving expense deduction will be allowable (under sec. 217).

The Act replaces the 20-mile test of prior law with a 50-mile [now 35-mile] test. Under the 50-mile [35-mile] rule, no deduction is allowed unless the taxpayer's new principal place of work is at least 50 miles [35 miles] farther from his former residence than was his former principal place of work. If the taxpayer has no former principal place of work, the deduction is allowed only if the distance between the new principal place of work and his former residence is at least 50 miles [35 miles]. In applying the 50-mile [35-mile] test, the distance between the two points is to be the shortest of the more commonly traveled routes between these two points.

Deductions are allowed under this provision only if the taxpayer during the 12-month period immediately following his arrival at his new principal place of work is a full-time employee for at least 39 weeks. However, in the case of self-employed persons (who did not qualify for any moving expense deduction under prior law) deductions are allowed if during the 24-month period immediately following their arrival at the new principal place of work they perform services on a full-time basis during at least 78 weeks, of which not less than 39 weeks occur during the 12-month period immediately following the arrival at their new place of work.[2] Whether a self-employed taxpayer performs services on a full-time basis depends upon the customary practices of his occupation. (These provisions do not include the semi-retired, part-time students, or other similarly situated self-employed taxpayers who work only a few hours each week.)

If a taxpayer has not satisfied his 39-week or 78-week test before the time for filing his income tax return for the year during which the moving expenses would be deductible, he may (as under prior law) nevertheless claim a deduction for these expenses incurred during the earlier taxable year if it is possible for him at the time of filing his return to still satisfy the test. If this condition is not satisfied at the close of the subsequent year in which the test period of time ends, an amount equal to the expenses which were deducted in the earlier taxable year must be included in the taxpayer's gross income for that subsequent year.

The 39-week test is waived if the employee is unable to satisfy it as a result of death, disability, or involuntary separation (other than for willful misconduct) from the service of, or transfer for the benefit of, an employer after obtaining full-time employment in which the taxpayer

2. The self-employed rule also applies to a person who has served both as an employee and in a self-employed capacity but who is unable to meet the 39-week employee test. [TRA (1976) added I.R.C. § 217(g), a special moving expense rule for members of the armed forces. See also Rev.Rul. 76–2, 1976–1 C.B. 82, Ed.]

could reasonably have been expected to satisfy the requirement. The new 78-week test is waived for self-employed individuals in the case of death or disability.

The term "self-employed individual" is defined as an individual who performs personal services as the owner of an entire interest in an unincorporated trade or business, or as a partner in a partnership carrying on a trade or business. Under the Act, an individual who commences work at a new principal place of work as a self-employed individual is treated as having obtained employment when he has made substantial arrangements to commence such work.

Effective Date.—These provisions generally apply with respect to taxable years beginning after December 31, 1969. * * *

PROBLEMS

1. Lawyer has been practicing law in Town X and he and his family live in Suburb of Town X ten miles away. He decides to open an office in Town Y. Consequently he moves himself and his family to a home in Town Y.

   (a) How far away from Suburb must Town Y be located in order for Lawyer to be allowed a moving expense deduction?

   (b) How far away from Suburb must Town Y be located in order for Lawyer to be allowed a moving expense deduction if Lawyer has just graduated from law school in Town X and he was not employed?

   (c) Assuming Lawyer is a sole practitioner what time requirements are imposed on him in order for § 217 to apply?

   (d) What difference in result in (c), above, if Lawyer joins a firm in Town Y as a partner?

   (e) What difference in result in (c), above, if Lawyer goes to work for a firm in Town Y but as an associate rather than a partner?

   (f) Assuming the necessary time and distance requirements are met, and that a joint return is filed, what is the amount of Lawyer's § 217 deduction if he incurs the following expenses: $400 in moving his family's belongings; $250 in transporting his family, including lodging and 80% of meals en route; $400 on an unsuccessful house hunting trip to Town Y and back prior to acquiring a job; $1200 in motel and 80% of meal expenses for a period of 25 days two months after finding his job and moving to Town Y, but prior to locating permanent housing; and $700 to buy out of his lease on their apartment in Suburb; $1200 in closing costs on their newly purchased home; and $400 in "points" (interest) on their mortgage on their new home?

   (g) Is there any difference in the result in (f), above, if Lawyer's wife also takes a job in Town Y and meets the necessary time and distance requirements?

(h) If Lawyer's firm reimburses Lawyer for $1000 of his expenses what tax consequences will the reimbursement have?

2. Tardy closed his law practice in Chicago on May 1, 1990, to seek greener pastures in Springfield, Illinois. He began work there on July 1, 1990, and has been there in active practice ever since, meeting the 78 week test of § 217(c)(2)(B) late in 1991. In his return for 1991 he claimed a deduction for his moving expenses in the amount of $4000. On April 10, 1994, the Commissioner issued a deficiency notice disallowing the claimed deduction. Any likely need at that time for speedy action by Tardy? See §§ 6072, 6511(a); and see Della M. Meadows, 66 T.C. 51 (1976).

3. When Employer moved her to Indianapolis, Ms. Keen bought a house for $140,000. Several years later her Employer asked her to move to San Francisco which she did. The best offer Ms. Keen could get for her house was $135,000 so, under her employment contract, Employer bought the house from her for $140,000 (her cost). He later resold it for $135,000. What are the tax consequences to Ms. Keen *and* to Employer. See Seth E. Keener, 59 T.C. 302 (1972).

4. Professor Bionic took a year's leave of absence from the Biology Department at a Louisiana college to teach biology at a college in Vermont. As planned, he left Louisiana in June, 1991, and returned in September, 1992. At a cost of $3000 he moved his modest apartment furnishings to Vermont and back, saving an estimated $1000 additional expense in Vermont. May he deduct the $3000 (and some other unidentified costs as well) under § 217? See Alvin L. Goldman, 32 TCM 574 (1973).

B. THE CONCEPT OF ADJUSTED GROSS INCOME

Internal Revenue Code: Sections 62; 86(a)–(c).

Regulations: Section 1.62–1T(b) and (d).

EXCERPT FROM SENATE FINANCE COMMITTEE REPORT NO. 885

78th Congress, 2d Session (1944).
1944 Cum.Bull. 858, 877.

Fundamentally, the deductions * * * permitted to be made from gross income in arriving at adjusted gross income are those which are necessary to make as nearly equivalent as practicable the concept of adjusted gross income, when that concept is applied to different types of taxpayers deriving their income from varying sources. Such equivalence is necessary for equitable application of a mechanical tax table or a standard deduction * which does not depend upon the source of income. For example, in the case of an individual merchant or store proprietor, gross income under the law is gross receipts less the cost of

---

* See Part E, infra.

goods sold; it is necessary to reduce this amount by the amount of business expenses before it becomes comparable, for the purposes of such a tax table or the standard deduction, to the salary or wages of an employee in the usual case. Similarly, the gross income derived from rents and royalties is reduced by the deductions attributable thereto * * * in order that the resulting adjusted gross income will be on a parity with the income from interest and dividends in respect of which latter items no deductions are permitted in computing adjusted gross income.

The deductions [attributable to a trade or business] are limited to those which fall within the category of expenses directly incurred in the carrying on of a trade or business. The connection contemplated by the statute is a direct one rather than a remote one. For example, property taxes paid or incurred on real property used in the trade or business will be deductible whereas state income taxes, incurred on business profits, would clearly not be deductible for the purpose of computing adjusted gross income. Similarly, with respect to the deductions [attributable to rents and royalties] the term "attributable" shall be taken in its restricted sense; only such deductions as are, in the accounting sense, deemed to be expenses directly incurred in the rental of property or in the production of royalties. Thus, for this purpose, charitable contributions would not be deemed to be expenses directly incurred in the operation of a trade or business, or in the rental of property or the production of royalties. * * *

This section creates no new deductions; the only deductions permitted are such of those allowed in Chapter 1 of the Code as are specified in any of the clauses [now (1) through (13) of Section 62(a)] above. The circumstance that a particular item is specified in one of the clauses and is also includible in another does not enable the item to be twice subtracted in determining adjusted gross income.

* * *

NOTE

The concept of adjusted gross income has relevance only with respect to individual taxpayers. It has no significance for corporate taxpayers, or estates, trusts or partnerships. With respect to individuals, it serves as a measuring device for computing the ceiling limitation on allowable charitable deductions [1] and the Section 469(i) rental real estate exemption, and it imposes a floor on the deductibility of medical expenses,[2] some casualty and theft losses,[3] and some other itemized deductions.[4] It acts as a measuring rod in the overall limitation on

---

1. I.R.C. § 170(b). This ceiling is now expressed in terms of "contribution base," but that term is defined with reference to adjusted gross income. § 170(b)(1)(E). See Chapter 23B, infra.

2. I.R.C. § 213(a)(1) and (b). See Part C, infra.

3. I.R.C. § 165(c)(3) and (h)(2). See Chapter 23C, infra.

4. I.R.C. § 67. See Part E, infra.

itemized deductions [5] and the phase-out of personal exemptions,[6] as well as other exclusions,[7] deductions,[8] and credits.[9]

Adjusted gross income also serves as the measuring device for computing the portion of social security benefits [10] which must be included in gross income under Section 86.[11] Social security benefits are subject to tax, if within a taxable year, the sum of the taxpayer's "modified adjusted gross income" plus one-half of social security benefits received exceeds a specified "base amount." [12] "Modified adjusted gross income" is an individual's adjusted gross income computed without reduction for certain exclusions,[13] and increased by the amount of the taxpayer's tax-exempt interest for the year.[14] The "base amount" is $25,000 for an individual and $32,000 for a married individual filing a joint return, but zero for married individuals filing separately who reside together during the taxable year.[15] If Section 86 applies, the amount required to be included in gross income is one-half of the *lesser* of (1) the total social security benefits received during the taxable year or (2) the modified adjusted gross income plus one-half of the social security benefits received less the base amount.[16] Thus a maximum of one-half of the social security benefits may be included in gross income. Taxpayers who receive lump sum social security benefit payments which are attributable to prior years may make a special election to limit the amount of tax in the current year to the amount of tax that would have been paid had the benefits been received in the prior years.[17]

In a very broad sense all deductions are from gross income and result in taxable income. However, in the statutory scheme, some items of deduction are spoken of as allowable "above the line" (those described in Section 62), while some are deductible "below the line" (those outside Section 62). In this regard, Section 62 does not *authorize*

---

5. I.R.C. § 68. See Chapter 27A, infra.

6. I.R.C. § 151(d)(3). See Chapter 27A, infra.

7. See, e.g., I.R.C. § 135(b)(2), (c)(4) and Chapter 11B,. supra.

8. See, e.g., I.R.C. § 469(i)(3)(A) and Chapter 17E, supra.

9. See, e.g., I.R.C. § 32(b)(1)(B)(ii) and Chapter 27B, infra.

10. The term "social security benefit" includes monthly benefits received under Title II of the Social Security Act or tier railroad retirement benefits. I.R.C. § 86(d) (1).

11. P.L. No. 98–21, § 121(a), 98th Cong., 1st Sess. (1983). The provision is applicable to benefits received after 1983. See McSteen, "Planning for the Taxation of Social Security Benefits," 63 Taxes 3 (1985).

12. I.R.C. § 86(b).

13. See I.R.C. § 86(b)(2)(A). The concept of modified adjusted gross income disregards any income under this section and the exclusions of I.R.C. §§ 135, 911, 931 and 933, thus including such exclusions in a modified gross income.

14. I.R.C. § 86(b)(2)(B).

15. I.R.C. § 86(c). Congress provides a zero base amount for married individuals in order to prevent couples whose incomes are relatively equal from substantially reducing benefits subject to tax by filing separate returns. H.Rep. No. 98–25, 98th Cong., 1st Sess., 25 (1983).

16. I.R.C. § 86(a).

17. I.R.C. § 86(e). Cf. I.R.C. § 1341.

any deduction. It simply *identifies* deductions, authorized elsewhere in the statute, which may be taken in arriving at adjusted gross income. Deductions that are not mentioned in Section 62 are possibly deductible, but these deductions are *from* adjusted gross income (so-called itemized deductions) and can be taken only as elective itemized deductions,[18] in lieu of the standard deduction.[19] Deductions described in Section 62 are allowed in their entirety without regard to use of the standard deduction.[20] and in this light they are especially favorable deductions.

These brief comments identify a matter of major significance which must be given some thought. The thinking process will be aided by the Problems that follow and the segment on the standard deduction in part E of this chapter.

PROBLEMS

1. Assume the following expenses are properly deductible. Does the deduction fall under § 62, or may it be claimed only as a § 63 deduction.

(a) Employee, a policeman, purchases a new uniform at his own expense.

(b) Employee Salesman (not "outside") pays the cost of entertaining purchasers in social circumstances that are directly related to his trade or business and is not reimbursed by Employer.

(c) Same as (b), above, except that Employer reimburses Employee for the exact cost incurred. How should Employee treat the expenses and reimbursement on his return? See Reg. § 1.162–17. What result to Employer?

(d) Same as (b), above, except that Employer, an individual, rather than Employee, entertained the purchasers.

(e) Employee, at his own expense, pays $500 tuition for a refresher course in Home Town to bring himself up to date on current business techniques relating to his employment.

(f) Employee makes payments for medical expenses and charitable contributions and for taxes on his residence and interest on a note secured by a mortgage on the residence.

(g) Same as (f), above, except that the taxes and interest relate to a residence that Employee rents to Tenant.

(h) Employee has a loss on the sale of some stock that he held for investment.

(i) Employer, whose business is unincorporated, pays his state income taxes.

---

18. See the I.R.C. § 67(a) limitation on the deductibility of some itemized deductions in Part E, infra.

19. See I.R.C. § 63 Part E, infra.

20. See Part E, infra.

(j) Single pays his ex-wife $6000 in alimony. Is this within the common thread of § 62 deductions?

(k) Employee incurs properly deductible moving expenses.

(*l*) Employee is a struggling actor who works in several acting jobs during the year earning $15,000 (his only gross income for the year) and who incurs $2000 of deductible business expenses in the year in conjunction with his acting jobs.

2. Retired, a single individual, receives $20,000 of social security benefits in the current year when his adjusted gross income is $30,000 and he has $10,000 of tax exempt interest. He has no § 86(b)(2)(A) deductions or exclusions. What is the amount, if any, of Retired's gross income inclusion under § 86?

C. EXTRAORDINARY MEDICAL EXPENSES

Internal Revenue Code: Sections 213(a), (b), (d)(1)–(4) and (9); 263(a)(1). See Sections 21; 152(c); 213(d)(5) and (e).

Regulations: See Section 1.213–1(a)(1) and (2), (e)(1)–(4)(i)(a).

RAYMON GERARD*

Tax Court of the United States, 1962.
37 T.C. 826.

MULRONEY, Judge:

[The Findings of Fact have been omitted. Ed.]

Opinion

Section 213(a)[1] as here applicable allows "as a deduction the * * * amounts of the expenses paid during the taxable year, * * * for medical care of the taxpayer, his spouse, or a dependent."

Section 213(e) defines the term "medical care" as follows:

SEC. 213. MEDICAL, DENTAL, ETC., EXPENSES.

(e) **Definitions.**—For purposes of this section—

(1) The term "medical care" means amounts paid—

(A) for the diagnosis, cure, mitigation, treatment, or prevention of disease, or for the purpose of affecting any structure or function of the body (including amounts paid for accident or health insurance), or

---

* The Tax Equity and Fiscal Responsibility Act (TEFRA) of 1982, in addition to making substantive changes in I.R.C. § 213, redesignated subsection 213(e) as subsection 213(d). Therefore the definition of "medical care" now appears in subsection (d) of § 213, not in (e). In the material that follows, references in the cases to subsection 213(e) should be read as references to the statutory definition of medical care. Ed.

1. All section references are to the Internal Revenue Code of 1954, as amended.

(B) for transportation primarily for and essential to medical care referred to in subparagraph (A).

It is well established that some form of control of temperature and humidity was a medical necessity in petitioners' home. Their daughter's illness made it dangerous for her to be exposed to dry, dusty air. The evidence shows petitioners had tried a room air-conditioning unit in their home in New Jersey but it was not satisfactory.[2] This restricted the child to one room for the entire day in order to get the beneficial effects and it was bad for her psychologically. It was the doctor who advised petitioners it would be better for the child to have the central unit so she could have the whole home as her restricted area. Children afflicted with cystic fibrosis have a special diet and they are treated with antibiotics given by mouth and by aerosols and they sleep every night in a tent which has additional antibiotics.

We think the expenditure of $1,300 for installing the air-conditioning unit was an expenditure for medical care for petitioners' dependent, within the scope of the above-quoted statute. But there is another statute which must be considered because of the nature of this expenditure.

Section 263(a)(1) provides in part: "No deduction shall be allowed for * * * Any amount paid out * * * for permanent improvements or betterments made to increase the value of any property."

The general rule, expressed in respondent's regulation and numerous cases, is that a medical care expenditure for what is a capital expenditure in the nature of a permanent improvement to the taxpayer's home is not deductible as medical expense. Frank S. Delp, 30 T.C. 1230; John L. Seymour, 14 T.C. 1111; sec. 1.213–1(e)(1)(iii), Income Tax Regs. However, it has been held, and respondent admits, that the mere fact that a medical care expenditure is also a capital expenditure is not always sufficient to disqualify it for medical deduction. When the medical care expenditure is for a permanent addition to the taxpayer's home, deductibility as a medical expense depends upon whether it increases the value of the home. In Berry v. Wiseman, 174 F.Supp. 748 (W.D.Okla.1958), the court held the cost ($4,400) of installing an elevator in taxpayer's home was deductible as medical expense. There the housewife petitioner suffered from acute coronary insufficiency and the elevator was installed upon the advice of her physician. The court found that the elevator was permanent but "that it did not have the effect of increasing the value of the property." In Rev.Rul. 59–411, 1959–2 C.B. 100,[3] respondent announced he would follow the case of

---

2. Petitioner testified he took a medical deduction for this room air conditioner. Respondent's regulation sec. 1.213–1(e)(1)(iii) lists some capital expenditures which can be medical deductions and the list includes an expenditure for "an air conditioner which is detachable from the property and purchased only for the use of a sick person."

3. The said ruling states in part:

The Internal Revenue Service will follow the decision of the United States District Court for the Western District of Oklahoma in the case of James E. Berry et ux. v. Earl R. Wiseman (W.D.Okla.1958) 174 F.Supp. 748.

Berry v. Wiseman, supra, and his ruling indicates the significant fact in that case was the finding that the installation of the elevator did not increase the value of the house.

Prior to the above ruling, we had decided the *Delp* case in 1958. While the issue in Frank S. Delp, supra, was different (whether the electric air cleaner was permanently affixed to the home), there is an expression in the opinion indicating the extent of value increase is to measure medical deductibility. There we said speaking generally of medical care expenditures that represent permanent improvements to property:

> Such expenditures, to the extent the permanent improvement of the asset increases the value of the property, at least in a sense compensate for the expense of such improvement.

Respondent admits on brief where the taxpayer is able to show the medical care expenditure in the nature of a permanent addition to the residence does not increase the value of the home, it qualifies for medical deduction. We think it necessarily follows that where the taxpayer is able to show such increase in value is less than the expenditure, the amount in excess of value enhancement is deductible as medical expense. Here the parties stipulate the cost of installing the air-conditioning unit was $1,300 and the unit increased the value of the home in the sum of $800. It follows that the balance, or $500, qualifies for medical deduction. We so hold.

Reviewed by the Court.

Decision will be entered under Rule 50.

COMMISSIONER v. BILDER

Supreme Court of the United States, 1962.
369 U.S. 499, 82 S.Ct. 881.

Mr. Justice HARLAN delivered the opinion of the Court.

This case concerns the deductibility as an expense for "medical care," under § 213 of the Internal Revenue Code of 1954, 26 U.S.C.A. § 213, of rent paid by a taxpayer for an apartment in Florida, where he was ordered by his physician, as part of a regimen of medical treatment, to spend the winter months.[1]

The court ruled that the cost of an elevator installed in the taxpayers' residence was deductible as a medical expense. The elevator had been installed at a cost of some $4,400 on the advice of a doctor to alleviate an acute coronary insufficiency of Mrs. Berry.

Accordingly, expenditures made for medical purposes will not be disallowed merely because they are of a capital nature. However, it is the position of the Service that the capital nature of an expenditure will be a consideration in determining its de-ductibility. If such expenditures constitute amounts paid out for permanent improvements which *increase the value* of any property or estate, they will not be allowed as medical expense deductions.

Steps will be taken to modify outstanding rulings contrary to this court decision and to conform Treasury regulations promulgated under section 213 of the Internal Revenue Code of 1954.

1. [Quotations from I.R.C. § 213 are omitted. Ed.]

The taxpayer, now deceased, was an attorney practicing law in Newark, New Jersey. In December 1953, when he was 43 years of age and had suffered four heart attacks during the previous eight years, he was advised by a heart specialist to spend the winter season in a warm climate. The taxpayer, his wife, and his three-year-old daughter proceeded immediately to Fort Lauderdale, Florida, where they resided for the ensuing three months in an apartment rented for $1,500. Two months of the succeeding winter were also spent in Fort Lauderdale in an apartment rented for $829.

The taxpayer claimed the two rental payments as deductible medical expenses in his 1954 and 1955 income tax returns. These deductions were disallowed in their entirety by the Commissioner.[2] The Tax Court reversed the Commissioner's determination to the extent of one-third of the deductions, finding that proportion of the total claimed attributable to the taxpayer's own living accommodations. The remaining two-thirds it attributed to the accommodations of his wife and child, whose presence, the Tax Court concluded, had not been shown to be necessary to the medical treatment of the taxpayer's illness. 33 T.C. 155.

On cross-appeals from the decision of the Tax Court, the Court of Appeals held, by a divided vote, that the full rental payments were deductible as expenses for "medical care" within the meaning of § 213. 289 F.2d 291. Because of a subsequent contrary holding by the Court of Appeals for the Second Circuit, Carasso v. Commissioner, 292 F.2d 367, and the need for a uniform rule on the point, we granted certiorari to resolve the conflict. 368 U.S. 912, 82 S.Ct. 193.

The Commissioner concedes that prior to the enactment of the Internal Revenue Code of 1954 rental payments of the sort made by the taxpayer were recognized as deductible medical expenses. This was because § 23(x) of the Internal Revenue Code of 1939, though expressly authorizing deductions only for "amounts paid for the diagnosis, cure, mitigation, treatment, or prevention of disease,"[3] had been construed to include "travel primarily for and essential to * * * the prevention or alleviation of a physical or mental defect or illness," Treasury

---

2. The Commissioner concedes that the taxpayer's sojourn in Florida was not for vacation purposes but was "a medical necessity and * * * a primary part of necessary medical treatment of a disease" from which the taxpayer was suffering, i.e., atherosclerosis. 33 T.C., at 157. The taxpayer also claimed in each of his tax returns a $250 deduction for his transportation between Newark and Fort Lauderdale. Although the Commissioner initially disallowed this deduction he thereafter acquiesced in its allowance by the Tax Court.

3. Section 23(x) was added to the Internal Revenue Code of 1939 by § 127(a) of the Revenue Act of 1942, 56 Stat. 825. It provided, in pertinent part:

"[In computing net income there shall be allowed as deductions] * * * expenses paid during the taxable year, not compensated for by insurance or otherwise, for medical care of the taxpayer, his spouse, or a dependent * * * of the taxpayer. The term 'medical care,' as used in this subsection, shall include amounts paid for the diagnosis, cure, mitigation, treatment, or prevention of disease, or for the purpose of affecting any structure or function of the body (including amounts paid for accident or health insurance)."

Regulations 111, § 29.23(x)–1, and the cost of meals and lodging during such travel, I.T. 3786, 1946–1 Cum.Bull. 76. See, e.g., Stringham v. Commissioner, 12 T.C. 580, aff'd, 183 F.2d 597; Rev.Rul. 55–261, 1955–1 Cum.Bull. 307.

The Commissioner maintains, however, that it was the purpose of Congress, in enacting § 213(e)(1)(A) of the 1954 Code, albeit in language identical to that used in § 23(x) of the 1939 Code (* * * see note 3, supra), to deny deductions for all personal or living expenses incidental to medical treatment other than the cost of transportation of the patient alone, that exception having been expressly added by subdivision (B) to the definition of "medical care" in § 213(e)(1).

We consider the Commissioner's position unassailable in light of the congressional purpose explicitly revealed in the House and Senate Committee Reports on the bill. These reports, anticipating the precise situation now before us, state:

> "Subsection (e) defines medical care to mean amounts paid for the diagnosis, cure, mitigation, treatment, or prevention of diseases or for the purpose of affecting any structure or function of the body (including amounts paid for accident or health insurance), or for transportation primarily for and essential to medical care. The deduction permitted for 'transportation primarily for and essential to medical care' *clarifies existing law* in that it specifically *excludes deduction of any meals and lodging while away from home receiving medical treatment.* For example, if a doctor prescribes that a patient must go to Florida in order to alleviate specific chronic ailments and to escape unfavorable climatic conditions which have proven injurious to the health of the taxpayer, and the travel is prescribed for reasons other than the general improvement of a patient's health, the cost of the patient's transportation to Florida would be deductible *but not his living expenses while there.* However, if a doctor prescribed an appendectomy and the taxpayer chose to go to Florida for the operation not even his transportation costs would be deductible. The subsection is not intended otherwise to *change* the existing definitions of medical care, to deny the cost of ordinary ambulance transportation nor to deny the cost of food or lodging provided as part of a hospital bill." H.R.Rep. No. 1337, 83d Cong., 2d Sess. A60 (1954); S.Rep. No. 1622, 83d Cong., 2d Sess. 219–220 (1954).[4] (Emphasis supplied.)

Since under the predecessor statute, as it had been construed, expenses for meals and lodging *were* deductible as expenses for "medical care," it may well be true that the Committee Reports spoke in part inartistically when they referred to subsection (e) as a mere clarification of "existing law," although it will be noted that the report also

---

4. The substance of the rule set forth in both Reports has been embodied in the Treasury Regulations interpreting § 213. [See Reg. § 1.213–1(e)(1)(iv). Ed.]

referred to what was being done as a *pro tanto* "change" in "the existing definitions of medical care." Yet Congress' purpose to exclude such expenses as medical deductions under the new bill is unmistakable in these authoritative pronouncements, ibid.; cf. Budget Message of the President for the Fiscal Year 1955, H.R.Doc. No. 264, 83d Cong., 2d Sess. M17 (1954); Memorandum of Joint Committee on Internal Revenue Taxation, 1 Senate Hearings on the Internal Revenue Code of 1954, 83d Cong., 2d Sess. 24 (1954); Memorandum of the Under Secretary of the Treasury, id., at 103. It is that factor which is of controlling importance here.[5]

We need not consider whether we would be warranted in disregarding these unequivocal expressions of legislative intent if the statute were so written as to permit no reasonable construction other than that urged on behalf of the taxpayer. Compare Boston Sand & Gravel Co. v. United States, 278 U.S. 41, 48, 49 S.Ct. 52, 53; United States v. Dickerson, 310 U.S. 554, 561–562, 60 S.Ct. 1034, 1038; Harrison v. Norther Trust Co., 317 U.S. 476, 479, 63 S.Ct. 361, 362. See also Association of Westinghouse Salaried Employees v. Westinghouse Elec. Corp., 348 U.S. 437, 444, 75 S.Ct. 489, 491. Even the initial decision of the Tax Court under the 1939 Code respecting the deductibility of similar expenses under § 23(x) recognized that the language of that statute was "susceptible to a variety of conflicting interpretations," Stringham v. Commissioner, 12 T.C. 580, 583. The Tax Court's conclusion as to the meaning of § 23(x) of the earlier statute which was affirmed by the Court of Appeals, 183 F.2d 579, and acquiesced in by the Commissioner, necessarily rested on what emerged from a study of the legislative history of that enactment. So too the conclusion in this case, which turns on the construction of the identical words re-enacted as part of § 213, must be based on an examination of the legislative history of this provision of the 1954 Code. The Committee Reports foreclose any reading of that provision which would permit this taxpayer to take the rental payments for his Florida apartment as "medical care" deductions.

Reversed.

Mr. Justice DOUGLAS would affirm the judgment below for the reasons given by Judge Kalodner, 289 F.2d 291.

Mr. Justice FRANKFURTER took no part in the decision of this case.

Mr. Justice WHITE took no part in the consideration or decision of this case.

---

5. The explicitness of the Committee Reports renders it unnecessary to consider the Commissioner's alternative argument that the statute on its face precludes these deductions because (1) § 262 of the 1954 Code, 26 U.S.C.A. § 262, allows no deductions for "personal, living, or family expenses" "[e]xcept as otherwise expressly provided in this chapter," and (2) apart from the medical "transportation" expense provided in § 213(e)(1)(B), no other *express* exception can be found in the statute. And the equitable considerations which the respondent brings to bear in support of her construction of § 213 are of course beside the point in this Court, since we must give the statute effect in accordance with the purpose so clearly manifested by Congress.

MONTGOMERY v. COMMISSIONER *

United States Court of Appeals, Sixth Circuit, 1970.
428 F.2d 243.

CELEBREZZE, Circuit Judge.   This is an appeal from a judgment of the Tax Court of the United States by the Commissioner of Internal Revenue [hereinafter "Commissioner"] against Morris C. Montgomery [hereinafter "Taxpayer"] and his wife, who had filed a joint return for the taxable year 1961.   The Tax Court held, four judges dissenting, that the cost of meals and lodging of the Taxpayer and his wife, while en route from their home in Lawrenceburg, Kentucky, to Rochester, Minnesota, and return, on trips in 1961 for bona fide medical reasons, is included within the meaning of "transportation" expenses as used in Section 213(e)(1)(B) of the Internal Revenue Code of 1954; and therefore, such costs were deductible expenses for "medical care."

During 1961, the Taxpayer and his wife made three round trips to the Mayo Clinic, Rochester, Minnesota, from their legal residence in Lawrenceburg, Kentucky.   Each of these trips was for admittedly medical purposes and the Commissioner concedes that although the later two trips were for the medical treatment of Taxpayer's wife, the Taxpayer's accompaniment of his wife was required for medical reasons.   The Taxpayer and his wife made their first round trip by automobile and incurred certain itemized expenses, during their transportation, for food and lodging.   Subsequently, Taxpayer's wife traveled by train, pullman accommodations, and bus to the Mayo Clinic for an operation; and the Taxpayer traveled by automobile to the Clinic after the operation and accompanied his convalescing wife on her return to Lawrenceburg.   Thereafter, Taxpayer's wife made a final trip by plane to the Mayo Clinic where she was hospitalized.   At the time of her discharge from the Clinic, her husband again traveled by automobile to bring her home.   During these various trips, Taxpayer and his wife incurred a total expense for meals and lodging between Lawrenceburg and Rochester of $162.39.

The sole issue in the appeal is whether this $162.39 in expenses are deductible as expenses for "medical care" pursuant to Section 213 of the Internal Revenue Code of 1954.

The term "medical care" is defined under Section 213(e)(1) as amounts paid:

"(B) for transportation primarily for and essential to medical care referred to in subparagraph (A) [1], *   *   *."

The Commissioner contends that moneys paid for food and lodging en route to a place of medication are "traveling" expenses in excess of

---

* See the editor's footnote at page 532, supra.

There is a comment on this case in Johnson, "Medical Travel Expense," 16 S.Dak. L.Rev. 326 (1971). Ed.

[1].   Subparagraph (a) reads: "for the diagnosis, cure, mitigation, treatment or prevention of disease, or for the purpose of affecting any structure or function of the body."

the mere cost of "transporting" the person and baggage of the taxpayers to their place of destination. The Commissioner maintains that the use of the more narrow phrase "expenses for transportation," rather than "expenses * * * for traveling [to the place of medication]" indicates a plain intention to deny the deductibility of in-transit expenses for food and lodging. The Commissioner further contends that the cost of meals and lodging are "personal, living or family expenses" for which "no deduction shall be allowed, * * * [e]xcept as otherwise expressly provided." Internal Revenue Code, Section 262.

In response, the Taxpayer contends that "expenses * * * for transportation" includes, as the Tax Court held below, all expenses "required to bring the patient to the place of medication." 51 T.C. 410. Such expenses were deductible under the prior Internal Revenue Code of 1939, and the Tax Court found that the legislative history of the present Code, as well as the present Treasury Regulations, permit their continued deductibility. We agree.

Under the Internal Revenue Code of 1939, all food and lodging expenses of a patient on the way to the place of medication and at the place of medication were deductible. In Commissioner of Internal Revenue v. Bilder, 369 U.S. 499, 501, 82 S.Ct. 881 (1962), the United States Supreme Court denied the deductibility under the 1954 Code of lodging expenses at the place of medication. In doing so, it observed:

> "The Commissioner concedes that prior to the enactment of the Internal Revenue Code of 1954 rental payments of the sort made by the taxpayer were recognized as deductible medical expenses. This was because § 23(x) of the Internal Revenue Code of 1939, 26 U.S.C.A. 23(x) though expressly authorizing deductions only for 'amounts paid for the diagnosis, cure, mitigation, treatment, or prevention of disease,' had been construed to include 'travel primarily for and essential to * * * the prevention or alleviation of a physical or mental defect or illness,' Treasury Regulations 111, § 29.23(x)-1, and the cost of meals and lodging during such travel, I.T. 3786, 1946–1 Cum. Bull. 76. See, e.g. Stringham v. Commissioner, 12 T.C. 580, aff'd, 183 F.2d 579; Rev.Rule 55–261, 1955–1 Cum.Bull. 307."

Unfortunately, the liberal provisions of the 1939 Code for deductibility of "travel" expenses led to very significant abuses. Taxpayers would travel on doctors' orders to resort areas for the alleviation of a specific ailment and deduct all of the costs of their food and lodging while on such medical vacations. The legislative history of the Internal Revenue Code of 1954 indicates a specific intent to eliminate the resort area medication abuse. Both the House and Senate Committee Reports on the 1954 Code discuss the deductibility of medical care expenses. They state:

> "The deduction permitted for 'transportation primarily for and essential to medical care' clarifies existing law in that it specifically *excludes deduction of any meals and lodging while*

away from home receiving medical treatment. For example, if a doctor prescribes that a patient must go to Florida in order to alleviate specific chronic ailments and to escape unfavorable climate conditions which have proven injurious to the health of the taxpayer, and the travel is prescribed for reasons other than the general improvement of a patient's health, *the cost of the patient's transportation to Florida would be deductible but not his living expenses while there.* (Emphasis added) H.R.Rep. No. 1337, 83d Cong.2d Sess. A 60 (1954); S.Rep. No. 1622, 83d Cong., 2nd Sess. 219–220 (1954) U.S.Code Cong. & Admin.News, p. 4856."

The Treasury Department incorporated the substance of the above Reports in its Regulations interpreting Section 213. [See Reg. § 1.213–1(e)(1)(iv). Ed.]

* * *

It is apparent that the concern of Congress and the Treasury was to eliminate the abuse of "resort area" medication. Thus Congress eliminated the deductibility of food and lodging expenses at the actual place of medication.[2] Congress did not, however, eliminate the cost of transporting the patient to the place of medication.[3]

We believe that the legislative history and the accompanying regulations indicate a Congressional intent to maintain "existing law" with regard to the deduction of all costs required to transport the patient to the critical place of medication.

The abuse Congress sought to eliminate—the taking of ordinary living expenses "while there"—did not occur until after the patient arrived at the place of care. The effect of the regulations which deny deductibility for food and lodging expenses "while * * * receiving medical treatment" is to allow a deduction while traveling to the place of medical attention. If Congress had wished to exclude the costs for food and lodgings incurred in traveling to the place of medication, it could have so provided. The legislative history nowhere indicates an intention to exclude "all ordinary food and lodging expenses," nor does it limit transportation expenses "to the cost of transporting the patient and his baggage."

Food and lodging expenses incurred while traveling are likely to be substantially higher than the cost of living at home. We believe that Congress intended that these higher costs, required by the transporta-

---

2. Of course, expenses of meals and lodging incurred "as part of a hospital bill" are deductible. House and Senate Reports, infra, n. 3. Income Tax Regulations 1.213–1(e)(1)(iv) and (v).

3. As the House and Senate Reports state, the "cost of the patient's transportation to Florida would be deductible." H.R. Rep. No. 1337, 83rd Congress, 2nd Sess. A60 (1954); S.Rep. No. 1628, 83rd Cong., 2nd Sess., 219–220 (1954). Similarly, if a patient required a professional ambulance service to transport him to the place of medication, that portion of the professional fee attributable to the food and lodging expenses of the driver would be a deductible transportation expense. The Treasury Regulations also provide that nurse's services, "including nurses' board" paid by the taxpayer, are a deductible expense. Treasury Regulations 1.213–1(e)(1)(ii).

tion of a patient to the place of medical care, are to be deductible expenses for medical care under Section 213 of the 1954 Code.

Finally, we are not unmindful of the opinions of the four dissenting judges on the Tax Court. They correctly indicate that the word "transportation" has historically been given a narrower meaning than "travel." The former word has generally been used to cover the costs of transporting the person and his baggage, while the latter has been used in conjunction with the allowance of such amenities as food and lodging. See Internal Revenue Code of 1954 §§ 62(2)(B)(C), 162(a)(2), 217(b)(1)(B) and 274(d)(1). Further, it is clear that in passing the 1954 Code, Congress intended to retreat somewhat from its prior liberal attitude towards medical expenses. This is indicated by the inclusion of Section 262 requiring that "personal, living or family expenses" shall not be deductible "except as otherwise expressly provided," and the present regulations which state "deductions for expenditures for medical care * * * will be confined strictly to expenses incurred primarily for the prevention or alleviation of a physical or mental defect or illness." Treasury Regulations § 1.213–1(e)(1)(ii).

These two factors would be of great influence, but for our belief that the legislative history of Section 213(e) is clear in its import. Food and lodging expense while traveling to the place of medication and incurred prior to "receiving medical treatment" were to be maintained as deductible expenses. The use of the narrow term "transportation," rather than "travel" was indicative of Congress' intent to preclude food and lodging expenses after arrival at the place of medication. Cf. Commissioner v. Bilder, 369 U.S. 499, 82 S.Ct. 881 (1962). The phrase "expenses for traveling" might well have been construed to cover food and lodging expenses during periods of stay at the place of medical treatment; precisely the "abuse" Congress sought to eliminate by the 1954 Code.

We hold that the Taxpayer and his wife properly deducted under Section 213 food and lodging expenses required to bring them to the critical point of medical treatment. The judgment of the Tax Court is affirmed.

NOTE

Under the Internal Revenue Code of 1939, all food and lodging expenses of a patient en route to and from a place for medical care and at the place of medical care (i.e., at the hospital, not just in the vicinity) were deductible expenses. Off to Tucson for the winter?! No. The legislative history of the Internal Revenue Code of 1954 indicates congressional awareness of the prevalent abuses and an intention to deny a deduction for meals and lodging while merely away from home for medical treatment.[1] The Tax Reform Act of 1984 added Section

---

1. H.Rep. No. 1337, 83d Cong., 2d Sess. A60 (1954); S.Rep. No. 1662, 83d Cong., 2d Sess. 219–220 (1954).

213(d)(2) which specifically enlarges the medical expense definition to include amounts paid for certain lodging (but not meals) while away from home receiving medical treatment.[2]

Expenses for meals and lodging incurred as an in-patient in a hospital or similar institution are deductible medical expenses.[3] In Commissioner v. Bilder[4] the Supreme Court indicated that meals and lodging expenses incurred in the proximity of the place of medical care are nondeductible. However Section 213(d)(2) creates an exception to the *Bilder* conclusion with respect to some lodging expenses. Amounts paid for lodging while away from home are deductible if the lodging is required to enable the patient to be receiving medical care from a physician in a licensed hospital (or the equivalent of a licensed hospital). Thus lodging expenses in an outpatient capacity may be deductible. For example, if you go to Rochester, Minnesota and stay in one of the countless rooming houses or hotels unconnected with the Mayo Clinic while you get treatment at the Clinic, your lodging expenses (but not your meals) are deductible.

No deduction is allowed for lodging that is lavish or extravagent or for lodging that entails any significant element of personal pleasure or recreation. The lodging of a companion may be deducted, if the transportation expenses of the companion for the trip are deductible as medical expenses.[5] The amount of the deduction is limited to $50 per night for each eligible person. By silent implication, the new provision seals the door earlier closed on the question of the deductibility of *meals* in these circumstances.

A close question exists whether a taxpayer may deduct the cost of meals and lodging incurred while traveling *to and from* the place where medical care is received. In Montgomery v. Commissioner,[6] the Sixth Circuit, affirming the Tax Court, held that the cost of meals and lodging en route is included within the meaning of "transportation" expense as used in Section 213(d)(1)(B) and therefore is a deductible expense for medical care.[7] In Winoma Bell Hunt[8] on the other hand, it was held that meals and lodging expenses incurred during travel for medical reasons were not deductible; but in that case it is unclear whether the expenses were incurred at or en route to the place of care.

2. P.L. No. 98–369, § 423(b)(3), 98th Cong., 2d Sess. (1984).

3. Reg. § 1.213–1(e)(1)(v).

4. 369 U.S. 499, 82 S.Ct. 881 (1962). This conclusion is also supported by the Montgomery case at page 538 of the text. See also Max Carasso, 34 T.C. 1139 (1960), affirmed 292 F.2d 367 (2d Cir.1961), cert. denied 369 U.S. 874, 82 S.Ct. 1144 (1962), and Rose v. Commissioner, 485 F.2d 581 (5th Cir.1973).

5. H.Rep. No. 98–432, 98th Cong., 2d Sess. 1584 (1984).

6. 428 F.2d 243 (6th Cir.1970).

7. In Kelly v. Commissioner, 440 F.2d 307 (7th Cir.1971), although the deductibility of meals and lodging while traveling to the place of treatment was not at issue, the court indicated that the congressional purpose behind the changes in I.R.C. § 213 was to prevent "resort area" abuses and not absolutely to prohibit the deductibility of meals and lodging while traveling to a place for medical attention. A decision in accord with this dictum, unaided by the recent amendment will be either enlightened jurisprudence or judicial legislation, depending upon the viewers own philosophy.

8. 31 T.C.M. 1119 (1972).

The issue is not settled. By analogy to business travel it seems proper to allow a deduction for food and lodging expenses incurred while traveling to and from a place to receive medical care. These care-related expenses are likely to be substantially higher than the cost of living at home. However, meals and lodging are not easily squeezed into the term "transportation" and there is express language in the legislative history [9] which indicates Congress may not have intended that these expenses be allowed. Congress should resolve the *Montgomery* issue.

Meals and lodging expenses are not the only borderline expenditures that may or may not be deemed medical expenses. A large number of questionable items have been placed within the deductible category. Here are some examples: The cost of a wig was ruled deductible when as a result of disease a woman lost all of her hair, and a physician recommended the wig as needed to restore her mental health.[10] The costs of a son's clarinet and lessons to play it were ruled deductible when his orthodontist recommended them in order to alleviate a severe malocclusion of the son's teeth.[11] The cost of birth control pills prescribed by a physician,[12] the cost of a vasectomy,[13] and the cost of an operation performed on a woman to render her incapable of having children [14] qualify as deductible medical expenses. The cost of laetrile, where its use is legal, is deductible.[15] Although not all our criminal courts recognize drug addiction as an illness, amounts paid by a taxpayer to maintain a dependent in a therapeutic center for drug addicts have been held deductible.[16] Similarly, amounts paid for inpatient treatment at a therapeutic center for alcoholism and meals and lodging furnished incident to the treatment [17] and transportation costs incurred in attending meetings of Alcoholics Anonymous may be deducted.[18] Costs of acupuncture treatment [19] and medical transplants [20] are also deductible.

In a reversal of prior law,[21] Section 213(d)(9) now excludes cosmetic surgery or similar procedures from the definition of "medical care" unless the surgery or procedure is necessary to ameliorate a deformity arising from, or directly related to, a congenital abnormality, a personal injury resulting from an accident or trauma, or disfiguring disease[22].

9. Supra note 1.

10. Rev.Rul. 62–189, 1962–2 C.B. 88.

11. Rev.Rul. 62–210, 1962–2, C.B. 89.

12. Rev.Rul. 73–200, 1973–1 C.B. 140.

13. Rev.Rul. 73–201, 1973–1 C.B. 140.

14. Rev.Rul. 73–603, 1973–2 C.B. 76.

15. Rev.Rul. 78–325, 1978–2 C.B. 124.

16. Rev.Rul. 72–226, 1972–1 C.B. 96.

17. Rev.Rul. 73–325, 1973–2 C.B. 75.

18. Rev.Rul. 63–273, 1963–2 C.B. 112.

19. Rev.Rul. 72–593, 1972–2 C.B. 180.

20. Rev.Rul. 73–189, 1973–1 C.B. 139. See Note, "Tax Consequences of Transfers of Bodily Parts," 73 Col.L.Rev. 482 (1973).

21. See W.W. Mattes, 77 T.C. 650 (1981), acq. 1982–1 C.B.1; Rev.Rul. 76–332, 1976–2 C.B. 81; Rev.Rul. 82–111, 1982–1 C.B. 48.

22. I.R.C. § 213(d)(9)(A). The subsection is effective for years after 1990.

Under the provision procedures such as hair removal electrolysis, hair transplants, lyposuction, and face lifts are generally not deductible.[23]

Some borderline expenses have been disallowed. The cost of dancing lessons taken to benefit varicose veins in taxpayer's legs, but without the advice of a physician, is not deductible expense for medical care.[24] And a deduction for dancing lessons even recommended by a physician and admittedly beneficial to the taxpayer was denied because the activity was too personal.[25] The Service would disallow deductions for expenses to improve one's general health and well being as opposed to curing a specific ailment or disease. Recent rulings have denied deductions for the cost of programs to stop smoking [26] and to lose weight [27] where the programs are designed to improve a taxpayer's general health, even though recommended by a doctor. If, however, the recommendation is made to cure a particular problem of the taxpayer, the expense should be held deductible.[28]

Amounts expended for the "prevention" of disease also involve close questions. Where a dentist recommended the installation of a device for adding fluoride to a home water supply as an aid in the prevention of tooth decay, the expenses of installation and the monthly rental charges thereon were treated as deductible medical expenses.[29] But the taxpayer was too optimistic, and no deduction was permitted, where he purchased and drank bottled distilled water merely to avoid drinking city fluoridated water.[30] Since the possibility of disease from nuclear fallout is very remote, the cost of a fallout shelter is probably a nondeductible personal expense.[31]

Where doctors recommended guardianship proceedings and hospitalization of the taxpayer, the fees of an attorney for services performed in connection with the initiation and termination of the guardianship proceedings were held deductible under Section 213.[32] But a legal fee paid by a taxpayer to obtain a divorce recommended by his psychiatrist was not a deductible medical expense.[33] Although amounts paid by taxpayers for psychiatric treatment for sexual inadequacy are considered by the Commissioner to be deductible medical expenses,[34] fees paid to a clergyman to improve a taxpayer's marriage are not.[35]

---

23. I.R.C. § 213(d)(9)(B). See note 21, supra. If expenses for cosmetic surgery are not deductible under § 213(d)(9), the insurance costs for such expenses are not deductible under § 213 and reimbursement for such expenses is not excludable under an employer's health plan. Conf.Rep. No. 101–964, 101st Cong.2d Sess. 8 (1990).

24. Adler v. Commissioner, 330 F.2d 91 (9th Cir.1964).

25. J.J. Thoene, 33 T.C. 62 (1959). See also Schrayter v. Commissioner, 39 T.C.M. 205 (1979).

26. Rev.Rul. 79–162, 1979–1 C.B. 116.

27. Rev.Rul. 79–151, 1979–1 C.B. 116.

28. IRS Letter Ruling 8004111, 10–31–79.

29. Rev.Rul. 64–267, 1964–2 C.B. 69.

30. Rev.Rul. 56–19, 1956–1 C.B. 135.

31. F.H. Daniels, 41 T.C. 324 (1963).

32. Gerstacker v. Commissioner, 414 F.2d 448 (6th Cir.1969).

33. J.H. Jacobs, 62 T.C. 813 (1974).

34. Rev.Rul. 75–187, 1975–1 C.B. 92.

35. Rev.Rul. 75–319, 1975–2 C.B. 88.

The deductibility of various educational costs as medical expenses has been frequently litigated. In a case in which the taxpayer sent his two children to a boarding school to alleviate his wife's nervous condition and help her to recuperate from an illness, the tuition was held nondeductible as a medical expense, because it was considered a mere family expense analogous to wages paid to a cook.[36] Tuition paid by parents for their blind son to attend a private school was held not deductible, because the school did not have a direct or proximate therapeutic effect on his blindness.[37] However, an individual's condition may be such that the primary reason for his being in an institution is the availability of "medical care." In these circumstances a deduction for tuition should be permitted, as it was where an ear specialist recommended a school designed to mitigate and alleviate a deafness handicap of the taxpayer's son.[38]

A deduction for tuition expenses was allowed where a child of average or above average intelligence but with psychiatric problems was sent to a private school because she was incapable of functioning normally at a public school.[39] However, in a case in which the taxpayer's son was sent to a private school, to help cure his "neurotic block against learning," and to get an education, the cost was allocated between nondeductible tuition and deductible mental therapy.[40] If university tuition and other charges are broken down, an identifiable fee for medical care is deductible.[41]

That which is an uncertain Section 213 medical expense deduction may in some circumstances constitute an ordinary and necessary business expense under Section 162. If a taxpayer on a business trip undergoes an operation and is required, upon discharge from the hospital, to remain at a hotel in the vicinity for a time for post-operative care prior to returning home,[42] it may be argued that the additional costs are a part of his deductible travel expenses under Section 162, without regard to Section 213 limitations. When an actor's teeth were knocked out while filming a movie the cost of the dental work to replace them was held deductible as a business expense under Section 162.[43] Amounts paid for reader's services performed in connection with work of a blind individual are deductible under Section 162, not Section 213.[44]

Where it is questionable whether an expense is deductible as a business expense rather than a medical expense, Rev.Rul. 75–316 [45] indicates the expense may be deducted under Section 162 if the follow-

36. Ochs v. Commissioner, 195 F.2d 692 (2d Cir.1952), cert. denied 344 U.S. 827, 73 S.Ct. 28 (1952).

37. Arnold P. Grunwald, 51 T.C. 108 (1968). See also Fay v. Commissioner, 76 T.C. 408 (1981).

38. Donovan v. Campbell, Jr., unreported, 61–1 USTC ¶ 9357 (N.D.Tex.1961).

39. L.D. Greisdorf, 54 T.C. 1684 (1970), acq. 1970–2 C.B. XIX.

40. C. Fink Fischer, 50 T.C. 164 (1968), acq. 1969–2 C.B. XXIV.

41. Rev.Rul. 54–457, 1954–2 C.B. 100.

42. See Kelly v. Commissioner, supra note 6.

43. Reginald Denny, 33 B.T.A. 738 (1935), nonacq., XV–1 C.B. 30 (1936).

44. Rev.Rul. 75–316, 1975–2 C.B. 54.

45. 1975–2 C.B. 54.

ing three elements are present: (1) the nature of the taxpayer's work clearly requires that he incur a particular expense to satisfactorily perform such work, (2) the goods or services purchased by such expense are clearly not required or used, other than incidentally, in the conduct of the individual's personal activities, and (3) the Code and Regulations are otherwise silent as to the treatment of such expense.

PROBLEMS

1. Divorced Homeowner, who received neither alimony nor other support payments from her former husband, fully supported her 20 year old Daughter who had no income, lived with Homeowner and was a dependent of Homeowner under § 152. In the current year, Homeowner installed a central air conditioning system at a cost of $4100, which Dr. Watson said was an elementary requirement in caring for Daughter's respiratory problems. After installation, Homeowner's home had increased in value by $2100. Other medical expenses paid during the year by Homeowner and Daughter consisted of prescription medicine in the amount of $320 and doctors' bills in the amount of $400. Late in the year, she also paid $300 in premiums for health and accident insurance but received no reimbursements under the policy that year.

(a) If Homeowner's adjusted gross income is $12,000 for the year, what will be the amount of her medical expense deduction?

(b) Would it make better sense and, if so, be possible under the present statute to allow a deduction of $400 per year for the air conditioning expenditure, assuming the system has a 5 year life?

(c) If in the current year Homeowner incurs maintenance expenses of $300 on the air conditioning system can that be taken into account as a medical expense? Would a $150 deduction for those expenses be more supportable assuming, of course, Daughter is still there and still asthmatic? And what about an estimate that $400 of the year's electricity bill is attributable to running the air conditioning system?

2. A and B both went from their hometowns to Big City on business, each planning to return the next day, which A did. A incurred costs for transportation, meals and lodging in the amount of $200. B, however, became ill at the end of his business day and remained in his hotel for two extra days until he was well enough to return home. His expenses, which without the illness would have been the same as A's, came to $300. What may B deduct, and on what authority?

3. Sickly made frequent visits to his Psychiatrist. Late in the year he sent the doctor $6000, indicating it was to apply against future charges for services. Wobbly checked into a retirement home in the same year. He paid the home $20,000 for the lifetime right to live in the home and receive care, including medical care. The home gave him

a statement indicating, appropriately, that $6000 of the charge was for medical care. May either Sickly or Wobbly deduct the $6000 payments? Compare Robert S. Bassett, 26 T.C. 619 (1956), with Rev.Rul. 75–302, 1975–2 C.B. 86.

D. PERSONAL AND DEPENDENCY EXEMPTIONS

Internal Revenue Code: Sections 151; 152; 7703. See Sections 71(a), (c); 215; 6013(a), (d).

Regulations: Section 1.151–1(b) and (c)(2).

Almost every individual taxpayer has at least one automatic deduction, the so-called "personal exemption." [1] For 1989 the exemption amount was $2000. [2] Beginning in 1990, the deduction is adjusted annually to reflect changes in the Consumer Price Index. [3] Although the statute speaks somewhat confusingly of "allowance," "deduction" and "exemption," the amounts discussed here are simply subtractions from "adjusted gross income" (a term considered earlier in this chapter) in arriving at taxable income. [4]

The dollar amount is the amount of each personal exemption for which one qualifies regardless of whether it is an exemption for the taxpayer, the taxpayer's spouse, or a dependent of the taxpayer. [5] Almost every individual taxpayer is allowed an exemption for himself. However, if another taxpayer properly claimed the individual as a dependent, the individual is denied an exemption for himself. [6] A husband and wife filing a joint return constitute two taxpayers and they therefore are allowed two personal exemptions. [7] If they do not file a joint return, a spouse may claim an allowance for the other spouse only if the other has no gross income and is not the dependent of any other taxpayer. [8]

Students should note that the deduction provisions of Section 151 can be broken down into two main parts: Subsection (b) of Section 151 concerns the personal exemption for the taxpayer and his spouse. The second part of the statute, Section 151(c), governs additional personal exemptions for *dependents*. Section 152, defining the term "dependent", authorizes no deduction; it merely sets out precise rules for determining who is a dependent. Neither a husband nor a wife is ever a "dependent" of the other for federal tax purposes. Right? Right!

There are two principal requirements for "dependent" status and a third basic prerequisite for the dependency deduction. First, the taxpayer and the person to be claimed as a dependent must bear one of the relationships specifically listed under Section 152(a). Although gener-

---

1. Some individuals are denied a personal exemption. I.R.C. § 151(d)(2). See note 6, infra. Some (high income) individuals' personal exemptions are phased out. I.R.C. § 151(d)(3). See Chapter 27A, infra.

2. I.R.C. § 151(d)(1).

3. I.R.C. § 151(d)(4)(A).

4. I.R.C. § 63(b)(2).

5. I.R.C. § 151(b) and (c).

6. I.R.C. § 151(d)(2).

7. Reg. § 1.151–1(b).

8. I.R.C. § 151(b).

ally those relationships are by blood, nevertheless the section treats adopted or foster children the same as blood relatives [9] and includes as a dependent a non-related individual who lives in the taxpayer's house as a member of the household.[10] However, Section 152(b)(5) provides that if at any time during the taxable year the relationship between the taxpayer and an individual is in violation of local law the individual does not qualify as a dependent.[11]

Secondly, the taxpayer claiming the dependent must provide over one-half of the support for the person during the year.[12] Support in these circumstances may be difficult to determine. It includes clothing, meals, lodging, and other necessities furnished to the dependent but does not include the value of personal services rendered to the dependent by the taxpayer,[13] or non-necessities such as a boat.[14] The Code provides that a scholarship received by a student will not be considered as support in determining whether parents furnish sufficient support.[15] On the other hand, the statutory scholarship exclusion does not encompass student loans.[16]

In some situations, especially with respect to elderly persons, several members of a family may jointly contribute to the support of an individual. Section 152(c) provides that, if certain requirements are met, those supporting the individual may agree that one of the group will be treated as though he provided over half of the individual's support for the year for purposes of Section 152(a). One of the problems presented below calls for close examination of Section 152(c).

Support problems also arise with respect to the children of divorced or legally separated parents.[17] Amounts received by a divorced spouse which are included in gross income under Section 71(a) and are used for the support of the children are deemed support contributions by that spouse. If, however, the payments are not within the recipient's income because of Section 71(c), then the payments are support provided by the paying spouse. Under Section 152(e)(1) generally the custodial parent is entitled to the dependency deduction. If, however, the custodial parent signs a waiver that he or she will not claim the child as a dependent for the taxable year, the non-custodial parent is entitled to the deduction if he or she attaches the waiver to his or her return for the year.[18] The rules are slightly different for divorce decrees or

---

9. I.R.C. § 152(b)(2).

10. I.R.C. § 152(a)(9). Household membership also sometimes brings an individual within the classification "child of the taxpayer" for purposes of § 151(c). I.R.C. § 152(b)(2).

11. Leonard J. Eichbauer, 30 TCM 581 (1971); Estate of Daniel Buckley, 37 T.C. 664 (1962); Ensminger v. Commissioner, 610 F.2d 189 (4th Cir.1979). See also Leon Turnipseed, 27 T.C. 758 (1957), reaching this result before the enactment of § 152(b)(5). But see Shackelford v. U.S., 3 B.R. 42 (Bkrtcy.W.D.Mo.1980).

12. I.R.C. § 152(a).

13. Reg. § 1.152–1(a).

14. Flowers v. U.S., unreported, 1957–1 U.S.T.C. ¶ 9655 (D.C.Pa.1957). But see Rev.Rul. 77–282, 1977–2 C.B. 52, treating an automobile as an item of support.

15. I.R.C. § 152(d).

16. P. McCauley, 56 T.C. 48 (1971).

17. See I.R.C. § 152(e)(1)(A).

18. I.R.C. § 152(e)(2). If the waiver is for more than one year, a copy of the original waiver must be attached to the

separate maintenance agreements which were entered into before 1985. There, the non-custodial parent is entitled to the deduction only if the decree or agreement provides for it and the non-custodial parent provides at least $600 of support for the child.[19] These rules apply only if the parents have custody of the child for at least one half of the year,[20] if they provide more than one half of the child's support,[21] if they do not file a joint return,[22] and if the child is not the subject of a multiple support agreement.[23] However, for purposes of the Section 213 medical expense deduction, the child will be treated as a dependent of both parents.[24] Thus either parent may deduct medical expenses incurred on behalf of the child even though the dependency exemption is allowed to the other parent.

The third basic requirement for a dependency exemption is that the person claimed as a dependent may not have *gross income* in excess of the exemption amount for the year involved, i.e. $2000 in 1989.[25] For purposes of Section 151(c) gross income is defined the same as under Section 61, and therefore the income inclusion and exclusion sections apply in the determination of gross income.[26] The gross income limitation does not apply, however, if the dependent is a child of the taxpayer[27] *and* is either under the age of 19 at the close of the calendar year in which the taxpayer's taxable year begins or is a full-time student who has not attained age 24 at the end of such calendar year.[28]

No dependency exemption is allowed, even though the three requirements are met, if the dependent is married and files a joint return with his or her spouse.[29] The problems following illustrate the statutory requirements presented above; but, if a student is required to work them, it should be less to learn these statutory details than to learn how to deal with intricate tax language.

One should look again at Sections 62 and 63. The personal exemptions, not mentioned in Section 62, are deductible *from* adjusted gross income but, unlike the so-called itemized deductions, the personal exemptions are allowed without regard to whether the taxpayer itemizes deductions or uses the standard deduction.[30]

non-custodial parent's return for each of those years.

19. I.R.C. § 152(e)(4). Support provided by a spouse of a remarried parent is treated as support from that parent for purposes of § 152(e). I.R.C. § 152(e)(5).

20. I.R.C. § 152(e)(1)(B).

21. I.R.C. § 152(e)(1)(A). Cf. § 152(e)(5).

22. If a joint return is filed, the question of which parent is allowed the exemption is irrelevant.

23. I.R.C. § 152(e)(3).

24. I.R.C. § 213(d)(5).

25. I.R.C. § 151(c)(1)(A). See I.R.C. § 151(d)(1) and (3). A limited exception to

this requirement is provided by I.R.C. § 151(c)(5). If a dependent is permanently and totally disabled and works at a school which provides medical care to alleviate his or her disability, then whatever income he or she earns from the school is not taken into account in determining the gross income restriction.

26. Reg. § 1.151–2(a).

27. I.R.C. §§ 151(c)(1)(B) and (c)(3).

28. I.R.C. §§ 151(c)(1)(B) and (c)(4).

29. I.R.C. § 151(c)(2).

30. See I.R.C. § 63(b)(2).

Even though personal exemptions are allowed in computing taxable income nevertheless, beginning in 1991, they are phased out for taxpayers having adjusted gross income in excess of specified levels.[31] The phase-out is achieved by disallowance of a portion of the deductions.[32] It is considered in Chapter 27A which deals with tax rates.

PROBLEMS

1. In the following parts of this question, state the number of deductions for personal exemptions available. The following facts may be assumed unless otherwise indicated: T was married; T's spouse had no gross income during the year and was not a dependent of any other person; and T files a separate return. Treat each part separately unless otherwise indicated.

(a) T married W on December 31, and W's only income for the year was $50 of interest on tax exempt bonds.

(b) Same as (a), above, except that on December 31 W also received $100 as a wedding present from Uncle U.

(c) Same as (a), above, except that the $50 was a gain from the sale of the bonds in (a), above.

(d) Under the facts of (c), above, may T claim a dependency exemption for W if a spousal exemption is foreclosed?

(e) Same as (c), above, except that T and W file a joint return.

2. A and B were husband and wife and calendar year taxpayers. A died in the current year and B married C in the same year, six months after A's death. B had no gross income for the year.

(a) When A's executor files A's final return as a separate return of A, may he claim an exemption for B even though C does too? See Rev.Rul. 71–159, 1971–1 C.B. 50.

(b) If it were B (who had no income) who had died and A (who had lots of income) had married D, could A on a separate return (D also filing separately) claim an exemption for B? See Rev.Rul. 71–158, 1971–1 C.B. 50.

3. In each of the following parts state whether T was entitled to a "dependency" exemption for the particular person (i.e., X) involved. Assume the following facts for each of these parts, unless otherwise indicated: the taxable year is 1989; T was married but filed a separate return; and T furnished over one-half of the support for the particular person involved. Also assume, unless otherwise indicated, that such person earned less than $2000 gross income during the year, and did not live with T. Treat each part separately unless otherwise indicated.

(a) X was T's wife's brother.

---

31. I.R.C. § 151(d)(3). The phase-out is set to expire after December 31, 1995. I.R.C. § 151(d)(3)(E).

32. The phase-out is an "applicable percentage" of the exemption amount. The applicable percentage is 2 percentage points for each $2,500 (or fraction thereof) by which the taxpayer's adjusted gross income exceeds a "threshold amount." I.R.C. § 151(d)(3)(A)–(C).

(b) Same as (a), above, but assume further that:

   (1) T's wife died the year before.

   (2) T and W were divorced the year before. Cf. Steele v. Suwalski, 75 F.2d 885 (7th Cir.1935).

(c) X was T's wife's sister's husband.

(d) Same as (c), above, except that X lived with T the entire year.

(e) X is T's son who will be 19 next January 1st and who earned $2000 from summer jobs during the year but who is a full-time college student, except in the summer. See Reg. § 1.151–1(c)(2).

(f) X is T's 18 year old daughter who had only $500 of gross income during the year, but who married Y during the year with whom she files a joint return.

(g) Same as (f), above, but Y also had relatively little income from which tax was withheld and their return was filed only for purposes of obtaining a refund. See Rev.Rul. 65–34, 1965–1 C.B. 86.

(h) X was T's 18 year old son for whom T contributed $2000 in support while X, who had no gross income, applied $3000 out of gifts from Uncle U to his support.

(i) Same as (h), above, except that X's only contribution to his own support was a $3000 scholarship enabling him to attend Embraceable U.

4. T's father X, who has no gross income, was supported in the current year by T, T's two brothers (A and B), and C, an unrelated friend. A total of $4000 was spent for the father's support which was contributed in the following proportions by the above persons: X, 15%; T, 25%; A, 20%; B, 10%; and C, 30%. Which of these persons, if any, is entitled to claim X as a dependent and what procedures must they follow?

5. W, upon graduation from law school, decides to divorce H after 3 years of marriage. The divorce becomes final in the current year and W is awarded custody of their son H, Jr. Who is entitled to the dependency deduction in the following circumstances?

(a) W furnishes 40 percent of Jr.'s support and H furnishes 60 percent.

(b) Same as (a), above, except that W waives claiming any dependency deduction.

(c) Same as (a), above, except that Jr. lives with Grandpa for 9 months out of the year.

(d) Instead of getting divorced, W moves out of the house into her own apartment on May 1 of the current year and continues to reside there throughout the year. Jr. lives with H and both W and H equally provide for Jr.'s support.

6. In 1982, Mr. Kramer's long hours at his job begin to take their toll on the Kramer marriage. Eventually, Mrs. Kramer decides to "find herself" by leaving the homestead and filing for divorce. In the process of "finding herself," Mrs. Kramer loses custody of her son in the divorce decree which became final in 1983. Mr. Kramer is awarded custody of the child. Who is entitled to the deduction in the current year if:

(a) The divorce decree is silent as to who is entitled to the deduction, and both Mr. and Mrs. Kramer provide equally for their son's support?

(b) The divorce decree stipulates that Mrs. Kramer is entitled to the deduction. Both she and Mr. Kramer expend $500 each for the child's support in the current year.

(c) Same as (b), above, except Mrs. Kramer provides $1,000 for support and Mr. Kramer provides $2,000.

E. THE STANDARD DEDUCTION

Internal Revenue Code: Sections 63; 67; 7703. See Section 68.

Regulations: Section 1.67–1T(a).

———

Often in this course, as in any course, it is necessary to put things into perspective by considering where one has been and where one is going. We have basically pulled together the items to be included in gross income and have considered several deductions. We have also seen that some of those deductions are listed in Section 62 and are allowed in computing adjusted gross income and that under Section 63(b)(2) exemptions are deducted from adjusted gross income in computing taxable income; but what about the remaining deductions? What happens to them? Where do they go? Can we use them? They are commonly referred to as "itemized deductions," [1] and we may or may not be able to use them in computing taxable income. The road from adjusted gross income to taxable income is mapped out in Section 63, a section that answers the questions raised above. The utility of itemized deductions generally depends upon whether in the aggregate (after a 2 percent floor imposed on some itemized deductions [2] and a reduction in most itemized deductions of high-income taxpayers [3]) they exceed the "standard deduction," [4] a concept explained below.

The standard deduction came into the Code in 1944 [5] to simplify tax returns by according individuals an election to deduct, subject to a ceiling, an amount equal to 10% of their adjusted gross incomes, in lieu of some deductions otherwise to be itemized. This permits a taxpayer to deduct a specified amount without keeping records of various ex-

1. I.R.C. § 63(d).

2. I.R.C. § 67(a).

3. I.R.C. § 68.

4. I.R.C. § 63(b)(1) and (c).

5. Individual Income Tax Act of 1944, § 9, 58 Stat. 231, 236 (1944).

penditures and without specifically reporting a large group of deductions. The corresponding reduction in the administrative burden of the Internal Revenue Service is obvious. The standard deduction is an alternative to claiming deductions for items such as taxes, interest, extraordinary medical expenses, and any others not specified under Section 62.

In the 1950's and 1960's inflation and the congressional addition of some itemized expenses to the deductible list operated to reduce individual returns using the elective standard deduction from 82.2% in 1944 to an estimated 58.2% in 1969.[6] Recognition of this prompted Congress to increase both the percentage and the ceiling limitation on the standard deduction on several occasions between 1970 and 1976. In addition, the Revenue Act of 1964 added the "minimum standard deduction"[7] that put a floor under the standard deduction and was enacted especially to benefit large, low-income families.[8]

The 1977 Tax Act, in what a colleague described as a "hocus pocus sleight of hand trick," made the standard deduction disappear while at the same time producing a sort of "born again" standard deduction, the "zero bracket amount".[9] This device, now abandoned, was a further attempt to simplify a taxpayer's tax computation by using an automatic, rather than elective, amount to shield some otherwise taxable income from tax without requiring specific deductions.[10]

In years after 1986, Congress has reverted to the standard deduction but with no minimum standard deduction, zero bracket amount, or other such concept to complicate the computation.[11] Congress has substantially increased the amount of the standard deduction with the result that fewer taxpayers are expected to "itemize"[12] or to be required to pay taxes. The amount of the basic standard deduction is $5,000 for married individuals filing jointly and for surviving spouses, $4,400 for heads of households, $3,000 for single individuals, and $2,500 for married individuals filing separately.[13] Beginning in 1989 the amount of the standard deduction for 1988 is indexed for inflation.[14]

---

6. Staff of the Joint Committee on Internal Revenue Taxation, General Explanation of the Tax Reform Act of 1969, p. 216 (1970).

7. Revenue Act of 1964, § 112, 78 Stat. 19, 23 (1964).

8. The minimum standard deduction was increased over the years and was renamed the "low income allowance."

9. Pub.Law No. 95-30, 95th Cong., 1st Sess. § 102 (1977).

10. On the one hand Congress did away with the standard deduction thereby relieving taxpayers of the burden of computing and subtracting that amount in arriving at taxable income. At the same time it used approximately the same *amount* as a foundation or prop under the Section 1 rate tables to jack up the rates. Thus it

created a *zero bracket* rate for the lowest levels of taxable income but permitted the remaining rates of tax on taxable income to rise from the top of the zero bracket.

11. I.R.C. § 63.

12. See also I.R.C. § 67, which is discussed below.

13. I.R.C. § 63(c)(2). Classifications such as head of households, surviving spouse, etc. are defined in I.R.C. § 2 and are considered in Chapter 27A, infra.

For 1987 the standard deduction amounts were $3,760 for married individuals filing jointly and for surviving spouses, $2,540 for heads of households and single individuals, and $1,880 for married individuals filing separately. I.R.C. § 63(h).

14. I.R.C. § 63(c)(4).

Additional standard deductions are allowed for elderly and blind taxpayers. Six hundred dollars is allowed for an elderly person (one who has attained age 65 before the close of his taxable year) and $600 for a blind individual if, in either case, the person is married or a surviving spouse.[15] The additional deduction is $1,200 if an individual is both blind and age 65.[16] Unmarrieds, other than surviving spouses, are allowed an even larger additional standard deduction of $750 in each category ($1,500 if in both).[17] Beginning in 1989 the amount of the additional standard deduction is also indexed for inflation.[18]

A special limitation on the amount of the standard deduction is imposed if the taxpayer is claimed as a dependent under Section 151 by another taxpayer.[19] In such a situation the amount of the dependent taxpayer's basic standard deduction may not exceed the greater of that taxpayer's "earned income" or $500.[20]

The standard deduction automatically applies to an individual taxpayer in computing taxable income for the year unless the taxpayer elects on his tax return to itemize his deductions [21] or the taxpayer does not qualify for use of the standard deduction and must itemize his deductions.[22] One such denial occurs under Section 63(c)(6)(A) which disallows use of the standard deduction by a married taxpayer on that taxpayer's separate return if the taxpayer's spouse has itemized deductions on the spouse's separate return. The reason for this rule is that one spouse could pay and deduct all itemized items, while the other spouse could make full use of the standard deduction; and they would receive a double benefit. The statute precludes this type of double benefit through intra-family tailoring and also precludes use of the standard deduction in some other circumstances.[23]

In making the election to itemize considered above, one must first determine the amount of his itemized deductions. Generally, this is easy as one simply combines the amounts of all of his deductions (other than exemptions) that are left over after some are given "above the line" status under Section 62.[24] However, we become increasingly aware that nothing in taxation is *that* easy. Section 67 enacted in the 1986 legislation enters the scene and imposes a 2 percent floor under

---

15. I.R.C. § 63(f). Marital status is determined under I.R.C. § 7703. I.R.C. § 63(g). See note 13, supra. If the taxpayer has a spouse for whom he may claim a personal exemption under § 151(b) additional $600 deductions may be claimed if the spouse has attained the age of 65 or is blind. I.R.C. § 63(f)(1)(B) and (f)(2)(B).

16. I.R.C. § 63(f)(1)(A) and (2)(A).

17. I.R.C. § 63(f)(3).

18. I.R.C. § 63(c)(4). See Chapter 27A, infra.

19. I.R.C. § 63(c)(5). See Chapter 18D, supra.

20. Id. "Earned income" is defined in I.R.C. § 911(d)(2) as essentially income from services. The $500 amount is also indexed for inflation after 1989. I.R.C. § 63(c)(4).

21. I.R.C. § 63(b). See I.R.C. § 63(e). The original standard deduction in 1944 was elective, i.e., a taxpayer itemized his deductions unless he elected the standard deduction. Under the post–1986 rules, this is reversed.

22. I.R.C. § 63(c)(6).

23. See I.R.C. § 63(c)(6)(B)–(E).

24. See Chapter 18D, supra.

some (many) itemized deductions.[25]   Thus deductions other than those deductible under Section 62 (above the line), exemptions, and those specifically listed in Section 67(b)[26] are referred to as miscellaneous itemized deductions and they are allowed to be deducted as itemized deductions only to the extent that their total amount exceeds 2 percent of the taxpayer's adjusted gross income.   In determining whether or not to elect to itemize deductions, a taxpayer must first add up his itemized deductions not listed in Section 67(b) and subject that total to the 2 percent floor and add the resulting figure to his Section 67(b) itemized deductions.   To further complicate the computation, Section 68 requires high-income taxpayers to reduce the amount of their itemized deductions[27] by 3 percent of the excess of their adjusted gross income in excess of an applicable amount (generally $100,000)[28] but not in excess of 80 percent of the taxpayer's itemized deductions.[29]   This reduction is discussed in Chapter 27A, infra.   Finally, a taxpayer must then compare his total adjusted itemized deductions to the total amount of his basic and additional standard deductions.

PROBLEMS

1.   Single Taxpayer in the current year has $20,000 of adjusted gross income, a single personal exemption, and the following allowable itemized deductions: $1,000 in interest, $500 in taxes, $1,500 in unreimbursed employee travel expenses, $200 in tax preparation fees, and $300 bar association dues.   For simplicity, assume that there are no inflation adjustments after 1989.   See §§ 63(c)(4), 151(d)(3).

   (a)   What is Taxpayer's taxable income for the current year?

   (b)   What difference in result in (a), above, if Taxpayer's 65th birthday is January 1 of the succeeding year.   See Reg. § 1.151–1(c)(2).

   (c)   What difference in result under the facts of (a), above, if Taxpayer is a married couple filing a joint return?

   (d)   What difference in result under the facts of (c), above, if Taxpayers' deductible interest is $4,000 rather than $1,000?

2.   T, who is single, a child of X and a full-time law student has gross investment income of $4,000 in the current year and no § 62 or itemized deductions.   For simplicity assume that there are no inflation adjustments after 1989.   See §§ 63(c)(4), 151(d)(3).   X properly claims T as a dependent for the year.

25.   I.R.C. § 67(a).

26.   The I.R.C. § 67(b) deductions are not subject to the 2% floor.   Several of the § 67(b) deductions have previously been dealt with in this book.   § 163 (interest); § 164 (taxes);   § 213 (medical expenses); § 217 (moving expenses) and § 691(c) (related to income in respect of decedent). Other § 67(b) deductions are considered in later parts of the book.

27.   Some itemized deductions are excluded from the computation.   I.R.C. § 68(c).

28.   I.R.C. § 68(b)(1).   The amount is $50,000 for a married taxpayer filing a separate return.   Id.   The amount is adjusted for inflation for years after 1991. I.R.C. § 68(b)(2).

29.   I.R.C. § 68(a).   See note 27, supra.

(a) What is T's taxable income, if any, for the current year?

(b) What difference in result in (a), above, if instead T has $1,000 of earned income (§ 911(b)) and $3,000 of investment income?

(c) What difference in result in (a), above, if instead T has $4,000 of earned income and no investment income?

(d) What results in (a)–(c), above, if X neglects to claim T as a dependent?

3. A lives in New York and B in Florida. Both are single and have very substantial all-salary incomes of identical amounts in 1989. A pays state income tax in the amount of $4,000. B pays no state income tax. Assume (quite artificially) that neither has any other cost, expense, or expenditure that could be claimed as a deduction. Which, if either, should claim the standard deduction? Explain. Would your answer be different if the $4,000 paid by A was deductible alimony?

4. Husband and Wife file separate returns. Husband has substantial itemized deductions, but Wife has very few. Why does Congress prohibit the use of the standard deduction by Wife if Husband itemizes his deductions?

5. Husband and Wife are living apart and their children reside with Wife who pays all the household expenses from her own substantial income. Wife files a separate return for 1989 claiming a standard deduction of $3,000. Properly? If Husband also has substantial income, what is the ceiling on *his* standard deduction? (See § 7703(b) for both questions.)

6. X, Y, and Z supported their father F who lived alone but had no income. In the current year X paid $2,000 for Father's food. Y paid $2,000 for Father's lodging, and Z paid $2,000 for doctor and hospital expenses for Father. Under a multiple support agreement, X claimed Father as a dependent. What do you need to know to determine whether that was a serious mistake?

PART FIVE: THE YEAR OF INCLUSION OR DEDUCTION

CHAPTER 19. FUNDAMENTAL TIMING PRINCIPLES

A. INTRODUCTION

Internal Revenue Code: Sections 441(a) through (e); 442; 446; 451(a); 461(a). See Sections 448; 460.

Regulations: Section 1.446–1(a) through (c)(1).

Federal income taxes are computed on the basis of a net income figure (taxable income) for a twelve month period (the taxable year).[1] Preceding chapters have developed some of the principles under which it is determined whether and how various items may bear on the computation of taxable income. Assuming an item is significant in this respect, our question now is: *When,* for what taxable year, is the item taken into account? The taxable year is usually a twelve month period ending on the last day of a month.[2] A taxpayer may use the calendar year which of course ends on December 31st, or he may elect a fiscal taxable year which ends on the last day of any other month.[3] After a taxpayer has chosen an accounting period, approval of the Commissioner is required for a change of his accounting period.[4] Why does Congress require such approval?

Identification of the proper taxable year for reporting an item of income or for claiming a deduction can bear importantly on the taxpayer's tax liability. Obviously, it is not just a question whether he is taxed on an item in 1991 or 1992. Substantive changes in the law, changes in the tax rates, changes in the taxpayer's status, changes in who the taxpayer is, the running of the statute of limitations, and other financial activities of the taxpayer, including the time value of money, all may bear on the amount of liability if the item falls into one year rather than another.

---

1. I.R.C. § 441.

2. Sometimes a shorter period is treated as if it were a full taxable year, as upon the death of a taxpayer or the creation of a new taxable entity such as a corporation or a trust. I.R.C. § 443(a)(2). But, if a short period arises out of a change in a taxpayer's accounting period, income must be "annualized." I.R.C. § 443(b).

3. If a taxpayer fails to adopt a proper fiscal period he must use the calendar year. I.R.C. § 441(b)(2) and (g).

Trusts, other than wholly charitable trusts, are required to adopt a calendar year. I.R.C. § 645.

4. I.R.C. § 442. Cf. I.R.C. § 443(a)(1), (b).

Whether a taxpayer uses the calendar year or a fiscal year, the period for which he reports items of income or deduction is affected by the method of accounting that he has adopted. The principal accounting methods, which are examined in this chapter, are the cash receipts and disbursements method and the accrual method. The cash method of accounting, normally used by individuals, measures tax liability by including an item in income or allowing a deduction at the time that cash or its equivalent is received or paid. The accrual method of accounting is normally used and sometimes must be used by businesses. It measures tax liability by including an item in income at the time the taxpayer becomes entitled to it and allowing a deduction at the time a deductible obligation becomes fixed and certain, that is, when all events have occurred to fix the right to receive payment or to fix the duty to make payment but sometimes only after economic performance, where in either instance the amount can be determined with reasonable accuracy.[5]

Although the cash and accrual methods are the principal accounting methods, they are not the exclusive methods. The code approves some statutory variations in methods of accounting.[6] Approved variations include special rules relating to reporting income from installment sales under Section 453 [7] and special treatment of certain types of income and expense.[8]

With regard to the detailed implementation of any accounting method, the regulations state: [9]

> It is recognized that no uniform method of accounting can be prescribed for all taxpayers. Each taxpayer shall adopt such forms and systems as are, in his judgment, best suited to his need. However, no method of accounting is acceptable unless, in the opinion of the Commissioner, it clearly reflects income. A method of accounting which reflects the consistent application of generally accepted accounting principles in a particular trade or business in accordance with accepted conditions or practices in that trade or business will ordinarily be regarded as clearly reflecting income, provided all items of gross income and expense are treated consistently from year to year.

The student will find his analysis of tax accounting problems more interesting and less mechanical if he keeps in mind a "matching" concept familiar to accountants. We seek a net income figure for a specified period. But events and transactions affecting the computation do not all fall neatly within the beginning and end of the period

---

5. Reg. § 1.446–1(c)(1)(ii); and see Reg. § 1.461–1(a)(2) and I.R.C. § 461(h) discussed at page 609, infra.

6. The use of unspecified accounting methods is also permitted, subject to approval of the Commissioner. I.R.C. § 446(c).

7. See Chapter 24A, infra.

8. Statutory references appear at Reg. § 1.446–1(c)(1)(iii).

9. Reg. § 1.446–1(a)(2).

like episodes in a three-act play. And so, ideally, we attempt to take account of expenses incurred in producing income reportable for 1992 in the 1992 computations, even though such expenses represent expenditures actually made in 1991 or 1993. The cash method of accounting often fails miserably in this respect, but it is permitted to be used in most situations because of its essential simplicity. Other failures of tax accounting in this respect appear subsequently in this chapter.

In the 1986 legislation Congress specifically provided that some taxpayers may not use the cash method of accounting.[10] "Tax shelters"[11] may never use the cash method.[12] Generally, corporations other than S corporations[13] and partnerships in which such corporations are partners may not use the cash method.[14] There are exceptions which allow a normally disqualified corporation or partnership to use the cash method if it is in the farming or timber business,[15] is a qualified personal service corporation[16] or if its average gross receipts for years beginning in 1986 do not exceed five million dollars per year.[17] The rule is effective for years after 1986; entities formed prior to that date are required to change their accounting methods and are given statutory Commissioner approval for such a change.[18]

Use of the cash method is precluded in other circumstances.[19] As an introductory thought, consider this problem. T, a merchant, purchases 1000 widgets for sale in his business agreeing to pay $10,000 for them but not until 1992. He receives the widgets in 1991 and sells all of them that year for $20,000. In 1992 he pays the supplier the $10,000. Does he have gross income of $20,000 in 1991 (and maybe a $10,000 loss in 1992 if he goes out of business at the end of 1992)? or

10. I.R.C. § 448.

11. A "tax shelter" is defined by I.R.C. § 461(i)(3) as: (1) any enterprise (other than a C corporation) in which interests in such enterprise have been offered for sale in any offering required to be registered with a federal or state agency, (§ 461(i)(3)(A)); (2) any syndicate, i.e., partnership or other entity (other than a C corporation) if more than 35 percent of the losses of such entity are allocable to limited partners or limited entrepreneurs, (§§ 461(i)(3)(B) and 1256(e)(3)(B)); and (3) any partnership, entity, plan or arrangement, the principal purpose of which is the avoidance or evasion of taxes, (§§ 461(i)(3)(C) and 6662(d)(2)(C)(ii).

Additionally, the House Report indicates that, in determining whether an activity constitutes a tax shelter within the meaning of § 461(i), consideration should be given to whether there is a reasonable and significant expectation that either: (1) deductions exceeding income from such activity will be available to reduce income from other sources; or (2) credits exceeding the tax attributable to the activity will be available to off-set taxes on income from other sources. H.Rep. No. 98–432, 98th Cong., 2d Sess. 1260 (1984).

12. I.R.C. § 448(a)(3) and (d)(3).

13. I.R.C. § 1361. S corporations are essentially closely held corporations whose shareholders elect to be taxed as aggregates similar to partners in partnerships rather than as a corporate entity.

14. I.R.C. § 448(a)(1) and (2).

15. I.R.C. § 448(b)(1).   See I.R.C. § 448(d)(1).

16. I.R.C. § 448(b)(2). A qualified personal service corporation is not treated as a corporation for purposes of determining whether a partnership is disqualified from use of the cash method. Id. A qualified personal service corporation is defined in § 448(d)(2) under a test related to the function carried on by the corporation and an employee ownership test.

17. I.R.C. §§ 448(b)(3) and (c).

18. I.R.C. § 448(d)(7)(B).

19. See, for example, I.R.C. § 447.

should the $10,000 cost of the widgets reduce T's gross income for 1991 to $10,000, even though he made payment for the widgets in 1992? Actually, T is not permitted a cash method approach here,[20] and the latter approach is required. But the point here is that an expenditure related to the production of 1991 income is "matched" against income to be reported in that year.

The matching concept is behind some accepted departures from straight cash or accrual method accounting. For example, a business activity may involve the building and sale of major structures, such as hotels or bridges, work on which may extend over several years. In such situations, the "percentage of completion method" must be used.[21] Under this method, items of income and deduction are taken into account proportionately as work on the contract progresses.[22] However, in some such situations,[23] a taxpayer may use the "completed contract method" of accounting under which the taxpayer is permitted to determine and report his net profit on the project upon completion of the entire contract.[24]

Various hybrid methods of accounting, even combining cash and accrual concepts, may be used.[25] However, a basic statutory requirement is that the method used must clearly reflect income.[26] Materials that follow in this chapter show the kinds of controversies that are engendered by this requirement.

A taxpayer is not limited to the use of a single accounting method in computing his tax liability. She may use one accounting method for her trade or business and another for computing taxable income on items not connected with her trade or business,[27] and she may use different accounting methods for separate trades or businesses in which she is involved.[28]

Although a taxpayer may initially adopt any accounting method that clearly reflects income, nevertheless the consent of the Commissioner must be obtained in order to change accounting methods.[29] Approval is required so as to avoid distortion of one's income by means of an accounting method change, and one must generally show a business purpose for making the change. The definition of what

---

20. See note on Inventories, infra, this Chapter at page 603.

21. See I.R.C. § 460 which requires income or losses from such contracts to be partially reported under the percentage of completion method of accounting. There are exceptions to this rule. I.R.C. § 460(e). See note 23, infra. In addition, in using the percentage of completion method, a taxpayer may elect to defer income until a year in which 10% of the taxpayer's estimated costs have been incurred. I.R.C. § 460(b)(5).

22. See I.R.C. § 460(b) and (c) and Reg. § 1.451–3(c)(1).

23. I.R.C. § 460(e). There are exceptions for home construction contracts and contracts which will be completed within two years by a taxpayer whose average gross receipts for the three preceding taxable years do not exceed ten million dollars. I.R.C. § 460(e)(1).

24. Reg. § 1.451–3(b)(2).

25. See I.R.C. § 446(c)(4).

26. I.R.C. § 446(b).

27. Reg. § 1.446–1(c)(1)(iv)(b).

28. I.R.C. § 446(d).

29. I.R.C. § 446(e).

constitutes a change in accounting method and the procedures to be followed in seeking approval are stated in the Regulations.[30]

As a general principle each taxable year stands alone and each year's tax liability is computed separately, a concept spoken of as preserving the integrity of the taxable year.[31]　Thus, if one reported an item of income as accrued in 1992, and in 1993 it became apparent that collection would never be made, taxable income for 1992 is not to be adjusted (the year is not reopened) and, if uncollectibility is to affect tax liability, it will affect liability for 1993, rather than 1992.　Some exceptions to this strict approach to the taxable year concept are examined in Chapter 20, along with the related statutory provisions for income averaging and for the carryover or carryback to another year of some items of deduction.

In general, substantive provisions of the Code allowing deductions take account of both the cash and accrual method of accounting.　See Section 162(a) allowing a deduction for business expenses " * * * paid or incurred during the taxable year * * *;" Section 163(a) authorizing a deduction for * * * "interest paid or accrued within the taxable year * * *;" Section 164(a) authorizing a deduction for certain taxes " * * * paid or accrued * * *;" and similar language appears in Section 212.　There are other examples.　In contrast, other provisions of the statute force the cash method, even though the taxpayer may have properly adopted the accrual method of accounting.　See Section 170(a) concerning the charitable deduction, requiring *payment,* and Section 213(a) authorizing the deduction for medical expenses " * * * *paid* during the taxable year * * *."　Alimony inclusion and deduction is also put on a cash basis.　Sections 71(a), 215(a).　There are other examples.　But generally the Code accepts the taxpayer's cash or accrual method of accounting.[32]

B.　THE CASH RECEIPTS AND DISBURSEMENTS METHOD *

1.　RECEIPTS

Internal Revenue Code: Sections 446; 451(a).

Regulations: Sections 1.446–1(c)(1)(i); 1.451–1(a), –2.**

30.　Regs. § 1.446–1(e).　See also Rev. Proc. 72–52, 1972–2 C.B. 833.

31.　See Burnet v. Sanford & Brooks Co., 282 U.S. 359, 51 S.Ct. 150 (1931).

32.　But see part D of this Chapter which considers I.R.C. § 267(a)(2) which places an accrual method payor on the cash method with respect to expenses owed to a cash method payee and considers I.R.C. § 467 which is applicable to deferred

payments for the rental of property or for the performance of services forcing a matching of income and deduction by placing a cash method payor or payee on the accrual method.

* See Schapiro, "Prepayments and Distortion of Income Under Cash Basis Tax Accounting," 30 Tax L.R. 117 (1975).

** The doctrine of constructive receipt presented in this provision of the Regula-

LAVERY v. COMMISSIONER ***
United States Court of Appeals, Seventh Circuit, 1946.
158 F.2d 859.

EVANS, Circuit Judge. This appeal involves a dispute over the year a sum received by Lavery, the taxpayer, appellant herein, was taxable under the federal income tax law.

Mr. Lavery, the taxpayer, had been managing editor of the American Bar Association Journal. He was paid in full for his 1941 services. He terminated his services and the Board of Editors tendered him an honorarium, a check for $2,666.67, which he accepted as "payment in full satisfaction of all his claims against the said Association and the members of the said Board of Editors on account of his said employment as such Managing Editor and the termination of that position." The check represented four months' pay at the rate of $8,000 per annum.

The check was received December 30, 1941, and cashed January 2, 1942. December 30th fell on Tuesday.

Taxpayer reported on the cash receipts and disbursements basis.

[After quoting relevant provisions of the 1939 Code and corresponding regulations, not materially different from their current counterparts, the opinion continued.]

* * *

Taxpayer relies upon the case of Avery v. Commissioner, 292 U.S. 210, 54 S.Ct. 674. In the later case of Putnam v. Commissioner, 324 U.S. 393, 65 S.Ct. 811, 814, 158 A.L.R. 1426, the Court referred to its holding in the Avery case as follows: "Avery v. Commissioner * * * holds that dividends of a living taxpayer on the cash basis would not become his income on mere declaration but only when 'received,' that is, unqualifiedly made subject to the stockholder's demand *as by check* * * *." (Italics ours.)

The Court inferentially holds that receipt of a check is equivalent to the receipt of cash. The Avery case was decided on the fact hypothesis that the check was not received until January, following its execution in December.

There might perhaps be a distinction between the date of receipt of cash and the date of the receipt of a check which arrived the last day of the year and too late to be cashed by the payee on that day. In the instant case the taxpayer could have cashed the check on the day it was received by him, or at least on the next day. There was no doubt about the validity of the check or the solvency of the drawer.

Our conclusion is that the check was the equivalent of cash in this case, and this being so, we must hold it was received in 1941. Magill,

tions and involved in the Ross case, infra this Chapter, is broadly discussed in Finnegan, "Constructive Receipt of Income," 22 N.Y.U.Inst. on Fed.Tax. 367 (1964).

*** See generally Note, "Checks and Notes as Income When Received by a Cash Basis Taxpayer," 73 Harv.L.Rev. 1199 (1960). Ed.

Taxable Income, Rev.Ed., 1945, p. 179; Hedrick v. Commissioner, 2 Cir., 154 F.2d 90, 91.

Taxpayer also argues that the check was in payment of services by him rendered in 1942. While the fact assertion on which this argument is predicated is disputed, we dispose of this appeal on the theory that the date of the payment, not the date of the rendition of the services, is the determinative fact.

The decision of the Tax Court is affirmed.

CHARLES F. KAHLER

Tax Court of the United States, 1952.
18 T.C. 31.

[The Findings of Fact have been omitted. Ed.]

Opinion

RICE, Judge: The sole issue is when did the petitioner realize the income represented by the commission check delivered December 31, 1946. Was it in 1946, as determined by respondent, or in 1947, as claimed by petitioner? This, in turn, is based on the question whether the receipt of a check by a cash basis taxpayer after banking hours on the last day of the taxable period constitutes a realization of income.

Applicable provisions of the statute are set forth in the margin.[1]

In his brief, petitioner argues that "the mere receipt of a check does not give rise to income within the taxable year of receipt unless the check is received in sufficient time before the end of the taxable year so the check may be converted into cash within the taxable year." In support of such result, petitioner relies upon L.M. Fischer, 14 T.C. 792 (1950); Urban A. Lavery, 5 T.C. 1283 (1945), affd. (C.A.7, 1946) 158 F.2d 859; and Harvey H. Ostenberg, 17 B.T.A. 738 (1929).

In the *Fischer* case, we held that a check delivered to the taxpayer on December 31, 1942, which was not deposited until 1943, was not income in 1942 but in 1943, since the check was subject to a substantial restriction. At the time of delivery of such check, there was an oral agreement made between the drawer and the taxpayer that the latter would hold the check for a few days before he cashed it since the drawer was short of money in the bank. Such a situation is completely distinguishable from that in the instant case.

The *Lavery* and *Ostenberg* cases both decided that checks delivered to the taxpayers were income in the year of delivery. In the *Lavery* case delivery was on December 30, and in the *Ostenberg* case delivery was on December 31. Petitioner relies on the dicta appearing in these cases to the effect that the result might have been different had the petitioner in either case been able to show that he could not have

1. [The quoted sections of the 1939 Code, not materially different from their current counterparts, are omitted. Ed.]

cashed the check in the year drawn. We fail to see where there should be any difference in result just because it might be impossible to cash a check in the year in which drawn, where delivery actually took place in such year. Respondent's regulations provide that all items of gross income shall be included in the taxable year in which received by the taxpayer, and that where services are paid for other than by money, the amount to be included as income is the fair market value of the thing taken in payment.[2]

Analogous cases to the instant case are those which were concerned with the proper year in which deductions might be taken where a check was drawn and delivered in one year and cashed in a subsequent year. Under the negotiable instruments law, payment by check is a conditional payment subject to the condition that it will be honored upon presentation; and once such presentation is made and the check is honored, the date of payment relates back to the time of delivery. See Estelle Broussard, 16 T.C. 23 (1951); Estate of Modie J. Spiegel, 12 T.C. 524 (1949); and cases cited therein. In the *Spiegel* case we said, at page 529:

> It would seem to us unfortunate for the Tax Court to fail to recognize what has so frequently been suggested, that as a practical matter, in everyday personal and commercial usage, the transfer of funds by check is an accepted procedure. The parties almost without exception think and deal in terms of payment except in the unusual circumstance, not involved here, that the check is dishonored upon presentation, or that it was delivered in the first place subject to some condition or infirmity which intervenes between delivery and presentation.

Under such circumstances, we feel that it is immaterial that delivery of a check is made too late in the taxable year for the check to be cashed in that year. The petitioner realized income upon receipt of the commission check on December 31, 1946.

Reviewed by the Court.

Decision will be entered for the respondent.

MURDOCK, J., concurring: I agree with the result reached that the receipt of a check is regarded as payment and income unless it is subject to some restriction but feel that the petitioner's case is weaker in some respects than the majority opinion might indicate. A finding is made that the check in question was received by the petitioner "sometime after 5 p.m. on December 31, 1946." There is also evidence that he could not have obtained cash for the check at the drawee bank but he could have deposited the check in that bank, later on December 31, 1946. There was another bank in the town and the evidence does not show whether or not he could have cashed the check in that bank after regular banking hours. Furthermore he might have made some other

---

2. Treasury Regulations 111, sec. 29.22(a)–3, and sec. 29.41–2. [See Reg. §§ 1.61–2(d) and 1.446–1(a) and (c). Ed.]

use of the check during 1946. For example, he might have cashed it at some place other than at a bank or he might have used it to discharge some obligation, within the year 1946.

HARRON, J., agrees with this concurring opinion.

ESTATE OF COID HURLBURT

Tax Court of the United States, 1956.
25 T.C. 1286 (NA).

Opinion

MULRONEY, Judge: The Commissioner determined a deficiency in income tax in the amount of $4,555.07 for the calendar year 1947. The sole issue is whether certain contracts entered into by Coid Hurlburt, decedent, in the sale of certain parcels of real estate in 1947 were includible in income as amounts realized under section 111(b) of the 1939 Internal Revenue Code.

All of the facts have been stipulated and they are herein incorporated by this reference.

The decedent, Coid Hurlburt, and his wife, Merle Hurlburt, filed a joint income tax return for the year 1947 with the then collector of internal revenue for the district of Colorado.

In 1947 Coid Hurlburt sold three parcels of farm property located in Washington County, Colorado. The sales were accomplished by what we will call contracts of sale, which were documents entitled "Receipt and Option." The contracts called for a downpayment which was receipted for in the contract, one or two further payments in 1947, and annual payments thereafter over the next 10 to 18 years until the full purchase price, with interest, was paid. In one contract the vendor agreed to accept purchaser's $8,000 farm as a part of the purchase price. It was provided in two of the contracts that one copy of the contract, together with abstract and warranty deed, be deposited with the Citizen's National Bank of Akron, Colorado, "until payments have been completed as agreed." The other contract did not have this provision but all three contracts, abstracts, and warranty deeds were actually deposited with the bank. The purchasers all took immediate possession of the farms and there were no defaults in the payments.

The taxpayer makes some argument that the receipt and option documents were not contracts of sale but options. This is based on the absence of express language in the instruments obligating the purchasers to pay the purchase price—the language is that the purchasers were to receive the deeds when all of the payments were made. There is some language in some of the Colorado decisions cited in the brief interpreting similar instruments which might tend to support this argument of petitioner. But we do not go into the question for there is much general authority holding such a contract will be held to be one of purchase and sale when it appears the general intention was to consummate a sale. There is much law on the subject and it would be impossible to harmonize all of the decisions interpreting doubtful documents as contracts rather than options. The purchasers who signed the documents are not before us. We are content to assume the documents are valid contracts of sale and we will treat them as such for the purpose of this decision.

Section 111(a) of the 1939 Internal Revenue Code provides, in part: "The gain from the sale * * * of property shall be the excess of the amount realized therefrom over the adjusted basis * * *." Section 111(b) of the 1939 Internal Revenue Code provides: "The amount realized from the sale or other disposition of property shall be the sum of any money received plus the fair market value of the property (other than money) received."

There is no dispute over the vendor's adjusted base with regard to each of the three parcels and no dispute that in each instance it was more than the vendor received in money in the sale transaction in the year 1947, and no dispute that in each instance it was less than the full purchase price as stated in the contracts of sale. The vendor reported his income in 1947 on the cash basis without reporting any gain on the three contract sales. The Commissioner argues the sales were complete in 1947 when the contracts, abstracts, and warranty deeds were delivered to the bank, the initial payments made, and the purchasers took possession of the properties. The respondent then contends the contracts for the deferred payment of the purchase price had a fair market value in 1947 equal to the unpaid balances and the entire gain from the sale was realized in 1947 under section 111(b) of the 1939 Internal Revenue Code, supra.

The vital issue in this case is whether these contracts are to be valued in 1947 under section 111(b), supra, and that value included as "amount realized" by vendor in that year. It is stipulated that: "The purchasers executed no notes, bonds, and other evidence of indebtedness other than the 'Receipts and Options' hereinbefore mentioned and gave no additional security."

The contracts did nothing more than evidence the amounts due the vendor over a period of years and as such can be regarded as little more than accounts receivable. The vendor was a cash basis taxpayer and he did not receive any notes, bonds, mortgages, or other evidence of indebtedness such as normally would be considered amounts realized by a cash basis taxpayer.

In a like situation in Harold W. Johnston, 14 T.C. 560, where the only evidence of indebtedness was the contract for future payments, we held such a contract could not be valued by a cash basis taxpayer, and that value included in the "amount realized" under section 111(b). Cf. Estate of Clarence W. Ennis, 23 T.C. 799, appeal dismissed C.A.6; Nina v. Ennis, 17 T.C. 465.

In Harold W. Johnston, supra, we said:

"when the contract merely requires future payments and no notes, mortgages, or other evidence of indebtedness such as commonly change hands in commerce, which could be recognized as the equivalent of cash to some extent, are given and accepted as part of the purchase price * * * [it] creates accounts payable by the purchasers and accounts receivable by the sellers which those two taxpayers would accrue if they were using an accrual method * * *. But such an agreement to pay the balance of the purchase price in the future has no tax significance to either purchaser or seller if he is using a cash system. * * *"

It was stipulated that when the vendor died in 1948 these contracts were valued at the unpaid balances for Colorado State inheritance tax purposes, in the vendor's estate. That evidence is without significance in determining whether the contracts had possessed a fair market value in the hands of a cash basis taxpayer. Admittedly the contract rights were assets in the deceased vendor's estate. As such, they would be valued as of the date of death and this would be true even though they were not the type of asset which would be includible in the income of a cash basis taxpayer.

We hold, therefore, that the contractual obligations were not amounts realized in 1947, and that the only "amount realized" in 1947 by the decedent was the total of the cash payments actually received in that year. These payments were not in excess of the decedent's basis for the property sold, and consequently no gain was realized on such sales in the year 1947.

Decision will be entered for the petitioners.

COWDEN v. COMMISSIONER

United States Court of Appeals, Fifth Circuit, 1961.
289 F.2d 20.

JONES, Circuit Judge. We here review a decision of the Tax Court by which a determination was made of federal income tax liability of Frank Cowden, Sr., his wife and their children, for the years 1951 and 1952. In April 1951, Frank Cowden, Sr. and his wife made an oil, gas and mineral lease for themselves and their children upon described lands in Texas to Stanolind Oil and Gas Company. By related supplemental agreements, Stanolind agreed to make "bonus" or "advance royalty" payments in an aggregate amount of $511,192.50. On execution of the instruments $10,223.85 was payable, the sum of $250,484.31 was due "no earlier than" January 5 "nor later than" January 10, 1952, and $250,484.34 was stipulated to be paid "no earlier than" January 5 "nor later than" January 10, 1953. One-half of the amounts was to be paid to Frank Cowden, Sr. and his wife, and one-sixth was payable to each of their children. In the deferred payments agreements it was provided that:

"This contract evidences the obligation of Stanolind Oil and Gas Company to make the deferred payments referred to in subparagraphs (b) and (c) of the preceding paragraph hereof,

and it is understood and agreed that the obligation of Stanolind Oil and Gas Company to make such payments is a firm
and absolute personal obligation of said Company, which is not
in any manner conditioned upon development or production
from the demised premises, nor upon the continued ownership
of the leasehold interest in such premises by Stanolind Oil and
Gas Company, but that such payments shall be made in all
events."

On November 30, 1951, the taxpayers assigned the payments due
from Stanolind in 1952 to the First National Bank of Midland, of which
Frank Cowden, Sr. was a director. Assignments of the payments due in
1953 were made to the bank on November 20, 1952. For the assignment of the 1952 payments the bank paid the face value of the amounts
assigned discounted by $257.43 in the case of Frank Cowden, Sr., and
his wife, and $85.81 in the case of each of their children. For the
amounts due in 1953 the discounts were $313.14 for Frank Cowden, Sr.
and his wife, and $104.38 for each of their children. The taxpayers
reported the amounts received by them from the assignments as long-
term capital gains. The Commissioner made a determination that the
contractual obligations of Stanolind to make payments in future years
represented ordinary income, subject to depletion, to the extent of the
fair market value of the obligations at the time they were created. The
Commissioner computed the fair market value of the Stanolind obligations, which were not interest bearing, by the deduction of a discount of
four per cent. on the deferred payments from the date of the agreements until the respective maturities. Such computation fixed a 1951
equivalent of cash value of $487,647.46 for the bonus payments, paid in
1951 and agreed to be paid thereafter, aggregating $511,192.50. The
Commissioner determined that the taxpayers should be taxed in 1951
on $487,647.46, as ordinary income.

A majority of the Tax Court was convinced that, under the particular facts of this case, the bonus payments were not only readily but
immediately convertible to cash and were the equivalent of cash, and
had a fair market value equal to their face value. The Tax Court
decided that the entire amounts of the bonus payments, $511,192.50,
were taxable in 1951, as ordinary income. Cowden v. Commissioner of
Internal Revenue, 32 T.C. 853. Two judges of the Tax Court dissented.

The Tax Court stated, as a general proposition, "that executory
contracts to make future payments in money do not have a fair market
value." The particular facts by which the Tax Court distinguishes this
case from the authorities by which the general proposition is established are, as stated in the opinion of the majority.

      " *   *   * that the bonus payors were perfectly willing and
able at the time of execution of the leases and bonus agreements to pay such bonus in an immediate lump sum payment;
to pay the bonus immediately in a lump sum at all times
thereafter until the due dates under the agreements; that

Cowden, Sr., believed the bonus agreements had a market value at the time of their execution; that a bank in which he was an officer and depositor was willing to and in fact did purchase such rights at a nominal discount; that the bank considered such rights to be bankable and to represent direct obligations of the payor; that the bank generally dealt in such contracts where it was satisfied with the financial responsibility of the payor and looked solely to it for payment without recourse to the lessor and, in short, that the sole reason why the bonuses were not immediately paid in cash upon execution of the leases involved was the refusal of the lessor to receive such payments."

These findings are, in some respects, challenged by the taxpayers as being unsupported by the evidence. Our review of the record has led us to the conclusion that the findings of fact made by the Tax Court are sustained by substantial evidence. However, we must observe that the statement of Frank Cowden, Sr. that the contract obligations had "some market value" is not to be regarded as binding upon him and the other taxpayers with respect to the decisive issue in the case.

The dissenting opinion of the Tax Court minority states that the conclusion reached by the majority "is in effect that the taxpayers are not free to make the bargain of their choice," and one of the taxpayers' specifications of error is that the Tax Court "erred in holding that taxpayers are not free to make the bargain of their choice."

The Tax Court majority distinguishes the authorities cited and relied upon by the taxpayers upon several grounds. The Tax Court seemingly lays stress upon the fact, found to be here present, that the bonus payor was willing and able to make the entire bonus payment upon the execution of the agreement. It is said by the taxpayers that the Tax Court has held that a constructive receipt, under the equivalent of cash doctrine, resulted from the willingness of the lessee to pay the entire bonus on execution of the leases and the unwillingness of the taxpayers, for reasons of their own,[1] to receive the full amount. If this be the effect of the Tax Court's decision there may be some justification for the criticism appearing in the opinion of the minority and the concern expressed elsewhere.[2]

It was said in Gregory v. Helvering, 293 U.S. 465, 55 S.Ct. 266, and recently repeated in Knetsch v. United States, 364 U.S. 361, 81 S.Ct. 132, 135, "The legal right of a taxpayer to decrease the amount of what otherwise would be his taxes, or altogether avoid them, by means which the law permits, cannot be doubted." See Rupe Investment Corporation v. Commissioner of Internal Revenue, 5 Cir., 1959, 266 F.2d 624; Williams v. United States, 5 Cir., 1955, 219 F.2d 523. As a general rule a tax avoidance motive is not to be considered in determining the tax

---

1. It is not denied that a desire to save taxes was the sole purpose for the taxpayers' insistence that payment be postponed.

2. 9 Oil & Gas Tax Q. 122; 49 A.B.A.J. 1205; 59 Colum.L.Rev. 1237; 8 Tax Fortnightor 835; 11th Ann.S.W.Leg.Found. Inst.Oil & Gas Law & Taxation 651.

liability resulting from a transaction. Sun Properties v. United States, 5 Cir., 220 F.2d 171; Caldwell v. Campbell, 5 Cir., 1955, 218 F.2d 567; Roscoe v. Commissioner of Internal Revenue, 5 Cir., 1954, 215 F.2d 478. The taxpayers had the right to decline to enter into a mineral lease of their lands except upon the condition that the lessee obligate itself for a bonus payable in part in installments in future years, and the doing so would not, of itself, subject the deferred payments to taxation during the year that the lease was made. Nor would a tax liability necessarily arise although the lease contract was made with a solvent lessee who had been willing and able to pay the entire bonus upon the execution of the lease.

While it is true that the parties may enter into any legal arrangement they see fit even though the particular form in which it was cast was selected with the hope of a reduction in taxes, it is also true that if a consideration for which one of the parties bargains is the equivalent of cash it will be subjected to taxation to the extent of its fair market value. Whether the undertaking of the lessee to make future bonus payments was, when made, the equivalent of cash and, as such, taxable as current income is the issue in this case. In a somewhat similar case, decided in 1941, the Board of Tax Appeals stated that "where no notes, bonds, or other evidences of indebtedness other than the contract were given, such contract had no fair market value." Kleberg v. Commissioner, 43 B.T.A. 277, quoting from Titus v. Commissioner, 33 B.T.A. 928. In 1959 the Tax Court held that where the deferred bonus payments were evidenced by promissory notes the equivalent of cash doctrine might be applicable. Barnsley v. Commissioner, 31 T.C. 1260. There the Tax Court said:

> "It is, of course, possible under an oil and gas lease containing proper provisions to have a bonus payable and taxable in installments, Alice G.K. Kleberg, 43 B.T.A. 277. The case before us does not constitute such an arrangement. In the Kleberg case the contractual agreement was to pay a named amount in two payments as bonus. It was not a case like the one here where cash and negotiable notes, the latter being the equivalent of cash, representing the bonus were received in the same year by the taxpayer."

The test announced in Kleberg, from which Barnsley does not depart, seems to be whether the obligation to make the deferred payments is represented by "notes, bonds, or other evidences of indebtedness other than the contract". In this case, the literal test of Kleberg is met as the obligation of Stanolind to the Cowdens was evidenced by an instrument other than the contract of lease. This instrument is not, however, one of the kind which fall into the classification of notes or bonds. The taxpayers urge that there can be no "equivalent of cash" obligation unless it is a negotiable instrument. Such a test, to be determined by the form of the obligation, is as unrealistic as it is formalistic. The income tax law deals in economic realities, not legal abstractions,[3] and the reach of the income tax law is not to be delimited by technical refinements or mere formalism.[4]

A promissory note, negotiable in form, is not necessarily the equivalent of cash. Such an instrument may have been issued by a maker of doubtful solvency[5] or for other reasons such paper might be denied a ready acceptance in the market place. We think the converse of this principle ought to be applicable. We are convinced that if a promise to pay of a solvent obligor is unconditional and assignable, not subject to set-offs, and is of a kind that is frequently transferred to lenders or investors at a discount not substantially greater than the generally prevailing premium for the use of money, such promise is the equivalent of cash and taxable in like manner as cash would have been taxable had it been received by the taxpayer rather than the obligation. The principle that negotiability is not the test of taxability in an equivalent of cash case such as is before us, is consistent with the rule that men may, if they can, so order their affairs as to minimize taxes,[6] and points up the doctrine that substance and not form should control in the application of income tax laws.[7]

The Tax Court stressed in its findings that the provisions for deferring a part of the bonus were made solely at the request of and for the benefit of the taxpayers and that the lessee was willing and able to make the bonus payments in cash upon execution of the agreements. It appears to us that the Tax Court, in reaching its decision that the taxpayers had received equivalent of cash bonuses in the year the leases were executed, gave as much and probably more weight to those findings than to the other facts found by it. We are persuaded of this not only by the language of its opinion but because, in its determination of the cash equivalent, it used the amounts which it determined the taxpayers could have received if they had made a different contract, rather than the fair market value cash equivalent[8] of the obligation for which the taxpayers had bargained in the contracts which they had a lawful right to make. We are unable to say whether or not the Tax Court, if it disregarded, as we think it should have done, the facts as it found them as to the willingness of the lessee to pay and the unwillingness of the taxpayers to receive a full bonus on execution of the leases, would have determined that the deferred bonus obligations were taxable in the year of the agreements as the equivalent of cash. This question is primarily a fact issue. Glenn v. Penn, 6 Cir., 1958, 250 F.2d 507; Kasper v. Banek, 8 Cir., 1954, 214 F.2d 125. There should be a

3. Commissioner of Internal Revenue v. Southwest Exploration Company, 350 U.S. 308, 76 S.Ct. 395.

4. United States v. Joliet & Chicago Railroad Company, 315 U.S. 44, 62 S.Ct. 442.

5. Board v. Commissioner, 18 B.T.A. 650.

6. Cf. Atlantic Coast Line Railroad Company v. Phillips, 332 U.S. 168, 67 S.Ct.

1584; Bullen v. State of Wisconsin, 240 U.S. 625, 36 S.Ct. 473.

7. United States v. Phellis, 257 U.S. 156, 42 S.Ct. 63; Morsman v. Commissioner of Internal Revenue, 8 Cir., 1937, 90 F.2d 18, 113 A.L.R. 441.

8. Computed by the Commissioner by discounting the obligations at a 4 per cent rate.

remand to the Tax Court for a reconsideration of the questions submitted in the light of what has been said here.*

* * *

PAUL V. HORNUNG

Tax Court of the United States, 1967.
47 T.C. 428.

HOYT, Judge: Respondent determined an income tax deficiency against petitioner in the amount of $3,163.76 for the taxable year 1962. Petitioner having conceded an issue relating to a travel expense deduction, the questions remaining for decision are:

(1) Whether the value of a 1962 Corvette automobile which was won by petitioner for his performance in a professional football game should be included in his gross income for the taxable year 1962.

* * *

Findings of Fact

The stipulated facts are found accordingly and adopted as our findings.

Petitioner is a cash basis taxpayer residing in Louisville, Ky. For the taxable year 1962, petitioner filed his Federal individual income tax return (Form 1040) with the district director of internal revenue, Louisville, Ky. Petitioner is a well-known professional football player who was employed by the Green Bay Packers in 1962. Prior to becoming a professional, petitioner attended the University of Notre Dame and was an All-American quarterback on the university football team.

Issue 1. The Corvette

Sport Magazine is a publication of the McFadden-Bartell Corp., with business offices in New York City. Each year Sport Magazine (hereinafter sometimes referred to as Sport or the magazine) awards a new Corvette automobile to the player selected by its editors (primarily by its editor in chief) as the outstanding player in the National Football League championship game. This award was won by John Unitas of the Baltimore Colts in 1958 and 1959 and by Norm Van Brocklin of the Philadelphia Eagles in 1960. A similar annual award is made to outstanding professional athletes in baseball, hockey, and basketball. The existence of the award is announced several days prior to the sporting event in question, and the selection and announcement of the winner is made immediately following the athletic contest. The Corvette automobiles are generally presented to the recipients at a luncheon or dinner several days subsequent to the sporting event and a photograph of the athlete receiving the car is published in the maga-

---

* On remand the contractual obligations were held to be the equivalent of cash. Frank Cowden, Sr., 20 TCM 1134 (1961).

zine, together with an article relating to his performance during the particular athletic event. The Corvette awards are intended to promote the sale of Sport Magazine and their cost is deducted by the publisher for Federal income tax purposes as promotion and advertising expense.

The Corvette which is to be awarded to the most valuable player in the National Football League championship game is generally purchased by the magazine several months prior to the date the game is played, and it is held by a New York area Chevrolet dealer until delivered to the recipient of the award. In some years when the game is played in New York the magazine has had the car on display at the stadium on the day of the game.

On December 31, 1961, petitioner played in the National Football League championship game between the Green Bay Packers and the New York Giants. The game was played in Green Bay, Wis. Petitioner scored a total of 19 points during this game and thereby established a new league record. At the end of this game petitioner was selected by the editors of Sport as the most valuable player and winner of the Corvette, and press releases were issued announcing the award. At approximately 4:30 on the afternoon of December 31, 1961, following the game, the editor in chief of Sport informed petitioner that he had been selected as the most valuable player of the game. The editor in chief did not have the key or the title to the Corvette with him in Green Bay and petitioner did not request or demand immediate possession of the car at that time but he accepted the award.

The Corvette which was to be awarded in connection with this 1961 championship game had been purchased by Sport in September of 1961. However, since the game was played in Green Bay, Wis., the car was not on display at the stadium on the day of the game, but was in New York in the hands of a Chevrolet dealership. As far as Sport was concerned the car was "available" to petitioner on December 31, 1961, as soon as the award was announced. However, December 31, 1961, was a Sunday and the New York dealership at which the car was located was closed. Although the National Football League championship game is always played on a Sunday, Sport is prepared to make prior arrangements to have the car available in New York for the recipient of the award on that Sunday afternoon if the circumstances appear to warrant such arrangements—particularly if the game is played in New York. Such arrangements were not made in 1961 because the game was played in Green Bay, and, in the words of Sport's editor in chief, "it seemed a hundred-to-one that * * * [the recipient of the award] would want to come in [to New York] on New Year's Eve to take possession" of the prize.

On December 31, 1961, when petitioner was informed that he had won the Corvette, he was also informed that a luncheon was to be held for him in New York City on the following Wednesday by the publisher of Sport, at which luncheon his award would be presented. At that time petitioner consented to attend the luncheon in order to receive the Corvette. There was no discussion that he would obtain the car prior to the presentation ceremony previously announced. The lunch was held as scheduled on Wednesday, January 3, 1962, in a New York restaurant. Petitioner attended and was photographed during the course of the presentation of the automobile to him. A photograph of petitioner sitting in the car outside of the restaurant was published in the April 1962 issue of Sport, together with an article regarding his achievements in the championship game and the Corvette prize award. Petitioner was not required to attend the lunch or to pose for photographs or perform any other service for Sport as a condition or as consideration for his receipt of the car.

The fair market value of the Corvette automobile received by petitioner was $3,331.04. Petitioner reported the sale of the Corvette in his 1962 Federal income tax return in Schedule D attached thereto as a * * * gain as follows:

Kind of Property	Date Acquired	Date Sold	Gross Sales Price	Depreciation Allowed	Cost	Gain
1962 Corvette gift— Sport Magazine	1962	1962	3,331.04	0.00	0.00	None

* * *

Petitioner did not include the fair market value of this car in his gross income for 1962, or for any other year. McFadden-Bartell Corporation deducted its cost as a promotion and advertising expense.

* * *

Opinion

Issue 1. The Corvette

Petitioner alleged in his petition that the Corvette was received by him as a gift in 1962. However, at trial and on brief, he argues that the car was constructively received in 1961, prior to the taxable year for which the deficiency is being assessed. If this contention is upheld, the question of whether the car constituted a reportable item of gross income need not be considered. This argument is based upon the assertion that the announcement and acceptance of the award occurred at approximately 4:30 on the afternoon of December 31, 1961, following the game.

It is undisputed that petitioner was selected as the most valuable player of the National Football League championship game in Green Bay on December 31, 1961. It is also undisputed that petitioner actually received the car on January 3, 1962, in New York. Petitioner relies upon the statement at the trial by the editor in chief of Sport that as far as Sport was concerned the car was "available" to petitioner on December 31, 1961, as soon as the award was announced. It is therefore contended that the petitioner should be deemed to have received the value of the award in 1961 under the doctrine of constructive receipt.

The amount of any item of gross income is included in gross income for the taxable year in which received by the taxpayer unless such amount is properly accounted for as of a different period. Sec. 451(a).[3] It is further provided in section 446(c) that the cash receipts method, which the petitioner utilized, is a permissible method of computing taxable income. The doctrine of constructive receipt is developed by regulations under section 446(c) which provides as follows: [4]

> Generally, under the cash receipts and disbursements method
> * * * all items which constitute gross income (whether in the form of cash, property, or services) are to be included for the taxable year in which actually or constructively received.
>
> * * *

The regulations under section 451 elaborate on the meaning of constructive receipt.[5]

> Income although not actually reduced to a taxpayer's possession is constructively received by him in the taxable year during which it is credited to his account, set apart for him, or otherwise made available so that he may draw upon it at any time, or so that he could have drawn upon it during the taxable year if notice of intention to withdraw had been given. However, income is not constructively received if the taxpayer's control of its receipt is subject to substantial limitations or restrictions. * * *

The probable purpose for development of the doctrine of constructive receipt was stated as follows in Ross v. Commissioner, 169 F.2d 483, 491 (C.A.1, 1948):

> The doctrine of constructive receipt was, no doubt, conceived by the Treasury in order to prevent a taxpayer from choosing the year in which to return income merely by choosing the year in which to reduce it to possession. Thereby the Treasury may subject income to taxation when the only thing preventing its reduction to possession is the volition of the taxpayer. * * *

However, it was held in the *Ross* case, at page 496, that the doctrine of constructive receipt could be asserted by a taxpayer as a defense to a deficiency assessment even though the item in controversy had not been reported for the taxable year of the alleged constructive receipt:

> if these items were constructively received when earned they cannot be treated as income in any later year, * * * and, in the absence of misstatement of fact, intentional or otherwise,

---

3. All section references are to the Internal Revenue Code of 1954 unless otherwise indicated.

4. Sec. 1.446–1(c)(1)(i), Income Tax Regs.

5. Sec. 1.451–2(a), Income Tax Regs.

the petitioner cannot be estopped from asserting that the items were taxable only in the years in which constructively received.

The basis of constructive receipt is essentially unfettered control by the recipient over the date of actual receipt. Petitioner has failed to convince us that he possessed such control on December 31, 1961, over the receipt of the Corvette. The evidence establishes that the Corvette which was presented to petitioner on January 3, 1962, was in the possession of a Chevrolet dealer in New York City on December 31, 1961. At the time the award was announced in Green Bay, the editor in chief of Sport had neither the title nor keys to the car, and nothing was given or presented to petitioner to evidence his ownership or right to possession of the car at that time.

Moreover, since December 31, 1961, was a Sunday, it is doubtful whether the car could have been transferred to petitioner before Monday even with the cooperation of the editor in chief of Sport. The New York dealership at which the car was located was closed. The car had not been set aside for petitioner's use and delivery was not dependent solely upon the volition of petitioner. The doctrine of constructive receipt is therefore inapplicable, and we hold that petitioner received the Corvette for income tax purposes in 1962 as he originally alleged in his petition and as he reported in his 1962 income tax return.

* * *

[The Court held that the car was not received as a gift but was a prize or award specifically required to be included in ordinary income at its fair market value in 1962 under Section 74. The subsequent sale of the car was a separate transaction. Ed.]

2. DISBURSEMENTS *

Internal Revenue Code: Section 461(a) and (g).

Regulations: Section 1.461–1(a)(1).

———

REVENUE RULING 54–465
1954–2 Cum.Bull. 93.

A charitable contribution in the form of a check is deductible, in the manner and to the extent provided by section 23(*o*) and (q) of the Internal Revenue Code of 1939 [See I.R.C. (1986) Section 170(a). Ed.], in the taxable year in which the check is delivered provided the check is honored and paid and there are no restrictions as to time and manner of payment thereof. See Estate of Modie J. Spiegel v. Commissioner, 12 T.C. 524, acquiescence, C.B. 1949–2, 3.

---

* See Irwin, "Prepayments by a Cash Basis Taxpayer," 15 U.S.C. Tax Inst. 547 (1963).

NOTE ON CREDIT CARD PAYMENTS

Over the years we have moved from a cash-paying society to a check-paying society to a credit card society. In the first transition the tax law kept pace by treating payment by check essentially the same as payment in cash.[1] From the standpoint of a cash method taxpayer, he has paid a deductible expense when he hands over a check. In fact payment is effected when he places a check in the mail;[2] but of course this is qualified by the requirement that the check is honored and paid in due course when presented to the drawee bank.[3] If a purist can detect a departure from strict cash method doctrine here (recall for example that payment on a check may be stopped and its issuance does not constitute an irrevocable assignment of the drawer's funds), nevertheless the tax result comports with the way we all view things. We have "paid" the monthly bills when we mail out the checks. And it would be untidy to have to determine when a check was presented for payment.

Have we "paid" a bill when we sign a credit card chit? A doctrinal obstacle to an affirmative answer might seem to be that the card holder parts with no cash at that time. Nevertheless, he has "paid" the obligation to the principal creditor whose recourse thereafter is against the credit card company. At the same time he has incurred an obligation to the credit card company in accordance with his agreement with it. Should it not be viewed as if he had borrowed money and used it to pay his obligation, which would of course support an instant deduction?[4] For purposes of determining when federal taxes are "paid," the Treasury has given qualified acceptance to this view.[5] On the other hand, the Treasury at one time took the position in Rev.Rul. 71–216[6] that for purposes of the charitable deduction under Section 170, "payment" does not occur when a contribution is made with the use of a credit card until the contributor pays the credit card company, even if the charity is in receipt of the funds at an earlier time.

The use of a credit card is not analogous to borrowing money at the bank and receiving less than the amount of the loan, the difference representing interest. Such interest is not considered paid at that time.[7] But the use of a credit card presents a three party deal, and the obligation that is discharged is an obligation to a third party, not to the one who advances the money.

1. Witt's Estate v. Fahs, 160 F.Supp. 521 (S.D.Fla.1956).

2. Id. and cf. Reg. § 1.170–1(b).

3. Cf. Reg. § 301.6311–1(a)(1). See Brooks Griffin, 49 T.C. 253 (1967).

4. William J. Granan, 55 T.C. 753 (1971).

5. I.R.S. News Release No. 1005 (Jan. 16, 1970) indicated that " * * * if a check or other document issued by a bank or credit card company used by a taxpayer in payment of taxes is acceptable by the Federal Reserve District concerned as a negotiable instrument for banking purposes, it will be accepted [as payment] by the I.R.S."

6. 1971–1 C.B. 96.

7. Cathcart v. Commissioner, 36 T.C.M. 1321 (1977), infra at page 584.

Of course in this respect it is necessary to look at the exact nature of the credit arrangement. If a department store issues a credit card for use in purchases only at the store, no payment occurs until the store's bill is paid. This is a two-party deal. Whether a charge on a credit card issued by an oil company falls into the two-party or three-party area depends upon whether the obligation runs to the company or to an independent dealer, the gas station from which merchandise was purchased. Indeed, it is not safe to try to generalize here, as credit card arrangements are largely a matter of contract, which suggests possible wide variations in the relationships of the parties, and the legal consequences of the use of credit cards are not fully settled.[8]

If the use of a credit card did not produce an instant deduction, what would be the alternatives? It might be said that payment occurs only when the credit card company pays the taxpayer's bill. But this is so impractical a view as to require rejection. The taxpayer will seldom know when his chits are presented for payment. It is also irrelevant, if we view the matter as involving a three-party deal in which the taxpayer's obligation to a supplier is discharged when he signs the chit. The credit card company does not pay as his agent.

Nor would it be proper to say that the taxpayer has paid only when he pays the credit card company's bill. He is certainly not then paying the supplier. He is, instead, repaying a loan made by the credit card company, which is not the obligation for which a deduction may be claimed. Moreover, if we accept the settled treatment of checks as payment, we seem to have an *a fortiori* argument here. After the check-maker hands over his check he can still stop payment on it; it is not so clear that the credit card user is in a position to recall his "payment" to a supplier.[9]

Finally, the instant deduction approach to credit card transactions again comports with the way our society views these transactions. We think of the *air line* as paid when they have accepted the credit card, even though we know we will be hearing from the *credit card company* at the end of the month. And so it seems the tax law *should* follow our move to a credit card society. Good theory and, even more important, practical considerations require it. In fact, since an earlier edition of this book expressed the above positions [10] the Service has come around on this issue.[11] In Rev.Rul. 78–

---

8. The non-tax aspects of credit card transactions are thoughtfully examined in Nordstrom, Law of Sales, pp. 353–360 (West Hornbook Series 1970); see also South, "Credit Cards: a Primer," 23 Business Lawyer 327 (1968). As to the potential for different tax consequences between the use of two party vs. three part credit cards, see Londey, "Payments of Expenses by Credit Card: A Current Deduction for the Cash-Method Taxpayer?" 62 Taxes 239 (1984).

9. See Londey, "Payments of Expenses by Credit Card: A Current Deduction for the Cash-Method Taxpayer?" 62 Taxes 239 (1984); Brandel and Leonard, "Bank Charge Cards: New Cash or New Credit," 69 Mich.L.Rev. 1033 (1971).

10. See Freeland and Stephens, Fundamentals of Federal Income Taxation 519–521 (Foundation Press 1972).

11. Olson, "Bank Credit Cards and the Timing of Deductions Under Revenue Ruling 78–38: A Return to Consis-

38 [12] the Service gave "further study" to its prior position in Rev. Rul. 71–216 [13] and did an about face, reversing its prior Ruling, stating: [14]

> Since the cardholder's use of the credit card creates the cardholder's own debt to a third party, the use of a bank credit card to make a charitable contribution is equivalent to the use of borrowed funds to make a contribution.

> The general rule is that when a deductible payment is made with borrowed money, the deduction is not postponed until the year in which the borrowed money is repaid. Such expenses must be deducted in the year they are paid and not when the loans are repaid. Granan v. Commissioner, 55 T.C. 753 (1971).

> Accordingly, the taxpayer discussed in Rev.Rul. 71–216, who made a contribution to a qualified charity by a charge to the taxpayer's bank credit card, is entitled to a charitable contribution deduction under section 170(a) of the Code in the year the charge was made. * * *

In a companion ruling [15] the Service uses the same rationale to conclude that the use of a bank credit card to pay a Section 213 medical expense constitutes payment of the medical expense in the year the credit card charge is made regardless of when the bank is paid.

VANDER POEL, FRANCIS & CO., INC.
Tax Court of the United States, 1947.
8 T.C. 407.

Opinion

* * *

[This case involved the question whether a doctrine of "constructive payment" parallels the established doctrine of "constructive receipt." Some excerpts from the opinion will be informative. Ed.]

* * *

There is but one issue involved in this proceeding, and that is whether petitioner, a corporation which kept its books and made its income tax returns on the cash basis, is entitled to deduct the full amount of the salaries regularly and duly voted to its two officers, Vander Poel and Francis, and unconditionally credited to their respective accounts, notwithstanding it did not actually pay the full amount of these salaries in cash or other property during 1942.

* * *

They properly returned these salaries for taxation on their 1942 returns under the doctrine of "constructive receipt." * * * [T]he

tency" 35 Wash. and Lee L.Rev. 1089 (1978).

12. 1978–1 C.B. 68.

13. See note 6, supra.

14. Supra note 12.

15. Rev.Rul. 78–39, 1978–1 C.B. 73.

weight of authority as we interpret the authorities is against the doctrine that "constructive payment" is a necessary corollary of "constructive receipt." Mertens, in his Law of Federal Income Taxation, vol. 2, sec. 10.18, says:

> Constructive Payments as Deductions. Under the doctrine of constructive receipt a taxpayer on the cash basis is taxed upon income which he has not as yet actually received. Logically it would seem that where the payee is held to have constructively received an item as income, the payor should be entitled to deduct the same item as constructively paid, but the statute rather than logic is the controlling force in tax cases and so it is not surprising to find such reasoning often rejected. The difference is that the statute is presumed to reach and tax all income, and the doctrine of constructive receipt is an aid to that end. It must be remembered that the doctrine of constructive receipt is designed to effect a realistic concept of realization of income and to prevent abuses. Deductions, on the other hand, are a matter of legislative grace, and the terms of the statute permitting the particular deduction must be fully met without the aid of assumptions. "What may be income to the one may not be a deductible payment by the other." A review of the cases indicates that the courts will seldom support a doctrine of constructive payment in the sense in which it is used in this chapter, i.e., to determine when an item has been paid rather than who has paid it.

* * * If in any of our decisions, memorandum opinions or otherwise, we have said anything to the contrary of the above holdings, we think it is against the weight of authority and should not be followed. Therefore, following Martinus & Sons v. Commissioner [1] and other cases above cited, we sustain the Commissioner. See also our recent decision in Claude Patterson Noble,[2] in which among other things, we said:

> * * * No payment was made in 1942 by petitioner to her husband for his services; but the payment for services rendered in that year was made in 1943. Likewise the payment for 1943 services was not made until February 1944. It is argued that the custom was that petitioner's husband prepare all checks for her signature and that had he seen fit to do so, he could have received payment of the full amount of the salary at the close of each year for which the service was rendered. Thus it is said to follow that petitioner constructively paid and her husband constructively received payment of the salary for 1942 and 1943 at the close of each of those years. The fact remains, however, these checks were not prepared, signed, or delivered until after the close of those respective

---

1.　116 F.2d 732, affirming B.T.A. memorandum opinion.

2.　7 T.C. 960.

years. Accordingly there was no such payment or receipt in either case until after the close of the year. Massachusetts Mutual Insurance Co. v. United States, 288 U.S. 269; Martinus & Sons v. Commissioner, 116 F.2d 732; Cox Motor Sales Co., 42 B.T.A. 192; Sanford Corporation v. Commissioner, 106 F.2d 882.

*   *   *

COMMISSIONER v. BOYLSTON MARKET ASS'N

United States Court of Appeals, First Circuit, 1942.
131 F.2d 966.

MAHONEY, Circuit Judge. The Board of Tax Appeals reversed a determination by the Commissioner of Internal Revenue of deficiencies in the Boylston Market Association's income tax of $835.34 for the year 1936, and $431.84 for the year 1938, and the Commissioner has appealed.

The taxpayer in the course of its business, which is the management of real estate owned by it, purchased from time to time fire and other insurance policies covering periods of three or more years. It keeps its books and makes its returns on a cash receipts and disbursements basis. The taxpayer has since 1915 deducted each year as insurance expenses the amount of insurance premiums applicable to carrying insurance for that year regardless of the year in which the premium was actually paid. This method was required by the Treasury Department prior to 1938 by G.C.M. 13148, XIII–1 Cum.Bull. 67 (1934). Prior to January 1, 1936, the taxpayer had prepaid insurance premiums in the amount of $6,690.75 and during that year it paid premiums in an amount of $1082.77. The amount of insurance premiums prorated by the taxpayer in 1936 was $4421.76. Prior to January 1, 1938, it had prepaid insurance premiums in the amount of $6148.42 and during that year paid premiums in the amount of $890.47. The taxpayer took a deduction of $3284.25, which was the amount prorated for the year 1938. The Commissioner in his notice of deficiency for the year 1936 allowed only $1082.77 and for the year 1938 only $890.47, being the amounts actually paid in those years, on the basis that deductions for insurance expense of a taxpayer on the cash receipts and disbursements basis is limited to premiums paid during the taxable year.

We are asked to determine whether a taxpayer who keeps his books and files his returns on a cash basis is limited to the deduction of the insurance premiums actually paid in any year or whether he should deduct for each tax year the pro rata portion of the prepaid insurance applicable to that year. The pertinent provisions of the statute are Sections 23 and 43 of the Revenue Act of 1936,[1] 49 Stat. 1648, 26 U.S. C.A.Int.Rev.Acts, pages 813, 827, 839.

1. [§ 23, not materially different from I.R.C. (1986) § 162(a), and § 43, similar to I.R.C. (1986) § 461(a), are omitted. Ed.]

This court in Welch v. DeBlois, 1 Cir., 1938, 94 F.2d 842, held that a taxpayer on the cash receipts and disbursements basis who made prepayments of insurance premiums was entitled to take a full deduction for these payments as ordinary and necessary business expenses in the year in which payment was made despite the fact that the insurance covered a three-year period. The government on the basis of that decision changed its earlier G.C.M. rule, supra, which had required the taxpayer to prorate prepaid insurance premiums. The Board of Tax Appeals has refused to follow that case in George S. Jephson v. Com'r, 37 B.T.A. 1117; Frank Real Estate & Investment Co., 40 B.T.A. 1382, unreported memorandum decision Nov. 15, 1939, and in the instant case. The arguments in that case in favor of treating prepaid insurance as an ordinary and necessary business expense are persuasive. We are, nevertheless, unable to find a real basis for distinguishing between prepayment of rentals, Baton Coal Co. v. Commissioner, 3 Cir., 1931, 51 F.2d 469, certiorari denied 284 U.S. 674, 52 S.Ct. 129; Galatoire Bros. v. Lines, 5 Cir., 1928, 23 F.2d 676; See Main & McKinney Building Co. v. Commissioner, 5 Cir., 1940, 113 F.2d 81, 82, certiorari denied 311 U.S. 688, 61 S.Ct. 66; bonuses for the acquisition of leases, Home Trust Co. v. Commissioner, 8 Cir.1933, 65 F.2d 532; J. Alland & Bro., Inc. v. United States, D.C.Mass.1928, 28 F.2d 792; bonuses for the cancellation of leases, Steele-Wedeles Co. v. Commissioner, 30 B.T.A. 841, 842; Borland v. Commissioner, 27 B.T.A. 538, 542; commissions for negotiating leases, see Bonwit Teller & Co. v. Commissioner, 2 Cir., 1931, 53 F.2d 381, 384, 82 A.L.R. 325, and prepaid insurance. Some distinctions may be drawn in the cases cited on the basis of the facts contained therein, but we are of the opinion that there is no justification for treating them differently insofar as deductions are concerned. All of the cases cited are readily distinguishable from such a clear cut case as a permanent improvement to a building. This latter is clearly a capital expenditure. See Parkersburg Iron & Steel Co. v. Burnet, 4 Cir., 1931, 48 F.2d 163, 165. In such a case there is the creation of a capital asset which has a life extending beyond the taxable year and which depreciates over a period of years. The taxpayer regardless of his method of accounting can only take deductions for depreciation over the life of the asset. Advance rentals, payments of bonuses for acquisition and cancellation of leases, and commissions for negotiating leases are all matters which the taxpayer amortizes over the life of the lease. Whether we consider these payments to be the cost of the exhaustible asset, as in the case of advance rentals, or the cost of acquiring the asset, as in the case of bonuses, the payments are prorated primarily because the life of the asset extends beyond the taxable year. To permit the taxpayer to take a full deduction in the year of payment would distort his income. Prepaid insurance presents the same problem and should be solved in the same way. Prepaid insurance for a period of three years may be easily allocated. It is protection for the entire period and the taxpayer may, if he desires, at any time surrender the insurance policy. It thus is clearly an asset having a longer life than a single taxable year. The line to be drawn between capital expenditures and ordinary and necessary business expenses is not always an easy one, but we are satisfied that in treating prepaid insurance as a capital expense we are obtaining some degree of consistency in these matters. We are, therefore, of the opinion that Welch v. DeBlois, supra, is incorrect and should be overruled.

The decision of Board of Tax Appeals is affirmed.

NOTE

As indicated by the *Boylston Market Ass'n* case and as later set forth in the regulations,[1] an expenditure by a cash method taxpayer which results in the creation of an asset that has a useful life extending "substantially beyond" the close of the taxable year may not be fully deducted in the year payment is made. Instead, the expenditure must be capitalized and deductions may be taken only ratably over the asset's useful life. In determining whether an asset has a useful life extending "substantially beyond" the close of the taxable year, the court in Zaninovich v. Commissioner[2] adopted a "one-year" rule. Under this rule, prepaid expenses (other than those governed by a specific statute) may be deducted in the year they are paid, even though they span a period that touches two taxable years, as long as the expenses do not relate to a period greater than one year.

In some situations deductibility of expenses by cash method taxpayers is specifically provided for by statute.[3] For example, Section 461(g) requires cash method taxpayers to allocate deductions for prepaid interest to the periods to which they relate and to do so by way of capitalization and amortization.[4] The statute makes an exception for "points", a loan processing fee paid at the inception of a loan, which is treated as a current payment of interest.[5] However, the exception is limited to amounts customarily charged in connection with indebtedness incurred to purchase or improve a principal residence.[6] Thus, a taxpayer cannot easily manipulate these payments in such a way as to distort his income for a period.

Question may be raised whether Congress has gone far enough in Section 461(g). There is some possibility of distortion by way of deferring the payment of interest to a convenient later date when the corresponding tax deduction may be more beneficial. No statutory or common law rule forecloses this practice. However such deferrals may

1. Reg. § 1.461–1(a)(1).

2. 616 F.2d 429 (9th Cir.1980).

3. See I.R.C. § 461(g).

4. There were conflicting results prior to the enactment of I.R.C. § 461(g). See, e.g., John D. Fackler, 39 BTA 395 (1939), nonacq., 1968–2 C.B. 3, allowing the deduction for prepaid interest, Burck v. Commissioner, 533 F.2d 768 (2d Cir.1976), contra,

and Rev.Rul. 68–643, 1968–2 C.B. 76, generally limiting the deduction to interest for twelve months beyond the year of payment.

5. I.R.C. § 461(g)(2). See Rev.Rul. 69–188, 1969–1 C.B. 54, at page 456, supra. Cf. the *Cathcart* case which follows this note and involves withheld points.

6. Id.

be substantially restricted in a self-policing manner by impatient creditors.

CATHCART v. COMMISSIONER *

Tax Court of the United States, 1977.
36 T.C.M. 1321.

Opinion

The only issue we must resolve is whether petitioners are entitled to deduct points withheld from mortgage proceeds in the year petitioners obtained their mortgage.

On January 15, 1973, petitioners obtained a net proceeds mortgage loan from Southern Federal. The face amount of the mortgage was $57,600, bearing a 7 percent interest rate and having a duration of 29 years. As is common practice in net proceeds, mortgage loans, the amount ultimately disbursed to petitioners, $55,039.92, was less than the face amount of the mortgage. The difference withheld by Southern Federal, $2,560.08, was used to pay various services and to pay points totalling $1,086.60. Although points frequently represent a hidden service charge, in the case before us the parties agree that the points represent an interest charge. As such, their deductibility is governed by section 163.

Petitioners contend the entire $1,086.60 charged for points is fully deductible in 1973. In contrast, respondent contends the amount charged for points was not fully paid by petitioners in 1973, but rather payment is included in petitioners' monthly mortgage payments over the 29-year term. As such, respondent contends petitioners must prorate the points over the life of the loan. This method of prorating the charge over the life of the loan would entitle petitioners to an interest deduction of $34.34 for 1973.

Section 163(a) provides that "There shall be allowed as a deduction all interest paid or accrued within the taxable year on indebtedness." Despite the language of section 163(a), cash method taxpayers may not take interest expense deductions for prepaid interest if such deductions materially distort their income. Sandor v. Commissioner, 62 T.C. 469 (1974), affd. 536 F.2d 874 (9th Cir.1976); Cole v. Commissioner, 64 T.C. 1091 (1975); Resnik v. Commissioner, 66 T.C. 74 (1976), on appeal (7th Cir., June 30, 1976).

The Internal Revenue Service, and subsequently Congress, recognized an administrative exception to the material distortion of income argument when dealing with taxpayers who prepay interest or points on a home mortgage. See Rev.Rul. 69–582, 1969–2 C.B. 29; sec. 461(g) (2), added by sec. 208(a), Tax Reform Act of 1976, 90 Stat. 1541. Consequently, cash method taxpayers who prepay points on their home mortgages with funds not obtained from the lender are entitled to

* Footnotes omitted.

deduct the entire amount in the year paid. This rule, however, does not settle the case before us.

Although we have cash method taxpayers who obtained a mortgage loan secured by their personal residence, the points required in order to obtain the loan were *withheld* from the mortgage proceeds. Because the points were withheld from the loan proceeds, rather than *paid* by petitioners to Southern Federal, we conclude petitioners are not entitled to deduct the entire $1,086.60 in 1973. Our decision in this matter is controlled by Rubnitz v. Commissioner, 67 T.C. 621 (1977).

In *Rubnitz,* taxpayer owned an interest in Branham Associates (hereinafter Branham). In order to construct an apartment complex Branham, in 1970, obtained a $1,650,000 construction loan from a savings and loan association. Withheld from the proceeds of this loan was a "loan fee" of $57,750, which the parties agreed constituted interest under section 163(a). We concluded that the deduction or withholding of the loan fee from the loan proceeds did not constitute a "payment" of interest within the meaning of section 163(a), and therefore Branham was not entitled to deduct the full $57,750 as interest paid in 1970. Consequently, taxpayer was not entitled to the entire interest deduction he had claimed. In reaching this conclusion, we noted, at 628, Branham received $1,592,220 from the bank but it promised to repay $1,650,000 plus interest at a specified rate. Of the difference between these figures, $57,750 might well have represented additional interest charges. However, it is plain that Branham did not pay that interest in 1970. Instead, by signing a promissory note, it specifically chose to postpone paying that amount until sometime in the future. The entire $57,780 was to be paid ratably by the borrower over the life of the loan as one component of the monthly installments * * * which would ultimately result in the payment of the full $1,650,000. Therefore, Branham may not deduct the $57,750 as "interest paid" during 1970.

Similarly, we conclude that petitioners are not entitled to deduct their points, totalling $1,086.60, as "interest paid" during 1973. Rather, petitioners may only deduct $34.34, that pro rata portion of the points attributable to 1973.

To reflect the foregoing,

Decision will be entered under Rule 155.

PROBLEMS

1. Lender lends out money at a legal interest rate to Debtor. Debtor is required to pay $5000 interest each year on the loan which extends over a five year period with no reduction in the obligation to make the interest payments even if payment of the principal is accelerated. The interest is deductible by Debtor under § 163. The agreement calls for payment of each year's interest on December 31 of the year. Both parties are calendar year, cash method taxpayers. Discuss the tax consequences to both parties under the following alternatives:

(a) Debtor mails a check for $5000 interest to Lender on December 31, of year one. It is delivered to Lender on January 2 of year two.

(b) Debtor mails the check in (a), above, on December 30 of year one. It is delivered to Lender on December 31 of year one but after the banks are closed.

(c) Debtor pays all five years' interest ($25,000) to Lender in cash on December 31 of year one.

(d) Same as (c), above, but Debtor does so because Lender makes it a condition of extending Debtor another loan.

(e) Debtor pays year one's $5000 of interest in cash on January 2nd of year two and, as agreed, pays year two's interest on December 31 of year two.

(f) Debtor offers to pay Lender the $5000 interest due on December 31 of year one but Lender suggests that he pay it on January 2nd of year two, which he does.

(g) Debtor gives Lender a promissory note on December 31 of year one agreeing to pay year one's interest plus $50 on January 30 of year two. Debtor pays off the note on January 30 of year two.

2. Lawyer renders services to Client which are deductible to Client under I.R.C. § 162. What result to both Lawyer and Client if both are cash method, calendar year taxpayers in each of the following circumstances:

(a) Lawyer sends out a bill for $1000 on December 24 of year one. Client pays the bill on January 5 of year two.

(b) Lawyer sends out a bill for $1000 on November 15 of year one. Client immediately pays the bill using his American Express credit card and American Express pays Lawyer the $1000 on December 15 of year one. Client pays American Express the $1000 credit card bill on January 15 of year two.

(c) Prior to rendering the services Lawyer and Client agree that Lawyer will be paid $500 in year one and $500 in year two. Client pays Lawyer $500 of cash on December 24 of year one and $500 of cash on January 5 of year two.

(d) Client calls Lawyer at 4:00 p.m., December 31 of year one, saying he has Lawyer's fee statement, has made out check in full payment and, as he is about to leave for Europe, will leave check with desk clerk at Client's apartment. Lawyer is ill, has no one to send to pick up check, and finally picks it up on January 2 of year two. See Loose v. U.S., 74 F.2d 147 (8th Cir. 1934).

C. THE ACCRUAL METHOD

---

1. INCOME ITEMS

Internal Revenue Code: Section 451(a). See Sections 448(d)(5), 455, 456, and 458.

Regulations: Section 1.451–1(a). See Section 1.455–1.

SPRING CITY FOUNDRY CO. v. COMMISSIONER

Supreme Court of the United States, 1934.
292 U.S. 182, 54 S.Ct. 644, rehearing denied 292 U.S. 613, 54 S.Ct. 857, 1934.

Mr. Chief Justice HUGHES delivered the opinion of the Court.

[The taxpayer, petitioner in the Supreme Court, using the calendar year, accrual method of accounting, had sold goods in 1920 on open account. Before the end of the year the purchaser went bankrupt and a receiver was appointed. By the end of the year it was clear the taxpayer would not be paid in full for the goods. The question was how, if at all, the post-sale events affected the taxpayer's taxable income for the year.

In a portion of the opinion not reproduced here, the court upheld the Commissioner's disallowance of any bad debt deduction for the year. As now, under Section 166, the statute provided a bad debt deduction but only for debts that became worthless during the taxable year. There was then no provision for a deduction for *partially* worthless debts as is now provided by Section 166(a)(2), and the purchaser's obligation had not become wholly worthless in 1920. The bad debt deduction is considered in Chapter 23A, infra.

The alternate contention of the taxpayer was that the partial worthlessness of the purchaser's obligations in 1920 affected its *gross* income for that year. This contention was also rejected in the portion of the opinion that follows. Ed.]

* * *

Petitioner first contends that the debt, to the extent that it was ascertained in 1920 to be worthless, was not returnable as gross income in that year, that is, apart from any question of deductions, it was not to be regarded as taxable income at all. We see no merit in this contention. Keeping accounts and making returns on the accrual basis, as distinguished from the cash basis, import that it is the *right* to receive and not the actual receipt that determines the inclusion of the amount in gross income. When the right to receive an amount becomes fixed, the right accrues. When a merchandising concern makes sales, its inventory is reduced and a claim for the purchase price arises. Article 35 of Regulations 45 under the Revenue Act of 1918 provided: "In the case of a manufacturing, merchandising, or mining business 'gross income' means the total sales, less the cost of goods sold, plus any income from investments and from incidental or outside operations or sources." [1]

On an accrual basis, the "total sales," to which the regulation refers, are manifestly the accounts receivable arising from the sales, and these accounts receivable, less the cost of the goods sold, figure in the statement of gross income. If such accounts receivable become uncollectible, in whole or part, the question is one of the deduction which may be taken according to the applicable statute. See United States v. Anderson, 269 U.S. 422, 440, 441, 46 S.Ct. 131; American National Co. v. United States, 274 U.S. 99, 102, 103, 47 S.Ct. 520; Brown v. Helvering, 291 U.S. 193, 199, 54 S.Ct. 356; Rouss v. Bowers, 30 F.2d 628, 629. That is the question here. It is not altered by the fact that the claim of loss relates to an item of gross income which had accrued in the same year.

* * *

REVENUE RULING 70–151
1970–1 Cum.Bull. 116.

The purpose of this Revenue Ruling is to update and restate, under the current statute and regulations, the position set forth in I.T. 3165, C.B. 1938–1, 158.

The question presented is when income accrues under the circumstances described below.

The taxpayer, a domestic corporation reporting its income under the accrual method of accounting for Federal income tax purposes, instituted a suit against the United States in the United States Court of Claims for damages for alleged breach of contract. The taxpayer was awarded a judgment in 1968. A petition for writ of certiorari was filed by the United States and denied by the Supreme Court of the United States in 1969. No petition for rehearing was filed by the United States. No appropriation was made by Congress for the amount of the judgment in 1969.

Section 451 of the Internal Revenue Code of 1954 provides, in part, that any item of gross income shall be included in gross income for the taxable year in which received by the taxpayer unless, under the method of accounting used in computing taxable income, such amount is to be properly accounted for as of a different period.

Section 1.451–1(a) of the Income Tax Regulations provide, in pertinent part, that under the accrual method of accounting, income is includible in gross income when all events have occurred that fix the right to receive such income and the amount thereof can be determined with reasonable accuracy.

1. This provision has been carried forward in the regulations under the later revenue acts. See Regulations 77, Article 55.

In the instant case the right to receive the sum due as a result of the judgment was determined in 1969. The fact that Congress did not make an appropriation for the payment of such sum in 1969 does not govern since the judgment became an acknowledged liability of the United States in 1969.

Accordingly, the amount of the judgment must be included in the taxpayer's gross income in 1969 under the taxpayer's method of accounting.

I.T. 3165 is superseded, since the position set forth therein is restated under current law in this Revenue Ruling.

NORTH AMERICAN OIL CONSOLIDATED v. BURNET

Supreme Court of the United States, 1932.
286 U.S. 417, 52 S.Ct. 613.

Mr. Justice BRANDEIS delivered the opinion of the Court.

The question for decision is whether the sum of $171,979.22 received by the North American Oil Consolidated in 1917, was taxable to it as income of that year.

The money was paid to the company under the following circumstances. Among many properties operated by it in 1916 was a section of oil land, the legal title to which stood in the name of the United States. Prior to that year, the Government, claiming also the beneficial ownership, had instituted a suit to oust the company from possession; and on February 2, 1916, it secured the appointment of a receiver to operate the property, or supervise its operations, and to hold the net income thereof. The money paid to the company in 1917 represented the net profits which had been earned from that property in 1916 during the receivership. The money was paid to the receiver as earned. After entry by the District Court in 1917 of the final decree dismissing the bill, the money was paid, in that year, by the receiver to the company. United States v. North American Oil Consolidated, 242 F. 723. The Government took an appeal (without supersedeas) to the Circuit Court of Appeals. In 1920, that Court affirmed the decree. 264 F. 336. In 1922, a further appeal to this Court was dismissed by stipulation. 258 U.S. 633, 42 S.Ct. 315.

The income earned from the property in 1916 had been entered on the books of the company as its income. It had not been included in its original return of income for 1916; but it was included in an amended return for that year which was filed in 1918. Upon auditing the company's income and profits tax returns for 1917, the Commissioner of Internal Revenue determined a deficiency based on other items. The company appealed to the Board of Tax Appeals. There in 1927 the Commissioner prayed that the deficiency already claimed should be increased so as to include a tax on the amount paid by the receiver to the company in 1917. The Board held that the profits were taxable to the receiver as income of 1916; and hence made no finding whether the company's accounts were kept on the cash receipts and disbursements basis or on the accrual basis. 12 B.T.A. 68. The Circuit Court of Appeals held that the profits were taxable to the company as income of 1917, regardless of whether the company's returns were made on the cash or on the accrual basis. 50 F.2d 752. This Court granted a writ of certiorari. 284 U.S. 614, 52 S.Ct. 208.

It is conceded that the net profits earned by the property during the receivership constituted income. The company contends that they should have been reported by the receiver for taxation in 1916; that if not returnable by him, they should have been returned by the company for 1916, because they constitute income of the company accrued in that year; and that if not taxable as income of the company for 1916, they were taxable to it as income for 1922, since the litigation was not finally terminated in its favor until 1922.

First. The income earned in 1916 and impounded by the receiver in that year was not taxable to him, because he was the receiver of only a part of the properties operated by the company. Under § 13(c) of the Revenue Act of 1916,[1] receivers who "are operating the property or business of corporations" were obliged to make returns "of net income as and for such corporations," and "any income tax due" was to be "assessed and collected in the same manner as if assessed directly against the organization of whose business or properties they have custody and control." The phraseology of this section was adopted without change in the Revenue Act of 1918, 40 Stat. 1057, 1081, c. 18, § 239. The regulations of the Treasury Department have consistently construed these statutes as applying only to receivers in charge of the entire property or business of a corporation; and in all other cases have required the corporations themselves to report their income. Treas. Regs. 33, arts. 26, 209; Treas.Regs. 45, arts. 424, 622. That construction is clearly correct. The language of the section contemplates a substitution of the receiver for the corporation; and there can be such substitution only when the receiver is in complete control of the properties and business of the corporation. Moreover, there is no provision for the consolidation of the return of a receiver of part of a corporation's property or business with the return of the corporation itself. It may not be assumed that Congress intended to require the filing of two separate returns for the same year, each covering only a part of the corporate income, without making provision for consolidation so that the tax could be based upon the income as a whole.

Second. The net profits were not taxable to the company as income of 1916. For the company was not required in 1916 to report as

1. Act of September 8, 1916, 39 Stat. 756, 771, c. 463: "In cases wherein receivers, trustees in bankruptcy, or assignees are operating the property or business of corporations * * *, subject to tax imposed by this title, such receivers, trustees or assignees shall make returns of net income as and for such corporations * * *, in the same manner and form as such organizations are hereinbefore required to make returns, and any income tax due on the basis of such returns made by receivers, trustees, or assignees shall be assessed and collected in the same manner as if assessed directly against the organizations of whose business or properties they have custody and control." [See I.R.C. (1986) § 6012(b)(3). Ed.]

income an amount which it might never receive. See Burnet v. Logan, 283 U.S. 404, 413, 51 S.Ct. 550. Compare Lucas v. American Code Co., 280 U.S. 445, 452, 50 S.Ct. 202; Burnet v. Sanford & Brooks Co., 282 U.S. 359, 363, 51 S.Ct. 150. There was no constructive receipt of the profits by the company in that year, because at no time during the year was there a right in the company to demand that the receiver pay over the money. Throughout 1916 it was uncertain who would be declared entitled to the profits. It was not until 1917, when the District Court entered a final decree vacating the receivership and dismissing the bill, that the company became entitled to receive the money. Nor is it material, for the purposes of this case, whether the company's return was filed on the cash receipts and disbursements basis, or on the accrual basis. In neither event was it taxable in 1916 on account of income which it had not yet received and which it might never receive.

Third. The net profits earned by the property in 1916 were not income of the year 1922—the year in which the litigation with the Government was finally terminated. They became income of the company in 1917, when it first became entitled to them and when it actually received them. If a taxpayer receives earnings under a claim of right and without restriction as to its disposition, he has received income which he is required to return, even though it may still be claimed that he is not entitled to retain the money, and even though he may still be adjudged liable to restore its equivalent. See Board v. Commissioner, 51 F.2d 73, 75, 76. Compare United States v. S.S. White Dental Mfg. Co., 274 U.S. 398, 403, 47 S.Ct. 598. If in 1922 the Government had prevailed, and the company had been obliged to refund the profits received in 1917, it would have been entitled to a deduction from the profits of 1922, not from those of any earlier year. Compare Lucas v. American Code Co., supra.

Affirmed.

NEW CAPITAL HOTEL, INC.

Tax Court of the United States, 1957.
28 T.C. 706, affirmed per curiam 261 F.2d 437 (6th Cir.1958).

The respondent determined a deficiency in petitioner's income tax for the year 1949 in the amount of $11,724.50.

The sole issue is whether a $30,000 advance payment received in 1949 by the petitioner lessor, an accrual basis taxpayer, pursuant to lease contract is includible in gross income in 1949, as determined by the respondent, or in 1959, the year in which the advance payment is to be applied as rent.

[The findings of fact are omitted. Ed.]

Opinion

BLACK, Judge: The sole question involved here is whether the $30,000 advance payment received in 1949 by the petitioner is includible in its gross income for that year.

The petitioner lessor leased certain hotel property, which it owned, for a period of 10 years from January 1, 1950, to December 31, 1959. The lease contract provided that the lessee would pay rents as follows: $30,000 during each year of the lease and "for the last year of this lease, Lessee agrees to pay in advance the sum of Thirty Thousand Dollars ($30,000.00), the receipt of which is hereby acknowledged. Said sum, however, shall apply only on the rental for the last year of this lease." The lease also provided that if the building should be substantially destroyed during the period of the lease the lessor shall refund to the lessee all or part of the $30,000 as may not cover the rental of the property up to the time of such destruction, provided, however, that no rental is then in arrears.

The petitioner's president testified that the lessee preferred paying the last year's rent in advance rather than executing a performance bond, which the lessor was demanding. The lessee, during 1949, paid the above-mentioned $30,000 to the petitioner. There were no restrictions on the use of the $30,000; the petitioner had unfettered control over it.

The petitioner, an accrual basis taxpayer, reflected the advance rental payment in a liability account entitled "Deposit on lease contract" and contends that it should be reported as income in 1959, the year in which petitioner contends it would be considered as earned. The respondent determined that the $30,000 constituted gross income in 1949, the year of receipt, under section 22(a), Internal Revenue Code of 1939.[1]

It is clear from the record that the advance payment, although securing the lessee's performance of the covenants, was intended to be rent, was described in the lease contract as rent, and was primarily rent. Gilken Corporation, 10 T.C. 445, 451–456 (1948), affd. (C.A.6, 1949) 176 F.2d 141, 144–145. Since the rent was received in 1949, it would be includible in gross income in that year even though the rent is to be applied for the use of the property in 1959. Hirsch Improvement Co. v. Commissioner (C.A.2, 1944) 143 F.2d 912, affirming a Memorandum Opinion of this Court. This is so regardless of whether the taxpayer keeps his books and computes his income on a cash basis, see Edwin B. De Golia, 40 B.T.A. 845 (1939), or on an accrual basis, see Palm Beach Aero Corporation, 17 T.C. 1169, 1170, 1177–1178 (1952); Hyde Park Realty, Inc. v. Commissioner (C.A.2, 1954) 211 F.2d 462, affirming 20 T.C. 43 (1953).

The petitioner argues that its method of accounting clearly reflects its income and that the inclusion of the rent in gross income for the year 1949, rather than 1959, will distort its income for the 2 years because in 1959 it will incur approximately $23,000 in expenses incident to the earning of the $30,000 rent.[2]

---

1. SEC. 22. GROSS INCOME.

(a) General Definition.—"Gross income" includes gains, profits, and income derived from * * * rent, * * *

2. The petitioner, in its reply brief, apparently also contends that if the $30,000 is includible in its 1949 gross income it should be allowed a deduction of $23,000 for expenses to be incurred in 1959 in

We have recognized that the inclusion of prepaid income in gross income in the year of receipt of the item representing it, rather than in a subsequent year when it is considered earned, is not in accord with principles of commercial accounting. See Curtis R. Andrews, 23 T.C. 1026, 1033–1034 (1955); E.W. Schuessler, 24 T.C. 247, 249 (1955), reversed (C.A.5, 1956) 230 F.2d 722. We have, however, consistently held that the Commissioner has acted within the discretion granted him under section 41 of the 1939 Code in holding that prepaid income must be returned in the year received in order to clearly reflect income. Cf. Automobile Club of Michigan v. Commissioner, 353 U.S. 180, 188– 190 (1957). In the instant case the petitioner seeks to defer a nonrecurring advance rental payment[3] for a period of 10 years.[4] Under the circumstances detailed in our Findings of Fact we cannot say that the Commissioner abused the discretion granted him in section 41, Internal Revenue Code of 1939,[*] in determining that the $30,000 was includible in the petitioner's gross income in 1949.

Among the decisions which petitioner relies on in its brief in support of its contention that the $30,000 is not taxable in 1949, is John Mantell, 17 T.C. 1143 (1952). We think the facts of the instant case are clearly distinguishable from those present in the *Mantell* case. In the *Mantell* case our Findings of Fact made clear that the $33,320, which was involved there, was not meant to be paid as advance rental. It was paid primarily to be held as security to guarantee the performance by the lessees of the obligations and covenants contained in the lease. The next to the last paragraph of our Findings of Fact in the *Mantell* case enumerates the several things for which the $33,320 was to act as security to guarantee that the lessees would perform. Our Findings of Fact then conclude with the following final paragraph (p. 1147):

> The sum of $33,320 received by the petitioner upon the execution of the lease in 1946 was intended to be and was in fact a security deposit. It was not paid as prepaid rent and was not taxable income when received.

Manifestly, we could make no such finding in the instant case because the lease agreement itself provides:

> And, for the last year of this lease, Lessee agrees to pay in advance the sum of Thirty Thousand Dollars ($30,000.00), the receipt of which is hereby acknowledged. Said sum, however, shall apply only on the rental for the last year of this lease.

connection with the earning of the rent. This issue has not been properly pleaded and is not properly before us. Regardless, it has no merit. See Bressner Radio, Inc., 28 T.C. 378 (1957).

3. There is no contention that the Commissioner's action in this case will upset a consistent accounting system of long standing. Cf. Pacific Grape Products Co., 17 T.C. 1097 (1952), revd. (C.A.9, 1955) 219 F.2d 862.

4. Even under the liberalized provisions for reporting prepaid income under the short-lived section 452(b), Internal Revenue Code of 1954, a prepayment 10 years in advance, such as the one involved herein, would be includible in gross income ratably in the year of receipt and the next succeeding 5 years unless the Secretary or his delegate prescribed otherwise. See S.Rept. No. 1622, 83d Cong., 2d Sess. (1954), pp. 301, 302.

* See I.R.C. (1986) § 446(b). Ed.

That the $30,000 in question was paid by the lessee as advance rental for the year 1959 seems too clear for argument and, under the authorities cited, we must hold that it was taxable income to petitioner in the year 1949, when it was received.

Decision will be entered for the respondent.

ARTNELL CO. v. COMMISSIONER *

United States Court of Appeals, Seventh Circuit, 1968.
400 F.2d 981.

FAIRCHILD, Circuit Judge. The tax court upheld the commissioner's determination of deficiencies,[1] and Artnell Company, transferee taxpayer, seeks review. The main question is whether prepayments for services (proceeds of advance sales of tickets for baseball games and revenues for related future services) must be treated as income when received or whether such treatment could be deferred by the accrual basis taxpayer until the games were played and other services rendered.

Early in the 1962 baseball season, as in previous seasons, the White Sox team was operated by Chicago White Sox, Inc. It sold season tickets and single admissions for later games. It received revenues for broadcasting and televising future games, and it sold season parking books. Its taxable year would normally have run to October 31, 1962. It employed the accrual method of accounting for its own and for income tax purposes.

Before May 31, 1962, Artnell Company had acquired all the stock in White Sox. On that date White Sox was liquidated. Artnell became the owner of all the assets and subject to all the liabilities. It continued to operate the team.

As of May 31, the balance sheet of White Sox showed as deferred unearned income that part of the amount received for season tickets, advance single admissions, radio, television, and season parking books, allocable to games to be played after May 31. As the games were played Artnell took into income the amounts of deferred unearned income allocated to each.

The White Sox income tax return for the taxable year ending May 31, 1962 (because of the liquidation) was filed by Artnell as transferee. The return did not include the deferred unearned income as gross income. The commissioner decided it must be included and determined deficiencies accordingly.

When a business receives money in exchange for its obligation to render service or deliver goods and the costs of performance are incurred in a later accounting period, treatment of the receipt as

---

* See Malman, "Treatment of Prepaid Income—Clear Reflection of Income or Muddied Waters," 37 Tax L.Rev. 103 (1981); Cohen, "Prepaid Income for Future Services: When May an Accrual Basis Tax-payer Utilize the Deferral Technique?" 34 U.Fla.L.Rev. 776 (1982).

1. 48 T.C. 411.

income tends to reflect an illusory or partially illusory gain for the period of receipt. Accountancy has techniques (e.g. deferral of income, reserves for expenses) for achieving a more realistic reflection. The degree to which such techniques are available under income tax statutes is a vexing question.[2]

The commissioner urges the simple answer "that deferral of income is a matter for Congress to permit and, until Congress acts, deferral must be disallowed." He stands on "the established rule that an accrual basis taxpayer must include in gross income in the year of receipt prepaid items for which services will be performed in a later year. The rule implements the annual accounting principle which is at the heart of the federal taxing statute and which forbids transactional accounting for income tax purposes, however sound such methods might be for financial and other purposes under commercial accounting practice." [3]

Artnell relies upon statutory language which requires computation of taxable income under the accrual method of accounting regularly used by the taxpayer unless such method "does not clearly reflect income." [4] This language could call for a factual determination in the individual case whether an accrual system which employs the deferral of income technique clearly reflects income. Artnell contends that the White Sox system does so.

The commissioner's principal contention, which was sustained by the tax court, is that there is a rule of law which rejects deferral of income. Presumably he believes that any system in which prepaid income is deferred "does not clearly reflect income" and would consider the present statutory provisions for deferral in the case of prepaid subscription income [5] and prepaid dues of certain membership organizations [6] extensions of legislative grace.

One could reason from the statutory language that any deferral of prepaid income which fulfills standards of sound accounting practice could be employed by an accrual basis taxpayer, and the commissioner would not have power to reject it. Three Supreme Court decisions, *Automobile Club of Michigan*,[7] *American Automobile Association*,[8] and *Schlude* [9] have made it clear that this is not the law.

There are two other lines of reasoning reflected in the three decisions cited. All three held, upon consideration of the particular facts, that the commissioner did not abuse his discretion in rejecting a deferral of income where the time and extent of performance of future

2. See Aland, Prepaid Income and Estimated Future Expenses, Jan. 1968 ABA Journal 84; Annotation: Income Taxes— Prepayment—When Income, 9 L.Ed.2d 1191.

3. The quotations are from the commissioner's brief.

4. 26 U.S.C.A. sec. 446.

5. 26 U.S.C.A. sec. 455.

6. 26 U.S.C.A. sec. 456.

7. Automobile Club of Michigan v. Commissioner of Internal Revenue (1957), 353 U.S. 180, 77 S.Ct. 707.

8. American Auto. Ass'n v. United States (1961), 367 U.S. 687, 81 S.Ct. 1727.

9. Schlude v. Commissioner of Internal Revenue (1963), 372 U.S. 128, 83 S.Ct. 601.

services were uncertain. Thus in *Automobile Club of Michigan:* "The pro rata allocation of the membership dues in monthly amounts is purely artificial and bears no relation to the services which petitioner may in fact be called upon to render for the member." In *American Automobile Association:* "That 'irregularity,' however, is highly relevant to the clarity of an accounting system which defers receipt, as earned income, of dues to a taxable period in which no, some or all the services paid for by those dues may or may not be rendered." In *Schlude:* "The American Automobile Association Case rested upon an additional ground which is also controlling here. Relying upon Automobile Club of Michigan * * *, the Court rejected the taxpayer's system as artificial since the advance payments related to services which were to be performed only upon customers' demands without relation to fixed dates in the future. The system employed here suffers from that very same vice * * *." In *Schlude* the Court also found that certain expenses were deducted in the year the payments were received even though related income had been deferred to later periods.

The uncertainty stressed in those decisions is not present here. The deferred income was allocable to games which were to be played on a fixed schedule. Except for rain dates, there was certainty. We would have no difficulty distinguishing the instant case in this respect.

A second consideration is reflected in *American Automobile Association* and *Schlude.* It is that Congress is aware of the problem and that it is the policy of the Supreme Court to defer, where possible, to congressional procedures in the tax field. Thus in *American Automobile Association:* "At the very least, this background indicates congressional recognition of the complications inherent in the problem and its seriousness to the general revenues. We must leave to the Congress the fashioning of a rule which, in any event, must have wide ramifications. * * * Finding only that, in light of existing provisions not specifically authorizing it, the exercise of the Commissioner's discretion in rejecting the Association's accounting system was not unsound, we need not anticipate what will be the product of further 'study of this entire problem.'" In *Schlude:* "Plainly, the considerations expressed in American Automobile Association are apposite here. We need only add here that since the American Automobile Association decision, a specific provision extending the deferral practice to certain membership corporations was enacted * * * continuing, at least so far, the congressional policy of treating this problem by precise provisions of narrow applicability. Consequently, as in the American Automobile Association Case, we invoke the 'long-established policy of the Court in deferring, where possible, to congressional procedures in the tax field,' and, as in that case, we cannot say that the Commissioner's rejection of the studio's deferral system was unsound."

Has the Supreme Court left an opening for a decision that under the facts of a particular case, the extent and time of future performance are so certain, and related items properly accounted for with such clarity, that a system of accounting involving deferral of prepaid income is found clearly to reflect income, and the commissioner's rejection deemed an abuse of discretion? Or has it decided that the commissioner has complete and unreviewable discretion to reject deferral of prepaid income where Congress has made no provision? The tax court apparently adopted the latter view, for it concluded "that the Supreme Court would reach the same decision regardless of the method used by the taxpayer for deferring prepaid income."

It is our best judgment that, although the policy of deferring, where possible, to congressional procedures in the tax field will cause the Supreme Court to accord the widest possible latitude to the commissioner's discretion, there must be situations where the deferral technique will so clearly reflect income that the Court will find an abuse of discretion if the commissioner rejects it.

Prior to 1955 the commissioner permitted accrual basis publishers to defer unearned income from magazine subscriptions if they had consistently done so in the past. He refused to allow others to adopt the method.[10] In 1955 his refusal was held, by the tenth circuit, in *Beacon*,[11] to be an abuse of discretion. In *Automobile Club of Michigan*, the Supreme Court distinguished *Beacon*, on its facts, because "performance of the subscription, in most instances, was, in part, necessarily deferred until the publication dates after the tax year." The Court, however, expressed no opinion upon the correctness of *Beacon*. In 1958, Congress dealt specifically with the *Beacon* problem.[12] It is at least arguable that the deferral as income of prepaid admissions to events which will take place on a fixed schedule in a different taxable year is so similar to deferral of prepaid subscriptions that it would be an abuse of discretion to reject similar accounting treatment.

In any event the prepaid admission situation approaches much closer to certainty than the situations considered in *Automobile Club of Michigan, American Automobile Association,* or *Schlude.*

The instant case was presented to the tax court on a stipulation of facts. The parties agreed as to the amounts of prepaid revenue allocated to the games played after May 31. The stipulation does not set forth other facts from which it could be determined that all other relevant items were so treated in the White Sox method of accounting that the income attributable to the first seven months of its normal fiscal and taxable year was clearly reflected.

The commissioner now points out that Artnell failed to produce this evidence and argues here that we must affirm on that ground even if we disagree with the commissioner's primary contention.

We think, however, that the commissioner shares responsibility for the failure of proof, for he seems to have let the tax court judge believe that this was not an issue. The judge wrote: "Since the respondent

---

10. See I.T. 3369, 1940–1 Cum.Bull. 46, modified, Rev.Rul. 57–87, 1957–1 Cum.Bull. 507. See also Anno., 9 L.Ed.2d 1191, at 1201–03.

11. Beacon Publishing Company v. Commissioner of Internal Revenue (10th Cir., 1955), 218 F.2d 697.

12. 26 U.S.C.A. sec. 455.

does not contend that the petitioner's method for deferring the advance receipts fails to match properly income and related expenses, we must therefore decide whether prepaid income is taxable in the year received, regardless of the merits of the proposed method for deferring it."

We choose, however, not to base our decision on an inferred waiver of this issue by the commissioner. It is specially important in this area to have the facts carefully developed.

We conclude that the tax court erred in deciding that these revenues were income when received regardless of the merits of the method employed. There must be further hearing in the tax court to determine whether the White Sox method of accounting did clearly reflect its income in its final, seven month, taxable year.

*   *   *

The decision of the tax court is reversed and the cause remanded for further hearing consistent with this opinion.

[See note below for result on remand.   Ed.]

DEFERRED INCOME

As can be discerned from the opinion the *Artnell* case delivered a major jolt to long-standing and generally accepted Treasury policy requiring taxpayers, whether on the cash or accrual method, to include amounts received for goods and services to be furnished in a later year in income in the year of receipt. In *Artnell* on remand, the Tax Court concluded that the White Sox' method of accounting, while not perfect in matching income with related expenses, was more supportable than that proposed by the Commissioner and upheld the taxpayer's deferred reporting of a portion of its income.[1]

Undeniably, the immediate inclusion policy challenged by *Artnell* is at variance with business accounting principles. It is tempting therefore simply to say that it is wrong. Nevertheless, there is some respectable support for it, both as a practical matter and as regards precedent. From the practical point of view, while both business and tax accounting principles are designed to yield an annual net income figure, their objectives are not identical. The business world wants a periodic net income figure for purposes of determining profitability of the business and comparative profitability for various accounting periods. Congress wants a steady flow of tax revenue and assurance that taxpayers in fact pay tax on all elements of gain. With this second objective in mind a momentary gain, even if it may later be offset by related expenses in a later period, *can* be identified as income. Thus, the issue is one of statutory interpretation: *Has* Congress compelled this result? On the other hand, with an eye toward the graduated rate tables, there is a question whether the business accounting purpose of identifying net income for the critical period, reasonably taking account

1.   29 T.C.M. 403 (1970).

of subsequent related costs or expenditures, is not as important for tax accounting as for business accounting. These thoughts have a direct bearing both on the interpretation of the Code's accounting sections as they stand and on the congressional question whether present provisions need revision, and they are reflected in the history of the Treasury's immediate reporting policy.

The Treasury's strict inclusion policy appeared as early as 1938 in a memorandum [2] which, relying upon "claim of right" language in *North American Oil Consolidated,* stated that "amounts received * * * within the taxable year without restriction as to disposition, use, or enjoyment, for subscription service to be rendered in a succeeding year or years constitute income for the year in which received regardless of the fact that the taxpayer's books of account are kept on the accrual basis." The proposition received judicial support both before and after publication of the memorandum.[3]

In the enactment of the 1954 Code, Congress undertook to change the immediate inclusion rule to a tax accounting rule in keeping with business accounting principles. Under Section 452, accrual method taxpayers were permitted to report prepaid income from services or goods over the period in which the services were rendered or the goods were delivered up to a maximum period of five years subsequent to the year of receipt. At the same time, Section 462 was added to allow, at the Commissioner's discretion, accrual method taxpayers to establish a reserve for estimated future expenses.[4] Because of congressional fear that a substantial temporary loss of revenue would occur in the period immediately following enactment of the sections as a result of taxpayers deferring recognition of their prepaid income under Section 452 and accelerating deductions under Section 462,[5] both sections were retroactively repealed in 1955.[6]

Subsequent to the repeal of Sections 452 and 462 and until *Artnell,* the Commissioner has been largely successful in maintaining that, in order clearly to reflect income under Section 446, prepaid income of accrual method taxpayers for both goods and services must be included within income in the year of prepayment. In fairly recent times, several Supreme Court cases have endorsed this view, namely Automobile Club of Michigan v. Commissioner,[7] American Automobile Ass'n v. United States,[8] and Schlude v. Commissioner,[9] all of which are discussed and distinguished in *Artnell.*[10] In the meantime, limited statu-

---

2. GCM 20021, 1938–1 C.B. 157, 158.

3. E.g., Brown v. Helvering, 291 U.S. 193, 54 S.Ct. 356 (1934); South Dade Farms v. Commissioner, 138 F.2d 818 (5th Cir. 1943); South Tacoma Motor Co., 3 T.C. 411 (1944); Your Health Club, Inc., 4 T.C. 385 (1944), acq., 1945 C.B. 7; Curtis R. Andrews, 23 T.C. 1026 (1955). But see I.T. 3369, 1940–1 C.B. 46, and Beacon Pub. Co. v. Commissioner, 218 F.2d 697 (10th Cir. 1955).

4. See the *Schuessler* case and the note following, page 607, infra, this chapter.

5. See H.Rep. No. 293, 84th Cong., 1st Sess. (1955), 1955–2 C.B. 852, 853.

6. P.L. 74, 84th Cong., 1st Sess. (1955).

7. 353 U.S. 180, 77 S.Ct. 707 (1957).

8. 367 U.S. 687, 81 S.Ct. 1727 (1961).

9. 372 U.S. 128, 83 S.Ct. 601 (1963).

10. Lower court decisions to the same effect include, e.g., Services: R.C.A. Corp.

tory exceptions to the immediate inclusion rule were made in the case of income from newspaper, magazine, and periodical subscriptions under Section 455 [11] and prepaid club dues under Section 456.

It seems certain that *Artnell* has already had an impact on tax accounting principles and that it will play a role in subsequent developments.[12] For one thing, the Government did not petition for certiorari in *Artnell*. Moreover, since the decision the promulgation of a Revenue Procedure concerning prepayment for services and a change in the accounting regulations relating to prepayment for goods reflect a kind of hesitant, perhaps now stalled and, at most, creeping move toward the adoption of business accounting principles. In Rev.Proc. 70–21 [13] the Commissioner announced a new policy with respect to prepaid services.[14] The Procedure provides that, if there is a prepayment to an accrual method taxpayer for services to be rendered in the current and a succeeding year, income is required to be included in the current year only to the extent that services are rendered in that year and the remaining income need not be reported until the subsequent year. However, the ruling is restrictive in that no postponement is allowed if the prepayment is for services to be rendered beyond the end of the succeeding year or at an unspecified future date.[15] If the services were to have been rendered by the end of the succeeding year but they are not rendered by that time, any prepayment not previously reported is treated as gross income for the succeeding year. The Procedure is expressly inapplicable to prepaid interest or rent.[16]

Going back to *Artnell*, the continued immediate inclusion rule for interest and rent seems curious. The key question in *Artnell* was properly identified as whether the taxpayer's accounting method clearly reflects income.[17] Prepaid interest and rent are precisely allocable among accounting periods on the basis of elapsed time and thus are

v. United States, 664 F.2d 881 (2d Cir. 1981); Popular Library, Inc., 39 T.C. 1092 (1963); W.O. McMahon, Inc., 45 T.C. 221 (1965); Decision, Inc., 47 T.C. 58 (1966); Prichard Funeral Home, 25 T.C.M. 1434 (1966); Wide Acres Rest Home, Inc., 26 T.C.M. 391 (1967); Travis v. Commissioner, 406 F.2d 987 (6th Cir.1969). Goods: Fifth & York Co. v. U.S., 234 F.Supp. 421 (W.D. Ky.1964); Chester Farrara, 44 T.C. 189 (1965); Modernaire Interiors, Inc., 27 T.C.M. 1334 (1968); Hagen Advertising Displays, Inc. v. Commissioner, 407 F.2d 1105 (6th Cir.1969); S. Garber, Inc., 51 T.C. 733 (1969). But see Veenstra and De Haan Coal Co., 11 T.C. 964 (1948), holding that the prepayment was a mere deposit.

11. See also I.R.C. § 458, added by the Revenue Act of 1978, under which accrual method taxpayers who sell magazines, paperbacks and records may defer prepayments if the shipped goods can be returned by the buyer within specified periods after the end of the year.

12. See Boise Cascade Corp. v. U.S., 530 F.2d 1367 (Ct.Cls.1976), cert. den. 429 U.S. 867, 97 S.Ct. 176 in which the Court of Claims allowed an accrual method taxpayer in the construction business to defer prepaid income for services where the services were to be rendered at taxpayer's not recipient's discretion. The result is of questionable validity.

13. 1970–2 C.B. 501 (1970).

14. Rev.Proc. 71–21, 1971–2 C.B. 549, superseded Rev.Proc. 70–21, providing essentially the same rules.

15. The two-year limitation does not apply to prepayments for bus and streetcar tokens and photographic services.

16. For this purpose "rent" does not include payment for the use of property where significant services are rendered as in the case of hotels, boarding houses, and motels.

17. I.R.C. § 446(b).

seemingly likely prospects for deferred reporting. Consider the statutory amortization rule for the deduction of prepaid interest, Section 461(g).

The Court of Claims has recently taken a small step to disagree with the service's position in a case [18] in which plaintiff, an accrual method taxpayer, deferred the inclusion of prepaid interest from its gross income. After differentiating cases in which the prepayment was a condition of the loan, the court stated: [19]

> It is clear that the Commissioner has the power to change a taxpayer's method of tax accounting from a method which distorts income to a method that clearly reflects income. I.R.C. § 446; Treas.Reg. 1.446–1(a)(2); Automobile Club of Michigan v. Commissioner of Internal Revenue, 353 U.S. 180, 77 S.Ct. 707, 1 L.Ed.2d 746 (1957); American Automobile Association v. United States, 367 U.S. 687, 81 S.Ct. 1727, 6 L.Ed.2d 1109 (1961); Schlude v. Commissioner of Internal Revenue, 372 U.S. 128, 83 S.Ct. 601 (1963). However, where there is no distortion of income or potential for distortion under a method of tax accounting because the date income is earned is easily determinable, it is an abuse of the Commissioner's discretion to switch a taxpayer's method of tax accounting to a different method. Boise Cascade Corp. v. United States, 530 F.2d 1367, 208 Ct.Cl. 619, cert. denied, 429 U.S. 867, 97 S.Ct. 176 (1976); Artnell Co. v. Commissioner of Internal Revenue, 400 F.2d 981 (7th Cir.1968). Also, the Supreme Court has indicated that, when reviewing tax accounting questions, deference should be paid to accounting methods which a regulatory body or agency imposes upon a business or enterprise. See Commissioner of Internal Revenue v. Idaho Power Co., 418 U.S. 1, 15, 94 S.Ct. 2757 (1974); Commissioner of Internal Revenue v. Standard Life & Accident Co., 433 U.S. 148, 97 S.Ct. 2523 (1977).

> Upon first glance at the facts surrounding this issue, we are impressed with the de minimis nature of the prepaid interest plaintiff received in 1964 compared to the total taxable interest included in income ($165,739.75 compared to $126,000,000 reported interest income). This alone raises a question in our minds of whether there was or existed the potential for material income distortion under plaintiff's regular accrual tax accounting method.

> When we couple the de minimis nature of the amount of prepaid income plaintiff received with the fact that plaintiff consistently has reported it[s] prepaid interest on the regular accrual accounting method for many years, and the fact that the plaintiff was required to use the accrual method of account-

---

18. Morgan Guar. Trust Co. of New York v. U.S., 585 F.2d 988 (Ct.Cls.1978).

19. Id. at 997.

ing by the Federal Reserve Board, we find the conclusion inescapable that there was no material distortion of income occurring under plaintiff's regular accrual tax accounting method for prepaid interest, nor the potential for such distortion. We think this conclusion is further buttressed by the fact that the date upon which the prepaid interest was subsequently earned could be computed to the day. Such was not the case under the artificial accounting methods employed in Automobile Club of Michigan v. Commissioner, supra; American Auto. Ass'n v. U.S., supra; and Schlude v. Commissioner, supra. Accordingly, we hold that the Commissioner abused his discretion in this case when he switched plaintiff from its regular accrual tax accounting method to the cash basis method for purposes of accounting for its prepaid interest.

Admittedly *Morgan Guaranty* can be distinguished as a de minimis case or a case involving consistent taxpayer procedure.[20] And the prepayment related merely to the succeeding year. Yet the court recognizes that prepaid interest can be computed "to the day" and that the opposite result here would convert an accrual method taxpayer to the cash method. We applaud the result but, if other courts follow it in interest and rent situation, we are not unmindful of other problems. What dollar amounts might be involved? And what impact on the revenue would result if the treatment generally allowed under Rev. Proc. 70–21 were applied to interest and rents? Should courts perhaps limit the prepayment to only the succeeding year?

The reasoning in *Artnell* and *Morgan Guaranty* raises a question about the two-year rule of Rev.Proc. 70–21. If two-year spreading by way of deferral is within the statutes, why is three-year (or more) deferral not? One wonders whether restrictions in Rev.Proc. 70–21 may not rest more on concern for the revenue than on any nice legal distinctions and, if so, whether the restrictions can stand if the basic breakthrough in *Artnell* is accepted. One wonders further whether changes of this type, even if highly desirable, cannot be better engineered to accommodate all interests by Congress, rather than the administration and the courts.[21]

A companion development to Rev.Proc. 70–21 is an amendment to the accounting regulations which relates to prepayments for goods.[22] Under the provision a taxpayer may defer amounts received as prepayment for goods sold in the ordinary course of his trade or business until

---

20. Waldheim Realty and Inv. Co. v. Commissioner, 245 F.2d 823 (8th Cir.1967).

21. Rev.Proc. 70–21 is discussed in Battle, "Advance Payments for Services: Limited Deferral Permitted" 57 A.B.A.J. 182 (1971). Prepayments for both services and goods are discussed in Sobeloff, "New Prepaid Income Rule: IRS Reversal of Position will Aid Many Taxpayers," 33 J.Tax. 194 (1970).

22. See Reg. § 1.451–5. The basic tax accounting problems in this area are interestingly discussed in Pacific Grape Products Co. v. Commissioner, 219 F.2d 862 (9th Cir.1955); and see Poole, "The Taxation of Prepaid Sales of Goods," 24 Tax L.Rev. 375 (1969), which also preceded the amendment of the Regulations.

the year in which the payments are ordinarily accruable under the taxpayer's regular method of accounting.[23]   There is a complex two-year limitation, like that in Rev.Proc. 70–21, with respect to prepayments for goods that the taxpayer has in inventory or which are readily available through normal sources of supply.[24]

If services are to be performed in conjunction with the sale of goods, the regulations still apply if the performance of the services is an integral part of the sale.[25]   If the amount allocable to payment for services is less than 5% of the total price, the services obligation will automatically be considered an integral part of the sale of the goods.[26]

INVENTORIES

Whenever tax computations require the use of inventories, the accrual method of accounting must be used, at least with regard to purchases and sales.[1]   When must inventories be used?   Whenever "production, purchase, or sale of merchandise is an income-producing factor." [2]   Consequently, inventory accounting plays a very large role in the federal income tax.   It is required of the butcher, the baker, and the candlestick maker, but not of the attorney or the accountant.

The political science major who is frightened to death by mere mention of the term "inventory" can learn a comforting lot by a study of Amory and Hardee (Herwitz and Trautman revision), Materials on Accounting, c. 1, pp. 33–36, and c. 4, pp. 170–212 (Foundation Press, 1959).[3]   The accounting profession worries a great deal about proper treatment of inventories in its effort to develop generally accepted accounting principles.[4]   We eschew all the details that titillate accountants and attempt here only a very basic explanation of inventories and their general relationship to the determination of gross income and to the accounting period in which gross income must be reported, the subject of this chapter.

We already know that the general formula for determining gross income from the sale of property can be expressed as:

23. Reg. § 1.451–5(a)(1) and –5(b)(2). See Rev.Rul. 72–208, 1972–1 C.B. 129.

24. Reg. § 1.451–5(c).   The exception seems another part of the Treasury's reluctance to go too far too fast, perhaps again with the revenue in mind.   As a practical matter, however, if the goods sold for future delivery are in inventory, there may be a basis for recognizing the cost of goods sold prior to their later delivery, which overcomes a problem involving the treatment of gross receipts as gross income where goods sold for future delivery are not in any way identifiable.   See Veenstra and De Haan Coal Co., supra note 10, at 967.

25. Reg. § 1.451–5(a)(2).

26. Reg. § 1.451–5(a)(3).   Application of the regulations is illustrated at Reg. § 1.451–5(c)(4).   The history of tax problems in the sale of goods and an analysis of the new regulations is presented in Brody, "Advance Payment for Sales of Goods: New Regulations Permit Deferral" 57 A.B. A.J. 707 (1971).

1. Reg. § 1.446–1(c)(2).

2. Reg. § 1.471–1.

3. See also Fiflis and Kripke, Accounting for Business Lawyers, c. 1, pp. 43–54, and c. VI, pp. 234–278 (West 1971).

4. E.g., Accounting Research Bulletin No. 43, c. 4 "Inventory Pricing," set out in Amory and Hardee, supra, App. A, at 480–484.

Amount realized

Less   Adjusted basis

Equals   Realized gain

The parallel expression of this concept where property is sold in the course of a business, such as a haberdashery, is:

Gross sales

Less   Cost of goods sold

Equals   Gross profit from sales

Gross sales is obviously a fairly automatic figure, but how does a merchant (or a manufacturer) determine the cost of the goods that he has sold during an accounting period? It is here that inventories play their principal role. It is usually impracticable for a merchant separately to determine his gain or loss on each sale.[5] A device is needed that will produce the correct overall result by way of a kind of aggregate approach.

To overcome the problem suggested, the figure used for cost of goods sold is determined by (1) ascertaining the cost of goods on hand at the start of the accounting period, which is called "opening inventory;" (2) adding to that the cost of goods acquired during the accounting period, referred to in an abbreviated way as "purchases;" and (3) subtracting from that sum the cost of the goods still on hand at the end of the accounting period, "closing inventory." Thus:

Opening inventory

Plus   Purchases
Less   Closing inventory

Equals   Cost of goods sold

Some assurance that in the long run all gain or loss will be taken into account is achieved by the fact that the figure to be used as opening inventory for a particular period is the figure that was used for closing inventory for the preceding period. Play with the formula enough to see that, if an improperly low figure were used for closing inventory in 1992, it would tend to show a higher cost of goods sold and lower profit for that year; but in 1993 the improperly low opening inventory figure (which is closing inventory for 1992) would result in a lower cost of goods sold and higher profit for 1993. This is not intended to suggest that the taxpayer has the option to juggle these figures.[6]

In this inventory approach the most uncertain figure is closing inventory. "Opening inventory" is somewhat automatic, simply being carried over as closing inventory of the last year.[7] "Purchases" is

---

5. The used car dealer and others who make relatively few sales of large items are exceptions.

6. There are legitimate juggling opportunities which can be achieved, e.g., by selling down (i.e., not replacing) high cost Lifo inventories; but this is rare.

7. But see footnote comments below on uncertainties regarding what is included in closing inventory.

likewise somewhat automatic.[8]　But closing inventory involves both a determination of the quantity of goods (or each item of goods) on hand [9] and then properly "pricing" it.

The quantity of goods on hand at the end of an accounting period can be determined by observation—"taking inventory." [10]　However, the quantitative figure must be converted to a dollar figure, representing the *cost* of what is on hand.[11]　In a hardware store the brass screws in a box may have been purchased at several different times, some recently and some a year or more ago.　What was their price when purchased?　Nobody knows, but conventions answer the question.　If it is assumed that the earliest purchased screws were the one's first sold (the "first in-first out" convention), then those on hand are treated as the most recently purchased and are "priced" for inventory purposes in accordance with this assumption.　That is, if the last ten gross of screws acquired cost $14.40 and there are 1440 screws on hand, then each screw is included in closing inventory at one cent.　If there are 1500 on hand, 60 of them are priced in accordance with the cost of the next-to-last batch of screws acquired, and so forth.[12]

A less common alternative pricing convention is the "last in-first out" approach.　These conventions are commonly referred to as "Lifo" or "Fifo."　Work out for yourself the basic consequences of inventory pricing under the Lifo convention.[13]

A businessman may wish to show high earnings to creditors and shareholders but low earnings to employees and the Commissioner of Internal Revenue.　He can't of course do both, and *consistency* is a key requirement in accounting matters.[14]　Nevertheless, the gross profit on sales for any given year is affected by the pricing convention adopted. Try this:　Assume a merchandising business makes substantial

---

8.　A significant problem arises here as to when a purchase is taken into account; for example, does purchases include an item merely ordered or in transit to the taxpayer, or must it be received prior to the end of the accounting period?　Must it be paid for?　Note the parallel problems on sales and closing inventory.

9.　As in the case of purchases, question arises here whether goods should be treated as no longer on hand if ordered or en route to the buyer or only if delivered or paid for.　There is some flexibility, but the answer must be meshed with the approach taken to the question when a sale is included in gross sales.　A moment's reflection should indicate that distortion would result if goods considered to have passed out of closing inventory were not treated as sold for purposes of determining gross sales.

10.　The student should not envisage the calendar year haberdasher having to forego New Year's Eve revels to take inventory.　The job is accomplished at another time with suitable adjustment to achieve the year-end objective, or these days it may even be achieved electronically.

11.　A conservative business accounting maxim of never over-stating income has generated a "cost or market" variation here, under which inventory is priced at market, if that is less than cost, and this variation is permitted for tax accounting. See Reg. § 1.471–2 and –4.

12.　Note that inventory pricing is vastly more complicated in the case of a manufacturing rather than a mere merchandising business.　This gets into the area of "cost accounting" in which there must be added to materials costs both labor and other direct and indirect expenses, as regards finished products and so-called "work in process" as well.

13.　Cf. I.R.C. § 474.

14.　See Reg. § 1.471–2(b).　It should be noted that differences in business and tax accounting often do require the keeping of two sets of books.

purchases of goods annually but maintains a fairly steady stock of goods, quantitatively. If over a period of time prices are rising, will the business report more income for a particular period under the Fifo approach or under the Lifo approach?

It will now be seen that inventories play a timing roll as well as a measuring role for gross income. If the inventory pricing method followed tends to show a low *closing* inventory for the prior year, and the effect of the low figure is a greater cost of goods sold and a correspondingly lower profit on sales for that year, the effect is also to shift reportable income to a future year. That is because the lower *opening* inventory for the next year will result in a lower cost of goods sold and a correspondingly higher profit on sales in a subsequent period. In effect, given required consistency, the whole scheme operates within a kind of closed circle, and advantage now is bought only at the cost of disadvantage later, or vice versa.

Students should share the authors' recognition that even a thoughtful reading of the foregoing comments leaves them relatively uninformed about the intricacies of inventory accounting. Nevertheless, it may prepare them for further study as and if required or at least facilitate dialogue with members of the accounting profession.

2. DEDUCTION ITEMS

Internal Revenue Code: Section 461(a), (f), and (h).

Regulations: Section 1.461–1(a)(2).

REVENUE RULING 57–463

1957–2 Cum.Bull. 303.

Advice has been requested concerning the period in which interest is deductible by a taxpayer using the accrual method of accounting where, after consenting to an assessment for income taxes, penalties, and interest, the taxpayer, in a subsequent year, entered into a compromise agreement providing for deferred installment payments of the amount assessed plus additional interest on the deferred payments.

Section 461 of the Internal Revenue Code of 1954 provides the general rule that the amount of any deduction or credit allowed by Subtitle A shall be taken for the taxable year which is the proper taxable year under the method of accounting used in computing taxable income. A taxpayer keeping his accounts and filing his returns on the accrual method of accounting is entitled to deduct interest in the taxable year in which liability accrues. I.T. 3740, C.B.1945, 109. Interest on a deficiency in tax should be accrued in the year in which the liability for the deficiency is finally determined. G.C.M. 9575, C.B. X–1, 381 (1931).

In the instant case, the taxpayer's liability for the deficiencies became determined at the time the taxpayer consented to the assessment, and a deduction for interest to that date may be allowed for that taxable year. The compromise agreement merely fixed the rate of payment of the assessed amounts. Interest accruing on the deferred payments may be allowed as a deduction ratably as the taxpayer's liability for such interest accrues.

SCHUESSLER v. COMMISSIONER

United States Court of Appeals, Fifth Circuit, 1956.
230 F.2d 722.

TUTTLE, Circuit Judge. This is a petition for review of a decision by the Tax Court disallowing a deduction in 1946 of an item of $13,300.00, representing a reserve set up by taxpayers while keeping their books on the accrual basis, to represent their estimated cost of carrying out a guarantee, given with each of the furnaces sold by them during the year, to turn the furnace on and off each year for five years.

The opinion of the Tax Court treats the matter as though ample proof was offered by the taxpayer (hereafter the husband will be called "taxpayer") to raise the legal issue and we find the record warrants this treatment. Taxpayer was in the gas furnace business in 1946, during which he sold 665 furnaces, each with a guarantee that he would turn the furnace on and off each year for five years. The fact that such service, if performed, would cost $2.00 per call was amply established. The taxpayer, himself a bookkeeper and accountant prior to entering this business, testified to his keeping his books on the accrual method and claimed that the only way his income could be accurately reported was by charging against the cost of furnaces sold in 1946 the reserve representing the amount which he became legally liable to expend in subsequent years in connection with the sales. The proof was clear that he actually sold the furnaces for $20.00 to $25.00 more than his competitors because of his guarantee, which they did not give.

We think it quite clear that petitioner's method of accounting comes much closer to giving a correct picture of his income than would a system in which he sold equipment in one year and received an inflated price because he obligated himself, in effect, to refund part of it in services later but was required to report the total receipts as income on the high level of the sales year and take deductions on the low level of the service years. The reasonableness of taxpayer's action, however, is not the test if it runs counter to requirements of the statute.

We find that not only does it not offend any statutory requirement, but, in fact, we think it is in accord with the language and intent of the law.[1] Clearly what is sought by this statute is an accounting method that most accurately reflects the taxpayer's income on an annual accounting basis.[2]

---

1. [I.R.C. §§ 41 and 43 (1939), and Reg. 111 § 29.41–1 are omitted. Ed.]

2. This principle was early recognized in United States v. Anderson, 269 U.S. 422, 46 S.Ct. 131.

The decisions of the Tax Court and of the several Courts of Appeals are not uniform on this subject, some circuits requiring a mathematical certainty as to the exact amount of the future expenditures that cannot be satisfied in the usual case. Other circuits, seemingly more concerned with the underlying principle of charging to each year's income reasonably ascertainable future expenses necessary to earn or retain the income, have permitted the accrual of restricted items of future expenses. Two of this latter category are Harrold v. Commissioner [3] and Pacific Grape Products Co. v. Commissioner.[4]

In the Harrold case the taxpayer was permitted to deduct from its gross income in 1945 the estimated cost of back filling a tract of land which would be done under state law requirements in the year 1946. The Court there said:

> " * * * when all the facts have occurred which determined that the taxpayer has incurred a liability in the tax year, and neither the fact nor the amount of the liability is contested, and the amount, although not definitely ascertained, is susceptible of estimate with reasonable accuracy in the tax year, deduction thereof from income may be taken by a taxpayer on an accrual basis." Harrold v. Commissioner, 4 Cir., 192 F.2d 1002, 1006.

The Pacific Grape Products case is also, it seems to us, indistinguishable in principle from the case before us. There the taxpayer accrued the sales price of canned goods sold on December 31, and at the same time deducted the estimated cost of labeling and preparing the goods for shipping and brokerage fees to be paid the following year. The Tax Court, with six judges dissenting, accepted the Commissioner's view that the deductions should be disallowed. 17 T.C. 1097. The Court of Appeals reversed, saying:

> "Not only do we have here a system of accounting which for years has been adopted and carried into effect by substantially all members of a large industry, but the system is one which appeals to us as so much in line with plain common sense that we are at a loss to understand what could have prompted the Commissioner to disapprove it. Contrary to his suggestion that petitioner's method did not reflect its true income it seems to us that the alterations demanded by the Commissioner would wholly distort that income."

The case of Beacon Publishing Co. v. Commissioner [5] is considered by both parties here and was noted by the Tax Court as of especial significance. That case involved the treatment of prepaid income received by the Beacon Publishing Co. covering subscriptions to be furnished in subsequent years. The Tax Court in its decision here said:

---

3. 4 Cir., 192 F.2d 1002.

4. 9 Cir., 219 F.2d 862, 869.

5. 10 Cir., 218 F.2d 697.

" * * * This is essentially the same problem as the reporting of prepaid income in the year in which received for services to be performed in following years. The petitioner in fact, on brief, recognizes that the two problems are identical and cites Beacon Publishing Co. v. Commissioner, 10 Cir., 1955, 218 F.2d 697, in support of his argument that the reserve here in issue was a proper deduction in computing his income in 1946."

The Tax Court then simply declined to follow the Court in the Beacon case, preferring to adhere to its own views as expressed in Curtis A. Andrews v. Commissioner, 23 T.C. 1026. We prefer the reasoning as well as the conclusion reached by the Court in the Tenth Circuit. There the opinion correctly, we think, disposed of the "claim of right" theory advanced by the Commissioner and adopted by the Tax Court in this type of case.[6]

Finally we think the enactment in 1954 of Section 462 of the Internal Revenue Code of 1954 [7] and its subsequent repeal constitute no legislative history bearing on the construction of the provisions of the Internal Revenue Code of 1939.[8]

The record below amply supports the contention of the taxpayer that there was a legal liability created in 1946, when the purchase price was paid for the gas furnaces, for the taxpayer to turn the furnaces on and off for the succeeding five years; that the cost of such service as reasonably established at a minimum of $2.00 per visit; and that the payment of $20.00 to $25.00 extra by the purchasers fully proved their intention to call upon the taxpayer each year for the service. These facts authorized the setting up of a reserve out of the 1946 income to enable the taxpayer to meet these established charges in future years. The decision of the Tax Court is therefore in error and must be reversed.

Reversed with directions to enter judgment for the taxpayer.

NOTE

It is certain that accountants make the acquaintance early of Dr. Doolittle's marvelous quadruped, the Push Me-Pull You. They know almost instinctively that, if you push receipts of income forward to a future period when they are earned (as in *Artnell*),[1] related deductions, i.e., the costs of earning the receipts should be pulled forward to the same period, achieving a match-up that best determines a net income *for the period.* They also know that if you push receipts of income back

---

6. See Beacon Publishing Co. v. Commissioner, 218 F.2d 697, 699.

7. 26 U.S.C.A. § 462.

8. For an interesting discussion of the history of this legislation see Sen.Rep. No. 372, 84 Cong., 1st Sess., 1955 U.S.Code Congressional and Administrative News, p. 2046–2051. See also Sporrer, The Past and Future of Deferring Income and Reserving for Expenses, TAXES (Mag.) January 1956, 45.

1. See page 594, supra. See also Gunn, "Matching of Costs and Revenues as a Goal of Tax Accounting," 4 Virg.Tax Rev. 1 (1984).

to an earlier period in which they have been received but not yet been earned, logic requires that related deductions should be pulled back, too, along with the prepaid receipts. Congress, however, is not enchanted with the Push Me-Pull You, although this theory is at the heart of generally accepted business accounting principles.

Rather, Congress is motivated by revenue generating pressures which require treating receipts, even though not yet earned, as income for tax purposes. From a practical standpoint, this yields greater certainty that the tax on amounts received by a taxpayer will in fact be paid or collected. Similar concerns underlie the Service's historical reluctance to permit current deductions for anticipated future expenses such as the taxpayer's reserve method of accounting in *Scheussler*.[2] Uncertainty as to whether such costs will actually be paid and as to the accuracy of the taxpayer's estimates of such costs contributes to this concern.

In the 1984 Act Congress did not alter the income side of accrual transactions (*Artnell*), but it did make clarifications and changes to the deductions side. Prior to the 1984 Act, the law required as a predicate to the deduction of an anticipated expense by an accrual method taxpayer, that the expense satisfy an "all-events" test. The classic all events test makes an expense deductible only when: (1) all the events have occurred which establish the liability giving rise to the deduction; and (2) the amount of the liability can be established with reasonable accuracy.[3]

Judicial interpretation of the all-events test often led to controversy over whether an accrual was premature. Initially the courts held that under the accrual method expenses became deductible only at the time of actual performance of the activities which the taxpayer was required to perform.[4] But later cases were more liberal in determining when taxpayers met the all events test, allowing a deduction when only the taxpayer's obligation to perform was fixed.[5] For example, in *Harrold v. Commissioner*[6] the court held that, as surface mining reclamation costs can be estimated with reasonable accuracy, such costs are deductible at the time the land is stripped even though the land is not restored as required until a future year. However, the Service consistently maintained that an expense should not be deducted until there is a fixed liability to pay a specific amount.[7] The Service also

2. See, e.g., Simplified Tax Records, Inc., 41 T.C. 75 (1963), and cases cited therein.

3. Reg. § 1.461–1(a)(2).

4. See, e.g., Spencer, White & Prentis, Inc. v. Commissioner, 144 F.2d 45 (2d Cir. 1944), where a contractor required to restore property damaged in connection with a construction project was denied a deduction for the estimated costs of such restoration.

5. Cases allowing the accrual of an expense before performance of the required activity include Crescent Wharf & Warehouse Co. v. Commissioner, 518 F.2d 772 (9th Cir.1975) (accrual of workmens' compensation liability at the time the injury occurs), and Lukens Steel Co. v. Commissioner, 442 F.2d 1131 (3d Cir.1971) (accrual of contingent liability to fund a negotiated supplemental unemployment benefit plan).

6. 192 F.2d 1002 (4th Cir.1951).

7. Rev.Rul. 72–34, 1972–1 C.B. 132.

maintained that if a liability was contingent upon some future event, no deduction was allowable until that event actually occurred.[8]

Disagreement also arose between taxpayers and the Service as to when the *amount* of a liability is determinable with reasonable accuracy. In general, the courts held that this part of the all events test was satisfied when the liability could be estimated, not necessarily calculated, with reasonable accuracy.[9] The Service, on the other hand, took the position that in order to satisfy this requirement the exact amount of the liability had to be determinable by a computation based on known or knowable facts.[10]

The controversy regarding the all events test was increased by the concern of Congress over a further problem, the "time value of money." It simply is not sound to allow a one dollar deduction *now* for one dollar that is to be paid two years from now. If one has to pay one dollar of expenses in two years he can put, say, 80 cents (depending on interest rates) in the bank now and withdraw one dollar in two years to pay the expenses. Consequently he should be allowed either an 80 cent deduction now or a one dollar deduction two years from now, but not one dollar right now. In testimony before a Senate Finance Subcommittee preceding the enactment of the 1984 legislation, the Acting Tax Legislative Counsel of the Treasury Department explained the problem: [11]

> The high interest rates and inflation that we have experienced in recent years bring into question the economic assumptions that underlie certain provisions of the Internal Revenue Code. These high rates have resulted in a material increase in the "time value of money." In the simplest terms, the time value of money is the difference between the value of immediately available funds and the right to receive funds at some time in the future. In many respects the Code ignores time value of money concepts. For example, where an accrual basis taxpayer is entitled to accrue a $1 deduction, the Code permits a full $1 deduction, whether the $1 is paid today or ten years in the future. The failure of the Code to recognize this difference has led to numerous tax shelter transactions that enable taxpayers to produce substantial unintended tax benefits—at a substantial revenue loss to government * * * [w]e believe the time has come for a fundamental reexamination of several provisions of the Code that do not properly take time value of money concepts into account.
>
> * * *
>
> * * * One of the most fundamental and obvious time value of money issues is the determination of the proper amount of the deduction to be allowed where a liability arises today in

---

8. Id.

9. See, e.g., Kaiser Steel Corp. v. United States, 717 F.2d 1304 (9th Cir.1983).

10. Let.Rul. 7831003 (1978).

11. Testimony of Robert G. Woodard before the Senate Finance I.R.S. Oversight Committee on Tax Shelters, June 24, 1983.

connection with a payment to be made in the future. Assume, for example, that A, an accrual basis taxpayer, incurs in 1983 a legal obligation to pay $100 to B in 1990. ∗ ∗ ∗ If A is allowed to deduct $100 in 1983, a gross overstatement of the deduction will occur. As the $100 need not be paid for seven years, A can fund that liability today for much less than $100. Thus, if A set aside $57.23 in 1983, invested that amount at an 8 percent after-tax rate until 1990, he would in 1990 have exactly the $100 needed to satisfy his liability to B. ∗ ∗ ∗ From an economic point of view, therefore, A's deduction should be $57.23 in 1983 or $100 in 1990. In no case should A be permitted to deduct $100 in 1983.

The controversy regarding the all events test was alleviated by the 1984 enactment of Section 461(h),[12] albeit in a manner which does not benefit many taxpayers. In order to erase the time value of money distortion arising from the current accrual and deduction of the full amount of expenses to be incurred later and to resolve the prior judicial controversies, Congress added another event to the judicially created all events test.[13]

Section 461(h) provides that the all events test is not deemed to be met any earlier than when "economic performance" with respect to an item occurs.[14] In effect, under the economic performance test, one asks whether the taxpayer has completed his end of the transaction. Section 461(h)(2) mandates specific principles, which the Treasury may modify in forthcoming regulations, for determining when economic performance occurs. The Joint Committee explanation of those principles states: [15]

> The principles provided by the Act describe the two most common categories of liabilities: first, cases where the liability arises as a result of another person providing goods and services to the taxpayer and, second, cases where the liability requires the taxpayer to provide goods and services to another

12. P.L. No. 98–369, § 91, 98th Cong., 2d Sess. (1984). See Cunningham, "A Theoretical Analysis of the Tax Treatment of Future Costs," 40 Tax L.Rev. 1428 (1985).

13. H.Rep. No. 98–432, 98th Cong., 2d Sess. 1254 (1984); S.Rep. No. 98–169, 98th Cong., 2d Sess. 266 (1984). Theoretically, two options were available to Congress: allow taxpayers a current deduction for a discounted amount of the liability; or, postpone deduction of the full amount until the taxpayer has completed performance giving rise to the liability. Because a discounted valuation system would be extraordinarily complex and hard to administer, Congress opted for the latter approach.

I.R.C. § 461(h) is just one of a number of changes that were made by the Tax Re-

form Act of 1984 to take into account the time value of money. See I.R.C. §§ 1271–1275 and 483 (original issue discount and interest on deferred payments); §§ 1276–1278 (market discount bonds); § 7872 (below market interest rate loans); and § 467 (certain payments for the use of property or services).

14. I.R.C. § 461(h)(1). The all events test of Reg. § 1.461–1(a)(2) was codified in I.R.C. § 461(h)(4). See H.Rep. No. 98–432, 98th Cong., 2d Sess. 1255 (1984); S.Rep. No. 98–169, 98th Cong., 2d Sess. 267 (1984).

15. Jt.Comm. Explanation of the Tax Reform Act of 1984, pages 261 and 262 (1984).

person or undertake some activity as a result of its income-producing activities.

With respect to the first category of liabilities, if the liability arises out of the use of property, economic performance occurs as the taxpayer uses the property. If the liability requires a payment for the providing of property, economic performance occurs when the property is provided. However, Congress intended that the Treasury Department issue regulations providing that the time at which property is provided should include the time of delivery, shipment, or other time so long as the taxpayer accounts for such items consistently from year to year. If the liability of the taxpayer requires a payment to another person for the providing of services to the taxpayer by another person, economic performance generally occurs when such other person provides the services.

With respect to the second category of liabilities, if the liability of the taxpayer requires the taxpayer to provide property or perform services, economic performance occurs as the taxpayer provides the property or performs the services. For this purpose, property does not include money; that is, economic performance generally does not occur as payments are made except as specifically provided in the code or regulations. For example, if a contractor is engaged by a highway construction company to repair damaged properties, economic performance occurs as the contractor performs the work. Likewise, when the highway construction company itself repairs the damage, economic performance occurs as repairs are made.

Under a special rule for workers' compensation and tort liabilities requiring payments to another person, economic performance occurs as payments are made to that person. In the case of any other liability of the taxpayer, economic performance will occur at the time determined under regulations to be prescribed by the Treasury.

The enactment of Section 461(h) not only resolves the general controversy involving premature accruals, but it also resolves the uncertainty surrounding the use of estimated liabilities or reserve accounts such as the reserve in the *Schuessler* case. The economic performance test conclusively prohibits the use of such accounts,[16] except as specifically allowed by other provisions of the Code.[17]

---

16. I.R.C. § 461(h)(2)(B).

17. I.R.C. § 461(h)(5) provides that the economic performance test does not apply to deductions allowable under any provision of the Code specifically providing for a deduction for charges to a reserve for estimated expenses. In addition, the reports of both the House Ways and Means Committee and the Senate Finance Committee indicate exceptions to the economic performance test with respect to a liability of the taxpayer to provide benefits to his employees through a qualified pension, profit-sharing or bonus plan under §§ 404 or 404A and for contributions by a taxpayer to a funded welfare benefit plan under § 419. H.Rep. No. 98–432, 98th Cong., 2d Sess. 1255, 1256 (1984); S.Rep. No. 98–169, 98th Cong., 2d Sess. 268 (1984).

Section 461(h)(3) provides an exception to the economic performance test for certain "recurring items." The exception found its way
into the Code to provide a smooth transition from established business
tax practices to the harsher rule of economic performance.[18] Clearly
the most significant exception to the economic performance rule,[19] the
recurring item exception allows the accrual of a deduction before
economic performance occurs if four basic requirements are met. Generally: (1) the pre-1984 all events (but not economic performance) test
with respect to an item must be met during the taxable year;[20] (2)
economic performance must actually occur with respect to the item
within the shorter of a reasonable period [21] after the close of the taxable
year or eight and one-half months after the close of the taxable year;[22]
(3) the item must be recurring in nature and the taxpayer must
consistently treat items of this kind as incurred in the taxable year in
which the pre-1984 all events test is satisfied;[23] and, (4) either the item
must not be a material item or the accrual of the item in the taxable
year in which the pre-1984 all events test is met must more properly
match the item against the income that it generated than would the
accrual of the item in the taxable year in which economic performance
occurs.[24]

The Report of the Conference Committee sets guidelines to help
identify the expenses that will qualify for this exception. According to
these guidelines, materiality of the expense is to be determined by
taking into account the size of the item, both in absolute terms and
relative to the taxpayer's income and other expenses.[25] When considering the propriety of the matching of income and expenses, generally
accepted accounting principles are an important, but not controlling,

18. H.Rep. No. 98–861, 98th Cong., 2d
Sess. 873 (1984). I.R.C. § 461(h)(3)(C) prevents this "recurring items" exception
from applying to workers compensation
and tort liabilities.

19. Some of the exceptions of rather
narrow application include the deduction
of mining and solid waste reclamation expenditures, of closing costs associated with
the decommissioning of nuclear power
plants prior to economic performance and
of natural gas supplier refunds by utilities
under certain conditions. I.R.C. §§ 468,
468A. See H.Rep. No. 98–861, 98th Cong.,
2d Sess. 875–76 (1984). See also I.R.C.
§ 468B providing that a qualified payment
to a court-ordered settlement fund that
extinguishes a tort liability of the taxpayer
consititutes economic performance with respect to such liability.

The Tax Reform Act of 1984 also includes special provisions for net operating
loss carrybacks of statutory or tort liability
losses and nuclear power plant decommissioning losses, which are otherwise deferred by the application of the economic

performance rule. I.R.C. §§ 172(b)(1)(K),
172(k)(1) and (2).

20. I.R.C. § 461(h)(3)(A)(i).

21. There is no indication in the Code
and no suggestion in any of the Committee
reports of what constitutes a "reasonable
period."

22. I.R.C. § 461(h)(3)(A)(ii).

23. I.R.C. § 461(h)(3)(A)(iii).

24. I.R.C. § 461(h)(3)(A)(iv).

25. H.Rep. No. 98–861, 98th Cong., 2d
Sess. 873 (1984). If the item is classified as
material on the taxpayer's financial statements it is conclusively presumed to be
material for purposes of § 461(h). On the
other hand, if the financial statements
deem the item immaterial no presumption
attaches under § 461(h). I.R.C. § 461(h)(3)
(B). Whether an item is considered material for purposes of the recurring item exception is of no relevance as to whether it
is material under other provisions of the
Code. H.Rep. No. 98–861, 98th Cong., 2d
Sess. 874 (1984).

factor.[26] And, finally, the Report indicates that in determining whether an item is recurring in nature and treated consistently by the taxpayer, the frequency with which the item occurs and the manner in which it is reported for tax purposes should be considered.[27]

PROBLEMS

1. Lawyer renders services to Client which are deductible to Client under I.R.C. § 162. Lawyer sends Client a bill for $1,000 on December 24 of year one and Client pays the bill on January 5 of year two. Discuss the tax consequences to Lawyer and Client assuming, even if unlikely, that both are calendar year, accrual method taxpayers.

2. Lender lends out money at a legal rate to Debtor. Debtor is required to pay $5,000 interest each year on the loan which extends over a five year period. The interest is deductible by Debtor under § 163. The agreement calls for payment of each year's interest on December 31 of the year. The loan is made on January 1st of year one. Both parties are calendar year, accrual method taxpayers. Discuss the tax consequences to both parties under the following alternatives:

   (a) Debtor pays all five years' interest ($25,000) to Lender in cash on December 31 of year one.

   (b) Debtor pays the first two years' interest ($10,000) to Lender in cash on December 31 of year one.

   (c) Debtor pays year one's $5,000 of interest in cash on January 2d of year two.

   (d) On December 31 of year one Debtor who is having "serious financial trouble" fails to pay Lender.

   (e) On December 31 of year one Debtor does not pay the interest because of a legitimate dispute over his obligation to pay the first year's interest.

   (f) On December 15 of year one Debtor legitimately disputes his obligation to pay year one's interest but he does pay it, and in year two he sues to recover it.

3. Accrue, a calendar year, accrual method taxpayer, runs a dance school which offers lessons over 30 months with one lesson in each month. No make-up lessons are offered nor is the 30-month period extended for a participant who misses any scheduled lessons. The cost of the lessons is $300 which is required to be prepaid in January of the first year. Based on prior experience, Accrue has found that each lesson (including salaries, rent, utilities) costs her $4.00 per person. On January 1st of year one, 100 students sign up and pay for lessons which commence in January of year one. Discuss Accrue's tax consequences.

---

26. Id.

27. Id. This exception is to be available also to taxpayers just starting a trade or business and to taxpayers who do not incur the expense annually.

This exception is unavailable to tax shelters as defined in I.R.C. § 461(i)(3). I.R.C. § 461(i)(1). See note 11 at page 559, supra.

4. Discuss the tax consequences to the parties involved under the following alternatives:

(a) Widget Corporation, an accrual-basis taxpayer, orders $3,000 worth of carpet cleaning from Mr. Carpet Cleaner, a cash-basis taxpayer, on November 1 of year one. Widget receives and pays for the carpet cleaning on February 1 of year two. Assume that both Widget and Mr. Carpet Cleaner are calendar year taxpayers.

(b) Same as (a), above, except that Widget pays the $3,000 to Mr. Carpet Cleaner on December 1 of year one.

(c) Same as (a), above, except that the carpet cleaning occurs on December 1 of year one.

(d) Same as (a), above, except that you learned that Widget had sales of $2,000,000 and expenses of $1,500,000 in 1986, and typically orders $3,000 worth of carpet cleaning every ten months.

(e) Same as (d), above, except that Widget doesn't receive or pay for the carpet cleaning until October 1 of year two.

D. FORCED MATCHING OF METHODS

Internal Revenue Code: Sections 267(a)(2), (b) and (c); 467.

———

The use of different accounting methods by two or more taxpayers involved in the same transaction may lead to tax consequences that do not fairly reflect the substance of the transaction. This may be so even though each taxpayer is strictly adhering to the rules of his own accounting method. Sometimes when this occurs Congress enacts special rules to alter the accounting method of one of the taxpayers. Below, we examine two such sections. Section 267(a)(2) requires cash and accrual taxpayers both to use the cash method, and Section 467 essentially requires use of the accrual method.

Section 267(a)(2). It is clear that for an accrual method taxpayer the timing of a deduction for interest and other expenses generally does not turn on when the interest or expense is actually paid. The item, if otherwise deductible, is properly deducted when the liability to pay ripens.[1] It is equally clear that a cash method taxpayer is required to include an amount in gross income when received;[2] the right to receive, short of constructive receipt,[3] is generally a neutral consequence to a cash method taxpayer. With these basic principles in mind, one can understand that related taxpayers,[4] one using the accrual method and the other using the cash method, could effect a distortion of tax liability with respect to expenses and interest if no special rule

1. I.R.C. § 461(h) and Reg. § 1.461–1(a)(2).

2. Reg. § 1.446–1(c)(1)(i).

3. Reg. § 1.451–2(a).

4. I.R.C. § 267(b).

stood in the way. Thus, if an accrual method taxpayer owes interest to a cash method lender, the interest can generally be deducted by the accrual method debtor even though no payment is made to the cash method lender. The result is a deduction for the debtor without matching inclusion of income to the creditor. If the parties are related, it is possible the lender may never be paid, with the result, that despite the deduction, the amount is never reported as income or, at least, that payment (and tax on the interest income) may be long delayed.

Prior to the Tax Reform Act of 1984, the congressional response to this potential distortion [5] was to disallow the deduction to the accrual method taxpayer forever if payment was not made to the related payee within the taxable year or within two and one-half months after the close of the taxable year. The new approach to this problem area taken in the Tax Reform Act of 1984 is, as explained in the legislative history, more equitable and perhaps more effective than the antiseptic approach of prior law. The House Report [6] states:

> Under the bill, an accrual-basis taxpayer will be placed on the cash method of accounting with respect to deductions of business expenses and interest owed to a related cash-basis taxpayer. Thus, the accrual-basis taxpayer will be allowed to deduct business expenses or interest owed to a related cash-basis taxpayer when payment is made (whether or not paid within 2½ months after the close of the taxable year); in other words, the deduction by the payor will be allowed no earlier than when the corresponding income is recognized by the payee. This provision will apply to all deductible expenses (whether or not deductible under section 162, 163 or 212) the timing of which depends upon the taxpayer's method of accounting or upon the making of an election to expense an item. It will not apply, for example, to expenses such as the deductions for cost recovery or depreciation of an asset (other than an asset which is related to the performance (or nonperformance) of services by the payee).

Section 467. Prior to the enactment of Section 467 in 1984, the parties to a multi-year agreement for the rental of property or for the long-term performance of services were largely free to design payment terms to suit their wishes. Depending upon the tax status of the parties for example in the context of a lease, it might be advantageous to have the bulk of the payments made during the early years (frontloading) or, alternatively, in the later years (backloading). Typically, a backloaded arrangement (e.g., $1,000,000 per year, payable at the end of the fourth year) benefitted a cash method lessor by permitting him to defer income until the later year when he received payment,[7] even

---

5. See page 616, supra.

6. H.Rep. No. 98–432, 98th Cong., 2d Sess. 1578–79 (1984).

7. Reg. §§ 1.446–1(c)(1)(i) and 1.451–1(a). See pages 561–576, supra.

though the accrual method lessee was permitted deductions for rental expense ratably over the term of the lease.[8]

An additional benefit available to lessors of property was the conversion of ordinary income into capital gain by the use of agreements with progressively stepped up rental rates.[9] Under a so-called step-rate agreement the rent gradually increases (in "steps") over the term of the lease. Since property is obviously more valuable when it returns a higher rental, at some later time the lessor could sell the property at a price reflecting the higher rents due in the later years of the lease, thus effecting a conversion of essentially deferred ordinary rental income into capital gain. The tax advantage at the crossover could more than offset the lower rentals he would accept in the early years. With the enactment of Section 467 in the Tax Reform Act of 1984,[10] such manipulation of rental income (and rental expense) is no longer possible.[11] At least it is no longer possible in a big way; Section 467 steps in to alter tax results in property rentals only if the total consideration to be paid exceeds $250,000.[12]

This is probably a good place to say, too that, although we speak in terms of rental income just as the statute does, Section 467 may also apply to payments for services. It is not self-executing in that respect but subsection (g), rather ineptly, authorizes the promulgation of regulations to bring about that result.

The basic thrust of Section 467 is to put both parties to a "Section 467 rental agreement"[13] on a specially prescribed accrual method of accounting for that transaction. A Section 467 rental agreement is defined as any rental agreement covering the use of tangible property (calling for total consideration of more than $250,000) under which (1) an amount allocable to the use of property in one year is to be paid after the close of the year following the year in which that use occurs, or (2) the rent to be paid under the agreement increases over the term of the lease.[14] The accrual method prescribed applies present value concepts to the rent that accrues during each year and imposes interest on the amount of accrued but unpaid rent from prior years.[15] The discount rate and interest rate to be used under Section 467 is 110 percent of the applicable Federal rate determined under Section 1274(d), compounded semiannually.[16] The effect of this treatment is to require inclusion and deduction of the value of rentals in the year of use. Any difference between this amount and the cash changing hands

8. I.R.C. § 461(h); Reg. §§ 1.446–1(c)(1) (ii) and 1.461–1(a)(2). See pages 606–615, supra.

9. S.Rep. No. 98–169, 98th Cong., 2d Sess. 260 (1984).

10. P.L. No. 98–369, § 92, 98th Cong., 2d Sess. (1984).

11. See Whitesman, "Section 467: Tax Planning for Deferred-Payment Leases," 5 Virg.Tax Rev. 345 (1986); Hamilton and Comi, "The Time Value of Money: Section 467 Rental Agreements Under the Tax Reform Act of 1984," 63 Taxes 155 (1985).

12. I.R.C. § 467(d)(2).

13. I.R.C. § 467(d)(1).

14. I.R.C. § 461(d).

15. I.R.C. § 467(a).

16. I.R.C. § 467(e)(4). The applicable Federal rate is discussed at page 467, supra.

is, in effect, a loan between the taxpayers on which interest is imputed. That is, if in any year a lessor receives less than the value of a year's rental, the difference is treated as a loan by him to the lessee.

Section 467 sets forth alternative rules for calculating the amount of rent that accrues during a particular period. If the agreement itself purports to allocate rentals, the amount of rent that accrues for any period is determined in accordance with the rental agreement; present value principles are to be applied to any rent to be paid after the close of the period with which it is associated.[17] The exact manner in which present value concepts are to be applied is not yet clear. The Conference Committee Report implies that regulations may establish several methods for determining the rental accrual, which differ depending on the type of lease involved.[18]

If the rental agreement contains no rent allocation provision or if the transaction is a "disqualified leaseback or long-term agreement," a special rule providing for the "leveling" of rents determines accruals.[19] While it is easy enough to determine whether a lease contains a rent allocation clause, identifying a disqualified leaseback or long-term agreement may be difficult. A disqualified leaseback or long-term agreement must be either part of a leaseback transaction [20] or must be for a term exceeding 75 percent of the statutory recovery period [21] of the property in question; and, in either case, a principal purpose for providing for increasing rents under the agreement must be the avoidance of tax.[22] The Conference Committee Report seems uselessly to suggest that whether the requisite tax avoidance purpose exists is to be determined on the basis of all the facts and circumstances.[23] The Report does indicate, however, several factors that should be considered when making this determination. They are: whether the tax brackets of the lessor and the lessee differ, and if so, the amount of the disparity; [24] the involvement of a tax-exempt organization; [25] and whether the lessee has an option to renew the lease at an amount

---

17. I.R.C. § 467(b)(1).

18. H.Rep. No. 95–861, 98th Cong., 2d Sess. 892 (1984). We await promulgation of such regulations.

19. I.R.C. § 467(b)(2), (3).

20. A leaseback transaction is one that involves a leaseback to any person who had an interest in the property within the two years prior to the leaseback. I.R.C. § 467(e)(2).

21. I.R.C. § 467(e)(3)(A) sets forth the statutory recovery periods for the different classes of recovery (depreciable) property. Even if the property is not recovery property within the meaning of § 168(c)(1), it is treated as if it were recovery property for purposes of determining whether a long-term agreement exists. I.R.C. § 467(e)(3) (B).

22. I.R.C. § 467(b)(4).

23. H.Rep. No. 98–861, 98th Cong., 2d Sess. 893 (1984).

24. Id. at 893–894. The Conference Report further suggests that, where the lessor is in a higher tax bracket than the lessee, the motives of the lessor and lessee for entering into a step-rate rental agreement will be "closely scrutinized" and the taxpayers should have to show that market conditions or other business reasons justify the agreement. Id.

25. H.Rep. No. 98–861, 98th Cong., 2d Sess. 894 (1984). The Conference Committee was particularly worried about a transaction referred to as the "sandwich" lease. Such an arrangement occurs where a tax-exempt organization is interposed between two taxable parties as a lessee-sublessor in order to achieve income deferral for the lessor without sacrificing the deduction of the sublessee. Id.

significantly less than the amounts payable during the later years of the lease.[26]

Section 467 also directs the promulgation of regulations setting forth circumstances under which certain leaseback and long-term agreements are exempt from the special rent-leveling provisions.[27] The circumstances to be elaborated are to cover: (1) changes in rent paid determined by reference to price indices; [28] (2) rents based on a fixed percentage of lessee receipts; [29] (3) reasonable periods during which rent is forgiven or abated; [30] and (4) changes in amounts paid to unrelated third parties.[31] The Conference Committee also anticipates that future regulations would allow reasonable fluctuations in rent above or below the average rent payable over the term of the lease, permitting some commercial flexibility and planning without condoning tax avoidance.[32]

If the rental agreement is determined to be a disqualified leaseback or long-term agreement, the special rent-leveling rules apply. Simply stated, these rules determine a uniform rental for the lease period through the use of present value concepts. This uniform periodic rental is the "constant rental amount" [33] allocable to each lease period and is identified as the amount which, if paid at the close of each rental period under the agreement, will result in a present value equal to the present value of the aggregate payments required under the rental agreement.[34]

The operation of Section 467 may be seen through an example. First, consider a lease agreement, providing for a lump-sum payment of $4,000,000 at the end of a four year period, which contains no rent allocation provision. Because there is no provision allocating rents in the agreement, the rent leveling rule of Section 467(b)(2) applies. Assuming that 110 percent of the applicable Federal rate under Section 1274(d) is 12 percent, the constant rental accrual and associated interest would be calculated as follows:

26. H.Rep. No. 98–861, 98th Cong., 2d Sess. 894–895 (1984). This factor is given even more weight if the option rental amount is approximately equal to the amount that would be provided had the rent leveling provisions been in effect. Id.

27. I.R.C. § 467(b)(5).

28. I.R.C. § 467(b)(5)(A).

29. I.R.C. § 467(b)(5)(B).

30. I.R.C. § 467(b)(5)(C). The Conference Committee Report states that whether the length of a "rent holiday" is reasonable is to be determined by local commercial practices, but in no event should such period exceed 24 months. H.Rep. No. 98–861, 98th Cong., 2d Sess. 893 (1984).

31. I.R.C. § 467(b)(5)(D).

32. H.Rep. No. 98–861, 98th Cong., 2d Sess. 893 (1984). The Conference Report

also noted that in Rev.Rul. 75–21, 1975–1 C.B. 715, the Treasury ruled that a fluctuation of 10 percent is permissible in cases involving leases of personal property. The Conference Committee felt that such a standard might not be appropriate in cases involving real estate leases and that regulations might be promulgated in order to impose less restrictive standards for real estate leases. Id.

33. I.R.C. § 467(e)(1).

34. Id. If the lease provides for a lump-sum payment at the end of the lease term, the constant rental amount is that amount which, if paid at the close of each lease period together with interest thereon at the rates indicated in § 467(e)(4), would equal at the close of the lease period the amount of the lump-sum payment. S.Rep. No. 98–169, 98th Cong., 2d Sess. 262 (1984).

Year	Accrued Rent [35]	Interest [36]	Total
1	$ 832,536	—	$ 832,536
2	832,536	$102,902	935,438
3	832,536	218,522	1,051,058
4	832,536	348,432	1,180,968
	$3,330,144	$669,856	$4,000,000

Prior to Section 467, a cash method lessor would not recognize any income until he was required to report the $4,000,000 payment received at the end of year four, while the accrual method lessee would deduct $1,000,000 each year as rent expense. The table set forth above illustrates the significant changes brought about by the enactment of Section 467. Now the lessor must accrue $832,536 per year as rental income plus the corresponding interest income on the amount he is deemed to have loaned to the lessee; and the lessee may deduct $832,536 per year as rental expense, along with the phantom interest expense for the particular year.

Now suppose a lease agreement as just described (i.e., one providing for a $4,000,000 lump-sum payment at the end of a four year term) but one that contains a provision allocating $700,000 of the rent to year 1, $900,000 to year 2, $1,100,000 to year 3, and $1,300,000 to year 4. The sum of the allocation totaling $4,000,000 is to be paid at the end of the lease term. Assuming the same interest rate as used in the first example above, and assuming that this is not a disqualified leaseback or long-term agreement, the following table represents the effect of Section 467(b)(1) on the transaction:

Year	Rent Allocation	Accrued Rent [37]	Interest [38]	Total
1	$ 700,000	$ 493,472	—	$ 493,472
2	900,000	712,884	$ 60,993	773,877

35. The first step in arriving at the constant rental amount is to determine the present value of $4,000,000 payable four years in the future, using a discount rate of 12 percent compounded semiannually. This figure is the amount which, if invested now at an interest rate of 12 percent compounded semiannually, would produce an account balance of $4,000,000 after a period of four years. This figure turns out to be $2,509,650. Given this figure, the next step is to determine how much of an annuity $2,509,650 would buy over a four year period with annual payments given an interest rate of 12 percent compounded semiannually. This amount, $832,536, is the constant rental amount.

36. The interest is computed by multiplying the cumulative amounts in the "total" column by the appropriate interest rate. For example, the interest in year 2 is computed by multiplying $832,536 by 12.36 percent (12.36 percent is the same as

12 percent compounded semiannually), and the interest in year 3 is computed by multiplying $1,767,974 ($832,536 plus $935,438) by 12.36 percent.

37. The accrued rent column represents the present value of $700,000 three years in the future, the present value of $900,000 two years in the future, the present value of $1,100,000 one year in the future, and $1,300,000, using a discount rate of 12 percent compounded semiannually. However, it should be kept in mind that the Conference Committee Report anticipated that regulations would be issued providing for different methods of determining rental accrual depending on the type of lease involved. See page 620, supra.

38. The interest is computed by multiplying the cumulative amounts in the "total" column by a 12.36 percent interest rate (12 percent compounded semiannually).

Year	Rent Allocation	Accrued Rent	Interest	Total
3	$1,100,000	$ 978,996	$156,645	$1,135,641
4	1,300,000	1,300,000	297,010	1,597,010
Totals		$3,485,352	$514,648	$4,000,000

As in the first example, the lessor would have to recognize as income, and the lessee may claim as rental expense the amounts shown above in the accrued rent and interest columns.

These tables illustrate the differences under Section 467 between a disqualified leaseback or long-term agreement and a mere Section 467 rental agreement. Under the former the leveling rules find a uniform, or constant rental and apply it to every year of the lease. Under the latter, the present value reallocation of rents uses as a starting point the allocation of rents contained in the lease.

If a leaseback or long-term agreement is not subject to the rent-leveling provisions of Section 467(b)(2), a special recapture provision requires that a lessor who disposes of leased property subject to such an agreement recognize as ordinary income the lesser of the gain realized on the disposition or the amount of the "prior understated inclusions." [39] Prior understated inclusions is defined as the excess of the amount that would have been taken into account by the lessor if the rent-leveling rules had been applied over the amount of income actually recognized by the lessor.[40]

PROBLEMS

1. In each of the following situations, determine in what year the payor would be allowed a deduction and what year the payee would include the amount involved in his gross income:

(a) A, an accrual method taxpayer, ordered and received $500 worth of janitorial supplies in year one from B who is unrelated to A and who is a cash method taxpayer. The supplies are for use in his cleaning business. A makes the $500 payment to B sometime in year two.

(b) Same as (a), above, except that A and B are father and daughter, respectively.

(c) What result in (b), above, if A uses the cash method of accounting and B uses the accrual method of accounting?

2. Determine whether § 267(a)(2) would apply in the following situations:

(a) X Corporation, an accrual method taxpayer, leases a parcel of land from B, a cash method taxpayer. B owns 60 out of a total

---

39. I.R.C. § 467(c).

40. I.R.C. § 467(c)(3). The Conference Committee Report anticipates the Treasury will prescribe regulations that will provide exceptions to the rent recapture

rules similar to the exceptions provided under I.R.C. §§ 1245 and 1250. H.Rep. No. 98–861, 98th Cong., 2d Sess. 895 (1984). See, e.g., I.R.C. § 1245(b).

of 100 shares of X Corporation common stock issued and outstanding. X Corporation has no other classes of stock.

(b) Same as (a), above, except that B owns 40 shares of X, S, B's spouse, owns 15 shares of X, and the remaining shares are held by unrelated parties.

(c) Same as (a), above, except that B owns 20 shares of X, S, B's spouse, owns 15 shares of X, the B and Z partnership owns 40 shares of X, and the remaining shares are held by unrelated parties. B and Z, unrelated parties, each have a 50 percent interest in the capital and profits of the B and Z partnership.

(d) Same as (c), above, except that the B and Z partnership only owns 20 shares of X Corporation.

(e) Same as (a), above, except that B owns 20 shares in X, S, B's spouse owns 15 shares of X, the S and Z partnership owns 20 shares of X, and the remaining shares are held by unrelated parties. S and Z, an unrelated party, each own a 50 percent interest in the capital and profits of the S and Z partnership.

(f) Same as (a), above, except that B owns 30 shares of X, S, B's spouse owns 15 shares of X, S's brother owns 10 shares of X, and the remaining shares are held by unrelated parties.

CHAPTER 20. HOW INELUCTABLE IS THE INTEGRITY OF THE TAXABLE YEAR?

A. TAXPAYER'S RESTORATION OF PREVIOUSLY TAXED INCOME

Internal Revenue Code: Section 1341(a) and (b)(1) and (2) (first sentence).

Regulations: Section 1.1341–1(a), (b)(1)(i) and (ii).

UNITED STATES v. LEWIS
Supreme Court of the United States, 1951.
340 U.S. 590, 71 S.Ct. 522.

Mr. Justice BLACK delivered the opinion of the Court.

Respondent Lewis brought this action in the Court of Claims seeking a refund of an alleged overpayment of his 1944 income tax. The facts found by the Court of Claims are: In his 1944 income tax return respondent reported about $22,000 which he had received that year as an employee's bonus. As a result of subsequent litigation in a state court, however, it was decided that respondent's bonus had been improperly computed; under compulsion of the state court's judgment he returned approximately $11,000 to his employer. Until payment of the judgment in 1946, respondent had at all times claimed and used the full $22,000 unconditionally as his own, in the good faith though "mistaken" belief that he was entitled to the whole bonus.

On the foregoing facts the Government's position is that respondent's 1944 tax should not be recomputed, but that respondent should have deducted the $11,000 as a loss in his 1946 tax return. See G.C.M. 16730, XV–1, Cum.Bull. 179 (1936). The Court of Claims, however, relying on its own case, Greenwald v. United States, 102 Ct.Cl. 272, 57 F.Supp. 569, held that the excess bonus received "under a mistake of fact" was not income in 1944 and ordered a refund based on a recalculation of that year's tax. 117 Ct.Cl. 336, 91 F.Supp. 1017. We granted certiorari, 340 U.S. 903, 71 S.Ct. 279, because this holding conflicted with many decisions of the courts of appeals, see, e.g., Haberkorn v. United States, 173 F.2d 587, and with principles announced in North American Oil v. Burnet, 286 U.S. 417, 52 S.Ct. 613.

In the *North American Oil* case, we said: "If a taxpayer receives earnings under a claim of right and without restriction as to its disposition, he has received income which he is required to return, even though it may still be claimed that he is not entitled to retain the money, and even though he may still be adjudged liable to restore its equivalent." 286 U.S. at 424, 52 S.Ct. at page 615. Nothing in this

624

language permits an exception merely because a taxpayer is "mistaken" as to the validity of his claim. Nor has the "claim of right" doctrine been impaired, as the Court of Claims stated, by Freuler v. Helvering, 291 U.S. 35, 54 S.Ct. 308, or Commissioner v. Wilcox, 327 U.S. 404, 66 S.Ct. 546. The *Freuler* case involved an entirely different section of the Internal Revenue Code, and its holding is inapplicable here. 291 U.S. at 43, 54 S.Ct. at page 311. And in Commissioner v. Wilcox, supra, we held that receipts from embezzlement did not constitute income distinguishing *North American Oil* on the ground that an embezzler asserts no "bona fide legal or equitable claim." 327 U.S. at 408, 66 S.Ct. at page 549.

Income taxes must be paid on income received (or accrued) during an annual accounting period. Cf. I.R.C., §§ 41, 42; and see Burnet v. Sanford & Brooks Co., 282 U.S. 359, 363, 51 S.Ct. 150, 151. The "claim of right" interpretation of the tax laws has long been used to give finality to that period, and is now deeply rooted in the federal tax system. See cases collected in 2 Mertens, Law of Federal Income Taxation, § 12.103. We see no reason why the Court should depart from this well-settled interpretation merely because it results in an advantage or disadvantage to a taxpayer.*

Reversed.

Mr. Justice DOUGLAS, dissenting.

The question in this case is not whether the bonus had to be included in 1944 income for purposes of the tax. Plainly it should have been because the taxpayer claimed it as of right. Some years later, however, it was judicially determined that he had no claim to the bonus. The question is whether he may then get back the tax which he paid on the money.

Many inequities are inherent in the income tax. We multiply them needlessly by nice distinctions which have no place in the practical administration of the law. If the refund were allowed, the integrity of the taxable year would not be violated. The tax would be paid when due; but the Government would not be permitted to maintain the unconscionable position that it can keep the tax after it is shown that payment was made on money which was not income to the taxpayer.

THE MECHANICS OF SECTION 1341

The student should study the economics of the example below and then try to work it out through the Code.

Assume that T, an unmarried taxpayer and not head of a household, in 1991 had gross income (all from commissions) in the amount of $50,000. Assuming in both years (1991 and 1992) there is no post-1989

---

* It has been suggested that it would be more "equitable" to reopen respondent's 1944 tax return. While the suggestion might work to the advantage of this taxpayer, it could not be adopted as a general solution because, in many cases, the three-year statute of limitations would preclude recovery. I.R.C. § 322(b). [See I.R.C. (1986) § 6511(a). Ed.]

inflation,[1] his taxable income for the year 1991 was $39,450 on which T paid a tax of $8517.50.

For the next year 1992, T received gross income of $20,000 but, during the year, it was discovered that due to an accounting error on the employer's books, T's commissions for the prior year, 1991, were overstated by $5,000, meaning that T had been overpaid in the amount of $5,000 in 1991. T was required to and did repay $5,000 to his employer in 1992. Without regard to the repayment, T's taxable income for 1992, was $16,000 (gross income $20,000 less $4,000 in deductions).

Prior to the enactment of Section 1341 (1954), T could *only* deduct the $5,000 repayment in 1992, in computing his tax for that year. (See U.S. v. Lewis, above). This he can still do (Section 1341(a)(4)) but another, and perhaps more favorable, alternative is open to T under Section 1341(a)(5). That provision, by permitting the taxpayer to reduce his tax for the year of repayment by the amount of tax for the prior year attributable to the amount repaid, effects a result essentially similar to the objective sought by the taxpayer in U.S. v. Lewis.

The following example, using the above facts, illustrates (1) the deduction from year-of-repayment gross income approach and (2) the reduction in tax alternative.

1991 Taxable income $39,450 and a tax of $8517.50.

1992 Taxable income without regard to repayment is $16,000, but T repaid $5,000 received under claim of right in 1991.

T's tax liability for 1992, can be computed as follows:

(1) Simply a deduction from 1992 income:

Tax on ($16,000−$5,000) $11,000	$1,650

or

(2) Reduction in tax for 1992 by the amount of tax attributable to the $5,000 overpayment in 1991.

(A) Tax on $16,000 (1992 taxable income, without regard to repayment)		$2,400
(B) Tax (1991) on $39,450	$8,517.50	
(C) Less: Tax (1991) payable on ($39,450−$5,000) $34,450	$7,117.50	
(D) Tax (1991) attributable to $5,000 repayment	$1,400.00	
The amount in (D) offsets the tax computed in (A)		$1,400
T's tax liability for 1992		$1,000

CONCLUSION: Since the reduction in tax for 1992, by the amount of the 1991 tax attributable to the $5,000 repayment is of greater tax benefit than a deduction of the amount of the repayment from 1992 income ((1), above), the taxpayer will use the reduction of tax method ((2), above), effecting a tax saving of $650 ($1650−$1000).[2] In other circumstances the deduction from income alternative ((1) in the above example) might prove to be more beneficial, effecting a greater tax saving. When would that occur?

1. See I.R.C. § 1(f). 2. See I.R.C. § 6411(d).

JOSEPH P. PIKE

Tax Court of the United States, 1965.
44 T.C. 787.

[Petitioner was an attorney who handled legal matters before the Kentucky Department of Insurance. He was also a shareholder of the Cardinal Life Insurance Company. In 1957 he and other shareholders sold a part of their interest in the Company at a gain of about $20,000. An investigation of the transaction was conducted by a special counsel of the state (Wolford) who was of the opinion that the $20,000 gain properly belonged to the Cardinal Company. Although no suit was brought in 1958 several shareholders including petitioner paid their gains over to the Cardinal Company.

FORRESTER, Judge:

*   *   *

Petitioner believed that any continued controversy over the sale of Cardinal contract stock or any litigation resulting from such controversy would damage his status and his reputation with the insurance industry. Petitioner was not entirely convinced that the profits legally belonged to Cardinal. However, petitioner realized the possibility that, when the attorney general's office and a prominent attorney like Wolford were contesting his position, his view of the law might have been erroneous. Rather than allow further controversy to endanger his professional career, petitioner decided to pay over his profit to Cardinal. Petitioner thereafter continued to engage in the private practice of law and to work for life insurance companies.

*   *   *

We next consider petitioner's contention that he is entitled to relief under section 1341 [1] on account of the payment to Cardinal in 1958 of his profits from the sale of contract stock. Respondent attacks this contention on two fronts: (1) Petitioner's payment to Cardinal is not deductible in 1958 because allowance of a deduction would frustrate sharply defined public policy and because the payment was personal in nature; (2) it was not "established" that petitioner was not entitled to retain the profits. As a corollary to his second approach, respondent contends that the payment was voluntary on the part of petitioner and for this reason not deductible. We will deal with respondent's contentions in the order indicated.

Respondent asserts two separate reasons why petitioner's 1958 payment to Cardinal was not deductible. Respondent first argues that allowance of a deduction would frustrate the sharply defined public policy of the Commonwealth of Kentucky, because, according to respondent, petitioner's actions with respect to the registration of the contract stock violated the criminal provisions of the Kentucky Securities Act. Respondent cites Tank Truck Rentals v. Commissioner, 356 U.S. 30 (1958). Even if we agreed with respondent that petitioner had commit-

---

1. [I.R.C. § 1341(a) is omitted. Ed.]

ted a crime—and the evidence establishes no more than that the Kentucky attorney general had argued that the Securities Act had been violated—we would not for that reason disallow the deduction, because the payment in question was not made on account of and was not directly related to any such violation. Rather, it was made in response to the claim by the department of insurance that the profits from the sale of contract stock rightfully belonged to Cardinal. Tank Truck Rentals v. Commissioner, supra, is clearly distinguishable, since the deductions there disallowed were payments of fines for violations of State law, and allowance of deductions would have diluted the intended penalties. See Lawrence M. Marks, 27 T.C. 464 (1956); Rev.Rul. 61–115, 1961–1 C.B. 46.

Respondent's argument that petitioner's payment was a nondeductible personal expense is based upon the assertion that, in making the payment, petitioner was motivated by a desire to avoid criminal prosecution for violation of the Securities Act. There is no support in the record for this assertion. On the contrary, the evidence strongly supports petitioner's testimony that he paid over the money because he feared lest further controversy over the matter damage his status and reputation with the insurance industry and hence endanger his professional career, which was closely tied to that industry. We have so found. Nor do we think petitioner was unreasonable in his belief. No more is required for petitioner's payment to Cardinal to be deductible as an ordinary and necessary business expense under section 162(a). Lawrence M. Marks, supra; Rev.Rul. 61–115, supra; see Old Town Corporation, 37 T.C. 845 (1962), acq. 1962–2 C.B. 5; C. Doris H. Pepper, 36 T.C. 886 (1961).

Respondent's second objection to granting relief under section 1341 is that it was not sufficiently "established," in 1958 or any other year, that petitioner "did not have an unrestricted right to" the profits from the sale of the contract stock. Sec. 1341(a)(2). Respondent urges that there must be a clear showing, under State statutes or decisions, of petitioner's liability to Cardinal, before section 1341(a)(2) can be satisfied. Certainly, a judicial determination of liability is not required. See Rev.Rul. 58–456, 1958–2 C.B. 415, 418. However, we believe that it is necessary under section 1341(a)(2) for a taxpayer to demonstrate at least the probable validity of the adverse claim to the funds repaid. This position is supported by Rev.Rul. 58–456, supra, wherein the following language of the Court of Appeals for the Ninth Circuit is quoted with approval (Crellin's Estate v. Commissioner, 203 F.2d 812 (C.A.9, 1953), certiorari denied 346 U.S. 873, affirming 17 T.C. 781):

> In short, for tax purposes, it is that which the holding company could have compelled, not that in which the stockholders were willing to acquiesce, which controls. Otherwise, the taxpayers in this case could "lift the federal taxhand" to suit their convenience. * * *

Section 1341 was enacted to change the result reached in United States v. Lewis, 341 U.S. 590 (1951). See H.Rept. No. 1337, to accompany H.R. 8300 (Pub.L. 591), 83d Cong., 2d Sess., p. A294 (1954); Estate of Samuel Stein, 37 T.C. 945, 957 (1962). *Lewis* was a suit for refund of 1944 taxes paid on that part of an amount, received under claim of right as a bonus, which the taxpayer was required (under compulsion of a judgment) to restore in 1946. The Supreme Court held that no refund of the taxpayer's 1944 taxes was allowable. Consequently, the taxpayer was only entitled to a deduction in 1946, the year of the repayment.

We are of the opinion that, to become entitled to relief under section 1341, a taxpayer must prove by a preponderance of the evidence that he was not entitled to the unrestricted use of the amount received in the prior year. In other words (assuming that the Supreme Court had decided the *Lewis* case in taxpayer's favor) he must produce proof sufficient to have entitled him to an adjustment of the prior year's tax.

We do not believe that Congress intended to allow a credit based upon a recomputation of the prior year's tax in the absence of such a showing. This interpretation of the statute is supported by the use of the word "established" in section 1341(a)(2). For section 1341 to be applicable, it must be "*established* after the close of such prior taxable year (or years) that the taxpayer did not have an unrestricted right to such item." (Sec. 1341(a)(2). Emphasis supplied.) "Establish" means "to prove or make acceptable beyond a reasonable doubt." Webster's New International Dictionary (3d ed. 1961).

We are of the opinion that petitioner has not satisfied the requirements of section 1341(a)(2). Petitioner does not admit that he was not entitled to the profits he received in 1957. Indeed, he testified that he was not convinced the money belonged to Cardinal, though the formidable array of lawyers arguing the contrary raised some doubt in his mind. Petitioner was not compelled by legal process to make the payment. Finally, the record does not disclose the theory upon which Thurman and Wolford were basing their claim that the profits belonged to Cardinal; so we cannot say whether, under Kentucky law, such claim would have been upheld.

Petitioner relies upon Wetstone v. United States, an unreported case (D.Conn.1960, 5 A.F.T.R.2d 1486, 60–1 U.S.T.C. par. 9452), for the proposition that he need not prove the probable validity of the regulatory authorities' claim. The *Wetstone* case involved a year to which section 1341 was not applicable; it did not purport to construe section 1341. Although the court's reasoning seems questionable, we need not decide whether the case is correct on its own facts. Suffice it to say that the rule laid down therein is incompatible with our interpretation of the purpose and the language of section 1341. See Ernest H. Berger, 37 T.C. 1026, 1032.

Petitioner has not proved that he was not entitled to retain the profits from the sale of Cardinal contract stock. Accordingly, he does not meet the requirements for relief under section 1341. As previously pointed out, however, a bona fide claim was asserted against him, there was serious uncertainty as to the validity of the claim, and the payment in satisfaction of the claim was made for valid business reasons. The payment was not voluntary, in the sense of being gratuitous. It follows, then, that the payment is deductible under section 162(a) as an ordinary and necessary business expense. Lawrence M. Marks, supra.[2]

Decision will be entered under Rule 50.

NOTE

Section 1341 may be a good place to take note of the rule of the seven barrel staves. Apparently, it took seven barrel staves to make a vessel that would hold water; if one was missing, it was just a case of nothing done. A statutory provision that requires the coincidence of several requirements presents the same problem; if one is not met the provision is inapplicable. Note the three prerequisites expressed in Section 1341(a)(1) through (3).[1]

In *Pike*, set out above, the taxpayer fulfilled the first requirement, which appears at Section 1341(a)(1). He included an item in his gross income for 1957 because it appeared he had an unrestricted right to it. Indeed such inclusion was required under the *North American Oil* doctrine.[2] Application of this first test may not be difficult.[3] For example, an embezzler who later returned misappropriated funds would obviously fail it.[4]

In *Pike* the taxpayer also met the third test, which appears at Section 1341(a)(3); the amount in question exceeded $3000. One may wonder about this congressional insertion of a de minimis principle. But it probably does have the administrative advantage of relieving the Commissioner from the task of analyzing and cross-checking numerous

---

2. In his petition and amended petition, petitioner claimed a net operating loss carryback from 1958 to 1957. Respondent's objection to this claim was based upon the theory that the 1958 payment to Cardinal was not a deduction attributable to petitioner's trade or business. See sec. 172(d)(4). In view of our decision herein, respondent's objection is not well founded.

1. An additional limitation of § 1341 is found in § 1341(b)(2) which provides that the section "does not apply to any deduction allowable with respect to an item which was included in gross income by reason of the sale or other disposition of stock in trade of the taxpayer (or other property of a kind which would properly have been included in the inventory of the taxpayer if on hand at the close of the prior taxable year) or property held by the taxpayer primarily for sale to customers in the ordinary course of his trade or business."

2. The case is set out at page 589, supra. See also Reg. § 1.1341-1(a)(2), treating income included under a claim of right as "an item included in gross income because it appeared from all the facts available in the year of inclusion that the taxpayer had an unrestricted right to such item." See Dubroff, "The Claim of Right Doctrine," 40 Tax L.Rev. 729 (1985). An early, basic analysis of § 1341 appears in Webster, "The Claim of Right Doctrine: 1954 Version," 10 Tax L.Rev. 381 (1955) and see Emanuel, "The Scope of Section 1341," 53 Taxes 644 (1975).

3. See Rev.Rul. 68-153, 1968-1 C.B. 371.

4. See Rev.Rul. 65-254, 1965-2 C.B. 50.

Pike-like assertions that can have little impact on the revenue and are something less than cataclysmic to the taxpayer involved.

But the missing barrel stave in *Pike* was the requirement of Section 1341(a)(2), and this is where the most controversy has arisen. Although the taxpayer's act of turning over his gain to Cardinal was not wholly voluntary, it seems fair to say, as the Court did, that no obligation for him to do so was "established," as that term is used in the statute.

Note that the amount repaid must constitute an *allowable deduction* within the *Lewis* principle, if the Section 1341 alternatives are to be available. In *Pike* this test was met but, where a repayment fails to fit within the requirements of Section 162 or Section 212, it may not be.[5]

It is also clear that the taxpayer's lack of unrestricted right to the item must be established *after* the close of the year for which the item was included in gross income but on the basis of circumstances that existed *during* such prior year. The statutory test is whether the taxpayer "did not have" the right that was apparent in the year of receipt. Thus, a subsequent agreement to return an amount to which the taxpayer *was* entitled, no matter how binding on the taxpayer, will not invoke Section 1341. In George L. Blanton,[6] *after* receiving corporate fees for three years, the taxpayer entered into an agreement that any fees held to be excessive by the Internal Revenue Service (and so not deductible by the corporation) would be returned by him to the corporation. When the first three years' fees were found to be excessive, taxpayer returned the excess to the corporation and asserted a right to the benefits of Section 1341. The Tax Court held that the section did not apply because:[7]

> Under § 1341(a)(2), the requisite lack of an unrestricted right to an income item permitting deduction must arise out of the circumstances, terms, and conditions of the *original* payment of such item to the taxpayer and not out of circumstances, terms, and conditions imposed upon such payment by reason of some subsequent agreement between payor and payee.

The *Blanton* result raises the question whether Section 1341 would apply if *prior to receipt* an employee has entered into a valid contract with the employer under which he is obligated to repay amounts subsequently held not to be deductible by the employer. Is the answer indicated by the *Van Cleave* case which follows sound as a matter of statutory interpretation? As a matter of tax policy?

5. See Karl Hope, 55 T.C. 1020 (1971); and cf. U.S. v. Simon, 281 F.2d 520 (6th Cir.1960).

6. 46 T.C. 527 (1966), affirmed per curiam 379 F.2d 558 (5th Cir.1967).

7. Id. at 530. See Soled, "Reimbursement Agreements for Excessive Payments: Compensation and Other," 26 N.Y.U.Inst. on Fed.Tax. 1143 (1968).

VAN CLEAVE v. UNITED STATES

United States Court of Appeals, Sixth Circuit,* 1983.
718 F.2d 193.

Before ENGEL and KRUPANSKY, Circuit Judges and BROWN, Senior Circuit Judge.

BAILEY BROWN, Senior Circuit Judge.

This appeal involves a claim of favorable income tax treatment under 26 U.S.C. § 1341 by a taxpayer who in a subsequent year paid back excessive compensation to the corporation which employed him. The taxpayer included this excessive compensation in his return for the year the compensation was received. The government concedes that taxpayer is entitled to a deduction in the subsequent year. Taxpayer contends, however, that he should be allowed, pursuant to Section 1341, more favorable tax treatment by in effect excluding the excessive compensation from his income in the year received, thereby reducing his tax liability for that year and receiving a credit against his tax liability for the subsequent year. The district court, after a bench trial, entered judgment for the government in taxpayer's refund action and taxpayer appealed. We reverse and hold that taxpayer is entitled to the benefit of Section 1341.

BACKGROUND

The taxpayer, Eugene Van Cleave, was president and majority stockholder of VanMark Corporation throughout the time in question. In 1969, the corporation adopted a by-law requiring corporate officers who received from the corporation income determined by the Internal Revenue Service (IRS) to be excessive—and so not deductible by the corporation as a business expense—to pay back the amount determined to be excessive to the corporation. In addition, Mr. Van Cleave entered into a separate agreement requiring him to reimburse the corporation for nondeductible compensation.

Mr. Van Cleave received $332,000 in salary and bonuses in 1974. During 1975, the IRS audited the corporation's return, determined that $57,500 of Mr. Van Cleave's salary was excessive, and disallowed that portion of his salary as a deduction to the corporation. In December, 1975, pursuant to the corporation's by-law and the agreement between Mr. Van Cleave and the corporation, Mr. Van Cleave repaid the nondeductible $57,500.

Mr. Van Cleave reported the full compensation on his calendar year 1974 income tax return. On his 1975 return, prepared with the repayment to the corporation in mind, he calculated his tax liability by using 26 U.S.C. § 1341. The IRS audited the return, and allowed a deduction for 1975 but disallowed use of Section 1341, resulting in a tax

---

* See Bartelstein, "Van Cleave v. United States: Repayment Agreements and Section 1341" 38 Tax Lawyer 239 (1984), which is critical of the *Van Cleave* result and supportive of the District Court's contrary result in the case.

deficiency of $5,987.34. Mr. Van Cleave paid this deficiency and brought this action for a refund.

This case turns on the interpretation of Section 1341 of the Internal Revenue Code.

* * *

Section 1341 was enacted by Congress to mitigate the sometimes harsh result of the application of the "claim of right" doctrine. United States v. Skelly Oil Co., 394 U.S. 678, 681, 89 S.Ct. 1379, 1381 (1969); * * * Under the claim of right doctrine, a taxpayer must pay tax on an item in the year in which he receives it under a claim of right even if it is later determined that his right to the item was not absolute and he is required to return it. The taxpayer, however, is allowed to deduct the amount of the item from his income in the year of repayment. This result was held to be required because income and deductions are determined on an annual basis. *Skelly* at 681, 89 S.Ct. at 1381. But, as pointed out by the Supreme Court in *Skelly,* it is possible for a taxpayer to benefit less from the deduction in the year of repayment than he would benefit if he had been able to deduct the amount repaid from his income in the year of receipt. Id. This result of the claim of right doctrine could occur when, as was the case with Mr. Van Cleave, the taxpayer had been in a higher tax bracket in the year of receipt than he was in the year of repayment.

Section 1341 allows the taxpayer to choose the more favorable alternative as follows:

> If the taxpayer included an item in gross income in one taxable year, and in a subsequent taxable year he becomes entitled to a deduction because the item or a portion thereof is no longer subject to his unrestricted use, and the amount of the deduction is in excess of $3,000, the tax for the subsequent year is reduced by either the tax attributable to the deduction or the decrease in the tax for the prior year attributable to the removal of the item, whichever is greater. Under the rule of the *Lewis* case (340 U.S. 590, 71 S.Ct. 522 (1951)) [see infra], the taxpayer is entitled to a deduction only in the year of repayment. * * *

I.

The district court held that Section 1341 treatment was not available to Mr. Van Cleave because it determined that his repayment was voluntary. The district court determined that it was voluntary because Mr. Van Cleave owned a substantial majority of the stock and in that sense controlled the corporation. On appeal, however, the government does not contend that Section 1341 is inapplicable because the repayment was voluntary and indeed does not contend that the repayment in fact was voluntary.

The district court also seemed to be persuaded by the argument that, if Mr. Van Cleave were allowed Section 1341 treatment under these circumstances, this would open the door to tax avoidance in that taxpayers who controlled corporations could "test the waters" in setting their compensation without risk of an adverse tax result. We believe, however, that such possibility of tax avoidance is not a proper consideration in applying this statute, and that the consideration is a legislative rather than a judicial consideration. Moreover, as Mr. Van Cleave suggests, the possibility of tax avoidance could be reduced by requiring the corporation and recipient of compensation to state in their returns that such compensation was paid subject to an obligation to reimburse in the event a deduction is disallowed to the corporation.

II.

The leading case on the claim of right tax doctrine is North American Oil Consolidated v. Burnet, 286 U.S. 417, 52 S.Ct. 613 (1932). *North American Oil* involved a dispute over the year in which income, earned on property held by a receiver during a title dispute between the taxpayer and the government, was to be taxed. The possibilities were 1916, the year in which the income was earned; 1917, the year in which the district court ruled in favor of the taxpayer and the money was paid to the taxpayer; or 1922, the year the litigation was finally terminated in the taxpayer's favor. In an opinion by Justice Brandeis, the Court determined that 1917 was the year that the income must be reported and set forth the claim of right doctrine as follows:

> If a taxpayer receives earnings under a claim of right and without restriction as to its disposition, he has received income which he is required to return, even though it may still be claimed that he is not entitled to retain the money, and even though he may still be adjudged liable to restore its equivalent. Id. at 424, 52 S.Ct. at 615.

In a more recent case, Healy v. Commissioner, 345 U.S. 278, 73 S.Ct. 671 (1953), each of the taxpayers involved received excessive compensation from a closely-held corporation in which he was both a shareholder and an officer. The taxpayers reported that compensation as income in the year of receipt. In a subsequent year, the IRS determined that part of this compensation was excessive, disallowed the deduction to the corporation, and taxpayers, as transferees, were required to pay back the excess. The government conceded that the taxpayers could deduct the amount paid back from their taxable income, but argued that the deduction could only be taken in the year of repayment. Taxpayers, on the other hand, argued that they should be allowed to have their tax liability determined by taking a deduction in the year the excessive compensation was received. The Court held that, under the claim of right doctrine, the deduction could be taken only from the income of the year of repayment.

In a similar case, United States v. Lewis, 340 U.S. 590, 71 S.Ct. 522 (1951), taxpayer received a bonus from his employer in 1944 and reported it on his income tax return for that year. In a subsequent year, taxpayer paid back one half of the bonus pursuant to a state court judgment. As in *Healy,* taxpayer claimed that he should be able, in the year of repayment, to have his tax liability determined by taking a deduction in the year the excessive bonus was paid to him. The Court held, however, that, under the claim of right doctrine, the taxpayer could take a deduction only in the year of repayment. Justice Douglas dissented, noting that the effect of the Court's decision was to allow the government to exact tax on money that was not income to the taxpayer.

As previously noted, Section 1341 was enacted to alleviate the effect of the claim of right doctrine in cases such as *Lewis.* The government argues, however, that Section 1341 is not available to the taxpayer in the instant case. The government points out that Section 1341 provides for taxpayer relief only if "it *appeared* that the taxpayer had an unrestricted right" (emphasis added) to the excess salary and "it was established after the close of such prior taxable year * * * that the taxpayer did not have an unrestricted right to such item." Section 1341(a)(1) and (2). The government argues that Mr. Van Cleave had more than an *appearance* of an unrestricted right to the excess compensation in the year in which it was received, and that the right to the compensation became restricted only upon the occurrence of the IRS audit and determination in a subsequent year. The government maintains that, since Mr. Van Cleave had an unrestricted right to the compensation in the year of receipt, contingent only upon the happening of an event in a subsequent year, Section 1341 is not available to him.*

We reject this argument and hold that Section 1341 is available to Mr. Van Cleave. The fact that his ultimate right to the compensation was not determined until the occurrence of a subsequent event does not mean that Mr. Van Cleave had, in the statutory sense, an unrestricted right to the compensation when he received it. In Prince v. United States, 610 F.2d 350 (1980), the Fifth Circuit reversed a district court decision that the estate of a taxpayer was not entitled to Section 1341 tax adjustment. A state court had ruled that the decedent, a trust beneficiary, had received trust funds—and paid federal income tax on them—that should have gone to the trustee as part of its fee. The state court required the decedent's estate to return these funds to the trustee. The government's position in that case was identical to its stance in this case: Section 1341 was not available to the taxpayer's estate because the taxpayer had an unrestricted right to the income in the year of receipt, not just the appearance of a right. Id. at 352. In rejecting the government's argument, the court said:

> The Alabama judgment established, whether expressly or by implication, that the deductions from the trust income for the ten year fee had been miscalculated. As a result, [decedent]

* The government also maintains this position in Rev.Rul. 67–437, 1967–2 C.B. 296. See also Rev.Rul. 69–115, 1969–1 C.B. 50, which holds that the taxpayers would be allowed to deduct the payment as an I.R.C. § 162 deduction in the year of repayment. Ed.

had received more income from the trust than she was entitled to receive. This income had to be returned. The requirements of Section 1341 were thus clearly satisfied. [Decedent] appeared to have an unrestricted right to the income when she received it; it was established in a taxable year after she received it that she did not have such a right. Id.

We agree with the Fifth Circuit's reading of Section 1341 and hold that the fact that a restriction on a taxpayer's right to income does not arise until a year subsequent to the time of receipt does not affect the availability of Section 1341 tax adjustment. Therefore, Section 1341 tax adjustment is available to a taxpayer in this situation if the other requirements of the section are met. We are aided in this conclusion by our examination of cases involving the application of the claim of right doctrine, the effect of which the section was designed to alleviate. United States v. Lewis, 340 U.S. 590, 71 S.Ct. 522 (1951); Healy v. Commissioner, 345 U.S. 278, 73 S.Ct. 671 (1953). Acceptance of the government's reading of the statute would thwart the ameliorative purpose intended by Congress in enacting the section. * * * Accordingly, Mr. Van Cleave is entitled to a tax adjustment under Section 1341.

The judgment of the district court is reversed and the case is remanded for proceedings consistent with this opinion.

PROBLEMS

1. Section 1341 provides a statutory exception to the *Lewis* rule which employs the doctrine of strict annual accounting.

   (a) What requirements must be met in order to trigger § 1341?

   (b) If § 1341 applies what is the result to the taxpayer?

   (c) When is § 1341 more beneficial to the taxpayer than the *Lewis* case?

   (d) If the two years involved in a § 1341 situation are both a pre-1988 year and a post-1987 year, what is the likelihood that § 1341(a)(5) will apply to reduce a noncorporate taxpayer's tax below the *Lewis* (later year deduction under § 1341(a)(4)) result?

2. Payer received $40,000 in the form of advance and regular commissions on sales of goods for his employer in year one. Will § 1341 be applicable if:

   (a) In year two some customers return goods due to a breach of warranty and Payer repays Employer $10,000 of commissions that were prepaid as he is required to do under his contract?

   (b) The years are the same as in (a), above, except that Payer acquired by embezzlement the $10,000 that was subsequently returned?

(c) Payer acquired the $10,000 in the same manner as in part (a), above; however, he was not required by contract to return the excess contributions but did so voluntarily?

(d) Payer returned the $10,000 based on a return of merchandise by a customer of Payer in year two, under such circumstances that Payer's employer rescinded the contract with the customer, which, in turn, effected a reduced commission to Payer, requiring him to repay $10,000 to his employer?

B. THE TAX BENEFIT DOCTRINE *

Internal Revenue Code: Section 111(a). See Sections 111(b) and (c).

ALICE PHELAN SULLIVAN CORP. v. COMMISSIONER **

Court of Claims of the United States, 1967.
381 F.2d 399.

COLLINS, Judge. Plaintiff, a California corporation, brings this action to recover an alleged overpayment in its 1957 income tax. During that year, there was returned to taxpayer two parcels of realty, each of which it had previously donated and claimed as a charitable contribution deduction. The first donation had been made in 1939; the second, in 1940. Under the then applicable corporate tax rates, the deductions claimed ($4,243.49 for 1939 and $4,463.44 for 1940) yielded plaintiff an aggregate tax benefit of $1,877.49.[1]

Each conveyance had been made subject to the condition that the property be used either for a religious or for an educational purpose. In 1957, the donee decided not to use the gifts; they were therefore reconveyed to plaintiff. Upon audit of taxpayer's income tax return it was found that the recovered property was not reflected in its 1957 gross income. The Commissioner of Internal Revenue disagreed with plaintiff's characterization of the recovery as a nontaxable return of capital. He viewed the transaction as giving rise to taxable income and therefore adjusted plaintiff's income by adding to it $8,706.93—the total of the charitable contribution deductions previously claimed and allowed. This addition to income, taxed at the 1957 corporate tax rate of 52 percent, resulted in a deficiency assessment of $4,527.60. After payment of the deficiency, plaintiff filed a claim for the refund of $2,650.11, asserting this amount as overpayment on the theory that a

---

* See Lindsay, "An Asset-Based Approach to the Tax Benefit Rule," 72 Cal.L.Rev. 1257 (1984); White, "An Essay on the Conceptual Foundations of the Tax Benefit Rule," 82 Mich.L.Rev. 486 (1983). Bittker and Kanner, "The Tax Benefit Rule," 26 U.C.L.A.L.Rev. 265 (1978); Corlew, "The Tax Benefit Rule, Claim of Right Restorations, and Annual Accounting: A Cure for the Inconsistencies," 21 Vand.L.Rev. 995 (1968).

** There is a comment on *Sullivan* at 66 Mich.L.Rev. 381 (1967). Ed.

1. The tax rate in 1939 was 18 percent; in 1940, 24 percent.

correct assessment could demand no more than the return of the tax benefit originally enjoyed, i.e., $1,877.49. The claim was disallowed.

This court has had prior occasion to consider the question which the present suit presents. In Perry v. United States, 160 F.Supp. 270, 142 Ct.Cl. 7 (1958) (Judges Madden and Laramore dissenting), it was recognized that a return to the donor of a prior charitable contribution gave rise to income to the extent of the deduction previously allowed. The court's point of division—which is likewise the division between the instant parties—was whether the "gain" attributable to the recovery was to be taxed at the rate applicable at the time the deduction was first claimed or whether the proper rate was that in effect at the time of recovery. The majority, concluding that the Government should be entitled to recoup no more than that which it lost, held that the tax liability arising upon the return of a charitable gift should equal the tax benefit experienced at time of donation. Taxpayer urges that the *Perry* rationale dictates that a like result be reached in this case.

The Government, of course, assumes the opposite stance. Mindful of the homage due the principle of stare decisis, it bids us first to consider the criteria under which judicial reexamination of an earlier decision is justifiable. We are referred to Judge Davis' concurring opinion in Mississippi River Fuel Corp. v. United States, 314 F.2d 953, 958, 161 Ct.Cl. 237, 246–247 (1963), wherein he states that:

> * * * The question is not what we would hold if we now took a fresh look but whether we should take that fresh look.
>
> * * *

[We] examine anew the issue which this case presents.

A transaction which returns to a taxpayer his own property cannot be considered as giving rise to "income"—at least where that term is confined to its traditional sense of "gain derived from capital, from labor, or from both combined." Eisner v. Macomber, 252 U.S. 189, 207, 40 S.Ct. 189 (1920). Yet the principle is well engrained in our tax law that the return or recovery of property that was once the subject of an income tax deduction must be treated as income in the year of its recovery. Rothensies v. Electric Storage Battery Co., 329 U.S. 296, 67 S.Ct. 271 (1946); Estate of Black v. Commissioner, 39 B.T.A. 338 (1939), aff'd sub nom. Union Trust Co. v. Commissioner, 111 F.2d 60 (7th Cir.), cert. denied, 311 U.S. 658, 61 S.Ct. 12. The only limitation upon that principle is the so-called "tax-benefit rule." This rule permits exclusion of the recovered item from income so long as its initial use as a deduction did not provide a tax saving. California & Hawaiian Sugar Ref. Corp. v. United States, supra; Central Loan & Inv. Co. v. Commissioner, 39 B.T.A. 981 (1939). But where full tax use of a deduction was made and a tax saving thereby obtained, then the extent of saving is considered immaterial. The recovery is viewed as income to the full extent of the deduction previously allowed.[2]

2. The rationale which supports the principle, as well as its limitation, is that the property, having once served to offset taxable income (i.e., as a tax deduction)

Formerly the exclusive province of judge-made law, the tax-benefit concept now finds expression both in statute and administrative regulations. Section 111 of the Internal Revenue Code of 1954 accords tax-benefit treatment to the recovery of bad debts, prior taxes, and delinquency amounts.[3] Treasury regulations have "broadened" the rule of exclusion by extending similar treatment to "all other losses, expenditures, and accruals made the basis of deductions from gross income for prior taxable years * * *."[4]

Drawing our attention to the broad language of this regulation, the Government insists that the present recovery must find its place within the scope of the regulation and, as such, should be taxed in a manner consistent with the treatment provided for like items of recovery, i.e., that it be taxed at the rate prevailing in the year of recovery. We are compelled to agree.

Set in historical perspective, it is clear that the cited regulation may not be regarded as an unauthorized extension of the otherwise limited congressional approval given to the tax-benefit concept. While the statute, (i.e., section 111) addresses itself only to bad debts, prior taxes, and delinquency amounts, it was, as noted in Dobson v. Commissioner, 320 U.S. 489, 64 S.Ct. 239 (1943), designed not to limit the application of the judicially designed tax-benefit rule, but rather to insure against its demise. "A specific statutory exception was necessary in bad debt cases only because the courts reversed the Tax Court and established as matter of law a 'theoretically proper' rule which distorted the taxpayer's income [i.e., taxation of a recovery though no benefit may have been obtained through its earlier deduction]." 320 U.S. at 506, 64 S.Ct. at 249.

The *Dobson* decision insured the continued validity of the tax-benefit concept, and the regulation—being but the embodiment of that principle—is clearly adequate to embrace a recoverable charitable contribution. See California & Hawaiian Sugar Ref. Corp., supra, 311 F.2d at 239, 159 Ct.Cl. at 567. But the regulation does not specify which tax rate is to be applied to the recouped deduction, and this consideration brings us to the matter here in issue.

Ever since Burnet v. Sanford & Brooks Co., 282 U.S. 359, 51 S.Ct. 150 (1931), the concept of accounting for items of income and expense on an annual basis has been accepted as the basic principle upon which our tax laws are structured. "It is the essence of any system of taxation that it should produce revenue ascertainable, and payable to the government, at regular intervals. Only by such a system is it practicable to produce a regular flow of income and apply methods of accounting, assessment, and collection capable of practical operation." 282 U.S. at 365, 51 S.Ct. at 152. To insure the vitality of the single-

should be treated, upon its recoupment, as the recovery of that which had been previously deducted. See Plumb, "The Tax Benefit Rule Today," 57 Harv.L.Rev. 129, 131 n. 10 (1943).

3. [I.R.C. § 111 and Reg. § 1.111-1 is omitted. Ed.]

4. Id.

year concept, it is essential not only that annual income be ascertained without reference to losses experienced in an earlier accounting period, but also that income be taxed without reference to earlier tax rates. And absent specific statutory authority sanctioning a departure from this principle, it may only be said of *Perry* that it achieved a result which was more equitably just than legally correct.[5]

Since taxpayer in this case did obtain full tax benefit from its earlier deductions, those deductions were properly classified as income upon recoupment and must be taxed as such. This can mean nothing less than the application of that tax rate which is in effect during the year in which the recovered item is recognized as a factor of income. We therefore sustain the Government's position and grant its motion for summary judgment. Perry v. United States, supra, is hereby overruled, and plaintiff's petition is dismissed.

PROBLEMS

1. In year one Taxpayers filed a joint return showing gross income of $45,000 and deductions of $48,000, which included state real property taxes paid on their residence in the amount of $4,000. Contesting the amount of their liability for the state property taxes, Taxpayers successfully brought suit for a refund of those taxes. What result to Taxpayers in the following alternative circumstances?

(a) In year two, they get a judgment for and receive a $2,000 refund.

(b) In year two, they get a judgment for and receive a $4,000 refund.

(c) What result in (b), above, if they had no itemized deductions for year one other than the $4,000 in taxes and they claimed the standard deduction for year one?

2. Compare § 111 with § 1341. Which is friendlier to the taxpayer?

---

5. This opinion represents the views of the majority and complies with existing law and decisions. However, in the writer's personal opinion, it produces a harsh and inequitable result. Perhaps, it exemplifies a situation "where the letter of the law killeth; the spirit giveth life." The tax-benefit concept is an equitable doctrine which should be carried to an equitable conclusion. Since it is the declared public policy to encourage contributions to chari-table and educational organizations, a donor, whose gift to such organizations is returned, should not be required to refund to the Government a greater amount than the tax benefit received when the deduction was made for the gift. Such a rule would avoid a penalty to the taxpayer and an unjust enrichment to the Government. However, the court cannot legislate and any change in the existing law rests within the wisdom and discretion of the Congress.

C. INCOME AVERAGING

1. STATUTORY AVERAGING

The Internal Revenue Code of 1954, by way of Sections 1301 to 1305, generally allowed an individual taxpayer whose income in a year was more than 40 percent higher than the average of his or her income for the prior three years to subject the excess to tax at rates that would have applied if the excess had been earned in equal amounts over the four year period.[1] Thus, income averaging attempted to place an individual whose income varied greatly from year to year on a tax parity with an individual whose income was relatively stable over a period of time. With the 1986 introduction of the modified flat tax rates the need for statutory income averaging was so reduced that Congress repealed the statute.[2] Students who feel that they have been deprived of a beneficial tax-saving provision upon entering the work force should be aware that an individual was generally ineligible to income average for a year if he or she had been a full time student during any of the three prior years.[3] Some averaging is still available; see the next subparts of this Chapter.

2. DO–IT–YOURSELF AVERAGING

REVENUE RULING 60–31
1960–1 Cum.Bull. 174.

Advice has been requested regarding the taxable year of inclusion in gross income of a taxpayer, using the cash receipts and disbursements method of accounting, of compensation for services received under the circumstances described below.

(1) On January 1, 1958, the taxpayer and corporation X executed an employment contract under which the taxpayer is to be employed by the corporation in an executive capacity for a period of five years. Under the contract, the taxpayer is entitled to a stated annual salary and to additional compensation of $10x$ dollars for each year. The additional compensation will be credited to a bookkeeping reserve account and will be deferred, accumulated, and paid in annual installments equal to one-fifth of the amount in the reserve as of the close of the year immediately preceding the year of first payment. The payments are to begin only upon (a) termination of the taxpayer's employment by the corporation; (b) the taxpayer's becoming a part-time employee of the corporation; or (c) the taxpayer's becoming partially or

---

1. I.R.C. (1954) §§ 1301–1305. That excess had to exceed $3,000 for the provisions to apply. I.R.C. (1954) § 1301.

2. Pub.Law No. 99–514, 99th Cong., 2d Sess. § 141 (1986).

3. I.R.C. (1954) § 1303(d)(1) which was subject to an exception found in § 1303(d)(2).

totally incapacitated. Under the terms of the agreement, corporation X is under a merely contractual obligation to make the payments when due, and the parties did not intend that the amounts in the reserve be held by the corporation in trust for the taxpayer.

The contract further provides that if the taxpayer should fail or refuse to perform his duties, the corporation will be relieved of any obligation to make further credits to the reserve (but not of the obligation to distribute amounts previously contributed); but, if the taxpayer should become incapacitated from performing his duties, then credits to the reserve will continue for one year from the date of the incapacity, but not beyond the expiration of the five-year term of the contract. There is no specific provision in the contract for forfeiture by the taxpayer of his right to distribution from the reserve; and, in the event he should die prior to his receipt in full of the balance in the account, the remaining balance is distributable to his personal representative at the rate of one-fifth per year for five years, beginning three months after his death.

(2) The taxpayer is an officer and director of corporation A, which has a plan for making future payments of additional compensation for current services to certain officers and key employees designated by its board of directors. This plan provides that a percentage of the annual net earnings (before Federal income taxes) in excess of $4,000x$ dollars is to be designated for division among the participants in proportion to their respective salaries. This amount is not currently paid to the participants; but, the corporation has set up on its books a separate account for each participant and each year it credits thereto the dollar amount of his participation for the year, reduced by a proportionate part of the corporation's income taxes attributable to the additional compensation. Each account is also credited with the net amount, if any, realized from investing any portion of the amount in the account.

Distributions are to be made from these accounts annually beginning when the employee (1) reaches age 60, (2) is no longer employed by the company, including cessation of employment due to death, or (3) becomes totally disabled to perform his duties, whichever occurs first. The annual distribution will equal a stated percentage of the balance in the employee's account at the close of the year immediately preceding the year of first payment, and distributions will continue until the account is exhausted. However, the corporation's liability to make these distributions is contingent upon the employee's (1) refraining from engaging in any business competitive to that of the corporation, (2) making himself available to the corporation for consultation and advice after retirement or termination of his services, unless disabled, and (3) retaining unencumbered any interest or benefit under the plan. In the event of his death, either before or after the beginning of payments, amounts in an employee's account are distributable in installments computed in the same way to his designated beneficiaries or heirs-at-law. Under the terms of the compensation plan, corporation A is under a merely contractual obligation to make the payments when due, and the parties did not intend that the amounts in each account be held by the corporation in trust for the participants.

(3) On October 1, 1957, the taxpayer, an author, and corporation Y, a publisher, executed an agreement under which the taxpayer granted to the publisher the exclusive right to print, publish and sell a book he had written. This agreement provides that the publisher will (1) pay the author specified royalties based on the actual cash received from the sale of the published work, (2) render semi-annual statements of the sales, and (3) at the time of rendering each statement make settlement for the amount due. On the same day, another agreement was signed by the same parties, mutually agreeing that, in consideration of, and notwithstanding any contrary provisions contained in the first contract, the publisher shall not pay the taxpayer more than $100x$ dollars in any one calendar year. Under this supplemental contract, sums in excess of $100x$ dollars accruing in any one calendar year are to be carried over by the publisher into succeeding accounting periods; and the publisher shall not be required either to pay interest to the taxpayer on any such excess sums or to segregate any such sums in any manner.

(4) In June 1957, the taxpayer, a football player, entered into a two-year standard player's contract with a football club in which he agreed to play football and engage in activities related to football during the two-year term only for the club. In addition to a specified salary for the two-year term, it was mutually agreed that as an inducement for signing the contract the taxpayer would be paid a bonus of $150x$ dollars. The taxpayer could have demanded and received payment of this bonus at the time of signing the contract, but at his suggestion there was added to the standard contract form a paragraph providing substantially as follows:

The player shall receive the sum of $150x$ dollars upon signing of this contract, contingent upon the payment of this $150x$ dollars to an escrow agent designated by him. The escrow agreement shall be subject to approval by the legal representatives of the player, the Club, and the escrow agent.

Pursuant to this added provision, an escrow agreement was executed on June 25, 1957, in which the club agreed to pay $150x$ dollars on that date to the Y bank, as escrow agent; and the escrow agent agreed to pay this amount, plus interest, to the taxpayer in installments over a period of five years. The escrow agreement also provides that the account established by the escrow agent is to bear the taxpayer's name; that payments from such account may be made only in accordance with the terms of the agreement; that the agreement is binding upon the parties thereto and their successors or assigns; and that in the event of the taxpayer's death during the escrow period the balance due will become part of his estate.

(5) The taxpayer, a boxer, entered into an agreement with a boxing club to fight a particular opponent at a specified time and place. The place of the fight agreed to was decided upon because of the insistence

of the taxpayer that it be held there. The agreement was on the standard form of contract required by the state athletic commission and provided, in part, that for his performance taxpayer was to receive 16x percent of the gross receipts derived from the match. Simultaneously, the same parties executed a separate agreement providing for payment of the taxpayer's share of the receipts from the match as follows: 25 percent thereof not later than two weeks after the bout, and 25 percent thereof during each of the three years following the year of the bout in equal semiannual installments. Such deferments are not customary in prize fighting contracts, and the supplemental agreement was executed at the demand of the taxpayer. Upon the taxpayer's insistence, the agreements also provided that any telecast of the fight must receive his prior consent and that he was to approve or disapprove all proposed sales of radio and motion picture rights.

Section 1.451–1(a) of the Income Tax Regulations provides in part as follows:

> Gains, profits, and income are to be included in gross income for the taxable year in which they are actually or constructively received by the taxpayer unless includible for a different year in accordance with the taxpayer's method of accounting. * * *.

And, with respect to the cash receipts and disbursements method of accounting, section 1.446–1(c)(1)(i) provides in part—

> Generally, under the cash receipts and disbursements method in the computation of taxable income, all items which constitute gross income (whether in the form of cash, property, or services) are to be included for the taxable year in which actually or constructively received. * * *.

As previously stated, the individual concerned in each of the situations described above, employs the cash receipts and disbursements method of accounting. Under that method, as indicated by the above-quoted provisions of the regulations, he is required to include the compensation concerned in gross income only for the taxable year in which it is actually or constructively received. Consequently, the question for resolution is whether in each of the situations described the income in question was constructively received in a taxable year prior to the taxable year of actual receipt.

A mere promise to pay, not represented by notes or secured in any way, is not regarded as a receipt of income within the intendment of the cash receipts and disbursements method. See United States v. Christine Oil & Gas Co., 269 F. 458; William J. Jackson v. Smietanka, 272 F. 970, Ct.D. 5, C.B. 4, 96 (1921); and E.F. Cremin v. Commissioner, 5 B.T.A. 1164, acquiescence, C.B. VI–1, 2 (1927). Also C. Florian Zittel v. Commissioner, 12 B.T.A. 675, in which, holding a salary to be taxable when received, the Board said: "Taxpayers on a receipts and disbursements basis are required to report only income actually received no matter how binding any contracts they may have to receive more."

This should not be construed to mean that under the cash receipts and disbursements method income may be taxed only when realized in cash. For, under that method a taxpayer is required to include in income that which is received in cash or cash equivalent. W.P. Henritze v. Commissioner, 41 B.T.A. 505. And, as stated in the above-quoted provisions of the regulations, the "receipt" contemplated by the cash method may be actual or constructive.

With respect to the constructive receipt of income, section 1.451–2(a) of the Income Tax Regulations (which accords with prior regulations extending back to, and including, Article 53 of Regulations 45 under the Revenue Act of 1918) provides, in part, as follows:

> Income although not actually reduced to a taxpayer's possession is constructively received by him in the taxable year during which it is credited to his account or set apart for him so that he may draw upon it at any time. However, income is not constructively received if the taxpayer's control of its receipt is subject to substantial limitations or restrictions. Thus, if a corporation credits its employees with bonus stock, but the stock is not available to such employees until some future date, the mere crediting on the books of the corporation does not constitute receipt.

Thus, under the doctrine of constructive receipt, a taxpayer may not deliberately turn his back upon income and thereby select the year for which he will report it. The Hamilton National Bank of Chattanooga, as Administrator of the Estate of S. Strang Nicklin, Deceased, v. Commissioner, 29 B.T.A. 63. Nor may a taxpayer, by a private agreement, postpone receipt of income from one taxable year to another. James E. Lewis v. Commissioner, 30 B.T.A. 318.

However, the statute cannot be administered by speculating whether the payor would have been willing to agree to an earlier payment. See, for example, J.D. Amend, et ux., v. Commissioner, 13 T.C. 178, acquiescence, C.B. 1950–1, 1; and C.E. Gullett, et al., v. Commissioner, 31 B.T.A. 1067, in which the court, citing a number of authorities for its holding stated:

> It is clear that the doctrine of constructive receipt is to be sparingly used; that amounts due from a corporation but unpaid, are not to be included in the income of an individual reporting his income on a cash receipts basis unless it appears that the money was available to him, that the corporation was able and ready to pay him, that his right to receive was not restricted, and that his failure to receive resulted from exercise of his own choice.

Consequently, it seems clear that in each case involving a deferral of compensation a determination of whether the doctrine of constructive receipt is applicable must be made upon the basis of the specific factual situation involved.

Applying the foregoing criteria to the situations described above, the following conclusions have been reached:

(1) The additional compensation to be received by the taxpayer under the employment contract concerned will be includible in his gross income only in the taxable years in which the taxpayer actually receives installment payments in cash or other property previously credited to his account. To hold otherwise would be contrary to the provisions of the regulations and the court decisions mentioned above.

(2) For the reasons in (1) above, it is held that the taxpayer here involved also will be required to include the deferred compensation concerned in his gross income only in the taxable years in which the taxpayer actually receives installment payments in cash or other property previously credited to his account.

In arriving at this conclusion and the conclusion reached in case "(1)," consideration has been given to section 1.402(b)–1 of the Income Tax Regulations and to Revenue Ruling 57–37, C.B. 1957–1, 18, as modified by Revenue Ruling 57–528, C.B. 1957–2, 263. Section 1.402(b)–1(a)(1) provides in part, with an exception not here relevant, that any contribution made by an employer on behalf of an employee to a trust during a taxable year of the employer which ends within or with a taxable year of the trust for which the trust is not exempt under section 501(a) of the Code, shall be included in income of the employee for his taxable year during which the contribution is made if his interest in the contribution is nonforfeitable at the time the contribution is made. Revenue Ruling 57–37, as modified by Revenue Ruling 57–528, held, *inter alia,* that certain contributions conveying fully vested and nonforfeitable interests made by an employer into separate independently controlled trusts for the purpose of furnishing unemployment and other benefits to its eligible employees constituted additional compensation to the employees includible, under section 402(b) of the Code and section 1.402(b)–1(a)(1) of the regulations, in their income for the taxable year in which such contributions were made. These Revenue Rulings are distinguishable from cases "(1)" and "(2)" in that, under all the facts and circumstances of these cases, no trusts for the benefit of the taxpayers were created and no contributions are to be made thereto. Consequently, section 402(b) of the Code and section 1.402(b)–1(a)(1) of the regulations are inapplicable.

(3) Here the principal agreement provided that the royalties were payable substantially as earned, and this agreement was supplemented by a further concurrent agreement which made the royalties payable over a period of years. This supplemental agreement, however, was made before the royalties were earned; in fact, it was made on the same day as the principal agreement and the two agreements were a part of the same transaction. Thus, for all practical purposes, the arrangement from the beginning is similar to that in (1) above. Therefore, it is also held that the author concerned will be required to

include the royalties in his gross income only in the taxable years in which they are actually received in cash or other property.

(4) In arriving at a determination as to the includibility of the $150x$ dollars concerned in the gross income of the football player, under the circumstances described, in addition to the authorities cited above, consideration also has been given to Revenue Ruling 55–727, C.B. 1955–2, 25, and to the decision in E.T. Sproull v. Commissioner, 16 T.C. 244.

In Revenue Ruling 55–727, the taxpayer, a professional baseball player, entered into a contract in 1953 in which he agreed to render services for a baseball club and to refrain from playing baseball for any other club during the term of the contract. In addition to specified compensation, the contract provided for a bonus to the player or his estate, payable one-half in January 1954 and one-half in January 1955, whether or not he was able to render services. The primary question was whether the bonus was capital gain or ordinary income; and, in holding that the bonus payments constituted ordinary income, it was stated that they were taxable for the year in which received by the player. However, under the facts set forth in Revenue Ruling 55–727 there was no arrangement, as here, for placing the amount of the bonus in escrow. Consequently, the instant situation is distinguishable from that considered in Revenue Ruling 55–727.

In E.T. Sproull v. Commissioner, 16 T.C. 244, affirmed, 194 F.2d 541, the petitioner's employer in 1945 transferred in trust for the petitioner the amount of $10,500. The trustee was directed to pay out of principal to the petitioner the sum of $5,250 in 1946 and the balance, including income, in 1947. In the event of the petitioner's prior death, the amounts were to be paid to his administrator, executor, or heirs. The petitioner contended that the Commissioner erred in including the sum of $10,500 in his taxable income for 1945. In this connection, the court stated:

> * * * it is undoubtedly true that the amount which the Commissioner has included in petitioner's income for 1945 was used in that year for his benefit * * * in setting up the trust of which petitioner, or, in the event of his death then his estate, was the sole beneficiary * * *.

> The question then becomes * * * was "any economic or financial benefit conferred on the employee as compensation" in the taxable year. If so, it was taxable to him in that year. This question we must answer in the affirmative. The employer's part of the transaction terminated in 1945. It was then that the amount of the compensation was fixed at $10,500 and irrevocably paid out for petitioner's sole benefit. * * *."

Applying the principles stated in the *Sproull* decision to the facts here, it is concluded that the $150x$-dollar bonus is includible in the gross income of the football player concerned in 1957, the year in which the club unconditionally paid such amount to the escrow agent.

(5) In this case, the taxpayer and the boxing club, as well as the opponent whom taxpayer had agreed to meet, are each acting in his or its own right, the proposed match is a joint venture by all of these participants, and the taxpayer is not an employee of the boxing club. The taxpayer's share of the gross receipts from the match belong to him and never belonged to the boxing club. Thus, the taxpayer acquired all of the benefits of his share of the receipts except the right of immediate physical possession; and, although the club retained physical possession, it was by virtue of an arrangement with the taxpayer who, in substance and effect, authorized the boxing club to take possession and hold for him. The receipts, therefore, were income to the taxpayer at the time they were paid to and retained by the boxing club by his agreement and, in substance, at his direction, and are includible in his gross income in the taxable year in which so paid to the club. See the *Sproull* case, supra, and Lucas v. Guy C. Earl, 281 U.S. 111, 50 S.Ct. 241.

As previously stated, in each case involving a deferral of compensation, a determination of whether the doctrine of constructive receipt is applicable must be made upon the basis of the specific factual situation involved.

Consistent with the foregoing, the nonacquiescence published in C.B. 1952–2, 5, with respect to the decision in Commissioner v. James F. Oates, 18 T.C. 570, affirmed, 207 F.2d 711, has been withdrawn and acquiescence substituted therefor at page 5 of this Bulletin.

With respect to deductions for payments made by an employer under a deferred compensation plan, see section 404(a)(5) of the 1954 Code and section 1.404(a)–12 of the Income Tax Regulations.

In the application of those sections to unfunded plans, no deduction is allowable for any compensation paid or accrued by an employer on account of any employee under such a plan except in the year when paid and then only to the extent allowable under section 404(a). Thus, under an unfunded plan, if compensation is paid by an employer directly to a former employee, such amounts are deductible under section 404(a)(5) when *actually* paid *in cash or other property to the employee,* provided that such amounts meet the requirements of section 162 or section 212.

Advance rulings will not be issued in specific cases involving deferred compensation arrangements.*

NOTE

Circumstance (5) in the foregoing Revenue Ruling is similar to that in a controversy involving Sugar Ray Robinson. When the *Robinson* case was litigated, the Tax Court rejected the Commissioner's "joint venture" theory and held, further, that amounts not received within

---

* Despite the last sentence of Rev.Rul. 60–31, the Treasury later announced that it will entertain requests for rulings on deferred compensation arrangements. Rev.Rul. 64–279, 1964–2 C.B. 121. Ed.

the taxable year could not be treated as constructively received. Ray S. Robinson, 44 T.C. 20 (1965). The Commissioner has acquiesced in that decision. 1970–2 C.B. xxi. Moreover, the Commissioner has acknowledged that circumstance (5) in Rev.Rul. 60–31 does not reflect a joint venture and has proffered a modified circumstance (5) which does. Rev.Rul. 70–435, 1970–2 C.B. 100.

3.   STATUTORY DO–IT–YOURSELF AVERAGING

Averaging efforts described in Rev.Rul. 60–31 do not involve any statutory dispensation; instead, they merely show how a taxpayer may order his affairs so that the actual receipt of income that might be bunched in one year can be spread *forward* with attending averaging consequences under general statutory and tax common law principles. There are some additional averaging possibilities that involve both statutory dispensations and careful planning.[1] A detailed analysis of this category cannot reasonably be attempted in a course in fundamentals, but a general description of the area may be of interest.[2]

An employee who receives steady salary increases over his working career can arrange overall to pay less tax on his lifetime salary income if he makes an arrangement such as that described in circumstance (1) or circumstance (2) of Rev.Rul. 60–31. Under such an arrangement, some of his compensation is deferred to and taxed in his retirement years when his lower annual income, even after 1986, may attract lower tax rates. Can he *assure* such later payment, for example, by having his employer irrevocably pay the deferred amounts into an irrevocable trust for his employee's benefit, and still get the hoped-for tax deferral? Generally not if there is no substantial risk of forfeiture of the employee's interest.[3] Here, even without regard to questions of constructive receipt, the employee would be taxed on contributions to the trust as they were made.

Qualified Plans. BUT (and it is a *big but*) just such arrangements can be made, which combine assured payment with the desired tax deferral, if they are made in connection with a "qualified" pension plan that meets the requirements of Section 401(a). Contributions to a qualified plan may be made in an amount designed to achieve defined benefits. Other qualified plan contributions are geared directly to the employee's salary or in amounts varying with the profits of the business (a profit-sharing plan), and they may be made in cash or in

---

1. Actually a kind of averaging results from the application of a number of Code provisions; e.g., the annuity rules of I.R.C. § 72 (see Chapter 5, supra.), the installment sales provisions of I.R.C. § 453 (see Chapter 24A, infra.), and even from the application of some tax common law principles, e.g., Burnet v. Logan, 283 U.S. 404, 51 S.Ct. 550 (1931) (see Chapter 24B, infra.).

2. For a detailed discussion, see Boren, Qualified Deferred Compensation Plans, Callaghan and Company (1983).

3. I.R.C. § 402(b). See also I.R.C. § 83.

securities of the employer.[4] A glance at Section 401(a) will give at least a hint of the detailed criteria for qualification of a plan.

One key requirement is that the plan not discriminate in favor of "highly compensated employees."[5] A highly compensated employee is any employee who during the current or preceding year (1) was at any time a five percent owner, (2) received compensation in excess of $75,000 (to be indexed), (3) received compensation in excess of $50,000 (to be indexed) and whose compensation is in the upper 20 percent of all employees or (4) was an officer and received compensation in excess of $45,000 (to be indexed).[6]

From the point of view of the employee, two distinct tax advantages flow from participation in a qualified pension or profit-sharing plan:

1. The employee is not taxed on contributions for his benefit until amounts are distributed to him.[7] Thus, he pays tax later on this deferred compensation and, very likely, at lower rates because distributions are received over his retirement years.[8]

2. The trust to which contributions are made is exempt from tax.[9] Thus gains and losses and income earned by "pre taxed" (untaxed) compensation grow while held in the trust without the usual tax attrition.

Compare the tax consequences to the employee of compensation paid directly to him and placed by him in a savings account or in a private trust of his own creation using "after-tax" dollars.

Notwithstanding deferral of the tax to the employee for contributions to a qualified plan, the employer can deduct the contributions when paid.[10] But the statute virtually forecloses an immediate deduction for employer contributions to a funded pension plan which does not qualify under Section 401 and in which the employee's rights are

---

4. A plan may be set up which gives employees the option of receiving salary in cash or having it contributed to an employee trust. Under such a plan, known as a § 401(k) plan, amounts contributed to the trust and earnings and gains on such amounts are not taxed to the employee until withdrawn from the trust. The Tax Reform Act of 1986 limited § 401(k) salary deferrals to $7,000 per year. I.R.C. §§ 401(k), 402(a)(8) and 402(g). See Chip, "How the New Law Affects Saving for Retirement," 66 J.Tax'n 30 (1987), for a discussion of the effect of the 1986 Act on § 401(k) plans and other qualified deferred compensation arrangements.

5. I.R.C. § 401(a)(4). A plan will not be qualified if it discriminates in favor of highly compensated individuals.

6. I.R.C. §§ 414(q) and 415(b)(1)(A). An employee meeting the second through fourth criteria during the current year will

not be treated as a highly compensated employee unless he is also among the 100 employees who have received the highest compensation during such year. I.R.C. § 414(q)(2). Indexing of the $75,000, $50,000 and $45,000 amounts occurs pursuant to § 415(d).

7. I.R.C. § 402(a).

8. This is especially true for taxpayers who escaped the 50% bracket with respect to pre-1988 contributions who later receive distributions at a top 28% or 31% rate after 1990 (or maybe at a rate of only 15%). Post-1987 contributions are not subject to as great potential rate benefits. See the text at note 33, infra.

9. I.R.C. § 501(a) and (c)(17).

10. I.R.C. § 404(a). In addition to meeting the requirements of § 404(a), the contributions must also pass the ordinary and necessary tests of § 162 or § 212.

forfeitable. This might be an attractive way to reward specific employees outside the proscription against a discriminatory plan mentioned above. It would appear that the employee would get the benefit of deferral,[11] and it might seem the employer could claim a deduction for his contributions. The deferral is allowed, but if a plan of this type fails to qualify, and the employee's rights are forfeitable, the employer is allowed a deduction only at the time the employee reports gross income.[12] But if a plan is qualified, its overall advantages may be summarized as affording the employee the obvious advantages of tax deferral and growth of his savings without customary tax attrition,[13] while the employer secures the usual immediate deduction for compensation paid.

H.R. 10 Plans. It will be observed that the foregoing comments all relate to taxpayers who enjoy *employee* status; what about *self-employed persons*? They may qualify for what are commonly called H.R. 10 plans which are similar to qualified plans except that as the self-employed person makes contributions to an H.R. 10 plan, he takes an income tax deduction (rather than being allowed a gross income exclusion as in the case of a qualified plan).[14] Both plans are, in effect, funded with "pre-tax" dollars. As in the case of qualified plans, earnings on those dollars are exempt from tax until distribution to the self-employed person.[15] The Tax Equity and Fiscal Responsibility Act of 1982 [16] eliminated earlier basic differences between employer-employee plans and H.R. 10 plans which had allowed more tax advantages to the former than the latter. Since 1982 both employees and self-employed taxpayers have been subject to the same contribution and

---

11. See I.R.C. § 402(b). Deferred compensation arrangements of this type may be accomplished by way of an employer's purchase of annuities for employees. I.R.C. § 403(a). And, under some additional limitations, annuities purchased by certain tax exempt organizations, including state educational institutions, are accorded similar deferral advantages even if not a part of a qualified pension plan. I.R.C. §§ 403(b) and 404(a)(2).

There is discussion of non-statutory deferred compensation arrangements in Lefevre, Knight, and Danico, Tax Management Portfolio No. 20 3rd (BNA 1969), entitled "Deferred Compensation Arrangements" which, while stressing arrangements not within the special Code provisions, contains suitable references and some comment on the special statutory rules.

12. I.R.C. § 404(a)(5).

13. To the extent that lump sum distributions are attributable to post-1973 employer contributions, the distributions are ordinary income, although they are subject to a one-time-only five year averaging provision if received by an individual who has attained age 59½. I.R.C. § 402(e). Lump sum distributions attributable to pre-1974 employer contributions are eligible under transitional rules for long term capital gain treatment with no averaging. However, this capital gain treatment is being phased out over a six year period beginning in 1987. The percentages of the pre-1974 employer contributions eligible for capital gain treatment were 100% in 1987, 95% in 1988, 75% in 1989, 50% in 1990, and are 25% in 1991. By 1992, capital gains treatment will be entirely phased out. Taxpayers attaining age 50 by January 1, 1986 are eligible for other transitional rule elections. Pub.Law No. 99–514, 99th Cong., 2d Sess. § 1122(h) (1986). The diminishing significance of capital gain treatment will be apparent after a consideration of Chapter 21, infra.

14. I.R.C. §§ 401(c)(1), 404(a). These are favored "above the line" deductions. See I.R.C. § 62(a)(6).

15. I.R.C. §§ 404(a), 501(a) and (c)(17) and 402(a).

16. Pub.Law No. 97–248 97th Cong., 2d Sess. § 235 et seq. (1982).

benefit limits [17] and corresponding deduction allowances.[18]   In addition the same vesting [19] and coverage requirements [20] are applicable to both types of plans.   A few minor disadvantages remain for self-employed pension plans.   The H.R. 10 rules provide for more stringent discrimination testing for individuals who own more than one unincorporated trade or business [21] and provide "prohibited transactions" penalties [22] for loans to an owner-employee.

Individual Retirement Accounts.   The Economic Recovery Tax Act of 1981 made it possible for employees and self-employed persons, whether or not they were covered by a deferred compensation plan by their employers or an H.R. 10 plan of their own, to make deductible payments to an individual retirement account (IRA).[23]   An IRA is a retirement fund established by an individual for himself alone or for himself and his nonworking spouse.   It is similar to an H.R. 10 plan in that it allows the taxpayer a deduction for contributions, freedom from tax attrition during growth, and taxation only as distributions are made from the account.[24]   In general, payments to an IRA account are deductible in amounts up to 100 percent of an employee's compensation [25] or up to a self-employed individual's "earned income" but in either case not in excess of $2,000 for the year.[26]   However, these maximum figures are really misleading.   The Tax Reform Act of 1986 generally eliminates an individual's deduction for IRA contributions if he (or his spouse, if married) is covered by a qualified plan (including an H.R. 10 plan) and he (or he and his spouse, if a joint return is filed) has substantial adjusted gross income.[27]

17.   See I.R.C. § 415.

18.   See I.R.C. § 404.

19.   See I.R.C. § 411.

20.   See I.R.C. § 410.

21.   I.R.C. § 401(d)(1) and (2).

22.   I.R.C. § 4975.

23.   Pub.Law No. 97–34, 97th Cong., 1st Sess. § 311 (1981). See Langstraat, "The Individual Retirement Account: Retirement Help for the Masses, or Another Tax Break for the Wealthy?" 60 St.John's L. Rev. 437 (1986).

24.   I.R.C. §§ 219(g), 408(e) and 408(d). The deductions are favored "above the line" deductions. See I.R.C. § 62(a)(7).

25.   Alimony received by a divorced spouse is considered "compensation" for purposes of the 100 percent of compensation limit.   I.R.C. § 219(f)(1).   This enabling provision, added by the Tax Reform Act of 1984, permits a divorced spouse receiving alimony to enjoy the benefits of establishing an individual retirement account.   Pub.Law No. 98–369, 98 Cong., 2nd Sess. § 529(a) (1984).   Without this provision, a divorced spouse whose only source of income is alimony would be precluded

from the § 219(a) deduction.   This is so because § 219(b)(1) limits the deduction to the lesser of $2,000 or the amount of compensation includible in the spouse's income.   Thus, if the divorced spouse had no income other than alimony and alimony was not considered compensation, the divorced spouse would not be entitled to a deduction.

26.   I.R.C. § 219(a), (b) and (f)(1).   In the case of a taxpayer with a nonworking spouse, or a spouse who elects to be treated for the year as having no compensation, who is also benefited by the I.R.A., the maximum amount is $2,250.   I.R.C. § 219(c).

27.   I.R.C. § 219(g).   An individual's IRA deduction limit is phased out if the individual (or his spouse, if married) is covered by a qualified plan and the individual (or married couple if a joint return is filed) has adjusted gross income in excess of the "applicable dollar amount."   The "applicable dollar amount" is $40,000 for a married couple filing a joint return, $25,000 for an unmarried individual filing a single return and zero for a married couple filing separate returns.   The IRA deduction limit is phased out by an amount

If a taxpayer's IRA deduction is partially or totally denied, the taxpayer may make a non-deductible IRA contribution in an amount which, when added to his allowable deduction, does not exceed the maximum deduction for a taxpayer in his category.[28] The taxability of amounts later withdrawn from an IRA during a year is dependent on the mixture of deductible and nondeductible IRA contributions. If an individual withdraws an amount from an IRA to which there have been mixed contributions, part of the withdrawal is nontaxable.[29]

Incentive Stock Options. A related deferred compensation device for corporate employees is the incentive stock option (ISO).[30] An ISO is an option granted by an employer corporation to an employee to purchase stock in the corporation at a fixed or determinable price, if certain requirements are met. No income is recognized by the employ-

that bears the same ratio to the IRA deduction limit as the taxpayer's adjusted gross income in excess of the applicable dollar limit (or, in the case of a married couple filing a joint return, the couples' adjusted gross income in excess of the applicable dollar limits) bears to $10,000. Thus, if an employee is covered by a qualified plan, the IRA deduction limit is zero for individuals with adjusted gross income above $35,000, married couples filing a joint return with adjusted gross income above $50,000 and married couples filing separately if a spouse has adjusted gross income above $10,000. I.R.C. § 219(g).

28. I.R.C. § 408(o).

29. I.R.C. § 408(d). The amount excludible from gross income for the year is that portion of the amount withdrawn which bears the same ratio to the total amount withdrawn for the year as the amount of the individual's aggregate nondeductible IRA contributions bears to the aggregate of all IRA contributions of the individual. Id.

IRA's are taxed in a manner similar to annuities. I.R.C. § 72. See Chapter 7, supra. For purposes of calculating the taxable portion of an IRA, there are several specific rules. First, all individual retirement plans are treated as one contract. Second, all distributions during any year are treated as one distribution. Third, the value of the contract (calculated after adding back distributions during the year), income on the contract, and investment in the contract are computed as of the close of the calendar year with or within which the taxable year ends. Fourth, the aggregate amount of withdrawals excludible from income for all years cannot exceed the taxpayer's investment in the contract for all years. I.R.C. § 408(d)(2).

The following example taken from the legislative history illustrates the calcula-

tion of taxable income from the IRA distribution:

* * * assume that (1) an individual makes a $2,000 IRA contribution for the individual's 1987 tax year, $1,500 of which is deductible, (2) no withdrawals are made from the IRA during the taxable year, (3) the account balance at the end of the taxable year is $2,200, and (4) no prior IRA contributions have been made. The individual is required to report all such information on the individual's 1987 tax return. For 1988, assume (1) the individual makes a $2,000 IRA contribution to another IRA account, none of which is deductible, (2) no withdrawals are made from the IRA during the taxable year, and (3) the aggregate account balance at the of the end of the taxable year for both IRAs is $4,600. In the individual's 1989 taxable year, no IRA contributions are made and $1,000 is withdrawn from the IRA to which the individual contributed during the 1987 taxable year. At the end of the 1989 taxable year, the aggregate account balance of both IRAs is $4,000. The $1,000 withdrawn from an IRA during the 1989 tax year is treated as partially a return of nondeductible contributions, calculated as the percentage of $1,000 that the total nondeductible contributions ($500 plus $2,000) is of the total account balance ($4,000) at the end of the taxable year plus distributions during the year ($1,000). Thus, 2,500/5,000 or 1/2 of the $1,000 withdrawal is treated as a return of nondeductible contributions (and, is not taxable). Cong.Rep. No. 99–841, 99th Cong., 2d Sess., II–379–380 (1986).

30. Qualified stock options, the predecessor to ISOs, were generally eliminated by the Tax Reform Act of 1976. Pub.Law No. 94–455, 94th Cong., 2d Sess. § 603 (1976), and see I.R.C. § 83.

ee when the ISO is granted or even when the option is exercised.[31] Income is recognized by an employee who exercises the option only upon his subsequent sale of the stock acquired with the option.[32]

Several recent events have reduced the attractiveness of qualified plans, H.R. 10 plans, individual retirement accounts and ISOs. First, recent tax legislation since 1986 has dramatically lowered and flattened tax rates.[33] The lower modified flat tax rates decrease the incentive to defer the tax on income. In addition, tax brackets are now so compressed that much income deferred to later years will likely be taxed at the same rate as that at which it would have been taxed if there had been no deferral. However, there are still advantages. A taxpayer always enjoys having the use of pre-tax dollars with the collector merely chasing along behind. And pre-tax dollars are bigger, can earn more than after-tax dollars.

There is one nasty aspect to the use of deferred compensation tax plans. Perhaps more than in any other tax area, there are rapid, numerous, and complex changes in the tax rules governing deferred compensation. Increasing complexity of the rules threatens their future utility.

D. THE CARRYOVER AND CARRYBACK DEVICES

Internal Revenue Code: See Section 172.

Let us assume that a novelty merchandiser stocks up on teenage mutant ninja turtles, roller blades, Trivial Pursuit games, pet rocks, skate boards, cabbage patch dolls, or clackers (or some other symbol of a fleeting fad) and makes a killing in 1990, say $100,000 profit. In 1991 he redoubles his purchases, but the popular fancy has turned to roller skates, and ninja turtles, roller blades, Trivial Pursuit, pet rocks and the skate board have taken their places in history along side the buggy whip and the whiffle-tree. So perhaps he has a huge loss in 1991; let's say $50,000. Now, it's all very well to say that he *did* have $100,000 properly taxed in 1990 and that, as he had *no* taxable income for 1991, he should be grateful to be relieved of the obligation to pay any tax for that year. But our merchandiser, despite the much-touted integrity of the taxable year, can't help but take a little longer view of his operations. For the *two* years he sees aggregate net profits of $50,000 but especially with a view to graduated tax rates, the tax paid for the two years seems unconscionable. Congress agrees with his view and, by way of an exception to standard taxable year principles, we have long

---

31. I.R.C. §§ 421 and 422. The amount by which the fair market value of a share of stock in the year in which it is appropriately subject to tax under I.R.C. § 83 exceeds the option price is included in the employee's taxable income under the alternative minimum tax. I.R.C. § 56(b)(3). See Chap. 27C, infra.

32. Id. Any gain recognized is capital gain, provided certain holding period requirements are met.

33. See Chapter 27A, infra.

had statutory provisions that permit operating losses in one year to be utilized in a redetermination of tax liability for another year.

The device by which the relief suggested is accomplished is a provision that permits an operating loss in one year to be carried *back* and treated as a business deduction in one or more of three preceding taxable years; or, to the extent that income in such years will not absorb the loss, it is carried *forward* and treated as a business deduction in one or more of fifteen succeeding taxable years.[1] The year to which the loss is carried is not elective; of the eighteen years involved (three back and fifteen forward), the loss must be utilized, to the extent that it can be, in the earliest year, except that the Tax Reform Act of 1976 provided for an elective relinquishment of the carryback period with respect to a net operating loss for any taxable year ending after 1975.[2]

What is the effect of a net operating loss that results in a carryback to a prior year. Generally speaking, it may result in a determination that the tax for the earlier year was overpaid and, if so, the happy consequence is a tax refund. There is a collateral consequence here which is not unintended. The operation of the net operating loss provision is not limited to the extreme situation suggested at the outset of this note. Many conventional businessmen suffer momentary setbacks. When an operating loss threatens continuation of the business, a refund of prior years' taxes may supply cash to meet payrolls and otherwise keep the business afloat until the storm is weathered. Refunds arising out of carrybacks are handled expeditiously, outside the procedures prescribed for regular claims for refund.[3]

A net operating loss that cannot be carried back (for lack of income in the preceding three years) or which a taxpayer elects not to carry back simply moves forward as a deduction in the succeeding years. It is a momentary disaster but nearly money in the bank, because it represents an amount of otherwise taxable income that can be earned in effect tax free in later periods. Of course the potential advantage never reaches fruition unless the taxpayer in fact has commensurate earnings for later periods.

The foregoing comments present the net operating loss in broad outline, and no attempt is made here to deal with the many complexities of the provision. Nevertheless, it may be noted that a principal problem in working with Section 172 is the computation of the net operating loss for the year. Generally speaking, there is such a loss when deductions exceed gross income.[4] However, the statute contains

---

1. I.R.C. § 172(a) and (b)(1)(A). There are some exceptions to the three year carryback, fifteen year carryover rule found in § 172(b)(1)(B) through (E). See Asimow, "Detriment and Benefit of Net Operating Losses: A Unifying Theory," 24 Tax L.Rev. 1 (1968).

2. I.R.C. § 172(b)(2) and (b)(3).

3. See I.R.C. § 6411; and see Chapter 29, infra. See also § 6511(d)(2)(A) providing a special refund limitations period. Of course the government pays no interest on amounts refunded because of a net operating loss carryback. I.R.C. § 6611(f)(1).

4. I.R.C. § 172(c).

some refinements and, as the title of the section suggests, the objective is to identify the loss that is traceable to *business* operations. Thus, in the case of an individual the net operating loss for a year is essentially the excess of his trade or business deductions over gross income, including non-business income reduced by certain non-business deductions.[5]

It will be apparent that a net operating loss carryback may affect the computation of adjusted gross income for the year to which the loss is carried. And it will be recalled that some deductions are measured in part by adjusted gross income for the year. Whether a recomputation of the deductions so affected for purposes of measuring a refund or determining the net operating loss carryover to subsequent years[6] is required for the year to which the loss is carried depends upon the detailed provisions of the statute. The percentage limitation governing the medical expense deduction under Section 213, for example, must be recomputed[7] but generally not the limitation on the charitable deduction.[8] The principal reason why the charitable deduction limitation for a year is not permitted to be affected by an operating loss carried back to such year is to assure the taxpayer of the expected deduction for charitable contributions without regard to subsequent events.

Overall, Section 172 can properly be regarded as something of an income averaging device. While it does nothing to level off income when all the years are profitable years, it does at least permit a loss year to have a leveling effect on profit years within the nineteen year span.

Section 172 is by no means the only Code provision that makes use of the carryover concept as a kind of departure from strict annual accounting. We have previously seen the use of carryovers in Chapter 17 in conjunction with the at risk rules, the Section 280A(c)(5) rule, and the passive activity rules. It will also be seen for example in Chapter 21 that, when limitations on the deductibility of capital losses preclude the full tax use of such a loss in one year, the unused portion may be utilized in later years. And in Chapter 23 it will become apparent that a similar opportunity is sometimes afforded for a later deduction for charitable contributions that exceed the statutory ceiling on the deduction for the year in which the contribution is made.

---

5. The details are specified in I.R.C. § 172(d) where it will be seen, among other things, that neither the personal exemption under § 151 nor noncorporate capital losses in excess of capital gains enter into the computation. I.R.C. § 172(d)(3), (d)(2), respectively. A corporation's normal deductions are modified under § 172(d)(5) in measuring its net operating loss.

6. See also I.R.C. § 172(b)(2)(A).

7. Reg. § 1.172–5(a)(2)(ii). There is no special rule in § 213.

8. Ibid; and see I.R.C. § 170(b)(1)(F). An individual's charitable deduction carryover under § 170(d)(1) may be affected by the net operating loss deduction. See Reg. §§ 1.170A–8(e); 1.172–5(a)(2)(ii).

PART SIX: THE CHARACTERIZATION OF INCOME AND DEDUCTIONS

CHAPTER 21. CAPITAL GAINS AND LOSSES

A. INTRODUCTION

It must now be recognized that a mere quantitative approach to items of income and deduction is insufficient for federal income tax purposes; the quality of such items must also be considered. The thought is not entirely new at this point, for we have already recognized that some income which could be taxed escapes tax if it has a tax-exempt quality, such as interest on state or municipal bonds. We have also seen that some potential deductions are flatly disallowed. Here, however, we are concerned with items of income that are taxed but which, according to their character, are taxed under special rules, and with items of deduction which, while not flatly disallowed, are subject to important statutory limitations. In general it is "capital gain" that may qualify for special tax treatment and "capital loss" that may encounter special, restrictive, rules as to deduction. Thus, we must look at items qualitatively as well as quantitatively, a process referred to as the "characterization" of income and deduction items.

Whether a gain or loss is subject to special treatment, as "capital" as opposed to "ordinary", usually is dependent upon (1) whether it arises in a transaction involving a "capital asset," (2) whether the capital asset has been the subject of a "sale or exchange," and (3) how long the taxpayer has "held" the asset. In addition the student should be alert for statutory provisions that may artificially accord capital gain or loss treatment to some transactions which do not actually involve the sale or exchange of a capital asset.[1]

Parts D, E, and F of this Chapter deal with the basic problems of characterization of items of income and deduction. Parts B and C explore the statutory mechanics for the treatment of capital gains and losses. Before plunging into detail, brief consideration is given here to the history and general philosophy of the tax treatment accorded transactions in capital assets.

Capital Gains. It has always been clear that a merchant's sale of his stock in trade gives rise to gain or loss to be taken into account for tax purposes. However, when the first income tax was imposed follow-

1. Take a preliminary look at I.R.C. §§ 166(d)(1)(B) and 165(g)(1). See also the note at page 679, infra.

657

ing the adoption of the Sixteenth Amendment,[2] it contained no specific reference to gains or losses from dealing in property. What then of a sale of plant or equipment? of land held for investment? of securities? and so forth. Taxpayers were prompted to argue that gain on the sale of such properties was not income within the meaning of the Sixteenth Amendment or the federal taxing statute. In part the thought was that if one sold, say, securities and merely reinvested the proceeds in other securities (or even put the money in the bank), his financial position was unaltered; he had merely substituted the new securities (or the cash) for the securities previously owned and his investment continued. The notion was bolstered by the further thought that if there was gain of some sort in such transactions it might be largely illusory anyway, often traceable to mere changes in the price structure. These concepts gained substantial acceptance under the British Income Tax and, strangely, substantial vestiges persisted until 1965 when capital gains were first formally subjected to tax in England.[3]

Under the modern federal income tax the proposition that capital gains should not be taxed was never accepted.[4] In Merchants' Loan & Trust Co. v. Smietanka,[5] the Supreme Court held that capital gains were income within the meaning of that term in the Sixteenth Amendment. Relying in part on cases under the Corporate Excise Tax Act of 1909, the Court, quoting its opinion in Eisner v. Macomber,[6] said: [7]

> Income may be defined as the gain derived from capital, from labor, or from both combined, *provided it be understood to include profit gained through a sale or conversion of capital assets.*

While *Merchants' Loan* was the end of the constitutional issue *whether* capital gains were subject to tax, it marked only the beginning of congressional consideration of *how* such gains should be taxed.[8] In 1921, Congress enacted the first provisions giving preferential treatment to capital gains by way of a tax rate on such gains below those applicable to other types of income.[9] Reporting the bill, the Ways and Means Committee said: [10]

> The sale of * * * capital assets is now seriously retarded by the fact that gains and profits earned over a series of years are under the present law taxed as a lump sum (and the amount of surtax greatly enhanced thereby) in the year in which the

2. Revenue Act of 1916, 39 Stat. 756 (1916).

3. See Magill, Taxable Income, 82–103 (1945) and Finance Act 1965, Part III.

4. Cf. Gray v. Darlington, 15 Wallace Rep. 63 (1872), where the proposition that capital gains should not be taxed was accepted under the Civil War Income Tax Act, 14 Stat. 477–8 (1867).

5. 255 U.S. 509, 41 S.Ct. 386 (1921).

6. 252 U.S. 189, 207, 40 S.Ct. 189, 193 (1920).

7. 255 U.S. 509, 518, 41 S.Ct. 386, 388 (1921), emphasis added.

8. See, generally, Magill, Taxable Income, 103–113 (1945).

9. Revenue Act of 1921, § 106(a)(6), 42 Stat. 227, 232 (1921).

10. House Rep. No. 350, 67th Cong., 1st Sess., pp. 10–11, (1921) as quoted in Seidman, Legislative History of the Income Tax Laws, 1938–1861, 813 (1938).

profit is realized. Many such sales, with their possible profit taking and consequent increase of the tax revenue, have been blocked by this feature of the present law. In order to permit such transactions to go forward without fear of a prohibitive tax, the proposed bill * * * adds a new section * * * [placing a preferential rate on gains from the sale or dispositions of capital assets].

While it may be argued that capital gain is no different in kind from other income and is, perhaps, just as spendable, three factors have now been identified that seem to give it a different quality. That is, a disposition of a capital asset may involve only a continuation of an investment in a different form; gain said to be realized may merely or largely reflect only changes in the overall price structure; and the gain may have been some time in the making, raising the question whether it is fair to bunch it into a single taxable year with possible attending tax attrition through progressive rate tables. Although no one of these factors, nor indeed all three in combination, has ever prompted Congress wholly to *relieve* capital gains from tax, all have played a part in the congressional deliberations on *how* to tax gains on the disposition of property. And the factors have been considered relevant, not only in matters such as those in this Chapter which deals directly with capital gains and losses, but in other areas as well. Consider, for example, but not in detail at this point, the reasons for special provision for the taxation of installment sales (Section 453) and of gain on the disposition of property used in a trade or business (Section 1231), and for the nonrecognition of gain on certain exchanges (Section 1031) and involuntary conversions (Section 1033).

Over the years, Congress has seen fit on numerous occasions to vary the preferential treatment accorded capital gains. As originally enacted, the 1921 legislation imposed a maximum 12½ percent tax rate on gain from the disposition of capital assets held for more than two years. As the above committee report indicates, the principal policy reason prompting such preferential treatment was a recognition of the long period over which such gain accrued. This policy was more strongly reflected in the 1934 Revenue Act,[11] in which Congress favored capital gains by providing that sometimes less than the entire gain had to be included in income; the longer the property had been held, the smaller percentage of the gain includable. Under the provisions of that Act, no preference was accorded gain on the disposition of capital assets held for only one year or less but, thereafter, the amount of capital gain subject to inclusion in income was reduced on a sliding scale which went as low as 30 percent if the property was held for more than 10 years. The Revenue Act of 1938,[12] shortened the holding periods. In 1942 Congress abolished the sliding scale inclusion approach in favor of a flat preferential ceiling rate on gain from the disposition of capital

---

11. Revenue Act of 1934, § 117(a), 48 Stat. 680, 714 (1934).

12. Revenue Act of 1938, § 117(b), 52 Stat. 447, 500 (1938).

assets held for more than six months.[13] Although often challenged, the six months holding period remained in effect through 1976. It was increased to nine months for 1977 and to one year [14] from 1978 through June 22, 1984, when it reverted to the six months period to again be extended to one year in 1988.[15] Other parts of this chapter give substantial attention to the identification of "long-term" and "short-term" capital gains and losses and to the interrelationship of such gains and losses.

Changes in the treatment of capital gains have occurred, not only with regard to the holding period requirement, but also in the definition of capital assets and the maximum rates at which such gains may be taxed. These changes largely reflect shifts in congressional preoccupation with one or more of the factors that seem to set capital gains apart from other forms of income.[16]

The Tax Reform Acts of 1969 and 1976 reduced some of the advantages previously accorded capital gain transactions and raised the question whether further reductions would follow. Early in 1977, one could have speculated that preferential treatment for capital gains would be further reduced, because people speaking for the Carter administration were encouraging an elimination of all preferential treatment for capital gains. However, Congress turned the other way in 1978. Possibly because of increasing inflation, because of a taxpayer revolt against increasing taxes which began with California's passage of Proposition Thirteen, or for other reasons, Congress, in the Revenue Act of 1978, reversed the trend and generally lightened the tax burden on capital gains.[17] A further lightening of that burden occurred indirectly under the Economic Recovery Tax of 1981 when Congress reduced the maximum tax rate on capital gains.[18]

The Tax Reform Act of 1986 did an about-face and essentially eliminated the preferential treatment of capital gains for the first time since 1921. Just prior to the enactment of the Tax Reform Act of 1986, as a result of a 60 percent deduction for such gains, the ceiling rate of

---

13. Revenue Act of 1942, § 150(a), 56 Stat. 798, 843 (1942). Off and on these are indications that Congress may once again opt for a sliding scale.

14. See TRA (1976) § 1402. For a criticism of this aspect of capital gains see Lowndes, "The Taxation of Capital Gains and Losses Under the Federal Income Tax," 26 Texas L.Rev. 440, 442 (1948).

15. P.L. No. 98–369, § 1001(a), 98th Cong., 2d Sess. (1984).

16. The policy arguments both for and against preferential treatment for capital gains, which have been advanced over the years, including some not stated here, are collected in Blum, "A Handy Summary of the Capital Gain Arguments," 35 Taxes 247 (1957) and see Kutsoris, "In Defense of Capital Gains," 42 Fordham L.R. 1 (1973).

17. See I.R.C. § 1202. See also Surrey, "Reflections on the Revenue Act of 1978 and Future Tax Policy," 13 Geo.L.Rev. 687 at 693 (1979) for suggestions of other reasons for the reduction.

The Revenue Act of 1978 also simplified the mechanics of capital gains computations for noncorporate taxpayers by repealing the I.R.C. (1954) § 1202(b) alternative tax for individuals and other noncorporate taxpayers, the legislative history making reference to the strongest policy argument that would favor elimination of all preferential capital gains treatment, i.e., simplification of the federal taxing structure. Revenue Act of 1978, §§ 401(a) and (c) (1978).

18. Economic Recovery Tax Act of 1981, § 101(a) (1981).

tax applicable to capital gains was 20 percent,[19] the top rate on ordinary income being 50 percent.[20] The 1986 law reduced the ceiling rate on ordinary income to 28 percent and, by eliminating the special 60 percent deduction for capital gains,[21] it imposed the same 28 percent ceiling rate on capital gains as that imposed on ordinary income. Thus the 1986 Act abolished preferential treatment for capital gains as well as the rate disparity between ordinary income and capital gain; but in doing so, it did not outright abandon the familiar characterization of items of income as "ordinary income" or "capital gain".[22]

Some light is shed on this seeming paradox by the legislative history, which stated: [23]

> The committee believes that as a result of the bill's reduction of individual tax rates on such forms of capital income as business profits, interest, dividends, and short-term capital gains, the need to provide a reduced rate for net capital gain is eliminated. This will result in a tremendous amount of simplification for many taxpayers since their tax will no longer depend upon the characterization of income as ordinary or capital gain. In addition, this will eliminate any requirement that capital assets be held by the taxpayer for any extended period of time (currently 6 months) in order to obtain favorable treatment. This will result in greater willingness to invest in assets that are freely traded (e.g., stocks).

> The committee believes that the top rate on individual capital gains should not exceed the rates set forth in the bill, and therefore the bill provides that the maximum tax rate on capital gains will not exceed the top individual rate that the bill presently provides even if the top individual rate is increased during subsequent consideration of the bill.

The debate over taxation of capital gains was at the heart of the controversy in the 1990 budget deficit legislation. You didn't need to read his lips to know that President Bush wanted substantial reductions in the tax rate on capital gains. But the opposition to a reduction did not budge, and when Congress enacted an essentially 31 percent maximum tax rate on ordinary income,[24] they kept their 1986 word with respect to capital gains by imposing a 28 percent ceiling on such gains.[25]

19. An individual could deduct from gross income 60% of net capital gain (the excess of net long-term capital gain over any net short-term capital loss). I.R.C. (1954) § 1202. Since the maximum regular individual tax rate was 50%, the deduction meant that net capital gain was taxed at a maximum rate of 20% (i.e., 40% × 50%).

20. I.R.C. § 1.

21. The 1986 Act repealed I.R.C. (1954) § 1202. Pub.Law No. 99–514, 99th Cong., 2d Sess. § 301 (1986).

22. See Conf.Rep. No. 99–841, 99th Cong., 2d Sess. II–105 (1986).

23. Sen.Rep. No. 99–313, 99th Cong., 2d Sess. 169 (1986).

24. See I.R.C. § 1(a)–(e) and page 970, infra.

25. I.R.C. § 1(h). This subsection essentially parrots § 1(j) of the 1986 legislation. It is discussed in more detail at page 665, infra.

Capital Losses. The first limitation upon the deductibility of *capital losses* appeared in the Revenue Act of 1924.[26] The Ways and Means Committee, in suggesting a limitation on the rate and amount of deductions for capital losses, stated: [27]

> [Certain] considerations led Congress, in the revenue act of 1921, to provide that the tax on capital gains in the case of property acquired and held by the taxpayer for profit or investment for more than two years should be limited to 12½ per cent. But Congress failed to place a similar limitation on capital losses, so that to-day the taxpayer pays a maximum tax of 12½ per cent on gains derived from the sale of capital assets, but is allowed to deduct in full from his taxable income his net losses resulting from the sale of capital assets during the taxable year. The injustice to the Government is too obvious to require much comment. The taxpayer may refrain from taking his profits, or, if he does take them, pays but a 12½ per cent tax, whereas he is at liberty at any time to take advantage of any losses that may have been incurred and avail himself of a full deduction from his income. When we consider that the rate on the larger incomes runs as high as 58 per cent, it can readily be realized how great the advantage is. The Government can collect but 12½ per cent of a gain, but it is compelled to lighten the burden of the taxpayer to the extent of 58 per cent of his losses. Take, for example, the case of a man with an income of $350,000 a year. Assume that he bought in the year 1917 5,000 shares of stock X at par, and that he sells these shares in 1922 for $600,000, showing a profit of $100,000. By reason of this transaction he would pay, in addition to the tax on his regular income, $12,500 to the Government. But assume that instead of selling this stock at a profit, he sold it in 1922 at a loss of $100,000. He would then be entitled to deduct the $100,000 from his income of $350,000, and the loss to the Government by reason of that deduction would be $58,000. Is there any further argument needed?

The Revenue Act of 1924 and successive acts through 1932 provided a limitation on the deductibility of capital losses. The device first adopted was to foreclose any deduction from ordinary income for capital losses but to permit the tax, otherwise computed, to be reduced by an amount up to 12½ percent of qualified losses.[28] This produced a result more consonant with the maximum 12½ percent rate of tax on capital gains. Although changes have occurred, restrictions upon the deductibility of capital losses have continued to the present.[29]

26. Revenue Act of 1924, § 208(c), 43 Stat. 253, 262 (1924).

27. House Rep. No. 1388, 67th Cong., 4th Sess. (1923), as quoted in Seidman, Legislative History of the Income Tax Laws, 1938–1861, 721 (1938).

28. Revenue Act of 1924, supra, at § 208(c).

29. I.R.C. §§ 1211, 1212. An informative brief history of both the capital loss restrictions and the capital gains preferences appears in 3B Mertens, The Law of

The Revenue Reconciliation Act of 1990 continues restrictions on the deductibility of capital losses.[30] One may question why, if no preferential treatment is provided for capital gain, there should be any limitation on capital losses. The legislative history provides no answer, but timing is the essential point. Without such a limitation, taxpayers would be able without limit to use capital losses to wipe out ordinary income from other sources, creating a new type of tax shelter. Thus, taxpayers with the usual varied results in their investment portfolios could use capital losses to shelter ordinary income and hold capital gains for a step-up in basis at death.[31] Seemingly to avoid such a result, Congress retained the capital loss limitations which operate in a manner similar to the Section 469 passive activity loss limitations.[32]

The limitations upon the deductibility of capital losses work as an inducement to attempt to characterize gains as capital gains, even in the absence of preferential rate treatment for such gains. They can be absorbed dollar for dollar by capital losses. The more of the taxpayer's income that is characterized as capital gain, the greater the amount of capital loss the taxpayer can deduct in the current year.[33] There remains some, albeit limited, benefit in characterizing a gain as capital gain.

The retained dichotomy of ordinary income and capital gain with minimal preferential treatment for capital gains has one major disadvantage. It thwarts another congressional objective, *tax simplification*.[34] As you work your way through the remaining chapters of this book, consider how much simpler our tax laws would be if Congress had totally eliminated capital gain and loss characterization. Similar simplification would occur in other tax areas not within the scope of this book, such as the taxation of corporations and partnerships.[35] You may even want to consider how much simpler this course would be without the retained dichotomy.[36]

B. THE MECHANICS OF CAPITAL GAINS

Internal Revenue Code: Sections 1(a)–(e) and (h); 1222. See Sections 1201(a); 1221.

Federal Income Taxation, §§ 22.02–22.03 (1966 Rev.).

30. Id.

31. I.R.C. § 1014. Cf. I.R.C. §§ 1031, 1033 and 1034 and Chapter 26, infra.

32. See Chapter 17D, supra.

33. I.R.C. § 1211(b).

34. See Eisenstein, The Ideologies of Taxation 92–105 (1961).

35. See, e.g., I.R.C. §§ 304 and 751(b).

36. A philosophical consideration of the questions whether, when, and how capital gains should be taxed will be aided by a study of the following works: Surrey, "Definitional Problems in Capital Gains Taxation," 69 Harv.L.Rev. 985 (1956); Smith, Federal Tax Reform 151–155 (1961); Goode, The Individual Income Tax 199–207 (1964), all reprinted (the Surrey article with modifications) in Sander and Westfall, Readings in Federal Taxation (Foundation Press 1970) at pages 552–572, 537–541, and 529–537, respectively; Johnson, "Seventeen Culls From Capital Gains," 48 Tax Notes 1285 (1990).

Noncorporate taxpayers. After 1990, the Internal Revenue Code provides special, but only slightly preferential, tax treatment for "net capital gain" as defined by Section 1222(11). The pre-1987 preferential treatment fixed a ceiling tax rate of only 20 percent for net capital gain.[1] The current statute retains the characterization provisions of the prior law and even the same basic code structure, but it substantially removes preferential rate treatment. In general, the rates of tax applicable to net capital gain are the same as those applied to ordinary taxable income, although capital gain is subject to a 28 percent ceiling while ordinary income is subject to a 31 percent ceiling.[2] Thus for some, albeit limited, taxpayers there is a 3 percent rate differential.

There is a special statutory structure applicable to capital gain income, and it requires some deciphering in order to understand the mechanics of both capital gains (considered in this part) and capital losses (considered in the next part). Section 1222 provides a statutory netting mechanism. Sections 1222(1) through 1222(4) define short-term capital gain, short-term capital loss, long-term capital gain, and long-term capital loss, respectively.[3] Sections 1222(5) through 1222(8) then in essence provide for the netting of short-term losses against short-term gains and long-term losses against long-term gains in the following manner:

Short-term capital gain (§ 1222(1))	Long-term capital gain (§ 1222(3))
—Short-term capital loss (§ 1222(2))	—Long-term capital loss (§ 1222(4))
Net short-term capital gain or loss (§ 1222(5) and (6))	Net long-term capital gain or loss (§ 1222(7) and (8))

Next, the net shorts are netted against the net longs. If net gains exceed net losses in this final netting, we apply the rules discussed in this part. If net losses exceed net gains, we apply the rules discussed in the next part of this Chapter. In the final netting process, net gains can arise in three situations: (1) a net short-term gain in excess of a net long-term loss; (2) a net long-term gain in excess of a net short-term loss (the excess net long-term gain in this situation is classified by Section 1222(11) as *net capital gain*); and (3) a combination of a net short-term gain and a net long-term gain (with the net long-term gain again classified as net capital gain).

The Treasury takes some liberty with a literal reading of the statute in filtering the results of the above final netting process into

1. I.R.C. § 1202 (now repealed) provided a 60% deduction of net capital gain (the excess of net long-term capital gain over net short-term capital loss) from gross income. Since the maximum regular income tax was 50% the deduction meant the net capital gain was taxed at a maximum rate of 20% (i.e., 40% × 50%).

2. I.R.C. § 1(a)–(e), (h). See note 7, infra. From 1987 through 1990, there was no special preferential treatment for capital gains.

3. Note that each of the definitional subsections contained in I.R.C. § 1222 requires the presence of three factors in order for the gain or loss to be "capital" in nature: (1) a sale or exchange; (2) a capital asset; and (3) a holding for a specified period of time. Each of these three factors is examined later in this Chapter.

gross income on the income tax return (Schedule D of Form 1040).[4] If a taxpayer falls into one of the three types of final net gain situations above, only the amount of the net gain is included in gross income.[5]

An example is helpful in demonstrating this netting process. Assume that in 1991, T, a single individual taxpayer has a long-term capital gain (Section 1222(3)) of $30,000, a long-term capital loss (Section 1222(4)) of $10,000, and a short-term capital loss (Section 1222(2)) of $5,000. Assume T has other income, salary for example, of $50,000. Technically T's gross income is $80,000 computed as follows:

Salary	$50,000
Long-term capital gain	30,000
Gross income	$80,000

However, on his income tax return T will net his capital gains and losses on Schedule D and, as a result, we say that T has gross income of $65,000 computed as follows:

Salary			$50,000
Long-term capital gain	$ 30,000		
Long-term capital loss	−10,000		
Net long-term capital gain		$20,000	
Short-term capital gain	$ 0		
Short-term capital loss	−5,000		
Net short-term capital loss		$ 5,000	
Net capital gain			$15,000
Gross income (after capital loss)			$65,000

Prior to 1988 the netting process and the separation of long-term and short-term gains were crucial to the computation of tax liability. At that time preferential treatment was accorded the Section 1222(11) net capital gain which arose in the second and third of the three gain situations above, whereas no preferential treatment was accorded net short-term gains. Prior to 1987, the preference took the form of a deduction of 60 percent of the amount of net capital gain.[6] That deduction was repealed by the 1986 Act thereby treating net capital gain just like ordinary income with a qualification originally in Section 1(j), and now in Section 1(h), that if the rate of tax on ordinary income is increased beyond 28 percent, a 28 percent ceiling would be imposed

---

4. See Reg. § 1.162–17(b) taking similar statutory liberty in another context. See problem 3 at page 349, supra. If there is an overall net capital loss, then no capital gains are included in gross income.

5. The procedure used on the income tax return and in practice varies from the strict statutory formula which would require inclusion of all gains in gross income and deduction of losses. Although generally the variant procedure generates the same amount of adjusted gross income (See

§ 62(a)(3)), it is sometimes necessary to establish "the gross income stated in the return". E.g., I.R.C. § 6501(c), sometimes extending limitation periods where gross income is substantially omitted. In such circumstances the statutory formula is applied rather than the shortcut generally permitted on the return. See also Reg. § 1.162–17(b).

6. See now-repealed I.R.C. §§ 1202 and 62(3).

on net capital gain.[7] With the 1991 rate increase to 31 percent on ordinary income, Section 1(h) applies to a taxpayer in the 31 percent rate bracket who also has a net capital gain.

When Section 1(h) comes into play, net capital gains are generally treated as though they were the last taxable income received (i.e., the top incremented amounts of taxable income), and they are taxed just like ordinary income and net short-term capital gains (i.e., they may be taxed at the 15 percent rate); [8] however, they cannot be taxed at a rate greater than 28 percent. Thus, to the extent that they would be taxed at a 31 percent rate under the regular tax schedule, they are extracted from taxable income and subjected to a 28 percent rate ceiling.[9]

Tracking Section 1(h) as drafted by our legislative trapeze artists is more difficult than stating the rule of thumb above. To illustrate the application of the Section, return to the previous example involving T, a taxpayer with $50,000 of ordinary income and $15,000 of net capital gain and assume further that T is a single individual whose regular tax is computed under Section 1(c). Disregard all other deductions to which T might be entitled (e.g. the Section 63 standard deduction and the Section 151 exemption) so that T's taxable income is $65,000 and assume that there is no cost of living adjustment to the Section 1(c) rates under Section 1(f). T's tax is computed as follows:

Applying Section 1(h), we meet the "if" clause. Taxpayer T has net capital gain of $15,000. T also has ordinary income (salary) of $50,000. T's tax liability cannot exceed *the sum of:*

(A) a tax (without regard to Subsection (h)) on the greater of:
(i) $50,000: taxable income ($65,000) reduced by net capital gain ($15,000).

or

(ii) $19,450: taxable income, taxed (under Section 1(c)) at a rate below 28%.
The Section 1(c) tax on the ($50,000) greater amount is:

Plus $11,560.00 [10]

(B) a tax at a rate of 28% on the amount of taxable income ($65,000) in excess of the amount for which tax was determined in (A), above ($50,000). Thus 28% of $15,000 is: $ 4,200.00 [11]

Equals a total tax of: $15,760.00 [12]

Note that the initial tax computation is made to turn on the *greater* of (A) a partial tax on all taxable income other than net capital gain *or* (B) a tax on the amount of all taxable income taxed at a rate below 28

---

7. See page 661, supra.

8. I.R.C. § 1(h)(1)(B).

9. I.R.C. § 1(h)(2).

10. I.R.C. § 1(h)(1). Under § 1(c), this figure is $10,645.50 plus $914.50 (31% of $2950).

11. I.R.C. § 1(h)(2).

12. I.R.C. § 1(h).

percent.[13]   Under the statute the only situation in which the (B) alternative would be applicable is where all taxable income other than net capital gain is less than the bracketed ceiling for the applicable 15 percent rate.[14]   In that situation some, perhaps all, of the net capital gain would be taxed at a 15 percent rate.   For example, if in the above illustration T had $10,000 of salary and $15,000 of net capital gain, the salary and $9,450 of net capital gain would be taxed at the 15 percent rate with the remaining $5,550 of net capital gain taxed at the 28 percent rate.[15]

Net short-term capital gains, although identifiable in the Section 1222 grinder, were not accorded preferential rate treatment in the 1954 Code and they are not subject to the special ceiling rate provision of Section 1(h) of the 1986 Code.   Except for their usefulness in offsetting capital losses, net short-term capital gains are treated as any other ordinary income.

Corporations.   Corporations compute and net their capital gains just like noncorporate taxpayers.   In addition, no preferential tax treatment is provided for corporate net capital gains.   The 1986 Code reduced maximum corporate tax rates on ordinary income from 46 percent to 34 percent [16] with corporate capital gains being subject to the same maximum 34 percent tax rate.

Section 1(h), which provides the method of taxing capital gains of individuals and other noncorporate taxpayers, is not applicable to corporations; however, it has a corporate counterpart.   Section 1201(a), which is a fail-safe measure somewhat akin to Section 1(h), was erected as a hedge against anticipated increases in rates on regular corporate taxable income.[17]   Section 1201(a) imposes an alternative flat rate of tax at 34 percent on the net capital gain of corporations, but it applies *only* if the regular corporate tax rate is increased beyond the current 34 percent ceiling.

13.   The rate below 28% for years after 1987 is 15%.   See I.R.C. § 1(a)–(e).

14.   The 15% rate applies up to different ceiling amounts, of taxable income for different classifications of taxpayers.   The 15% rate runs up to $32,450 for married persons filing jointly and surviving spouses, $26,050 for heads of households, $19,450 for singles, $16,225 for married persons filing separately, and $3,300 for estates and trusts.   I.R.C. § 1(a)–(e).   Beginning in 1991, the ceiling amounts are indexed for inflation.   I.R.C. § 1(f).

15.   I.R.C. § 1(h)(1)(B).   Similarly, if T had no salary and no other ordinary income, and $15,000 of net capital gain, the tax would be computed solely on T's $15,000 of net capital gain at the 15% rate.

16.   I.R.C. § 11(b).   There are three stepped rate brackets, from a low of 15%

on taxable income up to $50,000, to 25% on taxable income from $50,000 to $75,000, and finally to 34% on all taxable income in excess of $75,000.   In addition, corporations with taxable income in excess of $100,000 for any taxable year must increase their tax liability by the lesser of 5% of taxable income in excess of $100,000 or $11,750.   See the flush sentence of I.R.C. § 11(b).   The effect of this provision is to eliminate the benefits of § 11 graduated rates for corporations.   All such benefits are eliminated for corporations with taxable income in excess of $335,000, in effect taxing *all* the taxable income at the 34% rate.

17.   Conf.Rep. No. 99–841, 99th Cong., 2d Sess., II–106 and 107 (1986).

PROBLEM

Compute a single taxpayer's tax liability for a year in which he has $50,000 salary, a $10,000 long-term capital gain, a $4,000 long-term capital loss, a $5,000 short-term capital gain and a $2,000 short-term capital loss assuming that there are no cost of living adjustments to the § 1(c) rates under § 1(f). Disregard any deductions to which taxpayer may be entitled, including the standard deduction and the personal exemption.

C. THE MECHANICS OF CAPITAL LOSSES

Internal Revenue Code: Sections 1211(b); 1212(b)(1), (2)(B)(i). See Sections 165(c) and (f); 1211(a); 1212(a); 1221; 1222.

————

Noncorporate Taxpayers. The losses discussed here are only *deductible* losses. Under Section 1222(2) and (4), the terms short-term capital loss and long-term capital loss are defined to include only such losses as are "taken into account in computing taxable income." Before we can discuss the mechanics of capital losses, we must therefore determine *whether* a loss is taken into account, that is, deductible. In the case of individuals, the primary Code section that determines whether a loss is deductible is Section 165(c), which should be reviewed. If a loss is deductible, then the provisions currently under examination determine *how* and to *what extent* the deduction may be utilized.

Capital losses are generally deductible only from or against capital gains. Capital losses, whether long-term or short-term, offset capital gains, long-term or short-term, dollar for dollar. In the case of a noncorporate taxpayer, however, capital losses in excess of capital gains can be deducted from ordinary income, but only to a limited extent. Any capital loss balance remaining is carried forward into succeeding taxable years, retaining its original character as either long-term or short-term capital loss. This carryover loss is applied against capital gains (and to a limited extent against ordinary income) in each succeeding year until fully utilized.[1]

The statutory mechanics of Section 1222, previously discussed in Part B of this Chapter, require the taxpayer first to "net out" his long-term transactions and short-term transactions, and then to "net out" net longs against net shorts.[2] Somewhat like the net gain situations previously discussed, the netting process results in three possible net *loss* situations. First, there may be a net short-term loss that reduces or eliminates, dollar-for-dollar, the amount of net long-term gain. Likewise, there may be a net long-term loss which reduces or eliminates, dollar-for-dollar, any net short-term gain. The third possibility, is net

1. See I.R.C. §§ 1211(b), 1212(b) and 1222(10).

2. If there are overall net gains, the net gains are afforded the treatment described in Part B, supra.

losses in both short-term and long-term categories. The double netting process, now familiar, presents a procedure under which capital losses are always fully utilized in any year to the extent that there are capital gains for the year. Implicit in all this is the previously discussed rationale for the continued dichotomy between capital gain and ordinary income;[3] capital gain has a limitless capacity for being offset by capital losses, whereas the reduction of ordinary income by capital losses is severely restricted. These restrictions and the possibly deferred utilization of capital losses that run afoul of them are the subject of this discussion.

The Section 1211(b) Limitation. The starting point for the treatment of capital losses is Section 1211(b). It provides, essentially, that capital losses are deductible only to the extent of capital gains plus, if such losses exceed such gains, an amount of ordinary income not to exceed the *lower* of $3,000 ($1,500 in the case of a married individual filing a separate return) or the excess of such losses over such gains.

An illustration of the operation of Section 1211(b) may be helpful. In this example all deductions except those concerning capital losses are disregarded. Assume that T, a single taxpayer, has salary income of $12,000. During the year, he has the following capital gains and losses:

Long-term gain	$400	Short-term gain	$400
Long-term loss	$1200	Short-term loss	$1000
Net long-term loss	($800)	Net short-term loss	($600)

The total of T's net long-term loss and net short-term loss is $1,400, well within the $3,000 limitation, and T can deduct this $1,400 amount from ordinary income.

Tracking the statute, we see that Section 1211(b) initially authorizes capital losses as deductions from capital gains. The initial offset is reflected in the paragraph above. If such losses exceed such gains, as they do here, then Section 1211(b) authorizes the deduction of the excess from ordinary income to the extent of the *lower* of: (1) $3,000 ($1,500 for a married taxpayer filing separately) or (2) the excess of such losses over such gains. In the example, the excess of the losses, whether long-term or short-term, is $1,400. This is less than the $3,000 dollar ceiling limitation of Section 1211(b)(1). Therefore, T's deduction from ordinary income is $1,400, and his adjusted gross income is $10,600 computed as follows:

Salary	$12,000
Less § 1211(b) deduction (see § 62(a)(3))	– 1,400
Adjusted gross income	$10,600

In the above example, if the amount of T's net long-term capital loss had been $2,000 and the amount of his net short-term capital loss had been $1,600, then the dollar limitation of Section 1211(b)(1) would

---

3.　See page 660, supra.

apply. In this circumstance, the deduction from ordinary income is limited by Section 1211(b)(1) to $3,000, the lower of the dollar ceiling ($3,000) or the excess of capital losses over capital gains ($3,600). Thus, of a total excess capital loss of $3,600, under Section 1211(b) the taxpayer can deduct only $3,000 from ordinary income. If the losses had not been capital losses but ordinary losses, T could have deducted the entire amount from ordinary income without limitation and without going through the grinder of Section 1222 and 1211(b).

Recall that long-term capital gains receive only minor favorable treatment and short-term capital gains receive no favorable treatment under the current statute. As in the case of gains, Congress has seen fit to retain the dichotomy for capital and ordinary losses. Can you see any reason for continuing the rigid (punitive?) restriction, limiting the deduction of capital losses against ordinary income?

If, applying the current statute, only $3,000 of the $3,600 excess capital loss is deductible from ordinary income, two questions now arise. First, what happens to the $600 ($3,600–$3,000) which exceeds the Section 1211(b) limitation? And second, of the net long-term loss of $2,000 and the net short-term loss of $1,600, totaling $3,600, which net loss (long-term or short-term) is first consumed against ordinary income within the limitation of Section 1211(b)? The key for unlocking the answer to both questions is found in Section 1212(b) relating to capital loss carryovers.

The Section 1212(b) Carryover. The carryover statute for noncorporate taxpayers, Section 1212(b), provides that capital losses not utilized in the year incurred are carried over into subsequent taxable years and treated as long-term or short-term losses, depending upon their original character.[4] Any carried over losses are treated as though they actually arose in the taxable year to which they are carried. Consequently, they are in effect reborn in succeeding taxable years indefinitely until finally utilized in accordance with the statute, or until their demise at the taxpayer's death.[5]

The character of a capital loss, whether long-term or short-term, remains the same in the year to which it is carried. If a taxpayer has only unused net long-term capital losses in a particular year, his carryover will be long-term loss. Similarly, if the taxpayer has only unused net short-term capital losses, his carryover will be short-term loss. But what if he has both net short-term and net long-term capital

---

4. The "if" clause at the beginning of I.R.C. § 1212(b)(1) makes the carryover provisions dependent upon the taxpayer having a "net capital loss," which is defined in I.R.C. § 1222(10) as "the excess of the losses from the sales or exchanges of capital assets over the sum allowed under section 1211."

The phrase "amount allowed" in I.R.C. § 1212(b)(2) creates some uncertainty. It is the Treasury's position that utilization of carryovers may not be deferred; the amount that can be used reduces the amount carried to the next year whether used or not. Rev.Rul. 76–177, 1976–1 C.B. 224.

5. I.R.C. § 1212(b). Carryover losses die with the taxpayer and are not passed on to his estate. However, I.R.C. § 642(h) passes along losses of an estate or trust to the beneficiaries upon termination of the estate or trust.

losses that are not fully exhausted in the year incurred? Should the short-term or long-term loss be used first in the year incurred with respect to the Section 1211(b) deduction from ordinary income? Which type of loss remains to be carried over?

Section 1212(b)(2) answers these questions by the effective but cryptic device of generating *constructive* short-term capital gain.[6] Note that the gain is simply short-term gain, not net short-term gain. When it is recalled that the determination of a net short-term capital loss requires the netting of short-term gains and losses, it will be seen that the creation of constructive short-term gain either reduces the amount of net short-term capital loss or increases the amount of net short-term capital gain. These computations are made prior to making the Section 1212(b)(1) carryover computations. *Thus, when working with the statute, one must complete the Section 1212(b)(2) computations first, before computing carryover losses under Section 1212(b)(1).*

The operation of Section 1212(b) is best understood by means of examples. First, if in year one T's total capital gains (long-term or short-term) equal his total capital losses (long-term or short-term) there will be no capital loss carryover; capital gains and losses, long or short, offset one another. All such losses are exhausted in the year incurred, and there is no deduction from ordinary income and no carryover.

Assume instead that T, a single taxpayer has a substantial salary (ordinary income), a net long-term capital gain of $2,000, and a short-term capital loss of $10,000 in year one. Here $2,000 of short-term loss can be used against the net long-term gain. T can also deduct $3,000 from ordinary income under Section 1211(b)(1),[7] leaving a $5,000 unused balance of net short-term capital loss. We turn to Section 1212(b) (specifically Section 1212(b)(1)(A) involving short-term capital loss carryovers) to compute T's loss carryover.[8] Section 1212(b)(2) constructs an additional $3,000 of short-term capital gain which is then used (backtracking, if you will) in the Section 1212(b)(1)(A) computation.[9] Under Section 1212(b)(1)(A) the net short-term capital loss (now $7,000 when it is netted with the $3,000 constructive short-term gain) exceeds the net long-term capital gain ($2,000) by $5,000, and that $5,000 is the

---

6. We disregard any consideration of I.R.C. § 1212(b)(2)(A)(ii) and (B). As a practical matter, these provisions generally permit a simple trust (essentially one required to distribute all of its income currently) to fully carry over its capital losses in excess of capital gains. It rarely applies to an individual taxpayer, and its application is disregarded in this note and problem.

7. In these circumstances, focusing on the I.R.C. § 1211(b) limitation, the amount of the net capital loss exceeds $3,000 and § 1211(b) permits a deduction from ordinary income to the extent of "* * * the lower of: (1) $3,000 * * *, or (2) the excess of such losses over such gains". Ac-

cordingly, here the excess of such loss ($10,000) over such gain ($2,000) is $8,000; since this exceeds the $3,000 dollar limit, the deduction from ordinary income is $3,000. I.R.C. § 1211(b)(1).

8. Under the precise language of the statute, I.R.C. § 1212(b) is applicable only "[i]f the taxpayer * * * has a net capital loss for [the] taxable year." Because T has a § 1222(10) net capital loss of $5,000, the "if" clause of § 1212(b) is satisfied and T will be allowed a carryover loss. See note 4, supra.

9. I.R.C. § 1212(b)(1) is meaningless without first computing *constructive* short-term capital gain under § 1212(b)(2).

unused loss balance to be carried into year two as a short-term capital loss in conformance with its original character.

The results under the precise language of the statute are:

Actual short-term gain:	$0		
Constructive (§ 1211(b)(1)) short- term gain:	3,000		
Total short-term gain:		$ 3,000	
Less short-term loss:		10,000	
Net short-term loss:			$7,000
Less net long-term gain:			2,000
Net short-term loss carried over:			$5,000[10]

Assume a more complicated set of facts. In year one T, a single taxpayer, has salary (ordinary income) of $12,000, and *both* net long-term and net short-term capital losses, as follows:

Long-term gain	$ 4,000	Short-term gain	$ 2,000
Long-term loss	$10,000	Short-term loss	$10,000
Net long-term loss	($6,000)	Net short-term loss	($8,000)

Under Section 1211(b)(1), T is allowed a $3,000 deduction from ordinary income;[11] but we are now faced with questions not encountered in the previous examples: must net short-term or net long-term loss be used to pay for this $3,000 deduction from ordinary income? And what losses remain to be carried into the subsequent taxable year?

These questions are again answered by the special rule of Section 1212(b)(2) read in conjunction with Section 1212(b)(1). First, we turn to Section 1212(b)(2), which generates $3,000 of constructive short-term gain.[12] Net short-term capital loss is thus reduced from $8,000 to $5,000, and under Section 1212(b)(1)(A) this excess is carried into year two as a short-term capital loss. Tracking Section 1212(b)(1)(A):

Actual short-term gain:	$2,000	
Constructive (§ 1211(b)(1) short-term gain):	3,000	
Total short-term gain:		$ 5,000
Less short-term loss:		$10,000
Net short-term loss:		$5,000
There is no net long-term gain:		0
Net short-term loss carried over:		$5,000

Under Section 1212(b)(1)(B), even after constructing $3,000 of short-term capital gain by way of Section 1212(b)(2) the net long-term loss of $6,000 stays intact, and the long-term capital loss carried to year two is the entire $6,000. The statutory computation of the long-term loss carryover is as follows:

10. If, instead, T had a long-term capital loss of $10,000 and a net short-term capital gain of $2,000, there again would be a $3,000 reduction in ordinary income as well as a $5,000 long-term capital loss carryover. I.R.C. §§ 1211(b), 1212(b).

11. See note 7, supra.

12. See note 9, supra.

Net long-term loss:		$6,000
Actual short-term gain:	$2,000	
Constructive (§ 1212(b)(1)) short-term gain:	3,000	
Total short-term gain:		$ 5,000
Less short-term loss:		10,000
Net short-term loss:		$ 5,000
Thus there is no net short-term gain:		0
Net long-term loss carried over:		$6,000

The net effect of the above computations is to show that net short-term capital loss is accorded priority in paying for the $3,000 deduction from ordinary income and no amount of the net long-term capital loss is used against this ordinary income. Under Sections 1212(b)(1)(A) and (B), respectively, the remaining $5,000 short-term and $6,000 long-term carryover losses will be carried into year two and treated as though they were recognized in that year. In the same manner, they may be carried over to succeeding taxable years until exhausted or until T's death.[13] The problems below illustrate these rules.

Corporations. The major difference in the treatment of capital losses of corporations and individuals is that Section 1211(b), authorizing noncorporate taxpayers a limited deduction of excess capital losses from ordinary income, is neither applicable to nor duplicated for corporations. In the case of a corporation, Section 1211(a) provides that losses from sales or exchanges of capital assets shall be allowed *only* to the extent of gains from such sales or exchanges. Should the Code be simplified by applying the corporate rule to individuals? A further important difference is that Section 1212(a) treats excess capital losses in a given year as a short-term capital loss carryback (regardless of its origin) to each of the three taxable years *preceding* the loss year and, to the extent not so used, as a short-term capital loss carryover (regardless of its origin) to each of the five taxable years *succeeding* the loss year.[14]

PROBLEMS

Here are two questions on capital losses incurred after 1991. The figure for taxable income given in column A reflects a single taxpayer's taxable income for each of two years *without* regard to his capital gains and losses. Note that in computing gross income (as adjusted) on the return (see page 664 of the text) no gains will be included, since capital losses exceed capital gains. In addition, the § 1211(b) excess amount will be a deduction reducing ordinary income.

A. Taxable Income	B. LTCG	C. LTCL	D. STCG	E. STCL
1. $10,000	$2,000	$ 6,000	$2,600	$1,000
2. 10,000	2,000	10,000	2,000	4,000

---

13. See note 5, supra.

14. I.R.C. § 1212(a)(1). The amount carried back may not increase or produce a net operating loss for the taxable year to which it is carried. I.R.C. § 1212(a)(1)(A)(ii).

For each year separately, without regard to computations for other years, determine the amount of the taxpayer's capital loss that is allowed as a deduction from ordinary income under § 1211(b)(1) or (2) and the amount and character of his capital loss carryover, if any, under § 1212(b).

D. THE MEANING OF "CAPITAL ASSET"

---

1. THE STATUTORY DEFINITION

Internal Revenue Code: Section 1221. See Sections 1234; 1236; 1237.

MAULDIN v. COMMISSIONER

United States Court of Appeals, Tenth Circuit, 1952.
195 F.2d 714.

Before HUXMAN, MURRAH and PICKETT, Circuit Judges.

MURRAH, Circuit Judge. This is an appeal from a decision of the Tax Court, holding that certain lots sold by petitioners during the taxable years 1944 and 1945, were "property held by the taxpayer primarily for sale to customers in the ordinary course of his trade or business" within the exclusionary clause of Section 117(a)(1) of the Internal Revenue Code, 26 U.S.C.A. § 117(a)(1).[1] If the gain from the sale of these lots was derived in this manner, it constituted ordinary income taxable under Section 22(a),[2] and not a capital gain taxable under Section 117(a)(1).[3] Petitioners, residents of the State of New Mexico, are husband and wife, and all income involved is community income. The two cases were therefore consolidated for trial and disposition. A summary of Mauldin's business activities is necessary to a determination of the issue presented.

C.E. Mauldin, a graduate veterinarian since 1904, who also engaged in some road contracting, moved to Albuquerque, New Mexico in 1916, where he organized a road construction company. While in Clovis, New Mexico in 1920, to bid on a sewer project, he decided to move there and engage in the cattle business. Later in the same year, he contracted to buy 160 acres of land one-half mile from the city limits of Clovis for $20,000.00. This land was particularly suitable for cattle feeding, but was not at that time considered suitable for residential development, because the City, with a population of 5000, was not growing in that direction.

By the time Mauldin finally received title to the land in June 1921, he decided that it was not the time to go into the cattle business because of drought, crop and bank failures, and a decline in the cattle

---

1. See I.R.C. (1986) § 1221(1). All footnotes in this opinion are by the editors.

2. See I.R.C. § 61(a).

3. See I.R.C. § 1221(1).

business which continued through 1924. He tried to sell the entire tract in 1924 for less than he paid for it, but was unable to do so, partly because a highway had been surveyed diagonally across the land, splitting it into two tracts and rendering it less suitable for cattle feeding. A real estate agent with whom he listed the property for sale advised him that they would have better success if he divided it into small tracts and blocks. The land was accordingly platted into 29 tracts and 4 blocks containing 88 lots each, and called the "Mauldin Addition". At the time the land was platted in 1924, there was still no demand for residential property in the area. In 1927, he built a home for himself near the center of the Addition.

There were no sales of any consequence until the land commenced to be included in the city limits of Clovis in 1931. By 1939, it was wholly within the city limits, and without Mauldin's request, the City began a paving program in the area, for which he was assessed approximately $25,000.00. When he was unable to pay this assessment, the City instituted suits on its paving liens, and in order to save his property, he divided some additional tracts into lots and devoted most of his time to the sale of the lots in the Addition. He listed the property with real estate agents and otherwise promoted sales through personal solicitations, signs, newspaper advertisements, and gifts of lots to a school and the builder of the first F.H.A. house in Clovis. He stated that at times he would "chase" a prospective purchaser "around the block". During 1939 and 1940, he sold enough lots to liquidate the paving indebtedness.

Mauldin testified that with the indebtedness to the City paid, he decided to hold the remaining portions of the original tract for investment purposes, and after 1940, did nothing to promote sales. He stated, "I cut it up and tried my best to sell it to clear it, and when I cleared it, I quit". From 1940 until 1949, when his health failed, Mauldin devoted full time to the lumber business he organized in 1939. During this period, he had no real estate office, no license to sell real estate, did not advertise the properties by newspapers or signs, had no fixed price for lots, and at times refused to sell certain lots, either because the prospective purchaser would not pay the asked price, or Mauldin did not wish to sell the particular property at that time. The only real estate purchased by Mauldin after acquiring the 160 acres in 1920 was one "unsightly" block of lots near his residence, and some commercial properties to be used in connection with his lumber business.

Due primarily to the location of war facilities nearby, the City of Clovis grew in population to 14,000 in 1940 and to 20,000 to 25,000 in 1945, and the lots, Mauldin Addition, were in great demand. By the end of 1945, Mauldin had disposed of all but 20 acres of his original 160 acre tract. This 20 acres was considered by him and real estate dealers to be his most valuable property. Mauldin's records show that he sold 2 lots in 2 transactions in 1941; 11 in 1942 in 2 transactions (6 lots were given to his daughter as a wedding present); 5½ in 1943 in 3 transactions; 5½ in 1944 in 3 transactions; 44½ in 1945 in 15 transactions; 39 in 1946, 1 in 1947 and 2 in 1948. For the taxable years in 1939 and 1940, the taxpayers' income tax returns showed income from real estate only; for each of the years 1941 and 1944 (returns for 1942 and 1943 not shown) they showed net income of approximately $3,000.00 from sales of real estate and approximately $12,000.00 from the lumber business; for the year 1945, $20,484.84 from real estate and $12,339.80 from lumber; and in 1946, $21,942.88 from real estate and $25,005.07 from lumber. On his 1940 return, Mauldin stated that the nature of his business was "real estate"; in 1943 it was shown as "lumber business"; in 1944 he did not designate the nature of his business; and in 1945 it was shown as "lumber and real estate".

In their income tax returns for the years 1944 and 1945, petitioners showed the lots sold during those years as long-time capital assets, and computed the tax accordingly. The Commissioner determined that the profit realized was ordinary income within the meaning of Section 117(a)(1) [4] of the Internal Revenue Code, and assessed the additional tax. This appeal is from the judgment of the Tax Court sustaining the Commissioner, and the only question is whether its judgment on these facts can be said to be clearly erroneous.

It is admitted by taxpayer that during 1939 and 1940, he was engaged in the business of selling the tracts and lots in Mauldin Addition. He earnestly contends, however, that after 1940, his business status was changed; that his full time thereafter was devoted to the lumber business, and held the remaining lots for investment purposes, selling them only through unsolicited offers when the price was right.

There is no fixed formula or rule of thumb for determining whether property sold by the taxpayer was held by him primarily for sale to customers in the ordinary course of his trade or business. Each case must, in the last analysis, rest upon its own facts. There are a number of helpful factors, however, to point the way, among which are the purposes for which the property was acquired, whether for sale or investment; and continuity and frequency of sales as opposed to isolated transactions. Dunlap v. Oldham Lumber Co., 5 Cir., 178 F.2d 781; Annot. 106 A.L.R. 254; Mertens, Vol. 3, Sec. 22.08. [5] And, any other facts tending to indicate that the sales or transactions are in furtherance of an occupation of the taxpayer, recognizing however that one actively engaged in the business of real estate may discontinue such business and simply sell off the remnants of his holdings without further engaging in the business. Snell v. Commissioner, 5 Cir., 97 F.2d 891. Thus, where residents of New York bought land in Florida and elsewhere from time to time for investment, a part of which was platted and improved, it was held that the occasional sale of lots through local brokers was not sufficiently frequent or engrossing to give the taxpayers the vocation of real estate dealers. Phipps v.

---

4. Ibid.

5. See Mertens, Vol. 3B, Sec. 22.15 (1973).

Commissioner, 2 Cir., 54 F.2d 469. And, in Foran v. Commissioner, 5 Cir., 165 F.2d 705, a taxpayer admittedly engaged as a broker of nonproducing oil and gas leases and royalties purchased a producing property which he sold within eighteen months. The profit realized therefrom was held to be income from a long-time capital asset, the court reasoning that since this was the first producing property purchased by the taxpayer, there was no occasion to disbelieve his statement that he acquired it for investment or his motive for selling it.

On the other hand, sale and exchange of lots in 1939 and 1940 from a 92 acre tract of land, partially subdivided in 1932, was held to be in the ordinary course of business where the taxpayer had been continuously engaged in the real estate business since 1908, and had divided a part of the tract into lots in order to facilitate the sale of the land. Gruver v. Commissioner, 4 Cir., 142 F.2d 363. So too was the sale of lots from a tract of land which had been originally purchased for and used as a lettuce farm, but subdivided into lots when it became too valuable for truck farming operations. Richards v. Commissioner, 9 Cir., 81 F.2d 369, 106 A.L.R. 249. See also Oliver v. Commissioner, 4 Cir., 138 F.2d 910. And, lots sold through sales agencies after reacquisition at a trustee's sale, were held to be in the ordinary course of trade or business, as against the contention that they were sold in furtherance of an orderly liquidation in Ehrman v. Commissioner, 9 Cir., 120 F.2d 607. While the purpose for which the property was acquired is of some weight, the ultimate question is the purpose for which it was held. Rollingwood Corp. v. Commissioner, 9 Cir., 190 F.2d 263.

Admittedly, Mauldin originally purchased the property for purposes other than for sale in the ordinary course of trade or business. When, however, he subdivided and offered it for sale, he was undoubtedly engaged in the vocation of selling lots from this tract of land at least until 1940. As against his contention that he ceased to engage in the business after 1940, the record evidence shows that he sold more lots in 1945 on a sellers market without solicitation than he did in 1940 on a buyers market. It seems fairly inferable from the record that at all times he had lots for sale, and that the volume sold depended primarily upon the prevailing economic conditions, brought on by wartime activities and their aftermath. It is true that he was in the lumber business, but his returns plainly show that a substantial part of his income was derived from the sale of the lots. In these circumstances, we cannot say that the Tax Court's conclusions are without factual bases.

The decisions are Affirmed.

MALAT v. RIDDELL *

Supreme Court of the United States, 1966.
383 U.S. 569, 86 S.Ct. 1030.

PER CURIAM. Petitioner [1] was a participant in a joint venture which acquired a 45-acre parcel of land, the intended use for which is somewhat in dispute. Petitioner contends that the venturers' intention was to develop and operate an apartment project on the land; the respondent's position is that there was a "dual purpose" of developing the property for rental purposes or selling, whichever proved to be the more profitable. In any event, difficulties in obtaining the necessary financing were encountered, and the interior lots of the tract were subdivided and sold. The profit from those sales was reported and taxed as ordinary income.

The joint venturers continued to explore the possibility of commercially developing the remaining exterior parcels. Additional frustrations in the form of zoning restrictions were encountered. These difficulties persuaded petitioner and another of the joint ventures of the desirability of terminating the venture; accordingly, they sold out their interests in the remaining property. Petitioner contends that he is entitled to treat the profits from this last sale as capital gains; the respondent takes the position that this was "property held by the taxpayer primarily for sale to customers in the ordinary course of his trade or business," [2] and thus subject to taxation as ordinary income.

The District Court made the following finding:

> The members of [the joint venture], as of the date the 44.901 acres were acquired, intended either to sell the property or develop it for rental, depending upon which course appeared to be most profitable. The venturers realized that they had made a good purchase price-wise and, if they were unable to obtain acceptable construction financing or rezoning * * * which would be prerequisite to commercial development, they would sell the property in bulk so they wouldn't get hurt. The purpose of either selling or developing the property continued during the period in which [the joint venture] held the property.

The District Court ruled that petitioner had failed to establish that the property was not held *primarily* for sale to customers in the ordinary course of business, and thus rejected petitioner's claim to capital gain treatment for the profits derived from the property's resale. The Court of Appeals affirmed, 347 F.2d 23. We granted certiorari (382 U.S. 900)

---

* See Bernstein, " 'Primarily for Sale': A Semantic Snare," 20 Stan.L.Rev. 1093 (1968). Ed.

1. The taxpayer and his wife who filed a joint return are the petitioners, but for simplicity are referred to throughout as "petitioner."

2. Internal Revenue Code of 1954, § 1221(1), 26 U.S.C.A. § 1221(1). * * *

to resolve a conflict among the courts of appeals [3] with regard to the meaning of the term "primarily" as it is used in § 1221(1) of the Internal Revenue Code of 1954.

The statute denies capital gain treatment to profits reaped from the sale of "property held by the taxpayer *primarily* for sale to customers in the ordinary course of his trade or business." (Emphasis added.) The respondent urges upon us a construction of "primarily" as meaning that a purpose may be "primary" if it is a "substantial" one.

As we have often said, "the words of statutes—including revenue acts—should be interpreted where possible in their ordinary, everyday senses." Crane v. Commissioner, 331 U.S. 1, 6, 67 S.Ct. 1047, 1051. And see Hanover Bank v. Commissioner, 369 U.S. 672, 687–688, 82 S.Ct. 1047, 1051; Commissioner v. Korell, 339 U.S. 619, 627–628. Departure from a literal reading of statutory language may, on occasion, be indicated by relevant internal evidence of the statute itself and necessary in order to effect the legislative purpose. See, e.g., Board of Governors v. Agnew, 329 U.S. 441, 446–448, 67 S.Ct. 411, 413–415. But this is not such an occasion. The purpose of the statutory provision with which we deal is to differentiate between the "profits and losses arising from the everyday operation of a business" on the one hand (Corn Products Co. v. Commissioner, 350 U.S. 46, 52, 76 S.Ct. 20, 24) and "the realization of appreciation in value accrued over a substantial period of time" on the other. (Commissioner v. Gillette Motor Co., 364 U.S. 130, 134, 80 S.Ct. 1497, 1500.) A literal reading of the statute is consistent with this legislative purpose. We hold that, as used in § 1221(1), "primarily" means "of first importance" or "principally."

Since the courts below applied an incorrect legal standard, we do not consider whether the result would be supportable on the facts of this case had the correct one been applied. We believe, moreover, that the appropriate disposition is to remand the case to the District Court for fresh fact-findings, addressed to the statute as we have now construed it.

Vacated and remanded.

NOTE

The *Mauldin* case, above, is typical in paying little heed to whether real property may be said to be held for sale "to customers." [1] Comparatively recently, we received the Supreme Court's exciting message that in Section 1221(1), "primarily" means "of first importance" or "principally." [2] As time goes on our education expands. In International

---

3. Compare Rollingwood Corp. v. Commissioner, 190 F.2d 263, 266 (C.A.9th Cir.); American Can Co. v. Commissioner, 317 F.2d 604, 605 (C.A.2d Cir.), with United States v. Bennett, 186 F.2d 407, 410–411 (C.A.5th Cir.); Municipal Bond Corp. v. Commissioner, 341 F.2d 683, 688–689 (C.A.8th Cir.). Cf. Recordak Corp. v. Unit-

ed States, 163 Ct.Cl. 294, 300–301, 325 F.2d 460, 463–464.

1. See Friedlander, " 'To Customers': The Forgotten Element in the Characterization of Gains on Sales of Real Property." 39 Tax L.Rev. 31 (1983).

2. Malat v. Riddell, supra page 678.

Shoe Machine Corp. v. U.S.,[3] we discover that, even though rental income from property exceeds income from its sale, the property can be considered held primarily for sale. After *Malat* this is tough medicine to take, unless washed down with a good gulp of "corn." [4] In any event, the court in *Mauldin,* the principal case above, is discouragingly correct in suggesting that the question whether property is held primarily for sale is not answerable by a "fixed formula"; and the opinion does recite some factors that aid analysis.

The meaning of a term in the Internal Revenue Code is not always to be determined in the manner in which the Court approached the meaning of "primarily" in *Malat,* with reference to dictionary definitions and supposed common usage. Congress may provide its own definition for the terms used.[5] In the capital gain and loss area there are many instances in which, in order to achieve a desired result, *Congress* itself ascribes meanings to terms which are quite at variance from their "ordinary everyday senses." It seems desirable here to direct attention to some of this congressional game-playing; but the comments that follow are intended to be only generally informative and not to be used as a basis for detailed study at this point.

Recall that capital gain or loss consequences require: (1) a transaction involving a capital asset, (2) a sale or exchange of that capital asset, and (3) a determination of how long the taxpayer has held the capital asset. Section 1221 defines the term capital asset but it is subject to both judicial and statutory exceptions.[6] The Section 1221 definition has been amended several times.[7]

If a transaction does not involve a capital asset, or if it does not constitute a sale or exchange, it will give rise only to ordinary income or to an ordinary deduction. It may be difficult to determine whether a transaction meets such tests. Consequently, at times Congress has seen fit to clarify the status of a transaction or artificially to accord to a transaction one or more of the essential elements. At other times Congress expressly deprives a capital asset transaction of its characterization. Varying policy reasons, some of which are related to the reasons previously identified for capital asset treatment, underlie such congressional decisions.

Instances in which Congress has seen fit to treat a transaction as though all three requirements are met, even though none or less than all may be met, include Section 1235, according long-term capital gain

3. 491 F.2d 157 (1st Cir.1974).

4. See Corn Products Refining Co. v. Commissioner, set out infra page 693; but see also Arkansas Best Corp. v. Commissioner, set out infra page 697.

5. The student should be aware of a number of general definitions contained in I.R.C. § 7701.

6. See pages 681 and 693, infra.

7. The Tax Reform Act of 1976 added a letter or memorandum (or a collection of such property) to other property excluded under I.R.C. § 1221(3). It also added I.R.C. § 1221(5), excluding from "capital assets" government publications received by a taxpayer without charge or at a reduced price. Under § 170(e) this effectively precludes a deduction for charitable contributions of such items. See Chapter 23B, infra.

consequences to certain dispositions of patent rights [8] and Section 166(d), classifying nonbusiness bad debts as short-term capital losses.[9] Conversely, even though certain transactions meet all three requirements, Sections 1239, 1245, 1250, 1252 through 1255 [10] convert some potential capital gains to ordinary income, and Section 1242 through 1244 accord ordinary loss treatment to some transactions which would generally produce capital losses.

In other situations, Congress artificially supplies only one of the three requirements to a transaction. For example, the "sale or exchange" requirement is supplied by statute when securities become worthless and there is no actual sale or exchange that would normally be needed to make the resulting loss a capital loss. Section 165(g).[11] Some casualties are similarly treated. Section 1231.[12] The retirement of a bond may be "considered as" an exchange of the bond, Section 1271, and a lessee's relinquishment of his lease may be "considered as" an exchange of the lease. Section 1241.[13] In other instances, Congress prescribes artificial holding periods at variance with the time that property disposed of is actually held. Section 1223.[14]

Similarly, there are times when Congress will treat property as a capital asset even though it is not within the Section 1221 definition. For instance, under Section 1231 property described in Section 1221(2) may or may not be accorded capital asset status.[15] When one sells, exchanges, or has a loss on the failure to exercise an option, the characterization of the transaction depends, not upon whether the option itself is a capital asset, but upon whether the property to which it relates so qualifies. This is the prescription of Section 1234, which was enacted to give the option itself a neutral status, recognizing that it is no more than a right to buy or sell property, and to make a more realistic characterization of the transaction on the basis of the character of the property subject to the option.[16]

Most of the provisions referred to above reappear for more detailed consideration in subsequent portions of this book. The two provisions discussed below, Sections 1236 and 1237, are not reconsidered and therefore warrant brief analysis here.

Prior to 1951, it was often uncertain whether one who was a dealer in securities held particular securities in that capacity or as an investor.[17] Thus, the status of the securities in his hands, as noncapital or capital assets, was often the subject of controversy. A dealer would be tempted to shift securities from investment status to inventory status or vice versa, to support his contention that ordinary gain should be

---

8. See page 713, infra.

9. See Chapter 23, infra at page 800.

10. See Chapter 22, infra at page 782.

11. See Chapter 23, infra at page 800.

12. See Chapter 22, infra at page 770.

13. See page 713, infra.

14. See page 733, infra.

15. See Chapter 22, infra at page 770.

16. See Problem 2, at page 738, infra.

17. See Reg. § 1.1236–1(d)(1)(ii). David C. Fitch, 34 TCM 233 (1975), reflects a narrow definition of "dealer," resting in part on Higgins v. Commissioner, 312 U.S. 212, 61 S.Ct. 475 (1941).

treated as capital gain or that capital loss should be treated as ordinary loss. Section 1236 was addressed to the problem.[18] In effect it restricts classification changes that would be convenient for the taxpayer by requiring an identification of the status of the security at the time of its acquisition. Thus, Congress has attempted to clarify the character of a security as a capital asset or not when its actual classification may be equivocal. Section 1236 provides that, if a dealer is to treat securities as capital assets, he generally must clearly indicate on his records before the close of the day on which the securities are acquired that the securities are held for investment purposes, and he cannot at anytime thereafter hold them for sale to customers.[19] Once the purpose is identified under Section 1236 as investment, the classification may not in any event be changed if the security is subsequently sold at a loss. The statute does not expressly foreclose reclassification of securities originally classified as investments if they are sold at a gain. Why?

Another instance in which it may be difficult to determine whether one holding property is a dealer or an investor is when a landowner subdivides real property and sells it.[20] Section 1237 sometimes renders such a determination unnecessary; but the statute is limited in its application. First of all it is wholly unavailable to dealers or to persons who actually become dealers, a requirement creating factual uncertainties that tend to dilute the effectiveness of the clarification purpose of the statute. In addition under Section 1237(a), the land in question (1) must never have been held primarily for sale to customers, (2) must not have been the subject of substantial improvement[21] and (3) unless inherited, must have been held by the taxpayer for at least five years. For example in the *Mauldin* case, supra, there was no question but that in 1939 and 1940 the taxpayer held the "Mauldin Addition" for sale to customers in the ordinary course of his business. This would in itself render Section 1237 inapplicable under Section 1237(a)(1).[22]

When Section 1237 *is* applicable it provides only partial capital asset treatment. Five parcels may be sold as capital gains but, for any year in which a sixth sale occurs and thereafter, gain in an amount up to 5 percent of the sale price on each parcel will be ordinary income.[23] Commissions paid to outside dealers may offset such ordinary income.[24]

Although Section 1237 is severely limited in application, nevertheless there are circumstances in which it can be of very great benefit to a

18. Sen.Rep. No. 781, 82d Cong., 1st Sess. (1951), 1951–2 C.B. 458 at 482.

19. An exception is made under I.R.C. § 1236(d) for securities exchange floor specialists who have a 7 business day grace period in which to make their designation.

20. See *Mauldin,* supra page 674. For further analysis of the relevant factors in making the dealer or investor determination in real estate transactions, see Emmanuel, "Capital Gains for Real Estate Operators," 12 U. of Fla.L.Rev. 280 (1959).

21. There is an exception for certain improvements. See I.R.C. § 1237(b)(3).

22. See also I.R.C. § 1237(a)(2)(C), disqualifying the Mauldin Addition (had § 1237 then been in effect) because of the substantial cost of the city paving which, because disqualified as a deductible tax by § 164(c)(1), would be a proscribed addition to the taxpayer's basis.

23. I.R.C. § 1237(b)(1).

24. I.R.C. § 1237(b)(2).

taxpayer. For instance, one who has appreciated realty that he has held for many years may make minimal subdivisional improvements on it and sell it off piece-meal, himself or through a broker. The minimum but important assurance that Section 1237 affords him is that his efforts in that transaction will not place him in a dealer category. Thus, except for the innocuous 5% rule, he may be able to count on capital gain treatment for all his sales. It should also be pointed out, however, that Section 1237 is not exclusive [25] and, even if a taxpayer does not qualify for its benefits, he may still maintain he is an investor in an attempt to classify all of his gain as capital gain.[26] Some suggest that Section 1237 is not available when needed and is not needed when available.

2. "INCOME" PROPERTY *

Internal Revenue Code: Sections 102(b); 273; 1001(e); 1241.
Regulations: Sections 1.1014–5; 1.1015–1(b), (c).

HORT v. COMMISSIONER

Supreme Court of the United States, 1941.
313 U.S. 28, 61 S.Ct. 757.

Mr. Justice MURPHY delivered the opinion of the Court.

We must determine whether the amount petitioner received as consideration for cancellation of a lease of realty in New York City was ordinary gross income as defined in § 22(a) of the Revenue Act of 1932 (47 Stat. 169, 178), and whether, in any event, petitioner sustained a loss through cancellation of the lease which is recognized in § 23(e) of the same Act (47 Stat. 169, 180).

Petitioner acquired the property, a lot and ten-story office building, by devise from his father in 1928. At the time he became owner, the premises were leased to a firm which had sublet the main floor to the Irving Trust Co. In 1927, five years before the head lease expired, the Irving Trust Co. and petitioner's father executed a contract in which the latter agreed to lease the main floor and basement to the former for a term of fifteen years at an annual rental of $25,000, the term to commence at the expiration of the head lease.

---

25. Reg. § 1.1237–1(a)(4); R.E. Gordy, 36 T.C. 855 (1961), acq., 1964–1 (part 1) C.B. 4.

26. His reason for making such an argument could be to avoid the 5% ordinary income characterization of § 1237(b)(1) or his failure to meet the requirements of § 1237(a). For cases treating subdivided land as a capital asset after the enactment of § 1237, see Bon v. U.S., unreported, 60–1 U.S.T.C. ¶ 9186 (D.Wyo.1960) and Barker v. U.S., unreported, 65–2 U.S.T.C. ¶ 9736 (S.D. Calif.1965). On § 1237 generally see

Repetti, "What Makes a Dealer under Section 1237," 17 N.Y.U.Inst. on Fed.Tax. 651 (1959), and Weithorn, "Subdivisions of Real Estate-'Dealer' v. 'Investor' Problem," 11 Tax.L.Rev. 157 (1959).

* See Del Cotto, " 'Property' in the Capital Asset Definition: Influence of 'Fruit and Tree'," 15 Buffalo L.Rev. 1 (1965). See also the Classic Articles of Professors Eustice and Lyon cited in a note in Chapter 12, "Assignment of Income," at page 289, supra.

In 1933, the Irving Trust Co. found it unprofitable to maintain a branch in petitioner's building. After some negotiations, petitioner and the Trust Co. agreed to cancel the lease in consideration of a payment to petitioner of $140,000. Petitioner did not include this amount in gross income in his income tax return for 1933. On the contrary, he reported a loss of $21,494.75 on the theory that the amount he received as consideration for the cancellation was $21,494.75 less than the difference between the present value of the unmatured rental payments and the fair rental value of the main floor and basement for the unexpired term of the lease. He did not deduct this figure, however, because he reported other losses in excess of gross income.

The Commissioner included the entire $140,000 in gross income, disallowed the asserted loss, made certain other adjustments not material here, and assessed a deficiency. The Board of Tax Appeals, affirmed. 39 B.T.A. 922. The Circuit Court of Appeals affirmed per curiam on the authority of Warren Service Corp. v. Commissioner, 110 F.2d 723, 112 F.2d 167. Because of conflict with Commissioner v. Langwell Real Estate Corp., 47 F.2d 841, we granted certiorari limited to the question whether, "in computing net gain or loss for income tax purposes, a taxpayer [can] offset the value of the lease canceled against the consideration received by him for the cancellation." 311 U.S. 641, 61 S.Ct. 174.

Petitioner apparently contends that the amount received for cancellation of the lease was capital rather than ordinary income and that it was therefore subject to §§ 101, 111–113, and 117 (47 Stat. 169, 191, 195–202, 207) which govern capital gains and losses. Further, he argues that even if that amount must be reported as ordinary gross income he sustained a loss which § 23(e) authorizes him to deduct. We cannot agree.

The amount received by petitioner for cancellation of the lease must be included in his gross income in its entirety. Section 22(a), copied in the margin,[1] expressly defines gross income to include "gains, profits, and income derived from * * * rent, * * * or gains or profits and income derived from any source whatever." Plainly this definition reached the rent paid prior to cancellation just as it would have embraced subsequent payments if the lease had never been canceled. It would have included a prepayment of the discounted value of unmatured rental payments whether received at the inception of the lease or at any time thereafter. Similarly, it would have extended to the proceeds of a suit to recover damages had the Irving Trust Co. breached the lease instead of concluding a settlement. Compare United States v. Safety Car Heating Co., 297 U.S. 88, 56 S.Ct. 353; Burnet v. Sanford, 282 U.S. 359, 51 S.Ct. 150. That the amount petitioner received resulted from negotiations ending in cancellation of the lease rather than from a suit to enforce it cannot alter the fact that basically the payment was merely a substitute for the rent reserved in the lease.

1. [I.R.C. (1939) § 22(a) is omitted. Ed.]

So far as the application of § 22(a) is concerned, it is immaterial that petitioner chose to accept an amount less than the strict present value of the unmatured rental payments rather than to engage in litigation, possibly uncertain and expensive.

The consideration received for cancellation of the lease was not a return of capital. We assume that the lease was "property," whatever that signifies abstractly. Presumably the bond in Helvering v. Horst, 311 U.S. 112, 61 S.Ct. 144, and the lease in Helvering v. Bruun, 309 U.S. 461, 60 S.Ct. 631, were also "property," but the interest coupon in *Horst* and the building in *Bruun* nevertheless were held to constitute items of gross income. Simply because the lease was "property" the amount received for its cancellation was not a return of capital, quite apart from the fact that "property" and "capital" are not necessarily synonymous in the Revenue Act of 1932 or in common usage. Where, as in this case, the disputed amount was essentially a substitute for rental payments which § 22(a) expressly characterizes as gross income, it must be regarded as ordinary income, and it is immaterial that for some purposes the contract creating the right to such payments may be treated as "property" or "capital."

For the same reasons, that amount was not a return of capital because petitioner acquired the lease as an incident of the realty devised to him by his father. Theoretically, it might have been possible in such a case to value realty and lease separately and to label each a capital asset. Compare Maass v. Higgins, 312 U.S. 443, 61 S.Ct. 631; Appeal of Farmer, 1 B.T.A. 711. But that would not have converted into capital the amount petitioner received from the Trust Co., since § 22(b)(3) [2] of the 1932 Act (47 Stat. 169, 178) would have required him to include in gross income the rent derived from the property, and that section, like § 22(a), does not distinguish rental payments and a payment which is clearly a substitute for rental payments.

We conclude that petitioner must report as gross income the entire amount received for cancellation of the lease, without regard to the claimed disparity between that amount and the difference between the present value of the unmatured rental payments and the fair rental value of the property for the unexpired period of the lease. The cancellation of the lease involved nothing more than relinquishment of the right to future rental payments in return for a present substitute payment and possession of the leased premises. Undoubtedly it diminished the amount of gross income petitioner expected to realize, but to that extent he was relieved of the duty to pay income tax. Nothing in § 23(e) [3] indicates that Congress intended to allow petitioner to reduce ordinary income actually received and reported by the amount of income he failed to realize. See Warren Service Corp. v. Commissioner, supra; Josey v. Commissioner, 104 F.2d 453; Tiscornia v. Commissioner, 95 F.2d 678; Farrelly-Walsh, Inc. v. Commissioner, 13 B.T.A. 923;

2. [I.R.C. (1939) § 22(b)(3) is omitted. See I.R.C. (1986) § 102(b)(1). Ed.]

3. [I.R.C. (1939) § 23(e) is omitted. See I.R.C. (1986) § 165(c). Ed.]

Goerke Co. v. Commissioner, 7 B.T.A. 860; Merckens v. Commissioner, 7 B.T.A. 32. Compare, United States v. Safety Car Heating Co., supra; Voliva v. Commissioner, 36 F.2d 212; Appeal of Denholm & McKay Co., 2 B.T.A. 444. We may assume that petitioner was injured insofar as the cancellation of the lease affected the value of the realty. But that would become a deductible loss only when its extent had been fixed by a closed transaction. Regulations No. 77, Art. 171, p. 46; United States v. White Dental Mfg. Co., 274 U.S. 398, 47 S.Ct. 598.

The judgment of the Circuit Court of Appeals is affirmed.

METROPOLITAN BLDG. CO. v. COMMISSIONER

United States Court of Appeals, Ninth Circuit, 1960.
282 F.2d 592.

MERRILL, Circuit Judge. The question presented by this case involves the owner of real property, his lessee and a sublessee. The sublessee wished to enter into a desirable arrangement directly with the owner and to this end to eliminate the intervening interest of the lessee-sublessor. He paid a sum of money to the lessee, in consideration of which the lessee released to the owner, his lessor, all his right and interest under his lease.

The question presented is whether the sum so paid to the lessee is to be regarded entirely as the equivalent of rent owed to the lessee and taxable to the lessee as income or whether it is to be regarded entirely as a sale by the lessee of a capital asset and taxable as capital gain. The Commissioner of Internal Revenue ruled that the payment was the equivalent of rental and taxable as income.

At issue is the amount of tax from Metropolitan Building Company, the lessee, for the taxable year ending June 30, 1953. Following the ruling of the Commissioner, this proceeding was instituted in the Tax Court by Metropolitan for redetermination of deficiencies in income and excess profits taxes for that year. The Tax Court affirmed the ruling of the Commissioner. Metropolitan has petitioned this Court for review, contending that the payment in question should be held to be capital gain. We have concluded that petitioner is correct in its contention and that the judgment of the Tax Court must be reversed.

The University of Washington owns real estate comprising about four city blocks in the downtown area of Seattle. In 1907 it executed a lease upon this property extending to November 1, 1954. This lease was acquired by petitioner Metropolitan Building Company on December 3, 1907.

On August 1, 1922, Metropolitan executed a sublease of the greater portion of one city block, extending to October 31, 1954, one day prior to the termination of the main lease. Under the terms of the sublease the sublessee was to construct a hotel upon the leased premises. Rental provided was $25,000.00 a year. In addition, the sublessee agreed to pay its just proportion of any ad valorem personal property taxes assessed against Metropolitan's leasehold. The Olympic Hotel was constructed upon the leased premises. On March 31, 1936, the sublease was acquired by The Olympic, Inc.

During the year 1952, the University of Washington, as fee owner, was attempting to arrange a long-term disposition of the Olympic Hotel property for the period following the expiration of Metropolitan's lease in November, 1954. To this end the University invited proposals for the lease of the hotel, and a number of highly competitive proposals were submitted by various large hotel operators. All these proposals, except that of The Olympic, Inc., necessarily contemplated a lease commencing November 1, 1954.

The proposal made by The Olympic, Inc., offered, at no cost or expense to the University, to procure from Metropolitan a release to the University of all Metropolitan's right, title and interest in and to the Olympic Hotel property under its lease. Olympic then offered the University to take a new lease directly from it for a term of approximately twenty-two years commencing forthwith. Under this proposal, additional rentals of $725,000.00 would accrue to the University during the period prior to November 1, 1954, which otherwise would not have been forthcoming.

The University was favorably disposed to this proposal and negotiations were undertaken with Metropolitan for the acquisition by the University of Metropolitan's leasehold interest. A letter was written on August 18, 1952, by the Board of Regents of the University to Metropolitan requesting Metropolitan to release to the University its leasehold rights with respect to the Olympic Hotel property. At a meeting of the Board of Directors of Metropolitan, held August 19, 1952, the following resolution was adopted:

> "Resolved, the President hereby is authorized to sell to the University of Washington our leasehold rights to that area of the Metropolitan Tract occupied by the Olympic Hotel, including the existing sub-lease provided an agreement can be reached which is approved by the company's accounting and legal counsel."

On September 8, 1952, an agreement was reached between Metropolitan and the State of Washington, acting through the Board of Regents of the University, whereby petitioner conveyed, quitclaimed, assigned and released to the State of Washington all of the right, title and interest of Metropolitan in and to that portion of the leasehold upon which the Olympic Hotel was located. For this assignment and transfer Metropolitan received from The Olympic, Inc., the sum of $137,000.00. The University then proceeded in accordance with its understanding to lease the property to The Olympic, Inc.

Metropolitan's president, asked as to how the sum of $137,000.00 had been computed, testified that roughly it covered $53,000.00 ground rent, $44,000.00 as Metropolitan's just proportion of the ad valorem personal property tax assessed against Metropolitan's leasehold, and $40,000.00 for increased taxes.

The Commissioner contends that this payment is taxable to Metropolitan as ordinary income. He relies upon Hort v. Commissioner, 1940, 313 U.S. 28, 31, 61 S.Ct. 757, where it is held:

"Where, as in this case, the disputed amount was essentially a substitute for rental payments which § 22(a) [26 U.S.C.A. § 22(a)] expressly characterizes as gross income, it must be regarded as ordinary income * * *."

In that case the petitioner owned a business building, a portion of which had been leased to the Irving Trust Company for a term of fifteen years at $25,000.00 a year. The Trust Company finding it unprofitable to maintain a branch office at that location, paid the petitioner $140,000.00 for cancellation of the lease.

In that case the Trust Company did not acquire any interest of its lessor. It simply compromised and liquidated its rental obligation under the lease. The sum received by the lessor was in lieu of the rentals which the Trust Company otherwise was obligated to pay and was not compensation for acquisition of any interest of the lessor.

In the case before us, the sums paid to Metropolitan were not simply a discharge of Olympic's obligation to pay rental. They were paid for the purchase of Metropolitan's entire leasehold interest. The case is not one of a liquidation of a right to future income as is Hort, but rather it is one of a disposition of income-producing property itself. The giving up of a lease by a tenant fits the legal requirements of a sale or exchange under Internal Revenue Code 1939, 117(j) 26 U.S.C.A. § 117(j) and a gain realized by the tenant on such a transaction is capital gain. Commissioner of Internal Revenue v. Golonsky, 3 Cir., 1952, 200 F.2d 72, certiorari denied 345 U.S. 939, 73 S.Ct. 830; Commissioner of Internal Revenue v. Ray, 5 Cir., 1954, 210 F.2d 300, certiorari denied 348 U.S. 829, 75 S.Ct. 53; Commissioner of Internal Revenue v. McCue Bros. & Drummond, Inc., 2 Cir., 1954, 210 F.2d 752, certiorari denied 348 U.S. 829, 75 S.Ct. 53; Walter H. Sutliff, 1942, 46 B.T.A. 446.

In Golonsky the court stated the problem of the case as follows:

"A tenant in possession of premises under a lease, upon receipt of payment by the landlord, and pursuant to an agreement made with the landlord, 'vacated and surrendered the premises' before the date at which the lease expired." 200 F.2d at page 73.

It was held that the proceeds of the transaction constituted capital gain.

The Commissioner would (and the Tax Court did) distinguish Golonsky upon the ground that in the instant case the consideration passed not from the lessor but from the sublessee, the very party obliged to pay rental to the recipient, and that such consideration represented the amount which the recipient felt it would otherwise have received under the sublease. Further, it is said, the value of the leasehold was fixed and limited by the rentals due under the sublease since the term of the sublease corresponded with that of the lease.

We are not impressed by this proposed distinction. The lease clearly had value over the amount of rentals due by virtue of the fact that its acquisition was of importance to Olympic. Irrespective of the method used by Metropolitan in arriving at the figure of $137,000.00, it is clear that Metropolitan did profit to some extent by the transaction. The Commissioner seems to concede that if the consideration had been paid by the University or if the lease had been assigned to a third party the transaction would have constituted a sale by the lessee.

It is not the person of the payor which controls the nature of the transaction in our view. Rather, it is the fact that the transaction constituted a bona fide transfer, for a legitimate business purpose, of the leasehold in its entirety. It did not constitute a release or transfer only of the right to future income under the sublease and the business purpose of the transaction would not have been met by such a release.

We conclude that the sum of $137,000.00, received by petitioner for release of its leasehold, must be held taxable as capital gain and not as ordinary income.

Reversed and remanded for redetermination, in accordance with this opinion, of deficiencies in income and excess profits taxes of petitioner for its taxable year ended June 30, 1953.

NOTE

With *Hort* in mind (we hope) as well as the modification of its message in *Metropolitan Building,* we approach the question of the tax consequences of the sale of a life or other term interest or of an income interest in a trust. For example, (and we shall use this example throughout this brief note) S transfers securities to T, as trustee, the income from the assets to be paid to L for life and then the securities to be distributed to R. We recall from Chapter 13, perhaps in a somewhat oversimplified way, that a trust of this type is viewed essentially as a conduit and that the income earned by the trust property which is distributable to L will be taxed to L. Suppose then that L *sells his interest to P.* Two questions are presented: (1) How is gain or loss to be measured? (2) How is gain or loss to be characterized?

Measurement of Gain. It may well be contended that L merely receives an advance payment of future income and, as in *Hort,* all that is received should be taxed. However, that argument runs into *Blair,*[1] which recognized an income interest in a trust as *property,* similar to the decision on the leasehold in *Metropolitan Building.* If this is a disposition of property and not simply an anticipatory assignment of income, then we must think in terms of basis as a subtraction from the amount realized to determine L's gain. And so we must, on good authority.[2]

1. Blair v. Commissioner, 300 U.S. 5, 57 S.Ct. 330 (1937), supra page 280.

2. E.g., Bell's Estate v. Commissioner, 137 F.2d 454 (8th Cir.1943); McAllister v. Commissioner, 157 F.2d 235 (2d Cir.1946), cert. denied 330 U.S. 826, 67 S.Ct. 864 (1947).

Three possibilities now appear. If one purchased a temporary interest, such as L's life interest, he would have a cost basis for it. The cost would be amortized, written off by way of deductions, over the expected duration of the interest. Upon sale of the interest, the adjusted basis would be subtracted from the amount received to determine gain. There is little doubt about this, but of course it does not answer L's question.

If a temporary interest in property is received by gift or bequest, it too is accorded a basis determined, as usual, with reference to Section 1015, Section 1014, or Section 1041. In a bequest situation, the basis for the temporary interest is a part of the Section 1014 basis for the underlying property. In the case of a lifetime gift, such as that received by L, the basis for the income interest is a part of the transferred basis of the donor under Section 1015 or Section 1041. Here (in both the bequest and the gift cases) we encounter the "uniform basis" concept and the phenomenon of a sharing of that basis in shifting percentages by those who have an interest in the property. The thought is that the basis of the property transferred remains uniform, except as it may be subject to adjustments such as for depreciation. But the separate interests in the property share the uniform basis in accordance with the changing *values* of their interests.[3]

Sections 273 and 102(b) are relevant here. The amortization deduction permitted one who *purchases* a temporary interest is denied to one such as L who acquires a life or other terminable interest by gift, and also to one acquiring a temporary interest by bequest or by inheritance. This is because Congress in Section 102 expresses a policy to exclude from gross income a gift or bequest of *property,* but not the income therefrom. The entire exclusion finds its form in the uniform basis. That entire basis will ultimately be passed on to R, the remainderman. That being so, it would be inappropriate to allow L an amortization deduction using a part of the uniform basis. So, in general in these cases the uniform basis remains intact but the bases for the several interests in the property change. When L's interest is worth 40 percent of the value of the property, the basis for this interest is 40 percent of the uniform basis and R's basis is the other 60 percent. As a life tenant grows older his interest diminishes in value. (Consider what you would pay for the right to income from a trust for the life of one 50 years of age and what you would pay if the life tenant were 80.) Thus, when L's interest declines to only 20 percent of the value of the property, his basis has also declined to only 20 percent of the uniform basis but R's basis (as he is now much closer to full ownership) has increased to 80 percent.

Now, are we going to let L assert his share of the uniform basis when he sells his interest to P? Several cases have held that he may,[4]

---

3. Reg. §§ 1.1015–1(b), 1.1014–5.

4. See *Bell's Estate* and *McAllister,* supra note 2.

and quite properly in the absence of statutory proscription. But it does create a distortion. If L's interest has a relative value that gives him 40 percent of the uniform basis, which he subtracts in determining his gain, it is still true that R will have 100 percent of the uniform basis when L's interest which P purchased ends.[5] Thus we've used 140 percent of the uniform basis which is violative of the policy embodied in Section 102(b). Yes, you say, but P invested new funds equal to the added basis. True, we say, *but* his amortization of that *cost* basis is not foreclosed by Section 273 as it is for someone like L who acquires the interest by gift. So we *had* (note the past tense) a distortion here.

In 1969, Congress added Section 1001(e) which requires L, upon the sale of his interest, to *disregard* his share of the Section 1015 (or Section 1014 or Section 1041) uniform basis. Zero basis for L taxes him on *all* that he receives as gain.

Section 1001(e)(3) makes an exception to the zero basis rule of Section 1001(e)(1) if there is a transfer of the entire interest in the property, such as a sale by L *and* R of their interests to P. In light of the preceding discussion, is the reason for this exception discernible?

Characterizing the Gain. If a life interest is property[6] and not within any of the exclusionary paragraphs of Section 1221, it is a capital asset. If it is sold, the gain is capital gain. If it has been held for more than one year, it is long-term capital gain. *All* that L gets is gross income, but it is characterized as capital gain. So be it! *Should* that be it? There may be competing policies here. What L receives is essentially a substitute for what would probably have come to him as ordinary income.[7] While we veer back pretty close to *Hort* with this thought, we find shelter again (for L) in the *Metropolitan Building.* And as a policy matter we might feel that to telescope all of L's receipts into one year would be harsh.[8] In any event, Congress left usual characterization rules intact at the time it changed the measuring device for gain or loss on sales of terminable interests.

PROBLEMS

1. Agent entered into a contract with a national insurance Company to manage its State office for a ten year period. After two years

---

5. Notice that there is no similar problem with regard to a sale of R's remainder. His purchaser will take a cost basis unaffected by the uniform basis rules. Thus, § 1001(e) is not made applicable to the remainder interest, as the uniform basis will just expire with the life beneficiary, and R *may* use his share of the uniform basis upon the sale of this interest. Cf. I.R.C. § 1001(e)(3).

6. See Blair v. Commissioner, supra note 1.

7. Note, however, the characterization rules of I.R.C. §§ 652(b) and 662(b); and

see Ferguson, Freeland and Stephens, The Federal Income Taxation of Estates and Beneficiaries, c. 7, page 468, "The Qualitative Measure."

8. See I.R.C. § 467(c) which requires a lessor of property which is subject to a leaseback or a long term agreement but not subject to the § 467(b)(2) rent leveling provision to recognize gain as ordinary income to the extent of the prior understated rental inclusions. See page 617, supra for a discussion of § 467.

Company decides to discontinue its State operations and agrees to pay Agent $50,000 to terminate his contract. What result to Agent?

2. Recall the *Stranahan* case at page 293, supra. What is the character of taxpayer's gain in that case?

3. Landlord L owns two contiguous parcels of land. He leases both parcels to Tenant T for $1,000 per month per parcel or a total of $24,000 per year; the rent is payable at the end of each year. The lease is for a 10 year period. Upon the following events, which occur more than one year after the lease is signed, what are the results:

(a) To L if he sells the right to the rents on both parcels, prior to any rental payments being due or paid, to a third party for $200,000?

(b) To L if T pays him $20,000 to cancel the leases on both parcels?

(c) To T if L pays him $20,000 to cancel the leases on both parcels?

(d) To T, if after subleasing one of the parcels of land to S for $1200 per month for a five year period, S pays him $10,000 for all T's rights in his lease on that parcel and L releases T from the lease and accepts S as the new tenant?

(e) To T if S subleases one parcel of land from T at $1200 per month for the remainder of T's ten year period?

4. Beneficiary B owns an income interest in a trust which he purchased several years ago. The remaining income interest has twenty years to run after the date of the sale described below and his adjusted basis in the remaining interest is $50,000. What result:

(a) If B sells the entire interest for $60,000?

(b) If B sells the right to one quarter of each year's income for $15,000?

(c) If B received the income interest as a gift (rather than by purchasing it, but assuming the same adjusted basis) and he sells his entire interest for $60,000?

(d) If B inherited the income interest and B and the remainder-man R both sell their interests to a third party with B receiving $60,000 for his interest?

(e) If R sells his remainder interest when it has an adjusted basis of $100,000 for $150,000?

3. THE CORN PRODUCTS DOCTRINE

CORN PRODUCTS REFINING CO. v. COMMISSIONER *

Supreme Court of the United States, 1955.
350 U.S. 46, 76 S.Ct. 20, rehearing denied 350 U.S. 943, 76 S.Ct. 297, 1956.

Mr. Justice CLARK delivered the opinion of the Court.

This case concerns the tax treatment to be accorded certain transactions in commodity futures.[1] In the Tax Court, petitioner Corn Products Refining Company contended that its purchases and sales of corn futures in 1940 and 1942 were capital-asset transactions under § 117(a) of the Internal Revenue Code of 1939. It further contended that its futures transactions came within the "wash sales" provisions of § 118. The 1940 claim was disposed of on the ground that § 118 did not apply, but for the year 1942 both the Tax Court and the Court of Appeals for the Second Circuit, 215 F.2d 513, held that the futures were not capital assets under § 117. We granted certiorari, 348 U.S. 911, 75 S.Ct. 298,[2] because of an asserted conflict with holdings in the Courts of Appeal for the Third, Fifth, and Sixth Circuits.[3] Since we hold that these futures do not constitute capital assets in petitioner's hands, we do not reach the issue of whether the transactions were "wash sales."

Petitioner is a nationally known manufacturer of products made from grain corn. It manufactures starch, syrup, sugar, and their byproducts, feeds and oil. Its average yearly grind of raw corn during the period 1937 through 1942 varied from thirty-five to sixty million bushels. Most of its products were sold under contracts requiring shipment in thirty days at a set price or at market price on the date of delivery, whichever was lower. It permitted cancellation of such contracts, but from experience it could calculate with some accuracy future orders that would remain firm. While it also sold to a few customers on long-term contracts involving substantial orders, these had little effect on the transactions here involved.[4]

---

* See Rabinovitz and Shashy, "Properties of Property: Indigestion from Corn Products," 27 U. of Fla.L.Rev. 964 (1975) and Cunnane, "Acquiring Capital Items for Non-Capital Purposes, or When is a Capital Asset Not a Capital Asset?" 29 N.Y.U. Inst. on Fed.Tax. 705 (1971).

1. A commodity future is a contract to purchase some fixed amount of a commodity at a future date for a fixed price. Corn futures, involved in the present case, are in terms of some multiple of five thousand bushels to be delivered eleven months or less after the contract. Cf. Hoffman, Future Trading (1932), 118.

2. The grant was limited to the following two questions:

"1. Are transactions in commodity futures which are not 'true hedges' capital asset transactions and thus subject to the limitations of Section 117 of the Internal Revenue Code of 1939, or do the resulting gains and losses from such transactions give rise to ordinary income and ordinary deductions?

"2. Are commodity futures contracts 'securities' and thus subject to the 'wash sales' provisions of Section 118 of the Internal Revenue Code of 1939?"

3. Makransky's Estate v. Commissioner, 154 F.2d 59 (C.A.3d Cir.); Commissioner v. Farmers & Ginners Cotton Oil Co., 120 F.2d 772 (C.A.5th Cir.); Trenton Cotton Oil Co. v. Commissioner, 147 F.2d 33 (C.A. 6th Cir.).

4. Petitioner had contracts with three consumers to furnish, for a period of ten years or more, large quantities of starch or

In 1934 and again in 1936 droughts in the corn belt caused a sharp increase in the price of spot corn. With a storage capacity of only 2,300,000 bushels of corn, a bare three weeks' supply, Corn Products found itself unable to buy at a price which would permit its refined corn sugar, cerelose, to compete successfully with cane and beet sugar. To avoid a recurrence of this situation, petitioner, in 1937, began to establish a long position in corn futures "as a part of its corn buying program" and "as the most economical method of obtaining an adequate supply of raw corn" without entailing the expenditure of large sums for additional storage facilities. At harvest time each year it would buy futures when the price appeared favorable. It would take delivery on such contracts as it found necessary to its manufacturing operations and sell the remainder in early summer if no shortage was imminent. If shortages appeared, however, it sold futures only as it bought spot corn for grinding.[5] In this manner it reached a balanced position with reference to any increase in spot corn prices. It made no effort to protect itself against a decline in prices.

In 1940 it netted a profit of $680,587.39 in corn futures, but in 1942 it suffered a loss of $109,969.38. In computing its tax liability Corn Products reported these figures as ordinary profit and loss from its manufacturing operations for the respective years. It now contends that its futures were "capital assets" under § 117 and that gains and losses therefrom should have been treated as arising from the sale of a capital asset.[6] In support of this position it claims that its futures trading was separate and apart from its manufacturing operations and that in its futures transactions it was acting as a "legitimate capitalist." United States v. New York Coffee & Sugar Exchange, 263 U.S. 611, 619, 44 S.Ct. 225, 227. It denies that its futures transactions were "hedges" or "speculative" dealings as covered by the ruling of General Counsel's Memorandum 17322, XV–2 Cum.Bull. 151, and claims that it is in truth "the forgotten man" of that administrative interpretation.

Both the Tax Court and the Court of Appeals found petitioner's futures transactions to be an integral part of its business designed to protect its manufacturing operations against a price increase in its principal raw material and to assure a ready supply for future manufacturing requirements. Corn Products does not level a direct attack on these two-court findings but insists that its futures were "property"

feed. In January 1940, petitioner had sold 2,000,000 bags of corn sugar, delivery to be made several months in the future. Also, members of the canning industry on the Pacific Coast had contracts to purchase corn sugar for delivery in more than thirty days.

5. The dispositions of the corn futures during the period in dispute were as follows:

	Sales of futures thousand bushels	Delivery under futures thousand bushels
1938	17,400	4,975
1939	14,180	2,865
1940	14,595	250
1941	2,545	2,175
1942	5,695	4,460

6. [I.R.C. (1939) § 117(a)(1) is omitted. See I.R.C. (1986) § 1221. Ed.]

entitled to capital-asset treatment under § 117 and as such were distinct from its manufacturing business. We cannot agree.

We find nothing in this record to support the contention that Corn Products' futures activity was separate and apart from its manufacturing operation. On the contrary, it appears that the transactions were vitally important to the company's business as a form of insurance against increases in the price of raw corn. Not only were the purchases initiated for just this reason, but the petitioner's sales policy, selling in the future at a fixed price or less, continued to leave it exceedingly vulnerable to rises in the price of corn. Further, the purchase of corn futures assured the company a source of supply which was admittedly cheaper than constructing additional storage facilities for raw corn. Under these facts it is difficult to imagine a program more closely geared to a company's manufacturing enterprise or more important to its successful operation.

Likewise the claim of Corn Products that it was dealing in the market as a "legitimate capitalist" lacks support in the record. There can be no quarrel with a manufacturer's desire to protect itself against increasing costs of raw materials. Transactions which provide such protection are considered a legitimate form of insurance. United States v. New York Coffee & Sugar Exchange, 263 U.S., at 619, 44 S.Ct. at page 227; Browne v. Thorn, 260 U.S. 137, 139–140, 43 S.Ct. 36, 37. However, in labeling its activity as that of a "legitimate capitalist" exercising "good judgment" in the futures market, petitioner ignores the testimony of its own officers that in entering that market the company was "trying to protect a part of [its] manufacturing costs"; that its entry was not for the purpose of "speculating and buying and selling corn futures" but to fill an actual "need for the quantity of corn [bought] * * * in order to cover * * * what [products] we expected to market over a period of fifteen or eighteen months." It matters not whether the label be that of "legitimate capitalist" or "speculator"; this is not the talk of the capital investor but of the far-sighted manufacturer. For tax purposes petitioner's purchases have been found to "constitute an integral part of its manufacturing business" by both the Tax Court and the Court of Appeals, and on essentially factual questions the findings of two courts should not ordinarily be disturbed. Comstock v. Group of Investors, 335 U.S. 211, 214, 68 S.Ct. 1454, 1456.

Petitioner also makes much of the conclusion by both the Tax Court and the Court of Appeals that its transactions did not constitute "true hedging." It is true that Corn Products did not secure complete protection from its market operations. Under its sales policy petitioner could not guard against a fall in prices. It is clear however, that petitioner feared the possibility of a price rise more than that of a price decline. It therefore purchased partial insurance against its principal risk, and hoped to retain sufficient flexibility to avoid serious losses on a declining market.

Nor can we find support for petitioner's contention that hedging is not within the exclusions of § 117(a). Admittedly, petitioner's corn futures do not come within the literal language of the exclusions set out in that section. They were not stock in trade, actual inventory, property held for sale to customers or depreciable property used in a trade or business. But the capital-asset provision of § 117 must not be so broadly applied as to defeat rather than further the purpose of Congress. Burnet v. Harmel, 287 U.S. 103, 108, 53 S.Ct. 74, 76. Congress intended that profits and losses arising from the everyday operation of a business be considered as ordinary income or loss rather than capital gain or loss. The preferential treatment provided by § 117 applies to transactions in property which are not the normal source of business income. It was intended "to relieve the taxpayer from * * * excessive tax burdens on gains resulting from a conversion of capital investments, and to remove the deterrent effect of those burdens on such conversions." Burnet v. Harmel, 287 U.S., at 106, 53 S.Ct., at page 75. Since this section is an exception from the normal tax requirements of the Internal Revenue Code, the definition of a capital asset must be narrowly applied and its exclusions interpreted broadly. This is necessary to effectuate the basic congressional purpose. This Court has always construed narrowly the term "capital assets" in § 117. See Hort v. Commissioner, 313 U.S. 28, 31, 61 S.Ct. 757, 758; Kieselbach v. Commissioner, 317 U.S. 399, 403, 63 S.Ct. 303, 305.

The problem of the appropriate tax treatment of hedging transactions first arose under the 1934 Tax Code revision.[7] Thereafter the Treasury issued G.C.M. 17322, supra, distinguishing speculative transactions in commodity futures from hedging transactions. It held that hedging transactions were essentially to be regarded as insurance rather than a dealing in capital assets and that gains and losses therefrom were ordinary business gains and losses. The interpretation outlined in this memorandum has been consistently followed by the courts as well as by the Commissioner.[8] While it is true that this Court has not passed on its validity, it has been well recognized for 20 years; and Congress has made no change in it though the Code has been re-enacted on three subsequent occasions. This bespeaks congressional approval. Helvering v. Winmill, 305 U.S. 79, 83, 59 S.Ct. 45, 46. Furthermore, Congress has since specifically recognized the hedging

---

7. Section 208(8) of the Revenue Act of 1924 limited "capital assets" to property held more than two years. This definition was retained until the Act of 1934. Since the rules of the various commodity exchanges required that futures contracts be closed out in periods shorter than two years, these contracts could not qualify as capital assets.

8. Stewart Silk Corp. v. Commissioner, 9 T.C. 174; Battelle v. Commissioner, 47 B.T.A. 117; Grote v. Commissioner, 41 B.T.A. 247. See Estate of Makransky v. Commissioner, 5 T.C. 397, 412, affirmed per curiam 154 F.2d 59 (3d Cir. 1946); Trenton Cotton Oil Co. v. Commissioner, 147 F.2d 33, 35 (6th Cir. 1945); Commissioner v. Farmers & Ginners Cotton Oil Co., 120 F.2d 772, 774 (5th Cir. 1941); Tennessee Egg Co. v. Commissioner, 47 B.T.A. 558, 560; G.C.M. 18383, 1937–2 Cum.Bull. 244, 245; I.T. 3137, 1937–2 Cum.Bull. 164, 166. Cf. Commissioner v. Banfield, 122 F.2d 1017, 1019–1020 (9th Cir. 1941); G.C.M. 18658, 1937–2 Cum.Bull. 77.

exception here under consideration in the short-sale rule of § 1233(a) of the 1954 Code.[9]

We believe that the statute clearly refutes the contention of Corn Products. Moreover, it is significant to note that practical considerations lead to the same conclusion. To hold otherwise would permit those engaged in hedging transactions to transmute ordinary income into capital gain at will. The hedger may either sell the future and purchase in the spot market or take delivery under the future contract itself. But if a sale of the future created a capital transaction while delivery of the commodity under the same future did not, a loophole in the statute would be created and the purpose of Congress frustrated.

The judgment is affirmed.

Mr. Justice HARLAN took no part in the consideration or decision of this case.

ARKANSAS BEST CORP. v. COMMISSIONER *
Supreme Court of the United States, 1988.
485 U.S. 212, 108 S.Ct. 971.

Justice MARSHALL delivered the opinion of the Court.

The issue presented in this case is whether capital stock held by petitioner Arkansas Best Corporation (Arkansas Best) is a "capital asset" as defined in § 1221 of the Internal Revenue Code regardless of whether the stock was purchased and held for a business purpose or for an investment purpose.

I

Arkansas Best is a diversified holding company. In 1968 it acquired approximately 65% of the stock of the National Bank of Commerce (Bank) in Dallas, Texas. Between 1969 and 1974, Arkansas Best more than tripled the number of shares it owned in the Bank, although its percentage interest in the Bank remained relatively stable. These acquisitions were prompted principally by the Bank's need for added capital. Until 1972, the Bank appeared to be prosperous and growing, and the added capital was necessary to accommodate this growth. As the Dallas real estate market declined, however, so too did the financial health of the Bank, which had a heavy concentration of loans in the local real estate industry. In 1972, federal examiners classified the

---

9. Section 1233(a) provides that gain or loss from "the short sale of property, other than a hedging transaction in commodity futures," shall be treated as gain or loss from the sale of a capital asset to the extent "that the property, including a commodity future, used to close the short sale constitutes a capital asset in the hands of a taxpayer." The legislative history recognizes explicitly the hedging exception. H.R.Rep. No. 1337, 83d Cong., 2d Sess., p. A278; S.Rep. No. 1622, 83d Cong., 2d Sess., p. 437: "Under existing law bona fide hedging transactions do not result in capital gains or losses. This result is based upon case law and regulations. To continue this result hedging transactions in commodity futures have been specifically excepted from the operation of this subsection."

* Some footnotes omitted.

Bank as a problem bank. The infusion of capital after 1972 was prompted by the loan portfolio problems of the bank.

Petitioner sold the bulk of its Bank stock on June 30, 1975, leaving it with only a 14.7% stake in the Bank. On its federal income tax return for 1975, petitioner claimed a deduction for an ordinary loss of $9,995,688 resulting from the sale of the stock. The Commissioner of Internal Revenue disallowed the deduction, finding that the loss from the sale of stock was a capital loss, rather than an ordinary loss, and that it therefore was subject to the capital loss limitations in the Internal Revenue Code.[1]

Arkansas Best challenged the Commissioner's determination in the United States Tax Court. The Tax Court, relying on cases interpreting Corn Products Refining Co. v. Commissioner, 350 U.S. 46 (1955), held that stock purchased with a substantial investment purpose is a capital asset which, when sold, gives rise to a capital gain or loss, whereas stock purchased and held for a business purpose, without any substantial investment motive, is an ordinary asset whose sale gives rise to ordinary gains or losses. See 83 T.C. 640, 653–654 (1984). The court characterized Arkansas Best's acquisitions through 1972 as occurring during the Bank's " 'growth' phase," and found that these acquisitions "were motivated primarily by investment purpose and only incidentally by some business purpose." Id., at 654. The stock acquired during this period therefore constituted a capital asset, which gave rise to a capital loss when sold in 1975. The court determined, however, that the acquisitions after 1972 occurred during the Bank's " 'problem' phase," ibid., and, except for certain minor exceptions, "were made exclusively for business purposes and subsequently held for the same reasons." Id., at 656. These acquisitions, the court found, were designed to preserve petitioner's business reputation, because without the added capital the Bank probably would have failed. Id., at 656–657. The loss realized on the sale of this stock was thus held to be an ordinary loss.

The Court of Appeals for the Eighth Circuit reversed the Tax Court's determination that the loss realized on stock purchased after 1972 was subject to ordinary-loss treatment, holding that all of the Bank stock sold in 1975 was subject to capital-loss treatment. 800 F.2d 215 (1986). The court reasoned that the Bank stock clearly fell within the general definition of "capital asset" in Internal Revenue Code § 1221, and that the stock did not fall within any of the specific statutory exceptions to this definition. The court concluded that Arkansas Best's purpose in acquiring and holding the stock was irrelevant to the determination whether the stock was a capital asset. We granted certiorari, 480 U.S. 930, and now affirm.

---

1. Title 26 U.S.C. § 1211(a) states that "[i]n the case of a corporation, losses from sales or exchanges of capital assets shall be allowed only to the extent of gains from such sales or exchanges." Section 1212(a) establishes rules governing carrybacks and carryovers of capital losses, permitting such losses to offset capital gains in certain earlier or later years.

II

Section 1221 of the Internal Revenue Code defines "capital asset" broadly, as "property held by the taxpayer (whether or not connected with his trade or business)," and then excludes five specific classes of property from capital-asset status. In the statute's present form, the classes of property exempted from the broad definition are (1) "property of a kind which would properly be included in the inventory of the taxpayer"; (2) real property or other depreciable property used in the taxpayer's trade or business; (3) "a copyright, a literary, musical, or artistic composition," or similar property; (4) "accounts or notes receivable acquired in the ordinary course of trade or business for services rendered" or from the sale of inventory; and (5) publications of the Federal Government. Arkansas Best acknowledges that the Bank stock falls within the literal definition of "capital asset" in § 1221, and is outside of the statutory exclusions. It asserts, however, that this determination does not end the inquiry. Petitioner argues that in *Corn Products Refining Co. v. Commissioner,* supra, this Court rejected a literal reading of § 1221, and concluded that assets acquired and sold for ordinary business purposes rather than for investment purposes should be given ordinary-asset treatment. Petitioner's reading of *Corn Products* finds much support in the academic literature [3] and in the courts.[4] Unfortunately for petitioner, this broad reading finds no support in the language of § 1221.

In essence, petitioner argues that "property held by the taxpayer (whether or not connected with his trade or business)" does not include property that is acquired and held for a business purpose. In petitioner's view an asset's status as "property" thus turns on the motivation behind its acquisition. This motive test, however, is not only nowhere mentioned in § 1221, but it is also in direct conflict with the parenthetical phrase "whether or not connected with his trade or business." The broad definition of the term "capital asset" explicitly makes irrelevant any consideration of the property's connection with the taxpayer's business, whereas petitioner's rule would make this factor dispositive.[5]

---

3. See, e.g., 2 B. Bittker, Federal Taxation of Income, Estates and Gifts ¶ 51.10.3, p. 51–62 (1981); Chirelstein, Capital Gain and the Sale of a Business Opportunity: The Income Tax Treatment of Contract Termination Payments, 49 Minn.L.Rev. 1, 41 (1964); Troxell & Noall, Judicial Erosion of the Concept of Securities as Capital Assets, 19 Tax L.Rev. 185, 187 (1964); Note, The *Corn Products* Doctrine and Its Application to Partnership Interests, 79 Colum.L.Rev. 341, and n. 3 (1979).

4. See, e.g., Campbell Taggart, Inc. v. United States, 744 F.2d 442, 456–458 (CA5 1984); Steadman v. Commissioner, 424 F.2d 1, 5 (CA6), cert. denied, 400 U.S. 869 (1970); Booth Newspapers, Inc. v. United States, 157 Ct.Cl. 886, 893–896, 303 F.2d 916, 920–921 (1962); W.W. Windle Co. v. Commissioner, 65 T.C. 694, 707–713 (1976).

5. Petitioner mistakenly relies on cases in which this Court, in narrowly applying the general definition of "capital asset," has "construed 'capital asset' to exclude property representing income items or accretions to the value of a capital asset themselves properly attributable to income," even though these items are property in the broad sense of the word. United States v. Midland–Ross Corp., 381 U.S. 54, 57 (1965). See, e.g., Commissioner v. Gillette Motor Co., 364 U.S. 130 (1960) ("capital asset" does not include compensation awarded taxpayer that represented fair

In a related argument, petitioner contends that the five exceptions listed in § 1221 for certain kinds of property are illustrative, rather than exhaustive, and that courts are therefore free to fashion additional exceptions in order to further the general purposes of the capital-asset provisions. The language of the statute refutes petitioner's construction. Section 1221 provides that "capital asset" means "property held by the taxpayer[,] . . . but does not include" the five classes of property listed as exceptions. We believe this locution signifies that the listed exceptions are exclusive. The body of § 1221 establishes a general definition of the term "capital asset," and the phrase "does not include" takes out of that broad definition only the classes of property that are specifically mentioned. The legislative history of the capital-asset definition supports this interpretation, see H.R.Rep. No. 704, 73d Cong., 2d Sess., 31 (1934) ("[T]he definition includes all property, except as specifically excluded"); H.R.Rep. No. 1337, 83d Cong., 2d Sess., A273 (1954) ("[A] capital asset is property held by the taxpayer with certain exceptions"), as does the applicable Treasury regulation, see 26 CFR § 1.1221–1(a) (1987) ("The term 'capital assets' includes all classes of property not specifically excluded by section 1221").

Petitioner's reading of the statute is also in tension with the exceptions listed in § 1221. These exclusions would be largely superfluous if assets acquired primarily or exclusively for business purposes were not capital assets. Inventory, real or depreciable property used in the taxpayer's trade or business, and accounts or notes receivable acquired in the ordinary course of business, would undoubtedly satisfy such a business-motive test. Yet these exceptions were created by Congress in separate enactments spanning 30 years.[6] Without any express direction from Congress, we are unwilling to read § 1221 in a manner that makes surplusage of these statutory exclusions.

In the end, petitioner places all reliance on its reading of Corn Products Refining Co. v. Commissioner, 350 U.S. 46 (1955)—a reading we believe is too expansive. In *Corn Products,* the Court considered whether income arising from a taxpayer's dealings in corn futures was entitled to capital-gains treatment. The taxpayer was a company that converted corn into starches, sugars, and other products. After droughts in the 1930's caused sharp increases in corn prices, the

rental value of its facilities); Commissioner v. P.G. Lake, Inc., 356 U.S. 260 (1958) ("capital asset" does not include proceeds from sale of oil payment rights); Hort v. Commissioner, 313 U.S. 28 (1941) ("capital asset" does not include payment to lessor for cancellation of unexpired portion of a lease). This line of cases, based on the premise that § 1221 "property" does not include claims or rights to ordinary income, has no application in the present context. Petitioner sold capital stock, not a claim to ordinary income.

6. The inventory exception was part of the original enactment of the capital-asset provision in 1924. See Revenue Act of 1924, ch. 234, § 208(a)(8), 43 Stat. 263. Depreciable property used in a trade or business was excluded in 1938, see Revenue Act of 1938, ch. 289, § 117(a)(1), 52 Stat. 500, and real property used in a trade or business was excluded in 1942, see Revenue Act of 1942, ch. 619, § 151(a), 56 Stat. 846. The exception for accounts and notes receivable acquired in the ordinary course of trade or business was added in 1954. Internal Revenue Code of 1954, § 1221(4), 68A Stat. 322.

company began a program of buying corn futures to assure itself an adequate supply of corn and protect against price increases. See id., at 48. The company "would take delivery on such contracts as it found necessary to its manufacturing operations and sell the remainder in early summer if no shortage was imminent. If shortages appeared, however, it sold futures only as it bought spot corn for grinding." Id., at 48–49. The Court characterized the company's dealing in corn futures as "hedging." Id., at 51. As explained by the Court of Appeals in *Corn Products*, "[h]edging is a method of dealing in commodity futures whereby a person or business protects itself against price fluctuations at the time of delivery of the product which it sells or buys." 215 F.2d 513, 515 (CA2 1954). In evaluating the company's claim that the sales of corn futures resulted in capital gains and losses, this Court stated:

> "Nor can we find support for petitioner's contention that hedging is not within the exclusions of [§ 1221]. Admittedly, petitioner's corn futures do not come within the literal language of the exclusions set out in that section. They were not stock in trade, actual inventory, property held for sale to customers or depreciable property used in a trade or business. But the capital-asset provision of [§ 1221] must not be so broadly applied as to defeat rather than further the purpose of Congress. Congress intended that profits and losses arising from the everyday operation of a business be considered as ordinary income or loss rather than capital gain or loss. . . . Since this section is an exception from the normal tax requirements of the Internal Revenue Code, the definition of a capital asset must be narrowly applied and its exclusions interpreted broadly." 350 U.S., at 51–52 (citations omitted).

The Court went on to note that hedging transactions consistently had been considered to give rise to ordinary gains and losses, and then concluded that the corn futures were subject to ordinary-asset treatment. Id., at 52–53.

The Court in *Corn Products* proffered the oft-quoted rule of construction that the definition of "capital asset" must be narrowly applied and its exclusions interpreted broadly, but it did not state explicitly whether the holding was based on a narrow reading of the phrase "property held by the taxpayer," or on a broad reading of the inventory exclusion of § 1221. In light of the stark language of § 1221, however, we believe that *Corn Products* is properly interpreted as involving an application of § 1221's inventory exception. Such a reading is consistent both with the Court's reasoning in that case and with § 1221. The Court stated in *Corn Products* that the company's futures transactions were "an integral part of its business designed to protect its manufacturing operations against a price increase in its principal raw material and to assure a ready supply for future manufacturing requirements." 350 U.S., at 50. The company bought, sold, and took delivery under the futures contracts as required by the company's manufacturing needs.

As Professor Bittker notes, under these circumstances, the futures can "easily be viewed as surrogates for the raw material itself." 2 B. Bittker, Federal Taxation of Income, Estates and Gifts ¶ 51.10.3, p. 51–62 (1981). The Court of Appeals for the Second Circuit in *Corn Products* clearly took this approach. That court stated that when commodity futures are "utilized solely for the purpose of stabilizing inventory cost[,] . . . [they] cannot reasonably be separated from the inventory items," and concluded that "property used in hedging transactions properly comes within the exclusions of [§ 1221]." 215 F.2d, at 516. This Court indicated its acceptance of the Second Circuit's reasoning when it began the central paragraph of its opinion: "Nor can we find support for petitioner's contention that hedging is not within the exclusions of [§ 1221]." 350 U.S., at 51. In the following paragraph, the Court argued that the Treasury had consistently viewed such hedging transactions as a form of insurance to stabilize the cost of inventory, and cited a Treasury ruling which concluded that the value of a manufacturer's raw-material inventory should be adjusted to take into account hedging transactions in futures contracts. See id., at 52–53 (citing G.C.M. 17322, XV–2 Cum.Bull. 151 (1936)). This discussion, read in light of the Second Circuit's holding and the plain language of § 1221, convinces us that although the corn futures were not "actual inventory," their use as an integral part of the taxpayer's inventory-purchase system led the Court to treat them as substitutes for the corn inventory such that they came within a broad reading of "property of a kind which would properly be included in the inventory of the taxpayer" in § 1221.

Petitioner argues that by focusing attention on whether the asset was acquired and sold as an integral part of the taxpayer's everyday business operations, the Court in *Corn Products* intended to create a general exemption from capital-asset status for assets acquired for business purposes. We believe petitioner misunderstands the relevance of the Court's inquiry. A business connection, although irrelevant to the initial determination of whether an item is a capital asset, is relevant in determining the applicability of certain of the statutory exceptions, including the inventory exception. The close connection between the futures transactions and the taxpayer's business in *Corn Products* was crucial to whether the corn futures could be considered surrogates for the stored inventory of raw corn. For if the futures dealings were not part of the company's inventory-purchase system, and instead amounted simply to speculation in corn futures, they could not be considered substitutes for the company's corn inventory, and would fall outside even a broad reading of the inventory exclusion. We conclude that *Corn Products* is properly interpreted as standing for the narrow proposition that hedging transactions that are an integral part of a business' inventory-purchase system fall within the inventory exclusion of § 1221.[7] Arkansas Best, which is not a dealer in securities,

7. Although congressional inaction is generally a poor measure of congressional intent, we are given some pause by the fact that over 25 years have passed since Corn

has never suggested that the Bank stock falls within the inventory exclusion. *Corn Products* thus has no application to this case.

It is also important to note that the business-motive test advocated by petitioner is subject to the same kind of abuse that the Court condemned in *Corn Products*. The Court explained in *Corn Products* that unless hedging transactions were subject to ordinary gain and loss treatment, taxpayers engaged in such transactions could "transmute ordinary income into capital gain at will." 350 U.S., at 53–54. The hedger could garner capital-asset treatment by selling the future and purchasing the commodity on the spot market, or ordinary-asset treatment by taking delivery under the future contract. In a similar vein, if capital stock purchased and held for a business purpose is an ordinary asset, whereas the same stock purchased and held with an investment motive is a capital asset, a taxpayer such as Arkansas Best could have significant influence over whether the asset would receive capital or ordinary treatment. Because stock is most naturally viewed as a capital asset, the Internal Revenue Service would be hard pressed to challenge a taxpayer's claim that stock was acquired as an investment, and that a gain arising from the sale of such stock was therefore a capital gain. Indeed, we are unaware of a single decision that has applied the business-motive test so as to require a taxpayer to report a gain from the sale of stock as an ordinary gain. If the same stock is sold at a loss, however, the taxpayer may be able to garner ordinary-loss treatment by emphasizing the business purpose behind the stock's acquisition. The potential for such abuse was evidenced in this case by the fact that as late as 1974, when Arkansas Best still hoped to sell the Bank stock at a profit, Arkansas Best apparently expected to report the gain as a capital gain. See 83 T.C., at 647–648.

III

We conclude that a taxpayer's motivation in purchasing an asset is irrelevant to the question whether the asset is "property held by a taxpayer (whether or not connected with his business)" and is thus within § 1221's general definition of "capital asset." Because the capital stock held by petitioner falls within the broad definition of the term "capital asset" in § 1221 and is outside the classes of property excluded from capital-asset status, the loss arising from the sale of the stock is a capital loss. *Corn Products Refining Co. v. Commissioner,* supra, which we interpret as involving a broad reading of the inventory exclusion of § 1221, has no application in the present context. Accordingly, the judgment of the Court of Appeals is affirmed.

It is so ordered.

Products Refining Co. v. Commissioner was initially interpreted as excluding assets acquired for business purposes from the definition of "capital asset," see Booth Newspapers, Inc. v. United States, 157 Ct.Cl. 886, 303 F.2d 916 (1962), without any sign of disfavor from Congress. We cannot ignore the unambiguous language of § 1221, however, no matter how reticent Congress has been. If a broad exclusion from capital-asset status is to be created for assets acquired for business purposes, it must come from congressional action, not silence.

PROBLEM

Taxpayer T was having difficulty obtaining a component part needed in his manufacturing process to produce a machine that he sells to customers. To assure a supply of the part, T purchased stock in Corporation X which produces it. The purchasing priority accorded Corporation X shareholders was T's principal purpose for purchasing the shares. Two years after the purchase of the shares at a cost of $200,000, T revamped his manufacturing process in such a way that the part was no longer needed. What result to T if he immediately sold the stock for $150,000?

E. THE SALE OR EXCHANGE REQUIREMENT

---

1. INTRODUCTION

Internal Revenue Code: Section 1222. See Sections 1235; 1241; 1253; 1271.

KENAN v. COMMISSIONER

United States Court of Appeals, Second Circuit, 1940.
114 F.2d 217.

AUGUSTUS N. HAND, Circuit Judge. The testatrix, Mrs. Bingham, died on July 27, 1917, leaving a will under which she placed her residuary estate in trust and provided in item "Seventh" that her trustees should pay a certain amount annually to her niece, Louise Clisby Wise, until the latter reached the age of forty, "at which time or as soon thereafter as compatible with the interests of my estate they shall pay to her the sum of Five Million ($5,000,000.00) Dollars." The will provided in item "Eleventh" that the trustees, in the case of certain payments including that of the $5,000,000 under item "Seventh", should have the right "to substitute for the payment in money, payment in marketable securities of a value equal to the sum to be paid, the selection of the securities to be substituted in any instance, and the valuation of such securities to be done by the Trustees and their selection and valuation to be final."

Louise Clisby Wise became forty years of age on July 28, 1935. The trustees decided to pay her the $5,000,000 partly in cash and partly in securities. The greater part of the securities had been owned by the testator and transferred as part of her estate to the trustees; others had been purchased by the trustees. All had appreciated in value during the period for which they were held by the trustees, and the Commissioner determined that the distribution of the securities to the niece resulted in capital gains which were taxable to the trustees under the rates specified in Section 117 of the Revenue Act of 1934, which limits the percentage of gain to be treated as taxable income on the "sale or exchange" of capital assets. On this basis, the Commissioner determined a deficiency of $367,687.12 in the income tax for the year 1935.

The Board overruled the objections of the trustees to the imposition of any tax and denied a motion of the Commissioner to amend his answer in order to claim the full amount of the appreciation in value as ordinary income rather than a percentage of it as a capital gain, and confirmed the original deficiency determination. The taxpayers contend that the decision of the Board was erroneous because they realized neither gain from the sale or exchange of capital assets nor income of any character by delivering the securities to the legatee pursuant to the permissive terms of the will. The Commissioner contends that gain was realized by the delivery of the securities but that such gain was ordinary income not derived from a sale or exchange and therefore taxable in its entirety. The trustees have filed a petition to review the order of the Board determining the deficiency of $367,687.12 and the Commissioner has filed a cross-petition claiming a deficiency of $1,238,841.99, based on his contention that the gain was not governed by Section 117, and therefore not limited by the percentages therein specified.

The amount of gain is to be determined under Section 111 of the Revenue Act of 1934, which provides:

> "(a) Computation of gain or loss. The gain from the sale or other disposition of property shall be the excess of the amount realized therefrom over the adjusted basis * * *.

> "(b) Amount realized. The amount realized from the sale or other disposition of property shall be the sum of any money received plus the fair market value of the property (other than money) received."

Section 113, 26 U.S.C.A. Int.Rev.Code, § 113, is claimed by the taxpayers to be relevant and provides:

> "(a) The basis of property shall be the cost of such property; except that—

> * * *

> "(5) Property transmitted at death. If the property was acquired by bequest, devise, or inheritance, or by the decedent's estate from the decedent, the basis shall be the fair market value of such property at the time of such acquisition."

The Taxpayer's Appeal

In support of their petition the taxpayers contend that the delivery of the securities of the trust estate to the legatee was a donative disposition of property pursuant to the terms of the will, and that no gain was thereby realized. They argue that when they determined that the legacy should be one of securities, it became for all purposes a bequest of property, just as if the cash alternative had not been provided, and not taxable for the reason that no gain is realized on the transfer by a testamentary trustee of specific securities or other property bequeathed by will to a legatee.

We do not think that the situation here is the same as that of a legacy of specific property. The legatee was never in the position occupied by the recipient of specific securities under a will. She had a claim against the estate for $5,000,000, payable either in cash or securities of that value, but had no title or right to the securities, legal or equitable, until they were delivered to her by the trustees after the exercise of their option. She took none of the chances of a legatee of specific securities or of a share of a residue that the securities might appreciate or decline in value between the time of the death of the testator and the transfer to her by the trustees, but instead had at all times a claim for an unvarying amount in money or its equivalent.

If there had merely been a bequest to the legatee of $5,000,000 and she had agreed with the trustees to take securities of that value, the transaction would have been a "sale or other disposition" of the securities under Suisman v. Eaton, 15 F.Supp. 113, affirmed, 2 Cir., 83 F.2d 1019, certiorari denied 299 U.S. 573, 57 S.Ct. 37. There, a will creating a trust provided that each of the testator's children was to receive $50,000 on attaining the age of twenty-five. The trustee transferred stock of the value of $50,000 to one of the children, Minerva, in satisfaction of her legacy. Judge Hincks said in the district court (15 F.Supp. at page 115), that the "property which the trust estate received from the 'sale or other disposition' of said stocks was the discharge of the corpus from Minerva's equitable right to receive $50,000 therefrom; the amount realized, i.e., the 'fair market value of the property (other than money) received,' * * * was $50,000; and the excess of the amount realized over the basis was properly computed by the Commissioner, legally assessed as part of the taxable income of the trust estate, and the tax thereon was legally collected."

In the present case, the legatee had a claim which was a charge against the trust estate for $5,000,000 in cash or securities and the trustees had the power to determine whether the claim should be satisfied in one form or the other. The claim, though enforceable only in the alternative, was, like the claim in Suisman v. Eaton, supra, a charge against the entire trust estate. If it were satisfied by a cash payment securities might have to be sold on which (if those actually delivered in specie were selected) a taxable gain would necessarily have been realized. Instead of making such a sale the trustees delivered the securities and exchanged them pro tanto for the general claim of the legatee, which was thereby satisfied.

It is said that this transaction was not such a "sale or other disposition" as is intended by Section 111(a) or was dealt with in Suisman v. Eaton, because it was effectuated only by the will of the trustees and not, as in Suisman v. Eaton, through a mutual agreement between trustee and legatee. The Board made no such distinction, and we are not inclined to limit thus the meaning of the words "other disposition" used in Section 111(a), or of "exchange" used in Section 117. The word "exchange" does not necessarily have the connotation of a bilateral agreement which may be said to attach to the word "sale." Thus, should a person set up a trust and reserve to himself the power to substitute for the securities placed in trust other securities of equal value, there would seem no doubt that the exercise of this reserved power would be an "exchange" within the common meaning of the word, even though the settlor consulted no will other than his own, although, of course, we do not here advert to the problems of taxability in such a situation.

The Board alluded to the fact that both here and in Suisman v. Eaton the bequest was fixed at a definite amount in money, that in both cases there was no bequest of specific securities (nor of a share in the residue which might vary in value), that the rights of the legatee, like those in the Suisman case, were a charge upon the corpus of the trust, and that the trustees had to part either with $5,000,000 in cash or with securities worth that amount at the time of the transfer. It added that the increase in value of the securities was realized by the trust and benefited it to the full extent, since, except for the increase, it would have had to part with other property, and it cited in further support of its position United States v. Kirby Lumber Co., 284 U.S. 1, 52 S.Ct. 4. Under circumstances like those here, where the legatee did not take securities designated by the will or an interest in the corpus which might be more or less at the time of the transfer than at the time of decedent's death, it seems to us that the trustees realized a gain by using these securities to settle a claim worth $5,000,000, just as the trustee in Suisman v. Eaton realized one.

It seems reasonably clear that the property was not "transmitted at death" or "acquired by bequest * * * from the decedent." Section 113(a)(5). It follows that the fears of the taxpayers that double taxation of this appreciation will result because the legatee will take the basis of the decedent under Brewster v. Gage, 280 U.S. 327, 50 S.Ct. 115, are groundless. It is true that under Section 113(a)(5) the basis for property "acquired by bequest, devise, or inheritance" is "the fair market value of such property at the time of such acquisition" and that under Brewster v. Gage, supra, the date of acquisition has been defined as the date of death of the testator. But the holding of the present case is necessarily a determination that the property here acquired is acquired in an exchange and not "by bequest, devise or inheritance," since Sections 117 and 113(a)(5) seem to be mutually exclusive. The legatee's basis would seem to be the value of the claim surrendered in exchange for the securities; and the Board of Tax Appeals has so held. Sherman Ewing v. Commissioner of Internal Revenue, 40 B.T.A. 911.

The Commissioner's Appeal

We have already held that a taxable gain was realized by the delivery of the securities. It follows from the reasons that support that conclusion that the appreciation was a capital gain, taxable at the rates specified in Section 117. Therefore, neither under Section 111(a) nor under Section 22(a), 26 U.S.C.A. Int.Rev.Acts, page 669, can the gain realized be taxed as ordinary income.

There can be no doubt that from an accounting standpoint the trustees realized a gain in the capital of their trust when they disposed of securities worth far more at the time of disposition than at the time of acquisition in order to settle (pro tanto) a claim of $5,000,000. It would seem to us a strange anomaly if a disposition of securities which were in fact a "capital asset" should not be taxed at the rates afforded by Section 117 to individuals who have sold or exchanged property which they had held for the specified periods. It is not without significance that the appeal of the Commissioner was plainly an afterthought. The original deficiency was determined on the theory that the capital gains rates were applicable and the Commissioner sought to amend his answer so as to claim that ordinary rates should be applied only after the case had been orally argued before the Board. The Board denied his motion to reopen the case for the consideration of this contention. Since we find that the Commissioner's cross-petition is unfounded on the merits, we have no reason to consider the technical question whether the denial of the motion to amend the answer was an abuse of discretion.

The purpose of the capital gains provisions of the Revenue Act of 1934 is so to treat an appreciation in value, arising over a period of years but realized in one year, that the tax thereon will roughly approximate what it would have been had a tax been paid each year upon the appreciation in value for that year. Cf. Burnet v. Harmel, 287 U.S. 103, 106, 53 S.Ct. 74. The appreciation in value in the present case took place between 1917 and 1935, whereas the Commissioner's theory would tax it as though it had all taken place in 1935. If the trustees had sold the securities, they would be taxed at capital gain rates. Both the trustees and the Commissioner, in their arguments as respondent and cross-respondents, draw the analogy between the transaction here and a sale, and no injustice is done to either by taxing the gain at the rates which would apply had a sale actually been made and the proceeds delivered to the legatee. It seems to us extraordinary that the exercise by the trustees of the option to deliver to the legatee securities, rather than cash, should be thought to result in an increased deficiency of enormous proportions.

Orders affirmed.

GALVIN HUDSON

Tax Court of the United States, 1953.
20 T.C. 734, affirmed sub nom. Ogilvie v. Commissioner, 216 F.2d 748 (6th Cir. 1954).

Findings of Fact

All the facts are stipulated and are so found.

Petitioners, residents of Memphis, Tennessee, filed their income tax returns for the year 1945 with the collector of internal revenue for the district of Tennessee. Galvin Hudson is in the lumber and cooperage business, and Hillsman Taylor is a practicing attorney.

On November 23, 1929, Mary Mallory Harahan obtained a judgment against Howard Cole in the amount of $75,702.12 in the Supreme Court of the State of New York. This judgment will hereinafter be referred to as the Cole judgment.

On June 30, 1943, the petitioners purchased the Cole judgment from the residuary legatees of Mary Mallory Harahan's estate; each petitioner acquired a 50 per cent interest in the judgment. Their aggregate cost of the judgment was $11,004; this included attorney fees and expenses of $1,004.

In May 1945 Howard Cole paid petitioners the sum of $21,150 as a full settlement of the judgment against him.

Each of the petitioners reported his profit on the settlement of the Cole judgment for income tax purposes as a long-term capital gain for 1945.

Respondent explained the adjustment to petitioners' net income as follows:

> (a) It is held that the profits realized on the collection of a judgment from Mr. Howard Cole is taxable as ordinary income. In your return your reported 50% of $5,073.00, or $2,536.50 as capital gain. Accordingly, ordinary net income is increased in the amount of $5,073.00. * * *

The gain resulting to petitioners from the settlement of the Cole judgment is ordinary income, as distinguished from a capital gain.

JOHNSON, Judge: Simply, the issue is whether the gain realized from the settlement of a judgment is ordinary income or capital gain when the settlement was made between the judgment debtor and the assignee or transferee of a prior judgment creditor. Petitioners contend that they are entitled to the benefits of section 117(a), Internal Revenue Code, with regard to the gain from the settlement of a judgment. Respondent has determined that the gain is ordinary income and taxable as such. There is no question about the bona fides of the transaction, nor is there any disagreement about the fact that the judgment, when entered and transferred, was property and a capital asset. The parties differ, however, on the question of whether there was a "sale or exchange of a capital asset." Section 117(a)(4). Petitioners and respondent both adhere to the principle that the words "sale or exchange" should be given their ordinary meaning. Petitioners, citing authority, define the word "sale" as follows:

> A sale is a contract whereby one acquires a property in the thing sold and the other parts with it for a valuable consideration * * * or a sale is generally understood to mean the transfer of property for money * * *.

Also, "Sell in its ordinary sense means a transfer of property for a fixed price in money or its equivalent."

We cannot see how there was a transfer of property, or how the judgment debtor acquired property as the result of the transaction wherein the judgment was settled. The most that can be said is that the judgment debtor paid a debt or extinguished a claim so as to preclude execution on the judgment outstanding against him. In a hypothetical case, if the judgment had been transferred to someone other than the judgment debtor, the property transferred would still be in existence after the transaction was completed. However, as it actually happened, when the judgment debtor settled the judgment, the claim arising from the judgment was extinguished without the transfer of any property or property right to the judgment debtor. In their day-to-day transactions, neither businessmen nor lawyers would call the settlement of a judgment a sale; we can see no reason to apply a strained interpretation to the transaction before us. When petitioners received the $21,150 in full settlement of the judgment, they did not recover the money as the result of any sale or exchange but only as a collection or settlement of the judgment.

It is well established that where the gain realized did not result from a sale or exchange of a capital asset, the gain is not within the provisions of section 117(a)(4). In R.W. Hale, 32 B.T.A. 356, affd. 85 F.2d 815, there was a compromise of notes for less than face value and the taxpayer claimed there was a sale or exchange of notes within the meaning of the capital gains provision of the Code. In deciding the issue against the taxpayer, we said:

> The petitioners did not sell or exchange the mortgage notes, and consequently an essential condition expressly required by the statute has not been met and no capital loss has been suffered. * * *

The *Hale* case was cited with approval in Pat N. Fahey, 16 T.C. 105. There, the taxpayer, an attorney, was assigned, for a cash consideration, an interest in a fee. Upon a successful settlement of the litigation, the taxpayer was paid his part of the fee. We held that his share was not capital gain because he did not sell or exchange anything. In another situation, a redemption of bonds before maturity by the issuing corporation was not a sale or exchange of capital assets. Fairbanks v. United States, 306 U.S. 436. In a similar situation in Bingham v. Commissioner, 105 F.2d 971, 972, the court said:

> What may have been property in the hands of the holder of the notes simply vanished when the surrender took place and the maker received them. He then had, at most, only his own obligations to pay himself. Any theoretical concept of a sale of the notes to the maker in return for what he gave up to get them back must yield before the hard fact that he received nothing which was property in his hands but had merely succeeded in extinguishing his liabilities by the amounts which were due on the notes. There was, therefore, no sale of the notes to

him in the ordinary meaning of the word and no exchange of assets for assets since the notes could not, as assets, survive the transaction. That being so, such a settlement as the one this petitioner made involved neither a sale nor an exchange of capital assets within the meaning of the statute. * * *

See also, Jack Rosenzweig, 1 T.C. 24, and Matilda S. Puelicher, 6 T.C. 300.

We have carefully considered the many cases cited by petitioners but we have found none of them controlling the issue before us. Cf. Commissioner v. Bookstein, 123 F.2d 996; United States v. Adamson, 161 F.2d 942; Isadore Golonsky, 16 T.C. 1450, affd. 200 F.2d 72; Louis W. Ray, 18 T.C. 438; McCue Bros. & Drummond, Inc., 19 T.C. 667. The respondent, therefore, must be sustained on this issue.

Reviewed by the Court.

Decisions will be entered under Rule 50.

NOTE

The disparate results in the two principal cases above, *Kenan* and *Hudson,* point up a distinction that must be kept in mind here. In those cases no really effective argument could be advanced that the taxpayer had not made a "disposition of property." And Section 1001 makes a disposition a taxable event. Moreover, the property disposed of was a capital asset. But in these cases the final crucial question is whether the disposition is in the nature of a "sale or exchange." Whether this requirement is met is clearly not determined by what the parties call the transaction; the answer will depend upon its substance.[1]

There is a superficial similarity between *Kenan* and *Hudson.* In one case a taxpayer obligor discharges his obligation and in the other a taxpayer obligee receives that to which he is entitled. However, in the former, the obligor is said to have made an exchange; in the latter the disposition by the obligee is not so characterized. The thought intrudes that we have come upon a unilateral exchange, where the goose's sauce is not for the gander. For the message of the cases is that, while a debt-discharging obligor may be engaged in an exchange, the payment-receiving obligee is not.

The rationale for this seeming anomaly, which is advanced in *Hudson,* rests on the extinguishment of the debt as it is received by the judgment debtor; thus, the taxpayer obligee is not involved in an exchange, because what he may be said to transfer ceases to exist in the transaction. But it might as well be said that in *Kenan* the taxpayer obligor received no property since the obligation disappears when he discharges it.

1. Cf. Starr's Estate v. Commissioner, 274 F.2d 294 (9th Cir.1959).

The rationale of *Hudson* fully applied could have yielded a rule that neither obligor nor obligee is engaged in a sale or exchange in transactions of this type. On the other hand, in both instances the obligation involved is property in the hands of the obligee and, if the courts had chosen to disregard the extinguishment of the obligation, both obligor and obligee might be viewed as engaged in an exchange. Either of these views might be easier to square doctrinally than the differentiation reflected in the principal cases. However there is some logic to the rules that have developed.

The doctrinal difficulty with these apparently conflicting results can probably best be eased by a realignment of the transactions. It is consistent with economic reality in *Kenan* to treat the transaction as if the obligor trustee had paid the obligation in cash and the obligee recipient, in turn, had used the cash to purchase the transferred property from the trustee. Thus, from the standpoint of the obligor trustee, the sale or exchange requirement is met. But the trust beneficiary obligee has made no sale or exchange, because he is seen as merely receiving a payment due and as using the receipt to make a purchase. Turning to *Hudson,* the obligee is seen to be in the same position as the recipient in *Kenan;* he has just received payment of the sum due. If we assume in a *Hudson* situation that the judgment debtor satisfied his obligation with appreciated property, his position would be analogous to the *Kenan* trustee, supporting sale or exchange treatment of the transaction. But the obligee taxpayer could still be viewed as merely receiving payment of a debt and making a purchase of property, so that as to him the transaction still would not constitute a sale or exchange. Thus, even on a doctrinal level, it is possible to view the cases as not in conflict.

The *Davis* case [2] (now neutralized by Section 1041) will be recalled, taxing a divorced husband upon his transfer of appreciated property in discharge of his wife's dower rights. The foregoing rationale supports sale or exchange treatment for his transfer, a point not at issue in *Davis.* Application of the *Kenan* principle can also produce a loss, if the amount of the obligation discharged is less than the basis of the property transferred to discharge it.[3]

The statute creates an interesting problem of identifying what constitutes a sale or exchange. The *Kenan* obligor's transfer, yes; the *Hudson* obligee's collection, no. However, question may be raised whether special preferential gain treatment or ordinary loss treatment should be made to turn on such an issue. If the *Hudson* creditor had sold the judgment debt to a third party, instead of collecting from the debtor, he would have reached the promised land.[4] Is sale to another really very different from what is in effect a sale to the debtor? Should characterization be governed, then, only by the nature of the asset and

2. U.S. v. Davis, 370 U.S. 65, 82 S.Ct. 1190 (1962).

3. See Rev.Rul. 74–178, 1974–1 C.B. 196.

4. Paine v. Commissioner, 236 F.2d 398 (8th Cir.1956).

its holding period, rather than in part by the nature of its disposition? While Congress has not seen fit to go so far as a general rule, special statutory provisions sometimes take liberties with the usual sale or exchange requirement.

If a lessee relinquishes his lease in exchange for a payment by the lessor, is the character of his gain affected by the fact that the lease is extinguished so that the lessee has made no exchange? Section 1241 specifically says no. Such receipts "are considered as amounts received in exchange for" the lease. Similarly, if a nonbusiness debt becomes bad or a security becomes worthless, the creditor or shareholder has made no actual sale or exchange, but Congress characterizes the losses involved by a statutory pretention that there was an exchange.[5] An uninsured, unreimbursed casualty loss involves no exchange, but Section 1231 sometimes treats it as such.[6] Four other special statutory sale or exchange rules appear in Sections 1234A, 1235, 1253 and 1271, all singled out for brief discussion here.

In general, under Section 1271 amounts paid upon the retirement of obligations issued by corporations, governmental units and entities other than natural persons[7] are treated as amounts received in exchange for such obligations. This is a statutory reversal of the *Hudson* principle, but only with respect to obligations issued by other than natural persons.[8] The reversal may well be applauded, even as we wonder whether the concept might be extended. However, even as an inequity is thus avoided, an additional problem is created, if the bond was issued at a discount. In such an instance some of the gain that accrues is essentially interest and should not be accorded capital gain consequences. The concept of original issue discount, along with other sections finding obscured interest, is considered in Chapter 24.[9]

Another provision that may artificially accord sale or exchange classification to a transaction is Section 1235. An invention, whether patented or not, is usually within the Section 1221 definition of capital assets.[10] A common method of exploiting an invention is for the inventor to license others to use it, often fixing the consideration in terms of a part of the proceeds from its use. Can this be regarded as a sale? For a "holder"[11] Section 1235 says it can, and that section generates long-term capital gain (regardless of the length of time the invention was held) out of a licensing arrangement, if the "holder" transfers all his substantial rights in the property.[12]

---

5. I.R.C. §§ 165(g), 166(d). See Chapter 23 at page 800, infra.

6. See Chapter 22 at page 770, infra.

7. I.R.C. § 1271(b)(1).

8. Id.

9. See page 893, infra.

10. However, note that a literary product of the inventive mind is not normally accorded capital asset treatment. I.R.C. § 1221(3). If a literary product is a capital asset the question whether its disposition is a sale or exchange as opposed to a mere royalty arrangement is subject to the same tests as a patent. Rev.Rul. 60–226, 1960–1 C.B. 26.

11. I.R.C. § 1235(b).

12. See Reg. § 1.1235–2(b). The retention of substantial rights, such as a right to terminate a license agreement after a period, Taylor-Winfield Corp., 57 T.C. 205 (1971), or the right to exploit the patent in

If one who is not a "holder" disposes of a patent in a manner different from an outright sale or exchange, i.e. by way of an exclusive licensing arrangement for a period coterminus with the life of the patent or for consideration measured by the licensee's profit, he may have capital gain treatment also. For a time the Treasury held he would not,[13] but with judicial prompting the Treasury has changed its position,[14] and now a non-"holder" who disposes of a patent is in much the same position as one who is within Section 1235, although he does not automatically satisfy the one year holding period for long-term gain.

The Economic Recovery Tax Act of 1981 added Section 1234A, which accords sale or exchange treatment to the cancellation, lapse, expiration, or other termination of a right or obligation with respect to "actively traded personal property".[15] Court decisions have held that a lapse, cancellation, or abandonment of such property lacks sale or exchange status and the disposition produces ordinary income or loss.[16] Congress enacted Section 1234A because it considered ordinary loss treatment inappropriate in transactions that are "economically equivalent to a sale or exchange of the contract," [17] such as the settlement or cancellation of a contract to deliver commodities. Therefore, Section 1234A applies to rights or obligations with respect to actively traded personal property other than stock, e.g., metals, foods, currency, and non-stock securities, but it applies only if the property is, or on acquisition would be, a capital asset in the hands of the taxpayer.

Finally, the Tax Reform Act of 1969 added Section 1253, concerning the disposition of franchises, trademarks, and trade names, which is aimed in part at a problem similar to that covered by Section 1235, dealing with patents. The common problem is whether a disposition is a sale or exchange or whether instead it should be viewed as a mere license. In contrast to the affirmative approach of Section 1235 (sale classification upon transfer of "all substantial rights"), Section 1253 provides only a negative rule. The transfer of a franchise, trademark, or trade name is not to be treated as a sale or exchange if the transferor retains any significant power, right or continuing interest in the property. Moreover, and quite contrary to principles adopted in Section 1235, under Section 1253 any amounts received or accrued which are dependent on the productivity, use, or disposition of the property are expressly denied capital gain treatment. Dispositions of franchises, trademarks, or trade names which are not so proscribed

geographical areas placed outside the agreement, Klein's Estate v. Commissioner, 507 F.2d 617 (7th Cir.1974), may defeat the application of I.R.C. § 1235. However, one may, within the section, sell an undivided interest, even a small interest, in all substantial rights. Reg. § 1.1235–2(c); Allen G. Eickmeyer, 66 T.C. 109 (1976). See Olson, "Federal Income Taxation of Patent and Know-How Transfers," 28 St. Louis U.L.J. 537 (1984).

13. Mim. 6490, 1950–1, C.B. 9; Rev.Rul. 55–58, 1955–1 C.B. 97.

14. Rev.Rul. 58–353, 1958–2 C.B. 408.

15. See I.R.C. § 1092(d)(1).

16. Leh v. Commissioner, 260 F.2d 489 (9th Cir.1958); Commissioner v. Pittston Co., 252 F.2d 344 (2d Cir.1958), cert. denied 357 U.S. 919, 78 S.Ct. 1360 (1958).

17. Sen.Rep. No. 97–144, 97th Cong., 1st Sess. pp. 170–71 (1981).

may qualify as sales or exchanges and for capital gain characterization if, of course, the property is a capital asset in the hands of the taxpayer.[18]

The proposed regulations seem to promise a strict interpretation of Section 1253. For example, among the listed agreement restrictions not expressed in the statute, which will defeat capital gain treatment on a transfer of a franchise, are: (1) "A right to prevent the transferee from removing equipment outside the territory in which the transferee is permitted to operate;" and (2) "Any other right which permits the transferor to exercise continuing, active, and operational control over the transferee's trade or business activities." [19]

YARBRO v. COMMISSIONER *

United States Court of Appeals, Fifth Circuit, 1984.**
737 F.2d 479.

JOHN R. BROWN, Circuit Judge:

This case presents the question of whether an individual taxpayer's loss resulting from the abandonment of unimproved real estate subject to a non-recourse mortgage exceeding the market value is an ordinary loss or a capital loss. Because the Commissioner may change an earlier interpretation of the law to another reasonable interpretation, we affirm the Tax Court's holding that an abandonment of real property subject to non-recourse debt is a "sale or exchange" for purposes of determining whether a loss is a capital loss.

Facts

James W. Yarbro (Taxpayer) has been a self-employed financial and tax consultant since 1969. In 1972, he acquired a real estate broker's license. In that year, he formed three joint ventures and negotiated a separate land purchase for each of the ventures. Only the land purchase for the last of the three joint ventures is at issue here.

The venture was formed by Taxpayer, together with five other persons, for the purpose of acquiring about 132 acres of undeveloped land on the northern limits of the city of Fort Worth, Texas. The purchase price was $362,132.08. About 10% was paid in cash, and the balance was covered by four non-recourse promissory notes secured by deeds of trust on the property. Taxpayer took title to the property as trustee, and under the terms of the joint venture agreement, was

---

18. The inherent obscurities of I.R.C. § 1253 foretell uncertainty and controversy in the area of its coverage for some time to come. An extensive critical analysis of the section appears in Andrews and Freeland, "Capital Gains and Losses of Individuals and Related Matters under the Tax Reform Act of 1969," 12 Ariz.L.Rev. 627, 666–677 (1970); see also Hall and Smith, "Franchising Under The Tax Reform Act," 4 Ind. Legal Forum 305 (1970).

19. Proposed Reg. § 1.1253–2(d)(7) and (9); see also Resorts Intern. Inc. v. Commissioner, 511 F.2d 107, n. 7 (5th Cir.1975), commenting on I.R.C. § 1253 although it did not apply to the tax years at issue.

* See Weinstein, "Tax Ideas: Yarbro Trouble for Taxpayers Who Litigate," 13 Real Est.L.J. 354 (1985).

** Some footnotes omitted.

responsible for managing the property. For his services as trustee and manager, Taxpayer received a one-time fee of $4,000. Taxpayer was also entitled to receive a 3% sales commission if the property were sold.

Each participant in the joint venture was required to contribute $4,100 in cash for each ten-percent interest purchased. One investor purchased a 50-percent interest, while the other investors, including taxpayer herein, each purchased a ten-percent interest. About six months after the joint venture was organized, taxpayer bought out one of the other ten-percent investors for $6,150, making his total investment in the joint venture a little over $10,000.

At the time the property was acquired, it was subject to a livestock grazing lease, and during the years the joint venture owned the property (1972 through 1976), it continued to be rented for grazing purposes at a rental of approximately $1,000 per year. The joint venture's only other income during those years was a small amount of interest. During that same period of time, the joint venture incurred expenses of about $23,000 each year for interest, taxes and insurance. Because these expenses greatly exceeded the income generated by the land, the participants were required to make annual pro-rata contributions to the venture. Taxpayer's contributions were about $4,500 per year.

Taxpayer acknowledged at trial that one of the primary purposes in purchasing the property was the expectation that the property would appreciate in value and that it could be sold at a later date for a substantial profit. Although the possibility of developing the property was considered, no definite development plans were drawn up, no improvements were ever made, and the joint venture participants were never asked to advance any funds for that purpose.[2]

In the summer of 1976, the City of Fort Worth decided to raise the real estate taxes on the joint venture's property by 435% from $770 per year to approximately $3,350 per year. At about the same time, real estate activity in the area completely dried up. As a consequence, by November of 1976, the property's fair market value had dropped below the face amount of the nonrecourse mortgage to which it was subject. When confronted with these facts, the joint venture participants decided to abandon the property and not to pay the real estate taxes for 1976 or the $22,811 annual interest payment for that year. Accordingly, on November 15, 1976, Taxpayer, as trustee, notified the Fort Worth National Bank (the trustee of the mortgages) that he was abandoning the property. Although the bank requested Taxpayer to reconvey the property to it, Taxpayer refused to do so, reasoning that he "had nothing to convey and would have nothing to do * * * with the property from that point on."

---

2. Other reasons taxpayer gave for purchasing the property were: (1) to further his property management business and to earn a $4,000 management fee, (2) to have the opportunity to earn a three-percent real estate commission if the property were ever sold, (3) to earn rental income, and (4) to become associated with Lawson Ridgeway, a local real estate developer who purchased a 50-percent interest in the joint venture.

In June, 1977, the bank obtained title to the property pursuant to foreclosure proceedings. None of the joint venture participants received any consideration from the foreclosure sale.

The Tax

On his 1976 federal income tax return, Taxpayer claimed an ordinary loss of $10,376 from the abandonment of the joint venture property. The Commissioner, however, determined that Taxpayer's loss was not an ordinary loss, but, rather, constituted a long-term capital loss. The Commissioner took the position that Taxpayer's abandonment of the property constituted a "sale or exchange" within the meaning of Sections 1211 and 1222 of the Code. The Commissioner further contended that Taxpayer held his own interest in the land as an investment and not for use in taxpayer's "trade or business" or "primarily for sale to customers in the ordinary course of business." Thus, the Commissioner contended that the abandonment was a "sale or exchange" of a "capital asset."

The Tax Court agreed with the Commissioner's analysis. Determining that Taxpayer acquired his interest in the property "primarily for investment purposes" the Tax Court held that the property was not used in Taxpayer's financial consulting and property management business within the meaning of Section 1231 of the Code. The Tax Court also concluded that the "casual" rental of the land for grazing purposes at a nominal fee did not evidence use of the land in a bona fide rental business, and that the evidence did not support a finding that the land was held primarily for sale to customers in the ordinary course of business. Finally, the Tax Court, following the course charted in Freeland v. Commissioner, 74 T.C. 970 (1980), and Middleton v. Commissioner, 77 T.C. 310 (1981), aff'd per curiam, 693 F.2d 124 (11th Cir.1982), held that an abandonment of property constituted a "sale or exchange" for purposes of Code Sections 1211 and 1222.

Statutory Context

Section 165(a) of the Internal Revenue Code of 1954 provides, as a general rule, that taxpayers may deduct "any loss sustained during the taxable year and not compensated for by insurance or otherwise." 26 U.S.C. § 165(a). The application of this general rule, however, is limited by Section 165(f), which provides that "losses from *sales or exchanges* of *capital assets* shall be allowed only to the extent allowed in §§ 1211 and 1212." 26 U.S.C. § 165(f) (emphasis added). Taxpayer, by arguing that the abandonment was not a "sale or exchange," and that the land in the hands of the joint venture was not a "capital asset," seeks to establish that the loss was an ordinary loss. If accepted, this position would allow Taxpayer to avoid the limitations imposed by §§ 1211 and 1212 on the deduction that may be taken for capital losses.[3]

"Sale or Exchange" by Abandonment

Taxpayer first argues that the Tax Court's decision that the abandonment of property subject to a non-recourse mortgage is a "sale or exchange" must be rejected because it is a reversal of the position previously taken by the Commissioner, the Tax Court, and other courts. Taxpayer adds that he relied on their earlier positions. In support of this proposition, Taxpayer cites Commissioner v. Hoffman, 117 F.2d 987 (2d Cir.1941); A.J. Industries v. United States, 503 F.2d 660 (9th Cir. 1974); Blum v. Commissioner, 133 F.2d 447, 448 (2d Cir.1943); Bickerstaff v. Commissioner, 128 F.2d 366 (5th Cir.1942); Helvering v. Gordon, 134 F.2d 685 (4th Cir.1943); Denman v. Brumback, 58 F.2d 128 (6th Cir.1932).

We point out that in these cases—except for *Blum*—the issue was not whether an abandonment is a "sale or exchange" for determining whether the loss is capital or ordinary. Instead, these cases decided in which year the loss is appropriately taken. The cases held that the loss was sustained in the year in which the property became worthless and was abandoned, rather than the year in which the taxpayer was technically divested of title. *Blum* held that the transaction in question was indeed a sale and not an abandonment, and concluded that there was a capital loss. In Commissioner v. Green, 126 F.2d 70 (3d Cir.1941) and Helvering v. Jones, 120 F.2d 828 (8th Cir.1941), the courts seem to assume that an abandonment was not a "sale or exchange," but nevertheless held that the loss was a capital loss because the taxpayers' interests in the property were not cut off until the later foreclosure sales, which themselves are "sales or exchanges." Helvering v. Hammel, 311 U.S. 504, 61 S.Ct. 368 (1941).

More recently, the Tax Court, in a case identical in material respects to this case, held that an abandonment of property subject to non-recourse debt is a "sale or exchange" resulting in capital loss treatment, and the Eleventh Circuit affirmed. Middleton v. Commissioner, 77 T.C. 310 (1981), aff'd, 693 F.2d 124 (11th Cir.1982). Assuming that *Middleton* was a departure from the prior position of the Commissioner and the Tax Court, we reject Taxpayer's argument that such a departure is improperly applied retroactively. The Supreme Court has recently held that the Commissioner may change an earlier interpretation of the law, even if such change is made retroactive in effect, and even though a taxpayer may have relied to his detriment upon the Commissioner's prior position. Dickman v. Commissioner, 465 U.S.

---

3. There are two requirements for the capital gain and loss provisions to be applicable: (1) there must be a "capital asset" or property that is treated like a capital asset under § 1231, and (2) there must be a "sale or exchange." 29 U.S.C. §§ 165(a), (f), 1211, 1212. 8 Standard Federal Tax Reporter ¶ 4717 (CCH 1984). Thus, in order to affirm the holding that the loss was a capital loss, we must affirm that there was both (1) a "sale or exchange," and (2) a "capital asset."

330, 104 S.Ct. 1086 (1984); Dixon v. United States, 381 U.S. 68, 85 S.Ct. 1301 (1965). The Commissioner is not required to assert a particular position as soon as the statute authorizes such an interpretation. Id.

The interpretation of an agency charged with the administration of a statute is entitled to a substantial degree of deference. Aluminum Co. of America v. Central Lincoln Peoples' Utility District, 467 U.S. 380, 104 S.Ct. 2472 (1984). To uphold an agency's interpretation, "we need not find that its construction is the only reasonable one. * * * We need only conclude that it is a reasonable interpretation of the relevant provisions." Id., quoting Unemployment Compensation Comm'n v. Aragon, 329 U.S. 143, 153, 67 S.Ct. 245, 250 (1946). As our discussion below indicates, the Commissioner in *Middleton* and in this case has given the statutory term "sale or exchange" a reasonable and practical interpretation in light of decisions more recent than the *Hoffman, Bickerstaff, Denman* line of cases. Moreover, the Tax Court, with its own expertise, has accepted that interpretation.

The term "exchange," in its most common, ordinary meaning implies an act of giving one thing in return for another thing regarded as an equivalent. Webster's New International Dictionary (2d ed. 1954). Thus, three things are required: a giving, a receipt, and a causal connection between the two. In the case of abandonment of property subject to nonrecourse debt, the owner gives up legal title to the property. The mortgagee, who has a legal interest in the property, is the beneficiary of this gift, because the mortgagee's interest is no longer subject to the abandoning owner's rights.

In *Middleton,* as in this case, the taxpayer argued that, because the debt was nonrecourse and he therefore had no personal liability for the debt, he received nothing in exchange for his relinquishment of title. In essence, the argument is that because the taxpayer personally had no obligation to repay the debt, the abandonment could not have relieved him of any obligation. This argument is inconsistent with several Supreme Court decisions.

The Supreme Court has held that regardless of the nonrecourse nature of the debt, the taxpayer does receive a benefit from the disposition of the property: he is relieved of his obligation to pay the debt and taxes and assessments against the property.

* * *

Although *Crane* and *Tufts* concerned the *amount* of the gain or loss and not the *character* of the gain or loss, their rationales support the Commissioner's position in the instant case to the extent that the concept of "amount realized" for computing gain or loss may be equated with the concept of consideration for "sale or exchange" purposes.

Indeed, the Supreme Court in two decisions has followed the same approach of *Crane* and *Tufts* in the "sale or exchange" context.

In Helvering v. Hammel, 311 U.S. 504, 61 S.Ct. 368 (1941), and Helvering v. Nebraska Bridge Supply & Lumber Co., 312 U.S. 666, 61 S.Ct. 827 (1941), the Court held that there had been a "sale or exchange" and a capital loss even though the taxpayer had received no boot or other consideration, other than relief from a debt. In *Hammel,* the Court looked to the legislative purpose and history of the capital gain and loss provisions and held that "sale or exchange" included foreclosure sales. The involuntary nature of the transaction and the lack of any surplus from the sale to be returned to the owner did not make the foreclosure any less a "sale or exchange." Soon after *Hammel,* the Supreme Court rendered a decision, the relevance of which to the recourse-nonrecourse "sale or exchange" issue was aptly explained by the Seventh Circuit:

> In Helvering v. Nebraska Bridge Supply & Lumber Co., 312 U.S. 666, 61 S.Ct. 827 (per curiam), the rationale of *Hammel* was extended. The taxpayer in *Nebraska Bridge Supply* owned property on which the real estate taxes were delinquent. The delinquency created no personal liability. The tax lien was thus like a nonrecourse mortgage. Arkansas bid in the property at a tax sale, acquiring it without paying anything. The state was thus like the holder of a nonrecourse mortgage foreclosing on property worth less than the mortgage. The Eighth Circuit had allowed the taxpayer to take an ordinary loss deduction because "[t]he transfer of title to the State is not only involuntary, but is without any consideration moving to the transferor." 115 F.2d 288, 291 (1940). The Supreme Court summarily reversed.

Laport v. Commissioner, 671 F.2d 1028 (7th Cir.1982). Based on the Supreme Court's reasoning in *Crane, Tufts* and *Nebraska Bridge Supply,* we approve the Tax Court's acceptance of the Commissioner's interpretation that one who abandons property subject to non-recourse debt receives a relief from the debt obligation when he gives up legal title. Moreover, it is clear that the relief from the debt is what causes the abandonment. It was advantageous, in the view of the Supreme Court, for the Taxpayer to relinquish title only because the debt of which he was relieved was greater than the market value. Thus, under the Supreme Court precedents, the abandonment in this case involved a giving in order to receive something in return as the equivalent,[5] and therefore fit within the ordinary meaning of "sale or exchange."

Moreover, an abandonment of property subject to non-recourse debts has the same *practical effect* as several other transactions which have each been held to be a "sale or exchange." The Supreme Court has held that an involuntary foreclosure sale of real estate was a "sale or exchange" and the loss a capital loss. Helvering v. Hammel, 311 U.S. 504, 61 S.Ct. 368 (1941). In *Nebraska Bridge Supply,* the Court held a tax forfeiture to be a "sale or exchange." In Laport v. Commissioner, 671 F.2d 1028 (7th Cir.1982), the Court held that the taxpayer's conveyance to the mortgagee by quitclaim deed in lieu of foreclosure

---

5. The mortgage agreement effectively treated the property and the debt as being equivalent in value.

was a "sale or exchange." In Freeland v. Commissioner, 74 T.C. 970 (1980), the Tax Court held that where the value of land sunk below the amount of a nonrecourse debt and the owner conveyed the land to the mortgagee by quitclaim, there was a "sale or exchange" and an ordinary loss.

The abandonment followed by the mortgagee's foreclosure in this case is the functional equivalent of the foreclosure sale in *Hammel*, the tax forfeiture in *Nebraska Bridge Supply*, and the quitclaims in lieu of foreclosure in *Laport* and *Freeland*. In all these transactions, the taxpayer-owner is relieved of his obligation to repay the debt and is relieved of title of the property. Because the mortgagee is legally entitled to recover title to the property in any of these cases, the fact that out of prudence he concludes he must go through foreclosure proceedings to formalize his interest in the land is not a rational basis for altering the character of the gain or loss realized by the taxpayer on the transaction. The differences in these transactions is not a difference in substance, but only in form.

The taxpayer who has decided that he cannot or should not make further payment on the nonrecourse loan can manipulate the form of the change in ownership of the property simply by either quitclaiming or abandoning the land before the mortgagee forecloses. Thus, the question is "whether a taxpayer can avoid the tax consequences of *Hammel* and *Nebraska Bridge Supply* by the simple expedient of [abandoning] the property before the mortgagee can foreclose. The *Freeland* Court saw no reason, nor do we, to put such a premium on artful timing." Laport v. Commissioner, 671 F.2d at 1033. Cf. Diedrich v. Commissioner, 457 U.S. 191, 102 S.Ct. 2414 (1982) (ignoring form of transaction in favor of the substance of the transaction).

Allowing taxpayers to manipulate the character of their losses from capital to ordinary by hastening to abandon rather than allowing foreclosure would frustrate the congressional purpose to treat capital gains and losses on a parity. As explained by the Supreme Court in *Hammel*, the *quid pro quo* of allowing generous tax treatment on capital gains is the limitation imposed on deductions for capital losses. 311 U.S. at 509–10, 61 S.Ct. at 370–371; 671 F.2d at 1033; 74 T.C. at 976. Thus, where the taxpayer would be eligible for capital gains treatment upon the sale of property had it appreciated in value, he should not be allowed to avoid the limitations on deductions for capital losses by using an artfully timed abandonment rather than a sale, voluntary reconveyance, or foreclosure. Accordingly, we affirm the Tax Court's holding that the Commissioner's interpretation of "sale or exchange" as including an abandonment of property subject to nonrecourse debt is a reasonable one.

No Help From the Regulations

Taxpayer argues that "use of the term 'abandonment' in Regulation 1.165–2, paragraph (a) and the exclusion in paragraph (b) of losses from the 'sale or exchange' of property" shows that the regulation recognizes that an abandonment is not a sale or exchange. Section 1.165–2 provides:

Obsolescence of Nondepreciable Property

(a) *Allowance of Deduction.* A loss incurred in a business or in a transaction entered into for profit and arising from the sudden termination of the usefulness in such business or transaction of any nondepreciable property, in a case where such business or transaction is discontinued or where such property is permanently discarded from use therein, shall be allowed as a deduction under section 165(a) for the taxable year in which the loss is actually sustained. For this purpose, the taxable year in which the loss is sustained is not necessarily the taxable year in which the overt act of abandonment, or the loss of title to the property, occurs.

(b) *Exceptions.* This section does not apply to losses sustained upon the sale or exchange of property, losses sustained upon the obsolescence or worthlessness of depreciable property, casualty losses, or losses reflected in inventories required to be taken from section 471. The limitations contained in sections 1211 and 1212 upon losses from the sale or exchange of capital assets do not apply to losses allowable under this section.

1984 Fed.Tax Regs., Vol. I, p. 707.

Initially, we point out that courts have held that the subject of the sentence referring to "act of abandonment" is the proper *timing* of the deduction for abandonment losses, and not the *character* of the loss. *Laport,* 671 F.2d at 1031, n. 5; A.J. Industries, Inc. v. United States, 503 F.2d 660, 666–70, n. 6, 6b (9th Cir.1974). Moreover, this Regulation is not applicable here, because subsection (b) of the Regulation provides that the Regulation "does not apply to losses sustained upon the sale or exchange of property * * *" This case falls within the "sale or exchange" exception of subsection (b), for the reasons stated above. Thus, our holding is not inconsistent with the implication that taxpayer draws from the use of "abandonment" in subsection (a) and the use of "sale or exchange" in the exception of subsection (b). While some abandonments that bring nothing in return, such as the scrapping of obsolete equipment, may not be sales or exchanges, cf., e.g., Louisville and Nashville R.R. Co. v. Commissioner, 641 F.2d 435 (6th Cir.1981); J.B.N. Telephone Co. v. United States, 638 F.2d 227 (10th Cir.1981), and thus subject to this Regulation, nevertheless, an abandonment that is deemed to bring in return relief from a nonrecourse debt is a sale or exchange. Thus, this case is excepted from Section 1.165–2 by subsection (b), and the allowance by subsection (a) of a deduction for certain other abandonments is not inconsistent with our ruling.

Capital Asset

Taxpayer argues alternatively that even if the abandonment is a sale or exchange, his loss was still ordinary because the land was not a "capital asset" in his hands. 26 U.S.C. § 1221. Specifically, he argues that the land was not held for investment, but instead was "used in his trade or business" of renting property.

This Court has recently held that our review on the question of a taxpayer's holding purpose is narrowly confined by the Rule 52(a) "clearly erroneous" rule, even though it is an ultimate question of fact in deciding "capital asset" status. Byram v. United States, 705 F.2d 1418 (5th Cir.1983).[7] "The choice of a standard will determine the outcome of many cases," and this is one such case. 705 F.2d at 1421.

The Tax Court held that Taxpayer was not in the trade or business of renting property, and his interest in the land was not bought or held for that purpose. The Court declared: "We think petitioner acquired his interest primarily for investment purposes. * * * We are not persuaded that the casual rental converts the tract into property used in a trade or business within the meaning of the statute." This finding was supported by Taxpayer's testimony acknowledging that one of the primary purposes in purchasing the property was to realize an appreciation in value of the land expected to occur as a result of the growth of nearby Fort Worth. The only rental of the land was for grazing, which brought in approximately $1000 annually. That income covered only a minute part of the partnership's yearly expenses of approximately $71,470 (taxes, insurance, and primarily interest) incurred in owning the land during the same period. Even ignoring these expenses, the $1000 yearly rental would represent a rate of return of far less than 1% on the $362,132 investment in the property. Moreover, there were no improvements made on the land, nor any definite plans to make improvements in the future.

The Tax Court also held that the Taxpayer's interest in the land was not property used in his trade or business of tax and financial consulting, stating that the connection between the business and the owning of the interest in the land was too tenuous and conjectural. Taxpayer argued that he participated in the venture "to show [to his partner-clients] good faith belief that it was a worthy investment." However, that position means only that he was showing his clients that it was a good investment by choosing it for himself *as a good investment*. Taxpayer's assertion, therefore, supports the Tax Court's finding that he held the property for investment, rather than for *use* in his trade or business.

* * *

Affirmed.

---

7. For criticism of the *Byram* holding, see Friedlander, "To Customers" The Forgotten Element in the Characterization of Gains on Sales of Real Property, 39 Tax.L. Rev. 31 (1983).

PROBLEM

Creditor purchases Debtor's $5,000 interest bearing note from a third party as an investment at a cost of $4,000. A year later Debtor pays off the principal of the note using General Motors stock which he purchased several years ago at a cost of $2,000 which is now worth $5,000. What are the tax consequences to Creditor and Debtor?

2. CORRELATION WITH PRIOR TRANSACTIONS

ARROWSMITH v. COMMISSIONER

Supreme Court of the United States, 1952.
344 U.S. 6, 73 S.Ct. 71, rehearing denied, 344 U.S. 900, 73 S.Ct. 273, 1952.

Mr. Justice BLACK delivered the opinion of the Court.

This is an income tax controversy growing out of the following facts as shown by findings of the Tax Court. In 1937 two taxpayers, petitioners here, decided to liquidate and divide the proceeds of a corporation in which they had equal stock ownership.* Partial distributions made in 1937, 1938, and 1939 were followed by a final one in 1940. Petitioners reported the profits obtained from this transaction, classifying them as capital gains. They thereby paid less income tax than would have been required had the income been attributed to ordinary business transactions for profit. About the propriety of these 1937–1940 returns, there is no dispute. But in 1944 a judgment was rendered against the old corporation and against Frederick R. Bauer, individually. The two taxpayers were required to and did pay the judgment for the corporation, of whose assets they were transferees. See Phillips-Jones Corp. v. Parmley, 302 U.S. 233, 235–236, 58 S.Ct. 497, 198. Cf. I.R.C. § 311(a). Classifying the loss as an ordinary business one, each took a tax deduction for 100% of the amount paid. Treatment of the loss as a capital one would have allowed deduction of a much smaller amount. See I.R.C. § 117(b), (d)(2) and (e). The Commissioner viewed the 1944 payment as part of the original liquidation transaction requiring classification as a capital loss, just as the taxpayers had treated the original dividends as capital gains. Disagreeing with the Commissioner the Tax Court classified the 1944 payment as an ordinary business loss. 15 T.C. 876. Disagreeing with the Tax Court the Court of Appeals reversed, treating the loss as "capital." 193 F.2d 734. This latter holding conflicts with the Third Circuit's holding in Commissioner v. Switlik, 184 F.2d 299. Because of this conflict, we granted certiorari. 343 U.S. 976, 72 S.Ct. 1075.

I.R.C. § 23(g) treats losses from sales or exchanges of capital assets as "capital losses" and I.R.C. § 115(c) requires that liquidation distributions be treated as exchanges. [See I.R.C. (1986) § 331(a). Ed.] The

---

* At dissolution the corporate stock was owned by Frederick P. Bauer and the executor of Davenport Pogue's estate. The parties here now are Pogue's widow, Bauer's widow, and the executor of Bauer's estate.

losses here fall squarely within the definition of "capital losses" contained in these sections. Taxpayers were required to pay the judgment because of liability imposed on them as transferees of liquidation distribution assets. And it is plain that their liability as transferees was not based on any ordinary business transaction of theirs apart from the liquidation proceedings. It is not even denied that had this judgment been paid after liquidation, but during the year 1940, the losses would have been properly treated as capital ones. For payment during 1940 would simply have reduced the amount of capital gains taxpayers received during that year.

It is contended, however, that this payment which would have been a capital transaction in 1940 was transformed into an ordinary business transaction in 1944 because of the well-established principle that each taxable year is a separate unit for tax accounting purposes. United States v. Lewis, 340 U.S. 590, 71 S.Ct. 522; North American Oil v. Burnet, 286 U.S. 417, 52 S.Ct. 613. But this principle is not breached by considering all the 1937–1944 liquidation transaction events in order properly to classify the nature of the 1944 loss for tax purposes. Such an examination is not an attempt to reopen and readjust the 1937 to 1940 tax returns, an action that would be inconsistent with the annual tax accounting principle.

The petitioner Bauer's executor presents an argument for reversal which applies to Bauer alone. He was liable not only by reason of being a transferee of the corporate assets. He was also held liable jointly with the original corporation, on findings that he had secretly profited because of a breach of his fiduciary relationship to the judgment creditor. Trounstine v. Bauer, Pogue & Co., 44 F.Supp. 767, 773; 144 F.2d 379, 382. The judgment was against both Bauer and the corporation. For this reason it is contended that the nature of Bauer's tax deduction should be considered on the basis of his liability as an individual who sustained a loss in an ordinary business transaction for profit. We agree with the Court of Appeals that this contention should not be sustained. While there was a liability against him in both capacities, the individual judgment against him was for the whole amount. His payment of only half the judgment indicates that both he and the other transferee were paying in their capacities as such. We see no reason for giving Bauer a preferred tax position.

Affirmed.

Mr. Justice DOUGLAS, dissenting.

I agree with Mr. Justice JACKSON that these losses should be treated as ordinary, not capital losses. There were no capital transactions in the year in which the losses were suffered. Those transactions occurred and were accounted for in earlier years in accord with the established principle that each year is a separate unit for tax accounting purposes. See United States v. Lewis, 340 U.S. 590, 71 S.Ct. 522. I have not felt, as my dissent in the *Lewis* case indicates, that the law made that an inexorable principle. But if it is the law, we should require observance of it—not merely by taxpayers but by the Government as well. We should force each year to stand on its own footing, whoever may gain or lose from it in a particular case. We impeach that principle when we treat this year's losses as if they diminished last year's gains.

Mr. Justice JACKSON, whom Mr. Justice FRANKFURTER joins, dissenting.

This problem arises only because the judgment was rendered in a taxable year subsequent to the liquidation.

Had the liability of the transferor-corporation been reduced to judgment during the taxable year in which liquidation occurred, or prior thereto, this problem, under the tax laws, would not arise. The amount of the judgment rendered against the corporation would have decreased the amount it had available for distribution, which would have reduced the liquidating dividends proportionately and diminished the capital gains taxes assessed against the stockholders. Probably it would also have decreased the corporation's own taxable income.

Congress might have allowed, under such circumstances, tax returns of the prior year to be reopened or readjusted so as to give the same tax results as would have obtained had the liability become known prior to liquidation. Such a solution is foreclosed to us and the alternatives left are to regard the judgment liability fastened by operation of law on the transferee as an ordinary loss for the year of adjudication or to regard it as a capital loss for such year.

This Court simplifies the choice to one of reading the English language, and declares that the losses here come "squarely within" the definition of capital losses contained within two sections of the Internal Revenue Code. What seems so clear to this Court was not seen at all by the Tax Court, in this case or in earlier consideration of the same issue; nor was it grasped by the Court of Appeals for the Third Circuit. Commissioner v. Switlik, 184 F.2d 299 (1950).

I find little aid in the choice of alternatives from arguments based on equities. One enables the taxpayer to deduct the amount of the judgment against his ordinary income which might be taxed as high as 87%, while if the liability had been assessed against the corporation prior to liquidation it would have reduced his capital gain which was taxable at only 25% (now 26%). The consequence may readily be characterized as a windfall (regarding a windfall as anything that is left to a taxpayer after the collector has finished with him).

On the other hand, adoption of the contrary alternative may penalize the taxpayer because of two factors: (1) since capital losses are deductible only against capital gains, plus $1,000, [See (1986) Section 1211(b)(1)(B), prior to 1976 amendments. Ed.] a taxpayer having no net capital gains in the ensuing five years would have no opportunity to deduct anything beyond $5,000 [But see (1986) Section 1212(b). Ed.]; and (2) had the liability been discharged by the corporation, a portion of it would probably in effect have been paid by the Government, since the corporation could have taken it as a deduction, while here the total liability comes out of the pockets of the stockholders.

Solicitude for the revenues is a plausible but treacherous basis upon which to decide a particular tax case. A victory may have implications which in future cases will cost the Treasury more than a defeat. This might be such a case, for anything I know. Suppose that subsequent to liquidation it is found that a corporation has undisclosed claims instead of liabilities and that under applicable state law they may be prosecuted for the benefit of the stockholders. The logic of the Court's decision here, if adhered to, would result in a lesser return to the Government than if the recoveries were considered ordinary income. Would it be so clear that this is a capital loss if the shoe were on the other foot?

Where the statute is so indecisive and the importance of a particular holding lies in its rational and harmonious relation to the general scheme of the tax law, I think great deference is due the twice-expressed judgment of the Tax Court. In spite of the gelding of Dobson v. Commissioner, 320 U.S. 489, 64 S.Ct. 239, by the recent revision of the Judicial Code, Act of June 25, 1948, § 36, 62 Stat. 991–992, I still think the Tax Court is a more competent and steady influence toward a systematic body of tax law than our sporadic omnipotence in a field beset with invisible boomerangs. I should reverse, in reliance upon the Tax Court's judgment more, perhaps, than my own.

UNITED STATES v. SKELLY OIL CO.

Supreme Court of the United States, 1969.
394 U.S. 678, 89 S.Ct. 1379.

Mr. Justice MARSHALL delivered the opinion of the Court: During its tax year ending December 31, 1958, respondent refunded $505,536.54 to two of its customers for overcharges during the six preceding years. Respondent, an Oklahoma producer of natural gas, had set its prices during the earlier years in accordance with a minimum price order of the Oklahoma Corporation Commission. After that order was vacated as a result of a decision of this Court, Michigan Wisconsin Pipe Line Co. v. Corporation Comm'n of Oklahoma, 355 U.S. 425, 78 S.Ct. 409 (1958), respondent found it necessary to settle a number of claims filed by its customers; the repayments in question represent settlements of two of those claims. Since respondent had claimed an unrestricted right to its sales receipts during the years 1952 through 1957, it had included the $505,536.54 in its gross income in those years. The amount was also included in respondent's "gross income from the property" as defined in § 613 of the Internal Revenue Code of 1954, the section which allows taxpayers to deduct a fixed percentage of certain receipts to compensate for the depletion of natural resources from which they derive income. Allowable percentage depletion for receipts from oil and gas wells is [was then] fixed at 27½% of the "gross income from the property." Since respondent claimed and the Commissioner allowed percentage depletion deductions during these years, 27½% of the receipts in question was added to the depletion allowances to which respondent would otherwise have been entitled. Accordingly, the actual increase in respondent's taxable income attributable to the receipts in question was not $505,536.54, but only $366,513.99. Yet, when respondent made its refunds in 1958, it attempted to deduct the full $505,536.54. The Commissioner objected and assessed a deficiency. Respondent paid and, after its claim for a refund had been disallowed, began the present suit. The Government won in the District Court, 255 F.Supp. 228 (D.C.N.D.Okla.1966), but the Court of Appeals for the Tenth Circuit reversed, 392 F.2d 128 (1968). Upon petition by the Government, we granted certiorari, 393 U.S. 820, 89 S.Ct. 121 (1968), to consider whether the Court of Appeals' decision had allowed respondent "the practical equivalent of double deduction," Charles Ilfeld Co. v. Hernandez, 292 U.S. 62, 68, 54 S.Ct. 596, 598 (1934), in conflict with past decisions of this Court and sound principles of tax law. We reverse.

I. The present problem is an outgrowth of the so-called "claim-of-right" doctrine. Mr. Justice Brandeis, speaking for a unanimous Court in North American Oil Consolidated v. Burnet, 286 U.S. 417, 424, 52 S.Ct. 613, 615 (1932), gave that doctrine its classic formulation. "If a taxpayer receives earnings under a claim of right and without restriction as to its disposition, he has received income which he is required to return, even though it may still be claimed that he is not entitled to retain the money, and even though he may still be adjudged to restore its equivalent." Should it later appear that the taxpayer was not entitled to keep the money, Mr. Justice Brandeis explained, he would be entitled to a deduction in the year of repayment; the taxes due for the year of receipt would not be affected. This approach was dictated by Congress' adoption of an annual accounting system as an integral part of the tax code. See Burnet v. Sanford & Brooks Co., 282 U.S. 359, 365–366, 51 S.Ct. 150, 152 (1931). Of course, the tax benefit from the deduction in the year of repayment might differ from the increase in taxes attributable to the receipt; for example, tax rates might have changed, or the taxpayer might be in a different tax "bracket." See Healy v. Commissioner, 345 U.S. 278, 284–285, 73 S.Ct. 671, 675 (1953). But as the doctrine was originally formulated, these discrepancies were accepted as an unavoidable consequence of the annual accounting system.

Section 1341 of the 1954 Code was enacted to alleviate some of the inequities which Congress felt existed in this area.[1] See H.R.Rep. No. 1337, 83d Cong., 2d Sess., 86–87 (1954); S.Rep. No. 1622, 83d Cong., 2d Sess., 118–119 (1954). As an alternative to the deduction in the year of repayment[2] which prior law allowed, § 1341(a)(5) permits certain tax-

1. [Section 1341(a) is omitted. Ed.] Section 1341(b)(2) contains an exclusion covering certain cases involving sales of stock in trade or inventory. However, because of special treatment given refunds made by regulated public utilities, both parties agree that § 1341(b)(2) is inapplicable to this case and that, accordingly, § 1341(a) applies.

2. In the case of an accrual-basis taxpayer, the legislative history makes it clear

payers to recompute their taxes for the year of receipt. Whenever § 1341(a)(5) applies, taxes for the current year are to be reduced by the amount taxes were increased in the year or years of receipt because the disputed items were included in gross income. Nevertheless, it is clear that Congress did not intend to tamper with the underlying claim-of-right doctrine; it only provided an alternative for certain cases in which the new approach favored the taxpayer. When the new approach was not advantageous to the taxpayer, the old law was to apply under § 1341(a)(4).

In this case, the parties have stipulated that § 1341(a)(5) does not apply. Accordingly, as the courts below recognized, respondent's taxes must be computed under § 1341(a)(4) and thus, in effect, without regard to the special relief Congress provided through the enactment of § 1341. Nevertheless, respondent argues, and the Court of Appeals seems to have held, that the language used in § 1341 requires that respondent be allowed a deduction for the full amount it refunded to its customers. We think the section has no such significance.

In describing the situations in which the section applies, § 1341(a)(2) talks of cases in which "a deduction is allowable for the taxable year because it was established after the close of [the year or years of receipt] that the taxpayer did not have an unrestricted right to such item * * *." The "item" referred to is first mentioned in § 1341(a)(1); it is the item included in gross income in the year of receipt. The section does not imply in any way that the "deduction" and the "item" must necessarily be equal in amount. In fact, the use of the words "a deduction" and the placement of § 1341 in subchapter Q—the subchapter dealing largely with side-effects of the annual accounting system—make it clear that it is necessary to refer to other portions of the Code to discover how much of a deduction is allowable. The regulations promulgated under the section make the necessity for such a cross-reference clear. Treas.Reg. § 1.1341–1 (1957). Therefore, when § 1341(a)(4)—the subsection applicable here—speaks of "the tax * * * computed with such deduction," it is referring to the deduction mentioned in § 1341(a)(2); and that deduction must be determined not by any mechanical equation with the "item" originally included in gross income, but by reference to the applicable sections of the Code and the case law developed under those sections.

II. There is some dispute between the parties about whether the refunds in question are deductible as losses under § 165 of the 1954 Code or as business expenses under § 162.[3] Although in some situations the distinction may have relevance, cf. Equitable Life Ins. Co. of Iowa v. United States, 340 F.2d 9 (C.A.8th Cir.1965), we do not think it makes any difference here. In either case, the Code should not be

that the deduction is allowable at the proper time for accrual. H.R.Rep. No. 1337, 83d Cong., 2d Sess., A294 (1954); S.Rep. No. 1622, 83d Cong., 2d Sess., 451–452 (1954).

3. The Commissioner has long recognized that a deduction under some section is allowable. G.C.M. 16730, XV–1 Cum. Bull. 179 (1936).

interpreted to allow respondent "the practical equivalent of double deduction," Charles Ilfeld Co. v. Hernandez, 292 U.S. 62, 68, 54 S.Ct. 596, 598 (1934), absent a clear declaration of intent by Congress. See United States v. Ludey, 274 U.S. 295, 47 S.Ct. 608 (1927). Accordingly, to avoid that result in this case, the deduction allowable in the year of repayment must be reduced by the percentage depletion allowance which respondent claimed and the Commissioner allowed in the years of receipt as a result of the inclusion of the later-refunded items in respondent's "gross income from the property" in those years. Any other approach would allow respondent a total of $1.27½ in deductions for every $1 refunded to its customers.

Under the annual accounting system dictated by the Code, each year's tax must be definitively calculable at the end of the tax year. "It is the essence of any system of taxation that it should produce revenue ascertainable, and payable to the Government, at regular intervals." Burnet v. Sanford & Brooks Co., supra, at 365. In cases arising under the claim-of-right doctrine, this emphasis on the annual accounting period normally requires that the tax consequences of a receipt should not determine the size of the deduction allowable in the year of repayment. There is no requirement that the deduction save the taxpayer the exact amount of taxes he paid because of the inclusion of the item in income for a prior year. See Healy v. Commissioner, supra.

Nevertheless, the annual accounting concept does not require us to close our eyes to what happened in prior years. For instance, it is well settled that the prior year may be examined to determine whether the repayment gives rise to a regular loss or a capital loss. Arrowsmith v. Commissioner, 344 U.S. 6, 73 S.Ct. 71 (1952). The rationale for the *Arrowsmith* rule is easy to see; if money was taxed at a special lower rate when received, the taxpayer would be accorded an unfair tax windfall if repayments were generally deductible from receipts taxable at the higher rate applicable to ordinary income. The Court in *Arrowsmith* was unwilling to infer that Congress intended such a result.

This case is really no different.[4] In essence, oil and gas producers are taxed on only 72½% of their "gross income from the property" whenever they claim percentage depletion. The remainder of their oil and gas receipts is in reality tax exempt. We cannot believe that Congress intended to give taxpayers a deduction for refunding money that was not taxed when received. Cf. Maurice P. O'Meara, 8 T.C. 622,

---

4. The analogy would be even more striking if in *Arrowsmith* the individual taxpayer had not utilized the alternative tax for capital gains, as they were permitted to do by what is now § 1201 of the 1954 Code. Where the 25% alternative tax is not used, individual taxpayers are taxed at ordinary rates on 50% of their capital gains. See § 1202. In such a situation, the rule of the *Arrowsmith* case prevents taxpayers from deducting 100% of an item refunded when they were taxed on only 50% of it when it was received. Although *Arrowsmith* prevents this inequitable result by treating the repayment as a capital loss, rather than by disallowing 50% of the deduction, the policy behind the decision is applicable in this case. Here it would be inequitable to allow a 100% deduction when only 72½% was taxed on receipt.

634–635 (1947). Accordingly *Arrowsmith* teaches that the full amount of the repayment cannot, in the circumstances of this case, be allowed as a deduction.

This result does no violence to the annual accounting system. Here, as in *Arrowsmith*, the earlier returns are not being reopened. And no attempt is being made to require the tax savings from the deduction to equal the tax consequences of the receipts in prior years.[5] In addition, the approach here adopted will affect only a few cases. The percentage depletion allowance is quite unusual; unlike most other deductions provided by the Code, it allows a fixed portion of gross income to go untaxed. As a result, the depletion allowance increases in years when disputed amounts are received under claim of right; there is no corresponding decrease in the allowance because of later deductions for repayments.[6] Therefore, if a deduction for 100% of the repayments were allowed, every time money is received and later repaid the taxpayer would make a profit equivalent to the taxes on $27\frac{1}{2}\%$ of the amount refunded. In other situations when the taxes on a receipt do not equal the tax benefits of a repayment, either the taxpayer or the Government may, depending on circumstances, be the beneficiary. Here, the taxpayer always wins and the Government always loses. We cannot believe that Congress would have intended such an inequitable result.

The parties have stipulated that respondent is entitled to a judgment for $20,932.64 plus statutory interest for claims unrelated to the matter in controversy here; the District Court entered a judgment for that amount. Accordingly, the judgment of the Court of Appeals is reversed and the case is remanded to that court with instructions that it be returned to the District Court for re-entry of the original District Court judgment.

Reversed.

The dissenting opinions of STEWART, J. (DOUGLAS and HARLAN, JJ., joining), and DOUGLAS, J., are omitted. Ed.

NOTE

The scope of the *Arrowsmith* doctrine remains uncertain.[1] The parent decision involved a question of characterization, holding that

---

5. Compare the analogous approach utilized under the "tax benefit" rule. Alice Phelan Sullivan Corp. v. United States, 381 F.2d 399 (Ct.Cl.1967); see Internal Revenue Code of 1954 § 111. In keeping with the analogy, the Commissioner has indicated that the Government will only seek to reduce the deduction in the year on repayment to the extent that the depletion allowance attributable to the receipt directly or indirectly reduced taxable income. Proposed Treas.Reg. § 1.613–2(c)(8), 33 Fed. Reg. 10702–10703 (1968).

6. The 10% standard deduction mentioned by the dissent, post, at n. 6, differs in that it allows as a deduction a percentage of adjusted gross income, rather than of gross income. See § 141; cf. §§ 170, 213. As a result, repayments may in certain cases cause a decrease in the 10% standard deduction allowable in the year of repayment, assuming that the repayment is of the character to be deducted in calculating adjusted gross income. See § 62.

1. See Rabinovitz, "Effect of Prior Year's Transactions on Federal Income

loss quite arguably ordinary for lack of any sale or exchange in the taxable year, was *capital loss* because of its relationship to transactions in a prior year. There is little doubt that a similar approach can convert potential capital gain to *ordinary income;* and that was the result in David Bresler,[2] where part of a settlement in an antitrust suit compensated the taxpayer for a loss on the sale of business property claimed as an ordinary loss in a prior year.

Other applications of the *Arrowsmith* doctrine seem to extend its reach. For example, T made a gain on the sale of oil and gas leases, which he reported as long-term capital gain. Later, accused of fraud on the ground that some wells were illegally slanted, he settled the claim and treated the payment as a deductible business expense incurred to avoid litigation, to save legal expenses and to preserve his business reputation. Not so, said the Fifth Circuit, supporting the Commissioner and a prior district court decision. Under *Arrowsmith,* the payment was so related to the taxpayer's prior capital gain as to require capital loss treatment.[3]

The recapture of "insider's" profits under section 16(b) of the Securities and Exchange Act of 1934 has produced numerous *Arrowsmith* controversies. An insider who makes short swing profits on the purchase and sale (or sale and purchase) of stock in his corporation is required to disgorge and to pay the profits over to the corporation for the benefit of *all* shareholders. Can his payment qualify as a business expense deductible from ordinary income?

It is theoretically possible for a taxpayer to have a *tax* loss on transactions in which he has *S.E.C.* "insider's" profits. A buys 100 shares of his corporation's stock in year one for $1000. In March of year three he sells the 100 shares for $700, replacing them in June of year three for $600. He must pay the corporation $100 (or so it is alleged), but he has a $300 tax loss. If his corporate payment is to protect his business reputation and his job, certainly *Arrowsmith* is not an obstacle to an ordinary deduction. No known case deals with just this problem. In the *litigated* cases, the taxpayer has had a long-term capital gain on the sale. What then about the section 16(b) payment where respectable evidence is presented relating the payment and the taxpayer's business?

The Courts of Appeal have uniformly held, despite the Tax Court's insistence that the payments are a business expense generating an ordinary deduction, that *Arrowsmith* is overpowering, and the characterization of the deduction depends upon the prior tax treatment of the transaction generating the payment.[4] It has been suggested that the

Tax Consequences of Current Receipts or Payments," 28 Tax L.Rev. 85 (1972).

2. 65 T.C. 182 (1975), acq. 1976–2 C.B. 1.

3. Kimbell v. U.S., 490 F.2d 203 (5th Cir.1974), cert. denied 419 U.S. 833, 95 S.Ct. 58.

4. Brown v. Commissioner, 529 F.2d 609 (10th Cir.1976); Cummings v. Commissioner, 506 F.2d 449 (2d Cir.1974), cert. denied 421 U.S. 913, 95 S.Ct. 1571 (1975); Anderson v. Commissioner, 480 F.2d 1304 (7th Cir.1973); Mitchell v. Commissioner, 428 F.2d 259 (6th Cir.1970), cert. denied 401

proper solution is to add the section 16(b) payment to the basis of the purchased shares,[5] but a court has yet to accept this alternative.[6] In this area the Tax Court looks rather like the nimble triple-threat back running out of running room [7] before he can reach the goal line. Zooks! Could it be the Tax Court is running the wrong way?

PROBLEM

What tax consequences to the taxpayers in the *Arrowsmith* case if both the liquidation and the payment of the judgment occurred after 1991, and the taxpayers were subject to the 31 percent ordinary income tax bracket?

F. THE HOLDING PERIOD

Internal Revenue Code: Section 1223(1), (2), (11). See Sections 1014(a); 1015(a); 1041(b)(2); 1222; 1233.

REVENUE RULING 66–7
1966–1 Cum.Bull. 188.

Advice has been requested as to when a capital asset will have been held for more than 6 months within the meaning of sections 1222(3) and (4) of the Internal Revenue Code of 1954, particularly where the asset was acquired on the last day of a calendar month which has less than 31 days.

Section 1222(3) of the Code provides, in part, that the term "long-term capital gain" means gain from the sale or exchange of a capital asset *held for more than 6 months* and section 1222(4) of the Code provides, in part, that the "long-term capital loss" means loss from the sale or exchange of a capital asset *held for more than 6 months*.

It is well and long established that, in computing a period of "years" or "months" prescribed, in a contract or statute, "from" or "after" a designated day, date, act, or other event, the day thus designated is excluded and the last day of the prescribed period is included, unless a different intent is definitely evidenced. See I.T. 3287, C.B. 1939–1 (Part 1), 138.

I.T. 3985, C.B. 1949–2, 51, states the position of the Internal Revenue Service that the determination of the holding period of "capital assets" under sections 117(a)(2), (3), (4), (5), and (h)(4), of the Internal Revenue Code of 1939, must be made with reference to calendar months

U.S. 909, 91 S.Ct. 868 (1971), reversing the Tax Court in each instance.

5. Lokken, "Tax Significance of Payments in Satisfaction of Liabilities Arising Under Section 16(b) of the Securities Exchange Act of 1934," 4 Ga.L.Rev. 298 (1970).

6. But see Drennen, J., agreeing in his dissent in Nathan Cummings, 61 T.C. 1, 4 (1973).

7. See Jack E. Golsen, 54 T.C. 742 (1970) in which the Tax Court indicates that in a specific case it will follow the view of the court of appeals to which an appeal lies.

and fractions thereof, rather than with reference to days. The ruling was concerned primarily with the determination of the total holding period of securities purchased and sold where the provisions of section 117(h)(4) of the 1939 Code, relating to "wash sales," were applicable. Although similar provisions are not involved in the instant case, the principles enunciated in that ruling apply here. Furthermore, although I.T. 3287 was not cited in I.T. 3985 the rule stated in the former was actually applied in all the appropriate illustrative examples of the latter, that is, in examples 1 through 6.

In view of the foregoing, it is concluded that the holding period of a capital asset begins to run on the day following the date of acquisition of the asset involved. Accordingly, a capital asset acquired on the last day of any calendar month, regardless of whether the month has 31 days or less, must not be disposed of until on or after the first day of the seventh succeeding month of the calendar in order to have been "held for more than 6 months" within the meaning of sections 1222(3) and (4) of the Code. For example, an asset acquired on April 30, 1963, must not have been disposed of before November 1, 1963, in order to have been held for more than 6 months.*

I.T. 3985, C.B. 1949–2, 51, is hereby amplified for the purpose of determining when a capital asset has been held for more than 6 months where the asset was acquired on the last day of a month having less than 31 days.

The same rule applies in determining holding periods of property for purposes of section 1231 of the Code.

Pursuant to authority contained in section 7805(b) of the Code the provisions of this Revenue Ruling will be applicable with respect to dispositions of property after April 10, 1966.

REVENUE RULING 66–97
1966–1 Cum.Bull. 190.

Advice has been requested regarding the holding period of debentures and as to whether there is a distinction between a trade effected on a registered securities exchange and a trade made in the "over-the-counter" market.

The taxpayer purchased for investment certain debentures on the same day in an "over-the-counter" trade and a trade effected on a registered securities exchange. There are two relevant dates in connection with such security transactions: (1) the "trade date"—the date on which the contract to buy or sell the security is made and (2) the "settlement date"—the date on which the security is delivered and payment is tendered. In many cases settlement takes place a fixed number of days after the trade. In transactions involving bonds, notes or other evidences of indebtedness, the buyer pays the interest accrued

---

* In Lena M. Anderson, 33 TCM 234 (1974), the taxpayer had short-term capital gain on stock purchased December 2, 1966 and sold on June 2, 1967. Ed.

on the security to the date of settlement as a part of the consideration for the transfer. However, bonds as well as stocks are considered acquired or sold on the respective "trade dates." See I.T. 3442, C.B. 1941–1, 212. I.T. 3287, C.B. 1939–1, 138, states that the period during which an asset was held is to be computed by excluding the day on which the asset was acquired and including the day upon which it was sold. See also I.T. 3705, C.B. 1945, 174, and Revenue Ruling 66–7, page 188, this Bulletin. This rule applies whether the trade is made on a registered securities exchange or in the "over-the-counter" market.

Accordingly, the holding period for debentures acquired by purchase, whether on a registered securities exchange or in the "over-the-counter" market, is to be determined by excluding the "trade date" on which the debentures are acquired and including the "trade date" on which the debentures are sold.

The same rule applies generally in determining the holding periods of stocks and securities acquired by purchase.

NOTE

Close questions with respect to holding periods are most likely to arise in the purchase and sale of stocks and bonds. In a broker's board room it will not be uncommon to hear a high-bracket taxpayer say, "I don't yet have my year in." The inference is of course that he has a gain on a security which he hopes will be taxable as long-term capital gain. He is anxious to sell and fearful the price will decline but not quite willing to accept the tax attrition attending short-term gain. There is an obvious need for care in such cases.

Although the holding period is usually governed by the "trade dates," as indicated in Rev.Rul. 66–97, above, there is a different approach to the determination of the year for which the gain or loss on such transactions should be reported. If a trade is made in the regular way on December 31, the settlement date will be several days later. If a cash method, calendar year taxpayer has a gain on such a transaction, the trade date ends his holding period; his gain should be included in gross income in the succeeding year, although the result is far from clear.[1] On the other hand a loss on such a transaction is treated as realized and deductible for the year in which the trade date fell.[2]

---

1. Theoretically we look to cash flow in the succeeding year, although some legislative history implies a contrary result. See S.Rep. No. 99–313, 99th Cong., 2d Sess. 131 (1986), 1986–3 C.B. (Vol. 3) 131, stating that "in the case of sales that are made on an established market, where cash settlement of transactions customarily occurs several business days after the date on which a trade is made, that gain or loss would be recognized for Federal income tax purposes by both cash or accrual method taxpayers on the day that the trade is executed." At one point, a taxpayer was allowed to take his choice of years. Rev. Rul. 82–227, 1982–2 C.B. 89, although that Ruling was prior to the enactment of I.R.C. § 453(k)(2)(A) precluding the application of § 453 to sales of stock or securities traded on an established securities market.

2. Rev.Rul. 70–344, 1970–2 C.B. 50. Although this proposition is doctrinally difficult to support, nevertheless the principle is well established. See G.C.M. 21503, 1939–2 C.B. 205.

These are principles fairly easily stated. But there are many transactions in securities that involve timing considerations not fully answered by these principles. For example, T buys 100 shares of A stock on February 1 and another 100 shares of A stock on July 1. On February 2 of the next year he sells 100 shares of A stock. Which 100 shares has he sold? This raises basically a question of identification but, if he is unable to identify which block was sold, the Regulations answer the question on a "first-in, first-out" basis.[3] Obviously, this has a bearing, not only on his holding period (Might he have been hoping for short-term treatment?), but on his basis as well, if the two blocks of A stock were acquired at different prices.

Suppose T thinks the price of B stock is going down. On January 5 of the current year he sells 100 shares of B stock "short." This means he sells the stock without owning it, borrowing it from someone else to whom he is obliged ultimately to repay the loan when he closes or "covers" the short sale. Of course he hopes to buy the stock later for this purpose at a price below that at which he sold and, thus, to realize a gain. The short sale itself is not a taxable transaction (What basis could he use to determine gain or loss?), but gain or loss is realized when the short sale is closed by delivery of the stock. In general, whether gain or loss is long-term or short-term is determined by the period for which the stock delivered has been held.[4] In the usual case, short-term gain or loss will therefore be the result.

Suppose now that T has 100 shares of C stock on which he has a substantial paper gain. He bought the stock on April 1, and "now" is December 15 of the same year. He is afraid the price might drop but disinclined to realize short-term gain and, in fact, not happy about adding to his current year's income at all. (What advantages, apart from converting his gain to long-term, might arise from carrying the transaction over to the succeeding year?) He decides upon what is termed a short sale "against the box." That is, he sells while "long" in (owning) C stock but with the idea that he will close the sale only later, delivering the C stock when he has held it more than one year. In pursuance of the plan he sells short December 15 of the current year, and effects delivery April 2 of the succeeding year. To what extent has he accomplished his objective? 1. He has nailed down his gain; he can be indifferent to subsequent market fluctuations. 2. He has deferred realization of his gain until the succeeding year, not increasing his current year's income, even though he assured his gain in that year. 3. But Section 1233(b) classifies his gain as short-term. Aimed at just this kind of monkey business, that section specifies short-term treatment if on the day of a short sale a taxpayer owns property substantially identical to that sold short, which he has held for only one year or less.

---

3. Reg. §§ 1.1012–1(c)(1), 1.1223–1(i). See Colgan, "Identification of Securities Sold or Transferred," 18 N.Y.U.Inst. on Fed.Tax. 323 (1960).

4. Reg. § 1.1233–1(a)(3).

Section 1233 has implications far beyond the problem presented in the preceding paragraph. And many securities transactions are much more sophisticated than those suggested above. The "put," the "call," the "straddle," and the options and future markets are exciting playthings for those whose securities dealings go beyond every-day investing,[5] but no attempt is made here to consider holding period and related problems that arise with respect to these and related transactions.[6] Note, however, that Congress acted in one area of the option market by amending Section 1234(b). In the case of a grantor of an option, any gain or loss on a closing transaction with respect to the option or any gain on the lapse of an option is classified as short-term capital gain.

Close questions with respect to holding periods may arise in the purchase and sale of real estate, although the problem is not as crucial in this area as in the stock area, because real estate is normally held for a longer period of time. Wide variations in real estate transactions [7] suggest several points of time at which acquisition or disposition might be deemed to occur.[8] The Service has taken the position that, in the case of an unconditional contract for sale, the holding period for purposes of both acquisition and disposition is measured by the earlier of the date upon which title passes or the date upon which delivery of possession occurs and the burdens and privileges of ownership pass.[9]

Usually the actual dates on which a taxpayer acquires and disposes of property determine his holding period for the property. But, just as there are statutory exceptions to the general definition of capital assets and to the general requirement of a sale or exchange, so are there statutory exceptions to the general holding period concept. One, Section 1233, was illustrated above. Attention is drawn to some other exceptions in the Problems that follow this note.

5. See Rev.Rul. 78–182, 1978–1 C.B. 265. A list of articles dealing with "options," aptly identified as "The Newest Game in Town" appears at 31 Tax L.Rev. 362 (1976).

The Economic Recovery Tax Act of 1981 enacted I.R.C. §§ 1092 and 1256 and amended other subsections; these measures were designed to prevent the tax avoidance aspects of commodity straddles.

6. Analysis of some of the transactions appears in the following articles: Mintz, "How to Use Short Sales and Stock Option Contracts to Produce Tax Savings," 24 J.Tax. 66 (1966); Bennion, "Current Developments in Tax Planning with Securities Transactions: 'Puts'; 'Calls'; 'Straddles'; 'Short Sales'; 'Arbitrage'," 13 U.S.C.Tax Inst. 489 (1961); Hariton, "Puts, Calls and Straddles," 18 N.Y.U.Inst. on Fed.Tax. 357 (1960); Lippitz, "Tax Guide for a Seller of Puts and Calls," 38 Taxes 829 (1960); Esks, "Federal Tax Advantages to Investors in the Use of Put and Call Options," 31 Tax L.Rev. 1 (1975); Kennedy, "Selecting the

Off-Beat Investments: Puts, Calls, Straddles, Warrants, Commodity Futures and Other Exotica," 32 N.Y.U.Inst. on Fed.Tax. 1093 (1974).

7. Vernon Hoven, 56 T.C. 50 (1971); Ted F. Merrill, 40 T.C. 66 (1963), affirmed per curiam, 336 F.2d 771 (9th Cir.1964); Boykin v. Commissioner, 344 F.2d 889 (5th Cir.1965).

8. Those possibilities include the date that an executory contract becomes binding, that title passes, that possession changes, and that the benefits and burdens of ownership pass. Withey, J., discusses this problem very well in Donald Borrelli, 31 TCM 876 (1972).

9. Rev.Rul. 54–607, 1954–2 C.B. 177. The holding period is deemed to commence on the date following the earliest of the two dates and to cease on the earliest of the two dates. Rev.Rul. 54–607 expressly indicates that a mere purchase option contract, as opposed to an unconditional contract to sell, is not within these rules.

PROBLEMS

1. Taxpayer, a cash method taxpayer, engaged in the following transactions in shares of stock. Consider the amount and character of his gain or loss in each transaction:

(a) T bought 100 shares of stock on January 15, 1991 at a cost of $50 per share. He sold them on January 16, 1992 at $60 per share.

(b) T bought 100 shares of stock on February 28, 1991 at a cost of $50 per share. He sold them on February 29, 1992 for $60 per share.

(c) T bought 100 shares at $50 per share on February 10, 1991 and another 100 shares at $50 per share on March 10, 1991. He sold 100 of the shares on February 15, 1992 for $60 per share. See Reg. §§ 1.1223–1(i) and 1.1012–1(c)(1).

(d) T told his broker to purchase 100 shares of stock on December 29, 1991 at a time when its price was $50 per share. The stock was delivered to T on January 3, 1992 when it was selling for $52 per share. T told his broker to sell the stock on December 30, 1992 when it sold for $60 per share, and it was delivered to Buyer on January 4, 1993 when it was selling for $63 per share.

(e) Same as (d), above, except that the value of the stock on December 30, 1992 was $45 per share and on January 4, 1993 was $48 per share.

(f) T's father bought 100 shares of stock on January 10, 1991 at $30 per share. On March 10, 1991 when they were worth $40 per share he gave them to T who sold them on January 15, 1992 for $60 per share (see § 1223(2)).

(g) T's father purchased 1000 shares of stock for $10 per share several years ago. The stock was worth $50 per share on March 1, 1991, the date of Father's death. The stock was distributed to T by the executor on January 5, 1992 and T sold it for $60 per share on January 15, 1992.

(h) Same as (g), above, except that T was executor of his father's estate and as such he sold the stock on January 15, 1992 for $60 per share to pay the estate's administration expenses.

2. Owner owned four acres of urban land which he leased to Tacker for 99 years at an agreed rental of $10,000 per year. In addition, Tacker acquired an option under which he or his assignee could purchase the property at any time during the life of the lease for $250,000, Tacker being permitted upon exercise of the option to apply against the purchase price $1,000 of prior rental for each year that rental payments had been made under the lease. Twenty-five years later Purchaser appeared on the scene ready, willing and able to buy the property for $300,000. What result to Tacker:

    (a) If he exercises the option and immediately sells to Purchaser for $300,000?

    (b) If he sells Purchaser his option for $75,000?

    3. T purchased unimproved land on April 1, 1991 and commenced construction of a personal residence, which was completed on January 1, 1993. Before T even moved in, and on that date, B offered him $60,000 for the house and land. T's cost basis for the land is $20,000 and for the house is $30,000, and the proposed purchase price is allocable $25,000 for the land and $35,000 for the house. It can also be established that construction of the house was 50% completed on December 31, 1991. What would be the consequences to T if the sale is effected on January 1, 1993? (See Paul v. Commissioner, 206 F.2d 763 (3d Cir.1953).)

CHAPTER 22. CHARACTERIZATION OF GAIN ON THE SALE OF DEPRECIABLE PROPERTY

A. DEPRECIATION

1. INTRODUCTION

Internal Revenue Code: Sections 167(a), (b), (c); 168(a), (b), (c), (e)(1) and (2), (f)(1) and (5), (g)(1), (2), and (7), (i)(1); 1016(a)(2). See Section 62(a)(1) and (4); 168(d); 169; 263(a); 263A.

Regulations: Sections 1.162–4; 1.167(a)–1(a) and (b), –3, –10; 1.167(b)–0(a), –1(a).

T leaves his position with a shoe manufacturing company to go into business by himself, making and selling shoes. He sets up shop in a garage on the back of his property and purchases an electric stitching machine for $1600, his only significant piece of equipment. For eight years he purchases each year $2000 worth of leather and other supplies and electricity that cost him $500. Each year he makes 200 pairs of shoes and sells them at $22.50 each.

He sees the following results each year:

Receipts	$4500
Less materials and supplies	2500
Profit for the year	$2000

And over the eight year period he considers he has made a profit of $16,000 (8 × $2000).

But now he learns that his stitching machine is worn out, has no salvage value, and must be replaced. Looking back he wonders about his profit. While it appears he made $16,000, he now sees that he has incurred another $1600 cost and has made only $14,400. But did he make only $400 for the first year (when he bought the machine) and $2000 each year for the next seven years? Or maybe $2000 for each of the first seven years and only $400 for the eighth year when the machine finally wore out? Neither possibility makes good sense, if he wishes to think (or must for tax purposes) in terms of annual profit. The sensible thing is to allocate cost for something like the stitcher over the period it is useful to him. And this is what depreciation is all about. Under the simplest approach to the problem, T can quickly be made to see that if he used up his $1600 stitcher over eight years of work it has been an added manufacturing cost to him of $200 each year. He now sees each year's results as:

Receipts		$4500
Less:		
Materials & supplies	2500	
Depreciation	200	
		2700
Profit for year		$1800

And his profit for eight years is $14,400 (8 $\times$ $1800), as before, but more appropriately determined on the basis of a like amount of profit each year. Should he worry, too, that his garage is eight years older?

For federal income tax purposes Sections 167 and 168 treat depreciation as if it were an operating expense by allowing an annual deduction for exhaustion and wear and tear (including predictable obsolescence) of property. The business community utilized the concept in the determination of annual profits even before there was a federal income tax.[1]

Prerequisites for Deduction. Sections 167(a) and 168(a) restrict the depreciation deduction to (1) property used in a trade or business and (2) property held for the production of income. Thus inventory and property held for sale to customers are placed outside the scope of the section. And so is property that is held for merely personal use, even though it too declines in value over a period of time. Why?

Only property that will be consumed, or will wear out, or will become obsolete, or will otherwise become useless to the taxpayer can qualify for the deduction. Thus, unimproved realty is said to be nondepreciable, meaning, in the tax sense, that it cannot be the subject of a depreciation deduction.[2] And if realty is improved, it is only the improvements that can qualify.[3]

The Useful Life Concept. It is only property that has an identifiable useful life to the taxpayer[4] which can qualify for the deduction. As is apparent in the shoemaker illustration above, depreciation is a cost spreading device, and the concept anticipates that cost will spread over the period the property is to be used. If property is such that no useful life is ascertainable it, too, is said to be nondepreciable. This requirement disqualifies goodwill which cannot be "written off" by way of depreciation[5] for lack of any ascertainable useful life, even though a

---

1. Knoxville v. Knoxville Water Co., 212 U.S. 1, 29 S.Ct. 148 (1909).

2. Reg. § 1.167(a)–2; but see comments on depletion under "Related Concepts," below and see Henderson, "Land Cost Expenditures: Recent Trend Shows Many Such Costs Are Now Depreciable," 38 J.Tax. 78 (1973). However, property need not be tangible to be depreciable. See Schenk, "Depreciation of Intangible Assets: The Uncertainty of Death and Taxes," 13 Wayne L.Rev. 501 (1967).

3. See, for example, Rev.Rul. 74–265, 1974–1 C.B. 56, allowing depreciation of the cost of landscaping an apartment complex over the life of the apartment buildings if replacement of the buildings will destroy the landscaping. If not, landscaping has no useful life and is not depreciable. See "The Useful Life Concept," below.

4. Under pre-ACRS Systems (see page 743, infra) property was depreciable to a taxpayer only for the number of years he intended to use the property not for the number of years of the property's life. Massey Motors, Inc. v. U.S., 364 U.S. 92, 80 S.Ct. 1411 (1960).

5. Reg. § 1.167(a)–3.

taxpayer may have purchased goodwill along with the other assets of another's business.[6] Similarly, if one purchases a franchise or other contractual right which is to continue for a stated period, his cost may not be depreciable for lack of a useful life, if the right is renewable and it is uncertain whether the period will be extended.[7]

Other intangibles may have an "economic" useful life.[8]

Useful life is not only a requirement for the depreciation deduction, it also plays a role in measuring the amount of the deduction. As the Supreme Court has said:[9]

> The amount of the allowance for depreciation is the sum which should be set aside for the taxable year, in order that, at the end of the useful life of the [asset] in the business, the aggregate of the sums set aside will (with the salvage value) suffice to provide an amount equal to the original cost.

If, as in the shoemaker example, the simplest depreciation method is adopted, the useful life pegs the so-called depreciation rate. That is, if the machine is to be used for eight years and if charges are to be spread equally over the eight years, the rate must be $12\frac{1}{2}$ percent in order for the entire cost to be taken into account over the life of the asset ($12\frac{1}{2}\%$ $\times$ \$1600 = \$200; and 8 $\times$ \$200 = \$1600).

It is obvious that the period of useful life with respect to any piece of property is speculative and a likely subject for disagreement between the Treasury and the taxpayer. In 1934 the burden of proving useful life was on the taxpayer,[10] and Treasury personnel took a restrictive approach to depreciation.[11] In an effort to alleviate such disagreements both the Treasury and Congress have provided various guidelines or requirements for the determination of normal useful lives which taxpayers may use as a shield against attack on audit. Over the years the

---

6. It is sometimes difficult to separate other assets from goodwill for depreciation purposes. Nevertheless, in KFOX, Inc. v. United States, 510 F.2d 1365 (Ct.Cl.1975), the cost of a radio station's personal service contracts were allowed to be separated from its cost of goodwill. The contracts were amortized over the life of the contract plus the period of the single renewal option. Similarly, in Computing and Software, Inc., 64 T.C. 223 (1975), a purchaser of a consumer credit information service was able to allocate part of the purchase price to credit information files (separate from goodwill).

7. Toledo TV Cable Co., 55 T.C. 1107 (1971) (renewable municipal franchises related to community antenna television); Westinghouse Broadcasting Co. v. Commissioner, 309 F.2d 279 (3d Cir.1962), cert. denied 372 U.S. 935, 83 S.Ct. 881 (1963) (renewable television network affiliation contract); Nachman v. Commissioner, 191

F.2d 934 (5th Cir.1951) (renewable liquor license). But see I.R.C. § 1253(d). Although the courts generally base these decisions on the useful life concept, it can be argued as well that salvage value may equal full initial cost, which would be an added reason for denial of any depreciation deduction.

8. In Computing and Software, Inc., supra note 6, credit information files were held to have an "economic" useful life of six years and in Rodeway Inns of America, 63 T.C. 414 (1974), acq., 1975–1 C.B. 2, an exclusive motel territorial agreement was determined to have a five year "economic" useful life.

9. U.S. v. Ludey, 274 U.S. 295, 300, 47 S.Ct. 608, 610 (1927).

10. T.D. 4422, XIII–1 C.B. 58 (1934).

11. Stephens, "Tax Amortization is the Key to the Stable Door," 5 U. of Fla.L.Rev. 261, 266–271 (1952).

general trend has been to shorten the recognized lives of assets.[12] In 1971 Congress enacted the asset depreciation range (A.D.R.) system[13] which set various class lives for property which were shorter lives than under prior depreciation rules. The Accelerated Cost Recovery System (ACRS), discussed in detail later,[14] generally provides for even shorter useful lives than under any prior system.[15] The word "cost" is used loosely here. One may have a machine that "cost" him nothing but which is subject to depreciation. If, for example, he acquired the machine by gift, Section 1015 accords him a basis for the property. And he is entitled to write off *that* basis by way of depreciation deductions.[16] Thus, it is cost or other basis which is deductible by way of depreciation.

Because cost or other basis fixes the overall limits of the depreciation deductions for any asset, an acquisition of a depreciable asset has the same ultimate impact on taxable income as any deductible expense; only the amount of the expenditure is deductible. When the depreciable cost of an asset is "recovered" (charged off by way of depreciation deductions) depreciation deductions stop.

Technically the cost of an asset must take into account not only acquisition cost but also the amount that may be recovered on disposition of the asset, commonly referred to as its salvage value. Thus, the deductions taken over the useful life should equal only net cost, i.e., cost less salvage value. Suppose the shoemaker who acquires a stitcher for $1600 anticipates its sale eight years later for $400. The 12½ percent depreciation rate suggested above might properly be applied to $1200 ($1600 cost less $400 salvage value), yielding annual depreciation deductions of $150 which, over eight years, would aggregate $1200. Over the years the determination of salvage value has led to substantial controversy; the ACRS, which is discussed below, simply disregards salvage value in the depreciation computation.[17]

Depreciation Methods. With respect to property used in one's business or held for the production of income, once the property's basis, useful life and, if necessary,[18] salvage value are known, several different methods of depreciation may be available to the taxpayer. These methods regulate the timing of depreciation deductions within the cost limitations indicated above. One can spread the depreciation deduction evenly over the life of his property, the so-called "straight-line" method used in the shoemaker illustration above. There are also several expressly authorized accelerated methods of depreciation which increase depreciation deductions in the early years of the asset's useful life and decrease them in later years. However, the total amount of

---

12. In 1942 the Treasury published revised Bulletin "F" providing normal useful lives for assets on an item by item basis. In Rev.Proc. 62–21, 1962–2 C.B. 418, the Treasury provided shorter guidelines for classification of assets.

13. I.R.C. § 167(m).

14. See page 747 infra.

15. See page 747, infra.

16. See I.R.C. § 167(c).

17. I.R.C. § 168(b)(4).

18. Salvage is disregarded under the ACRS. I.R.C. § 168(b)(4).

depreciation that can ultimately be claimed is generally the same under each of the methods. However, since salvage is disregarded under the ACRS, total depreciation on recovery property under that system may exceed total depreciation on non–ACRS property.[19]

In 1954 when statutory accelerated depreciation methods were first proposed under Section 167 the Senate Report explained some of the authorized depreciation methods as follows: [20]

> Subsection (b) [of Section 167] corresponds to the same provision of the House bill. Subsection (b) provides methods which, for taxable years ending after December 31, 1954, will be deemed to produce a reasonable allowance for depreciation of property described in subsection (c) so long as the useful life used in determining such allowance is accurate. Your committee has struck the word "one" from the phrase "an allowance computed in accordance with regulations prescribed by the Secretary or his delegate under one of the following methods:". This word was deleted to make it clear that more than one method may be used on various property or classes of property of a taxpayer. For example, a tax payer may use the straight-line method of depreciation on buildings while using the declining balance method on machinery. The methods described in subsection (b) are:
>
> (1) The straight-line method—
>
> Under this method, the cost or other basis of the property, less its estimated salvage value, is deducted in equal annual installments over the period of its estimated useful life. The depreciation deduction is obtained by dividing the amount to be depreciated by the estimated useful life. This may be expressed as a rate of depreciation computed by dividing the estimated life into 1. The deduction per taxable year may be arrived at by multiplying the cost or other basis (less salvage value) by the resulting rate.
>
> (2) Declining balance method—
>
> Under this method a uniform rate is applied to the unrecovered basis of the asset. Since the basis is always reduced by prior depreciation, the rate is applied to a constantly declining basis. The salvage value is not deducted from the basis prior to applying the rate, since under this method at the expiration of useful life there remains an undepreciated balance which represents salvage value. The rate to be used under this paragraph may never exceed twice the rate which would have been used had the deduction been computed under the method

---

19. If the non–ACRS property had a zero salvage value the totals would be equal.

20. Sen.Rep. No. 1622, 83rd Cong., 3rd Sess. pp. 201–202 (1954). The sum of the years-digits method is not included. See Kahn and Blum, "Debate on Accelerated Depreciation" 78 Mich.L.Rev. 1172 (1981).

described in paragraph (1). Under section 23(1) of the 1939 Code the declining balance method was allowed in certain instances but the rate was generally limited to 1½ times of the rate used under the straight-line method. If this method has been used for property acquired prior to December 31, 1953, it may continue to be used but the rate provided for in paragraph (2) will not be presumed to be reasonable with respect to such property.

In all instances, it is important to bear in mind, as explained above, that the depreciation deduction is merely a method of cost allocation which recognizes that to the extent buildings, equipment, and other items are consumed in profit-making activities, the value consumed represents a cost to be spread over the item's life and taken into account in determining a net income or loss for each year in the life of the item. Neither for business nor for tax accounting is any effort made to determine the exact value shrinkage in each accounting period as a means of determining an asset's cost for the period. Nor is it intended that cost less depreciation reflect *value* at any given point of time; "adjusted basis" and "value" are not synonymous. The cost-spreading methods described above are conventions, which operate mechanically and quite differently, depending upon the method selected. Watch for this in some of the special problems (particularly characterization of gain on the disposition of depreciable property) arising in subsequent assignments, which are traceable to the depreciation deduction.

The three principal methods which are illustrated are not applicable to all types of property [21] and are not exclusive. Other methods of depreciation are accorded recognition by Section 168(f)(1). Depreciation methods may be used which make depreciation dependent upon the percentage of total income flow with respect to the property in any year, upon the percentage of production which occurs in a year as compared to expected production over the asset's life, or upon the percentage of hours a machine is used in relation to the number of hours it will be used.[22]

The depreciation deduction is an ordinary deduction generally reducing gross income in arriving at adjusted gross income.[23]

The Relationship of Depreciation to Basis

When a taxpayer claims depreciation on property, the deduction is attended by a commensurate reduction in his basis for the property. Thus, the cost or other basis for depreciable property may be likened to a limited supply of deductions from which the taxpayer may draw in accordance with various methods until the supply is used up. If the supply is to be tapped over a period of several years, there must be a device for keeping track of the supply. Basis is the device, although of

21. I.R.C. § 168(f).

22. I.R.C. § 168(f)(1).

23. I.R.C. § 62(a)(1) and (4).

course it serves other purposes as well. As deductions are claimed, downward basis adjustments effect a shrinkage of the supply, and "adjusted" basis reflects the remaining amount that can be claimed as deductions. In a tax sense the taxpayer thus achieves a "return" of his capital as he "expenses" his capital expenditure piecemeal over the period during which depreciation deductions are claimed.

Basis adjustments arising out of depreciation are governed by Section 1016(a)(2). The downward adjustment required is at least the amount of depreciation deduction permitted ("*allowable*") under the depreciation method employed by the taxpayer. This is because depreciation is in the nature of a continuing expense, unaffected by the success or failure of the taxpayer's business, and Congress does not permit a taxpayer to time his depreciation deductions for his own convenience any more than he can time his deductions for rent or salary. Thus, while depreciation does not involve a current pay-out, as salary expense may, it is properly viewed as a continuing expense each year, just as if it were salary expense paid or accrued. Consequently, basis is reduced even if the taxpayer claims no depreciation deduction. The amount of depreciation allowable is determined in accordance with the depreciation method that has been adopted by the taxpayer. If he has claimed no depreciation and has therefore adopted no method, the statute specifies that allowable depreciation is to be determined under the straight-line method.

It may be that a taxpayer will claim depreciation deductions in excess of those permitted. This could come about, for example, by his erroneous use of too high a basis for an asset or by his assumption of an improperly short useful life. What should be the effect on basis of his claiming excessive deductions? If the amount claimed is not challenged (and is therefore "*allowed*"), should the full amount claimed work to reduce basis, even though it exceeds the amount permitted by the statute (the amount "allowable")? Congress has said that it should, the sensible notion being that if the taxpayer's taxable income has been reduced by the deduction, even improperly, he has had the use of his capital expenditure to that extent. Thus, in general, the plan has been to call for downward basis adjustment for depreciation "allowed" but not less than the amount "allowable".

Before the statute took its present form a taxpayer unsuccessfully challenged the "allowed or allowable" approach in a case in which excessive deductions claimed and allowed had accorded the taxpayer no advantage, because losses left no potentially taxable income against which the excess deductions could be used.[24] Although the law at the time afforded no relief in such circumstances, Congress recognized the need for a modification of the "allowed" concept, which now appears in Section 1016(a)(2)(B). With this change, while "allowable" depreciation always works a reduction in basis, depreciation allowed in excess of the

---

24. Virginian Hotel Corp. v. Helvering, 319 U.S. 523, 63 S.Ct. 1260 (1943).

amount allowable effects a basis reduction only to the extent that the excess resulted in a reduction of the taxpayer's taxes.

The Accelerated Cost Recovery System

Congress seems to be constantly tinkering with the depreciation system. The basic underlying concepts of the system which are discussed above (useful life, depreciable cost, depreciation methods, and basis adjustments) are applicable to all types of depreciable property— real and personal, tangible and intangible, and new and used. Yet different detailed rules apply to the different types of property and the rules are subject to frequent change. The most recent overhaul of the depreciation system is the Accelerated Cost Recovery System (ACRS), found in Section 168, which was a major part of the Economic Recovery Tax Act of 1981.[25] Congress has tinkered with the ACRS system several times since 1981;[26] the system was substantially revised in the Tax Reform Act of 1986.[27] Because the 1986 changes were so substantial, we will refer to the pre–1987 rules as *old* ACRS and the post–1986 rules as *current* ACRS.[28]

ACRS is mandatory,[29] not elective, although some elections may be made *within* the system.[30] ACRS applies to most tangible depreciable property.[31] Intangible property [32] does not qualify for ACRS treatment. The statute also excludes from ACRS property depreciated under a method not expressed in terms of time of utility, such as property depreciated under the unit-of-production method.[33] If for any reason ACRS does not apply, Section 167 applies and a separate set of rules comes into play.[34] Thus, ACRS is not the exclusive depreciation deduction section; it is mandatory when it applies, but if it is inapplicable, Section 167 is used.[35]

Recovery Periods. ACRS varies from the previously considered Section 167 rules in several respects. Under ACRS taxpayers recover

25. See Gehan, "Appreciating Depreciation," 40 N.Y.U. Inst. of Fed. Tax. Ch. 26 (1982).

The Act also repealed the I.R.C. § 263(e) mechanical "Reasonable Repair Allowance" which helped distinguish between repairs and capital expenditures. See page 355, supra.

26. See, e.g., P.L. No. 97–248, 97th Cong., 2d Sess. §§ 205(a), (b), 206 (1982); P.L. No. 98–369, 98th Cong., 2d Sess. §§ 111, 179 (1984).

27. P.L. No. 99–514, 99th Cong., 2d Sess. § 201 (1986).

28. Property placed in service by the taxpayer after December 31, 1986 is subject to *current* ACRS. P.L. No. 99–514, note 27 supra, § 203(a)(1)(A). *Old* ACRS is generally applicable to property placed in service after December 31, 1980 and before January 1, 1987.

29. I.R.C. § 168(a).

30. But see notes 53, 54 and 56, infra.

31. I.R.C. § 168(a).

32. Intangible property is amortized over its life. See note 72, infra.

33. I.R.C. § 168(f)(1). See also I.R.C. § 168(f)(2)–(4) listing some other property that does not qualify for ACRS.

34. Some of those rules are considered in the general rules discussed supra at pages 740 through 747, supra, and some rules specifically related to personal property as discussed at page 759, infra.

35. In addition the "anti-churning" rules, considered below, may make the *current* ACRS rules inapplicable bringing either *old* ACRS or Section 167 into play. See the text at note 61, infra.

the entire cost of tangible depreciable property over lives known as "recovery periods" that are, for the most part, shorter [36] than the useful lives employed under Section 167.[37] This is accomplished by assigning all such property to one of several classes with predetermined useful lives or recovery periods. A happy consequence is elimination of controversy between government and taxpayer over the useful life of the property.[38] Furthermore, ACRS completely disregards salvage value in the computation of depreciation, both simplifying the computation and alleviating controversy.[39] ACRS also varies from Section 167 by providing for the use of the same schedules whether the property is new or used property.[40]

Under *current* ACRS each item of property is assigned to one of several classifications which is generally dependent upon the property's class life under the A.D.R. system.[41] Under each *classification* items of property are assigned to an applicable *recovery period* which becomes the period of time over which that property is depreciated.[42] Most personal property is classified as either "3–year", "5–year" or "7–year" property which has respective recovery periods of 3, 5, or 7 years.[43] Some property specifically listed in Section 168(e)(3) is subject to special classification. For example, automobiles are specifically placed within the 5–year class with a 5 year recovery period.[44] Almost all depreciable real property is assigned either a 27.5 year or a 31.5 year recovery period.[45]

In our example above, if the shoemaker acquires a stitcher, it has a 11 year class life under the A.D.R. system.[46] It is classified as 7–year property under ACRS and has a 7 year recovery period.[47] If shoemaker buys it for $1600 and places it in service in 1991, he uses the 7–year recovery period even though he actually plans to use the stitcher for a shorter or longer period. Also since ACRS disregards salvage value,

---

36. However, see the *current* ACRS recovery periods assigned to real property. I.R.C. § 168(c). See page 766, infra.

37. The recovery periods assigned to property under ACRS are generally shorter than the lives under the A.D.R. system. See note 13, supra. For example, office furniture now depreciable over 7 years was depreciable over 10 years under the A.D.R. system. See Rev.Proc. 83–35, 1983–1 C.B. 745 at 746.

38. The system also eliminates any controversy over the requirement that the property be depreciated over its useful life *to the taxpayer.* See Massey Motors, Inc. v. U.S., note 4, supra.

39. I.R.C. § 168(b)(4) and (g)(2)(A).

40. Compare I.R.C. § 168(a) with § 167(a) and see Rev.Rul. 57–352, 1957–2 C.B. 150.

41. I.R.C. § 168(e)(1) and (i)(1). But see I.R.C. § 168(e)(2) and (3) establishing sepa-

rate classifications of most real property and special classifications for some other types of property.

Recall that the property's class life under the A.D.R. system also establishes its useful life for I.R.C. § 167 depreciation. See note 13, supra.

42. I.R.C. § 168(c).

43. 3–year property includes property with a class life under the A.D.R. system of 4 years; 5–year property is property with an A.D.R. class life of 5 through 9 years; and 7–year property is property with an A.D.R. class life of 10 through 15 years. I.R.C. § 168(e)(1).

44. I.R.C. § 168(c) and (e)(3)(B)(i).

45. I.R.C. § 168(c)(1). See I.R.C. § 168(e)(2).

46. Rev.Proc. 83–85, supra note 37 at 752.

47. I.R.C. § 168(c)(1) and (e)(1).

the shoemaker is permitted to recover the entire cost of the stitcher over 7 years, even if he hopes to sell it for $400 after 10 years.[48]

Depreciation Methods. Current ACRS provides that the type of depreciation methods available with respect to property also depends upon the classification of property.[49] Residential rental property and nonresidential real property qualify only for the straight-line method of depreciation.[50] With regard to the other classes, property that is within the 3–year, 5–year, 7–year, or 10–year classifications qualifies for the 200% declining balance method of depreciation with a switch to the straight-line method for the year when that method yields a greater depreciation allowance; [51] and 15–year and 20–year property qualifies for the 150% declining balance method with a similar ultimate switch to the straight-line method.[52] With respect to the above classifications of 3–year to 10–year property, the taxpayer may elect to use the 150% declining value method for all property within that class placed in service in the year of the election.[53] In addition, with respect to the above classifications of 3–year to 20–year property, the taxpayer may elect to use the straight-line depreciation method for all property within that class placed in service in the year of the election.[54]

Under Section 168(g), *current* ACRS also provides an alternative depreciation system that that is required for some properties [55] and may be elected for any other ACRS property.[56] Generally, the alternative system uses straight-line depreciation with longer lives than the ACRS rules above causing, of course, a slower depreciation of assets. Why, you may ask, would a taxpayer elect to use slower depreciation? In the formative years of a business or, indeed, in any period of losses, one considers the deferral of deductions to a period for which they will save taxes. Otherwise, although one would rarely elect to use the alternative system, it is required in some cases.[57] Moreover, the alternative system is used in the computation of the alternative minimum tax which is considered later in this course [58] and in the computation of "earnings and profits," a matter beyond the scope of this course, which is a concept of importance in the income taxation of corporations and their shareholders.

Conventions. The ACRS system also adopts certain "conventions," administrative rules of convenience which, for depreciation purposes, treat property as if it were placed in service at a set point in time during a year rather than on the specific date its use commences. There are separate conventions for personal and real property which

---

48. Cf. I.R.C. §§ 1245 and 1250 and the concept of recapture beginning at page 788, infra.

49. See I.R.C. § 168(b) and (e).

50. I.R.C. § 168(b)(3)(A) and (B). See also I.R.C. § 168(e)(2).

51. I.R.C. § 168(b)(1).

52. I.R.C. § 168(b)(2).

53. I.R.C. § 168(b)(2)(D) and (5).

54. I.R.C. § 168(b)(3)(C) and (5).

55. I.R.C. §§ 168(g)(1)(A)–(D) and 280F(b)(1). See page 763, infra.

56. I.R.C. § 168(g)(1)(E).

57. Note 55, supra.

58. See Chapter 27C, infra.

are considered later in this Chapter.[59] The convention rules also apply on the disposition of depreciable property.[60]

Anti-churning Rules. *Current* ACRS also provides a series of "anti-churning" rules [61] that are designed to prevent taxpayers from bringing within the *current* ACRS rules property they or "related persons" [62] used before the *current* ACRS rules applied. ACRS is intended to encourage new capital investment, and Congress does not want taxpayers merely to churn their old investments to take advantage of the more rapid *current* ACRS writeoffs. Therefore the anti-churning rules apply if, *and only if,* the *current* ACRS rules allow the taxpayer a more rapid writeoff (more depreciation) in the first year the property is placed in service than depreciation allowed for that year by the rules under which the property was being depreciated by the related person.[63] For example, if in 1991 a taxpayer acquires property from a "related person" who owned or used the property and who acquired it after 1980 but prior to 1987, (so that *old* ACRS applied), the taxpayer cannot use *current* ACRS but must use *old* ACRS *if* in the first year of his use *current* ACRS would allow more generous depreciation allowances than *old* ACRS.[64] Similarly, if the taxpayer acquires property from a related person who owned or used the property prior to 1981 (so that the Section 167 rules applied), the taxpayer may not use *current* ACRS depreciation and must use the Section 167 rules if, and again only if, the *current* ACRS rules would result in a greater writeoff than the Section 167 rules in the year the property is placed in service by the taxpayer.[65] Furthermore, in this latter case the property is "used" property, and Section 167 placed additional restrictions on its depreciation.[66]

For purposes of the anti-churning rules, "related persons" include family members of the taxpayer including spouses, brothers, sisters, ancestors and descendants and entities such as corporations, partnerships and trusts in which the taxpayer has an interest.[67] The anti-churning rules apply to property acquired not only by purchase but in various other transactions, including some leasing transactions, sale leasebacks, property exchanges that qualify for nonrecognition of

---

59. I.R.C. § 168(d). See Parts 2 and 3, infra.

60. I.R.C. § 168(d)(4) parentheticals.

61. I.R.C. § 168(f)(5). Actually most of the anti-churning rules are found in § 168(e)(4) of the 1954 Code and § 168(f)(5) merely incorporates them by reference.

62. See the discussion below.

63. I.R.C. § 168(f)(5)(B). The half-year convention is used in making all the calculations. I.R.C. § 168(f)(5)(B)(ii)(II).

64. I.R.C. § 168(f)(5)(A). Conf.Rep. No. 99–841, 99th Cong., 2d Sess. II–54 (1986). The anti-churning rules are inherently in-

applicable to most real property and are also inapplicable to some other property. I.R.C. § 168(f)(5)(B)(i) and (ii), respectively.

65. I.R.C. § 168(f)(5).

66. Again, most real property is not subject to these anti-churning rules. I.R.C. § 168(f)(5)(B)(i). But most personal property is subject to them. See now-repealed I.R.C. § 167(c) related to personal property. See also Rev.Rul. 57–352, 1957–2 C.B. 150, allowing either the 150% declining balance or the straight-line method of depreciation for used personal property.

67. I.R.C. § 168(e)(4)(D).

gain,[68] and property acquired in any transaction one of whose principal purposes is avoiding the anti-churning rules.[69]

Collateral Effects

Congressional adjustments in the depreciation deduction are by no means based solely on a search for the best way to determine a net income for the taxable year. Congress made the liberalizing changes in 1954, and in 1981 in an effort to stimulate the economy. Congress has made adjustments in the depreciation deduction in the hope of inducing sociological improvements and ecological advances. For example, changes made by the Tax Reform Act of 1969 were undertaken to stimulate investment in rehabilitating low income housing by allowing certain expenditures in that area to be deducted over a short sixty-month period.[70] In addition under the Revenue Act of 1971 Congress added now expired Section 188 providing for an elective sixty-month amortization of capital expenditures relating to the acquisition, construction, or rehabilitation of on-the-job training and child care facilities. And in 1969 Congress also provided a rapid write-off for pollution control facilities, obviously with an eye toward our ecology.[71] These provisions reflect a departure from the useful life concept, as they permit cost "amortization" [72] over an artificial period.

The Related Concept of Depletion

Those who drill oil, mine natural resources, or cut timber may encounter a phenomenon somewhat like the shoemaker's exhaustion of his stitcher. Or perhaps their situation should be likened to a merchant who gradually sells off his stock in trade. In either event, it is pretty clear that in a business operation they are using up or otherwise parting with something for which they probably have a tax basis. Question arises how the "depletion" of their resource should affect their tax liability.

The problem was not anticipated in the enactment of the Corporate Excise Tax Act of 1909 the precursor of our current income tax.[73] Deciding a case under that Act on a procedural ground, the Supreme Court refused to permit any allowance for the wasting of gold and other precious metals in determining the net income from the taxpayer's mining operation.[74]

---

68. See generally I.R.C. § 168(e)(4)(A)–(C) and Ch. 26A and B, infra.

69. I.R.C. § 168(e)(4)(F).

70. This I.R.C. § 167(k) deduction has been replaced by a credit. See I.R.C. § 42 and page 768, infra.

71. I.R.C. § 169.

72. Amortization is essentially the same as depreciation but it relates to intangible property or, as here, an accelerated life. It requires use of an equal annual write-off the same as straight-line depreciation.

73. § 38, 36 Stat. 112 (1909).

74. Stratton's Independence, Ltd. v. Howbert, 231 U.S. 399, 34 S.Ct. 136 (1913). The opinion contains an inference that, had the amount been properly determined, an allowance might have been made under the statutory "depreciation" deduction.

But Congress legislated specifically on the problem in the enactment of the first modern income tax statute. The Revenue Act of 1913 permitted "cost" depletion.[75] The effect of this provision was very much like the current depreciation deduction, allowing a recovery of cost or other basis as the wasting asset was consumed by its exploitation. The deduction was limited, however, to an amount not in excess of 5% of the value of the product mined.[76] World War I prompted a liberalization of the depletion deduction. To encourage mining activities, Congress abandoned the cost approach to depletion or, more accurately, added to it an alternative "discovery value" approach to the problem.[77]

In essence, what this meant was that, without regard to cost or other basis, a taxpayer could establish a *value* for certain natural resources at the time of their discovery, or within thirty days thereafter, and then write off that *value* as he exploited the resources. Although there was thus a limit beyond which depletion deductions could not be taken, the variation from the depreciation deduction, where allowances can never exceed cost or other basis, is apparent. Of course, under either early method the depletion deduction had to be spread differently from the depreciation deduction; no useful life concept was relevant, but the recoverable amount was spread with reference to the assumed portion of recoverable units recovered during the year.

Discovery value depletion persisted for many years,[78] but was dropped upon the enactment of the Internal Revenue Code of 1954. Cost depletion is still a part of the tax law.[79] A more controversial depletion provision appeared in 1924, when Congress invented "percentage depletion." The concept gets its name from the fact that the amount of the deduction, annually, is determined by a stated percentage of the "gross income from the property" subject to the allowance.[80] There is no ceiling on the amount of the deductions that can be claimed over the years—no limitation to cost or other basis or even to discovery value. Section 613(b) presents a long list of the types of property that are subject to percentage depletion.[81] For each a percentage of gross income is stated, which measures the amount of the deduction. After some reduction in percentage figures in the Tax Reform Act of 1969, the figures range from 5 percent to 22 percent.[82]

---

75. Revenue Act of 1913, § 11B, 38 Stat. 166, 167 (1913).

76. Ibid.

77. Revenue Act of 1918, § 214(a)(10), 40 Stat. 1057, 1067 (1918).

78. See I.R.C. § 23(m).

79. See I.R.C. §§ 611, 612.

80. I.R.C. § 613.

81. In Heisler v. United States, 463 F.2d 375 (9th Cir.1972), cert. denied 410 U.S. 927, 93 S.Ct. 1358 (1973) the court denied percentage depletion on taxpayers bodies because they did not constitute "other natural deposits" within I.R.C. § 613(b).

82. A discussion of depletion, touching on problems not alluded to above, appears in Bittker and Lokken, Federal Taxation of Income Estates and Gifts, Ch. 24 (2d Ed. 1989). A detailed analysis of some aspects of the depletion deduction will be found in Menge, "The Role of Taxation in Providing for Depletion of Mineral Reserves," House Committee on Ways and Means, 2 Tax Revision Compendium 967 (1959), reprinted in Sander and Westfall, Readings in

Prior to 1975 oil and gas wells led the parade qualifying across the board for the maximum 22 percent depletion rate; but in 1975 Congress eliminated percentage depletion for major oil companies.[83] They did continue the 22 percent rate for some types of oil and gas [84] and they partially continued oil and gas depletion for independent producers,[85] although the percentage rate of depletion for independents gradually dropped from 22 percent in phases to 15 percent in 1984 and thereafter.[86]

SHARP v. UNITED STATES

District Court of the United States, District of Delaware, 1961.
199 F.Supp. 743, affirmed 303 F.2d 783, 3d Cir.1962.

LAYTON, District Judge.   This is a ruling on cross motions for summary judgment under Rule 56 [1] by taxpayers and defendant in these two actions brought by taxpayers to recover alleged overpayments of federal income taxes for the calendar year 1954. The two actions were consolidated previously on stipulation of counsel.

Plaintiffs, Hugh R. Sharp, Jr., and Bayard Sharp, were equal partners in a partnership which on December 17, 1946, purchased a Beechcraft airplane at a cost of $45,875. From 1948 to 1953, additional capital expenditures were made with respect to the airplane in the amount of $8,398.50. Thus, the total cost of the airplane, including capital expenditures, was $54,273.50. Title was held by the partnership. During the period of ownership, the airplane was used by the partnership 73.654% for the personal use of the partners and 26.346% for business purposes.[2] Therefore, the partnership was allowed depreciation on the basis of only $14,298.90, or 26.346% of the airplane's total cost. Depreciation taken by the partnership and allowed on this basis during the period totaled $13,777.92. During 1954, the airplane was sold by the partnership for $35,380. At issue here is the amount of gain or loss realized by the partnership on the sale of the airplane.

Federal Taxation, 348–360 (1970), and Statement of Robert G. Dunlop (President, Sun Oil Company), Hearings on T.R.A. 1969 before the Sen.Fin.Comm., 91st Cong. 1st Sess., pt. 5, at 4455–65 (1969), reprinted in Sander and Westfall, supra at 361.

83. I.R.C. § 613(d).

84. See I.R.C. § 613A(b).

85. Under I.R.C. § 613A(c)(3) independents may deplete their first 1000 barrels a day.

86. I.R.C. § 613A(c)(1).

1. 28 U.S.C.A. F.R.Civ.P. 56.

2. The stipulation is not precise as to the exact nature of the division into percentages of personal and business use. It was assumed in the briefs and at oral argument, and therefore it is assumed in this opinion, that the parties are agreed, for purposes of ruling on these motions, that the airplane was used from the beginning, and throughout its ownership by taxpayers, approximately ¼ for business and ¾ for pleasure, without variations. Other considerations might apply if the nature of the ¼–¾ division of use had been different. Suppose, for example, during the total 8 years of ownership, that for the first 6 years the plane had been used exclusively for pleasure, and that for the last 2 years it had been used exclusively for business. Under such circumstances, gain or loss might depend not only on the original cost and the depreciation taken but also on the value of the plane when it was converted to a business use. See Treasury Regulations § 1.165–9(b).

The taxpayers earnestly contend that, if anything, they suffered a loss on the sale, but certainly that they realized no gain. They contend that the relevant statutes permit no other conclusion. Taxpayers point out that the basis of property is its cost.[3] The total cost of the airplane was $54,273.50. For determining gain or loss, numerous adjustments in this basis are permissible, including subtracting from the cost basis the amount of depreciation allowed.[4] Since the depreciation allowed on the airplane was $13,777.92, taxpayers have subtracted this amount from $54,273.50, giving an adjusted basis of $40,495.58. The Code explicitly states that the loss recognized on the sale of property is the excess of the adjusted basis over the amount realized from the sale of the property.[5] The selling price of the airplane was $35,380. Accordingly, taxpayers subtracted this amount from the adjusted basis of $40,495.58 and compute their loss on the sale of the airplane as being $5,115.58. The taxpayers, as the Court understands their argument, do not seek to deduct any part of this loss. Their only claim is that no gain was realized on the sale.

The government theory is grounded in the fact that the airplane was used by the partnership 73.654% for pleasure and 26.346% for business purposes. Both the adjusted basis and the proceeds of sale of the plane are allocated in these proportions, giving in effect two sales. A gain on the business part of the sale is balanced against a non-deductible loss on the personal part, producing a net gain. More detail will clarify the government theory. It will be recalled that in computing depreciation, the cost basis was allocated so that depreciation was allowed on only 26.346% of the cost basis, i.e., $14,298.90.[6] The remainder of the cost basis, i.e., $39,974.60, was allocated to the personal use of the airplane and no depreciation was allowed. The government has adjusted only the business basis, by subtracting from $14,298.90 the depreciation allowed, i.e., $13,777.92, producing an adjusted business basis of $520.98. Now that the airplane is being sold, the government takes the view that this same allocation should be continued for purposes of gain or loss computation on the sale. Accordingly, the proceeds from the sale of the airplane, i.e., $35,380, have been allocated in accordance with the percentages of past business and personal use into portions of $9,321.21 and $26,058.79, respectively. The government then subtracts the adjusted business basis of $520.98 from the proceeds of the sale which were allocated to the business use of the airplane, $9,321.21, and concludes that the taxpayers realized a gain of $8,800.23 on the sale. Any loss on the personal use of the airplane is not deductible because of its personal nature and is disregarded. The taxpayers, being equal partners, have each been assessed with a taxable gain on one-half of $8,800.23, or $4,400.11.

3. 26 U.S.C.A. § 1012.

4. 26 U.S.C.A. § 1016(a)(2)(A).

5. 26 U.S.C.A. § 1001(a).

6. See 26 U.S.C.A. § 167(a).

Counsel for the government have said this is the first challenge by a taxpayer to Rev.Rul. 286, 1953–2 Cum.Bull. 20,[7] and that if the position argued for by the taxpayers be sustained, it would "produce serious and far reaching inequities in the administration of the internal revenue laws."

While research has disclosed no decided case in which an allocation has been made in accordance with percentages of past business and personal use of property, taxpayers are clearly in error if it is their contention that courts will not regard a thing, normally accepted as an entity, as divisible for tax purposes. There are numerous decisions in which the sale proceeds from an orange grove, for instance, have been allocated between the trees (capital gain) and the unharvested crop (income),[8] or where the proceeds from the sale of an interest in a partnership have been allocated between the earned but uncollected fees,[9] or income producing property [10] (income), and the other assets of the business (capital gain). A different sort of allocation was ordered in a leading Third Circuit case, Paul v. Commissioner.[11] In Paul, taxpayer, who was in the business of holding rental property for investment purposes, bought a partially completed apartment building in May, which he sold more than six months later, in November. The issue was whether the taxpayer could treat the entire gain or any part thereof as long term capital gain, under Section 117(j) of the Internal Revenue Code of 1939.[12] The Court held that a portion of the gain must be allocated to the part of the building erected more than six months before the sale and given long term treatment.[13] The remainder of the proceeds allocable to the construction between May and November was taxed as short term gain.

The closest analogy to the case at bar is the sale of depreciable and non-depreciable property as a unit—the sale of a building and land together, for instance. In United States v. Koshland,[14] a hotel caught fire and was destroyed. At issue in the case was the amount of the casualty loss deduction permissible under the circumstances. However, in the course of its opinion, the Court discussed the allocation problem

---

7. The relevant portion of Rev.Rule 286, 1953–2 Cum.Bull. 20, reads as follows:

"Only that part of a loss resulting from the sale of property used for both personal and income-producing purposes that can be allocated to the income-producing portion of the property constitutes a loss within the meaning of § 23(e) of the Internal Revenue Code [26 U.S.C.A. (I.R.C.1939), § 23(e)]. In determining the gain or loss on the sale, there must be an actual allocation of the amounts which represent cost, selling price, depreciation allowed or allowable, and selling expenses to the respective portions of property in the same manner as if there were two separate transactions."

8. See e.g., Watson v. Commissioner, 345 U.S. 544, 73 S.Ct. 848 (1953); Smyth v. Cole, 218 F.2d 667 (9th Cir.1955).

9. Tunnell v. United States, 259 F.2d 916 (3d Cir.1958); United States v. Snow, 223 F.2d 103 (9th Cir.1955).

10. Williams v. McGowan, 152 F.2d 570 (2d Cir.1945).

11. 206 F.2d 763 (3d Cir.1953); see also Commissioner v. Williams, 256 F.2d 152 (5th Cir.1958).

12. 26 U.S.C.A. (1939) § 117(j).

13. 206 F.2d at 766.

14. 208 F.2d 636 (9th Cir.1954).

directly, noting that the hotel was depreciable whereas the land on which it stood was not.

"* * * The result is that there is no single 'adjusted basis' for the land and building as a unit. The depreciation allowed or allowable on the building reduces the basis of the building only. No depreciation is allowed on the land, and the original basis of the land therefore remains unaffected. The adjusted basis of the building and the basis of the land cannot be combined into a single 'adjusted basis' for the property as a whole, for to do so would in effect be reducing the basis of the whole, by depreciation allowed or allowable only as against the building, a part.

"Thus, for tax purposes, upon a sale of the property as a whole the selling price must be allocated between the land and building and the gain or loss separately determined upon each, by reference to the adjusted basis of each." [15]

This principle has been recognized in other cases without discussion.[16] The taxpayers point out that an airplane is not capable of separation into business and personal uses in the same way that a hotel is separable from the land on which it stands, or in the same way that the unharvested crop may be separated from the trees of the grove, or the accounts receivable from the other partnership assets. There were not two airplanes, say the taxpayers—a business airplane and a personal airplane—there was one airplane. There were not two sales; there was but one sale, one adjusted basis and one selling price. Any division or allocation, therefore, involves resorting to fiction, which is anathema to the tax law.

The taxpayers' argument against allocation in this case has superficial appeal. The whole idea of allocation is lacking in explicit authority from the literal words of the relevant sections in the Code. Since the situation here is not covered literally by the Statute, perhaps any interstices in statutory coverage should be filled by Congress not the Court. But this argument ignores the basic fact that no tax statute can encompass every situation which may arise. The Statute is phrased in general terms leaving it to the Commissioner by regulation or ruling and the Courts by interpretation to solve problems arising under unusual and novel facts. Merely because Congress did not specifically provide for the facts presented here does not mean it intended to exempt profits arising from the sale of property used both for business and pleasure. The taxpayers' argument also overlooks the fact that allocation has long been accepted by the courts in other cases. In dealing with another allocation problem, the Third Circuit Court of Appeals has said:

15. 208 F.2d at 640.

16. See, e.g., Crane v. Commissioner, 331 U.S. 1, 4–5, 67 S.Ct. 1047 (1947); Tracy v. Commissioner, 53 F.2d 575, 577 (6th Cir. 1931); Belle Isle Creamery Co. v. Commissioner, 14 B.T.A. 737, 738 (1928); C.D. Johnson Lumber Corp. v. Commissioner, 12 T.C. 348, 356, 365 (1949).

"The federal revenue laws are to be construed in the light of their general purpose 'so as to give a uniform application to a nation-wide scheme of taxation.' Burnet v. Harmel, 1932, 287 U.S. 103, 110, 53 S.Ct. 74; United States v. Pelzer, 1941, 312 U.S. 399, 402, 61 S.Ct. 659; Lyeth v. Hoey, 1938, 305 U.S. 188, 194, 59 S.Ct. 155." [17]

But if taxpayers' theory prevails, there will be lack of uniformity in tax treatment between those who use property partially for business and pleasure on the one hand, and those who use property exclusively for business on the other. To use round figures, if property used exclusively for business has an adjusted basis of $500 ($14,000 cost less $13,500 depreciation) and it is sold for $9,000, nobody will deny that a taxable gain of $8,500 has been realized. Now, suppose that a larger piece of property is used only ¼ for business purposes and ¾ for pleasure, but that the adjusted basis of the business part is the same as in the first example, namely $500, and that depreciation figures and cost of the business part are also the same. Taxes levied on the business segment of the larger property should not be different from taxes levied on the other property used exclusively for business. To put it another way, taxpayers having two business properties with the same cost and depreciation should pay the same taxes, if the properties are sold for the same price. The fact that one of the properties was also used for pleasure should make no difference.

Under the government's allocation theory, uniformity is achieved; under the taxpayers', it is not. If the government's theory involves, as the taxpayers suggest, "dividing" the plane up, it can only be replied that this is precisely what was done in calculating the depreciation deduction to which the taxpayers acquiesced. There is no greater peculiarity in doing the same thing when computing gain or loss on a sale. The depreciable business use and non-depreciable personal use of the airplane are not essentially different from the depreciable hotel and non-depreciable land discussed in the Koshland case, supra.

The fairness of the government's theory can be seen more easily using a different analysis. This different analysis involves allocation of loss instead of sale proceeds and cost basis. Continuing the use of round numbers, the $20,000 loss on the sale of the airplane (cost of $55,000 less sale proceeds of $35,000) can be allocated ¾ to the personal use and ¼ to the business use. If the property had not been depreciable, but used in the same fashion, it would seem proper that the taxpayer should be allowed to deduct $5,000 as a business loss—no more, no less. Since depreciation deductions were taken in our case with respect to the business use of the airplane of about $13,500, and whereas the actual loss on this part of the plane's use was only $5,000, it would appear that taxpayer has received fortuitously the benefit of depreciation deductions equal to the difference between $13,500 and

17. Paul v. Commissioner, 206 F.2d 763, 765–766 (3d Cir.1953).

$5,000, or $8,500. Even though all depreciation was allowed or allowable, it is the government's position that the "excessive" depreciation should be taxed.[18] This Court agrees.

Application of the rationale and certain of the language of Paul v. Commissioner [19] to the instant case compels the following conclusion. Allocation of the proceeds from the sale of this plan in accordance with its percentages of business and personal use is "practical and fair." This Court believes that Rev.Rule 286, 1953–2 Cum.Bull. 20, as applied here, represents a reasonable exercise by the Commissioner of his rule making power. There is no reason to make this an "all or nothing proposition." It is realistic to recognize that there are "gradations" between the percentage of business and personal use of a piece of property. It is concluded here that it is "proper that those gradations have tax significance."

The taxpayers' motion for summary judgment is denied and the government's is granted. Let an order be submitted in conformity herewith.

PROBLEMS

1. If the *Sharp* "divided airplane" was purchased after 1978 and was used for non-entertainment business purposes, would the facility limitation of § 274(a)(1)(B) deny the depreciation deduction? Cf. John L. Beckley, 34 TCM 235 (1975).

2. Section 263(a) provides "no deduction shall be allowed for any amount paid out for new buildings. . . ." Thus if one pays for salaries or for painting etc. in construction of a building, the expenses are capitalized and the total cost of the building is then depreciated assuming the § 167 or § 168 requirements are met.

   (a) If Company owns trucks that are used during the year exclusively in constructing a new storage plant for the Company, is Company allowed a depreciation deduction for the trucks during the year? Consider what tax alternative there might be and then see Commissioner v. Idaho Power Co., 418 U.S. 1, 94 S.Ct. 2757 (1974).

   (b) Are interest on loans connected with property and taxes on the property which are paid during the construction period currently deductible? See § 263A.

---

18. Assuming that taxpayers are in a high tax bracket, it may be noted that complete equalization of tax benefits is not accomplished in the government's theory. Taxpayer took the $8,500 "excess" depreciation as ordinary deductions. Taxpayers are now being taxed on this amount at only capital gain rates. It would seem that taxpayers are still ahead.

19. 206 F.2d 763, 766 (3d Cir.1953).

2. SPECIAL DEPRECIATION RULES ON PERSONAL PROPERTY

Internal Revenue Code: Sections 167(a)–(c); 168(a)–(c), (d)(1), (3) and (4)(A) and (C), (e)(1) and (3), (f)(1) and (5), (g)(1), (2), (3)(D), and (7), (i)(1); 179 (omit (d) (4)–(9)); 280F(a), (b), (d) (omit (d)(6)(C) and (D)).

The income tax deduction for depreciation of personal property is claimed under a variety of methods which are examined below. Temporarily disregarding special provisions or limitations, there are essentially three sets of general rules. Most personal property acquired after 1986 is subject to *current* ACRS rules, the Accelerated Cost Recovery System. However, the anti-churning rules can toss such property either into *old* ACRS (the Accelerated Cost Recovery System as it existed before the 1986 amendments) or into Section 167 (the long-standing depreciation rules). If post–1986 personal property does not qualify for ACRS treatment because it is intangible property or otherwise excluded under the *current* ACRS rules,[1] Section 167 again comes into play. We begin our consideration of this area with a discussion of *current* ACRS. We then examine so-called first-year bonus depreciation under Section 179 and Section 280F limitations on allowances above and finish with a brief comment on the now-repealed investment credit.

Current ACRS Under Section 168. As previously indicated, *current* ACRS applies to most tangible personal property placed in service after December 31, 1986. Under *current* ACRS if the applicable recovery period is not in excess of ten years, the system employs the 200% (double) declining balance method of depreciation which disregards salvage value; and if it is more than ten years, the system employs the 150% declining balance method, which also disregards salvage.[2] *Current* ACRS calls for a switch to the straight-line method in the first year in which that method results in a greater amount of depreciation than the applicable declining balance method.[3]

Three elective alternatives are available to a taxpayer who qualifies for *current* ACRS: (1) If he qualifies for the 200% declining balance method, he may use the 150% declining balance method (disregarding salvage) over the recovery period of the property,[4] (2) regardless of whether he qualifies for the 150% or 200% declining balance method, he may use the straight-line method (still disregarding salvage) over the recovery period of the property,[5] or (3) he may use the straight-line method [6] with a generally extended life [7] under the Section 168(g) alternative depreciation system. If any of the alternatives is elected,

---

1. I.R.C. § 168(f)(1)–(4).

2. I.R.C. § 168(b)(1), (2) and (4).

3. I.R.C. § 168(b)(1)(B) and (b)(2). When this occurs, the one-half year convention extends the life of the property an additional one half of a year. See note 10, infra.

4. I.R.C. § 168(b)(2)(C), (b)(5).

5. I.R.C. § 168(b)(3)(D), (b)(5).

6. I.R.C. § 168(g)(2)(A).

7. I.R.C. § 168(g)(2)(C).

the election is applied to *all* ACRS property within the same *class* which is placed in service during the year of election.[8]

Current ACRS uses the "half-year convention". The "half-year convention" is an administrative rule of convenience which, for depreciation purposes, treats property as if it were placed in service at the midpoint of the year no matter when during the year it is actually placed in service. Thus, one-half of a year's depreciation is allowed for the year the property is acquired regardless of whether the property is placed in service on January 1 or December 31 of the year. The half-year convention is applicable to all the methods of depreciation under consideration.[9] In determining the deduction under the straight-line method (or in a switch from an accelerated method to the straight-line method), a half-year deduction is necessitated for the year following the end of the normal recovery period.[10] That is to say that if we think of an asset with a normal recovery period of five years, the allowance of a half-year for year one and a half-year for year six and a full allowance for each of the four other years results in a full five years of depreciation.

The comparative results under *current* ACRS can be seen by a reconsideration of a hypothetical situation using numbers similar to the ones used with respect to the shoemaker and his stitching machine. Assume that a taxpayer on January 1 purchases new manufacturing equipment with a $1,600 cost, that the taxpayer intends to use it for an 8 year period, and that the equipment will have no salvage value at the end of the 8 years. The equipment also has an A.D.R. class life of 8 years and is therefore classified as 5–year property with a 5 year recovery period under *current* ACRS.[11] The comparative depreciation results are illustrated in the following chart:

Current ACRS:

Year	200% D.B.		Straight–Line		Alternative Depreciation	
	Annual	Cumulative	Annual	Cumulative	Annual	Cumulative
1	320	320	160	160	100	100
2	512	832	320	480	200	300
3	307	1139	320	800	200	500
4	184	1323	320	1120	200	700
5	184 [12]	1507	320	1440	200	900
6	92	1600	160	1600	200	1100
7	0	1600	0	1600	200	1300
8	0	1600	0	1600	200	1500
9					100	1600

8. I.R.C. § 168(b)(5) and (g)(7). This rule is inapplicable to nonresidential real property and residential rental property. Id.

9. I.R.C. § 168(a)(3), (d)(1), (g)(2)(B).

10. See the chart below.

11. I.R.C. § 168(c)(1), (e)(1). Assistance in making the computations below is provided by the Service in Rev.Proc. 87–57, 1987–2 C.B. 687. See especially Tables 1 and 8 at pages 696 and 703, respectively.

12. A switch to straight line depreciation occurs here where that method results in a greater allowance than the double declining balance method.

To forestall abuse by a taxpayer who tries to take advantage of the half-year convention rule by loading up on personal property late in the year, the statute substitutes a special "mid-quarter" convention.[13] If more than 40 percent of the cost of all ACRS personal property acquired during a year is placed in service in the fourth quarter of the year, the mid-quarter rule is invoked.[14]

If *current* ACRS personal property is disposed of prior to completion of the recovery period, the half-year convention (or mid-quarter convention if it applied on acquisition) applies in computing the depreciation for the year of disposition.[15] Thus if half-year convention personal property with a 5–year recovery period is disposed of on the last day of the fourth year of its recovery period, a depreciation deduction is allowed for only one half of year four.

However, *current* ACRS is not always applicable. If ACRS is inapplicable to property [16] or a taxpayer elects out of Section 168 to use the unit of production or some comparable method,[17] Section 167 controls.

As previously stated [18], the anti-churning rules aimed at preventing taxpayers from churning their old investments to take advantage of more rapid *current* ACRS write-offs can take personal property out of *current* ACRS and toss it into *old* ACRS (if it was acquired by a related person after 1980) or into Section 167 (if it was acquired by a related person prior to 1981).[19] Such maneuvering occurs only if the first year depreciation in the system to which the property is tossed is less than first year depreciation under *current* ACRS.[20] Although the text does not discuss the intricacies of those prior systems, note that the anti-churning rules work to the taxpayers' disadvantage providing slower depreciation than that allowed under *current* ACRS.

Section 179 Bonus Depreciation. The foregoing analysis of depreciation of personal property does not provide a complete picture. In addition to the above rules, personal property may qualify for bonus depreciation under Section 179.[21] In order to encourage investment, Section 179 allows taxpayers to elect to write off a part of the cost of some depreciable personal property as an ordinary deduction in the year in which the property is placed in service. However, taxpayers are limited to $10,000 as the amount of such bonus depreciation they may deduct in a year.[22] The limit applies, not to each piece of property,

---

13. I.R.C. § 168(d)(4)(C).

14. I.R.C. § 168(d)(3)(A). Note that nonresidential real estate and residential rental property are disregarded in making the 40% determination. I.R.C. § 168(d)(3)(B).

15. I.R.C. § 168(d)(4)(A) and (C) parentheticals. While this result appears harsh, allowing the deduction would generally only result in a wash. See I.R.C. §§ 1001(b), 1016(a)(2), and 1245(a).

16. See I.R.C. § 168(f)(2)–(4).

17. I.R.C. § 168(f)(1).

18. See page 750, supra.

19. I.R.C. § 168(f)(5)(A).

20. I.R.C. § 168(f)(5)(B).

21. Technically, the statute treats the I.R.C. § 179 amount as an expense, thus allowing a current deduction.

22. I.R.C. § 179(b)(1). The limits are generally cut in half if spouses file separate returns. I.R.C. § 179(b)(4).

but to all qualifying property a taxpayer places in service during the year; [23] and the $10,000 limitation is reduced by one dollar for each one dollar of total cost of Section 179 property placed in service during the year in excess of $200,000.[24] In addition, the Section 179 deduction may not exceed the amount of taxable income derived from the taxpayer's active conduct of a trade or business during the year.[25] The effect of Section 179 is to allow additional depreciation in the year property is placed in service; but, as will be seen in the pages ahead, the benefit is not granted without exacting some cost.[26]

Not all depreciable personal property qualifies for the Section 179 election.[27] The section is applicable only to property qualifying under ACRS [28] which is "section 1245 property" [29] and which is acquired by "purchase" for use in the active conduct of the taxpayer's trade or business.[30] The term "purchase" is defined by Section 179(d)(2) to include all acquisitions of property other than acquisitions from certain related persons [31] and other than acquisitions in certain non-recognition transactions,[32] by gift,[33] or from a decedent (if the basis is determined under Section 1014).[34]

Just as the basis of property must be reduced by Section 167 or Section 168 depreciation deductions,[35] the basis must also reflect a Section 179 deduction which is, in essence, a depreciation deduction. The basis of the Section 179 property must be reduced before the property is depreciated under the Section 168 ACRS.[36] The reduction precludes a double depreciation deduction.[37]

23. I.R.C. § 179(b)(1).

24. I.R.C. § 179(b)(2). Thus if the total of such property placed in service for the year were $210,000 there could be no § 179 deduction for the year.

25. I.R.C. § 179(b)(3)(A). Taxable income is computed without regard to the I.R.C. § 179 deduction. I.R.C. § 179(b)(3)(C). Any amount allowed by § 179(b)(1) and (2) but disallowed by § 179(b)(3)(A) is carried over to subsequent years. I.R.C. § 179(b)(3)(B).

26. Since the § 179 reduction is in essence a depreciation deduction, it is subject to § 1245(a) recapture. See page 788, infra.

27. Some real property also qualifies as "section 179 property." The definition is not limited to personal property but applies to "section 1245 property" which includes some real property. See I.R.C. § 1245(a)(3).

28. I.R.C. § 179(d)(1).

29. This is property which is defined in I.R.C. § 1245(a)(3). See page 791, infra. This includes some real property. See note 27, supra.

30. I.R.C. § 179(d)(1). Property merely held for the production of income does not qualify for § 179 expensing.

31. I.R.C. § 179(d)(2)(A) and (B).

32. I.R.C. § 179(d)(2)(C)(i). See I.R.C. §§ 362(a); 723.

33. Id. See I.R.C. §§ 1015 and 1041.

34. I.R.C. § 179(d)(2)(C)(ii).

35. I.R.C. § 1016(a)(2). See page 745, supra.

36. Cf. I.R.C. § 1016(a)(2) and I.R.C. § 168(d)(1)(A)(ii)(II). Again a technical amendment is necessary to clarify this adjustment.

37. If the property is held for its full recovery period I.R.C. § 179 does not change the total amount of deductions a taxpayer may take with respect to a particular piece of property; it simply changes the timing of the taxpayer's cost recovery. Thus, if property is held for its full recovery period, a taxpayer will recover its entire cost, and no more, whether or not § 179 is elected. For example, assume that in 1991, a taxpayer places a machine in service which costs $10,000 and is eligible for the § 179 deduction, and the taxpayer purchases no other eligible property during the year. He may elect to treat the

If Section 179 property is not used predominantly in the taxpayer's trade or business before the end of the property's recovery period, recapture of the Section 179 amount is required in the year of conversion.[38]

Section 280F Limitations on "Luxury" Automobiles. The *current* ACRS system fixes a five-year recovery period for automobiles;[39] but Congress has decided that depreciating expensive, "luxury" cars over such a short period is too much of a good thing. So by Section 280F(a), the life of such cars is in effect extended by allowing a maximum of $12,800 adjusted for inflation for years after 1988[40] of cost recovery over the usual five-year period. This may be claimed $2,560 in year one, $4,100 in year two, $2,450 in year three, and $1,475 in year four and in year five.[41] To the extent that a car is luxurious (costs more than $12,800), a maximum amount of $1,475 can be written off in each year following the first five years during which the taxpayer continues to use the car in a depreciable capacity,[42] until of course the acquisition basis is exhausted. If in any year of its depreciable life the car is used only a portion of the time for business,[43] only that portion of the potential deduction is allowed.[44]

Section 280F "Limitations on Listed Property". Section 280F also limits ACRS deductions allowed on certain other "listed property" that has a business use of 50 percent or less[45] (i.e., is not used predominantly for business purposes in the taxable year). "Listed property" includes: passenger automobiles and other property used as a means of transportation; property of a type generally used for entertainment, recreation, or amusement purposes; computers not used exclusively at a regular business establishment; and cellular phones or similar telecommunications equipment.[46] In general, any use of listed property in

entire $10,000 cost of the machine as a § 179 deduction. However, because the "adjusted basis" of the machine will be zero, the taxpayer has no further basis to depreciate and can take no § 168 deductions. If the machine costs $30,000, the taxpayer can elect to deduct $10,000 under § 179, and compute his § 168 deductions using an "adjusted basis" of $20,000.

38. I.R.C. § 179(d)(10).

39. I.R.C. § 168(e)(3)(B)(i).

40. The $12,800 limitation is to be adjusted by an "automobile price inflation adjustment" rounded to the nearest $100 for years after 1988. I.R.C. § 280F(d)(7). For example, in 1989 the amount was $13,100. See Rev.Proc. 89–64, 1989–2 C.B. 783.

41. I.R.C. § 280F(a)(2)(A). These mysterious numbers are arrived at by using the double declining balance method (with a half-year convention) to depreciate the $12,800 "cost" and by switching to the straight-line method for year five and the

first half of year six. These numbers are adjusted for inflation after 1988. See note 40, supra.

Any deduction allowable under § 179 is considered to be a § 168 deduction and is also subject to the § 280F limitations. Temp.Reg. § 1.280F–2T(b)(4).

42. I.R.C. § 280F(a)(2)(B). See also note 44, infra.

43. If the portion is 50% or less, the listed property limitations come into play. See the discussion below.

44. Cf. Sharp v. United States, 199 F.Supp. 743 (D.Del.1961), affirmed 303 F.2d 783 (3d Cir.1962). Any nondepreciable portion related to nonbusiness use may not be written off as a deduction in a succeeding year.

45. I.R.C. § 280F(b).

46. I.R.C. § 280F(d)(4). The regulations may add similar types of property to the list. I.R.C. § 280F(d)(4)(A)(vi).

connection with the performance of services by an employee is not considered business use, unless the use is for the convenience of the employer and is required as a condition of employment.[47] Listed property with a business use of 50 percent or less, can be depreciated using only the alternative depreciation system of Section 168(g).[48] For example, five-year property used less than 50 percent in business must be depreciated using the straight-line method over a recovery period generally equal to its A.D.R. class life of between five and nine years.[49] There are several special rules here.[50] For example, automobiles continue to be specifically assigned a 5–year recovery period for the alternative depreciation system.[51]

To add to the pain, if the *more-than-50 percent* test is met for the year that a listed property is placed in service, but is not met in a subsequent year, all excess depreciation claimed in the first and subsequent years over the depreciation that would have been allowed using the alternative depreciation system is recaptured as ordinary income in the subsequent year.[52]

The Service appropriately requires that taxpayers substantiate the use of listed property by adequate, contemporaneous records. If a taxpayer does not keep such records he loses the benefits of the depreciation deduction and may be vulnerable to added liability for negligence or possibly even fraud.[53] The records must reflect with substantial accuracy the business use of the property and indicate its business purposes, unless the purpose is clear from the surrounding circumstances. For example, in regard to automobiles, logs must be kept which show the date and mileage of trips for business purposes.

The Now Repealed Regular Investment Credit. Prior to January 1, 1986, the tax approach to depreciation of personal property could not be fully examined without consideration of the loosely related regular investment *credit.*[54] The regular investment credit was a device that Congress used to stimulate business. Generally, the credit was equal to 10 percent of the qualified investment in property.[55] Congress turned the investment credit on and off over the years (or altered its rates) to help stimulate or slow down business and, in turn, the economy. But

---

47. I.R.C. § 280F(d)(3).

48. I.R.C. § 280F(b)(1).

49. I.R.C. § 168(g)(2)(C). See I.R.C. § 168(e)(1).

50. I.R.C. § 168(g)(3).

51. I.R.C. § 168(g)(3)(D).

52. I.R.C. § 280F(b)(3).

53. I.R.C. §§ 274(d)(4); 6662; 6663. See T.D. 8009, 1985–1 C.B. 82, announcing the Service's intent to ease the record keeping requirements for automobiles.

54. This is the first practical exposure in this book to a credit. Credits are considered in Chapter 27B, infra. A credit directly reduces a taxpayer's income tax liability by reducing his tax after it has been computed under the rate tables. Compare a deduction which is merely a reduction of the tax base prior to imposition of tax rates.

55. I.R.C. § 46(b)(1) (now repealed). However, if the property had a recovery period of less than five years, essentially only a 6% credit was allowed. I.R.C. § 46(c)(7) (now repealed). Generally, a basis reduction in the property was required prior to computation of ACRS depreciation. I.R.C. § 48(q)(1) (now repealed); but see I.R.C. § 48(q)(4) (now repealed). If the property was prematurely disposed of, there was a recapture of the investment credit. I.R.C. § 47(a) (now repealed).

in 1986 Congress repealed it, for property acquired after 1985.[56] As it is not unreasonable to predict its resurrection in some future year if there is an economic downturn, we make brief mention of it here.

Additional thoughts. We have explored numerous intricate rules with respect to depreciation of personal property. The problems below test your ability to apply those rules. But first, take a moment to reflect both on Congressional policy in this area and on the interrelationship of the relevant sections.

Under the Economic Recovery Tax Act of 1981 Congress introduced a very generous ACRS and retained an equally generous regular investment credit whose operations were at the heart of a trickle-down economic theory. Between 1981 and 1984, Congress backed away from its generous stance both under the ACRS system as a whole and in the potentially abusive areas dealt with in Section 280F. In 1986 it repealed the regular investment credit while allowing more generous ACRS depreciation on much (but not all) depreciable personal property. Are these moves sound? Where do we go next? Is the regular investment credit merely on hold until the next major economic downturn?

The following suggested procedure may aid in working the computations in the problems below:

(1) **Section 179.** Determine if you are dealing with property under ACRS. Section 179 is applicable only to such property and, to the extent a Section 179 write-off is taken, property does not receive the benefit of the regular ACRS depreciation.[57] Thus one should first make any Section 179 computation.

(2) **Regular depreciation.** Compute depreciation deductions under either Section 168 or Section 167. All of the above computations are subject to the principles of the *Sharp* case [58] which allows depreciation only on that portion of the property which is used in a trade or business or for the production of income.

(3) **Section 280F.** As a final step, if Section 280F imposes limitations on the amount of depreciation or a recapture of depreciation, the limitation or recapture should be determined and applied to the computations.

PROBLEMS

1. On January 2 in a year after 1986 for $100,000 Depreciator purchases new equipment for use in his business. The purchase is made from an unrelated person. The equipment has a 6–year class life and is 5–year property under § 168(c). Depreciator plans to use the equipment for seven years, and expects it to have a salvage value of

---

56. I.R.C. § 49 (now repealed). There is still an investment credit, but it is much more limited than the regular investment credit. I.R.C. § 46. See Chapter 27B, infra.

57. See note 36, supra.

58. See page 753, supra.

$10,000 at the end of that time. Depreciator is a single, calendar year taxpayer, and he uses the equipment *only* in his business.

In the following problems compute the depreciation deductions with respect to the equipment in each year of its use and Depreciator's adjusted basis for the property each year.

(a) Depreciator elects under § 168(b)(5) to use the straight-line method for the equipment and all other property in its class placed in service during the year.

(b) Depreciator uses the accelerated ACRS method provided by § 168(a).

(c) Same as (b), above, except that Depreciator disposes of the equipment on December 1 of year five.

(d) What differences from (b), above, if Depreciator also elects to use § 179? What additional facts do you need to know?

(e) The equipment has a 6–year life and Depreciator elects to use the § 168(g) alternative depreciation system for the equipment and all other property in its class placed in service during the year.

(f) Same facts as (b), above, except that instead of buying the equipment new, Depreciator bought it used from his sister. She bought the equipment in 1980 and immediately placed it in service depreciating it over its eight year useful life to her. In general (without computations) what results to Depreciator?

2. Hi Roller buys a "luxury" automobile for business and personal use at a cost of $15,000 in the current year. Assume for simplicity that there is no inflation in the CPI automobile component after October, 1987. See § 280F(d)(7).

(a) Compute the maximum depreciation deductions available to Hi assuming no § 179 election is made and there is no personal use of the car.

(b) What results to Hi under the facts of (a), above, if the car is used for business purposes the following percentages of the time in the following years: year one 70%; year two 80%; year three 70%; year four and later 60% each year.

(c) What general result (no computations) to Hi in (b), above, if in years four and following the automobile is used only 50% for business use?

3. SPECIAL RULES ON REALTY

Internal Revenue Code: Sections 168(a), (b)(3)(A) and (B) and (4), (c), (d)(2) and (4)(B), (e)(2), (f)(5)(B)(i), (g)(1)(E) and (2). See Sections 42; 46(1); 47.

Prior to the 1986 legislation, real estate had a good thing going. It provided major tax sheltering possibilities—interest deductions on mortgages, no at-risk limitations, generally low capital gains rates on sale, *Crane* principle for basis determination, *and* accelerated depreciation [1] and a short depreciable life. The 1986 legislation went a long way toward demolishing the real estate tax shelter: It subjected some real estate to the at-risk rules,[2] imposed a major passive investment activities limitation on the sheltering of investment real estate,[3] and drastically altered the rules for the depreciation of real estate.

Immediately prior to the 1986 legislation, most new or used real estate qualified for *old* ACRS treatment.   Under *old* ACRS it was assigned a 19–year recovery period [4] and qualified for either accelerated (175 percent declining balance) or straight-line depreciation.[5] The 1986 legislation, applicable to property placed in service after December 31, 1986, changed these rules dramatically.   It classified real estate as either "residential rental property" [6] or "nonresidential real property." [7] Both types of real property must be depreciated using only the straight-line method [8] and in making the straight-line computation, residential rental property is assigned a 27.5–year life while nonresidential real property is assigned a 31.5–year life.[9] The alternative depreciation system may be elected with respect to both types of property and both are assigned a 40–year life under that system.[10] As always under ACRS, salvage value is disregarded.[11]

Rental property is classified as "residential" only if 80 percent or more of the gross rental income from a building is from dwelling units.[12] The Code further provides that "dwelling units" do not include units in a building, such as a hotel, in which more than one-half of the units are used on a transient basis.[13] Generally, all other depreciable real estate falls into the nonresidential real property classification.[14]

The depreciation of these two classifications of real property under ACRS varies in several ways from the depreciation of personal property. As seen above, only the straight-line depreciation method is available to real estate.[15] An election to use the alternative depreciation system is made on a property by property not a class by class basis.[16] In addition, for the year such real property is placed in service, rather

1. But see I.R.C. § 1250 in Part B4, infra.

2. See page 493, supra.

3. See page 503, supra.

4. Between 1980 and 1986, real estate was first assigned a 15–year recovery period and, later, an 18–year recovery period, prior to the 19–year period.

5. See now-amended I.R.C. § 168(b)(2).

6. See I.R.C. § 168(e)(2)(A).

7. See I.R.C. § 168(e)(2)(B). Only real property with a class life of less than 27.5 years is not included within one of these two definitions.

8. I.R.C. § 168(b)(3)(A) and (B).

9. I.R.C. § 168(c)(1).

10. I.R.C. § 168(g)(2)(C). Recall that only straight-line depreciation is available under the alternative depreciation system.

11. I.R.C. § 168(b)(4) and (g)(2)(A).

12. I.R.C. § 168(e)(2)(A)(i).

13. I.R.C. § 168(e)(2)(A)(ii)(I).

14. I.R.C. § 168(e)(2)(B). Some real property used in business may be assigned a class life of less than 27.5–years; it is not subjected to the above rules. I.R.C. § 168(e)(2)(B)(ii). See Rev.Rul. 83–35, 1983–1 C.B. 745.

15. I.R.C. § 168(b)(3)(A) and (B).

16. I.R.C. § 168(g)(7)(A). Cf. I.R.C. § 168(b)(5).

than applying the half-year convention, which generally applies to personal property, depreciation deductions are allowed for the property according to a "mid-month convention" allowing depreciation beginning in the middle of the month for the month that the property is first placed in service.[17] Similarly, such real property is depreciable in the year of disposition only for the months during which the property was held by the taxpayer (again using a mid-month convention).[18] Finally, the longer lives and the mandatory straight-line depreciation method applicable to these two classifications of real estate provide no incentive to churn such property. Accordingly, the *current* ACRS anti-churning rules have been made inapplicable to such real property.[19]

Congress has traditionally provided two additional sets of rules to encourage investment in special types of real estate to achieve two quite different goals. The first goal is to encourage investment in the rehabilitation of older real estate. Costs incurred in the restoration of older depreciable real property qualify for an investment credit [20] if various requirements are met.[21] Congress allows a credit equal to 20 percent [22] of the "qualified rehabilitation expenditures" [23] of restoration of a "certified historic structure," [24] and there is a 10 percent credit for such costs incurred in rehabilitating buildings built before 1936 even if they are not certified historic structures.[25] Sections 47(c)(1) and (3) impose various requirements related to the amount and the cost of reconstruction of the property. If a rehabilitation credit is allowed, the basis of the property is reduced by the full amount of the credit prior to its depreciation under ACRS.[26]

The second set of rules is aimed at encouraging investment in low income housing. The rules allow credits for costs incurred by owners of residential rental property which qualifies as "low income housing." The low income housing credit is subject to myriad rules [27] but, if both the property and the expenditure qualify, the owner of the property qualifies for a substantial tax benefit. For construction costs of new property or rehabilitation costs of used property placed in service in 1987, a credit of 9 percent *per* year is allowed for each of 10 years if the low income units are not financed with tax exempt bonds or similar federal subsidies; [28] otherwise, a credit of 4 percent per year for 10 years is allowed.[29] If such costs are incurred on property that is placed in service after 1987, a credit equal to either 70 percent or 30 percent of

---

17. I.R.C. § 168(d)(2) and (4)(B).

18. I.R.C. § 168(d)(4)(B) parentheticals.

19. I.R.C. § 168(f)(5)(B)(i).

20. I.R.C. § 46(1). The investment credit is subject to a number of special rules and is itself a part of the general business credit. I.R.C. § 38. See page 985, infra.

21. I.R.C. § 47(c).

22. I.R.C. § 47(a)(2).

23. I.R.C. § 47(c)(2).

24. I.R.C. § 47(c)(3).

25. I.R.C. § 47(a)(1). See I.R.C. § 47(c)(1) and (2).

26. I.R.C. § 50(c)(1).

27. See generally I.R.C. § 42. See Callison, "New Tax Credit for Low-Income Housing Provides Investment Incentive," 66 J.Tax'n 100 (1987).

28. I.R.C. § 42(a), (b)(1)(A), and (f)(1).

29. I.R.C. § 42(a), (b)(1)(B)(i), and (f)(1).

such qualified costs is allowed, depending again on how the property is financed.[30] Again, the credit is spread over a 10–year period.[31] In addition, another 4 percent credit of the aggregate acquisition cost (as opposed to construction and rehabilitation costs) is allowed over a 10–year period for costs of acquiring used property.[32] An indirect benefit here is that the property's basis for depreciation purposes is not reduced by the credits claimed.[33] Thus the full cost qualifies for depreciation deductions as well. Pay dirt?! The credit would be no more than a fitting reward for mastering the reams of statute involved! Not quite. Certainly the credit is a good deal, *but* not quite so good as it looks. As stated above, there are lots of technical requirements which must be satisfied.[34] Among them, stringent limits are imposed on the rents one can charge for the use of such property.[35] Thus, the tax advantages, which are tremendous, may be balanced by reduced revenues from the investment. Nevertheless, if we are to depart from purely revenue objectives for the tax laws, we have here a commendable Congressional goal for which investors still may be well rewarded.

Both of the above credits are part of the general business credit which is considered in Chapter 27B, infra and which imposes further possible limits upon their utility. Additionally, both are potentially subject to the passive investment activities credit limitation, considered in Chapter 17D, supra and Chapter 27B, infra.

PROBLEMS

1. On January 1, 1991 Depreciator purchases a piece of new improved real property at a cost of $130,000 of which $100,000 is attributable to the building and $30,000 to the land. Depreciator immediately rents the property to others. Compute Depreciator's depreciation in 1992 in the following situations:

(a) The building is an apartment building.

(b) The building is an office building.

(c) The buildings in (a) and (b), above, are used, not new, property and were purchased from Depreciator's sister who originally purchased them in 1982.

(d) Depreciator elects the alternative depreciation system with respect to the buildings in (a) and (b), above.

(e) $100,000 is spent to rehabilitate the buildings in (a) and (b), above, which are certified historic structures built in 1940.

(f) The $100,000 is spent in rehabilitating the office building in (b), above, which is not a certified historic structure but was built in 1930.

---

30. I.R.C. § 42(b)(2)(B).

31. Id.

32. I.R.C. § 42(a), (b)(1)(B)(ii), and (f)(1).

33. Conf.Rep. No. 99–841, 99th Cong., 2d Sess. II–103 (1986), reprinted in 1986–3

C.B. Vol. 4 at 103. Cf. I.R.C. § 50(c)(1) and (3).

34. See generally I.R.C. § 42(c)(2), (g), (h), (i), (k) and (*l*).

35. I.R.C. § 42(g)(1).

B. SALES AND EXCHANGES OF DEPRECIABLE
PROPERTY

---

1. THE SECTION 1231 HOTCHPOT

Internal Revenue Code: Section 1231. See Sections 1(h); 1060; 1211(b); 1221; 1222.

Section 1231 is complicated; after all, it is a part of the Internal Revenue Code. The function of Section 1231 is exclusively characterization. Although Section 1231 is complicated, it really is not as difficult as it first appears, or at least it may come to seem that way because of its taxpayer orientation. There is fun here for some taxpayers, but tempered a bit by the recent addition of a recapture, "gotcha," rule in subsection (c).

As stated above, the function of Section 1231 is simply one of characterization. Generally, Section 1231 provides that, if during the taxable year, the gains on the disposition of certain types of property exceed the losses on the disposition of the same types of property, all the gains and losses are treated as long-term capital gains and long-term capital losses, respectively.[1] Conversely, if the losses on the disposition of these properties equal or exceed the gains, all the gains and losses are treated as ordinary.[2] Taking some liberties with the statutory scheme,[3] in general a net figure is determined by throwing all relevant gains and losses into the "hotchpot." If there is a net gain, we say a long-term capital gain of the net amount emerges from the hotchpot to be considered for computation purposes with other capital gains and losses. If a loss nets out, the loss is ordinary for computational purposes.

The Section 1231 Main Hotchpot. Section 1231 applies to (grabs for the hotchpot) any recognized gain or loss from the *sale or exchange* of depreciable business property held for more than one year and real property used in business [4] which has been held for more than one year. It also applies to any recognized gain or loss from the *compulsory or involuntary conversion* [5] of any depreciable business property or real property held for more than one year and of any capital asset held for more than one year, if the asset is held in connection with a trade or

---

1. I.R.C. § 1231(a)(1).

2. I.R.C. § 1231(a)(2).

3. Literally and appropriately because in very limited circumstances it can make a difference (such as computation of gross income), the statute precludes any such netting.

4. I.R.C. § 1231(b) contains a definition of the term "property used in the trade or business," which is not simply descriptive.

See also the *Stephen P. Wasnok* case which follows this note.

5. The statute expressly contemplates that compulsory or involuntary conversion can result from destruction in whole or in part, theft or seizure, or an exercise of the power of requisition or condemnation or the threat or imminence thereof. I.R.C. § 1231(a)(3)(A)(ii).

business or a transaction entered into for profit. Thus Section 1231 is applicable only to property connected with a trade or business or a profit-seeking activity.[6] This combination of transactions is brought together in the Section 1231 hotchpot, and gains in the hotchpot are compared with losses in the hotchpot. If the gains exceed the losses, then *all* the gains and losses are treated as long-term capital gains and losses.[7] If the losses exceed the gains then *all* the gains and losses are characterized as ordinary gains and losses.[8]

Historically Section 1231 has been a pro-taxpayer section. Without its hotchpot principles, almost all the items [9] affected by it would lack either capital asset [10] or sale or exchange attributes.[11] Thus, generally, all the gains and losses would be ordinary gains and losses. Fortunately for the taxpayer, this (ordinary) treatment applies if Section 1231 losses exceed gains. But if gains exceed losses, Section 1231 comes to the taxpayer's aid and characterizes all such gains and losses as long-term capital gains and losses, except to the extent that subsection (c) applies. Prior to 1988 except to the extent that subsection (c) applied, the net gains were potentially accorded substantial preferential treatment.[12] After 1990 there is some preference for net capital gains,[13] and in some circumstances Section 1231 may act in an additional way to a taxpayer's benefit. If apart from any section 1231 items, a taxpayer has net capital losses that may not be deductible in the current year for lack of capital gains[14] the characterization of Section 1231 gain in excess of loss as long-term capital gain and loss will generate net capital gain[15] against which the losses may be used. In other words, the device may increase the deductibility of non-Section 1231 net capital losses in the current year.[16] Thus, Section 1231 remains a pro-taxpayer provision.

6. Prior to the 1984 Act, I.R.C. § 1231 also applied to compulsory or involuntary conversions of "personal" capital assets, i.e., assets unrelated to any profit-seeking activity. Those assets which were removed from § 1231 now may be within § 165(h)(2), still another subhotchpot that now characterizes so-called personal casualty gains and losses. See Chapter 23 C, infra.

7. I.R.C. § 1231(a)(1). See note 3, supra.

8. I.R.C. § 1231(a)(2). See note 3, supra.

9. A compulsory conversion of a capital asset would lack neither sale or exchange nor capital asset status.

10. See I.R.C. § 1221(2).

11. See pages 704–724, supra.

12. See I.R.C. (1954) § 1202. The long-term capital gains and losses generated under § 1231 were netted against the tax-payer's conventional capital gains and losses to determine whether § 1202 was applicable.

13. I.R.C. § 1(h).

14. I.R.C. § 1211(b).

15. I.R.C. § 1222(11).

16. For example, assume a taxpayer had $50,000 of taxable income and, in addition, $3,000 of capital gain and $10,000 of capital loss and $4,000 of I.R.C. § 1231 gain. Without § 1231, the $4,000 of § 1231 gain would be ordinary income and § 1211(b) would limit the deductibility of capital losses to $6,000 ($3,000 capital gain plus $3,000) with a $4,000 § 1212(b) loss carryover. Thus the current year's taxable income would be $51,000 ($50,000 plus $4,000 less the § 1211(b) excess of $3,000). With the assistance of § 1231 (assuming § 1231(c) is inapplicable), the $4,000 of § 1231 gain becomes capital gain resulting in a total of $7,000 of capital gain. Under § 1211(b) there would be full deductibility of the losses in the current year (loss would be deductible to the extent of gain plus $3,000) and no carryovers. Thus taxpayer would have only $47,000 of current taxable

The Section 1231(a)(4)(C) Subhotchpot. There are two special rules that cut across the otherwise simple Section 1231 process. The first is a pro-taxpayer exception to the "main" hotchpot rule considered above. It creates a "subhotchpot" rule that must be applied prior to consideration of main hotchpot consequences. Section 1231(a)(4)(C) provides that, before any gains and losses from *involuntary* conversions (from fire, storm, etc. or from theft) are to be included in the main hotchpot, gains from such conversions must equal or exceed losses from such conversions. Consequently, a taxpayer first compares his allowable involuntary casualty gains and losses from trade or business or profit seeking assets. If gains exceed losses, then all these gains and losses are routed into the main hotchpot. If losses in the subhotchpot exceed gains, then Section 1231 does not apply to any of such gains or losses; they all remain ordinary gains and losses, never entering the main hotchpot. Preservation of the *ordinary* character of this net amount of loss in the subhotchpot is to the taxpayer's advantage. Why?

The Section 1231(c) Lookback Recapture Rule. Other than on compulsory or involuntary conversions, taxpayers could maximize the benefits of the Section 1231 main hotchpot by timing all losses to fall in one year and all gains in another year thereby characterizing all gains as long-term capital gains and all losses as ordinary losses. Seemingly to preclude such use of Section 1231, in the Tax Reform Act of 1984 Congress enacted a second special rule which imposes a limitation upon the benefits of the Section 1231 main hotchpot rule. Section 1231(c) establishes a "lookback rule" which, if applicable, overrides the main hotchpot rule and recharacterizes some or all of a main hotchpot *net* gain for the current year from long-term capital gain to ordinary income. The rule requires such a recharacterization to the extent that there are unrecaptured Section 1231 main hotchpot net losses for any of the preceding five years. Such losses are the sum of net losses established by the main hotchpot over the prior five years which have not been offset as ordinary income by subsequent net main hotchpot gains.[17] Hence, if in year 3, the current year, there is a Section 1231 main hotchpot net gain of $10,000, but in years 1 and 2, there were Section 1231 main hotchpot net losses of $5,000 and $3,000, respectively, the recharacterization rule requires $8,000 of the year 3 net gain to be characterized as ordinary income, and only the remaining $2,000 gain will retain its Section 1231 long-term capital gain character. All of the above rules are illustrated in problem 1 of the problems for this section.

income ($50,000 less the § 1211(b) excess of $3,000) and no carryovers.

17. The legislative history indicates the losses are recaptured in the chronological order in which they arose (i.e. first in, first out). Conf.Rep. No. 98–861, 98th Cong., 2d Sess. 1034 (1984).

The lookback recapture rule is discussed in Cash, "The Erosion of Section 1231," 62 Taxes 789 (1984).

STEPHEN P. WASNOK

Tax Court of the United States, 1971.
30 T.C.M. 39.

SACKS, Commissioner: Respondent determined deficiencies in the income tax of petitioners for the taxable years and in the amounts set forth below:

Petitioner	Taxable Year	Amount
Stephen P. Wasnok	1967	$195.70
Mary Alice Wasnok	1967	158.66
Stephen P. and Mary Alice Wasnok	1968	54.46

The sole issue for decision is whether petitioners' disposition of certain real property at a loss constitutes an ordinary loss fully deductible in 1965, the year in which the loss was sustained, or a capital loss, deductible as a loss carryover in 1967 and 1968.

Findings of Fact

Most of the facts have been stipulated by the parties. Their stipulation, together with attached exhibits, is incorporated herein by this reference.

Stephen P. and Mary Alice Wasnok, sometimes hereinafter referred to as petitioners or as Stephen and Mary, are husband and wife who resided in Fullerton, California at the time of the filing of their petition herein. Their separate income tax returns for the taxable year 1967 and their joint income tax return for the taxable year 1968 were filed with the district director of internal revenue, Los Angeles, California.

In 1960 petitioners were residing in Cincinnati, Ohio. Sometime during that year they purchased a home there located at 5654 Sagecrest Drive, hereinafter referred to as the Sagecrest property. A substantial portion of the purchase price of this property was borrowed on a promissory note secured by a first mortgage on the property from Spring Grove Avenue Loan and Deposit Company (hereinafter referred to as Spring Grove Loan Co.).

Early in 1961 petitioners decided to move to California. They listed the Sagecrest property with its builder for sale, but without result since the market at the time was extremely poor. Finally, on June 15, 1961 petitioners leased the property for a monthly rental of $225.00 and thereafter departed for California.

Between June 15, 1961 and May 7, 1965 petitioners leased the Sagecrest property to various tenants at an average rental of $200.00 per month. Such tenants were located by advertising the property for rent in Cincinnati newspapers and by referrals from former neighbors. During this period petitioners on two occasions listed the property for sale with brokers, in each case, however, for only a ninety day period of time. Neither listing generated an offer for more than the amount due on the mortgage.

By 1965 petitioners found themselves unable to continue payments due on their note on the Sagecrest property to Spring Grove Loan Co. Spring Grove thereafter notified petitioners that they would either have to deed the property back or the company would have to institute foreclosure proceedings. On May 7, 1965 petitioners executed a deed conveying their interest in the Sagecrest property to Spring Grove Loan Co. in satisfaction of the then balance due on their note in the amount of $24,421.04.

For the taxable years 1961 through 1964 petitioners filed federal income tax returns reporting thereon rental income and claiming various expenses, including depreciation, on the Sagecrest property. Their return for 1961 was examined by the Internal Revenue Service and the cost basis of the land and improvements was agreed upon in the amount of $32,729.70. Total depreciation on the improvements claimed and allowed for the taxable years 1961 through 1964 was $4,697.42.

Petitioners did not file federal income tax returns for the taxable years 1965 and 1966 on the premise that no returns were required because no tax appeared to be due.

For 1965, however, petitioners had gross income in the amount of $5,603.21 and for 1966, in the amount of $3,180.00.

On their separate returns for the taxable year 1967, petitioners for the first time each claimed a capital loss carry-forward deduction in the amount of $1,000.00 which was predicated upon their disposition in 1965 of the Sagecrest property to Spring Grove Loan Co. Thereafter, on their joint return for 1968, petitioners claimed a further capital loss carry-forward deduction of $389.00, computed as follows:

Cost of Sagecrest property	$32,729.70
Less: depreciation taken	4,697.42
Adjusted basis	$28,032.28
Sale on May 7, 1965	24,421.04
Capital Loss	$ 3,611.24
Claimed in 1967 (separate return)	2,000.00
Sub-total	1,611.24
Claimed in 1968	$ 389.00 [1]
Balance to carry-over	$ 1,222.24

In his notices of deficiency, respondent disallowed to petitioners the claimed capital loss carry-over deductions for the taxable years 1967 and 1968 on the ground that the loss involved was an ordinary loss

---

1. The amount necessary to balance income with itemized deductions and exemptions for 1968.

deductible in the year sustained (1965) rather than a capital loss subject to the carry-over provisions of the Internal Revenue Code of 1954.

Petitioners' disposition of the Sagecrest property at a loss constitutes an ordinary loss fully deductible in 1965, the year in which the loss was sustained and not a capital loss.

Opinion

It is petitioners' position herein that the Sagecrest property was a capital asset in their hands, and that its disposition at a loss resulted in a capital loss which they properly deferred deducting on their returns until 1967 and 1968 when they had sufficient income to file returns.

Respondent contends that the property in question was not a capital asset in petitioners' hands, but an asset of the type described in section 1231 of the Code [2] losses upon the disposition of which are ordinary in nature and required to be deducted, to the extent that there is gross income, in the year in which sustained. Since petitioners' gross income in 1965 was more than sufficient to absorb the loss in that year, no deduction of any kind is allowable in the years here at issue.

Section 1221 of the Code defines the term "capital asset" as any property held by the taxpayer, *excluding however,* "property used in his trade or business, of a character which is subject to the allowance for depreciation * * * or real property used in his trade or business." With respect to "property used in the trade or business" of a taxpayer, section 1231 provides that while net gains on sales or exchanges of such property shall be treated as capital gains, net losses are not to be treated as *capital* losses, but as *ordinary* losses.

The evidence presented to the Court is not complex. Simply stated, it shows that when petitioners moved from Ohio to California in 1961 they could not sell their residence in Ohio and therefore rented it to various tenants until May, 1965, when it was deeded back to the mortgagee because petitioners could no longer make the mortgage payments and did not desire the mortgagee to foreclose. It further shows that during the period 1961 through 1964 petitioners received rents of about two hundred dollars per month except for brief periods when the property was vacant. Their return for 1961 was examined by respondent and the tax basis for the property agreed upon. Depreciation was claimed on the improvements during the period 1961 to 1964 and, after reducing basis by the amount of depreciation claimed, the difference between the adjusted basis and mortgage balance produced a loss of $3,611.24.

In our view petitioners' activity in renting out the Sagecrest property for a fairly continuous period of four years between 1961 and 1965, at a substantial rental, together with the concurrent claiming on their income tax returns for these years of the expenses incurred in

---

2. [I.R.C. § 1231 is omitted. Ed.]

such rental activity, including depreciation, establishes the use of such property in a "trade or business." Leland Hazard, 7 T.C. 372 (1946).

We therefore find that the property in question was not a capital asset in petitioners' hands at the time of its disposition, but an asset of the kind described in section 1231. The loss sustained on the disposition of such an asset is an ordinary loss. Since such loss was sustained in 1965, when petitioners had gross income sufficient to entirely absorb it, no loss is allowable to petitioners in either 1967 or 1968.

Reviewed and adopted as the report of the Small Tax Case Division.

Decision will be entered for respondent.

NOTE

Stephen P. Wasnok is merely a current reaffirmation of a principle initially announced by the Tax Court in Leland Hazard,[1] one of the "name" cases in this area. Whether it is a sound principle may be judged in part against the competing view of the Second Circuit, expressed as follows in Grier v. U.S.,[2] another well-known case:

> In this case [quite similar to Wasnok Ed.] the activities with relation to this single dwelling, although of long duration, were minimal in nature. Activity to rent and re-rent was not required. No employees were regularly engaged for maintenance or repair.
>
> Lacking the broader activities stressed in [cases other than Hazard which reached the 'business' result Ed.], the real estate in this case appears to partake more of the nature of property held for investment than property used in a trade or business. The property in this case, although used for the production of income, shall not be considered as used in the taxpayer's trade or business.

Attention should be called as well to Section 62(a)(4) permitting an allowance in the determination of adjusted gross income of deductions, including losses, attributable to property held for the production of rent, even if such deductions do not come within Section 62(a)(1) as attributable to a trade or business of the taxpayer. Is there at least a negative inference here that not all rental activity constitutes business activity?

It would be a good time to reconsider the several classifications of profit-seeking activity as involving the conduct of a "trade or business,"[3] property "held for the production of income,"[4] or a "transaction entered into for profit."[5] For example, under the *Hazard* principle

---

1. 7 T.C. 372 (1946), acq., 1946–2 C.B. 3.

2. 218 F.2d 603 (2d Cir.1955); the quotation is from the opinion of the District Judge, 120 F.Supp. 395 (D.Conn.1954), adopted by the Court of Appeals in a per curiam affirmance.

3. See, e.g., Imbesi v. Commissioner, 361 F.2d 640 (3d Cir.1966).

4. See, e.g., Bowers v. Lumpkin, supra, at page 423.

5. See, e.g., William C. Horrmann, supra, at page 444.

how would the taxpayer in *Horrmann* [6] have fared if he had been successful in attempts to rent the property in question?

And can you ever succeed in business (classification) by only really trying? If T opens up a new automobile dealership in December, of the current year, but makes no sales until January, was he carrying on a trade or business in the current year? What about a young lawyer who hangs up his shingle in December but is carefully avoided by clients until the following year? [7]

WILLIAMS v. McGOWAN

United States Court of Appeals, Second Circuit, 1945.
152 F.2d 570.

L. HAND, Circuit Judge. This is an appeal from a judgment dismissing the complaint in an action by a taxpayer to recover income taxes paid for the year 1940. [After holding that attorneys' fees incurred in obtaining an income tax refund were deductible under an earlier version of Section 212, the opinion moved to a second issue. Ed.]

Williams, the taxpayer, and one, Reynolds, had for many years been engaged in the hardware business in the City of Corning, New York. On the 20th of January, 1926, they formed a partnership, of which Williams was entitled to two-thirds of the profits, and Reynolds, one-third. They agreed that on February 1, 1925, the capital invested in the business had been $118,082.05, of which Reynolds had a credit of $29,029.03, and Williams, the balance—$89,053.02. At the end of every business year, on February 1st, Reynolds was to pay to Williams, interest upon the amount of the difference between his share of the capital and one-third of the total as shown by the inventory; and upon withdrawal of one party the other was to have the privilege of buying the other's interest as it appeared on the books. The business was carried on through the firm's fiscal year, ending January 31, 1940, in accordance with this agreement, and thereafter until Reynolds' death on July 18th of that year. Williams settled with Reynolds' executrix on September 6th in an agreement by which he promised to pay her $12,187.90, and to assume all liabilities of the business; and he did pay her $2,187.98 in cash at once, and $10,000 on the 10th of the following October. On September 17th of the same year, Williams sold the business as a whole to the Corning Building Company for $63,926.28— its agreed value as of February 1, 1940—"plus an amount to be computed by multiplying the gross sales of the business from the first day of February, 1940 to the 28th day of September, 1940," by an agreed fraction. This value was made up of cash of about $8100, receivables of about $7000, fixtures of about $800, and a merchandise inventory of about $49,000, less some $1000 for bills payable. To this was added about $6,000 credited to Williams for profits under the

6. Supra note 5.

7. See, Cf., Morton Frank, supra, at page 357.

language just quoted, making a total of nearly $70,000. Upon this sale Williams suffered a loss upon his original two-thirds of the business, but he made a small gain upon the one-third which he had bought from Reynolds' executrix; and in his income tax return he entered both as items of "ordinary income," and not as transactions in "capital assets." This the Commissioner disallowed and recomputed the tax accordingly; Williams paid the deficiency and sued to recover it in this action. The only question is whether the business was "capital assets" under § 117(a)(1) of the Internal Revenue Code, 26 U.S.C.A. Int.Rev.Code, § 117(a)(1).

It has been held that a partner's interest in a going firm is for tax purposes to be regarded as a "capital asset." Stilgenbaur v. United States, 9 Cir., 115 F.2d 283; Commissioner v. Shapiro, 6 Cir., 125 F.2d 532, 144 A.L.R. 349. We too accepted the doctrine in McClellan v. Commissioner, 2 Cir., 117 F.2d 988, although we had held the opposite in Helvering v. Smith, 2 Cir., 90 F.2d 590, 591, where the partnership articles had provided that a retiring partner should receive as his share only his percentage of the sums "actually collected" and "of all earnings * * * for services performed." Such a payment, we thought, was income; and we expressly repudiated the notion that the Uniform Partnership Act had, generally speaking, changed the firm into a juristic entity. See also Doyle v. Commissioner, 4 Cir., 102 F.2d 86. If a partner's interest in a going firm is "capital assets" perhaps a dead partner's interest is the same. New York Partnership Law §§ 61, 62(4), Consol.Laws N.Y. c. 39. We need not say. When Williams bought out Reynolds' interest, he became the sole owner of the business, the firm had ended upon any theory, and the situation for tax purposes was no other than if Reynolds had never been a partner at all, except that to the extent of one-third of the "amount realized" on Williams' sale to the Corning Company, his "basis" was different. The judge thought that, because upon that sale both parties fixed the price at the liquidation value of the business while Reynolds was alive, "plus" its estimated earnings thereafter, it was as though Williams had sold his interest in the firm during its existence. But the method by which the parties agreed upon the price was irrelevant to the computation of Williams' income. The Treasury, if that served its interest, need not heed any fiction which the parties found it convenient to adopt; nor need Williams do the same in his dealings with the Treasury. We have to decide only whether upon the sale of a going business it is to be comminuted into its fragments, and these are to be separately matched against the definition in § 117(a)(1), or whether the whole business is to be treated as if it were a single piece of property.

Our law has been sparing in the creation of juristic entities; it has never, for example, taken over the Roman "universitas facti"; [1] and

---

1. "By universitas facti is meant a number of things of the same kind which are regarded as a whole; e.g. a herd, a stock of wares." Mackeldey, Roman Law § 162.

indeed for many years it fumbled uncertainly with the concept of a corporation.[2]   One might have supposed that partnership would have been an especially promising field in which to raise up an entity, particularly since merchants have always kept their accounts upon that basis.   Yet there too our law resisted at the price of great and continuing confusion; and, even when it might be thought that a statute admitted, if it did not demand, recognition of the firm as an entity, the old concepts prevailed.   Francis v. McNeal, 228 U.S. 695, 33 S.Ct. 701.   And so, even though we might agree that under the influence of the Uniform Partnership Act a partner's interest in the firm should be treated as indivisible, and for that reason a "capital asset" within § 117(a)(1), we should be chary about extending further so exotic a jural concept.   Be that as it may, in this instance the section itself furnishes the answer.   It starts in the broadest way by declaring that all "property" is "capital assets," and then makes three exceptions.   The first is "stock in trade * * * or other property of a kind which would properly be included in the inventory"; next comes "property held * * * primarily for sale to customers"; and finally, property "used in the trade or business of a character which is subject to * * * allowance for depreciation."   In the face of this language, although it may be true that a "stock in trade," taken by itself, should be treated as a "universitas facti," by no possibility can a whole business be so treated; and the same is true as to any property within the other exceptions.   Congress plainly did mean to comminute the elements of a business; plainly it did not regard the whole as "capital assets."

As has already appeared, Williams transferred to the Corning Company "cash," "receivables," "fixtures" and a "merchandise inventory."   "Fixtures" are not capital because they are subject to a depreciation allowance; the inventory, as we have just seen, is expressly excluded.   So far as appears, no allowance was made for "good-will"; but, even if there had been, we held in Haberle Crystal Springs Brewing Company v. Clarke, Collector, 2 Cir., 30 F.2d 219, that "good-will" was a depreciable intangible.   It is true that the Supreme Court reversed that judgment—280 U.S. 384, 50 S.Ct. 155—but it based its decision only upon the fact that there could be no allowance for the depreciation of "good-will" in a brewery, a business condemned by the Eighteenth Amendment.   There can of course be no gain or loss in the transfer of cash; and, although Williams does appear to have made a gain of $1072.71 upon the "receivables," the point has not been argued that they are not subject to a depreciation allowance.   That we leave open for decision by the district court, if the parties cannot agree.   The gain or loss upon every other item should be computed as an item in ordinary income.

Judgment reversed.

2. "To the 'church' modern law owes its conception of a juristic person, and the clear line that it draws between 'the corporation aggregate' and the sum of its members." Pollack & Maitland, Vol. 1, p. 489.

FRANK, Circuit Judge (dissenting in part).

I agree that it is irrelevant that the business was once owned by a partnership. For when the sale to the Corning Company occurred, the partnership was dead, had become merely a memory, a ghost. To say that the sale was of the partnership's assets would, then, be to indulge in animism.

But I do not agree that we should ignore what the parties to the sale, Williams and the Corning Company, actually did. They did not arrange for a transfer to the buyer, as if in separate bundles, of the several ingredients of the business. They contracted for the sale of the entire business as a going concern. Here is what they said in their agreement: "The party of the first part agrees to sell and the party of the second part agrees to buy, *all of the right, title and interest* of the said party of the first part *in and to the hardware business* now being conducted by the said party of the first part, *including* cash on hand and on deposit in the First National Bank & Trust Company of Corning in the A.F. Williams Hardware Store account, in accounts receivable, bills receivable, notes receivable, merchandise and fixtures, including two G.M. trucks, good will and all other assets of every kind and description used in and about said business.[1] * * * Said party of the first part agrees not to engage in the hardware business within a radius of twenty-five miles from the City of Corning, New York, for a period of ten years from the 1st day of October 1940."

To carve up this transaction into distinct sales—of cash, receivables, fixtures, trucks, merchandise, and good will—is to do violence to the realities. I do not think Congress intended any such artificial result. * * *

PROBLEMS

1. Hotchpot engaged in (or encountered) the following transactions (or events) in the current year. Determine separately for each part (a) through (i) how the matters indicated will be characterized for the current year, assuming in all parts other than (g)–(i) that § 1231(c) is inapplicable.

(a) Hotchpot sells some land used in his business for several years for $20,000. It had cost him $10,000. He also receives $16,000 when the State condemns some other land that he had purchased for $18,000 which he has leased to a third person for several years.

(b) Same as (a), above, including the same bases, except that both pieces of land were inherited from Hotchpot's Uncle who died three months before the dispositions.

(c) Hotchpot sells a building used for several years in his business, which he depreciated under the straight-line method. The sale price is $15,000 and the adjusted basis $5,000. His two year

1. Emphasis added.

old car, used exclusively in business, is totally destroyed in a fire. The car had a $6,000 adjusted basis but was worth $8,000 prior to the fire. He received $4,000 in insurance proceeds.

(d) In addition to the building and the car in (c), above, assume that Hotchpot had a painting that he had purchased two years ago which was held in connection with his business and which was also destroyed in the fire. The painting had been purchased for $4,000 and he received $8,000 in insurance proceeds.

(e) In addition to the building sale, car loss, and painting gain in (c) and (d), above, assume Hotchpot sells land used for several years in his business for $30,000. The land, which he had hoped contained oil, had been purchased for $50,000.

(f) Would Hotchpot be pleased if the Commissioner successfully alleged that the land in problem (e), above, was held as an investment rather than for use in Hotchpot's business?

(g) What result under the facts of (d), above (building gain, car loss, and painting gain), if four years before the fire Hotchpot had had a $5,000 net § 1231 loss and three years before a $3,000 net § 1231 loss, and he had had no other § 1231 transactions in other years.

(h) Same as (g), above, except that in addition two years before the tax year Hotchpot had a $6,000 net § 1231 loss.

(i) Same as (h), above, except that one year before the tax year Hotchpot had had a $10,000 net § 1231 gain.

2. Car Dealer uses some cars for demonstration purposes. Are the cars depreciable? Disregarding § 1245 if they are held long-term does gain on their sale qualify for § 1231(a) main hotchpot treatment? See Rev.Rul. 75–538, 1975–2 C.B. 34.

3. Merchant who has been in business for several years sells his sole proprietorship consisting of the following assets, all of which, except for the inventory, have been held for more than one year.

	Adjusted Basis	Fair Market Value
Inventory	$ 8,000	$16,000
Goodwill	0	20,000
Land (used in business)	30,000	20,000
Building (used in business)	15,000	20,000
Machinery & Equipment (used in business)	12,000	14,000
Total	$65,000	$90,000

Merchant also agrees, for an additional $10,000 that he will not compete in the same geographical area during the succeeding ten years.

(a) Disregarding any consideration of §§ 1245 and 1250, which are considered in the succeeding subchapters of the text, what are the tax consequences to Merchant on his sale of the Business for $100,000?

(b)　What difference in result if Merchant's business is incorporated, he is the sole shareholder, and he has a $70,000 basis in the stock which he sells for $90,000, assuming that he is again paid an additional $10,000 for his covenant not to compete?

2.　CHARACTERIZATION UNDER SECTION 1239

Internal Revenue Code: Sections 267(b)(3), (10), (11) and (12) and (c); 318(a)(3)(B)(i); 1239.

UNITED STATES v. PARKER *

United States Court of Appeals, Fifth Circuit, 1967.
376 F.2d 402.

GOLDBERG, Circuit Judge: The protesting and unhappy taxpayers, Curtis L. Parker and his wife, Martha, owned a wholesale and retail oil and gasoline business. On April 1, 1959, Parker and B.K. Eaves, a longtime employee, formed a Louisiana corporation incorporating Parker's business. The corporation had an authorized capital stock of 1,000 shares.

Parker subscribed to 800 shares and paid for them by transferring to the corporation certain property valued at $93,400.00 to be used in the corporation's business. Eaves subscribed to the remaining 200 shares. He paid $7,500.00 cash and agreed to pay the balance of $23,350.00 over a period of 5 years.

At the first meeting of the corporation's board of directors a resolution was passed accepting Eaves's subscription. He was issued stock certificates for the amount of stock paid for at that time (64.239 shares), and the board of directors resolved that the remainder of Eaves's stock certificates would be issued as their purchase price was paid. The Articles of Incorporation included a provision stating that none of the stock of the corporation might be transferred unless the stock were first offered to the corporation at the same price offered by the proposed transferee. (If the corporation did not accept the offer, another stockholder could.)

Parker and Eaves also entered into a stockholders' agreement which provided that whenever Eaves's employment should terminate for any reason, including death, his shares would then be purchased by Parker at a price to be governed by the fair market value per share of the corporation's assets, specifically excluding good will "or any other intangible asset." The value per share was set at $116.75 for the first year of the corporation's existence (until April 1, 1960), and thereafter

---

* Some footnotes are omitted, others renumbered. Ed.

the price was to be set by agreement between Parker and Eaves, with arbitration if they could not agree.

The face of all stock certificates issued to Parker and Eaves carried notice of the restriction on sale created by the Articles of Incorporation. Only the stock certificates issued to Eaves carried a legend that they were subject to the Eaves-Parker buy-and-sell agreement.

Also, at the first meeting of the board of directors, Parker sold to the corporation certain other assets which were depreciable property (such as motor vehicles, furniture and fixtures, and other equipment which Parker had apparently used in the business before the incorporation) worth $95,738.70. The corporation was to pay for this property in ten annual installments with interest of 5 per cent. Parker elected to treat the sale as a capital transaction, and reported the gain from it as long term capital gain. IRC § 1231.

The present suit arises because the Internal Revenue Service treated the gain as ordinary income under IRC § 1239, based upon the contention that the taxpayers owned more than 80 per cent "in value" of all outstanding stock of the corporation at the time of sale. The Service assessed deficiencies for the calendar years 1959, 1960, and 1961. Taxpayers paid the assessments under protest and sued in district court for a refund. 28 U.S.C.A. § 1346(a). The district court granted summary judgment for the taxpayers, and the government appeals. We reverse.

* * *

[T]he government argues that even if the full 20 per cent of the shares allotted to Eaves was "outstanding" at the time of the sale, "the restrictions placed upon those shares and their inherent limitations made them worth less per share than Parker's." We * * * agree.

Section 1239 prevents capital gain treatment of a "sale or exchange" of depreciable property to a controlled corporation or a spouse. Without this section a taxpayer who had property which had been depreciated to a low basis could sell that property to a controlled corporation or spouse and pay only capital gains rates on the gain. The transferee (who is virtually identical to the transferor in the proscribed area) could then redepreciate the property, using the sale price as a new basis. The depreciation, of course, would be deducted from ordinary income.[1] Section 1239 renders such a scheme profitless by taxing the gain on the transfer at ordinary rather than capital rates.

---

1. The net effect may be shown graphically in a hypothetical case: R, the transferor, holds property depreciated to a value of $2,000. R sells the property for $6,000 to E, his controlled corporation. R pays a maximum capital gains tax of 25 per cent on the $4,000 gain, or a tax of $1,000. E, with a basis of $6,000 on the property takes depreciation deductions from ordinary income. After four or five years of these deductions E has depreciated the property back to the $2,000 basis. (See depreciation guidelines in Rev.Proc. 62–21; rates of depreciation in Rev.Proc. 65–13, Appendix I, Table A.) E has by then deducted $4,000 in depreciation from ordinary income. If E is in the 50 per cent bracket, the $4,000 in depreciation deductions has saved him $2,000 in income taxes. R has therefore paid a $1,000 capital gains tax and has saved E $2,000 in income taxes. If R and E are identical (and in cases covered by § 1239 they certainly may

The issue here, of course, is whether Parker's corporation is sufficiently Parker's slave to justify invocation of § 1239. We have concluded that Parker owned, for purposes of § 1239, exactly 80 per cent of the corporation's outstanding stock. The decisive question now is whether this 80 per cent is, under § 1239, "more than 80 per cent *in value* of the outstanding stock." [emphasis added]

We first note what § 1239 does not say. It does not use the standard of § 368(c) which is invoked by § 351 for transfers to a controlled corporation in exchange for that corporation's stock or securities. Control is defined by § 368(c) as

> "ownership of stock possessing at least 80 percent of the total combined *voting power* of all classes of stock entitled to vote and at least 80 percent of the total *number* of shares of all other classes of stock of the corporation." [emphasis added]

By contrast, § 1239 says "more than 80 per cent *in value.*" The words "in value" in § 1239 must have some meaning. Trotz v. Commissioner of Internal Revenue, 10 Cir.1966, 361 F.2d 927, 930. We cannot indulge in statutory interpretation by excision. Statutory explication may be an art, but it must not be artful. Further, we cannot say that by using "in value" Congress intended us to consider only the factors of voting power or number of shares. "If the 80% determination is to be [merely] on the basis of the number of shares outstanding, no reason exists for the use of the words 'in value'." Trotz v. Commissioner of Internal Revenue, supra, 361 F.2d at 930. Or, if number of shares and voting power were the sole indicia, Congress could have limited § 1239 by using terms similar to those which § 351 draws from § 368(c) in an analogous situation within the Code's framework. "In value" is a broader phrase, and we think that it calls for the familiar, though difficult, process of fair market valuation.[2]

> "The value of property is an underlying factor in a great number of income tax cases, particularly in such areas of the law as those involving the receipt of income, the computation of gain or loss, depreciation and depletion." 10 Mertens, Law of Federal Income Taxation § 59.01 (1964 revision). Value is not a strange or alien concept in tax law, and we have held that "There is no distinction, for most purposes * * *, in the meaning of fair market value as used in an estate tax case and

be considered so), then R has avoided $2,000 in taxes by paying only $1,000.

2. The district judge stated his findings of fact and conclusions of law with explicitness. He concluded, as do we, that market valuation was the proper test for § 1239. He found as a matter of law, however, that neither the restrictions on salability of the Eaves stock nor its minority position reduced its value per share, and it is here that we disagree. However, partly because of the peculiar circumstances of this case, but largely because the district judge stated his findings and conclusions so clearly and distinctly and isolated with precision the ground for his holding, we have been able to render unnecessary the remand which would usually be required. Even though we disagree on one point, the opinion of the district judge epitomizes the result sought by Rule 52(a), and thereby promotes the "just, speedy, and inexpensive determination of every action" sought by Rule 1.

one involving income tax." Champion v. Commissioner, 5 Cir. 1962, 303 F.2d 887, 892–893.

We next note that in the present case Eaves owned exactly 20 per cent of the outstanding stock, and Parker owned exactly 80 per cent. Therefore, if any fact can be found which shows that the value per share of Parker's stock exceeded by any amount, no matter how small, the value per share of Eaves's, then Parker owned more than 80 per cent in value of the outstanding stock. While it is true that Parker and Eaves owned the same class of stock, Eaves's stock was burdened with impedimenta from which Parker's stock was free. We hold that as a matter of law these impedimenta must have decreased the value per share of Eaves's stock, and as we need only show that this value per share was lower by any indeterminate amount, no matter how miniscule, than the value per share of Parker's stock, we are able to render judgment here without remand.[3]

The impedimenta which depress the value spring from two sources.

A. *The Restrictions on Transfer of Stock.* Eaves's stock was encumbered by two kinds of restrictions. First, the articles of incorporation stated that the corporation had the right of first refusal of any offer to sell to a third party. Second, Eaves's agreement with Parker stated that if Eaves left the employ of the corporation for any reason, he must sell all of his stock to Parker at a price representing the value per share of the assets, specifically excluding good will. Notice to the world of these restrictions, like the mark of Cain, was on the face of Eaves's stock certificates.

The practical effect of these restrictions was to reduce the number of opportunities for Eaves to sell or give away the stock and to place a limit (the duration of his employment) upon the period when he might hold the stock. "A commodity freely salable is obviously worth more on the market than a precisely similar commodity which cannot be freely sold." Judge Woodbury for the First Circuit in Worcester County Trust Co. v. Commissioner of Internal Revenue, 1 Cir.1943, 134 F.2d 578, 582.

The alienability of Parker's stock was restricted only by the limitation imposed by the articles of incorporation. Whether this limitation, in the light of Parker's complete control, had any real effect on alienability we need not consider, for Eaves's stock was burdened not only by the articles but also by the extra and potent limitation of the buy-sell agreement. Even if we consider the Eaves and Parker stock as identically limited by the articles, Parker's stock was not affected by

---

3. In this aspect the present case differs from Trotz v. Commissioner of Internal Revenue, supra. There, the taxpayer Trotz owned 79 per cent of the outstanding stock and the lesser shareholder owned 21 per cent. The Tenth Circuit remanded the case for a factual determination by the Tax Court of whether any difference between the values per share of the large and small blocks brought Trotz's holding above 80 per cent in value. In contrast, in the present case any extra value per share in Parker's stock will bring his holding above 80 per cent in value. No determination is needed of how much more per share Parker's stock is worth.

the buy-sell agreement; Eaves's was. "In our view it must be said that the restriction necessarily has a depressing effect upon the value of the stock in the market." Worcester County Trust Co., supra, 134 F.2d at 582. That such an extra limitation on alienability would depress market value to some greater extent is a well-recognized proposition: Mailloux v. Commissioner of Internal Revenue, 5 Cir.1963, 320 F.2d 60; James v. Commissioner of Internal Revenue, 2 Cir.1945, 148 F.2d 236; Kirby v. Commissioner of Internal Revenue, 5 Cir.1939, 102 F.2d 115; Mathews v. United States, E.D.N.Y.1964, 226 F.Supp. 1003; Baltimore National Bank v. United States, D.Md.1955, 136 F.Supp. 642. "Separation of the power of alienation from the ownership of property, or other forms of restriction against transfer, have in numerous cases been held to lessen the value of property." 10 Mertens, Law of Federal Income Taxation § 59.20 (1964 Rev.).

B. *The Lack of Control.* Eaves owned only 20 per cent of the stock. This left Parker in sole control of the corporation's affairs. Parker could, without Eaves, elect and remove directors and officers, amend the articles, and promulgate by-laws. He could dissolve the corporation. 5 LSA–R.S. § 12:54. With these powers, Parker controlled without possibility of challenge the entire operation from the smallest detail to the largest. He exercised so much power that the corporation was his alter ego, or his slave. This is the situation at which § 1239 aims.

Any purchaser of Eaves's stock would not be buying any degree of control over the corporation. The voting power which technically inhered in Eaves's stock was in reality worthless; Parker owned all of the real voting stock.

We hold that this disability which inhered in Eaves's stock reduced its value per share below that of Parker's stock as a matter of law. Cravens v. Welch, S.D.Cal.1935, 10 F.Supp. 94; Irene de Guebriant, 14 T.C. 611 (1950), rev'd on other grounds sub nom. Clafin v. Commissioner of Internal Revenue, 2 Cir.1951, 186 F.2d 307; Mathilde B. Hooper, 41 B.T.A. 114 (1940). See Mathews v. United States, supra; Worthen v. United States, D.Mass.1961, 192 F.Supp. 727.

> "Even absent any contemplated change in management, control increases the value of an investment by protecting it. The power to change the management, even while unexercised, protects the investor with control against an abrupt change by someone else and against a gradual deterioration of the incumbent management. Therefore, in a sense, controlling shares are inherently worth more than noncontrolling shares for reasons relating solely to investment value. When control is diffused, the same reasoning establishes, to a lesser degree, that shares enabling their holder to participate in control are worth more than those that do not. This is the strongest part of any argument against a broad reading of [Perlman v. Feldmann, 2 Cir.1955, 219 F.2d 173, cert. denied 349 U.S. 952, 75

S.Ct. 880 (1955)]. It is the kernel of truth in the assertion that a premium paid for controlling shares only shows that a premium paid for controlling shares only shows that controlling shares are inherently worth more than minority shares." Andrews, The Stockholder's Right to Equal Opportunity in the Sale of Shares, 78 Harvard L.Rev. 505, 526 (1965).[4]

In the vast majority of cases, courts of appeals have remanded where, as here, the lower courts failed to take into account all of the existing impedimenta on market value. For instance, in Kirby v. Commissioner of Internal Revenue, supra, we said:

> "The Board [of Tax Appeals] * * * declined to make any allowance against the value [of the stock] for the burden of the contract under which the stock had been bought and held. The result was neither, a true nor a fair, [sic] determination of value. The finding which mirrors that result cannot stand.

> "Therefore * * * we reverse the order of the Board, and remand * * * for a redetermination * * *." 102 F.2d at 118.

We reiterate that in the present case it is sufficient for the rendering of judgment to note that the restriction on Eaves's stock and its minority qualities combine to have some depressing effect, no matter how small, on its value per share. We hold, therefore, that Parker owned more than 80 per cent in value of the corporation's stock, and that any gain on the sale of the depreciable property was properly taxed at ordinary rates. We render judgment for the government.

Reversed and rendered.

PROBLEMS

1. Depreciator is a shareholder of Redepreciation Corporation and owns 20% of its stock. Depreciator's Spouse owns 10% of the stock and his adult Son owns 10%. The remaining stock is owned by unrelated persons. In the current year Depreciator sells to Redepreciation for $110,000 a building used in his business and depreciated on the straight line method with a $40,000 adjusted basis and an $80,000 value and the land underlying it with a $10,000 adjusted basis and $30,000 value. The building will be used in the business of Redepreciation.

(a) What is the amount and character of the gain on the sale?

(b) What result if Spouse owns 20% of the stock, Son owns 20%, and the remaining stock is owned by unrelated persons?

---

4. This entire article is concerned with the inherent disparity of value between controlling and non-controlling shares. Professor Andrews proposes a remedy to allow minority shareholders to share in the premium paid for controlling stock, but that remedy is not part of the law of Louisiana; the article's call for a remedy demonstrates how real the problem is.

(c) What result if Spouse owns 10% of the stock, Spouse's brother owns 10%, Son owns 20% and the remaining stock is owned by unrelated persons?

(d) What result in (b), above, if the sale is made by Other Corporation (in which Depreciator owns 100% of the stock) to Redepreciation Corporation?

(e) What result if the sale is between Depreciator and a trust in which Depreciator's Spouse is the income beneficiary? The trust will rent the property to a third party.

(f) What result in (e), above, if the property was the residence of Depreciator and spouse and they live in a rental apartment after the sale?

(g) Do your answers suggest the purpose and scope of § 1239?

3. RECAPTURE UNDER SECTION 1245

Internal Revenue Code: Sections 64; 1245(a)(1)–(3), (b)(1) and (2), (c), (d). See Sections 179(d)(10); 1041(b); 1222; 1231.

Regulations: Section 1.1245–1(a)(1), (b), (c)(1), (d), –2(a)(1) through (3)(i) and (7), – 6(a).

––––––––

    Section 1245 (as well as Section 1250) is predominantly a *characterization* provision converting what is possibly capital gain to ordinary income. We learn here also that Sections 1245 and 1250 are not merely characterization provisions. As will be discovered later in Chapter 26, they are also *recognition* sections which sometimes require recognition of a gain that otherwise might not be taxed. Thus, both sections have significance beyond the area of characterization into the area of nonrecognition.

    The problem dealt with here comes about as follows: In Sections 167 and 168 Congress has authorized a deduction for depreciation on property used in a trade or business or held for the production of income. Under Section 1016(a)(2), the price paid for such deductions is a reduction of basis. It is a fair price; depreciation deductions are viewed as a tax recovery of cost. If depreciable property is sold at a gain, *quantitatively* the prior depreciation that reduced taxable income is offset at the time of sale by a corresponding increase in the gain on the sale. But Section 1231 enters the picture with respect to property used in a trade or business. If in the year of sale Section 1231 gains exceed such losses, the gain gets capital gains treatment. Gains on property held for the production of income also get capital gain treatment. Whereas the gains are normally *capital gains* the depreciation deductions previously taken reduced *ordinary* income. In this light the come-uppance supposedly fostered by Section 1016 basis adjustments succeeds quantitatively but it has weaknesses *qualitatively*. Historically, and to some extent currently, a taxpayer would gladly have accepted an *ordinary* deduction now at a cost of a corresponding increase in *capital gain* later. The scope of the problem is enlarged by express congressional approval of accelerated depreciation methods, especially under ACRS and so-called bonus depreciation under Section 179. The concept of recapture, the "Gotcha," is the principal congressional answer to this problem. To the extent that the recapture provisions apply they convert what would normally be Section 1231 gain or capital gain to Section 64 ordinary income. The Code sections providing for recapture, the most important of which are Sections 1245 and 1250, are complicated and far from flawless, both from a policy standpoint and with regard to drafting details. The strength of the congressional policy behind the sections is evidenced by the fact that they are made applicable "notwithstanding" any other Code section;[1] they simply override other Code sections, except where the recapture provisions themselves expressly say otherwise.[2]

Section 1245 must of course be carefully examined. Nevertheless, such an examination will be facilitated by a consideration of its scope and purpose as revealed in the legislative history of the section. The Senate Finance Committee Report stated in part:[3]

* * *

In general, the new section provides for the inclusion in gross income (as ordinary income) of the gain from the disposition of certain depreciable property, to the extent of depreciation deductions taken in periods after December 31, 1961, which are reflected in the adjusted basis of such property.

Section 1245. Gain from Dispositions of Certain Depreciable Property

(a) *General Rule*—Paragraph (1) of section 1245(a) provides the general rule that if "section 1245 property" is disposed of, the amount by which the lower of "recomputed basis" or the amount realized (or the fair market value in transactions in which no amount is realized) exceeds the adjusted basis of the property is to be treated as gain from the sale or exchange of property which is neither a capital asset nor property described in section 1231. [Amendments made by TRA (1976) now substitute "ordinary income," defined in Section 64, for this cumbersome phrase. Ed.] The term "disposed of" includes any transfer or involuntary conversion. * * *

Paragraph (2) of section 1245(a), under the bill as passed by the House, defined "recomputed basis" as the adjusted basis of the property recomputed by adding thereto all adjustments, for taxable years beginning after December 31, 1961, reflected in such adjusted basis on account of deductions for deprecia-

---

1. See I.R.C. §§ 1245(d) and 1250(h).

2. See I.R.C. §§ 1245(b) and 1250(d).

3. Sen.Rep. No. 1881, 87th Cong., 2d Sess. (1962), 1962–3 C.B. 703, 984–985. See

Schapiro, "Recapture of Depreciation and Section 1245 of the Internal Revenue Code," 72 Yale L.J. 1483 (1963).

tion, or for amortization * * * whether in respect of the same or other property and whether allowed or allowable to the taxpayer or any other person. Your committee amendments provide that such adjustments shall be added thereto for all periods after December 31, 1961. For example, if a taxpayer, who reports his income on the basis of a fiscal year ending November 30, purchases section 1245 property on January 1, 1962, at a cost of $10,000 and the taxpayer takes depreciation deductions of $2,000 (the amount allowable) before making a gift of the property to his son on October 31, 1962, the son's adjusted basis in the property for purposes of determining gain would, under the provisions of sections 1015 (relating to the basis of property acquired by gift) and 1016 (relating to adjustments to basis), be the same as his father's adjusted basis ($8,000) and the recomputed basis of the property in the son's hands would be $10,000 since the $2,000 of depreciation deductions taken by the father are reflected in the son's basis in the property. Thus, if the son later sells the property during a taxable year of the son beginning after December 31, 1962, for $10,000, he would have $2,000 of gain to which section 1245(a) applies. Moreover, if the son himself takes $1,000 in depreciation deductions (the amount allowable) with respect to the property and then sells it for $10,000, he would have $3,000 of gain to which section 1245(a) applies.

While recomputed basis is determined with respect to adjustments to basis for deductions for depreciation (and for amortization * * *) which were either allowed or allowable, if the taxpayer can establish by adequate records or other sufficient evidence that the amount allowed for any taxable year was less than the amount allowable, the amount to be added for such taxable year is the amount allowed. For example, assume that in the year 1967 it becomes necessary to determine the recomputed basis of property, the adjusted basis of which reflects an adjustment of $1,000 with respect to depreciation deductions allowable for the calendar year 1962. If the taxpayer can establish by adequate records or other sufficient evidence that he had been allowed a deduction of only $800 for 1962, then in determining the recomputed basis, the amount added to adjusted basis with respect to the $1,000 adjustment to basis for 1962 will be only $800.

Paragraph (1) of section 1245(a) further provides that gain is to be recognized notwithstanding any other provision of subtitle A of the 1954 Code. Thus, other nonrecognition sections of the code are overridden by the new section. [See Chapter 26, infra. Ed.] * * *

In the case of a disposition of section 1245 property in which an amount is realized (a sale, exchange, or involuntary conversion), the gain to which section 1245(a) applies is the amount by which the amount realized or the recomputed basis, whichever is lower, exceeds the adjusted basis of the property. In the case of any other disposition, the gain to which section 1245(a) applies is the amount by which the fair market value of the property on the date of disposition or its recomputed basis, whichever is lower, exceeds its adjusted basis. [The recapture bite under Section 1245(a) will be easily understood if it is recognized to be the lower of two alternative amounts—viz:

(1) In case of a sale or exchange or involuntary conversion

Recomputed Basis		Amount Realized
–Adjusted Basis	or	–Adjusted Basis

(2) In case of other dispositions

Recomputed Basis		Fair Market Value
–Adjusted Basis	or	–Adjusted Basis

But carefully check these suggestions against the language of the statute. Ed.]

For example, if section 1245 property has an adjusted basis of $2,000 and a recomputed basis of $3,300 and is sold for $2,900, the gain to which section 1245(a) applies is $900 ($2,900 minus $2,000). If the property is sold for $3,700, the gain is $1,700, of which $1,300 ($3,300 minus $2,000) is gain to which section 1245(a) applies. If, on the other hand, the property is distributed by a corporation to a stockholder in a distribution to which section 1245(a) applies and at a time when the fair market value of the property is $3,100, the gain recognized to the corporation upon such disposition is $1,100 ($3,100 minus $2,000); if the fair market value is $3,800 at the time of such disposition, the gain to which section 1245(a) applies is $1,300 ($3,300 minus $2,000).

* * *

Both the intrinsic nature and the use of property may have a bearing on whether it is subject to Section 1245. Although Congress defines Section 1245 property in Section 1245(a)(3) uncertainties inherent in the definition have been the subject of some of the sharpest criticism leveled at the provision. An aggravation is that Section 1250 property, subject to different recapture rules considered later in this chapter, is defined residually as depreciable realty, other than Section 1245 property.[4] The scope of Section 1245 in this respect is a serious problem for practicing lawyers and accountants.[5] It is not a matter to which law students should address much attention and it is therefore not discussed in detail; but the Senate Finance Committee did state:[6]

4. I.R.C. § 1250(c).

5. See "Depreciation Recapture Revisited: A Critique," 3 Real Property Probate, and Trust Journal, No. 4, Winter (1968).

6. Sen.Rep. No. 1881, supra note 3 at 985–986.

Paragraph (3) of section 1245(a) defines "section 1245 property." Section 1245 property is any property * * * of a type described in subparagraph (A) or (B) of such paragraph (3) which is or has been property of a character subject to the allowance for depreciation provided in section 167. Even though the property may not be subject to the allowance for depreciation in the hands of the taxpayer, such property is nevertheless subject to the provisions of section 1245(a) if the property was subject to the allowance for depreciation in the hands of any prior holder, and if such depreciation is taken into account in determining the adjusted basis of the property in the hands of the taxpayer.

* * * [T]he term "personal property" in subparagraph (A) of section 1245(a)(3) is intended to include not only "tangible personal property" * * * but also intangible personal property.

* * *

Since the enactment of Section 1245 in 1962, the principal changes made in the section which remain a part of the Code have been to extend it to some additional property. Congress added Subsections 1245(a)(3)(C)–(F) to bring in some other types of property. In addition, Subsection 1245(a)(4) now provides special rules for the determination of the recomputed basis of players' contracts for purposes of recapture upon the sale of sports franchises.[7]

The Section 179 bonus depreciation deduction is treated as an amortization deduction for purposes of Section 1245.[8] Furthermore if Section 179 bonus depreciation is taken on property and prior to the end of the property's recovery period the property's use is changed and it is not used predominantly in one's trade or business, the Section 179 bonus depreciation is recaptured as ordinary income in the year of conversion.[9]

Section 1245 is not only a characterization provision. It may force a recognition of gain which, without it, would go unrecognized. But this is not the invariable result; there are some limited exceptions to its application found in § 1245(b). Some of the exceptions will be relevant only as subsequent chapters are considered. In explaining § 1245(b) and (d) the Senate Committee Report stated in part:[10]

Subsection (b) of section 1245 sets forth certain exceptions and limitations to the general rule provided in subsection (a). Paragraph (1) provides that subsection (a) will not apply to a

---

7. Sales of player contracts were subjected to § 1245 gain prior to T.R.A. 1976. Rev.Rul. 67–380, 1967–2 C.B. 291. The provision has the effect of converting additional gain on the sale of a sports franchise to ordinary income to account for the greater of previously unrecaptured depreciation on player contracts acquired at the time of acquisition of the franchise or on player contracts involved in the transfer itself.

8. I.R.C. § 1245(a)(2)(C).

9. I.R.C. § 179(d)(10). Compare Rev. Rul. 69–487 at page 793, infra.

10. Sen.Rep. No. 1881, supra note 3 at 986–988 and 989.

disposition by gift. [See also Section 1041(b)(1). Ed.] Paragraph (2) provides that, except as provided in section 691, subsection (a) will not apply to a transfer at death.

* * *

(d) *Application of Section.*—Subsection (d) of section 1245 provides that the section is to apply notwithstanding any other provision of subtitle A of the code. Thus, section 1245 overrides any nonrecognition provision of subtitle A or any "income characterizing" provision. For example, the gain to which section 1245(a) applies might otherwise be considered as gain from the sale or exchange of a capital asset under section 1231, (relating to property used in the trade or business and involuntary conversions). Since section 1245 overrides section 1231, the gain to which section 1245(a) applies will be treated as ordinary income, and only the remaining gain, if any, from the property may be considered as gain from the sale or exchange of a capital asset if section 1231 is applicable. For example, assume that a taxpayer sells for $130 section 1245 property with an adjusted basis of $40 and a recomputed basis of $100. The excess of the recomputed basis over adjusted basis, or $60, will be treated as gain under section 1245(a). The excess of the selling price over recomputed basis, or $30, may be considered under section 1231 as gain from the sale of a capital asset.

REVENUE RULING 69–487 *
1969–2 Cum.Bull. 165.

An individual taxpayer operating a business as a sole proprietorship converted to personal use an automobile that had been used solely for business purposes. At that time, the fair market value of the automobile was substantially higher than its adjusted basis.

Held, for the purposes of section 1245 of the Internal Revenue Code of 1954, the conversion to personal use is not a "disposition" of the automobile. Accordingly, there is no gain to be recognized by the taxpayer upon the conversion to personal use. However, the provisions of section 1245 of the Code would apply to any disposition of the automobile by the taxpayer at a later date.

PROBLEMS

1. Recap, a calendar year taxpayer, owns a piece of equipment that he uses in his business. The equipment was purchased in 1988 for $100,000, is "5–year property" within the meaning of § 168(c), and Recap has taken the ACRS deductions on it allowed by § 168. Recap did not elect § 179. Assume Recap has no net § 1231 losses in prior years.

---

* See I.R.C. § 179(d)(10) and note 9 at page 792, supra.

(a) What result to Recap if he sells the equipment to Buyer on December 31, 1994 for $30,000?

(b) What difference in result if Recap had elected to use § 179?

(c) What result if as a result of a scarcity of equipment Recap is able to sell the equipment to Desperate for $110,000?

(d) What result to Recap in (a), above, if he had failed to take any depreciation deductions on the equipment? Would he be content to let things be or would he want to seek a refund based on depreciation allowable for prior years?

(e) What result to Recap in (c), above, if in addition he sold some land used for storage in his business for $9,000? He had owned the land for three years and it had a $20,000 adjusted basis.

(f) Same as (e), above, but the sale price of the land is $15,000?

(g) What results in (a), above, if Recap sells the equipment to his wife?

2. Do you see a significant relationship between § 1245(a)(2) and the transferred basis rules of § 1015 and § 1041(b)(2)? Does the statute sanction assignment of "fruit" in these circumstances?

4. RECAPTURE UNDER SECTION 1250

Internal Revenue Code: Section 1250(a)(1)(A) and (B)(v); (b)(1), (3) and (5); (c); (d)(1) and (2); (g); and (h). See Sections 64; 1222; 1231.

Regulations: Section 1.1250–1(a)(1) through (a)(3)(ii); –1(c)(1) and (4); –1(e)(1) and (2); –2(a)(1); –2(b)(1).

———

Section 1245, dealing mainly with personal property, came into the Code in 1962; but it was not until 1964 that Congress enacted Section 1250 which, with substantial differences, first extended the recapture concept to dispositions of real property. The following excerpt from the 1964 Report of the Senate Finance Committee [1] reveals some of the reasons for the delay as well as for the different approach to the realty problem in Section 1250.

* * *

(b) General Reasons for Provisions—Since * * * depreciation deductions are taken against ordinary income while any gain on the sale of the property is treated as a capital gain, there is an opportunity under present law in effect to convert ordinary income into capital gain. This occurs whenever the depreciation deductions allowed reduce the basis of the property faster than the actual decline in its value.

1. Sen.Rep. No. 830, 88th Cong., 2d Sess. (1964), 1964–1 (Part 2) C.B. 505, 635–637.

Congress in the Revenue Act of 1962 recognized the existence of this same problem in the case of gains from the disposition of depreciable machinery and other personal property. In that act, the Congress provided that any gain realized on the sale of these assets in the future would be ordinary income to the extent of any depreciation deductions taken in 1962 and subsequent years with respect to the property.

In the case of real estate, this problem is magnified by the fact that real estate is usually acquired through debt financing and the depreciation deductions allowed relate not only to the taxpayer's equity investment but to the indebtedness as well. Since [under the gross basis concept of *Crane* (Ed.)] the depreciation deductions relate to the indebtedness as well as the equity in the property, this may permit the tax-free amortization of any mortgage on the property. As a result in such cases there is a tax-free cash return of a part of the investment which may in fact enable the taxpayer to show a loss for several years which he may offset against income for tax purposes.

In 1962, Congress did not include real property in the recapture provision applicable to depreciable personal property because it recognized the problem in doing so where there is an appreciable rise in the value of real property attributable to a rise in the general price level over a long period of time. The bill this year takes this factor into account. It makes sure that the ordinary income treatment is applied upon the sale of the asset only to what may truly be called excess depreciation deductions. It does this first by providing that in no event is there to be a recapture of depreciation as ordinary income where the property is sold at a gain except to the extent the depreciation deductions taken exceed the deduction which would have been allowable had the taxpayer limited his deductions to those available under the straight-line method of depreciation.[2] Secondly, a provision has been added which in any event tapers off the proportion of any gain which will be treated as ordinary income so that it disappears gradually over a 10-year holding period for the real estate. As a result, under the bill, no ordinary income will be realized on the sale of real estate held for more than 10 years.[3]

(c) General Explanation of Provisions —In view of the considerations set forth above, the House and your committee

---

2. This is technically incorrect. If property is sold within one year of its acquisition all depreciation deductions are recaptured as ordinary income. See I.R.C. § 1250(b)(1). Ed.

3. Although the statute still speaks in terms of the "applicable percentage" of gain or other tainted amount to be accorded ordinary income treatment, this diminution of the recapture amount is a vanishing concept, as the "applicable percentage" is now almost always *one hundred* percent. See I.R.C. § 1250(a)(1)(B). Ed.

have amended present law to provide that when depreciable real estate is sold after December 31, 1963, in certain cases a proportion of any gain realized upon the sale of the property is to be treated as ordinary income; that is, previous depreciation deductions against ordinary income are to be "recaptured" from the capital gains category.

The bill accomplishes this result by treating as ordinary income a certain percentage of what is called "additional" depreciation or the amount of gain realized on the sale of the property, whichever is smaller. Generally, the "additional" depreciation referred to here is that part of the depreciation deductions which exceeds the depreciation deductions allowable under the straight-line method. The depreciation deductions taken into account, however, are only those taken after December 31, 1963. Thus, they are the excess of any depreciation deductions taken under the double-declining balance method, sum-of-the-years-digits method, or other method of rapid depreciation, over the depreciation which would have been taken under the straight-line method. In the case of property held for 1 year or less, however, the deductions recaptured are to include not only the excess over straight-line depreciation, but rather the entire depreciation deductions taken.

The bill limits the depreciation recapture to the excess over straight-line depreciation because it is believed that only to this extent could the depreciation taken appropriately be considered in excess of the decline in the value of the property which occurs over time. If a gain still occurs, it is believed that this is attributable to a rise in price levels generally rather than to an absence of a decline in the value of the property. The portion representing the rise in value is comparable to other forms of gains which quite generally are treated as capital gains.

* * *

In 1969 and again in 1976 Congress tightened the Section 1250 screws by subjecting additional depreciation on almost all Section 1250 property to a 100 percent applicable percentage.[4] The Economic Recovery Tax Act of 1981 made no mechanical changes in the Section 1250 recapture computation. As a result of the 1986 legislation, real property qualifies only for straight-line depreciation.[5] This makes Section 1250 pretty much a dead letter with respect to property acquired after 1986 because the amount of "additional depreciation" will generally be zero.[6] But that is not always the case; if such real property is held for a period of one year or less, all depreciation allowed is treated as additional depreciation.[7] In addition, Section 1250 is potentially appli-

---

4. I.R.C. § 1250(a)(1)(B)(v). See I.R.C. § 1250(a)(1)(B)(i)–(iv).

5. I.R.C. § 168(b)(3).

6. I.R.C. § 1250(b)(1).

7. Id.

cable to real property depreciated under Section 167 or *old* ACRS using accelerated depreciation.[8] Thus there remains some vitality in the old workhorse; although with the repeal of most preferential treatment for capital gains, Section 1250 now mostly adds a belt to a job already accomplished by suspenders.

PROBLEMS

1. To what extent does § 1250 apply to real property placed in service after 1986?

2. On January 1, 1986 Owner purchased a new residential building for use in his business for $450,000 of which $380,000 was properly allocated to the building and $70,000 to the land. Owner properly elected to use the straight-line method over a 19–year recovery period. On December 31, 1991 (six years later) Owner sold the building for $680,000, of which $580,000 was allocable to the building and $100,000 to the land.

   (a) Disregarding the mid-month convention and assuming a full six year's depreciation, what is the amount and character of Owner's gain on the sale?

   (b) What results in (a), above, if instead the building was depreciated using the 175% declining balance method which was allowed during that period and, as a result, Owner had the following depreciation deductions on the building: 1986: $33,440; 1987: $31,920; 1988: $28,880; 1989: $26,220; 1990: $23,940; 1991: $21,660. At the end of 1991 Owner had total depreciation deductions of $166,060 and an adjusted basis of $213,940 for the building.

   (c) What results in (a) and (b), above, if the building is nonresidential property?

   (d) What *general* differences in the amounts of depreciation and the results if the property in (b), above, was placed in service in 1988 and sold four years later?

5.   OTHER RECAPTURE CONCEPTS

Internal Revenue Code: See Sections 1252; 1254; 1255.

Congress has extended the recapture concept, applying it to assumed past overcharges arising out of deductions other than the depreciation (or related amortization) deduction. Section 1252, which bears

8. We say potentially applicable because the property may have been held for its full useful life and be fully depreciated in which event total accelerated depreciation would not exceed total straight-line depreciation.

For a short period from 1981 to 1986 nonresidential real property depreciated under *old* ACRS using accelerated depreciation was subject to the I.R.C. § 1245(a)(5). This rule was repealed by the 1986 legislation. Pub.Law No. 99–514, 99th Cong., 2d Sess. § 201(d)(11)(D) (1986).

a direct relationship to Section 175 and now repealed Section 182, presents a somewhat simpler recapture rule. Section 175 permits expenditures for soil and water conservation and to prevent soil erosion to be expensed, not merely charged to capital account. Section 182 sometimes accorded similar treatment to expenditures made for the purpose of clearing farm land. Thus, as explained by the Staff of the Joint Committee: [1]

> The current deduction allowed for soil and water conservation expenditures and land clearing expenditures with respect to farm land, combined with the capital gains treatment allowed under prior law on the sale of the farm land permitted high-income taxpayers to convert ordinary income into capital gains. These taxpayers could purchase farm land, deduct these expenditures from their high-bracket nonfarm income, and then receive capital gain treatment on the sale of the farm land.

Under Section 1252, if farm land is sold and it has been held for less than 10 years and has been the subject of deductions from ordinary income under Sections 175 or 182, gain on the sale to the extent of such deductions may be recaptured as ordinary income. [2] If the land has been held for only five years or less, the amount of the Section 175 and 182 deductions fixes the amount of the gain subject to ordinary income treatment. [3] If a sale takes place in the sixth year only 80% of the amount of such deductions is recaptured; and there are corresponding 20% reductions in each succeeding year so that, in effect, Section 1252 becomes inapplicable to land held for more than 10 years. [4]

Section 1254, added by the Tax Reform Act of 1976 and expanded by the 1986 tax legislation taxes as ordinary income some gain on the disposition of oil, gas and mineral property. [5] Section 1254 recaptures two types of deductions with respect to property placed in service after 1986. First, to the extent that prior depletion deductions [6] resulted in a reduction of the adjusted basis of such property, gain on the sale of the property is recaptured as ordinary income. [7] In addition, if intangible drilling and development expenditures on the property, normally capital expenditures, have been expensed (currently deducted) as permitted by Sections 263(c), 616, or 617, the amount of the deductions are also recaptured as ordinary income to the extent of the gain on such property. [8]

Another addition to the growing list of recapture provisions, Section 1255, was added by the Revenue Act of 1978. Under that Act

---

1. General Explanation of the Tax Reform Act of 1969, Staff of the Joint Comm. on Int.Rev.Tax, 95 (1970).

2. I.R.C. § 1252(a)(1).

3. I.R.C. § 1252(a)(1), (3).

4. I.R.C. § 1252(a)(3).

5. I.R.C. § 1254(a)(3).

6. See page 751, supra.

7. I.R.C. § 1254(a)(1)(A)(ii).

8. I.R.C. § 1254(a)(1)(A)(i). Total recapture under both recapture rules cannot exceed the gain on the property. I.R.C. § 1254(a)(1)(B).

Congress also added Section 126, which excludes from gross income certain payments received under a number of federal and state cost-sharing conservation programs. Under Section 1255, if property acquired, improved, or otherwise modified with Section 126 excluded grants is disposed of within 10 years of receipt of the grant, the amount of the grant is potentially recaptured as ordinary income.[9] The amount of recapture is phased out by being reduced by 10 percent per year for each year after the first 10 years; thus there is no recapture on dispositions of property 20 years after receipt of the grant.[10] Both Sections 1254 and 1255 adopt a form that will appear familiar from prior study of Sections 1245 and 1250.

---

9. I.R.C. § 1255(a)(1).

10. I.R.C. § 1255(a)(3). The recapture gain cannot exceed the gain on the property. I.R.C. § 1255(a)(1)(B).

CHAPTER 23. DEDUCTIONS AFFECTED BY CHARACTERIZATION PRINCIPLES

A. BAD DEBTS AND WORTHLESS SECURITIES

Internal Revenue Code: Sections 165(g)(1) and (2); 166(a) through (e); 6511(d) (1). See Sections 62; 111(a); 271(a); 448(d)(5).

Regulations: Sections 1.165–5(a) through (c); 1.166–1(c)–(g), –2(a) and (b), –5(a)–(c).

Reconsider briefly the approach to deductions in general. If a deduction is to be claimed a Code section must specifically provide for it.[1] Even then, it must also be determined whether any other statutory or common law principle disallows or in some manner restricts the deduction.[2] If these hurdles are taken, a question arises whether the deduction can be taken into account in the computation of adjusted gross income.[3] Finally the deduction, like an item of income, must be characterized as capital or ordinary, a process which may affect the other issues raised above.[4] Characterization presents a special problem under the bad debt deduction. As a similar problem arises with respect to the charitable deduction and the deduction for casualty losses to property held for personal use, both are considered in the subsequent parts of this chapter.

HOWARD S. BUGBEE

Tax Court of the United States, 1975.
34 T.C.M. 291.

Memorandum Findings of Fact and Opinion

STERRETT, Judge: The respondent determined a deficiency in petitioner's federal income tax for the taxable year 1966 in the amount of $7,242.68. Other issues having been conceded, the sole remaining issue [1] is whether petitioner has established the existence of a debtor-creditor relationship with respect to funds advanced by petitioner to one Paul Billings and thereby validated his claim to a short-term

---

1. Cf. I.R.C. § 63.

2. See, e.g., I.R.C. §§ 165(f), 262 through 280H.

3. I.R.C. § 62.

4. I.R.C. §§ 1221, 1222.

1. Petitioner also avers respondent has erred in disallowing a medical expense de-duction claimed on the same tax return. However, this disallowance was due solely to the increase in petitioner's adjusted gross income caused by the disallowance of the claimed short-termed capital loss in issue. Petitioner has made no substantive allegations with respect to this disallow-ance.

capital loss under sections 166(a) and 166(d), Internal Revenue Code of 1954.[2]

Findings of Fact

Some of the facts have been stipulated and are so found. The stipulation of facts, together with the exhibits attached thereto, are incorporated herein by this reference.

Petitioner, Howard S. Bugbee (hereinafter petitioner), resided in Honolulu, Hawaii at the time of filing his petition herein. Petitioner filed a "married filing separately" federal income tax return for the taxable year 1966 with the district director of internal revenue at Los Angeles, California.

At all relevant times herein, petitioner was president and majority stockholder of Poop Deck, Inc., a California corporation operating a beer parlor in Hermosa Beach, California. The corporation's other shareholders were petitioner's then spouse Nancy Bugbee and William G. Garbade.

Petitioner first met Paul Billings (hereinafter Billings) at his beer parlor in 1957. Their relationship was first that of proprietor and customer. Over a period of time their friendship grew and they talked of business ventures that Billings might pursue. Billings became godfather to one of petitioner's children.

As a result of their conversations petitioner was impressed with Billings' abilities and thought he could turn his ideas into successful business ventures. Based on this impression, petitioner began to advance money to Billings. These advances were first evidenced by informal notes which were periodically consolidated into larger, more formal notes. There were 11 notes in all representing $19,750 advanced by petitioner to Billings.

These notes were all unconditional, unsecured demand notes signed by Billings between September, 1958 and December, 1960, and evidenced money actually received by Billings from petitioner.[3] The notes provided for interest at a rate of at least 6 percent, however no interest was ever actually paid. Billings has never repaid any part of the principal represented by these notes, although at trial he acknowledged these advances were still outstanding and evidenced an intention to repay them if possible.

2. All statutory references are to the Internal Revenue Code of 1954 as amended, unless otherwise indicated.

3. A typical note provided as follows: $1000.00 September 30, 1959 ON DEMAND after date (without grace). I promise to pay to the order of Howard S. Bugbee One Thousand and no/100 ****** Dollars, for value received with interest at Six per cent per _____ from This Date until paid, interest payable Quarterly both principal and interest payable in lawful money of the United States.

(signed) Paul Billings
Paul Billings
1402 Strand
Hermosa Beach, Calif.

No. _____ Due On Demand.

During this period when the advances were made Billings was unemployed and he was basically unemployed between 1960 and 1966. Although petitioner knew Billings was unemployed between 1958 and 1960, petitioner neither investigated nor did he have any personal knowledge of Billings' financial position.

Billings used the funds received from the petitioner to investigate various business ventures, although in fact much of the money was used by Billings for personal living expenses.

Petitioner was aware of Billings' activities with respect to these ventures, but he did not participate in them. Petitioner's then spouse, Nancy Bugbee, was also aware that petitioner had advanced funds to Billings. Some of her personal funds represented the source of some of these advances. In 1966 petitioner and his spouse were divorced. In the interlocutory judgment of divorce entered June 23, 1966, by which the rights of the parties were established, no mention of the funds advanced by Nancy Bugbee was made.

Petitioner expected to be repaid after Billings established one of these ventures, but such repayment was not conditioned on the success of any of these ventures. Through 1967 petitioner had periodic personal contact with Billings and requested repayment of the notes without success.

Petitioner, on his 1966 tax return, reported a "Personal Bad Debt-Paul Billings" and claimed a $19,750 short-term capital loss. This loss was used in its entirety to offset long-term capital gain recognized that year from other sources. Respondent disallowed this loss as follows:

(b) It is determined that the bad debt deduction which you claimed on your return resulting from loans to Paul Billings is not allowable under Section 166 of the Internal Revenue Code because it has not been established that a debtor-creditor relationship was intended by the loans, the amount of the loans have not been established and it has not been established that the money loaned was your property.

After the trial respondent filed a Motion for Leave to File Amended Answer to Conform the Pleadings to the Proof, pursuant to Rule 41(b) of the Rules of Practice and Procedure of this Court. In this motion respondent asserted that the testimony presented at trial raised the additional issue of whether the claimed bad debts became worthless in 1966. Respondent also filed an Amendment to Answer in which he requested that his original answer be amended to include the above issue of worthlessness as a ground for denying petitioner's claim.

Petitioner objected to this motion arguing that this issue was not raised at trial. Petitioner also objected on the grounds that this issue was not stated in the "Explanation of Adjustments" in the statutory notice received by the petitioner and that it should not be raised at this time. Petitioner asserted that if properly apprised of this issue, additional evidence with respect to it could have been presented at trial. Respondent's motion was denied by this Court.

In his reply brief, respondent has conceded that the amount of the advances has been established, and that the money advanced was the petitioner's property.

Opinion

The case at bar presents for our determination the sole issue of whether petitioner is entitled to claim a short-term capital loss within the terms of sections 166(a) and 166(d)[4] and the accompanying regulations as a result of Billings' failure to repay the funds he had advanced him. Other requirements of these provisions having been previously disposed of, the only remaining factual issue is whether a debtor-creditor relationship existed between Billings and petitioner at the time these advances were made.

To qualify under section 166 there first must exist a bona fide debt which arises from a debtor-creditor relationship based upon a valid and enforceable obligation to pay a fixed and determinable sum of money. Section 1.166–1(c), Income Tax Regs. "Whether a transfer of money creates a bona fide debt depends upon the existence of an intent by both parties, substantially contemporaneous to the time of such transfer, to establish an enforceable obligation of repayment". Delta Plastics Corp., 54 T.C. 1287, 1291 (1970). This determination then is a question of fact to which the substance and not the form of the relationship between petitioner and Billings must be applied. Delta Plastics Corp., supra.

Looking beyond the formal relationship between the petitioner and Billings, respondent has pointed out several factors that he believes amply illustrate his position. Respondent first argues that in reality these advances represented the money necessary to investigate prospective business ventures in which both men would share in the potential profits and as such do not represent loans.

Petitioner's testimony with respect to this matter is not entirely clear. At one point he stated that, if any of these ventures materialized, he "would be a part of it." Later, he stated that, although he expected to be repaid after one of these ventures was established, these advances were personal loans to Billings and that they were to be repaid from whatever sources Billings might have. Billings' testimony is more direct. He clearly stated that these advances were for his personal business ventures and that petitioner was not involved in them. Billings also acknowledged liability for these advances and evidenced an intention to repay if possible. There is also no indication in the record of an agreement under which petitioner would be entitled to share in the profits of any of these ventures. We reject this contention of the respondent.

Respondent next argues that bona fide debts never existed since these advances were worthless when made and petitioner did not have

4. [I.R.C. §§ 166(a) and 166(d) are omitted. Ed.]

a reasonable expectation that they would be repaid. In support respondent points out that during this period Billings was unemployed and had no independent means of support, that the loans were unsecured, that despite the failure of Billings to make interest payments on the first notes additional funds were advanced, that the nature of Billings' proposed ventures was purely speculative, and that petitioner never sought repayment in court.

Respondent does not question the wisdom of these advances. Anyway that determination could only be made with the use of hindsight, which in this instance is not an appropriate tool. As noted earlier our task is to determine the intent of the parties as it existed when the advances were made. Delta Plastics Corp., supra. See Santa Anita Consolidated, Inc., 50 T.C. 536, 554 (1968).

The record in this case does indicate that Billings was in poor financial condition when these advances were made. However this Court has said that this factor does not preclude a finding of the existence of a bona fide debt. Santa Anita Consolidated, Inc., supra, at 553; Richard M. Drachman, 23 T.C. 558 (1954). The use of unsecured notes reflects the nature of the risk involved that petitioner accepted. Any unsecured debt involves some risk, however this factor is not determinative. Santa Anita Consolidated, Inc., supra at 552.

This Court has said, "For the advance to be a loan, it is not necessary that there be an unqualified expectation of repayment." Richard M. Drachman, supra at 562. In the final analysis the repayment of any loan depends on the success of the borrower. "The real differences lie in the debt-creating intention of the parties, and the genuineness of repayment prospects in the light of economic realities", Santa Anita Consolidated, Inc., supra at 552. See also Earle v. W.J. Jones & Son, 200 F.2d 846, 851 (9th Cir.1952).

We have found that petitioner made these advances because he believed Billings could be successful and that he would be subsequently repaid. After a careful review of the record, we believe petitioner's motives were genuine and that they existed throughout the period during which these advances were made.

Respondent maintains that, since Billings was in poor financial condition, in reality any repayment was conditioned on Billings' business success and, since that condition was never fulfilled, there never was an enforceable repayment obligation. For support respondent cites Zimmerman v. United States, 318 F.2d 611 (9th Cir.1963). In that case the taxpayer advanced money to an organization he was initiating. Repayment was to be made out of the dues collected from the members of this new organization. The organization faltered and the taxpayer was not repaid. The court held that the contingent nature of the repayment obligation alone precluded the finding of a bona fide debt. See also Alexander & Baldwin v. Kanne, 190 F.2d 153, 154 (9th Cir. 1951) (repayment " 'only when, if and to the extent that,' after all the indebtedness and liquidation costs of Waterhouse Company had been paid, there remained an excess of assets."); Bercaw v. Commissioner, 165 F.2d 521, 525 (4th Cir.1948), affirming a memorandum decision of this Court (" * * * oral agreement under which petitioner agreed to advance the money necessary to carry on the litigation and the guardian agreed to pay petitioner from any funds recovered * * *.")

The facts in the case at bar do not reveal that any repayments by Billings were conditioned on his ultimate success. Although petitioner expected to be repaid after Billings had established one of his ventures, we have found that petitioner was to be repaid from any assets that Billings might have. Billings himself testified that these advances were personal, unconditional loans for which he was liable.

Respondent finally argues that, since petitioner and Billings were close personal friends, these advances might be classified as gifts. Although the parties were friends, their relationship did not have a long history. There also was no blood relationship, although Billings was named godfather to one of the Bugbee children.

Although the record does not indicate petitioner's financial condition during the period 1958–1960, the divorce decree issued in 1966 only describes assets of moderate value. We do not believe that petitioner's financial condition was such that he could make these advances without expectation of repayment. The facts do not support respondent's contention that these advances were gifts. Commissioner v. Duberstein, 363 U.S. 278 (1960).

We believe that petitioner has established the existence of a debtor-creditor relationship and that respondent's determination must be denied.

Decision will be entered under Rule 155.

NOTE

The best approach to the bad debt deduction is to raise three questions: (1) Is there a debt? (2) Is it a bad debt? (3) Is it a business bad debt?

The first question which is raised in the *Bugbee* case, above, is most likely to arise with respect to individuals, although it has a corporate counterpart. There is a presumption that transfers between relatives or close friends do not constitute loans.[1] For example, if F "lends" $1000 to S, his son, this may or may not give rise to a debt, depending upon the subjective intention of the parties at the time of the "loan" and their ability to overcome the presumption. If there is no intention that the "debt" ever be repaid, that which takes the form of a loan is in fact a gift.[2] Of course, at the outset it makes no difference for income tax purposes, as neither loan nor gift is deductible and neither is income to the recipient. But if a bad debt deduction is later asserted, it

1. See Jacob Grossman, 9 B.T.A. 643, (1927); Carolyn C. Marlett, 35 T.C.M. 456 (1976).

2. See note 1, supra.

cannot be supported unless the original transaction was in fact a loan. The obvious uncertainties inherent in this situation are behind the restrictive treatment accorded nonbusiness debts. When the forerunner of Section 166(d) was enacted in 1942, the committee reports indicated: [3]

> The present law gives the same treatment to bad debts incurred in nonbusiness transactions as it allows to business bad debts. An example of a nonbusiness bad debt would be an unrepaid loan to a friend or relative * * *. This liberal allowance for nonbusiness bad debts has suffered considerable abuse through taxpayers making loans which they do not expect to be repaid. This practice is particularly prevalent in the case of loans to persons with respect to whom the taxpayer is not entitled to a credit for dependents. The situation has presented serious administrative difficulties because of the requirement of proof.

Secondly, as regards the *bad* debt question, gratuitous forgiveness of a loan generates no deduction. A transaction that starts out as a loan may be converted to a mere non-deductible gift. The deduction arises only when the debt becomes uncollectible, "bad". This concept does not require proof of an unsatisfied judgment. The Regulations [4] indicate the degree of pessimism permitted the taxpayer in a determination that a debt is a bad debt.

Finally, the business or nonbusiness dichotomy of Section 166 must be taken into account. Identify the two ways in which a business debt is or may be accorded different treatment from a nonbusiness debt when uncollectibility looms. The somewhat involved residual definition of a nonbusiness bad debt in Section 166(d)(2)(A) and (B) will be better understood having in mind the following fragment of legislative history: [5]

> If a debt at the time it becomes worthless is not directly related to the taxpayer's trade or business, under present law it is treated as a nonbusiness bad debt. This rule is applied even though the debt was related to the taxpayer's trade or business at the time it was created. For example, a taxpayer is not permitted to treat as a business bad debt, which is fully deductible, an account receivable which proves uncollectible after the taxpayer has gone out of business. [See Section 166(d)(2)(B). Ed.]
>
> The bill eliminates this harsh treatment by permitting the taxpayer to deduct as a business bad debt an obligation which becomes worthless, whether or not it is directly related to the trade or business at that time, if it was a bona fide business

---

3. H.Rep. No. 2333, 77th Cong., 1st Sess. (1942), 1942–2 C.B. 372, 408.

4. Reg. § 1.166–2.

5. Sen.Rep. No. 1622, 83rd Cong., 2d Sess., p. 24 (1954).

asset at the time it was created or acquired. [See Section 166(d)(2)(A). Ed.]

A policy reason for the business-nonbusiness bad debt classifications created by Congress in 1942[6] was "to put nonbusiness investments in the form of loans on a footing with other nonbusiness investments."[7] With this reason in mind, the courts have been strict in interpreting the trade or business requirement.[8]

One problem has been that of loans by a shareholder-employee of a corporation to the corporation. In a leading case, Whipple v. Commissioner,[9] the taxpayer, who had for many years been promoting both corporate and noncorporate businesses, formed a corporation in which he was an 80 percent shareholder and subsequently made loans to it. The corporation failed and he attempted to treat the loans as business bad debts. Unsuccessful in the Tax Court[10] and the Court of Appeals,[11] he finally reached the Supreme Court where he fared no better. A corporation's business is of course not that of its shareholder,[12] and the business classification of the loan therefore depended upon the taxpayer's own business. Working from that premise, the Supreme Court said, in part:[13]

> Petitioner, therefore, must demonstrate that he is engaged in a trade or business, and lying at the heart of his claim is the issue upon which the lower courts have divided and which brought the case here: That where a taxpayer furnishes regular services to one or many corporations, an independent trade or business of the taxpayer has been shown. But against the background of the 1943 amendments and the decisions of this Court in the *Dalton, Burnet, duPont* and *Higgins* cases, petitioner's claim must be rejected.

> Devoting one's time and energies to the affairs of a corporation is not of itself, and without more, a trade or business of the person so engaged. Though such activities may produce income, profit or gain in the form of dividends or enhancement in the value of an investment, this return is distinctive to the

---

6. Revenue Act of 1942, § 124(a)(4), 56 Stat. 798, 821 (1942). There is another distinction between business and nonbusiness bad debts. Partially worthless business bad debts are deductible to the extent properly charged off (I.R.C. § 166(a)(2)).

7. Putnam v. Commissioner, 352 U.S. 82, 92, 77 S.Ct. 175 (1956). Cf. Bittker and Eustice, Federal Income Taxation of Corporations and Shareholders, 4–35 n. 121 (5th Ed. Warren Gorham & Lamont 1987). For a consideration of the distinction between property held for investment and property used in a trade or business see Chapter 15 at page 422.

8. In addition to Putnam, supra note 7, see Commissioner v. Smith, 203 F.2d 310 (2d Cir.1953), cert. denied, 346 U.S. 816, 74 S.Ct. 27 (1953).

9. 373 U.S. 193, 83 S.Ct. 1168 (1963).

10. A.J. Whipple, 19 T.C.M. 187 (1960).

11. Whipple v. Commissioner, 301 F.2d 108 (5th Cir.1962).

12. A.J. Whipple, supra note 10 at 192. See Knickerbocker, "What Constitutes a Trade or Business for Bad Debt Purposes: 'Stockholder' as a Business," 23 N.Y.U.Inst. on Fed.Tax. 113 (1965).

13. 373 U.S. 193, 201–203, 83 S.Ct. 1168, 1173–1174 (1962). Footnotes omitted.

process of investing and is generated by the successful operation of the corporation's business as distinguished from the trade or business of the taxpayer himself. When the only return is that of an investor, the taxpayer has not satisfied his burden of demonstrating that he is engaged in a trade or business since investing is not a trade or business and the return to the taxpayer, though substantially the product of his services, legally arises not from his own trade or business but from that of the corporation. Even if the taxpayer demonstrates an independent trade or business of his own, care must be taken to distinguish bad debt losses arising from his own business and those actually arising from activities peculiar to an investor concerned with, and participating in, the conduct of the corporate business.

If full-time service to one corporation does not alone amount to a trade or business, which it does not, it is difficult to understand how the same service to many corporations would suffice. To be sure, the presence of more than one corporation might lend support to a finding that the taxpayer was engaged in a regular course of promoting corporations for a fee or commission, see Ballantine, Corporations (rev.ed. 1946), 102, or for a profit on their sale, see Giblin v. Commissioner, 227 F.2d 692 (C.A.5th Cir.), but in such cases there is compensation other than the normal investor's return, income received directly for his own services rather than indirectly through the corporate enterprise, and the principles of *Burnet, Dalton, duPont* and *Higgins* are therefore not offended. On the other hand, since the Tax Court found, and the petitioner does not dispute, that there was no intention here of developing the corporations as going businesses for sale to customers in the ordinary course, the case before us inexorably rests upon the claim that one who actively engages in serving his own corporations for the purpose of creating future income through those enterprises is in a trade or business. That argument is untenable in light of *Burnet, Dalton, duPont* and *Higgins,* and we reject it. Absent substantial additional evidence, furnishing management and other services to corporations for a reward not different from that flowing to an investor in those corporations is not a trade or business under § 23(k)(4). We are, therefore, fully in agreement with this aspect of the decision below.

Although the courts have held that loans by shareholder-employees are generally nonbusiness, investment-type loans, in some such circumstances business bad debt deductions have been allowed. A shareholder who is an employee of a corporation is engaged in business as an employee.[14] If such a taxpayer makes a loan to his corporation *to*

14. Cf. I.R.C. § 62(a)(1) and (2).

insure his continued employment, the loan may properly be classified as one arising out of the conduct of his trade or business, that of performing services as an employee. In a leading case [15] adopting this rationale, the taxpayer was required by the majority shareholders of the corporation in which he was a minority shareholder to make loans to the corporation in order to retain his employment status. He was discharged later upon his refusal to make further loans. When the corporation subsequently failed and the loans become uncollectible, the taxpayer was allowed a business bad debt deduction.[16]

A loan to a corporation by a shareholder-employee, even if not made to preserve his job, may get business classification if it bears the required proximate relationship to a separate unincorporated business of the taxpayer.[17] In one case,[18] Abe Saperstein who, before his death, owned the Harlem Globetrotters outright, made loans to the now defunct American Basketball League, in which he owned an interest and for which he served, uncompensated, as commissioner. The loans later became worthless. The court held the loans were not mere investments but were proximately related to Mr. Saperstein's separate Globetrotter business. It was enough that the taxpayer had made the loans to the A.B.L. in the hope that it would provide competition and playing sites for the Globetrotter team.

It is generally accepted that business classification turns on the question whether loans are "proximately related" [19] to the taxpayer's trade or business. However the application of this test has not been uniform. The problem is that one can have both investment and business motives for making loans. In such cases is it enough that business is a significant motive for the loan? Or must it be the primary motive?

The Supreme Court has now set the requirement that business be the dominant motive for the loan.[20]

CHARLES J. HASLAM
Tax Court of the United States, 1974.
33 T.C.M. 482.

Memorandum Findings of Fact and Opinion

FORRESTER, Judge: Respondent determined a deficiency in petitioners' Federal income tax for the taxable year 1967 in the amount of

---

15. Trent v. Commissioner, 291 F.2d 669 (2d Cir.1961).

16. Several cases have followed and extended this rationale. See B.A. Faucher, 29 T.C.M. 950 (1970); Maurice Artstein, 29 T.C.M. 961 (1970).

17. In Whipple, supra note 9, the Supreme Court remanded the case to the Tax Court for a determination whether the loans bore the requisite relationship to a

separate real estate business of the taxpayer. The case was settled prior to a decision on remand. See Knickerbocker, supra note 12.

18. Estate of A.M. Saperstein, 29 T.C.M. 916 (1970).

19. Reg. § 1.166–5(b).

20. U.S. v. Generes, 405 U.S. 93, 92 S.Ct. 827 (1972).

$979.01 and a penalty pursuant to section 6651(a)[1] in the amount of $244.75.

The only issue for our decision is whether petitioners are entitled to business or nonbusiness deductions for losses arising from their guarantee of debts of Charles J. Haslam's wholly owned corporation.[2]

Findings of Fact

Some of the facts have been stipulated and are so found.

Petitioners, Charles J. Haslam and Harriet S. Haslam, are husband and wife who, at the time of the filing of the petition herein, resided in Slingerlands, New York. They filed their Federal joint income tax return for 1967 on April 15, 1969, with the district director of internal revenue in Albany, New York.

From 1948 to 1954 Charles J. Haslam (hereinafter referred to as petitioner) was employed by the Dupont Company in their explosives division as a sales and technical representative. Prior to this time, he had worked a great deal with explosives in the army as a captain in the corps of combat engineers, and had received additional training in explosives at Michigan College of Mining and Technology where he received a bachelor of science degree in 1948.

In 1954 petitioner and Earl Canavan (Canavan) established Northern Explosives, Inc. (Northern), a corporation engaged in the sale and distribution of explosives. Petitioner and Canavan each owned 50 percent of the stock in Northern, each having an investment of $10,000.

Petitioner managed the corporate business of Northern and was also employed by the corporation as a salesman, while Canavan took no active part in the corporate operations. Northern had three employees in addition to petitioner, two truck drivers and a part-time secretary.

In 1957, petitioner bought out Canavan's interest in Northern for $10,000, thereafter owning 100 percent of the stock with an investment of $20,000.

In 1960, Northern encountered financial difficulties and required additional cash to continue its operations. Thereafter petitioner guaranteed loans in the total amount of $100,000 made to Northern by the National Commercial Bank and Trust Company of Albany, New York (Commercial). To secure these guarantees petitioner pledged certain marketable securities and his personal residence.

At the time petitioner guaranteed the loans, he was devoting his full time and effort to his employment with Northern. His salary was approximately $250 to $300 per week and, in addition, he received an automobile, funds for its maintenance and insurance, medical insurance, and other employee benefits. With the exception of stock divi-

1. All statutory references are to the Internal Revenue Code of 1954, as amended, unless otherwise specified.

2. Petitioners have conceded that the delinquency penalty imposed by respondent is warranted if there is a deficiency in their income tax for 1967.

dends of $4,000 to $5,000 per year (said dividends from securities of petitioner other than his stock in Northern), petitioner had no other source of income.

Despite the loans to the corporation, Northern continued to experience financial difficulties. The corporation went into chapter XI status under the Federal Bankruptcy Act in 1961, and went bankrupt in 1964. Northern was unable to repay the loans guaranteed by petitioner, and in 1967 Commercial sold the securities pledged by petitioner for $70,464.58. Commercial applied $55,956 of this amount to the debt of Northern guaranteed by petitioner, and the remaining $14,508.58 to petitioner's liability on another debt obligation.

Petitioner remained an employee of Northern until it went bankrupt in 1964. In June 1964 he obtained employment as a salesman of steel castings for Falvey Steel Castings, Inc. (Falvey). Petitioner's gross income from his draw against commissions from Falvey during the years 1964 to 1968 are as follows:

Year	Draw Against Commissions
1964	$ 2,900.00
1965	14,025.00
1966	11,307.00
1967	10,704.06
1968	11,213.42

During the years 1965 and 1966 petitioner's actual earned commissions were only approximately $10,000 per year. Sums petitioner received in excess of these amounts were cash advances against future commissions.

On their joint Federal income tax return for 1967 petitioners claimed a business bad debt in the amount of $55,956 on the loss sustained on petitioner's guarantee of the Northern loans. Respondent disallowed petitioners' claimed loss as a business bad debt, determining that it was deductible only as a nonbusiness bad debt.

Opinion

The sole issue for our decision is whether petitioners are entitled to a business or nonbusiness bad debt deduction for losses arising from their guarantee of debts of a corporation in which petitioner Charles J. Haslam was both an employee and an investor.

A bad debt loss, deductible under section 166, is created where a taxpayer sustains a loss upon payment on the guarantee of a debt, and the debtor is unable to satisfy the guarantor. Putnam v. Commissioner, 352 U.S. 82 (1956); Stratmore v. United States, 420 F.2d 461 (C.A.3, 1970); Estate of Martha M. Byers, 57 T.C. 568, 574 (1972), affirmed per curiam 472 F.2d 590 (C.A.6, 1973); Robert E. Gillespie, 54 T.C. 1025, 1031, affirmed by an unpublished order [72–2 USTC ¶ 9742] (C.A.9,

1972). Thus, petitioners sustained a bad debt loss upon payment of their guarantee of Northern debts subsequent to its bankruptcy.

Under section 166, business bad debt losses are deductible against ordinary income, while nonbusiness bad debt losses are deductible only as short-term capital losses. Petitioners argue that their bad debt loss is deductible as a business bad debt, while respondent argues that it is deductible only as a nonbusiness bad debt.

The character of a bad debt loss is determined by the relationship it bears to the taxpayer's trade or business. A debt will only qualify as a business bad debt if it bears a direct relationship to the taxpayer's trade or business (Hogue v. Commissioner, 459 F.2d 932, 939, fn. 11 (C.A.10, 1972), affirming a Memorandum Opinion of this Court [Dec. 30,733(M)]; Estate of Martha M. Byers, 57 T.C. 568, 577 (1972); Oddee Smith, 55 T.C. 260, 268 (1970), vacated and remanded per curiam 457 F.2d 797 (C.A.5, 1972), opinion on remand 60 T.C. 316 (1973)), and such relationship is a proximate one. I. Hal Millsap, Jr., 46 T.C. 751, 754, fn. 3 (1966), affd. 387 F.2d 420 (C.A.8, 1968); Stratmore v. United States, 420 F.2d 461 (C.A.3, 1970); sec. 1.166–5(b), Income Tax Regs. In the instant case, petitioners argue that their guarantees to Northern bear such a relationship to petitioner's trade or business as an employee of that corporation.

It is clear that being an employee may constitute a trade or business for the purposes of section 166. Trent v. Commissioner, 291 F.2d 669 (C.A.2, 1961); cf. David J. Primuth, 54 T.C. 374 (1970). It is also clear that the debt obligations in the instant case were directly related to petitioner's trade or business as an employee, in that petitioners' guarantees were required for Northern to obtain the funds needed to continue its operations and petitioner's employment. The determination of whether the guarantees were proximately related to petitioner's trade or business as an employee, however, presents a more difficult question, in that petitioner also had an interest in Northern as its sole shareholder. Being an investor in a corporation does not constitute a trade or business, and losses resulting from guarantees made to protect a taxpayer's investment are not deductible as a business bad debt. Whipple v. Commissioner, 373 U.S. 193 (1963).

Where a taxpayer sustains a loss on a guarantee to a corporation in which he has both an employee and stockholder interest, a proximate relationship between the taxpayer's trade or business as an employee and his loss is established only if the taxpayer's dominant motivation in entering into the guarantees was to protect the employee interest. United States v. Generes, 405 U.S. 93 (1972). Petitioners, therefore, must prove that their dominant motivation in guaranteeing the loans to Northern was to protect petitioner's employment in order to establish the requisite proximate relationship.

The determination of taxpayer's dominant motivation is a factual question on which the taxpayer bears the burden of proof. Oddee Smith, 60 T.C. 316, 318 (1973). The trier of fact must determine the taxpayer's overriding reason for incurring the obligation and, in so doing "compare the risk against the potential reward and give proper emphasis to the objective rather than to the subjective." United States v. Generes, supra at 104.

In *Generes* the employee-shareholder had an initial investment of approximately $40,000 in his corporation. He worked six to eight hours a week for the corporation at an annual salary of $12,000, and had full-time employment outside of the corporation as the president of a savings and loan association at an annual salary of $19,000. His annual gross income was approximately $40,000 per year. Other members of the taxpayer's family also had employment and investment interests in the corporation. The Supreme Court held that these factors would not support a finding that the taxpayer's dominant motivation in guaranteeing loans to his corporation was to protect his employment with the corporation. In its holding, the Supreme Court disregarded the taxpayer's testimony that his dominant motivation was related to his employment, determining that his testimony was self-serving and not supported by the facts.

In the instant case, petitioner testified that his dominant motivation in guaranteeing loans to Northern was to protect his employment. It is our conclusion that the facts support his testimony, and accordingly we hold that petitioner's loss is deductible as a business bad debt.

Unlike the taxpayer in *Generes,* petitioner was a full-time employee of his corporation and he had no other employment. His salary from Northern was his major source of income. We note that petitioner's skills as an explosives' expert were not apparently readily marketable and that subsequent to Northern's bankruptcy petitioner obtained employment in a field unrelated to explosives at a salary less than he earned at Northern.

Viewing the facts in the record realistically, we think it much more likely that petitioner was more interested in preserving his position as an employee rather than as an investor in Northern. It is clear that petitioner made the guarantees in the hope of preserving Northern's corporate existence. From his position as an investor, it is clear that the preservation of the corporation would at best afford him some prospect of saving the $20,000 he had invested in the corporation. From his position as an employee however, such preservation would assure petitioner's continued employment at an annual salary of approximately $15,000. In our opinion, an assured salary of $15,000 per year over a period of years was a more valuable interest to petitioner than the mere possibility of recouping the already invested $20,000 in Northern, and the prospect of such continued employment was petitioner's dominant motivation in guaranteeing the loans to Northern. We thus decide the sole remaining issue for petitioner, but because of concessions.

Decision will be entered under Rule 155.

PROBLEMS

1. In year one Lawyer performs legal services for Client and bills him $1000. Client does not pay Lawyer. In year six it becomes evident the debt will never be paid.

>   (a) What else must be known in order to determine whether Lawyer is entitled to a bad debt deduction? Cf. I.R.C. § 448(d)(5). What will the character of any allowed deduction be?

>   (b) Assuming that the Commissioner asserts (and Lawyer cannot show otherwise) that the debt in fact became worthless in year two, is Lawyer's use of the bad debt deduction necessarily foreclosed by the statute of limitations?

>   (c) Assuming Lawyer was allowed a deduction for year six, what tax consequences to Lawyer if in year seven Client inherits some money and pays the $1000 obligation? What consequences upon payment in year seven if Lawyer properly was not allowed the deduction in year six?

2. Without regard to the transactions or events described below, Cher Holder, who is a single taxpayer, has gross ordinary income of $60,000, § 62 and § 63 deductions of $20,000, and taxable income of $40,000 in the current year. Consider together the following further facts and then answer questions (a) through (d) which follow:

>   (1) Cher owns a $5,000 "note" of Flibinite Corporation which she got from the Corporation for a loan of that amount and which is supposed to pay nine percent interest each year. Flibinite goes bankrupt and Cher's "note" is worthless. The Commissioner successfully asserts that Cher's "note" represents an equity contribution to Flibinite. Cher acquired the "note" two years ago.

>   (2) Cher owns common stock in Flibinite which also becomes worthless in the current year. She paid $3,000 for the stock the year before.

>   (3) Two years ago Cher loaned her friend Mooney $2,600. That loan becomes worthless in the current year. (What factors would be considered in determining if the loan created a bona fide debt?) Assume the debt was bona fide.

>   (4) Cher owned some tax exempt state bonds which she purchased for $8,000 four years ago. When they were worth $12,000 they were stolen and Cher received $12,000 in insurance proceeds in the current year.

>   >   (a) To what extent will the above transactions reduce Cher's taxable income for the year?

>   >   (b) What, if any, is Cher's capital loss carryover to the succeeding year?

(c) If, in addition, Cher had sold some stock for $20,000 which she had purchased more than six months earlier for $9,400, what is her taxable income for the current year? (Assume her other § 62 and § 63 deductions are still $20,000).

(d) Assuming the facts of all parts including part (c) in the above problem, must Cher report any income (and if so what character of income) if in the following year Mooney inherits some money and repays her $2,600 obligation to Cher?

B. THE CHARITABLE DEDUCTION

Internal Revenue Code: Sections 170(a)(1), (b)(1)(A), (B), (C), (D), and (F), (b)(2), (c), (e)(1), (2), and (5), (i) and (j); 1011(b). See Sections 67(b)(4); 162(b); 170(d)(1)(A), (f)(1)–(4), (g), (j), (*l*); 501(k).

REVENUE RULING 83–104

1983-2 Cum.Bull. 46.

ISSUE

Is the taxpayer entitled to a deduction for a charitable contribution under section 170 of the Internal Revenue Code in each of the situations described below?

FACTS

In each of the situations described below, the donee organization operates a private school and is an organization described in section 170(c) of the Code. In each situation a taxpayer who is a parent of a child who attends the school makes a payment to the organization. In each situation, the cost of educating a child in the school is not less than the payments made by the parent to the organization.

Situation 1. Organization S, which operates a private school, requests the taxpayer to contribute $400x for each child enrolled in the school. Parents who do not make the $400x contribution are required to pay $400x tuition for each child enrolled in the school. Parents who neither make the contribution nor pay tuition cannot enroll their children in the school. The taxpayer paid $400x to S.

Situation 2. Organization T, which operates a private school, solicits contributions from parents of applicants for admission to the school during the period of the school's solicitation for enrollment of students or while the applications are pending. The solicitation materials are part of the application materials or are presented in a form indicating that parents of applicants have been singled out as a class for solicitation. With the exception of a few parents, every parent who is financially able makes a contribution or pledges to make a contribution to T. No tuition is charged. The taxpayer paid $400x to T, which amount was suggested by T.

Situation 3. Organization U, which operates a private school, admits or readmits a significantly larger percentage of applicants whose parents have made contributions to U than applicants whose parents have not made contributions. The taxpayer paid $400x to U.

Situation 4. Organization V, a society for religious instruction, has as its sole function the operation of a private school providing secular and religious education to the children of its members. No tuition is charged for attending the school, which is funded through V's general account. Contributions to the account are solicited from all society members, as well as from local churches and nonmembers. Persons other than parents of children attending the school do not contribute a significant portion of the school's support. Funds normally come to V from parents on a regular, established schedule. At times, parents are personally solicited by the school treasurer to contribute funds according to their financial ability. No student is refused admittance to the school because of the failure of his or her parents to contribute to the school. The taxpayer paid $40x to V.

Situation 5. Organization W, operates a private school that charges a tuition of $300x per student. In addition, it solicits contributions from parents of students during periods other than the period of the school's solicitation for student enrollments or the period when applications to the school are pending. Solicitation materials indicate that parents of students have been singled out as a class for solicitation and the solicitation materials include a report of W's cost per student to operate the school. Suggested amounts of contributions based on an individual's ability to pay are provided. No unusual pressure to contribute is placed upon individuals with children in the school, and many parents do not contribute. In addition, W receives contributions from many former students, parents of former students, and other individuals. The taxpayer paid $100x to W in addition to the tuition payment.

Situation 6. Church X operates a school providing secular and religious education that is attended both by children of parents who are members of X and by children of nonmembers. X receives contributions from all of its members. These contributions are placed in X's general operating fund and are expended when needed to support all church activities. A substantial portion of the other activities is unrelated to the school. Most members of X do not have children in the school, and a major portion of X's expenses are attributable to its nonschool functions. The methods of soliciting contributions to X from church members with children in the school are the same as the methods of soliciting contributions from members without children in the school. X has full control over the use of the contributions that it receives. Members who have children enrolled in the school are not required to pay tuition for their children, but tuition is charged for the children of nonmembers. Taxpayer, a member of X and whose child attends X's school, contributed $200x to X during the year for X's general purposes.

LAW AND ANALYSIS

Section 170(a) of the Code provides, subject to certain limitations, for the allowance of a deduction for charitable contributions or gifts to or for the use of organizations described in section 170(c), payment of which is made during the taxable year.

A contribution for purposes of section 170 of the Code is a voluntary transfer of money or property that is made with no expectation of procuring a financial benefit commensurate with the amount of the transfer. (See section 1.170A–1(c)(5) of the Income Tax Regulations and H.R.Rep. No. 1337, 83rd Cong., 2d Sess. A44 (1954).) Tuition expenditures by a taxpayer to an educational institution are therefore not deductible as charitable contributions to the institution because they are required payments for which the taxpayer receives benefits presumably equal in value to the amount paid. (See Channing v. United States, 4 F.Supp. 33 (D.Mass), aff'd per curiam 67 F.2d 986 (1st Cir. 1933), cert. denied, 291 U.S. 686 (1934).) Similarly, payments made by a taxpayer on behalf of children attending parochial or other church-sponsored schools are not allowable deductions as contributions either to the school or to the religious organization operating the school if the payments are earmarked for such children. (See Rev.Rul. 54–580, 1954–2 C.B. 97.) However, the fact that the payments are not earmarked does not necessarily mean that the payments are deductible. On the other hand, a charitable deduction for a payment to an organization that operates a school will not be denied solely because the payment was, to any substantial extent, offset by the fair market value of the services rendered to the taxpayer in the nature of tuition.

Whether a transfer of money by a parent to an organization that operates a school is a voluntary transfer that is made with no expectation of obtaining a commensurate benefit depends upon whether a reasonable person, taking all the facts and circumstances of the case into account, would conclude that enrollment in the school was in no manner contingent upon making the payment, that the payment was not made pursuant to a plan (whether express or implied) to convert nondeductible tuition into charitable contributions, and that receipt of the benefit was not otherwise dependent upon the making of the payment.

In determining this issue, the presence of one or more of the following factors creates a presumption that the payment is not a charitable contribution:[1] the existence of a contract under which a taxpayer agrees to make a "contribution" and which contains provisions ensuring the admission of the taxpayer's child;[2] a plan allowing taxpayers either to pay tuition or to make "contributions" in exchange for schooling;[3] the earmarking of a contribution for the direct benefit of a particular individual;[4] or the otherwise-unexplained denial of admission or readmission to a school of children of taxpayers who are financially able, but who do not contribute.

In other cases, although no single factor may be determinative, a combination of several factors may indicate that a payment is not a charitable contribution. In these cases, both economic and noneconomic pressures placed upon parents must be taken into account. The factors that the Service ordinarily will take into consideration, but will not limit itself to, are the following: (1) the absence of a significant tuition charge; (2) substantial or unusual pressure to contribute applied to parents of children attending a school; (3) contribution appeals made as part of the admissions or enrollment process; (4) the absence of significant potential sources of revenue for operating the school other than contributions by parents of children attending the school; (5) and other factors suggesting that a contribution policy has been created as a means of avoiding the characterization of payments as tuition.

However, if a combination of such factors is not present, payments by a parent will normally constitute deductible contributions, even if the actual cost of educating the child exceeds the amount of any tuition charged for the child's education.

HOLDINGS

Situation 1. The taxpayer is not entitled to a charitable contribution deduction for the payment to Organization S. Because the taxpayer must either make the contribution or pay the tuition charge in order for his or her child to attend S's school, admission is contingent upon making a payment of $400x. The taxpayer's payment is not voluntary and no deduction is allowed.

Situation 2. The taxpayer is not entitled to a charitable contribution deduction for the payment to Organization T. Because of the time and manner of the solicitation of contributions by T, and the fact that no tuition is charged, it is not reasonable to expect that a parent can obtain the admission of his or her child to T's school without making the suggested payments. Under these circumstances, the payments made by the taxpayer are in the nature of tuition, not voluntary contributions.

Situation 3. The taxpayer is not entitled to a charitable contribution deduction for contributions to Organization U. The Service will ordinarily conclude that the parents of applicants are aware of the preference given to applicants whose parents have made contributions. The Service will therefore ordinarily conclude that the parent could not reasonably expect to obtain the admission of his or her child to the school without making the transfer, regardless of the manner or timing of the solicitation by U. The Service will not so conclude, however, if the preference given to children of contributors is principally due to some other reason.

Situation 4. Under these circumstances, the Service will generally conclude that the payment to Organization V is nondeductible. Unless contributions from sources other than parents are of such magnitude that V's school is not economically dependent upon parents' contributions, parents would ordinarily not be certain that V's school could provide educational benefits without their payments. This conclusion is further evidenced by the fact that parents contribute on a regular, established schedule. In addition, the pressure placed on parents throughout the personal solicitation of contributions by V's school treasurer further indicates that their payments were not voluntary.

Situation 5. Under these circumstances, the Service will generally conclude that the taxpayer is entitled to claim a charitable contribution deduction of $100x to Organization W. Because a charitable organization normally solicits contributions from those known to have the greatest interest in the organization, the fact that parents are singled out for a solicitation will not in itself create an inference that future admissions or any other benefits depend on a contribution from the parent.

Situation 6. The Service will ordinarily conclude that the taxpayer is allowed a charitable contribution deduction of $200x to Organization X. Because the facts indicate that X's school is supported by the church, that most contributors to the church are not parents of children enrolled in the school, and that contributions from parent members are solicited in the same manner as contributions from other members, the taxpayer's contributions will be considered charitable contributions, and not payments of tuition, unless there is a showing that the contributions by members with children in X's school are significantly larger than those of other members. The absence of a tuition charge is not determinative in view of these facts.

* * *

REVENUE RULING 67–246

1967–2 Cum.Bull. 104.

Advice has been requested concerning certain fund-raising practices which are frequently employed by or on behalf of charitable organizations and which involve the deductibility, as charitable contributions under section 170 of the Internal Revenue Code of 1954, of payments in connection with admission to or other participation in fund-raising activities for charity such as charity balls, bazaars, banquets, shows, and athletic events.

Affairs of the type in question are commonly employed to raise funds for charity in two ways. One is from profit derived from sale of admissions or other privileges or benefits connected with the event at such prices as their value warrants. Another is through the use of the affair as an occasion for solicitation of gifts in combination with the sale of the admissions or other privileges or benefits involved. In cases of the latter type the sale of the privilege or benefit is combined with solicitation of a gift or donation of some amount in addition to the sale value of the admission or privilege.

The need for guidelines on the subject is indicated by the frequency of misunderstanding of the requirements for deductibility of such payments and increasing incidence of their erroneous treatment for income tax purposes.

In particular, an increasing number of instances are being reported in which the public has been erroneously advised in advertisements or solicitations by sponsors that the entire amounts paid for tickets or other privileges in connection with fund-raising affairs for charity are deductible. Audits of returns are revealing other instances of erroneous advice and misunderstanding as to what, if any, portion of such payments is deductible in various circumstances. There is evidence also of instances in which taxpayers are being misled by questionable solicitation practices which make it appear from the wording of the solicitation that taxpayer's payment is a "contribution," whereas the payment solicited is simply the purchase price of an item offered for sale by the organization.

Section 170 of the Code provides for allowance of deductions for charitable contributions, subject to certain requirements and limitations. To the extent here relevant a charitable contribution is defined by that section as "a contribution or gift to or for the use of" certain specified types of organizations.

To be deductible as a charitable contribution for Federal income tax purposes under section 170 of the Code, a payment to or for the use of a qualified charitable organization must be a gift. To be a gift for such purposes in the present context there must be, among other requirements, a payment of money or transfer of property without adequate consideration.

As a general rule, where a transaction involving a payment is in the form of a purchase of an item of value, the presumption arises that no gift has been made for charitable contribution purposes, the presumption being that the payment in such case is the purchase price.

Thus, where consideration in the form of admissions or other privileges or benefits is received in connection with payments by patrons of fund-raising affairs of the type in question, the presumption is that the payments are not gifts. In such case, therefore, if a charitable contribution deduction is claimed with respect to the payment, the burden is on the taxpayer to establish that the amount paid is not the purchase price of the privileges or benefits and that part of the payment, in fact, does qualify as a gift.

In showing that a gift has been made, an essential element is proof that the portion of the payment claimed as a gift represents the excess of the total amount paid over the value of the consideration received therefor. This may be established by evidence that the payment exceeds the fair market value of the privileges or other benefits received by the amount claimed to have been paid as a gift.

Another element which is important in establishing that a gift was made in such circumstances, is evidence that the payment in excess of the value received was made with the intention of making a gift. While proof of such intention may not be an essential requirement under all circumstances and may sometimes be inferred from surrounding circumstances, the intention to make a gift is, nevertheless, highly relevant in overcoming doubt in those cases in which there is a question whether an amount was in fact paid as a purchase price or as a gift.

Regardless of the intention of the parties, however, a payment of the type in question can in any event qualify as a deductible gift only to the extent that it is shown to exceed the fair market value of any consideration received in the form of privileges or other benefits.

In those cases in which a fund-raising activity is designed to solicit payments which are intended to be in part a gift and in part the purchase price of admission to or other participation in an event of the type in question, the organization conducting the activity should employ procedures which make clear not only that a gift is being solicited in connection with the sale of the admissions or other privileges related to the fund-raising event, but, also the amount of the gift being solicited. To do this, the amount properly attributable to the purchase of admissions or other privileges and the amount solicited as a gift should be determined in advance of solicitation. The respective amounts should be stated in making the solicitation and clearly indicated on any ticket, receipt, or other evidence issued in connection with the payment.

In making such a determination, the full fair market value of the admission and other benefits or privileges must be taken into account. Where the affair is reasonably comparable to events for which there are established charges for admission, such as theatrical or athletic performances, the established charges should be treated as fixing the fair market value of the admission or privilege. Where the amount paid is the same as the standard admission charge there is, of course, no deductible contribution, regardless of the intention of the parties. Where the event has no such counterpart, only that portion of the payment which exceeds a reasonable estimate of the fair market value of the admission or other privileges may be designated as a charitable contribution.

The fact that the full amount or a portion of the payment made by the taxpayer is used by the organization exclusively for charitable purposes has no bearing upon the determination to be made as to the value of the admission or other privileges and the amount qualifying as a contribution.

Also, the mere fact that tickets or other privileges are not utilized does not entitle the patron to any greater charitable contribution deduction than would otherwise be allowable. The test of deductibility is not whether the right to admission or privileges is exercised but whether the right was accepted or rejected by the taxpayer. If a patron desires to support an affair, but does not intend to use the tickets or exercise the other privileges being offered with the event, he can make an outright gift of the amount he wishes to contribute, in which event he would not accept or keep any ticket or other evidence of any of the privileges related to the event connected with the solicitation.

The foregoing summary is not intended to be all inclusive of the legal requirements relating to deductibility of payments as charitable contributions for Federal income tax purposes. Neither does it attempt to deal with many of the refinements and distinctions which sometimes arise in connection with questions of whether a gift for such purposes has been made in particular circumstances.

The principles stated are intended instead to summarize with as little complexity as possible, those basic rules which govern deductibility of payments in the majority of the circumstances involved. They have their basis in section 170 of the Code, the regulations thereunder, and in court decisions. The observance of these provisions will provide greater assurance to taxpayer contributors that their claimed deductions in such cases are allowable.

Where it is disclosed that the public or the patrons of a fund-raising affair for charity have been erroneously informed concerning the extent of the deductibility of their payments in connection with the affair, it necessarily follows that all charitable contribution deductions claimed with respect to payments made in connection with the particular event or affair will be subject to special scrutiny and may be questioned in audit of returns.

In the following examples application of the principles discussed above is illustrated in connection with various types of fund-raising activities for charity. Again, the examples are drawn to illustrate the general rules involved without attempting to deal with distinctions that sometimes arise in special situations. In each instance, the charitable organization involved is assumed to be an organization previously determined to be qualified to receive deductible charitable contributions under section 170 of the Code, and the references to deductibility are to deductibility as charitable contributions for Federal income tax purposes.

Example 1:

The *M* Charity sponsors a symphony concert for the purpose of raising funds for *M*'s charitable programs. *M* agrees to pay a fee which is calculated to reimburse the symphony for hall rental, musicians' salaries, advertising costs, and printing of tickets. Under the agreement, *M* is entitled to all receipts from ticket sales. *M* sells tickets to the concert charging $5 for balcony seats and $10 for orchestra circle seats. These prices approximate the established admission charges for concert performances by the symphony orchestra. The tickets to the concert and the advertising material promoting ticket sales emphasize that the concert is sponsored by, and is for the benefit of *M* Charity.

Notwithstanding the fact that taxpayers who acquire tickets to the concert may think they are making a charitable contribution to or for the benefit of *M* Charity, no part of the payments made is deductible as a charitable contribution for Federal income tax purposes. Since the payments approximate the established admission charge for similar events, there is no gift. The result would be the same even if the advertising materials promoting ticket sales stated that amounts paid for tickets are "tax deductible" and tickets to the concert were purchased in reliance upon such statements. Acquisition of tickets or other privileges by a taxpayer in reliance upon statements made by a charitable organization that the amounts paid are deductible does not convert an otherwise nondeductible payment into a deductible charitable contribution.

Example 2:

The facts are the same as in *Example 1*, except that the *M* Charity desires to use the concert as an occasion for the solicitation of gifts. It indicates that fact in its advertising material promoting the event, and fixes the payments solicited in connection with each class of admission at $30 for orchestra circle seats and $15 for balcony seats. The advertising and the tickets clearly reflect the fact that the established admission charges for comparable performances by the symphony orchestra are $10 for orchestra circle seats and $5 for balcony seats, and that only the excess of the solicited amounts paid in connection with admission to the concert over the established prices is a contribution to *M*.

Under these circumstances a taxpayer who makes a payment of $60 and receives two orchestra circle seat tickets can show that his payment exceeds the established admission charge for similar tickets to comparable performances of the symphony orchestra by $40. The circumstances also confirm that that amount of the payment was solicited as, and intended to be, a gift to *M* Charity. The $40, therefore, is deductible as a charitable contribution.

* * *

HERNANDEZ v. COMMISSIONER *

Supreme Court of the United States, 1989.**
490 U.S. 680, 109 S.Ct. 2136.

Justice MARSHALL delivered the opinion of the Court.

Section 170 of the Internal Revenue Code of 1954, 26 U.S.C. § 170 (Code), permits a taxpayer to deduct from gross income the amount of a "charitable contribution." The Code defines that term as a "contribution or gift" to certain eligible donees, including entities organized and

---

* See "The Supreme Court, 1988 Term," 103 Harv.L.Rev. 40, 361 (1989), and see Stewart, Gardner, and Duncan, "*Hernandez* and *Davis*: Has the U.S. Supreme Court Resolved the Controversy Involving Charitable Contributions?" 15 Rev.Tax'n of Ind. 39 (1991).

** Some footnotes omitted.

operated exclusively for religious purposes. We granted certiorari to determine whether taxpayers may deduct as charitable contributions payments made to branch churches of the Church of Scientology (Church) in order to receive services known as "auditing" and "training." We hold that such payments are not deductible.

I

Scientology was founded in the 1950's by L. Ron Hubbard. It is propagated today by a "mother church" in California and by numerous branch churches around the world. The mother church instructs laity, trains and ordains ministers, and creates new congregations. Branch churches, known as "franchises" or "missions," provide Scientology services at the local level, under the supervision of the mother church. Church of Scientology of California v. Commissioner, 823 F.2d 1310, 1313 (CA9 1987), cert. denied, 486 U.S. 1015, 108 S.Ct. 1752 (1988).

Scientologists believe that an immortal spiritual being exists in every person. A person becomes aware of this spiritual dimension through a process known as "auditing." [2] Auditing involves a one-to-one encounter between a participant (known as a "preclear") and a Church official (known as an "auditor"). An electronic device, the E-meter, helps the auditor identify the preclear's areas of spiritual difficulty by measuring skin responses during a question and answer session. Although auditing sessions are conducted one-on-one, the content of each session is not individually tailored. The preclear gains spiritual awareness by progressing through sequential levels of auditing, provided in short blocks of time known as "intensives." 83 T.C. 575, 577 (1984), aff'd, 822 F.2d 844 (CA9 1987).

The Church also offers members doctrinal courses known as "training." Participants in these sessions study the tenets of Scientology and seek to attain the qualifications necessary to serve as auditors. Training courses, like auditing sessions, are provided in sequential levels. Scientologists are taught that spiritual gains result from participation in such courses. 83 T.C., at 577.

The Church charges a "fixed donation," also known as a "price" or a "fixed contribution," for participants to gain access to auditing and training sessions. These charges are set forth in schedules and prices vary with a session's length and level of sophistication. In 1972, for example, the general rates for auditing ranged from $625 for a 12½-hour auditing intensive, the shortest available, to $4,250 for a 100-hour intensive, the longest available. Specialized types of auditing required higher fixed donations: a 12½-hour "Integrity Processing" auditing intensive cost $750; a 12½-hour "Expanded Dianetics" auditing intensive cost $950. This system of mandatory fixed charges is based on a central tenet of Scientology known as the "doctrine of exchange," according to which any time a person receives something he must pay

---

2. Auditing is also known as "processing," "counseling," and "pastoral counsel-ing." 83 T.C. 575, 577 (1984), aff'd, 822 F.2d 844 (CA9 1987).

something back. Id., at 577–578. In so doing, a Scientologist maintains "inflow" and "outflow" and avoids spiritual decline. 819 F.2d 1212, 1222 (CA1 1987).

The proceeds generated from auditing and training sessions are the Church's primary source of income. The Church promotes these sessions not only through newspaper, magazine, and radio advertisements, but also through free lectures, free personality tests, and leaflets. The Church also encourages, and indeed rewards with a 5% discount, advance payment for these sessions. 822 F.2d, at 847. The Church often refunds unused portions of prepaid auditing or training fees, less an administrative charge.

The petitioners in these consolidated cases each made payments to a branch church for auditing or training sessions. They sought to deduct these payments on their federal income tax returns as charitable contributions under § 170. Respondent Commissioner of the Internal Revenue Service (Commissioner or IRS) disallowed these deductions, finding that the payments were not charitable contributions within the meaning of § 170.

. . . Before trial, the Commissioner stipulated that the branch churches of Scientology are religious organizations entitled to receive tax-deductible charitable contributions under the relevant sections of the Code. This stipulation isolated as the sole statutory issue whether payments for auditing or training sessions constitute "contribution[s] or gift[s]" under § 170.[4]

. . . [T]he [Tax] [C]ourt upheld the Commissioner's decision. 83 T.C. 575 (1984). It observed first that the term "charitable contribution" in § 170 is synonymous with the word "gift," which case law had defined "as a *voluntary transfer* of property by the owner to another *without consideration* therefor." Id., at 580, quoting DeJong v. Commissioner, 36 T.C. 896, 899 (1961) (emphasis in original) aff'd, 309 F.2d 373 (CA9 1962). It then determined that petitioners had received consideration for their payments, namely, "the benefit of various religious services provided by the Church of Scientology." 83 T.C., at 580.

. . .

The Court of Appeals for the First Circuit in petitioner Hernandez' case, and for the Ninth Circuit in Graham, Hermann, and Maynard's

---

4. The stipulation allowed the Tax Court to avoid having to decide whether the particular branches to which payments were made in these cases qualified under § 170(c)(2) and § 501(c)(3) of the Code as tax-exempt organizations entitled to receive charitable contributions. In a separate case decided during the pendency of this litigation, the Tax Court held that the mother church in California did not qualify as a tax-exempt organization under § 501(c)(3) for the years 1970 through 1972 because it had diverted profits to its founder and others, had conspired to impede collection of its taxes, and had conducted almost all activities for a commercial purpose. Church of Scientology of California v. Commissioner, 83 T.C. 381 (1984). The Court of Appeals for the Ninth Circuit affirmed, basing its decision solely on the ground that the Church had diverted profits for the use of private individuals. It did not address the other bases of the Tax Court's decision. Church of Scientology of California v. Commissioner of Internal Revenue, 823 F.2d 1310 (CA9 1987), cert. denied, 486 U.S. 1015, 108 S.Ct. 1752 (1988).

case, affirmed. The First Circuit rejected Hernandez' argument that under § 170, the IRS' ordinary inquiry into whether the taxpayer received consideration for his payment should not apply to "the return of a commensurate *religious* benefit, as opposed to an *economic or financial* benefit." 819 F.2d, at 1217 (emphasis in original). The court found "no indication that Congress intended to distinguish the religious benefits sought by Hernandez from the medical, educational, scientific, literary, or other benefits that could likewise provide the *quid* for the *quo* of a nondeductible payment to a charitable organization." Ibid. The court also rejected Hernandez' argument that it was impracticable to put a value on the services he had purchased, noting that the Church itself had "established and advertised monetary prices" for auditing and training sessions, and that Hernandez had not claimed that these prices misstated the cost of providing these sessions. Id., at 1218.

* * *

We granted certiorari, 485 U.S. 1005, 108 S.Ct. 1467 (1988); 486 U.S. 1022, 108 S.Ct. 1994 (1988), to resolve a circuit conflict concerning the validity of charitable deductions for auditing and training payments.[5] We now affirm.

II

For over 70 years, federal taxpayers have been allowed to deduct the amount of contributions or gifts to charitable, religious, and other eleemosynary institutions. See 2 B. Bittker, Federal Taxation of Income, Estates and Gifts ¶ 35.1.1 (1981) (tracing history of charitable deduction). Section 170, the present provision, was enacted in 1954; it requires a taxpayer claiming the deduction to satisfy a number of conditions. The Commissioner's stipulation in this case, however, has narrowed the statutory inquiry to one such condition: whether petitioners' payments for auditing and training sessions are "contribution[s] or gift[s]" within the meaning of § 170.

The legislative history of the "contribution or gift" limitation, though sparse, reveals that Congress intended to differentiate between unrequited payments to qualified recipients and payments made to such recipients in return for goods or services. Only the former were deemed deductible. The House and Senate Reports on the 1954 tax bill, for example, both define "gifts" as payments "made with no expectation of a financial return commensurate with the amount of the gift." S.Rep. No. 1622, 83d Cong., 2d Sess., 196 (1954); H.R.Rep. No. 1337, 83d Cong., 2d Sess., A44 (1954). Using payments to hospitals as an example, both Reports state that the gift characterization should not

---

5. Compare Christiansen v. Commissioner of Internal Revenue, 843 F.2d 418 (CA10 1988), (holding payments not deductible) cert. pending, No. 87–2023; Miller v. IRS, 829 F.2d 500 (CA4 1987) (same), cert. pending, No. 87–1449 with Neher v. Commissioner of Internal Revenue, 852 F.2d 848 (CA6 1988) (holding payments deducti-ble); Foley v. Commissioner of Internal Revenue, 844 F.2d 94 (CA2 1988) (same), cert. pending, No. 88–102; Staples v. Commissioner of Internal Revenue, 821 F.2d 1324 (CA8 1987) (same), cert. pending, No. 87–1382. The rulings for the taxpayer in the *Neher, Foley,* and *Staples* cases rested on statutory, not constitutional, grounds.

apply to "a payment by an individual to a hospital *in consideration of* a binding obligation to provide medical treatment for the individual's employees.　It would apply only if there were no expectation of any quid pro quo from the hospital."　S.Rep. No. 1622, supra, at 196 (emphasis added); H.Rep. No. 1337, supra, at A44 (emphasis added).[7]

In ascertaining whether a given payment was made with "the expectation of any quid pro quo," S.Rep. No. 1622, supra, at 196; H.Rep. No. 1337, supra, at A44, the Internal Revenue Service (IRS) has customarily examined the external features of the transaction in question.　This practice has the advantage of obviating the need for the IRS to conduct imprecise inquiries into the motivations of individual taxpayers.　The lower courts have generally embraced this structural analysis. . . .　We likewise focused on external features in United States v. American Bar Endowment, 477 U.S. 105, 106 S.Ct. 2426 (1986), to resolve the taxpayers' claims that they were entitled to partial deductions for premiums paid to a charitable organization for insurance coverage; the taxpayers contended that they had paid unusually high premiums in an effort to make a contribution along with their purchase of insurance.　We upheld the Commissioner's disallowance of the partial deductions because the taxpayers had failed to demonstrate, at a minimum, the existence of comparable insurance policies with prices lower than those of the policy they had each purchased.　In so doing, we stressed that "[t]he *sine qua non* of a charitable contribution is a transfer of money or property *without adequate consideration*."　Id., at 118, 106 S.Ct., at 2434 (emphasis added in part).

In light of this understanding of § 170, it is readily apparent that petitioners' payments to the Church do not qualify as "contribution[s] or gift[s]."　As the Tax Court found, these payments were part of a quintessential *quid pro quo* exchange: in return for their money, petitioners received an identifiable benefit, namely, auditing and training sessions.　The Church established fixed price schedules for auditing and training sessions in each branch church; it calibrated particular prices to auditing or training sessions of particular lengths and levels of sophistication; it returned a refund if auditing and training services went unperformed; it distributed "account cards" on which persons who had paid money to the Church could monitor what prepaid services they had not yet claimed; and it categorically barred provision of auditing or training sessions for free.　Each of these practices reveals the inherently reciprocal nature of the exchange.

Petitioners do not argue that such a structural analysis is inappropriate under § 170, or that the external features of the auditing and training transactions do not strongly suggest a *quid pro quo* exchange.

---

7. The portions of these Reports explicating the term "gifts" actually address a closely related provision of the Code, § 162(b), which refers specifically to § 170. Section 162(b) provides, in pertinent part, that a taxpayer may not deduct as a trade or business expense a "contribution or gift" which would have been deductible under § 170 were it not for the fact that the taxpayer had already met the maximum amount (measured as a percentage of income) which § 170(b) permits to be deducted.

Indeed, the petitioners in the consolidated *Graham* case conceded at trial that they expected to receive specific amounts of auditing and training in return for their payments. 822 F.2d, at 850. Petitioners argue instead that they are entitled to deductions because a *quid pro quo* analysis is inappropriate under § 170 when the benefit a taxpayer receives is purely religious in nature. Along the same lines, petitioners claim that payments made for the right to participate in a religious service should be automatically deductible under § 170.

We cannot accept this statutory argument for several reasons. First, it finds no support in the language of § 170. Whether or not Congress could, consistent with the Establishment Clause, provide for the automatic deductibility of a payment made to a church that either generates religious benefits or guarantees access to a religious service, that is a choice Congress has thus far declined to make. Instead, Congress has specified that a payment to an organization operated exclusively for religious (or other eleemosynary) purposes is deductible *only* if such a payment is a "contribution or gift." 26 U.S.C. § 170(c). The Code makes no special preference for payments made in the expectation of gaining religious benefits or access to a religious service. Foley v. Commissioner of Internal Revenue, 844 F.2d 94, 98 (CA2 1988) (Newman, J., dissenting), cert. pending, No. 88–102. The House and Senate Reports on § 170, and the other legislative history of that provision, offer no indication that Congress' failure to enact such a preference was an oversight.

Second, petitioners' deductibility proposal would expand the charitable contribution deduction far beyond what Congress has provided. Numerous forms of payments to eligible donees plausibly could be categorized as providing a religious benefit or as securing access to a religious service. For example, some taxpayers might regard their tuition payments to parochial schools as generating a religious benefit or as securing access to a religious service; such payments, however, have long been held not to be charitable contributions under § 170. 844 F.2d, at 98, citing Winters v. Commissioner of Internal Revenue, 468 F.2d 778 (CA2 1972); see id., at 781 (noting Congress' refusal to enact legislation permitting taxpayers to deduct parochial school tuition payments). Taxpayers might make similar claims about payments for church-sponsored counseling sessions or for medical care at church-affiliated hospitals that otherwise might not be deductible. Given that, under the First Amendment, the IRS can reject otherwise valid claims of religious benefit only on the ground that a taxpayers' alleged beliefs are not sincerely held, but not on the ground that such beliefs are inherently irreligious, see United States v. Ballard, 322 U.S. 78, 64 S.Ct. 882, 88 L.Ed. 1148 (1944), the resulting tax deductions would likely expand the charitable contribution provision far beyond its present size. We are loath to effect this result in the absence of supportive congressional intent. Cf. United States v. Lee, 455 U.S. 252, 259–261, 102 S.Ct. 1051, 1056–1057 (1982).

* * *

Accordingly, we conclude that petitioners' payments to the Church for auditing and training sessions are not "contribution[s] or gift[s]" within the meaning of that statutory expression.[10]

* * *

V

For the reasons stated herein, the judgments of the Courts of Appeals are hereby

Affirmed.

Justice BRENNAN and Justice KENNEDY took no part in the consideration or decision of these cases.

Justice O'CONNOR, with whom Justice SCALIA joins, dissenting.

The Court today acquiesces in the decision of the Internal Revenue Service (IRS) to manufacture a singular exception to its 70–year practice of allowing fixed payments indistinguishable from those made by petitioners to be deducted as charitable contributions. Because the IRS cannot constitutionally be allowed to select which religions will receive the benefit of its past rulings, I respectfully dissent.

The cases before the Court have an air of artificiality about them that is due to the IRS' dual litigation strategy against the Church of Scientology. As the Court notes, . . . the IRS has successfully argued that the mother Church of Scientology was not a tax-exempt organization from 1970 to 1972 because it had diverted profits to the founder of Scientology and others, conspired to impede collection of its taxes, and conducted almost all of its activities for a commercial purpose. See Church of Scientology of California v. Commissioner, 83 T.C. 381 (1984), aff'd, 823 F.2d 1310 (CA9 1987), cert. denied, 486 U.S. 1015, 108 S.Ct. 1752 (1988). In the cases before the Court today, however, the IRS decided to contest the payments made to Scientology under 26 U.S.C. § 170 rather than challenge the tax-exempt status of the various branches of the Church to which the payments were made. According to the Solicitor General, the IRS challenged the payments themselves in order to expedite matters. . . . See also Neher v. Commissioner, 852 F.2d 848, 850–851 (CA6 1988). As part of its litigation strategy in these cases, the IRS agreed to several stipulations which, in my view, necessarily determine the proper approach to the questions presented by petitioners.

The stipulations . . . established that Scientology was at all relevant times a religion; that each Scientology branch to which payments were made was at all relevant times a "church" within the meaning of § 170(b)(1)(A)(i); and that Scientology was at all times a "corporation" within the meaning of § 170(c)(2) and exempt from

---

10. Petitioners have not argued here that their payments qualify as "dual payments" under IRS regulations and that they are therefore entitled to a partial deduction to the extent their payments exceeded the value of the benefit received. See American Bar Endowment, 477 U.S., at 117, 106 S.Ct., at 2433 (citing Rev.Rul. 67–246, 1967–2 Cum.Bull. 104). We thus have no occasion to decide this issue.

general income taxation under 26 U.S.C. § 501(a). See . . . 83 T.C. 575, 576 (1984), aff'd, 822 F.2d 844 (CA9 1987). As the Solicitor General recognizes, it follows from these stipulations that Scientology operates for " 'charitable purposes' " and puts the "public interest above the private interest." Brief for United States 30. See also *Neher,* 852 F.2d, at 855. Moreover, the stipulations establish that the payments made by petitioners are fixed donations made by individuals to a tax-exempt religious organization in order to participate in religious services, and are not based on "market prices set to reap the profits of a commercial money-making venture." Staples v. Commissioner, 821 F.2d 1324, 1328 (CA8 1987), cert. pending, No. 87–1382. The Tax Court, however, appears to have ignored the stipulations. It concluded, perhaps relying on its previous opinion in *Church of Scientology,* that "Scientology operates in a commercial manner in providing [auditing and training]. In fact, one of its articulated goals is to make money." 83 T.C., at 578. The Solicitor General has duplicated the error here, referring on numerous occasions to the commercial nature of Scientology in an attempt to negate the effect of the stipulations. . . .

It must be emphasized that the IRS' position here is *not* based upon the contention that a portion of the knowledge received from auditing or training is of secular, commercial, nonreligious value. Thus, the denial of a deduction in these cases bears no resemblance to the denial of a deduction for religious-school tuition up to the market value of the secularly useful education received. See Oppewal v. Commissioner, 468 F.2d 1000 (CA1 1972); Winters v. Commissioner, 468 F.2d 778 (CA2 1972); DeJong v. Commissioner, 309 F.2d 373 (CA9 1962). Here the IRS denies deductibility solely on the basis that the exchange is a *quid pro quo,* even though the *quid* is exclusively of spiritual or religious worth. The Government cites no instances in which this has been done before, and there are good reasons why.

When a taxpayer claims as a charitable deduction part of a fixed amount given to a charitable organization in exchange for benefits that have a commercial value, the allowable portion of that claim is computed by subtracting from the total amount paid the value of the physical benefit received. If at a charity sale one purchases for $1,000 a painting whose market value is demonstrably no more than $50, there has been a contribution of $950. The same would be true if one purchases a $1,000 seat at a charitable dinner where the food is worth $50. An identical calculation can be made where the *quid* received is not a painting or a meal, but an intangible such as entertainment, so long as that intangible has some market value established in a noncontributory context. Hence, one who purchases a ticket to a concert, at the going rate for concerts by the particular performers, makes a charitable contribution of zero even if it is announced in advance that all proceeds from the ticket sales will go to charity. The performers may have made a charitable contribution, but the audience has paid the going rate for a show.

It becomes impossible, however, to compute the "contribution" portion of a payment to a charity where what is received in return is not merely an intangible, but an intangible (or, for that matter a tangible) that is not bought and sold except in donative contexts so that the only "market" price against which it can be evaluated is a market price that always includes donations. Suppose, for example, that the charitable organization that traditionally solicits donations on Veterans' Day, in exchange for which it gives the donor an imitation poppy bearing its name, were to establish a flat rule that no one gets a poppy without a donation of at least $10. One would have to say that the "market" rate for such poppies was $10, but it would assuredly not be true that everyone who "bought" a poppy for $10 made no contribution. Similarly, if one buys a $100 seat at a prayer breakfast—receiving as the *quid pro quo* food for both body and soul—it would make no sense to say that no charitable contribution whatever has occurred simply because the "going rate" for all prayer breakfasts (with equivalent bodily food) is $100. The latter may well be true, but that "going rate" *includes* a contribution.

Confronted with this difficulty, and with the constitutional necessity of not making irrational distinctions among taxpayers, and with the even higher standard of equality of treatment among *religions* that the First Amendment imposes, the Government has only two practicable options with regard to distinctively religious *quids pro quo:* to disregard them all, or to tax them all. Over the years it has chosen the former course.

Congress enacted the first charitable contribution exception to income taxation in 1917. War Revenue Act of 1917, ch. 63, § 1201(2), 40 Stat. 330. A mere two years later, in A.R.M. 2, 1 Cum.Bull. 150 (1919), the IRS gave its first blessing to the deductions of fixed payments to religious organizations as charitable contributions:

> "[T]he distinction of pew rents, assessments, church dues, and the like from basket collections is hardly warranted by the act. The act reads 'contributions' and 'gifts.' It is felt that all of these come within the two terms.
>
> "In substance it is believed that these are simply methods of contributing although in form they may vary. Is a basket collection given involuntarily to be distinguished from an envelope system, the latter being regarded as 'dues'? From a technical angle, the pew rents may be differentiated, but in practice the so-called 'personal accommodation' they may afford is conjectural. It is believed that the real intent is to contribute and not to hire a seat or pew for personal accommodation. In fact, basket contributors sometimes receive the same accommodation informally."

The IRS reaffirmed its position in 1970, ruling that "[p]ew rents, building fund assessments and periodic dues paid to a church . . . are all methods of making contributions to the church and such payments are deductible as charitable contributions." Rev.Rul. 70–47, 1970–1 Cum.Bull. 49. Similarly, notwithstanding the "form" of Mass stipends as fixed payments for specific religious services, . . . the IRS has allowed charitable deductions of such payments. See Rev.Rul. 78–366, 1978–2 Cum.Bull. 241.

These rulings, which are "official interpretation[s] of [the tax laws] by the [IRS]," Rev.Proc. 78–24, 1978–2 Cum.Bull. 503, 504, flatly contradict the Solicitor General's claim that there "is no administrative practice recognizing that payments made in exchange for religious benefits are tax deductible." . . . Indeed, an Assistant Commissioner of the IRS recently explained in a "question and answer guidance package" to tax-exempt organizations that "[i]n contrast to tuition payments, religious observances generally are not regarded as yielding private benefits to the donor, who is viewed as receiving only incidental benefits when attending the observances. The primary beneficiaries are viewed as being the general public and members of the faith. Thus, payments for saying masses, pew rents, tithes, and other payments involving fixed donations for similar religious services, are fully deductible contributions." IRS Official Explains New Examination–Education Program on Charitable Contributions to Tax–Exempt Organizations, B.N.A. Daily Tax Report for Executives 186:J–1, 186:J–3 (Sept. 26, 1988). Although this guidance package may not be as authoritative as IRS rulings, . . . in the absence of any contrary indications it does reflect the continuing adherence of the IRS to its practice of allowing deductions for fixed payments for religious services.

There can be no doubt that at least some of the fixed payments which the IRS has treated as charitable deductions, or which the Court assumes the IRS would allow taxpayers to deduct . . . are as "inherently reciprocal" . . . as the payments for auditing at issue here. In exchange for their payment of pew rents, Christians receive particular seats during worship services. . . . Similarly, in some synagogues attendance at the worship services for Jewish High Holy Days is often predicated upon the purchase of a general admission ticket or a reserved seat ticket. . . . Religious honors such as publicly reading from Scripture are purchased or auctioned periodically in some synagogues of Jews from Morocco and Syria. . . . Mormons must tithe ten percent of their income as a necessary but not sufficient condition to obtaining a "temple recommend," i.e., the right to be admitted into the temple. . . . A Mass stipend—a fixed payment given to a Catholic priest, in consideration of which he is obliged to apply the fruits of the Mass for the intention of the donor—has similar overtones of exchange. According to some Catholic theologians, the nature of the pact between a priest and a donor who pays a Mass stipend is "a bilateral contract known as *do ut facias*. One person agrees to give while the other party agrees to do something in return." . . . A finer example of a *quid pro quo* exchange would be hard to formulate.

This is not a situation where the IRS has explicitly and affirmatively reevaluated its longstanding interpretation of § 170 and decided to analyze *all* fixed religious contributions under a *quid pro quo* standard. There is no indication whatever that the IRS has abandoned its 70–year practice with respect to payments made by those other than Scientologists. In 1978, when it ruled that payments for auditing and training were not charitable contributions under § 170, the IRS did not cite— much less try to reconcile—its previous rulings concerning the deductibility of other forms of fixed payments for religious services or practices. See Rev.Rul. 78–189, 1978–1 Cum.Bull. 68 (equating payments for auditing with tuition paid to religious schools).

Nevertheless, the Government now attempts to reconcile its previous rulings with its decision in these cases by relying on a distinction between direct and incidental benefits in exchange for payments made to a charitable organization. This distinction, adumbrated as early as the IRS' 1919 ruling, recognizes that even a deductible charitable contribution may generate certain benefits for the donor. As long as the benefits remain "incidental" and do not indicate that the payment was actually made for the "personal accommodation" of the donor, the payment will be deductible. It is the Government's view that the payments made by petitioners should not be deductible under § 170 because the "unusual facts in these cases . . . demonstrate that the payments were made primarily for 'personal accommodation.' " . . . Specifically, the Solicitor General asserts that "the rigid connection between the provision of auditing and training services and payment of the fixed price" indicates a *quid pro quo* relationship and "reflect[s] the value that petitioners expected to receive for their money." . . .

There is no discernable reason why there is a more rigid connection between payment and services in the religious practices of Scientology than in the religious practices of the faiths described above. Neither has the Government explained why the benefit received by a Christian who obtains the pew of his or her choice by paying a rental fee, a Jew who gains entrance to High Holy Day services by purchasing a ticket, a Mormon who makes the fixed payment necessary for a temple recommend, or a Catholic who pays a Mass stipend, is incidental to the real benefit conferred on the "general public and members of the faith," . . . while the benefit received by a Scientologist from auditing is a personal accommodation. If the perceived difference lies in the fact that Christians and Jews worship in congregations, whereas Scientologists, in a manner reminiscent of Eastern religions, . . . gain awareness of the "immortal spiritual being" within them in one-to-one sessions with auditors, . . . such a distinction would raise serious Establishment Clause problems. See Wallace v. Jaffree, 472 U.S. 38, 69–70, 105 S.Ct. 2479, 2497 (1985) (opinion concurring in judgment); Lynch v. Donnelly, 465 U.S. 668, 687–689, 104 S.Ct. 1355, 1366–1367 (1984) (concurring opinion). The distinction is no more legitimate if it is based on the fact that congregational worship services "would be said anyway," . . . without the payment of a pew rental or stipend or tithe by a particular adherent. The relevant comparison between Scientology and other religions must be between the Scientologist undergoing auditing or training on one hand and the congregation on the other. For some religions the central importance of the congregation achieves legal dimensions. In Orthodox Judaism, for example, certain worship services cannot be performed and Scripture cannot be read publicly without the presence of at least ten men. . . . If payments for participation occurred in such a setting, would the benefit to the tenth man be only incidental while for the personal accommodation of the eleventh? In the same vein, will the deductibility of a Mass stipend turn on whether there are other congregants to hear the Mass? And conversely, does the fact that the payment of a tithe by a Mormon is an absolute prerequisite to admission to the temple make that payment for admission a personal accommodation regardless of the size of the congregation?

* * *

I would reverse the decisions below.

NOTE

Introduction. Section 170(a) provides a deduction for any contribution to a qualified charity made within a taxable year.[1] Congress encourages contributions to charitable organizations by providing taxpayers with this deduction.[2] This relieves some of the economic responsibilities that would otherwise fall on the federal government if not met by private funding.[3]

Consideration of this deduction provision has been postponed until now because comprehension of the charitable deduction rules requires, among other things, an understanding of the characterization provisions.[4] This note provides a road map to the subsections of Section 170 not in their alphabetical order, but instead, in the order in which they should be considered to properly determine the amount of the current year's charitable deduction as well as any charitable deduction carryovers.

Qualified Charitable Donees. In order for a charitable contribution to be deductible, it must be made to a qualified organization.[5] Section

---

1. See Year of Deduction, infra. Articles providing an overview of I.R.C. § 170 include Taggart, "The Charitable Deduction," 26 Tax L.Rev. 63 (1970); Sorlien and Olsen, "Analyzing the New Charitable Contributions Rules: Planning, Pitfalls and Problems," 32 J. Tax'n 218 (1970); Wittenbach and Milani, "A Flowchart Focusing on the Individual Charitable Contribution Deduction Provisions," 66 Taxes 285 (1988).

2. This deduction is an itemized deduction. See Chapter 18E.

3. Policy articles considering I.R.C. § 170 include McDaniel, "Federal Matching Grants for Charitable Contributions: A Substitute for the Income Tax Deduction,"

27 Tax L.Rev. 377 (1972); Bittker, "Charitable Contribution: Tax Deduction or Matching Grants?" 28 Tax L.Rev. 37 (1972); McNulty, "Public Policy and Private Charity: A Tax Policy Perspective," 3 Va.Tax Rev. 229 (1984); Wiedenbeck, "Charitable Contributions: A Policy Perspective," 50 Mo.L.Rev. 85 (1985); Gergen, "The Case for a Charitable Contributions Deduction," 74 Va.L.Rev. 1393 (1988).

4. See The Amount of the Contribution, infra.

5. See I.R.S. Pub. No. 78 (Cumulative List of Organizations Described in Section 170(c)) for a list of organizations that qualify for deductible charitable contributions.

170(c) provides five classifications of qualified organizations:[6] (1) a federal, state or local governmental entity;[7] (2) certain religious,[8] charitable, scientific, literary, educational, amateur sports and prevention of cruelty to children and animals organizations;[9] (3) certain war veterans' organizations;[10] (4) domestic fraternal societies, orders, or associations operating under the lodge system where gifts are used exclusively for the purposes listed in classification (2) above (other than amateur sports);[11] and (5) non-profit cemetery companies and corporations.[12]

Section 170 essentially divides charitable organizations into two classifications. The first, referred to as "public charities," are charities substantially funded by the general public.[13] The second classification, "private charities," are private foundations funded by smaller groups of private individuals or families.[14] Some privately funded charitable organizations are treated as public charities where contributions or net earnings of the organization are distributed for qualified charitable uses within a limited period beyond the end of the year.[15]

Contributions. In order to qualify for a charitable deduction, one must make a "contribution . . . to or for the use of" a charity.[16] A contribution has been defined as "a voluntary transfer of money or property made with no expectation of procuring a financial benefit commensurate with the amount of the transfer."[17] As the Rulings and

---

6. In addition, I.R.C. § 170(g) treats unreimbursed amounts paid to maintain a non-dependent and non-related foreign exchange student in the twelfth grade or lower as a member of a taxpayer's household as a contribution for the use of a public charity. I.R.C. § 170(g)(1). Cf. I.R.C. § 170(b)(1)(B). The deduction is permitted only if there is a written agreement between the taxpayer and a charity described in § 170(c)(2), (3) or (4) to implement such an educational program. I.R.C. § 170(g)(1)(A). The deductible amount is limited to a maximum of $50 a month for the number of months the student is maintained. I.R.C. § 170(g)(2)(A).

7. I.R.C. § 170(c)(1). Included also are political subdivisions of such entities and United States possessions, but only if the contribution or gift is to be used exclusively for public purposes.

8. See Bittker, "Churches, Taxes and the Constitution," 78 Yale L.J. 218 (1970); Schwarz, "Limiting Religious Tax Exemptions: When Should the Church Render Unto Caesar?" 29 U.Fla.L.Rev. 50 (1976).

9. I.R.C. § 170(c)(2). The charity can be a corporation, trust or community chest, fund or foundation created or organized in the United States, a state of the United States, the District of Columbia or a United States possession, none of whose net earnings inure to the benefit of any private shareholder or individual and which does not attempt to influence legislation or become involved in political campaigns. Id. In addition, a contribution is deductible only if it is to be used in the United States or one of its possessions exclusively for one of the above purposes. Id.

10. I.R.C. § 170(c)(3). The organizations must be organized in the United States or one of its possessions and none of its net earnings may inure to the benefit of a private shareholder or individual. Id.

11. I.R.C. § 170(c)(4).

12. I.R.C. § 170(c)(5). No part of the net earnings of such company or corporation may inure to the benefit of any private shareholder or individual. See Whalen, "A Grave Injustice: The Uncharitable Federal Tax Treatment of Bequest to Public Cemeteries," 58 Fordham L.Rev. 705 (1990).

13. Cf. I.R.C. § 170(b)(1)(A).

14. Cf. I.R.C. § 170(b)(1)(B).

15. I.R.C. § 170(b)(1)(A)(vii), (b)(1)(E).

16. I.R.C. § 170(c). The words "or gift" are omitted from the quote, as a contribution encompasses a gift. The term "for the use of" is considered at notes 78–79, infra.

17. Rev.Rul. 83–104, 1983–2 C.B. 46, 47.

Hernandez case just considered illustrate, if a taxpayer receives a *quid pro quo* for a transfer to a charity, there is no "contribution," [18] and no charitable deduction is allowed. In some instances the transferor may be allowed a Section 162 business expense deduction, even though a *quid pro quo* is received.[19]

If cash or its equivalent [20] is given to a charity and partial consideration is received from the charity, then only the excess of the amount of the cash over the amount of the consideration received qualifies as a charitable deduction.[21] For example, if taxpayer pays $100 for a ticket to a charitable dinner the value of which is $40, the taxpayer may deduct only the balance, $60, as a charitable contribution.[22]

If property other than cash is transferred to a charity for partial consideration, a part-gift, part-sale transaction occurs.[23] Recall that in the event of a noncharitable part-gift, part-sale transaction, the Service questionably treats the gift and sale transactions as a single transfer.[24] However, when a *charitable* part-gift, part-sale transaction occurs, the transaction is sensibly divided into two simultaneous transfers, one a sale and the other a gift.[25] For the sale part of the transaction, the amount realized is the partial consideration received from the charity on the transfer; the gain on the sale is measured by the amount realized less the portion of the adjusted basis of the transferred property which bears the same ratio to the total adjusted basis of the property transferred as the consideration received from the charity bears to the total fair market value of the property transferred.[26] The remaining fair market value of the property is treated as the part-gift contribution to charity with the property having an adjusted basis equal to the remaining adjusted basis of the property.[27]

A classic example of a part-gift, part-sale to charity is a transfer of property encumbered with debt.[28] Another example is a transfer to charity for some amount of monetary consideration. For example, assume that Donor transfers some land with an adjusted basis of

---

18. See Hernandez v. Commissioner, Rev.Rul. 83–104, and Rev.Rul. 67–246 at pages 815–823, supra.

19. Reg. § 1.170A–1(c)(5). See also United States v. Jefferson Mills, Inc., 367 F.2d 392 (5th Cir.1966); Singer Co. v. United States, 449 F.2d 413 (Ct.Cl.1971); Sarah Marquis, 49 T.C. 695 (1968), acq. 1971–2 C.B. 3. But cf. I.R.C. § 162(b).

20. See infra note 31.

21. Rev.Rul. 67–246, 1967–2 C.B. 104. Cf. Rev.Proc. 90–12, 1990–1 C.B. 471.

See also I.R.C. § 170(1) allowing an 80% deduction for amounts transferred to higher education institutions when the transferor becomes entitled to purchase tickets to athletic events at the institution. See Childress, "Taxes, Tickets and the TAMRA," 20 Tax Adviser 625 (1989).

22. See Rev.Rul. 67–246, supra note 21.

23. See Lichter, "The Federal Tax Rules and Theory of Bargain Sale Gifts to Charity," 12 Tax Manager Est., Gifts, and Tr.J. 172 (1987); Teitell, "Making Charitable Gifts of Mortgaged Property: A Bargain Sale with Capital Gains Considerations," 125 Tr. & Est. 54 (1986).

24. See Reg. §§ 1.1001–1(e) and 1.1015–4. See also Chapter 6B2 problem 2 and Chapter 6C, supra.

25. See I.R.C. §§ 170(e)(2) and 1011(b) and Reg. §§ 1.170A–4(c)(2) and 1.1011–2.

26. I.R.C. § 1011(b), Reg. § 1.1011–2. See the Amount of the Contribution, infra.

27. I.R.C. § 170(e)(2); Reg. § 1.170A–4(c)(2).

28. See Guest v. Commissioner, 77 T.C. 9 (1981).

$120,000 and a fair market value of $180,000 to a charity and that the property is either subject to a liability of $120,000 or the property is unencumbered but the charity pays Donor $120,000 cash for it.[29] There would essentially be two transactions, a sale of two thirds ($120,000/$180,000) of the property and a gift of the remaining one-third ($180,000—$120,000/$180,000) of the property. The sale property would have an $80,000 adjusted basis [30] resulting in a $40,000 gain to Donor on the part-sale transaction. In addition, Donor is considered to have made a charitable gift of the remaining property worth $60,000 having an adjusted basis of $40,000.[31]

The Amount of the Contribution. To the extent that a "contribution" is made to or for the use of a qualified charitable donee, the amount treated as contributed to the charity must be determined.

Cash. To the extent the contribution is in cash, the amount of the contribution is the amount of the donated cash. A gift made by check or a charge to a credit card which is paid in due course is the equivalent of cash and the amount of the check or the credit card charge is the amount of the contribution.[32]

Property. If property other than cash is contributed to a charity, the fair market value of the property contributed is the potential amount of the contribution.[33] However, if the property is appreciated property, the amount of the contribution may be reduced by some or all of the amount of the built-in gain.[34] To determine whether a reduction occurs, it is first necessary to determine the character of the gain which would be recognized if the property were sold by the donor.

If the gain would be other than long-term capital gain, the amount of the contribution is reduced by the total amount of the lurking ordinary income or gain other than long-term capital gain.[35] Throughout Section 170 any reference to long-term capital gain includes Section 1231 gain.[36] Thus, if an individual donates inventory with a basis of $100 and a value of $250 to charity, the amount of the contribution is only $100, the $250 fair market value of the inventory less its $150 of lurking ordinary gain.[37] Similar results would apply if the property

---

29. This example should appear familiar. See problem 2 on page 135, supra.

30. I.R.C. § 1011(b); Reg. § 1.1011–2. The computation is equal to the fraction of the consideration received over the fair market value of the property transferred ($120,000/$180,000) times the adjusted basis of the property transferred ($120,000).

31. I.R.C. § 170(e)(2); Reg. § 1.170A–4(c)(2). The gifted property would have an adjusted basis equal to the fraction of the gift amount over the fair market value of the property transferred ($60,000/$180,000) times the adjusted basis of the property transferred ($120,000). The full $60,000 amount may or may not be deductible. See the Amount of the Contribution, infra, and Reg. § 1.170A–4(c)(2)(i).

32. Cf. Rev.Rul. 54–465, 1954–2 C.B. 93, and Rev.Rul. 78–38, 1978–1 C.B. 67.

33. Reg. § 1.170A–1(c).

34. See I.R.C. § 170(e).

35. I.R.C. § 170(e)(1)(A).

36. See I.R.C. §§ 170(e)(1) last sentence, 170(b)(1)(C)(iv) last sentence and Reg. § 1.170A–4(b)(4). I.R.C. § 1231 property is treated as a capital asset for determination of the amount of the contribution, except to the extent the donor would have recognized gain from sale as ordinary income under §§ 617(d)(1), 1245(a), 1250(a), 1251(c), 1252(a), or 1254(a).

37. See I.R.C. § 1221(1).

were short-term capital gain property, Section 1245 or Section 1250 property, or Section 1231–type property held for less than one year.[38]

But, even if the property is long-term capital gain property (including Section 1231 gain property),[39] the amount of the contribution may be reduced. If the property is tangible personal property donated to a public charity and the use of the property is unrelated to the charity's function [40] or if the property is given to a private charity,[41] the amount of the contribution must be reduced by the amount of the long-term capital gain.[42] For example, if an individual gives a painting worth $10,000, which cost the individual $4,000 to a public charity and the painting is used by the charity in its charitable function (e.g., if the gift is to an art museum which includes the painting in its collection),[43] the individual makes a $10,000 contribution.[44] However, if the painting is not used in the public charity's charitable function or is given to a private charity, the amount of the contribution is $4,000 ($10,000 less the painting's $6,000 built-in long-term gain).[45]

There is one exception to the private charity long-term capital gain reduction rule. If there is a gift to a private charity of "qualified appreciated stock," there is no reduction of the long-term capital gain amount.[46] Qualified appreciated stock is publicly traded stock the sale of which would result in long-term capital gain to the taxpayer,[47] but only to the extent that taxpayer or his family's [48] total contributions of such stock to private charities do not exceed 10 percent of the value of the stock of the corporation.[49] Thus, if the individual in the prior example had transferred AT & T stock (instead of the painting) with a $4,000 basis and $10,000 value to a private charity, the amount of the contribution would be $10,000.

Partial Interests in Property. If a taxpayer gives less than his entire interest in property to a charity, a series of special rules come into play. Congress enacted special rules for transfers of partial interests such as a charitable income interest or a charitable remainder interest out of a concern that a donor or trustee could deprive the

---

38. See Reg. § 1.170A–4(b)(1).

39. See note 36, supra.

40. I.R.C. § 170(e)(1)(B)(i).   See Reg. § 1.170A–4(b)(3).

41. I.R.C. § 170(e)(1)(B)(ii).

42. I.R.C. § 170(e)(1)(B).

43. Reg.   § 1.170A–4(b)(3).   See Anthoine, "Deductions for Charitable Contributions of Appreciated Property—the Art World" 35 Tax L.Rev. 239 (1980); Bell "Changing I.R.C. Sec. 170(e)(1)(A): For Art's Sake," 37 Case West.Res.L.Rev. 536 (1988).

44. Even if no amount of reduction occurs under the regular income tax, an indirect reduction of the amount of long-term capital gain may occur under the alterna-

tive minimum tax. I.R.C. § 57(a)(6) and Chap. 27C, infra.

45. I.R.C. § 170(e)(1)(B). If tangible depreciable personal property were given to a charity, the property could be subject to both I.R.C. § 1245 and I.R.C. § 1231 gain. The fair market value of the property would be reduced by the § 1245 gain and it might also be reduced by the § 1231 gain.

46. I.R.C. § 170(e)(5)(A). This exception is currently applicable only through December 31, 1994. I.R.C. § 170(e)(5)(D).

47. I.R.C. § 170(e)(5)(B).

48. Family is defined by I.R.C. § 267(c)(4). I.R.C. § 170(e)(5)(C)(ii).

49. I.R.C. § 170(e)(5)(C).

charity of its benefits by investing in nonincome producing assets or wasting assets respectively.[50]

If the partial interest is a charitable remainder interest in a trust, the value of the remainder qualifies for a charitable deduction [51] only if the interest is in the form of a charitable remainder annuity trust,[52] a charitable remainder unitrust,[53] or a pooled income fund.[54] If an income interest in a trust is contributed to charity, it qualifies for a deduction only if the amount distributed to charity is a guaranteed annuity or a fixed percentage of the fair market value of the trust property determined annually and the grantor is treated as the owner of such interest under Section 671.[55] These trust limitations are designed to prevent abuses and to ensure that the charity actually receives an adequate amount of contribution in relation to the income tax deduction which is allowed.[56]

If a charitable gift of a partial interest in property to charity is not in trust, the contribution will qualify as a charitable contribution only if the partial interest in property would be deductible if contributed in a trust, i.e. a qualified remainder interest or qualified income interest,[57] or if the contribution is a remainder interest in a personal residence or farm,[58] a contribution of an undivided portion of a taxpayer's entire interest in property,[59] or a "qualified conservation contribution." [60]

For example, a transfer of a right to use a building to a charity for a limited or indefinite period is a partial interest in property that does

---

50. See Stephens, Maxfield, Lind and Calfee, *Federal Estate and Gift Taxation* ¶ 5.05[7] and [8] (6th Ed. Warren, Gorham & Lamont 1991).

51. I.R.C. § 170(f)(2)(A).

52. I.R.C. § 664(d)(1). A charitable remainder annuity trust is a trust that meets three requirements: (1) a fixed amount (not less than 5% of the value of the property at the time it is transferred to the trust) must be paid at least annually to recipients (at least one of which does not qualify under § 170(c)) for a term of years (not more than 20 years) or for the life or lives of living individuals; (2) no other amounts can be paid for uses or to organizations other than those qualified for the income tax deduction; and (3) when the payments described in (1) above terminate, the remainder must be paid to or for the use of an organization qualified for the income tax charitable deduction, or retained by the trust for such a use. Id.

53. I.R.C. § 664(d)(2). A charitable remainder unitrust is a trust that meets three requirements: (1) a fluctuating amount fixed in terms of a percentage (not less than 5%) of the annual value of the trust assets must be paid at least annually to a non-qualified recipient for a term of

years (not more than 20 years) or for the life or lives of living individuals; (2) and (3) are identical to requirements (2) and (3) in note 52, supra. Id.

54. I.R.C. § 642(c)(5). A pooled income fund is a fund controlled by the charity entitled to the remainder. Property transferred to the fund is commingled with that of other donors, no donor or beneficiary of an income interest of the fund is a trustee, and the private income beneficiary receives distributions that are determined by the rate of return on the entire fund. Id.

55. I.R.C. § 170(f)(2)(B). See Stephens, Maxfield, Lind and Calfee, supra note 50 at ¶ 5.05[9], and Chapter 13B, supra.

56. See note 50, supra.

57. I.R.C. § 170(f)(3)(A). See the text at notes 51–56, supra.

58. I.R.C. § 170(f)(3)(B)(i).

59. I.R.C. § 170(f)(3)(B)(ii).

60. I.R.C. § 170(f)(3)(B)(iii). A qualified conservation contribution is a contribution of "a qualified real property interest" to a "qualified organization" exclusively for "conservation purposes." I.R.C. § 170(h)(1). Those terms are defined in I.R.C. § 170(h)(2)–(6).

not qualify for a charitable deduction.[61] This disallowance result is sensible if one thinks of the use of such property as a contribution of rental property with a zero basis which generates ordinary income.[62] Similarly, if a person transfers rental land to a trust that provides that all income from the land is to be distributed to a private individual for her life with a remainder to charity, the charitable remainder does not qualify for a charitable deduction because it is not a qualified remainder interest.[63] If the land were transferred to a trust with a charitable remainder which satisfied the requirements of a charitable remainder annuity trust, a charitable remainder unitrust or a pooled income fund, the value of the remainder would qualify for a charitable deduction.[64] Finally, an outright transfer of a fractional interest in the parcel of land, say a one-third interest, would qualify for a charitable deduction.[65]

Services. Services rendered to a charity are not property and consequently do not qualify as charitable contributions.[66] Services might be compared to ordinary income property with a zero adjusted basis, which if contributed to charity would result in a zero amount of contribution.[67] However, while services do not qualify for a charitable deduction, unreimbursed expenses incurred incident to the rendering of such services may constitute a charitable contribution.[68] Thus, a teacher's aid's cost of materials purchased and used in conjunction with the teaching assistance and the cost of transportation to and from the school constitute a charitable contribution.[69] If the expenses incident to rendering services are for traveling expenses (including meals and lodging) while away from home, they are deductible as charitable contributions only if there is no significant element of pleasure, recreation or vacation in such travel.[70]

Limitations on Charitable Contributions of Individual Taxpayers. After determining whether there is a *contribution* to or for the use of a *qualified charitable donee* and the *amount of the contribution,* the total

61. Rev.Rul. 70–477, 1970–2 C.B. 62.

62. See I.R.C. § 170(e)(1)(A). Cf. notes 35–38, supra.

63. See I.R.C. § 170(f)(2)(A) and notes 51–54, supra.

64. Id.

65. I.R.C. § 170(f)(3)(B)(ii). This represents an undivided portion of the entire interest in the property. The amount of the contribution may be reduced if the property is appreciated property. See notes 33–45, supra.

66. Reg. § 1.170A–1(g). See Grant v. Commissioner, 84 T.C. 809 (1985), affirmed 800 F.2d 260 (4th Cir.1986). The Service has ruled that a gift of blood is a nondeductible gift of services. Rev.Rul. 53–162, 1953–2 C.B. 127.

67. I.R.C. § 170(e)(1)(A); see notes 35–38, supra.

68. Reg. § 1.170A–1(g). See Luckey, "Taxation: Deduction of Expenses Incurred by Another in the Performance of a Service to a Charitable Organization," 17 U.Balt.L.Rev. 524 (1988).

69. Id. Cf. I.R.C. § 170(i) which allows a standard mileage rate of 12 cents per mile for transportation costs as a charitable deduction. Cf. Rev.Proc. 90–59, 1990–2 C.B. ___, allowing a 27.5 cents per mile standard mileage rate deduction under § 162, on or after January 1, 1991. Such costs are treated as a contribution "to" and not merely "for the use of a charity." Rev. Rul. 84–61, 1984–1 C.B. 39. See notes 80–83, infra.

70. I.R.C. § 170(j). See Chapter 14C2. See also Charles L. McCollum, 37 T.C.M. 1817 (1978), where a family attempted to deduct the cost of ski trips as members of a ski patrol. This case was decided prior to the enactment of I.R.C. § 170(j).

amount that a taxpayer will be allowed to deduct in a taxable year must be determined. Congress imposes various ceilings on the total amount that a taxpayer may deduct in any taxable year.[71] Contributions in excess of any of the ceilings are permitted to be carried over to the five succeeding years.[72]

We first consider the ceilings on the total amount of an individual taxpayer's contributions.[73] The amount of the ceiling is determined by a combination of factors including the type of charity (public or private), the character of the property transferred (whether the property is appreciated long-term capital gain property), whether the transfer is to or merely for the use of the charity, and the taxpayer's contribution base.

All of the ceilings are determined by computing some percentage of an individual taxpayer's "contribution base." [74] A contribution base is the taxpayer's adjusted gross income [75] computed without regard to any Section 172 net operating loss carryback to the year of the contribution.[76]

Contributions to Public Charities. An individual may deduct contributions made during the year *to a* public charity to the extent that such contributions do not exceed 50 percent of the taxpayer's contribution base.[77] The 50 percent ceiling is inapplicable if the contribution is merely "for the use of" a public charity.[78] A contribution is "for the use of" a charity if it is a contribution of an income interest in property (regardless of whether it is in a trust) or if (after all non-charitable interests expire) the property is held in trust for the benefit of a charity.[79]

Contributions for the use of Public Charities and to or for Private Charities. Contributions for the use of public charities [80] and all contributions to or for private charities are subject to a general limitation of 30 percent of the taxpayer's contribution base for the year.[81] These contributions are considered immediately after the gifts that qualify for the 50 percent ceiling.[82] However, the amount of such contributions may not exceed 50 percent of the contribution base less the amount of property contributed to public charities; [83] thus, such contributions are limited to the lesser of (1) 30 percent of the taxpayer's contribution base or (2) the excess of 50 percent of the taxpayer's contribution base over the contributions to public charities.[84]

71. I.R.C. § 170(b).

72. I.R.C. § 170(b)(1)(B), (b)(1)(C)(ii), (b)(1)(D)(ii), (d)(1).

73. In general, an estate or trust in not subject to any limitation on its charitable contributions. I.R.C. § 642(c)(1).

74. I.R.C. § 170(b)(1).

75. I.R.C. § 62. See Chapter 18B, supra.

76. I.R.C. § 170(b)(1)(F).

77. I.R.C. § 170(b)(1)(A).

78. I.R.C. § 170(b)(1)(A); Reg. § 1.170A–8(b).

79. Reg. § 1.170A–8(a)(2). Cf. I.R.C. § 170(f)(1).

80. I.R.C. § 170(b)(1)(B). Cf. Reg. § 1.170A–8(c).

81. I.R.C. § 170(b)(1)(B)(i).

82. Reg. § 1.170A–8(c)(2)(ii).

83. I.R.C. § 170(b)(1)(B)(ii).

84. I.R.C. § 170(b)(1)(B).

Contributions of Appreciated Capital Gain Property. After the above ceilings are imposed, there are further ceilings on gifts of appreciated capital gain property. A contribution *to* a public charity of appreciated property which if sold would result in long-term capital gain (or Section 1231 gain)[85] and which does not have its long-term capital gain amount reduced because it is not unrelated to the charitable function[86] is subject to a further ceiling equal to 30 percent of the taxpayer's contribution base.[87] A taxpayer may elect to reduce the amount of the contribution by the amount of the property's long-term capital gain (converting the property to non-appreciated property) so that it is then subject only to the 50 percent ceiling.[88]

Finally, gifts of any other appreciated (non-reduced) long-term capital gain property for the use of a public charity or to or for a private charity are subject to a ceiling of 20 percent of the taxpayer's contribution base, but not in excess of 30 percent of taxpayer's contribution base reduced by any unreduced long-term capital gain property given to a public charity.[89]

To the extent that an individual taxpayer's total charitable contributions for any taxable year exceed any of the limitations considered above, the excess amounts are carried over and treated as contributions of the same character (e.g., long-term capital gain property) to the same classification of donee (e.g., public or private charity) in each of the succeeding five years.[90] Any carryover is used up first in time (earliest years first) but only after taking into account the actual charitable contributions in the carryover year.[91] Any carryover unused at the end of the five year period expires and is wasted.

To illustrate some of the rules described above, assume T, an individual, with a $100,000 contribution base gives $10,000 cash and a building with an adjusted basis of $40,000 and worth $100,000 (subject to $20,000 Section 1250 gain and $40,000 Section 1231 gain) to a public charity. The amount of T's contribution is $90,000: $10,000 (cash) and $80,000 (building).[92] Since the gift is to a public charity the 50 percent ceiling applies and T is limited to a $50,000 deduction.[93] However, the transfer of the building is also subject to the 30 percent ceiling for appreciated property contributed to a public charity[94] and only a $30,000 portion of the building is currently deductible, with the remaining $50,000 treated as a carryover contribution of unreduced long-term capital gain property in the subsequent year.[95] Thus, T's total Section 170 deduction for the current year is $40,000. As an alternative to the above consequences, T may elect to reduce the amount of the building

85. I.R.C. § 170(b)(1)(C)(iv).

86. I.R.C. § 170(e)(1)(B)(i).

87. I.R.C. § 170(b)(1)(C)(i).

88. I.R.C. § 170(b)(1)(C)(iii).

89. I.R.C. § 170(b)(1)(D)(i).

90. I.R.C. § 170(b)(1)(B) flush language, (b)(1)(C)(ii), (b)(1)(D)(ii), (d)(1).

91. Id.

92. I.R.C. § 170(e)(1)(A). There is no § 170(e)(1)(B) reduction.

93. I.R.C. § 170(b)(1)(A).

94. I.R.C. § 170(b)(1)(C).

95. I.R.C. § 170(b)(1)(C)(ii), (d)(1).

contribution by its long-term capital gain (Section 1231 gain) from $80,000 to $40,000,[96] with the result that the full $10,000 of cash and $40,000 of unappreciated building would be subject to and within the Section 170(b)(1)(A) 50 percent ceiling. If the election were made, T would have $50,000 of total contributions for the current year and no carryover.[97] As a result of the election, T would increase her current year's charitable deduction by $10,000, but lose the potential benefit of the $50,000 carryover amount of building in the succeeding five years.

Assume instead that T, again with a $100,000 contribution base, gives $5,000 cash to a public charity, AT & T stock with an adjusted basis of $20,000 and value of $35,000 to a public charity, $15,000 cash to a private charity, and AT & T stock with an adjusted basis of $5,000 and value of $10,000 to a private charity. T's total contributions to the public charities ($5,000 of cash and $35,000 of AT & T stock) are within the 50 percent limit.[98] Since all of T's gifts to public charity are considered prior to the gifts to private charities,[99] T is limited to a deduction of $10,000 to the private charity.[100] Taxpayer's $35,000 gift of AT & T stock to the public charity would be further limited to 30 percent of taxpayer's contribution base or $30,000.[101] The $10,000 gift of stock to the private charity would not be deductible in the current year.[102] Thus taxpayer would be allowed a $45,000 charitable deduction in the current year with nondeductible contributions being carried over to the succeeding year.[103] As an alternative, T could elect to reduce the AT & T stock given to public charity by the amount of its long-term capital gain from $35,000 to $20,000.[104] If the election were made, T could deduct the total $25,000 of gifts to public charity ($5,000 of cash and $20,000 of AT & T stock),[105] the $15,000 cash gift to the private charity,[106] and the $10,000 AT & T stock gift to the private charity.[107] If the election were made, T's total charitable deduction for the year would be $50,000, but T would not have any carryover amounts in the succeeding years.[108]

96. I.R.C. § 170(b)(1)(C)(iii).

97. Since the total amount of contributions ($50,000) does not exceed 50% of T's contribution base ($50,000), there is no carryover under I.R.C. § 170(b)(1)(D).

98. I.R.C. § 170(b)(1)(A).

99. Reg. § 1.170A–8(c)(2)(ii).

100. I.R.C. § 170(b)(1)(B)(ii). The $10,000 amount represents the lesser of $30,000 (30% of taxpayer's contribution base) and $10,000 (50% of taxpayer's contribution base less gifts to public charities without regard to the § 170(b)(1)(C) 30% limit, or $50,000 less $40,000 of cash and stock). Cf. Reg. § 1.170A–8(f) Example (2).

101. I.R.C. § 170(b)(1)(C)(i).

102. I.R.C. § 170(b)(1)(D)(i)(II). This is equal to the lesser of $20,000 (20% of taxpayer's contribution base) and zero (30% of

taxpayer's contribution base less contributions of capital gain property to which § 170(b)(1)(C) applies, or $30,000 less $30,000).

103. I.R.C. § 170(b)(1)(B), (b)(1)(C)(ii), and (b)(1)(D)(ii). The nondeductible carryover contributions would include $5,000 of cash to the private charity, $5,000 of AT & T stock to the public charity, and $10,000 of AT & T stock to the private charity.

104. I.R.C. § 170(b)(1)(C)(iii).

105. I.R.C. § 170(b)(1)(A).

106. I.R.C. § 170(b)(1)(B)(ii).

107. Id. I.R.C. § 170(b)(1)(D)(i)(II).

108. T would have used up all of his charitable contributions ($50,000 after the reduction in the AT & T stock to a public charity) with none remaining to be carried over.

In summary, Section 170(b) essentially imposes a 50 percent ceiling on individual gifts to public charities and 30 percent ceiling on gifts for the use of public charities and to private charities. It imposes additional limitations on gifts of long-term capital gain property. Excess contributions in any of the above categories are subject to the five-year carryover rule.

Limitations on Charitable Contributions by Corporate Taxpayers. The total deductions allowed to a corporation may not exceed 10 percent of the corporation's taxable income subject to several adjustments. The corporation's taxable income is computed without regard to any charitable deduction under Section 170, the capital loss carryback of Section 1212(a)(1), the net operating loss carryback of Section 172, and the deductions allowed under Section 241 through 250 (other than Section 248).[109] Corporate contributions in excess of the 10 percent ceiling are subject to a five-year carryover rule similar to the rule applicable to excess contributions made by individual taxpayers.[110] None of the special rules which apply to contributions by individuals (i.e., whether the charity is public or private, whether the property is long-term capital gain property, or whether the contribution is to or for the use of public charities) are applicable to corporate contributions.[111] However, there are some special corporate rules relating to the timing of corporate contributions[112] and the amount of corporate contributions.[113]

Year of Deduction. A deduction for a charitable contribution may be taken only for the year in which the contribution is actually made, or when treated as actually made in a carryover year. Thus for Section 170 purposes, a taxpayer is on the cash method of accounting, even if the taxpayer otherwise uses the accrual method of accounting.[114] As a result, if a pledge is made to make a contribution in a future year, a contribution may not be deducted until the year in which the pledge is paid.[115] A credit card contribution, being the equivalent of cash, is deductible in the taxable year a charge is made to the credit card.[116] A contribution by check is deductible in the taxable year in which the check is delivered, provided that it is honored and paid and there are no restrictions as to time and manner of payment.[117] Gifts of property generally occur on the delivery of the property (or its title) to the donee.[118] Gifts of stock occur when the stock is transferred on the corporate books.[119]

109. I.R.C. § 170(b)(2).

110. I.R.C. § 170(d)(2).

111. Cf. I.R.C. § 170(b)(1).

112. I.R.C. § 170(a)(2).

113. I.R.C. § 170(e)(3) and (4).

114. Reg. § 1.170A–1(a).

115. Id. Mann v. Commissioner, 35 F.2d 873 (D.C.Cir.1929).

116. Rev.Rul. 78–38, note 32, supra.

117. Rev.Rul. 54–465, note 32, supra.

118. Johnson v. United States, 280 F.Supp. 412 (N.D.N.Y.1967).

119. J.W. Londen, 45 T.C. 106 (1965).

Verification. A charitable contribution is allowed as a deduction only if it is properly verified.[120] If a contribution is in cash or its equivalent,[121] appropriate records must be kept (receipts, cancelled checks, etc.).[122] The subjective element of fair market value of non-cash property presents verification difficulties. The impossibility of detecting overvaluation and the concept of "audit lottery" has led to further verification requirements with respect to gifts of property.[123] If a contribution is made in property other than money, the taxpayer must obtain a receipt from the donee.[124] If the property (other than publicly traded securities) has a claimed value in excess of $5,000 ($10,000 in the case of non-publicly traded stock), the donor must in addition obtain a formal qualified appraisal by an independent appraiser[125] which must be attached to the taxpayer's return.[126] Moreover, there are substantial penalties for underpayment of income tax as a result of overvaluation of property.[127]

PROBLEMS

1. T's contribution base for the year of the following gifts is $150,000. During the year T makes contributions to Suntan U., an organization within § 170(b)(1)(A)(ii) and (c)(2), or to Private Foundation, which is within § 170(c)(2) but not within § 170(b)(1)(A)(vii). In each of the following circumstances determine T's § 170 deduction for the current year, and what effect, if any, § 170(d)(1)(A) will have:

   (a) T gives $100,000 cash to Suntan U.

   (b) T gives $100,000 cash to Private Foundation.

   (c) T gives $60,000 cash to Suntan U. and $40,000 to Private Foundation.

   (d) T gives $20,000 to Suntan U. and $80,000 to Private Foundation.

   (e) T has a freshman daughter who attends Suntan U. and he pays $3,000 tuition for her and makes a $10,000 Sponsors' Club contribution. Children of members of the Sponsors' Club are automatically admitted to Suntan U.

2. This problem involves transfers of property by T, an individual, to Suntan U. and Private Foundation both as described in 1, above, in a year after 1990. Assume that in the current year T has a $200,000 "contribution base," and unless otherwise stated he makes no other

---

120. See I.R.C. § 170(a)(1) last sentence. See Kalick and Buechler, "Charitable Contributions: Substantiation and Valuation Requirements," 20 Tax Adviser 242 (1989); Wood, "Qualified Appraisal Rules," 13 J. Real Estate Tax'n 385 (1986).

121. See note 31, supra.

122. Reg. § 1.170A–13(a). In the absence of a cancelled check or written receipt from the donee organization, other reliable written records showing the name of the donee and the amount and date of the contribution will suffice for verification. Id.

123. Expl. of Sen. Fin. Comm., 98th Cong., 2d Sess. 444 (1984).

124. Reg. § 1.170A–13(b).

125. Reg. § 1.170A–13(c)(2).

126. Id.

127. See I.R.C. § 6662(a), (b)(3), (e). But see I.R.C. § 6664(c).

charitable gifts. T owns property with a basis of $70,000 and a value of $90,000.

(a) If the property is inventory and he contributes it to Suntan U., what will T's charitable deduction be?

(b) If the property is inventory and he contributes it to Private Foundation, what will T's charitable contribution be?

(c) If the property is corporate stock held for more than one year and he contributes it to Suntan U. what will T's charitable contribution be?

(d) Same as (c), above, except the stock has been held only five months.

(e) Same as (c), above, except that the stock was given to Private Foundation rather than Suntan U. Assume the stock is not publicly traded. Cf. § 170(e)(5).

(f) Same as (e), above, except that the stock is § 170(e)(5) "qualified appreciated stock."

(g) What result under the facts of (c), above, if T exercises the election proffered by § 170(b)(1)(C)(iii)?

(h) What result if T gives Suntan U. § 1250 property which if sold would be subject to $10,000 of § 1250 recapture?

3. After completing his term of office Publius Maximus who has been in a high office for several years donates his private working papers to Charity U. The papers are properly valued at $100,000.

(a) Will Publius be allowed a charitable deduction for the gift? See § 1221(3).

(b) Publius also teaches Sunday School at his church. Will he be allowed a charitable deduction for the value of his services? See Reg. § 1.170A–1(g).

(c) Publius donates blood (worth $100) during the year to the blood bank. Deductible? Consider Rev.Rul. 53–162, 1953–2 C.B. 127, and Green v. Commissioner, 74 T.C. 1229 (1980).

(d) Publius allows the United Way Crusade to use an office in a building that he owns; the office has a fair market value of $100 per month. Is he allowed a deduction for the value of the use of the office? See § 170(f)(3)(A) and note § 170(f)(2)(B). See also Rev.Rul. 70–477, 1970–2 C.B. 62, and § 170(f)(3)(B)(iii) and (h).

(e) Publius volunteers for the National Ski Patrol. He travels each weekend to a ski resort incurring costs of travel, meals and lodging. Deductible? See § 170(k).

4. Planner has held for several years some stock that he purchased at a cost of $60,000. In the current year when his contribution base (prior to the "sale" below) is $50,000 and the stock is now worth $80,000, he "sells" it for $60,000 to Charity U., an organization within § 170(b)(1)(A)(ii) and (c)(2).

(a) What is the amount of his gain or loss on the sale?

(b) What is his charitable deduction?

(c) Same questions as (a) and (b), above, except that the property is § 1250 property with a $60,000 adjusted basis and if the property were sold there would be $10,000 of § 1250 gain.

C. CASUALTY AND THEFT LOSSES

1. NATURE OF LOSSES ALLOWED *

Internal Revenue Code: Section 165(a), (c).

Regulations: Section 1.165–1(e), –7(a)(1), (3), (5), –8(a)(1), (d).

Losses incurred by a taxpayer may have an impact on his tax liability. As indicated in Chapter 14, losses are generally deductible under Section 165(a). Subsection (c) imposes some limitations regarding individuals. Losses incurred in the taxpayer's trade or business are deductible under Section 165(a) and (c)(1) without regard to how they arise. Deductions claimed in this category may be challenged as not really incurred in business, a problem to which Section 183 is addressed. Chapter 15 reflects another possible ground on which a taxpayer may claim a loss deduction without regard to how the loss arises, namely that the loss is within Section 165(a) and (c)(2) as one incurred in a transaction entered into for profit, although not in a trade or business. Although deductible, both business and profit-seeking activity losses are restricted sometimes under Section 165(f), which allows capital losses only to the extent allowed under Sections 1211 and 1212.[1]

A loss may of course occur outside the taxpayer's business and in a transaction not entered into for profit. Generally these losses are not deductible, in keeping with the philosophy of Section 262 which forecloses deductions for personal, living or family expenses. The statute does not expressly foreclose these deductions; it simply does not provide for them. It will be recalled that a taxpayer gets no deduction for a loss on the sale of his residence unless after he converts it to property held for profit he sustains a loss. However, subject to limitations, Section 165(c)(3) permits a deduction for some losses unconnected with business and not involved in an attempt to make a profit. What losses? "Casualty" and "theft" losses. Casualty or theft business losses or profit seeking losses may and should be treated under Section 165(c)(1) or Section 165(c)(2), respectively, without regard to Section 165(c)(3).

---

* See Note, "The Casualty Loss Deduction and Consumer Expectation: Section 165(c)(3) of the Internal Revenue Code," 36 U.Chi.L.Rev. 220 (1968); the statutory concepts are attacked in Epstein, "The Consumption and Loss of Personal Property under the Internal Revenue Code," 23 Stan.L.Rev. 454 (1971).

1. See Chapter 21C at page 668, supra.

Those losses are characterized under Section 1231.[2] Section 165(c)(3) losses are characterized under Section 165(h), which is considered below.

Nevertheless, we are concerned here with losses arising out of a casualty or by theft which *need* Section 165(c)(3) to make the scene. They are losses with respect to purely personal items of property. These losses raise first a question of the scope of the statutory concepts of "casualty" and "theft." We must also then consider: Second, the time at which (taxable year for which) these losses are to be deducted and, Third, the measurement and characterization of casualty and theft losses. For the most part, the answers to the timing and measurement questions are the same whether the losses concern business or profit-seeking or merely personal property.

REVENUE RULING 63–232
1963–2 Cum.Bull. 97.

The Internal Revenue Service has re-examined its position with regard to the deductibility of losses resulting from termite damage, as set forth in Revenue Ruling 59–277, C.B. 1959–2, 73.

Revenue Ruling 59–277 stated that the Service would follow the rule of George L. Buist, et ux. v. United States, 164 F.Supp. 218 (1958); Martin A. Rosenberg v. Commissioner, 198 F.2d 46 (1952); and Joseph Shopmaker et al. v. United States, 119 F.Supp. 705 (1953), only in those cases where the facts were substantially the same. The courts in these cases held that damage caused by termites over periods up to 15 months after infestation constituted a deductible casualty loss under section 165 of the Internal Revenue Code of 1954.

Revenue Ruling 59–277 further stated that in other cases, the Service would follow the rule announced in Charles J. Fay et al. v. Helvering, 120 F.2d 253 (1941); United States v. Betty Rogers, et al., 120 F.2d 244 (1941); and Leslie C. Dodge et ux. v. Commissioner, 25 T.C. 1022 (1956). In the latter cases the termite infestation and subsequent damage occurred over periods of several years.

An extensive examination of scientific data regarding the habits, destructive power and other factors peculiar to termites discloses that the biological background of all termites found in the United States is generally the same, with one notable exception. The subterranean or ground dwelling termite attacks only wood which is in contact with the ground, while the other types of termites attack wood directly from the air.

Leading authorities on the subject have concluded that little or no structural damage can be caused by termites during the first two years after the initial infestation. It has been estimated that under normal conditions, if left unchecked, depending upon climate and other factors, an infestation of three to eight years would be required to necessitate

2. See page 770, supra.

extensive repairs. Even under extreme conditions, the period would be from one to six years. See "Our Enemy the Termite" by Thomas Elliott Snyder; "Termite and Termite Control" by Charles A. Kofoid; "Insects Their Ways and Means of Living" by Robert Evans Snodgrass; and other authorities.

Such authorities agree that termite infestation and the resulting damage cannot be inflicted with the suddenness comparable to that caused by fire, storm or shipwreck.

Accordingly, it is the position of the Service, based on the scientific data available in this area, that damage caused by termites to property not connected with the trade or business does not constitute an allowable deduction as a casualty loss within the meaning of section 165(c)(3) of the Code. Such damage is the result of gradual deterioration through a steadily operating cause and is not the result of an identifiable event of a sudden, unusual or unexpected nature. Further, time elapsed between the incurrence of damage and its ultimate discovery is not a proper measure to determine whether the damage resulted from a casualty. Time of discovery of the damage, in some situations, may affect the extent of the damage, but this does not change the form or the nature of the event, the mode of its operation, or the character of the result. These characteristics are determinative when applying section 165(c)(3) of the Code.

The Internal Revenue Service will no longer follow the decisions of *Buist, Rosenberg,* and *Shopmaker,* supra. The only real distinction between these cases and the decisions of *Rogers, Fay* and *Dodge,* supra, is the time in which the loss was discovered.

Under the authority contained in section 7805(b) of the Code, Revenue Ruling 59–277, C.B. 1959–2, 73, is revoked for all taxable years beginning after November 12, 1963.

PULVERS v. COMMISSIONER *

United States Court of Appeals, Ninth Circuit, 1969.
407 F.2d 838.

CHAMBERS, Circuit Judge. Can taxpayers on their federal income tax return take a deduction for an "other casualty loss" when as a consequence of a nearby landslide that ruined three nearby homes, but did no physical damage to the property of taxpayers, with a resultant loss of value because of common fear the mountain might attack their residence and lot next? (There is yet no substantial impairment of ingress or egress on the street serving their home.) We agree with the tax court that they cannot.

* * *

* Cf. I.R.C. § 165(k) discussed at page 853, infra. The subsection does not alter the result in this case. Ed.

The tax court affirmed the commissioner's determination that the taxpayers incurred no actual loss: that they suffered a hypothetical loss or a mere fluctuation in value.

It may be that the loss is all in the heads of taxpayers and of prospective purchasers, but that circumstance has resulted in a very substantial depreciation of value. (Of course, if the rest of the hill or mountain remains quiet for many years, some or most of the value would come back.) But we would agree with the Los Angeles County assessor that the value certainly went down. And, the finding that the loss was a "mere" fluctuation in value is enough to aggravate any taxpayer.

We think their loss is one that the Congress could not have intended to include in Sec. 165(c)(3). The specific losses named are fire, storm, shipwreck, and theft. Each of those surely involves physical damage or loss of the physical property. Thus, we read "or other casualty," in para materia, meaning "something like those specifically mentioned." The first things that one thinks of as "other casualty losses" are earthquakes and automobile collision losses, both involving physical damage losses.

One trouble with the construction of taxpayers on "other casualty" is that the consequences are limitless. Think of the thousands of claims that could be made for loss of value because of shift of highways, but still involving no lack of ingress.

If one is over the San Andreas fault in California, an authentic report (if one could be had) that it is about to slip would depreciate one's property value before the event.* A notorious gangster buying the house next door would depreciate the value of one's property.

It is difficult to imagine the consequences of taxpayers' reading of the statute. The internal revenue service now has an army of tax gatherers and it always claims it does not have enough. Think of the number this door, if opened, would add. We will not imply that the Congress intended such a thing. Of course, if the courts would so imply, the Congress would straighten us out very quickly.

We agree with the Fourth Circuit case of Citizens Bank of Weston v. Commissioner, 252 F.2d 425. Also, our reading of United States v. White Dental Co., 274 U.S. 398, 47 S.Ct. 598, indicates the result we reach here.

Some day we may get a case where a condition has arisen of such certain future consequences that the taxpayer in good sense has absolutely abandoned his property. It might call for a different result, but we shall not reach it here. Neither do we reach the case where egress and ingress have been lost for the foreseeable future or materially impaired.

* Cf. Lewis F. Ford, 33 TCM 496 (1974), denying deduction for loss in value because of fear of future storms. Ed.

The taxpayers' argument is appealing. The ingenuity is admirable. But the language is such that we do not think the Congress intended the contended for construction.

The decision of the Tax Court is affirmed.

MARY FRANCES ALLEN

Tax Court of the United States, 1951.
16 T.C. 163.

Petitioner contests respondent's adjustment disallowing a deduction for loss by theft, accounting for a deficiency of $1,800.16 in income tax for 1945.

* * *

Opinion

VAN FOSSAN, Judge: * * * Stripped to essentials, the facts are that petitioner owned a brooch which she lost in some manner while visiting the Metropolitan Museum of Art in New York. She does not, and cannot, prove that the pin was stolen. All we know is that the brooch disappeared and was never found by, or returned to, petitioner.

Petitioner has the burden of proof. This includes presentation of proof which, absent positive proof, reasonably leads us to conclude that the article was stolen. If the reasonable inferences from the evidence point to theft, the proponent is entitled to prevail. If the contrary be true and reasonable inferences point to another conclusion, the proponent must fail. If the evidence is in equipoise preponderating neither to the one nor the other conclusion, petitioner has not carried her burden.

In the case at bar we cannot find as a fact that a theft occurred. The reasonable inferences from the evidence point otherwise. It is noted that there is no evidence as to the nature of the clasp by which the pin was fastened to petitioner's dress. We do not know whether it was a "safety clasp" or merely a simple clasp. Nor is there any evidence that petitioner was jostled in the crowd (the usual occurrence when a theft from the person is attempted). If the pin was properly equipped (as may be assumed from its value) with a safety clasp and securely fastened to petitioner's dress, the question arises as to how it could have been removed without damage to the dress, there being no testimony as to any such damage. If it were essential to the disposition of this case that we find either that the pin was lost by theft or was lost by inadvertence, our finding on the record made would be that it was lost by some mischance or inadvertence—not by theft. The inference that such was true is the more readily drawn. However, we need not go so far. We need only hold that petitioner, who had the burden of proof, has not established that the loss was occasioned by theft, a *sine qua non* to a decision in her favor under section 23(e)(3).

We see no merit in petitioner's argument based on the New York Criminal Statutes which hold that the finder of a lost article shall report the finding and make certain efforts toward locating the owner. These statutes are neither binding nor persuasive here. There is no evidence that the pin was ever found and thus the New York statute could not be invoked against anyone. This argument but emphasizes the lack of proof which characterizes the record in this case.

We sustain the respondent's determination.

Reviewed by the Court.

Decision will be entered for the respondent.

OPPER, J., dissenting: As the hearer of the evidence, I would find the fact to be that petitioner's brooch was stolen. I would do so for the very reason that the Court now finds otherwise; that is, that of all the possibilities, the most probable is a loss by theft.

This conclusion presupposes that we believe the testimony of the witnesses. Having heard them testify, I have no reservations in this respect. If the evidence is believed, petitioner had the brooch pinned on her dress at about 4:30 in the afternoon. She was present only in well lighted rooms so constructed that no article could reasonably be lost—especially in view of the subsequent search which the record shows. At 5 o'clock she discovered that the brooch was missing, having in the meantime mingled with a crowd of 5,000 people preparing to leave the museum.

Accepting this evidence, the three possibilities are thus: that the brooch dropped off and has never been found; that it was found but not turned in, and that it was stolen by some person in the crowd. The first may be disregarded as not a reasonable probability; the second would be impossible if the finder were honest. It assumes a virtual concealment which in the case of so valuable an object would actually amount to a theft. Taken with the third, it necessarily points to theft as the only reasonable cause of disappearance.

The suggestion that failure to show the condition of the clasp is fatal to petitioner's case seems to me to prove too much. If the clasp were so difficult to open as to make its removal unlikely, it is even more improbable that it could have fallen off by itself; and if it could open accidentally so as to allow the brooch to fall off, it must have been easy game for a competent sneak thief. Since the clasp in any condition would make removal more likely than mere accidental opening, it is only on the assumption that she was not being candid that petitioner's failure to produce such evidence could be the ground for the result now reached.

Absolute proof by an eye witness is so improbable that the burden now being imposed upon taxpayers virtually repeals *pro tanto* section 23(e)(3). Ever since Appeal of Howard J. Simons, in 1 B.T.A. at page 351, the rule has been otherwise. Without regard to the New York penal law, to which, however, resort would appear to be authorized by the precedents,[1] the probabilities of theft have been demonstrated as completely as such circumstances could ever permit. I see no reason now for departing from principles so well settled and so long established.

LEECH and TIETJENS, JJ., agree with this dissent.

2. TIMING CASUALTY LOSSES

Internal Revenue Code: Section 165(c)(3), (e), (i), (k).

Regulations: Section 1.165–1(d)(1) through (3), –7(a)(1), –8(a)(2), –11(a) and (d).

Once it is determined that there is a casualty or theft loss, the questions arise: When did the loss occur and for what year is a deduction allowed?[1] Casualty losses are deductible for the year in which the loss is sustained.[2] This may be the year of the casualty or a later year in which the amount of the loss is ascertained, in a case where the full extent of the loss was not or by its very nature could not be known until a subsequent year.[3]

Under a limited statutory alternative, the deduction may be allowed for a year prior to the casualty. Under Section 165(i) if a casualty loss is attributable to a disaster in an area subsequently declared by the President to warrant assistance under the Disaster Relief Act of 1974, the taxpayer may elect to claim the deduction for the year immediately before the year in which the casualty occurred. The Section 165(i) timing rule is also applicable to a taxpayer whose residence is in a federally declared disaster area if the residence is rendered unsafe for use as a residence as a proximate result of the disaster or if the taxpayer is ordered by the government to demolish or relocate such residence.[4]

Theft losses are generally a deduction for the year in which the theft is discovered.[5] It has been held that when a theft is discovered in year one the loss must be deducted in year one and, if in subsequent years the taxpayer recalls additional items that were taken, their loss must be deducted in year one by means of an amended return or refund claim, rather than in the subsequent years.[6] However, the timing rule is generally helpful to taxpayers. For example, an embezzlement that occurred in 1984 but which is discovered in 1988, gives rise to a 1988 deduction. If the reverse were true, use of the 1984 deduction would be foreclosed by statutes of limitation.[7]

---

1. Morris Plan Co. of St. Joseph, 42 B.T.A. 1190, 1195; Earle v. Commissioner, (CCA–2) 72 F.2d 366.

1. The broad treatment of tax timing principles appears in this book at Chapters 19 and 20, supra.

2. Reg. § 1.165–7(a)(1).

3. Rose Licht, 37 B.T.A. 1096 (1938), acq., 1963–2 C.B. 4; Donald H. Kunsman, 49 T.C. 62 (1967).

4. I.R.C. § 165(k).

5. I.R.C. § 165(e).

6. Jane U. Elliot, 40 T.C. 304 (1963), acq., 1964–1 (Part 1) C.B. 4.

7. See Chapter 29, infra.

The Regulations recognize an exception to the general timing rules for both casualties and thefts. If in the year of the casualty or discovery of the theft there exists a reasonable prospect of recovery of the loss, the portion of the loss with respect to which there is a recovery prospect is not deductible unless or until it becomes clear there will be no recovery.[8] It is possible, however, that a loss is properly claimed for year one because no "reasonable prospect of recovery" exists in that year. In year two reimbursement is unexpectedly received. With what consequences? The amount recovered is treated as income when received in year two; the tax for year one is *not* recomputed.[9] This is a part of the tax benefit doctrine previously considered in Chapter 20, supra.

3. MEASURING THE LOSS

Internal Revenue Code: Sections 67(b)(3); 123; 165(b), (h).

Regulations: Section 1.165–7(a)(2), (b)(1) and (3) Example (1), –8(c).

HELVERING v. OWENS

Supreme Court of the United States, 1939.
305 U.S. 468, 59 S.Ct. 260.

Mr. Justice ROBERTS delivered the opinion of the Court.

The courts below have given opposing answers to the question whether the basis for determining the amount of a loss sustained during the taxable year through injury to property not used in a trade or business, and therefore not the subject of an annual depreciation allowance, should be original cost or value immediately before the casualty.[1] To resolve this conflict we granted certiorari in both cases.

In No. 180 the facts are that the respondent Donald H. Owens purchased an automobile at a date subsequent to March 1, 1913, and prior to 1934, for $1825, and used it for pleasure until June 1934 when it was damaged in a collision. The car was not insured. Prior to the accident its fair market value was $225; after that event the fair market value was $190. The respondents filed a joint income tax return for the calendar year 1934 in which they claimed a deduction of $1635, the difference between cost and fair market value after the casualty. The Commissioner reduced the deduction to $35, the difference in market value before and after the collision. The Board of Tax Appeals sustained the taxpayers' claim and the Circuit Court of Appeals affirmed its ruling.

In No. 318 it appears that the taxpayers acquired a boat, boathouse, and pier in 1926 at a cost of $5,325. In August 1933 the

---

8. Reg. §§ 1.165–1(d)(2), 1.165–1(d)(3). See Katherine Ander, 47 T.C. 592 (1967); Ramsay Scarlett & Co., Inc., 61 T.C. 795 (1974); Frank Hudock, 65 T.C. 351 (1975).

9. John E. Montgomery, 65 T.C. 511 (1975). Cf. I.R.C. § 111(a).

1. Helvering v. Owens, 95 F.2d 318; Helvering v. Obici, 97 F.2d 431.

property, which had been used solely for pleasure, and was uninsured, was totally destroyed by a storm. Its actual value immediately prior to destruction was $3905. The taxpayers claimed the right to deduct cost in the computation of taxable income. The Commissioner allowed only value at date of destruction. The Board of Tax Appeals held with the taxpayers but the Circuit Court of Appeals reversed the Board's ruling.

Decision in No. 180 is governed by the Revenue Act of 1934,[2] in No. 318 by the Revenue Act of 1932.[3] The provisions of both statutes touching the question presented are substantially the same and we shall refer only to those of the 1934 Act.* Section 23(e)(3) permits deduction from gross income of losses "of property not connected with the trade or business" of the taxpayer, "if the loss arises from * * * casualty." Subsection (h) declares that "The basis for determining the amount of deduction for losses sustained, to be allowed under subsection (e) * * *, shall be the adjusted basis provided in section 113(b)." Section 113 is entitled "Adjusted basis for determining gain or loss"; in subsection (a) it provides that "The basis of property shall be the cost of such property," with exceptions not material. Subsection (b), to which 23(h) refers, is: "*Adjusted basis.*—The adjusted basis for determining the gain or loss from the sale or other disposition of property, whenever acquired, shall be the basis determined under subsection (a), adjusted as hereinafter provided. (1) *General rule.*—Proper adjustment in respect of the property shall in all cases be made—(B) in respect of any period since February 28, 1913, for exhaustion, wear and tear, obsolescence, amortization, and depletion, to the extent allowed (but not less than the amount allowable) under this Act or prior income tax laws."

The income tax acts have consistently allowed deduction for exhaustion, wear and tear, or obsolescence only in the case of "property used in the trade or business." The taxpayers in these cases could not, therefore, have claimed any deduction on this account for years prior to that in which the casualty occurred. For this reason they claim they may deduct upon the unadjusted basis,—that is,—cost. As the income tax laws call for accounting on an annual basis; as they provide for deductions for "losses sustained during the taxable year"; as the taxpayer is not allowed annual deductions for depreciation of nonbusiness property; as § 23(h) requires that the deduction shall be on "the adjusted basis provided in section 113(b)," thus contemplating an adjustment of value consequent on depreciation; and as the property involved was subject to depreciation and of less value in the taxable year, than its original cost, we think § 113(b)(1)(B) must be read as a limitation upon the amount of the deduction so that it may not exceed cost, and in the case of depreciable non-business property may not exceed the amount of the loss actually sustained in the taxable year,

---

2. c. 277, 48 Stat. 680, §§ 23(a)(f)(h)(1), 24(a)1, 41, 113; 26 U.S.C.A. §§ 23, 24, 41, 113.

3. c. 209, 47 Stat. 169, §§ 23(e)(f)(g)(h), 24(a)1, 113.

* The parallel current provisions are I.R.C. (1986) §§ 165(c)(3), 165(b), 1012, 1011, and 1016(a)(2), respectively. Ed.

measured by the then depreciated value of the property. The Treasury rulings have not been consistent, but this construction is the one which has finally been adopted.[4]

In No. 180 judgment reversed.

In No. 318 judgment affirmed.

NOTE

The rules of Reg. § 1.165–7(b) present a fairly clear picture of the determination of the initial amount of common casualty and theft [1] losses. Study them. As the regulation indicates, the amount is generally the same whether the loss is incurred in a trade or business or in a transaction entered into for profit or is merely personal. Under all such circumstances questions of valuation may create difficulty.[2] There are three important differences however. First, business or profit classification makes inapplicable the $100 floor [3] which, on a de minimis principle similar to avoidance of trivial insurance claims, disallows the first $100 of loss from a casualty regarding purely personal assets. These losses can be claimed under Section 165(c)(1) or (2), escaping the Section 165(h)(1) limitation which applies only to (c)(3) losses. Second, the regulations incorporate the *Owens* result to provide that losses of a purely personal nature never exceed the difference in value of the property before and after the casualty. The same rule generally applies to business and profit-making property. However, in the case of business or profit making property that is totally destroyed the loss deduction is for the full adjusted basis of the property (less reimbursements) even if that amount exceeds the *value* of the property before the casualty. Can you rationalize this distinction?

The third difference is that the Section 1231 hotchpot rules apply to characterize only business and profit-making property losses. The deductibility of theft and casualty losses of such property is limited only if the losses are capital and then only by Sections 1211 and 1212. Section 165(h)(2) contains a separate hotchpot to characterize personal casualty gains and losses, and it sometimes limits the deductibility of such losses. In order to understand Section 165(h)(2), recognize first that one may have gains as well as losses from theft or casualty. For example, if a thief steals a ring with a cost basis of $1,000 which is worth $10,000 and the owner collects $10,000 of insurance, the result is a $9,000 gain to the owner. If total personal gains from theft or casualty for a year exceed such losses (after the $100 floor for each loss), Section 165(h)(2)(B) characterizes all such gains and losses as capital

---

4. Treasury Regulations 86, Arts. 23(e)–1, 23(h)1, 113(b)1; G.C.M. XV 1, Cumulative Bulletin 115–118.

1. See also Reg. § 1.165–8(c).

2. See Reg. § 1.165–7(a)(2).

Cf. Smith's Estate v. Commissioner, 510 F.2d 479 (2d Cir.1975), cert. denied 423 U.S. 827, 96 S.Ct. 44 (1975), valuing nonrepresentational art objects for estate tax purposes; Bernard Eiferman, 35 T.C.M. 790 (1976).

3. See I.R.C. § 165(h)(1) and Reg. § 1.165–7(b)(4).

gains and losses and imposes no restrictions on the deductibility of the losses.[4] If these losses exceed gains both gains and losses remain ordinary (due to a lack of a sale or exchange), but Section 165(h)(2)(A)(i) allows the losses to be deducted, first, only to the extent of gains;[5] and then, any losses in excess of the gains are deductible only to the extent they exceed 10% of the taxpayer's adjusted gross income for the year.[6]

REVENUE RULING 68–531
1968–2 Cum.Bull. 80.

Advice has been requested concerning the computation of the casualty loss deduction under the circumstances stated below.

The taxpayer owns a citrus grove and is engaged in the business of growing and selling citrus fruit. In 1967 a hurricane damaged all of the citrus trees in the grove and totally destroyed the fruit ripening on the trees. The taxpayer's basis in the trees was 100x dollars. The trees had a value of 200x dollars (including the value of the fruit) immediately before the casualty. Immediately after the casualty the trees had a value of 120x dollars. The ripening fruit had a value immediately before the casualty of 20x dollars. The specific question is whether the value of the fruit may be included in determining the amount of the casualty loss deduction.

Section 165(a) of the Internal Revenue Code of 1954 provides that there shall be allowed as a deduction any loss sustained during the taxable year and not compensated for by insurance or otherwise.

Section 165(c) of the Code provides that in the case of an individual the deduction under subsection (a) shall be limited to certain classes of losses, including losses incurred in a trade or business.

Section 1.165–7(b)(1) of the Income Tax Regulations requires casualty losses to be measured by the lesser of (1) the amount equal to the fair market value of the property immediately before the casualty reduced by the fair market value of the property immediately after the casualty, or (2) the amount of the adjusted basis for determining the loss from the sale or other disposition of the property involved. Section 1.165–7(b)(2) of the regulations requires in the case of property used in a trade or business that a separate computation be made with respect to each identifiable property damaged or destroyed.

Section 1.165–6(c) of the regulations provides that the total loss by frost, storm, flood or fire of a prospective crop being grown in the business of farming shall not be allowed as a deduction under section 165(a) of the Code.

---

4. But see I.R.C. §§ 165(f), 1211(b), 1212(b).

5. I.R.C. § 165(h)(2)(A)(i).

6. I.R.C. § 165(h)(2)(A)(ii). See I.R.C. § 165(h)(4)(A) treating such losses to the extent of gains as deductible under § 62.

Such treatment is for the purpose of measuring adjusted gross income under § 165(h)(2)(A)(ii) and also for computing the taxpayer's taxable income. To the extent deductible, losses in excess of gains are itemized deductions.

In the instant case, since the cost of growing the fruit was deductible by the taxpayer as a business expense, he had no basis in the ripening fruit. Further, the difference between the cost of a growing crop and its prospective sales price is only anticipated income and the loss of anticipated income is not deductible.

Accordingly, the value of the fruit is to be excluded in determining, under section 165(a) of the Code, the amount of the casualty loss deduction.

However, with respect to the citrus trees damaged by the hurricane, the amount of the deductible loss is measured by the difference between the fair market value of the trees (not including the fruit) immediately before the casualty and the fair market value of the trees (not including the fruit) immediately after the casualty, but that amount may not exceed the adjusted basis of the trees for determining loss. In the instant case, the amount deductible for the damage to the trees is limited to 60x dollars, which is the difference between the fair market value of the trees immediately before the casualty (200x dollars less 20x dollars) and their fair market value immediately after the casualty (120x dollars).

PROBLEMS

1. Prone slammed the car door on his wife's hand. Quick examination showed a slightly injured pinky but her diamond ring seemingly intact. Later that night they discovered the diamond had slipped out of its prongs, seemingly damaged by the car door. It was never found and the ring was uninsured.

   (a) May Prone claim a casualty loss deduction? See J. P. White, 48 T.C. 430 (1967).

   (b) Does the *White* case suggest an alternative argument Mary Francis Allen's attorney could have made in her case in order to obtain a deduction? See Rev.Rul. 72–592, 1972–2 C.B. 101.

2. At a cost of $10,000, Sleepy purchased a car in 1988 for personal use. In 1991 he dozed off one night while driving and the car attached itself to a tree. Before the accident, the car was worth $8,000 but, after the accident, only $1,000. At the time of the accident Sleepy was taking a vase, a decorative ornament in his home, to a dealer to have it appraised. It had been purchased several years earlier for $10,000, and it was totally destroyed in the accident. Sleepy recovered $1,000 in insurance for the car and $20,000 for the vase. Disregarding the above transactions Sleepy has an adjusted gross income of $30,000.

   (a) What is the amount of Sleepy's personal casualty loss on the car for the year?

   (b) What is the amount of Sleepy's personal casualty gain on the vase for the year?

   (c) What is the character of those gains and losses?

   (d) To what extent are Sleepy's losses deductible?

(e) Is the deduction an itemized deduction?

(f) What results in (a)–(e), above, if Sleepy recovers only $12,000 in insurance for the vase?

(g) What differences in the results above if Sleepy avoids the insurance company and does not collect the $1000 of auto insurance because he fears the company will cancel his policy? See § 165(h)(4)(E).

3. Shaky's house is damaged in an earthquake and he and his family are required to live in a motel and eat their meals in a restaurant while repairs are made. Shaky's insurance policy pays the total cost of the repairs and, additionally, pays $1200 of the family's meals and lodging expenses which total $1800 during the repair period. Normally Shaky would pay only $1000 for these expenses during the period. What tax consequences to Shaky? See § 123.

PART SEVEN: DEFERRAL AND NON-RECOGNITION OF INCOME AND DEDUCTIONS

CHAPTER 24. THE INTERRELATIONSHIP OF TIMING AND CHARACTERIZATION

A. TRANSACTIONS UNDER SECTION 453

Internal Revenue Code: Sections 453(a) through (g) and (i) through (k); 453A; 453B(a) through (c) and (g). See Sections 483; 1038; 1041; 1239; 1245; 1250.

Regulations: Sections 1.453–4(c)–9(a) and (b); 15A.453–1(a), 1(b)(1), –(3)(i), (4), (5) Examples (1)–(3), –1(c)(1), –1(c)(2)(i)(A), –1(c)(3)(i), –1(c)(4). (The section 453 Reg. references are even more important than the usual Reg. citations in working the Problems at the end of this segment.)

Introduction. A simple example illustrates the need for Section 453. Assume Seller purchased a parcel of land as an investment many years ago at a cost of $40,000 and it is now worth $400,000. Buyer approaches Seller and wants to purchase the property, but Buyer has little cash available. Seller agrees to sell the property to Buyer, who will pay Seller $400,000 in four years. In the meantime, Buyer will make adequate interest payments [1] on the outstanding $400,000 obligation. As a result of the transaction Seller has a $360,000 realized gain. Were it not for the Section 453 installment sale provisions, Seller would recognize the entire gain in the current year.[2] Obviously, Seller has a problem; he currently has received no cash from the transaction with which to pay an income tax generated by the sale of the property. Congress, recognizing Seller's plight enacted Section 453, the installment sales provision, to provide Seller relief from this liquidity problem.[3] In general, under Section 453 Seller's gain is included in his gross income only as payments are received from Buyer,[4] thereby providing Seller with the necessary liquidity to pay the tax on his gain. Substantial amendments were made to Section 453 by the Installment

---

1. See I.R.C. § 483 considered at Chapter 24C.

2. I.R.C. § 1001(a) and (c). See Chapter 24B, infra.

3. Cf. H.Rep. No. 91–413, pt. 1, 91st Cong., 1st Sess. 107 (1969), 1969–3 C.B. 267.

4. See I.R.C. § 453(a), (c).

Sales Revision Act of 1980 [5] providing most of the current installment sales rules.

Section 453 essentially is a timing provision, available to both cash and accrual-method taxpayers. This topic technically could have been previously discussed in Chapter 19. Since installment sales are substantially interrelated with characterization of income,[6] consideration of the installment sales provision has been deferred from the timing rules of Chapter 19 to this Chapter. Not only is Section 453 an important provision, it is also the culmination of many of the concepts learned earlier in this course.[7] Therefore it provides an opportunity to revisit several concepts and rules previously discussed.

The General Rule. An "installment sale" of property occurs when at least one payment of the total purchase price is to be received after the close of the taxable year in which the disposition occurs.[8] When an installment sale occurs, Section 453 allows the gain to be spread over the payment period by requiring a percentage of each payment to be included in gross income in the year of receipt. Section 453(c) provides the method for calculating the percentage of each payment [9] to be included in the seller's gross income as each payment is received. The percentage is the ratio of the "gross profit" [10] to the "total contract price." [11] The gross profit is the gain on the sale of the property that will be realized over the life of all of the payments, and the total contract price is generally the selling price [12] of the property.[13] In addition, adequate interest must be paid on the obligation.[14]

Returning to the example above, assume that Seller and Buyer agree that Buyer will pay Seller $100,000 per year for four years, with adequate interest on any unpaid balance. The sale results in a gross

---

5. Pub.Law No. 96–471, 94 Stat. 2247 (1980). Articles discussing I.R.C. § 453 after the Installment Sales Revision Act of 1980 include: Emory and Hjorth, "An Analysis of the Changes Made by the Installment Sales Revision Act of 1980," 54 J. Tax'n 66–71 and 130–137 (1981); Ginsburg, "Future Payment Sales After the 1980 Revision Act," 39 N.Y.U.Inst. on Fed.Tax. Ch. 43 (1981); Mylan, "Installment Sales Revision Act of 1980," 17 Willamette L.Rev. 303 (1981). For an article proposing the subsequently enacted 1980 changes, see Ginsburg, "Taxing the Sale for Future Payment," 30 Tax L.Rev. 469 (1975).

6. See Chapter 21 supra.

7. See, e.g., the concept of assignment of income considered in Chapter 14 supra.

8. I.R.C. § 453(b)(1).

9. Generally the term "payment" does not include the receipt of evidences of indebtedness of the person acquiring the property. I.R.C. § 453(f)(3). However, receipt of evidences of indebtedness which are payable on demand, or are issued by corporations and government entities and readily tradeable will be treated as payments. I.R.C. § 453(f)(4). See Reg. § 15A.453–1(b)(3).

10. Reg. § 15A.453–1(b)(2)(v).

11. Reg. § 15A.453–1(b)(2)(iii).

12. Reg. § 15A.453–1(b)(2)(ii). Selling price means the gross selling price without reduction for any existing indebtedness on the property. For installment sales in taxable years ending after October 19, 1980, selling expenses are not deducted from the selling price, but are added to the adjusted basis for purposes of determining the gross profit ratio.

13. See Reg. § 15A.453–1(b)(2)(iii). The contract price is adjusted for any qualified indebtedness assumed or taken subject to by the buyer. Id. See notes 62–68, infra.

14. Cf. I.R.C. § 483. Interest payments are taxed under the Seller's method of accounting separate from the payment of the principal obligation.

profit of $360,000 ($400,000 amount realized on the property over the life of the payments less the $40,000 adjusted basis) and a total contract price of $400,000. As each $100,000 payment is made, the ratio of the gross profit to the total contract price ($360,000/$400,000) or 90 percent of the payment received is included in Seller's gross income. Thus there is $90,000 of gross income as each payment is made with the result that Seller's $360,000 gain realized on the sale is spread over the four year payment period. The total gain realized on the sale is eventually included in Seller's gross income, but the timing of the inclusion depends upon the timing of Buyer's payments.[15]

Consistent with the policy of spreading the gain over the life of the payments, the character of the gain recognized is governed by the character of the gain which would have been recognized if the property had been sold for its full fair market value in cash.[16] Thus, because Seller's investment land was a capital asset held for longer than one year, each $90,000 inclusion in gross income constitutes a long-term capital gain.[17]

A taxpayer may affirmatively elect not to use Section 453 installment sales treatment.[18] The election must be made on or before the due date (including extensions) of the taxpayer's income tax return for the taxable year in which the sale or other disposition of the property occurs.[19] The consequences of an election-out are considered in the next subpart of this Chapter.[20] Why would a taxpayer ever want to elect out of Section 453 treatment?

Contingent Sales Price. Prior to 1980 it was sometimes to a taxpayer's advantage to postpone the gain on a sale of property by providing a contingency under a sales contract thereby precluding the applicability of Section 453. In the Installment Sales Revision Act of 1980, Congress provided that even sales with a contingent sale price were to be subject to Section 453 treatment.[21] The Senate Committee Report of the 1980 legislation reported the change in the law as follows: [22]

---

15. If the amount of payments is unequal, then the amounts included in gross income are also unequal. For example, if Buyer paid Seller $100,000 in year one, $50,000 in years two and three and $200,000 in year four, Seller would include 90% ($360,000/$400,000) of each payment in gross income or $90,000 in year one, $45,000 in years two and three and $180,000 in year four. The result is total gross income inclusion of $360,000.

16. Cf. I.R.C. § 453(i) for the recognition of recapture income under § 1245 or § 1250.

17. I.R.C. § 1222(3).

18. I.R.C. § 453(d)(1). In the absence of election, § 453 automatically applies to all installment sales.

19. I.R.C. § 453(d)(2). See Rev.Rul. 90–46, 1990–1 C.B. 107, providing guidance as to when the Service will allow a late election out of I.R.C. § 453. The election may be revoked only with the Secretary's consent. I.R.C. § 453(d)(3).

20. See Chapter 24B, infra.

21. I.R.C. § 453(j)(2). The Secretary has authority to prescribe regulations necessary to determine ratable basis recovery in transaction where the sales price or gross profit percentage cannot be determined on the date of sale. See Reg. § 15A.453–1(c).

22. S.Rep. No. 96–1000, 96th Cong., 2d Sess. 1, 22–24 (1980), 1980–2 C.B. 494, 506–507.

Present Law.—As a general rule, installment reporting of gain from deferred payments is not available where all or a portion of the selling price is subject to a contingency. The case law holds that the selling price must be fixed and determinable for section 453(b) to apply.[23] An agreement, however, to indemnify the purchaser for breach of certain warranties and representations by offset against the purchase price will not disqualify an installment sale under section 453(b).[24] Exactly how broad such contingencies can be is unclear.

Where an installment sale is subject to a contingency with respect to the price and the installment method is not available, the taxpayer is required to recognize all of the gain in the year of the sale with respect to all of the payments to be made, even though such payments are payable in future taxable years. In the case of a cash-method taxpayer where the future payments have no readily ascertainable fair market value, the taxpayer may treat the transaction with respect to those payments as "open" and use the cost-recovery method under *Burnet v. Logan,* 283 U.S. 404 (1931).[25]

* * *

Explanation of Provision.—The bill permits installment sale reporting for sales for a contingent selling price. In extending eligibility, the bill does not prescribe specific rules for every conceivable transaction. Rather, the bill provides that specific rules will be prescribed under regulations.[26]

However, it is intended that, for sales under which there is a stated maximum selling price, the regulations will permit basis recovery on the basis of a gross profit ratio determined by reference to the stated maximum selling price.[27] For purposes of this provision, incidental or remote contingencies are not to be taken into account in determining if there is a stated maximum selling price. In general, the maximum selling price would be determined from the "four corners" of the contract agreement as the largest price which could be paid to the taxpayer assuming all contingencies, formulas, etc., operate in the taxpayer's favor. Income from the sale would be reported on a pro rata basis with respect to each installment payment using the maximum selling price to determine the total contract price and gross profit ratio. If, pursuant to standards prescribed by regulations, it is subsequently determined that the contingency will not be satisfied in whole or in part, thus reducing the maximum selling price, the taxpayer's income from the sale would be recomputed.[28] The taxpayer

---

23. Gralapp v. U.S., 458 F.2d 1158 (10th Cir.1972); In re Steen, 509 F.2d 1398 (9th Cir.1975).

24. See Rev.Rul. 77–56, 1977–1 C.B. 135.

25. [See Chapter 24B1, infra. Ed.]

26. [See I.R.C. § 453(j)(2). Ed.]

27. [See Reg. § 15A.453–1(c)(2)(i). Ed.]

28. [Id.]

would then report reduced income, as adjusted, with respect to each installment payment received in the taxable year of adjustment and subsequent taxable years. If the maximum price is reduced in more than one taxable year, e.g., because of successive changes in the status of the contingency, each such year of reduction would constitute an adjustment year.

Where the taxpayer has reported more income from installment payments received in previous taxable years than the total recomputed income, the taxpayer would be permitted to deduct the excesses in the adjustment year as a loss.

In cases where the sales price is indefinite and no maximum selling price can be determined but the obligation is payable over a fixed period of time, it is generally intended that basis of the property sold would be recovered ratably over the fixed period.[29] In a case where the selling price and payment period are both indefinite but a sale has in fact occurred, it is intended that the regulations would permit ratable basis recovery over some reasonable period of time.[30] Also, in appropriate cases, it is intended that basis recovery would be permitted under an income forecast type method.[31]

The creation of a statutory deferred payment option for all forms of deferred payment sales significantly expands the availability of installment reporting to include situations where it has not previously been permitted. By providing an expanded statutory installment reporting option, the Committee believes that in the future there should be little incentive to devise convoluted forms of deferred payment obligations to attempt to obtain deferred reporting. In any event, the effect of the new rules is to reduce substantially the justification for treating transactions as "open" and permitting the use of the cost-recovery method sanctioned by Burnet v. Logan, 283 U.S. 404 (1931). Accordingly, it is the Committee's intent that the cost-recovery method not be available in the case of sales for a

---

29. [See Reg. § 15A.453–1(c)(3)(i). Ed.]

30. [The basis is to be prorated over a 15 year period unless the taxpayer can establish that such a period "would substantially and inappropriately defer recovery of the taxpayer's basis." Reg. § 15A.453–1(c)(4). Ed.]

31. In general, the income forecast method for basis recovery is considered appropriate for a transaction with respect to which it may be demonstrated that receipts will be greater for the earlier years of the payment period and then decline for the later years of the payment period. It is intended that the regulations will deal with the application of this method with respect to sales of property qualifying for depreciation under the income forecast method (e.g. movies, mineral rights) when the selling price is based on production, a sale under which the amount payable to the seller is based on a declining percentage of the purchaser's revenues, and similar sales. In developing these regulations, the Committee intends that the Treasury Department will prescribe rules for this method to avoid, whenever possible, leaving a seller with an unrecovered basis in the obligation, and thereby creating a capital loss, after the final payment is received. For qualifying transactions, a more rapid basis recovery under this method is to be allowed even if there is a fixed period over which payments are to be received. [See Reg. § 15A.453–1(c)(6). Ed.]

fixed price (whether the seller's obligation is evidenced by a note, contractual promise, or otherwise), and that its use be limited to those rare and extraordinary cases involving sales for a contingent price where the fair market value of the purchaser's obligation cannot reasonably be ascertained.[32]

Situations in Which Section 453 is Inapplicable. There are several situations to which Section 453 does not apply. To the extent the provision is inapplicable, gain or loss must be recognized in the year of disposition.[33]

Sales at a Loss. If property is sold at a loss, no tax is due as a result of the sale. Thus no liquidity problem arises on the sale and the Service has appropriately ruled that Section 453 is inapplicable.[34]

Dealer Dispositions. Section 453 is inapplicable to dealer dispositions [35] and to dispositions of personal property which is inventory of the selling taxpayer.[36] A dealer disposition is a disposition of personal property by a person who regularly sells personal property on the installment plan,[37] or a disposition of real property which is held for sale to customers in the ordinary course of the seller's trade or business.[38] Dealer dispositions are generally [39] not subject to the installment sales rules.[40]

Recapture Income. The installment method is inapplicable to the extent of any Section 1245 or 1250 recapture gain which is required to be recognized on the sale.[41] Such gain is required to be recognized in the year of the disposition.[42] If there is any remaining Section 1231 gain or long-term capital gain on the sale of the recapture property, that remaining gain does qualify for installment treatment under a *recomputed* gross profit to total contract price ratio that reflects the recognized recapture gain.[43] For example, if in the example above (where the property had an adjusted basis of $40,000 and was sold for four $100,000 installments) the property sold was depreciable real property with $60,000 of Section 1250 recapture gain and $300,000 of Section 1231 gain, Seller would recognize the $60,000 of recapture gain in the year of sale. As a result, the gross profit ratio would have to be recomputed to reflect the $60,000 recognition of recapture gain. The gross profit for the ratio calculation would now be the remaining gain to be recognized $300,000, and the total contract price would remain $400,000. This results in ¾ ($300,000/$400,000) of each $100,000

32. See Chapter 24B, infra and Reg. § 15A.453–1(d)(2)(iii).

33. See Chapter 24B, infra.

34. Rev.Rul. 70–430, 1970–2 C.B. 51.

35. I.R.C. § 453(b)(2)(A).

36. I.R.C. § 453(b)(2)(B).

37. I.R.C. § 453(*l*)(1)(A).

38. I.R.C. § 453(*l*)(1)(B).

39. I.R.C. § 453(*l*)(2) creates exceptions (making § 453 applicable) for farm proper-

ty as defined in § 2032A(e)(4) or (5) and certain timeshares and residential lots.

40. See Chapter 24B, infra.

41. I.R.C. § 453(i)(1). Installment treatment is also inapplicable to recapture income indirectly recognized on the sale of a partnership interest under § 751. I.R.C. § 453(i)(2).

42. I.R.C. § 453(i)(1)(A).

43. I.R.C. § 453(i)(1)(B).

payment, or $75,000, being recognized as Section 1231 gain when each of the four $100,000 payments are received by Seller.[44]

Sale of Depreciable Property to a Controlled Entity. Section 453 generally does not apply to a disposition of depreciable property[45] between a taxpayer and a related person as defined in Section 1239(b).[46] In general, under Section 1239(b) a related person is a greater than 50% controlled entity, either a corporation where more than 50% of the stock is owned directly or indirectly by attribution by the Seller, or a partnership where more than 50% of the capital interest or profits interest is owned directly or indirectly by attribution by the Seller or two such controlled entities which have such 50% common ownership.[47] In addition, a related person includes a trust in which the taxpayer or his spouse has a beneficial interest.[48] However, family members are not treated as related persons under this rule.[49]

The depreciable property rule is inapplicable if the disposition did not have the avoidance of income tax as one of its principal purposes.[50] If Section 453(g) is applicable, the rule effectively places the seller on the accrual method,[51] and the gain is generally all ordinary income.[52]

Sales of Publicly Traded Stock or Securities. Section 453 treatment is denied to sales of stock or securities which are traded on an established securities market.[53] Because the seller could easily have sold such property for cash on the open market, the usual liquidity problem which Section 453 is intended to alleviate is not present and Section 453 is inapplicable.[54] All payments on such sales are treated as received in the year of the sale.[55] Regulations may extend the coverage of this exception to include similar types of property other than stock or securities traded on an established market.[56]

Sales of Personal Property on a Revolving Credit Plan. Installment treatment is also denied to sales of personal property on a

44. Thus, $135,000 ($60,000 (ordinary income) + $75,000 (§ 1231 gain)) is gain recognized in the year of sale, with $75,000 (§ 1231 gain) being recognized in each of the remaining 3 years. Total gain recognized is still the $360,000.

45. Such property must be depreciable in the hands of the related party transferee. I.R.C. § 453(f)(7).

46. I.R.C. § 453(g)(1) and (3).

47. I.R.C. § 1239(b)(1) and (c). See also I.R.C. §§ 267(b)(3), (10), (11) and (12) and 707(b)(1)(B).

48. I.R.C. § 1239(b)(2).

49. Cf. I.R.C. §§ 267(b)(1) and 1239(b).

50. I.R.C. § 453(g)(2).

51. I.R.C. § 453(g)(1)(B)(i). An exception is created for contingent payments whose fair market value is not reasonably ascertainable. As to such payments, the basis is to be recovered ratably. I.R.C. § 453(g)(1)(B)(ii).

52. I.R.C. § 1239(a).

53. I.R.C. § 453(k)(2)(A).

54. S.Rep. No. 313, 99th Cong., 2d Sess. 124 (1986), 1986–3 C.B. (Vol. 3) 124.

55. I.R.C. § 453(k) (flush language).

56. I.R.C. § 453(k)(2)(B).

revolving credit plan.[57]　As above, all payments related to such sales are deemed received in the year of sale.[58]

Nonrecognition Sales.　To the extent a sale is treated as a nonrecognition transaction under the Code,[59] only the gain required to be recognized is taxed and potentially may be subject to Section 453 treatment.[60]　For example, to the extent that there is an interspousal installment sale of property under Section 1041 (providing a general rule that no gain or loss is to be recognized on transfers between spouses or between former spouses if such transfer is incident to a divorce), no gain is recognized to the seller spouse and no installment treatment is needed even though the sale is in the form of an installment sale.[61]

Special Rules Related to Section 453.　There are several special rules which alter the general Section 453 installment sale rule.　These rules apply to situations where there is a liquidity problem or where there effectively is no liquidity problem.

Liabilities.　If property which is sold on the installment method is subject to a liability, under the *Crane* principle [62] the liability is included in the amount realized on the sale.　Relief from the liability occurs in the year of the sale and under the installment sale rules, the amount of relief should be treated as a payment in the year of the sale. However, the relief is not an actual cash payment and, as a result, the taxpayer may not have the necessary liquidity with which to pay the resulting tax liability.　The regulations partially alleviate this problem by treating relief from a liability as a nonpayment [63] as long as the amount of the liability does not exceed the adjusted basis of the property.[64]　However, to ensure sufficient recognition of gain, the ratio of gross profit to the total contract price that is used in measuring the Section 453 gain must be adjusted.　The total contract price, or denominator of the fraction, is reduced by the amount of the liability not in excess of the amount of the adjusted basis.[65]　The overall effect of this adjustment is to disregard the liability (up to the amount of the

57. I.R.C. § 453(k)(1). The regulations define a revolving credit plan to include "cycle budget accounts, flexible budget accounts, continuous budget accounts, and other similar plans or arrangements for the sale of personal property under which the customer agrees to pay each billing-month . . . a part of the outstanding balance of the customer's account." Reg. § 1.453A–2(c)(1). See also Reg. § 1.453A–2(c)(6)(vi) describing the methodology in allocating gross income to the appropriate tax years as payments are received under a revolving credit plan.

58. I.R.C. § 453(k) (flush language).

59. See Chapter 26, infra.

60. See I.R.C. § 453(f)(6) and Rev.Rul. 75, 1953–1 CB 83.

61. See Chapters 6B3 and 10B, supra.

62. See Crane v. Commissioner, supra page 143.

63. Reg. § 15A.453–1(b)(2)(iv) makes the following rules inapplicable to "[a]ny obligation created subsequent to the taxpayer's acquisition of the property and incurred or assumed by the taxpayer or placed as an encumbrance on the property in contemplation of disposition of the property. . . . if the arrangement results in accelerating recovery of the taxpayer's basis in the installment sale."

64. Reg. § 15A.453–1(b)(3)(i). If the liability exceeds the adjusted basis, the excess is treated as a payment received in the year of disposition. Id.

65. Reg. § 15A.453–1(b)(2)(iii). See also Reg. § 1.453–4(c).

adjusted basis) as a payment, while at the same time treating a greater portion of the cash payments as gain from the Section 453 sale.

For example, assume the property in the example above ($40,000 adjusted basis, $400,000 fair market value) was land subject to a $40,000 liability. If Buyer assumed the liability and paid Seller $90,000 (rather than $100,000) in each of the four years, Seller's gain would still be $360,000. Under the special liability rule, none of the liability assumed by Buyer would be treated as a payment in the year of the sale because it is not in excess of the adjusted basis of the property. However, the Section 453 ratio would be adjusted as follows: the total contract price would be reduced by $40,000, to $360,000, with the result that the gross profit/total contract price ratio would be increased to $360,000/$360,000 or one. As a result, the full $90,000 of each year's payment would be gain included in Seller's gross income. Thus, over the four year period the full $360,000 gain would still be recognized by Seller.[66]

If the amount of the liability relief exceeds the adjusted basis of the property, then the excess of the liability over the adjusted basis continues to be treated as a payment in the year of sale.[67] Using the rule above, at the point when the liability equals the adjusted basis, the ratio of gross profit to total contract price becomes one. Since the Service does not want to increase the ratio above one, the Service simply treats any excess liability as a payment in the year of the sale.[68]

Dispositions of Installment Sales Obligations. The Section 453 rules are intended to alleviate potential liquidity problems; accordingly, the rule should not be applicable if there is no potential liquidity problem. For example, if the seller of property under the installment method subsequently disposes of the Section 453 installment obligations by selling them, should Section 453 rules continue to apply? Clearly there is no longer a liquidity problem.

Similarly, a disposition of the installment obligations by gift potentially creates the opportunity for other tax avoidance schemes. For example, the seller of property, having made a sale under the installment method could make a gift of the buyer's obligations to a third person, possibly a member of his family in a lower tax bracket. As a result, the vendor would escape tax and his donee would be taxed less heavily.[69] Such avoidance possibilities and such lack of liquidity prompted the enactment in 1928 of the forerunner of Section 453B.[70]

---

66. See also Reg. § 15A.453–1(b)(5) Example (2).

67. See note 64, supra.

68. For an illustration of this rule, see Reg. § 15A.453–1(b)(5) Example (3).

69. Wallace Huntington, 15 B.T.A. 851 (1929). See H.R.Rep. No. 2, 70th Cong., 1st Sess. 16 (1928) reported in Seidman, Legislative History of Income Tax Laws 1938– 1961 at 521 (1938). Other avoidance possibilities were identified in the Report.

Thus, in 1928, prior to the enactment of § 42 of the Revenue Act of 1934, and prior to the enactment of present § 691, which was first enacted in 1942, the death of one who had made an installment sale eliminated all income tax on gain on such a sale not previously reported. But see I.R.C. §§ 453B(c) and 691(a)(4) and see Susie Salvatore, at page 284 supra.

70. Revenue Act of 1928, § 44(d), 45 Stat. 791, 806 (1928). See Roche, "Disposi-

Section 453B taxes the seller on previously untaxed gain, upon his disposition of an installment obligation. The amount of gain so taxed is either the amount realized (in the case of a satisfaction, sale or exchange) or the fair market value of the obligation (at the time of any other type of disposition, such as a gift) less the taxpayer's basis in the Section 453 obligation.[71] The basis of an installment obligation is the face amount of the obligation less the amount of income that the taxpayer would have to include in gross income if the obligation were paid off in full.[72] Test the propriety of this basis rule in the light of the reporting rules of Section 453. For example, if Seller in our prior example ($40,000 adjusted basis and four $100,000 notes) sold the notes for $400,000 prior to collecting any of them, Seller would have a $360,000 Section 453B gain [73] at the time of the sale of the notes. And properly so, because he has the cash with which to pay the tax.

In 1934 Congress added a characterization provision to what is now Section 453B. It provides that the gain or loss on the disposition of an installment obligation is to be treated as arising from a sale or exchange of the property for which the obligation was received.[74] Initially designed to accord the taxpayer an advantage under the sliding scale approach to the inclusion of capital gains in income, which was then in effect,[75] the provision is still important in characterization situations under the 1986 Code.

The term "disposition" in Section 453B is broadly interpreted. It generally includes gifts no matter the nature of the donee,[76] transfers to and from trusts,[77] and in rare circumstances even the assignment of the obligation as security for a loan,[78] but not mere changes in the terms of

---

tions of Installment Obligations," 41 Tax L.Rev. 1 (1985); Emory, "Disposition of Installment Obligation: Income Deferral, 'Thou Art Lost and Gone Forever'," 54 Iowa L.Rev. 945 (1969).

71. I.R.C. § 453B(a).

72. I.R.C. § 453B(b).

73. The gain is the difference between the amount realized on the notes ($400,000) less the bases of the obligations $40,000 ($400,000 less $360,000 of income returnable if the obligations were satisfied in full).

74. Revenue Act of 1934 § 44(d), 48 Stat. 680, 695 (1934). See I.R.C. § 453B(a) last sentence.

75. For example, the sale of an installment obligation held short-term but received upon a sale of capital asset property held long-term gets long-term capital gain treatment.

76. See I.R.C. § 453B(f); Rev.Rul. 55–157, 1955–1 C.B. 293. Thus Susie Salvatore could not have avoided the result in her case by making an installment sale of

her property and then giving the installment sales obligations to her children. See page 284 supra. But see I.R.C. § 453B(g).

77. Cases and rulings dealing with transfers to a trust include Marshall v. U.S., 26 F.Supp. 580 (S.D.Cal.1939); Springer v. United States (unreported), 69–2 U.S.T.C. ¶ 9567 (N.D.Ala.1969); Rev.Rul. 67–167, 1967–1 C.B. 107. If the transfer is to a revocable trust it does not constitute a § 453B "disposition." Rev.Rul. 74–613, 1974–2 C.B. 153. On transfers from a trust to a beneficiary, see Rev.Rul. 55–159, 1955–1 C.B. 391.

78. Rev.Rul. 65–185, 1965–2 C.B. 153. But see Elmer v. Commissioner, 65 F.2d 568 (2d Cir.1933); Town and Country Food Co., 51 T.C. 1049 (1969), acq., 1969–2 C.B. XXV; United Surgical Steel Company, Inc., 54 T.C. 1215 (1970), acq., 1971–2 C.B. 3; Rev.Rul. 68–246, 1968–1 C.B. 198. Query whether these are valid authorities under current law in view of the enactment of I.R.C. § 453A(a), (b), and (d) considered infra.

the obligation itself.[79] The statute removes from the disposition rules, the transmission of installment obligations at death,[80] their distribution in certain corporate liquidations,[81] and their transfer under Section 1041 (other than in trust) between spouses and ex-spouses if incident to their divorce.[82]

If real property is sold under the installment sales provisions of Section 453, a repossession of the property by the vendor upon default by the purchaser constitutes a Section 453B disposition of the installment obligations.[83] Absent other statutory provisions, the amount of gain to be reported would be the difference between the fair market value of the property, which is treated as the consideration received upon disposition of the obligations, and the vendor's basis for the obligations, with proper adjustment for any costs incurred by the vendor.[84] Still, in economic reality the vendor has only received his original property back. With an interruption, it is fair to say that there is essentially a continuation of the vendor's original investment, a circumstance that Congress has frequently treated as a situation in which gain should not be recognized. Section 1038, a nonrecognition provision, now applies here.[85]

Related Party Sales. The rather complicated rule of Section 453(e) is aimed at taxpayers who attempt to take advantage of Section 453 even though there is liquidity generated within the scope of persons related to the Seller.[86] The Senate Report gives the background and rules of the Section: [87]

> **Present Law.**—Under present law, the installment sale statutory provision does not preclude installment sale reporting for sales between related parties. . . .
>
> Under the existing statutory framework, taxpayers have used the installment sale provision as a tax planning device for intra-family transfers of appreciated property, including marketable securities.[88] There are several tax advantages in making intra-family installment sales of appreciated property. The seller would achieve deferral of recognition of gain until the related buyer actually pays the installments to the seller, even if cash proceeds from the property are received within the

---

79. Rev.Rul. 68–419, 1968–2 C.B. 196. Cf. Rev. Rul 75–457, 1975–2 C.B. 196. But see Rev.Rul. 77–294, 1977–2 C.B. 173.

80. I.R.C. § 453B(c). But see I.R.C. § 691(a)(4).

81. I.R.C. § 453B(d). Cf. I.R.C. § 453(h).

82. I.R.C. § 453B(g).

83. Reg. § 1.453–5(b)(2).

84. The same result follows if, instead of a mere repossession, the vendor reacquires the property upon a foreclosure sale, applying the purchaser's obligation against the purchase price. Reg. § 1.453–5(b)(2).

85. However, the nonrecognition concept is reserved for Chapter 26, infra, and a brief note on I.R.C. § 1038 appears there at page 964.

86. See Emory and Hjorth, "Installment Sales Act Part II: Cost Recovery, Liquidations, Related Party Dispositions," 54 J. Tax'n 130, 133–34 (1981).

87. S.Rep. No. 96–1000, supra note 22, at 12–17, 500–502.

88. Another technique used for intra-family transfers involves the so-called "private annuity" arrangement. The bill does not deal directly with this type of arrangement.

related party group from a subsequent resale by the installment buyer shortly after making the initial purchase. In addition to spreading out the gain recognized by the seller over the term of the installment sale, the seller may achieve some estate planning benefits since the value of the installment obligation generally will be frozen for estate tax purposes. Any subsequent appreciation in value of the property sold, or in property acquired by reinvestment of the proceeds from the property sold on the installment basis, would not affect the seller's gross estate since the value of the property is no longer included in his gross estate.

With respect to the related buyer, there is usually no tax to be paid if the appreciated property is resold shortly after the installment purchase. Since the buyer's adjusted basis is a cost basis which includes the portion of the purchase price payable in the future, the gain or loss from the buyer's resale would represent only the fluctuation in value occurring after the installment purchase. Thus, after the related party's resale, all appreciation has been realized within the related group but the recognition of the gain for tax purposes may be deferred for a long period of time.

In the leading case, Rushing v. Commissioner,[89] the test was held to be that, in order to receive the installment benefits, the "seller may not directly or indirectly have control over the proceeds or possess the economic benefit therefrom." In this case, a sale of corporate stock was made to the trustee of trusts for the benefit of the seller's children. Since the sales were made to trusts created after the corporations had adopted plans of liquidation, the Government made an assignment of income argument. The Court upheld installment sale treatment for the stock sold to the trustee under the "control or enjoyment" test because the trustee was independent of the taxpayer and owed a fiduciary duty to the children. The Court rejected the assignment of income argument because it found that no income was being assigned.

* * *

Explanation of Provision.—The bill prescribes special rules for situations involving installment sales to certain related parties who also dispose of the property. . . .[90]

Under the bill, the amount realized upon certain resales by the related party installment purchaser will trigger recognition of gain by the initial seller, based on his gross profit ratio, only to the extent the amount realized from the second disposition exceeds actual payments made under the installment

---

89. 441 F.2d 593 (5th Cir.1971), affirming 52 T.C. 888 (1969).

90. [See I.R.C. § 453(e)(1). Ed.]

sale.[91] Thus, acceleration of recognition of the installment gain from the first sale will generally result only to the extent additional cash and other property flows into the related group as a result of a second disposition of the property. In the case of a second disposition which is not a sale or exchange, the fair market value of the property disposed of is treated as the amount realized for this purpose. . . .[92]

The excess of any amount realized from resales over payments received on the first sale as of the end of a taxable year will be taken into account. Thus, the tax treatment would not turn on the strict chronological order in which resales or payments are made. If, under these rules, a resale results in the recognition of gain to the initial seller, subsequent payments actually received by that seller would be recovered tax-free until they have equaled the amount realized from the resale which resulted in the acceleration of recognition of gain.[93]

In the case of property other than marketable securities, the resale rule will apply only with respect to second dispositions occurring within 2 years of the initial installment sale. . . .[94]

In the case of marketable securities, the resale rule would apply without a time limit for resales occurring before the installment obligation is satisfied. For this purpose, the term "marketable security" means any security for which, as of the date of disposition, there was a market on an established securities market, or otherwise.[95]

The bill also contains several exceptions to the application of these rules. . . .[96] [T]he resale rules will not apply in any case where it is established to the satisfaction of the Internal Revenue Service that none of the dispositions had as one of its principal purposes the avoidance of Federal income taxes.[97]

In the exceptional cases to which the nonavoidance exception may apply, it is anticipated that regulations would provide definitive rules so that complicated legislation is not necessary to prescribe substituted property or taxpayer rules which would not be of general application. In appropriate cases, it is anticipated that the regulations and rulings under the nontax

---

91. [See I.R.C. § 453(e)(3). Thus, if the initial seller received a $100,000 cash down payment and the related party also made a $100,000 second disposition, I.R.C. § 453(e) would not apply. Ed.]

92. [See I.R.C. § 453(e)(4). Ed.]

93. [See I.R.C. § 453(e)(5). Ed.]

94. [See I.R.C. § 453(e)(2)(A). Ed.]

95. [Footnote omitted. After 1986, I.R.C. § 453 is inapplicable to installment

sales of marketable securities. I.R.C. § 453(k)(2). See note 53, supra. Thus this rule would apply only to pre–1987 installment sales of such property. Ed.]

96. [See I.R.C. § 453(e)(6)(A)–(C). Ed.]

97. [See I.R.C. § 453(e)(7). See also Roche, "Satisfying the Secretary: Demonstrating Lack of Tax Avoidance Motivation in Related Party Installment Sales," 5 Vir. Tax Rev. 91 (1985). Ed.]

avoidance exception will deal with certain tax-free transfers which normally would not be treated as a second disposition of the property, e.g., charitable transfers, like-kind exchanges, gift transfers and transfers to a controlled corporation or a partnership. Generally it is intended that a second disposition will qualify under the nontax avoidance exception when it is of an involuntary nature, e.g., foreclosure upon the property by a judgment lien creditor of the related purchaser or bankruptcy of the related purchaser. In addition it is intended that the exception will apply in the case of a second disposition which is also an installment sale if the terms of payment under the installment resale are substantially equivalent to, or longer than, those for the first installment sale. However, the exception would not apply if the resale terms would permit significant deferral of recognition of gain from the initial sale when proceeds from the resale are being collected sooner.

Under the bill, the period for assessing a deficiency in tax attributable to a second disposition by the related purchaser will not expire before the day which is 2 years after the date the initial installment seller furnishes a notice that there was a second disposition of the property.[98] The notice is to be furnished in the manner prescribed by regulations. Under the bill, a protective notification may be filed to prevent the tolling of the period of limitations for assessing a deficiency in cases where there are questions as to whether a second disposition has occurred (e.g., a lease which might be characterized as a sale or exchange for tax purposes) or whether there is a principal purpose of Federal income tax avoidance.

For purposes of the related party rules, the bill adopts a definition of related parties which will include spouses, children, grandchildren, and parents. . . . [99]

In the case of a corporation, it will be considered to be related to another taxpayer if stock which is or might be owned by it is or would be treated as owned by the other taxpayer under the general corporate attribution rules (Code Section 318). Generally, a related corporation will be one in which a person directly or indirectly owns 50 percent or more in value of the stock in the corporation. Also for this purpose, the principles of the general corporate stock ownership attribution rules (Code Section 318) will apply in determining the related party status of partnerships, trusts, and estates.[100]

It is to be understood that the provisions governing the use of the installment method to report sales between related parties, and the definition of such relationships, are not intend-

98. [See I.R.C. § 453(e)(8). Ed.]

99. [See I.R.C. §§ 453(f)(1), 318(a), 267(b). Ed.]

100. [The 1986 Act extended the related persons definition to include I.R.C. § 267(b) relationships. Ed.]

ed to preclude the Internal Revenue Service from asserting the proper tax treatment of transactions that are shams.

As an illustration of the above rules, assume that Seller sold land with a $40,000 adjusted basis to his Daughter in exchange for a $400,000 note to be paid off in 4 payments in years 5–8, but that in year 2, Daughter sold one-half of the land to a third party for $200,000 of cash. Under Section 453(e)(1), Seller would be treated as receiving a $200,000 payment in year 2 and would recognize a $180,000 long-term capital gain under Section 453 in that year.[101] When Seller received the first two $100,000 payments from Daughter in years 5 and 6, Seller would recognize no gain.[102] When Seller received Daughter's two final $100,000 payments in years 7 and 8, Seller would recognize a further $90,000 long-term capital gain in each of those years.[103]

Section 453A. Section 453A indirectly relates to the liquidity situation under Section 453. The section involves two rules that apply only to nondealer sales of property [104] under the installment method where the sale price exceeds $150,000.[105] The Section 453A rules apply in two diverse situations.[106]

The first rule, found in Section 453A(c), is applicable in very limited situations and is related to the "time value of money" concept.[107] Since the use of the installment method essentially defers payment of Seller's tax liability, taxpayers in effect are borrowing money tax-free from the federal government. In limited circumstances, the first rule requires that interest be paid on the amount of tax which is deferred (the amount of that loan).

This rule requires a taxpayer receiving nondealer installment obligations to pay as tax in a year an amount equal to the interest the taxpayer would have had to pay if he had an underpayment of tax liability for the year in an amount equal to the tax liability deferred as a result of the installment sale.[108] The amount of the presumed underpayment of tax is the product of "deferred tax liability" and the "applicable percentage." [109] The deferred tax liability is the deferred gain which has not been recognized at the close of the taxable year [110] on the Section 453 sale multiplied by top tax rate in effect under Section 1 or Section 11 for the taxable year, depending upon the noncorporate or corporate status of the taxpayer.[111] The applicable percentage is equal to the face amount of obligations under this section

101. I.R.C. § 453(e)(1), (2)(A), (3). The $180,000 amount is the $200,000 payment multiplied by the original sale's gross profit ratio of 90% ($360,000/$400,000).

102. I.R.C. § 453(e)(5).

103. I.R.C. § 453(a).

104. Dealer dispositions do not qualify for I.R.C. § 453. See notes 35 and 40, supra.

105. I.R.C. § 453A(b)(1). Some further exceptions are found in I.R.C. § 453A(b)(3) and (4).

106. See Olchyk, "Nondealer Installment Sales Less Benefical After TAMRA," 70 J. Tax'n 132 (1989).

107. See pages 611–612, supra and pages 893–901 infra.

108. I.R.C. § 453A(c)(1).

109. I.R.C. § 453A(c)(2)(A).

110. I.R.C. § 453A(c)(3)(A).

111. I.R.C. § 453A(c)(3)(B).

outstanding as of the close of the taxable in excess of $5 million divided by the entire face amount of such obligations outstanding at the close of the taxable year.[112] The interest on the underpayment is computed at rates in effect under Section 6621(a)(2), the section used to compute interest on tax deficiency payments.[113]

Section 453A(b)(2) provides an important exception to the above rule, making it applicable only to that portion of a taxpayer's total face amount of nondealer real property installment obligations that both arise in a year and are outstanding as of the close of the year that are in excess of $5 million. Thus, if a nondealer makes $5 million of such sales in year one, Section 453A(c) is inapplicable.[114] If $15 million of such sales are made in year two and are outstanding at the end of the year, two-thirds of the $15 million of obligations is subject to the underpayment interest rule.[115] Furthermore the two-thirds, or any unpaid portion continues to be subject to the rule until the full $15 million of obligations is discharged.[116] If another $5 million of such sales is made in year three, the year three obligations are again within the exception and are not subject to Section 453A(c).[117]

Although the interest payment is treated as a tax liability under Section 453A(c)(1), it is essentially an interest payment and it is therefore subject to the general rules regarding the deductibility of interest on an underpayment of tax.[118]

The second rule, found in Section 453A(d), applies if a nondealer installment obligation is pledged as security [119] for an indebtedness.[120] Since the proceeds of the indebtedness create liquidity for the holder of the installment obligation, the net proceeds of the indebtedness are treated as a Section 453 payment.[121] The Section 453A(d) rule bears similarity to the Section 453B disposition rule. The amount of imputed payment may not exceed the remaining total contract price left to be paid under the installment obligation.[122] And once a payment is imputed under Section 453A(d), then no actual installment obligation payments are included as Section 453 payments until the previously imputed amount is recovered.[123]

---

112. I.R.C. § 453A(c)(4).

113. I.R.C. § 453A(c)(2)(B). Thus the amount treated as additional tax imposed is equal to the product of the deferred tax liability times the applicable percentage times the underpayment rate.

114. I.R.C. § 453A(b)(2).

115. See I.R.C. § 453A(c)(4). The two-thirds ratio is a fraction computed as follows: $15 million less $5 million/$15 million.

116. I.R.C. § 453A(c)(1) to (3).

117. I.R.C. § 453A(b)(2).

118. I.R.C. § 453A(c)(5).

119. See I.R.C. § 453A(d)(4).

120. Again, the installment obligation must arise in a sale whose price exceeds $150,000. I.R.C. § 453A(b)(1).

121. I.R.C. § 453A(d)(1).

122. I.R.C. § 453A(d)(2).

123. I.R.C. § 453A(d)(3). Cf. I.R.C. § 453(e)(5) (1986).

PROBLEMS

1.   Seller owns a parcel of land which he purchased five years ago for $2000.   He sells it to Buyer under an arrangement where buyer pays him $2000 cash in the current year and gives him four 12 percent interest bearing notes to be paid off in each of the succeeding four years.   Each note has a $2000 face amount and a $1750 fair market value.   Disregarding the tax consequences of any interest payments, what results to Seller in each of the five years if in the alternative:

(a)   Seller is a cash method taxpayer who makes no § 453(d) election.

(b)   Seller is an accrual method taxpayer who makes no § 453(d) election.

(c)   What result to Seller in (b), above, if the property was instead an office building on which Seller had claimed depreciation and the § 1250 recapture on the building amounted to $3000? See § 453(i).

(d)   What result to Seller in part (b), above, if the property is a building (not including the land underlying it) which Seller rented to a third person and depreciated on the straight-line method and the sale is to Corporation 100% of whose stock is owned by Seller and Corporation continues to rent the property to the third person?

(e)   What result to Seller in (b), above, if prior to collecting any of the notes he sells them to a third party for their fair market value of $7000?

(f)   What result to Seller in (b), above, if prior to collecting any of the notes he gives them to his Daughter?   Assume the notes are still worth $1750 each.   What results to Daughter when she receives full payment of the notes?

(g)   What results to Seller in part (b), above, if the property was subject to a $2000 mortgage which Buyer assumed and Buyer gave Seller only three of the $2000 notes?

(h)   What results to Seller in part (b), above, if the property was subject to a $3000 mortgage which Buyer assumed and Buyer gave Seller two $2000 notes to be paid in each of the succeeding two years and a $1000 note to be paid in the fourth year?

(i)   What result in part (a), above, if the sale is made to Daughter who immediately resells the property to Buyer for $10,000? See § 453(e).

(j)   What result in part (i), above, if instead Daughter resold the property for $11,000 in the *succeeding year* before the note for that year was paid?   Subsequently, the note for the year was timely paid by Daughter.

(k) What result if the resale price in (j), above, was $9,000?

(*l*) What result to Seller under the facts of parts (i) and (k), above, on his collection of the remaining notes from Daughter?

2. Client has a rental building that he acquired several years ago and depreciated using the straight-line method. It currently has an adjusted basis of $200,000 and a value of $500,000. Buyer purchases the building giving Client five $100,000 12% interest bearing notes, one to be paid in each of the five succeeding years (years two through six). In the year of sale (year one), Client borrows $200,000 pledging the $500,000 of Buyer's notes as security. What tax consequences to Client in the current year and each of the succeeding five years?

3. Taxpayer, a cash method taxpayer, owned all the stock in a company that owned all the rights in a new type of X-ray scanning device which had an extremely speculative value. She had owned the stock for several years and had a $100,000 cost basis in it. She sold the stock to a big electronics firm for 10 percent of the earnings generated by the scanning device over the succeeding 25 years. Although her right to earnings was speculative, she received $15,000 in each of the 25 succeeding years.

(a) What are the tax consequences to Taxpayer in each year?

(b) Would your result in (a), above, be altered if Taxpayer is an accrual method taxpayer?

(c) What result in (a), above, if the maximum stated sales price is $300,000, and after 20 years having paid $300,000 the electronics firm terminates their payments?

B. TRANSACTIONS ELECTED OUT OF SECTION 453

---

1. OPEN TRANSACTIONS

Internal Revenue Code: Sections 453(d); 1001(a) through (c); 1011(a). Regulations: Section 1.1001–1(a).

BURNET v. LOGAN

Supreme Court of the United States, 1931.
283 U.S. 404, 51 S.Ct. 550.

Mr. Justice McREYNOLDS delivered the opinion of the Court.

These causes present the same questions. One opinion, stating the essential circumstances disclosed in No. 521, will suffice for both.

Prior to March, 1913, and until March 11, 1916, respondent, Mrs. Logan, owned 250 of the 4,000 capital shares issued by the Andrews & Hitchcock Iron Company. It held 12% of the stock of the Mahoning Ore & Steel Company, an operating concern. In 1895 the latter corporation procured a lease for 97 years upon the "Mahoning" mine and since then has regularly taken therefrom large, but varying, quantities of iron ore—in 1913, 1,515,428 tons; in 1914, 1,212,287 tons; in 1915, 2,311,940 tons; in 1919, 1,217,167 tons; in 1921, 303,020 tons; in 1923, 3,029,865 tons. The lease contract did not require production of either maximum or minimum tonnage or any definite payments. Through an agreement of stockholders (steel manufacturers) the Mahoning Company is obligated to apportion extracted ore among them according to their holdings.

On March 11, 1916, the owners of all the shares in Andrews & Hitchcock Company sold them to Youngstown Sheet & Tube Company, which thus acquired, among other things, 12% of the Mahoning Company's stock and the right to receive the same percentage of ore thereafter taken from the leased mine.

For the shares so acquired the Youngstown Company paid the holders $2,200,000 in money and agreed to pay annually thereafter for distribution among them 60 cents for each ton of ore apportioned to it. Of this cash Mrs. Logan received 250/4000ths—$137,500; and she became entitled to the same fraction of any annual payment thereafter made by the purchaser under the terms of sale.

Mrs. Logan's mother had long owned 1100 shares of the Andrews & Hitchcock Company. She died in 1917, leaving to the daughter one-half of her interest in payments thereafter made by the Youngstown Company. This bequest was appraised for federal estate tax purposes at $277,164.50.

During 1917, 1918, 1919 and 1920 the Youngstown Company paid large sums under the agreement. Out of these respondent received on account of her 250 shares $9,900.00 in 1917, $11,250.00 in 1918, $8,995.50 in 1919, $5,444.30 in 1920—$35,589.80. By reason of the interest from her mother's estate she received $19,790.10 in 1919, and $11,977.49 in 1920.

Reports of income for 1918, 1919 and 1920 were made by Mrs. Logan upon the basis of cash receipts and disbursements. They included no part of what she had obtained from annual payments by the Youngstown Company. She maintains that until the total amount actually received by her from the sale of her shares equals their value on March 1, 1913, no taxable income will arise from the transaction. Also that until she actually receives by reason of the right bequeathed to her a sum equal to its appraised value, there will be no taxable income therefrom.

On March 1, 1913, the value of the 250 shares then held by Mrs. Logan *exceeded* $173,089.80—the total of all sums actually received by her prior to 1921 from their sale ($137,500.00 cash in 1916 plus four annual payments amounting to $35,589.80). That value also exceeded original cost of the shares. The amount received on the interest devised by her mother was less than its valuation for estate taxation; also less than the value when acquired by Mrs. Logan.

The Commissioner ruled that the obligation of the Youngstown Company to pay 60 cents per ton had a fair market value of $1,942,111.46 on March 11, 1916; that this value should be treated as so much cash and the sale of the stock regarded as a closed transaction with no profit in 1916. He also used this valuation as the basis for apportioning subsequent annual receipts between income and return of capital. His calculations, based upon estimates and assumptions, are too intricate for brief statement.* He made deficiency assessments according to the view just stated and the Board of Tax Appeals approved the result.

The Circuit Court of Appeals held that, in the circumstances, it was impossible to determine with fair certainty the market value of the agreement by the Youngstown Company to pay 60 cents per ton. Also, that respondent was entitled to the return of her capital—the value of 250 shares on March 1, 1913, and the assessed value of the interest derived from her mother—before she could be charged with any taxable income. As this had not in fact been returned, there was no taxable income.

We agree with the result reached by the Circuit Court of Appeals.

The 1916 transaction was a sale of stock—not an exchange of property. We are not dealing with royalties or deductions from gross income because of depletion of mining property. Nor does the situation demand that an effort be made to place according to the best available data some approximate value upon the contract for future payments. This probably was necessary in order to assess the mother's estate. As annual payments on account of extracted ore come in they can be readily apportioned first as return of capital and later as profit. The liability for income tax ultimately can be fairly determined without resort to mere estimates, assumptions and speculation. When the

---

* In the brief for petitioner the following appears:

"The fair market value of the Youngstown contract on March 11, 1916, was found by the Commissioner to be $1,942,111.46. This was based upon an estimate that the ore reserves at the Mahoning mine amounted to 82,858,535 tons; that all such ore would be mined; that 12 percent (or 9,942,564.2 tons) would be delivered to the Youngstown Company. The total amount to be received by all the vendors of stock would then be $5,965,814.52 at the rate of 60 cents per ton. The Commissioner's figure for the fair market value on March 11, 1916, was the then worth of $5,965,814.52, upon the assumption that the amount was to be received in equal annual installments during 45 years, discounted at 6 per cent, with a provision for a sinking fund at 4 per cent. For lack of evidence to the contrary this value was approved by the Board. The value of the 550/4000 interest which each acquired by bequest was fixed at $277,164.50 for purposes of Federal estate tax at the time of the mother's death.

"During the years here involved the Youngstown Company made payments in accordance with the terms of the contract, and respondents respectively received sums proportionate to the interests in the contract which they acquired by exchange of property and by bequest.

"The Board held that respondents' receipts from the contract, during the years in question, represented 'gross income'; that respondents should be allowed to deduct from said gross income a reasonable allowance for exhaustion of their contract interests; and that the balance of the receipts should be regarded as taxable income."

profit, if any, is actually realized, the taxpayer will be required to respond. The consideration for the sale was $2,200,000.00 in cash and the promise of future money payments wholly contingent upon facts and circumstances not possible to foretell with anything like fair certainty. The promise was in no proper sense equivalent to cash. It had no ascertainable fair market value. The transaction was not a closed one. Respondent might never recoup her capital investment from payments only conditionally promised. Prior to 1921 all receipts from the sale of her shares amounted to less than their value on March 1, 1913. She properly demanded the return of her capital investment before assessment of any taxable profit based on conjecture.

> "In order to determine whether there has been gain or loss, and the amount of the gain, if any, we must withdraw from the gross proceeds an amount sufficient to restore the capital value that existed at the commencement of the period under consideration." Doyle v. Mitchell Bros. Co., 247 U.S. 179, 184, 185, 83 S.Ct. 467, 469. Rev.Act 1916, § 2, 39 Stat. 757, 758; Rev.Act 1918, c. 18, 40 Stat. 1057. Ordinarily, at least, a taxpayer may not deduct from gross receipts a supposed loss which in fact is represented by his outstanding note. Eckert v. Commissioner of Internal Revenue, ante, p. 140, 51 S.Ct. 373. And, conversely, a promise to pay indeterminate sums of money is not necessarily taxable income. "Generally speaking, the income tax law is concerned only with realized losses, as with realized gains." Lucas v. American Code Co., 280 U.S. 445, 449, 50 S.Ct. 202.

From her mother's estate Mrs. Logan obtained the right to share in possible proceeds of a contract thereafter to pay indefinite sums. The value of this was assumed to be $277,164.50 and its transfer was so taxed. Some valuation—speculative or otherwise—was necessary in order to close the estate. It may never yield as much, it may yield more. If a sum equal to the value thus ascertained had been invested in an annuity contract, payments thereunder would have been free from income tax until the owner had recouped his capital investment.* We think a like rule should be applied here. The statute definitely excepts bequests from receipts which go to make up taxable income. See Burnet v. Whitehouse, ante, p. 148, 51 S.Ct. 374.

> The judgments below are affirmed.

---

* Current statutory rules tax a portion of each annuity payment as received. See I.R.C. § 72, supra page 169. Moreover, a 1942 change would preclude the annuity-type treatment the court suggests for the disposition of the shares the taxpayer received from her mother. The mother's right to payment would be foreclosed from receiving a date-of-death basis by I.R.C. § 1014(c); and the recipient of payments attributable to the mother's rights would have income in respect of a decedent under § 691. See page 321, supra. None of this, however, affects the viability of the *Logan* principle regarding open transactions suggested by the treatment of payment for the shares owned originally by the taxpayer. Ed.

NOTE

Recall from Chapter 6 that under Section 1001(a) gain or loss is the difference between the "amount realized" on a disposition and the "adjusted basis" of the property relinquished. If either the "amount realized" or the "adjusted basis" is incapable of being measured then the gain or loss on a transaction is unknown as well. This simple concept is now well established as the doctrine of Burnet v. Logan,[1] or the "open transaction" doctrine.

An open transaction arises in two different types of situations. It may involve a situation like Burnet v. Logan where the amount realized is unknown; if an election is made under Section 453(d),[2] the doctrine leaves these transactions "open" to see what is actually received in subsequent years. As amounts are received they initially constitute a recovery of capital. Once an amount equal to the adjusted basis of the transferred property is received capital has been recovered, and any further receipts constitute income in the year received. These are all concepts considered in Chapter 6 and a student may be asking: Why defer consideration of the open transaction doctrine until now? The answer is: The doctrine not only has measurement and timing consequences, it has characterization aspects as well. If the doctrine of Burnet v. Logan applies and a transaction is left open then subsequently recognized gain (or loss) is seen to arise out of the original transfer and is characterized by that transfer. Thus any gain Mrs. Logan subsequently recognized was long term capital gain. If, however, the doctrine is inapplicable because an "amount realized" can be determined then the transaction is "closed" and gain or loss based on that determination is immediately recognized. That gain is characterized by the original transaction but, if the amount actually realized over the years exceeds the initial determination, the excess is ordinary income and is not characterized by the nature of the original sale or exchange.[3] The rationale is that, while the initial gain arose out of the sale, the later gain is merely attributable to "payment" of an obligation with a basis less than the amount received.[4] Ironically, however, if the actual receipts are less than the estimate the loss that results may take its character from the original sale. Why?

The second situation in which the open transaction doctrine applies is where the "adjusted basis" of property disposed of is unknown, rather than the "amount realized" on its disposition. No Section 453(d) election is necessary in this situation; generally payment is made in the current year and is not postponed, but even if it is, no Section 453(d)

---

1. The doctrine is applicable to both cash and accrual method taxpayers. The open transaction doctrine is given statutory application in the limited area of patent sales. I.R.C. § 1235.

2. If no I.R.C. § 453(d) election is made, § 453 strains to tax the gain. See page 862, supra.

3. Waring v. Commissioner, 412 F.2d 800 (3d Cir.1969); see Stephen H. Dorsey, 49 T.C. 606 (1968).

4. See Galvin Hudson, supra page 708.

election is required. For example, in Inaja Land Co., Ltd.,[5] the taxpayer which owned some land with a basis of approximately $61,000 sold an easement for $50,000, giving the buyer the right to divert water across the taxpayer's property. The court concluded that, as it could not determine what portion of the property was being taken, there was no way to allocate a portion of the taxpayer's basis for use in the gain or loss formula. Accordingly gain or loss was impossible to compute, and the receipt of the $50,000 was treated as a mere recovery of capital, reducing the property's basis to $11,000 but giving rise to no gain. The court stated: [6]

* * *

Capital recoveries in excess of cost do constitute taxable income. Petitioner has made no attempt to allocate a basis to that part of the property covered by the easements. It is conceded that all of petitioner's lands were not affected by the easements conveyed. Petitioner does not contest the rule that, where property is acquired for a lump sum and subsequently disposed of a portion at a time, there must be an allocation of the cost or other basis over the several units and gain or loss computed on the disposition of each part, except where apportionment would be wholly impracticable or impossible. Nathan Blum, 5 T.C. 702, 709. Petitioner argues that it would be impracticable and impossible to apportion a definite basis to the easements here involved, since they could not be described by metes and bounds; that the flow of the water has changed and will change the course of the river; that the extent of the flood was and is not predictable; and that to date the city has not released the full measure of water to which it is entitled. In Strother v. Commissioner, 55 F.2d 626, the court says:

* * * A taxpayer * * * should not be charged with gain on pure conjecture unsupported by any foundation of ascertainable fact. See Burnet v. Logan, 283 U.S. 404, 51 S.Ct. 550.

This rule is approved in the recent case of Raytheon Production Corporation v. Commissioner, supra. Apportionment with reasonable accuracy of the amount received not being possible, and this amount being less than petitioner's cost basis for the property, it can not be determined that petitioner has, in fact, realized gain in any amount. Applying the rule as above set out, no portion of the payment in question should be considered as income, but the full amount must be treated as a return of capital and applied in reduction of petitioner's cost basis. Burnet v. Logan, 283 U.S. 404.

* * *

But some words of caution are needed. Although the doctrine of Burnet v. Logan is well-established in tax law, its importance should

---

5. 9 T.C. 727 (1947), acq. 1948–1 C.B.   **6.** Id. at 735–736.

not be overemphasized. Section 1001(b) provides that the "amount realized" on a disposition of property is the amount of money received plus the fair market value of any property *received*. But recall from the *Philadelphia Park Amusement* case in Chapter 6[7] that if the value of what is received cannot be ascertained in any arm's length transaction, it will be assumed that it is equal to the value of the property given up. Thus for the open transaction doctrine to apply on the ground that the amount realized cannot be ascertained, both the value of the property transferred and the value of the property received must be unknown.

Additionally, the doctrine should not be overemphasized because, as the regulations properly state:[8] "The fair market value of property is a question of fact, but only in *rare and extraordinary* cases will property be considered to have no fair market value." Thus only in "rare and extraordinary circumstances" will courts cry "uncle" and give up on estimating fair market value. When they do, it does not mean it is completely impossible to make some sort of studied guess at value. Witness the fact that in the Burnet v. Logan case the mother's right to payment was in fact "valued" for estate tax purposes in 1917 even though her right then involved the amount of future payments to be expected which was the subject of controversy in the later income tax case. Nevertheless, the right to future payment was said to be incapable of being valued for income tax purposes. Why the difference?

A more recent example of an application of the open transaction doctrine occurred in Stephen H. Dorsey[9] where in return for their stock in a pinsetting company the taxpayers became entitled to receive one percent of all receipts by AMF from the sale or lease of its automatic pinsetting machines. The courts applied Burnet v. Logan because of the uncertainties and contingencies existing at the time of the transfer stating:[10]

* * *

Here, as in Burnet v. Logan, supra, the petitioners received a "promise of future money payments wholly contingent upon facts and circumstances not possible to foretell with anything like fair certainty." A fair preponderance of the evidence in this record supports the position of petitioners that their contract rights with AMF had no ascertainable fair market value on September 16, 1954. Among the principal uncertainties and contingencies which existed on September 16, 1954, were:

1. *Conditions Prevalent in the Bowling Industry,* particularly the unsavory past reputation of bowling and its unknown future potential.

---

7. See page 124, supra.

8. Reg. § 1.1001–1(a); see also Reg. § 15A.453–1(d)(2)(ii) and (iii).

9. Supra note 3.

10. Id. at 629.

2. *Obstacles to the Success of Automatic Pinsetters Within the Bowling Industry,* including the uncertainty as to their acceptance by the public and by bowling proprietors, their unproven status as a unique new product, and marketing problems.

3. *Problems Facing the AMF Pinsetter,* such as patent infringement suits, the quantity and quality of competition, especially from Brunswick Corp., the fact that AMF was a newcomer to the bowling industry in 1954, and the pinsetter's unproven character.

4. *Difficulties of Ascertaining How Much of Any Success Would Actually Redound to the Participating Certificate Holders,* this being a consequence of AMF's control and constant changing of pinsetter prices, AMF's control of all marketing and management decisions, and the possibility that AMF could have operated its own pinsetting machines rather than sell or lease them, in which event the petitioners would have received no payments.

In short, without relying solely on any specific factor, we believe that the participating certificates had no ascertainable fair market value on September 16, 1954, and that the transaction before us must be treated as an "open" transaction.

* * *

PROBLEMS

Taxpayer, a cash method taxpayer, owned all the stock in a company that owned all the rights in a new type of X-ray scanning device which had an extremely speculative value. She had owned the stock for several years and had a $100,000 cost basis in it. She sold the stock to a big electronics firm for $50,000 cash and 2 percent of the earnings generated by the scanning device over the succeeding life of the electronics firm and she made a § 453(d) election. Although her right to earnings is speculative, she receives $2000 in each of the succeeding years.

(a) What are the tax consequences to Taxpayer in each year?

(b) Would your result in (a), above, be altered if Taxpayer is an accrual method taxpayer?

2. CLOSED TRANSACTIONS

a. Cash Method Taxpayers

Regulation: Section 15A.453–1(d)(1) and (2).

———

WARREN JONES CO. v. COMMISSIONER

United States Court of Appeals, Ninth Circuit, 1975.
524 F.2d 788.

ELY, Circuit Judge: During its taxable year ending on October 31, 1968, the Warren Jones Company, a cash basis taxpayer, sold an apartment building for $153,000. In return, the taxpayer received a cash downpayment of $20,000 and the buyer's promise in a standard form real estate contract, to pay $133,000, plus interest, over the following fifteen years. The Tax Court held, with three judges dissenting, that the fair market value of the real estate contract did not constitute an "amount realized" by the taxpayer in the taxable year of sale under section 1001(b) of the Internal Revenue Code.[1] Warren Jones Co., 60 T.C. 663 (1973) (reviewed by the full Court). The Commissioner of Internal Revenue has appealed, and we reverse.

I. Background

On May 27, 1968, the taxpayer, a family-held corporation chartered by the State of Washington, entered into a real estate contract for the sale of one of its Seattle apartment buildings, the Wallingford Court Apartments, to Bernard and Jo Ann Storey for $153,000. When the sale closed on June 15, 1968, the Storeys paid $20,000 in cash and took possession of the apartments. The Storeys were then obligated by the contract to pay the taxpayer $1,000 per month, plus 8 percent interest on the declining balance, for a period of fifteen years. The balance due at the end of fifteen years is to be payable in a lump sum. The contract was the only evidence of the Storeys' indebtedness, since no notes or other such instruments passed between the parties. Upon receipt of the full purchase price, the taxpayer is obligated by the contract to deed the Wallingford Apartments to the Storeys.

The Tax Court found, as facts, that the transaction between the taxpayer and the Storeys was a completed sale in the taxable year ending on October 31, 1968, and that in that year, the Storeys were solvent obligors. The court also found that real estate contracts such as that between the taxpayer and the Storeys were regularly bought and sold in the Seattle area. The court concluded, from the testimony before it, that in the taxable year of sale, the taxpayer could have sold its contract, which had a face value of $133,000, to a savings and loan association or a similar institutional buyer for approximately $117,980. The court found, however, that in accordance with prevailing business practices, any potential buyer for the contract would likely have required the taxpayer to deposit $41,000 of the proceeds from the sale of the contract in a savings account, assigned to the buyer, for the purpose of securing the first $41,000 of the Storeys' payments. Consequently,

---

1. Unless otherwise stated, all section references are to the Internal Revenue Code of 1954, 26 U.S.C. (1970).

the court found that in the taxable year of sale, the contract had a fair market value of only $76,980 (the contract's selling price minus the amount deposited in the assigned savings account).

On the sale's closing date, the taxpayer had an adjusted basis of $61,913 in the Wallingford Apartments. In determining the amount it had realized from the sale, the taxpayer added only the $20,000 down-payment and the portion of the $4,000 in monthly payments it had received that was allocable to principal. Consequently, on its federal income tax return for the taxable year ending October 31, 1968, the taxpayer reported no gain from the apartment sale. The taxpayer's return explained that the corporation reported on the cash basis and that under the Tax Court's holding in Nina J. Ennis, 17 T.C. 465 (1951), it was not required to report gain on the sale until it had recovered its basis. * * *

* * * The question presented is whether section 1001(b) requires the taxpayer to include the fair market value of its real estate contract with the Storeys in determining the "amount realized" during the taxable year of the sale.[3]

Holding that the fair market value of the contract was not includable in the amount realized from the sale, the Tax Court majority relied on the doctrine of "cash equivalency." Under that doctrine, the cash basis taxpayer must report income received in the form of property only if the property is the "equivalent of cash." See generally 2 J. Mertens, The Law of Federal Income Taxation §§ 11.01–11.05 (Malone rev. 1974).

The Tax Court majority adopted the following as its definition of the phrase, "equivalent of cash":

> * * * if the promise to pay of a solvent obligor is unconditional and assignable, not subject to set-offs, and is of a kind that is frequently transferred to lenders or investors at a discount not substantially greater than the generally prevailing premium for the use of money, such promise is the equivalent of cash * * *

Warren Jones Co., supra at 668–69, quoting Cowden v. Commissioner, 289 F.2d 20, 24 (5th Cir.1961). Applying the quoted definition, the Tax Court held that the taxpayer's contract, which had a face value of $133,000, was not the "equivalent of cash" since it had a fair market value of only $76,980. Had the taxpayer sold the contract, the discount from the face value, approximately 42 percent, would have been "sub-

---

3. Several commentators have addressed the question. See, e.g., 2 J. Mertens, The Law of Federal Income Taxation § 11.07 (Malone rev. 1974); J. Sneed, The Configurations of Gross Income 39–62 (1967); Levin & Javaras, Receipt of Notes and Other Rights to Future Payments by a Cash-Basis Taxpayer, 54 A.B.A.J. 405 (1968); Comment, The Doctrine of Cash Equivalency, 22 U.C.L.A.L.Rev. 219 (1974); Comment, Realization of Income in Deferred-Payment Sales, 34 Mo.L.Rev. 357 (1969).

stantially greater than the generally prevailing premium for the use of money." [4]

The Tax Court observed that requiring the taxpayer to realize the fair market value of the contract in the year of the sale could subject the taxpayer to substantial hardships. The taxpayer would be taxed in the initial year on a substantial portion of its gain from the sale of the property, even though it had received, in cash, only a small fraction of the purchase price. To raise funds to pay its taxes, the taxpayer might be forced to sell the contract at the contract's fair market value, even though such a sale might not otherwise be necessary or advantageous. Most importantly in the Tax Court's view, if the taxpayer were required to realize the fair market value of the contract in the year of the sale, the sale transaction would be closed for tax purposes in that year; hence, the taxpayer's capital gain on the transaction would be permanently limited to the difference between its adjusted basis and the contract's fair market value plus the cash payments received in the year of sale. If the taxpayer did retain the contract, so as to collect its face value, the amounts received in excess of the contract's fair market value would constitute ordinary income. The Tax Court also noted that requiring the cash basis taxpayer to realize the fair market value of the real estate contract would tend to obscure the differences between the cash and accrual methods of reporting.

The Commissioner does not dispute the Tax Court's conclusion that the taxpayer's contract with the Storeys had a fair market value of $76,980, or any other of the court's findings of fact.[5] Rather, the Commissioner contends that since, as found by the Tax Court, the contract had a fair market value, section 1001(b) requires the taxpayer to include the amount of that fair market value in determining the amount realized.[6]

4. The taxpayer's argument on appeal that to be a cash equivalent, a debt instrument must be negotiable is untenable. See, e.g., Heller Trust v. Comm'r, 382 F.2d 675, 681 (9th Cir.1967); Cowden v. C.I.R., 289 F.2d 20, 24 (5th Cir.1961).

5. Relying primarily on Bedell v. Comm'r, 30 F.2d 622 (2d Cir.1929), the taxpayer disputes the Tax Court's finding that the sale of the Wallingford Apartments was a completed transaction in the taxable year ending October 31, 1968. The question whether a particular sale is completed is ordinarily a question of fact, Clodfelter v. Comm'r, 426 F.2d 1391 (9th Cir.1970), and the disputed finding in the present case is most assuredly not clearly erroneous.

6. The Commissioner's theoretical approach to the result for which he contends is not altogether clear. He may be rejecting the doctrine of cash equivalency altogether, cf. *Warren Jones Co.*, supra at 673–74 (Quealy, J., dissenting), or he may be contending that any property with a fair market value is the equivalent of cash in the amount of its fair market value. See Comment, The Doctrine of Cash Equivalency, supra n. 3 at 225–26; but see M. Levine, Real Estate Transactions, Tax Planning and Consequences § 731 (1973). Since as to a cash basis taxpayer, with which we are here concerned, both theories would achieve the same result, we need not distinguish between them.

The taxpayer contends that the basic question before us is one of fact. We disagree. The question is essentially one of statutory construction and it therefore presents an issue of law.

II. Statutory Analysis

*   *   *

*   *   * We cannot avoid the conclusion that in 1924 Congress intended to establish the more definite rule for which the Commissioner here contends and that consequently, if the fair market value of property received in an exchange can be ascertained, that fair market value must be reported as an amount realized.

Congress clearly understood that the 1924 statute might subject some taxpayers to the hardships discussed by the Tax Court majority. In the Revenue Act of 1926, ch. 27, § 212(d), 44 Stat. 23, Congress enacted the installment basis for reporting gain that is now reflected in section 453 of the current Code. Under section 453, a taxpayer who sells real property and receives payments in the year of sale totaling less than 30 percent of the selling price may elect to report as taxable income in any given year only

> that proportion of the installment payments actually received in that year which the gross profit, realized or to be realized when payment is completed, bears to the total contract price.

26 U.S.C.A. § 453(a)(1).

By providing the installment basis, Congress intended " *   *   * to relieve taxpayers who adopted it from having to pay an income tax in the year of sale based on the full amount of anticipated profits when in fact they had received in cash only a small portion of the sales price." Commissioner v. South Texas Lumber Co., 333 U.S. 496, 503, 68 S.Ct. 695, 700 (1948). For sales that qualify, the installment basis also eliminates the other potential disadvantages to which the Tax Court referred. Since taxation in the year of the sale is based on the value of the payments actually received, the taxpayer should not be required to sell his obligation in order to meet his tax liabilities. Furthermore, the installment basis does not change the character of the gain received. If gain on an exchange would otherwise be capital, it remains capital under section 453. Finally, the installment basis treats cash and accrual basis taxpayers equally.

We view section 453 as persuasive evidence in support of the interpretation of section 1001(b) for which the Commissioner contends. The installment basis is Congress's method of providing relief from the rigors of section 1001(b). In its report on the Revenue Act of 1926, the Senate Finance Committee expressly noted that in sales or exchanges not qualifying for the installment basis, "deferred-payment contracts"

> *   *   * are to be regarded as the equivalent of cash if such obligations have a fair market value. In consequence, that portion of the initial payment and of the fair market value of such obligations which represents profit is to be returned as income as of the taxable year of the sale.

S.Rep. No. 52, 69th Cong., 1st Sess. (1926), reproduced at 1939–1 Cum. Bull. (Part 2) 332, 347.

* * *

III. Case Law

The prior decisions of our own court support the conclusion we have reached. On several occasions, we have held that if the fair market value of a deferred payment obligation received in a sale or other exchange can be ascertained, that fair market value must be included as an amount realized under section 1001(b). Most recently, in In re Steen, 509 F.2d 1398, 1404–05 (9th Cir.1975), we held that the fair market value of an installment payment contract received in exchange for shares of stock was ascertainable and that consequently, that fair market value was an amount realized in the year of the sale. In Heller Trust v. Commissioner, 382 F.2d 675, 681 (9th Cir.1967), our court affirmed a Tax Court decision requiring a taxpayer to include the fair market value of real estate contracts as an amount realized in the year of a sale, even though the fair market value of the contracts there involved was only 50 percent of their face value. See also Clodfelter v. Commissioner, 426 F.2d 1391 (9th Cir.1970); Tombari v. Commissioner, 299 F.2d 889, 892–93 (9th Cir.1962); Gersten v. Commissioner, 267 F.2d 195 (9th Cir.1959).[9]

There are, of course, "rare and extraordinary" situations in which it is impossible to ascertain the fair market value of a deferred payment obligation in the year of sale. See Treas.Reg. § 1.1001–1(a). The total amount payable under an obligation may be so speculative, or the right to receive any payments at all so contingent, that the fair market value of the obligation cannot be fixed. See Burnet v. Logan, 283 U.S. 404, 51 S.Ct. 550 (1931); In re Steen, 509 F.2d 1398, 1403–04 (9th Cir.1975) (right to payment depended on favorable judicial decision on novel question of state law); Westover v. Smith, 173 F.2d 90 (9th Cir.1949). If an obligation is not marketable, it may be impossible to establish its fair market value. See Willhoit v. Commissioner, 308 F.2d 259 (9th Cir. 1962) (uncontradicted testimony that there was no market for high risk

---

9. Accord, McCormac v. United States, 424 F.2d 607, 191 Ct.Cl. 483 (1970); Kaufman v. Comm'r, 372 F.2d 789, 793–94 (4th Cir.1966); Campagna v. United States, 290 F.2d 682 (2d Cir.1961); 2 J. Mertens, supra n. 3; J. Sneed, supra n. 3 at 48–49.

The Tax Court adopted as its definition of "cash equivalency" certain language from the opinion in Cowden v. Comm'r, 289 F.2d 29 (5th Cir.1961). In our view, the holding in Cowden does not conflict with the prior decisions of our court or with our present decision. In Cowden, the Fifth Circuit held that the Tax Court had overemphasized one of its findings of fact in reaching its decision and remanded the case for the Tax Court's reconsideration. The language adopted by the Tax Court appears within the context of the Fifth Circuit's discussion, in Cowden, of the taxpayer's contention that the deferred payment obligation he had received in exchange for an oil and gas lease could have no realizable value because it was not negotiable. In rejecting the taxpayer's contention, the Cowden court appears to have written the language adopted by the Tax Court principally as a description of the obligation involved in that case. See Dennis v. Comm'r, 473 F.2d 274, 285 (5th Cir.1973), in which the Fifth Circuit, citing Cowden, states that when property received in a sale or exchange has a fair market value, that value constitutes an amount realized.

contracts); Phillips v. Frank, 295 F.2d 629 (9th Cir.1961) (uncontradicted testimony that highly speculative contracts could not have been sold in the year of sale). But see United States v. Davis, 370 U.S. 65, 71–74, 82 S.Ct. 1190 (1962) (wife's release of her marital rights in a property settlement agreement held to have a fair market value equal to the value of property that her husband transferred to her in exchange); Gersten v. Commissioner, supra at 197 ("It is not necessary to find any actual sales of like articles to establish a fair market value.")

The Tax Court found, as a fact, that the taxpayer's real estate contract with the Storeys had a fair market value of $76,980 in the taxable year of sale. Consequently, the taxpayer must include $76,980 in determining the amount realized under section 1001(b). As previously noted, however, the Commissioner has conceded that the taxpayer is eligible to report on the installment basis and has calculated the taxpayer's deficiency accordingly.

The decision of the Tax Court is reversed, and on remand, the Tax Court will enter judgment for the Commissioner.[10]

Reversed and remanded, with directions.

NOTE

If a cash method taxpayer in a *closed* transaction elects out of Section 453 under Section 453(d) and receives obligations that are for a fixed amount regardless of whether they have a cash equivalent, the fair market value of the obligations is treated as an amount realized in the year of sale.[1] What are the tax consequences on collection of the full amount of the obligations and what character will the amounts not previously taxed have?[2] Again, with a timing exception, we run parallel to a concept presented earlier.

The problem is perhaps best illustrated by a further example. Assume a cash method taxpayer sells a parcel of land, a capital asset held long-term in which he has a $20,000 basis, for a purchase price of $100,000. He receives from the buyer $50,000 cash in the year of sale and an interest bearing obligation under which the buyer agrees to pay $10,000 a year in each of the succeeding five years. Assume further that the obligation has a $40,000 fair market value.[3] If the taxpayer elects under Section 453(d), he would recognize a $70,000 long term capital gain in the year of the sale, the difference between the $90,000

10. The taxpayer has not here challenged, and we have not examined, the Commissioner's calculation of the taxpayer's gain under section 453. The Tax Court may examine those calculations on remand, if the taxpayer so requests.

1. Reg. § 15A.453–1(d)(2)(ii) and (iii). For a critical discussion of the regulations, see Karjala, "Sales of Property Outside Section 453," 64 Taxes 153 (1986).

2. This note disregards discussion of any interest paid on such obligations.

3. Reg. § 15A.453–1(d)(2)(ii) provides that "in no event will the fair market value of the installment obligation be considered to be less than the fair market value of the property sold (minus any other consideration received by the taxpayer on the sale)." The validity of this requirement is questioned by Schler, "The Sale of Property for a Fixed Payment Note: Remaining Uncertainties," 41 Tax L.Rev. 209, 212 (1986).

amount realized and the $20,000 adjusted basis. But what happens when he receives $10,000 as the first payment on the obligation in the year after the sale? The Shafpa Realty Corp. case [4] holds in effect that the difference between face and market values which went untaxed in the year of the sale must be amortized over the life of the payments. The taxpayer has an obligation with a $40,000 basis (determined by the amount he previously included as a part of the amount realized) which may be amortized over the period during which payment is to be made. Thus in each of the five years the taxpayer will have an $8,000 recovery of capital and $2,000 of income.

If the obligation were to pay an indefinite amount for a specified period, say a percentage of income earned by the property for five years, but having an estimatable fair market value of $40,000 (i.e., no Burnet v. Logan situation) then, if a Section 453(d) election is made, for the year of sale the amount realized would be $90,000 ($50,000 cash and other property worth $40,000) [5] and taxpayer would have the same $70,000 long-term capital gain. However, since the total recovery is indefinite no income would be taxed as payments were made on the obligation itself until the $40,000 tax cost basis was recovered. Any excess recovery over the $40,000 would be income as received. [6] Consequently if (quite unrealistically) the percentage of the income came to $10,000 a year for five years, taxpayer would recover capital in the first four years and would have $10,000 of income in year five. This same rule has been applied in a situation where although the principal amount to be paid is definite, nevertheless it is highly speculative whether the payments under obligation will be made. [7]

Regardless of when the excess is taxed the remaining question is what is the character of the excess? Since the original transaction was closed in the year of sale, the receipt of any excess does not arise out of any sale or exchange. There is a mere extinction of the obligation and the excess regardless of when it is taxed is ordinary income. [8]

b. Accrual Method Taxpayers

Regulation: Section 15A.453–1(d)(1) and (2).

———

Under the accrual method of accounting there is no equivalency of cash question; the receipt of cash or its equivalent is not significant. If an accrual method taxpayer in a closed transaction elects out of Section 453 under Section 453(d) and the payments are fixed in amount, the total amount payable under the installment obligation is included in

4. 8 B.T.A. 283 (1927).

5. Reg. § 15A.453–1(d)(2)(iii).

6. Cf. Stephen H. Dorsey, 49 T.C. 606 (1968).

7. Commissioner v. Liftin, 317 F.2d 234 (4th Cir.1963).

8. Waring v. Commissioner, 412 F.2d 800 (3d Cir.1969); cf. Galvin Hudson, supra page 708.

the amount realized in the year of the sale.[1] As the Supreme Court stated in Spring City Foundry Co. v. Commissioner:[2]

> Keeping account and making returns on the accrual basis, as distinguished from the cash basis, import that it is the *right* to receive and not the actual receipt that determines the inclusion of the amount in gross income.

That quotation dealt with a question of timing: When, for what period, is an item to be included? But it relates as well to the question of the amount of inclusion. Under Section 1001(b) an "amount realized" is the "sum of any money received plus the fair market value of property (other than money) received." We are concerned with the right to receive something in the future; consequently it is the amount of money or the value of property *to be* received which is included in gross income. Thus if an accrual method taxpayer in the year of a sale receives the purchaser's obligation to pay $10,000 a year over a five year period, even if the obligation has a fair market value of only $40,000, if Section 453(d) is elected he is required to treat the $50,000 face amount of the obligation, the amount *to be* received, as part of the amount realized in the year of the sale.[3] The Tax Court has stated this principle as follows: [4]

> Section 1001(b) of the Code provides that the amount realized from the sale or other disposition of property shall be the sum of any money received plus the fair market value of the property (other than money) received. However, an accrual basis taxpayer does not treat an unconditional right to receive money as property received, but rather as money received to the full extent of the face value of the right. See Key Homes, Inc., 30 T.C. 109, affirmed per curiam (C.A.6) 271 F.2d 280. The fact that there is always the possibility that a purchaser or debtor may default in his obligation is not sufficient to defer the accruing of income that has been earned. Spring City Foundry Co. v. Commissioner, 292 U.S. 182, 54 S.Ct. 644.

If a payment to an accrual method taxpayer is *not fixed* in amount and if a Section 453(d) election is made, the results are the same as the results to a cash method taxpayer to whom payments are not fixed in amount.[5] Generally, the fair market value of the contingent payments is included in the amount realized in the year of the sale (with identical consequences as to a cash method taxpayer as actual amounts are received),[6] unless the open transaction Burnet v. Logan doctrine applies to the entire sale.[7]

1. Reg. § 15A.453–1(d)(2)(ii).

2. 292 U.S. 182, 54 S.Ct. 644 (1934).

3. George L. Castner Co., 30 T.C. 1061 (1958).

4. First Sav. and Loan Ass'n, 40 T.C. 474, 487 (1963).

5. Reg. § 15A.453–1(d)(2)(iii).

6. See notes 5–8 at page 891, supra.

7. See page 877, supra.

PROBLEMS

1. Seller owns a parcel of land which he purchased five years ago for $2000. He sells it to Buyer under an arrangement where buyer pays $2000 cash in the current year and gives him four ten percent interest bearing notes to be paid off in each of the succeeding four years. Each note has a $2000 face amount and a $1750 fair market value. Disregarding the tax consequences of any interest payments, what results to Seller in each of the five years if in the alternative:

   (a) Seller is an accrual method taxpayer and he makes a § 453(d) election.

   (b) Seller is a cash method taxpayer and makes a § 453(d) election.

   (c) Same as (b), above, except that Buyer's notes are nonassignable and therefore have no equivalency of cash.

C. THE ORIGINAL ISSUE DISCOUNT RULES AND OTHER UNSTATED, HIDDEN, AND IMPUTED INTEREST

Internal Revenue Code: See Sections 483; 1271 through 1286.

————————

Interest of course is an amount paid for the use or forebearance of money. But it does not always jump out and, as John Houseman would say, bite you on the bottom and assert, "I am interest!" It may be stated, but maybe not accurately stated. It may be concealed, distorted, lightly veiled, artificially found, fixed or limited by statute, phantom, implied, imputed or presumed—to offer a few possibilities. As it is ordinary income to the payee and qualifiedly deductible by the payor, its elusive qualities make it a challenge to tax administration. The subject is broad, and we take on here only some of its principal features.

When an imputed interest question arises it is likely to drag with it a whole panoply of familiar tax issues. In Chapter 16 we took up Section 7872, the gift-interest boomerang for interest-free or below-market interest rate loans, and we saw that Congress sometimes artificially presumes, creates or imputes interest in order to tax more appropriately the parties involved.[1] Congress has also made several other changes to generate unconventional interest income and deductions.

The provisions may be more manageable if examined with their four related concepts (imputation, recharacterization, timing, and compounding); it is useful also to trace parallel concepts under pre–1984 law. For example, if A sells B a capital asset on terms that require total payments of $50,000 and $10,000 of that amount is required to be *imputed* (treated) as interest, the $10,000 amount is *recharacterized* as

1. See page 464, supra.

ordinary income to A and as a potential ordinary deduction for B, and only the remaining $40,000 is an amount realized on the sale of a capital asset. The *timing* concepts in this scenario are not quite so simple. For what year do we tax A on the interest? For what year do we allow B a deduction? Do income and deduction consequences occur as the interest accrues or as it is paid? Finally, how do we *compute* such interest? Here we revert back to the concept of the time value of money which was discussed in Chapter 19.[2] For if we find interest where none is stated, we must determine the method of computing the interest income and its related deduction. Should we impute simple interest evenly over the stated time; or should we impute compound interest, in effect adding interest on the interest determined periodically?[3]

The recent tax provisions and the four concepts considered above to some extent grew out of pre–1984 Code sections. First of all, in 1964 Congress had enacted the predecessor of current Section 483. The section treated as interest, even though not so designated, an appropriate percentage of the principal amount of obligations that were consideration for the sales of property. Under that section, if insufficient interest in a tax sense was to be paid on an obligation arising out of a sale of property, the section imputed to the transaction interest[4] compounded semiannually.[5] Of course this recharacterization of part of the payments as interest reduced the amount of principal payments.

The second set of prior Code provisions was the original issue discount rules of Sections 1232 and 1232A, both now replaced by broader rules.[6] The old rules recognized that if a debtor borrowed $40,000 from a lender but was required to repay $50,000 in three years when the obligation was due, the $10,000 difference was really interest which should be characterized as ordinary income to the lender and as potentially deductible interest by the debtor. The former Code provisions accepted the difference, termed original issue discount, as the amount of interest without concern for the rate of interest in the transaction. However, Sections 1232 and 1232A did contain specific timing rules that applied to both lender and debtor regardless of their accounting methods. Under those rules both taxpayers were effectively placed on the accrual method and the interest was accrued daily at compounded rates over the life of the obligation.[7]

2. See page 611, supra.

3. For example, the $10,000 of imputed interest to A in a three-year transaction might be designated either simple interest of $3,333 in each of the 3 years, or compounded interest with say, roughly, $3,072 of interest in year one, $3,333 in year two, and $3,595 in year three. The latter assumption reflects the concept of the time value of money, which is conceptually sound but computationally difficult.

4. Immediately prior to the 1984 Act if less than 9% simple interest was to be paid, interest was imputed at a 10% rate compounded semiannually.

5. Reg. § 1.483–1. Of course, it should be understood that we are talking about the make-believe world of federal taxation. Congress is powerless to redraft a contract. The section purports to say only how the agreement will be treated for tax purposes.

6. See I.R.C. §§ 1271–1275.

7. Sections 1232 and 1232A were limited in scope and applied only to debt instruments for cash issued by corporations and some government units. The sections were

Thus, both pre–1984 rules had the effect of relabeling some payments as interest and of recharacterizing those payments. However, while Section 483 operated to impute interest, it neglected timing; and, while Sections 1232 and 1232A both compounded interest and considered timing, they did not impute interest; they simply dealt with interest that was already there.

The current provisions on original issue discount seek out obscured interest and provide related principal consequences in many more situations than their predecessors. They use the classic concepts (imputing, recharacterizing, timing and compounding) in varying degrees in one of the most complex set of rules in the Code. The following is a summary of some of those rules.[8]

Section 1274: Debts for Property. The most important and most sweeping of the original issue discount rules is Section 1274,[9] which sometimes establishes what may be called *tax* interest on a debt instrument issued for the purchase of property.[10] Section 1274 recognizes the economic reality that when one buys property from another promising to pay money in the future, he has effectively borrowed money the repayment of which includes both an interest and a principal component. Under Section 1274 Congress establishes the required method for measuring the interest component. If Section 1274 applies it may invoke a combination of the tax concepts previously mentioned: imputing interest, recharacterizing payments, timing both parties under the accrual method, and compounding interest. Thus, if insufficient (as Congress sees it) interest is stated under a debt instrument issued for property, the interest amount is recomputed at semiannually compounded rates; and it is accrued (to be reported) annually for both income and deduction purposes. In addition, the recomputed principal amount of the debt is redetermined for income tax purposes to measure gain and loss, to determine Section 453 installment sale consequences, to establish the cost basis, and to compute depreciation. However, take note of Section 1275(b)(1) which makes Sections 1274 and 483 inapplicable to a buyer of personal use property.

The first question to be addressed under the Section 1274 rules is whether there is sufficient interest required to be paid with respect to

---

inapplicable to debt instruments issued by individuals, to obligations issued for property, and to obligations not held as capital assets. See Canellos and Kleinbard, "The Miracle of Compound Interest: Interest Deferral and Discount After 1982," 38 Tax L.Rev. 565 (1983).

8. See New York State Bar Assn's Ad Hoc Comm. on Original Issue Discount and Coupon Stripping, "Original Issue Discount and Coupon Stripping," *reprinted in* 22 Tax Notes 993 (Mar. 5, 1984).

9. See Davis, "Buying and Selling Property: The Determination and Treatment of Imputed Interest," 44 N.Y.U.Tax Inst. Ch.

33 (1986); and for pre–1985 law, see Sheffield, "Debt Issued for Traded and Nontraded Property," 62 Taxes 1022 (1984); Goldberg, "Tax Planning for Interest After TRA 1984: Unstated Interest and Original Issue Discount," 43 N.Y.U.Inst. on Fed. Tax'n 23 (1985); Helfand, "The Impact of Time Value of Money Concepts on Deferred and Prepaid Items," 43 N.Y.U.Inst. on Fed.Tax'n 41 (1985).

10. Similar rules were enacted in 1984 to add imputed interest to debts for the use of property or services. See I.R.C. § 467 discussed at page 617, supra.

the debt obligation. To make this determination, the actual rate charged under the terms of the instrument is compared with the "applicable Federal rate." [11] Generally, if the rate of interest to be paid over the life of the debt obligation is equal to the applicable Federal rate, then no interest is imputed under Section 1274.[12] If the rate to be paid is not within this "safe harbor," then interest is generally imputed at the applicable Federal rate, compounded semiannually.[13] Such interest is considered the specified interest for tax purposes. Under Section 1274, interest is computed on a daily basis and is generally included in (or deductible from) income annually under accrual concepts applied to both parties.[14] Imputation of the interest effectively reduces the income-tax-recognized purchase price of the property. In a situation where there is insufficient interest and Section 1274 applies, all of the four concepts above (imputing, recharacterizing, timing and compounding) potentially come into play.

A basic numerical example may help to illustrate the Section 1274 rules. Assume that Seller sells land to Buyer for $5,000,000 payable at the end of three years. Buyer gives Seller a note for $5,000,000 with simple interest payable annually at the end of each year over the three years at a rate of 10%. Assume further in this and in all subsequent examples that the applicable Federal rate is 12%.

First, one must test the instrument for adequate stated interest to determine whether it is necessary to impute interest. Since the 10% interest fixed by the instrument is less than the safe harbor applicable Federal rate, interest must be imputed at the 12% applicable Federal rate, compounded semiannually. To determine how much interest to impute, one must first redetermine the income-tax-recognized purchase price of the property (the "issue price"). Under Section 1274(b), the issue price equals the sum of the present values of the payments, discounted at the 12% imputed rate, compounded semiannually. So

* * *

Year	Actual Payments	Present Value at 12% Compounded Semiannually
1	$ 500,000	$ 445,000
2	500,000	396,000
3	5,500,000	3,877,300
	$6,500,000	$4,718,300

As the table indicates, the issue price becomes $4,718,300, and the next question is the amount and timing of imputed interest. The amount of

---

11. I.R.C. § 1274(d). Separate rates are determined for short-term (less than three years), mid-term (between three and nine years), and long-term (over nine years) notes. See page 467, supra.

12. I.R.C. § 1274(a), (b)(2)(B), and (c). But see I.R.C. § 1274(e) using a 110% of the applicable Federal rate in sale-leaseback transactions. See also I.R.C. § 1274A(a).

13. I.R.C. § 1274(a), (b) and (c).

14. I.R.C. § 1272(a)(3) and (4). But see I.R.C. § 1274A(c).

original issue discount (hereinafter OID), which is phantom but includable and deductible interest, equals the interest on the issue price at a rate of 12% per year compounded semiannually less the amount of interest actually to be paid in each year. Again in tabular form:

Year	Adjusted Issue Price [15]	Yield at 12% (compounded semiannually)	Actual Interest Paid	OID Taxed
1	$4,718,300	$ 583,200	$ 500,000	$ 83,200
2	4,801,500	593,500	500,000	93,500
3	4,895,000	605,000	500,000	105,000 [16]
		$1,781,700	$1,500,000	$281,700

Thus, in the above example where the stated and actual purchase price is $5,000,000 with 10% simple interest to be paid annually, Section 1274 applies and for tax purposes adjusts the sales price to $4,718,300. In addition, Section 1274 creates and taxes Seller on $83,200 of additional interest in year one, $93,500 in year two, and $105,000 in year three. Complementary results accrue to Buyer—a reduction in his cost basis to $4,718,300 but additional potential interest deductions over the three years in the amounts of OID on which the seller is taxed.

The original issue discount rules apply differently to a debt for property situation where sufficient interest is stated but all the interest is payable at the end of the contract period. In that case, no interest is imputed but Section 1272(a)(1) [17] requires accrual of the stated interest annually for both parties' tax computations. Thus, if a debt for property meets the safe harbor applicable Federal rate but the interest on the debt is not paid as it accrues, no interest is *imputed* but original issue discount *timing* rules do come into play.

Another example illustrates this situation. Assume Seller sells land to Buyer for $5,000,000 under a three-year note with interest at 12%, compounded semiannually over the three years. The note and all interest are payable at the end of year three. The total amount, including interest, payable in year three is $7,092,595.

As the rate of interest on the note equals the safe harbor 12% applicable Federal rate (previously assumed),[18] there is adequate stated interest. The case is thus distinguishable from the prior examples and no interest is imputed. However, the interest must still be accrued (reported) annually, both as income and as a deduction. Since there is adequate stated interest, the issue price (the purchase price of the property which is the "amount realized" by the seller and the "cost basis" of the buyer) is equal to the principal amount of $5,000,000.

---

15. This is the issue price increased by the previous year's OID.

16. In this calculation, OID should and does equal the difference between the stated redemption price (see § 1273(a)(2)) and the adjusted issue price (see § 1272(a)(4)). See I.R.C. § 1273(a)(1).

17. See also I.R.C. §§ 1272(a)(3) and 1273.

18. See I.R.C. § 1274(c)(2).

The amount of OID taxed annually equals the annual interest on the issue price at a rate of 12% per year, compounded semiannually, less the interest actually paid in that year.

Year	Adjusted Issue Price [19]	Yield at 12% (compounded semiannually)	Actual Interest Paid	OID Taxed
1	$5,000,000	$ 618,000	-0-	$ 618,000
2	5,618,000	694,385	-0-	694,385
3	6,312,385	780,210		780,210
		$2,092,595	-0-	$2,092,595

Finally, in a third possible debt for property situation, if the taxpayer meets both the 100% safe harbor interest rules and the interest is paid annually, the original issue discount rules are inapplicable; even for tax purposes, the stated interest is interest and the stated principal is principal. There is no OID.

The debt for property rules do not apply to all sales of property. Section 1274A, examined below, creates some special exceptions. In addition, Section 1274(c)(3) contains several exceptions, including sales of property for less than $250,000; [20] sales of principal residences; [21] sales of farms for $1,000,000 or less by individuals, estates, testamentary trusts and small businesses; [22] sales of debt instruments that are publicly traded or issued for publicly traded property; [23] some sales of patents; [24] and sales of land between family members at a price not in excess of $500,000.[25]

As originally enacted, Section 1274 was far reaching and controversial. In 1985, Congress amended Section 1274 and enacted Section 1274A which created two major exceptions to the Section 1274 rules.

The first exception relates to the interest rate which must apply to trigger Section 1274. Section 1274A imposes a cap on imputed interest of 9 percent per annum compounded semiannually.[26] Thus, if a 9 percent interest rate is less than the applicable Federal rate, taxpayers need use only the 9 percent rate to escape adverse consequences under Section 1274.[27] This rule applies only to a "qualified debt instrument" which is a debt instrument given for property (other than new Section 38 property as defined in Section 48(b)) where the stated principal amount of the instrument does not exceed $2,800,000.[28]

---

19. See note 15, supra.

20. I.R.C. § 1274(c)(3)(C); see especially § 1274(c)(3)(C)(iii). Cf. I.R.C. § 1274A(a).

21. I.R.C. § 1274(c)(3)(B). Cf. I.R.C. § 483(a) and (e).

22. I.R.C. § 1274(c)(3)(A).

23. I.R.C. § 1274(c)(3)(D).

24. I.R.C. § 1274(c)(3)(E).

25. I.R.C. § 1274(c)(3)(F). See I.R.C. § 483(e).

26. I.R.C. § 1274A(a).

27. This exception also applies to I.R.C. § 483, which is considered below. I.R.C. § 1274A(a).

28. I.R.C. § 1274A(b). The property may not be new I.R.C. § 38 property as defined in § 48(b) as in effect prior to the enactment of the Revenue Reduction Act of 1990. Id. The $2,800,000 amount is indexed for inflation for years after 1989. I.R.C. § 1274A(d)(2). The exception contains an aggregation provision to prevent taxpayers from creating several obligations

The second Section 1274A exception allows taxpayers to elect to use the cash method of accounting, rather than the accrual method, to alter the timing rules of Section 1274 if the debt obligation is a "cash method debt instrument." [29] This type of instrument is one in which the principal amount of the obligation does not exceed $2 million,[30] the lender-seller does not use the accrual method of accounting and is not a dealer in the property sold, the property is not new Section 38 property, an election is made by both parties to use this rule and, but for the election, Section 1274 would have applied.[31] Thus, the cash method may be used if it is used by both electing parties.

Under prior law, there was substantial "creative" financing in sales of property (lower-than-market interest, balloon principal payments, balloon interest payments, and so forth) which generally avoided the application of existing statutory tax restrictions and gave arms-length buyers and sellers a lot of flexibility in arranging transactions. Despite some exceptions, the current complex rules encourage persons to state sufficient and timely interest payments to avoid the Section 1274 thicket.

Section 483: Debts for Property. Section 483 generally applies to sales of property which fall within the exception provisions of Section 1274, including a Section 1274A(c) election out of Section 1274, if payments are to be made more than one year after the date of the sale. Section 483 sometimes imputes the same amounts of interest [32] and uses the same safe harbor rule as Section 1274.[33] However, in most circumstances Section 483 employs the 9 percent cap of Section 1274A, and in limited circumstances it uses a 6 percent cap.[34] Unlike Section 1274 and Section 1274A, Section 483 does not compel annual accrual. It lets the timing consequences depend upon a taxpayer's accounting method.[35] Section 483 also is subject to some exceptions.[36]

to avoid the dollar limitation. I.R.C. § 1274A(d)(1).

29. I.R.C. § 1274A(c)(1). If an election is made then I.R.C. § 483 applies. See Garlock, A Practical Guide to the Original Issue Discount Regulations pp. 3–5 (1990 Supp.).

30. The aggregation rule of I.R.C. § 1274(d)(1) also applies here.

31. I.R.C. § 1274A(c)(2). See also I.R.C. § 1274A(b).

32. I.R.C. §§ 483(b) and 1274A.

33. I.R.C. § 483(c)(1)(B).

34. I.R.C. § 483(e) uses a 6% cap for sales of land between members of the same family if all sales for the year between the parties do not exceed $500,000 and if neither party is a nonresident alien. Cf. I.R.C. § 267(c)(4).

35. For example, assume the facts are generally the same as in the example at page 896, supra, except that the amounts are only 1% of the amounts used in the

example and the property *is § 38 property* so that the 9% ceiling rule of § 1274A is inapplicable. If A sells B property for $50,000 paying interest at an annual rate of 10% and the applicable Federal rate is 12%, I.R.C. § 483, not § 1274, is applicable because the selling price is less than $250,000. I.R.C. § 1274(c)(4)(C). Assume that B is an accrual method taxpayer and A is a cash method taxpayer. Similar to the § 1274 example using a rate of 12% compounded semiannually, a total of $2,817 of interest will be imputed (1% of the amounts in the example at page 896, supra). Since B is an accrual method taxpayer, he *may* be able to deduct the OID interest annually or $832 in year one, $935 in year two and $1,050 in year three. If so, the timing results to him are identical to the I.R.C. § 1274 timing results.

There is some disagreement as to whether the accrual basis taxpayer may take the interest deduction as it accrues. The pro-

36. See note 36 on page 900.

Sections 1272 and 1273: Debts for Cash. Debts for cash (loans), which were the subject of now repealed Sections 1232 and 1232A, now appear in Sections 1272 and 1273. Subject to a de minimis exception,[37] these rules simply treat original issue discount as interest accruing annually both for income and deduction purposes. Unlike the Section 1274 rules, however, Sections 1272 and 1273 do not impute interest. They simply identify and treat excess repayment amounts as what they are, *interest.*[38] There are several types of debts for cash which are not subject to the rules;[39] for example, tax exempt obligations, U.S. savings bonds, short-term (one-year or less) obligations,[40] and non-trade and non-business loans not in excess of $10,000 between natural persons.[41]

Other Rules. Other provisions that convert what would be capital gain to interest or ordinary income, which bear some similarity to the rules discussed above, are summarized here.

Sections 1276–1278: Market Discount Rules. If one purchases a bond issued after July 18, 1984, at a discount (at a figure below its stated redemption price) then, subject to a de minimis exception,[42] the discount is prorated over the life of the bond[43] to maturity and is treated as interest. Cash method taxpayers are not taxed on an accrual basis[44] but, if the bond is subsequently disposed of, under Section 1276 the prorated amount is treated as ordinary (in essence interest) income on disposition of the bond.[45] Furthermore, deductions for interest on a loan to purchase such a bond are generally deferred until disposition of the bond, except for conventional interest not attributable to the original issue discount.[46]

---

posed regulations under I.R.C. § 483 are unclear as to the result. See Garlock, A Practical Guide to the Original Issue Discount Regulations, supra note 29 at page 207, for the position that interest is deducted as it accrues. A contrary view is that interest is deducted only as payments fall due, see Lokken, "The Time Value of Money Rules," 42 Tax L.Rev. 1, 137 (1986).

Since A is a cash method taxpayer, he will not be taxed on the total $2,817 of OID until it is paid in year three. Thus, A is able to defer recognition of the imputed interest.

36. I.R.C. § 483(d)(2) through (4).

37. I.R.C. § 1273(a)(3).

38. Thus, as seen at page 894, supra, if A loans B $40,000 and B agrees to repay A $50,000 in three years, the $10,000 excess is interest and it accrues annually in a compounded manner to both parties in an amount equal to $3,072 in year one, $3,333 in year two, and $3,595 in year three. We reemphasize that the rate of interest is not compared to any Federal rate and is disregarded.

39. I.R.C. § 1272(a)(2).

40. With respect to short term obligations, I.R.C. § 1281 requires the difference between their issue price or purchase price and their face amounts to be accrued ratably and included in income by some taxpayers. Some interest on loans to purchase short term obligations, which is not included under § 1281, must be deferred under § 1282.

41. But see I.R.C. § 1272(a)(2)(E)(ii).

42. I.R.C. § 1278(a)(2)(C) creates a statutorily presumed zero discount.

43. Some bonds are exempt. I.R.C. § 1278(a)(1)(B).

44. An election can be made to treat the interest as taxable annually. I.R.C. § 1278(b).

45. I.R.C. § 1276(a)(1). I.R.C. § 1276(d) provides exceptions to the rule similar to the exceptions of § 1245(b). See page 792, supra.

46. I.R.C. § 1277.

Sections 1281–1283: Discounts on Short Term Obligations. Short term obligations (less than one year) are not subject to either the Section 1272 original issue discount rules [47] or the market discount rules.[48] But some such obligations [49] are subject to an accrual-of-interest rule to the extent of their acquisition discount [50] (redemption price less taxpayer's basis). The acquisition discount is interest, and it is deemed to accrue ratably on a daily basis as ordinary income to the holder of the bond.[51] If a short-term bond is *not* subject to the above rule,[52] then interest on a loan to purchase the bond is not deductible to the extent of the amount of interest that would have been taxed under Section 1281 if the obligation had been subject to that section.[53]

Section 1286: Stripped Bonds. A taxpayer can "strip" a coupon bond by ripping off all of its interest coupons and keeping them when selling the bond. Obviously the bond will be sold at a double discount, at a price below its maturity price (a time value concept) and also reduced because it will earn no interest while held. It is a hunk of rock redeemable for cash at a future date. Still there will be an income element in the discount. The amount taxed as interest is the total amount of discount from face value. The taxable amount of the discount is based on interest rates and the time to maturity. Thus, that amount is interest to the purchaser and the original issue discount rules of Sections 1272 and 1273 are applicable.[54]

47. I.R.C. § 1272(a)(2)(C).

48. I.R.C. § 1278(a)(1)(B)(i).

49. See I.R.C. §§ 1281(b) and 1283(a)(1)(B).

50. I.R.C. § 1283(a)(2).

51. I.R.C. § 1281(a)(1). Any other interest payable on the obligation is also included in gross income. I.R.C. § 1281(a)(2).

52. See note 49, supra.

53. I.R.C. § 1282.

54. I.R.C. § 1286(a). See the text at notes 38 through 41, supra. As to the tax consequences to the seller, see § 1286(b) treating some of the coupon interest as ordinary income. See McGrath, "Coupon Stripping Under Section 1286: Trees, Fruits and Felines," 38 Tax Lawyer 267 (1985).

CHAPTER 25. DISALLOWANCE OF LOSSES

A. LOSSES BETWEEN RELATED TAXPAYERS

Internal Revenue Code: Sections 267(a)(1), (b), (c), (d), (g). See Section 1041.
Regulations: Section 1.267(d)–1(a), (c)(3).

McWILLIAMS v. COMMISSIONER

Supreme Court of the United States, 1947.
331 U.S. 694, 67 S.Ct. 1477.

Mr. Chief Justice VINSON delivered the opinion of the Court.

The facts of these cases are not in dispute. John P. McWilliams, petitioner in No. 945, had for a number of years managed the large independent estate of his wife, petitioner in No. 947, as well as his own. On several occasions in 1940 and 1941 he ordered his broker to sell certain stock for the account of one of the two and to buy the same number of shares of the same stock for the other, at as nearly the same price as possible. He told the broker that his purpose was to establish tax losses. On each occasion the sale and purchase were promptly negotiated through the Stock Exchange, and the identity of the persons buying from the selling spouse and of the persons selling to the buying spouse was never known. Invariably, however, the buying spouse received stock certificates different from those which the other had sold. Petitioners filed separate income tax returns for these years, and claimed the losses which he or she sustained on the sales as deductions from gross income.

The Commissioner disallowed these deductions on the authority of § 24(b) of the Internal Revenue Code,[1] which prohibits deductions for losses from "sales or exchanges of property, directly or indirectly * * * Between members of a family," and between certain other closely related individuals and corporations.

On the taxpayers' applications to the Tax Court, it held § 24(b) inapplicable, following its own decision in Ickelheimer v. Commissioner,[2] and expunged the Commissioner's deficiency assessments.[3] The Circuit Court of Appeals reversed the Tax Court[4] and we granted certiorari[5] because of a conflict between circuits[6] and the importance of the question involved.

1. [I.R.C. (1939) § 24(b) is omitted. See I.R.C. (1986) § 267(a)(1), (b)(1), and (c)(4). Ed.]

2. 45 B.T.A. 478, affirmed, 132 F.2d 660 (C.C.A.2).

3. 5 T.C. 623.

4. 158 F.2d 637 (C.C.A.6).

5. 330 U.S. 814, 67 S.Ct. 868. In No. 946, the petition for certiorari of the Estate

6. See note 6 on page 903.

Petitioners contend that Congress could not have intended to disallow losses on transactions like those described above, which, having been made through a public market, were undoubtedly bona fide sales, both in the sense that title to property was actually transferred, and also in the sense that a fair consideration was paid in exchange. They contend that the disallowance of such losses would amount, *pro tanto,* to treating husband and wife as a single individual for tax purposes.

In support of this contention, they call our attention to the pre-1934 rule, which applied to all sales regardless of the relationship of seller and buyer, and made the deductibility of the resultant loss turn on the "good faith" of the sale, i.e., whether the seller actually parted with title and control.[7] They point out that in the case of the usual intra-family sale, the evidence material to this issue was peculiarly within the knowledge and even the control of the taxpayer and those amenable to his wishes, and inaccessible to the Government.[8] They maintain that the only purpose of the provisions of the 1934 and 1937 Revenue Acts—the forerunners of § 24(b)[9]—was to overcome these evidentiary difficulties by disallowing losses on such sales irrespective of good faith. It seems to be petitioners' belief that the evidentiary difficulties so contemplated were only those relating to proof of the parties' observance of the formalities of a sale and of the fairness of the price, and consequently that the legislative remedy applied only to sales made immediately from one member of a family to another, or mediately through a controlled intermediary.

We are not persuaded that Congress had so limited an appreciation of this type of tax avoidance problem. Even assuming that the problem was thought to arise solely out of the taxpayer's inherent advantage in a contest concerning the good or bad faith of an intra-family sale, deception could obviously be practiced by a buying spouse's agreement or tacit readiness to hold the property sold at the disposal of a selling spouse, rather more easily than by a pretense of a sale where none

of Susan P. McWilliams, the deceased mother of John P. McWilliams, was granted at the same time as the petitions in Nos. 945 and 947, and the three cases were consolidated in this Court. As all three present the same material facts and raise precisely the same issues, no further reference will be made to the several cases separately.

6. The decision of the Circuit Court of Appeals for the Second Circuit in Commissioner v. Ickelheimer, supra, note 2, is in conflict on this point with the decision of the Circuit Court of Appeals for the Sixth Circuit in the present case, and also with that of the Circuit Court of Appeals for the Fourth Circuit in Commissioner v. Kohn, 158 F.2d 32.

7. Commissioner v. Hale, 67 F.2d 561 (C.C.A.1); Zimmermann v. Commissioner,

36 B.T.A. 279, reversed on other grounds, 100 F.2d 1023 (C.C.A.3); Uihlein v. Commissioner, 30 B.T.A. 399, affirmed, 82 F.2d 944 (C.C.A.7).

8. See H.Rep. No. 1546, 75th Cong., 1st Sess., p. 26 (1939–1 Cum.Bull, (Part 2) 704, 722–723). See also cases cited in note 7, supra.

9. The provisions of § 24(b)(1)(A) and (B) of the Internal Revenue Code originated in § 24(a)(6) of the Revenue Act of 1934, 48 Stat. 680, 691. These provisions were reenacted without change as § 24(a) (6) of the Revenue Act of 1936, 49 Stat. 1648, 1662, and the provisions of § 24(b) (1)(C), (D), (E), and (F) of the Code were added by § 301 of the 1937 Act, 50 Stat. 813, 827.

actually occurred, or by an unfair price. The difficulty of determining the finality of an intra-family transfer was one with which the courts wrestled under the pre-1934 law,[10] and which Congress undoubtedly meant to overcome by enacting the provisions of § 24(b).[11]

It is clear, however, that this difficulty is one which arises out of the close relationship of the parties, and would be met whenever, by prearrangement, one spouse sells and another buys the same property at a common price, regardless of the mechanics of the transaction. Indeed, if the property is fungible, the possibility that a sale and purchase may be rendered nugatory by the buying spouse's agreement to hold for the benefit of the selling spouse, and the difficulty of proving that fact against the taxpayer, are equally great when the units of the property which the one buys are not the identical units which the other sells.

Securities transactions have been the most common vehicle for the creation of intra-family losses. Even if we should accept petitioners' premise that the only purpose of § 24(b) was to meet an evidentiary problem, we could agree that Congress did not mean to reach the transactions in this case only if we thought it completely indifferent to the effectuality of its solution.

Moreover, we think the evidentiary problem was not the only one which Congress intended to meet. Section 24(b) states an absolute prohibition—not a presumption—against the allowance of losses on any sales between the members of certain designated groups. The one common characteristic of these groups is that their members, although distinct legal entities, generally have a near-identity of economic interests.[12] It is a fair inference that even legally genuine intra-group transfers were not thought to result, usually, in economically genuine realizations of loss, and accordingly that Congress did not deem them to be appropriate occasions for the allowance of deductions.

The pertinent legislative history lends support to this inference. The Congressional Committees, in reporting the provisions enacted in 1934, merely stated that "the practice of creating losses through transactions between members of a family and close corporations has been frequently utilized for avoiding the income tax," and that these provisions were proposed to "deny losses to be taken in the case of [such] sales" and "to close this loophole of tax avoidance."[13] Similar language was used in reporting the 1937 provisions.[14] Chairman Doughton of the Ways and Means Committee, in explaining the 1937 provisions to

---

10. Cf. Shoenberg v. Commissioner, 77 F.2d 446 (C.C.A.8); Cole v. Helburn, 4 F.Supp. 230; Zimmermann v. Commissioner, supra, note 7.

11. See H.Rep. No. 1546, 75th Cong., 1st Sess., p. 26, supra, note 8.

12. See the text of [§ 267(b). Ed.]

13. H.Rep. No. 704, 73d Cong., 2d Sess., p. 23 (1939–1 Cum.Bull. (Part 2) 554, 571);

S.Rep. No. 558, 73d Cong. 2d Sess., p. 27 (1939–1 Cum.Bull. (Part 2) 586, 607).

14. The type of situations to which these provisions applied was described as being that "in which, due to family relationships or friendly control, artificial losses might be created for tax purposes." H.Rep. No. 1546, 75th Cong., 1st Sess., p. 28 (1939–1 Cum.Bull. (Part 2) 704, 724).

the House, spoke of "the artificial taking and establishment of losses where property was shuffled back and forth between various legal entities owned by the same persons or person," and stated that "these transactions seem to occur at moments remarkably opportune to the real party in interest in reducing his tax liability but, at the same time allowing him to keep substantial control of the assets being traded or exchanged." [15]

We conclude that the purpose of § 24(b) was to put an end to the right of taxpayers to choose, by intra-family transfers and other designated devices, their own time for realizing tax losses on investments which, for most practical purposes, are continued uninterrupted.

We are clear as to this purpose, too, that its effectuation obviously had to be made independent of the manner in which an intra-group transfer was accomplished. Congress, with such purpose in mind, could not have intended to include within the scope of § 24(b) only simple transfers made directly or through a dummy, or to exclude transfers of securities effected through the medium of the Stock Exchange, unless it wanted to leave a loop-hole almost as large as the one it had set out to close.

Petitioners suggest that Congress, if it truly intended to disallow losses on intra-family transactions through the market, would probably have done so by an amendment to the wash sales provisions,[16] making them applicable where the seller and buyer were members of the same family, as well as where they were one and the same individual. This extension of the wash sales provisions, however, would bar only one particular means of accomplishing the evil at which § 24(b) was aimed, and the necessity for a comprehensive remedy would have remained.

Nor can we agree that Congress' omission from § 24(b) of any prescribed time interval, comparable in function to that in the wash sales provisions, indicates that § 24(b) was not intended to apply to intra-family transfers through the Exchange. Petitioners' argument is predicated on the difficulty which courts may have in determining whether the elapse of certain periods of time between one spouse's sale and the other's purchase of like securities on the Exchange is of great enough importance in itself to break the continuity of the investment and make § 24(b) inapplicable.

Precisely the same difficulty may arise, however, in the case of an intra-family transfer through an individual intermediary, who, by pre-arrangement, buys from one spouse at the market price and a short time later sells the identical certificates to the other at the price prevailing at the time of sale. The omission of a prescribed time

---

15. 81 Cong.Rec. 9019. Representative Hill, chairman of a House subcommittee on the income-tax laws, explained to the House with reference to the 1934 provisions that the Committee had "provided in this bill that transfers between members of the family for the purpose of creating a loss to be offset against ordinary income shall not be recognized for such deduction purposes." 78 Cong.Rec. 2662.

16. [I.R.C. (1939) § 118 is omitted. See I.R.C. (1986) § 1091. Ed.]

interval negates the applicability of § 24(b) to the former type of transfer no more than it does to the latter. But if we should hold that it negated both, we would have converted the section into a mere trap for the unwary.[17]

Petitioners also urge that, whatever may have been Congress' intent, its designation in § 24(b) of sales "between" members of a family is not adequate to comprehend the transactions in this case, which consisted only of a sale of stock by one of the petitioners to an unknown stranger, and the purchase of different certificates of stock by the other petitioner, presumably from another stranger.

We can understand how this phraseology, if construed literally and out of context, might be thought to mean only direct intra-family transfers. But petitioners concede that the express statutory reference to sales made "directly or indirectly" precludes that construction. Moreover, we can discover in this language no implication whatsoever that an indirect intra-family sale of fungibles is outside the statute unless the units sold by one spouse and those bought by the other are identical. Indeed, if we accepted petitioners' construction of the statute, we think we would be reading into it a crippling exception which is not there.

Finally, we must reject petitioners' assertion that the *Dobson* rule [18] controls this case. The Tax Court found the facts as we stated them, and then overruled the Commissioner's determination because it thought that § 24(b) had no application to a taxpayer's sale of securities on the Exchange to an unknown purchaser, regardless of what other circumstances accompanied the sale. We have decided otherwise, and on our construction of the statute, and the conceded facts, the Tax Court could not have reached a result contrary to our own.[19]

Affirmed.

Mr. Justice BURTON took no part in the consideration or decision of these cases.

NOTE

The application of Section 267 may not depend entirely on the relationship between the seller and the one to whom title is transferred. In Julius Long Stern,[1] the Tax Court agreed with the Commissioner that Section 24(b) of the 1939 Code (similar to present Section 267)

---

17. We have noted petitioners' suggestion that a taxpayer is assured, under the wash sales provisions, of the right to deduct the loss incurred on a sale of securities, even though he himself buys similar securities thirty-one days later; and that he should certainly not be precluded by § 24(b) from claiming a similar loss if the taxpayer's spouse, instead of the taxpayer, makes the purchase under the same circumstances. We do not feel impelled to comment on these propositions, however,

in a case in which the sale and purchase were practically simultaneous and the net consideration received by one spouse and that paid by the other differed only in the amount of brokers' commissions and excise taxes.

18. Dobson v. Commissioner, 320 U.S. 489, 64 S.Ct. 239 (1944).

19. Cf. Trust of Bingham v. Commissioner, 325 U.S. 365, 65 S.Ct. 1232 (1945).

1. 21 T.C. 155 (1953).

disallowed a loss deduction. The taxpayer had converted his residence to rental property and then, after a time, transferred it for consideration in an amount less than his basis to his daughter and son-in-law, as tenants by the entirety. The Court of Appeals reversed, allowing the claimed deduction, saying, in part:[2]

> Applying [the] statutory provisions to the case before us it will be seen that the loss, if any, which the taxpayer suffered upon the sale of the West River Street property was deductible by him for income tax purposes unless it was a sale between himself and his daughter, Claire Guttman. If it was a sale between himself and his son-in-law, Dr. Guttman, the loss was deductible, since a son-in-law is not within the class defined by section 24(b)(2)(D). We are in complete accord with views expressed by Judge Hill in his dissenting opinion that the sale in this case was between the taxpayer and Dr. Guttman and that no sale in fact took place to Claire Guttman who supplied no part of the consideration for the sale and received her interest in the property as a tenant by the entirety purely as a gift from her husband. Indeed the findings of fact of the Tax Court compel this conclusion for the court found: "Dr. Guttman decided to, and did, purchase the house from the petitioner at a price of $30,000. * * * The petitioner's daughter did not participate in any of these negotiations, nor was she a party to them."
>
> The opinion filed by Judge Opper is based upon the proposition that under the law of Pennsylvania Claire Guttman became the owner of the entire property as a tenant by the entirety and accordingly was vendee of her father as to the whole property. The premise may be admitted but the conclusion sought to be drawn does not follow. For the fact that Mrs. Guttman acquired an estate by the entirety in the property under Pennsylvania law as a result of the direction of her husband that she be included as a grantee in the deed of conveyance did not make her, what in actual fact she was not, the purchaser of the property on a sale by her father, within the meaning of the Internal Revenue Code. As Judge Hill well said in his dissenting opinion, 21 T.C. 155, "the majority relies upon legal fiction in the effort to establish that a sale between the petitioner and his daughter was accomplished as a matter of law. The fiction relied upon belongs to the law of real property. It had its roots in the common law and was born centuries before income taxation was a gleam in the fiscal eye of government. This fiction argues that husband and wife are one. In the enactment and administration of revenue laws, fact rather than fiction is made to prevail." See Wisotzkey v.

2. Stern v. Commissioner, 215 F.2d 701, 705 (3d Cir.1954).

Commissioner of Internal Revenue, 3 Cir.1944, 144 F.2d 632, 636.

Moreover, the contention proves too much. For if Mrs. Guttman is to be regarded as grantee of the whole property under the Pennsylvania law of tenancy by the entirety and therefore as sole purchaser from the taxpayer, her husband, Dr. Guttman, must likewise under the same law be regarded as grantee of the whole and, therefore, likewise sole purchaser. It is obvious that at this point the fiction of the Pennsylvania law breaks down so far as concerns its usefulness to solve the tax question which is before us and that the question can only be solved upon a practical view of the actual facts of the case, disregarding the fictions of the ancient law of real property.

The student will recall that Section 267 is by no means the only reason why a sale of property for a price less than basis may give rise to no tax deduction. The individual taxpayer's initial hurdles are to show that the loss was incurred either in his "trade or business," Section 165(c)(1), or in "a transaction entered into for profit," Section 165(c)(2). For these reasons two types of transactions yield no deduction even if Section 267 is wholly inapplicable to them: (1) A sale of property held for merely personal use, such as the taxpayer's residence, fails the initial tests;[3] and (2) Even if the property is business or income-producing property, if the purported sale is in reality some sort of arrangement among parties with common interests which cannot be viewed as an arm's length transaction, again the initial tests are not met. Clearly not a loss in "business," such purported sales have also been held not to arise in a "transaction entered into for profit."[4]

PROBLEMS

1. Father purchased some corporate stock several years ago for $50,000. On January 15 of the current year he sells the stock to his Daughter for $40,000, its fair market value. What result if:

(a) Daughter resells the stock to a third party for $45,000 on February 15 of the current year?

(b) Daughter resells the stock to a third party for $55,000 on February 15 of the current year?

(c) Daughter resells the stock to a third party for $35,000 on February 15 of the current year?

(d) Daughter gives the stock to Son on February 15 of the current year when it is worth $45,000 and Son sells it on March 15 for $48,000?

2. If the *McWilliams'* transactions had occurred after 1984, would § 1041(a) apply? If so, what results to the parties?

3. David R. Pulliam, 39 T.C. 883 (1963), affirmed on other grounds 329 F.2d 97 (10th Cir.1964).

4. Estate of Minnie Miller v. Commissioner, 421 F.2d 1405 (4th Cir.1970).

3. Loser purchased corporate stock in 1960 for $90,000. Loser died when the stock was worth $100,000. During the administration of the estate, the value of the stock declined to $50,000 and at that time in order to pay administration expenses the estate sold the stock to Loser's daughter for $50,000. What are the income tax consequences to the estate?

4. Taxpayer T owns some land that he purchased as an investment ten years ago for $10,000. In the current year he sells it to Corporation C for $5000, which is its fair market value. Will § 267 preclude a loss deduction for T if C is owned:

(a) 10% by T.

20% by T's son S.

30% by equal partnership TX (X unrelated).

40% by others?

(b) 30% by T's son S.

30% by equal partnership TX (X unrelated).

40% by others?

(c) 30% by T's son S.

30% by equal partnership SX (X unrelated).

40% by others?

5. Taxpayer owns stock which is seized by the government and sold at public auction at a loss to pay delinquent taxes. Taxpayer's brother purchases the stock at the sale. Does § 267 apply to disallow the loss? Consider the Supreme Court's discussion of the legislative history of § 267 in *McWilliams* and compare Merritt v. Commissioner, 400 F.2d 417 (5th Cir.1968) with McNeill v. Commissioner, 251 F.2d 863 (4th Cir.1958).

B. WASH SALES

Internal Revenue Code: Sections 1091(a), (d); 1223(4). See Section 1041.

Regulations: Section 1.1091–1(g), –2.

———

NOTE

As indicated in Chapter 6, the mere decline in the value of property, without more, does not give rise to a deductible loss. Such loss is not "realized" for tax purposes until the property is sold or otherwise disposed of. Thus where a taxpayer holds stock that has declined in value, he may have a paper loss but the loss is not given tax effect until he disposes of the stock. If the taxpayer has substantial capital gains for the year, he might want to sell stock that has declined in value and apply the resulting capital loss to reduce his capital gains. But what if in other circumstances the taxpayer wishes to hold on to the stock because he believes the stock will eventually appreciate? Can he sell the stock at a loss, decrease his capital gains to that extent, and immediately reacquire the (loss) shares in the market? In this way the taxpayer might seem to realize a tax loss without, in essence, changing his investment position. Right? Wrong! Section 1091 disallows losses on "wash sales." In substance, Section 1091 provides that losses from the sale or disposition of stock or securities, including contracts or options to acquire or, sell stock or securities,[1] are non-deductible if within thirty days before or after the sale, the taxpayer acquires "substantially identical" securities.[2] As with Section 267, Section 1091 disallows losses on transactions that technically give rise to losses but in substance result in no economic loss because the taxpayer has maintained a similar investment status.

Although at first glance Section 1091 appears to be sweeping in scope, several limitations narrow its application. Section 1091 pertains only to *losses* on wash sales; gains from the sale of stock or securities that are reacquired within the sixty-one day period are not affected by Section 1091. Further, the provision does not apply to taxpayers who are dealers and are holding the securities for purchase or sale in their trades or businesses.[3] Most importantly, the loss is disallowed only if "substantially identical"[4] stock or securities are acquired. Notably, the service has ruled that securities of different corporations, even if in the same industry, are not substantially identical.[5]

It is important to note that Section 1091 may not actually "disallow" a loss, but may merely postpone it until the reacquired shares are subsequently disposed of. This result is achieved by way of Section 1091(d) which, in essence, increases the basis of the reacquired shares by the amount of the loss initially disallowed and Section 1223(4) which tacks the holding period of the original stock onto the holding period of the new stock for purposes of characterizing the gain or loss on disposition of the new stock. How may this perhaps usual result be altered by Section 1014?

PROBLEMS

1. On December 1 of the current year Taxpayer sold 1000 shares of X Corporation stock for $50,000. He had purchased the stock exactly

---

1. I.R.C. § 1091(a) last sentence. See also Reg. § 1.1091–1(f).

2. I.R.C. § 1091(a).

3. See the last clause of I.R.C. § 1091(a). Cf. I.R.C. § 1236.

4. Rev.Rul. 58–211, 1958–1 C.B. 529 states that "[securities are] substantially identical * * * if they are not substantially different in any material feature * * * or because of differences in several material features considered together." With respect to bonds, a material feature is the interest rate. See Rev.Rul. 60–195, 1960–1 C.B. 300. Differences in maturity dates are considered relatively insubstan-

tial. Frick v. Driscoll, 129 F.2d 148 (3d Cir.1942). See also Rev.Rul. 58–210, 1958–1 C.B. 523 (interest payment date and issuance date not material).

Regarding stock of the same company, see Rev.Rul. 77–201, 1977–1 C.B. 250, where convertible preferred stock was held substantially identical to common stock of same company because there were no restrictions on convertibility and both stocks had the same voting rights and dividend restrictions. See generally, Krane, "Losses from Wash Sales of Stock or Securities," 4 J.Corp.Tax. 226, 229–232 (1977).

5. Rev.Rul. 59–44, 1959–1 C.B. 205.

two years earlier for $60,000. On December 15, of the current year he purchased another 1000 shares of identical X corporation stock for $55,000.

(a) What are the tax consequences of the December 1 sale?

(b) What is Taxpayer's basis for the newly acquired shares?

(c) What is Taxpayer's holding period for the newly acquired shares as of January 1 of the next year?

(d) What result to Taxpayer in (a)–(c), above, (gain or loss, basis and new holding period), if the December 1 sale had been for $75,000 and he had repurchased 1000 shares of X stock on December 15 for $65,000?

(e) Is there any difference in result to Taxpayer in part (a), above, if he purchased the new shares on December 1 for $55,000 and sold the old shares on December 15 for $50,000?

(f) If the facts are the same as in (a), above, except that Taxpayer sold his original shares on December 1 to Daughter, what result to Daughter when she sells those shares on March 15 of the next year for $55,000? Consider the consequences to both Taxpayer and Daughter. See § 267(d), last sentence.

(g) Are the Wash sale sanctions more or less stringent than those of § 267? Explain.

2. On June 1 of the current year, Short borrowed 100 shares of B stock and sold it short for $9000. Owning no B shares, Short purchased 100 shares of identical B stock on June 15 for $10,000 and "closed" the sale. On July 5 of the same year, Short again purchased 100 shares of identical B stock at a price of $9500.

(a) Does § 1091 apply to disallow Short's loss? See Reg. § 1.1091–1(g).

(b) What result if Short closed the sale on June 15 with identical B stock which he had purchased on March 1 of the current year?

CHAPTER 26. NONRECOGNITION PROVISIONS

A. INTRODUCTION

A precise use of language is an aid to, if not an outright prerequisite for, accurate thinking. The precise use of language includes the proper use of terms in accordance with their meaning in the context in which they are used. Thus, as seen in earlier chapters, it is essential to avoid the use of the term "value" when "basis" is what is meant. A new term now appears: "recognition" or, as the case may be, "nonrecognition." It crops up in the case of some transactions in which gain or loss is "realized;" but "realization" does not necessarily connote "recognition."

Gain (or loss) has no income tax significance as long as it is represented by a mere increase (or decrease) in the value of the taxpayer's property. Something more must occur, as for example a sale or an exchange of the property, before the gain (or loss), is said to be "realized." If gain is realized, is it subject to tax? Not necessarily. The message of the sections considered in this Chapter is that not all realized gains (or losses) are to be accorded immediate consideration in the determination of taxable income. Of course, that is the consequence of *deferred reporting* of gains, permitted under Section 453, and of the *disallowance* of some losses, as in Sections 267 and 1091. But the sections presently under consideration provide that certain other gains and losses, although admittedly realized, shall simply go unrecognized, at least for the time being. The effect is that gain which clearly could be taxed is excluded from gross income, and loss that could be deducted loses its potential for reducing taxable income. The question must therefore always be raised whether a "realized" gain or loss is "recognized."

In approaching these provisions it would be well to keep in mind that Section 453 is a mere timing device, that Section 267 is an outright disallowance provision tempered only by the limited relief rules of Section 267(d), and that Section 1091 is a disallowance rule which is ameliorated substantially by the substitute basis provisions of Section 1091(d). All the nonrecognition sections of this Chapter have related basis provisions, much like Section 1091(d), which must be carefully examined in appraising the purpose and scope of these sections. The student should approach the nonrecognition rules of this Chapter curious as to why Congress spells out these additional exceptions to the usual treatment of realized gains and losses.

If a taxpayer who owns investment real estate with a basis of $100,000 and fair market value of $175,000 sells the property for cash, his realized gain of $75,000 is gross income and the tax consequences are immediate. Of course, if instead the sale is an installment sale under Section 453, the gain may then be reported ratably over the years that payments are received, in that proportion which the profit on the sale bears to the contract price. But even so the entire gain ultimately is recognized. There is simply no way and no reason to apply the nonrecognition rules, because the taxpayer has closed out his investment by sale. Similarly, if the taxpayer exchanges his land for a yacht worth $175,000, his realized gain is all subject to immediate tax consequences. Although the yacht is property, it is clear that the taxpayer has closed out his real estate investment in exchange for the yacht. Section 1001(a) and (c).

If in other circumstances the taxpayer should exchange investment real estate for another parcel of real estate worth $175,000 to be held by him for investment, his realized gain is still $75,000. But can we question whether he has really closed out his investment when the only changed circumstance is the different location of the new tract of land? In substance, the taxpayer's economic position after the exchange is the same as before. In these circumstances a special nonrecognition rule becomes applicable.

The nonrecognition provisions are all predicated on the notion that realized gain, or a loss that otherwise would qualify as a deductible loss, is sensibly deferred when the taxpayer has retained his investment in property that is essentially the same type as the originally held property. These rules are not universally applicable to all types of property. The statute provides nonrecognition to selective transactions, and it must be carefully examined. While the example here relates to an exchange that is accorded nonrecognition treatment under Section 1031, some other types of transactions, not involving exchanges as such, also are accorded nonrecognition treatment under other sections. The philosophy underlying the nonrecognition rules of these other provisions will be seen to be similar to the philosophy underlying Section 1031.

This is not your first introduction to a nonrecognition provision. Recall that in Chapters 6 and 10 we dealt with Section 1041 which applies to transfers of property between spouses and transfers between former spouses if they are incident to a divorce. Section 1041 (note its location in the Code) is a typical nonrecognition provision. Even though gain or loss is realized, Section 1041(a) provides that it is not recognized. Consistent with the treatment of gain or loss, Section 1041(b)(2) provides that the transferee, who in essence steps into the shoes of the transferor, takes the property with a *transferred* basis (the transferor's basis carries over to the transferee). See also Sections 1223(2) and 7701(a)(43). Many of the nonrecognition provisions (all of them in this Chapter) involve only one taxpayer who is seen to have a continuing investment despite the change in property. Nonrecognition generally carries with it an *exchanged* basis (which is in essence a substituted basis) and a tacked holding period for the new property.

See, for example, Sections 1031(d), 1223(1), and 7701(a)(44). If the difference between Section 1041 nonrecognition and nonrecognition under the sections considered in this chapter troubles you, remember the theory underlying transfers between spouses and former spouses incident to a divorce is that such parties constitute a single economic unit for federal tax purposes so that, in another sense, there is a continuing investment.

As a broad proposition, the nonrecognition rules and their attending basis provisions are so interrelated as to effect only a postponement of the tax on gain or the deduction of loss that initially goes unrecognized. To be sure, the date-of-death value basis rule of Section 1014 may intervene to convert mere postponement to outright amnesty (or final disallowance) if, after a transaction in which gain (or loss) goes unrecognized, the taxpayer dies. Consequently, except for this possibility, the nonrecognition rules are largely rules of deferral. Take a further look at Section 1231(a), which limits the hotchpot ingredients to *recognized* gains and losses. See again also Section 1222, limiting the definition of short and long-term capital gains and losses to such gains and losses as are " * * * taken into account in computing taxable income."

B. LIKE KIND EXCHANGES

1. THE LIKE KIND EXCHANGE REQUIREMENTS

Internal Revenue Code: Sections 1001(c); 1031; 1223(1). See Sections 453(f)(6); 1245(b)(4); 1250(d)(4).

Regulations: Sections 1.1031(a)–1; 1.1031(b)–1(b) Example (1); 1.1031(d)–1.

At the outset, it should be stated that the "if" clause of Section 1031(a) is strewn with hurdles to be taken. First, with respect to the nature of the property transferred, it must be " * * * *property held for productive use in a trade or business or for investment * * *,*".[1] Moreover, the statute expressly excludes inventory and the like and also excludes *inter alia* stocks, bonds, interests in a partnership,[2] certificates of trust, and choses in action. Second, the disposition must qualify as an *exchange*. Finally, the consideration received must be property of *like kind* to be held for productive use in a trade or business or for investment.[3] All three criteria must be met.

---

1. Emphasis added.

2. This does not include an interest in a partnership which has in effect a valid election under I.R.C. § 761(a). Such an interest is treated as an interest in each of the assets of the partnership. I.R.C. § 1031(a)(2), flush language.

3. If as part of a transaction otherwise qualifying under I.R.C. § 1031, the taxpayer, pursuant to pre-arranged plan, disposes of the property received in the exchange, § 1031 does not apply. This is so because the property received is not *to be held* for productive use in his trade or business or for investment. See Rev.Rul. 75–292,

Depending on the nature of the controversy, taxpayer nonrecognition of gain or government effort to disallow loss,[4] the vast majority of the cases has been concerned with the question whether the transaction constitutes an *exchange* of like kind properties.

BLOOMINGTON COCA–COLA BOTTLING CO. v. COMMISSIONER

United States Court of Appeals, Seventh Circuit, 1951.
189 F.2d 14.

* * *

A "sale" is a transfer of property for a price in money or its equivalent. "Exchange" means the giving of one thing for another. That is to say, in a sale, the property is transferred in consideration of a definite price expressed in terms of money, while in an exchange, the property is transferred in return for other property without the intervention of money. True, "Border-line cases arise where the money forms a substantial part of the adjustment of values in connection with the disposition of property and the acquisition of similar properties. The presence in a transaction of a small amount of cash, to adjust certain differences in value of the properties exchanged will not necessarily prevent the transaction from being considered an exchange. * * * Where cash is paid by the taxpayer, it may be considered as representing the purchase price of excess value of 'like property' received." 3 Mertens, Law of Federal Income Taxation, § 20.29, pp. 143, 144.

* * *

COMMISSIONER v. CRICHTON

United States Court of Appeals, Fifth Circuit, 1941.
122 F.2d 181.

HUTCHESON, Circuit Judge. In 1936, respondent and her three children, owning, in undivided interests, a tract of unimproved country land and an improved city lot, effected an exchange of interests. Her children transferred to respondent their undivided interest in the city lot. Respondent transferred to her children, as of equal value, an undivided $3/12$ interest in the "oil, gas and other minerals, in, on and under, and that may be produced from" the country land. The $1/2$ interest conveyed to respondent had a value of $15,357.77. The interest respondent transferred to her children had a cost basis of zero.

Respondent treating the exchange as one of property for property of like kind and therefore nontaxable under Section 112(b)(1),[1] Revenue Act of 1936, 26 U.S.C.A.Int.Rev.Acts, page 855, did not report any profit therefrom. The commissioner, of the opinion that the exchange result-

---

1975–2 C.B. 333, and compare Rev.Rul. 75–291, 1975–2 C.B. 332.

4. See e.g., 124 Front Street, Inc., 65 T.C. 6 (1975). To the extent that a transaction falls within I.R.C. § 1031, no loss on

that transaction is *ever* recognized. I.R.C. § 1031(c). See e.g., Valley Title Co., 34 T.C.M. 312 (1975).

1. [I.R.C. (1939) § 112(b) is omitted. See I.R.C. (1986) § 1031(a). Ed.]

ed in a capital gain of $15,357.71, under Section 117, Revenue Act of 1936, 26 U.S.C.A.Int.Rev.Acts, page 873, determined a deficiency of $628.66 accordingly.

The Board [2] of the opinion that the exchange was "solely in kind", disagreed with the commissioner and on redetermination fixed the deficiency at $86.46. The commissioner is here insisting that the Board has wrongfully decided the question. We do not think so. We agree with the Board that whatever difficulty there might have been, if the statute stood alone, in determining the meaning of the very general words it uses, as applied to the facts of this case, that difficulty vanishes in the light of Treasury Regulation 94,[3] if that regulation is valid, and we think it quite clear that it is. As was the case with regard to the statute considered in Helvering v. Reynolds Tobacco Co., 306 U.S. 110, 113, 59 S.Ct. 423, 425, so here, the section "is so general in its terms as to render an interpretative regulation appropriate."

As was the case there, so here, "the administrative construction embodied in the regulation has [for many years], been uniform with respect to each of the revenue acts, * * *, as evidenced by Treasury rulings and regulations, and decisions of the Board of Tax Appeals."

The commissioner concedes, as he must, that under Louisiana law, mineral rights are interests not in personal but in real property, and that the rights exchanged were real rights. In the light therefore of the rule the regulation lays down, of the examples given in the illustrations it puts forth, and of the construction which, under its interpretation, the statute has been given throughout this long period, it will not do for him to now marshal or parade the supposed dissimilarities in grade or quality, the unlikenesses, in attributes, appearance and capacities, between undivided real interests in a respectively small town hotel, and mineral properties. For the regulation and the interpretation under it, leave in no doubt that no gain or loss is realized by one, other than a dealer, from an exchange of real estate for other real estate, and that the distinction intended and made by the statute is the broad one between classes and characters of properties, for instance, between real and personal property. It was not intended to draw any distinction between parcels of real property however dissimilar they may be in location, in attributes and in capacities for profitable use.

The order of the Board was right. It is affirmed.

NOTE

The regulations interpret "like kind" to ". . . have reference to the nature or character of the property and not to its grade or quality. One kind or class of property may not, under [Section 1031], be exchanged for property of a different kind or class." [1]

---

2. 42 B.T.A. 490.

3. [The provisions in the current regulations which correspond to earlier provisions quoted here are at Reg. § 1.1031(a)–1(b) and (c). Ed.]

1. Reg. § 1.1031(a)–1(b).

As the *Crichton* case illustrates, the term "like kind" is interpreted very broadly when applied to real estate transactions. Parcels of real property, however dissimilar, are like kind properties.[2] The Service has tried to limit the term's scope to parcels of real estate.[3] Query whether the Service will be successful if the issue is litigated. There is one definite limitation to the broad "like kind" interpretation in real estate swaps. The statute specifically provides that real property located in the United States and real property located outside the United States are not like kind property.[4]

The like kind test set out in the regulations[5] applies to personal property as well as real property, but when personal property is exchanged, the term "like kind" is interpreted narrowly.[6] The Service has held that an exchange of gold bullion for silver bullion, both held for investment, is not an exchange of like kind property because they are intrinsically different metals used primarily in different ways.[7] More recently, the Service has proposed regulations[8] related to exchanges of tangible depreciable personal property.[9] Under the regulations the like kind test for tangible depreciable personal property is liberalized. Such property may satisfy either the old like kind test or a new "like class" test.[10] The term "like class" is defined as property either within the same "General Business Asset Class"[11] or, if property is not listed within a General Business Asset Class, within the same "Product Class."[12] The proposed regulations list some examples:[13] a personal computer exchanged for a printer (both held for productive use in a trade or business) are in the same General Business Asset Class and are, therefore, of a like class;[14] whereas an airplane exchanged for a general purpose truck (both held for productive use in a business) are

2. See page 915, supra. See also Carl E. Koch, 71 T.C. 54 (1978), parcels of real estate subject to 99–year condominium leases and unencumbered parcels of real estate are like kind.

3. See, e.g., Rev.Rul. 67–255, 1967–2 C.B. 270, and Rev.Rul. 76–390, 1976–2 C.B. 243 (land and mere improvements to land were not like kind properties under I.R.C. § 1033(g)(1)), as well as Rev.Rul. 71–41, 1971–1 C.B. 223 (mere improvements to land and land with improvements were not like kind properties, also under I.R.C. § 1033(g)(1)). I.R.C. § 1033(g) uses the term "like kind," and its meaning under § 1033 should be identical to its meaning under § 1031(a).

4. I.R.C. § 1031(h).

5. See note 1, supra.

6. See Prop.Reg. § 1.1031(a)–2. The statute hints of a narrow interpretation in providing that livestock of different sexes are not property of a like kind. I.R.C. § 1031(e).

7. Rev.Rul. 82–166, 1982–2 C.B. 190. But see Rev.Rul. 82–96, 1982–1 C.B. 113, exchange of gold bullion for Canadian Maple Leaf gold coins (not a circulating medium of exchange) are like kind.

8. The proposed regulations supplement Reg. § 1.1031(a)–1.

9. Prop.Reg. § 1.1031(a)–2. See Bogdanski, "On Beyond Real Estate: The New Like–Kind Exchange Regulations" 48 Tax Notes No. 7, 903 (1990).

10. Prop.Reg. § 1.1031(a)–2(a), (b)(1).

11. Prop.Reg. § 1.1031(a)–2(b)(2) relies on the definition of General Business Asset Classes found in Rev.Proc. 87–56, 1987–2 C.B. 674 at 00.11 through 00.28 and 00.4. The classes contain several different types of property that are used in businesses such as: office furniture, fixtures and equipment; information systems (computers); automobiles; and buses.

12. Prop.Reg. § 1.1031(a)–2(b)(3). Product Classes are defined in a Product Code issued by the Commerce Department.

13. Prop.Reg. § 1.1031(a)–2(b)(6).

14. Prop.Reg. § 1.1031(a)–2(b)(6) Example (1).

in different General Business Asset Classes and are not of a like class.[15] Exchanges of intangible personal property, nondepreciable personal property, and personal property held for investment must continue to satisfy only the traditional like kind test to attain nonrecognition treatment.[16]

LESLIE CO. v. COMMISSIONER

United States Court of Appeals, Third Circuit, 1976.
539 F.2d 943.

GARTH, Circuit Judge: This appeal involves the tax consequences of a sale and leaseback arrangement. The question presented is whether the sale and leaseback arrangement constitutes an exchange of like-kind properties, on which no loss is recognized, or whether that transaction is governed by the general recognition provision of Int.Rev.Code § 1002.[1] The Tax Court, on taxpayer's petition for a redetermination of deficiencies assessed against it by the Commissioner, held that the fee conveyance aspect of the transaction was a sale entitled to recognition, and that the leaseback was merely a condition precedent to that sale. The Tax Court thereby allowed the loss claimed by the taxpayer. For the reasons given below, we affirm.

I. Leslie Company, the taxpayer, is a New Jersey corporation engaged in the manufacture and distribution of pressure and temperature regulators and instantaneous water heaters. Leslie, finding its *Lyndhurst*, New Jersey plant inadequate for its needs, decided to move to a new facility. To this end, in March 1967 Leslie purchased land in Parsippany, on which to construct a new manufacturing plant.

Leslie, however, was unable to acquire the necessary financing for the construction of its proposed $2,400,000 plant. Accordingly, on October 30, 1967, it entered into an agreement with the Prudential Life Insurance Company of America, whereby Leslie would erect a plant to specifications approved by Prudential and Prudential would then purchase the Parsippany property and building from Leslie. At the time of purchase Prudential would lease back the facility to Leslie. The property and improvements were to be conveyed to Prudential for $2,400,000 or the actual cost to Leslie, whichever amount was less.

The lease term was established at 30 years,[2] at an annual net rental of $190,560, which was 7.94% of the purchase price. The lease agreement gave Leslie two 10-year options to renew. The annual net rental during each option period was $72,000, or 3% of the purchase

---

15. Prop.Reg. § 1.1031(a)–2(b)(6) Example (2).

16. Prop.Reg. § 1.1031(a)–2(c). In determining whether intangible personal property is of like kind to other such property, both the type of intangible right involved and the underlying property to which the intangible property relates are considered. Id.

1. All references are to the Internal Revenue Code of 1954. [Footnotes have been edited and renumbered. Ed.]

2. The parties stipulated, and the Tax Court found accordingly, that the useful life of the building Leslie constructed was 30 years.

price. The lease also provided that Leslie could offer to repurchase the property [3] at five year intervals, beginning with the 15th year of the lease, at specified prices as follows:

At the end of the

(15th year	$1,798,000
(20th year	1,592,000
(25th year	1,386,000
(30th year	1,180,000

Under the lease Prudential was entitled to all condemnation proceeds, net of any damages suffered by Leslie with respect to its trade fixtures and certain structural improvements, without any deduction for Leslie's leasehold interest.

Construction was completed in December, 1968, at a total cost to Leslie (including the purchase price of the land) of $3,187,414. On December 16, 1968 Leslie unconditionally conveyed the property to Prudential, as its contract required, for $2,400,000. At the same time, Leslie and Prudential executed a 30-year lease.

Leslie, on its 1968 corporate income tax return, reported and deducted a loss of $787,414 from the sale of the property.[4] The Commissioner of Internal Revenue disallowed the claimed loss on the ground that the sale and leaseback transaction constituted an exchange of like-kind properties within the scope of Int.Rev.Code § 1031. That section of the Code, if applicable, provides for nonrecognition (and hence nondeductibility) of such losses.[5] Rather than permitting Leslie to take the entire deduction of $787,414 in 1968, the Commissioner treated the $787,414 as Leslie's cost in obtaining the lease, and amortized that sum over the lease's 30-year term. Accordingly, Leslie was assessed deficiencies of $383,023.52 in its corporate income taxes for the years 1965, 1966 and 1968.

Leslie petitioned the Tax Court for a redetermination of the deficiencies assessed against it, contending that the conveyance of the Parsippany property constituted a sale, on which loss is recognized. The Tax Court agreed.[6]

Although the Tax Court found as a fact that Leslie would not have entered into the sale transaction without a leaseback guarantee, * * * it concluded that this finding was not dispositive of the character of the transaction. Rather, it held that to constitute an exchange under Int.Rev.Code § 1031 there must be a reciprocal transfer of properties, as distinguished from a transfer of property for a money consideration only, * * * citing Treas.Reg. § 1.1002–1(d). Based on

---

3. See note 10 infra.

4. The $787,414 was the difference between Leslie's actual cost of $3,187,414 and the $2,400,000 which Prudential paid Leslie for the property. This 1968 loss resulted in a net operating loss for that year of $366,907, which was carried back to 1965.

5. The Commissioner characterizes the instant transaction as an exchange of real property for a 30-year lease plus cash ($2,400,000). (Appellant's Brief at 2). Thus, in the Commissioner's view, Int.Rev. Code § 1031(c) applies.

6. 64 T.C. 247 (1975).

its findings that the fair market value of the Parsippany property at the time of sale was "in the neighborhood of" the $2,400,000 which Prudential paid, and that the annual net rental of $190,560 to be paid by Leslie was comparable to the fair rental value of similar types of property in the Northern New Jersey area,[7] the Tax Court majority reasoned that Leslie's leasehold had no separate capital value which could be properly viewed as part of the consideration paid. Accordingly, Leslie having received $2,400,000 from Prudential as the sole consideration for the property conveyed, the Tax Court held that the transaction was not an exchange of like-kind properties within the purview of Int.Rev.Code § 1031, but was rather a sale, and so governed by the general recognition provision of Int.Rev.Code § 1002.

Six judges of the Tax Court dissented from this holding. Judge Tannenwald, in an opinion in which Judges Raum, Drennen, Quealy and Hall joined, agreed with the Tax Court majority that the conveyance was a sale, but would have disallowed a loss deduction, reasoning that the leasehold had a premium value to Leslie equal to the $787,414 difference between cost and sales price.[8] This dissent reasoned that since Leslie would not have willingly incurred the loss but for the guaranteed lease, this amount should be treated as a bonus paid for the leasehold, and should be amortized over the leasehold's 30-year term.

Judge Wilbur, in a separate dissent with which Judges Tannenwald and Hall agreed, 64 T.C. at 257, declined to decide whether the conveyance was a sale or an exchange. His concern was that the Tax Court majority was permitting the taxpayer to "write off 25 per cent of the costs of acquiring the right to use a building for one-half a century that was constructed for its [Leslie's] own special purposes." He, like Judge Tannenwald, would hold the loss incurred was attributable to the acquisition of the leasehold interest rather than to the construction of the building.

The Commissioner's appeal from the decision of the Tax Court followed.

II. The threshold question in any dispute involving the applicability of Int.Rev.Code § 1031 is whether the transaction constitutes an

---

7. These findings were based on the testimony of a witness presented by the Commissioner, who testified that the sale price of the property and the rental established by the lease were comparable to their respective fair market values. This testimony, as might be expected, was uncontroverted by the taxpayer.

8. Judge Quealy also filed a separate dissent, 64 T.C. at 257, in which he pointed to Leslie's reservation of a favorable option to repurchase the property as further support for the position that the petitioner incurred no loss upon sale.

We are hard pressed to agree with this characterization of Leslie's very limited rights of repurchase under the lease as "favorable." The repurchase right is set forth in * * * the lease * * *. Leslie is given the right to terminate the lease after the 15th, 20th, 25th and 30th years. To do so, however, it must make an offer to repurchase the property back from Prudential, at specified prices. * * * Prudential need not accept the offer, although nonacceptance does not prejudice Leslie's rights of termination. Thus Leslie's option to offer to repurchase may be exercised only at the risk of losing the right to use the property for the remainder of the lease term.

exchange. This is so because § 1031 nonrecognition applies only to exchanges. Section 1031 does not apply where, for example, a taxpayer sells business property for cash and immediately reinvests that cash in other business property even if that property is "like-kind" property. Bell Lines Inc. v. United States, 480 F.2d 710 (4th Cir.1973). Hence, our inquiry must center on whether the Leslie-Prudential transaction was a sale, as Leslie contends, or an exchange, as the Commissioner argues. If a sale then, as stated, § 1031 is inapplicable and we need not be concerned further with ascertaining whether the other requirements of that section have been met. See Jordan Marsh Co. v. Commissioner, 269 F. 453, 455 (2d Cir.1959). If an exchange, then of course we would be obliged to continue our inquiry to determine if the properties involved were "like-kind."

The Tax Court's conclusion that the Leslie conveyance resulted in a sale was predicated almost totally on an analysis of the applicable Treasury Regulations. Noting that Treas.Reg. § 1.1002–1(b) requires a strict construction of § 1031, the Tax Court tested the instant transaction against the definition of "exchange" contained in Treas.Reg. § 1.1002(d):

> (d) Exchange. Ordinarily, to constitute an exchange, the transaction must be a reciprocal transfer of property as distinguished from a transfer of property for a money consideration only.

Based on its conclusion that the leasehold had no capital value, the Tax Court held that it was not a part of the consideration received but was merely a condition precedent to the sale. Thus, the conveyance to Prudential was "solely for a money consideration" and therefore was not an "exchange." The Tax Court cited Jordan Marsh Co. v. Commissioner, supra, in support of its result. In light of its holding, it specifically declined to consider or resolve any possible conflict between *Jordan Marsh*, a decision of the Second Circuit, and the Eighth Circuit decision in Century Electric Co. v. Commissioner, 192 F.2d 155 (8th Cir. 1951), cert. denied 342 U.S. 954, 72 S.Ct. 625 (1952).

The Commissioner, relying on *Century Electric*, argues that the Tax Court erred in holding the Leslie-Prudential conveyance to be a sale. He could not, and does not, dispute the Tax Court's findings as to the fair market value and fair rental value of the property. Rather, he argues that value in this context is irrelevant and that the only appropriate consideration is whether the conveyance of the fee and the conveyance of the leasehold were reciprocal.[9] The Commissioner, without regard to his own regulations which define an "exchange," then seeks to support his position by reference to the legislative purpose giving rise to the enactment of the nonrecognition provision. He argues that this provision (§ 1031 and its predecessors) was adopted

---

9. As noted above, the Tax Court found that this element of reciprocity *was* present.

primarily to eliminate any requirement that the government value the property involved in such exchanges.[10] Alternatively, the Commissioner argues that even if the conveyance is held to be a sale and thereby not within Int.Rev.Code § 1031, any expenditure incurred by Leslie over and above the selling price of $2,400,000 was not a loss as claimed, but rather a premium or bonus which Leslie paid to obtain the leasehold. Such an expenditure is a capital expenditure, the Commissioner argues, and therefore should be amortized over the 30-year lease term.

Leslie, on the other hand, urges affirmance of the Tax Court's holding, relying on Jordan Marsh Co. v. Commissioner, supra, and stresses, as does the Tax Court, that the initial issue to be resolved is the character of the transaction. * * *

In Century Electric Co. v. Commissioner, supra, the Eighth Circuit held a sale and leaseback arrangement to be a like-kind exchange governed by the nonrecognition provision. * * * Its holding that no loss was to be recognized was based solely on its finding that the sale and leaseback transactions were reciprocal. The Eighth Circuit read the legislative history of [§ 1031] as evidencing a Congressional purpose to relieve the government of the administrative burden of valuing properties received in like-kind exchanges. Thus the Court stated * * * that:

> the market value of the properties of like kind involved in the transfer does not enter into the equation.

By contrast, in Jordan Marsh v. Commissioner, supra, a case construing the same code provision as *Century Electric,* the Second Circuit held that a similar sale and leaseback transaction resulted in a *sale,* on which loss was recognized. The facts in *Jordan Marsh* were similar to the facts here. Jordan Marsh, the taxpayer, had sold two parcels of land for cash in the sum of $2.3 million an amount which was stipulated to be equal to the fair market value of the property. Simultaneously, the premises were leased back to Jordan Marsh for a term of 30-plus years, with options to renew. The rentals to be paid by Jordan Marsh were "full and normal rentals", so that the Court found that the leasehold interest had no separate capital value.

The Court, in examining the legislative history of [§ 1031] took issue with the Eighth Circuit's interpretation of the Congressional purpose behind the nonrecognition provision. The Second Circuit said that:

10. The Commissioner takes the position that:

"The statute was intended to be corrective legislation of three specific shortcomings of prior Revenue Acts, viz—(1) the administrative burden of valuing property received in a like-kind exchange; (2) the inequity, in the case of an exchange, of forcing a taxpayer to recognize a paper gain which was still tied up in a continuing investment; and (3) the prevention of taxpayer from taking colorable losses in wash sales and other fictitious exchanges. Preliminary Report of a Subcommittee of the House Committee on Ways and Means on Prevention of Tax Avoidance, 73d Cong., 2d Sess. (1933).

Congress was primarily concerned with the inequity, in the case of an exchange, of forcing a taxpayer to recognize a paper gain which was still tied up in a continuing investment of the same sort.

It reasoned further that, if gains were not to be recognized on the ground that they were theoretical, then neither should losses, which were equally theoretical, be recognized. Analyzing the *Jordan Marsh* transaction in the light of this interpretation of Congressional purpose, the Second Circuit, finding Jordan Marsh had liquidated its investment in realty for cash in an amount fully equal to the value of the fee, concluded that the taxpayer was not "still tied up in a continuing investment of the same sort." Accordingly, the Court held that there was no exchange within the purview of § 112(b), but rather a sale.

Thus we may interpret the essential difference between *Jordan Marsh* and *Century Electric* as centering on their respective views of the need to value property involved in a sale and leaseback.[11] *Jordan Marsh* viewing the Congressional purpose behind the nonrecognition provision as one of avoiding taxation of paper gains and losses, would value the properties involved in order to determine whether the requirements of an "exchange" have been met. *Century Electric,* on the other hand, viewing the legislative enactment as one to relieve the administrative burden of valuation, would regard the value of the properties involved as irrelevant.

We are persuaded that the *Jordan Marsh* approach is a more satisfactory one. First, it is supported by the Commissioner's own definition of "exchange" which distinguishes an exchange from a transfer of property *solely* for a money consideration. Treas.Reg. § 1.1002–1(d) (emphasis added).[12] Second, if resort is to be had to legislative history, it appears to us that the view of Congressional purpose taken by the *Jordan Marsh* court is sounder than that of the Eighth Circuit in *Century Electric.* As the Court in *Jordan Marsh* said in discounting the purpose attributed to Congress by the Commissioner and by *Century Electric:*

> Indeed, if these sections had been intended to obviate the necessity of making difficult valuations, one would have expected them to provide for nonrecognition of gains and losses in all exchanges, whether the property received in exchanges were 'of a like kind' or *not* of a like kind. And if such had

11. The Court in *Jordan Marsh* also distinguished *Century Electric* on its facts, since in that case there had been no finding that the cash received by the taxpayer was the full equivalent of the value of the fee which had been conveyed. Nor had there been a finding that the leaseback was at a rental which was a fair rental for the premises.

Indeed, as noted in *Jordan Marsh,* the record in *Century Electric* indicated that the sales price was substantially less than the fair market value. There was also evidence from which the Court could have found that the leasehold had a separate capital value, since the conveyance to a non-profit college avoided considerable tax liabilities on the property.

12. It was this definition on which the Tax Court relied in large part in holding the Leslie conveyance to be a sale for $2,400,000.

been the legislative objective, [§ 1031] providing for the recognition of gain from exchanges not wholly in kind, would never have been enacted. ＊ ＊ ＊

It seems to us, therefore, that in order to determine whether money was the sole consideration for a transfer the fair market value of the properties involved must be ascertained. Here, the Tax Court found that Leslie had sold its property unconditionally for cash equal to its fair market value, and had acquired a leasehold for which it was obligated to pay fair rental value. These findings, not clearly erroneous, are binding on this Court. ＊ ＊ ＊

Nor do we think the Tax Court erred in concluding that the leasehold acquired by Leslie had no capital value. Among other considerations, the rental charged at fair market rates, the lack of compensation for the leasehold interest in the event of condemnation, and the absence of any substantial right of control over the property all support this conclusion. On this record, we agree with the Tax Court that the conveyance was not an exchange, "a reciprocal transfer of property," but was rather "a transfer of property for a money consideration only," and therefore a *sale.* ＊ ＊ ＊

The Commissioner's evidence that the rentals charged to Leslie under its lease were at fair market value, leading to our conclusion that the leasehold had no capital value, also disposes of the Commissioner's alternative argument on appeal that Leslie's excess cost of $787,414 was not a loss. ＊ ＊ ＊

The decision of the Tax Court will be affirmed.

NOTE

The sale and leaseback transaction has generated substantial Section 1031 litigation. In the *Leslie* case, the Commissioner relied on his position taken in the regulations that a leasehold of 30 years or more is of a like kind to outright ownership [1] in an attempt to recharacterize the sale and leaseback as a Section 1031 exchange. If successful, the Commissioner would have been able to deny *Leslie* an immediate deduction of his loss on the transfer. The Court in *Leslie* cites the *Century Electric* case [2] which reached a result opposite to *Leslie*. In *Century Electric,* the taxpayer transferred a foundry building of uncertain value in return for $150,000 of cash and a leaseback of the building for a maximum 95 year period. The Court agreed with the Commissioner's position in the regulations,[3] and treated the transaction as a Section 1031 like kind exchange denying taxpayer's loss. However, in Jordan Marsh Co. v. Commissioner,[4] a case factually to *Leslie,* the Second Circuit distinguished *Century Electric* in a situation in which the taxpayer transferred two parcels of loss property for $2,300,000 in

1. Reg. § 1.1031(a)–1(c).

2. Century Electric Co. v. Commissioner, 192 F.2d 155 (8th Cir.1951), cert. denied 342 U.S. 954, 72 S.Ct. 625 (1952).

3. Reg. § 1.1031(a)–1(c).

4. 269 F.2d 453 (2d Cir.1959).

cash, representing the fair market value of the properties. At the same time, the taxpayer entered into a lease of the same property for 30 years with an option to renew for another 30 years. The Second Circuit concluded that the transaction was a sale and leaseback, not a Section 1031 exchange. The Commissioner indicated he will not follow the *Jordan Marsh* decision, stating: [5]

> It is the position of the Service that a sale and leaseback under the circumstances here present constitute, in substance, a single integrated transaction under which there is an 'exchange' of property of like kind with cash as boot.

The Commissioner has asserted the doctrine of substance over form in other circumstances to attempt to invoke the provisions of Section 1031. In Revenue Ruling 61-119,[6] the taxpayer sold some old equipment used in his trade or business to a dealer at a gain. In a separate transaction he purchased new equipment from the same dealer. The Service looked to the fact that the sale and purchase were reciprocal and mutually dependent transactions and concluded that, in substance, they constituted a Section 1031 exchange. Why did the taxpayer set up two separate transactions? Would the Commissioner be as interested in Section 1031 applying in the above circumstances today as he was in 1961?

2.   THREE–CORNERED EXCHANGES

Internal Revenue Code: Section 1031(a)(3).

Proposed Regulations: Sections 1.1031(a)–3(a), (b), (c)(1) and (4)(i), (f), and (g)(6).

REVENUE RULING 77–297
1977–2 Cum.Bull. 304.

Advice is requested whether the transaction described below is an exchange of property in which no gain or loss is recognized pursuant to section 1031(a) of the Internal Revenue Code of 1954.

A entered into a written agreement with *B* to sell *B* for 1,000*x* dollars a ranch (the "first ranch") consisting of land and certain buildings used by *A* in the business of raising livestock. Pursuant to the agreement, *B* placed 100*x* dollars into escrow and agreed to pay at closing an additional 200*x* dollars in cash, to assume a 160*x* dollar liability of *A*, and to execute a note for 540*x* dollars. The agreement also provided that *B* would cooperate with *A* to effectuate an exchange of properties should *A* locate suitable property. No personal property was involved in the transaction. *A* and *B* are not dealers in real estate.

---

5. Rev.Rul. 60–43, 1960–1 C.B. 687, 688. See also Rev.Rul. 76–301, 1976–2 C.B. 241.

As Rev.Rul 60–43 preceded the *Leslie* case, the Third Circuit in the *Leslie* case obviously disagrees with the Commission-er's position. See also Crowley, Milner & Co. v. Commissioner, 689 F.2d 635 (6th Cir. 1982).

6. 1961–1 C.B. 395.

A located another ranch (the "second ranch") consisting of land and certain buildings suitable for raising livestock. The second ranch was owned by *C*. *B* entered into an agreement with *C* to purchase the second ranch for 2,000*x* dollars. Pursuant to this agreement, *B* placed 40*x* dollars into escrow, agreed to pay at closing an additional 800*x* dollars, assume 400*x* dollars liability of *C*, and execute a note for 760*x* dollars. No personal property was involved in the transaction. *C* could not look to *A* for specific performance on the contract, thus, *B* was not acting as *A*'s agent in the purchase of the second parcel of property.

At closing, *B* purchased the second ranch as agreed. After the purchase, *B* exchanged the second ranch with *A* for the first ranch and assumed *A*'s liability of 160*x* dollars. With *C*'s concurrence, *A* assumed *C*'s 400*x* dollar liability and *B*'s note for 760*x* dollars. *C* released *B* from liability on the note. The escrow agent returned the 100*x* dollars to *B* that *B* had initially placed in escrow. This sum had never been available to *A*, since the conditions of the escrow were never satisfied.

Section 1031(a) of the Code provides that no gain or loss shall be recognized if property held for productive use in trade or business or for investment (not including stock in trade or other property held primarily for sale, nor stocks, bonds, notes, choses in action, certificates of trust or beneficial interest, or other securities or evidence of indebtedness or interest) is exchanged solely for property of a like kind to be held either for productive use in trade or business or for investment.

Section 1031(b) of the Code states that if an exchange would be within the provisions of subsection (a) if it were not for the fact that the property received in exchange consists not only of property permitted by such provisions to be received without the recognition of gain, but also of other property or money, then the gain, if any, to the recipient shall be recognized, but in an amount not in excess of the sum of such money and the fair market value of such other property.

Section 1.1031(b)–1(c) of the Income Tax Regulations states that consideration received in the form of an assumption of liabilities is to be treated as "other property or money" for the purpose of section 1031(b) of the Code. However, if, on an exchange described in section 1031(b), each party to the exchange assumes a liability of the other party, then, in determining the amount of "other property or money" for purposes of section 1031(b), consideration given in the form of an assumption of liabilities shall be offset against consideration received in the form of an assumption of liabilities.

Ordinarily, to constitute an exchange, the transaction must be a reciprocal transfer of property, as distinguished from a transfer of property for a money consideration only.

In the instant case *A* and *B* entered into a sales agreement with an exchange option if suitable property were found. Before the sale was consummated, the parties effectuated an exchange. Thus, for purposes of section 1031 of the Code, the parties entered into an exchange of property. See *Alderson v. Commissioner,* 317 F.2d 790 (9th Cir.1963), in which a similar transaction was treated as a like-kind exchange of property even though the original agreement called for a sale of the property. In addition, *A* 's 160*x* dollar liability assumed by *B* was offset by *B* 's liabilities assumed by *A,* pursuant to section 1.1031(b)–1(c) of the regulations.

Accordingly, as to *A,* the exchange of ranches qualifies for nonrecognition of gain or loss under section 1031 of the Code. As to *B,* the exchange of ranches does not qualify for nonrecognition of gain or loss under section 1031 because *B* did not hold the second ranch for productive use in a trade or business or for investment. See Rev.Rul. 75–291, 1975–2 C.B. 332, in which it is held that the nonrecognition provisions of section 1031 do not apply to a taxpayer who acquired property solely for the purpose of exchanging it for like-kind property.

However, in the instant case, *B* did not realize gain or loss as a result of the exchange since the total consideration received by *B* of 2,160*x* dollars (fair market value of first ranch of 1,000*x* dollars plus *B* 's liabilities assumed by *A* of 1,160*x* dollars) is equal to *B* 's basis in the property given up of 2,000*x* dollars plus *A* 's liability assumed by *B* of 160*x* dollars. See section 1001 of the Code and the applicable regulations thereunder.

NOTE

Sometimes taxpayers can avoid adverse tax consequences by way of what are commonly referred to as "three-cornered transactions." [1] As it requires an exchange, Section 1031 does not apply if property is sold and the proceeds are reinvested in property of a like kind.[2] In the basic three-cornered transaction, essentially sanctioned by the Service in Revenue Ruling 77–297, A has property (property X) that B wants and C has property (property Y) that A wants. Assume C's basis for his property Y is equal to its fair market value, but A's basis for his property X is much less than fair market value. Further, assume that the properties are of like kind and also that they are of equal value. Of course, A could sell property X to B and with the proceeds buy property Y from C. This would probably be all right with everyone except A who, in the process, would incur tax on his large gain on the sale of property X. So why not: (1) have B buy property Y from C (without adverse consequences to C because his basis in property Y is equal to its fair market value) and (2) then have A exchange property X with B for property Y, tax-free under Section 1031?

As regards A who has a large realized gain on the exchange, the transaction is rendered tax-free by Section 1031. The fact that B

---

1. W.D. Haden Co. v. Commissioner, 165 F.2d 588 (5th Cir.1948); see Dean, "Three–Party Exchanges of Real Estate," 17 Tulane Tax Inst. 131 (1967) and Winokur, "Real Estate Exchanges: The Three Cornered Deal," 28 N.Y.U.Inst. on Fed.Tax. 127 (1970), for general discussions of three-cornered transactions.

2. Compare I.R.C. § 1033(a)(2), infra at page 933.

acquired property Y for the very purpose of making the exchange has no effect on A. A has held property X, let's say for investment, and he exchanges it for property Y to be held for investment. There is no doubt this fits squarely within the statute.[3]

It is just as clear, however, that B is not within Section 1031. He does not have property held for productive use or for investment which he exchanges for property of a like kind. He has newly purchased property Y that he uses to effectuate the exchange. Thus Section 1031 does not apply to him.[4] Of course, on our facts B wouldn't give a four letter-word whether he was within or without Section 1031, because he has a new cost basis for property Y, presumably equal to the fair market value of property X, that he received in the exchange. Consequently, the transaction is neutral to him for tax purposes.

Revenue Ruling 77–297 is a variation on this basic three-cornered transaction,[5] because B transfers money into escrow prior to his acquisition of C's property. The Service sanctions the transaction because "[b]efore the sale was consummated, the parties effectuated an exchange."[6]

A further variation that was previously successful involved non-simultaneous exchanges of like kind property. Such transactions received judicial approval in Starker v. United States.[7] In *Starker,* taxpayer A, in our hypothetical above, transferred appreciated real estate to B in return for B's promise to locate and purchase parcels of real estate for A within a five-year period and to pay any outstanding balance due in cash. To the extent that A subsequently received qualifying property within the five-year period, the Court held that Section 1031 was applicable. The *Starker* court held that simultaneous transfers are not required in a Section 1031 exchange and, in response to the government's like kind argument, stated:[8]

> [A] contractual right to assume the rights of ownership should not, we believe, be treated as any different than the ownership rights themselves. Even if the contract right includes the possibility of the taxpayer receiving something other than

3. See Mercantile Trust Co. of Baltimore, 32 B.T.A. 82 (1935), acq. XIV–1 C.B. 13 (1935); Alderson v. Commissioner, 317 F.2d 790 (9th Cir.1963); Rev.Rul. 75–291, 1975–2 C.B. 332; Earlene Barker, 74 T.C. 555 (1980), involving a four party transaction.

4. See Rev.Rul. 75–292, 1975–2 C.B. 333.

5. In another variation, property subject to an option of sale was transferred by the taxpayer in escrow in exchange for like kind property. When the option holder exercised the option prior to escrow closing, the option holder, rather than the taxpayer's transferee, wound up with the property. The Tax Court held the taxpayer had sold his property and that § 1031 did not apply. John M. Rogers, 44 T.C. 126 (1965), affirmed per curiam 377 F.2d 534 (9th Cir.1967).

6. See page 926, supra. The Ruling adds that the cash in escrow had never been available to A because the conditions of the escrow were never satisfied. Had the cash been available to A, there would have been a constructive receipt of the cash and § 1031 would have been inapplicable, even though A might ultimately receive like kind property. See Prop.Reg. § 1–1031(a)–3(f), especially 3(f)(3). Example (i) and (ii).

7. 602 F.2d 1341 (9th Cir.1979).

8. Id at 1355.

ownership of like-kind property, we hold that it is still of a like kind with ownership for tax purposes when the taxpayer prefers property to cash before and through the executory period, and only like-kind property is ultimately received.

The use of nonsimultaneous exchanges was sharply curtailed by the Tax Reform Act of 1984.[9] The Act added Section 1031(a)(3), which allows an outright transfer but limits the taxpayer to relatively short periods of time within which to identify and receive Section 1031 property. The property received in the exchange must be identified within 45 days after the date the taxpayer transfers the property he is relinquishing ("the identification period").[10] The taxpayer must also receive the new property either within 180 days after the date he transfers the old property or by the due date (including extensions) of his tax return for the year of the transfer, whichever is earlier, ("the exchange period").[11]

The identification requirement does not always demand that the taxpayer know precisely the property he will receive in the exchange.[12] However, if the taxpayer identifies multiple properties, the maximum number of properties that may be identified is either 3 properties without regard to the fair market value of the properties ("the 3–property rule") or any number of properties as long as their aggregate fair market value does not exceed 200 percent of the aggregate fair market value of the relinquished properties ("the 200–percent rule").[13] If one of these rules is not met, the taxpayer is generally treated as though no property is identified and Section 1031 is inapplicable.[14] However, even if the taxpayer runs afoul of either of these rules, the identification requirement is met (1) to the extent that replacement property is actually received before the end of the identification period [15] and (2) to the extent that before the end of the exchange period, the taxpayer actually receives timely identified replacement property constituting at least 95 percent of the aggregate fair market values of the identified properties.[16]

Section 1031 is inapplicable to the extent that a transferor receives cash or other property.[17] This rule applies to both the actual and the *constructive receipt* of cash or other property before the receipt of like kind replacement property, regardless of the taxpayer's accounting method.[18] Examples of the constructive receipt rule are found in the regulations [19] and in problem 4 at the end of this subpart.

9. See Sommers, "Deferred Like–Kind Exchanges under Section 1031(a)(3) After *Starker*," 68 J.Tax. 92 (1988); Cuff and Wasserman, "Understanding the New Regulations on Deferred Exchanges," 68 Taxes 475 (1990).

10. I.R.C. § 1031(a)(3)(A).

11. I.R.C. § 1031(a)(3)(B).

12. See Prop.Reg. § 1.1031(a)–3(c)(4).

13. Prop.Reg. § 1.1031(a)–3(c)(4)(i).

14. Prop.Reg. § 1.1031(a)–3(c)(4)(ii).

15. Prop.Reg. § 1.1031(a)–3(c)(4)(ii)(A).

16. Prop.Reg. § 1.1031(a)–3(c)(4)(ii)(B).

17. I.R.C. § 1031(a) and (b).

18. Prop.Reg. § 1.1031(a)–3(f). The regulations use their regular definition of constructive receipt. Prop.Reg. § 1.1031(a)–3(f)(2). See Reg. § 1.451–2(a).

19. Prop.Reg. § 1.1031(a)–3(f)(3).

3. OTHER SECTION 1031 ISSUES

Internal Revenue Code: Sections 1031; 1223(1).

Regulations: Sections 1.1031(d)–2.

Section 1031 is a two edged sword—it applies to defer both *gains* and *losses.* In addition, it is a *non-elective* provision: if its requirements are satisfied, it automatically applies. Typical of all nonrecognition provisions, Section 1031 is accompanied by an exchanged basis [1] and a tacked holding period for the newly acquired like kind property.[2]

Section 1031(a) applies to exchanges solely for like kind property. If some boot (cash or other non-like kind property) is received (as is often the case), Sections 1031(b) or (c) may apply. In addition, Section 1031(a) is generally [3] inapplicable if the like kind exchange is between related persons [4] and either of the related persons disposes of their like kind property within two years [5] of the exchange.[6] The tax recognition consequences occur on the date of the disposition.[7]

Many like kind exchanges (especially of real estate) involve property subject to liabilities. If the other party in the exchange assumes a liability of the transferor or acquires property subject to a liability, the amount of the liability assumption or acquisition is treated as cash boot received by the transferor in the transaction.[8] However, if property on both sides of the exchange is encumbered, the amounts of the liabilities are offset against one another and only the net amount is treated as cash boot.[9] Things become more complicated if, as is commonly the case, cash is injected into the transaction. If a taxpayer transfers cash along with mortgaged like kind property he can net the cash against the mortgage in determining the amount of boot received.[10] However, if the taxpayer receives cash he may not net it against the liabilities received in determining his amount of boot.[11]

Section 1031 often involves the exchange of more than one parcel or piece of property. Proposed regulations provide a series of rules where there are exchanges of multiple properties.[12] These lengthy and complex proposed regulations may result in some unexpected tax conse-

1. I.R.C. § 1031(d).

2. I.R.C. § 1223(1).

3. But see I.R.C. § 1031(f)(2).

4. I.R.C. § 1031(f)(3).

5. The two-year period is suspended in some circumstances. See I.R.C. § 1031(g).

6. I.R.C. § 1031(f)(1). See Fellows and Yuhas, "Like–Kind Exchanges and Related Parties Under New Section 1031(f)," 68 Taxes 352 (1990).

7. I.R.C. § 1031(f)(1), last clause.

8. I.R.C. § 1031(d), last sentence. See Reg. § 1.1031(d)–2 Example (1) for an example of this rule.

9. Reg. § 1.1031(b)–1(c). Proposed regulations amending the cited regulations appropriately precluded such netting to the extent of any liabilities incurred by the taxpayer in anticipation of the I.R.C. § 1031 exchange. Prop.Reg. § 1.1031(b)–1(c).

10. Reg. § 1.1031(d)–2 Example 2(c).

11. Reg. § 1.1031(d)–2 Example 2(b). See problem 5, below, for an application of the liability rules.

12. Prop.Reg. § 1.1031(f)–1. See Levine, "New Personal Property and Multi-Asset Exchange Regs. May Increase Taxable Gain," 73 J.Tax. 16 (1990).

quences especially with regard to multiple asset exchanges involving liabilities and other forms of boot.[13]

Finally, before doing the problems dealing with the substantive rules of Section 1031, think for a moment about the benefits the like kind exchange rules may provide to taxpayers. Section 1031 applies to an exchange (a taxpayer initiated event) of like kind property (a term broadly defined, at least in the case of real property) to allow deferral of gain. A taxpayer can make an unlimited number of exchanges and hold property until she dies when the property receives a stepped-up basis [14] and totally avoids the income tax on its prior appreciation. In a time of tax base broadening and loophole closing, will Section 1031 with its generous taxpayer initiated tax deferral possibilities be the next provision to be excised by Congress? [15] Or will a strong real estate lobby continue to pressure Congress to retain the provision? Keep an eye on the Revenue Acts of 1991, 1992, 1993, or whenever for the answer.

PROBLEMS

1. X leased a twenty story building, as lessee for a period of 60 years. The first five floors of the building were used by X as a retail clothing store. The balance of the building X subleased to others. X had a basis in the entire lease of $15,000. The fair market value of the lease was only $10,000. Z paid X $10,000 for the entire leasehold. Thereafter Z subleased the first five floors to X. What are the tax consequences to X? See Rev.Rul. 76–301, 1976–2 C.B. 241.

2. T has 100 acres of unimproved land which he farms. Its cost basis is $10,000 but its value much greater. He trades it to B for a city apartment building worth $70,000, which has a basis to B of $30,000, and B transfers to T, as well, $4000 in cash and 100 shares of X Corp. stock for which B's basis is $40,000 but which have a fair market value of $26,000. None of the property involved is mortgaged, and B always claimed straight line depreciation on the apartment.

    (a) As regards T:

        (1) What is his realized gain on the exchange?

        (2) What is his *recognized* gain on the exchange?

        (3) What is his basis for the stock?

        (4) What is his basis for the apartment building?

        (5) Test whether your conclusions seem sensible by determining what the tax consequences to T would be if, immediately after the exchange, he sold the apartment building for $70,000 and the stock for $26,000 (taking account also of

---

13. See, e.g., Prop.Reg. § 1.1031(f)–1(d) Example (4).

14. I.R.C. § 1014.

15. For articles critical of I.R.C. § 1031, see Kornhauser, "Section 1031: We Don't Need Another Hero," 60 U.S.C.L.Rev. 397 (1987); Jensen, "The Uneasy Justification for Special Treatment of Like Kind Exchanges," 4 Amer.J.Tax.Pol. 193 (1985).

the amount on which he was taxed on the exchange), and comparing this with a straight sale of his farm land (instead of the exchange) for $100,000 cash.

(b) As regards B:

(1) What is his realized gain and loss on the exchange?

(2) What is his *recognized* gain or loss on the exchange?

(3) What is his basis for the farm land acquired?

(4) Could § 1250 affect B on these facts if, instead of straight line, B had claimed accelerated depreciation on the apartment?

(5) Test your conclusions about B by seeing whether a sale of the farm by him for $100,000 immediately after the exchange (and taking account of the tax treatment of the disposition of the stock on the exchange) will yield the same overall results as if initially, instead of making the exchange, he had sold the apartment building for $70,000 and the stock for $26,000.

Note: B's problems are a bit more intricate than T's. It is apparent that he has realized $100,000, the *value* of the farm land. But this amount must be allocated $4000 to the cash paid, $26,000 to the stock (its value) and $70,000 to the apartment building (its value). See Reg. § 1.1031(d)–1(e), Example. Is it clear that the $4000 cash paid by B will affect his adjusted basis, as otherwise determined, for the farm land?

3. T purchased a building and land at a cost of $500,000, $300,000 allocable to the building and $200,000 allocable to the land. The property is held as an investment. At a point when the building has been totally depreciated (under the straight-line method), T transfers the building and the land now worth $800,000 for another building and land also to be held as an investment. The fair market value of the replacement building is $400,000, and the fair market value of the replacement land is $400,000. As regards T:

(a) Does § 1031 apply to the exchange?

(b) Is T entitled to take depreciation deductions with respect to the building?

4. Buyer wants to acquire Seller's investment land. Seller has a substantial gain on the land, hates to pay tax on such gains, and would like to convert his investment to commercial real estate in a tax-free exchange. Discuss the results to Seller in the following alternative situations:

(a) Buyer pays cash for the land and Seller reinvests the proceeds in commercial property.

(b) Seller agrees to sell the land to Buyer who puts cash in an amount equal to the value of the land in an escrow account. The escrow provides for Seller to select commercial property equal in value to the land. Buyer will then acquire the commercial property with the escrowed cash and transfer the property to Seller. If Seller fails to find adequate property, the deal collapses. One year after the escrow account is opened, Seller selects commercial property that Buyer acquires with the escrowed cash and transfers it to Seller in exchange for the land.

(c) Seller, a calendar year taxpayer, transfers the land to Buyer on January 1 of the current year. Buyer puts cash in an amount equal to the value of the land in an escrow account. Seller is to select the like kind property he wants and Buyer is to acquire it with the escrowed cash. If at any time Buyer fails to meet his obligations, Seller may demand the cash. On February 15, Seller identifies 3 properties, any one of which he is willing to accept, and on June 15, Buyer acquires one of the properties (having a value equal to the land) and transfers it to Seller.

(d) Same as (c), above, except that after Seller's transfer of the land to Buyer and Buyer's transfer of the cash to the escrow account but prior to replacement property being acquired, Seller may at any time opt to take the cash, rather than replacement property.

5. A owns some investment real estate with an adjusted basis of $200,000, worth $500,000 and subject to a mortgage of $100,000.

(a) Discuss the results to A and B if A transfers his property to B in exchange for B's investment real estate worth $400,000 with an adjusted basis of $100,000.

(b) Discuss the results to A and B if, instead, A transfers his property to B in exchange for B's investment real estate worth $470,000 with an adjusted basis of $100,000 and subject to a $70,000 mortgage.

(c) Discuss the results to A and B under the facts of (a), above, if A's investment real estate subject to the liability is worth only $450,000 and A transfers $50,000 of cash in addition to his investment real estate to B in exchange for B's investment real estate.

C. INVOLUNTARY CONVERSIONS *

Internal Revenue Code: Sections 1001(c); 1033(a)(1), (a)(2), (b) last sentence, (g) (1), (2) and (4); 1223(1). See Sections 1231; 1245(b)(4); 1250(d)(4).

Regulations: Section 1.1033(b)–1(b).

---

* Two general articles in this area are Schaff, "Tax Consequences of an Involuntary Conversion," 46 Taxes 323 (1968); Gannet, "Tax Advantages and Risks in Real Property Exchanges: Voluntary and Involuntary," 25 N.Y.U.Inst. on Fed.Tax. 1 (1967).

NOTE

In the preceding section of this chapter you encountered a special nonrecognition provision relating to like kind *exchanges*. The notion there and applicable here is that the taxpayer, although in possession of replacement property, has not changed his economic position. An exchange of like kind properties is a voluntary transaction. Section 1033 permits the nonrecognition of *gain* in certain circumstances in which property is *involuntarily* converted. The involuntary conversion may be the result of destruction, theft, seizure, requisition or condemnation or threat or imminence thereof. Earlier, in another chapter we considered virtually identical language in another Code section. Take another close look at Section 1231.

The general message of Section 1033 can be simply stated. When property is involuntarily converted into money, if the taxpayer so elects,[1] gain is recognized only to the extent that the amount realized as a result of the conversion exceeds the cost of the replacement property.[2] The price of the nonrecognition ticket is that the replacement property must be "similar or related in service or use" to the converted property and the replacement must occur within the time limit of the statute.[3] The provision does not apply to losses resulting from involuntary conversions.[4] Students should be alert to a corresponding basis adjustment resulting from nonrecognition of gain. The basis of the replacement property is the cost of such property, reduced by the gain that is not recognized.[5] Except to the extent that Section 1014 intercedes, this is simply a deferral of tax to the future.

The complexity and controversy in the application of Section 1033 has centered around the meaning of the phrase, "similar or related in service or use."[6]

HARRY G. MASSER

Tax Court of the United States, 1958.
30 T.C. 741(A).

[The Findings of Fact have been omitted. Ed.]

1. In John McShain, 65 T.C. 686 (1976), the Tax Court held the § 1033 election to be irrevocable.

2. Moving expenses received as part of a lump sum condemnation award have been treated as a nonseverable part of the award itself and therefore as qualifying for § 1033 nonrecognition. E.R. Hitchcock Co. v. United States, 514 F.2d 484 (2d Cir. 1975); Graphic Press, Inc. v. Commissioner, 523 F.2d 585 (9th Cir.1975).

3. I.R.C. §§ 1033(a)(2); 1033(g)(4).

4. See I.R.C. §§ 165(c) and 1231.

5. I.R.C. § 1033(b), last sentence.

6. As to *condemned* real estate held for productive use in a trade or business or for investment, see § 1033(g) substituting "like kind" criteria. But see M.H.S. Company, Inc., 35 T.C.M. 733 (1976), in which the taxpayer reinvested a real estate condemnation award in new real estate with a third party as tenants in common, as a joint venture. Under state law the interest is considered a partnership interest which again under state law is *personal* property. Therefore, domino fashion, the Tax Court concluded that the replacement property is not "like kind," holding § 1033 inapplicable. Cf. I.R.C. § 1033(a)(2)(E).

Opinion

KERN, Judge: The question presented by this case is whether section 112(f)(1) of the Internal Revenue Code of 1939 [1] is applicable to the facts here before us. Those facts may be summarized as follows: Petitioner, who operated an interstate trucking business, bought at one time two pieces of property situated across a street from each other, one improved by a building (including offices and a bunkhouse) to be used for the loading and unloading of trucks, and the other to be used as space in which the trucks could be parked pending their loading and unloading. The two pieces of property were used together as an economic unit, constituting petitioner's terminal facilities serving the New York metropolitan area. It is conceded that the parking area was "involuntarily converted" by petitioner as the result of the threat or imminence of condemnation. If petitioner retained the improved property, the closest available space for a parking area would have been approximately a mile and a half away. For petitioner to have operated his truck terminal with his parking area that far from the building where the loading and unloading of his trucks took place and where his offices were located would have been physically possible, but would have been economically impractical because (1) it would have entailed considerable direct expense in connection with the additional labor required, (2) it would have resulted in increasing the hazards of traffic accidents and cargo thefts, (3) it would have resulted in such delays in deliveries as to have affected adversely petitioner's customer relations, and (4) it would have presented complicated problems in connection with traffic management. Because of the involuntary sale of the parking area as a result of the threat of condemnation, petitioner decided in good faith and in the exercise of prudent business judgment to sell the improved property also and to use the proceeds of both properties to buy property in the same general locality suitable for similar use as a truck terminal. Under these circumstances, was the sale of the improved property an involuntary conversion as a result of the threat or imminence of condemnation?

We are not aware of any authorities directly in point as to the question presented, and the legislative history of section 112(f) and its predecessor sections is not helpful.

Bearing in mind two basic principles, that "[t]axation * * * is eminently practical," Tyler v. United States, 281 U.S. 497, 503, and that a relief provision "should be liberally construed to effectuate its purpose," Massillon-Cleveland-Akron Sign Co., 15 T.C. 79, 83, we are of the opinion that when two pieces of property, practically adjacent to each other, were acquired for the purpose of being used and were used in a taxpayer's business as an economic unit, when one of the pieces of property was involuntarily sold as a result of the threat of condemna-

---

1. [I.R.C. (1939) § 112(f)(1) is omitted. See I.R.C. (1986) § 1033(a)(2). Ed.]

tion, when it was apparent that the continuation of the business on the remaining piece of property was impractical, and as a result of the involuntary sale of the one piece of property the taxpayer in the exercise of good business judgment sold the other piece of property, and when the proceeds of both sales were expended in the acquisition of property similar to the economic unit consisting of the two properties sold, the transaction, considered as a whole, constitutes an involuntary conversion of one economic property unit within the meaning of section 112(f).

Decision will be entered for petitioners.

CLIFTON INV. CO. v. COMMISSIONER

United States Court of Appeals, Sixth Circuit, 1963.
312 F.2d 719, cert. denied 373 U.S. 921, 83 S.Ct. 1524, 1963.

BOYD, District Judge. Petitioner is a real estate investment corporation organized and existing under the laws of the State of Ohio, with headquarters in Cincinnati. In 1956 the petitioner sold to the City of Cincinnati under its threat of exercising its power of eminent domain a six-story office building, known as the United Bank Building, located in the downtown section of that city, which building was held by petitioner for production of rental income from commercial tenants. The funds realized from the sale of this property to the city were used by the petitioner to purchase eighty percent of the outstanding stock of The Times Square Hotel of New York, Inc., also an Ohio corporation, which had as its sole asset a contract to buy the Times Square Hotel of New York City. The purchase of the hotel was effected by the corporation. The taxpayer-petitioner contends herein that the purchase of the controlling stock in the hotel corporation was an investment in property "similar or related in service or use" to the office building it had been forced to sell, thus deserving of the nonrecognition of gain provisions of Section 1033(a)(3)(A), Internal Revenue Code of 1954 (Title 26 U.S.C.A. Section 1033(a)(3)(A).[1] More specifically, the taxpayer contends that since both the properties herein were productive of rental income, the similarity contemplated by the statute aforesaid exists. The Commissioner ruled to the contrary, holding that any gain from the sale of the office building was recognizable and a deficiency was assessed against the taxpayer for the year 1956 in the amount of $19,057.09. The Tax Court agreed with the Commissioner, finding that the properties themselves were not "similar or related in service or use" as required by the statute. 36 T.C. 569. From the decision of the Tax Court this appeal was perfected.

In order to determine whether the requisite similarity existed under the statute between the properties herein, the Tax Court applied the so-called "functional test" or "end-use test." This it seems has been the Tax Court's traditional line of inquiry, when similar cases under the within statute have been considered by it. This approach takes

---

1. See [I.R.C. § 1033(a)(2). Ed.]

into account only the actual physical end use to which the properties involved are put, whether that use be by the owner-taxpayer or by his tenant; that is, whether the taxpayer-owner is the actual user of the property or merely holds it for investment purposes, as in the case of a lessor. We reject the functional test as applied to the holder of investment property, who replaces such property with other investment property, as in the case at bar.

The Tax Court in this case relied in part on its earlier decision in Liant Record, Inc. v. Commissioner, 36 T.C. 224 and chiefly on the decision of the Court of Appeals for the Third Circuit in McCaffrey v. Commissioner, 275 F.2d 27, 1960, cert. denied 363 U.S. 828, 80 S.Ct. 1598, the latter case approving and applying the aforesaid functional test in such a case as here presented. However, the Court of Appeals for the Second Circuit has since reversed the Tax Court's decision in Liant, 303 F.2d 326, 1962, and in so doing advanced what we consider to be the soundest approach among the number of decisions on this point. We need not here review all the relevant decisions, since this is done in the recent cases of Loco Realty Company v. Commissioner, 306 F.2d 207 (C.A.8) 1962, and Pohn v. Commissioner, 309 F.2d 427 (C.A.7) 1962, both of which decisions approved the Second Circuit Court's approach in Liant, the court in the Pohn case relying specifically on the Liant decision.

Congress must have intended that in order for the taxpayer to obtain the tax benefits of Section 1033 he must have continuity of interest as to the original property and its replacement in order that the taxpayer not be given a tax-free alteration of his interest. In short, the properties must be reasonably similar in their relation to the taxpayer. This reasonableness, as noted in the Liant case, is dependent upon a number of factors, all bearing on whether or not the relation of the taxpayer to the property has been changed. The ultimate use to which the properties are put, then, does not control the inquiry, when the taxpayer is not the user of the properties as in the case under consideration. As exemplary of the factors which are relevant the Liant decision mentions the following, after advancement of its "relation of the properties to the taxpayer" test:

> "In applying such a test to a lessor, a court must compare, inter alia, the extent and type of the lessor's management activity, the amount and kind of services rendered by him to the tenants, and the nature of his business risks connected with the properties."

Thus, each case is dependent on its peculiar facts and the factors bearing on the service or use of the properties to the taxpayer must be closely examined. The Tax Court employed an erroneous test in this case, but on examination of the record, the correctness of the result is manifest.

The record before us discloses that the United Bank Building and the Times Square Hotel both produced rental income to the taxpayer.

However, examination of what the properties required in the way of services to the tenants, management activity, and commercial tenancy considerations reveals an alteration of the taxpayer's interest. The record herein shows that the taxpayer corporation itself managed the United Bank Building, but deemed it necessary to procure professional management for the Times Square Hotel. There were primarily two employees for the United Bank Building, who afforded elevator and janitorial services to the tenants. In the Times Square Hotel between 130 and 140 employees were necessary to attend the hotel operation and offer services to the commercial tenants and hotel guests. Approximately 96% of the rental income from the hotel was from the guest room facilities and the large number of transients required daily services of varying kinds. Furniture, linens, personal services of every description were furnished the hotel guests, which were not furnished the commercial tenants of the United Bank Building. The hotel guests reside in the hotel rooms and that is obviously the only reason they are tenants. In the office building herein several tenants also used parts of the premises for living quarters, but were clearly not furnished the typical services the hotel guest demands. There was no great limitation placed on the types of commercial tenants to whom space was rented in the United Bank Building, but as the enumeration of commercial tenants of the hotel building reveals, space therein was leased for the most part and primarily with an eye to how such a business operation might fit in with the operation of a hotel, how it relates to the hotel guests. It is common experience that the services offered by a lessee of business premises in a hotel will reflect in the minds of its guests on the service they associate with the hotel itself. If a leased restaurant in a hotel offers good or bad service, there is a tendency to think of the food service at the hotel as good or bad. A number of unique business considerations enter when leasing commercial space in a hotel which do not apply to an office building.

We consider there to be, then, a material variance between the relation of the office building in question and the within hotel operation of the taxpayer, in the light of the relevant inquiry found in the Liant case. It is true that what the taxpayer derived from both properties herein was generally the same, rental income. But what the properties demanded of the taxpayer in the way of management, services, and relations to its tenants materially varied. That which the taxpayer receives from his properties and that which such properties demand of the taxpayer must both be considered in determining whether or not the properties are similar or related in service or use to the taxpayer.[2]

The decision of the Tax Court is affirmed.

2. Congress has since provided that replacement of property held for productive use in trade or business or for investment purposes with property of "like kind" satisfies the "similar or related in service or use" requirement. However, the acquisition of controlling interest in stock of a corporation holding property was specifically excepted from the relaxation of the test. Title 26 U.S.C.A. Section 1033(g)(1) and (2). (Technical Amendments Act of 1958).

SHACKELFORD MILLER, JR., Circuit Judge (concurring).

I concur in the result reached in the majority opinion.

However, I am not willing to adopt, without some modification thereof, the test adopted and applied in Liant Record, Inc. v. Commissioner, 303 F.2d 326, C.A.2d, upon which the majority opinion relies. I think that the investment character of the properties involved should be given more consideration than what seems to me is given by the ruling in the Liant case, although I do not think that investment basis alone is sufficient to comply with the statute, as Steuart Brothers, Inc. v. Commissioner, 261 F.2d 580, C.A.4th, might be construed as holding. As pointed out in Loco Realty Co. v. Commissioner, 306 F.2d 207, 215, C.A.8th, the statute was not intended to penalize but to protect persons whose property may be taken on condemnation and, accordingly, should be construed liberally. I agree with the standard adopted in the opinion in that case, although for our present purposes I do not think that it results in a reversal of the decision of the Tax Court.

REVENUE RULING 64-237
1964-2 Cum.Bull. 319.

The Internal Revenue Service has reconsidered its position with respect to replacement property that is "similar or related in service or use" to involuntarily converted property within the meaning of section 112(f) of the Internal Revenue Code of 1939 and section 1033(a) of the Internal Revenue Code of 1954 in light of the decision of the United States Court of Appeals for the Second Circuit in the case of Liant Record, Inc. v. Commissioner, 303 Fed. (2d) 326 (1962), and other appellate court decisions.

In previous litigation, the Service has taken the position that the statutory phrase, "similar or related in service or use," means that the property acquired must have a close "functional" similarity to the property converted. Under this test, property was not considered similar or related in service or use to the converted property unless the physical characteristics and end uses of the converted and replacement properties were closely similar. Although this "functional use test" has been upheld in the lower courts, it has not been sustained in the appellate courts with respect to investors in property, such as lessors.

In conformity with the appellate court decisions, in considering whether replacement property acquired by an investor is similar in service or use to the converted property, attention will be directed primarily to the similarity in the relationship of the services or uses which the original and replacement properties have to the taxpayer-owner. In applying this test, a determination will be made as to whether the properties are of a similar service to the taxpayer, the nature of the business risks connected with the properties, and what such properties demand of the taxpayer in the way of management, services and relations to his tenants.

For example, where the taxpayer is a lessor, who rented out the converted property for a light manufacturing plant and then rents out the replacement property for a wholesale grocery warehouse, the nature of the taxpayer-owner's service or use of the properties may be similar although that of the end users change. The two properties will be considered as similar or related in service or use where, for example, both are rented and where there is a similarity in the extent and type of the taxpayer's management activities, the amount and kind of services rendered by him to his tenants, and the nature of his business risks connected with the properties.

In modifying its position with respect to the involuntary conversion of property held for investment, the Service will continue to adhere to the functional test in the case of owner-users of property. Thus, if the taxpayer-owner operates a light manufacturing plant on the converted property and then operates a wholesale grocery warehouse on the replacement property, by changing his end use he has so changed the nature of his relationship to the property as to be outside the nonrecognition of gain provisions.

REVENUE RULING 76–319
1976–2 Cum.Bull. 242.

Advice has been requested whether, under the circumstances described below, property qualifies as replacement property for purposes of section 1033 of the Internal Revenue Code of 1954.

The taxpayer, a domestic corporation, was engaged in the operation of a recreational bowling center prior to the center's complete destruction by fire on June 30, 1974. The bowling center had consisted of bowling alleys, together with a lounge area and a bar. The center was fully insured against loss by fire. As a result of such insurance coverage the taxpayer received insurance proceeds in compensation for the destruction of the bowling center in an amount that exceeded the taxpayer's basis in the property. On its Federal income tax return for 1974, the taxpayer elected to defer recognition of the gain under the provisions of section 1033 of the Code.

Within the period specified in section 1033(a)[(2)](B) of the Code, the taxpayer invested the insurance proceeds in a new recreational billiard center. In addition to billiard tables, this center includes a lounge area, and a bar.

Section 1033(a) of the Code provides, in part, that if property (as a result of its destruction in whole or in part) is involuntarily converted into money, the gain shall be recognized except as provided in section 1033(a)[(2)](A). Section 1033(a)[(2)](A) provides, in part, that if the taxpayer during the period specified purchases other property similar or related in service or use to the property so converted, at the election of the taxpayer the gain shall be recognized only to the extent that the amount realized on the conversion exceeds the cost of such other property.

The specific question is whether the recreational billiard center (replacement property) is "similar or related in service or use" to the recreational bowling center (involuntarily converted property) within the meaning of section 1033(a) of the Code.

Rev.Rul. 64–237, 1964–2 C.B. 319, states that, with respect to an owner-user, property is not considered similar or related in service or use to the converted property unless the physical characteristics and end uses of the converted and replacement properties are closely similar.

In the instant case, the involuntarily converted property was a bowling center that consisted of bowling alleys together with a lounge area and a bar. The replacement property consists of a billiards center that included billiard tables, a lounge area, and a bar. The physical characteristics of the replacement property are not closely similar to those of the converted property since bowling alleys and bowling equipment are not closely similar to billiard tables and billiard equipment.

Accordingly, in the instant case, the billiard center is not similar or related in service or use to the bowling center within the meaning of section 1033(a)[(2)](A) of the Code. Therefore the billiard center does not qualify as replacement property for purposes of section 1033.

REVENUE RULING 67–254
1967–2 Cum.Bull. 269.

Advice has been requested whether the nonrecognition-of-gain benefits under the provisions of section 1033 of the Internal Revenue Code of 1954 apply where the proceeds of a condemnation award are used to rearrange plant facilities on the remaining portion of the plant property. Additionally, the question is raised as to whether such benefits apply if the taxpayer uses part of the award to erect a building on land he presently owns.

A State condemned a portion of the land upon which the taxpayer's manufacturing plant was situated. The condemned portion had been used as a storage area for the taxpayer's product and also contained thereon a garage which housed the plant's delivery trucks. The taxpayer received an award for the condemned property, none of which was compensation for damages to the portion of the property which he retained.

Because of the prohibitive cost of acquiring land in the area suitable for storage, the taxpayer used part of the proceeds of the condemnation award in the year of its receipt to rearrange the layout of his plant facilities on the remainder of his land in order to create a new storage area. He used the remainder of the award to build a new garage (to house the plant's delivery trucks) on a small plot of land located nearby, which he had owned for several years.

Section 1033(a)[(2)](A) of the Code provides, in effect, that if property is compulsorily or involuntarily converted into money and the taxpayer, during the period specified, purchases other property similar or related in service or use to the property so converted, at the election of the taxpayer the gain shall be recognized only to the extent that the amount realized upon such conversion exceeds the cost of such other property.

Accordingly, based on these facts, to the extent that the taxpayer expended the condemnation proceeds in restoring the plantsite so that it could be used in the same manner as it was used prior to the condemnation, he has acquired property similar or related in service or use to the property converted for purposes of section 1033(a)[(2)](A) of the Code. Whether all of the expenditures made by the taxpayer were necessary to restore the plantsite to its original usefulness is a question of fact to be determined upon examination of his income tax return for the year in which the transaction occurred.

In addition, the garage erected on land already owned qualifies under section 1033(a)[(2)](A) of the Code as property similar or related in service or use to the garage that was condemned.

REVENUE RULING 71–41
1971–1 Cum.Bull. 223.

Advice has been requested whether the investment of condemnation proceeds, under the circumstances set forth below, qualifies for the nonrecognition of gain provisions of section 1033 of the Internal Revenue Code of 1954.

The taxpayer, an individual, owned a warehouse which he rented to third parties. The warehouse and the land upon which it was located were condemned by the State and a gain was realized by the taxpayer on the condemnation. The condemnation proceeds were used by the taxpayer to erect a gas station on other land already owned by the taxpayer. The taxpayer rented the gas station to an oil company.

Section 1033(a) of the Code provides, in part, that if property is, as a result of condemnation, compulsorily or involuntarily converted into money and the taxpayer, during the period specified, purchases other property *similar or related in service or use* to the property so converted, at the election of the taxpayer the gain shall be recognized only to the extent that the amount realized upon such conversion exceeds the cost of the replacement property.

Section 1033(g) of the Code provides, in part, as follows:

(1) Special rule—For purposes of subsection (a), if real property * * * held for productive use in trade or business or for investment is * * * compulsorily or involuntarily converted, property of a *like kind* to be held either for productive use in a trade or business or for investment *shall be treated* as property similar or related in service or use to the property so converted.

The taxpayer in the instant case did not qualify for the special rule under section 1033(g) of the Code as the replacement property (gas station) and the property converted (land and warehouse) were not properties of a "like kind." The specific question is whether the taxpayer can qualify for treatment under section 1033(a) even though he fails to qualify under section 1033(g) of the Code.

Revenue Ruling 64–237, C.B.1964–2, 319, in applying section 1033(a) of the Code, states that in considering whether replacement property acquired by an investor for the purpose of leasing is similar in service or use to the converted property, attention will be directed primarily to the similarity in the relationship of the service or uses which the original and replacement properties have to the taxpayer-owner. In applying this test a determination will be made whether the properties are of a similar service to the taxpayer, the nature of the business risks connected with the properties, and what such properties demand of the taxpayer in the way of management, services, and relations to his tenants.

With respect to the property converted by the State, the taxpayer in the instant case was an investor for the production of rental income. As to the property acquired as replacement, the taxpayer is also an investor for the production of rental income. The mere fact that the taxpayer did not qualify under section 1033(g) of the Code does not preclude the taxpayer from the nonrecognition of gain provisions of section 1033 of the Code if the taxpayer is able to demonstrate that the replacement property is actually similar or related in service or use to the property converted within the meaning of section 1033(a) of the Code.

Accordingly, under the facts of the instant case, it is held that the gas station is property similar or related in service or use within the meaning of section 1033(a) of the Code. The taxpayer at his election will recognize gain upon the involuntarily converted property only to the extent that the amount realized upon such conversion exceeds the cost of the replacement property, provided, the actual replacement took place within the period of time prescribed by section 1033(a)[(2)](B) of the Code.

PROBLEMS

1. T was in the laundry and dry cleaning business. In the current year a fire completely destroyed the automatic dry cleaning equipment in his plant. Several years earlier the equipment in his plant had cost him $40,000 and, since its acquisition, T had properly claimed straight-line depreciation on the equipment in the amount of $16,000. After the fire and within the current year, T received $28,000 as insurance covering the loss.

   (a) If the dry cleaning end of the business has been unprofitable and T invests the $28,000 in securities, rather than replacing the equipment, what will be the tax consequences?

(b) If the capacity of the old equipment was in excess of T's needs and T replaces the old with smaller new equipment at a cost of $26,000

    (1) What will be the immediate tax consequences to T?

    (2) What will be T's basis for the purpose of claiming depreciation on the new equipment?

    (3) What would be the tax consequences to T if he made a quick change of plans and sold the newly acquired equipment for $26,000 before any depreciation became allowable with respect to it?

2. Would the court have reached the same result in *Harry G. Masser* if a single piece of business property had been damaged and, even though the property could still have been used in the business, the owner of the property "in the exercise of good business judgment" decided, nevertheless, to sell it and use the sale and insurance proceeds to purchase a piece of replacement property? See C.G. Willis, Inc., 41 T.C. 468 (1964), affirmed per curiam 342 F.2d 996 (3d Cir.1965).

3. The *Clifton Investment* case reflects a common problem regarding the scope of the term "similar or related in service or use." But suppose in *Clifton Investment* the taxpayer had bought a hotel rather than stock in a hotel corporation. Would the result in the case be different?

4. Rev.Rul. 70–399, 1970–2 C.B. 164, deals with the repurchase of a new hotel with the insurance proceeds received when an old hotel was destroyed by fire. Despite the intrinsic identity of the properties, the case is placed outside the protective covering of § 1033. The owner had leased the old hotel to others to operate but undertook to operate the new hotel himself. Thus the new property was not similar or related in service or use. Why would § 1033(g) be of no help here?

5. The two questions immediately preceding are concerned with some of the differences in the definition of "like kind" under §§ 1031 and 1033(g) and "similar or related in service or use" under § 1033(a). In enacting § 1033(g) the Senate Finance Committee Report stated:

> Both in the case of property involuntarily converted and in the case of the exchange of property held for productive use in trade or business or for investment, gain is not recognized because of the continuity of the investment. Your committee sees no reason why substantially similar rules should not be followed in determining what constitutes a continuity of investment in these two types of situations where there is a condemnation of real property. Moreover, it appears particularly unfortunate that present law requires a closer identity of the destroyed and converted property where the exchange is beyond the control of the taxpayer than that which is applied in the case of the voluntary exchange of business property.

As a result your committee has added a new subsection to the involuntary conversion (sec. 1033) provision of present law. In this new subsection it has added the 'like kind' test of the voluntary exchange of business property rule of present law as an alternative in the case of involuntary conversions for the rule requiring the substitution of property 'similar or related in service or use.' The 'like kind' rule in this case applies, however, only in the case of real property, does not include inventory or property held primarily for sale, and is limited to seizures, requisitions, condemnations, or the threat of imminence thereof. Nor does it apply in the case of the purchase of stock in acquiring control of a corporation. * * * Sen.Rep. No. 1893, 85th Cong., 2d Sess. (1958), 1958–3 C.B. 922, 993–4.

Is the restriction of § 1033(g) to condemnations of real property too narrow? Should the two tests of §§ 1031 and 1033 be made alternatives under both sections?

D. SALE OF A PRINCIPAL RESIDENCE *

Internal Revenue Code: Sections 121(a) through (c), (d)(1) and (7); 1034(a) through (e), (i), and (j); 1223(7).

Regulations: Section 1.1034–1(a), (b), (c)(3) and (4).

EXCERPT FROM HOUSE REPORT NO. 586
82d Cong., 1st Sess. (1951).
1951–2 C.B. 357, 377–378.

Section 303 of this bill amends the present provisions relating to a gain on the sale of a taxpayer's principal residence so as to eliminate a hardship under existing law which provides that when a personal residence is sold at a gain the difference between its adjusted basis and the sale price is taxed as a capital gain. The hardship is accentuated when the transactions are necessitated by such facts as an increase in the size of the family or a change in the place of the taxpayer's employment. In these situations the transaction partakes of the nature of an involuntary conversion. Cases of this type are particularly numerous in periods of rapid change such as mobilization or reconversion. For this reason the need for remedial action at the present time is urgent.

Section 303 of this bill [current Code Section 1034. Ed.] provides that when the sale of the taxpayer's principal residence is followed within a period of 1 year by the purchase of a substitute, or when the substitute is purchased within a year prior to the sale of the taxpayer's principal residence, [The periods have been extended to 2 years. Ed.]

---

* See Margolis, "Tax-Free Sales and Exchanges of Residences," 17 U.S.C. Tax.Inst. 483 (1965).

gain shall be recognized only to the extent that the selling price of the old residence exceeds the cost of the new one. Thus, if a dwelling purchased in 1940 for $10,000 is sold in 1951 for $15,000, there would ordinarily be a taxable gain of $5,000 under existing law. Under this bill no portion of the gain would be taxable provided a substitute "principal residence" is purchased by the taxpayer within the stated period of time for a price of $15,000 or more. If the replacement cost is less than $15,000, say $14,000, the amount taxable as gain will be $1,000.

This special treatment is not limited to the "involuntary conversion" type of case, where the taxpayer is forced to sell his home because the place of his employment is changed. While the need for relief is especially clear in such cases, an attempt to confine the provision to them would increase the task of administration very much.

The adjusted basis of the new residence will be reduced by the amount of gain not recognized upon the sale of the old residence. Thus, if the replacement is purchased for $19,000, the old residence cost $10,000 and was sold for $15,000, the adjusted basis of the new residence will be $19,000 minus $5,000 or $14,000. This is equal to the cost of the old residence plus the additional funds invested at the time the new residence is purchased. If the second residence had been purchased for $14,000, so that $1,000 of gain on the sale of the old residence would be recognized, its basis would be $14,000 minus $4,000, or $10,000.

For the purpose of qualifying a gain as a long-term capital gain the holding period of the residence acquired as a replacement in a set of transactions which qualify under the terms of this section of the bill will be the combined period of ownership of the successive principal residences of the taxpayer.

*　　*　　*

The taxpayer is not required to have actually been occupying his old residence on the date of its sale. Relief will be available even though the taxpayer moved into his new residence and rented the old one temporarily before its sale. Similarly, he may obtain relief even though he rents out his new residence temporarily before occupying it.

The special treatment provided under this section of the bill can be availed of only with respect to one sale or exchange per year [now each two years. Ed.] except when the taxpayer's new residence is involuntarily converted. *　*　*

Section 303 of this bill applies to cases where one residence is exchanged for another where a replacement residence is constructed by the taxpayer rather than purchased, and where the replacement is a residence which had to be reconstructed in order to permit its occupancy by the taxpayer. However, in cases where the replacement is built or reconstructed, only so much of the cost is counted as an offset against the selling price of his old residence as is properly chargeable against capital account within a period beginning 1 year prior to date of the sale of the old residence and ending 1 year after such date. [The ending periods have been extended to 2 years. Ed.]

The ownership of stock in a cooperative apartment corporation will be treated as the equivalent of ownership of a residence, provided the purchaser or seller of such stock uses the apartment which it entitles him to occupy as his principal residence.

Regulations will be issued under which the taxpayer and his spouse acting singly or jointly may obtain the benefits of section 303 even though the spouse who sold the old residence was not the same as the one who purchased the new one, or the rights of the spouses in the new residence are not distributed in the same manner as their rights in the old residence. These regulations will apply only if the spouses consent to their application and both old and new residences are used by the taxpayer and his spouse as their principal residence.

Where the taxpayer's residence is part of a property also used for business purposes, as in the case of an apartment over a store building or a home on a farm, and the entire property is sold, the provisions of section 303 will apply only to that part of the property used as a residence, including the environs and outbuildings relating to the dwelling but not to those relating to the business operations.

These provisions apply to a trailer or houseboat if it is actually used as the taxpayer's principal residence.

In order to protect the Government in cases where there is an unreported taxable gain on the sale of the taxpayer's residence, either because he did not carry out his intention to buy a new residence, or because some of the technical requirements were not met, the period for the assessment of a deficiency is extended to 3 years after the taxpayer has notified the Commissioner either that he has purchased a new residence, or that he has not acquired or does not intend to acquire a new residence within the prescribed period of time.

NOTE

The Economic Recovery Tax Act of 1981 [1] increased the Section 1034(a) replacement period with respect to a principal residence (initially one year) from eighteen months to two years generally for sales after July 20, 1981.[2] This period begins two years prior to the sale of the old residence and ends two years thereafter.[3]

The statute expressly requires that both the former residence and the new residence qualify as the taxpayer's principal residence. Thus if a taxpayer resides with his family in a New York City apartment during the week, using a country house only on weekends, the sale of

1. Pub.Law No. 97–34, § 122 (1981).

2. The Tax Reduction Act of 1975 had increased the replacement period to 18 months; however, if the new residence was constructed, the period was two years after the former residence was sold.

3. The statutory period cannot be extended. See e.g., Rev.Rul. 75–438, 1975–1 C.B. 334; Rev.Rul. 74–411, 1974–2 C.B. 270.

the old, followed by the purchase of another country house will not meet the test of the statute. This is so because the apartment is considered the principal residence.[4] In other circumstances, if both the former residence and the new residence otherwise qualify as the principal residence, the House Report and the Regulations expressly sanction temporary rental of either dwelling.[5] Therefore, if at the time the owner moves out, the former dwelling qualifies as the principal residence, it remains qualified even though it is temporarily rented. In *Robert G. Clapham*,[6] the taxpayer rented his former residence for three years prior to selling it. The Tax Court, holding for the taxpayer, concluded that the former residence qualified as the principal residence. " * * * [The] dominant motive was to sell the property at the earliest possible date rather than to hold the property for the realization of rental income. Under the facts and circumstances here present, the lease was therefore for a temporary period contemplated by the legislative history and the regulations, * * *."[7] The question whether a residence is the principal residence is a fact issue. If, in contrast to the facts in *Clapham*,[8] the taxpayer converts a residence to income-producing property, making every effort to rent with little or no attempt to sell, the dwelling will no longer qualify as the principal residence at the time it is eventually sold. In these circumstances, Section 1034 will not apply. This was the result in *Richard T. Houlette*.[9] In that case, the taxpayer moved out of his then principal residence. The dwelling was leased on five separate occasions for over six years. Two of the leases were for two year periods and sales efforts were minimal.

Quantitatively, a principal residence can include surrounding vast acreage, so long as it is not used for profit.[10]

Although the statute allows a fairly lengthy replacement period, the new residence must be *used* as the taxpayer's principal residence within the time period allotted by the statute.

If a taxpayer "rolls over" principal residences too frequently not all the residential sales qualify for nonrecognition. In general, Section 1034(d) provides that if a taxpayer sells a principal residence at a gain, similar subsequent sales within a two year period do not qualify for nonrecognition under subsection (a). However, if a subsequent sale and purchase are job related in conjunction with the commencement of work at a new job location and the taxpayer meets the Section 217(c) time and distance requirements, there is an exception, and the nonrecognition rules of subsection (a) apply.[11]

---

4. William C. Stolk, 40 T.C. 345 (1963), affirmed per curiam 326 F.2d 760 (2d Cir. 1964).

5. H. Rep. No. 586, 82d Cong., 1st Sess. (1951), p. 926, supra; Reg. § 1.1034–1(c)(3).

6. 63 T.C. 505 (1975). See also Rev.Rul. 78–146, 1978–1 C.B. 260.

7. Id. at 512.

8. Note 6, supra.

9. 48 T.C. 350 (1967).

10. See e.g., Clayburn M. Bennett v. U.S., 61–2 U.S.T.C. ¶ 9697 (D.C.No.Ga. 1961).

11. I.R.C. § 1034(d)(2).

LOKAN v. COMMISSIONER

Tax Court of the United States, 1979.
39 T.C.M. 168.

Memorandum Findings of Fact and Opinion

SCOTT, Judge: Respondent determined deficiencies in petitioners' income tax for the calendar years 1973 and 1974 in the amounts of $2,387.54 and $71.90, respectively, and an addition to tax under section 6653(a), I.R.C.1954,[1] for the year 1973 in the amount of $119.38.

Some of the issues raised by the pleadings have been disposed of by agreement of the parties, leaving for our decision the following:

(1) Was a new home, constructed by petitioners during the years 1973 through 1976, used by them as their principal residence within a period of 18 months from the date of sale of their old residence so as to entitle them to the benefit of the nonrecognition of gain provisions of section 1034 with respect to the gain realized on the sale of their old residence.

(2) If the house constructed by petitioners was not used by them as their principal residence within the 18-month period so as to entitle them to the nonrecognition provisions of section 1034 with respect to the cost of that house, should the cost to petitioners of a trailer purchased by them within one year after the sale of their old residence, which respondent concedes was a new principal residence of petitioners', include the entire seven and one-half acres of land purchased by petitioners or only the one and one-half acres that were not used by them in a farming operation.[2]

Findings of Fact

Most of the facts have been stipulated and are found accordingly.

Petitioners, husband and wife, who resided in New Port Richey, Florida, at the time of the filing of their petition in this case, filed a joint Federal income tax return for the calendar year 1973 with the Internal Revenue Service, Southeast Region, Chamblee, Georgia.

1. Unless otherwise indicated, all statutory references are to the Internal Revenue Code of 1954, as amended and in effect in the years in issue.

2. At the trial, the question arose as to why petitioners were not entitled to use of the installment method provided by sec. 453 in reporting income with respect to the sale of their old residence if respondent is sustained in his position that petitioners did not use the home they constructed in New Port Richey as a principal residence within the period of 18 months from the sale of the old residence and for this reason were not entitled to use of the provisions of sec. 1034 with respect to the new house.

The parties agreed to discuss this matter and petitioners were granted leave to file an amended petition claiming use of the installment method. The parties filed a supplemental stipulation of facts incorporating petitioners' pleading and the facts necessary to a computation under sec. 453. On brief, respondent conceded petitioners' right to use of the installment method and stated that the stipulated facts were sufficient for a computation on that basis and would be advantageous to petitioners. Because of respondent's concession in this respect, no issue is in this case in this regard, but the matter can be handled in a recomputation under Rule 155.

In April 1973 petitioners were living in a residence they owned in Clearwater, Florida. They took out a first mortgage on this residence and with the proceeds purchased seven and one-half acres of land in the New Port Richey, Florida, area for $20,500 (approximately $2,733 per acre). In May 1973 petitioners began construction of a new home on this land in the New Port Richey area. In November 1973 petitioners sold their then personal residence in Clearwater, Florida, for $48,500. Petitioners incurred $4,034 of expenses in connection with the sale of their Clearwater residence. Their adjusted basis in this residence was $24,778, so that petitioners realized a net gain on the sale of the old residence of $19,688.

Petitioners were required to vacate their Clearwater home in December 1973. At that time they purchased a house trailer for $2,109 which they situated on the land they had purchased in New Port Richey very close to the new house which was under construction. In December petitioners moved from their home in Clearwater to New Port Richey and moved into the house trailer. Petitioners incurred other expenses of $2,636 with respect to the house trailer situated on the New Port Richey property so that their total cost with respect to the trailer, aside from land, cost when they moved into it was $4,745.

At the time petitioners moved into the house trailer on the New Port Richey property, they had four children. Although petitioners had been working on the new home, it was far from completed. They promptly completed one of the upstairs bedrooms in the new home and a downstairs bath so that three of their children could sleep in the new residence while the remainder of the family slept in the trailer. Three of petitioners' children moved into the unfinished residence in New Port Richey at the time the family moved to New Port Richey and petitioners and the other child moved into the house trailer. The kitchen and dining room facilities of the trailer were used by the entire family for family meals. After approximately one month, one of petitioners' children who was living in the house moved back to the Clearwater area. About six months later, another one of the children moved out of the unfinished house and moved back to the Clearwater area. Petitioners' youngest son, Mark Lokan, lived in the new house which was under construction from December 1973 until the house was substantially completed in September 1976. Petitioners and their daughter occupied the house trailer right next to the new residence until the downstairs of the new residence was completed in September 1976 and the balance was sufficiently completed for petitioners to move into it and live there. Petitioners and the daughter who had also occupied the house trailer as sleeping quarters moved into the new house in September 1976.

By early 1974 petitioners had partially installed electricity, heat, lights and water in their new residence in New Port Richey. Appliances were also installed in early 1974 and the kitchen was completed by September 1976. Petitioners did all electric and plumbing work on their new residence in New Port Richey themselves.

In 1974 and 1975 petitioners used six acres of their land in the New Port Richey area in the business of farming. Their farming business consisted primarily of raising cattle. Petitioners on their 1974 and 1975 joint Federal income tax returns showed the use of these six acres of property for the business of farming.

Petitioners on their 1973 joint Federal income tax return reported no realized gain from the sale of their Clearwater residence in November 1973. Respondent in his notice of deficiency determined that petitioners had a long-term capital gain on the sale of their Clearwater residence in 1973 in the amount of $19,688 of which $9,844 was taxable, and increased petitioners' reported income for the year 1973 by the amount of this $9,844. In explaining the adjustment, respondent stated that petitioners did not meet the requirements of section 1034 for nonrecognition of gain on the sale of their personal residence.

Opinion

Section 1034, as applicable to the year 1973, provides that if property used by a taxpayer as his principal residence (old residence) is sold by him and within a period beginning one year before the date of such sale and ending one year after such date property is purchased and used by the taxpayer as his principal residence (new residence), gain from the sale of the old residence shall be recognized only to the extent that the taxpayer's adjusted sales price of the old residence exceeds the taxpayer's cost of purchasing the new residence. The section further provides (section 1034(c)(5)) that where construction of a new residence is commenced by the taxpayer before the expiration of one year after the date of the sale of the old residence, the section will apply if the new residence is occupied within a period of 18 months after the date of the sale of the old residence.[3]

Petitioners here have shown a sale of their old residence and the commencement of construction of a new residence within [a] period of one year after the sale of the old residence. However, in order to meet the requirements of section 1034 they must also show that they occupied the new residence as their principal residence within a period of 18 months following the sale of their old residence. Petitioners' old residence was sold in November 1973; therefore, this 18-month period would expire in May 1974. The record here is clear that petitioners themselves had not in any way occupied the new house which was under construction during this period and, in fact, did not occupy it until September 1976. Petitioners argue that because they were building the house themselves they could not occupy it until September 1976 since the house was not sufficiently completed, but that they did the next best thing by getting a trailer which they placed adjacent to the house, occupying the trailer with one of their children and moving three of their children into the house while it was under construction. Petitioners argue that for this reason the trailer should not be consid-

---

3. [I.R.C. § 1034 is omitted. Ed.]

ered as a separate home but a part of the new home they were building, and therefore they should be considered as occupying their new residence as a principal residence within the required period.

It is clear from the record, however, that neither petitioner lived in the building which was to be the new residence within the required time and that the trailer, though near to the new home, was a separate abode from the new home and that it was the trailer which was petitioners' principal residence until September 1976.

As was pointed out in Bayley v. Commissioner, 35 T.C. 288, 295 (1960), the use in the statute of the phrase "used by the taxpayer[s] as * * * [their] principal residence," with respect to a new residence means the physical occupancy of that residence by the owners. In other words, it means that the owners, who here are petitioners, must live in that new residence. In the *Bayley* case we discussed at some length the legislative history of section 1034 and the reason for our conclusion that "used as a principal residence" meant physical occupancy. Our holding in the *Bayley* case has been consistently followed by this Court and other courts. In Elam v. Commissioner, 58 T.C. 238 (1972), affd. per curiam 477 F.2d 1333 (6th Cir.1973), we held that where taxpayers purchased property on which they erected a guest house into which they moved within the period required by section 1034 for occupying a new residence and commenced construction of a main house, which they did not occupy within that period, they had not used the main house as a principal residence within the required period, and therefore only the guest house might be considered as the taxpayers' new residence in determining the amount of gain which should be reported on the sale of the old residence.

Respondent here has conceded that the trailer was a new residence for petitioners which was occupied by them as their principal residence within the required period.

In United States v. Sheahan, 323 F.2d 383 (5th Cir.1963), the Court held that even though the taxpayers' daughter had spent some time in the new house within the required period, even having her lunches there occasionally, the taxpayers had not occupied the new residence as their principal residence within the required period. A strict construction of the requirements of section 1034, regardless of the good faith or intent of the taxpayers, as set forth in the *Bayley, Elam* and *Sheahan* cases has been consistently followed by this Court. We, therefore, conclude that petitioners did not occupy the new house they were constructing at New Port Richey as a principal residence within the period of 18 months following the sale of their old residence. Therefore, the provisions of section 1034 are not applicable with respect to this residence.

Respondent recognizes that the trailer was a new principal residence of petitioners' and the only issue with respect to the proper adjustment under section 1034 with respect to the trailer is whether the cost of the entire seven and one-half acres of land purchased by petitioners should be considered as a part of the cost of the new trailer principal residence or only the one and one-half acres of that property not used by petitioners in their business of farming during 1974 and 1975.

Section 1.1034–1(c)(3)(ii), Income Tax Regs., provides in part follows:

> If the new residence is used only partially for residential purposes only so much of its cost as is allocable to the residential portion may be counted as the cost of purchasing the new residence.

Here, the record shows that petitioners used six acres of the land acquired in New Port Richey in their business of farming. Where property is used both as a taxpayer's residence and as a farm, the cost of the portion of the land properly allocable as a part of the residence is considered to be part of the cost of the residence and the cost of the balance of the land is considered to be a part of the property not used as a residence. See Spivey v. Commissioner, 40 T.C. 1051, 1053 (1963). We, therefore, conclude on the basis of this record that only one and one-half acres of the property acquired by petitioners is properly to be considered as a part of their trailer residence in computing the portion of the gain on the sale of their old residence which is subject to nonrecognition under section 1034.

Decision will be entered under Rule 155.

BOLARIS v. COMMISSIONER

United States Court of Appeals, Ninth Circuit 1985.
776 F.2d 1428.

CYNTHIA HOLCOMB HALL, Circuit Judge:

I. FACTS

The taxpayers, Stephen and Valerie H. Bolaris (the "Bolarises"), purchased a home in San Jose, California, in April 1975 for $44,000 and used it as their principal residence until October 1977, when they moved into a new home they had constructed at a cost of $107,040. They attempted to sell their old home continuously from July 1977 until it was sold in August 1978 for $70,000.

In the beginning, the Bolarises tried unsuccessfully for 90 days to sell their old home. At that point they rented the home on a month-to-month basis (to "lessen the burden of carrying the property") at a fair rental value in an arm's length transaction. After eight months the Bolarises asked the tenant to leave in the hopes of improving the saleability of the house. To that end they cleaned and repainted the home. About six weeks after the original tenant left, and after the house was improved, the Bolarises received their first offer to buy the old home, which the Bolarises accepted. Because the purchasers were having difficulty obtaining financing, the Bolarises agreed to rent the old home to the buyers until they obtained financing. The buyers rented the home for about one month, and finally bought it on August 14, 1978 for $70,000.

The Bolarises filed joint income tax returns reporting salaries of $29,021 and interest of $281 in 1977 and salaries of $33,355 and interest of $286 in 1978. In addition, they received rent from their old home of $1,271 in 1977 and $2,717 in 1978. From this income they deducted depreciation of $373 in 1977 and $1,120 in 1978 and rental expenses of $1,365 in 1977 and $3,607 in 1978. The IRS disallowed the depreciation and rental expense (except interest and real estate taxes of $486 in 1977 and $2,915 in 1978). The reason given in the statutory notice for disallowing the depreciation and rental expenses was that the rental of the home "was not entered into as a trade or business or for the production of income." These disallowances, along with a disallowed IRA deduction and California State Disability Insurance deduction, resulted in deficiencies of $486 in 1977 and $408 in 1978.

The Bolarises filed a pro se petition in the Tax Court under the simplified procedure for small tax cases. I.R.C. §§ 7456(d)(3), 7463. On the day of trial the IRS filed an amended answer asserting an increased deficiency of $3,339 and raising for the first time the issue of whether the Bolarises were entitled to deferred recognition of the gain from the sale of their old home under I.R.C. section 1034. The IRS contended that if the Bolarises were entitled to deferred gain on the sale of their old home under § 1034, they were not entitled to depreciation or rental expenses on the old home under §§ 167 and 212. As far as we have been able to determine, this is an issue of first impression. The Tax Court, in a reviewed decision,[4] permitted deferred recognition of the gain from the sale of the old home, but denied the Bolarises' claimed depreciation and rental expense under I.R.C. sections 167 and 212, accepting the IRS's theory that depreciation and rental expenses, and deferred recognition of gain were mutually exclusive as a matter of law. The Bolarises appealed pro se to this Circuit.

II. DELAYED RECOGNITION OF GAIN

The first issue is whether the Bolarises are entitled to delayed recognition of gain on the sale of their old home under section 1034. As the Tax Court stated, the IRS "does not seriously challenge the applicability of section 1034 to the sale in question, stating that 'the best view of the facts of this case is that [the Bolarises] qualify for section 1034 treatment. [Section 1034] is available because [the Bolarises] never converted the house from personal use.'" Bolaris v. Commissioner, 81 T.C. 840, 844 (1983). The Tax Court held that the Bolarises rental of their old residence prior to its sale did not preclude the applicability of section 1034, citing Clapham v. IRS, 63 T.C. 505 (1975). Bolaris, 81 T.C. at 845–47.

---

4. This case was tried before a Special Trial Judge who wrote an opinion; that opinion was reviewed by the full Tax Court, with a majority of those judges participating in the review adopting the opinion of the Special Trial Judge, two judges concurring, and four judges dissenting.

The Tax Court's findings regarding whether the Bolarises were entitled to nonrecognition of gain on the sale of their old home are subject to a clearly erroneous standard of review. See Crocker v. Commissioner, 571 F.2d 338, 338 (6th Cir.1978). We agree for the reasons stated by the Tax Court that the rental of the Bolarises' old home prior to its sale does not preclude the nonrecognition of gain realized on the sale of the old home. See Bolaris, 81 T.C. at 844–47. The legislative history of section 1034 supports the nonrecognition of gain in this case by stating:

> The term "residence" is used in contradistinction to property used in trade or business and property held for the production of income. Nevertheless, the mere fact that the taxpayer temporarily rents out either the old or the new residence may not, in the light of all the facts and circumstances in the case, prevent the gain from being not recognized. For example, if the taxpayer purchases his new residence before he sells his old residence, the fact that he rents out the new residence during the period before he vacates the old residence will not prevent the application of this subsection.

H.R.Rep. No. 586, 82d Cong., 1st Sess. 109, *reprinted in* 1951 U.S.Code Cong. & Ad.News 1781, 1896. See also Clapham v. Commissioner, 63 T.C. 505, 509–12 (1975). We affirm the Tax Court's decision permitting deferred recognition of gain from the sale of the Bolarises' old home.

III. DEDUCTIONS FOR PROPERTY HELD FOR THE PRODUCTION OF INCOME

A more difficult question is raised by the Tax Court's denial of depreciation and other rental expense deductions. Section 167 permits depreciation deductions for "property held for the production of income." I.R.C. § 167(a)(2). Section 212 permits deductions for insurance and miscellaneous maintenance expenses. *See id.* § 212 (permitting deductions for "ordinary and necessary expenses" relating to "the management, conservation, or maintenance of property held for the production of income").

A. Effect of Nonrecognition of Gain

The Tax Court accepted the IRS's argument that a residence which qualifies for nonrecognition of gain under section 1034 cannot, as a matter of law, also be held for the production of income under sections 167 or 212. *Bolaris*, 81 T.C. at 848–49. We review de novo this legal question involving statutory interpretation. Dumdeang v. Commissioner, 739 F.2d 452, 453 (9th Cir.1984).

The IRS's argument isolates the sentence in the legislative history of section 1034 quoted above that "[t]he term 'residence' is used in contradistinction to property used in trade or business and property held for the production of income." H.R.Rep. No. 586, supra. However, this sentence must be read in context with the remainder of the legislative history and in light of the historical background of sections 167, 212, and 1034. In 1942 Congress enacted the statutory predecessors to sections 167 and 212 which for the first time permitted deductions for expenses involving property held for the production of income. See 1 B. Bittker, Federal Taxation of Income, Estates and Gifts, ¶¶ 20.1.2 & 23.2.1 (1981). The following year the Tax Court held that property which has been abandoned as a residence and which has been diligently listed for rent or sale qualifies as property held for the production of income for purposes of obtaining rental expense deductions. See Robinson v. Commissioner, 2 T.C. 305, 307 (1943). This was true even though the property in *Robinson* was never rented. Id. at 307, 309.

Section 1034 was enacted in 1951. Congress was presumably aware of the *Robinson* decision at the time section 1034 was enacted. As noted above, the legislative history of section 1034 begins by stating that " 'residence' is used in contradistinction to * * * property held for the production of income." H.R.Rep. No. 586, supra. However, despite Congress' presumed awareness that an abandoned residence which was rented could qualify as property held for the production of income, the legislative history further states that "*[n]evertheless,* the mere fact that the taxpayer temporarily rents out either the old or the new residence may not, in light of all of the facts and circumstances in the case, prevent the gain from being not recognized." Id. (emphasis added). Thus, we read the legislative history of section 1034 as stating that a former residence could qualify for nonrecognition of gain even if the residence was temporarily rented and also qualified as being held for the production of income. This interpretation has never been questioned until this lawsuit.

The IRS apparently has now come to the conclusion that permitting both rental expense deductions and nonrecognition of gain provides an improper "windfall" to taxpayers. Our response is three-fold. First, not all rentals of former residences will qualify for rental expense deductions. For example, a rental for less than fair market value will most likely not qualify as property being held for the production of income. See Jasionowski v. Commissioner, 66 T.C. 312, 322 (1976) ("voluntary acceptance of rent at an amount substantially below fair market value is a clear indication" of a lack of profit-motive). Second, to the extent any "windfall" exists it is limited to a period of two years, the time within which the old residence must be sold to qualify for nonrecognition of gain. See I.R.C. § 1034(a). Third, if Congress had intended to prevent a "windfall" to taxpayers, it easily could have included a provision stating that application of section 1034 precluded rental expense deductions under sections 167 and 212. Congress did not draft such a provision and we refuse to imply one. We therefore reject the IRS's argument that a residence which qualifies for nonrecognition of gain cannot also be held for the production of income. If the IRS wants such a rule, it should ask Congress to enact it.

NONRECOGNITION PROVISIONS

B. Entitlement to Rental Expense Deductions

The remaining issue is whether the Bolarises are entitled to the claimed deductions in this case. An individual is entitled to deductions under sections 167 and 212 if "the individual [engaged] in the activity with the predominant purpose and intention of making a profit." *Allen* v. Commissioner, 72 T.C. 28, 33 (1979). See I.R.C. § 183. The burden of proving a profit motive is on the petitioner. Allen, 72 T.C. at 34. The existence of a profit motive is a factual question subject to clearly erroneous review. Jackson v. Commissioner, 708 F.2d 1402, 1405 (9th Cir.1983).

The Tax Court recently set forth a non-exhaustive list of five factors to be considered in determining whether an individual has converted his residence to property held for the production of income. See Grant v. Commissioner, 84 T.C. 809 (1985). The five factors, which we adopt, are as follows:

> (1) the length of time the house was occupied by the individual as his residence before placing it on the market for sale; (2) whether the individual premanently [sic] abandoned all further personal use of the house; (3) the character of the property (recreational or otherwise); (4) offers to rent; and (5) offers to sell.

Id. 825. See also Newcombe v. Commissioner, 54 T.C. 1298, 1300–01 (1970).[5] No one factor is determinative and all of the facts and circumstances of a particular case must be considered. See § 1.183–2(a), Income Tax Regs. (26 C.F.R.).

Several factors strongly support the conclusion that the Bolarises possessed the requisite profit-motive based upon their rental of the old home.[6] First, this case involves both offers to rent and offers to sell. More importantly, the Bolarises actually rented their old home at fair market rental. As the Tax Court's majority opinion recognized, "renting the residence at its fair market value would normally suggest that the taxpayer had the requisite profit objective." *Bolaris*, 81 T.C. at 849. See also Eisenstein v. Commissioner, 47 T.C.M. (P–H) ¶ 78,095, at 78– 442 (1978) ("If [the taxpayers'] primary motive was profit, they would

---

5. Section 1.183–2(b) of the Income Tax Regulations (26 C.F.R.) contains a separate list of nine factors to be considered in determining whether an activity is engaged in for profit. As the Tax Court has noted, however, the factors listed in section 1.183–2(b) "are more relevant to farming and hobbies than to rental property." See Smith v. Commissioner, 50 T.C.M. No. 366, 1985 T.C.M.Dec. (CCH) 42,444 (1985); *Jasionowski*, 66 T.C. at 321 n. 6. The section 1.183–2(b) factors provide general guidance but are not as helpful in this case as those set forth in *Grant*.

6. The Bolarises also contend that they intended to make a profit from the appreci-

ation on the old home during the time it was being rented. However, immediately upon leaving the old home, the Bolarises placed the home on the market hoping to sell it as soon as possible. "The placing of the property on the market for immediate sale, at or shortly after the time of its abandonment as a residence, will ordinarily be strong evidence that a taxpayer is not holding the property for postconversion appreciation in value." *Newcombe*, 54 T.C. at 1302. We therefore reject the Bolarises' contention that they were holding the old home for postconversion appreciation.

certainly have tried to maximize that profit by renting at the highest possible price.").

Second, the Bolarises permanently abandoned the old home when they moved to their new residence. Even if the Bolarises had wanted to return to the old home, they would have been unentitled legally to do so because the home was rented almost continually from the time they vacated the home until it was sold. See Langford v. Commissioner, 50 T.C.M. (P–H) ¶ 81,532, at 81–2061 (1981).

Third, the old home offered no elements of personal recreation. As stated in the Income Tax Regulations, "a profit motivation may be indicated where an activity lacks any appeal other than profit." § 1.183–2(b)(9), Income Tax Regs. (26 C.F.R.). See *Allen*, 72 T.C. at 36; *Langford*, 50 T.C.M. (P–H) at 81–2061.[7]

We view the Bolarises' ancillary desire to sell the old home as an insignificant factor in determining their profit-motive. See *Bolaris*, 81 T.C. at 854 (Wilbur, J., dissenting) (citing cases). Our conclusion is supported by Sherlock v. Commissioner, 31 T.C.M. (CCH) 383 (1972). In *Sherlock*, the taxpayers abandoned their old residence in November 1964 and offered it for sale for the first ninety days. *Id.* at 385. When no offers to buy were received the old residence was offered for rent or sale until it was finally sold in November 1966. The rental price sought was found to be reasonable but the home was never actually rented. *Id.* at 384. The Tax Court permitted rental expense deductions under sections 167 and 212 even though the taxpayers intended to sell the home. The court stated that "[i]t is completely understandable that petitioners desired to turn this potential expense eater [the old residence] into an income-producing asset during [the] waiting period [prior to sale]." *Id.* at 385.

The IRS argues that the Bolarises could not have intended to make a profit because the rental payments they received were less than their mortgage payments. Sustained unexplained losses are probative of a lack of profit motive but they present only one non-determinative factor to be considered. *Jasionowski*, 66 T.C. at 319; *Langford*, 50 T.C.M. (P–H) at 81–2060. We believe that the other factors discussed above outweigh the existence of short-term losses experienced by the Bolarises.

In denying the Bolarises' rental expense deductions, the Tax Court relied upon the IRS's new theory that a residence which qualifies for nonrecognition of gain cannot also be held for the production of income. In light of the factors discussed above indicating that the Bolarises possessed the requisite profit motive, we conclude that the Tax Court

---

7. We find the remaining *Grant* factor, the length of time the house was occupied as a residence before placing it on the market for sale, to be unhelpful in this case. The Bolarises occupied the old home as their principal residence from August 1975 to October 1977. This length of occu-pancy is too short to adequately indicate "the personal nature of expenses subse-quently incurred while holding the proper-ty for postoccupancy sale" but is too long to adequately indicate that such expenses are non-personal. *Newcombe*, 54 T.C. at 1300.

clearly erred in denying the deductions claimed under sections 167 and 212.

IV. CONCLUSION

The Tax Court's decision permitting deferred recognition of gain from the sale of the Bolarises' old home is AFFIRMED. The decision denying depreciation and rental expense deductions is REVERSED AND REMANDED for redetermination of the deficiencies.

REINHARDT, Circuit Judge, concurring and dissenting:

While I agree that the Bolarises are entitled to deferred recognition of the gain on the sale of their home under I.R.C. § 1034, I cannot agree that they are also entitled to take deductions under I.R.C. §§ 167 and 212 for the period during which they were attempting to sell that property. Under section 1034, deferred recognition of gain is allowed only if the property sold is the taxpayer's "principal residence." § 1034; Treas.Reg. § 1.1034–1(c)(3). On the other hand, under sections 167 and 212 deductions can be taken for depreciation and maintenance expenses only if the property is "held for the production of income." The two phrases are mutually exclusive as are the respective forms of tax treatment.

Courts have long recognized the difference between a residence and income producing property. It has been well-established law for over 40 years that deductions are not allowable under sections 167 and 212 for expenses incurred with respect to a taxpayer's residence, whether principal or not. Brady v. Commissioner, 1983 T.C.M. (P–H) ¶ 83,163, aff'd mem. 729 F.2d 1445 (3d Cir.), cert. denied, 469 U.S. 1074, 105 S.Ct. 569, 83 L.Ed.2d 509 (1984); Meredith v. Commissioner, 65 T.C. 34 (1975); Robinson v. Commissioner, 2 T.C. 305 (1943); Treas.Reg. §§ 1.167(a)–2, 1.212–1(h).

It would seem that the words of the statute as well as the interpretations of the courts compel the conclusion that if the sale of a "principal residence" results in a deferral of gain under section 1034, then the seller is barred from taking deductions under sections 167 and 212 for expenses incurred with respect to that property. Given the clarity of statutory language and the consistency of judicial interpretation, there would seem to be no reason to turn, as the majority does, to the legislative history.[2]

In any event, the legislative history is plain and unambiguous.[3] It states: "[t]he term 'residence' is used in contradistinction to * * * property held for production of income." H.R.Rep. No. 586, 82d Cong., 1st Sess. 109, *reprinted in* 1951 U.S.Code Cong. & Ad.News 1781, 1896.

---

2. See Focht v. Commissioner, 68 T.C. 223, 244 (1977) (Hall, J., dissenting): "It has been said, with more than a grain of truth, that judges in tax cases these days tend to consult the statute only when the legislative history is ambiguous."

3. Cf. Bluff v. Father Gray (H.L.) per Lord Mildew: "If Parliament does not mean what it says it must say so." (Quoted in A.P. Herbert, The Uncommon Law: The Employment Tax (1935)).

Thus, the legislative history confirms what we have already noted: "residence" and "property held for the production of income" are mutually exclusive terms.

The legislative history also states that the fact that the taxpayer rents out his old house may not, in light of all the facts and circumstances, be inconsistent with a finding that the old house is still the taxpayer's residence. *Id.* See Treas.Reg. § 1.1034–1(c)(3). The majority seizes on the statement that the temporary renting out of a home does not deprive it of its character as the taxpayer's principal residence. On the basis of this rather benign proposition and without any particular further explanation, the majority leaps to the conclusion that a taxpayer's home can at once be *both* a residence and property held for the production of income. In fact, as has been demonstrated above, the legislative history provides compelling support for precisely the opposite conclusion. Contrary to the majority's assertion, the proposition that "residence" and "income producing property" are antithetical terms is not novel: it has been advanced by the Commissioner and accepted by the Tax Court, either expressly or impliedly, on a number of occasions. See, e.g., Trisko v. Commissioner, 29 T.C. 515, 520 (1957); Stolk v. Commissioner, 40 T.C. 345, 353–54 (1963), aff'd mem. 326 F.2d 760 (2d Cir.1964); Daves v. Commissioner, 54 T.C. 170, 175 (1970); Barry v. Commissioner, 1971 T.C.M. (P–H) ¶ 71,179;[4] Rogers v. Commissioner, 1982 T.C.M. (P–H) ¶ 82,718.[5]

Moreover, a holding that the Bolarises cannot take deductions under sections 167 and 212 does not mean that they are not entitled to any deductions at all for expenses relating to their home. Under sections 163, 164, and 183(b)(1) the Bolarises were entitled to, and did, deduct in full the mortgage interest and real estate taxes that they paid. In addition, section 183(b)(2) authorizes the deduction of the depreciation and maintenance expenses to the extent that the income from the rental of the house exceeds the amount of the mortgage interest and real estate tax payments. It is only because the Bolarises' rental income was less than the amount of those payments that they

---

4. While it appears that in *Trisko* and *Barry* the taxpayers were allowed to take certain deductions for depreciation as well as take advantage of § 1034, neither case held that a taxpayer can take deductions under §§ 167, 212 when § 1034 is also applicable. First, in neither case did the Commissioner challenge the taking of the deductions; rather he challenged only the availability of § 1034. In the case before us, of course, the Commissioner is challenging both. Second, in both *Trisko* and *Barry* the court explicitly held that the taxpayers' old house was not held for the production of income. The Bolarises, however, will be entitled to deductions under §§ 167, 212 only if their old house *was* held for the production of income. *Trisko* and

Barry both stated that § 1034 was not applicable if the taxpayers' old house was held for the production of income.

5. The majority relies heavily on *Robinson*, supra, in reaching its conclusion. However, *Robinson* merely holds that if the taxpayer has actually *abandoned* his residence, the property can then become property held for the production of income. Thus, it provides no support for the majority's conclusion. It follows therefore that there is no validity to the majority's theory that the existence of *Robinson* at the time Congress enacted § 1034 demonstrates that Congress intended homeowners to receive the benefit of both § 1034 and §§ 167, 212 simultaneously.

cannot deduct at least some portion of the maintenance and depreciation expenses they incurred.[6]

Because I believe that the judgment of the Tax Court should be affirmed in its entirety, I respectfully dissent.

EXCERPT FROM HOUSE REPORT NO. 95–1445

95th Congress, 2d Session (1978).
1978–3 vol. 1 Cum.Bull. 307.

4. Exclusion of gain on sale of residences (secs. 405 of the bill and secs. * * * 121 * * * of the Code)

Present law

* * *

Individuals Age 65 and Over

Under present law, an individual who has attained the age of 65 may elect to exclude from gross income, on a one-time basis, the entire gain realized on the sale of his or her principal residence if the adjusted sales price is $35,000 or less (sec. 121). If the adjusted sales price exceeds $35,000, the amount excludible is that portion of the gain which is determined by multiplying the total gain by a fraction, the numerator of which is $35,000, and the denominator of which is the adjusted sales price of the residence. The exclusion is not available unless the property was owned and used by the taxpayer as his or her principal residence for 5 years or more during the 8-year period preceding the sale.

If an individual who has attained the age of 65 makes an election to exclude from gross income gain realized from the sale of his or her principal residence, and also purchases and uses a new principal residence within the period beginning 18 months before, and ending 18 months after, the sale date of the old residence, the amount realized, for rollover purposes, is reduced by the amount of gain excluded from the taxpayer's income. As a result, the amount which must be invested in a new residence to satisfy the rollover provisions is reduced by the amount of gain not included in the taxpayer's gross income. Similarly, the amount of reduction in the basis of the new residence attributable to the unrecognized gain on the sale of the old residence does not reflect the amount of gain excluded from gross income.

Reasons for Change

The committee believes that the taxes imposed upon an individual with respect to gain realized on the sale or exchange of a principal residence, in many instances, may be unduly high, especially in view of recent inflation levels and the increasing cost of housing. In most situations, however, the committee believes that the rollover provision

---

6. For a fuller explanation of the somewhat complicated workings of § 183(b), see Judge Korner's concurrence in the Tax Court's opinion in this case, 81 T.C. at 850–52.

of present law operates adequately to allow individuals to move from one residence to another without recognition of gain or payment of tax. Where an individual has a basis in his or her principal residence that is significantly lower than its current market value either because the residence has been owned for a number of years or because the rollover provision has applied to one or more sales of previous residences, the tax due on the gain recognized on the sale of the residence may be quite high in the event that the taxpayer replaces the residence with a less expensive dwelling or moves to rental quarters. While the provisions of present law relating to the exclusion of gain by taxpayers who have attained the age of 65 may ameliorate this situation somewhat, the committee believes that the current dollar limits and age restriction are unrealistic in view of increased housing costs and lower retirement ages.

Explanation of Provision

The committee bill repeals the provision of present law relating to gain realized on the sale of a principal residence by a taxpayer 65 and over. It provides that an individual * * * [who has attained the age of 55 Ed.] may elect to exclude from gross income up to [$125,000 Ed.] ([$62,500 Ed.] in the case of married individuals who file separate returns) of any gain realized on the sale or exchange of his or her principal residence (including both condominiums and shares of stock by a tenant-shareholder in a cooperative housing corporation). The exclusion applies only once in a taxpayer's lifetime. Additionally, the provisions of section 1033 (relating to involuntary conversions) and 1034 (relating to rollover of gain on the sale of a principal residence) shall * * * apply to any sale or exchange of the principal residence with respect to which this election is made. * * * [I]f a taxpayer previously made an election under section 121 (relating to elections by taxpayers who have attained the age of 65) before the effective date of the bill, an election also may be made to exclude gain under this new provision with respect to another sale of a principal residence. Where this is the case, there is to be no reduction in the amount of gain excludible due to the prior election.

In addition, the exclusion applies only with respect to gain realized on the sale or exchange of a principal residence which the taxpayer has owned and occupied as his or her principal residence for periods aggregating [three Ed.] years out of the [five Ed.] year period which immediately precedes the sale. For purposes of determining the length of time that a principal residence was owned and occupied by a taxpayer making this election, only that period of time which the particular principal residence that is being sold or exchanged was owned and occupied will be taken into account. There would be no "tacking" of the holding period for replacement property. For example, the holding period for an old residence would not be taken into account even if gain had been rolled over into a new residence. As under present law, the ownership and occupancy rule may be satisfied only by the taxpayer, or by the taxpayer's spouse in the case of married individuals.

For purposes of the exclusion contained in the bill, the definition of a taxpayer's principal residence is that presently used for the rollover provision (sec. 1034). Therefore, whether property qualifies as an individual's principal residence, or what portion of a large property qualifies, will depend upon the facts and circumstances in each case, including the taxpayer's good faith. Similarly, the facts and circumstances test is to apply to determine which residence is a taxpayer's principal residence where he or she has owned and occupied more than one residence for the [three Ed.] year period preceding the sale in question.

* * *

There is to be only one lifetime election with respect to married taxpayers. In other words, the election does not apply separately to each spouse. If, however, each of two parties have made elections independently prior to becoming married, there is to be no recapture of the taxes attributable to the gain excluded with respect to the sale of one of the residences.

If spouses make an election during marriage, and subsequently become divorced, no further elections are available to either of them or to their spouses should they marry. The election provided in the bill must be made in accordance with regulations prescribed by the Secretary.

Effective Date

This provision is effective for sales of personal residences after July 26, 1978.

* * *

PROBLEMS

1. In the current year for $165,000 (the "adjusted sales price") Homeowner sold property which he had used as his principal residence for 20 years. His adjusted basis for the residence was $30,000. In the same year he acquired and occupied a new condominium which cost him $100,000 and which he used as his principal residence.

  (a) If Homeowner is 50 years of age,

    (1) What are the tax consequences of the sale?

    (2) What is his basis for the new condominium?

    (3) What is his holding period for the condominium four months after its acquisition?

  (b) If Homeowner is 70 years old at the time of sale,

    (1) To what extent may he avoid tax on the gain realized on the sale?

    (2) If he seeks maximum nonrecognition of gain, what will be his basis for the condominium?

(3) And what will be his holding period for the condominium two months after its acquisition?

(c) The facts are the same as in part (b), above, except that several years ago Homeowner who was over 65 sold his principal residence using the old (pre-July 26, 1978) § 121 election and § 1034 and as a result his basis and tacked holding period for the replacement residence, which he has owned and used for four years, are $30,000 and 20 years. What results to Homeowner if he engages in the transaction in (b), above?

(d) What result under § 453 to Homeowner in (a), above, in the current and succeeding nine years if Buyer pays him $16,500 cash in the current year and Buyer gives him a note under which Buyer agrees to (and does) pay him $16,500 in each of the succeeding nine years, paying 10% interest on the unpaid balance? See Rev.Rul. 75, 1953–1 C.B. 83.

2. Several years ago, Resident paid $60,000 for his residence and the six acres of land which surrounded it. In the current year he spends $5000 repairing the home to make it more saleable and two months later he sells it for $100,000. After real estate commissions he receives $95,000. Resident moves into a motel and three months later he purchases a lot for $20,000 and begins construction of a new home. Twenty-four months after the original sale, even though construction is not completed Resident and his family move into the new residence when construction costs on it total $50,000. Construction is completed six months later at a total cost of $75,000.

(a) What is Resident's recognized gain on the sale of the old residence? See Kern v. Granquist, 291 F.2d 29 (9th Cir.1961).

(b) What is Resident's basis for the new residence?

E. OTHER NONRECOGNITION PROVISIONS

Internal Revenue Code: See Section 1038.

———

Congress applies the nonrecognition concept to several transactions that fall outside the scope of this book and to some others which, while within, are accorded only brief mention here. For example, a transfer of property to a new corporation in exchange for its shares is a transaction in which gain or loss is clearly realized; and so is a transfer of property to a partnership in exchange for a partnership interest. Nevertheless, such corporate and partnership transactions are usually accorded tax neutrality by way of a nonrecognition provision.[1] Some partnership distributions are similarly treated,[2] as are some limited distributions in liquidation by corporations.[3] Gain or loss goes unrecog-

---

1. As regards corporations, see I.R.C. §§ 351, 358, 362; and as regards partnerships, see I.R.C. §§ 721, 722, 723. Cf. I.R.C. §§ 704(c), 724.

2. I.R.C. §§ 731, 732, 733.

3. I.R.C. §§ 332, 334(b).

nized upon a corporation's transfer of its own shares whether for money or other property, even if the shares are treasury stock.[4] A shareholder's exchange of stock for like stock in the same corporation may be of no immediate tax significance whether he has a realized gain or loss on the exchange.[5] And numerous corporate reorganizations that involve potentially taxable exchanges of stock and other property escape immediate tax consequences to the corporation or the shareholders involved.[6] As in the sections studied, the usual price for nonrecognition is some type of transferred or exchanged basis, although the basis rule is of course a compensating advantage where loss is not recognized.

Outside the area of business organizations, the Code provides for nonrecognition of gain or loss upon some exchanges of life insurance, endowment or annuity contracts for similar contracts [7] and upon the exchange of some United States obligations for other such obligations.[8] It may be a comforting thought that there is sufficient similarity in the nonrecognition provisions so that an understanding of one or several is a great help grasping the significance of another.

It will be recalled that, if an installment sale of property under Section 453 is followed by a default and reacquisition of the same property, the vendor's tax liability may be accelerated by the disposition rules of Section 453B. Nevertheless, he is, in a sense, merely restored to the same position he was in prior to the sale. A nonrecognition provision now may provide some relief from the acceleration of tax liability otherwise arising out of a disposition of Section 453 obligations. Section 1038 [9] provides for nonrecognition (or only partial recognition) of gain in certain repossessions, which sometimes would be within the disposition rules of Section 453B.[10] Section 1038 applies only to sales of real property, and only if the obligation was secured by the real property and the vendor reacquires the same property in partial or full satisfaction of the purchaser's indebtedness.[11] Under Section 1038, the general effect is to treat amounts previously received on the sale (such as initial and subsequent cash payments) as income, except to the extent that the receipts have previously been reported as income, for example, under Section 453(c).[12] But amounts so treated cannot exceed the gain realized on the original sale, reduced by gain previously reported.[13] What this provision seeks to do is to isolate out the amount

---

4. I.R.C. § 1032.

5. I.R.C. § 1036; but see § 1031(a)(2)(B).

6. I.R.C. §§ 354, 356, 358, 361, 362(b), 368, 1032.

7. I.R.C. § 1035.

8. I.R.C. § 1037.

9. See Hauser, "Effect of Repossessions under Section 1038," 25 N.Y.U.Inst. on Fed.Tax. 47 (1967); Willis, "Repossession of Real Property—Application of Section 1038," 18 U.S.C.Tax Inst. 601 (1966).

10. I.R.C. § 1038 is not limited to § 453 installment sales and may apply to other deferred payment sales of real property, e.g., where § 453(d) is elected. Sen.Fin. Comm.Rep.No. 1361, 88th Cong., 2d Sess. (1964) 1964–2 C.B. 831. See Handler, "Tax Consequences of Mortgage Foreclosures and Transfers of Real Property to the Mortgagee," 31 Tax L.Rev. 193, 215 (1976).

11. I.R.C. § 1038(a).

12. I.R.C. § 1038(b)(1).

13. I.R.C. § 1038(b)(2). Any further investment by the reacquiring vendor also reduces the income reportable under this provision.

that the reacquiring vendor has withdrawn from his original investment and to tax him on that amount (but not in excess of the amount of his original gain), to the extent that such withdrawals have previously escaped tax.

If the vendor's property has been returned to him, does he acquire it with the same basis as it had before he sold it? Clearly that would be inappropriate if in the sale and reacquisition he has withdrawn some of his initial investment without being taxed on the entire withdrawal. Section 1038(c), in keeping with other nonrecognition provisions, lays down a special basis rule which takes account of all facets of the sale and reacquisition. The basis for the reacquired property is determined with reference to the vendor's basis for the obligations relinquished in the reacquisition.[14] This will be seen to represent the vendor's basis for the property sold, reduced by prior receipts that went untaxed (for example under Section 453(c)) which are in effect a return of capital. To this is added (1) the amount on which the vendor is taxed under Section 1038(b),[15] because *taxed* gain should obviously not again be taxed when the reacquired property is sold, and (2) the amount of any payment the vendor made in connection with the reacquisition,[16] because this represents an actual additional cost of or investment in the property.

These remarks are not intended as a comprehensive analysis of Section 1038, which can present some complications not discussed. Nevertheless, they touch the main points, and the principles discussed above may be seen at work in the following basic illustration.

Assume T sold a piece of real estate with a basis to him of $60,000 for $100,000. $20,000 was paid in cash in the year of sale and the balance of the price was reflected in a note for $80,000, on which $20,000 was payable in each of the succeeding four years with interest on the unpaid balance (We now dismiss the interest, assuming it to be paid and taxed as due). The $80,000 note was secured by a mortgage on the property. Before any principal payments were made on the note and when the property had appreciated in value to $110,000 the buyer defaulted. T agreed to accept a reconveyance of the property in full satisfaction of the note and to pay the buyer an additional $30,000.[17] If there were no Section 1038, T would have had to report $32,000 of income on the disposition, computed as follows:

14. Cf. I.R.C. § 453B(b).

15. I.R.C. § 1038(c)(1).

16. I.R.C. § 1038(c)(2).

17. It is assumed here that T is paying full value to reacquire the property ($80,000 of purchaser's obligations, plus $30,000 cash equals $110,000). Realistically, the purchaser might accept less, because a forced sale, the alternative to the voluntary arrangement, probably would yield less than the fair market value of the property. See Reg. § 1.1038–1(h), Example (1); and Cf., Reg. § 20.2031–1(b), differentiating "fair market value" and "forced sale price."

Portion of fair market value of property received for obligations on reacquisition ($30,000 was received for cash)	$80,000
Less basis for Section 453 obligations (Section 453B(b))	48,000
Income reportable	$32,000

This is the same amount as would have been reported if the purchaser had paid the obligations in full.[18]

T's basis for the reacquired property would be $110,000. As this is a fully taxable transaction T reacquires the property as if by purchase for a consideration equal to its fair market value at the time of acquisition.[19]

However, under Section 1038(b)(1), T's taxable gain is only $2,000, computed as follows:

Money and fair market value of property (other than obligations) received prior to the reacquisition	$20,000
Less prior taxed gain (Section 453(c) gain on the $20,000 was 40,000/100,000 × $20,000 = $8,000)	8,000
Gain taxed (Before the Section 1038(b)(2) limitation)	$12,000

On these facts, however, Section 1038(b)(2) limits the gain upon which T is taxed on the reacquisition to $2,000, computed as follows:

Excess of sale price over adjusted basis		$40,000
Reduced by:		
Gain taxed before reacquisition	$ 8,000	
Money paid by T upon reacquisition [20]	30,000	
		38,000
Gain taxed on reacquisition		$ 2,000

Thus under Section 1038 T reports only $2,000, instead of the $32,000 otherwise reportable. The cost of this relief is a lower basis for the reacquired property, computed under Section 1038(c) as follows:

Basis for the obligations (Section 453B(b))	$48,000
Plus gain taxed on the reacquisition (Section 1038(b))	2,000
Plus amount paid by the vendor in connection with the reacquisition of the property (Section 1038(b)(2)(B))	30,000
Basis	$80,000

---

18. Reg. § 1.453–5(b)(2).

19. Reg. § 1.453–5(b)(6). As all of T's gain in the property ($40,000) has been taxed and T has invested another $10,000, the result is the same as if he had originally sold the property for $100,000 cash and has then added $10,000 to purchase new property at a cost of $110,000. (Note that he has taken out $20,000 and put in $30,000 more for a net $10,000 increase in his investment.)

20. This part of the limitation is not especially easy to understand. But notice that, if T had paid upon reacquisition only the same amount as he had withdrawn prior thereto ($20,000), the § 1038(b)(2) limitation would merely equal the amount taxable under § 1038(b)(1) ($40,000 less $8,000, less $20,000 equals $12,000). To the extent that he reinvests more than he has withdrawn, the amount taxed is reduced, because he has increased his net investment, rather than having made a net cash bail-out.

A review of the entire transaction and its tax consequences to T will demonstrate the propriety of his new $80,000 basis for the property, which now has a fair market value of $110,000 and a potential $30,000 gain to T upon its sale. At the time of the sale, T had property in which he had a potential $40,000 gain (F.M.V. $100,000 less basis $60,000). He withdrew $20,000 of his original investment of $60,000 but he was taxed on $10,000 of the amount withdrawn ($8,000 at time of sale plus $2,000 upon reacquisition). This should effect a net reduction of $10,000 in his original investment (and basis) because only the $10,000 tax free withdrawal was in the nature of a return of his capital. At this point his basis would have been $50,000 (original $60,000 less $10,000 return of capital). But he has also added $30,000 to his investment ($10,000 of which took account of the post-sale appreciation). Thus his basis becomes $80,000, and T remains potentially taxable on $30,000, the amount of his gain on the original sale which, so far, has gone untaxed.

PART EIGHT: CONVERTING TAXABLE INCOME INTO TAX LIABILITY
CHAPTER 27. COMPUTATIONS

A. CLASSIFICATION OF TAXPAYERS AND RATES

Internal Revenue Code: Sections 1; 2; 68; 151(d)(3) and (4); 6013(a) and (d). See Sections 3; 63; 66; 73; 6012; 6013(c) and (e); 7703.

A grasp of the concepts and principles presented in the preceding chapters of this book makes possible an intelligent look at the determination of a taxpayer's actual tax liability. Still deferring rules of tax procedure, this Chapter considers the conversion of taxable income into tentative tax liability, which then is reduced by various credits and measured against an alternative minimum tax to reach a determination of the actual liability for tax.

Briefly to recapitulate what has gone before, we have examined the profile of gross income, deductions allowed in arriving at taxable income, assignments of income, rules of timing (accounting !), characterization, and some principles of disallowance and nonrecognition. The 1986 Act made some substantial changes to the rules of the game. To broaden the tax base, Congress increased the lists of items specifically included within gross income. For example, more prizes and awards are taxable, and unemployment compensation is brought within the tax collector's grasp.[1] Congress also reduced statutory exclusions from gross income; fewer scholarships and fellowships escape[2] and, by express provision in the Code, employer gifts to employees are no longer excludible from employees' gross income.[3] The most significant increase in the amount to which the tax rates are applied (the tax base) is the result of congressional disallowance in whole or in part of previously deductible items. Some disallowances are direct: the repeal of the capital gains deduction,[4] the restriction of deductions for personal interest,[5] the limitation of deductions for the depreciation of real estate,[6] the 80 percent ceiling on the deduction of business meals and entertainment,[7] and the disallowance of the personal sales tax deduction,[8] just to name a few. Other deduction disallowances are less

1. I.R.C. §§ 74 and 85.

2. I.R.C. § 117.

3. I.R.C. § 102(c). Cf. I.R.C. §§ 74 and 132.

4. See I.R.C. (1954) § 1202. But see notes 62–66, infra.

5. I.R.C. § 163(h).

6. I.R.C. § 168(b)(3) and (c).

7. I.R.C. § 274(n).

8. I.R.C. § 164(a).

direct, viz: the 2 percent floor under certain itemized deductions [9] and the passive investment activity limitation.[10]

Of course, we discover (we've really known it all along!) that the disadvantage to taxpayers of base broadening can be offset by the major advantage of a reduction in overall tax rates. The 1986 legislation reduced tax rates across the board. Prior to 1981, noncorporate taxpayers were taxed at progressive tax rates [11] up to 70 percent and between 1981 and 1986, at progressive rates up to 50 percent. The 1986 legislation replaced progressive rates with modified flat tax rates and, generally, imposed a 28 percent rate ceiling on noncorporate taxpayers.[12]

In an effort to reduce the budget deficit, Congress in the 1990 tax legislation added a 31 percent tax rate for upper income noncorporate taxpayers.[13] Further, by imposing phase-outs of itemized deductions and personal exemptions, Congress effectively imposes an even higher tax rate on some upper income noncorporate taxpayers.[14] However, Congress did retain a 28 percent tax rate ceiling on noncorporate net capital gains.[15]

Classifications of Taxpayers.   Before we look more closely at the rates, specifically the points at which the 28 and the 31 percent rates are applicable, we must examine the classification of taxpayers. Prior to the 1986 legislation, the taxable income levels at which different sets of progressive rates were imposed depended upon the classification (by personal circumstances) of the taxpayer. These classifications, which determined the particular set of rates a taxpayer used, remain in the statute and are used now to determine the level at which the 28 percent and 31 percent rates apply.

Individual taxpayers are grouped into four classifications:

1.   Married Individuals Filing Joint Returns and Surviving Spouses; [16]

---

9. I.R.C. § 67(a).

10. I.R.C. § 469.

11. The purpose behind progressive rates is to increase the proportionate tax burden as taxable income increases. See Blum and Kalven, "The Uneasy Case for Progressive Taxation," 19 U. of Chi.L.Rev. 417 (1952); Smith, "High Progressive Tax Rates: Inequity and Immorality?" 20 U. of Fla.Rev. 451 (1968).

12. The 15 percent and 28 percent rates were not the exclusive noncorporate tax rates. Congress legislated against *any* of the income of high income taxpayers being taxed at a mere 15 percent rate. Further, Congress determined that taxpayers with even higher taxable income should not be allowed the benefits of personal exemptions. But the attack here was sneaky, and the objectives were achieved indirectly by way of a surtax bubble payment. Con-

gress imposed a 5 percent surtax on taxpayers in high income ranges, resulting in a 33 percent tax rate. The 5 percent surtax was phased out after the advantages of the 15 percent rate and the exemptions had been "paid for." Thus, a greater than 28 percent rate on taxable income applied to the extent that the 5 percent surtax phased out personal exemptions.

13. I.R.C. § 1(a)–(e).

14. I.R.C. §§ 68, 151(d)(3). See notes 47–61, infra. Additionally, if the alternative minimum tax applies to a taxpayer, a tax of greater than 31 percent of *taxable income* may be imposed because although the minimum tax uses a lower 24 percent rate, it taxes a potentially broader tax base.

15. I.R.C. § 1(h). See page 665, supra.

16. I.R.C. § 1(a).

2.　Heads of Households; [17]

3.　Unmarried Individuals (not falling within the first two classifications as surviving spouses or heads of households); [18]

4.　Married Individuals Filing Separate Returns. [19]

There is a separate schedule for trusts and estates; [20] and corporate taxpayers are taxed under an entirely different set of rates.[21]

The four classifications of individual taxpayers listed above are the same as they were prior to 1987. They are puzzling enough to invite the question: How did we get to the point of having the various classifications?

For many years all individuals were taxed under a single set of tax rates. In 1930, however, the Supreme Court held that in community property states earnings and other income of either spouse were taxable one-half to each spouse.[22] Under the then single progressive tax rate table, this splitting of income between community property state spouses gave married persons subject to those state laws a major tax advantage over married persons in common law states. The nature of the advantage should be clear. Not to be outdone, a movement began in common law states to adopt the community property system.[23] But, as there had always been many more common law states than community property states, it is not surprising that broad relief from the inequality eventually came from Congress. In 1948, the 1939 Code was amended so as to allow a married couple to split their aggregate taxable income for purposes of rate determination. Their tax liability then became twice the tax determined at rates fixed by one-half the amount of their combined income, often escaping the higher reaches of the table.[24] When the Bill reached the Senate, the Finance Committee Report stated in part: [25]

> This section amends ＊　＊　＊ the Code, relating to surtax on individuals, by adding a new subsection ＊　＊　＊ which

17.　I.R.C. § 1(b).

18.　I.R.C. § 1(c).

19.　I.R.C. § 1(d).

20.　I.R.C. § 1(e).

21.　I.R.C. § 11. See the text at note 87, infra.

22.　Poe v. Seaborn, 282 U.S. 101, 51 S.Ct. 58 (1930). While post-marital earnings are split, either spouse may have noncommunity property, the earnings from which are his or hers, separately.

See I.R.C. § 66(a), enacted in 1980, which in limited circumstances taxes community property earned income to the spouse whose services gave rise to the income, rather than one-half to each spouse. I.R.C. § 66 applies only if the spouses are living apart at all times during the year involved, they file separate returns, and no portion of the earned income is transferred be-

tween them. See also § 66(b), enacted in 1984, which allows the service to treat one spouse as the owner of community property income if that spouse acts as if he or she is solely entitled to the income and fails to notify the other spouse of the income. Cf. I.R.C. § 66(c).

See Miller, "Federal Income Taxation and Community Property Law: The Case for Divorce," 44 S.W.L.J. 1087 (1990).

23.　Sen.Rep. No. 1013, 80th Cong., 2d Sess. (1948), 1948–1 C.B. 301–303. There were also advantages to the community property states under the Estate and Gift Tax provisions which were eliminated by the Rev.Act of 1948. See I.R.C. §§ 2056, 2513, 2523.

24.　I.R.C. (1939) §§ 12(d) and 51(b).

25.　Sen.Rep. No. 1013, supra note 23 at 1948–1 C.B. 326.

provides for computation of tax under the plan for the so-called income splitting between husband and wife. This subsection applies only if a joint return for the taxable year involved is made. * * * Under the provisions * * * the combined normal tax and surtax * * * in the case of the husband and wife making the joint return shall be twice the combined normal tax and surtax that would be determined if the net income and the applicable credits * * * were reduced by one-half.

The early concept is identifiable in present Section 1(a). As was true initially, the special rates are available only if a joint return is filed. Use of the joint return by married persons is elective and is allowed only if the requirements of Section 6013(a) are satisfied. A consequence of filing a joint return is joint and several liability, not only for the tax reported, but also for deficiencies and interest and possibly civil penalties.[26] In many circumstances the income-splitting advantage of a joint return will result in less tax liability for the spouses than filing separate returns.[27] But the important thing here is the origin of the split-income device.

In 1954, the "surviving spouse" was fitted into the married joint return classification and remains there.[28] Surviving spouses, as defined in Section 2(a), are widows or widowers who for the two years following the year of their spouse's death do not remarry but do maintain certain dependents in their home. One is not a statutory "surviving spouse" for the year of the spouse's death. If the Section 2(a) requirements are met surviving spouses are allowed to use the Section 1(a) rates which, as indicated, are the income-splitting rates that are available to married couples filing joint returns.

In 1951, Congress created another set of rates applicable to another category of taxpayers known as "heads of households". The reason for according this new class of taxpayers preferential rates was stated in the House Report: [29]

> It is believed that taxpayers, not having spouses but nevertheless required to maintain a household for the benefit of other individuals, are in a somewhat similar position to married couples who, because they may share their income, are treated under present law substantially as if they were two single individuals each with half of the total income of the

---

26. I.R.C. § 6013(d)(3); see, however, the innocent spouse rules of §§ 6013(e) and 6653(b) and see page 1031, infra. Cf. I.R.C. § 66(c).

27. If the spouses have equal taxable incomes, there is no income-splitting advantage in filing a joint return. In addition, at both the lower and upper income levels, there may also be no such advantage. At the lower rate, whether split or not, income may be taxed only at the low-

est rate. At the upper rate, if each spouse has sufficient income to reach the maximum rate, a shift by way of the elective splitting provision may still leave the maximum rate applicable to the same amount of income.

28. I.R.C. § 1(a)(2).

29. H.Rep. No. 586, 82d Cong., 1st Sess. (1951), 1951–2 C.B. 364.

couple. The income of a head of household who must maintain a home for a child, for example, is likely to be shared with the child to the extent necessary to maintain the home, and raise and educate the child. This, it is believed, justifies the extension of some of the benefits of income splitting. The hardship appears particularly severe in the case of the individual with children to raise who, upon the death of his spouse, finds himself in the position not only of being denied the spouse's aid in raising the children, but under present law also may find his tax load heavier.

However, it was not deemed appropriate to give a head of household the full benefits of income splitting because it appears unlikely that there is as much sharing of income in these cases as between spouses. In the case of savings, for example, it appears unlikely that this income will be shared by a widow or widower with his child to the same extent as in the case of spouses. As a result only one-half of the benefits of income splitting are granted to heads of households.

Under the current provisions of the Code, "heads of households" are defined in Section 2(b) much in line with the comments just quoted.[30] But head of household status is not limited to widows or widowers. It can also apply, for example, to a divorced or legally separated person who maintains as his home a household in which unmarried descendants reside.[31] In 1954, the provision was expanded so as to include a taxpayer who maintains a household for others, including parents, if the others enjoy dependency status under Section 151.[32] In 1969, the head of household status was again enlarged so as to permit a person who is actually married to obtain the benefit of that classification, if he would otherwise qualify for head of household status, where the taxpayer and his spouse are physically separated even though not divorced or legally separated.[33] The rates under Section 1(b), applicable to heads of households effecting a smaller amnesty, fall between the rates for single persons and the rates for married couples filing joint returns.

And now we have come full circle. In the past, individuals not within the special classes described above and married persons filing separately shared the distinction of paying taxes in accordance with a third schedule of rates, the highest of the three. But in 1969, Congress determined this third schedule was too burdensome for the *unmarried individual* who was not a surviving spouse or a head of household. There emerged a revised third classification and schedule now found in Section 1(c), less preferential than the first two, but preferential never-

---

30. Taxpayer's home must constitute the child or other dependent's principal place of abode for more than one-half of such year. I.R.C. § 2(b)(1)(A).

31. I.R.C. § 2(b)(1)(A), (2)(B) and (C), and (c).

32. I.R.C. § 2(b)(1)(A)(ii) and (B).

33. I.R.C. §§ 2(c) and 7703(b).

theless. The Staff of the Joint Committee on Internal Revenue Taxation explains the development as follows: [34]

> Under prior law, the tax rates imposed on single persons
> were quite heavy relative to those imposed on married couples
> at the same income level; at some income levels a single
> person's tax was as much as 42.1 percent higher than the tax
> paid on a joint return with the same amount of taxable income.
> The Congress believed that some difference between the rate of
> tax paid by single persons and joint returns was appropriate to
> reflect the additional living expenses of married taxpayers but
> that the prior law differential of as much as 42 percent (the
> result of income splitting) could not be justified on this basis.

> The Act provides a new lower rate schedule for single
> persons effective in 1971.

*   *   *

> The prior law rate schedule for single persons will contin-
> ue to be used for married couples filing separate re-
> turns. . . .   The prior law single person rate schedule was
> retained for married persons filing separate returns because if
> each spouse were permitted to use the new tax rate schedule
> for single persons, many (especially those in community prop-
> erty states) could arrange their affairs and income in such a
> way that their combined tax would be less than that on a joint
> return.

> With the new rate schedule for single persons, married
> couples filing a joint return will pay more tax than two single
> persons with the same total income. This is a necessary result
> of changing the income splitting relationship between single
> and joint returns. Moreover, it is justified on the grounds that
> although a married couple has greater living expenses than a
> single person and hence should pay less tax, the couple's living
> expenses are likely to be less than those of two single persons
> and therefore the couple's tax should be higher than that of
> two single persons.

As the above quoted remarks indicate, the tagender in the rate
parade is now the married taxpayer who files separately. The 28 and
31 percent rates kick in at a lower level for that taxpayer than any of
the other individual classifications.[35]

As a result of these rate schedules has Congress imposed a tax on
virtue? If A and B have equal incomes, or if both have more than
nominal incomes, they may be better off living together and filing
separate returns than marrying. For instance if in 1991 Jane has
taxable income of $17,000 and John has the same taxable income of
$17,000 and they merely live together and file separately, their total

---

34. General Explanation of the Tax Reform Act of 1969, Staff of the Joint Comm.
on Int.Rev.Tax., pp. 222–223 (1970).

35. I.R.C. § 1(d). But see note 27, supra.

tax liability is $5,100.[36] If they enter the bonds of holy matrimony and file a joint return, their total tax liability increases to $5301.50.[37]

One rather glamorous way for married persons to avoid what is commonly referred to as the "marriage penalty" is for spouses to travel to a winter vacation resort at the end of the year, obtain a divorce and desirable single tax status by New Year's Eve, and return home to a remarriage after the New Year, suntanned, happy, reconciled and having paid for part of the excursion with the tax savings generated by single taxpayer status.[38] Not surprisingly, the Service frowns upon such divorces, considering them sham transactions.[39] In the first judicial confrontation on the question the Commissioner was successful, although the Court did not adopt a sham transaction approach.[40] The Court concluded that as both parties were domiciled in their home state its courts would not recognize their divorces, because the foreign courts lacked subject matter jurisdiction.

Under pre-1987 law, the potential amount of "marriage penalty" was significantly greater than under the post-1986 rates, i.e., the amounts were large enough for the savings to pay the full cost of the divorce excursion. So for years between 1981 and 1987, Congress provided a partial alleviation of the marriage penalty,[41] allowing two earner married couples a special deduction of up to a maximum of $3,000 of earned income.[42] The deduction significantly, but not totally, alleviated the marriage penalty. In the 1986 legislation, Congress repealed the section[43] for 1987 and later years by concluding there was less possibility for a marriage penalty under the lower post-1986 rates.[44]

The rate discrepancy can be a problem for separated persons who are not divorced. In many instances they do not file jointly, to avoid the risks inherent in joint and several tax liability, and they just use the rates applicable to married taxpayers filing separately.[45] But in some cases the spouse with whom the children reside can now file as

36. I.R.C. § 1(c) rates on two taxable incomes of $17,000 equals $5,100. Mapes v. United States, 576 F.2d 896 (Ct.Cl.1978) cert. denied 439 U.S. 1046, 99 S.Ct. 722 (1978), upheld the constitutionality of the § 1(c) rates even in view of the rate disparity. See also Johnson v. United States, 422 F.Supp. 958 (N.D.Ind.1976), affirmed per curiam 550 F.2d 1239 (7th Cir.1977), cert. denied 434 U.S. 1012, 98 S.Ct. 725 (1978).

37. I.R.C. § 1(a) rates on a single taxable income of $34,000 equals $5301.50. If the married taxpayers filed separate returns, the total tax would also be $5301.50 since they have equal incomes. I.R.C. § 1(d).

38. Boyter v. Commissioner, 74 T.C. 989 (1980), taxpayers journeyed to Haiti one year and the Dominican Republic the next for their annual government financed divorce vacation.

39. Rev.Rul. 76–255, 1976–2 C.B. 40.

40. Boyter v. Commissioner, supra note 38, added on appeal of the *Boyter* case, the Fourth Circuit remanded the case to the Tax Court for a determination whether the sham transaction doctrine was applicable. 668 F.2d 1382 (4th Cir.1981).

41. I.R.C. (1954) § 221. See Gann, "The Earned Income Deduction: Congress's 1981 Response to the 'Marriage Penalty' Tax," 68 Cornell L.Rev. 468 (1983).

42. See I.R.C. § 221(a)(2).

43. Pub.Law No. 99–514, 99th Cong., 2d Sess. § 131 (1986).

44. They also concluded that there was less discrepancy because of the standard deduction employed in the current law. Sen.Rep. No. 99–313, 99th Cong., 2d Sess. 41 (1986).

45. Cf. I.R.C. § 66 discussed at note 22, supra.

head of household even though legally married.[46] Review the above Joint Committee Staff's comments to determine whether the policies underlying the rate variances are justified. Would it be fairer simply to allow married persons to use the lesser of the Section 1(a) or Section 1(c) rates?

Rate Schedules. The above consideration of classifications leads us to a comparison of the various rate schedules imposed under Section 1 of the Code. Skimming Sections 1(a) through 1(d), and 1(e) which involves estates and trusts, it can be seen that the 28 and 31 percent rates take over at different levels. The schedule of the rates is as follows:

(a) Married individuals filing joint returns and surviving spouses:

If taxable income is:	*The tax is:*
Not over $32,450	15% of taxable income.
Over $32,450 but not over $78,400	$4,867.50, plus 28% of the excess over $32,450.
Over $78,400	$17,733.50, plus 31% of the excess over $78,400.

(b) Heads of households:

Not over $26,050	15% of taxable income.
Over $26,050 but not over $67,200	$3,907.50, plus 28% of the excess over $26,500.
Over $67,200	$15,429.50, plus 31% of the excess over $67,200.

(c) Unmarried individuals (other than surviving spouses and heads of households):

Not over $19,450	15% of taxable income.
Over $19,450, but not over $47,050	$2,917.50, plus 28% of the excess over $19,450.
Over $47,050	$10,645.50, plus 31% of the excess over $47,050.

(d) Married individuals filing separate returns:

Not over $16,225	15% of taxable income.
Over $16,225 but not over $39,200	$2,433.75, plus 28% of the excess over $16,225.
Over $39,200	$8,866.75, plus 31% of the excess over $39,200.

(e) Estates and trusts:

Not over $3,300	15% of taxable income.
Over $3,300 but not over $9,900	$495, plus 28% of the excess over $3,300.
Over $9,900	$2,313, plus 31% of the excess over $9,900.

---

46. I.R.C. §§ 2(c) and 7703(b). See text at note 29, supra.

Indirect Rate Increase. In the 1990 legislation, Congress indirectly increased the tax rates of upper-income noncorporate taxpayers by disallowing some deductions by means of a phase-out of personal exemptions and certain itemized deductions. This deduction disallowance is a further broadening of the tax base to generate revenue to reduce the budget deficit.

In years 1991 through 1995 [47] if a taxpayer's adjusted gross income exceeds a threshold amount, then the total amount of personal exemptions is reduced.[48] The threshold amount is $150,000 for marrieds filing joint returns and surviving spouses, $125,000 for heads of households, $100,000 for unmarrieds not within the above categories, and $75,000 for marrieds filing separately.[49] After 1991, the threshold amount is adjusted for inflation.[50] The amount of reduction is an applicable percentage of the exemption amount [51] and the applicable percentage generally is 2 percentage points for each $2,500 (or fraction thereof) by which the taxpayer's adjusted gross income exceeds the threshold amount.[52] The phase-out does not affect the taxpayer who is allowed to claim an exemption.[53]

For example, assume in 1991 a married couple has two children, they qualify for $8,000 of personal exemptions,[54] and they have $199,000 of adjusted gross income. Their adjusted gross income exceeds the threshold amount of $150,000 by $49,000, and they must reduce their exemptions by 40 percent (2 percent times 20 ($49,000 excess divided by $2,500 or fraction thereof)). Thus, the couple's personal exemptions are reduced by (and taxable income is increased by) $3,200 (40 percent of $8,000) to $4,800.

Along similar lines, in years 1991 through 1995 [55] an individual taxpayer [56] whose adjusted gross income exceeds a threshold amount of $100,000 ($50,000 for marrieds filing separately) [57] is required to reduce most itemized deductions by 3 percent (up to a maximum of 80 percent) of the amount by which adjusted gross income exceeds the threshold amount.[58] Certain itemized deductions (medical expenses, investment interest and wagering losses) are not subject to the reduction.[59] The reduction occurs only after all other limitations on itemized deductions [60] and the threshold amount is adjusted for inflation for years after 1991.[61]

47. I.R.C. § 151(d)(3)(E).

48. I.R.C. § 151(d)(3).

49. I.R.C. § 151(d)(3)(C).

50. I.R.C. § 151(d)(4)(B).

51. I.R.C. § 151(d)(3)(A).

52. I.R.C. § 151(d)(3)(B). For marrieds filing separately, the $2,500 amount is reduced to $1,250. Id. In no case may the phase-out exceed 100 percent. Id.

53. I.R.C. § 151(d)(3)(D). See I.R.C. § 151(c)(2), (d)(2).

54. This assumes no adjustment for inflation in the $2,000 exemption amount after 1989. See I.R.C. § 151(d)(4)(A).

55. I.R.C. § 68(f).

56. Section 68 is inapplicable to estates and trusts. I.R.C. § 68(e).

57. I.R.C. § 68(b)(1).

58. I.R.C. § 68(a).

59. I.R.C. § 68(c).

60. I.R.C. § 68(d).

61. I.R.C. § 68(b)(2).

If an unmarried individual in 1991 had total itemized deductions (which included no medical expenses, investment interest, or wagering losses) of $20,000 after all other limitations on such deductions and if the taxpayer also had $150,000 of adjusted gross income, the individual's itemized deductions would be reduced by 3 percent of $50,000 ($150,000 less $100,000) or $1,500 to $18,500. If the individual's adjusted gross income was $650,000, the itemized deductions would be reduced by 3 percent of $550,000 ($16,500), but the reduction is limited to a maximum of 80 percent of the amount otherwise allowable (80% times $20,000) or $16,000.

Rate Limitation on Net Capital Gains. As a part of the 1986 legislation, Congress raised the maximum rate on net capital gains to equate them to ordinary income.[62] But in 1986 Congress stated that if the rates on ordinary income were subsequently increased to a greater than 28 percent rate, a ceiling of 28 percent should be imposed on net capital gain.[63] Thus when the 1990 legislation imposed a 31 percent maximum rate on ordinary income,[64] the 28 percent ceiling was retained on net capital gains.[65] Under the current taxing scheme net capital gains are taxed as ordinary income unless the income falls into the 31 percent bracket in which event the net capital gains may not be taxed at a greater than 28 percent rate.[66]

The Kiddie Tax. Congress added a special "kiddie tax" in the 1986 legislation, aimed at preventing avoidance tactics of assignment of income to some minors. The rule applies to the net unearned income (generally unearned income in excess of $1,000) of a child who is under the age of 14 at the close of the taxable year.[67] Previously, unearned income attributed to a child as a result of interest from bank accounts or notes, dividends from stocks, and other such unearned income was taxed at the child's applicable tax rate. This section requires net unearned income [68] of a child under the age of 14 to be taxed at the higher of the child's regular rate or the rate at which it would be taxed to the parents if added to their other income.[69] Accordingly, the child's regular tax will not be less than the additional tax that would have been due on the parents' return if the net unearned income had been reported by the parents on their return at their top rate bracket.[70] Net unearned income is the unearned income in excess of $1,000 plus, if the child itemizes deductions, the amount of itemized deductions in excess of $500 connected with the production of the unearned income.[71] The

---

62. See note 4, supra.

63. I.R.C. § 1(j)(1), as enacted by the 1986 Act.

64. I.R.C. § 1(a)–(e).

65. I.R.C. § 1(h).

66. Id. See page 665, supra.

67. I.R.C. § 1(g)(2)(A). The provision is inapplicable if both parents are dead at the close of the taxable year. I.R.C. § 1(g)(2)(B).

68. I.R.C. § 911(d)(2) defines unearned income. I.R.C. § 1(g)(4)(A)(i).

69. I.R.C. § 1(g)(1). The amount of net unearned income so taxed may not exceed the child's taxable income for such year. I.R.C. § 1(g)(4)(B).

70. I.R.C. § 1(g)(3). There is a special allocation rule if more than one child is subject to the rate rule. I.R.C. § 1(g)(3)(B).

71. I.R.C. § 1(g)(4)(A).

source of the underlying property generating the income is of no consequence; nor is the date of the property transfer. Special rules determine which parent's rates apply if the parents are divorced or are married but file separate returns.[72] An elective provision enables the parents of a child having unearned interest and dividend income of less than $5,000 to report such income on the parents' return, thus precluding the need for the child to file a return.[73] If the election is made, the parents must include the child's income in excess of $1,000 in their income for the taxable year, and they must also increase their resulting tax liability by the lesser of $75 or 15 percent of the child's income in excess of $500.[74]

Bracket Creep. In recent years, much attention has been focused on the effect of inflation on the rate structure.[75] To the extent that a taxpayer's increase in income pushes him into a higher tax bracket and is merely a reflection of rising inflation, the taxpayer is left with less real income after taxes than he had before his increase in income. Adjustments for "bracket creep," first introduced in 1981 tax legislation are continued in the 1990 Act for years after 1990.[76] Similar inflation adjustments apply to the personal exemption,[77] the standard deduction,[78] and the adjusted gross income levels at which the limitations on personal exemptions and itemized deductions are phased in.[79]

Tax Tables. In order to provide low-income individual taxpayers who use the standard deduction [80] a simplified method of computing their taxes, the Code has traditionally called for the administrative preparation of tax tables that yield automatic tax determination without arithmetic computation.[81] The tables are in regulations promulgated pursuant to the Code and in the instructions that accompany individual tax returns. These tables do not reflect a further different set of individual rates. Instead, they are designed to yield an instant tax figure, determined under the relevant Section 1 rates.[82] Entering the table for his proper rate classification, a taxpayer finds his tax by reference to his taxable income and total number of personal exemptions. The tables are available only to taxpayers with taxable income less than a ceiling amount (not less than $20,000) to be determined by

72. I.R.C. § 1(g)(5).

See Schmolka, "The Kiddie Tax Under the Tax Reform Act of 1986: A Need for Reform While the Ink Is Still Wet," 11 Rev.Tax'n of Ind. 99 (1987).

73. I.R.C. § 1(g)(7).

74. I.R.C. § 1(g)(7)(B). The latter amount is to account for child's income from $500 to $1,000 that would otherwise be taxed to child at the 15 percent rate.

75. See e.g., Kelly *et al.* "Indexing for Inflation," 31 Tax Lawyer 17 (1978) where the authors quote Lewis Carroll's Red Queen on the problem, "Now here, you see, it takes all the running you can do to keep in the same place. If you want to go

somewhere else, you must run twice as fast as that."

76. I.R.C. § 1(f)(1).

77. I.R.C. § 151(d)(4)(A). This indexing occurs only in years after 1989. Id.

78. I.R.C. § 63(c)(4).

79. I.R.C. §§ 151(d)(4)(A), 68(b)(2).

80. I.R.C. § 3(a)(1)(A). But see I.R.C. § 3(a)(3) allowing the Commissioner to require use of the tables by persons who itemize.

81. I.R.C. § 3.

82. Some rounding off of tax liability occurs because of the bracket approach in the tables.

the Secretary.[83]   Use of the tables, no longer optional, is required of the taxpayers for whom they are available.[84]

Filing Requirement.   Related to tax rates and classifications is the Section 6012 requirement to file an income tax return.   Most persons are required to file, but, not all.   As a result of the standard deduction and personal exemptions, persons with low levels of gross income may automatically have zero taxable income.[85]   For example, if a married couple filed a joint return in 1988, they automatically got a $5,000 standard deduction and $3,900 in personal exemptions.   If their gross income did not exceed $8,900 they had no taxable income and no tax liability.   Section 6012 relieved them from the burden of even having to file a tax return.   The Service annually provides information indicating the levels of gross income at which taxpayers in varying classifications are required to file returns.[86]

Corporate Taxpayers.   Although this book is concerned with the taxation of noncorporate taxpayers, most of the fundamental principles and many of the Code sections considered apply to corporate taxpayers as well.   Except for special rules, you should be able to compute the taxable income of a corporation.   In conjunction with such computation, examine Section 11 which provides the tax rates applicable to corporations.   Like noncorporate rates, corporate rates were reduced under the 1986 legislation.   The top corporate rate was reduced from 46 percent to 34 percent, imposed by way of a three step graduated rate table.[87]   For corporate taxable income in excess of $100,000, an additional 5 percent surtax applies to amounts taxed below the 34 percent rates.   The surtax applies until the surtax collects $11,750,[88] and it applies a flat 34 percent tax rate.[89]

PROBLEMS

1.   Taxpayer is a calendar year taxpayer.   In each of the following subparts you are to compute his tax liability (before credits) assuming he has $100,000 of taxable income in 1991 (when no inflation occurs— see § 1(f)(1)).

(a)   Taxpayer is unmarried and has no special status.

(b)   On December 31 of the current year he married Wife, a calendar year taxpayer who has no income for the year, and they file a joint return.

83.   I.R.C. § 3(a)(1)(B) and (2).

84.   I.R.C. § 3(a)(1).

85.   This would not be so if the taxpayer were the dependent of another taxpayer. Cf. I.R.C. §§ 63(c)(5) and 151(d)(2).

86.   See the Instructions for Form 1040.

87.   Corporate rates are not indexed for inflation.

88.   I.R.C. § 11(b).   The amount is equal to a 19 percent benefit on the first $50,000

of taxable income and a 9 percent benefit on the next $25,000 of taxable income;   19 percent of $50,000 ($9,500) plus 9 percent of $25,000 ($2,250) equals the magic $11,750 amount.

89.   The surtax is similar to the individual 5% surtax applicable to noncorporate taxpayers from 1987 through 1990.   See note 12, supra.

(c) Taxpayer was married and two minor children supported by him lived with him and Wife, but Wife, who had no income in the year, died on January 15 of the current year.

(d) Same as (c), above, except that Wife died on December 31 of the prior year.

(e) Same as (c), above, except that Wife died on December 31, three years earlier.

(f) Same as (c), above, except that Taxpayer remarried on December 31 of the current year and he and New Wife file separate returns for the current year.

2. Husband and Wife, both under 65 and with good eyesight, have two dependent children. In 1991 (when no inflation occurs), they file a joint return. They have no § 62 deductions. Using the rate tables and assuming the exemption amount is $2,000 and the standard deduction for marrieds filing jointly is $5,000, compute their tax liability before credits if:

(a) They have $220,000 of gross income, $2,000 in state property taxes and $6,500 in miscellaneous employee business expenses.

(b) They have $220,000 of gross income, $3,000 in state income taxes and $30,600 in miscellaneous employee business expenses.

(c) The facts are the same as in (b), above, except that the $220,000 of gross income includes $100,000 of net capital gain.

3. Joe, age 12, is the beneficiary of a trust. In 1991, the trust pays him $5,000 of dividend income. His parents, whose 1991 taxable income is $40,000, file a joint return, claiming Joe as a dependent. Disregarding any cost of living adjustments in any year after 1988, what are the tax consequences of each of the following to Joe in 1991?

(a) The trust income is Joe's only income.

(b) In addition to the trust income of $5,000, Joe also earns $5,000 washing cars.

(c) Same as (a), above, except that Joe is 15 years of age.

(d) Same as (a), above, except that Joe's older sister, Jane, age 13, also receives $5,000 from the trust.

(e) Same as (a), above, except Joe's itemized deductions directly connected with the production of the trust income are $800.

B. CREDITS AGAINST TAX *

Internal Revenue Code: See Sections 21 through 53.

---

* See Hoff, "The Appropriate Role for Tax Credits in an Income Tax System," 35 Tax Lawyer 339 (1983); Weidenbaum, "Shifting from Income Tax Deductions to Credits," 51 Taxes 462 (1973).

The amount that must be paid by the taxpayer when she files her income tax return may be less than her computed tax liability for the year, because the potential payment is often reduced by credits against the tax. A credit is more advantageous to the taxpayer than a deduction because it reduces tax liability dollar-for-dollar, whereas a deduction reduces only taxable income with a corresponding but smaller reduction in tax liability. Tax legislation at one time reflected some movement away from deductions toward credits, possibly because of a policy decision that credits are fairer; however, with the adoption of modified flat tax rates, further movement from deductions to credits appears less likely. Deductions effect greater tax savings as the taxpayer's tax rate increases;[1] in contrast, credits have the same dollar saving for all taxpayers who otherwise would pay tax, regardless of their tax brackets.

Recent tax legislation has restructured the credit provisions of the Code, assigning the credits to five groups. Four groups of credits are said to be "nonrefundable;" even if they exceed the amount of tax computed, they do not generate a refund. They are personal credits, general business credits, certain miscellaneous credits, and the minimum tax credit. The fifth group of credits are "refundable" in the sense that the amount by which they exceed the tax liability computed may be refunded to the taxpayer. Within the credit provisions themselves, the order in which they are consumed may be important. It is obviously best that refundable credits be consumed last, after allowance of other credits, because this will maximize the amount of any refund.[2] The order in which the four classifications of nonrefundable credits are consumed is also significant, although not discretionary, because some nonrefundable credits qualify for carryovers to the extent they are not used in the year in which they arise. The statute fixes the pecking order of nonrefundable credits by providing that credit provisions are to be used to reduce tax liability in the order in which they appear in the Code. We consider the nonrefundable credits in their order in the Code too, and will consider refundable credits last.

In considering the credit calculations, the taxpayer must also take into consideration the passive loss limitation under Section 469[3] as it applies to some of the credits prior to considering the limitations above. In general, a taxpayer will not be allowed a reduction in tax liability for any "passive activity credit."[4] The "passive activity credit" is defined as the amount by which the sum of all credits from passive activities[5] exceed the regular tax liability[6] allocable to all the taxpayer's passive activities for the taxable year.[7] Thus, the amount of credits from passive activities is generally limited to the tax liability generated

---

1. See page 455, supra.

2. I.R.C. § 6401(b)(1). Cf. I.R.C. § 35.

3. See page 503, supra.

4. I.R.C. § 469(a)(1)(B).

5. I.R.C. § 469(d)(2)(A). See I.R.C. §§ 27(b), 28, 29, 38 (which includes

§§ 40(a), 41(a), 42(a), 43(a), 44(a), 46, and 51(a)).

6. See I.R.C. § 26(b).

7. I.R.C. § 469(d)(2). But see I.R.C. § 469(i) and (j)(4) for an exception for certain real estate activities.

by these passive activities; and if there are excess passive activity losses (in excess of income) for the year, the taxpayer will generally have no current benefit from the credits produced by the passive activities.[8] The entire amount of any disallowed credit may be carried forward indefinitely, but not carried back.[9]

A quick glimpse at Part IV of the Code (Sections 21 through 53) indicates that the credit sections are extremely detailed. The objective here, in most instances, is to present the general picture of the types of expenditures that qualify for the credits and to indicate how the various credits interrelate. As a student moves from tax adolescence to tax maturity he must seek the ability to distill from a new tax statute the messages needed to deal with a new tax problem. In this process an initial comprehension of the big picture is always a necessary beginning.

1. NONREFUNDABLE PERSONAL CREDITS

The nonrefundable personal credits are used first to reduce tax payable for a taxable year. The tax liability that may be so discharged is, generally, one's regular income tax liability. Liability for various special taxes beyond the scope of this course is disregarded in the computation.[10] The credits that fall into this classification are as follows:

Section 21: Credit for Dependent Care Expenses. This credit is allowed for "employment related expenses,"[11] that are incurred for household services or day care of a "qualifying individual,"[12] if incurred to enable the taxpayer to be gainfully employed.[13] Generally, a "qualifying individual" is a dependent relative of the taxpayer under the age of 13 or a mentally or physically handicapped dependent or spouse of the taxpayer.[14] To qualify for the credit, the taxpayer or his spouse[15] must furnish more than one-half the cost of maintaining a household in which one or more qualifying individuals reside.[16] The

8. There was a phase-in of the credit disallowance. The disallowance is 35 percent of the passive activity credit disallowance in 1987, 60 percent in 1988, 80 percent in 1989, 90 percent in 1990, and 100 percent after 1990. I.R.C. § 469(m).

9. I.R.C. § 469(b).

10. I.R.C. § 26(b)(2). See also § 55(c) for the relationship of credits to the alternative minimum tax. See page 997, infra; cf. I.R.C. § 26(a).

11. I.R.C. § 21(b)(2). Payments to relatives, including grandparents, may qualify as employment related expenses, subject to some § 21(e)(6) limitations.

12. I.R.C. § 21(b)(1). In 1981 Congress provided an exclusion from gross income for certain employer-provided dependent care services which, if paid for by the employee, would be considered employment

related expenses under § 21(b)(2). I.R.C. § 129. Amounts excluded under § 129 are ineligible for the credit under § 21. I.R.C. § 129(e)(7).

13. Expenses for care outside the home may be taken into account only for dependents under the age of 13 or dependents who regularly spend at least 8 hours each day in the taxpayer's household. I.R.C. § 21(b)(1)(A), (2)(B).

14. I.R.C. § 21(b)(1).

15. If married, the taxpayer must file a joint return with his spouse. I.R.C. § 21(e)(2); but see § 21(e)(4).

16. I.R.C. § 21(a)(1) and (e)(1). If divorced parents provide over one half of the support of a qualifying child and they have custody over him for more than one-half of the year, then the parent who has custody

credit is equal to an "applicable percentage," [17] which may not exceed 30 percent, of the taxpayer's employment-related expenses; [18] the employment-related expenses cannot exceed $2400 if there is one qualifying individual in the taxpayer's household, and $4800 if there are two or more such individuals.[19] Thus, as the applicable percentage never exceeds 30 percent, the credit may never exceed $720 or $1,440, respectively.

Section 22: Credit for the Elderly and Disabled. This credit is designed to provide tax relief to low and middle income elderly and retired disabled persons. The credit is the "section 22 amount," basically $5000, $7500, or $3750, depending on marital status,[20] for persons over age 64 and for retired persons who are disabled. That amount is intricately reduced by some social security, retirement, pension, and disability benefits.[21] In addition, the amount of the credit is phased out as an elderly or disabled person's adjusted gross income exceeds stipulated amounts, thus restricting the benefits of the credit to low and middle income elderly and disabled persons.[22]

Section 25: Credit for Interest on Certain Home Mortgages. This credit is allowed to low income taxpayers for a portion of their interest payments on mortgages related to their principal residence.[23] It applies only if the state in which they are located elects not fully to utilize its authority to issue tax-exempt mortgage subsidy bonds.[24] There are lots of requirements for states to meet; if met, a qualifying homeowner in the state may claim a credit up to a maximum of $2,000.[25] But the taxpayer is not permitted a double benefit; any interest qualifying for the credit is not deductible under Section 163(a).[26] This credit terminates after 1991.[27] The personal credits in Sections 21, 22 and 25 are

for the greater portion of the year is entitled to the credit. I.R.C. § 21(e)(5).

17. The applicable percentage is 30%, reduced (but not below 20%) by one percentage point for each $2,000 (or fraction thereof) by which the taxpayer's adjusted gross income exceeds $10,000. I.R.C. § 21(a)(2). Thus the applicable percentage levels off at 20% when the taxpayer's adjusted gross income exceeds $28,000.

18. See I.R.C. § 21(d) generally limiting such expenses to the amount of the taxpayer's earned income.

19. I.R.C. § 21(c).

20. See I.R.C. § 22(c)(2). The initial § 22 amount is as follows: single individuals are subject to a $5000 maximum as are married persons filing joint returns where only one has reached age 65. Married persons filing jointly if both have reached age 65 have a $7500 maximum, and there is a $3750 limit on married persons filing separately.

21. I.R.C. § 22(c)(3).

22. I.R.C. § 22(d)(1). The phase-out is $1 for each $2 of adjusted gross income in excess of $7500 for a single person, in excess of $10,000 for married persons filing jointly and in excess of $5000 for married persons filing separately. In general, the credit is fully phased out; (1) for a single person with adjusted gross income of $17,500; (2) for married persons filing jointly if both spouses are either over 65 or disabled with adjusted gross income of $25,000 ($20,000 if only one is qualified); and (3) for a married person filing separately with adjusted gross income of $12,500.

23. I.R.C. § 25(b)(2).

24. I.R.C. § 25(c)(2). This attempt to tease the states away from issuing mortgage subsidy bonds appears more intended as a restriction on the well-heeled tax-exempt investor than on the low-income home purchaser.

25. I.R.C. § 25(a)(2).

26. I.R.C. § 163(g).

27. I.R.C. § 25(h).

nonrefundable, but an excess Section 25 credit may be carried forward for three years.[28]

2. MISCELLANEOUS NONREFUNDABLE CREDITS

A second group of provisions (Sections 27 through 29) contains some miscellaneous credits that reduce the amount of tax to be paid (again, according to their numerical order in the Code), but they are nonrefundable and they do not qualify for any carryover. The credits in this group are:

Section 27: The Foreign Tax Credit. Income taxes imposed by foreign countries may be deducted under Section 164(a)(3) by the one who has paid the taxes. However, the taxpayer has an alternative of claiming foreign taxes as a credit.[29] The rules applicable to the credit are found in Section 901, which is modified by Section 904(a), in general limiting the amount of foreign tax qualifying for the credit to the amount equal to the United States tax liability multiplied by the ratio of the taxpayer's foreign source taxable income over his entire taxable income. Obviously the deduction and credit cannot both be claimed.[30] Generally, the credit provision will be more advantageous. Why?

Section 28: Clinical Testing of Certain Drugs. This provision allows a 50 percent credit for expenses incurred and not defrayed by grant or otherwise for clinical testing of drugs for rare diseases and conditions.[31]

Section 29: Credit for Producing Fuel From a Nonconventional Source. During the energy crisis Congress enacted several provisions designed to encourage the conservation of existing fuel supplies and the development of alternative energy sources. This energy crisis provision encourages taxpayers to develop alternative energy sources, such as shale oil, biomass fuel, coal-derived synthetic fuels, wood fuels, and steam-produced agricultural byproduct fuels.[32]

3. THE NONREFUNDABLE GENERAL BUSINESS CREDIT

The single "general business" credit allowed by Section 38 is a combination of credits that to the extent that they were in existence at the time, were treated separately prior to 1984. Each of the credits is initially computed separately and then they are combined[33] and examined for special limitations and carryovers.

28. I.R.C. § 25(e)(1).

29. I.R.C. §§ 27 and 901(a). See Isenbergh, "The Foreign Tax Credit: Royalties, Subsidies, and Creditable Taxes," 39 Tax L.Rev. 227 (1984).

30. I.R.C. § 275(a)(4). See I.R.C. § 901(a).

31. See I.R.C. § 28(a), (d)(1). No deduction is allowed to the extent there is a § 28

credit. I.R.C. § 280C(b). This credit expires after 1991. I.R.C. § 28(e). See Richardson, "The Orphan Drug Credit: An Inadequate Response to an Ill–Defined Problem," 6 Amer.J.Tax Pol. 135 (1987).

32. I.R.C. § 29(c). This credit applies to expenditures made prior to 1993. I.R.C. § 29(f).

33. I.R.C. § 38(b).

The general business credit reduces tax required to be paid [34] after applying the other nonrefundable credits [35] but prior to the utilization of the refundable credits.[36] Generally, the ceiling on the credit is $25,000 of tax liability after the credits allowed by Sections 21 through 29 plus 75 percent of such tax liability in excess of $25,000.[37] If the general business credit for the year is not fully utilized because of the above limitation, any unused portion may be carried back three years and forward fifteen years.[38] The credits that make up the general business credit are:

Section 40: The Alcohol Fuels Credit. This credit is another example of congressional policy on energy; it is aimed at encouraging the production of gasohol and ethanol. Under it taxpayers are allowed a credit for alcohol used as a fuel or combined in a mixture for fuel or for sale as fuel and for the production of ethanol.[39] As a price for the credit, Section 87 requires the taxpayer to include the amount of the credit in gross income.

Section 41: Credit for Increasing Research Activities. Congress has provided a credit to stimulate private sector research and development activities.[40] Section 41(a) allows a credit for 20 percent of a taxpayer's "qualified research expenses" [41] in the current year in excess, generally, of the average of such expenses over a four year base period [42] and a credit for 20 percent of qualifying "basic research payments" in excess of a special base amount.[43] The section provides definitions, limitations [44] and rules with respect to the interrelationship of the two 20 percent amounts.[45]

Section 42: The Low Income Housing Credit. This credit which is even more technical than the research activities credit, is considered in conjunction with the depreciation of real estate in Chapter 22A3.[46]

34. See I.R.C. § 26(b) and note 10, supra.

35. I.R.C. § 38(c)(1), last sentence. See I.R.C. §§ 21–29.

36. I.R.C. § 38(c)(1). See I.R.C. §§ 31–35.

37. I.R.C. § 38(c)(1). If the alternative minimum tax is applicable (see Chapter 27C, infra), there is a more complicated computation of the general business credit. Id.

38. I.R.C. § 39 provides that carrybacks and carryovers to the current year are combined with the current year's general business credit and *all* such amounts are used (i.e. consumed) to wipe out tax liability on a first-in, first-used basis. See I.R.C. § 38(a).

39. I.R.C. § 40(a).

40. The credit applies to expenditures made before January 1, 1992. I.R.C. § 41(h)(1).

41. I.R.C. § 41(b) and (c).

42. I.R.C. § 41(c). Base period research expenses are generally the average amount of qualified research expenses incurred by the taxpayer over the immediately preceding four years, but not less than 50 percent of the expenditures for the current year.

43. I.R.C. § 41(e)(1)(A). Basic research payments are essentially payments by a corporation to some third party. I.R.C. § 41(e)(2). The base period amount is defined in § 41(e)(3)–(6). See also I.R.C. § 41(e)(7).

44. See especially I.R.C. § 41(d)-(f).

45. I.R.C. § 41(e)(7)(C).

46. See page 768, supra.

Section 43: Enhanced Oil Recovery Credit. This credit is 15 percent of a taxpayer's "qualified enhanced oil recovery costs" in a year.[47] Such costs include various exploration and production costs incurred in domestic oil projects.[48] No deduction, basis increase, or other credit is allowed for the same expense or expenditure.[49]

Section 44: The Credit for Expenditures to Provide Access to Disabled Individuals. This section allows an eligible small business [50] a credit for 50% of eligible access expenditures [51] incurred in a year in excess of $250 and up to $10,250.[52] The credit is allowed for expenditures incurred to make a business accessible to disabled persons.[53] No deduction, basis increase, or other credit is allowed to the extent a disabled access credit is allowed.[54]

Section 46: The Investment Credit. As discussed briefly in Chapter 22, the "regular investment credit" that was applicable primarily to depreciable personal property was repealed by the 1986 legislation.[55] However, the investment credit applies to other types of investments. Costs incurred on rehabilitation of old buildings, expenditures for certain energy property, and certain costs incurred in reforestation still qualify for a varying-percentage investment credit.[56] The rehabilitation credit, equal to 10 or 20 percent of certain costs, was considered in conjunction with depreciation of real property [57]. The energy credit allows a 10 percent credit [58] for the cost of certain energy property [59] placed in service during the year.[60] The reforestation credit is a 10 percent credit for the amortizable basis of qualified timber property acquired during the year.[61]

Section 49 adds an "at-risk" limitation to the amount of the overall investment credit [62] similar to the Section 465 limitation on business loss deductions.[63] The investment credit at-risk limitations apply to the same business activities as are covered by Section 465.[64] Generally, the amount subject to the credit is determined by using rules similar to Section 465,[65] and the amount does not include amounts protected against loss through nonrecourse financing, guarantees, or other agree-

47. I.R.C. § 43(a). The credit is phased-out if crude oil prices exceeds certain amounts. I.R.C. § 43(b).

48. I.R.C. § 43(c).

49. I.R.C. § 43(d). A taxpayer may elect to make the credit inapplicable in any year. I.R.C. § 43(e).

50. An eligible small business is one which in the prior year had gross receipts of less than $1 million or not more than 30 full time employees. I.R.C. § 44(b).

51. I.R.C. § 44(c).

52. I.R.C. § 44(a). Thus the maximum credit in any year is $5,000.

53. Examples of such expenditures are found in § 44(c)(2).

54. I.R.C. § 44(d)(7).

55. See page 764, supra.

56. I.R.C. § 46.

57. I.R.C. § 47. See page 768, supra.

58. I.R.C. § 48(a)(2)(A).

59. I.R.C. § 48(a)(3).

60. I.R.C. § 48(a)(1).

61. I.R.C. § 48(b). See I.R.C. § 194.

62. See I.R.C. § 49(a)(1)(C).

63. See pages 492–494, supra.

64. I.R.C. § 49(a)(1)(B)(ii).

65. I.R.C. § 49(a)(1).

ments or arrangements.[66] There are also special rules for increases and decreases in such nonrecourse financing.[67]

Section 50 adds further special rules applicable to the investment credit. These include a recapture of a portion of the credit if the property is disposed of within 5 full years of being placed in service [68] and a reduction in the adjusted basis of property qualifying for the credit.[69]

Section 51: The Targeted Jobs Credit. This credit is provided in a congressional attempt to stimulate the hiring of members of certain designated groups,[70] called "disadvantaged", such as welfare recipients, economically subnormal Vietnam-era veterans, and low income youths, to lead them from the welfare rolls to economic independence. The credit provision is complex and applies to a percentage of a portion of wages paid to qualified employees in their first two years of employment.[71] It expires for workers commencing work after 1991.[72]

4. THE NONREFUNDABLE MINIMUM TAX CREDIT

Section 53: Credit for Prior Minimum Tax Liability. In the next subpart of this chapter, we consider the Alternative Minimum Tax (AMT). If a taxpayer is subject to the AMT for years after 1986, a credit for some of the tax is allowed in subsequent years [73] subject, of course, to some technical rules. Only a part of the prior year's AMT liability qualifies for the credit.[74] The credit is a nonrefundable credit which is computed only after taking into account all other nonrefundable credits.[75] It is allowed in any year only to the extent that regular tax liability less other nonrefundable credits for that year exceed that year's tentative minimum tax.[76] The carryover is for an unlimited period.[77]

5. REFUNDABLE CREDITS

Sections 31 through 35 contain a group of credits which are considered only after all other credits. They not only reduce tax liability after it has been reduced by the other credits, but they can also generate a tax refund. Some permit repayment of prepayments of tax

---

66. I.R.C. § 49(a)(1)(D)(iii).

67. I.R.C. § 49(a)(2), (b).

68. I.R.C. § 50(a).

69. I.R.C. § 50(c).

70. See I.R.C. § 51(d).

71. The targeted jobs credit is generally applicable to 40% of the first $6000 of "qualified first year wages". See I.R.C. § 51(a), (b), and (i).

72. I.R.C. § 51(c)(4). No deduction is allowed to the extent there is a § 51 credit if the employee satisfies a minimum employment period. I.R.C. § 280C(a).

73. I.R.C. § 53(a).

74. See, i.e., I.R.C. § 53(d)(1)(B). Essentially this rule limits the amount of credit to the amount of AMT attributable to tax preferences which are deferral preferences as opposed to permanent exclusion preferences. See page 997, infra.

75. I.R.C. § 53(c)(1).

76. I.R.C. § 53(c)(2).

77. I.R.C. § 53(b). See I.R.C. §§ 53(d)(2) and 55(c).

so that the refund is in the nature of a deposit recovery. Others are more generous. The credits within this classification are:

Section 31: Credit for Withholding on Wages. The most widely applicable credit provision is Section 31. It provides a credit for tax withheld by an employer.[78] This credit simply recognizes that such withholding is in the nature of a prepayment of tax.[79] The withholding requirements originated in the Current Tax Payment Act of 1943. An initial effect was a limited acceleration of revenue collections in a time of need during World War II. Their continuing function is to facilitate collection. One wonders whether the current broadly based income tax, even with its recently reduced rates, could be administered if all payments were to be made by the taxpayer only at the end of the year.

Section 3402(a) requires an employer to act as a tax collector and withhold from an employee an amount of tax generally based upon the employee's wages, exemptions, and tax classification. The Regulations contain tables[80] to guide employers in determining the amount to withhold, and the employer is personally liable for these amounts just as if it were tax imposed on him.[81] The tax applies only if there is an employment relationship[82] and is imposed on "wages"[83] which are broadly defined.[84] Under statutory changes made in 1969, an employer has alternative methods of determining the amount of tax to be withheld[85] and, if an employee certifies he had no tax liability for the prior year and expects to have none in the current year, he is exempt from withholding.[86]

A second part of the Current Tax Payment Act of 1943 provided for the payment of estimated tax by persons who were not wage earners or by wage earners with outside income.[87] Such payments are still generally required;[88] and, if required they are made on a quarterly basis; for most calendar year taxpayers the due dates are April 15, June 15, September 15, and January 15.[89] There are penalties for failure to pay the estimated tax.[90] Estimated tax payments are similar to withholding of taxes on wages because they also constitute a prepayment of tax. For that reason the Service treats them the same as the Section 31 credit on Form 1040.[91]

78. I.R.C. § 3402.

79. Cf. I.R.C. § 6401(b).

80. Reg. § 31.3402(b)–1 directs employers to the withholding tables contained in Circular E (Employer's Tax Guide).

81. I.R.C. § 3403.

82. See Reg. § 31.3401(c)–1.

83. I.R.C. § 3402(a)

84. See I.R.C. § 3401(a) and (f).

85. E.g., I.R.C. § 3402(c).

86. I.R.C. § 3402(n). See also § 3402(m), reducing amounts to be withheld in some circumstances.

87. See I.R.C. §§ 6315 and 6654.

88. See I.R.C. § 6654(e)(1) which protects taxpayers from penalties for failure to pay small amounts of estimated tax.

89. I.R.C. § 6654(c). The amount of required payments is determined under § 6654(d).

90. I.R.C. § 6654(a).

91. Technically, overpayment of estimated taxes is an overpayment of tax for which a credit is provided under I.R.C. § 35, considered infra. See I.R.C. §§ 6315 and 6401.

An excessive amount withheld for social security taxes is also treated as if it were withheld as income tax and thus qualifies for the Section 31 credit.[92] Excessive withholding often occurs when an individual changes jobs during the year and withholding in the aggregate by two or more employers exceeds amounts required to be withheld.

Section 32. Earned Income Credit. Section 32 allows a credit on "earned income"[93] to "eligible individuals."[94] In order to qualify for the credit, a taxpayer must have at least one "qualifying child."[95] The credit is a percentage[96] of earned income up to a flat dollar amount.[97] The credit is, however, phased out by a percentage of the amount by which the greater of earned income or adjusted gross income of the taxpayer exceeds a flat dollar amount.[98] The credit has recently been expanded to include a supplemental credit for health insurance premiums[99] and for a young child.[100] Subsection 32(f) directs the Service to issue tables to aid a taxpayer in determining the amount of the credit. An eligible individual may elect to receive advance payments of the credit from his employer.[101]

Section 33: Credit for Withholding on Nonresident Aliens and Foreign Corporations. Principles similar to those under Section 31 apply to withholding on income of nonresident aliens and foreign corporations.[102]

Section 34: Credit for Certain Uses of Gasoline and Special Fuels. This credit is allowed to the ultimate purchaser of gasoline and other fuels for the manufacturer's excise tax on such fuels where the fuel is used on a farm, for other non-highway purposes, by local transit systems, by the operators of intercity, local or school buses for nontaxable purposes, or for diesel-powered vehicles.[103]

Section 35: Credit for Overpayment of Tax. A refund is allowed for any overpayment of tax.[104]

92. I.R.C. § 31(b).

93. I.R.C. § 32(c)(2).

94. I.R.C. § 32(c)(1).

95. Id. The term qualifying child is defined in § 32(c)(3) and it involves relationship, residency and age tests. Id.

96. I.R.C. § 32(b)(1)(C). The percentage is increased if there is more than one qualifying child and is increased for future years. Id.

97. I.R.C. § 32(b)(1)(A). The original amount was $5,714, but it is adjusted for post–1984 inflation. I.R.C. § 32(i). The amount in 1990 was $6,810.

98. I.R.C. § 32(b)(1)(B). The original flat dollar amount was $9,000, but it is adjusted for post–1984 inflation. I.R.C. § 32(i). The amount in 1990 was $10,730. The phase-out percentage is increased if there is more than one qualifying child and is increased in future years. I.R.C. § 32(b) (1)(C).

99. I.R.C. § 32(a)(2), (b)(2). To qualify for this supplemental credit, the taxpayer must have at least one qualifying child. I.R.C. § 32(b)(2)(B)(ii). A taxpayer must reduce his § 213 medical expense deduction by any credit allowed for health insurance under § 32. I.R.C. § 213(f).

100. I.R.C. § 32(b)(1)(D).

101. See I.R.C. §§ 32(g) and 3507. The election allows employers to reduce their liability for income tax withholding and FICA taxes for the aggregate amount of advance payments made to employees in any pay period.

102. See I.R.C. § 1441 et seq.

103. I.R.C. § 34(a). See I.R.C. §§ 6420, 6421 and 6427.

104. See I.R.C. § 6401 and Chapter 29, infra.

PROBLEM

Taxpayer has $100,000 of tax liability in the current year prior to consideration of certain credits. None of the credits is subject to the passive activity credit limitation. Taxpayer is not subject to the alternative minimum tax. Determine tax payable or refundable after the credits and whether he is allowed any carrybacks or carryovers of credits. The credits are:

§ 21	Child care credit	$ 500
§ 27	Foreign tax credit	14,500
§ 31	Withholding credit	20,000
§ 41	Research credit	2,000
§ 46	Investment credit for re-habilitation expenses	80,000

C. THE ALTERNATIVE MINIMUM TAX

Internal Revenue Code: Sections 55; 56(a)(1), (2), (4), (6), and (7); (b)(1) and (3); 57(a)(5), (6) and (7); 58(b).

Prior to 1969, Congress was concerned that some taxpayers had been taking advantage of various relief provisions, not improperly or illegally, largely or entirely to avoid tax, even though they had thousands or even hundreds of thousands of dollars of gross income. To remedy an apparent abuse of relief provisions, Congress in 1969 introduced a special treatment of certain tax-favored items of income and deductions by imposing a "Minimum Tax for Tax Preferences." Separate minimum taxes were imposed for corporate and non-corporate taxpayers. Over the years Congress has sought to refine its attack on the tax, now known as the alternative minimum tax (AMT), and the 1990 legislation continued this effort. As a result of the Section 1 rate reductions since 1969 and an extension of the base for the alternative minimum tax in the 1986 legislation, it is likely that many more individuals will be subject to the alternative minimum tax. Thus, today even more than in the past, both noncorporate and corporate taxpayers and their tax advisors must be conscious of this lurking exaction.

Computation of noncorporate alternative minimum tax liability depends initially upon a determination of "alternative minimum taxable income" (AMTI). AMTI, generally speaking, is the taxpayer's regular taxable income with certain adjustments called for in Sections 56 and 58 and the addition of various so-called "tax preference" items that are listed in Section 57. In general, the AMTI amount is reduced by an exemption, and the balance is taxed at a flat 24 percent rate.[1] The approach is essentially an either/or one. When the alternative

----

1. The statute uses the term "tentative minimum tax." See I.R.C. § 55(a)(1) and (b). We choose to refer to it as the alternative minimum tax.

minimum tax is larger than tax computed in the regular way, the alternative minimum tax in essence becomes *the* tax for the year.

Sections 56 and 58 Adjustments.   Sections 56 and 58 call for various adjustments to be made to regular taxable income in computing AMTI.   They are so far-reaching they require an essential redetermination of taxable income.   Some of the adjustments involve complex tax areas beyond the scope of this course; [2] some others, in more familiar territory, are summarized below.

Depreciation.   A taxpayer owning depreciable property placed in service after 1986 will generally be required to keep two sets of books for depreciation of the property, the first set for regular taxable income [3] and a second set for the AMTI computation.   In the long run, the total depreciation amount is the same;   however, the AMTI deduction, which is computed using the alternative depreciation system of Section 168(g), is generally spread over a longer life than the regular depreciation deduction, resulting in smaller amounts of depreciation deductions in the early years of the asset's use.   If property is tangible personal property that is depreciated using the 200 percent or 150 percent declining balance method [4] for regular taxable income, the 150 percent declining balance method and a longer useful life [5] must generally be used in computing AMTI.[6]   Real and personal property depreciated under the straight-line method for regular taxable income [7] is depreciated again using the straight-line method but with a longer useful life in determining AMTI.[8]   All post–1986 property of the taxpayer is subject to the different depreciation methods, and the *net* difference in total depreciation on *all* such property is an increase or decrease to regular tax taxable income in computing AMTI.[9]

For example, if Taxpayer owns a nonresidential building placed in service after 1986 which cost $315,000, her Section 168 depreciation (disregarding the mid-month convention and in the absence of an election to use the alternative depreciation system) would be computed using a 31.5 year life and the straight-line method, and the amount of annual depreciation would be $10,000.[10]   But in computing AMTI, Taxpayer would use a forty-year life under the alternative depreciation straight-line method and the depreciation amount would be only $7,875 each year.   Thus there would be a $2,125 increase ($10,000 less $7,875) to regular taxable income in computing the AMTI.[11]   If Taxpayer

---

2.   See, i.e., I.R.C. §§ 56(a)(2), (5) and (8), (b)(2);   58(a) and (c).

3.   See Chapter 22A, supra.

4.   I.R.C. § 168(b)(1) and (2).

5.   But see I.R.C. § 56(a)(1)(B).

6.   I.R.C. § 56(a)(1)(A).

7.   I.R.C. § 168(b)(3).

8.   I.R.C. § 56(a)(1)(A)(i).

9.   A similar rule applies to the write off of post-1986 pollution control facilities to which I.R.C. 169 applies.   I.R.C. § 56(a)(5).

10.   I.R.C. § 168(b)(3) and (c)(1).   See problem 1(b) at page 769, supra.

11.   However, if this continues to be taxpayer's only piece of depreciable property and she holds it over 32 years, there would be a $7,875 *decrease* from her regular taxable income in computing her AMTI in years 33 through 40.

owned more than one piece of such depreciable property, there would be a net adjustment from each in computing her AMTI.

As post–1986 property generally is depreciated using a depreciation method under the AMT different from that under the regular tax, its adjusted basis for AMT purposes is also different from its adjusted basis for the regular tax.[12] The adjusted basis will be larger. Thus if such property is sold prior to the expiration of its AMT life, the amount of gain included in gross income under the AMTI is generally smaller than the gain under the regular tax. For example, in the hypothetical above, if Taxpayer held the building for 3 years and sold it at its original $315,000 cost, disregarding any mid-month convention, taxpayer would have a $30,000 gain in computing regular taxable income, but only a $23,625 gain in computing AMTI.

The above rules are inapplicable to property placed in service prior to 1987. However, the depreciation of pre–1987 property may result in a Section 57 tax preference item.[13]

Long-Term Contracts. A taxpayer using a long-term contract method of accounting [14] for any contract entered into after February 28, 1986 is required to use the percentage-of-completion method of accounting in computing AMTI.[15]

Net Operating Losses. The Section 172 net operating loss deduction under the regular tax,[16] is essentially recomputed under the AMTI to take account of the differences in losses as a result of the Section 56 through 58 adjustments.[17] In addition, any carryover of the recomputed net operating loss amount generally reduces AMTI by only 90 percent in a carryover year (as opposed to a 100 percent reduction of regular taxable income).[18] The general effect of this rule on net operating losses is to allow fewer losses and carryovers in computing AMTI than in computing regular taxable income.

Installment Sales of Section 1221(1) Property. Recall that dealer dispositions generally do not qualify for installment sale treatment.[19] However, some Section 1221(1) property does qualify for such Section 453 treatment [20] under the regular tax. With one minor exception,[21] installment sale treatment is unavailable to any Section 1221(1) property under the AMT.[22] As a result, the full amount of gain on such property is included in AMTI in the year of sale, resulting in a corresponding increase in AMTI over regular taxable income.

Itemized Deductions. Only limited itemized deductions are allowed in the computation of AMTI and no standard deduction or personal

---

12. I.R.C. § 56(a)(7).

13. See the text at note 43, infra.

14. See I.R.C. § 460(e) and page 560, supra.

15. I.R.C. § 56(a)(3). See I.R.C. § 460(b).

16. See page 654, supra.

17. I.R.C. § 56(a)(4) and (d)(2).

18. I.R.C. § 56(d)(1)(A).

19. See page 865, supra.

20. See I.R.C. §§ 453(l)(1)(A) and (l)(2).

21. I.R.C. § 56(a)(6) last sentence.

22. I.R.C. § 56(a)(6).

exemptions are allowed.[23] No miscellaneous itemized deductions [24] (those which are subject to the 2 percent floor) are allowed,[25] and there are special restrictions on several of the remaining itemized deductions (those listed in Section 67(b)). No deduction is allowed for state, local or foreign taxes.[26] Medical expenses are subject to a 10 percent floor, rather than the 7½ percent floor for the regular tax.[27] The rules related to deductibility of interest under Section 163(d) and (h) are also altered.[28] The remaining itemized deductions listed in Section 67(b), such as personal casualty and theft losses, wagering losses, charitable contributions, and moving expenses, are treated identically in computing regular taxable income and AMTI. Finally, the overall limitation on itemized deductions is not applicable in computing AMTI.[29]

Passive Activity Losses. The passive activity loss limitation rules of Section 469 apply in computing AMTI, and the scope of the limitations is generally the same.[30] However, similar to net operating losses, a separate computation of income and loss after the Section 56 and Section 57 adjustments is made to determine the amount of the AMTI passive activity limitation.[31]

Incentive Stock Options. As seen earlier, the 1986 legislation limited or eliminated most tax shelters but left deferred compensation as an important shelter. Section 421 working with Section 422 provides an important deferral on the exercise of certain stock options by excluding the excess of the fair market value of the stock at the time of the exercise, less the option price, from gross income.[32] However, that amount, the excess value over the option price, *is* a tax preference item

23. I.R.C. § 56(b)(1)(E).

24. I.R.C. § 67(b).

25. I.R.C. § 56(b)(1)(A)(i).

26. I.R.C. § 56(b)(1)(A)(ii). Correspondingly, no recovery of any nondeductible tax is included in AMT gross income. I.R.C. § 56(b)(1)(D).

27. I.R.C. § 56(b)(1)(B).

28. I.R.C. § 56(b)(1)(C) and (e). The alterations are: (1) The deductibility of "qualified residential interest" under § 163(h)(2)(D) and (3) of the regular tax is replaced by deductibility of a more limited "qualified housing interest," as defined in § 56(e) under AMTI. A major difference here is that in refinancing property under the AMTI test, interest on the principal amount of refinanced debt in excess of the principal amount of the original debt at the time of refinancing is not deductible. I.R.C. § 56(e)(1), last sentence. I.R.C. § 56(b)(1)(C)(i). Thus interest on "home equity indebtedness" does not qualify for a deduction. I.R.C. § 163(h)(3)(C)(i); (2) The § 163(d)(6) and (h)(5) phase-ins were disal-

lowed. I.R.C. § 56(b)(1)(C)(ii); (3) Interest which is exempt from tax under the regular tax but is taxed as a preference item under AMTI (see § 57(a)(5)) and related deductions are allowed as income and deductions in the § 163(d) limitation under the AMT. I.R.C. § 56(b)(1)(C)(iii); (4) "Qualified housing interest" rather than "qualified residence interest" is excluded from the term investment interest under § 163(d)(3)(B)(i). I.R.C. § 56(b)(1)(C)(iv); And (5) the adjustments of §§ 56–58 are applied in determining § 163(d) net investment income. I.R.C. § 56(b)(1)(C)(v).

29. I.R.C. § 56(b)(1)(F). See I.R.C. § 68 which is discussed at page 977, supra.

30. See, however, I.R.C. § 58(b)(2), which disallowed the § 469(m) phase-in.

31. I.R.C. § 58(b)(1).

32. The option price is the taxpayer's cost of the property and establishes the taxpayer's cost basis for determining gain or loss on a subsequent sale of the stock under the regular income tax.

which is included in computing AMTI, in the year when it is appropriately subject to tax under Section 83.[33]

Section 57 Tax Preference Items. The second step in computing AMTI is to increase the amount determined under Sections 56 and 58 by the amount of tax preference items listed in Section 57(a). The effect is to increase the minimum tax base by some or parts of deductions or exclusions for which Congress perceives the treatment in computing regular taxable income is too favorable. As in the Section 56 and Section 58 computations, some of the preference items are too technical for discussion here.[34] However, some of the items are familiar and have a significant impact on the AMTI computation. They are considered below.

Tax Exempt Interest on Private Activity Bonds. The interest from *some* tax exempt bonds which is excluded from gross income under Section 103(a) in computing regular taxable income is a tax preference item under the AMT. This is a major change from pre–1986 law and its potential effect is to tax some otherwise exempt interest. Subject to some exceptions,[35] the interest that is taxed here is interest from most "qualified bonds"[36] which are private activity bonds issued after August 7, 1986.[37] Since the interest on the bonds is included in AMTI, the deduction of expenses related to such interest, which is precluded in computing regular taxable income, is allowed in computing AMTI.[38]

Unrecognized Gain on Charitable Contribution Property. The fair market value of property generally establishes the amount potentially deductible as a charitable contribution. However, recall that all ordinary income and appreciation in the form of short-term capital gain and *some* appreciation in the form of long-term capital gain and Section 1231 gain on property contributed to charity reduces the fair market value amount of the charitable contribution.[39] Where the amount of the contribution is not reduced by long-term capital gain and Section 1231 appreciation, that amount of appreciation is a tax preference item.[40] For example, if a person contributes investment stock purchased for $1,000 and worth $10,000 and held more than six months to

---

33. I.R.C. § 56(b)(3). Under § 83 a taxpayer generally must report excess fair market value from a stock option when his rights in the option are freely transferable or when his rights are not subject to a substantial risk of forfeiture. I.R.C. § 83(a). In determining the basis of the stock acquired through such an exercise, the fair market value of the stock (used in computing the preference item) is the stock's basis for AMTI purposes. Id. As in the case of depreciation of post–1986 property, this requires keeping a double set of books, one for computation of regular taxable income and the other for computation of AMTI.

34. I.R.C. § 57(a)(1), (2), and (4).

35. I.R.C. § 57(a)(5)(C)(ii)–(iv).

36. I.R.C. § 141(e).

37. I.R.C. §§ 103(a), (b)(1); 141. See page 257, supra.

38. I.R.C. § 57(a)(5)(A). See I.R.C. § 265(a)(1) and (2).

39. I.R.C. § 170(e)(1)(A) and (B). Cf. I.R.C. § 170(b)(1)(C)(iii). See page 837, supra.

40. I.R.C. § 57(a)(6)(A). Long-term capital gain property includes § 1231(b) business property. I.R.C. § 57(a)(6)(B). A one year exception during taxable years commencing in 1991 applies to contributions of tangible personal property such as works of art. Id. See Rev.Rul. 90–111, 1990–2 C.B. ___.

an educational institution, the full $10,000 amount is deductible (subject to a ceiling equal to 30 percent of the contribution base).[41] The $9,000 of long-term capital gain appreciation does not reduce the amount of the charitable contribution, but it is a tax preference item.[42] If only a portion of the property qualifies for a current regular tax deduction because of the contribution base ceiling, only that portion of the appreciation is a tax preference item for the year.

Accelerated Depreciation on pre–1987 Depreciable Property. The special AMTI rules for recomputing depreciation on property placed in service after 1986 [43] are of course inapplicable to property placed in service prior to 1987. Nevertheless, depreciation on pre–1987 property may constitute a Section 57 tax preference item. The excess of accelerated depreciation on property for a year over the amount that would have been deductible on the property for the year if the straight-line method were used may constitute an item of tax preference.[44] The excess amount is a preference item *only* if the property is of a type that constituted a tax preference item prior to the 1986 legislation. Such property includes real property [45] and leased personal property.[46] The amount of any tax preference is here determined separately with respect to each piece of property.

Exemptions. Once the Section 56, Section 57 and Section 58 adjustments are made and the AMTI is calculated, the amount of AMTI is generally reduced by an exemption,[47] the amount of which depends upon the taxpayer's classification. The exemption is $40,000 for married persons filing jointly and for surviving spouses, $30,000 for unmarried persons who are not surviving spouses, and $20,000 for married persons filing separately and estates and trusts.[48] However, the exemption is phased-out as a taxpayer's AMTI exceeds certain levels: $150,000 for married persons filing jointly and surviving spouses, $112,500 for unmarried persons who are not surviving spouses, and $75,000 for married persons filing separately and estates and trusts.[49] The phase-out is 25 percent of the amount by which AMTI exceeds those levels.[50] Thus the exemption is fully phased-out as AMTI reaches the following levels: $310,000 in the first category,[51] $232,500 in the second category, and $155,000 in the third category.

41. I.R.C. § 170(b)(1)(C). See also I.R.C. § 170(b)(1)(D) and (e)(5).

42. I.R.C. § 57(a)(6)(A). Only property actually contributed after August 15, 1986, not carryovers of deductions prior to that date, are subject to the rule. P.L. No. 99–514, 99th Cong., 2d Sess. § 701(f)(4) (1986).

43. I.R.C. § 56(a)(1) and (5).

44. I.R.C. § 57(a)(7).

45. I.R.C. (1954) § 57(a)(2).

46. I.R.C. (1954) § 57(a)(3).

47. I.R.C. § 55(b)(1)(A).

48. I.R.C. § 55(d)(1).

49. I.R.C. § 55(d)(3).

50. Id.

51. This $310,000 amount is computed as follows: $310,000 less $150,000 equals $160,000. Twenty-five percent of $160,000 is $40,000. At $310,000 AMTI, the phase-out will equal the $40,000 exemption, leaving no further exemption to phaseout.

Computation. A 24 percent tax is imposed on AMTI less any applicable exemption.[52] If the amount of tax so computed exceeds the "regular tax," [53] the excess is the alternative minimum tax, and the taxpayer must pay both the regular tax and the alternative minimum tax for the year.[54] Another way of looking at this is that, in general, the *greater of* either the taxpayer's regular tax liability or his total alternative minimum tax liability (not reduced by the regular tax) is his tax liability for the year.

Seemingly, as always, there is a slight catch. Generally, in computing one's regular tax liability, taxes are reduced by credits in determining actual tax to be paid.[55] However, in the alternative minimum tax scheme the only credits allowed are the Section 27 foreign tax credit and the refundable credits.[56] Other credits do not enter into the Section 55 alternative minimum tax computation. Stated technically, such credits are allowed only to the extent of the excess of a taxpayer's regular tax liability over his alternative minimum tax.[57] Thus, if a taxpayer has Section 1 tax liability of $30,000 with $10,000 of nonrefundable credits (other than a foreign credit) but $50,000 of AMT, his total tax for the year is $50,000, $20,000 under Section 55 and $30,000 under Section 1 with no reduction for credits. To the extent that any nonrefundable credits are unused, a carryover of the credits is allowed against the regular tax in succeeding years.[58]

Corporate Alternative Minimum Tax. Although this is a course in individual income tax, it is important to have a basic understanding of how a basic concept such as the AMT affects corporations. Prior to the 1986 Act, corporations were subject to a minimum tax of 15 percent. But in 1986 the corporate AMT rate was raised to 20 percent.[59] In 1986, Congress also raised the amount of the corporate AMT exemption from $10,000 to $40,000,[60] although the corporate exemption is also subject to a 25 percent phase-out which begins at $150,000 of AMTI.[61]

The corporate minimum tax is similar in structure to the noncorporate minimum tax. However, it provides some different Section 56 and Section 58 adjustments which, as they are even more complicated than the noncorporate adjustments, are not explored here.[62]

Credit for AMT Liability. As seen in the credits discussion earlier in this Chapter, in the 1986 legislation Congress invented Section 53 which provides that a minimum tax determined for any year is carried

---

52. I.R.C. § 55(b)(1)(A). Between 1987 and 1990, the AMT was imposed at a 21 percent rate. See I.R.C. § 55(b)(1)(B) which allows reduction of the tax by an alternative minimum foreign tax credit as defined in § 59.

53. I.R.C. § 55(c).

54. I.R.C. § 55(a).

55. See Part B, supra.

56. See page 985, supra; see pages 988–990 supra.

57. I.R.C. §§ 26(a), 28(d)(2), 29(b)(6) and 38(c).

58. Conf.Rep. No. 99–841, 99th Cong., 2d Sess. II–261 (1986).

59. I.R.C. § 55(b)(1).

60. I.R.C. § 55(d)(2).

61. I.R.C. § 55(d)(3). The exemption is fully phased-out at $310,000.

62. See, e.g., I.R.C. § 56(c) and (g).

over as a credit against regular tax liability in subsequent years to the extent that regular tax liability for that year exceeds minimum tax liability for that year. The credit may be asserted only against minimum taxes payable on *deferral* preferences, e.g., depreciation, but not to *exemption* preferences, e.g., (i.e., tax exempt interest and appreciation on capital gain contributions.) [63]

PROBLEM

Taxpayer is a single, calendar year taxpayer. Assume that the following occurred in 1991 and, for simplicity assume the personal exemption amount is $2,000. She has $200,000 of gross income and $50,000 of deductions not including the depreciation below, which are deductible under § 62. In January of the year she purchases an apartment house with inherited funds at a cost of $650,000, $100,000 of which is for the land. In your computation disregard any mid-month convention. She gives some investment land, worth $30,000 that was purchased several years ago for $10,000, to her alma mater. She receives $3,750 of interest on a "qualified bond" under § 141(e)(1)(B) which is a private activity bond but is exempt from regular income tax under § 103(a). She also owns an unencumbered building acquired prior to 1987 on which she properly takes $30,000 of depreciation during the year when straight-line depreciation would have been only $20,000. She has $10,000 of miscellaneous expenses above the 2 percent floor and she pays state and local property taxes of $10,000 on her personal use property. She has no business or investment indebtedness. Compute her tax liability for the year.

---

63. I.R.C. § 53(d)(1)(B). Thus, to the extent the AMT is attributable to § 56(b)(1) adjustments as well as to § 57(a)(1), (5), and (6) tax preference items, no credit is allowed.

PART NINE: FEDERAL TAX PROCEDURE

CHAPTER 28. INTRODUCTION

No attempt is made in this book to present a full analysis of procedures involved in the determination and enforcement of federal income tax liability. Many procedural principles are introduced in earlier chapters where the emphasis, however, is on substantive tax law. Here the effort is to present procedural fundamentals in one place for more systematic consideration. The broad questions to consider are: (1) When and how can the taxpayer recover tax that was improperly paid (i.e., successfully assert a right to a refund)? (2) When and how can the government exact additional tax that should have been paid (i.e., successfully assert a deficiency)? (3) What means are available to the taxpayer to resist deficiency assertions? (4) What are the basics of criminal prosecution for tax fraud? Answers to these questions involve all three branches of government. Congress provides the statutory framework. The administration of the law is assigned primarily to the Internal Revenue Service, a branch of the Treasury Department; but the Justice Department enters the picture in some civil and criminal cases. The courts perform their usual role of deciding controversies.

A. CIVIL LIABILITY FOR TAX

Tax liability is determined initially by the taxpayer. Under our system of self-assessment, a potentially taxable individual is required to file an income tax return annually [1] and, upon filing, to pay any amount of tax shown on the return to be due. [2] Taxes so reported are automatically assessed. "Assessment" takes place when the assessment officer in the District Director's office or a Service Center signs the summary record of assessment. [3]

Billions of dollars pour into the Treasury by way of this quasi-voluntary method of tax determination and payment by the taxpayer

---

1. I.R.C. §§ 6012(a), 6072(a); and see Johnson, "An Inquiry Into the Assessment Process," 35 Tax L.Rev. 285 (1980). Interestingly, the well-known "Form 1040" came into existence with the inception of the modern income tax in 1913.

Civil or criminal penalties, or both, may result from a taxpayer's failure to file any required return, including, if applicable, the familiar Form 1040. See I.R.C. §§ 6651, 7203.

2. I.R.C. § 6151(a). Similar rules apply to taxpayers other than individuals, such as corporations, trusts and estates, and to other taxes, such as estate and gift taxes.

Of course large amounts of tax are collected by way of withholding by taxpayers' employers and by quarterly advance payments by taxpayers pursuant to their declarations of estimated tax, as noted at page 989, supra.

3. Reg. § 301.6203–1.

himself. Yet, the burden placed on the taxpayer is very great. Even just a little experience with the intricacies of substantive tax law should suggest that, quite apart from negligence or any intentional wrong-doing, many mistakes will be made by the taxpayer.

Human error may be at its worst with regard to the simple arithmetic required in the preparation of a return. The statute permits this kind of error to be corrected summarily. If upon examination of a return it is found that tax liability is understated because of a mathematical error appearing on the return, the amount of the tax with the error corrected can be forthwith assessed and the taxpayer billed for the underpayment.[4] Sometimes, on the other hand, a taxpayer is agreeably surprised to receive an automatic refund when the Service discovers he has made an arithmetical error to his disadvantage. If either the government or the taxpayer subsequently asserts that other types of errors appear on the return both administrative and judicial procedures, later discussed, are available to test the validity of such assertions and to enforce the appropriate adjustments.

Controversy over Tax Liability. It taxes credulity to think that a system of voluntary tax payment would work if the government invariably simply accepted the taxpayer's own appraisal of his liability, even after correcting arithmetical errors. This is not the plan. The initial steps in tax payment and collection should be thought of in terms of the following dialogue between the taxpayer and the government:

Taxpayer (the return): "This is what I propose to pay, and why. Check enclosed."

Government (no actual response, but this unstated message):

"We've checked your arithmetic, which is O.K. and, since we're pretty busy, we'll call it square."

But at a later date there may be additional *alternative* responses by the government, if the taxpayer's return is selected for audit. How will it be so selected? We cannot be certain. It is the government's policy, perhaps analogous to that behind the unmarked patrol car, to keep taxpayers somewhat in the dark in this respect.[5] The *in terrorem* effect is doubtless a boost to taxpayer integrity. Generally, it is more profitable for the government to audit returns reporting large amounts of income, because errors found there may produce much larger amounts of revenue. However, sufficient numbers of very small returns are subjected to scrutiny (particularly as to certain items, such as depen-

---

4. I.R.C. § 6213(b)(1); Reg. § 301.-6213–1(b)(1). The same instant assessment authority exists with respect to an underpayment arising out of an overstatement of income tax withheld or estimated income tax paid. I.R.C. § 6201(a)(3).

5. Audits are made both manually and by computer. Computer audits are made under the DIF system (discriminant function system). The Comptroller General has issued a report entitled "How the In-ternal Revenue Service Selects Individual Income Tax Returns for Audit" (GGD–76–55, 1976). The audit selection process is discussed in Saltzman, IRS Practice and Procedure, ¶ 8.03 (Warren, Gorham & Lamont 2d Ed. 1991); Wedick, "Looking for a Needle in a Haystack—How the I.R.S. Selects Returns for Audit," 83 Tax Adviser 673 (1983); Premis, "The Audit Review Process," 11 Creighton L.Rev. 755 (1978).

dency deductions) so that each taxpayer must wonder whether he is next.[6] Computers now play a role in the selection of returns for audit, for example, by turning up discrepancies between the amount of dividends reported on the return and the amount reported by the paying corporation as paid to the particular taxpayer,[7] but problems seem to persist in matching available data.

Silence is golden, after the filing of a return. If there is any response, it will be to identify some disagreement with the taxpayer's assertions (although it is possible the reply will indicate the taxpayer overpaid his tax).

Tax audits take several forms. A return may be reviewed by officials in an audit division of a regional Service Center and questions raised by way of correspondence.[8] This may be the source of the tax counterpart of the old familiar draft board "Greetings!" which may come by phone or by letter. In turn, the case may be referred to a District Director's office [9] where it is likely the taxpayer may be asked to appear for an interview,[10] and possibly to bring records. In such an interview (really at any time) the taxpayer may take the offensive and claim he has overpaid.[11] Finally, there is a chance of a field audit where the taxpayer and his records may get a going over on his premises.[12]

Taxpayers do not generally enjoy being called onto the carpet any more than schoolboys enjoy a command appearance in the principal's office. But they have little choice. Congress has armed tax officials with extensive authority to inquire into matters affecting tax liability and, with judicial assistance, to compel the cooperation of taxpayers and others who may have relevant information.[13] As in some other situations, inevitability suggests a somewhat quiescent and cooperative attitude; and the attitude of an agent is quite likely to reflect that of the taxpayer.

---

6. See I.R.C. § 6103(b)(2) which permits the Secretary to refuse to disclose the data and standards used in the selection of returns for audit when the Secretary determines that the disclosure would seriously impair enforcement of the internal revenue laws. This provision was probably enacted in response to taxpayer efforts to obtain I.R.S. audit standards under the Freedom of Information Act.

7. I.R.C. § 6042; and see Cohen, "Automation and Tax Administration," 28 Ohio St.L.J. 69 (1967); Meek, "A.D.P.'s Tax Administration Revolution: Its Advantages, Effects, and Problems," 24 J.Tax. 304 (1966); Caplin, "Automatic Data Processing of Federal Tax Returns," 7 The Practical Lawyer 43 (1961).

8. Reg. § 601.105(b)(2).

9. There are sixty one District Directors scattered over the United States. See I.R.C. § 7621; [1991] 12 Stand.Fed.Tax Rep. (CCH) ¶ 45075.

10. Reg. § 601.105(b)(2)(ii).

11. Id.

12. Reg. § 601.105(b)(3).

13. See generally, I.R.C. §§ 7602–7604; and see Caplin, "How to Handle a Federal Income Tax Audit," 28 Wash. and Lee L.Rev. 331 (1971); Pearson and Schmidt, "Successful Preparation and Negotiation May Reduce the Time and Breadth of an I.R.S. Audit" 40 Tax'n Accts. 234 (1988). Under a Supreme Court opinion, the business records even of an individual may be seized subject to a search warrant without offending his privilege against self-incrimination. Andresen v. Maryland, 427 U.S. 463, 96 S.Ct. 2737 (1976).

In the 1988 tax legislation Congress enacted a number of procedural provisions collectively known as the Taxpayer Bill of Rights.[14] The provisions were enacted in an attempt to provide taxpayers with necessary information about the Service's audit and tax collection procedures and to ensure that the tax laws are administered in a fair and equitable manner. The Act requires the Treasury Department to prepare a statement, written in simple and nontechnical terms, which describes the rights of the taxpayer and the obligations of the IRS during an audit, the procedure to be used in appealing a decision (administrative or judicial) of the IRS, the manner in which a taxpayer may request a tax refund or file a complaint, and the procedures which the IRS may use in enforcing assessments, jeopardy assessments, levy and distraint and liens.[15] The IRS employee conducting an interview with a taxpayer in connection with an audit or with collection efforts must review these rights and obligations with the taxpayer.[16] The IRS is now required to permit a taxpayer to make audio recordings of any in-person interview and, after notifying the taxpayer, the IRS may also make a recording of the interview provided the taxpayer is provided with a transcript of the recording on request.[17] During such an interview, if the taxpayer requests to be represented by an attorney or other enrolled representative, the interview must be suspended and the taxpayer must be allowed to seek such representation.[18]

One possible consequence of an audit is a "no change" letter [19] indicating that, after consideration, no adjustments are required. The alternative (disregarding a possible conclusion that there has been an overpayment) is a statement or letter indicating required adjustments and the amount of additional tax to be paid.[20] The taxpayer may very well disagree with the adjustments proposed by the examining agent. If so, the District Director sends the taxpayer a preliminary or "30-day letter".[21] The 30-day letter is a form letter which states the proposed adjustments and is accompanied by a copy of the examining agent's report explaining the bases for these proposals. The preliminary 30-day letter also informs the taxpayer that within a stated period, usually 30 days, he may request an administrative review of issues not settled with the Examiner.[22] It is important to note here that the taxpayer is not required to take this administrative step as a pre-condition to a

---

14. Pub.Law No. 100–647 §§ 6226–6247 (1988). See Adler, "TAMRA: Changes in the Income Taxation of Individuals," 13 Rev. Tax of Individuals 291–300 (1989); Saubert and O'Neil, "The New Taxpayer Bill of Rights," 67 Taxes 211 (1989); Kafka, "Taxpayer Bill of Rights Expands Safeguards and Civil Remedies," 70 J.Tax 4 (1989).

15. Pub.Law No. 100–647, supra note 14 at § 6627.

16. I.R.C. § 7521(b)(1).

17. I.R.C. § 7521(a).

18. I.R.C. § 7521(b)(2).

19. Reg. § 601.105(d). But see Rev. Proc. 85–13, 1985–1 C.B. 514.

20. Id.

21. Id. The terms of this letter are not prescribed by statute; indeed, it may emerge as a fifteen-day letter. It is not to be confused with the statutory notice of deficiency, commonly referred to as the "ninety-day letter."

22. The taxpayer does not always have the right to an Appeals Office conference. See Reg. § 601.106(b). This is explained in the thirty-day letter.

suit. The objective of the review presumably is to limit costly litigation, whenever practicable, over issues not settled.

The administrative review, if requested properly and granted,[23] is conducted by Appeals Offices which are established in each of the seven regions headed by a Regional Commissioner of Internal Revenue.[24] Prior to September 30, 1978, the Internal Revenue Service had provided taxpayers two opportunities for administrative review of disputed tax matters. The first step was a conference at the District Director's level at which the district conferee's settlement authority was limited. Then, if issues remained unresolved, the taxpayer could request a conference in the Appellate Division which operates directly beneath the Office of the Regional Commissioner. The officers of the Appellate Division generally had full settlement authority over most of the tax controversies brought before them. Today, the one-stop administrative review of the Appeals office has replaced the two tier system which preceded it. The Service merged the prior procedures in the belief that the one-stop system will benefit taxpayers by providing them with the opportunity to obtain full settlement of their disputes at the first administrative conference, thereby saving the time, effort, and expense previously required in participating in two conferences which, for the most part, were duplicate procedures.[25]

The two levels of negotiation described (examining officer and Appeals Office) probably act pretty effectively, overall, in resolving by agreement as many issues as possible and thus settling disagreements that otherwise might ripen into litigation. But there will probably always be room for improvement.[26]

Running the described administrative gauntlet usually would be a futile thing if the contested tax liability turned on an issue of law which, for example, was the subject of a Revenue Ruling adverse to the position of the taxpayer. But he need not run it. In deficiency matters, he has a right to refuse to enter into administrative negotiations or to break them off at any stage and to seek judicial intervention. After the 1986 legislation, however, a cautionary note is in order. The Tax Court has discretionary authority under Section 6673 to impose a penalty on the taxpayer for frivolous, groundless, or dilatory proceedings in the Court. By amendment to Section 6673, the Tax Court now has authority to consider any unreasonable failure by the taxpayer to pursue available administrative remedies as an additional factor in imposing the Section 6673 penalty. Conceivably, then, any forebearance or refusal to run any stage of the gauntlet may come back later to haunt the taxpayer in Tax Court.

23. Reg. § 601.106(a)(1). In some instances, the Appeals Office's jurisdiction can be invoked only by way of a formal written protest.

24. [1991] 12 Stand.Fed.Tax.Rep. (CCH) ¶ 45,070.

25. 43 Fed.Reg. 44,484–6 (1978).

26. See Wright, Needed Changes in Internal Revenue Service Conflict Resolution Procedures (1970); Cohen "Appellate Procedures in Tax Administration," 21 U.S.C. Tax Inst. 1 (1969).

Refund Controversies. Before litigation is discussed, a brief look should be taken at administrative procedures where the shoe is on the other foot; the taxpayer asserts a right to a refund. Although a draftee never had any such reciprocal opportunity, a taxpayer can sometimes properly send his "Greetings!" to the government. One way in which this possibility arises is for the taxpayer to make a mistake on his return to his own disadvantage and then to discover it later, maybe talking to you at a cocktail party. His next question will be: What can I do about it? In general what he can do, if his action is timely, is to file a refund claim; and if his claim is not allowed, he can then sue for a refund. Chapter 29 gives you some guidance in refund matters.

A refund suit may also arise in another way. As indicated above, the taxpayer can elect utter inactivity in response to deficiency assertions, although he will then have to pay the asserted tax. But payment does not necessarily foreclose the recovery of the very tax that he decided initially not to contest. If he has not cut off this possibility,[27] he may still take administrative and judicial steps to contest the liability through a refund claim and suit.

In either case the procedure starts with a claim made by an individual on Form 1040X or on an amended Form 1040.[28] The claim is generally filed in the Service Center serving the Internal Revenue district in which the tax was paid.[29] When filed it commences administrative procedures, including optional review procedures, which parallel those available in the case of deficiency controversies.[30] After rejection (or after waiting a stated period of time) the taxpayer may be able to give up on administrative relief and seek judicial intervention by way of a refund suit.

Until 1924 when the Board of Tax Appeals (now the United States Tax Court) was created,[31] the word invariably was pay first—litigate later. The government's need for a steady flow of revenue is so great that the taxpayer was restricted to the "refund route" if he wished to contest federal tax liability in the courts. But now for half a century he has been accorded an alternative. He stands at the crossroads when he receives a statutory notice of deficiency; he must then decide upon the form and forum for his suit to contest liability.

Tax Litigation. In general, except in the case of waiver [32] and jeopardy assessment,[33] assessment or collection of an income tax deficiency is barred until a statutory notice of deficiency, the "ninety-day letter," has been sent to the taxpayer.[34] The taxpayer has a right to this notice, whereas the 30-day letter is not mandatory,—need not be

27. See Finality in Tax Controversies, Chapter 30, infra at page 1040.

28. See Reg. §§ 601.105(e); 301.6402–3.

29. Reg. § 301.6402–2(a)(2).

30. Reg. § 601.105(e)(2).

31. Revenue Act of 1924, § 900, 43 Stat. 253 at 336 (1924).

32. See I.R.C. § 6213(d).

33. See I.R.C. §§ 6213(a) and 6861.

34. I.R.C. § 6213(a). See, generally, Worthy, "The Tax Litigation Structure," 5 Ga.L.Rev. 248 (1971); Ferguson, "Jurisdictional Problems in Federal Tax Controversies," 48 Iowa L.Rev. 312 (1963).

sent. Moreover, the required terms of this notice give the taxpayer ninety days within which to file a petition in the Tax Court for a "redetermination" of the asserted deficiency;[35] assessment and collection continue to be barred for that period and, if the taxpayer files a petition, until the decision of the Tax Court becomes final.[36] Limitation periods that otherwise run against the assessment or collection of tax are suspended for the ninety day period and, if a Tax Court petition is filed, for the litigation period and, in either event, for an additional 60 days after that period.[37]

In the light of all this, efforts to get the taxpayer to agree to the asserted deficiency during the administrative deficiency steps described above are presented in terms of a request that he execute Form 870, which is an authorized waiver of his statutory right to receive a ninety-day letter prior to assessment.[38]

The government may first determine there to be a deficiency close to the time when assessment would be barred by a statute of limitations. As indicated above, the government's position *could* then be protected by the issuance of the ninety-day letter tolling the statute, but this would tend to foreclose customary negotiations toward an agreed settlement. In such circumstances the taxpayer will be asked to execute a Form 872, which is an authorized extension of the limitation period.[39] As a practical matter a request to sign this extension presents the taxpayer with a Hobson's choice. Refusal to sign will simply bring on the statutory deficiency notice.

Suppose now a taxpayer has received the statutory notice of deficiency giving him ninety days in which to file a petition in the Tax Court. If he files such a petition, he relinquishes all other administrative and judicial remedies otherwise available, except his right to appeal the Tax Court's decision.[40] What he relinquishes specifically is the alternative of permitting the tax to be assessed, paying it, filing a claim for refund and then a suit in either the District Court or the Claims Court. Thus, receipt of the ninety-day letter places the taxpayer at the cross-roads, if he is determined to litigate.

Upon the mutual consent of the Service and the taxpayer, a notice of deficiency issued on or after January 1, 1986, may be rescinded.[41] When rescinded, the notice is treated as if it never existed,[42] and

---

35. Id. The 90-day period is extended to 150 days, if the notice is mailed to a person abroad. Id.

36. Id. The Tax Court generally has jurisdiction to redetermine the correct amount of the deficiency, even if the amount so redetermined is greater than the amount of the original deficiency. I.R.C. § 6214. The 1986 legislation confirmed the earlier view that such jurisdiction exists as to any addition to the tax, including additions for failure to pay the tax. Sen.Rep.No. 313, 99th Cong., 2d Sess. 200 (1986).

37. I.R.C. § 6503(a).

38. I.R.C. § 6213(d). The execution of a Form 870AD at the Appeals Office level may have further consequences. See Finality in Tax Controversies, Chapter 30, infra at page 1040.

39. I.R.C. § 6501(c)(4).

40. I.R.C. § 6512(a); and see Emma R. Dorl, 57 T.C. 720 (1972), affirmed per curiam 507 F.2d 406 (2d Cir.1974).

41. I.R.C. § 6212(d).

42. Id.

limitations regarding credits, refunds, and assessments relating to the rescinded notice are void. The parties are returned to their rights and obligations existing prior to issuance of the withdrawn notice.[43] Of course the Service may subsequently issue a notice of deficiency in an amount greater or less than the amount stated in the rescinded notice.[44]

A suit for refund cannot be filed in the Tax Court whose jurisdiction is in general limited to the redetermination of deficiencies in income, estate and gift taxes.[45] However, if the Tax Court's jurisdiction is properly invoked in response to a deficiency notice the Court can, in addition to finding that there is no deficiency, determine there has been an overpayment to be refunded to the taxpayer.[46] On the other hand, neither the District Court nor the Claims Court is given jurisdiction to redetermine deficiencies; tax litigation commenced in those courts rests on the taxpayer's suit for a refund. But of course a refund suit also is a comprehensive determination of income tax liability for the year in question and, where a counterclaim is possible,[47] may result in a deficiency determination.

The losing party in a deficiency proceeding in the Tax Court or in a refund suit in the District Court or Claims Court may appeal the decision (as of right) to the Court of Appeals, with the further possibility of review on certiorari to the Supreme Court.[48] A taxpayer who prevails in any civil tax proceeding may be awarded reasonable litigation costs.[49]

If a taxpayer decides to litigate a tax controversy, he discovers that the government is represented by counsel who are not a part of the Internal Revenue Service organization. Tax Court cases are tried by attorneys in the office of the Chief Counsel *for* the Internal Revenue Service, which is a unit in the Legal Division of the Treasury Department not under the Commissioner of Internal Revenue. Much of the work of the Chief Counsel's office is conducted in the offices of seven Regional Counsel and in the offices of Assistant Regional Counsel located in the district offices. In general, with respect to cases docketed

---

43. H. Rep. No. 426, 99th Cong., 1st Sess. 843 (1985).

44. Id.

45. See Rules of Practice and Procedure, United States Tax Court, Rule 13. Jurisdiction (1984). It has been questioned whether the Tax Court's jurisdiction should not be extended to refund suits. See Griswold, Federal Taxation, page 91, note 1. (Foundation Press 1966). In 1969 Senator Tydings proposed a bill which would have given the Tax Court exclusive jurisdiction over tax refund suits as well as deficiency suits. S.1974, 91st Cong., 1st Sess. (1969).

46. I.R.C. § 6512(b). But as regards enforcement of a Tax Court determination of overpayment, see Thelma Rosenberg, 29 TCM 888 (1970).

47. E.g., I.R.C. § 7422(e).

48. See I.R.C. § 7482. See page 28, supra. In specified circumstances, and at the discretion of the Court of Appeals, the taxpayer may appeal an interlocutory order of the Tax Court involving a controlling question of law. I.R.C. § 7482(a)(2). This is the result of an amendment in the 1986 legislation statutorily addressing a contrary holding in Shapiro v. Commissioner, 632 F.2d 170 (2d Cir. 1980). Conf.Rep.No. 99–841, 99th Cong., 2d Sess. II–806 (1986).

49. I.R.C. § 7430. Such costs include attorneys' fees. Id. Attorneys fees are limited to $75.00 per hour or such higher amount as justified upon the court's review. I.R.C. § 7430(c)(1)(B)(iii). See also I.R.C. §§ 7432, 7433.

in the Tax Court, settlement authority is either delegated to Regional Counsel or shared by Regional Counsel and the Appeals Office.[50] In the past, a great many so-called "session" cases were settled by Regional Counsel just before the Tax Court trial because many taxpayers would wait until Regional Counsel had exclusive settlement authority before pushing for a settlement. Thus, a great deal of time and effort was wasted on trial preparation. As a result, the Service promulgated new procedures that generally grant exclusive settlement authority to Regional Counsel at an earlier date in the belief it will induce earlier settlements.[51]

Other services performed by the Chief Counsel's office, such as participation in the drafting of proposed legislation and the promulgation of rulings and regulations, make it an attractive spot for some young lawyers with an interest in federal taxes.

If a Tax Court decision is appealed, there is a further shift in governmental personnel. The government's decision whether to appeal a Tax Court decision is made by the Solicitor General of the United States with participation by the Chief Counsel's office.[52] Whoever appeals a Tax Court decision, the appeal is handled for the government by attorneys in the Tax Division of the Department of Justice. And, of course, the Solicitor General also has the responsibility for tax cases that reach the Supreme Court by writ of certiorari.

The Court of Appeals is authorized to review decisions of the Tax Court "in the same manner and to the same extent as decisions of the district courts in civil actions tried without a jury." [53] This procedure for judicial review only appears to be tidy and logical. In fact, the decisions of the Tax Court, a centralized national tribunal, fan out into eleven non-unified appellate bodies. As a result, conflicting interpretations of the statute emerge in the various circuits, destroying in part what the Tax Court believes to be a principal purpose for its establishment, an effort toward uniform national administration of the tax laws. The further review of tax cases by the Supreme Court can respond to petitions for certiorari only in a very limited number of cases. Against this background, it is not surprising that over the years there have been repeated proposals for the creation of an intermediate appellate Court of Tax Appeals designed to do away with the present inverted pyramid.[54]

---

50. Reg. § 601.106(a)(2). See, generally, Cohen, "The Chief Counsel's Office," 42 Taxes 191 (1964).

51. Rev.Proc. 87–24, 1987–1 C.B. 720.

52. See Saltzman, IRS Practice and Procedure ¶ 3.04[4][a] (2d Ed. Warren, Gorham & Lamont 1991); Walters, "The Role of the Department of Justice in Tax Litigation," 23 So.Car.L.Rev. 193 (1971).

53. I.R.C. § 7482(a).

54. See Craig, "Federal Income Tax and the Supreme Court: The Case Against a National Court of Tax Appeals," 1983 Utah L.Rev. 679 (1983); Del Cotto, "The Need for a Court of Tax Appeals: An Argument and a Study," 12 Buffalo L.Rev. 5 (1962); Griswold, "The Need for a Court of Tax Appeals," 57 Harv.L.Rev. 1153 (1944); Surrey, "Some Suggested Topics in the Field of Tax Administration," 25 Wash. U.L.Rev. 399, 414–423 (1940). Geier, "The Emasculated Rule of Judicial Precedent in the Tax Court and the Internal Revenue Service," 39 Okla.L.Rev. 427 (1986).

Tax litigation that takes the form of refund suits in the district courts and the Claims Court is also handled by attorneys in the Tax Division of the Justice Department.

Procedures Generally Unavailable. The injunction and the declaratory judgment might appear to be especially promising remedies in tax controversies. Indeed, the injunction has played something of a role in the history of tax litigation. In an early case, before the ratification of the Sixteenth Amendment, a shareholder successfully enjoined his corporation from paying an income tax that he claimed was unconstitutional.[55] While the use of the injunction in tax cases is not now completely outlawed,[56] its utility is very limited.[57]

It is not difficult to think of circumstances in which a taxpayer might wish to get a declaratory judgment of his tax liability. However, the federal Declaratory Judgments Act [58] provides for such judgments in cases of actual controversy, *except* "with respect to federal taxes." Nevertheless, both the Tax Reform Act of 1976 and the Revenue Act of 1978 authorize various courts to render declaratory judgments in specific situations.[59] For example, Section 7478 authorizes the Tax Court to render declaratory judgments with regard to the tax-exempt status of prospective issues of government obligations under Section 103(a). Yet, despite these enactments, the availability of such a remedy remains extremely limited. Whether it may be possible to get a declaratory judgment as to rights and obligations that underlie liability for a federal tax is not entirely clear.[60]

On the other hand, there are circumstances in which a taxpayer can obtain a declaratory *ruling.* This has reference to an administrative determination of tax liability, perhaps before a return is filed or before a transaction is undertaken. Numerous Revenue Rulings appear in earlier chapters of this book. Their significance is further explored in a later chapter.[61]

Collection of Taxes. As a general rule, valid assessment of tax is a prerequisite to the government's right to collect the tax.[62] It is the act

---

55. Pollock v. Farmers' Loan & Trust Co., 157 U.S. 429, 15 S.Ct. 673 (1895).

56. E.g., I.R.C. § 6213(a), last sentence, is a statutory exception to § 7421(a).

57. Compare Enochs v. Williams Packing and Navigation Co., Inc., 370 U.S. 1, 82 S.Ct. 1125 (1962), with Miller v. Standard Nut Margarine Co., 284 U.S. 498, 52 S.Ct. 260 (1932), and Commissioner v. Shapiro, 424 U.S. 614, 96 S.Ct. 1062 (1976). Also, see Lynch, "Nontaxpayer Suits; Seeking Injunctive and Declaratory Relief Against IRS Administrative Action," 12 Akron L.Rev. 1 (1978). Andrews, "The Use of the Injunction as a Remedy for an Invalid Federal Tax Assessment," 40 Tax L.Rev. 653 (1985).

58. 28 U.S.C.A. § 2201 as amended by § 405 of the Revenue Act of 1935.

59. See I.R.C. §§ 7428, 7476.

60. See King v. U.S., 182 Ct.Cl. 631, 390 F.2d 894 (1968), granting such a judgment; reversed 395 U.S. 1, 89 S.Ct. 1501 (1969), on the basis of the limited jurisdiction of the Claims Court not unavailability of the remedy.

61. See Finality in Tax Controversies, Chapter 30, infra, at page 1040.

62. See I.R.C. § 6502. There is some authority supporting collection by suit without assessment. Cf. U.S. v. Ayer, 12 F.2d 194 (1st Cir.1926), sustaining a suit to collect estate tax without assessment. However, with respect to deficiencies there are parallel obstacles to both assessment and collection, see I.R.C. § 6213(a), and, when the tax can be assessed, it will be.

of assessment that establishes the taxpayer's debt to the government. An analogy might be a board of directors' declaration of a dividend, which creates a corporate debt to the shareholder. The statute expressly authorizes the Secretary of the Treasury and officials designated by him to collect assessed federal taxes [63] with substantial latitude as to method of collection.[64]

After proper assessment, the government has six years (or longer by agreement with the taxpayer) within which to collect the tax.[65] This limitation period for *collection* should not be confused with limitation periods within which *assessment* must be made, discussed in Chapter 30.

As might be expected, methods afforded the government for the collection of tax go beyond those available to private creditors. A conventional suit for collection may be brought [66] which, if successful, converts the taxpayer to a judgment debtor. But, additionally, the government may resort to the extraordinary remedies of levy and distraint.[67] This is to say that without judicial intervention the taxpayer's property may be seized and sold to satisfy the tax obligation.[68] Finally, an unpaid federal tax becomes a lien on the taxpayer's property [69] which, when perfected,[70] may be enforced to collect the tax.

A taxpayer cannot thwart the tax gatherer by giving away all his property to avoid payment, or even by dying. Of course, if a tax lien has attached to one's property, it will follow the property into the hands of the donee.[71] Otherwise the liability of the transferee depends upon state law. The Internal Revenue Code invokes state law by permitting enforcement of a taxpayer's tax liability against his transferee, to the extent of the transferee's liability "at law or in equity." [72] Liability "at law" may arise, for example, when a continuing corporation assumes the tax liability of a merging corporation.[73] A transferee's liability "in equity" is likely to be less clear cut, raising as it does conventional problems of creditors' rights.[74] In either event, subject to variation as to such matters as limitation periods [75] and burden of

---

63. I.R.C. § 6301. See Thrower, "Current Collection Problems and Procedures," 24 Tax Lawyer 217 (1971).

64. I.R.C. § 6302; see Reg. § 601.104(c). See Phelan, "A Summary of Extensive Tax Collection Powers of the I.R.S.," 9 Virg.Tax Rev. 405 (1990).

65. I.R.C. § 6502(a).

66. 28 U.S.C.A. § 1396.

67. I.R.C. § 6331; and see note 64, supra. The Taxpayer Bill of Rights, see supra note 14, imposed some limitations and restrictions on the government's ability to place liens on or seize property. See I.R.C. §§ 6326, 6331(a), 6334.

68. See, e.g., Martinon v. Fitzgerald, 306 F.Supp. 922 (S.D.N.Y.1968), affirmed per curiam, 418 F.2d 1336 (2d Cir.1969).

69. I.R.C. § 6321.

70. See I.R.C. § 6323(f); Reg. § 601.104(c).

71. E.g., U.S. v. Bess, 357 U.S. 51, 78 S.Ct. 1054 (1958). See Plumb, "Federal Liens and Priorities," 77 Yale L.J. 228, 605, 1104 (1967 and 1968).

72. I.R.C. § 6901.

73. E.g., Turnbull, Inc., Transferee, 22 T.C.M. 1750 (1963); a supplemental opinion at 42 T.C. 582 (1964) was affirmed 373 F.2d 91 (5th Cir.1967), cert. denied 389 U.S. 842, 88 S.Ct. 72 (1967).

74. See Commissioner v. Stern, 357 U.S. 39, 78 S.Ct. 1047 (1958), and cases there cited.

75. I.R.C. § 6901(c).

proof,[76] a transferee who is liable for another's tax is placed pretty much in the shoes of the principal taxpayer as regards assessment, payment, and collection of the tax.[77]

This note is intended to be only a general description of civil procedures involved in Federal Income Tax cases. The following books deal in a more comprehensive fashion with these matters: When You Go to the Tax Court (Commerce Clearing House, frequently revised); Saltzman, IRS Practice and Procedure (Warren, Gorham & Lamont 2d Ed. 1991); Garbis, Junghans and Struntz, Federal Tax Litigation (Warren, Gorham & Lamont 1985); Morgan, Tax Procedure and Tax Fraud (West Pub. 1990); Bittker and Lokken, Federal Taxation of Income, Estates and Gifts Vol. 4 (Warren, Gorham & Lamont 1981); Quiggle and Redman, Procedure Before the Internal Revenue Service (A.L.I. and A.B.A. 1984); Taylor, et al., Tax Court Practice (A.L.I. and A.B.A. 1990).

B. THE PROFILE OF A TAX FRAUD CASE

This Part B of this chapter is based on a paper prepared by George D. Crowley of the Illinois Bar for presentation in 1973 at the Southern Federal Tax Institute and later published in the Journal of Taxation.[1] Mr. Crowley and the Journal have agreed to adaptation and updating by the authors of this book to serve the purposes of this chapter.

GENERAL DESCRIPTION OF PROCEDURES

The hierarchy of enforcement personnel in the Internal Revenue Service is essentially as follows:

Director [now an Assistant Commissioner. Ed.] Criminal Investigation Division, National Office

Assistant Regional Commissioner, Criminal Investigation Division

Chief, Criminal Investigation Division, District Director's Office

Special Agents (including certain other "technical positions.")[2]

Special Agents of the Internal Revenue Service operate out of the Criminal Investigation Division of the district office. When a tax fraud investigation is approved by the Criminal Investigation Division,[3] a Revenue Agent is assigned by Audit Division for a joint investigation,[4] but he is specifically under the control of the Special Agent and, until

---

76. I.R.C. § 6902(a).

77. I.R.C. § 6901(a).

1. Crowley, "The Role of the Practitioner When His Client Faces a Criminal Tax Fraud Investigation," 40 J.Tax. 18 (1974). Mr. Crowley is coauthor of Crowley and Manning, Criminal Tax Fraud—Representing the Taxpayer before Trial (PLI 1976).

2. [1990] 6 Int.Rev. Manual Ad. (CCH) § 9111, at 28,015.

3. Among other things, informer's tips, discoveries by revenue agents, and suspicion of classes of taxpayers may indicate the need to investigate.

4. See Randall, "The Tax Man Cometh Back—with a Friend," 5 U. of Toledo L.Rev. 44 (1973).

the criminal aspects of the case are terminated, no civil negotiation concerning the amount of the tax will be allowed.

It is important that a taxpayer's representative recognize a tax fraud investigation is being conducted at the earliest possible time. There is no absolute answer to this problem and some experienced practitioners, in the end, look to their own visceral reactions as to the method by which an audit is being conducted. The most usual time of acquiring knowledge of a tax fraud investigation is when a Special Agent introduces himself into the case and seeks an interview with the taxpayer. This interview is usually preceded by *Miranda* [5] type warnings [6] and is sought for the purpose of obtaining an initial statement from the taxpayer, which is almost invariably damaging. Among various other indications that a taxpayer may be suspected of fraud is the service of an administrative summons upon the taxpayer's accountant before any other contact by a Special Agent.

When the Special Agent has completed his investigation, if he recommends prosecution, he will do so in a detailed report. This report is similar to the Revenue Agent's Report and contains all necessary facts to support the recommendation. The report is reviewed by the Special Agent's Group Chief.

As a matter of policy, the Service will provide the taxpayer or his representative a "district Criminal Investigation conference" with the Special Agent and his Group Chief before the report is approved,[7] but no "right" to this conference exists.[8] Regulation § 601.107(b)(2) provides that at the conference the Service conferee will inform the taxpayer's representative of the alleged fraudulent features of the case by a general oral statement and the Service will disclose the criminal adjustments and methods used by the Service. The taxpayer will, however, not be furnished a copy of the Special Agent's Report. Useful information may be obtained at this conference which, however, is viewed by the Service chiefly as a vehicle to button up loose ends in its case and to obtain further information. The amount of information obtained by taxpayer's representative will vary with the conferee.

The Special Agent's Report, if approved by the Criminal Investigation Division, is forwarded to the Regional Counsel's office in the region where the Criminal Investigation Division is located and the taxpayer is so notified, unless of course the case is in the hands of the United States Attorney.[9] Another conference is afforded to the taxpayer or his representative at this level; notice of conference is given in letter form by the Regional Counsel's office. Regional Counsel's analysis of the file is basically limited to a determination (1) that the taxpayer is in fact

---

5. Miranda v. Arizona, 384 U.S. 436, 86 S.Ct. 1602 (1966).

6. See Handbook for Special Agents § 242.13: Duty to Inform Individual of his Constitutional Rights.

7. See Reg. § 601.107(b)(2).

8. U.S. v. Goldstein, 342 F.Supp. 661 (E.D.N.Y.1972), reversed on other grounds 479 F.2d 1061 (2d Cir.1973), cert. denied 414 U.S. 873, 94 S.Ct. 151 (1973). This case does not reflect the current regulation.

9. Reg. § 601.107(c).

guilty of violating one or more specific criminal statutes and (2) that there is a reasonable probability of securing a conviction.

If the Regional Counsel approves the Special Agent's report, the report with the recommendation by Regional Counsel for criminal prosecution is forwarded to the Department of Justice, Tax Division, Criminal Section. Again, it is the policy of Justice to offer the taxpayer or his attorney one conference. The standards for review at Justice are quite similar to those of the Regional Counsel, although the Justice attorneys are more concerned with local prosecution problems and the geographic structure of income tax prosecutions.[10]

If the Department of Justice recommends prosecution, the case is forwarded to the appropriate United States Attorney's office, usually with instructions to secure an indictment. While conferences do take place at the United States Attorney's office prior to indictment, they are not routinely granted. The United States Attorney's office usually has no authority to stop criminal cases in advance of indictment, but will on occasion return the matter to the Service or to Justice for further investigation, or present it to a Grand Jury for examination of unreliable witnesses.

THE EXAMINATION OF WITNESSES AND RECORDS

Section 7602 authorizes the Internal Revenue Service to examine any books, papers, or records, to summon the person liable for the tax or any person [11] having possession or custody or care of relevant books and records to produce them and give relevant testimony, and to take any such testimony under oath of the person summoned as may be relevant or material to the inquiry. In many instances the taxpayer will be notified of the summons since the Tax Reform Act of 1976 adopted Section 7609 which granted taxpayers the right to notice when an administrative summons is served on a "third party record keeper." Generally, such record keepers are limited to include only banks, credit unions, savings and loan institutions, credit reporting agencies, issuers of credit cards, stock brokers, attorneys and accountants. The purpose of the notice is to inform the taxpayer whose records are being summoned that he has a statutory right to stay compliance with the summons and to intervene in any proceeding to enforce the summons. This power under Section 7602 may also be exercised to ascertain the correctness of any return and to determine any tax liability, or to collect any tax due. Section 6020 also authorizes the Service to make a return if the taxpayer has filed none. Under Section 7608(b), "a criminal investigator of the Criminal Investigation Division" is authorized to execute and serve search warrants and to serve subpoenas and summonses. The taxpayer may not enjoin the Commissioner from issuing the summons.[12]

---

10. For a more detailed discussion of the difference between the two reviews, see Balter, Tax Fraud and Evasion, ¶'s 3.04[6] and 3.05 (5th Ed. 1983).

11. Footnote omitted.

12. Reisman v. Caplin, 375 U.S. 440, 84 S.Ct. 508 (1964).

The administrative summons is not self-executing and the Agent or hearing examiner has no power to enforce it if the person summoned refuses, or is enjoined from, compliance. The Service must apply to a district court for enforcement by filing an *ex parte* petition. The district court will enter an order directing the person summoned to show cause why the summons should not be enforced and cause the order and the petition to be served. The "show cause" proceeding is a civil and adversary proceeding to which the Federal Rules of Civil Procedure apply.[13] Both the person summoned and anyone affected by a potential disclosure (having a proprietary interest in records sought) may appear or intervene before the district court.[14] The constitutional and other grounds for objection to enforcement of a summons are asserted in the enforcement proceeding and the district court will then either grant or deny enforcement.[15]

If the district court enters an order enforcing the summons, an appeal may be taken to the Court of Appeals. If the district court refuses to stay its order enforcing the summons pending appeal, the taxpayer or person summoned may appeal to the Court of Appeals for a stay of execution of the district court's order. Good faith objections may be raised in the judicial proceedings, whereas contumacious refusal to appear and object to an administrative summons may, upon conviction, subject the person summoned to a $1,000 fine or one year in prison or both.[16]

RESISTING A SUMMONS

A court will not enforce a summons issued for an improper purpose, such as harassment of the taxpayer,[17] pressure to settle a collateral dispute, or any other purpose reflecting on the good faith of a particular investigation,[18] nor one where the leads to the records in question were obtained in an unlawful search and seizure.[19]

The purposes for which a summons may be properly issued do not include the prosecution of tax crimes, but often civil investigation leads to suspicion of fraud. In Donaldson v. United States,[20] the Court held that a summons under Section 7602 may be issued, if it is issued in good faith,[21] prior to a recommendation for criminal prosecution. A recommendation for criminal prosecution made after issuance of the sum-

---

13. U.S. v. Powell, 379 U.S. 48, 85 S.Ct. 248 (1964).

14. Reisman v. Caplin, supra note 12.

15. Nonconstitutional objections are discussed in Crowley and Manning, supra note 1, at ¶ 8.5.

16. I.R.C. § 7210.

17. I.R.C. § 7605(b) requires that a taxpayer be subject to only one examination for any taxable year unless he or she is notified in writing by the Service that a further inspection is necessary.

18. U.S. v. Powell, supra note 13.

19. U.S. v. Bank of Commerce, 405 F.2d 931 (3rd Cir.1969), but see McGarry's, Inc. v. Rose, 344 F.2d 416 (1st Cir.1965), enforcing a summons where the records were known to the government prior to and independently of an illegal search.

20. 400 U.S. 517, 91 S.Ct. 534 (1971).

21. In resisting the summons for lack of good faith, the taxpayer must prove the Service had no valid purpose concerning civil tax collection or civil tax determination when it issued the summons, U.S. v. LaSalle Nat. Bank, 437 U.S. 298, 98 S.Ct. 2357 (1978).

mons but before enforcement is sought does not invalidate the summons.[22] In United States v. LaSalle Nat'l Bank,[23] the court held that the critical recommendation occurs when the Service forwards the case to the Department of Justice.

Despite the opinions focusing on recommendation dates, it is clear that a recommendation for prosecution is not the only test for proving that a summons was issued for an improper purpose. The question whether a summons is issued in good faith may be raised entirely separately from whether a recommendation for prosecution has been made.[24] Thus, if it can be shown that a firm decision to recommend prosecution has been made, even without any formal recommendation, or if the taxpayer's civil liability has already been determined, presumably the summons has been issued for an improper purpose and is not authorized by Section 7602.[25] The burden, though, is a difficult one for the taxpayer to meet in that the Special Agent's intent is not the controlling factor. The taxpayer instead must prove that the Service, *in an institutional sense,* had abandoned its pursuit of civil tax liability.[26]

If the person summoned intends to comply and the taxpayer has a protectible interest in the records or testimony sought, he may apply to the Federal courts for an injunction enjoining compliance by the person summoned. The result will usually be a petition for enforcement by the Service and an attempt by the taxpayer to intervene in that proceeding. The taxpayer has a statutory right to intervene in situations encompassed by Section 7609.[27] If that provision is not applicable and the person summoned refuses to comply, the taxpayer may intervene in an enforcement proceeding pursuant to Federal Rules of Civil Procedure 24(a)(2), but only if he has a proprietary interest in the records sought which is "significantly protectable".[28]

It appears from *Donaldson* that the same test will be applied to determine a taxpayer's rights to injunctive relief and to intervention. But they also appear to be very narrow rights; for example, in order to assert a valid 5th Amendment claim the taxpayer must be the owner or

22. U.S. v. Cromer, 483 F.2d 99 (9th Cir. 1973).

23. U.S. v. LaSalle Nat. Bank, supra note 21. The holding is now codified in I.R.C. § 7602(c)(1).

24. U.S. v. Lafko, 520 F.2d 622 (3d Cir. 1975); cf. U.S. v. Wright Motor Co., Inc., 536 F.2d 1090 (5th Cir.1976).

25. U.S. v. Wall Corp., 475 F.2d 893 (D.C.Cir.1972). I.R.C. § 7602(b) authorizes the issuance of a summons for the purpose of inquiring into any offense connected with the administration or enforcement of the Internal Revenue Code.

26. U.S. v. LaSalle Nat. Bank, supra note 21.

27. The procedures under I.R.C. § 7609 were amended by TEFRA to make it more difficult for a taxpayer to avert compliance by a third party record keeper who has been summoned to produce the taxpayer's records. The provision shifts the burden of initiating litigation concerning the validity of a third party summons to the taxpayer. If litigation is not commenced by the taxpayer within 20 days after he receives notice of the summons, the third party must comply with the summons and he is granted immunity from liability to the taxpayer. The Secretary still has the burden of persuasion if the taxpayer commences litigation.

28. Donaldson v. United States, supra note 20.

possessor of the records sought,[29] or there must be a privileged relationship (attorney-client) with the possessor of the records or the one whose testimony is sought.[30]

GENERALLY ADDITIONAL TAX MUST BE DUE

Proof of a tax deficiency is ordinarily an essential element in proving tax fraud. The practice has developed of obtaining indictments for filing false returns under Section 7206(1), which does not require proof of a deficiency. But in other instances, though case law is clear that the demonstration of a mere understatement of taxable income does not prove tax fraud, it is also clear from experience that if the Government can prove sizable understatements of taxable income for a number of years, they are a long way toward proving tax fraud to a judge or jury.

It is important to realize that several options are available to the Service to prove a deficiency, especially in the early stages of an investigation. Answers to seemingly innocent questions such as "Did you have any cash on hand (i.e., cash other than in bank account) at the beginning of 1975?" or "What bank accounts did you maintain throughout 1974?" can lead to successful prosecution in criminal and civil tax fraud cases. It is therefore essential that a taxpayer's representative be familiar with the methods of proving a deficiency in order to determine the direction of investigation and the problem areas involved.

The Service is not limited to proving a tax deficiency through the taxpayer's own books and records; the Commissioner is empowered to use less direct methods of proving income. In advanced courses students study methods that involve an increase in net worth, a review of bank deposits, an analysis of cash expenditures and available funds, and other indirect methods, such as the "normal markup," "unit of sales" or "unit of profit" methods.[31] For example, in Agnellino v. Commissioner [32] the Service was permitted to reconstruct a taxpayer's income from a motel and restaurant operation by analyzing the number of bed sheets that were rented from a laundry supply company.

Most tax fraud cases that are stopped before indictment are stopped in the early stages of the Criminal Investigation Division's investigation. By and large, this is not because the evidence indicates the taxpayer is innocent but because there is not enough evidence to prove him guilty. The first step any tax advisor should take, where legally possible, is to stop the flow of information and evidence to the Special Agent.

---

29. See Couch v. United States, 409 U.S. 322, 333, 93 S.Ct. 611, 618 (1973).

30. See Fisher v. United States, 425 U.S. 391, 403–405, 96 S.Ct. 1569, 1577 (1976).

31. See Balter, supra note 10, ¶ 10.04[10].

32. 20 T.C.M. 100 (1961), affirmed in part 302 F.2d 797 (3d Cir.1962).

MEETING THE SPECIAL AGENT

Virtually every successful tax fraud prosecution contains statements made by the taxpayer to the Special Agent. These statements are almost invariably damaging. If the statements are true, they often amount to a confession or provide damaging elements of the prosecution's case. If the statements are untrue, the Government may go to great efforts to prove they were untrue so as to offer such false exculpatory statements as evidence of *willfulness*, often an essential element of the crime charged.[33] The rationale is the taxpayer would not have lied if he had not had the guilty knowledge. Moreover, a taxpayer's false statements may themselves constitute an offense punishable under Section 7207 or 18 U.S.C.A. § 1001. The latter statute is a general non-Code provision that makes it a criminal violation to knowingly give false information or a false statement to any representative of a government agency.

Under no circumstances should the taxpayer be permitted to give a statement to the Special Agent except possibly in voluntary disclosure cases, discussed below. If the taxpayer has previously given a statement to a Special Agent, it is essential to learn what was said. In all but the most routine audits, communications with the Service should be through the taxpayer's representative. It is best that the taxpayer not even be present at any meeting or conferences.

Special Agents are instructed to tell a taxpayer, upon their initial visit, of their function as criminal investigators, and to advise the taxpayer that anything he says may be used against him, that he does not have to incriminate himself by answering questions or producing any documents, and that he may have the assistance of an attorney.[34]

At least two courts have held that this administrative requirement of modified *Miranda* warnings, even if self-imposed and not required by the Constitution itself, is binding on the Service.[35] In Beckwith v. United States[36] the Supreme Court held that a special agent who is investigating suspected criminal tax fraud need not give full *Miranda* warnings unless the taxpayer is taken into custody or the interview is inherently coercive. However, the Special Agent in *Beckwith* had given the warnings mentioned above, required by the Special Agent's manual, so the question remains open (not decided by the Supreme Court) whether the taxpayer has a right to the administrative *Miranda*-type warnings.

---

33. E.g., I.R.C. §§ 7201–7203.

34. Handbook for Special Agents § 242.13, Duty to Inform Individual of his Constitutional Rights. This policy with modification dates back to October 3, 1967 when the IRS issued News Release No. 897.

35. United States v. Heffner, 420 F.2d 809 (4th Cir.1969); United States v. Leahey, 434 F.2d 7 (1st Cir.1970).

36. 425 U.S. 341, 96 S.Ct. 1612 (1976).

CONSTITUTIONAL PROTECTION

The Fifth Amendment privilege against self-incrimination applies to an individual's oral testimony and to documentary communications; this includes the personal and business tax records of an individual.[37] The Fifth Amendment privilege does not apply, however, to corporate records, or those of a partnership.[38] The custodian of corporate records is required to turn them over, upon appropriate summons, even if they incriminate him, but not to testify regarding missing records if his testimony might incriminate him.[39] There is no requirement that unrequested corporate records be volunteered to the Service, nor should irrelevant documents be furnished in response to a summons.

An individual taxpayer's books and records have long been legally subject to seizure under the Fourth Amendment if "instrumentalities of a crime," [40] and in Warden v. Hayden,[41] the Supreme Court sustained the seizure of "mere evidence" of a crime, against an assertion of privilege. Now the Supreme Court has held that an individual's Fifth Amendment privilege against self-incrimination does not protect his business records from seizure pursuant to a valid search warrant.[42] There would appear to be little ground left for challenging a search warrant for a taxpayer's books and records.

Unauthorized inspection of records by an Agent constitutes a violation of the Fourth Amendment and the material inspected may be suppressed.[43] However, if a taxpayer fails to make a timely assertion of his rights he may be held to have waived them.[44]

The Special Agent in a fraud investigation will very quickly contact the taxpayer's accountant and attempt to obtain a detailed statement of the taxpayer's record-keeping practices, method of preparing return and handling of specific transactions. While a taxpayer has no way to silence the accountant, at least two things should be done immediately. First, obtain all of the taxpayer's personal books, records and documents in the accountant's possession (including workpapers) over which the taxpayer can assert an ownership interest. Second, advise the accountant that he is under no obligation to cooperate with the Special Agent and if the Special Agent wants his testimony, he should be required to issue a formal summons to compel the accountant's appearance and testimony. The accountant summoned has ten days to

37. Bellis v. United States, 417 U.S. 85, 94 S.Ct. 2179 (1974).

38. Id.

39. See Curcio v. United States, 354 U.S. 118, 77 S.Ct. 1145 (1957).

40. United States v. Stern, 225 F.Supp. 187 (S.D.N.Y.1964).

41. 387 U.S. 294, 87 S.Ct. 1642 (1967).

42. Andresen v. Maryland, 427 U.S. 463, 96 S.Ct. 2737 (1976).

43. U.S. v. Young, 215 F.Supp. 202 (E.D. Mich.1963); Application of Leonardo, 208 F.Supp. 124 (N.D.Cal.1962).

44. Rife v. Commissioner, 356 F.2d 883 (5th Cir.1966), taxpayer waived right by failure to timely object to second inspection of his books; accord Moloney v. U.S., 521 F.2d 491 (6th Cir.1975), cert. denied 423 U.S. 1017, 96 S.Ct. 452 (1975).

respond to the summons in which time any legal theory or argument to prohibit the testimony may be developed by the taxpayer's attorney.

In Couch v. United States[45] the Supreme Court held that personal books and records of a taxpayer, which had been turned over to an independent accountant and maintained in the accountant's office for a considerable period of time, must be produced upon a proper summons to the accountant issued by the Special Agent and that the taxpayer did not have constructive possession of the documents. The solution to the *Couch* situation may be not to leave the records with the accountant, but to require the accountant to work on those records in the taxpayer's place of business.

As a result of the Supreme Court decisions in *Fisher*[46] and *Andresen*[47] the following tests must be met in order for a taxpayer to be able constitutionally to protect his books and records. In the case of a subpoena for production of the records, the taxpayer will have a valid Fifth Amendment privilege if he or she has possession of the records.[48]

If the records are in the hands of a third party there must be a privileged relationship, such as attorney-client, between the parties in order to prevent enforcement of the summons. These tests are to be applied to the facts as they exist at the date of the issuance of the summons, rather than at the time of a subsequent transfer. If a search warrant is used, the taxpayer will not have a Fifth Amendment privilege to prevent seizure of the records and he or she can contest the validity of the search warrant only on the grounds that it violates his Fourth Amendment privilege.[49]

For any accounting work done during an investigation, the accountant should be retained as an agent of the attorney and not the taxpayer. The work should be performed in the attorney's office. All workpapers and memoranda prepared by the accountant should never leave the possession of the attorney. In United States v. Brown[50] the Seventh Circuit held that a Special Agent could require a major accounting firm to produce in response to a summons: (1) a memorandum prepared by the taxpayer's attorney which was retained in the accounting firm's file and (2) a memorandum prepared by an accountant summarizing the accounting advice given by the accountant at a meeting with the taxpayer and his attorney. Because a search warrant is more difficult to obtain than a subpoena, no information of any kind should be retained by the accountant in a tax fraud investigation; if he desires to maintain memoranda, they should be given to the taxpayer and kept in a file in the taxpayer's or his attorney's office where the accountant may consult them.

45. Supra note 29.

46. Supra note 30.

47. Supra note 42.

48. While *Couch* left open the possibility that "temporary and insignificant" relinquishment of possession would not defeat the privilege, under the circumstances it would be unwise to rely on such a nebulous exception to this rule.

49. Andresen v. Maryland, supra note 42.

50. 478 F.2d 1038 (7th Cir.1973).

COOPERATION BY THE TAXPAYER

Any doubts about cooperation with the Special Agent should be resolved against cooperation. The fact that a taxpayer has fully cooperated with the Service is of minor importance to the Service in determining whether to recommend prosecution.[51] As previously indicated, the overwhelming number of fraud cases that are won without trial are stopped because there is insufficient evidence to prove guilt, not because there is sufficient evidence to prove innocence.

If a practitioner has decided to cooperate and during the course of the investigation he discovers that the advantages sought are no longer present, he should stop cooperating. Cooperation should be constantly assessed; nothing should be turned over to the Agent unless it has been reviewed and approved by counsel. Cooperation is in order of course to the extent of providing documents or information that the investigator can obtain elsewhere. Otherwise, the taxpayer's attorney should courteously but firmly refuse to turn over information not otherwise available to the Agent until the material has been fully reviewed and specific advantages of cooperation determined.

From 1946 to 1952 the Internal Revenue Service had a formal policy regarding voluntary disclosure. In brief, the policy provided that, if prior to audit a taxpayer voluntarily disclosed to a responsible official of the Internal Revenue Service either that he had willfully failed to file his return or had filed a false return, the criminal phase of the case would be forgiven. Voluntary disclosures appear to be effective now only in failure to file cases, if then, and the disclosure must be made in advance of an audit or other Service contact. Voluntary disclosures in regard to fraudulent returns are, quite frankly, a guess and a gamble; this is a determination that should be made only by an attorney who is experienced in the tax fraud area.

ADMINISTRATIVE REVIEW

There will usually be an opportunity for conferences with the Group Chief of the investigating Special Agent (the "district criminal investigation conference").

The taxpayer is provided a conference at the office of Regional Counsel and at the Department of Justice, Tax Division, Criminal Section, prior to the referral to the local United States Attorney's office with directions to secure an indictment. A limited number of cases are stopped at both of these levels, so it is important to know what standards of evaluation are employed by the reviewers and what the substance of a typical conference is.

Regional Counsel. When the case is forwarded to Regional Counsel by the district director, it is assigned to the Assistant Regional Counsel, Enforcement. He then assigns it to one of his assistants. Shortly after

51. See Balter, supra note 10, c. 6.

he receives the Special Agent's report, he will receive from the Audit Division of the district director's office the original tax returns and the cooperating Revenue Agent's Report. The possession of the original returns prevents any civil tax action from taking place unless it is cleared with Regional Counsel.

It is the function of the Regional Counsel to provide legal advice to the Criminal Investigation Division. He is expected to evaluate evidentiary or other legal problems and to solve them. If they are unsolvable or problematical in important respects, he may return the matter to Criminal Investigation for further investigation or he may decline to recommend prosecution. The questions formally presented to Regional Counsel are: (1) is the taxpayer in fact guilty of violating a criminal statute? and (2) is his conviction a reasonable probability? In actual practice the only real question seems to be the latter, as it encompasses the former.

Conference in the office of the Regional Counsel is not considered a discovery proceeding. The assistant Regional Counsel will usually disclose the statutory violations, the theory of the case (e.g., specific item, net worth, bank deposits, etc.), and the amounts involved. Under these circumstances defense counsel should be very careful in the areas he discusses to avoid substantial discovery by the Government. A memorandum should be prepared outlining the history of the case and the points the defense wishes to raise. These arguments are best addressed to legal problems involved in the case or the sufficiency or admissibility of the proofs either generally or specifically.

Normally, officials in the office of Regional Counsel will begin by disclosing the items discussed above and then sit back and await comments. They do not take the position that the criminal case must be substantiated and defended to taxpayer's representative; the conference is for the purpose of permitting the taxpayer to offer argument and evidence on his behalf. Arguments regarding the taxpayer's health or his excellent reputation, offered as they usually are in mitigation of the offense, will have no effect at this stage. The arguments must convince the government attorneys that real difficulties exist in prosecution. Thus, if there was misconduct on the part of the investigating Agents that would result in the suppression of evidence, or if impeachment evidence is available against a principal Government witness, or if important parts of the Service's proof of willfulness can be explained away by other circumstances, such arguments should be pressed forcefully with detailed factual recitals and legal arguments. Once a legitimate issue is before them, a frank discussion of its merits is usually forthcoming.

A decision by Regional Counsel not to prosecute can be protested by the District Director or Criminal Investigation Division. If the Assistant Regional Commissioner for Criminal Investigation concurs in the protest, the case is forwarded to Washington where it is determined either by the Director, Enforcement Division, in the Commissioner's office, or by the Director, Enforcement Division, in the Chief Counsel's Office. The judgment of the latter division is final and not subject to appeal.

Department of Justice. The taxpayer may request a conference at Justice. The Justice Department does not uniformly solicit such a conference but will grant one upon request. The conference is usually held in Washington, D.C. The Justice Department's attorney may make the following recommendations on the case: (1) prosecute; (2) forward to U.S. Attorney with instructions for a grand jury investigation of recalcitrant witnesses; (3) forward to U.S. Attorney with instructions that he exercise discretionary judgment in light of local factors that may have serious jury impact; (4) return case to Service for further specific investigation; or (5) no prosecution.

Most cases referred to Justice are recommended for prosecution. The standards for prosecution are the same as in the Regional Counsel's office. However, as attorneys in the Criminal Section of the Tax Division are often called upon to try cases that they recommend be prosecuted, presumably they are more sensitive to evidentiary problems and jury factors than Regional Counsel. The Chief Counsel's Office may appeal a no prosecution decision by the Justice Department. The Justice Department makes the final decision after reviewing the protest.

TO TRIAL

When the investigation has been completed and, even after administrative review, there is a recommendation of criminal prosecution, the case is forwarded to the appropriate United States Attorney's office, usually with instructions to secure an indictment. The case is then in a trial status and to achieve the best results for the taxpayer the case should long have been in the hands of an experienced criminal trial lawyer. If it is only by this time that tax counsel realizes the matter no longer comes within his specialized understanding of law and legal process but should be under the control of a different expert, he is much too late. Tax counsel should at least be in close cooperation with a tax fraud expert long before the trial begins.

CHAPTER 29.   REFUND PROCEDURES

Internal Revenue Code:

§ 6402   Authority to make credits or refunds
§ 6511   Limitations on credit or refund
    (a) Period of limitation of filing claim
    (b) Limitation on allowance of credits and refunds
    (c) Special rules * * * extension of time by agreement
    (d)(1) and (2) Special rules applicable to income taxes
§ 6512   (a) Limitations in case of petition to Tax Court
§ 6513   Time return deemed filed and tax considered paid
    (a) Early return or advance payment of tax
    (b) Prepaid income tax
§ 6532   (a) Periods of limitation on suits
§ 6611   (a) Interest on overpayments
§ 6621   Determination of rate of interest
§ 7422   Civil actions for refund
    (a) No suit prior to filing claim for refund
    (b) Protest or duress
    (e) Stay of proceedings
    (f) Limitations on right of action for refund
§ 7502   (a) Timely mailing * * * timely filing and paying

Federal tax procedure is discussed broadly in the introductory note in Chapter 28. In this chapter somewhat more detailed consideration is given to the matter of refunds; Chapter 30 looks at deficiencies. Significant statutory provisions that bear on refunds are listed above; they should be read and then examined closely in connection with the problems following this note. Other provisions cited in the footnotes may be viewed as time permits. It is anticipated that the principal learning activity in this area (as in Chapter 30) will come from a thoughtful examination of important provisions in the statute. It is acknowledged elsewhere, however, that just reading the statute in cold blood is pretty tough going; the problems afford some relief.

In any event, if one riffles through the Code pages of Subtitle F— Procedure and Administration—(beginning with Section 6001), some idea of the scope of the procedural rules may be gathered. It seems hardly necessary, therefore, to point out that we have singled out what *may* be some of the most important provisions from which an overview of federal tax procedure may be gained; the treatment is far from comprehensive.

It is axiomatic to say that if a taxpayer seeks a tax refund he must have paid the tax that he seeks to have refunded. However, what constitutes payment is not always so clear. Payments made by an individual in connection with his declaration of estimated tax[1] may

---

1.   I.R.C. § 6654.

give rise to a right to a refund, as such payments are treated as payments on account of the tax for the year.[2] Similarly, even though there is no direct payment by the taxpayer, excessive withholding from a taxpayer's salary or wages [3] is treated as an overpayment for these purposes.[4] Of course in these circumstances the refund due is generally claimed on the return filed for the year and paid in due course, or applied against prepayments of tax for the following year.[5]

In the course of an audit a taxpayer may make a payment against the amount of a prospective deficiency to stop the running of interest. The Code permits the assessment of any amount paid as tax.[6] Generally, if the amount of the deficiency can be ascertained, the amount paid will be assessed.[7] But if the amount is not assessed the payment may be treated as a cash bond to assure future payment and, as such, it cannot be the subject of a claim for refund.[8]

The taxpayer's procedural choices when a deficiency is asserted will be recalled (to contest in the Tax Court or to pay and follow the refund route). For a time, taxpayers preferring to litigate in the District Court or Claims Court, rather than the Tax Court, but also wishing not to pay the entire asserted deficiency prior to litigation, undertook to pay a part of the deficiency and then to file a refund claim and suit for that part. A favorable decision would of course in effect be an adjudication that there was no deficiency. The Commissioner challenged the device, and in Flora v. United States[9] the Supreme Court, in agreement with the Commissioner, stated the "full payment" rule, which requires that the entire amount of an asserted deficiency be paid before a refund suit may be maintained.[10] If the taxpayer chooses to pay less than the deficiency asserted, his remedy is a deficiency proceeding in the Tax Court.

In *Flora,* the Supreme Court viewed resort to the refund suit by way of partial payment as destructive of "the harmony of our carefully structured twentieth century system of tax litigation." [11] The Court need hardly have worried. If only part of an asserted deficiency is paid, a deficiency notice can be issued. If the taxpayer does not then petition the Tax Court, the deficiency can be assessed and, if assessed,

---

2. I.R.C. § 6315.

3. See I.R.C. § 3402.

4. I.R.C. § 6401(b). On the content of refund claims, see Adams, "The Imperfect Claim for Refund," 22 The Tax Lawyer 309 (1969); Note, "What Should a Refund Claim Contain to Be Effective," 4 Taxation for Accountants 18 (1969).

5. See Reg. § 301.6402–3.

6. I.R.C. § 6213(b)(4).

7. Rev.Proc. 84–58, 1984–2 C.B. 501.

8. Ibid. Such amounts will be returned upon request, and they cannot be the subject of a refund claim that would support a suit for refund to determine tax liability.

See Farnsworth & Chambers Co., Inc. v. Phinney, 279 F.2d 538 (5th Cir.1960).

9. 357 U.S. 63, 78 S.Ct. 1079 (1958), on rehearing 362 U.S. 145, 80 S.Ct. 630 (1960).

10. Consider the plight of the taxpayer who lets the 90-day period expire and then cannot fully pay because, whether seized or voluntarily liquidated for payment, his assets are insufficient. See Ferguson, "Jurisdictional Problems in Federal Tax Controversies," 48 Iowa L.Rev. 312, 335 (1963): Nevertheless, this is the current rule. See, e.g., Nogle v. United States, unreported, 33 AFTR 2d 74–1314 (S.D.Ohio 1974).

11. 362 U.S. 145, 176, 80 S.Ct. 630, 646 (1960).

the tax must be paid, unless of course the taxpayer has no assets. On the other hand, if the taxpayer files a Tax Court petition in response to the deficiency notice, he gives up his refund suit, and the Tax Court takes jurisdiction of the entire controversy.[12]

The allowance of a refund claim does not assure the taxpayer of a receipt of cash. The Code expressly permits the government to credit any overpayment against any internal revenue tax liability of the taxpayer who otherwise would be entitled to a refund.[13] The statute does not seem to permit an overpayment to be credited against a taxpayer's possible tax liability for another year where that liability is contested and the tax has not yet been assessed. However, there is some authority that in such circumstances payment of the refund may be delayed until the question of liability for the other year has been finally determined.[14]

The Code sections cited at the beginning of this Chapter indicate administrative authority to refund overpayments of an individual's income tax.[15] They also suggest, at least by inference, that if one is unsuccessful in his administrative claim for refund, he may properly think in terms of judicial intervention.[16] In either event, a prerequisite to suit is an administrative refund claim [17] and either (1) a six months period of patience, or (2) prior adverse action on the claim.[18]

The requirement of an administrative claim prior to suit is a facet of the doctrine of exhaustion of administrative remedies. If the Internal Revenue Service is going to be principally responsible for administering the tax laws, it should be given a chance to sort out difficulties before the courts are cluttered up with more controversies. This is "old hat" to any casual student of administrative law; still in the tax refund setting (and probably others, too) a question can arise whether the claim filed properly supports the suit subsequently brought.[19] The hornbook-type message here is that the statutory prerequisite to suit is

12. I.R.C. §§ 6512(a), 7422(e); see Lore, "Supreme Court in Flora Decision Reveals Weakness in Rule Established," 12 J.Tax. 371 (1960).

13. I.R.C. § 6402(a); Reg. § 301.-6402–3(a)(6). As a matter of fact, various claims the United States may have against the taxpayer may be set off against the amount otherwise to be refunded. I.R.C. § 6402(d). See Garbis and Frome, Procedures in Federal Tax Controversies, 16.16 (1968); Saltzman, I.R.S. Practice and Procedure ¶11.07 (2d Ed. Warren, Gorham & Lamont 1991).

14. See U.S. ex rel. Cole v. Helvering, 73 F.2d 852 (D.C.Cir.1934).

15. I.R.C. § 6402.

16. I.R.C. § 7422. Suit in the district court against the United States is authorized by 28 U.S.C.A. § 1346. An alternative is a suit against the United States in the Claims Court which is authorized by 28 U.S.C.A. § 1491.

17. I.R.C. § 7422(a).

18. I.R.C. § 6532(a)(1).

19. Compare the tax deficiency setting in which, after the 1986 Act, a taxpayer's unreasonable failure to pursue available administrative remedies may be considered by the Tax Court in its determination whether to impose the discretionary § 6673 penalty for dilatory, groundless or frivolous proceedings. See Controversy over Tax Liability, supra at page 1000.

satisfied only if the claim filed gives notice of the nature of the suit which is subsequently brought.[20] The classic failure to meet this requirement was an administrative claim based on a special provision for relief from the World War I Excess Profits Tax, followed by a suit in which the taxpayer asserted as the only ground for a refund a *substantively good* claim for a deduction on account of obsolescence of patents. Failure to assert the valid patent ground in the earlier refund claim nullified the suit.[21]

Taxpayers sometimes fare better where a comprehensive claim is subsequently held to encompass a ground later more specifically asserted in court.[22] Nevertheless, a refund claim should in a sense be viewed as if it were a pleading. Failure to assert grounds on which the taxpayer may later wish to rely in a suit may by procedural error squander a valuable right.

The same precaution must be exercised where a refund claim once filed is sought to be amended. If the amendment in effect involves the assertion of a new ground for recovery, a new claim must be filed rather than a mere amendment to the original claim, and of course the new claim must also be filed within the period set by the statute of limitations.[23]

Another fundamental principle is that a taxpayer is entitled to an income tax refund only if he has in fact overpaid his tax for the year.[24] The proposition may seem obvious but actually defeats what might otherwise be an interesting ploy. Toward the end of the period within which a tax deficiency may be asserted, which usually corresponds to the period within which a refund claim may be filed, the taxpayer might assert a refund claim with respect to an item that he had treated erroneously to his disadvantage on the return for the year. For example, the taxpayer might have failed to claim depreciation in the amount of $1000. Assume if you will that on the same return he innocently but erroneously deducted prepaid interest in the amount of $2000. If the commissioner fails to assert a timely deficiency but the taxpayer nips in at the eleventh hour with a timely refund claim, may he isolate the depreciation item and get a refund for tax that would have been saved if the depreciation deduction had been claimed? The answer is no, as he has not overpaid his tax for the year, even though it is now too late for the Commissioner to assert a deficiency with respect to the improperly claimed interest deduction.

This is a hard and fast rule not to be confused with the equitable defense of recoupment sometimes asserted by the government in a refund suit. The statute of limitations may not stand in the way of the

20. U.S. v. Felt and Tarrant Mfg. Co., 283 U.S. 269, 51 S.Ct. 376 (1931); see also Susskind v. U.S., 1976–1 U.S.T.C. ¶ 9200 (E.D.N.Y.1976), holding "taxpayers may not change or raise new fact issues or shift to a new legal theory in the District Court."

21. Ibid.

22. See Ford v. United States, 402 F.2d 791 (6th Cir.1968), and cases cited therein.

23. See I.R.C. § 6511(a).

24. Lewis v. Reynolds, 284 U.S. 281, 52 S.Ct. 145 (1932).

government's assertion of a right to recoupment if the taxpayer has given a different tax treatment to the same transaction in different years. This is an equitable doctrine not always applied mechanically [25] which is to some extent codified now in the statutory provisions concerning "Mitigation of Effect of Limitations * * *," [26] about which a word must be said.

The statutory mitigation rules are highly complex and, while very important and a suitable subject for a graduate course in tax procedure, they cannot be given detailed consideration in an elementary tax course.[27] It may be well to know, however, that the provisions are two-edged and are as likely to work seriously to the taxpayer's disadvantage as they are to benefit him. By way of example, consider the following situation.

T is an accrual method calendar year lawyer. In 1988 he completed a job for a client and billed him $5,000, which the client paid in 1989. T erroneously included the $5,000 in his return for 1989, not reporting it for 1988, as he should have. In January, 1992, he files a timely claim for refund for 1989, on the ground his income for that year was overstated by $5,000. The Commissioner accepts T's position, which is of course inconsistent with his (T's) initial erroneous exclusion of the item for 1988. See Section 1311(b). If limitation periods now foreclose the assertion of a deficiency for 1988 (Are they likely to?), can T get his refund for 1989 and never pay tax on the fee? Not by a long shot. Allowance of T's claim for refund is a "determination" within the meaning of Section 1311(a), which in these circumstances has the general effect of reopening the year 1988. The year is reopened only briefly, however, affording the Commissioner only one year in which to take corrective action. Moreover, the year is reopened only for correction of the item in question. Thus, on our facts, there could be a redetermination of tax for 1988 taking account of the $5,000 fee. See Section 1314. Nevertheless, if T's income for 1988 was subject to higher rates than for 1989, instead of securing a refund T may wind up paying additional tax. It will be noted that on the facts considered the additional tax could not have been collected by unilateral action of the Commissioner. The possibility arises only because T's refund claim, asserting a position inconsistent with his prior treatment of the item, resulted in a determination that activates the Code provisions mitigating the statute of limitations. See Section 1312(3)(A).

More dramatic illustrations might be given. But the message here is that Sections 1311–1315 are *must* reading prior to embarking on any of the tax procedures discussed.

25. See Dysart v. United States, 340 F.2d 624 (Ct.Cl.1965).

26. I.R.C. (26 U.S.C.A.) § 1311 et seq. See Scheifly, "Internal Revenue Code Sections 1311–14: Resurrection of the Tax Year," 11 Gonzaga L.R. 457 (1976); Willis, "Some Limits of Equitable Recoupment, Tax Mitigation, and Res Judicata: Reflections Prompted by Chertkof v. United States," 38 Tax Lawyer 625 (1985).

27. An excellent basic analysis appears in Maguire, Surrey, and Traynor, "Section 820 of the Revenue Act of 1938," 48 Yale L.J. 719 (1939).

PROBLEMS

In each of the questions set out below determine what you believe to be the correct answer, indicate the statutory basis for your answer and, to the extent possible and appropriate, determine the reason Congress has adopted the statutory provision that is applied.

1. Differentiate a refund claim from a refund suit and state the procedural prerequisites for a suit for refund.

2. Tex Player, a calendar year taxpayer, learns that he has overpaid his tax for the year 1990 in the amount of $500. What is the latest date on which he may file a claim for refund if:

(a) He filed his 1990 return on April 1, 1991?

(b) Player's 1990 return was filed late on May 1, 1991?

(c) Player's 1990 return was timely filed, but the overpayment arose out of an erroneous deficiency assertion by a revenue agent, disallowing a $500 deductible casualty loss, which Player responded to with immediate payment on June 1, 1992?

(d) Same as (c), above, except that the $500 loss was not a casualty loss but was incurred when XYZ stock for which Player had a $500 basis became worthless during 1990?

3. With regard to problem 2(b), above, is Player's refund claim timely if, while not received by the Service until May 15, 1994, the claim is postmarked May 1, 1994?

4. Refunder filed her claim for refund on March 1, 1992.

(a) If the Service takes no action on her claim, when may she file suit?

(b) If her claim is denied on March 1, 1993, when must she file a suit for refund in order for the suit to be timely?

(c) How would your answer to (b), above, be affected by Refunder's waiver of notice of disallowance made at the time she filed the claim?

(d) Can you think of a circumstance in which the taxpayer would benefit by the waiver permitted in § 6532(a)(3)?

5. In a suit for refund can the government successfully assert as a defense that the taxpayer paid the amount of tax voluntarily and not under duress or in response to any claim by the government?

6. If a taxpayer is successful in his refund suit will he recover anything other than the actual amount of overpaid tax?

CHAPTER 30. DEFICIENCY PROCEDURES

(e) Stay of proceedings

§ 7482   Courts of review

A. INTRODUCTION

The broad outline of tax procedures presented in Chapter 28 encompasses in part the government's assertion of deficiencies. If a formal deficiency notice is issued it is prepared in the form of a determination by the Commissioner of Internal Revenue, the principal officer of the Internal Revenue Service. If the taxpayer files a Tax Court petition in response to a deficiency notice, the Commissioner is the respondent in the Tax Court proceeding and is of course the opposing party in any review of the Tax Court's decision. The early practice, now abandoned, of using the name of the Commissioner in the style of the case explains the prominence in tax litigation of "Helvering." Guy T. Helvering was the Commissioner for a substantial period; and of course uninformed students get less credit than they may think for citing the *Helvering* case on examinations.

In this chapter an attempt is made to afford the student a better grasp of rights and obligations in the deficiency area. The Code sections listed above should be read and then studied in connection with the problems at the end of this chapter. As in Chapter 29, the captions of the various Code provisions cited are set out. It is expected that this will be helpful in working the problems and perhaps at the time of review, especially here where a fairly large number of provisions is examined. The precaution offered in Chapter 28 again applies. The fairly large number of deficiency problems considered really only scratches the surface; perhaps a good overview may be obtained, but the presentation does not come close to being comprehensive.

B. ADDITIONS TO TAX

Although the Code must be the principal source for learning about deficiency procedures, some comments are presented in text form here either for purposes of emphasis or because they involve matters not easily or even possibly derived from a study of the statute alone.

It should be noticed at the outset that, if the taxpayer loses a deficiency controversy, either by suit or by settlement, he may be required to pay more than the bare amount of the asserted deficiency. For one thing, interest runs against him from the date the amount should have been paid.[1] Before the 1986 Act, the taxpayer generally

---

1. I.R.C. § 6601(a). Prior to the 1986 legislation, the rate of interest payable on a deficiency was the same as that receivable on a refund, which was determined annually with reference to the prime rate under I.R.C. § 6621. See Rev.Rul. 79–366, 1979–2 C.B. 402, and Rev.Rul. 81–260, 1981–2 C.B. 244. The amendments of the 1986 legislation change the interest rate for computations after December 31, 1986, to the Federal short-term rate plus 2 points for overpayments, or plus 3 points for underpayments. I.R.C. § 6621(a), (b). See I.R.C. § 6621(c) imposing a plus 5 points for corporate underpayments exceeding $100,000.

could deduct any such interest he paid,[2] somewhat mitigating its effect. For tax years beginning after December 31, 1986, such interest is "personal interest," [3] subject to the general overall disallowance of the deduction for personal interest for non-corporate taxpayers.[4] In addition to interest on the deficiency, the taxpayer may be subject to penalties. For example, failure to file a return or failure to pay the tax shown on a return when due, unless occasioned by some reasonable cause, invites penalties.[5] The penalty for failure to file a return is five percent of the tax per month.[6] The penalty for failure to pay the tax is one half of one percent of the tax per month,[7] in general increased to one percent per month after the Service notifies the taxpayer that it will levy upon his assets.[8] In either the failure to file or the failure to pay situation, Section 6651(a) provides that the total penalty may not exceed 25 percent of the tax. If there is a fraudulent failure to file a return, the penalty is increased to 15 percent of the tax per month with a maximum of 75 percent of the tax.[9] The 1989 tax legislation attempted to provide a fairer, more uniform and less complex civil penalty system.[10] Under the legislation, a uniform accuracy-related penalty is imposed for various taxpayer acts including: negligence resulting from the failure to make a reasonable attempt to comply with the provisions of the Code and from the careless, reckless or intentional disregard of rules and regulations; a substantial understatement of income tax; and a substantial valuation misstatement.[11] The penalty is equal to 20 percent of the portion of the taxpayer's underpayment attributable to such acts.[12] If any part of the underpayment is due to fraud, the penalty is 75 percent of the underpayment.[13] The Tax Court in its discretion also may assess a penalty of up to $5,000 on a taxpayer who asserts a frivolous or groundless position.[14] These are civil, not criminal, sanctions,[15] and in each instance the penalty is simple "added

2. I.R.C. (1954) § 163.

3. I.R.C. § 163(h)(2).

4. See page 475, supra.

5. I.R.C. § 6651(a).

6. I.R.C. § 6651(a)(1). See Brookens, "The Section 6651(a)(1) Penalty for Late Filed Tax Returns; Reasonable Cause and Unreasoned Decisions," 35 Case West.Res. L.Rev. 183 (1984–5).

7. I.R.C. § 6651(a)(2). See the limitation on this penalty, I.R.C. § 6651(c)(1). I.R.C. § 6651(a)(3) imposes a penalty of .5% per month for failure to pay the amount of tax due within ten days of the date of notice and demand therefore unless such failure is due to reasonable cause and not due to willful neglect. There is a minimum § 6651(a) penalty equal to the lesser of $100 or the amount of tax due, unless failure to file is due to reasonable cause and not to willful neglect. I.R.C. § 6651(a), flush language.

8. See I.R.C. § 6651(d).

9. I.R.C. § 6651(f).

10. Pub.Law No. 101–239 §§ 7711–7743 (1989). See Stark, "IMPACT Makes Fundamental Changes in Civil Penalties," 72 J.Tax 132 (1990).

11. I.R.C. § 6662(b).

12. I.R.C. § 6662(a).

13. I.R.C. § 6663(a). If any portion of the underpayment is attributable to fraud, the entire underpayment is treated as attributable to fraud, except as the taxpayer otherwise may establish. I.R.C. § 6653(b)(2).

14. I.R.C. § 6673. Cf. Charles S. Greenberg, 73 T.C. 806 (1980). See also I.R.C. §§ 6702 and 7482(c)(4) dealing with frivolous returns and frivolous appeals, respectively, and Howard v. United States, 84–1 U.S.T.C. ¶ 9443 (E.D.Wash.1984); Lamb v. Commissioner, 733 F.2d 86 (10th Cir.1984), modified by 744 F.2d 1448 (1984).

15. Helvering v. Mitchell, 303 U.S. 391, 58 S.Ct. 630 (1938).

to the tax" and therefore collected as tax. But the possibility of criminal sanctions exists as well, as indicated in Chapter 28, supra. Of course, criminal penalties are imposed only upon conviction.

Proof of fraud for purposes of sustaining the Commissioner's imposition of the civil fraud penalty may require something less than the proof beyond a reasonable doubt required for conviction for a crime.[16] In Shirley E. Kub v. Commissioner,[17] the Tax Court sustained the 50 percent penalty, saying: "Mrs. Kub's consistent omission of [similar income items received in three consecutive years] from her returns, her attempts to conceal the payments, and the fact that she had no reason to believe that they were not taxable income constitute clear and convincing evidence of fraud for all three years."[18] Obviously, perhaps, acquittal of a fraud charge in a criminal proceeding does not foreclose the imposition of the civil fraud penalty.[19]

For purposes of measuring the fraud penalty an individual's income tax return is never considered just a teensy weensy bit fraudulent. The penalty is 75 percent of *the underpayment* if "any portion" of the underpayment is attributable to fraud.[20]

C. THE INNOCENT SPOUSE

It will be recalled that, if a joint income tax return is filed by husband and wife, both are generally jointly and severally liable for the tax.[1] In the past this sometimes created such an unjust situation that some judges suggested Congress change the law.[2] For example, a widow who had filed a joint return with her deceased husband might suddenly be confronted with a large deficiency, including the 50 percent fraud penalty arising out of her husband's transgressions that were wholly unknown to her.

In 1971, limited relief was provided under the Section 6013(e)[3] innocent spouse rule which was amended in 1984.[4] The innocent spouse rule applies if the one claiming benefit of the rule (1) filed a

16. See Helvering v. Mitchell, supra note 15.

17. 33 T.C.M. 1282 (1974).

18. Id. at 1296. But compare Wiseley v. Commissioner, 185 F.2d 263 (6th Cir. 1950), with Owens v. United States, 197 F.2d 450 (8th Cir.1952).

19. Helvering v. Mitchell, supra note 15.

20. I.R.C. § 6663(b). Cf. Romm v. Commissioner, 255 F.2d 698 (4th Cir.1958), cert. denied 358 U.S. 833, 79 S.Ct. 54 (1958), reaching this result under less compelling language of prior law. The case may also be of interest as an example of a successful assertion of fraud circumventing the presumptive three-year statute of limitations. See I.R.C. § 6501(c)(1) and (2).

1. I.R.C. § 6013(d)(3).

2. E.g., Louise M. Scudder, 48 T.C. 36, 41 (1967).

3. P.L. No. 91–679, § 1, 91st Cong., 2d Sess. (1971). See I.R.C. § 6013(e)(5) dealing with income from community property. I.R.C. § 6013 is retroactive to all years affected by the Internal Revenue Code of 1954. Wissing v. Commissioner, 441 F.2d 533 (6th Cir.1971); but see United States v. Maxwell, 330 F.Supp. 1253, 1257 (N.D.Tex. 1971), affirmed 459 F.2d 22 (5th Cir.1972), holding that the new provision "does not open a year which has been closed by the statute of limitations, res judicata, or otherwise."

4. P.L. No. 98–369, § 424, 98th Cong., 2d Sess. (1984). See Beck, "Looking for the Perfect Woman: The Innocent Spouse in the Tax Court," 15 Rev.Tax of Ind. 3 (1991).

joint return on which there was a substantial (over $500) understatement [5] of tax attributable to grossly erroneous items of the other spouse; (2) establishes that in signing the return he or she did not know there was a substantial understatement; and (3) shows that he or she could not equitably be held liable for the tax attributable to the substantial understatement.[6] If these requisites are satisfied the statute grants amnesty for tax liability, interest and penalties attributable to the grossly erroneous items.[7]

A substantial understatement can arise as the result of an omission of an item from gross income [8] or any improperly claimed deduction, credit, or basis amount.[9] However to the extent that the liability results from a deduction, credit, or basis error (as opposed to an omission of income) [10] it must exceed a specified portion of the innocent spouse's adjusted gross income [11] in the taxable year preceding the year in which the deficiency notice is mailed (preadjustment year).[12]

In a similar provision, a non-fraudulent spouse is relieved of the 75 percent fraud penalty [13] arising from a fraudulent joint return of the spouses, unless some part of the underpayment is due to the fraud of each spouse.[14] However, fraud of the other spouse may open a year otherwise closed by the statute of limitations and leave an innocent spouse liable for the tax and interest and penalties (other than for fraud), unless the fraudulent situation invokes the broader relief of Section 6013(e).[15]

D. THE TAX COURT IN THE JUDICIAL HIERARCHY

The Golsen Doctrine.   The Tax Court is briefly introduced in Chapter 1, page 19, supra. By now its substantial role in the development of tax law is probably clear from the large number of Tax Court cases set out or cited earlier in this book. In this chapter the Tax Court is of course front and center, as it is the only tribunal in which the taxpayer may challenge the Commissioner's determination of an income tax deficiency without first paying the tax. The routine role of the Court will emerge from an examination of the Code provisions cited at the beginning of this chapter. A word is in order here, however, regarding its relationship to the United States Court of Appeals.

5. I.R.C. § 6013(e)(3).

6. I.R.C. § 6013(e)(1).

7. Id.

8. I.R.C. § 6013(e)(2)(A).

9. I.R.C. § 6013(e)(2)(B).

10. I.R.C. § 6013(e)(4)(E).

11. If the innocent spouse's adjusted gross income for the pre-adjustment year is $20,000 or less, the liability resulting from the deduction, credit or basis error must exceed 10 percent of that adjusted gross income figure. If the adjusted gross income of the innocent spouse is more than $20,000 in the pre-adjustment year the liability must be greater than 25 percent of such adjusted gross income.   I.R.C. § 6013(e)(4)(A) and (B).

12. I.R.C. § 6013(e)(4)(C).

13. I.R.C. § 6653(a) and (b).

14. I.R.C. § 6663(c).

15. See S.Rep. 91–1537, 91st Cong., 2d Sess. (1970), 1971–1 C.B. 606, 608.

The losing party in a Tax Court case may appeal (as of right) to the United States Court of Appeals.[1] The manner and scope of review generally are the same as in the review of civil, nonjury cases in the district court.[2] Further review is only by way of certiorari to the Supreme Court.[3]

In point of fact, the Court of Appeals is several courts inasmuch as the eleven numbered circuits and the Court of Appeals for the District of Columbia and for the Federal Circuit operate independently from each other. Upon review Tax Court decisions fan out in all directions, and some have made reference to this arrangement as an inverted pyramid. Perhaps a mirrored pyramid is closer as things come back together at the Supreme Court; but of course relatively few cases go that far.

Usually, if an individual taxpayer seeks review of a Tax Court decision he or she must appeal to the Court of Appeals for the circuit in which his or her residence is located.[4] For example, a Florida taxpayer would appeal to the 11th Circuit and a New Yorker to the 2nd.[5] Against this background, the question is: If the Court of Appeals to which an appeal may be taken has decided an issue that arises in a Tax Court case, must the Tax Court conform to that decision? For a very long time the Tax Court's stance was one of independence.[6]

*   *   *

One of the difficult problems which confronted the Tax Court, soon after it was created in 1926 [sic] as the Board of Tax Appeals, was what to do when an issue came before it again after a Court of Appeals had reversed its prior decision on that point. Clearly, it must thoroughly reconsider the problem in the light of the reasoning of the reversing appellate court and, if convinced thereby, the obvious procedure is to follow the higher court. But if still of the opinion that its original result was right, a court of national jurisdiction to avoid confusion should follow its own honest beliefs until the Supreme Court decides the point. The Tax Court early concluded that it should decide all cases as it thought right.

*   *   *

The Tax Court feels that it is adequately supported in this belief not only by the creating legislation and legislative history but by other circumstances as well. The Tax Court never knows, when it decides a case, where any subsequent appeal from that decision may go, or whether there will be an appeal. It usually, but not always, knows where the return of a taxpayer was filed, and therefore, the circuit to which an

---

1. I.R.C. § 7482(a). In limited circumstances, such right includes a right to appeal from a Tax Court interlocutory order. I.R.C. § 7482(a)(2).

2. Ibid.

3. Ibid.

4. Ibid.

5. By stipulation the taxpayer and the Commissioner may agree upon review in a different circuit. Ibid.

6. Arthur L. Lawrence, 27 T.C. 713, 716 and 718 (1957).

appeal could go, but the law permits the parties in all cases to appeal by mutual agreement to any Court of Appeals. Sec. 7482(b)(2), I.R.C.1954. Furthermore, it frequently happens that a decision of the Tax Court is appealable to two or even more Courts of Appeals.

* * *

Although the Tax Court had some examples of its single decisions being appealable to two or more circuits, its comment seems almost prophetic as to the difficulty that could be encountered in a departure from its independent position. In 1970, it adopted the opposite, earlier rejected view in deciding Jack E. Golsen,[7] and since then has decided cases in accordance with decisions in the circuits to which appeal probably would be taken. Since then two cases,[8] appearing back to back in the report of memorandum decisions, have reached opposite results on an identical issue under the *Golsen* principle. Deciding *Puckett,* the Court said:[9]

* * *

It having been stipulated that Finance was not a personal holding company within the definition of section 542 during its taxable years ended October 31, 1962 and 1963, we hold that its election under section 1372(a) was not terminated by reason of its receipt of interest, under section 1372(e)(5), House v. Commissioner, 453 F.2d 982 (C.A.5 1972), reversing a Memorandum Opinion of this Court.

We hasten to add that this decision does not reflect the thinking of this Court on the issue resolved hereby. * * * Most recently in Kenneth W. Doehring, T.C.Memo. 1974–234 a case arising out of the instant facts, we held that Finance's election under section 1372(a) for the years in issue had terminated under section 1372(e)(5).

However, as an appeal from the case at bar would be made to the Fifth Circuit, we consider the precedent established by that circuit in *House* to be controlling.

* * *

Some of us "die-hards" still light up when the *Golsen* button is punched.

If the *Golsen* answer to a difficult situation seems only to point up a dilemma, how about a United States Court of Tax Appeals?[10]

---

7. 54 T.C. 742 (1970), affirmed 445 F.2d 895 (10th Cir.1971), cert. denied 404 U.S. 940, 92 S.Ct. 284 (1971). See also the brief comment in Chapter 1, supra at page 19.

8. Kenneth W. Doehring and Paul E. Puckett, 33 TCM 1035 and 1038 respectively (1974).

9. Id. at 1040.

10. For early and more recent commentary see, respectively, Griswold, "The Need for a Court of Tax Appeals," 57 Harv.L.

Rev. 1153 (1944) and Del Cotto, "The Need for a Court of Tax Appeals: An Argument and a Study," 12 Buffalo L.Rev. 5 (1962).

Consider Arthur L. Lawrence, supra note 6, footnote 2: "The United States Customs Court and the Court of Claims are other national courts operating on the trial court level, but they do not have similar problems since the appeals in each case go to [the Court of Customs and Patent Appeals and the Supreme Court, respectively] an

Concurrent Refund and Deficiency Suits.   Perhaps Section 7422(e), which is cited at the beginning of this chapter, needs no explanation.   Even so, here is a word.   Having studied Chapter 29, you are generally acquainted with how and when a taxpayer may have properly filed suit for a refund of income tax in the district court or the Claims Court.   When you are well into this chapter and the Code sections cited here you will know, too, that after a refund suit is commenced the Commissioner *may* still be able to issue a notice of deficiency.   You will also know that the receipt of that notice opens up to the taxpayer another trial forum, the Tax Court.   Suppose that, having commenced the refund suit in the district court or claims court, the taxpayer now *also* files a petition for a redetermination of the deficiency in the Tax Court?   At one time, this created the strange picture of two judicial machines engaged in a race to decision, because a decision in one court would render the matter decided *res judicata* in the other.

Section 7422(e) now presents a more orderly picture when the possibility arises of overlapping refund and deficiency suits.   With this much background, little more need be said.   The statutory answer is to stay the refund suit for the time within which the taxpayer may file the Tax Court petition, leaving with the taxpayer the customary choice of forum.   However, the stay is extended a further 60 days so that, if the taxpayer disdains the Tax Court, the Commissioner may file a counterclaim in the refund suit.

Has Congress only half-assayed the problem?   Suppose the taxpayer has filed a timely and otherwise proper Tax Court petition but then, deciding he has really overpaid his tax, he begins to think in terms of a refund claim and suit.   Can the race to judgment now blocked by Section 7422(e) in other circumstances proceed without impediment here?   The answer, which is negative, lies somewhat buried in the verbiage of Section 6512(a); the timely filing of a Tax Court petition bars the refund suit with only three limited exceptions stated in the separately numbered paragraphs of Section 6512(a).

Invoking Tax Court Jurisdiction.   The statute clearly makes the issuance of a notice of deficiency [11] a prerequisite to a Tax Court suit.   It is within ninety days of the mailing of such notice that the taxpayer may file a petition with the Tax Court for a redetermination of the deficiency.[12]

Section 6861 authorizes jeopardy assessments in cases where the usual cumbersome procedures might threaten to impede collection of

appellate court which also has a nation-wide jurisdiction." [This has been changed. See Chapter 1D2 supra. Ed.]

11. See I.R.C. § 6212. Note, however, I.R.C. § 6212(d), allowing the taxpayer and the I.R.S. to agree mutually to rescind the statutory notice of deficiency. See Chapter 28, supra at page 1005. I.R.C. § 6212(d).

12. I.R.C. § 6213. A longer period is provided if the notice is mailed to a taxpayer outside the United States.

the tax.[13] In these cases the tax *may* be assessed and collected before issuance of a deficiency notice. It is congressional policy, however, not to foreclose resort to the Tax Court as one of three trial forums in these cases. Accordingly, Section 6861(b) requires the issuance of the statutory deficiency notice within sixty days after the mailing of the jeopardy assessment, assuring the taxpayer of his ticket to the Tax Court.

A companion provision to the jeopardy assessment section, Section 6851, authorizes the Commissioner immediately to make a determination of tax for the current or immediately preceding year, and to make an immediate demand for payment, if he finds the taxpayer designs to take action that may prejudice the collection of income tax for such year or years. For many years it was not clear whether in these cases a taxpayer is assured an opportunity to litigate liability in the Tax Court if he chooses to do so. In Laing v. United States [14] the Supreme Court terminated the uncertainty. It held that the assessment and demand for payment under Section 6851 creates a deficiency and, further, that in such circumstances the taxpayer has the right to a formal deficiency notice as provided in Section 6861(b) for jeopardy assessments.[15] Congress, though, responded to *Laing* in the Tax Reform Act of 1976 by amending Section 6851 to provide that the making of a termination assessment does not terminate a taxable year, create a deficiency, or require the Service to give the taxpayer a notice of deficiency within sixty days of the assessment (in contrast to the sixty day period of Section 6861(b) with regard to jeopardy assessments).[16] Nevertheless, Congress did support the *Laing* case to the extent that both Congress and the Court feel it is appropriate to allow a taxpayer who has been subjected to a termination assessment to litigate liability in the Tax Court [17] and, hence, amended Section 6851(b) requires the Service to send such a taxpayer a notice of deficiency within sixty days after the later of the due date or the actual filing date of the tax return for the taxable year involved.

The consequences of requiring statutory notices of deficiencies in the context of jeopardy and termination assessments are twofold: (1) If the notice of deficiency is not issued, the taxpayer *may* enjoin enforcement; he is within an expressed exception to the Section 7421(a) proscription of injunctions found in Section 6213(a), third sentence.[18] This was the holding in *Laing*. (2) Demand for payment under Section 6851(a) is not itself a deficiency notice, so that a taxpayer who petition-

13. See I.R.C. § 7429(a). See also I.R.C. § 6867.

14. 423 U.S. 161, 96 S.Ct. 473, 493 (1976).

15. See Roberts, "*Laing* Down a Challenge: The Future of Due Process and Tax Collections," 11 Gonzaga L.Rev. 369 (1976), and Rosenthal, "Jeopardy and Termination Assessments after *Laing* and *Hall:* Jeopardizing The Fourth Amendment," 31 Tax L.Rev. 317 (1976).

16. S.Rep. No. 938, 94th Cong., 2d Sess. 1976, 1976–3 C.B. 405.

17. Ibid.

18. Although rarely allowed, there are some situations in which jeopardy assessments will be enjoined under a judicially-created exception to § 7421(a). See Commissioner v. Shapiro, 424 U.S. 614, 96 S.Ct. 1062 (1976).

ed the Tax Court on the basis of such demand had misconceived his remedy; he should have sought to enjoin collection.[19]

Section 7429 was added to the Code by the Tax Reform Act of 1976. It enables a taxpayer who is subject to a jeopardy or termination assessment to obtain an almost immediate administrative and judicial review of both the reasonableness of the making of the assessment and the appropriateness of the amount of the assessment. Federal district courts are the proper forum for the judicial review, and the determination made pursuant to Section 7429 is not reviewable by any other court.[20]

Two further comments might be made regarding access to the Tax Court. Filing a petition within the specified ninety days may be accomplished by a timely *mailing* of the petition.[21] But this is only so if the petition is properly addressed, and the rule was held inapplicable when a petition was addressed to the Court at a New York address where it had office space, rather than to Washington, D.C.[22] Whether the mailing is timely may depend upon the "postmark" on the petition.[23] In a case in which the uncertainty was the date of mailing of the notice of deficiency, which *starts* the running of the 90–day period for timely filing, the Court held that certain so-called "line dates" put on a deficiency notice in a Florida post office were not "postmarks" on which the taxpayer could rely to determine the date of mailing; proof of earlier mailing was accepted to render the taxpayer's petition untimely.[24] Apparently this same question could arise regarding the time of a taxpayer's mailing of his petition. The case cited offers some learning on the question: What is a postmark?

E. SMALL TAX CASES

In 1968 the Tax Court on its own announced a new procedure for the handling of small tax cases. The purpose was to afford taxpayers an opportunity for a speedy adjudication of controversies with the Treasury Department where the taxpayer may not be able to afford or the case does not warrant the expenditures that normally attend a trial. There are many instances in the law in which it is just too expensive for a person to take the judicial steps needed to enforce his rights.[1] After the Tax Court made an initial effort to help the small taxpayer, the Tax Reform Act of 1969, by the addition of Section 7463, codified, elaborated, and made some changes in the procedure at first

---

19. See Musso, Sr. v. Commissioner, 531 F.2d 772 (5th Cir.1976).

20. I.R.C. § 7429(f).

21. I.R.C. § 7502.

22. Abbott Hoffman, 63 T.C. 638 (1975). The opinion calls attention to the standard 90–day letter form which gives Box 70, Washington, D.C. 20044 as the address. But a CCH blurb on this case gives 400 Second Street, N.W., Washington, D.C. 20217. Are both correct?

23. Separate provisions apply to registered and certified mail. See I.R.C. § 7502(c). And see Fred Sylvan, 65 T.C. 548 (1975).

24. Duane M. Traxler, 63 T.C. 534 (1975).

1. Cf. Nora Payne Hill, 13 T.C. 291 (1949), where taxpayer later went to the Court of Appeals and was reversed and remanded to the Tax Court, in which the deficiency involved was $57.52. She won?

administratively adopted. In general, a "small" tax case within this section is an estate or gift or income tax case in which the amount of the deficiency placed in dispute does not exceed $10,000, and the Tax Court is authorized to conduct such cases in accordance with simplified rules of procedure.[2] The section can be invoked at the taxpayer's election with the concurrence of the court.[3] Decisions under it are not subject to appeal and do not serve as precedents.[4]

It seems likely the Tax Court will tend to support the taxpayer's desire to use the small case procedure over objections by the Commissioner[5] but, in some situations, the court might properly remove a case from the small tax procedure so that it can be consolidated with a regular case involving common facts or a common issue of law.[6] Similarly, removal may be appropriate where a regular decision could provide a precedent for the disposition of a substantial number of other cases.[7]

Another feature of a small tax case is that most of them are handled by special trial judges appointed by the chief judge of the Tax Court.[8] Once appointed, their authority is intended to parallel that of a Tax Court judge in regard to administering oaths, issuing subpoenas and examining witnesses.[9]

F. BURDEN OF PROOF

In deficiency cases the government is really the moving party, seeking to get money from the taxpayer. Nevertheless, from the standpoint of evidentiary requirements the position of the parties seems to be reversed. The Tax Court Rules provide in general:[1]

> The burden of proof shall be upon the petitioner, except as otherwise provided by statute or determined by the Court; and except that, in respect of any new matter, increases in deficiency, and affirmative defenses, pleaded in his answer, it shall be upon the respondent. As to affirmative defenses, see Rule 39.[2]

2. I.R.C. § 7463(a).

3. Id.

4. Early comments on the procedure appear in an article by William M. Drennen, then Chief Judge of the Tax Court, entitled "Procedural Changes Affecting United States Tax Court," 4 Indiana Legal Forum 53, 58–67 (1970). See also Drennen, "The Tax Court's New Look: A View of the New Powers and Small Tax Procedure." 34 J.Tax. 82 (1971). Drennen, "New Rules of Practice and Procedure of the Tax Court: How are they Working?" 27 U.Fla.L.Rev. 897, 913 (1975).

5. See John Dressler, 56 T.C. 210 (1971).

6. H.Rep. No. 1800, 95th Cong., 2d Sess. 1978, 1978–3 C.B. 611.

7. Ibid.

8. See I.R.C. § 7443A.

9. I.R.C. § 7443A.

1. Rules of Practice and Procedure, United States Tax Court, Rule 142(a), as amended through January 16, 1984.

2. Rule 39 states: "A party shall set forth in his pleading any matter constituting an avoidance or affirmative defense, including res judicata, collateral estoppel, estoppel, waiver, duress, fraud, and the statute of limitations. A mere denial in a responsive pleading will not be sufficient to raise any such issue."

There are other situations in which by statute the burden of proof is on the Commissioner. For instance, Section 6902(a) provides:

> In proceedings before the Tax Court the burden of proof shall be upon the Secretary to show that a petitioner is liable as a transferee of property of a taxpayer, but not to show that the taxpayer was liable for the tax.[3]

And Section 7454(a) states:

> In any [Tax Court] proceeding involving the issue whether the petitioner has been guilty of fraud with intent to evade tax, the burden of proof in respect of such issue shall be upon the Secretary.[4]

The Commissioner also has the burden of proving a major omission from gross income to make applicable the extended statute of limitations for asserting a deficiency.[5]

The shift of the burden on new matters to the Commissioner provided by Rule 142(a) may be cold comfort to the taxpayer. Sometimes in the preparation for a Tax Court trial the Commissioner will turn up new issues on which he can easily meet the burden. The case of Joseph B. Ferguson[6] began with a petition regarding an asserted $1200 deficiency but ended with the Commissioner's successful assertion of several hundred thousand dollars of tax liability.

Does the taxpayer have an easier row to hoe if he contests asserted liability by way of a suit for refund? Under Lewis v. Reynolds[7] a taxpayer must prove that he overpaid his tax. Forbes v. Hassett[8] emphasizes that in a refund suit the taxpayer must prove, not only that the Commissioner was wrong, but also the essential facts upon which a correct determination of liability can be made. Thus, it is sometimes said that the taxpayer has a double burden in refund suits. In the Tax Court, according to the Supreme Court in Helvering v. Taylor,[9] the taxpayer must show that the Commissioner's determination of a deficiency is wrong, but he is not required to show the correct amount of the tax.

Of course in any Tax Court case the taxpayer may present evidence sufficient to establish a prima facie case. If he does, the presumption of correctness that usually or initially attaches to the deficiency notice vanishes, shifting the burden to the Commissioner. If he cannot present evidence to the contrary, the Commissioner cannot win simply by virtue of the lost presumption.[10]

---

3. See T.C. Rule 142(d).

4. See T.C. Rule 142(b).

5. See I.R.C. § 6501(e) and, e.g., C.A. Reis, 1 T.C. 9 (1942). See also I.R.C. § 183(d) hobby losses; § 534 and T.C. Rule 142(e), accumulated earnings tax; and § 7454(b), and T.C. Rule 142(c), foundation managers, for other situations in which the burden of proof is borne by the Commissioner.

6. 47 T.C. 11 (1966).

7. 284 U.S. 281, 52 S.Ct. 145 (1932).

8. 124 F.2d 925 (1st Cir.1942).

9. 293 U.S. 543, 55 S.Ct. 106 (1935).

10. Paul J. Byrum, 58 T.C. 731 (1972), allowing a contested deduction for stock becoming worthless in 1967. See also Efrain T. Suarez, 61 T.C. 841 (1974), reaching a similar result where the petitioner's

G. FINALITY IN TAX CONTROVERSIES

One may agree wholeheartedly with Mr. Justice Jackson's analysis of the terminal role of the Supreme Court: "We are not final because we are infallible; but we are infallible only because we are final." [1] But, if there is any question why, there is at least no question whether the Supreme Court is the end of the line. On the other hand, some potential tax controversies come to rest by way of specific statutory provisions, or by administrative action, or by decisions of lower federal courts. This note explores some of these aspects of finality in tax matters.

Statutory Finality. Some principles of finality operate to preclude controversy, rather than to settle a developed controversy. This is often the result of statutes of limitation such as are identified in these chapters on procedure. The presumptive three-year limitation periods on refund claims and deficiency assertions [2] give rise to the phenomenon of the "closed" year. Of course the year may turn out only to be zippered if, for example, there are subsequent assertions of fraud [3] or major omissions of gross income. [4] And, as has been indicated, even a year that is seemingly nailed shut at times is subject to a partial reopening. [5]

In some instances outside the limitation periods the statute forecloses the development of an otherwise possibly controversial issue. For example, if prior to 1981 a taxpayer and the government agreed upon the useful life of a depreciable asset, the agreed life was generally not subject to subsequent challenge. [6]

Administrative Finality. The Code expressly authorizes administrative officials to enter into binding agreements with taxpayers with regard to their liability for taxes. [7] In general such agreements, called "closing agreements," are "final and conclusive." [8]

Many years ago a closing agreement could be executed for the government only by one of the top officials in the Treasury Department. [9] The 1954 Code conferred such authority on "the Secretary."

---

deficiency notice lost its presumption of correctness because it was found to rest on evidence obtained in an illegal search and seizure.

For an excellent article discussing this entire area see Martinez, "Tax Collection and Populist Rhetoric: Shifting the Burden of Proof in Tax Cases," 39 Hastings L.J. 239 (1988).

1. Jackson, J., concurring in Brown v. Allen, 344 U.S. 443, 540, 73 S.Ct. 397, 427 (1953).

2. I.R.C. §§ 6511(a) and 6501(a).

3. I.R.C. § 6501(c)(1) and (2).

4. I.R.C. § 6501(e).

5. I.R.C. § 1311; and see Chapter 29 at page 1026.

6. See, now-repealed I.R.C. § 167(d); and cf. § 2504(c), sometimes foreclosing a valuation issue for gift tax purposes.

7. I.R.C. § 7121.

8. Ibid. They may be upset upon a showing of fraud or malfeasance or of misrepresentation of a material fact but, otherwise, must be accorded full effect by taxpayers, the administrators, and the judiciary. I.R.C. § 7121(b)(1) and (2).

9. See I.R.C. (1939) § 3760, requiring participation by the Secretary of the Treasury or the Under Secretary or an Assistant Secretary.

Subject to various restrictions regarding the nature of the agreement, the authority has been delegated pretty well down the line to the point where District Directors may execute some closing agreements.[10] The Treasury says that most closing agreements are signed by Chiefs and Associate Chiefs of Regional Appeals Offices.[11]

Closing agreements are of two kinds. The agreement may, for example, fix the income tax liability of a taxpayer for a particular taxable year.[12] On the other hand, the agreement may relate only to one or two questions, such as the fair market value of property received as compensation for services.[13] The latter type of agreement may be useful in situations in which statutes of limitation will afford the taxpayer no all-time assurance on a particular point. For example, whether property was received as compensation and the value of such property might determine the taxpayer's basis for the property which, upon its sale many years later, would determine his gain or loss.[14]

Closely akin to the government's closing agreement authority is its authority to compromise tax controversies.[15] The Treasury views its authority to compromise as limited to two situations: (1) doubt as to liability or (2) doubt as to collectibility, or both.[16] As in the case of a closing agreement, a valid compromise must conform to strict statutory and administrative requirements.[17] In line with the jurisdictional shift from Treasury to Justice which may take place in the course of a tax controversy,[18] the statute provides for action by the "Attorney General or his delegate" in the compromise of a controversy that has been referred to the Department of Justice for prosecution or defense.[19]

Over the years there has been substantial question whether an agreement that did not comply with the rules for the execution of a closing or compromise agreement was binding on either the taxpayer or the government.[20] While there is authority for strict compliance with

---

10. See, e.g., Commissioner's Delegation Order No. 97 (Rev. 10), 36 F.R. 13161 (1971).

11. Rev.Proc. 68–16, § 5.03 1968–1 C.B. 770, 775.

12. Such agreements are executed on Form 866, entitled "Agreement On Final Determination of Tax Liability."

13. Such agreements are executed on Form 906, entitled "Closing Agreement as to Final Determination Covering Specific Matters."

14. Cf. United States v. Frazell, 335 F.2d 487 (5th Cir.1964).

15. I.R.C. § 7122.

16. Rev.Proc. 80–6, § 4, 1980–1 C.B. 586, 588.

17. Jurisdictional and procedural requirements for compromise settlements are set out in Rev.Proc. 80–6, supra note 16. The compromise authority of District Directors was expanded by Commissioner's Delegation Order No. 11 (Rev. 6), 36 F.R. 9571 (1971).

18. See Chapter 28, Introduction, supra at page 999.

19. I.R.C. § 7122.

20. See Emmanuel, "The Effect of Waivers in Federal Income Tax Cases," 3 U.Fla.L.Rev. 176, 179 (1950). Congressional and administrative steps such as extensive sub-delegation, which tend to facilitate the execution of de jure closing or compromising agreements, may work toward a reduction of such controversies.

such rules,[21] there are also cases in which flawed agreements have been accorded finality on estoppel principles.[22]

Form 870, even Form 870AD,[23] by means of which a taxpayer agrees to the assessment of tax without receipt of a statutory deficiency notice, expressly acknowledges that it is not a closing agreement under Section 7121. However, Form 870AD does have language of finality which is observed by the government. Uncertainty as to the binding effect on the taxpayer of such language clearly suggests that one who wishes only to relinquish his right to go to the Tax Court, and to maintain his right to litigate in the District Court or the Claims Court should amend any proffered Form 870AD expressly to preserve his right to file claim and suit for refund.[24]

What is the status of the taxpayer who has requested and received an administrative ruling on a question of federal income tax liability? The best answers to this question can be found in an article by Mitchell Rogovin written when he was Chief Counsel for the Internal Revenue Service.[25] In very brief summary, there is no statutory obstacle to the Service's reneging on a ruling if the matter has not been handled so as to conform with the requirements for a closing or compromise agreement.[26] However, it is only in "rare or unusual circumstances" that the Treasury will apply retroactively its revocation of a ruling so as to upset the expectations of the one to whom the ruling was issued.[27] For this reason, taxpayers feel they can rely on rulings issued to them and, even though procedures have been streamlined, rather rarely seek closing agreements. On the other hand, a "determination letter" is a kind of ruling that is issued by the District Director, which is limited to the tax aspects of transactions that have been completed. Inasmuch as the letter relates only to past transactions and action is not taken by a taxpayer in reliance on such a letter, revocation is automatically retroactive, unless the Commissioner specifically exercises his authority to apply the change only prospectively.[28] As a general rule, oral communication by Service personnel and various Service publications, such as the popular "Your Federal Income Tax," have no more final effect on the determination of tax liability than the opinion of private tax counsel.[29]

21. E.g., Botany Worsted Mills v. U.S., 278 U.S. 282, 49 S.Ct. 129 (1929).

22. E.g., Backus v. United States, 59 F.2d 242 (Ct.Cl.1932), cert. denied 288 U.S. 610, 53 S.Ct. 402 (1933).

23. See Reg. § 601.106(d)(2).

24. In a case in which the taxpayer expressly agreed to file no refund claim, a compromise effected by way of a Form 870AD was held to estop him from filing a later claim, even though the Form 870AD did not meet the requirements of a closing or compromise agreement. Stair v. United States, 516 F.2d 560 (2d Cir.1975). See also Saltzman, IRS Practice and Procedure ¶ 9.08 (2d Ed. Warren, Gorham & Lamont 1991).

25. Rogovin, "Four R's: Regulations, Rulings, Reliance and Retroactivity," 43 Taxes 756, 763 et seq. (1965).

26. Cf. Dixon v. United States, 381 U.S. 68, 85 S.Ct. 1301 (1965).

27. Rev.Proc. 91–1, 1991–1 C.B. ___.

28. See I.R.C. § 7805(b).

29. Elliott, 30 T.C.M. 1030 (1971); Becker v. Commissioner, 751 F.2d 146 (3d Cir. 1984). See Rogovin, supra note 25 at 774; and see Kragen, "The Private Ruling: An Anomaly of Our Internal Revenue System," 45 Taxes 331 (1967).

Judicial Finality. The familiar doctrine of res judicata is of course fully applicable to tax controversies.[30] If a taxpayer has won a judgment in a district court in a refund suit, imagine what his reaction would be if told that the Commissioner is now asserting additional income tax liability for the same year and that he must again go to court to preserve his victory. But he need not, of course, because his liability for that year is res judicata.[31] The judgment is controlling not only with respect to the issues litigated but to all issues that could have been raised which bear on the determination of liability for the year.[32] Neither the form of the litigation (refund suit or deficiency proceeding) nor the forum in which the case is tried (Tax Court, District Court, or Claims Court) makes any difference. While the doctrine is dependent upon a prior adjudication of a controversy between the same parties or their privies, the same parties requirement is satisfied by the proposition that the contest is between the taxpayer and the government, whether the official party to the proceeding is the United States itself or the Commissioner of Internal Revenue.[33] Moreover, while the Tax Reform Act of 1969 has cured any doubt,[34] even when the Tax Court was an administrative agency,[35] an adjudication by the Tax Court or its predecessor the Board of Tax Appeals, invoked the doctrine.[36]

The related doctrine of collateral estoppel or estoppel by judgment is especially likely to be of importance in tax cases. The landmark opinion outlining the scope of the doctrine of collateral estoppel is that in Commissioner v. Sunnen.[37] A single controversial circumstance may have a bearing on income tax liability for several years. If a judgment fixes liability for one of the years, the broad doctrine of res judicata forecloses only the reopening of that liability. But the related doctrine of collateral estoppel forecloses the relitigation of issues that were in fact raised and decided in the earlier litigation, even when they arise in a new cause of action, such as a dispute as to liability for a later year.[38]

A simple example of the estoppel concept may be helpful. Assume that T is the income beneficiary of a trust. He assigns half his interest gratuitously to his son. The Commissioner asserts that T remains taxable on all the trust income under the fruit-tree doctrine.[39] T successfully contests his liability for tax on half the 1990 trust income in a Tax Court case which is not appealed. Now comes the Commissioner with the same assertion for the year 1991. Res judicata does not protect T, because the cause of action is not the same, i.e., his 1991 tax liability obviously was not decided in the case that involved the 1990

---

30. Tait v. Western Maryland Ry. Co., 289 U.S. 620, 53 S.Ct. 706 (1933).

31. Even this firm doctrine is subject to exception under the mitigation rules of I.R.C. § 1311 et seq.

32. Cf. Cromwell v. Sac County, 94 U.S. (4 Otto) 351, 352 (1876).

33. Ibid; and see I.R.C. § 7422(c).

34. I.R.C. § 7441.

35. See I.R.C. § 7441, prior to its amendment in 1969.

36. Tait v. Western Maryland Ry. Co., supra note 30, and see I.R.C. § 7481.

37. 333 U.S. 591, 68 S.Ct. 715 (1948); and see Goldstein, "Res Judicata and Collateral Estoppel," 54 A.B.A.J. 1131 (1968).

38. See IB Moore, Federal Practice, 718 at 724–725 (1984).

39. See Chapter 12, supra at page 289.

year. But T may be protected by collateral estoppel. Both doctrines reflect a policy that matters judicially determined should not be open for subsequent consideration; and collateral estoppel extends the notion of res judicata to cover a specific issue that has been decided.

However, there are limits to the doctrine. As the Supreme Court has said: [40]

> It must be confined to situations where the matter raised in the second suit is identical in all respects with that decided in the first proceeding and where the controlling facts and applicable legal rules remain unchanged.

The *Sunnen* case itself involved a fruit-tree controversy. But the *Clifford-Horst* line of cases [41] intervened between the first and second controversies. On this ground the Court held in *Sunnen* that the "legal atmosphere" had so changed as to render the doctrine of collateral estoppel inapplicable.

Collateral estoppel may of course work against the taxpayer. For example, a conviction in a criminal case for tax fraud under Section 7201 forecloses argument by the taxpayer that he is not liable for the civil fraud penalty under Section 6653(b).[42]

PROBLEMS

1. T is a calendar year taxpayer. When can the Commissioner make a timely assertion of an income tax deficiency against T for the year 1991, without resort to special limitation periods, if T filed his return for 1991 on:

(a) April 1, 1992?

(b) May 1, 1992?

(c) If T filed no return for 1991?

2. On essentially the same facts as those in problem 1, and assuming that T filed a return on April 1, 1992; what different result would you reach if:

(a) The deficiency asserted rests on an alleged omission of a $20,000 fee for T's services which, if reported, would have increased the gross income reported on the return to $60,000? or

(b) The deficiency asserted rests on an alleged omission from gross income, whatever the amount, done by T with the deliberate attempt to evade tax? (May T be in more than mere financial difficulty? See and broadly differentiate §§ 7201 and 7206(1).)

---

40. Commissioner v. Sunnen, supra note 37 at 599–600 and 720–721.

41. Chapters 12 and 13, supra.

42. See Nathaniel M. Stone, 56 T.C. 213 (1971), and cases there cited. On the other hand, an acquittal of the taxpayer in a preceding criminal case does not foreclose assertion of the civil fraud penalty. Helvering v. Mitchell, 303 U.S. 391, 58 S.Ct. 630 (1938).

(c) Mr. and Mrs. T filed a joint return under § 6013 even though they are separated and in the process of getting a divorce. The Commissioner, in a deficiency notice, asserts an understatement of $1,000 of tax attributable to an item of income omitted from Mr. T's gross income. Appraise Mrs. T's liability for tax, interest, and penalties. See § 6013(e).

3. The Commissioner sent Deficient a ninety day letter dated March 28, 1991. The "letter" was mailed at the post office by the Service on March 29, 1991 and the Service received certified mail notice dated March 29, which also bore the postmark date of March 29, 1991.

(a) Is Deficient's petition timely if it is properly mailed and postmarked on June 27, 1991 and arrives at the Tax Court on July 1, 1991?

(b) What result in (a), above, if the petition is properly mailed on June 29, 1991, but the post office stamps that date on it but fails to postmark it and it arrives at the Tax Court on July 1, 1991? See Duane M. Traxler, 63 T.C. 534 (1975).

(c) Is Deficient's petition timely in (a), above, if it was mailed and postmarked June 27, 1991, but was improperly addressed to the I.R.S. who forwarded it to the Tax Court and it arrived at the Tax Court on July 5, 1991? See Abbott Hoffman, 63 T.C. 638 (1975).

(d) Assume in (a), above, Deficient lived in Town X when the return for the year in question was filed and reported Town X as his address on his return and six months later he moved to Town Y and all subsequent returns show Town Y as his address. If the Commissioner sends the ninety day letter to Town X on the dates above but it is not forwarded to Deficient until April 15, 1991, will Deficient's petition be timely if it is filed by July 10, 1991? See § 6212(b)(1), Rev.Proc. 90–18, 1990–1 C.B. 491, and Mulvania v. Commissioner, 81 T.C. 65 (1983).

(e) If in any case above Deficient's petition is not timely and there is no Tax Court jurisdiction has Deficient completely lost his "day in court"?

4. If under § 6501(c)(4) T is asked to execute a Form 872, extending the time for assessment of a deficiency, what practical consideration will affect his response?

5. If under § 6213(d) T executes a simple Form 870, waiving restrictions on assessment of tax, to what extent has he capitulated, i.e., relinquished further opportunities to contest his liability?

6. If the Commissioner makes a jeopardy assessment prior to the issuance of a statutory notice of deficiency, will T lose his right to litigate the question of liability in the Tax Court?

7. Several judicial alternatives are open to taxpayers in tax litigation situations. In the following situations which procedure would the taxpayer be likely to use?

(a) The taxpayer has a factual issue as to which he feels a jury would be favorably disposed.

(b) The taxpayer has no money with which to pay an asserted deficiency.

(c) The taxpayer wishes to stop the running of interest but at the same time litigate the issues. (Consider this carefully).

(d) The litigation involves a very difficult tax law issue.

(e) The litigation involves a legal issue on which there is a split of authority among the circuits. The court of appeals in the circuit in which the taxpayer resides has decided the issue in the government's favor.

Are there further factors that a taxpayer might take into consideration in determining his judicial remedy and forum? See Quiggle and Redman, Procedure Before the Internal Revenue Service, § 4.04 (A.L.I. and A.B.A. 1984).

INDEX